June 17–20, 2014
Aarhus, Denmark

I0027529

**Association for Computing Machinery**

*Advancing Computing as a Science & Profession*

**IDC** 2014

INTERACTION DESIGN
and CHILDREN

Editors:
**Ole Sejer Iversen**
**Panos Markopoulos**
**Christian Dindler**
**Franca Garzotto**
**Christopher Frauenberger**
**Anja Zeising**

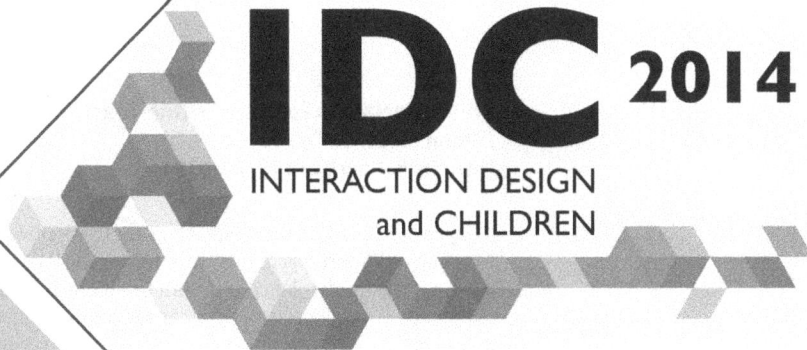

# IDC'14
## Proceedings of the 2014 Conference on Interaction Design and Children

*Sponsored by:*
**Aarhus University**

*In cooperation with:*
**The LEGO Foundation**

*Support from:*
**Intel, IT-Vest Networking Universities, University of Southern Denmark, & Aalborg University**

**Association for
Computing Machinery**

*Advancing Computing as a Science & Profession*

**The Association for Computing Machinery**
2 Penn Plaza, Suite 701
New York, New York 10121-0701

**Notice to Past Authors of ACM-Published Articles**
ACM intends to create a complete electronic archive of all articles and/or other material previously published by ACM. If you have written a work that has been previously published by ACM in any journal or conference proceedings prior to 1978, or any SIG Newsletter at any time, and you do NOT want this work to appear in the ACM Digital Library, please inform permissions@acm.org, stating the title of the work, the author(s), and where and when published.

**ISBN:** 978-1-4503-2272-0 (Digital)

**ISBN:** 978-1-4503-3091-6 (Print)


Additional copies may be ordered prepaid from:

**ACM Order Department**
PO Box 30777
New York, NY 10087-0777, USA

Phone: 1-800-342-6626 (USA and Canada)
+1-212-626-0500 (Global)
Fax: +1-212-944-1318
E-mail: acmhelp@acm.org
Hours of Operation: 8:30 am – 4:30 pm ET




Printed in the USA

# IDC 2014 Chairs' Welcome

Welcome to the 13th international conference on Interaction Design & Children, June 17–20, 2014, in Aarhus, Denmark. The mission of the IDC conference is to bring together researchers, designers and educators to explore new forms of technology, design and engaged learning among children. The conference incorporates papers, presentations, speakers, workshops, participatory design experiences and discussions on how to create better interactive experiences for children. IDC 2014 offers wide-ranging program, supporting and facilitating the exchange of ideas within and between all of these communities. The theme of this year's conference is 'Building Tomorrow's Technology – Together'.

We live in a global society where digital artefacts have become part of the everyday lives of children. Be it education, sports activities, rehabilitation or play, technology has come to play an important role in the way children relate to their physical, social and cultural surroundings. IDC 2014 invites researchers and practitioners to share their work on how technology affects children's well-being and sense-making in a global context and how children, their parents, teachers and peers can contribute to the design of new technology. We invite researchers and participants to share thoughts on emerging technology, new theoretical perspectives, design methods and approaches, and the understanding of these ideas for the benefit of children's development by questioning how we can build tomorrow's technology – together.

In Denmark, the Interaction Design and Children community is forged from research institutions and leading industry partners exploring aspects of children's play, learning and leisure as a foundation for technology design. For the IDC 2014, Aarhus University (AU), The LEGO® Foundation and INTEL have come together to create a venue for researchers and practitioners to work with theoretical, practical and methodological challenges in IDC.

Director of Transformative Learning Technologies Lab at Stanford University, Paulo Blikstein opens the IDC 2014 conference with a keynote on the designers' mission in the age of ubiquitous technology. According to Paulo Blikstein, we need to design devices, environments, and activities that reflect children's multiple epistemological resources and heuristics. The keynote is followed by two days of 18 full paper presentations, 44 short papers and 21 demos carefully selected through a double blind review process by the IDC program committee.

A new feature of IDC 2014 is a full day interactive forum for all conference attendees around the topic: How does the interaction with digital creative tools support child development? The focus in this session is on how children will develop with digital technologies and the ways we can inspire them to create their own digital tools. Different aspects of this question is addressed in groups prior to the workshop. Professor Marilyn Fleer from Monash University kicks off the session with a keynote on the relations between play and learning in digital environments – the significance of motives and demands. The keynote is followed by a challenge session facilitated by The LEGO® Foundation and LEGO® employees from different parts of the research and product development groups. The day ends with a closing panel session where topics from the challenge sessions and the IDC 2014 Conference in general are discussed and elaborated by people from research and industry. The interactive workshop day is hosted by The LEGO Foundation in their headquarters in Billund, Denmark. The LEGO Foundation provides IDC 2014 attendees an opportunity to go on an exclusive factory tour as part of the IDC closing program.

**Ole Sejer Iversen**
*General Chair*
*Aarhus University,*
*Denmark*

**Bo Stjerne Thomsen**
*Conference Co Chair*
*The LEGO Foundation,*
*Denmark*

**Lars Elbæk**
*Conference co-chair*
*University of Southern*
*Denmark, Denmark*

# Table of Contents

## Session: Keynote Address
Session Chairs: Bo Stjerne Thomsen *(LEGO Foundation)*, Bieke Zaman *(KU Leuven)*

## EMBODIED INTERACTION (Full Paper Session)
Session Chair: Janet C. Read *(University of Central Lancashire)*

## INTERACTING TOGETHER (Full Paper Session)
Session Chair: Svetlana Yarosh *(University of Minnesota)*

## DESIGNING FOR & WITH CHILDREN (Full Paper Session)
Session Chair: Mona Leigh Guha *(University of Maryland)*

## CRAFTING INTERACTIONS (Full Paper Session)
Session Chair: Narcís Parés *(Pompeu Fabra University)*

## APPLICATIONS FOR LEARNING (Full Paper Session)
Session Chair: Chris Quintana *(University of Michigan)*

## Wednesday Short Papers
Session Chair: Anja Zeising *(University of Bremen)*

## Thursday Short Papers
Session Chair: Christopher Frauenberger

## Closing Panel

Session Chair: Mitchel Resnick *(MIT Media Lab)*

## Author Index

# About the IDC Conference

Interaction Design and Children (IDC) is the premiere international conference for researchers, educators and practitioners to share the latest research findings, innovative methodologies and new technologies in the areas of inclusive child-centered design, learning and interaction. The annual conference incorporates papers, presentations, speakers, workshops, participatory design experiences and discussions on how to create better interactive experiences for children.

This volume is the formal proceedings of the IDC 2014 conference. IDC 2014 offers a wide-ranging program, supporting and facilitating the exchange of ideas within and between various communities committed to creating better interactive experiences for children. Participants often come from a variety of fields, including computer science, communication, child development, engineering, digital media, game design, educational psychology and learning sciences.

IDC 2014 builds on the strong and dedicated community that has developed around this annual conference for the past 13 years. Recent venues include New York, USA, in 2013, Bremen, Germany, in 2012, Ann Arbor, USA, in 2011, Barcelona, Spain, in 2010, and Como, Italy, in 2009. The 13th international conference on Interaction Design and Children (IDC 2014) is presented by Aarhus University and The LEGO® Foundation in Aarhus, Denmark, from June 17–20, 2014, supported by INTEL.

While the IDC community continues to grow and diversify each year, it remains a welcoming place to exchange ideas on inclusive design, learning and interactive technology for children everywhere.

This volume includes the archival material presented at the conference, namely full papers and short papers, as well as abstracts provided by the keynote speakers. Papers have been accepted through a rigorous, double blind review process where each paper has been reviewed by 3-5 expert reviewers. Associate chairs have provided meta-reviews, and the final selection of papers was decided by associate chairs and program chairs, who discussed each submission individually. The acceptance rates were as follows:

- Full Papers: 18 accepted out of 60 submitted (30%)
- Short Papers: 44 accepted out of 103 submitted (43%)

The IDC 2014 conference also included 21 demonstrations, 5 workshops, and 4 tutorial sessions and a doctoral consortium resulting in a 4-day program.

## About Aarhus University

Aarhus University (AU) in Denmark offers an education and research environment for 40,000 students, 1,600 PhD students and 11,000 members of staff. In 2012 Aarhus University was number 89 at the QS World University Ranking and number 116 of 17,000 universities on the Times Higher Education World University Ranking. The Child-Computer Interaction Group at the Center for Participatory IT has been actively engaged in the IDC environment since the first conference in Eindhoven, 2002. The Center for Participatory IT (pit.au.dk) has strong roots in the Scandinavian tradition for Participatory Design (PD), which combines the areas of technology development and use with a broader interest in participative practices at the workplace. In an Interactive Design and Children perspective, this approach suggests that involving children, their parents, educators and caretakers in the design process, significantly improves the quality of new IT.

## About The LEGO Foundation

The LEGO® Foundation, endowed by the founding family of the LEGO® Group, and built on their enduring values, was founded in 1986. The LEGO Foundation is committed to develop and share knowledge about the power of play in learning, and shares the mission of the LEGO Group: to inspire and develop the builders of tomorrow. The Foundation is dedicated to build a future where learning through play empowers children to become creative, engaged, lifelong learners. Its work is about re-defining play and re-imagining learning to ensure the value of play for children's learning and development is understood, embraced and acted upon. In collaboration with thought leaders, influencers, educators and parents the LEGO Foundation aims to equip, inspire and activate champions for play. www.LEGOFoundation.com

# Conference Organization

**General Chair:** Ole Sejer Iversen *(Aarhus University, DK)*

**Conference Co-Chairs:** Lars Elbæk *(University of Southern Denmark, DK)*
Bo Stjerne Thomsen *(The LEGO Foundation, DK)*

**Program Chairs:** Panos Markopoulos *(Eindhoven University of Technology, NL)*
Franca Garzotto *(Politecnico Di Milano, IT)*
Christian Dindler *(Aarhus University, DK)*

**Associated Paper Chairs:** Narcis Pares *(Universitat Pompeu Fabra, Barcelona, SP)*
Mona Leigh Guha *(University of Maryland, USA)*
Chris Quintana *(University of Michigan, USA)*
Eva Eriksson *(Chalmers University of Technology, SE)*
Janet C Read *(University of Central of Lancashire, UK)*
Svetlana Yarosh *(University of Minnesota, USA)*

**Short Paper Chairs:** Christopher Frauenberger *(Vienna University of Technology, AT)*
Anja Zeising *(University of Bremen, DE)*

**Workshop Chairs:** Bieke Zaman *(iMinds KU Leuven, BE)*
Mikael Skov *(Aalborg University, DK)*

**Tutorial Chair:** Juan Pablo Hourcade *(University of Iowa, USA)*

**Demo Chairs:** Martin Brynskov *(Aarhus University, DK)*
Mark Gross *(Carnegie Mellon University, USA)*

**Doctorial Consortium Chairs:** Tilde Bekker *(Eindhoven University of Technology, NL)*
Helle Karoff *(Aalborg University, DK)*

**Conference Advisor:** Allison Druin *(University of Maryland, USA)*

**Local Arrangements Chairs:** Aviaja Borup Lynggaard *(Aarhus University, DK)*
Stine Liv Johansen *(Aarhus University, DK)*
Rikke Toft Nørgård *(Aarhus University, DK)*
Jonas Fritsch *(Aarhus University, DK)*
Tina Holm Sørensen *(The LEGO Foundation, DK)*
Marianne Dammand Iversen *(Aarhus University, DK)*
Ann Eg Mølhave *(Aarhus University, DK)*
Gitte Grønning Munk *(Aarhus University, DK)*
Janne Bach Sørensen *(Aarhus University, DK)*
Louise Kjærgaard *(Aarhus University, DK)*
Kasper Ostrowski *(Aarhus University, DK)*
Rachel Charlotte Smith *(Aarhus University, DK)*
Klaus Thestrup *(Aarhus University, DK)*

**Program Committee:**

Dor Abrahamson
June Ahn
Alyssa M. Alcorn
Meryl Alper
Lisa Anthony
Alissa Antle
Carmelo Ardito
Zeina Atrash
Saskia Bakker
Mara Balestrini
Emilia Barakova
Wolmet Barendregt
Tilde Bekker
Laura Benton
Matthew Berland
Paulo Blikstein
Elizabeth Bonsignore
Paul Brna
Martin Brynskov
Pasquina Campanella
Antonio Camurri
Lorenzo Cantoni
Brendan Cassidy
Timothy Charoenying
Gene Chipman
Leslie Chipman
Daniel Churchill
Tamara Clegg
Luca Colombo
Joshua Danish
Antonella De Angeli
Linda de Valk
Nicoletta Di Blas
Christian Dindler
Nadine Dittert
Jordana Drell
Sarah Eagle
Elizabeth Eikey
Mike Eisenberg
Eva Eriksson
Jerry Alan Fails
Leah Findlater
Shalom Fisch
Dan Fitton

Beth Foss
Christopher Frauenberger
Natalie Freed
Franca Garzotto
Katie Gaudion
Helene Gelderblom
Michail Giannakos
Lorna Gibson
Shuli Gilutz
Timo Goettel
Evan Golub
Judith Good
Dimitris Grammenos
Mark Gross
Mona Leigh Guha
Libby Hanna
Bart Hengeveld
Davinia Hernández-Leo
Raymond Holt
Mike Horn
Matt Horton
Katy Howland
Kori Inkpen Quinn
Ole Sejer Iversen
Izdihar Jamil
Stine Liv Johansen
Sergi Jorda
Yasmin Kafai
Shaun Kane
Helle Karoff
Eva Sophie Katterfeldt
Alex Kuhn
Chronis Kynigos
Jean Baptiste Labrune
Kristin Lamberty
Monica Landoni
Rosa Lanzilotti
Linda Little
Michelle Lui
Michael Lund
Leilah Lyons
Olga Lyra
Andrew Macvean
Thor Magnusson

**Program Committee (continued):**

Laura Malinverni
Andrew Manches
Regan Mandryk
Gabriela Marcu
Panos Markopoulos
Patrizia Marti
Emanuela Mazzone
Lorna McKnight
Brenna McNally
Emma Mercier
Andrew Miller
Marcelo Milrad
Pejman Mirza-Babaei
Jaime Montemayor
Christiane Moser
Helen Pain
Narcis Pares
Tamara Peyton
Kaisa Pihlainen-Bednarik
Ana Lucia Pinto
Fabio Pittarello
Taciana Pontual
Erika Poole
Sara Price
Chris Quintana
Iulian Radu
Hayes Raffle
Dimitrios Raptis
Janet C Read
Emily Reardon
Simos Retalis
Glenda Revelle
Jochen Rick
Judy Robertson
Yvonne Rogers
Eric Rosenbaum
Maria Roussou

Elisa Rubegni
Nitin Sawhney
George Schafer
Heidi Schelhowe
Ben Schouten
Susanne Seitinger
Gavin Robert Sim
Mikael Skov
Iris Soute
Daniel Spikol
Anastopoulou Stamatina
Tony Stockman
Janienke Sturm
Masanori Sugimoto
Cristina Sylla
Anthony Tang
Anuj Tewari
Mike Tissenbaum
Cathy Tran
Chia-Wen Tsai
Edward Tse
Claudia Urrea
Vero Vanden Abeele
Lilia Villafuerte
Greg Walsh
Jillian Warren
Sabrina Wilske
Thomas Winkler
Svetlana Yarosh
Nikoleta Yiannoutsou
Jason Yip
Bieke Zaman
Massimo Zancanaro
Anja Zeising
Isabel Zorn
Oren Zuckerman

# IDC 2014 Sponsor & Supporters

**Sponsor:**

AARHUS UNIVERSITY

**In cooperation with:** The **LEGO** Foundation

**Supporter:** intel®

**Institutional Supporters:** **it**-vest
networking universities

UNIVERSITY OF SOUTHERN DENMARK

BREAKING NEW GROUND
AALBORG UNIVERSITY

# Re-empowering Powerful Ideas: Designers' Mission in the Age of Ubiquitous Technology

Paulo Blikstein
Stanford University
520 Galvez Mall
Stanford, CA, 94305
paulob@stanford.edu

## ABSTRACT

The project of universal, high-quality education is a new human endeavor. Not many decades ago, the mainstream view was that only a small elite required advanced education, and vocational training would suffice for everyone else. The need to educate all students in very different disciplines—many of them quite complex and advanced—is generating demands that the extant educational system cannot meet. Technology has been touted as one answer to these new demands, but has failed so far to escape a century-old cycle of inflated expectations. Our mission as designers of interactive technologies and environments is crucial to move out of this cycle, but it will require our community to make a convincing argument that technologies in education are not simply delivery media, but artifacts that extend human cognition in multiple ways. The adaptivity of computational media enables an acknowledgement of epistemological diversity which enables students to concretize their ideas and projects with motivation and engagement. Thus, the goal of providing rich educational experiences for all students will depend upon our ability to design devices, environments, and activities that are accepting of children's multiple epistemological resources and heuristics.

## Categories and Subject Descriptors

K.3.1 [Computers and Education]: Computers Uses in Education

## Keywords

Education, interaction design, physical computing, robotics, constructionism, constructivism, makers' movement

## Bio

Paulo Blikstein is an assistant professor in the Stanford University Graduate School of Education as well as in the Computer Science Department (by courtesy), where he directs the Transformative Learning Technologies Lab. Blikstein's academic research focuses on the capacity of new technologies to powerfully transform and facilitate the learning of science, engineering, and mathematics. He researches and designs educational technologies, including computer modeling, robotics, and digital fabrication, and develops hands-on learning environments in which children learn science and mathematics through the construction of sophisticated projects and devices. He also focuses on the application of data-mining and machine learning for the assessment of hands-on, project-based learning. Blikstein has spearheaded the FabLab@School project, building advanced digital fabrication labs in middle and high-schools in many countries. A recipient of the National Science Foundation Early Career Award, he holds a PhD. from Northwestern University and a MSc. from the MIT Media Lab.

## Introduction

The project of universal education is a relatively new human endeavor. Not many decades ago, the mainstream view was that only a small elite required advanced education, and vocational training would suffice for everyone else. As a case in point, the United States took nearly a century even to offer universal access. In the 1850s the school year lasted only four months, and in the early 1900s only 6% of students received high school diplomas. If today we criticize traditional schooling for its mass production of students, we often forget that this was precisely the intention—the outcome of an explicit policy to achieve universal access at a cost that society could afford (or was willing to finance) in training the masses for the job market. Elwood Cubberly, the father of "modern" school management, stated in the first decade of the 20th century that "[Schools should be factories] in which raw products, children, are to be shaped and formed into finished products... manufactured like nails, under specifications from government and industry. […] We should give up the exceedingly democratic idea that all are equal. […] One bright child may easily be worth more to the National Life than thousands of those of low mentality." Within this not-so-politically-correct mindset, reformers of the 19th and early 20th century such as Horace Mann placed a great emphasis on standardization and the establishment of a meritocracy which would identify the "geniuses" hidden in the masses.

In the beginning, therefore, the goal was to build a system to promote, at a low cost, a very basic education for the vast majority, and a high-quality, advanced education for the few. The organization of schools and the methods employed in classrooms were driven by these concerns, and they generated a genetic code that has been extremely resilient (Tyack & Cuban, 1995). At its best, the traditional classroom might be able to teach basic content and skills, either through systematic repetition, or by driving lower performing students out of school. However, in recent decades, we have become much more ambitious about what we expect from schooling, and it is no longer considered a legitimate option to simply exclude low performers from the process. Similarly, we desire more than arithmetic and basic literacy, and we want this for all students. We want children to learn physics, chemistry, advanced mathematics, engineering, problem solving, critical thinking, communication, programming, and many other topics that were or would have been deemed impossible by the 19th century pioneers.

This poses a serious problem: we built a system that accomplished its basic job – to deliver basic education to the masses – but this system was not designed for a 21st century mandate. We have, for decades, lived in a limbo of extremely ambitious demands, in which we turn to schools to solve all sorts of societal problems, but refuse to accept that schools need to change to deliver on our demands.

## 1. Technology: the eternal solution

A common solution for this problem has been to employ technology. Educational technologies have, for a long time, been part of the cycle of inflated expectations in schools (Cuban, 1986), and our fascination is easy to understand. Technology embodies the connotation of sudden and irresistible change, with apparently very little effort—a perfect combination. In 1922, Thomas Edison opined that motion pictures would soon replace textbooks, allowing the educational system to run at "100 percent efficiency." This was in the same era of progressive reform that saw the widespread adoption of radio, "the textbooks of the air," and, later, educational television. Since then, the cycles of innovation in educational technology have turned ever more rapidly to include computer labs, laptops, interactive whiteboards, internet, online video, personalized tutors, mobile phones, and tablets.

Many of the educational technologists' solutions for the school of the 21st century have been to apply Cubberly's paradigm with new tools: digitize the lecture, computerize the test, automatize the feedback. Despite the hype and the large amounts of money poured into these initiatives over the decades, the results have been dismal.

For decades we have tried to investigate how different tools, machines, and systems might impact teaching and learning, but much of this research has ignored that the effects of any medium will always be confounded with the methods employed in its utilization (Clark, 1983, 1994). In other words, it is impossible to identify whether an intervention that uses laptops is better than one that lacks them, because such an intervention uses methods intertwined with the very idea of what laptops can and cannot do; and the same limitations would apply for any no-laptop intervention. Different technologies have different characteristics and are able to create, sustain, and support very different learning designs. As such, one usually finds that studies focused on identifying the best between two interventions, no matter how controlled, show no significant differences or results. Consequently, it is more often than not impossible to determine any quantifiable advantage. It appears that identifying which approach works "best" for learning and whether or not technology "improves performance" are not questions of direct effect but, rather, considerations whose advantages are assessed in terms of availability and efficiency, as well as if they expand what students can do in schools, and allow for more complex content to be learned. Despite the fact that a given instructional method might be the "active ingredient" in effecting learning, current research

approaches place excessive emphasis on results but too little consideration on process and context. Sometimes the real learning is in the process, but can hardly be detected in the outcome. A child may learn a great deal by building a terribly dysfunctional robot. Oftentimes, also, this traditional approach to evaluating the efficiency of technology generates a tautology: what is the best way to learn robotics—with or without a robotics kit?

Consequently, much of the research on technology-in-education occupies itself with what seems to be a theoretically flawed question: does a given technology improve learning performance? This is equivalent to asking if a pencil improves writing performance in the absence of other options—obviously, it does because you cannot write without one. But would pencils in the classroom improve student's memorization skills? It is likely that they would not, because they make memorization less necessary. Thus if memorization is important for our hypothetical pre-pencil society, pencils would be deemed as expensive distractions which do not improve learning.

## 2. Technology and constructivism

Papert was amongst the first to say that technology should be used to teach the "new" stuff rather than repackaging the old for cheaper delivery. Papert's work entered mainstream consciousness in 1980, with the publication of the seminal "Mindstorms: Children, Computers and Powerful Ideas" (Papert, 1980). Over several decades, his students and researchers brought the "new" stuff to millions of children: programming, robotics, multi-agent modeling, cybernetics, system dynamics, and digital fabrication. This work also set the tone for other ways to understand technology in education: learning *from* vs. learning *with* technology (Jonassen & Reeves, 1996), and technological artifacts as objects we think with (Turkle & Papert, 1990) and might not be able to *sense* without (Ihde, 2004).

Returning to the pencil analogy, as extensions of our cognitive process, these technological objects could make traditional knowledge less useful and important—and thus effect a drop in performance when measured by the extant metrics. The availability of a calculator will most likely lead to a reduced facility for mental calculation, but it will also free up time and resources for more sophisticated procedures. Thus progressive educators such as Papert advocate the use of technology in schools not to optimize traditional education, but, rather, as a set of emancipatory tools that would put the most powerful construction materials in the hands of children. These protean technologies would enable students to design, engineer, and construct, and they would cater to a variety of forms of working, expressing, and building. The virtually limitless adaptivity of computational technologies permits the acknowledgement and fostering of different learning styles and epistemologies, engendering a convivial environment in which students can concretize their ideas and projects through intense personal engagement.

But the constructionist promise of technology has yet to penetrate the educational mainstream. For the most part, despite the ubiquity of technology, schools have adopted computers as tools to empower extant curricular subtexts – i.e., as informational devices or as teaching machines.

Nevertheless, just when we were about to give up on the constructionist project, after the gradual removal of Logo from school curricula, there were new developments. The first was the creation of Scratch, the graphical programming language that radically facilitated the learning of programming (Resnick,

Maloney, Monroy-Hernández et al., 2009). The second was the Open Hardware movement, which year after year generated ever newer, more capable, and less expensive devices, such as robotics boards, construction kits, and 3D printers, and started to make possible in a larger scale experiments that educators were doing in their labs and schools (Resnick, Berg, & Eisenberg, 2000; Eisenberg, 2002; Blikstein, 2008; Sipitakiat, 2000; Sipitakiat, Blikstein, & Cavallo, 2004; Millner & Resnick, 2005). Finally, the FabLab/Maker movement began to take shape: first with FabLabs spreading globally; followed by the Maker Faire and the awakening of the do-it-yourself ethos; and, most recently, Maker and Hackerspaces have been popping up everywhere, in schools, libraries, and community centers (Blikstein, 2013). The combination of an easy to learn programming language, low cost hardware, and multiple kinds of new spaces for "making" and building was just the right recipe to rekindle the hearts of progressive educators, constructionists included.

There were also other societal and academic transformations happening: several countries realized that they needed to strengthen their contingent of engineers and scientists to survive in the knowledge economy. In the United States, even government officials started to advocate that getting children excited and motivated about science was an important component of that process. Corporations, hungry for innovation and innovative workers, also started to support and incentivize alternatives to traditional education. Hundreds of ed-tech startup companies were created, producing a myriad of innovative games, robotics kits, and mobile apps. Social entrepreneurs founded non-profit organizations by the hundreds, with the sole goal of offering enrichment programs in robotics, programming, and hands-on science. The need for diversity in STEM fields gained popularity and alternative materials and technologies were developed, such as e-textiles (Buechley & Eisenberg, 2008). Also, theorists have advanced the discussion about the prospects of indigenous (or local) knowledge (Freire, 1974; Ladson-Billings, 1995; Lee, 2003; Moll, Amanti, Neff, & González, 1992), and it became increasingly accepted to value that kind of knowledge instead of the official curriculum as a way to simultaneously tap into students' existing representations and make the content relevant to their lives.

Taken together, these processes generated an unprecedented combination of support and infrastructure towards progressive approaches in education—funding, societal support, low-cost technologies, and the diversification of learning spaces and experiences. Nevertheless, I argue that one crucial element—design—will decide if this opportunity will result in sustainable change in schools. Still, a significant part of these technologies have been designed within the 19th century paradigm that deems impossible to teach advanced science and engineering content for all. Many of them are still not gender neutral, and are culturally-biased. Their design is often geared towards teaching students professional skills rather than augmenting their repertoire of expressive tools. Many schools have 3D printers, but in the absence of appropriated software, children are being exposed to infinitely complex computer aided design software that do not necessarily highlight the powerful ideas in 3D design. The same happens with several robotics and physical computing kits, which force middle-schoolers to learn Java or C even before they can make a light blink (see Figure 1). Instead of exploring the powerful ideas in robotics, they spend hours trying to grasp when to use a semi-colon and what "void" means.

The justification for the provision of such professional languages and devices for use by children was that a mere exposure of students to engineering was thought in itself to be sufficient. Arguably, for engineers and hobbyists, learning a "serious" programming language and the function of resistors and capacitors was crucial to do robotics properly. From this perspective, it is unproblematic to expose children to this level of raw detail and complexity. However, this focus impeded the goal of exposing students to powerful ideas, because much more time had to be spent on the technicalities of making things work or understanding the syntax of C code. Given the time constraints of schools, this factor became much more than a mere logistical factor—it effectively excludes a large number of students from the process. These unnecessary technicalities were exactly what the previous generations of designers attempted to hide from students, because they ended up being considerable barriers for novices. An "undesigned" technology that is hard to learn is a tool for educational elitism and exclusion.

**Arduino C**

```
void setup()    {
   pinMode(ledPin, OUTPUT);
}

void loop()
{
   digitalWrite(ledPin, HIGH);
   delay(1000);
   digitalWrite(ledPin, LOW);
   delay(1000);
}
```

**Cricket Logo**

```
forever [
        a, on
        wait 10
        a, off
        wait 10
    ]
end
```

**Figure 1. A comparison of two programs that make a light blink, in Arduino C (designed for adults and professionals) and Cricket Logo (designed for children).**

Not by coincidence, much of the effort to design appropriate tools have originated within the interaction design for children community. But it is not yet the mainstream voice. It is our role, as designers, researchers, and activists, to break the "Cubberlian" mindset of marginalization and privilege, and show the world that all children can learn and express themselves using technology, given tools that highlight powerful ideas and expressiveness over mere technique and utility.

## 3. References

[1]    Blikstein, P. (2008). Travels in Troy with Freire: Technology as an Agent for Emancipation. In P. Noguera & C. A. Torres (Eds.), *Social Justice Education for Teachers: Paulo Freire and the possible dream* (pp. 205-244). Rotterdam, Netherlands: Sense.

[2]    Blikstein, P. (2013). Digital Fabrication and 'Making' in Education: The Democratization of Invention. In J. Walter-Herrmann & B. C. (Eds.), *FabLabs: of Machines, Makers and Inventors*. Bielefeld: Transcript Publishers.

[3]    Buechley, L., & Eisenberg, M. (2008). The LilyPad Arduino: toward wearable engineering for everyone. IEEE Pervasive Computing, 7(2), 12-15.

[4]    Clark, R.E. (1983). Reconsidering research on learning from media. *Review of Educational Research, 53*(4), 445-459.

[5]    Clark, R.E. (1994). Media will never influence learning. *Educational Technology Research and Development, 42*(2), 21-30.

[6] Cuban, L. (1986). *Teachers and machines: The classroom use of technology since 1920.* New York: Teachers College Press.

[7] Eisenberg, M. (2002). Output Devices, Computation, and the Future of Mathematical Crafts. International Journal of Computers for Mathematical Learning, 7(1), 1-43.

[8] Freire, P. (1974). *Pedagogy of the oppressed.* New York: Seabury Press.

[9] Ihde, D. (2004). A Phenomenology of Technics. In D. M. Kaplan (Ed.), *Readings in the Philosophy of Technology.* New York: Rowman & Littlefield.

[10] Jonassen, D. H., & Reeves, T. C. (1996). Learning with technology: Using computers as cognitive tools. In D. H. Jonassen (Ed.), *Handbook of research for educational communications and technology* (pp. 693-719). New York: Macmillan.

[11] Ladson-Billings, G. (1995). Toward a theory of culturally relevant pedagogy. *American Education Research Journal, 35,* 465 – 491.

[12] Lee, C. D. (2003). Literacy, Technology and Culture. In G. Hatano & X. Lin (Eds.), *Technology, Culture and Education, Special Issue of Mind, Culture and Activity.*

[13] Millner, A., & Resnick, M. (2005). *Tools for Creating Custom Physical Computer Interfaces.* Paper presented at the 4th International Conference for Interaction Design for Children, Boulder, CO.

[14] Moll, L. C., Amanti, C., Neff, D., & González, N. (1992). Funds of knowledge for teaching: Using a qualitative approach to connect homes and classrooms. *Theory into Practice, 31*(2), 132-141.

[15] Papert, S. (1980). *Mindstorms: children, computers, and powerful ideas.* New York: Basic Books.

[16] Resnick, M., Berg, R., & Eisenberg, M. (2000). Beyond black boxes: Bringing transparency and aesthetics back to scientific investigation. Journal of the Learning Sciences, 9(1), 7-30.

[17] Resnick, M., Maloney, J., Monroy-Hernández, A., Rusk, N., Eastmond, E., Brennan, K., . . . Silverman, B. (2009). Scratch: programming for all. *Communications of the ACM, 52*(11), 60-67.

[18] Sipitakiat, A. (2000). *Digital Technology for Conviviality: making the most of learners' energy and imagination.* (MSc. thesis), Massachusetts Institute of Technology, Cambridge.

[19] Sipitakiat, A., Blikstein, P., & Cavallo, D. P. (2004). *GoGo Board: Augmenting Programmable Bricks for Economically Challenged Audiences.* Paper presented at the International Conference of the Learning Sciences, Los Angeles, USA.

[20] Turkle, S., & Papert, S. (1990). Epistemological Pluralism: Styles and Voices within the Computer Culture. *Signs,* 16(1), 128-157.

[21] Tyack, D., & Cuban, L. (1995). *Tinkering towards utopia: a century of public school reform.* Cambridge: Harvard University Press.

# Closing Keynote

# The Relations between Play and Learning in Digital Environments – the Significance of Motives and Demands

Marilyn Fleer
Monash University, Australia

## ABSTRACT

Although a great deal has been written about children's play, less attention has been directed to the relations between play and learning in digital environment (e.g. Falloon, 2013; Kennewell and Morgan, 2006). What we do know is that much of the research into play and learning in the early years has been conceptualized from a maturational point of view (e.g. Roopnarine, 2011) and this view of development appears to also underpin the design process in digital contexts (e.g Giest, 2012; Parette, Quesenberry and Blum, 2010), even though other perspectives are being introduced (e.g. Iversen and Brodesen, 2008). What has dominated the longstanding theories of play has been a theory of development that focuses on predetermined stages or milestones. Central to this conceptualization of development has been the age of the child. That is, age determines what kind of play might be expected or what might develop. In this reading, age determines when and how children play (e.g. object play, solitary play, parallel play, fantasy play, see Pellegrini, 2011 for an overview). Much of this thinking tends to consider play and development as universal, intrinsic to the child, biologically deterministic, and unfolding in predictable ways. But what has been absent from these theories of development is how play and learning are related within digital environments.

It is argued in this presentation that theories of play and development that are conceptualised in relation to milestones are not helpful for understanding how new settings such as digitally interactive environments afford new ways of playing and learning. What we know is that the virtual play of young children appears to invite a new kind of play (e.g. Albin-Clark, Howard and Anderson, 2011; Marsh, 2010; Singer and Singer, 2005), creating new demands upon children, and developing new motives that need to be better understood. What is not known is how digital contexts actually create these demands on children's play and learning in everyday preschool settings and what this affords for children's development. To capture the demands and motives for play and learning in these simultaneously virtual and concrete settings, I draw upon cultural-historical theory as first introduced by Vygotsky.

Vygotsky's (1998) theory conceptualizes development as a dialectical relation between the child and his or her environment, where a change in conditions can lead to a new motive orientation. Here a child's engagement in their concrete and virtual environment is experienced in relation to the child's social situation of development (Bozhovich, 2009). It is argued by

Vygotsky (1994) that the same environment will be experienced differently depending upon the child's social situation of development. This revolutionary view of development does not focus on the age of the child to determine how the child might play in the digital context, but rather it examines the relations between the child and the social and material environment. It is argued that a cultural-historical reading of play (Vygotsky, 1966) and development (Vygotsky, 1998) gives new ways of studying the demands and motives of children as they engage in digital contexts.

This presentation reports on the findings of a study which sought to examine the microgenetic movements within a concrete activity setting of a preschool where an iPad and movie making software program were introduced to the children (n=65). The children were aged between three and four years (n=53; range of 3.3 to 4.4; mean of 3.8 years). The preschoolers were followed over an eight week period where the storytelling of the classical fairytale Goldilocks and the 3 bears featured, alongside of using digital tablets. The telling and re-telling, dramatization and role-playing of the fairytale were introduced to the children, and these experiences supported the children in creating a slowmation (Hoban, 2007) of the fairytale. The children also made porridge, investigated how porridge cooled and was cooked, and set up and investigated a porridge cooling machine to subvert the need for Goldilocks to enter the three bears' house.

The focus of the data gathering was the everyday play and learning practices of the children and the three teachers (degree qualified teacher, a two year trained technically qualified teacher and a volunteer). A total of 232 hours of video observations were generated. Two cameras were positioned to capture the play and learning activities associated with the production of the slowmation, but also the dramatization and cooking experiences which were foundational concrete experiences for supporting the making of the slowmation.

The activity setting as introduced by Hedegaard (2012) is used in the research as an analytical concept to study the perspective of the children in relation to their motives, the demands they meet, and the competencies they bring to the creation of the slowmation. It is through a holistic analysis of a children's participation in the preschool, where a new activity setting was introduced, that we gain insights into how children meet these new demands for successfully making a slowmation.

Hedegaard's (2012) conceptualization of demands and motives were drawn upon for the microgenetic analysis of the nature of the play and learning associated with the use of the digital tablets in the activity setting. It has been argued by Hedegaard (2002) that the goals for education and the teacher's motive for supporting children's learning in a particular activity setting may not match the motives of the children. Play may be the dominating motive for one child and learning may be the motive for another. Therefore how two children in the same activity setting will experience the social and material environment may differ depending upon their leading motive (see Leontiev, 1978).

Through an analysis of the video observations, it was found that how children respond to the digital environment depends upon their motive orientation and this then determines if the activity setting creates new demands for affording learning. Taking the children's perspective has allowed for an analysis of how a child moves between play and learning within the same activity setting. It is argued in this presentation that the introduction of digital tablets create new demands in play based settings affording new possibilities for both play and learning, and the identified microgenetic movements show a new kind of relations between play and learning.

The findings have also shown that even in play based settings which afford dimensions of learning, how children take up learning is dependent upon the child's social situation of development. Children do not take up the learning goals of an activity setting when their leading activity is play. Analysing the new demands created through the introduction of digital tablets in the play-based setting gave the possibilities for understanding this new dimension of learning in play not previously discussed in the literature (Fleer, 2014).

## Categories and Subject Descriptors

A.0 General Literature, GENERAL: Conference proceedings

## Keywords

cultural-historical; young children; design; iPad; slowmation

## Bio

Professor Marilyn Fleer (PhD, MEd, MA, BEd) holds the Foundation Chair of Early Childhood Education and Development at Monash University, Australia, and is the President of the International Society for Cultural Activity Research (ISCAR). Her research interests focus on early years learning and development, with special attention on play, pedagogy, culture, science and technology education. She draws upon cultural-historical theory to inform her research.

## References

[1] Albin-Clark, A., Howard, T.L.J. and Anderson, B. (2011). Real-time computer graphics simulation of blockplay in early childhood, Computers and Education, 57, 2496-2504.

[2] Bozhovich, L. I. (2009). The social situation of child development. Journal of Russian and East European Psychology, 47, 59–86.

[3] Falloon, G. (2013). Young students using iPads: App design and content influences on their learning pathways, Computers and Education, 68, 505-521.

[4] Fleer, M. (2014). The demands and motives afforded through digital play in early childhood activity settings, Learning, Culture and Social Interaction, http://dxdoi.org/10.1016/j.lcsi.2014.02.012

[5] Giest, E.A. (2012). A qualitative examination of tow year-olds interaction with tablet based interactive technology, Journal of Instructional Psychology, 39 (1), 26-35.

[6] Hedegaard, M. (2002). Learning and child development: A cultural-historical study. Aarhus, Denmark: Aarhus University Press.

[7] Hedegaard, M. (2012). Analyzing children's learning and development in everyday settings from a cultural-historical wholeness approach. Mind, Culture, and Activity, 19, 127-138.

[8] Hoban, G. (2007). Using Slowmation for engaging preservice elementary teachers in understanding science content knowledge. Contemporary Issues in Technology and Teacher Education, 7(2), 1-9.

[9] Iversen, O.S. and Brodersen, C. (2008). Building a BRIDGE between children and users: a socio-cultural approach to child-computer interaction, Cognition Technology and Work, 10 (20), 83-93, DOI 10.1007/210111-007-0064-1

[10] Kennewell, S. and Morgan, A. (2006). Factors influencing learning through play in ICT settings, Computers and Education, 46, 265-279.

[11] Leontiev, A.N. (1978). Activity, consciousness, and personality. Englewood Cliffs, N.J.: Prentice-Hall Marsh, J. (2010). Young children's play in online virtual worlds, Journal of Early Childhood Research, 8 (10), 23-39.

[12] Parette, H.P., Quesenberry, A.C. and Blum, C. (2010). Missing the boat with technology usage in early childhood settings: A 21st century view of developmentally appropriate practices, Early Childhood Education Journal, 37: 335-343.

[13] Pellegrini, A. D. (Ed.). (2011). The Oxford Handbook of the development of play. Oxford UK: Oxford University Press.

[14] Roopnarine, J. L. (2011). Cultural variations in belief about play, parent-child play, and children's play: Meaning for childhood development. In A. D. Pellegrini (Ed.), The Oxford Handbook of the development of play (pp. 19-37). Oxford UK: Oxford University Press.

[15] Singer, D.G. and Singer, J.L. (2005). Imagination and play in the electronic age, Cambridge: Harvard University Press.

[16] Smilansky, S. (1968). The effects of sociodramatic pay on disadvantaged preschool children. John Wiley and Sons, Inc New York: US.

[17] Vygotsky, L.S. (1994). The problem of the environment. In J. Valsiner & R. vander Veer (Eds.), The Vygotsky reader (pp. 347-348). Oxford: Blackwell

[18] Vygotsky, L. S. (1966). Play and its role in the mental development of the child. Voprosy psikhologii, 12(6), 62–76.

[19] Vygotsky, L. S. (1998). Child Psychology (M. J. Hall, Trans.). In R. W. Rieber (Ed.), The collected works of L. S. Vygotsky (vol. 5). New York: Kluwer Academic and Plenum Publishers.

# Interpreting Data from Within: Supporting Human-Data Interaction in Museum Exhibits Through Perspective Taking

**Jessica Roberts**
University of Illinois at Chicago
1240 W. Harrison St. Ste 1570
Chicago, IL, USA
jrober31@uic.edu

**Leilah Lyons**
University of Illinois at Chicago/New York Hall of Science
1240 W. Harrison St. Ste. 1570
Chicago, IL, USA
llyons@uic.edu

**Francesco Cafaro**
University of Illinois at Chicago
851 S. Morgan St. M/C 152
Chicago, IL, USA
fcafar2@uic.edu

**Rebecca Eydt**
New York Hall of Science
47-01 111th St., Corona, NY, USA
reydt@nysci.org

## ABSTRACT

As data rather than physical artifacts become more commonly the product of modern scientific endeavor, we must attend to human-data interactions as people reason about and with representations of data increasingly being presented in museum settings. Complex data sets can be impenetrable for novices, so the exhibit presented here was designed to give visitors control over a personalized "slice" of the data set as an entry point for exploration. Personalized control and collaboration can often be at odds in exhibits, however. This paper presents a study of two alternate approaches to designing an embodied interaction control for the exhibit that serves both needs. The results demonstrate that interaction design can affect children's perspective taking as they interact with a Census data map museum display, and that the perspective taken by individuals is correlated with their operation of the interactive exhibit and the kinds of reasoning they employ while investigating data.

## Categories and Subject Descriptors

H.1.2 [**Information Systems**]: User/Machine Systems – *human factors, human information processing*; K.3.1 [**Computers and Education**]: Computer uses in Education – *collaborative learning*

## General Terms

Design, Human Factors

## Keywords

Museum exhibit design, embodied interaction, data interpretation, personalized interaction, actor perspective, GIS.

## 1. INTRODUCTION

Museums can serve many societal purposes: as places of scholarship, as homes of conservation, as places to gather, as sites of public outreach, and as cradles of informal learning. Given the diversity of museums it can be hard to make generalizations about their missions, but science museums, in particular, are often engaged in bringing the general public into contact with emerging

scientific artifacts and practices [47]. Science has been evolving away from a purely material culture to embrace a virtual culture, where the "stuff" of science is no longer limited to vitrines of taxonomically organized artifacts, but can also be large data sets. Concomitantly, scientific practices have grown to include visualizing and interpreting these data sets. If large data sets are the artifacts of modern science, museums need to learn how to exhibit them to a diverse audience.

Data are rarely presented to people, particularly the general public, in raw form; instead they are abstracted into more accessible formats, often visualizations. New ways of visualizing data are constantly emerging, but one of the oldest and still most popular formats is the data map. Spatially referenced data are increasingly presented as maps shared online, in the news, and in textbooks, yet even though these maps have been used to convey information for more than a hundred years, people still have a hard time interpreting them correctly. Now thanks to the proliferation of easily accessible geographic information systems (GIS) tools, many of these maps are made by individuals without in-depth understanding of GIS and data representation, resulting in authoritative-looking maps that grossly distort their underlying data [24]. Since maps touch on so many activities that are relevant to our daily lives, the skills required for data map interpretation should be encouraged in the general population.

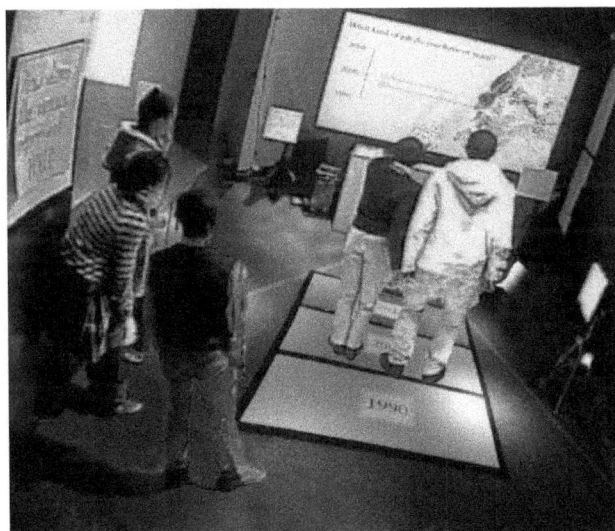

**Figure 1. Museum visitors interacting with CoCensus**

We do not yet know how people, especially children, reason about the data presented in these maps. Particularly, we know very little about how these maps are interpreted collectively in informal environments like museums, where the social aspect of the experience is one of the prime components of the visit for many visitors. Sociocultural perspectives on learning stress the importance of communication for learning, positing that concepts must be articulated in the social space before they can be truly incorporated into an individual's understanding [52]. Museums are thus an ideal setting for the collaborative exploration of ideas. Collaboration is defined by [46] as being "a coordinated, synchronous activity that is the result of a continued attempt to construct and maintain a shared conception of a problem." They constructed their definition in the service of studying in-school problem solving, but many of the component activities – coordination, the construction and maintenance of a shared understanding – are also common to the shared use of museum exhibits. When we describe the collaborative use of an exhibit, then, we refer to activities that involve coordination and which lead to the development of a shared understanding.

The CoCensus project (see Figure 1) described in this paper leverages embodied interaction to allow museum visitors to collaboratively explore the U.S. census on an interactive data map. We hypothesized that we could provide an "entry point" into this large data set by encouraging visitors to identify exclusively with a much smaller subset of the data and that we could in turn help visitors identify with "their" data subset by utilizing the affordances of embodied interaction over a large shared display [44]. Visitors are "reflected" on a map as scaled centroids showing the locations in the region of other people sharing their responses to census questions. The dynamic interface allows visitors to explore the data with the other visitors in the room, not just those with whom they are attending the museum. The emergent discussions that visitors have with one another as they compare and contrast "their own" data sets against the data sets of others in a common interaction space affords a type of collective, collaborative meaning-making that would be highly unlikely to occur with an exhibit that presented similar data via a single-user interface.

In this paper we discuss the interface design strategies we used to encourage visitors to collaboratively and interactively interpret large data sets in a museum. In particular, we will describe how we explored different methods to promote engagement with the data through perspective-taking and to encourage collective reasoning about the data, and the changes in user behaviors these design strategies produced during *in situ* testing at a mid-size science museum. In our discussion of our findings, we present some recommendations for how designers can affect perspective-taking and data reasoning within an interactive experience through embodied interaction design.

## 2. BACKGROUND AND PRIOR WORK

The aim of CoCensus is to support reasoning about census data by providing access to an accessible "slice" of the data that is mapped over the local environment and presented in a collaborative, social setting. It is widely accepted that a goal in museum educational communities is to move visitors from knowledge-based, fact-regurgitation exercises to richer ways of engaging with content like synthesis, interpretive reasoning, and inquiry, e.g. [11, 39, 40, 1]. When dealing with large data sets such as the United States census, the sheer size and complexity can be overwhelming to people not familiar with this type of data. The myriad of ever-changing categories used by the census to count people over time makes for a "high floor" for understanding the data, and it is likely that many museum visitors will be

unwilling to do the work to engage deeply with the data in an informal social setting. Children are especially challenged when confronted with census data, because in addition to the difficulties of decoding a data map in general, they are likely to be unfamiliar with this particular data set, making it even more difficult to bridge the gap between their current knowledge about the world and what the map is depicting. Lack of understanding about the purposes of the census may translate to lack of motivation in exploring its data, thereby making deep reasoning difficult.

## 2.1 Facilitating Personalization and Perspective-Taking

### 2.1.1 Customized Profile Creation

When presenting esoteric topics, museums often try to show visitors a connection between their personal lives or interests and the presented content. To enhance the ability of visitors to personally connect to the data, we allowed them to take a simplified "mock census" survey that we developed as a mobile tablet application (see Figure 2) which would be used to customize the data set they controlled within the exhibition. This customization process involves creating a mini-profile comprised of four categories of data collected by the census: your race or ancestry, the number of people in your household, your housing type (e.g. single family home, apartment building with 50+ units), and the industry in which you work or want to work. These questions were chosen from the available census categories because they are applicable to both children and adults, they connect in some way to identity or lifestyle, and they are relatively self-explanatory. The available options were simplified somewhat from the full array provided by the census, such as by trimming the over 250 reported race and ancestry groups to a moderately more manageable 67 options.

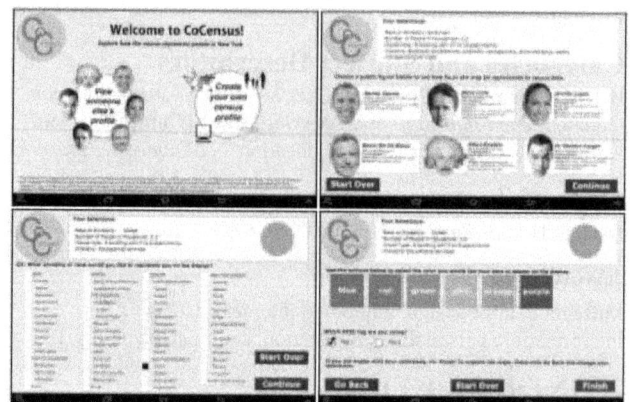

**Figure 2. Screenshots from CoCensus profile selection tablet application. Visitors had the choice of selecting a preconfigured profile or answering four census questions themselves to view personalized data.**

This tablet application for our "mini-census" allowed participants to select not only their own answers to questions but also the color they wished to have represent their data sets on the display. In order to provide a quicker access option to visitors, and to allow visitors to engage with census data without sharing their own information if they wished, we added an additional feature of preconfigured tags of public figures that people could select easily to allow them to proceed more quickly to the interaction. While not fully customized, we reasoned that selecting a favored public figure would still rely on personal preference and thus engender something of a personal connection to that personage's data set. The options initially tested were politicians President Barack

Obama and Mayor Bill de Blasio, scientists Marie Curie and Albert Einstein, celebrity Jennifer Lopez, and fictional character Dr. Sheldon Cooper.

Regardless of whether they chose a preconfigured or custom profile, visitors were allowed to select the color they wished to have represent them on the display. Based on work showing that the personalization of avatars in video gaming led to stronger connection and engagement, e.g. [49], we posited that this small extra personalization would increase children's feeling of connection while relieving them of the extra work of interpreting a key to determine "who is who."

### 2.1.2 Embodiment and Perspective-Taking

Our prior work with adult visitors [47] demonstrated that encouraging visitors to take a personalized perspective on census data increased the depth of their interest in the data maps, and affected the way they went about interpreting the data maps. In particular, establishing a physical connection through motion sensing technologies altered the way visitors positioned their perspective with respect to the data set [47]. Whereas in pilot testing when the embodied interaction components were not in place, visitors spoke of the data exclusively from an *Onlooker* or third-person perspective (e.g. "The Germans are all over the North Side."), once visitors were physically embodying individual data sets, some took on an *Actor* perspective, speaking from the perspective of someone in the map, for example, "I'm along the Lake."

In some cases, visitors used their Actor positioning as a springboard for creating stories about the "characters" they were embodying. This creative playful talk led to deep engagement in the data and helped them move past simple data interpretation to hypothesis generation and inference making. This type of rich engagement is the type of interaction CoCensus is hoping to support. There is some evidence that perspective-taking in general, and a first-person or personalized perspective-taking in particular, may hold special benefit for reasoning about data, as the next section will discuss.

### 2.2 Perspective-Taking and Data Interpretation

One linguistic tactic utilized by expert scientists when interpreting their complex data is to alter the perspective they use when discussing their phenomena. For example, [41] found that expert physicists talking about a graph representing data collected about a particular particle they were studying utilized what they termed a *blended identity* "composed of both the animate physicist and the inanimate entity" in order to interpret findings. Rather than discussing an inanimate entity in the third person, for example by saying, "When it comes down, it is in the domain state" when discussing this particle, [41] noted the lead physicist on the project saying, "When *I* come down, *I'm* in the domain state. (*emphasis added)"* In this utterance, this expert physicist (the principle investigator of the project) uses the personal pronoun "I" to describe what the inanimate object (the particle) is doing – coming down – and its state – the domain state. This type of *indeterminate reference* is found to be common among physicists, "used non-problematically by scientists in their everyday interpretive work." Looking at their data from multiple perspectives – as a physicist examining a particle and as the particle itself – aided the scientists in reasoning about the complex data.

Furthermore, Enyedy et al. note that children investigating physics phenomena in an embodied classroom simulation employed similar linguistic tactics in interpreting their friction models [20]. As they physically embodied a ball undergoing forces in a simulation, students utilized a first-person perspective in order to discuss and make sense of the physical forces at play. This affordance was a deliberate design decision by the researchers because the resulting perspectives "created a qualitatively different set of resources from which to reason and were found to be productive in model and theory building" [20]. Therefore an exhibit that affords this type of perspective-taking where the visitor "becomes" part of the data – hereafter called the *Actor perspective,* as used by [12] – has the potential to facilitate reasoning about data in the museum environment. It also holds the possibility of enhancing collaborative reasoning – taking an actor perspective, especially when one's actor perspective is unique, is very much like the museum experiences that assign roles to visitors, a strategy known to encourage collaborative interactions.

### 2.3 Support for Collaborative Meaning-Making in Museums

Personalization may motivate an individual's interest in an interactive experience, but it can complicate the interaction design when the experience is intended to be shared amongst multiple simultaneous users. There is inherent tension between designing an experience which is particular to each user while still supporting shared use, especially when each user is expected to have some degree of control over the exhibit.

Of course, not all museum exhibit experiences need to be shared [9], but one of the most powerful ways visitors can learn at museums is through meaning-making conversations with their companions [33, 40, 57]. Unfortunately, the designs of many digital "interactives" in a museum promote machine-human interactions while simultaneously limiting the social interactions of visitors [25]. In the early days of computers in museums, this lack of support for collaborative use was understandable – the form factor of kiosks with trackballs and small displays limited how well a digital interactive could include multiple visitors in the experience [17]. As the scope of interactive technologies has widened, there are fewer technical constraints on support for collaborative use, so the continued presence of exhibits that do not support collaborative interactions amongst visitors during exhibit use [25] suggest that the challenges seem to lie in designing for collaborative museum experiences. Here we review some of the design strategies that have been explored for supporting collaborative meaning-making during digital museum experiences.

### 2.3.1 Divide-and-Conquer Strategies

A common approach is to give visitors a shared challenge and parcel it out to participants, as a shared problem is known to provide opportunities for collaborative meaning-making [46]. One such strategy is to engage visitors in role playing with the goal of inducing interdependence among visitors, and which designers often facilitate with mobile devices [13, 32, 35]. A more specific role-play strategy involves engaging some visitors in interaction while others, usually parents, are in supervisory roles [7, 50]. Another approach to engaging visitors in a shared task is to divide the challenge itself up into parallel tasks, in the form of multi-question quizzes [26, 55] or via collaborative games with large shared displays that visitors use to coordinate their actions [29, 18].

All of the strategies described so far have been built around exhibits that have clearly defined goals, but others have addressed the challenge of how to engage visitors in experiences that are more about shared exploration than shared achievement. For example, there are a number of exhibits that allow visitors to explore shared virtual realities, like re-created archaeological ruins [55], or Augmented Reality (AR) visualizations of physical phenomena [56]. Others have employed technologies like AR [53] and laser pointers [37] to let visitors collectively reveal hidden aspects of artifacts. In all of these examples, however, though the interaction is exploratory in nature, the exhibits have been designed to lead groups of learners to specific museum-defined outcomes or discoveries.

### 2.3.2 Parallelization Strategies

Other designers have looked into the problem of how to support collaborative meaning-making while visitors explore their own personal interests, as opposed to pursuing goals defined by the museum. One strategy is to help visitors coordinate the tandem pursuit of their individual interests. With PEACH, visitors used mobiles to configure profiles of their individual interests, so that when a group approaches an exhibit, different members of the group may receive content specialized to their interests [48]. Receiving differential content can encourage visitors to share what they have individually learned with one another. A related strategy is to create privileged channels of audio communication [6, 55] so that visitors can separate and visit different places within a museum while still being able to share their experiences with one another verbally.

### 2.3.3 Aggregation as a Means to Share Control

When visitors attempt to follow their personal interests within a shared interaction space, though, there is always a risk of inducing conflict, as visitors' agendas for what to do with an exhibit may differ. While it can be possible for users interfering with each other to be productive for learning [21], this seems to be true mostly for scenarios where the opportunities for controlling the shared state of the exhibit are distributed amongst participants. Conflict over different personal goals is far less productive when one user "hogs" control of the interactive exhibit [51]: mutually-exclusive controls are a bad idea.

In our exhibit design, CoCensus, while we intend the experience to be exploratory, we are also borrowing the idea of "lightly" inducing interdependence to encourage collaborative meaning-making. True interdependence arises from imposing a shared goal. Since our exhibit is open-ended, we give no fixed "goal" to visitors, but the fact that the presence of each new visitor adds a new data subset to the shared display means that the actions of visitors still impact one another. Their presence and actions change and broaden the nature of the observations, comparisons, and questions that the data visualization can support in what we dub an "aggregational" fashion [36].

## 2.4 Discoverability, Usability, and Design Metaphors for Embodied Interaction in Museums

As mentioned above, we found in our prior work that when we allowed visitors to control data sets with their body movements they seemed to take on a more personalized, Actor perspective [47]. Embodied interactions [19] have been gaining popularity in museums, partly due to the novelty of the interactive technologies that support such interactions, partly because many designs do not require visitors to use devices (e.g., trackballs, light pens, etc.) which may get damaged or lost, but also because of the ability of such controls to promote interactive learning and sociability. By moving the site of interaction away from the virtual space of a screen and into the physical and social space of the exhibit

gallery, designers can exploit the natural performative characteristic of museum visits [38], where visitors are known to watch what one another do in galleries [51].

Developing embodied interaction designs that are easily discoverable is a nontrivial problem, however. As we expanded the set of controls possible with our exhibit, we knew that we would need to address the discoverability challenge. In standard WIMP (Windows Icon Menu Pointer) interfaces, available control activities are discoverable and often distributed in meaningful spatial patterns on the screen. For many embodied interaction experiences, especially whole-body interaction experiences, available control activities are hidden, as they are literally embedded in the body of the user. This means designers run the risk of creating a system which is not highly discoverable. This is a particular problem for a museum context, where visitors need to be able to quickly learn how to use the interface lest they give up and walk away [29]. For this reason, with CoCensus we opted to frame at least some of the control actions in a visible, spatial way: by using the labeling regions of the floor of the exhibit gallery to allow it to serve as a "control surface" of sorts. Other whole-body interaction exhibits have also successfully used the strategy of making the floor part of the interface [50]. Marking the control areas on the floor can help make the interface more discoverable, but may not be enough to make it usable. To help us tackle the usability challenge, we turned to a design principle from Human-Computer Interaction literature: consistency.

### 2.4.1 Designing Embodied Interfaces with Consistency

One commonly accepted design principle for making interfaces more usable is known as "Consistency" [42]. The idea is to make it easier for a learner to figure out what control actions he or she might initiate by making a new interface consistent with existing user expectations. These user expectations may be developed by interacting with other parts of the interface (internal consistency), or by interacting with prior interfaces (external consistency), or via users' interactions with analogically similar situations (metaphorical consistency). Internal consistency is most useful for rich interfaces with many related control activities – since most museum exhibits have relatively limited control sets, we deemed it not very applicable.

### 2.4.2 Metaphorical Consistency and Embodied Metaphors

Metaphorical consistency succeeds when users are easily able to detect the underlying analogical metaphor. An alternative approach for embodied interaction design that many embodied interaction designers have begun relying on is a special version of metaphorical consistency called embodied metaphors [8, 3, 4, 5, 27]. The core theory underlying embodied metaphors is that humans develop strong kinesthetic metaphors via their early childhood, constructivist explorations of the physical world [30]. For example, people often conflate physical concepts like "balance" with more abstract concepts like "justice." In our case, one of the control design challenges we faced was how to allow visitors to change the year of the Census data they were viewing. We were particularly interested to see if the embodied metaphors people bring to their conceptions of time could be used to design an embodied control of the time of the data sets being viewed.

People often refer to events in time using reasoning patterns that commonly apply to space: space and time share "enough relational structure" to allow spatial "schemata" [28] to be used in alternative to temporal schemata [10]. As described in [22], there are two common metaphorical mappings between space and time in English: (1) the "ego-moving" metaphor, in which a person (the "observer") progresses along a time-line towards his/her future, where the future is ahead; (2) the "time moving" metaphor, in which time is seen as a conveyor belt on which events are moving from the future to the past. People use ordered words such as "front" and "back" (rather than symmetric terms such as "right" or "left"), when spatial terms are used in the domain of time [22]. We know that these metaphors can be influential because people who are primed with different space to time metaphors exhibit different reasoning patterns [22]. For instance, in the study presented in [10], participants who were primed with the "ego-moving" metaphor thought that a meeting scheduled on Monday was actually on Friday, while those primed with the "time moving" metaphor exhibited the opposite bias [10]. It is worth noting that the metaphor chosen should be kept constant: as illustrated in [22], moving from one metaphorical system to the other slows down people in fulfilling their task.

We designed a time control strategy using this "ego moving" embodied metaphor for time (hereafter called the Vertical (V) strategy). Visitors move forward in the exhibition gallery towards the display to move the date of their data set forward in time, and step backwards to move the date of their data set backwards (see Figure 3, left). We hypothesized that the design of the interaction space may strongly influence not only the usability of the embodied exhibit, but also further enhance users' personal identification with "their" data sets. By using an ego-moving metaphor, we suspected that visitors would come to personally identify with their data sets more strongly. Egocentric perspective-taking is a concept also successfully used in an exhibit on orbital mechanics [34], and we thought it might be helpful for reasoning about data. This design does offer risks, however: foremost that visitors still might not find it usable (owing to their lack of prior experience with a similar interface designs). The other risk is that by allowing each visitor to control the time of his or her data separately, visitors might engage in meaningless data interpretation (e.g., attempting to compare the distribution of Finance jobs in 2010 to the distribution of Service jobs in 1990). For this reason, we also explored a time control strategy using a different approach based on external consistency.

**Figure 3. The two CoCensus configurations. Left: Vertical (V); Right: Horizontal (H)**

### 2.4.3 Embodied Interfaces and External Consistency
External consistency has been a very successful design strategy for WIMP interfaces, since users usually have had so many prior experiences with WIMP interfaces. Unlike WIMP interfaces, however, there are far fewer accepted schemas for mapping user movements into system controls [54], so designers might need to look to other familiar, but non-embodied, interfaces for exemplars. We reasoned that most users would be very familiar

with the concept of a horizontal timeline – with years marked as "ticks," moving from older years to the left to newer years towards the right of the scale. The timeline is itself a metaphor, but it is such a common interface element, using it fulfills both the principles of external and metaphorical consistency. We implemented this control scheme by literally marking out a timeline horizontally (parallel to the display) on the exhibit floor, and echoing it in the visualization display (see Figure 3, right). We intentionally designed the system to be mutually exclusive (only one user can set the decade on display at a time), so it would be more in keeping with existing timeline controls (external consistency), and to prevent users from making nonsensical cross-decade comparisons (e.g. comparing two different data sets at two different points in time). We felt confident that users would find this control scheme (hereafter called the Horizontal (H) configuration) usable, but given the known issues with mutually-exclusive controls potentially leading to non-productive interactions at exhibits, we thought it would pose an interesting contrast to compare against the V configuration.

## 3. INVESTIGATION AND METHODS
The two layout configurations discussed here were tested over two days in mid December 2013 *in situ* at a mid-sized urban science museum. Participants were recruited off the museum floor by members of the research team and asked to test out a new display showing census data. Due to the nature of the display, recruitment was limited to visitors who appeared to be age ten or older, and due to the social nature of the exhibit, visitors were recruited in groups of two or more. Each visitor used a tablet running the survey application (Figure 2) to complete the "mini-profile" configuration, asking questions of the researcher as necessary. Upon completion of the configuration, the visitors' responses were sent to the display's server via PHP in order to allow the display to show personalized information. Visitors were then given a lanyard to wear around their necks which held both an RFID card to associate them with the data [15] and a clip microphone for audio recording and were sent into the interaction space in a room separated from the main museum floor by a partial wall.

Researchers stayed outside the room to allow naturalistic interactions. In some cases participants called the researchers in to address a particular problem (such as the wrong information being displayed if the system had failed to reset for a new user) or general confusion about how the system worked. In those instances the researcher answered questions and offered explanations to the satisfaction of the participants and then left the room. The exception is that one member of the research team stayed in the room but out of sight of the participants in order to implement the changing of the question (ancestry, household size, etc.) being displayed. Participants were told to clap twice to change the data set, but as the automated control was not yet implemented, we utilized a "Wizard of Oz" approach for this feature.

Participants were allowed to interact with the system as long as they wanted, and upon leaving were asked to complete a one-page survey to gauge their perceptions of control and enjoyment of the display, comprised of 5-point Lickert scales and open-ended comment sections. Visitors typically explored the exhibit for 2-3 minutes, which is typical for interactive science museum exhibits [16]. Interactions were recorded using five video cameras and a microphone mounted in the space.

## 3.1 Sessions and Participants

Recordings were split into sessions, with the beginning of a session marked by the entrance of the first visitor into the interaction space and the end when the final overlapping visitor exited the space or removed his RFID tag. Over the course of two days, 35 sessions were recorded. Sessions in which visitors entered the space without RFID tags and sessions consisting of only one user were discarded from this analysis, as were those comprised of adult visitors, museum staff, and sessions in which one of the researchers answered more than trivial questions and ended up playing a major role in interpretation for the visitors. Fifteen sessions were transcribed and analyzed, though one session was later discarded from the analysis because it consisted of five users in multiple overlapping groups and could not be considered comparable with the other cases. The remaining fourteen sessions ranged in duration from 33 seconds to over 5 minutes, with an average duration of 2.51 minutes. Each session consisted of a pair of users for a total of 28 participants. Six of the sessions (12 participants) interacted with the V condition and eight sessions (16 participants) used the H condition. Each pair in this analysis consisted of two student classmates recruited from school groups ranging in age from 10 to 14 years old. Because the paired students were classmates, they were similar to each other in age and knew each other prior to the interaction.

## 3.2 Transcriptions and Coding

Fifteen sessions were transcribed for speech using Inqscribe and for interactivity using NVivo and Inqscribe. Videos were coded for interaction by recording instances of clapping (the means of switching between census categories) and timeline control (when visitors stepped into the control regions marked on the floor). Verbal transcripts were coded for perspective-taking and data interpretation.

Perspective codes marked instances of visitors making statements about the data from either an Onlooker perspective in which data were referred to in the third person, for example, "There are so many Puerto Ricans," or from an Actor perspective in which visitors used first-person pronouns to describe the data, such as, "We are totally not even a minority. We're like less than that."

Interpretation coding was meant to elucidate the reasoning children were doing about the data. While there are a number of ways of componentizing reasoning about spatialized data, (e.g. [23, 24, 31], in analyzing visitors' reasoning around our display, we drew upon work analyzing students' reasoning about GIS census maps in classrooms [43], as it was a close analogue to the types of reasoning found in our exhibit. An initial round of coding looked for eight unique codes related to data interpretation.

After reviewing the resultant coding, researchers refined the scope to a set of three codes that most clearly articulated the types of interpretive acts in which children were engaging in the space:

- Comparison across **Time** (periodicity, growth, development, change): Remarks that indicate an acknowledgement of difference (or lack of difference) between one decade and another. Marked by words like "now," "back then," "still," "used to," "before." Not including statements about control such as "I'm stepping in 1990" or "Go to 2010."
- Comparison between **Datasets**: Remarks discussing similarities or differences between two data sets, such as the number of single family homes compared to apartments. Can include comparisons of their quantities (e.g. "I slaughter you") or distributions ("You're by the lake and I'm not")

- **Spatial** Characterization or Comparison: Remarks related to location (e.g. Manhattan or the west side), distance ("far apart," "all grouped together"), distribution ("spread out" "all in Manhattan"), can be relative to location of other data set ("I'm here and you're there")

Findings related to the interplay among perspective-taking, interaction, and data interpretation are discussed below.

## 4. FINDINGS

Analysis of the visitors' sessions focuses on the relationships between the three types of codes: interaction, perspective, and data interpretation. In each case, the analysis relies on frequencies, not counts, of codes to account for the varying length of sessions. Here we will discuss in detail our three key findings: 1) The perspective taken by visitors is correlated with the data interpretation remarks visitors made during the interaction, with the Actor perspective strongly correlated with a higher incidence of both temporal reasoning and comparisons between data sets; 2) The configuration of the space and the distribution of control directly impacted the perspective taken by visitors in using the display; 3) The Actor perspective is significantly correlated with timeline use, while the Onlooker perspective is not correlated with either use of the timeline or clapping to change the data set.

## 4.1 Role of Perspective in Data Interpretation

Of key interest to this analysis was whether the perspectives taken by each visitor correlated with the frequencies of data interpretation statements made by that participant during the interaction. A Pearson product-moment correlation coefficient was computed to assess the relationship between frequency of perspective taking (Actor or Onlooker) and data interpretation statements (Time, Dataset, and Spatial reasoning). As expected, there was a positive correlation between taking an Actor perspective and the overall frequency of data interpretation statements ($r = 0.822$, $n = 28$, $p < 0.000$). Interestingly, Onlooker perspective was also significantly correlated, although to a lesser degree, with data interpretation overall ($r = 0.433$, $n = 28$, $p < 0.021$). See Table 1 for complete correlation statistics.

**Table 1. Pearson's Correlation for Perspective-taking and Data Interpretation Statements, all cases (N = 28 individuals)**

|  | Actor Perspective | Onlooker Perspective |
|---|---|---|
| **Total Data Interpretation** | 0.828** | 0.433* |
| Time Comparison | 0.705** | 0.048 |
| Dataset Comparison | 0.837** | 0.474* |
| Spatial Characterization | -0.143 | 0.463* |
| ** Correlation is significant at the 0.01 level (2-tailed). | | |
| * Correlation is significant at the 0.05 level (2-tailed). | | |

Looking more deeply, we find that the Actor Perspective is highly correlated with dataset comparison, ($r = 0.837$, $n = 28$, $p < 0.000$) nearly twice as much as the Onlooker perspective, ($r = 0.474$, $n = 28$, $p < 0.011$), which is what we would expect given that we were intentionally asking visitors to personalize their datasets so that they might identify more strongly and thus engage more deeply with "their" datasets. The Actor perspective is also strongly correlated with comparisons across time ($r = 0.705$, $n = 28$, $p < 0.000$), while there is no correlation between an Onlooker perspective and time comparison, an interesting contrast that will be returned to in the next section. There is no correlation with an Actor perspective and spatial reasoning, even though there is a correlation between the Onlooker perspective and spatial reasoning, ($r = 0.463$, $n = 28$, $p = 0.013$), which is again what we would expect, since the types of remarks we coded for spatial properties required the visitors to "take a step back" and be sensitive to the entirety of the data represented on the map, and not just a personalized portion of the data. It is important to note, however, that only three instances of spatial characterizations were coded throughout the sessions. This suggests that though spatial characterizations were occasionally made, they were too infrequently used to be able to draw deep conclusions from this data set. It also suggests that the current design of the display does not adequately afford the types of spatial characterizations we would hope to elicit, an issue that is being addressed by ongoing design work. Still, these results show that perspective-taking and data reasoning are clearly tightly linked, and that the *type* of perspective-taking is linked to different types of data interpretation.

## 4.2 Role of Control Configuration in Data Interpretation and Positioning

This study compared children's perspective taking and interpreting data in two conditions: the Vertical (V) condition in which each user was able to individually manipulate the data year for his personally embodied data set by moving front to back, and the Horizontal (H) condition in which a single user controlled the timeline for all users in the space by moving side to side on a timeline. This section discusses impacts of the two configurations on both data reasoning and perspectives.

### 4.2.1 Configuration and Data Interpretation

The 16 sessions utilizing the H configuration contained a total of 20 statements coded as data interpretation, compared to 36 data interpretation statements coded in the 12 V sessions. This contrast is especially striking when considering that the H sessions were overall longer than the V sessions, with the mean duration of H sessions at 2.90 minutes, compared to 2.12 minutes average for the V configuration sessions. Frequencies of data reasoning statements by condition are illustrated in Figure 4. These differences were significant for overall data interpretation $t(26)=2.33$, $p<0.03$, as well as time comparison $t(26)=2.00$, $p < 0.04$, and dataset comparison $t(26)=2.00$, $p < 0.03$.

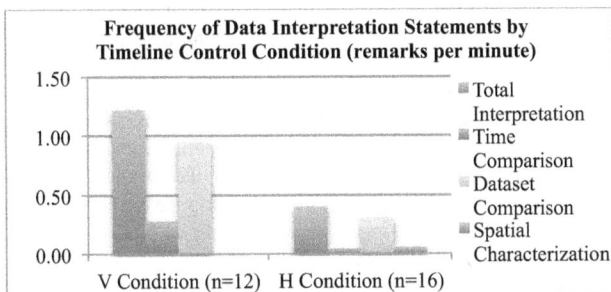

**Figure 4. Participants in the vertical (V) condition had higher frequencies of time comparison and dataset comparison statements compared to the horizontal (H) condition.**

### 4.2.2 Configuration and perspective-taking

Multiple independent-samples t-tests were conducted to compare frequencies of each perspective (Actor and Onlooker) in the two conditions (V and H). The frequencies of each are shown in Figure 5.

Participants used the Actor perspective significantly more in the V condition ($M = 1.1$, $SD = 1.3$) than the H condition ($M = 0.2$, $SD = 0.4$), $t(26) = 3.22$, $p = 0.00$. There was no significant difference in the frequency of the Onlooker perspective between the V ($M =$

0.4, $SD = 0.7$) and H ($M = 0.2$, $SD = 0.4$) conditions, $t(26) = 1.00$, $p = 0.35$.

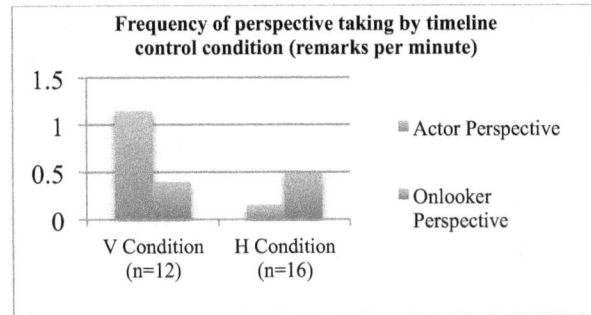

**Figure 5. The Vertical condition elicited significantly higher frequencies of actor positioning than the Horizontal setup.**

## 4.3 Relationship between Perspective and Control Actions

While the Actor perspective has been shown to enhance reasoning about the data set, as the exhibit is designed to be interactive it is crucial to understand the relationship between visitors' perspectives and their interactions with the display. Table 2 shows the correlations between visitors' perspectives and their control actions.

Given the significantly higher frequency of Actor perspective-taking in the V condition (see Section 4.2.2), and the significant correlation between the V condition and overall data interpretation frequency (see Section 4.2.1), one might wonder if the significant correlation seen here between the Actor perspective and total control actions is due to visitors in the V condition. In fact, for the V condition Actor perspective-taking is not significantly correlated with interacting with the exhibit overall, which seems surprising until one digs more deeply. The Actor perspective *is* correlated with time change actions in the V condition ($n=12$, $r=.767$, $p < 0.004$), while there is, if anything, a negative (although non-significant) correlation with data change interaction events. This suggests that visitors who make use of the timeline also take on the Actor perspective, while those who change the data set are less likely to have an Actor perspective, which is exactly the effect our design intended to produce. There is no correlation with the Onlooker perspective and any interaction activity, suggesting that there is no relationship between engaging in exhibit control actions and taking an Onlooker perspective on the data, which is what we would expect in an exhibit that is attempting to personalize data exploration via interaction design.

**Table 2. Pearson's correlations between control actions and perspective-taking, for all cases (N = 28 individuals)**

| | Total Actions | Data Change Actions | Time Change Actions |
|---|---|---|---|
| Actor Perspective | .489** | 0.044 | .637** |
| Onlooker Perspective | -0.093 | 0.041 | -0.16 |
| ** Correlation is significant at the 0.01 level (2-tailed). | | | |

## 5. DISCUSSION

Based on prior work we expected that locating control of the display within the body of the user would elicit the Actor perspective in visitors [45], and that this perspective could potentially facilitate reasoning about the data, as it has been shown to do for expert physicists [41] and students [20]. We found that children interacting with CoCensus engaged in two primary kinds of reasoning about the census data: comparisons over time and comparisons across data sets. Analysis of the dialogue between children while interacting demonstrated a strong correlation between instances of those reasoning utterances and the Actor perspective.

These findings underscore the value of utilizing personalization and embodiment to give children an access point to understand an otherwise complex and overwhelming data set.

## 5.1 A Tight Tie between User and Locus of Interaction Elicits Actor Perspective

The richness of the learning experience offered by embodied interaction exhibits is directly affected by how much control visitors have over the interaction, and the transparency of that control [2]. However, controlling the exhibit with gestures and body movements, rather than with traditional input devices (such as a keyboard or mouse) can be a challenge. As illustrated in [14], part of the problem lies in the separation between the locus of the interaction (the user's body) and the focus of the interaction (the screen). In traditional WIMP (Windows, Icon, Mouse, Pointer) interfaces, user's interaction was framed by the input device and the interface. Mouse movements, for instance, are generally mapped to cursor movements on the screen. Users can typically rely on prior experiences with the same software (internal consistency) or with other software (external consistency) or on analogies (metaphorical consistency) to help them figure out what control actions are possible and the effects of those actions.

With the horizontal timeline (H), which relied mostly on external consistency, the user was the "input device": like a mouse, she/he had to select the year that she/he wanted to explore. The user's body was used as a mouse cursor, to select a decade on a timeline on the floor; and the floor was the locus of that interaction. Similarly, with the vertical timeline (V), which relied more strongly on metaphorical consistency, the user her/himself was the input device; however, the locus of interaction was no longer on the floor: it was the user's body itself. Children no longer selected a decade by stepping on a specific, button-like spot on the floor, but instead did so by moving their body through space (under V, the floor markings function more like guidelines than controls). Visitors needed to embody a timeline, and to directly control the focus of the interaction (i.e. the data on the screen) by walking back and forth within the interaction space (i.e. "forward" and "backward" in time). Visitors easily adopted this mode of interaction. By choosing an embodied metaphor to establish metaphorical consistency, we also served to reinforce the users' sense of "self" within the interactive space, which seemed to result in the marked increase in Actor perspective-taking.

## 5.2 The Value of Multiple Perspectives

Though some of the data interpretation we hope to support with this exhibit is strengthened by the Actor perspective, this work also demonstrates that adopting an Onlooker perspective is associated with other types of desirable reasoning, like spatial reasoning. The very few instances of spatial characterizations, for example, were all correlated only with Onlooker perspective-taking. These findings strengthen the need to support multiple perspectives, even by a single user. In this study, 18 of the 28 participants took on at least one perspective during the interaction, and six participants utilized both perspectives during their interactions. It is worth noting that the 10 participants who took on neither an Actor nor an Onlooker perspective also contributed no remarks coded under any of the data interpretation categories. Given the benefits of these perspectives, especially the Actor perspective, demonstrated here, design considerations moving forward should seek to further support this perspective-taking, as well as to explore other types of perspective-taking.

## 6. CONCLUSIONS AND FUTURE WORK

It was expected based on prior work that supporting visitors in taking an Actor perspective as they engaged with the display would support their reasoning about the data presented in the exhibit. The extent of this correlation, and the dramatic differences between the two design approaches in inducing this perspective, however, were unexpected. This strongly suggests that embodied interface design can play a large role in helping shift the way learners might interpret an interactive experience.

Visitors were able to easily make use of the vertical timeline (V) to explore the data representations. This interaction design seemed to encourage visitors to take on an Actor perspective much more strongly, which in turn affected the ways they reasoned about the data. We suspect that the tight tie between the User and the Locus of Interaction in V, and the alignment of this embodied metaphor with the visitors' data set personalization, may have been the reason for the children's increased use of the Actor perspective. It may also explain the lack of difficulty visitors had with using the timeline control in V, despite the design not echoing existing designs as H did (external consistency). Reflecting on this, it seems part of reason may be related to the design principle we initially deemed irrelevant: internal consistency. Although encountering the embodied timeline control is hardly like encountering a new tool in the Adobe Photoshop tool palette (a common example of internal consistency), it was much more in keeping with the personalization theme the rest of the exhibit was encouraging (e.g., via data set customization). The lesson for embodied interaction design is twofold: (1) designers should consider the internal consistency of their embodied interaction designs even if the set of possible actions is quite small, and (2) that internal consistency need not just reside in the embodied interaction modality – it can and should span other aspects of the interface design as well.

Future work seeking to facilitate reasoning about data should seek to provide opportunities for users to adopt multiple perspectives. For example, were we to engage visitors with data without data set customization, e.g., by asking them to control different aspects of the visualization style (like the scaling or colorization of data representations), combined with other interaction metaphors, one might see better success at inducing an Onlooker perspective. The value of multiple perspectives for encouraging learners to tap into different types of reasoning also needs to be explored, as some have also begun to do for other problem spaces. For example, [34] is using perspective-taking to encourage an understanding of orbital mechanics, and [20] is exploring its use in physics education. Both of these learning environments provide interactive simulacra of real phenomena, however. We suspect that because data visualizations are themselves abstract representations, there are even wider opportunities for taking advantage of embodied metaphors, since the expectations for the control actions to conform to the "physics" of a simulated world do not apply in the same way.

## 7. ACKNOWLEDGMENTS

This material is based upon work supported by the National Science Foundation under NSF INSPIRE 1248052.

# 8. REFERENCES

[1] Allen, S. 2002. Looking for learning in visitor talk: A methodological exploration. *Learning conversations in museums*, 259-303.

[2] Allen, S. 2004. Designs for learning: Studying science museum exhibits that do more than entertain. *Science Education 88*, S1, 2004, S17-S33.

[3] Antle, A.N., Droumeva, M., and Corness, G. 2008. Playing with The Sound Maker: Do Embodied Metaphors Help Children Learn? *Proceedings of the 7th int'l conference on Interaction Design & Children IDC 08*, 178–185.

[4] Antle, A.N., Corness, G., Bakker, S., Droumeva, M., Van Den Hoven, E., and Bevans, A. 2009. Designing to support reasoned imagination through embodied metaphor. *Proceeding of the seventh ACM conference on Creativity and cognition CC 09*, 275.

[5] Antle, A.N., Corness, G., and Bevans, A. 2011. Springboard: Designing image schema based embodied interaction for an abstract domain. *Human-Computer Interaction Series*: *Whole Body Interaction*, Springer, 7-18.

[6] Aoki, P. M., Grinter, R. E., Hurst, A., Szymanski, M. H., Thornton, J. D., & Woodruff, A. 2002. Sotto voce: exploring the interplay of conversation and mobile audio spaces. In *Proc of the SIGCHI Conf on Human Factors in Computing Systems*. CHI '02. ACM, New York, NY, 431-438.

[7] Asai, K., Sugimoto, Y., and Billinghurst, M. 2010. Exhibition of lunar surface navigation system facilitating collaboration between children and parents in science museum. In *Proceedings of the 9th ACM SIGGRAPH Conference on Virtual-Reality Continuum and its Applications in Industry*, ACM, New York, NY, 119-124.

[8] Bakker, S., Antle, A. N., & Van Den Hoven, E. 2012. Embodied metaphors in tangible interaction design. *Personal Ubiquitous Comput., 16*, 4, 433–449.

[9] Ballantyne, R., & Packer, J. 2005. Solitary vs. Shared: Exploring the Social Dimension of Museum Learning. *Curator, 48*, 2, 177-192.

[10] Boroditsky, L. 2000. Metaphoric structuring: understanding time through spatial metaphors. *Cognition, 75*, 1, 1–28.

[11] Borun, M., Chambers, M., & Cleghorn, A. 1996. Families are learning in science museums. *Curator, 39*(2), 262-270.

[12] Brunyé, T. T., Ditman, T., Mahoney, C. R., Augustyn, J. S., & Taylor, H. A. 2009. When you and I share perspectives pronouns modulate perspective taking during narrative comprehension. *Psychological Science, 20*(1), 27-32.

[13] Cabrera, J. S., Frutos, H. M., Stoica, A. G., Avouris, N., Dimitriadis, Y., Fiotakis, G., et al. 2005. Mystery in the museum: collaborative learning activities using handheld devices. In the *Proceedings of the 7th international conference on Human computer interaction with mobile devices & services*. ACM, New York, NY.

[14] Cafaro, F., Lyons, L., Kang, R., Radinsky, J., Roberts, J., and Vogt, K. 2013. Framed Guessability: Using Embodied Allegories to Increase User Agreement on Gesture Sets. *Procs of the 8th Int'l Conference on Tangible, Embedded and Embodied Interaction*, ACM, 197–204.

[15] Cafaro, F., Panella, A., Lyons, L., Roberts, J., and Radinsky, J. 2013. I see you there!: developing identity-preserving embodied interaction for museum exhibits. *Proceedings of the 2013 ACM annual conference on Human factors in computing systems*, ACM, 1911–1920.

[16] Carlisle, R. W. 1985. What Do School Children Do at a Science Center? *Curator, 28*(1).

[17] Diamond, J., Bond, A., Schenker, B., Meier, D., & Twersky, D. 1995. Collaborative multimedia. *Curator 38*, 3, 137-149.

[18] Dini, R., Paternò, F., & Santoro, C. 2007. An environment to support multi-user interaction and cooperation for improving museum visits through games. In the *Proceedings of the 9th international conference on Human computer interaction with mobile devices and services*. ACM, New York, NY.

[19] Dourish, P. 2001. *Where the action is: the foundations of embodied interaction*. Cambridge, MA, USA: MIT Press.

[20] Enyedy, N., Danish, J. A., DeLiema, D. 2013. Constructing and Deconstructing Materially-Anchored Conceptual Blends in an Augmented Reality Collaborative Learning Environment (full paper). In S. Puntambekar, N. Rummel, M. Kapur M. Nathan (Eds.), Proceedings of the 10th International Conference on Computer Supported Collaborative Learning. Madison, WI.

[21] Falcão, T. P., & Price, S. 2009. What have you done! The role of 'interference' in tangible environments for supporting collaborative learning. In Proceedings of the *Conference on Computer Supported Collaborative Learning*. CSCL'09. ISLS, 324-334.

[22] Gentner, D., Imai, M., & Boroditsky, L. 2002. As time goes by: Evidence for two systems in processing space → time metaphors. *Language and Cognitive Processes*, 17, 5, 537-565.

[23] Golledge, R. G. 1995. Primitives of Spatial Knowledge. In Nyerges T. L., D. M. Mark, R. Laurini, & M. J. Egenhofer (Eds.), *Cognitive Aspects of Human-Computer Interaction for Geographic Information Systems* (pp. 29-44), Dordrecht: Kluwer Academic Publishers.

[24] Goodchild, M. F., & Janelle, D. G. 2010. Toward critical spatial thinking in the social sciences and humanities. *GeoJournal*, 75(1), 3-13.

[25] Heath, C., & Vom Lehn, D. 2008. Configuring 'Interactivity' Enhancing Engagement in Science Centres and Museums. *Social Studies of Science*, 38(1), 63-91.

[26] Hope, T., Nakamura, Y., Takahashi, T., Nobayashi, A., Fukuoka, S., Hamasaki, M., et al. 2009. Familial collaborations in a museum. In the *Proceedings of the SIGCHI Conference on Human Factors in Computing Systems*. CHI '09. ACM, New York, NY.

[27] Hurtienne, J. and Israel, J.H. 2007. Image schemas and their metaphorical extensions. *Tangible and Embedded Interaction*, ACM Press 127.

[28] Janelle, D.G. and Goodchild, M.F. 2011. Concepts, Principles, Toolse, and Challenges in Spatially Integrated Social Science. In Nyerges, T.L., H Couclelis, and R. McMaster (Eds.) The Sage Handbook of GIS & Society. Sage Publications. pp 27-45

[29] Jimenez, P. and Lyons, L. 2011. An Exploratory Study of Input Modalities for Mobile Devices Used with Museum Exhibits. In *Proceedings of the 29th international conference*

*on Human factors in computing systems*. CHI '11. ACM, New York, NY, 895-904.

[30] Johnson, M. 1987. *The Body in the Mind. The body in the mind*. The University of Chicago Press.

[31] Kaufman, M. M. 2004. Using Spatial-Temporal Primitives to Improve Geographic Skills for Preservice Teachers. *Journal of Geography,* 103(4), 171-181

[32] Klopfer, E., Perry, J., Squire, K., & Jan, M. 2005. Mystery at the Museum – A Collaborative Game for Museum Education. In the *Proceedings of the Conference on Computer Supported Collaborative Learning*. CSCL '05. ISLS, 316-320.

[33] Leinhardt, G., Crowley, K., & Knutson, K. (Eds.). 2002. *Learning Conversations in Museums*. Mahwah, New Jersey: Lawrence Erlbaum.

[34] Lindgren, Robb. 2012. Generating a learning stance through perspective-taking in a virtual environment. *Comput. Hum. Behav.* 28, 4 (July 2012), 1130-1139.

[35] Lyons, L. 2009. Designing Opportunistic User Interfaces to Support a Collaborative Museum Exhibit. In Proceedings of the *Conference on Computer Supported Collaborative Learning*. CSCL '09. ISLS, 375-384.

[36] Lyons, L., Cafaro, F., Radinsky, J., Roberts, J., Vogt, K. (2014). Aggregating Agency to Support Collaborative Learning in a Museum Exhibit at Chicago. Paper presented at *American Education Research Association (AERA '14)*. Philadelphia, PA, USA.

[37] Macedonia, M. 2003. Revitalizing museums with digital technology. *Computer 36*(2), 94-96.

[38] Meisner, R., Lehn, D.V., Heath, C., Burch, A., Gammon, B., and Reisman, M. 2007. Exhibiting Performance: Co-participation in science centres and museums. *International Journal of Science Education, 29*, 12, 1531 - 1555.

[39] National Research Council. 2007. Taking science to school: Learning and teaching science in *grades K-8*. Committee on science learning, kindergarten through eighth grade. R. A. Duschl, H. A. Schweingruber, & A. W. Shouse (Eds.). Board on Science Education, Center for Education. Division of Behavioral and Social Sciences and Education. Washington, D.C.: The National Academies Press.

[40] National Research Council. 2009. *Learning Science in Informal Environments: People, Places, and Pursuits*. The National Academies Press, Washington, DC.

[41] Ochs, E., Gonzales, P., & Jacoby, S. 1996. "When I come down I'm in the domain state": grammar and graphic representation in the interpretive activity of physicists. *Studies in Interactional Sociolinguistics, 13*, 328-369.

[42] Olson, D.R. 2010. *Building Interactive Systems: Principles for Human Computer Interaction (1st Ed.)*. Florence, KY: Cengage Learning.

[43] Radinsky, J., Melendez, J., Roberts, J. 2012. Do the Data Strike Back? Students' Presentations of Historical Narratives about Latino Communities using GIS. In Josh Radinsky (Chair), Tools for Constructing Historical Narratives: Teaching African American and Latino Histories With GIS Census Maps. Symposium conducted at the meeting of the American Educational Research Association, Vancouver, B.C., Canada.

[44] Roberts, J., Lyons, L., Radinsky, J., Cafaro, F. 2012. Proceedings from ICLS 2012. *Connecting Visitors to Exhibits through Design: Exploring United States census data with CoCensus*. Sydney, Australia.

[45] Roberts, J., Cafaro, C., Kang, R., Vogt, K., Lyons, L., & Radinsky, J. 2013. That's Me and That's You: Museum visitors' perspective-taking around an embodied interaction data map display. In *Proceedings of the 10$^{th}$ International Conference on Computer-Supported Collaborative Learning*. Madison, WI, USA. 343-344.

[46] Roschelle, J., & Teasley, S. 1995. The construction of shared knowledge in collaborative problem solving. In C. O'Malley (Ed.), *Computer-Supported Collaborative Learning* (pp. 69-197). Berlin: Springer-Verlag.

[47] Semper, R. 2008. Science museums as environments for learning. *Physics Today* 43, 11 (Jan. 2008), 50–56.

[48] Stock, O., Zancanaro, M., Busetta, P., Callaway, C., Kruger, A., Kruppa, M., et al. 2007. Adaptive, intelligent presentation of information for the museum visitor in PEACH. *User Modeling and User-Adapted Interaction, 17*, 3, 257 - 304.

[49] Suh, K. S., Kim, H., & Suh, E. K. (2011). What if your avatar looks like you? dual congruity perspectives for avatar use. *MIs Quarterly, 35*(3), 711-730.

[50] Tscholl, M., Lindgren, R., and Johnson, E. 2013. Enacting orbits: refining the design of a full-body learning simulation. In *Proc of the 12th Int'l Conference on Interaction Design & Children*. IDC '13. ACM, New York, NY, 451-454.

[51] vom Lehn, D., Heath, C., & Hindmarsh, J. 2001. Conduct and Collaboration in Museums and Galleries. *Symbolic Interaction, 24*, 2, 189-216.

[52] Vygotsky, L. 1987. Zone of proximal development. Mind in Society: The Development of Higher Psychological Processes, 52-91.

[53] Wagner, D., Schmalstieg, D., & Billinghurst, M. 2006. Handheld AR for Collaborative Edutainment. Proceedings of the International Conference on Artificial Reality and Telexistence. ICAT '06. IEEE, 85-96.

[54] Wobbrock, J.O., Morris, M.R., and Wilson, A.D. User-defined gestures for surface computing. 2009. In *Proc of the SIGCHI Conference on Human Factors in Computing Systems*. CHI '09. ACM, New York, NY, 1083–1092.

[55] Yatani, K., Sugimoto, M., & Kusunoki, F. 2004. *Musex: A System for Supporting Children's Collaborative Learning in a Museum with PDAs*. Paper presented at the the 2004 IEEE International Workshop on Wireless and Mobile Technologies in Education, Taoyuan, Taiwan.

[56] Yoon, S. A., Elinich, K., Wang, J., Steinmeier, C., & Tucker, S. 2012. Using augmented reality and knowledge-building scaffolds to improve learning in a science museum. *International Journal of Computer-Supported Collaborative Learning, 7*(4), 519-541.

[57] Zimmerman, H. T., Reeve, S., & Bell, P. 2010. Family sense-making practices in science center conversations. *Science Education, 94*(3), 478-505

# Designing and Evaluating Touchless Playful Interaction for ASD Children

Laura Bartoli [(1)], Franca Garzotto [(2)], Mirko Gelsomini [(2)], Luigi Oliveto [(2)], Matteo Valoriani [(2)]

[(1)] Associazione Astrolabio (Firenze), [(2)] Politecnico di Milano

[(1)] lbartoli101@gmail.com, [(2)] name.surname@polimi.it

## ABSTRACT

Limited studies exist that explore motion-based touchless applications for children with ASD (Autism Spectrum Disorder) and investigate their design issues and the benefits they can bring to this target group. The paper reports a structured set of design guidelines that distill our experience gained from empirical studies and collaborations with therapeutic centers. These heuristics informed the design of three touchless games that were evaluated in a controlled study involving medium functioning ASD children at a therapeutic center. Our findings confirm the potential of motion-based touchless applications games in technology-enhanced interventions for this target group.

## Categories and Subject Descriptors

K.3.0 [Computers and Education]: General; H.5.2 [Information Interfaces and Presentation]: Multimedia Systems, User Interfaces

**General Terms:** Design, Human Factors

## Keywords

Autistic children, motion-based touchless interaction, learning, therapy

## 1. BACKGROUND

The Autistic Spectrum Disorder (ASD) is a general term for a group of complex disorders of brain development, characterized, in varying degrees, by difficulties in social interaction, verbal and nonverbal communication and repetitive behaviors often accompanied by sensorimotor impairments. Autism, estimated to affect 1 of every 88 children, is marked by the presence of impairments along a triad of dimensions: social interaction, communication, and imagination. Children with autism show a great variance of symptoms, ranging from a delay or a total lack of spoken language to a severe impairment in the use of nonverbal behaviors that regulate social interaction, to a failure to develop peer relationships appropriate to age. ASD children also show imagination inability, manifested in the difficulty to generalize between environments, in a limited range of imaginative activities and in a difficulty in figuring out future events and abstract ideas. This reflects to a lack of spontaneous make-believe play or social imitative play and tendency to repetitive and stereotyped patterns of activity. Other behavioral symptoms include hyperactivity, short attention span, impulsivity, aggressiveness, self-injurious behavior, and temper tantrums.

Studies conducted to consider the effectiveness of digital technologies for ASD children reveal that these tools are in general well received [16]. A digital environment provides stimuli that are more focused, predictable, and replicable than conventional tools. It also reduces the confusing, multi-sensory distractions of the real world that may induce anxiety and create barriers to social communication. In addition, digital tools can exploit the benefits of visually based interventions adopted in existing therapeutic practices such as video modeling [6]. Existing products and prototypes for autistic children exploit a variety of technologies and interaction modes, from desktop to multitouch mobile devices, tangibles and digitally augmented objects, robots [11], and more recently, touchless motion based environments, enabling users to interact using body movements without any physical contact with digital tools.

The goal of our research is to design, develop and evaluate touchless motion based games that can be used for educational and therapeutic purposes in different contexts - school, therapeutic center, home - to improve autistic children's skills in the motor, cognitive, and social sphere. In previous papers [2][3], we reported a survey and a discussion of the state of the art on touchless motion-based interactive technology for autistic children [29][15][23][14]. This review pinpoints that the number of empirical studies in this field is small, the understandings of the neurological mechanisms underlying autism are limited, and the theoretical underpinnings are controversial [17][8][13][5]. Little is known about how touchless motion-based interaction works for autistic children and how it can be designed to promote specific skills. This papers provides an overview of our activities in this field (section 2) and presents our recent contributions to the above research issues, which include: i) a set of *design guidelines* (section 3) for motion-based touchless games for autistic children; ii) *three new motion-based touchless games* for low-medium functioning autistic children that were designed according to these guidelines (section 4); iii) *empirical evidence of the learning potential* of these games (sections 5 and 6).

## 2. THE WOKFLOW

Our research on motion-based touchless technology for ASD children involved the research and development team at our lab (3 HCI engineers, 1 interaction designer, 1 psychologist) and … from 3 different therapeutic centers: Centro Benedetta D'Intino in Milan (CBD), Associazione Astrolabio in Florence (AA) and San Camillo Hospital in Turin (SC). Overall, 18 specialists (6 neuropsychiatric doctors, 4 language therapists, 4 motor therapists, 4 special educators) and 19 autistic children have participated in our research so far. Children can be deemed as "medium-low functioning", for their cognitive level and for the severity of their deficits in at least one of the three ASD dimensions (social interaction, communication, imagination). Our overall work unfolded along various steps: field observations of children's normal daily activities (i.e., without any technology) at CBD; a first empirical investigation at AA of children interacting with *commercial* motion based touchless games (discussed in [2]); a partial replication of this study at CBD; definition of design guidelines; development of three new games designed according to the above guidelines; iterative evaluation of progressive

*IDC'14*, June 17–20, 2014, Aarhus, Denmark.
Copyright 2014 ACM 978-1-4503-2272-0/14/06…$15.00
http://dx.doi.org/10.1145/2593968.2593976

prototypes; summative evaluation of the final version of these games at AA.

Observing children's activities in their normal context enabled us to understand what happens in their real life context and where the opportunity lies for technology. We attended as observers 5 afternoon sessions at CBD in which 10 autistic children participated in their normal activities at the center. All sessions were videotaped and videos were discussed with CBD experts.

Four commercial Kinect games were then installed initially at AA (as reported in [2]) and later at CBD, in both cases for a period of two and a half months. Overall, these products were used by 15 children (5 at AA and 10 at CBD) who were videotaped during play, enabling us to collect over 30 hours of videos. The games, belonging to the "packages" *MS Kinect Sports* and MS *Rabbids Alive & Kicking,* were selected by therapists, after the analysis of over 150 entertainment products available on the market. At AA, observations and video recordings of children's play were complemented with standardized therapeutic tests on attention, as discussed in [2] and [3]. For each study, the gathered materials (videos, therapists', observers' notes, clinical measures) were initially analyzed independently by our team and by each local team of specialists; then focus groups were organized at each therapeutic center to discuss and compare design observations and results. This work on the field enabled us to assess the learning benefits of motion based touchless gaming in relationship to attentional skills and emotional or behavioral aspects. From these studies we also constructed a more accurate description of how children behave during gameplay, what works, what doesn't, which are the points of strength and weakness of the products used. This knowledge was distilled into a preliminary set of *design guidelines*. They informed the design of *three new games* that have similar game logic as the commercial games used but revised UX characteristics. The progressive prototypes of these games were evaluated at 3 therapeutic centers, involving overall 15 medium-low functioning children, leading to design revisions and refinements of our guidelines. The final version of the design guidelines are reported in the following section. The final version of the games was evaluated in a controlled study performed at AA, as discussed in sections 5 and 6.

## 3. DESIGN GUIDELINES

Our guidelines take into account the specificity of ASD, particularly in relationship to medium-low functioning children, the characteristics motion-based touchless interaction, and the learning potential of this paradigm. We have defined general and goal specific guidelines. *General guidelines* consider high-level design principles and concern general interface/ interaction features. *Goal specific guidelines* focus on design features related to specific learning goals. As such, they are classified in 3 categories, respectively associated to learning skills in the motor, cognitive, and social dimension.

## 3.1 General Guidelines

### One game per child

There is no such thing as an "average" child with autism. Each child manifests unique strengths and skill deficits. Things that are reinforcing or rewarding to one individual may be unpleasant for another person [26]. Any play activity must therefore be oriented to addressing the unique capability and needs of each individual child, which implies that a game must support a high degree of *customizability*. It must enable caregivers to adapt a gaming experience to the individual skills and preferences of each child,

customizing multimedia contents, rewards, play time, body movements.

### Evolving tasks

To support the evolving needs of a child over time, game should support *increasing* levels of motor and cognitive complexity of game tasks [20]. It should enable the progression along a continuum of game sessions involving activities that are similar but, when the child has acquired and consolidated the proper skills, are progressively more demanding in terms of motor, cognitive and social skills required.

### Unique goal

Within a play session, children should have a unique, explicit, well focused game goal to reach (e.g. "hit as many moving objects as possible", "avoid as many falling asteroids as possible"). The goal should be associated to one single task and a clear set of movements the child can afford (e.g. 'moving arms to hit objects') to promote the cognitive process related of organizing movements to achieve a given objective.

### Instructions

Understanding the goal and tasks should be facilitated before playing and should be reinforced during the whole game session. Children, especially those with a delay in or a total lack of verbal language, can benefit from visual means for communication, like PCSs (Picture Communication Symbols) and iconic images representing the movements to be performed and the body parts to be used.

### Rewarding

After a good performance, offering a rewarding stimulus which is "valued" or "liked" by the child increases motivation, enhances player's engagement and implicitly improves her skills [24]. In our experience, medium-low functioning autistic children might not value much quantitative performance results (e.g., points or extra time won) as rewards. What seems to act as a stronger motivator and a positive reinforcement is a video or audio effect that creates fun, e.g., the play of cartoon videos, funny animations, cheerful music, and applauses. In case of scarce game performance, these elements should not be necessarily removed at all, but can be reduced and completed with something that fosters children to do better, e.g., visual instructions, in order to help managing frustration issues.

### Repeatability and Predictability

Autistic subjects appear to have a well-established affinity with interactive technologies. Repeatability plays an important role to achieve mastery and provide control of the rate of learning. Repeating the same routines (tasks) improves not only individuals' mastery but also gives them the predictability they need as well as clear expectations of the next future.

### Transitions

The same game is typically played many times in the same configuration. Eventually, the child will need to move from a level in which she has proved to be successful to the next one, which unlocks new challenges and opportunities. It must be *very easy* for the caregiver and the child to repeat a game, as well as to move to the "next level". The time of restarting a session or switching from one level to the next one must be minimized, to reduce the risk of a child's loss of concentration during the transition.

### Minimalistic graphics

Visual items should be cheerful and aesthetically nice, but always strictly functional to the goal. Children may be distracted from visual elements that are not strictly relevant for the current task and may lose attention. In addition, too many visual stimuli may induce anxiety as children may not be able to discriminate and interpret single elements within a group. Graphic elements should have clearly distinguishable shapes and should not overlap. For some children, the use of colors may need to be reduced. Some subjects, for example, can work with black and white images only, getting very nervous when dealing with other colors.

### Clear audio

Sound or music can be used not only to provide feedbacks on actions. They should be played during moments when nothing happens on the screen or there is a transition from one game configuration to another, or at the end of the game to complement visual rewards effects. At the same time, it is important to remember that autistic children easily reach a point in which too many audio stimuli are perceived just as a mass of noise that they cannot interpret and creates extra stress. Hence similar principles mentioned for visual elements (see "Minimalistic Graphics") apply to sound: Sound elements should be cheerful, clear, simple, and functional to the game task and to the need of keeping children's attention.

### Dynamic stimuli

Dynamic stimuli such as animations and music should be provided along the entire game session. When visual elements remain static and nothing else happens, the child may lose concentration and move her attention to something outside the game. A prolonged static situation may trigger abnormal behaviors, such as stereotyped movements or motor rigidity (e.g. motionless gazing at the static image on the screen), which typically must be "unlocked" by a caregiver's intervention.

### Serendipity

In any game activity and for any, enjoyment increases when visual or audio effects create wonder or surprise. This is also true, at some degree, for autistic children. For these subjects sensory stimuli should balance phenomena that are more predictable and consistent with the ongoing task (e.g., audio feedbacks on child's movements) with serendipitous effects (e.g., a new different object appears and disappear on the screen), always having in mind the risk of attention loss.

### Avateering

An avatar is a virtual representation of the child inside the game that offers an immediate visual feedback to a player's actions [1]. It enforces the perception of "self" ("It looks *like me!*" – a child during our experiments). The game space becomes like a "virtual mirror" where the player sees herself, establishes a connection between her movements and the system's reaction, and develops imitative abilities (see also Guideline "Developing imitative abilities" in sect 3.3). In addition, avatars can be a means to direct children's focus of attention on the effects of their movements rather than the body movements per se, to promote static and dynamic motor skills (see General Guideline "Motor control through "external" attention"). Hence avatars should be incorporated in a game even when they are not strictly functional to the game narrative structure, e.g., they do not represent characters of a "story".

We identified three different kinds of Avatars:

- *Articulated Avatar:* all parts of the body are represented using simple shapes (points, lines, circles...) and follow players' movements
- *Pointing Avatar:* the user is represented by a single image that follows the movements of a single part of the user's body.

- *Real Avatar:* the user is shown as a silhouette of her body, which can be filled with the image of the child captured by the color camera.

## 3.2 Goal specific guidelines: Motor skills

### Motor control through "external" attention

To promote static and dynamic motor skills (i.e., movement control, balance, or postural control) it is important to provide audio-visual stimuli associated to each movement or still position needed to perform a game task, in order to direct a child focus of attention on the effects of her movements rather than the body movement per se. This guideline is also grounded on a number of studies on non-disabled persons pinpoint that fostering "external" attention focus (on the effects of one's movements) rather than on the action itself ("internal" attention focus) can boost motor learning. [21] found an increase in motor performance when directing an individual's attention "externally" compared to directing attention "internally". The advantage of focusing attention on the movement effect might be that it allows unconscious or automatic processes to control the movements required to achieve this effect. When persons focus on their body they might be more likely to consciously intervene in these control processes and may inadvertently disrupt the coordination of a number of relatively automatic (reflexive and self-organizing) processes that normally control the movement.

### Increasing gross motor skills

Gross motor skills enable such functions as walking, jumping, kicking, sitting upright, lifting, throwing, as well as head control, trunk stability, maintaining balance, balancing position from one foot to the other [19]. To promote the development of these skills, interaction can comprise the actions above and in general, movements that involve the large muscle groups and the whole body. As motor skills generally develop from the center to the body outward and head to tail, the progression of tasks (see General Guideline "Evolving Task") should include a progression of movements initially involving the whole body and then increasingly more peripheral parts.

### Increasing postural stability

To promote postural balance and control, the game can involve tasks that require to maintain still positions (e.g., keeping head or arms steady), to keep the line of gravity of the body with minimal sway, or to balance position from one foot to the other. Task complexity can be increased by requiring alternating dynamic movements and static gestures, or progressively augmenting the time during which motion-less positions must be maintained (offering appropriate rewards as time proceeds).

### Increasing coordination

Various types of tasks can promote motor coordination [9][25]:

- Tasks that involve coordinated movement of different parts of the body, or eye-rest of the body coordination. For example, to hit a virtual object, still or moving, in different positions or with varying speed, the child can use legs and arms alternation, shift of left and right arm/leg, or the combination of both arms/legs.
- Tasks that require distinguishing left/right or forward/backward, determining the distance between objects, combining movements into a controlled sequence, remembering the next movement in a sequence
- Tasks that require to apply visuo-spatial memory, which concerns to perception of spatial relationships among objects (e.g., in jigsaw puzzles) and is thought to be associated to coordination deficits.

## 3.3 Goal specific guidelines: Cognitive Skills

*Promoting perceptual learning and attention skills*

Perceptual learning forms important foundations of complex cognitive processes (i.e., language) and is defined as "the process of learning improved ability to respond to the environment" [27]. These improvements range from simple sensory discriminations - focusing on, and discriminating between, certain stimuli - to identification of items as belonging to the same or different category, to complex categorizations of spatial and temporal patterns relevant to real-world expertise. Perceptual learning is widely seen as tightly coupled with various forms of attention: sustained attention - the ability to direct and focus cognitive activity on specific stimuli; selective attention - the process by which a person can selectively pick out one message from a mixture of messages occurring simultaneously; weighted attention, which entails making a distinction between relevant and irrelevant stimuli. Different types of tasks and visual contents can promote perceptual learning:

- Tasks that require the child to stabilize her gaze and track with her body moving objects on display (sustained attention)
- Tasks that require moving the entire body or some body parts to hit or avoid specific moving objects (sustained attention).
- Tasks that involve movements to express simple sensory discriminations, e.g., distinguishing colors, shapes, sizes, position of objects (selective attention)
- Tasks that require to recognize a visual shape among multiple shapes or to reproduce a similar shape with the body (a body position (selective attention)
- Tasks and visual contents that require the child to focus on similarities or on differences such as pointing to and gripping visual elements that represent different food types or the same food type (selective attention)
- Tasks that involve more complex categorizations of spatial and temporal properties of the objects on display in situations relevant to a child's own life, e.g., "What do you eat at breakfast? Grasp only the food you eat at breakfast") (weighted attention)
- Tasks that require the child to select information relevant for a task, and ignore irrelevant information, e.g., hitting only "target" elements among various falling objects (weighted attention)

*Increasing space awareness*

Space awareness can be increased by tasks that involve moving in and out a constrained space (e.g., defined by a circle drawn on the floor) or rotating the body to change perspective on a virtual 3D space on the screen.

*Increasing body awareness*

To increase awareness of body and body structure, multimedia contents and movements should emphasize the identification of body parts, how they work and how they fit together. For example:

- Playing songs that focus on body parts, such as head, shoulders, knees and toes, and asking the child (while singing) to touch the parts of the body in the song, or to move and shake them (clapping, stopping and head nodding)
- Involving more than one child and requiring children doing interactions while certain body parts are touching the whole time, such as hands, elbows or heads, proving feedbacks when a player disconnects (see also Guideline "Engaging in human-human interaction")

*Developing imitative capability*

Autistic children show limited imitative capability, which is manifested by the lack of spontaneous make-believe play or social imitative play [10]. The (realistic or schematized) shape of the player's body and her movements in the game virtual space are fundamental to promote the development of imitative skills (see also General Guideline "Avateering"). Other means are the inclusion of tasks like: imitating the movements of characters on display; forming static shapes using the body that correspond to shapes or images on display; performing gross and fine motor movements that animate characters on the screen (objects, animals, vegetables, humans), e.g., in a storytelling contexts; imitating the movements of co-players (adults or peers).

## 3.4 Goal specific guidelines: Social Skills

*Not only multiplayer*

Most touchless games can be developed for being played by both a single individual and two or more persons without changing game logic. However, moving together in front of a display and performing independent or complementary tasks do not necessarily trigger social interaction. This is especially true for autistic children [28] who do not engage with others spontaneously. Social interaction must be supported "by design", with multiplayer tasks that are explicitly conceived to promote and exert social skills (see next guidelines).

*Motivating human-human interaction*

The game should include tasks that require movements of more than one player to be completed, i.e., jumping together to overcome an obstacle, creating a body shape that simulates a character on the screen with 3 legs and 4 arms. Visual elements and rewards should emphasize the concept of "together" and acknowledge the benefits of doing things cooperatively. Also avatars can act as a social cue that may influences children's perceptions, leading them to perceive the experience as more "social".

*Motivating communication*

Children with ASD are often self-absorbed and seem to exist in a private world where they are *unable* to successfully communicate with others. It is important to give them a motivation to make the effort of sending and receiving messages. To this end, a task that requires players to give verbal and non-verbal *mutual* instructions to reach a goal (e.g., "while I move here you have move there") offers a motivating opportunity for communication.

*Increasing joint attention*

Joint attention is the intentionally shared focus and interest of two individuals on the same object or event. It is achieved for example when one individual alerts another to an object by means of eye-gazing, pointing, or other verbal or non-verbal indications, and the other person looks back to her after looking at the object. Joint attention abilities are important for many aspects of language development, socio-emotional development and the ability to take part in normal relationships, and are negatively affected by autism. To support joint attention it is important to include tasks where one or more of the situations below take place:

- one child has to call the attention of another child, or an adult, toward a target objects, e.g., through a pointing gesture
- two children have to coordinate each other in order to find a target object and catch it simultaneously
- two children have to alternate in the same or different tasks ("turn taking") and regulate one's behavior to the one of the co-player.

## 4. OUR GAMES

Using the guidelines described in the previous sections, three different motion-based games have been designed and developed: *Bubble Game*, *Space Game* and *Shape Game*.

All games are strongly customizable according to the characteristics and learning needs of the specific child that plays with the system. This feature leads to a large number of playing opportunities even within the same game. The customization can be done by the therapist during the treatment sessions or by the children's parents at home, due to the simplicity and ease of use of the configuration functions and interface. The most relevant parameters that can be modified are game speed, object density and enabled body parts. Games can also be personalized using different graphic themes for background and graphic elements or adding specific multimedia reward.

The games automatically collect the scores obtained by players and the information relative to the played configuration, and generate a session report that can be used to evaluate or tune the treatment.

### 4.1 Bubble Game

The clinical goal of this game is to improve children speed and accuracy of movements and motor-visual coordination between visual elements. The body parts which can be used are head, one or two hands, one or two feet.

The children have to catch as many appearing objects as possible. They are free to play until time expires; at the end of the game the resulting score is shown on screen, representing the total number of collected objects. A more positive final reward (e.g. an applause and a golden cup) is given when the score is greater than a threshold calculated considering the various parameters (e.g. the total number of elements and the children allowed body parts).

The child avatar is an *Articulated Avatar*; it helps the child to recognize all body parts in order to better link her body with the stick figure on the screen and to improve the body awareness.

**Figure 1: Bubble Game**

Figure 1 shows a child playing a particular level of Bubble Game where she can use all body parts to catch and burst the appearing bubbles. On top of the screen the information about the total game time, the current score and the enabled body parts are displayed.

The game levels can be personalized using various parameters, the most relevant are: total game time; total number of elements; fade time of objects; objects size; objects position; body part to be used to hit (head, left hand, right hand, left foot, right foot or a combination of them) and graphic background.

### 4.2 Space Game

The main goal of this game (Figure 2) is to increase speed and accuracy of movements coordination and selective and sustained attention. This activity also elicits movement coordination and pace. The child has to move her entire body to avoid falling objects. She is represented by a *Pointing Avatar* that can move only horizontally from a side of the screen to the other, following her position. This kind of avatar has been chosen because children use only one point of their body (e.g. the hand) or the body as a whole to interact with the game space and do not need an articulated stick figure. They can concentrate only on falling objects, reducing the noise generated by useless body part movements and it also allows children with special motor disabilities to play the game.

The player has an initial number of "lives" and if she loses all of them before the game time is elapsed, she loses the game. If the child still has at least one life when the time runs out, she wins the game and the relative reward is shown on screen. Beside the falling objects to be avoided, some special award elements can be caught in order to gain additional lives (e.g. stars). The number of these objects can be defined by therapists according to the overall level of difficulty.

Game configurations are determined by multiple parameters such as game total time, total number of elements, objects falling time, number of initial lives, number of additional lives, body part to be used to hit (body, left hand, right hand), objects dimensions (small/medium/large), and graphic background.

In Figure 2 the top-left of the screen presents the remaining lives and time, while on the right side the current score is shown.

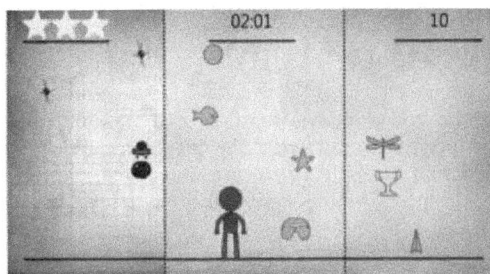

**Figure 2: Space Game**

### 4.3 Shape Game

The main goal of this game is to promote the following skills: identification of the correlation between the body and the shown image; body awareness and limits; body consciousness in the space; abstraction ability; imitative skills and motor control auto-regulation.

In Shape game children have to replicate a particular shape shown on screen using their body. While the motion sensor captures the user's silhouette, the child must overlay the shape until a certain threshold level (predefined for each game level) and within a certain time limit. Moreover, the child has to keep the correct position for a given time frame. The game can be played by a single child or by two children who have to collaborate together to mimic the shape on the screen. If time elapses before children correctly overlay the shape, the game ends without any particularly cheerful reward; when children overlay the shape at the expended degree, the game ends showing a multimedia reward.

**Figure 3: Shape Game**

A *Real Avatar* helps children to recognize themselves on the screen and improves body awareness and body schema.

As shown in Figure 3, the left part of the screen contains the graphic element representing the remaining time and indicates the coverage percentage level.

Therapists can create customized shapes in order to address different children's needs or to stimulate them in performing some specific body movements. For customization purposes, shapes can be extracted from any pre-existing image and edited with classical digital paint tools (brush and eraser) or can be generated on the fly by children or therapists using the shape capturing tool integrated in the game, as illustrated in Figure 4.

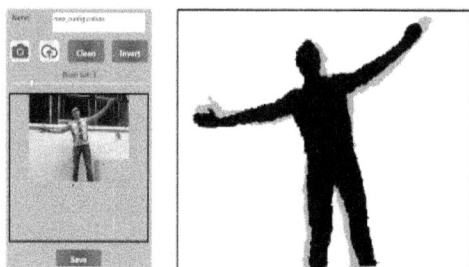

**Figure 4: Shape Game Capturing Tool**

# 5. EMPIRICAL STUDY

In order to validate the effectiveness of our games, we led an empirical controlled study. Our first goal was to evaluate the benefits of our games monitoring the improvement of the abilities of children. Our second goal was to compare the effectiveness of our games respect to the commercial ones, used in the previous study [2].

## 5.1 Study Variables

The variables considered in the evaluation phase can be divided into two different categories: *Performance* and *Clinical* variables.

The *Performance Variable* measures how better the child complete a specific task; this measure is related to the specific game that is played by the child.

The *Clinical Variables* include attention aspects and the capability of integrating visual and motor skills. For attention, we analyzed two variables [7] [27]:

- *Selective Attention*, the capability to focus on an important stimulus ignoring competing distractions
- *Sustained Attention*, the capability to hold the attention for the time needed to conclude an activity

In order to evaluate the capability of children to integrate visual and motor skills, we investigate:

- *Visual Perception*, the ability the mind and eye to interpret the surrounding environment by objectively processing visual information
- *Motor Coordination*, the harmonious functioning of body parts that involve movement, including gross motor movement, fine motor movement, and motor planning.
- *Visuo-Motor* Integration, the ability to control body movement guided by vision.

## 5.2 Participants

We recruited 10 medium-low functional children who can be considered as homogenous from a clinical perspective. In addition, information was collected using questionnaires compiled by parents, in order to confirm that all children have comparable behavioral characteristics (e.g., a very limited set of favorite activities and similar stereotyped behaviors, both verbal and motor).

The children (9 males, 1 female, aged 6-8 years) were randomly assigned either to the treatment group (G1) or the control group (G2). Both groups had regular therapeutic treatments during the study period. The treatment group G1 attended extra sessions during which they used our games. During the entire testing period, parents of all children were warned not to let them play with motion-based game consoles such as Nintendo Wii nor Xbox with Kinect at home.

## 5.3 Procedures

The study was performed at the therapeutic center AA (Association Astrolabio) in order to investigate behavioral reactions and social, motor and cognitive skills before and after the use of our games.

Before the game treatment, a preliminary phase (T0) took place, when both groups G1 and G2 were subjected to standardized clinical tests to define the initial functional profile and to establish the "starting point" of each child. While G2 continued its regular activities, G1 attended regular meetings and additional therapeutic sessions using our games and, at the end of the testing period (T1), both groups were evaluated.

G1 had been analyzed along a 3-months period (from October to December 2013) for a total amount of 10 individual weekly meetings of 45 minutes. Initial and final assessment needed 2 individual meetings. For each session, children played each game for 10 minutes, gradually increasing the level difficulty. The meetings were video-recorded, using two cameras placed in front and on the back of the children, simultaneously capturing children movements and the game visual interface respectively. A total of 15 hours of video recording were collected.

During the game sessions, the therapist was sitting or standing aside the child and outside the Kinect sensing area, taking notes and intervening when needed. All sessions took place in the same room without modification of the environment settings.

### 5.3.1 Assessment

In order to evaluate the Performance variable, we propose a *Global Weighted Score* (GWS) represents a weighted score depending on the specific game parameters.

### *Global Weighted Score (GWS)*

Each game has different tasks to achieve, so three different GWS variables have been defined.

*Bubble Game GWS = #Collected_Bubble * Difficulty_Level*

Where the *#Collected_Bubble* represents the number of hit items, while the *Difficulty_Level* is the category assigned by the therapist to the played configuration.

*Space Game GWS = #Item_Avoided * Difficulty_Level*

Where the *#Item_Avoided* represents the number of avoided objects during the game.

*Shape Game GWS = (Difficulty_Level * Steady_Time * Coverage_Threshold * (1 – (Final_Time / Max_Time))*

Where the *Steady_Time* is the time in which children have to maintain their position to cover the shape; *Coverage_Threshold* is the percentage of the shape that the children have to cover in order to win; *Final_Time* is the time spent to correctly cover the shape and *Max_Time* is the total time available for the specific level.

For the clinical variables we adopted 3 evaluation tests: Modified Bells Test (MBT), Subtest Wisc_IV and Visual-Motor Integration (VMI).

### *Modified Bell Test (MBT)*

The Modified Bells Test, adopted in many therapeutic centers in our country, is a child-oriented adaptation of the method proposed in [12][4] and consists in a sequence of cancellation tasks. In each task, a child marks as many similar items as possible from a paper of cluttered items. Target stimuli (images or shapes, e.g., of bells, with equal size and orientation) are randomly intermixed with other different ones. The evaluation of the attention process is based on the measurement of two indicators: accuracy (the total number of target items, identified in the maximum time – normally 2') and speed (the number of target items identified in the first 30").

### *Supplementary Subset Wisc IV*
The Wechsler Intelligence Scale for Children (WISC) [22] is an individually administered intelligence test for children that can be completed without reading or writing. The supplementary subset, one of the 15 Wisc IV subsets, evaluates in particular the selective attention. The test consists of a random deletion and a structured deletion task. For each trial of 45 seconds the child has to find and mark the requested figures of a given topic (e.g. animals).

### *Developmental test of Visual-Motor Integration (VMI)*
Visual-Motor Integration Test [18] is commonly used to identify significant difficulty in visual-motor integration and to determine the most appropriate intervention plan. This test was designed to measure both the integration between visual perception and motor coordination, and each of these two components separately. VMI is a paper-pencil based task, consisting in 27 items in which the subject copies a developmental sequence of geometric shapes in a predefined time frame. Since it does not need particular knowledge (numbers, letters) it is particularly suitable for ASD children.

### *5.3.2 Games Configurations*
All of the games were set with an initial homogeneous setup for all children. In each session, the child started from the level which he played the previous session, with the goal to redeem confidence and reach a satisfactory concentration level. All games configurations are divided in 5 levels with growing difficulty. Table 1 summarizes Bubble Game configurations.

**Table 1: Bubble Game configurations**

| Levels | Enabled body parts | Time [sec] | Time fade [sec] | #Elements | Appear after burst |
|---|---|---|---|---|---|
| 1 | Head, hands, feet | 120 | infinite | 90 | on |
| 2 | Hands, feet | 120 | 8 | 120 | off |
| 3 | Hands, feet | 120 | 5 | 180 | off |
| 4 | Hands | 120 | 4 | 180 | off |
| 5 | Head, feet | 120 | 4 | 180 | off |

Table 2 Space Game configurations. In the first 3 levels the graphical theme is "space" thus children have to avoid black satellites, planets and meteorites. The fourth level theme is "air" showing butterflies, airplanes and flowers, while the fifth level, displaying bubbles, shells and starfishes, has the "water" theme. The different graphic setting, especially in the last two levels, requires different degrees of difficulty in the identification of objects of different semantic values (star space vs. starfish), where the first increases life points and the second one decreases them.

**Table 2: Space Game configurations**

| Level | # Lives | Max Time [sec] | Time fall down [sec] | # Objects | # Bonus | Dimensions | Graphic theme |
|---|---|---|---|---|---|---|---|
| 1 | 5 | 90 | 6 | 25 | 15 | medium | space |
| 2 | 4 | 90 | 5 | 50 | 10 | medium | space |
| 3 | 3 | 90 | 4 | 60 | 7 | medium | space |
| 4 | 2 | 90 | 3 | 90 | 6 | small | air |
| 5 | 1 | 90 | 3 | 110 | 5 | small | water |

We also decided to augment the objects' density, increasing the number of flows of falling items, from 4 flows in level 1 to 10 in level 5.

Table 3 summarizes the experiment configurations of Shape. Each level is progressively more demanding in terms of cognitive and motor skills. In particular, L4 focuses on improving static balance skills while L5 involves motor planning abilities, since most of the figures in this level do not have a human shape.

**Table 3: Shape Game configurations**

| Level | Coverage | Pose time [sec] | Game time [sec] | Additional difficulties |
|---|---|---|---|---|
| 1 | 60% | 2 | 30 | No |
| 2 | 60% | 2 | 30 | No |
| 3 | 70% | 3 | 30 | No |
| 4 | 80% | 3 | 30 | Static balance |
| 5 | 90% | 3 | 40 | Abstraction |

## 6. RESULTS

### 6.1 Results of Clinical Test
Comparing the evaluation between the initial (T0) and final (T1) time, the use of our games shows important improvements of the treatment Group (G1) in terms of attention and visuo-motor abilities. In addition, surveys, compiled by parents during clinical meetings, according to the standardized tests and clinical observations, highlight an improvement of children's daily activities and skills.

### *6.1.1 Attention parameters*
Figure 5 and 6 show each child score at the beginning (T0) and at the end (T1) of the test phase. Children from c01 to c05 belong to the treatment group (G1) while from c06 to c10 apply to the control group (G2).

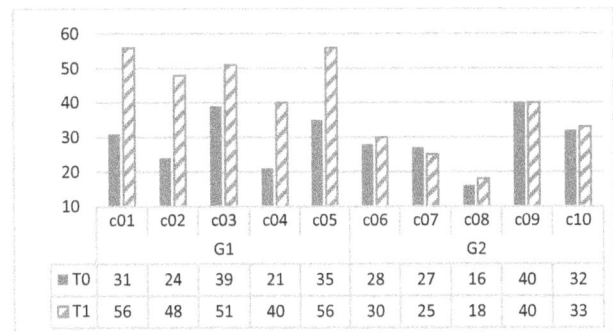

| | c01 | c02 | c03 | c04 | c05 | c06 | c07 | c08 | c09 | c10 |
|---|---|---|---|---|---|---|---|---|---|---|
| | | | G1 | | | | | G2 | | |
| T0 | 31 | 24 | 39 | 21 | 35 | 28 | 27 | 16 | 40 | 32 |
| T1 | 56 | 48 | 51 | 40 | 56 | 30 | 25 | 18 | 40 | 33 |

**Figure 5: Bell Test - Selective Attention**

The treatment group G1, between T0 and T1, has an average percentage increase of selective attention +72.38% [+14.43% average increase on the reference scale] and a sustained attention's one of +33.48 [+19.29% average increase on the reference scale]. On the contrary, G2 was not subjected to considerable variations and it remained steady on the investigated variables (the average percentage increase of selective attention is +3.07% [0.43% average increase on the reference scale] and of sustained attention of +11.23% [+6.86% average increase on the reference scale]).

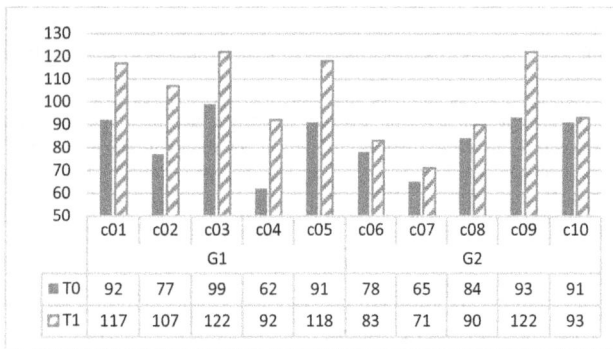

**Figure 6: Bell Test - Sustained attention**

| | c01 | c02 | c03 | c04 | c05 | c06 | c07 | c08 | c09 | c10 |
|---|---|---|---|---|---|---|---|---|---|---|
| T0 | 92 | 77 | 99 | 62 | 91 | 78 | 65 | 84 | 93 | 91 |
| T1 | 117 | 107 | 122 | 92 | 118 | 83 | 71 | 90 | 122 | 93 |

The clinically significant results on G1 were confirmed by the deletion subtest of WISC IV, obtaining an average percentage increase of 32.38% [+14.00% average increase on the reference scale] (Figure 7).

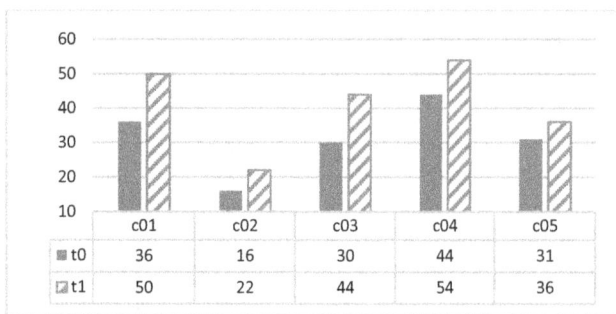

| | c01 | c02 | c03 | c04 | c05 |
|---|---|---|---|---|---|
| t0 | 36 | 16 | 30 | 44 | 31 |
| t1 | 50 | 22 | 44 | 54 | 36 |

**Figure 7: Wisc IV – Selective Attention**

### 6.1.2 Visuo-motor Integration

Overall general trends of G1 show a rise in the evaluated parameters during the entire testing period. Contrarily to G1, G2 do not obtain a significant variation (Table 4).

**Table 4: Comparison between Treatment and Control groups**

| TEST | | G1 | G2 |
|---|---|---|---|
| VMI | Avg. increase | 138.92% | 8.14% |
| | Avg. increase (ref. scale) | 13.61% | -0.14% |
| MOTOR COORDINATION | Avg. increase | 1136.42% | 18.80% |
| | Avg. increase (ref. scale) | 91.67% | 1.21% |
| VISUAL PERCEPTION | Avg. increase | 820.71% | 62.92% |
| | Avg. increase (ref. scale) | 11.4% | 3.73% |

Concerning the visuo-motor integration skill, G1 shows uneven trends due to each child's individual peculiarity.

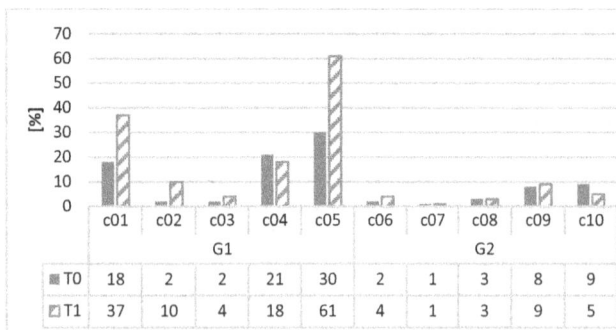

| | c01 | c02 | c03 | c04 | c05 | c06 | c07 | c08 | c09 | c10 |
|---|---|---|---|---|---|---|---|---|---|---|
| T0 | 18 | 2 | 2 | 21 | 30 | 2 | 1 | 3 | 8 | 9 |
| T1 | 37 | 10 | 4 | 18 | 61 | 4 | 1 | 3 | 9 | 5 |

**Figure 8: VMI Test – Integrated result**

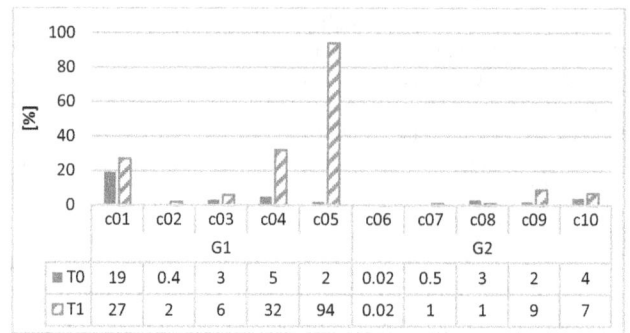

**Figure 9: VMI Test - Motor coordination skill**

| | c01 | c02 | c03 | c04 | c05 | c06 | c07 | c08 | c09 | c10 |
|---|---|---|---|---|---|---|---|---|---|---|
| T0 | 19 | 0.4 | 3 | 5 | 2 | 0.02 | 0.5 | 3 | 2 | 4 |
| T1 | 27 | 2 | 6 | 32 | 94 | 0.02 | 1 | 1 | 9 | 7 |

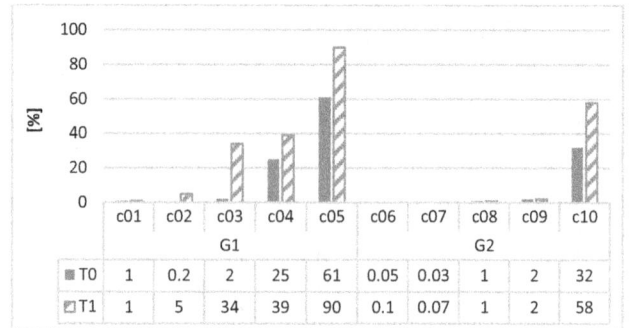

**Figure 10: VMI Test - Visual-Perception skill**

| | c01 | c02 | c03 | c04 | c05 | c06 | c07 | c08 | c09 | c10 |
|---|---|---|---|---|---|---|---|---|---|---|
| T0 | 1 | 0.2 | 2 | 25 | 61 | 0.05 | 0.03 | 1 | 2 | 32 |
| T1 | 1 | 5 | 34 | 39 | 90 | 0.1 | 0.07 | 1 | 2 | 58 |

## 6.2 Play Performance

Children have been progressively able to deal with complex play levels and improve their scores during their treatment period.

### 6.2.1 Bubble

Global Weighted Score (average per session) still increases for every child except c05 who experienced complications in L4 and L5 (Figure 11). Overall, the average number of hit bubbles from level L1 through L5 increases until L3 and decreases after L4. This means that L3 can be considered as the game *"sweet spot"*.

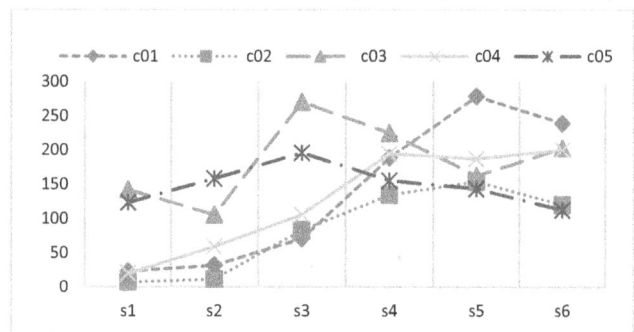

**Figure 11: Bubble - GWS average per session**

**Table 5: average # collected bubbles per difficulty level**

| Session | L1 | L2 | L3 | L4 | L5 |
|---|---|---|---|---|---|
| S1 | 30 | 91 | 52 | | |
| S2 | 24 | 76 | 91 | | |
| S3 | 27 | 59 | 75 | 58 | |
| S4 | 37 | 64 | 79 | 49 | 38 |
| S5 | | | 94 | 57 | 26 |
| S6 | | | | 64 | 33 |

### 6.2.2 Space

For all children, 28% of plays ended before completing the level because the number of collisions with objects that had to be avoided surpassed the number of life points and bonus items to collect.

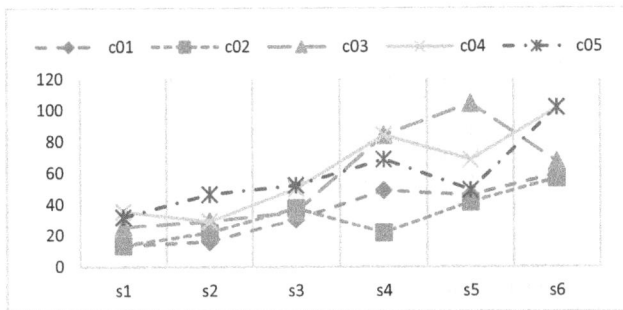

**Figure 12: Space - GWS average per session**

However, along the entire period, the Global Weighted Score (average per session) linearly increased and collisions (objects not avoided) decreased or remained constant.

### 6.2.3 Shape

Our findings show that the time for completing the tasks at a specific level of difficulty decreases with the treatment. After a first initial phase, children began understanding new and creative strategies combining them to complete the tasks. Overall Global Weighted Score (average per session) increases over the time for all the children with predictable fluctuations (Figure 13).

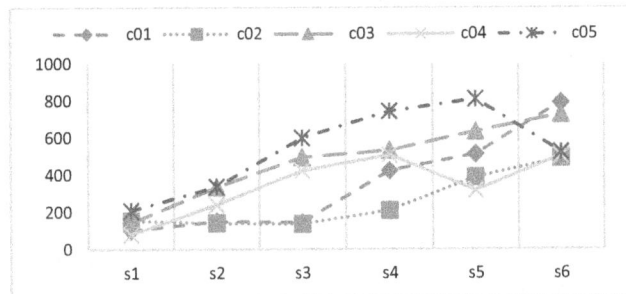

**Figure 13: Shape – GWS average per session**

### 6.2.4 Further Observations

The systematic analysis of the qualitative data gathered during the study (13 hours of video recording, therapist's and observers' notes, questionnaire-based feedbacks from parents) is still ongoing. Still, some facts have already emerged that are worth to be mentioned. During the first play sessions of Space Game, some children did not have a correct understanding of the correlation between their body and their virtual representation on the screen, in that *they identified themselves too much with avatars*: every time an avatar was hit by a falling object (which instead should be avoid) they said "Ahia!!" as if they were really hit and felt pain. This behavior is not surprising; the mechanisms for correct coupling perception/action are weak in cognitive disorders like autism. What is interesting is that the perceptual identification "own-body/avatar" gradually mitigated up to disappearing with the progression of game sessions. Another observed behavior is the *eye triangulation* that eventually occurs during play between the child, the therapist and game screen. This phenomenon was judged very positively by therapists, because the marked impairment in eye-to-eye gaze is a typical symptom of the social interaction deficits that characterizes autism.

Finally, parents filled questionnaires after the study and reported evident improvements in their children' motor skills, execution of daily tasks at home, and attitude towards social play with peers. The positive comments about the so called "Kinect treatment" spread by word of mouth among many families attending the therapeutic center, and many parents asked explicitly to organize an additional study and to have their children involved.

## 6.3 Discussion

Our findings provide empirical evidence that motion-based touchless games have a learning potential for autistic children, to promote attention, (integration of) motor and visual skills. This is witnessed by clinical tests and by the increasing level of play performance manifested with the progression of the treatment. Some observations arise from the comparison of the outcomes of the study reported here, hereinafter referred to as "Study 2", with our previous study reported in [2][3], hereinafter referred to as "Study 1", where we used commercial games with similar game logic. Both studies were performed at the same therapeutic center, with the same setting, number and duration of sessions. In Study 1 the children exposed to the game treatment had a slightly higher clinical profile (medium functioning) than participants of Study 2. Clinical variables considered in Study 1 were selective and sustained attention and were measured using Bell Test only. The most crucial difference of Study 1 is the use of *commercial* Kinect games. Study 1 showed positive results in the attention sphere that Study 2 confirms using a more robust research design, i.e., involving a control group and suing more than one standard method to measure the clinical variables.

**Table 4: Comparison between Study 1 and Study 2**

|  | TEST | Study 1 | Study 2 |
|---|---|---|---|
| Selective Attention | Avg increase | 43.40% | 72.38% |
|  | Avg. increase (ref. scale) | 14.71% | 14.43% |
| Sustained Attention | Avg increase | 15.29% | 33.48% |
|  | Avg. increase (ref. scale) | 10.43% | 19.29% |

The attention effects measured in Study 2 are more evident than in Study 1, as shown in Table 4. The average percentage increase of selective attention is higher in Study 2 (from 43.4% to 72.38%) while the average percentage relative to the reference scale is substantially the same in the two studies. In Study 2 both measures of sustained attention are higher. The percentage increase relative to the reference scales in Study 2 is even more relevant if we consider that participants have lower capabilities than those in Study 1. In conclusions, the comparison between the two studies seems to suggest that the games developed according to our guidelines are more effective than the commercial games used in the first study, which have a similar game logic but are not explicitly designed for autistic children. In this respect, Study 2 can support the effectiveness of our design heuristics.

The study reported in this paper certainly has a number of limitations. Tests were administered only once before and after the whole period of intervention. Autistic children's behavior may considerably vary depending on various circumstances of the day. We could only control for the local contextual factors during game sessions (e.g., the physical setting). Repeated test could have offered more reliable results. The tester sample included five children only. This small size is comparable to of most existing research addressing autistic children in relationship to technology, and is not much lower than the participants' size in most behavioral studies involving disabled children. Still, results measured on such a small number of subjects can only indicate a trend, and require further validation. In addition, the profile of our participants is considered "homogenous from a clinical perspective" (medium-low functioning subjects with low-moderate levels of cognitive deficit, sensory-motor dysfunction, and motor autonomy) but each autistic child has unique characteristics, as it is evident from the different measures of the clinical parameters at the beginning of the study. Hence many subjective variables that are difficult to control may have affected our results, and the heterogeneity of the target group makes meaningful comparative measures near impossible. Still, the therapists involved in our study were impressed by *each subject's* increment relative to her starting point and relative to the reference scale of each measured parameter that according to their experience, tells us more about the learning potential of an intervention than absolute increments and their average values.

## 7. FINAL REMARKS

This paper provides various contributions to the current state of the art in motion touchless technology for autistic children. We define a set of *design guidelines* for touchless games devoted to this target group that, to our knowledge, are novel. They are grounded on a vast experience on the field, distilling the know-how of many specialists - neurological doctors, therapists, educators, and our team. These guidelines have informed the design of *3 highly customizable touchless games*. These tools have been used in a controlled *empirical study* devoted to assess the learning benefits of our tools and also to indirectly validate the effectiveness of our design guidelines. The results from this study *confirm* and *extend* the findings of prior research [2][3], providing additional empirical evidence that touchless gaming does have a strong potential to improve attention and motor/ visual skills in medium-low functioning autistic children.

Still, all our results have to be considered as tentative and deserve further research. Considering the complexity of autism and the little we know about this disorder, our set of design guidelines should certainly be improved, refined, and validated. Additional empirical studies are needed to confirm the effectiveness of touchless interaction for autistic children's learning. In particular, more complex longitudinal studies should be performed to assess the persistency of benefits and their generalization to environments outside the treatment one, and to address some key research questions: to which degree are the skill improvements we measured a long-term achievement? to which degree can they be translated to other contexts and moments of participants' life?

Our games are freely available on http://www.m4allproject.eu/ or by contacting the authors. We hope the IDC community will help us disseminate them to families with ASD children and therapeutic centers. We also hope that other researchers will replicate our study, to address the above research questions, or to perform new studies that consider different profiles of autistic children or explore different learning variables other than the ones considered in our study.

## 8. ACKNOWLEDGMENTS

This work is partially supported by by the European Commission under grant *"M4ALL-Motion Based Interaction for All"* (# 2012-3969-531219 - Life Long Learning Program 2012). The authors are grateful to the children and families from Associazione Astrolabio, Centro Benedetta D'Intino, and San Camillo Hospital who participated in our studies.

## 9. REFERENCES

[1] Alcorn, A., Pain, H. et al. 2011. Social Communication between Virtual Characters and Children with Autism. Volume 6738, 2011, pp 7-14, Springer.

[2] Bartoli L., Corradi C., Garzotto F., Valoriani M. 2013. Exploring Motion-based Touchless Games for Autistic Children's Learning. *IDC 2013, 102-111*

[3] Bartoli L., Garzotto F., Valoriani M. 2014 Touchless Motion-based Interaction for Therapy of Autistic Children. In Ma M., Jain L., Anderson P. (eds) *Virtual, Augmented Reality and Serious Games for Healthcare 1, Springer, – to appear*

[4] Biancardi A., Stoppa E. 1997. Modified Bell Test. Erikson.

[5] Broaders S. C. et al. 2007. Making children gesture brings out implicit knowledge and leads to learning. *J. Experimental Psychology* 136 (4), 2007, 539-550. Springer.

[6] Blum-Dimaya, A., et al. Teaching children with autism to play a video game using activity schedules and game-embedded simultaneous video modeling. *Education and Treatment of Children*, 33(3), 2010, 351-370

[7] Brickenkamp, R., Zillmer, E. 1998. *The d2 test of attention*. Hogrefe & Huber Pub.

[8] Evans, M. 2012. Gestural Interfaces in Learning. *Proc. Of Int. Conf. on Society for Information Technology & Teacher Education* 2012, 3337-3340. AACE.

[9] Fabio R. 2003. *L'Attenzione – fisiologia, patologie e interventi riabilitativi*. Franco Angeli.

[10] Farneti P., Savelli L. 2013. *La mente imitativa*. Franco Angeli.

[11] Ferrari E., Robins E., Dautenhahn K. 2009. Therapeutic and educational objectives in robot assisted play for children with autism. *Proc. RO-MAN 2009*, 108-114, IEEE

[12] Gauthier L, Dehaut F, Joanette Y 1989. The bells test: A quantitative and qualitative test for visual neglect. *Int. J. of Clinical Neuropsychology*, 11, 49-54. APA.

[13] Grandhi, S. A., Joue, G., Mittelberg, I. 2011. Understanding naturalness and intuitiveness in gesture production: insights for touchless gestural interfaces. *Proc. CHI 2011*, 821-824. ACM.

[14] Herrera G., Casas X., Sevilla J., Rosa L., Pardo C., Plaza J., Jordan R., Le Groux S. 2012, Pictogram Room: Natural Interaction Technologies to Aid in the Development of Children with Autism. *Annuary of Clinical and Health Psychology* (8), 2012, 39-44. ACPS.

[15] Hsueh H.L., Ly A. Socio-emotional Learning Through Play and Reflection - http://memu.leehsueh.com/

[16] Kaliouby R., Robinson, P. 2005. The Emotional Hearing Aid: an Assistive Tool for Children with Asperger Syndrome. *Universal Access in the Information Society*, 4 (2), 121-134. Springer.

[17] Keay-Bright W., Howarth I., 2012, Is simplicity the key to engagement for children on the autism spectrum? *Personal and Ubiquitous Computing*, 16 (2), 2012, 129-141. Springer.

[18] Keith E. Beery. 2008. *VMI Developmental Test of Visual-Motor Integration*. Giunti O.S.

[19] Kurtz L. 2007. *Understanding Motor Skills in Children with Dyspraxia, ADHD, Autism, and Other Learning Disabilities*. Jessica Kingsley Publishers.

[20] Lee W. J., Huang C. W., Wu C. J., Huang S. T., Chen G. D. 2012. The Effects of Using Embodied Interactions to Improve Learning Performance. *Proc. ICALT 2012*, 557-559. IEEE

[21] McNevin, N. H., Shea, C. H., & Wulf, G. 2003. Increasing the distance of an external focus of attention enhances learning. *Psychological Research*, Feb. 2012, 67, 22–29. Springer.

[22] Orsini A., Pezzuti L., Picone L. 2012. *WISC-IV Wechsler Intelligence Scale for Children-IV*. Giunti O.S.

[23] Pares N., Masri P. van Wolferen, G., Creed C. 2005. Achieving dialogue with children with severe autism in an adaptive multisensory interaction: the "MEDIATE" project. *IEEE Trans. Visualization and Computer Graphics*, 11, 734-743. IEEE.

[24] Sylva K., Jolly A., Bruner, J. S. 1976. *Play: its role in development and evolution*. Penguin.

[25] Sugden D., Henderson S., 2007, *Movement Assessment Battery for Children*, 2nd Edition. Pearson

[26] Toner N., 2008, *Conducting Preference Assessments on Individuals with Autism and other Developmental Disabilities*.

[27] Van Zomeren, A. H., Brouwer, W. H. 1994. *Clinical neuropsychology of attention*. Oxford University Press.

[28] Xaiz C., Micheli E. 2008. *Gioco e interazione sociale nell'autismo*. Erickson.

[29] Zalapa, R. and M. Tentori, 2013. "Movement-based and tangible interactions to offer body awareness to children with autism". *Proc. of UCAmi '13*, 1-6. Springer.

# "Child as the Measure of all Things":
# The Body as a Referent in Designing a Museum Exhibit to Understand the Nanoscale

Joan Mora-Guiard, Narcis Pares
Universitat Pompeu Fabra
Cognitive Media Technologies group, ICT Department
c. Roc Boronat, 138
+34 93 542 2201
joan.mora / narcis.pares @upf.edu

## ABSTRACT

The nanoscale, despite being something "present" in our everyday life, is actually an abstract concept given the impossibility of having a direct perception of it. This article presents the design process and analysis of an interactive exhibit called "NanoZoom" for a temporary exhibition for the science museum of Barcelona. The goal of the exhibit was to help users understand how small objects are in the nanoscale by designing a full-body interactive experience. The hypothesis behind the design of the system was based on the idea that our body is our constant referent to allow us to understand issues of scale, proportions, distances, etc. Hence, taking the body of the user as a referent should help users better understand how small objects in the nanoscale are. The approach was based on a contemporary view on the Vitruvian Man in full-body interaction; i.e. based on modern theories that claim that embodied interaction can foster a better learning of our environment. Experimental assessment was carried out with 64 children, comparing the full-body interactive experience with a desktop adaptation of it. Results showed better performance on children's memorability and classification of objects (ranging from the size of centimeters to the nanoscale) for those who used the full-body experience with respect to those in the desktop system.

## Categories and Subject Descriptors

H.5.1 **[Information interfaces and presentation]**: Multimedia Information System – Artificial, augmented and virtual realities; H.5.2 **[User Interfaces]** (D.2.2, H.1.2; I.3.6) Ergonomics. K.3 **[Computers and Education]:** Computer Uses in Education.

## General Terms

Design, Human Factors, Performance, Theory

## Keywords

Embodied Interaction, Embodied Cognition, Full-body Interaction, Nanoscale, Children, Interaction Design, Virtual Learning Environment.

## 1. INTRODUCTION

At the end of the 15th century Leonardo da Vinci created the representation of the Vitruvian Man. This drawing was based on the proposal that the Roman architect Vitruvius made to take the human body as the source and reference of proportion in architecture. The work by Vitruvius, *De Architectura*, [19] can be considered one of the first (15BC) in which the human body was considered the referent for the design process. According to Vitruvius, making the human body the referent would lead to better architectural designs, thus creating spaces better suited for humans.

Recent years have seen a growing interest to explore and understand the capabilities of the body as an important part of human computer interaction (HCI) alongside the interest for embodied cognition. One example of the former is Krueger's Videoplace [15]. Krueger pursued the creation of systems where users had the "illusion that their actions were taking place" within a Virtual Environment. Another example of the importance of the body in HCI is the CAVE, in which, according to Cruz-Neira, "the body is implicit - the body appears physically and does not require rendering" [8, p5]. In both Virtual Reality (VR) systems, the body gained protagonism in new interaction paradigms that fostered gross motor habilities rather than fine motor skills.

In a more conceptual approach, Bill Buxton [4] wrote in 1986 that we should "pay more attention to the 'body language' of human computer dialogues" and that "computer systems make extremely poor use of the potential of human's sensory and motor systems".

These examples show how the body started to gain relevance in the history of interaction design, leading to a continuous evolution of the theoretical framework around the importance of the body in interaction. The adoption of psychological and cognitive theories on embodied cognition by the field of full-body interaction has given a central role to the body when designing new interactive experiences.

### 1.1 Background on the Role of the Body

The design of our interactive exhibit was based on the theories that pose that embodied experiences can reinforce learning and understanding. This idea comes from the theories that claim that human cognition is mediated by the body [4]; known as embodied cognition.

Phenomenology studies how subjective consciousness and knowledge arise from how we perceive, experience and act within the world mediated by our own body [7]. Dourish [10] derives the concept of embodied cognition from phenomenology. One of the major lessons he draws - is that embodiment is about the relationship between action and meaning [10, p. 126]. Embodiment is not just about being physically in the world, but also being in a "participative status" within it.

The relation between environment and physical experience is reflected in Piaget's Constructivist Theory. Piaget proposes that cognitive development is based on the "detachment" of knowledge from the world of concrete objects to the world of abstract and symbolic objects. The changes in children's construction and acquisition of knowledge emerge as a result of their activity within the world [1]. This idea of action, or activity, is also found in Leontiev's Activity Theory [15, 20]. Activity Theory states that psychological processes (i.e. cognitive processes) emerge from the activity of humans in the social environment and the artifacts within it. Inter-psychological processes, those that take place in the physical world, are necessary for the development of intra-psychological processes. Vygotsky called this process "Internalization" [21], which is in consonance with Piaget's constructivist model. These theories ground the importance of the body on the construction of cognitive processes and hence, on the learning and acquisition of knowledge.

Alongside these theories, the importance of the body has been fostered also by the evolution of computers and devices. As Grudin [11] proposed, the history of computing is that of "the computer reaching out". In this history, new kinds of sensors, such as multi-touch screens (led nowadays by smart-phones and tablets), Microsoft's Kinect™, Nintendo's Wii™ or Leap Motion™, have helped in the process. New hardware has lead to new ways of achieving communication between computing devices and users. Nowadays more natural interactions are being explored. Multi-touch surfaces allow *direct manipulation* of virtual objects as windows to virtual environments, while advances in tracking interfaces (e.g. accelerometers, infrared cameras, 3D tracking systems, etc.) have opened the door to full-body interaction, where the whole body can take part in the interactive process between computers and humans.

## 1.2 Problem Statement
In 2012 the CosmoCaixa Science Museum commissioned the research team to design an interactive exhibit to help visitors of an exhibition understand how small the nanoscale is. In this exhibition visitors learn about four different converging technologies: Neuroscience, Information and Communication Technologies, Biotechnology and Nanotechnology.

CosmoCaixa designs its exhibits for an archetypal visitor who is 10 to 12 years old. Therefore, our goal was to design an exhibit to help children of this age understand the nanoscale. Given the complexity of the abstract notion of the nanoscale and that it is not a well known concept by children of that range of ages; we took an approach of using the body as a referent. Hence, we developed a full-body interaction Virtual Learning Environment (VLE) for teaching the concept of nanoscale.

In the following sections we present and discuss work related to explaining the nanoscale. We then discuss different approaches on VLEs based on embodied cognition. We describe the design process of the museum exhibit we developed to help understand the notion of the nanoscale. While describing the design process we will also describe the interactive installation. This design is based on the role of the body as a referent. Finally, we describe the experimental assessment of the benefits that the full-body interactive experience may have for helping in the learning of the nanoscale.

## 2. RELATED WORK
## 2.1 Explaining the Nanoscale
The concept of the nanoscale is commonly taught in high school in the Mathematics subject. Students are introduced to the concept of scale alongside that of exponentiation and other scientific concepts such as atoms and molecules. In general traditional educational approaches of the concept are passive cognitive processes.

There have been a few attempts in the past to innovate with educational approaches using audiovisual and interactive means to try to explain the notion of nanoscale. One such example is the movie "Molecules to the Max" for IMAX theatres. This movie shows a journey into the molecular level. IMAX theatres offer unique visualization possibilities which would seem useful to explain and describe nanoscale objects, however, the spectator does not have a clear relation of scale and the zooming visual strategies make the spectator quickly lose reference of previous scales.

In this line we can find other approaches such as the "Understandingnano" [12] website. This website provides many videos that explain the nanoscale in order to better understand specific topics on nanotechnology. Again, as in the movie, clear referents to the viewer in the transition process from human scale to the nanoscale are not supported.

Only a few works have been found that explain the concept of the nanoscale to children from a more interactive point of view. One example is NanoCancer [2] which is a VLE in which users can prepare doses of drugs to attack a cancer tumour by manipulating different molecules on a large display. By trying out different combinations users can learn about the properties of each component and discover how these interact with the body at a nano level. However, there is no transition in the exhibit from a known human scale to the nanoscale to better show how small medical nanotechnology is.

The web application by Cary Huang, "The Scale of the Universe 2" [13], represents another interactive approach to better understand how small the nanoscale is. In this application, users can navigate through different objects that are representative of different scales. They can navigate from the scale of the Observable Universe to the scale of a Proton (i.e. the femto scale) by using a slider in the GUI. Navigation starts at a scale of everyday objects and can move either towards larger or smaller scales. Despite starting with everyday objects at the human scale, which are meant to act as referents, their representation depends on the size of the display in which users are visualizing them; almost always a desktop standard computer or laptop monitor. Moreover, users cannot manipulate these objects and therefore do not have a chance to become familiar with them.

## 2.2 Embodiment in VLEs
According to Dillenbourg [9] VLEs refer to systems that create an information environment designed to help teachers in the educational processes they follow. In these environments students can participate by "interacting with data". Dillenbourg stresses the fact that virtual and physical worlds must be closely linked to achieve good results in the understanding of the concepts portrayed in the VLEs.

Significant research exists on how digital technology positively helps learning and fosters user attention and attitude towards the learning experience [3, 14]. Some projects have applied embodied cognition theories to VLEs, adding to their potential the advantages of technology as learning experience mediators [6, 16, 17].

One of the first full-body VLE projects where interaction with the environment is essential is NICE (Narrative Immersive Constructionist / Collaborative Environment) [23]. Based on embodiment theories, this interactive VLE aims to teach children the effects of sunlight and rainfall in plants, the growth and recycling of vegetation and other similar biological concepts of a simple garden. Children enter the environment wearing stereo glasses, which allow them to see the real and virtual world, and they then use a wand to interact with virtual objects. They can plant seeds, watch the plants grow, and take care of them to obtain a successful crop. This way, the children learn from their own actions and personal experiences with and within this world.

Experiments carried out with NICE [23, 13] presented results that are still very important for the design and development of other interactive VLEs. The most important conclusion for our purposes is that there is a clear relationship between interactivity and engagement in VLEs. This can have a positive effect on the learning process and on the careful management of the balance between fun and learning tasks such that users do not lose focus on these learning tasks. Observed results showed an increase in children's engagement, which positively influenced the outcomes of the learning process of everyday and abstract concepts.

Another important related project is The KidsRoom [3], developed in 1996. According to their authors, the KidsRoom was "a perceptually-based, interactive, narrative playspace for children." Visual and sound effects, as described by the authors, were used to "transform a normal child's bedroom into a fantasy land where children are guided through a reactive adventure story". It allowed children to interact with the space without having to wear special devices, making interaction more natural. The goal was to build a digitally enhanced environment where the activity took place in the real physical environment, rather than in the virtual screen environment and where multiple users were simultaneously supported. Studies on the system revealed that multi-user interaction fostered children communication during the experience, for example helping one another in coordination. This approach stresses Vygotsky's idea that cognitive processes arise from social interaction processes.

The embodiement that both examples provided, and their use of space to convey the stimuli and content, are important referents for our design work as described in the following section.

## 3. FULL-BODY INTERACTION DESIGN

The exhibit that we designed for the "Tecnorevolution" Exhibition at CosmoCaixa was called "NanoZoom" (Figures 1, 2 and 3). We will now describe the requirements, challenges and goals of the exhibit, specify how we addressed them in our design process, and then present our final proposal for the interactive system.

## 3.1 Requirements, Challenges and Goals

Requirements were initially captured in interviews with experts and curators from CosmoCaixa who stressed the importance of achieving an exhibit that successfully helped visitors understand how small objects in the nanoscale are. The reason for this being

that this specific exhibit should help users better understand other sections of the exhibition which were related to nanotechnology.

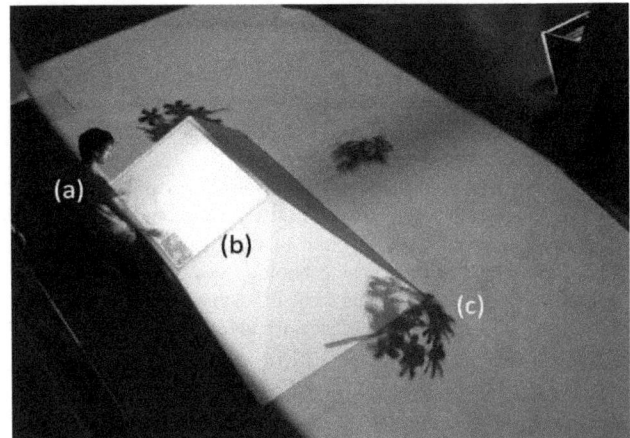

**Figure 1. The exhibit seen from above: a user (a) is interacting with the virtual objects on the table (b) while three objects are already on the floor (c).**

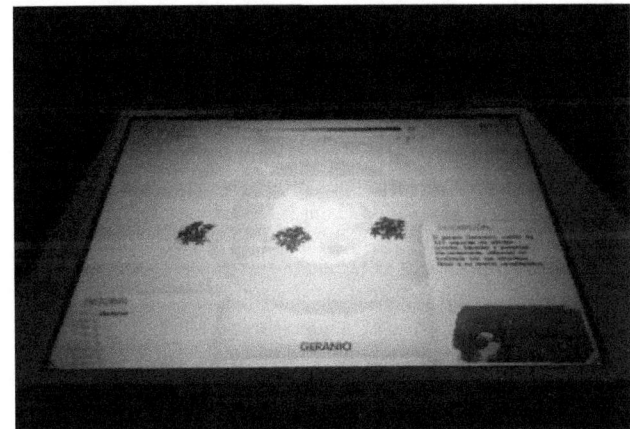

**Figure 2. Close up of the table. The picture shows the interactive content and the lateral slopes.**

From our analysis of multimedia and interactive applications related to the nanoscale we identified some recurrent issues that could affect understanding of the nanoscale concept.

First, analyzed work provided no solid referent for the spectators or users to compare the objects in the different scales; i.e. scales were either not clearly related to each other and hence their objects became unrelated too, or the scales were quickly lost from sight. Second, the display of the experience lacked a link to a global scale; i.e. to understand each scale some sort of global referent is needed and these works did not provide one explicitly. And third, the user had no, or only indirect, interaction with the objects; i.e. the user could not become familiarized with each object.

Since the design of the experience demanded us to focus on how the user was to be confronted with the virtual environment through the attitudes and relations that the user would adopt at every point in the experience we decided to follow the interaction-driven design strategy [18]. This allowed us to design the physical interfaces and their meaning in the construction of the experience based on the attitude we needed from the user.

## 3.2 Making the body of the user the referent

The main hypothesis behind our design was that taking the body of the user, as the referent, would help the user to better understand and perceive the abstract concept of the nanoscale. Because of this, we designed an exhibit in which the body of the user was the central element. The body linked all the experience and set a 1:1 relationship with the objects in the environment. Indeed, from birth, our own body is our best referent. We start learning through proprioception and kinesthesia and learn about our body parts and where they are located, and about our motion capabilities and our body position in space and its relation with the surrounding world. In our technology design the body of the user is the only constant known element throughout the experience (the physical interfaces are also constant but they are not well known to the user).

Our second hypothesis was that providing the users with the capacity to manipulate the objects at each scale would enhance this 1:1 relationship and knowledge between body and environment. Hence, we used an interactive multi-touch table (Figure 1b and 2) on which the users could see and play with the virtual objects at a human scale (Figure 1c).

According to these premises, on starting the experience the users find a set of virtual objects at the scale of centimeters on the initial menu of the multi-touch table. Users can then interact with everyday virtual objects (selected with the assistance of experts and the "Tecnorevolution" exhibition curators) such as a chicken egg, a geranium flower, a wisdom tooth, a human bone and a Euro coin. Users can select one object from the initial menu and obtain scientific information about it through a GUI on the table surface. They can "throw" the selected object onto the centre of the table (the play arena) by sliding a finger or two over the object. Users obtain three instances of the selected object in 3D on the play arena. They can manipulate and play with objects by "touching" or "pushing" through sliding hands and finger gestures over the multi-touch table.

Manipulation of these 3D objects in the play area can be considered a full-body interaction for a number of reasons. First, because in this initial level (at a scale of centimeters), the objects are represented at a 1:1 scale with respect to the users hands and rest of their body (Figures 1 and 2) and as they are well known objects we strengthen this known relation in this level of the experience. Second, the size of the multi-touch table (120x90cm) stimulates and requires users to make large arm gestures while interacting with the interface as they must often lean over the table to play with the objects as they move toward the opposite side of the play arena. These bodily actions provide a full-body experience to the user that enhances their understanding and increases their awareness of the properties of the objects with respect to size, scale and proportions. Based on the Constructivist Model and the way in which knowledge is "detached" through the manipulation of objects, this *direct* manipulation of virtual data benefits the perception and understanding of the virtual environment.

## 3.3 Miniaturizing the user

At any moment after having selected an object to manipulate, users can zoom in to move "down" to a smaller scale in the virtual environment. Users do this through a zoom gesture which has them placing their hands together at any point on the table and separating them out while dragging them on the surface. This full-body zoom gesture - as well as those for manipulating the objects - was based on the findings of a number of tests that we conducted with approximately 50 users to verify which gestures were deemed more natural for each task or goal.

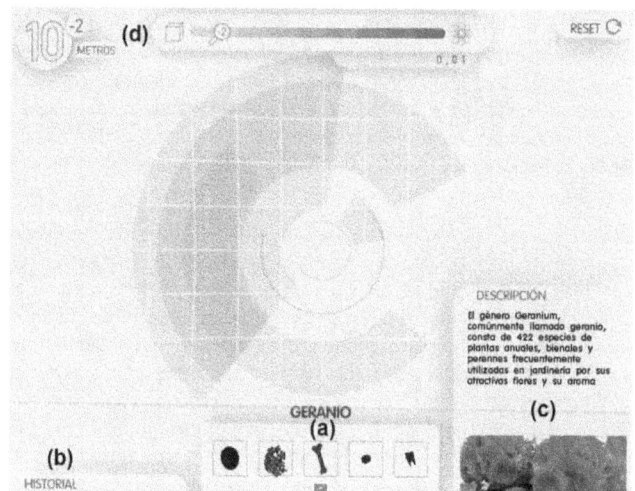

**Figure 4. GUI. Obect menus (a). History of navigation (b). Description of actual selected object (c). Scale gauges (d)**

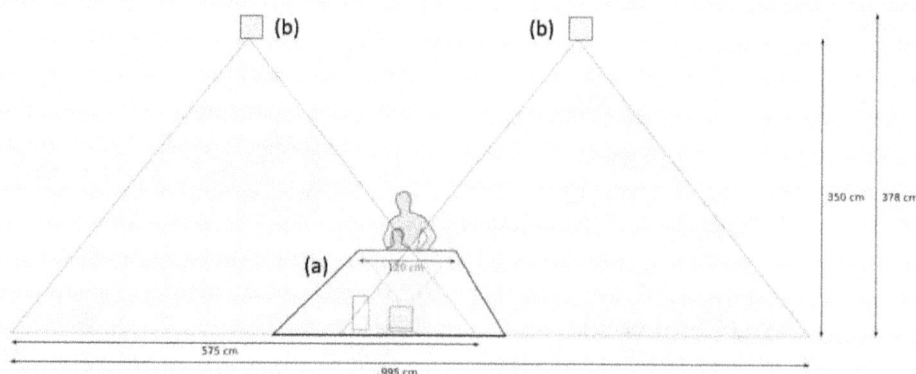

**Figure 3. Front elevation of the exhibit: multi-touch table (a), two projectors (b) for the 10 meters wide floor projection.**

Figure 5. Gauges detail. To the left one can see the base 10 exponential indicator. In the right there is the scale ruler and decimal indicator

After the first zoom gesture, the user moves from the centimeter scale to the millimeter scale (this is shown by a set of information gauges on the GUI of the table, Figure 4d and 5). The effect of the zooming in action is that objects grow ten times in size. This effect may also be perceived as shrinking the body of the user by a factor of ten. This change in relation of scale occurs at every zooming action and hence the body of the users is gradually "miniaturized". Nonetheless, in this process, the body of the user is maintained as a referent of scale and proportions for the user and allows him or her to relate to the sizes of the new discovered objects in the new scale level.

## 3.4 Maintaining the referent

As objects grow to ten times their size during the enlargement of the environment triggered by each zooming gesture, they no longer fit on the table. To avoid them disappearing from the field of view of the users and making them lose this new scale referent, the natural option was to make the virtual objects "fall" off the table to the floor onto an area around the table (Figures 1c and 2). We designed the table such that its laterals formed a truncated irregular pyramid (Figures 1b, 2 and 3) which then allowed the virtual objects to flow out of the table's surface and slide seamlessly down to the floor. Once on the floor, the users could still see the objects around them and could even go and walk over them and understand their new scale in relation with their newly "miniaturized" body.

Objects on the floor, a part from being a scale referent for the user at the table, also caught the attention of other visitors and motivated them to get closer to the interactive exhibit (Figure 6). Additionally, these objects could foster communication between the user at the table and the surrounding people, thus creating a social space from which knowledge could arise thanks to the inter-psychological processes being triggered in this space. As we have seen in previously commented embodied VLEs, collaboration between different participants is key for the learning process.

As items fall to the floor, on the table, a new set of objects of the new scale level is offered to the users. These users can again chose an object to play with and in so doing they assume a new scale of their own while seeing the "old" large objects floating around the floor. The body is again the referent of scale and proportion for the user.

As an example, let us suppose a user is now manipulating an ant on the play arena of the table, which fits comfortably in his or her hand. A user who had not gone through the previous phases of the experience, could think that ants are a few centimeters in size. However, the typical user will have first passed through other objects and related to them. Hence, potentially having initially manipulated a geranium flower, which would be known from personal experience to be a few centimeters in size, the user would have then zoomed in to see the geranium grow ten times and fall off the table to the floor. Then in the next level on selecting the ant from the menu of objects belonging to the

millimeter scale, the user would be very aware that the object now being held is a much smaller object. Moreover, the size of the ant on the table can be compared with the huge geraniums on the floor.

**Figure 6. In the picture one can see some users interacting with the multi-touch table while some people interact with the objects (chicken eggs) lying on the floor.**

When the objects on the table grow to ten times their current size the objects on the floor also grow by a factor of ten. Hence, they become huge objects with respect to the user. The floor projection was designed large enough (Figure 2) to always show objects that at least have been enlarged to 100 times their original size on the table (i.e. have suffered two zooming actions). This way, users always have a visual reference of at least three scale levels: one on the table and two on the floor. This is an important reinforcement of how the body becomes a referent in the global experience and in this way, the body of the user is always maintained as the measure of all objects and is the fixed known referent that allows a better understanding of how small everything becomes in the navigation towards the nanoscale.

## 3.5 Exhibit design

The final design of NanoZoom is composed of a multi-touch workbench with a large top surface of 120x90cm which is slightly tilted towards the main user for comfortable viewing and interaction by children (Figure 2). It is based on a rear-projection and an artificial vision system based on IR reflection for tracking user interaction, both of which are located inside the table. The interface of the table has a GUI that provides information on the current scale, a "scroll-up" (as opposed to "drop-down") window showing a description of the selected objects, a "scroll-up" window showing the historical list of selected objects during navigation (as a breadcrumb track) and a reset "button" in case a new user comes in when a previous user has left a navigation session halfway through. The floor projection is ~10x4.5m (~33x15feet) to provide a huge visualization area, which is achieved by two projectors mounted above the exhibit. The projection system is software controlled to hide the seam between the two projectors on the floor and to perfectly match the projection on the table and allow seamless transitions of the objects from table to floor.

# 4. ASSESSING THE SUCCESS OF THE EXHIBIT

## 4.1 Experimental Design

As we wanted to assess whether the full-body interaction design was indeed successful in the experience and as we also wanted to see if the use of the body as the referent allowed the user to better understand the relations of scale, we defined an experimental set-up to study these claimed benefits. Therefore, for this assessment we decided to define a comparative study where we confronted user interaction and learning results between the full-body interactive exhibit and a version of it that was adapted for desktop use with a regular monitor, keyboard and mouse interaction, which is detailed below in section 4.2.

We defined the following two main hypotheses:

- Users have better recall results when using the full-body experience than when using the desktop application.

- The users have a better sense of scale and relation of sizes when using the full-body experience than when using the desktop application.

The experiment comparative analysis tested two groups of children in two experimental conditions. Children were randomly chosen from within school groups visiting the science museum and hence had no idea they would be participating in such tests, which made up a convenience sample. One group of children used the full-body interaction VLE designed for the exhibition. This group was the experimental condition group. The other, control group, used the desktop application.

The demography of the experiment was 64 children aged between 11 and 13 years old. The population was evenly balanced with 33 girls and 31 boys and both experimental groups were composed of 32 subjects (Table 1).

Table 1. Sample distribution of the experimental subjects.

| Table Group | | | PC Group | | |
|---|---|---|---|---|---|
| Sex | | Age | Sex | | Age |
| Female | Male | Mean | Female | Male | Mean |
| 14 | 18 | 12 | 19 | 13 | 12 |

The experimental program was as described below (Figure 7), each session taking around 25 minutes maximum per child:

1. The school teacher in charge of the students signed an informed consent authorizing the participation of the children. Teachers had the authorization of the parents to decide upon the participation of children in any activity held within the CosmoCaixa museum. Hence, teachers signed the informed consent for each child to participate in our study. This consent authorized us to use the anonymous data collected from each child's interaction. The child also provided oral consent.

2. Children were guided to a table close to the exhibit area to do a pre-test with the following structure:

   o Children were asked for their age and gender, their literacy in computers and their technology habits related to multi-touch technology. We also tested for basic knowledge on the nanoscale.

   o Children were asked to do an 8 card sorting exercise to capture a baseline knowledge and ability related to scale of objects. Each card had an image and the name of an object that belonged to a different scale from centimeters to nanometers (Figure 6).

   o The pre-test lasted for 5 minutes maximum.

3. Children were then guided to either the interactive exhibit or to a computer with the desktop application. The desktop application was close to the full-body interactive experience to maintain the same kind of experimental context for both conditions. In either case, children were debriefed on how to use and interact with the application. They were then asked to experience it by themselves going through all the possible scales, from centimeters to nanometers.

4. During the experiment, quantitative data about user interaction was stored by the application in log files. This data would be used to analyze their list of selected objects. This interaction with the virtual environment lasted for 10 minutes maximum.

5. Finally, children were conducted again to the table to do a post-test:

   o Children were given a set of 40 different cards. Each card had the image and name of one of the 40 objects that were available in the experience (5 objects for each of the 8 levels from cm to nm). They were asked to select and separate the 8 objects they had chosen during their experience. This was to test their recall after the experience.

   o They were then asked to sort those objects by scale from centimeters to nanometers.

   o The post-test was 6 minutes long, giving a maximum of 3 minutes for each task.

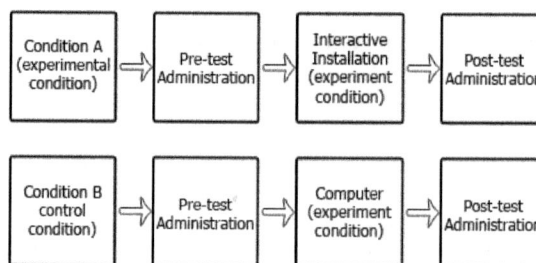

Figure 7. Experimental design procedure.

Both groups did the experiment inside the exhibition hall.

## 4.2 Desktop environment

As stated previously, the assessment was carried out by comparing the use of the full-body interactive experience designed for the museum exhibition, with respect to a desktop version of the interactive installation.

For the desktop application we adapted the multi-touch controls of the interactive experience to a mouse-based interaction on a regular 21 inch monitor placed on a regular office-like table. The selection, manipulation and zooming actions of the multi-touch table were translated in the following way:

1. Clicking left mouse button:

    a. Selecting objects in the menu (but not launching them onto the play area). Users must click on them with the mouse, versus having to press on them in the multi-touch table.

    b. Accessing object description and historical record of chosen objects. Users must click on the tabs with the mouse to display/hide them.

    c. Reset of experience. Users must click on the reset button for resetting the whole experience.

2. Dragging with left mouse button pressed:

    a. Launching objects in the menu onto the play arena. Users must "drag" the menu objects with the mouse having the left button pressed and finally release the mouse button.

    b. Manipulating objects on the play arena. Users may drag the objects around the table with the mouse and left button pressed and then release button to let object free again.

3. Double click of the left mouse button:

    a. Zoom-in action on the environment. Users may double click on the play arena to achieve the equivalent of the "zoom in" gesture on the multi-touch table.

We wanted our desktop application to be comparable to other applications developed in the past by other researchers (described in section 2.1). Therefore, we decided to use a single desktop screen (21 inch) as a standard desktop configuration. Because of this, we only showed the content of the multi-touch screen on the desktop screen and hence there was no feedback of the objects that grew too large to be displayed. In any case, it would have made little sense to attempt showing those objects since they would not fit in the screen..

## 4.3 Evaluation Tools

The system recorded children's activity in activity log files during the use of the full-body interaction exhibit or the desktop application. These activity logs saved which objects were selected by users during the experimental sessions. These log files also saved data on where on the multi-touch surface the users had interacted with the objects.

For the memorability test, we analyzed the recall of the eight objects selected by the children during the interactive experience. We therefore compared these eight objects with those that the children selected in the post-test with the cards. This was computed by the *intersection coefficient*, which relates the list of objects ready selected by users during the experience, with the list of objects with the cards. The higher the score, the better the children performed. Thus, the score we obtained was the intersection coefficient of how many objects were remembered correctly.

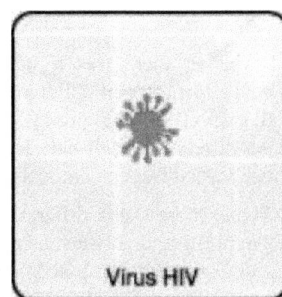

**Figure 8: Sample card for the HIV virus. The card depicts the image of the virus as represented in the virtual environment.**

For the second test, the acquisition of the notion of scale, we calculated *Kendall's tau* distance as a measure of the difference in the sorting of objects by the children with respect to the correct sorting of those same objects. In this case, the lower the score, the better the children performed.

## 5. RESULTS

Once we calculated Kendall's tau distances for the sorting of objects in the pre and post-tests and calculated the intersection coefficient for the post-test, we proceeded to analyze the data.

Our data was tested for normal distribution using Shapiro-Wilk's test since the groups were small (32 coefficients for each condition). The tests showed that the data was not normally distributed. Hence, we used Mann-Whitney U and Wilcoxon W non-parametric tests to verify our hypotheses.

## 5.1 Memorability

We first tested whether there was a significant difference between the memorability of children who used the desktop application and those who used the exhibit. The memorability score, operationalized as the intersection coefficient, was measured through a Matlab script that checked the number of coincidences between the application log and subject responses. The statistical analysis using Mann-Whitney U and Wilcoxon W non-parametric tests of two independent samples showed that, although the group that used the exhibit had a higher rank than the group on the desktop application, there was no significant difference between the two groups regarding memorability for the recall of objects used ($p < 0.164$) (see Table 2 and Table 3).

**Table 2. Memorability mean ranks**

| Group | N | Mean Rank | Sum of Ranks |
|---|---|---|---|
| **Exhibit** | 32 | 35.69 | 1142.00 |
| **Desktop** | 32 | 29.31 | 938.00 |
| **Total** | 64 | | |

**Table 3. Memorability test statistics**

| | Memory |
|---|---|
| **Mann-Whitney U** | 410.00 |
| **Wilcoxon W** | 938.00 |
| **Z** | -1.393 |
| **Asymp. Sig (2-tailed)** | .164 |

## 5.2 Sorting

We then compared whether there was a statistical significant difference between the performance of children in each of the two groups (control and exhibit) in the pre-test sorting task. As expected there was no difference at all between them and hence we can say both groups started from an equivalent notion of scale.

We then checked whether there was a difference in performance in the sorting task from pre-test to post-test using Friedman's test. This performance comparison was based on Kendall's tau distance, which measures the distance between the cards list and the objects list from the experience. For the desktop application we obtained no significant difference ($p < 0.25$). However, we did find a significant difference between pre-test and post-test results for the children who used the exhibit with $p < 0.012$ (see Table 4).

**Table 4. Friedman's test between pre-test and post-test for Exhibit group for the sorting**

| N | 32 |
|---|---|
| Squared-chi | 6.259 |
| gl | 1 |
| Asymp. Sig | .012 |

**Table 5. Friedman's test for post-tests between Table and Desktop groups for the sorting**

| N | 32 |
|---|---|
| Squared-chi | 4.172 |
| gl | 1 |
| Asymp. Sig | 0.041 |

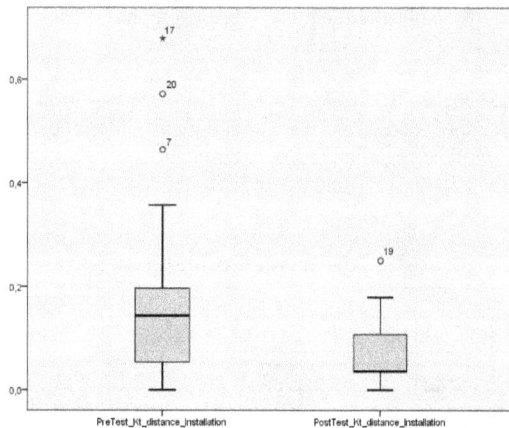

**Figure 9: Boxplot showing the values of Kendall's tau distance, which measures the distance between childrens' card sorting and the correct object list. The lower the value, the better the perfomance on the sorting activity. Left box is pre-test sorting, right box is the post-test sorting.**

To verify whether there was a difference between the two conditions, desktop and exhibit, Friedman's test was used to compare the post-test results of both groups. We indeed obtained a significant difference showing the children that had used the exhibit achieved better results ($p < 0.041$) (see Table 5). As stated previously on the evaluation tools subsection, we measured subjects' performance by using Kendall's tau distance between the application logs and response. In this case, the lower the distance, the better the sorting of the cards by the subjects (see Figure 9).

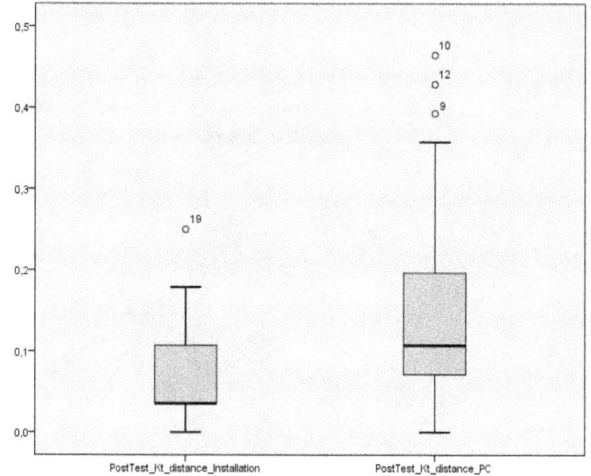

**Figure 10: Boxplot showing the values of Kendall's tau distance, comparing childrens' performance in post-test between exhibition (left) and desktop PC (right).**

Table 6 shows a summary of the improvement on scale understanding of children who used the exhibit over children who used the desktop application (the lower the distance the better).

**Table 6. Means of the different Kendall's tau distances (the lower the better).**

| Post-Test K dist | Mean | Std. Dev. |
|---|---|---|
| Exhibit | 0.0681 | 0.06 |
| Desktop | 0.1507 | 0.12756 |

## 6. DISCUSSION

Despite there being no statistical significance, we believe that the direct manipulation of objects compared to the mouse helped children to better relate with virtual environment objects. As children in the range of age of our subjects are typically not familiar with some of the objects seen in the smaller scales this may have accounted for these results. Having little knowledge makes it harder for children to remember those objects compared to more familiar objects (like the ones in larger scales, such as an egg or an ant).

Results do show that there seems to be a change in children's capacity for sorting objects depending on whether they used the exhibit or the desktop application; i.e. those who used the VLE performed better in sorting the objects. We can infer from these results that the full-body activity has an influence on cognitive processes related to learning, such as dealing with concepts of scale, for example helping children better sort the objects in the post-test. We believe the better results of the full-body interaction paradigm over a desktop interface are due to the fact that when interacting with the virtual environment with the whole body, the user is taking full advantage of the mediation of the body in the cognitive processes related to learning. This relates to the different cognitive theories we have discussed earlier that pose the body as a key part of learning processes.

# 7. CONCLUSIONS AND FUTURE WORK

Focusing on the active role that the body plays in mediating knowledge acquisition, according to current theories on embodied cognition, we have designed a full-body interaction Virtual Learning Environment based on these theories as an exhibit for a museum exhibition. This VLE helps children understand how small the nanoscale really is. First, our approach has been based on how the body of the user becomes the main referent of scale and the measure of all objects (as the Roman architect Vitruvius proposed in 15BC). Second, we have designed a 1:1 representation of the virtual objects and VE such that users better understand each scale level. Third, users can directly manipulate objects within the virtual environment to become familiarized with them and gain awareness of the scale relation with their bodies. Fourth, users can navigate from "human" scale (centimeters) to the nanoscale while having always at least three scale levels within view to maintain the scale referent.

The design approach used in the NanoZoom exhibit, based on full-body interaction and its potential advantages related to embodied cognition, has achieved very good results in memorability and scale-related abilities. We have experimentally shown that this approach helps children to better identify different sizes of objects when asked to sort them. Better relating of objects in the different scales can lead to a better understanding of the nanoscale by making it easier for learners to understand the difference between scales. The results from a comparative study between a group that used the full-body interactive exhibit and a control group using an equivalent adaptation for a regular desktop system show that the children who used the exhibit might have a better understanding of how small the nanoscale is, thus helping them better understand the concept.

This study shows that in interactive museum exhibits, it is not only fundamental to have an adequate content for the exhibit, but also to carefully analyze the type of educational approach used, the mediation role of the technology and its configuration, and how the body of the user can contribute to the unfolding of this mediation. Hence, full-body interaction is not necessarily always the best approach, but we have seen that, for example, using it as a referent for grounding knowledge and experience may help children in some learning processes.

Nonetheless, there are still many issues to be addressed in full-body interaction design. For example, future work could explore whether fostering the involvement of other users during the experience, thanks to the enlarged objects on the floor display, might enhance or rather disturb the learning process of the users. Another interesting aspect to assess would be to compare the use of the full-body interactive experience for the museum to a multi-touch experience on a handheld, where interactive gestures remain the same, but the full-body experience is lost. Finally, it could also be interesting to see how older children, who have already been introduced to the topic of the nanoscale, benefit from the VLE.

# 8. ACKNOWLEDGEMENTS

We would like to thank the La Caixa Foundation and the CosmoCaixa Science Museum, the expert in nano-bio-technology Dr. Victor Puntes and all the children that participated in the study.

# 9. REFERENCES

[1] Ackerman, E. K. 2004. Constructing Knowledge and Transforming the World. *Al learning zone of one's own: Sharing representations and flow in collaborative learning environments*. M. Tokoro and L. Steels (Eds). IOS Press, 2004. part 1. Chapt 2. pp 15-37.

[2] Alcaraz, S., Pares, N. and Mora, J. 2010. Interactive Learning Experience on Nanotechnology. ITS '10 ACM International Conference on Interactive Tabletops and Surfaces. P 301. DOI=10.1145/1936652.1936729.

[3] Bobick, A. F., Davis, J., Intille, S., Baird, F., cambell, L., Ivanov, Y., Pinhanez, c., Schutte, A. and Wilosn, A. 1996. The KidsRoom: A Perceptually-Based Interactive and Immersive Story Environment. In PRESENCE: Teleoperators and Virtual Environments, 8(4), August 1999. pp 369-393. DOI=10.1162/105474699566297.

[4] Borghi, A. M. and Cimatti, F. 2010. Embodied cognition and beyond: Acting and sensing the body. Neuropsychologia 48 (3): 763–773.

[5] Buxton, W. 1986. There's More to Interaction than Meets the Eye: Some Issues in Manual Input. In Norman, D. A. and Draper, S. W. (Eds.), *User Centered System Design: New Perspectives on Human-Computer Interaction*. Lawrence Erlbaum Associates, Hillsdale, New Jersey. Pp 319-337.

[6] Carreras A. and Pares, N. 2004. Designing an Interactive Exhibit for Children to Experience Abstract Concepts in New Trends on Human-Computer Interaction. Springer.

[7] Cerbone, D. R. 2006. Understanding Phenomenology. Acumen. Understanding Movements in Modern Thought Series.

[8] Cruz-Neira, C., Sandin, D. J., DeFAnti, T.A., Kenyon, R.V. and Hart, J.C. 1992. The CAVE: audio visual experience automatic virtual environment. Communications of the ACM Volume 35 Issue 6, June 1992. pp 64-72. DOI=10.1145/129888.129892

[9] Dillenbourg, P. 2000. Virtual Learning Environments. Proceedings of EUN Conference on "Learning in the New Millenium: Building New Education Strategies for Schools"

[10] Dourish, P. (2001) Where the Action Is: The Foundations of Embodied Interaction. MIT Press

[11] Grudin, J. 1990. The Computer Reaches Out: The historical continuity of interface design. Chi'90 Proceedings of the SIGCHI Conference on Human Factors in Computing Systems. Pp 261-268. DOI=10.1145/97243.97284

[12] Hawk's Perch Technical Writing, LLC. www.understandingnano.com

[13] Huag, C. The Scale of The Universe http://scaleofuniverse.com/

[14] Johnson, A. E., Roussos, M., Leigh, J., Vasilakis, C., Barnes, C. and Moher, T. G. 1998. The NICE Project: Learning

Together in a Virtual World. In the proceedings of VRAIS '98, Atlanta, Georgia, March 14-18, 1998. pp 176-183. DOI=10.1109/VRAIS.1998.658487

[15] Jonassen, D. H. and Rohrer-Murphy, L. 1999. Activity theory as a framework for designing constructivist learning environments. Educational Technology Research and Development, 47(1), 62-79.

[16] Krueger, M., Gionfriddo, T. and Hinrichsen, K. 1985. VIDEOPLACE - An Artificial Reality. CHI '85 Proceedings of the SIGCHI Conference on Human Factors in Computing Systems. Pp 35-40. DOI = 10.1145/1165385.317463

[17] Kynigos, C., Smyrnaiou, Z. and Roussou, M. 2010. Exploring rules and underlying concepts while engaged with collaborative full-body games. In Proceedings of the 9th International Conference on Interaction Design and Children (IDC '10). ACM, New York, NY, USA. pp 222-225. DOI=10.1145/1810543.1810576

[18] Lindgren, R. and Moshell, J. M.  2011. Supporting children's learning with body-based metaphors in a mixed reality environment. In Proceedings of the 10th International Conference on Interaction Design and Children (IDC '11).

ACM, New York, NY, USA, 177-180. DOI=10.1145/1999030.1999055

[19] Pares, N. and Pares, R. 2001. An Interaction-driven Strategy for Virtual Reality Applications. *Abstract Proceedings of the VR World Congress, El.pub, IST, EC.* (Barcelona, 2001)

[20] Roussou, M., et al. 1998. Learning and Building Together in an Immersive Virtual World In Presence vol 8, no 3, June, 1999, special issue on Virtual Environments and Learning; edited by William Winn and Michale J Moshell., MIT Press, pp. 247-263 and the cover.

[21] Vitruvius 15 BC. De Architectura III. Temples and orders of architecture.

[22] Wertsch, J. 1985. Vygotsky and the Social Formation of Mind. Harvard University Press.

[23] Wertsch, J. 1981. The Concept of Activity in Soviet Psychology. Armonk, New York: Sharpe, M. E

# Emergent Dialogue: Eliciting Values during Children's Collaboration with a Tabletop *Game for Change*

Alissa N. Antle, Jillian L. Warren, Aaron May, Min Fan, Alyssa F. Wise*

School of Interactive Arts & Technology
Simon Fraser University
250 -13450 102 Avenue
Surrey, B.C. Canada V3T 0A3

*Department of Education
Simon Fraser University
2400 Central City
Surrey, B.C., Canada V3T 2W1

[aantle, jlw29, amay, minf, afw3]@sfu.ca

## ABSTRACT

*Games for Change* (G4C) is a movement and community of practice dedicated to using digital games for social change[1]. However, a common model of persuasion built into most G4C, called Information Deficit, assumes that supporting children to learn facts will result in behavior change around social issues. There is little evidence that this approach works. We propose a model of game play, called *Emergent Dialogue*, which encourages children to discuss their values during interaction with factual information in a G4C. We summarize a set of guidelines based on our Emergent Dialogue model and apply them to the design of Youtopia, a tangible, tabletop learning game about sustainability. Our goal was to create a game that provided opportunities for children to express and discuss their values around sustainable development trade-offs during game play. We evaluate our design using video, survey and questionnaire data. Our results provide evidence that our model and design guidelines are effective for supporting value-based dialogue during collaborative game play.

## Categories and Subject Descriptors

H.5.m. Information interfaces & presentation (e.g., HCI): Misc.

## Keywords

Tangible computing; multi-touch interaction; digital tabletop; sustainability; games for change; collaboration; children.

## 1. INTRODUCTION

Children's educational games are designed to support children to meet specific learning outcomes. When the topics of these games involve social issues (e.g. antibiotic overuse, bullying, sustainability, social justice) then the goal is for children to learn not just facts but to eventually behave in line with social values. Games for Change (G4C) are digital games that purport to change or influence people's attitudes or behaviors around specific issues. Many G4C are developed based on implicit knowledge or assumptions about how external persuasion can influence attitudes and/or behaviours. This set of assumptions is called a model of persuasion. Hundreds of games have been created but there is little evidence that many of them contribute to either

learning facts, or influencing attitudes and/or behaviors [21]. One of the contributions of this paper is to make these models of persuasion explicit and to present a new model, called *Emergent Dialogue*, which is grounded in empirical work and translated into design strategies for digital games for learning around social issues in which we hope to influence children's attitudes and behaviors.

Elementary school curricula around sustainability often focus on key concepts such as balancing conservation and consumption. However, most learning activities do not explicitly expose the role that children's values have in learning or on their longer term behavior. For example, most children know that recycling is "good" and that they "ought" to do it. However, many children and adults do not consistently recycle. Thirty years of research in sustainability education has shown that telling people the "right thing to do" rarely results in the longer-term behavior changes we hope to encourage [21]. In particular, when values and attitudes contradict what we "should do", people often align their attitudes with their behaviors to justify the behavior [17].

We see these issues as an opportunity to contribute to both G4C and educational game design research. Our research question is then, *How can we design a children's educational G4C around sustainability that explicitly supports children to think about and discuss their values and attitudes about sustainable living?* For example, most children would say that they support preservation of forests but if this requires them to live in denser housing units, what then? Where do their values lie?

To address these challenges we first introduce different models of persuasion that have been used for G4C design. We point out the deficits of these models and briefly outline a new model, called *Emergent Dialogue,* put forward in [21]. This model originated in public workshops associated with environmental education and policy making [17]. Based on our work in [2], we summarize how the Emergent Dialogue model was translated into actionable design guidelines for digital games. We next describe *Youtopia*, a tangible, multi-touch tabletop sustainability game for elementary school-aged children, which we developed using these guidelines. The goal of playing Youtopia is to experience the challenges of balancing environmental and human needs in terms of food, shelter, energy and pollution while creating a world you would like to live in. A user study of Youtopia was designed to evaluate if children discussed their values during collaborative activity using Youtopia. We collected and analyzed video data from twenty sessions with forty children in order to identify sequences of value-rich dialogue and conflict between children during play sessions. We also analyzed interview and survey data to investigate if children were aware that they were discussing their values during interaction. We conclude with actionable recommendations for designing to support value-laden dialogue

[1] www.gamesforchange.org

around social issues in G4C and games for learning for children. The main contribution of this paper is our evaluation of Youtopia and the subsequent revision of our design guidelines for Emergent Dialogue based on designing a system and our study results.

## 2. BACKGROUND

There are many models of persuasion – more than we can discuss in one paper. We delimit our work by focusing on two common models and a new model, called Emergent Dialogue, which we derived from environmental education and policy workshops [2]. The most common model for attitude and behavior change seen in G4C is the Information Deficit model, summarized in [10]. The Information Deficit model persuades through "correct information". Our review of over thirty G4C found evidence of this model in most G4C. This model likely originated as "best practices" were mapped uncritically from educational games focused on teaching facts to G4C. We are now suggesting we should revisit the design of educational games with a more informed understanding of how learning facts, changing attitudes and influencing behaviors are all required in social issues education. The second model of persuasion, called Procedural Rhetoric, recently emerged from the games studies community as an alternative to the Information Deficit model, and possibly a more effective approach to serious game design [6]. The Procedural Rhetoric model focuses on persuasion through interaction or experiencing the consequences of one's actions. The third model, Emergent Dialogue, focuses on the role of dialogue around personal values in social issues education [21].

There is no empirical evidence that any one model is more effective than any other [21]. Each may have a role to play in both education and persuasion depending on the specifics of the social issue at stake. However, we think the practice of developing G4C can be made more effective if designers are explicitly aware of the persuasion model they are using. We propose that the Emergent Dialogue model may be effective at facilitating dialogue around personal values. When it is "designed into" an educational game for children, it may facilitate children to discuss their values in conjunction with learning facts about social issues and, in the long term, lead to better social outcomes. Before we can evaluate long term effects we must discover how to design G4C that support children to participate actively in discussion about their values during game play. This is the focus of our paper.

### 2.1 The Information Deficit Model

The *Information Deficit* model assumes that providing correct knowledge or facts about social issues will lead to desirable behaviors. Many approaches to sustainability education are based on this model. The Information Deficit model suggests that providing information will influence or change people's *values*, and that value change drives changes in their *attitudes*; which in turn drives changes in their *behaviors* [10]. For example, it is common for local governments and organizations to run community workshops and lectures intended to educate participants in the benefits of recycling, conservation, reuse and other environmentally friendly practices. These types of events are mirrored in most elementary school curricula. This approach is based on the assumption that unsustainable behaviors arise from a lack of knowledge.

The Information Deficit model assumes a top-down model of sustainable behavior change where some authoritative entity or organization (such as a curriculum, government, or NGO) already

has determined the *core message*. This information-centric model assumes that by using best new media practices to communicate the right information, behavior change will follow. Quiz games are the quintessential form of Information Deficit oriented G4C. For example, NASA's Recycle This![2] and Global Climate Change quizzes[3] are based on the Information Deficit model.

### 2.2 The Procedural Rhetoric Model

The *Procedural Rhetoric* model of behavior change emerged from game studies as a response to the criticism that many G4C, most based on the Information Deficit model, were either ineffective, unappealing or both [21]. Bogost coined the term Procedural Rhetoric to describe the practice of authoring arguments (i.e. rhetoric) through game mechanics (i.e. procedures) that result in pre-defined kinds of interactions [6]. In this model the argument of persuasion (i.e. the core message of the game) is not represented through information but through interactive processes. The rules of interaction in the game mechanics are in line with an argument for influencing attitudes or behaviors. Instead of simply providing players with facts or rewarding players for knowing facts, players are given an opportunity to interact with the core messages of the game through experiencing the consequences of their choices and actions during game play.

For example, in a simulation style environmental G4C, using a lot of energy usually results in high energy prices, environmental degradation or energy shortages. The implicit message is often that these effects are "bad" or negative. Cultural values around sustainability and responsible energy use are communicated to the player through the game rules, triggered by their choices through interaction. Rhetoric refers to the value-laden and culturally specific argument that behaviors which reduce energy use are good or right. Procedural refers to the rules programmed into a game through mechanics, algorithms and other forms of code. *Futura: The Sustainable Futures Game*[4] is an example of a simulation in which players experience the consequences of their actions through value-laden content. For example, if players create many energy plants, the colour palette of the world map changes to brown-grey and the ambient sound turns ominous. Users experience the core game message – that energy consumption and pollution are wrong – through interaction.

An underlying assumption of the Procedural Rhetoric model used in G4C is that by creating a set of game rules (procedures) that enable children to experience – through their interactional choices – particular events, they will modify their (future) behavior in line with the claims of the argument being made. In the case of both the Information Deficit and Procedural Rhetoric models, a top-down approach to content and information design is taken. Both models are based on the assumption that the desired outcome is a known quantity that must be advanced through the core message of the game, delivered through either facts or interactions.

### 2.3 The Emergent Dialogue Model

In [21] we introduced a model of persuasion for G4C called *Emergent Dialogue*. We suggested that this model could be applied in the design of digital media games. The model was taken from environmental education research about creating and running policy workshops with the general public. We worked to

[2] http://climatekids.nasa.gov/recycle-this

[3] http://climate.nasa.gov/interactives/quizzes

[4] http://www.antle.iat.sfu.ca/Futura

develop our model with sustainability social scientist John Robinson, who developed the core concepts of Emergent Dialogue in response to extensive critiques of the Information Deficit model. In [2] we presented the Emergent Dialogue model as an alternative approach to designing digital games for change and learning about social issues that may address the failure of existing models to elicit or influence future behaviors through learning facts or through interaction.

Robinson suggests that the previous conception of a unidirectional flow from information to behaviors is incorrect. Instead, he has found that people often bring their attitudes in line with their behaviors, rather than the other way around [17]. Because social issues are value laden, multiple conflicting views of sustainability exist and these cannot be easily reconciled. There is no one answer or set of facts or behaviors that is "correct". He suggests sustainability education should reveal that multiple conflicting values, moral positions and belief systems are involved in all issues of sustainability [17].

In this light, we suggest that when learning through game play is about influencing behavior around social issues, then success requires not only information and interaction but also and most importantly personally meaningful *participation* in dialogue. This is the fundamental premise of our work. In this paper, we apply and evaluate the Emergent Dialogue model in an educational G4C for children about sustainable living called Youtopia.

## 3. DESIGN METHODOLOGY

To date the Emergent Dialogue model has only appeared in public policy workshops and facilitated sessions with adults [21]. The challenge of the Emergent Dialogue approach is to find ways to support it through design decisions about content, procedures, rules and rewards in children's digital games. The elementary years International Baccalaureate curriculum[5] is pedagogically committed to participation, dialogue, and understanding the differences between facts, values and opinions. We use this as evidence to suggest that the Emergent Dialogue approach may be age-appropriate for elementary school-aged children.

## 3.1 From Model to Design

In order to design a game based on a model of persuasion we need ways to translate the model to actionable design decisions. In particular we needed a way to translate Emergent Dialogue into guidelines for a G4C for children. To understand how to apply the Emergent Dialogue model in G4C, we adapted a humanities research methodology called *Close Reading*, which has been used to understand important factors in video games [5]. Analysis of existing G4C was used to reveal some of the ways that persuasion models were implemented in games. We chose ten web and DVD G4C suitable for children on the topic of sustainability. Our close reading analysis identified six ways that persuasion models showed up in G4C. We call these *design markers* because they mark or provide evidence that a particular persuasion model has been instantiated into a game through the design process [2]. Design markers related to specific decisions made about content, how the player will interpret that content, how that content is communicated to the player, the goal of the game, what is rewarded in the game, and how the player can progress through the game to the final outcome. For each model: Information Deficit, Procedural Rhetoric and Emergent Dialogue we described markers that can be used to identify a model of persuasion at work. We delimited our study by focusing on G4C related to issues of sustainability and the environment, but we suggest that the results are applicable to other educational G4C around social issues where the core objective is learning that influences current or future attitudes and behaviors. A full description of our design marker derivation is available in [2].

We propose that design markers can be used as *design guidelines* for G4C based on each model of persuasion. This is possible since we explicitly identified relationships between each model of persuasion and designable game elements. In the next section, we define six design markers for the Emergent Dialogue model and describe how they can be used as guidelines to design a G4C.

## 3.2 Design Markers for Emergent Dialogue

For each marker we provide a definition and describe how it can be instantiated in game design decisions. The six markers are described individually, but we found that they are inter-related.

### 3.2.1 Content

The Content marker is about the information, meaning or "text" of the game or the message the game is trying to communicate. It is one of the most important markers because it deals with the *What?* of the game. What is the *core message* of the game?

The Emergent Dialogue model deals with the player's personal narratives about the content domain, rather than an authored or encoded message or judgment. This content is not present in the game; rather, the game provides opportunities to reflect and discuss personal meanings and values outside the mechanics of the game. For Emergent Dialogue to occur, the game artifact serves as a means of *eliciting* a player's perspective on the content domain using content, game mechanics or other forms of motivation. In contrast to the Information Deficit and Procedural Rhetoric models, in which the core message is directly encoded into the game, the player is invited to participate in discussion about their values about the content.

### 3.2.2 Interpretation

The Interpretation marker is about how the designers of the game intend the core message (content) to be interpreted by children. Do children reach their own interpretation of the core message as they experience the results of their actions in the game play? Or are they left to form their own interpretation of what the core message of the game was? Interpretation can fall anywhere on a continuum between "closed" or forced to "open" or unenforced.

In the Emergent Dialogue model, content and mechanics are used to create opportunities for children to create their own interpretations and perspectives about what content and experiences mean, based on their personal meaning-making process. This is in contrast to the Information Deficit model, in which content interpretation is fixed or closed since the content reflects what is "right" or "correct" in terms of sustainable behaviors. It contrasts with the Procedural Rhetoric model, in which players interpret the core message through their interactions and experiences in the game, leaving interpretation of the core message somewhat but not completely open.

### 3.2.3 Mode of Communication

This marker deals with *how* content is communicated through the game to the player. Are children told or shown the core message through text, graphics or sound? The mode of communication is a comparatively simple marker and is largely a function of the interaction of the previous two markers.

[5]http://www.ibo.org/diploma/curriculum
https://www.bced.gov.bc.ca/irp/plo.php

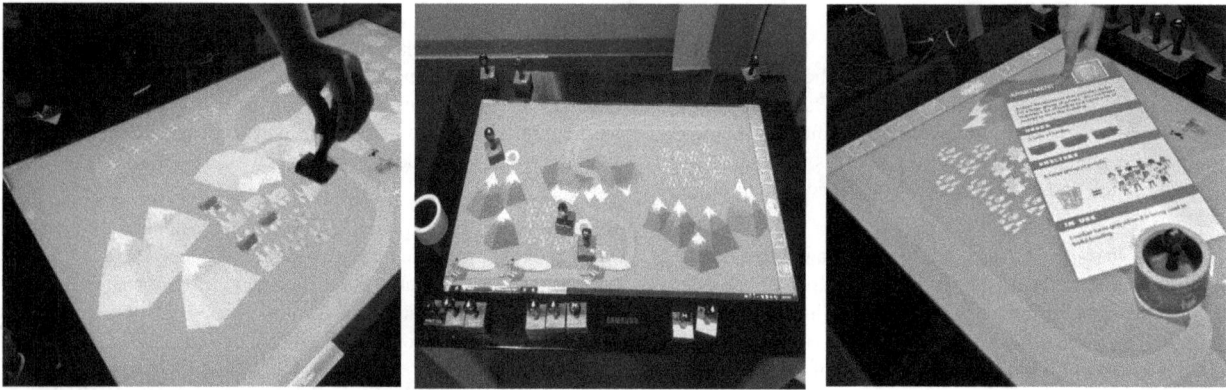

**Figure 1 (a) Stamping trees into lumber (b) Groups of related tree & wrench stamps (c) Placing stamp into Info "ring" displays Info card that describes land use type, what it needs, what it produces and how it contributes to the world.**

In Emergent Dialogue the system does not communicate the core message directly. Children should experience the core message through their dialogue in the context of game play. The system should give opportunities to participate in this process. This can be through the game interface or mechanics indirectly or through content directly (e.g. through a question: What do you think about ...?). This contrasts with the Information Deficit model, where the core message is directly communicated through content and feedback, and Procedural Rhetoric, where the message is communicated through specific system responses to player choices and actions.

### 3.2.4 Game Goals
Most contemporary definitions of games include some notion of winning and losing and both Information Deficit and Procedural Rhetoric adhere to this. By definition, a game is a system in which players engage in artificial conflict, defined by rules, which results in a quantifiable outcome [19]. In the Emergent Dialogue model, the goal is to arrive at some shared narrative around the social issue. In design this calls for open-ended tools or opportunities throughout the game to encourage players to discuss and share ideas and values, and most importantly through supporting players to determine their own game goals.

### 3.2.5 Motivation and Rewards
This marker is closely related to game goals. How does the game motivate the player to take specific action? What types of rewards are provided to encourage the player? In Emergent Dialogue oriented design there are no pre-defined objectives that the system can easily measure quantitatively. Therefore feedback should focus on the *process*, providing incentives and reward for authentic participation and honest engagement in the experience. For most social issues, children may bring their own sense of right and wrong and find the desire to "do good" provides internal motivation and reward independent of the game. This is in contrast to the other models in which what is right or good is encouraged by game mechanics and the game reward system.

### 3.2.6 Game Path and Outcomes
Our final marker is concerned with the path children take through the game, and the nature of the game's outcome. In the Emergent Dialogue model, the path to be navigated is less clear and there are no predetermined outcomes for the player to encounter. Players should be able to move in different directions and take different pathways through the game space, and it is up to the player to determine his or her own stopping point(s). In the other two models, there may be several paths but often these are uni-directional and

converge on a preset outcome, such as finishing a level or winning the game.

## 4. SYSTEM DESCRIPTION
Youtopia is a hybrid tangible and multi-touch land use planning game for elementary school aged children [4]. It was implemented on a Microsoft PixelSense digital tabletop. A short video of functionality is available at (www.antle.iat.sfu.ca/Youtopia). The main method of interaction is through physical stamp objects that children use to "stamp" different land use types onto an interactive map (Figure 1a). Youtopia was developed to investigate issues around tangibility, collaborative learning and G4C based on Emergent Dialogue. In this paper, we focus on exploring design to support Emergent Dialogue.

### 4.1 Learning Goals
Our system was designed to meet learning outcomes for the B.C. (Canada) Prescribed Learning Outcomes and the International Baccalaureate (IB) grade 5 unit on the environment and sustainability (ages 10-11)[5]. Sample learning outcomes include:

- Analyze the relationship between the economic development of communities and their available resources;
- Analyze data to determine if a resource is renewable or non-renewable;
- Understand that some resources are constantly available and are considered to be renewable resources (e.g. hydropower);
- Describe potential environmental impacts of using living and non-living resources.

Our preliminary results (below) indicated that all children successfully met the learning outcomes.

### 4.2 System Functionality
With Youtopia children work together to explore how their land use decisions either support or do not support a small or large population with shelter, food and energy. There are different types of shelter, food and energy sources as well as nature reserves, each with different benefits and limitations. Pollution results from human developments. The map is of a small area of land including mountains, forests, grasslands and a river. There are four maps, each with equivalent resources. Only the terrain elements are arranged differently. Together, the different populations and maps add sufficient complexity to the application so that children can play for long sessions. The underlying system model was designed to reflect real world relations between resources and developments. It was then calibrated to make it difficult to satisfy human needs without some pollution in the small population model, and impossible to do so with a larger population.

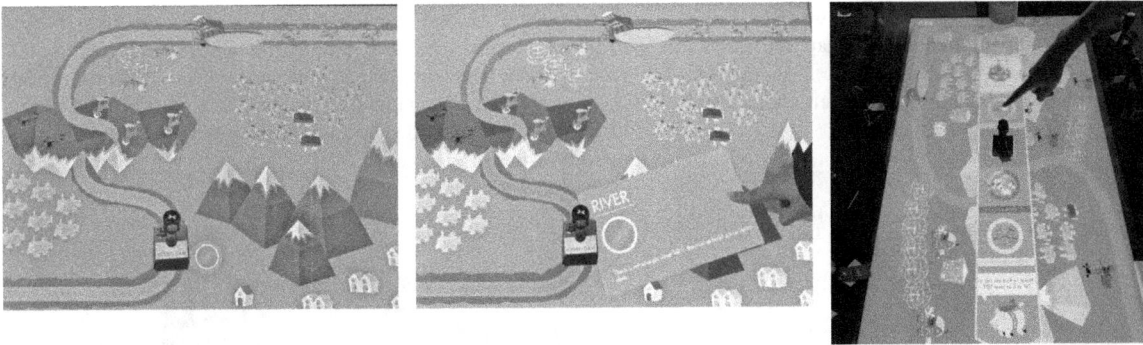

**Figure 2 (a) Learning tab appears (b) Pulling tab reveals message (c) Impact tool & touch display world state information.**

Natural resource and human developments are two main kinds of stamps, designated with a tree or a wrench on the top of the stamp handle. Each is also labeled with a picture and text to designate the land use type. To help children understand the relationships between lands uses related stamps are labeled with like colours. For example, irrigation, farms and garden stamps, which are all related to food production, are all colour-coded green (Figure 1b).

Another set of tools includes: erase, Info (information) ring (Figure 1c), impact (Figure 2c) and a 3D pig. The erase stamp enables "undo" without consequences. When a land use stamp is placed in the circular Info ring the system displays an information card about what the land use requires, produces and contributes to the world and constraints on usage, such as legal locations. For example, placing the apartment stamp in the ring displays how much lumber is needed to produce an apartment complex, how many people the structure can shelter and that it can be built in grasslands (Figure1c). Information is provided both textually and pictorially. When the Info tool is in use, the map is frozen and greyed out, so that no other children can interact at that time. The impact stamp also freezes interaction (Figure 2c). It displays an overlay showing the current state of the world in terms of what proportion of the population has its need met for shelter, food and energy, and how polluted the world is (expressed as partially filled-in rings, see Figure 4 below). The pig (Figure 1c, bottom of image) asks "Is this the world you want to live in?" Touching any circle highlights all the resources and developments contributing to that state on the map. For example, touching the food ring causes the system to highlight irrigation, farms and gardens (Figure 1c). A 3D pig object is used to create printable images of the current state of the world map, and the impact display.

## 4.3 Learning Feedback

If a child places a stamp in an illegal location then one of five types of learning tabs will appear (Figure 2a). For example, if the hydroelectric dam is placed on the river but there isn't enough water left (because it has been used up with other developments or reserves), then the "resource used up" orange tab appears (Figure 2a). A child can use their finger to drag the tab away from the stamp to display a message (Figure 2b). Messages are focused on explaining land use relationships and providing information that enables legal placement of a land use type. A child can resize or rotate the message so other children can see it.

## 4.4 Support for Collaboration

Researchers studying interaction with multi-user tabletops have suggested that even coherent groups of users may not immediately work together on collaborative applications [15]. To support collaboration we designed inputs that are co-dependent [3]. While each stamp is sensed individually, to successfully build anything requires two or more stamps placed in sequence. Typically, this is one or more natural resource stamps followed by a human development stamp. For example, since developments like the farm or garden require water, irrigation must first be placed on the map adjacent to the river. However, the river's water levels can be depleted so developments that depend on its usage may be limited due to this constraint. In this case, a development that uses water has to be removed, then irrigation placed, and then a farm or garden placed. We expected this strategy would require children to coordinate stamps and actions, and in doing so, negotiate what they want to achieve. Our preliminary results (below) indicated that children largely collaborated. More detailed analysis of collaboration is beyond the scope of this paper, outside of how it relates to Emergent Dialogue.

## 4.5 Applying Design Markers for Emergent Dialogue

In this section we describe the ways we incorporated the Emergent Dialogue model into the design of Youtopia for each type of design marker. Our goal was to use the six markers as guidelines to create a system that encouraged value-rich dialogue about sustainable land use planning.

### 4.5.1 Content

Content in the Emergent Dialogue model focuses on eliciting a dialogue that contains personal values about the content domain (sustainability) between the system and children, and ideally beyond the game into the classroom. The core message of Youtopia is that the children are responsible for making choices to develop and preserve the land to reflect the kind of world they want to live in. Because our system is a simulation style game, children can iteratively experiment with the consequences of their decisions, providing an opportunity to reflect on the effects of different choices. We also expected that requiring co-dependence of stamp inputs would encourage discussion about coordinating resources and developments. When children place the impact stamp tool anywhere on the map, they find out how much of their population's needs are met. The tool freezes the interface, displays a graphical overlay with images and text. This overlay is touch-sensitive and provides an opportunity to further explore the current world state by touching the food, shelter, energy and pollution rings to see all the land uses associated with that state. This provides another opportunity for children to discuss how their decisions are impacting the world that they are creating. After they have completed the game, children can use the 3D pig to create printable images of their final world map and impact display. The 3D Pig feature provides images that provide opportunities for children to continue to discuss their choices and values within the community of their classroom.

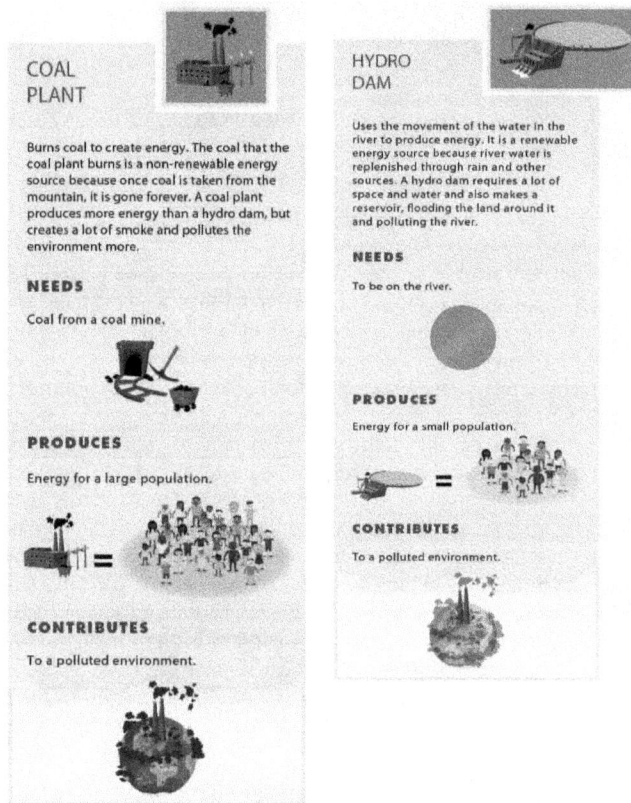

**Figure (3a) Info card for coal plant (3b) and hydro dam.**

### 4.5.2 Interpretation

We encourage open interpretation throughout our game. First, content (e.g. Info cards, learning tab cards) was all written without reference to any value judgments. For example, the Info card that explains how much energy and pollution a coal plant produces does not suggest that the pollution created by burning coal is "bad" or "wrong" or that cleaner solutions should be sought (see Figure 3a). We found this task harder than one might imagine, largely because values are routinely embedded into such content in source materials.

The interpretation of consequences of children's actions is also open since there is no winning or losing (see game Goals below). Children use the impact tool (Figure 2c) to display the state of the world. The system provides graphical information about food, shelter, energy and pollution levels using value-free means such as the proportion of rings filled, as shown in Figure 4. We used words that communicated general quantity but not quality or value judgment, such as "Most of the population has shelter." and "There is some pollution in the world."

### 4.5.3 Communication Mode

This marker deals with how content is communicated through the game. In our system children are not told the core message. Much of the content is accessed when they want it using the learning tabs or Info ring. They can choose to access Info cards

on any land use stamp by placing that stamp in the Info ring. This freezes the game and graphically displays images and text that are descriptive and value-free (Figure 3). Based on the children's values about balancing human and natural needs, they can decide how to proceed. The game does not tell them what or how to play correctly; they must discuss this and in doing so experience the core message of the game.

**Figure 4. Using graphical means to show proportion of population sheltered (left) and pollution levels (right).**

### 4.5.4 Game Goals

There is no explicit goal or "winning state" in our game, challenging the definition of it as a game. Children are invited to create a world they want to live in. It is open to the children to choose a map, decide the size of the population, how much of the population's needs they will or will not support, and how much pollution they can tolerate. They can use different types of shelter, food and energy as well as nature reserves, each with different benefits and limitations. The goal is for children to explore, through game play, how to create a world they would like to live in, which reflects their personal preferences, opinions and values. The impact stamp gives children information they can compare to their own personal goals for the game, rather than an absolute end state (since filling all the rings is very difficult).

### 4.5.5 Motivation and Rewards

Without a winning state it is difficult to know how to motivate children. We thought children might be motivated by the challenge of the task (intrinsic motivation), or by being able work together (external motivation). We also hoped the reward would come, in part, from being able to work through how to create a world that reflected their personal values. In the game there was no reward for meeting the population's needs without over-polluting the world. And conversely, not meeting the population's needs or creating pollution was not associated with right or wrong judgments or values. The activity ended when the children decided they were satisfied with their world. However, children knew they would have to print out their final map and impact display to later present it to their classmates. We thought this would provide external motivation to participate authentically.

### 4.5.6 Game Path and Outcomes

Using our system, children can play forward and backward through hundreds of game paths, each resulting in a slightly different outcome. At any time, they can start over, change the map, change the population, erase land uses and continue playing. We expect that providing multi-directional pathways and an underdetermined end outcome may encourage children to engage in dialogue. For example, they need to decide which natural resources to use at any point, which to preserve, which and where to put development and when they are satisfied with the game outcome (current state of their world).

# 5. USER STUDY METHODOLOGY

We evaluated Youtopia using a mixed methods user study at a local school with forty children, aged 10 and 11. We set up two identical systems on tabletops in pull-out rooms to ensure sound isolation and reduce distractions created by the novelty of the systems. Each room had two HD video cameras: one hung from the ceiling, the other on a tripod with a viewing angle that captured two children, the facilitator and the tabletop. In each room, we captured video and log data, and two additional researchers took still photographs and observational notes using structured observation sheets. We followed each session with a short survey and interviews which we recorded and transcribed. Two weeks later students presented their map and final world in a class presentation that was also recorded with video and assessed against learning outcomes by teachers using a standardized rubric.

In this paper we focus on using data to explore if Emergent Dialogue occurred and how specific design decisions for each design marker type may have encouraged it. We used coded video data to identify segments of Emergent Dialogue, which we summarize both quantitatively and with quotes. We augment this data with quantitative results from survey data related to Emergent Dialogue, and qualitative data from interviews in which children reflect on how their values played out in the sessions. Sample survey and interview questions appear in the results section. We did not notice observer effects, possibly because the research team interacted with the children informally outside of sessions to reduce such tension, and the main researcher was known to the children through other events. Although there may have been novelty effects in terms of enthusiasm for game play, we do not think that enthusiasm led to more or less discussion about values.

Children were grouped by their teachers into pairs with similar abilities and who worked well together. This pairing strategy was chosen to optimize chances of successful interaction and collaboration. The facilitator began each session with a preamble and tutorial about basic system functionality including how to use stamps, touch menus and tools. Children were instructed to "Create a world you would like to live in." Twenty minutes into the session they were told they had about seven minutes left.

## 5.1  Data Analysis

To verify that children successfully met learning outcomes we analyzed scores from a rubric developed by the teachers based on IB[5] learning outcomes. The average score for combined "content" and "reflection" categories was 4.8 out of 5 (SD =0.4). To date, most video coding of collaboration within the HCI literature involves looking at equality of participation – both verbal and physical (e.g. [9, 18]). Recent work has focused on mechanisms of negotiation and coordination (e.g. [1, 8]) and the interplay of physicality, space and conflict (e.g. [16]). Within the Learning Sciences literature the focus is more on the cognitive and socio-cultural processes supporting learning, resulting in fairly complex coding schemata. For example, Higgins et al. [11] developed a schema based on hierarchical categorisation that identifies increasing complexity in reasoning. Koschmann et al. [12] focus on microanalysis of small group meaning-making in the learning process. Dillenbourg and Evans [7] present an excellent summary of work in this area. However, none of the schemata presented are

suitable to identify instances of dialogue about personal values in their reasoning. As such we developed our own schema.

To verify that children collaborated (including verbal and physical participation) our coding began with a category called *working together* that involved both children working on a shared element of the task. This initial coding revealed that children almost exclusively collaborated throughout the sessions. We then created two non-mutually exclusive categories related to Emergent Dialogue: *in-depth* and *conflict*, both of which are subsets of *working together*. Refinement of these two categories and training of coders followed a standard process, which was repeated once for *in-depth* and later for *conflict*. The group included three coders as well as the principal researchers who did not code but oversaw the process and helped the coders refine categories. First the entire group met to define and agree on prototypical examples taken from observational notes. The three coders then worked together to code short segments of a training video. This led to refinement and further examples for both categories. This process continued until coders reached a Cohen's kappa value, $K > .75$ on the training video. *Cohen's kappa* is an estimation of the degree of consensus between raters.

*In-depth* includes events in which one or both children talk about decisions about what resources and developments to use. An *in-depth* event involves a sense of the world or individual values, which differs from simple preference. It must also involve reasoning using those values, typically around tradeoffs between human and natural needs. So the statement, "I think we should have houses not trees" is preference and would not be coded. However, the statement, "No, let's build houses instead of apartments because they use less lumber, and we can make more trees into nature reserves." would be coded *in-depth* because it involves values in the context of reasoning about tradeoffs.

*Conflict* includes verbal and/or physical disagreement with another person's action or utterance related to sustainability domain. *Conflict* requires an objection or stance on an issue. Presenting available options or suggestions is not *conflict*. *Conflict* may result in resolution, abandonment (unresolved) or uni-lateral decision-making.

After we developed our schema on the training video, we coded the 20 session videos in three rounds. First, three videos were coded by one person and cross-checked by another person ($K > .75$). Next, five videos were coded by one person and two of these were cross-checked by another person ($K > .75$). Finally, the remaining 12 videos were coded by one person and four were cross-checked ($K > .75$). After we coded *in-depth* and *conflict*, we ran descriptive statistics. Rather than looking exclusively for quantitative evidence at this early stage, we used video coding to identify segments in which children participated in Emergent Dialogue. We analyzed these segments in detail and triangulated with other data sources so that we could develop rich examples (following best practices in [11]) rather than only counting types of events within or across sessions.

# 6. RESULTS

Our results show clear evidence that children met learning outcomes and also engaged in discussion, negotiation and conflict about tradeoffs between human and environmental concerns that reflect their individual values. Sessions lasted on average 23 minutes (SD=4:23 minutes). On average there were about 10 *in-depth* (Emergent Dialogue) events per session. These tended to be short (10 seconds or less) although the longest lasted a full minute. These kinds of discussions comprised about 5% of the total collaboration time. Our video analysis revealed that children had significant *conflict* about 2.5 times per session, lasting on average 17 seconds. Of these we identified cases where children had conflict because of their different values. Sometimes they resolved differences, other times not. Overall the proportion of session time spent in these in-depth value-laden discussions and conflicts was small. However, we suggest that these segments of interaction were rich and that these kinds of interactions have the potential to transform children's understandings of the interplay of facts, values, and attitudes in social issues.

## 6.1 The Core Message

In the interviews all of the children reflected on the issues and tradeoffs they faced balancing human and natural needs, which is part of the core message of our game. They rated this issue as important, with an average score of 4.4 out of 5 (SD=0.6). In the interviews, one child said, "How I would think about it is …. I kind of anticipate what would happen before I put the stamp down … like I think about if I put the human down it would help them or I can put the nature reserves down will it help humans and nature." And their partner said, "Yes, like I would think like what would it do for us that would be what we really need, like if you don't do it, it won't be the end of the world." Another child said, "Probably we want to kind of even it out because humans are no better than any other animal and they can take the world for granted just because they are kind of bigger and we can do that; if we can do it then we have …… to space it out with animals because the animals have as much right as we do."

All the children grappled with the core message despite never being told what it was, or being rewarded for enacting it. They experienced it, prompted by opportunities within the game mechanics to reflect and discuss their values and choices to develop and preserve the land area in order to reflect the kind of world they wanted to live in.

## 6.2 Emergent Interpretation

Children used the erase, Info ring and impact tools repeatedly in sessions to understand the effects of different choices. These tools and their effects on the game provided opportunities for children to discuss their values in the context of reasoning about their actions. For example, after P1 placed the impact tool, the pair looked at the food, energy, shelter and pollution rings, and discussed the trade-off between pollution and housing levels, comparing to their own values for what was "good."

> P1: There is no pollution, all people have food, most people have shelter, all people have energy.
> P2: This is a good world.
> P1: You know what … it says most people .. I think if we add one more house. (*Uses eraser tool to erase a forest reserve to free up lumber*).
> P2: What! Why are you erasing it? (*Continues to protest*)
> P1. There's little pollution – it's OK.
> P2: No … wait.

P1 thinks that a little pollution is OK if all the population can have shelter. P2 disagrees and thinks a good world should have no pollution even if some people have no housing. With value-free content, their interpretation of what is good or enough emerges in the context of interaction; it is up to the children, and their differences prompt discussion (and compromise) about the kind of world they want to live in.

We often saw *in-depth* events when there were enough developments to support "most" but not "all" of the population.

Often, one child felt that this was fine but the other had a personal game goal to support all of the population. For example, P1 and P2 were working on shelter and placed the impact tool.

> P1: Let's see if all people have shelter.
> P2: Most people have shelter. That's good.
> P1: Let's think about it more … wait."
> P2: It's good enough. *Starts to do something else*

Our language choice of "some" and "all" was made to avoid value-laden words. However, because these words are subjective and there was no objective winning state, different interpretations emerged about what was "enough", which in turn prompted discussion and compromise. This idea of compromise inherent in this sequence is promising since compromise is at the heart of environmental planning.

One concern with using open interpretation in a learning game is that children may make false connections between their actions, system responses and the reasons for such responses. For example, they might think they have enough housing but too much pollution and so delete housing to impact pollution. However, in our case the impact tool provided evidence that pollution had not changed since deleting housing may free up trees but does not noticeably impact pollution.

## 6.3 Conflict as Motivation

Some pairs had little conflict, others had more. We observed that pairs that had conflict discussed their reasons for their choices, which sometimes involved using the Info ring or impact tool to present their case with facts and sometimes involved values. The impact stamp that triggered the world state overlay often resulted in reflection and discussions involving conflict about what to do next. Thus, conflict was beneficial in motivating discussion that involved values and further game play to try out alternatives. This finding is consistent with seminal work by Malone [13], who suggests that conceptual conflict is intrinsically motivating. Unlike a competitive game where conflict drives competition between two players, in our game conflict motivated negotiation and compromise during collaboration.

In the interviews when asked *If you had to do this activity on your own would your world have been different?* one child said, "She's leaning slightly towards natural resources and I'm leaning towards human side; like I said before I wanted to change some of it to apartments and she said no we should keep some more ….. but I eventually managed to get her to where she could change it all to apartments. Should I let her do that right away?" The facilitator then asked, *Would you have cut more trees down? Or did you have a debate about that as well?* The child said, "Yes, we had a little debate but I know that the trees are very, very, very important …" The children's conflict over the value of trees versus shelter motivated discussion, furthered game play and enabled them to make progress towards self-determined goals.

## 6.4 When do values emerge?

In many of the sessions we identified *in-depth* discussions about values in the latter half of the session when resources were running low and children were told they had seven minutes left. At the beginning of most sessions, resources were still in abundance so compromise was not yet needed. However, later the task became harder. For example, this late-game segment shows both *in-depth* dialogue and *conflict* about trying to create adequate shelter while conserving trees.

> P1: Most people have shelter. Are you kidding me?
> P2: What? No, no – most people can have shelter.

P1: No we have to try and do what we did before.
P2: There's only like only ... four more trees!!
P1: It's ok, it's ok.
P2: Four more trees ...

To address P2's concerns, P1 says, "Kill some of the houses" and erases most of the houses, to get trees back and builds higher capacity apartments, which still does not satisfy P2, who says, "What? People can't just live in apartments all their lives!"

We noticed that this type of value-laden conflict typically increased with time pressure when the pair had not yet created a world they were both satisfied with. This ties in to the issue of game challenge level.

## 6.5 Challenge as Motivation

We designed our system so that it was impossible meet all of a population's needs and have no pollution. However, it was possible to come very close to this state. Our *in-depth* analysis revealed that when children had difficulty, they were motivated to work together to find solutions, which in turn often resulted in *in-depth* discussions. For example, after P1 placed the impact tool,

P1: The world has to have some pollution if we're going to have all of those (*Points to all the developments*).
P2: No, No. I don't take that.
P1: What?
P2: Keep trying. (*Uses erase to try different approaches*)
P1: (*Eventually joins in*)

Challenge motivated Emergent Dialogue. This finding is also consistent with Malone [13], who suggests that appropriate challenge level is intrinsically motivating.

## 6.6 Emergent Dialogue is fun!

While conflict might be construed as negative, all children said they enjoyed working together. They also said working together helped them learn about balancing human and natural needs, rating this statement 3.7 of out 5 (SD=0.9). Children also said working together helped them understand their partner's values, rating this statement 4.0 out of 5 (SD=1.0). In response to the interview question, *How did having to work together affect the kind of world you created?* One child said. "Well we both had different ideas so we kind of liked different ideas .... we'd like something better so that's how it worked together." And the other child added, "I think that we both had different input and different views on this so if we both worked together two heads are better than one."

## 7. DISCUSSION

Overall we suggest that the design of our system was effective at eliciting collaboration and participation around deciding what kind of world the children wanted to live in, learning about the tradeoffs required, and encouraging some value-laden dialogue. In particular we think the ways we created opportunities for children to experience and discuss issues related to the core message worked well. Using value-free content combined with no right or wrong feedback or game goal meant children had to discuss their pathways through the game, use information and impact tools to discuss tradeoffs, and decide when to end the game. We suggest that it is largely the interplay of Emergent Dialogue design markers – rather than any one particular marker – that worked well to support the kinds of rich dialogue and productive conflict we saw. Compared to earlier work [1], we saw more heads-up inter-personal interaction.

Our initial assumptions were that children would only collaboratively work together some of the time. However, our first pass at coding showed they almost exclusively worked together. While we did not focus on the tangibility of the stamps in our design rationale, we suggest that having a set of sixteen physical objects, which were used for input and control, created situations where children were prompted to share the stamps and, in doing so, often discussed their reasons for wanting one stamp or another, or they discussed their plans based on the stamps they were looking or asking for, or about to use. Sometimes one child would reach to take a stamp before it was used by the other child, which also prompted conflict and subsequent discussion. Our video coding results showed this kind of overlap between *conflict* and *in-depth* discussion. This mirrors findings reported in [8] around productive conflict in tabletop learning. However, it is unclear if this pattern would have emerged if we had used only multi-touch buttons rather than physical "stamps". Speelpenning et al. found more evidence of dialogue around sharing tangible tools than equivalent touch tools in a sustainability game [20]. Olsen et al. found similar results when comparing tangible and touch toolbars [16]. Another factor that may have supported productive conflict is that there was only one of each stamp type. This may be similar to findings reported in [9] that suggest a single-touch interface requires more negotiation than multi-touch. We suggest that the combination of multiple unique input objects with the Emergent Dialogue design markers supported collaboration and productive conflict rather than non-productive conflict such as that reported in [14] in which children develop strategies to "own" input buttons and fight to gain control.

Children set their own winning state during game play. All children tried to meet the population's needs with as little pollution as possible and repeatedly checked to see if they had achieved this difficult task. Since it was not possible, *In-depth* dialogue and productive *conflict* often arose as they iteratively negotiated trade-offs and goals based on their own values throughout the game. We see this as similar to the way children iteratively discuss and modify game goals and rules in playground games such as tag, or hide and seek. No two games are alike. We suggest the openness of our system design in terms of content, game paths and lack of explicit goals enables this kind of organic determination of play. More work is needed to determine if more rigorous game rules and goals would eliminate this openness to interpretation.

We revised our markers based on our results and for clarity. We added two new markers (challenge level, tangibility), and separated marker six into two markers (multiple pathways and outcomes). In summary we present our revised guidelines:

1. **Content**: Enable children to experience the core message through system-generated opportunities that require discussion related to that message (e.g. overlays provide information about game world and current game state to encourage discussion but do not tell children what is "right" or what to do or how to win);

2. **Interpretation**: Use value-free information and consequences that are open to interpretation; but also provide a way for children to check their assumptions about causes and effects to avoid reinforcing misconceptions (e.g. impact tool enables them to see if changing developments impact pollution);

3. **Mode of Communication**: Provide on-demand content to support learning rather than forcing children through content (e.g. Info Ring, learning tabs, impact tool);

**4. Goals**: Enable children to determine their own game goals in line with their personal values;

**5. Challenge**: Calibrate challenge level difficulty so that it motivates discussion around how to achieve goals;

**6. Tangibility**: Use multiple unique physical inputs that require coordination (e.g. through co-dependent input design);

**7. Reward**: Rely on intrinsic motivation and provide mechanism to reward authentic participation (e.g. printout to share game outcomes with peers);

**8. Multiple Pathways**: Provide "no cost" opportunities to explore the consequences of a range of choices;

**9. Outcomes:** Enable game to finish when outcomes are in line with personal values and game goals.

## 8. CONCLUSION

We see this work as a first step at incorporating the Emergent Dialogue model into the design of children's G4C for social issues education. Our contributions include: encouraging designers to explicitly use one or another model of persuasion; providing an illustrated case of how to design using Emergent Dialogue guidelines in a G4C about sustainability; validating our design rationale with a robust mixed-methods user study; and providing a refined list of design guidelines to support Emergent Dialogue. We see this as a starting point for this work, and encourage other educational game designers to apply, validate and refine design markers for other styles of games, and social issue topics.

## 9. ACKNOWLEDGMENTS

Funded by NSERC, SSHRC, PICS and GRAND. We gratefully acknowledge the contributions of John Robinson, Allen Bevans, Anna Macaranas, Rachael Eckersley, Saba Nowroozi, Perry Tan, Amanda Willis and the fantastic school we worked with.

## 10. REFERENCES

[1] Antle, A.N., Bevans, A., Tanenbaum, J., Seaborn, K. and Wang, S. Futura: Design for collaborative learning and game play on a multi-touch digital tabletop. In *Proc. Conference on Tangibles, Embodied and Embedded Interaction*, ACM Press, (2011) 93-100.

[2] Antle, A.N., Tanenbaum, J., Macaranas, A. and Robinson, J. Games for Change: Looking at Models of Persuasion Through the Lens of Design. In Nijholt, A.(ed.) *Playful User Interfaces: Interfaces that Invite Social and Physical Interaction*, Springer, 2014, 163-184.

[3] Antle, A.N. and Wise, A.F. Getting down to details: Using learning theory to inform tangibles research and design for children. *Interacting with Computers 25*, 1, (2013) 1-20.

[4] Antle, A.N., Wise, A.F., Hall, A., Nowroozi, S., Tan, P., Warren, J., Eckersley, R. and Fan, M. Youtopia: A collaborative, tangible, multi-touch, sustainability learning activity In *Proc. Conference on Interaction Design for Children Conference*, ACM Press, (2013) 565-568.

[5] Bizzocchi, J. and Tanenbaum, J. Well Read: Applying Close Reading Techniques to Gameplay Experiences. In Davidson, D.( ed.) *Well Played 3.0: Video Games, Value, and Meaning*, ETC-Press, Pittsburgh, USA, 2011, 262 - 290.

[6] Bogost, I. *Persuasive Games: The Expressive Power of Video Games*. The MIT Press, Cambridge, 2007.

[7] Dillenbourg, P. and Evans, M. Interactive tabletops in education. *Int. Journal of Computer-Supported Collaborative Learning 6*, 4, (2011) 491–514.

[8] Fleck, R., Rogers, Y., Yuill, N., Marshall, P., Carr, A., Rick, J. and Bonnett, V. Actions speak loudly with words: unpacking collaboration around the table. In *Proc. Conference on Interactive Tabletops and Surfaces*, ACM Press, ( 2009) 189-196.

[9] Harris, A., Rick, J., Bonnett, V.J., Yuill, N., Fleck, R., Marshall, P. and Rogers, Y. Around the table: Are multiple-touch surfaces better than single-touch for children's collaborative interactions. In *Proc. of Computer Supported Collaborative Learning*, ( 2009) 335-344.

[10] He, H.A., Greenberg, S. and Huang, E.M. One size does *not* fit all: Applying the Transtheoretical Model to energy feedback technology design. In *Proc. Conference on Human Factors in Computing Systems*, ACM Press, (2010) 927-936.

[11] Higgins, S., Mercier, E., Burd, E. and Joyce-Gibbons, A. Multi-touch tables and collaborative learning. *British Journal of Educational Technology 43*, 6, (2012) 1041–1054.

[12] Koschmann, T., Stahl, G. and Zemel, A. The video analyst's manifesto. In Goldman, R., Pea, R., Barron, B. and Derry, S. (eds.) *Video Research in the Learning Sciences*, Lawrence Erlbaum, 2007, 133-143.

[13] Malone, T.W. Toward a theory of intrinsically motivating instruction. *Cognitive Science 5*, 4, (1981) 333-369.

[14] Marshall, P., Fleck, R., Harris, A., Rick, J., Hornecker, E., Rogers, Y., Yuill, N. and Dalton, N.S. Fighting for control: Children's embodied interactions when using physical and digital representations. In *Proc. Conference on Human Factors in Computing Systems*, ACM Press, (2009) 2149-2152.

[15] Marshall, P., Morris, R., Rogers, Y., Kreitmayer, S. and Davies, M. Rethinking 'multi-user': An in-the-wild study of how groups approach a walk-up-and-use tabletop interface. In *Proc. Conference on Human Factors in Computing Systems*, ACM Press, (2011) 3033-3042.

[16] Olson, I.C., Leong, Z.A., Wilensky, U. and Horn, M.S. It's just a toolbar!: Using tangibles to help children manage conflict around a multi-touch tabletop. In *Proc. Conference on Tangible, Embedded, and Embodied Interaction*, ACM Press, (2010) 29-36.

[17] Robinson, J. Squaring the Circle? Some thoughts on the idea of sustainable development. *Ecological Economics 48*, (2004) 369-384.

[18] Rogers, Y., Lim, Y., Hazelwood, W. and Marshall, P. Equal Opportunities: Do shareable interfaces promote more group participation than single user displays? *Human-Computer Interaction 24*, 2, (2009) 79-116.

[19] Salen, K. and Zimmerman, E. *Rules of Play: Game Design Fundamentals*. MIT Press, Cambridge, MA, USA, 2004.

[20] Speelpenning, T., Antle, A.N., Doring, T. and van den Hoven, E. Exploring how a tangible tool enables collaboration in a multi-touch tabletop game. In *Proc. INTERACT*, ACM Press, (2011) 605-621.

[21] Tanenbaum, J., Antle, A.N. and Robinson, J. Three perspectives on behavior change for serious games In Proc. of *Conference on Human Factors in Computing Systems*, ACM Press, (2013) 3389-3392.

# Designing Digital Peer Support for Children: Design Patterns for Social Interaction

Susanne Lindberg[1,3], Pontus Wärnestål[1,3], Jens Nygren[2,3], Petra Svedberg[2,3]

[1]Halmstad University
School of Information Science
P.O. 823, Halmstad, Sweden
+46 35 16 76 54
{susanne.lindberg,
pontus.warnestal}@hh.se

[2]Halmstad University
School of Social and Health Sciences
P.O. 823, Halmstad, Sweden
+46 35 16 78 63
{jens.nygren,
petra.svedberg}@hh.se

[3]The CHIPS Study Group
Halmstad University
P.O. 823, Halmstad, Sweden
chips@hh.se

## ABSTRACT

Children who have survived a life-threatening disease like cancer benefit from social support from other children with a similar background. However, these children are often geographically dispersed and have little opportunity to meet. We investigate the design and development of Digital Peer Support Services (DPS), which may overcome this problem. Peer support is a kind of social support that brings together peers with similar experiences to help their adjustment to a disease. The aim of this paper is to develop design patterns for social interaction that can be implemented in a DPS for children surviving cancer. We conducted four sets of design workshops with children, from which emerged clusters relating to peer support and friendship that were broken down into triads. From these, six design patterns for social interaction were developed. The patterns delineate different aspects of social interaction for children and are illustrated with examples from DPS prototypes and concepts. The patterns are organized into a hierarchy, comprising the beginning of a design pattern language for social interaction for children. An essential aspect of the patterns is providing users with transparency and control of the extent to which their social interaction is public or private.

## Categories and Subject Descriptors

H.5.2 [**User Interfaces**]: User-Centered Design.

K.4.2 [**Social Issues**]: Assistive technologies for persons with disabilities.

## General Terms

Design, Human Factors

## Keywords

Design Patterns, Children, Social Interaction, Digital Peer Support Service, Interaction design

*IDC'14*, June 17–20, 2014, Aarhus, Denmark.
Copyright © 2014 ACM 978-1-4503-2272-0/14/06…$15.00.
http://dx.doi.org/10.1145/2593968.2593972

## 1. INTRODUCTION

Social support is imperative when recovering from and dealing with the ramifications of a life-threatening disease such as cancer [26]. Children who have experienced cancer at a young age can for example lack social skills in comparison to other children their age, yet be more mature in other respects [22]. Furthermore, it is likely that worries, questions and concerns emerge as the child enters adolescence [12; 22]. The need for social support thus remains long after the treatment has ended.

Peer support is a kind of social support that brings peers, people with similar backgrounds and experiences, together through interpersonal communication, emotional empathy and trust [28]. It contributes to the health and well-being of the participants and is valuable for promoting adjustment to a disease [18]. However, there are limitations with face-to-face peer support interaction due to geographical distances, time constraints or individual ability [15]. These would benefit from the advent of Digital Peer Support Services (DPS). Yet, DPS for adults are often based on discussion forums. Children, who are less inclined to written social interaction [29], need ways to access DPS that are commensurable with their capabilities and preferences for social interaction.

A design pattern is a description of a design problem and how it can be solved [6]. It is a way to organize design knowledge [31], providing designers and users with readily applicable solutions to similar problems. They are for example utilized in participatory approaches [7], which incidentally are considered beneficial for designing with children [9; 25].

When designing a DPS for children, it is necessary to find one or more ways to design social interaction suitable for children. Based on our work with designing a DPS for children, we aim to specify design patterns that begin to express how social interaction in an online platform for children can be designed. We hope that these can be useful when designing social interaction for and together with children.

## 2. BACKGROUND

### 2.1 Digital Peer Support

The concept of peer support is based on the fact that in certain situations, people with shared experiences can better provide social support to each other than health care professionals can [21]. The nature of peer support interaction varies; it can be provided between two people or in groups, in different milieus, and be professionally moderated or peer-led [8].

A limitation with face-to-face peer support is the difficulty of attendance [15]. Participants may have a long distance to travel, not have the time to attend, or be physically unable to participate [27]. Creating a DPS can overcome some of these difficulties and bring together peers who otherwise would not have been able to meet [21]. Furthermore, DPS can offer anonymity and remove social factors like age, gender and appearance [21]. Sensitive issues can thus be easier to discuss [27].

While three out of four children with cancer survive [17], it does not mean that these children return to being the same as before the disease. Physical changes, such as scars and weight change occur. Also, adolescents who have had cancer as children often experience a feeling of being different from others, having experiences that many of their friends have not [12].

During their disease, it is typical that children develop strong bonds with their families and close friends [26]. The experience of cancer seems to give rise to long, strong relationships. Yet, it can be difficult for these children to start up new friendships with children who do not know or understand what they have been through [12]. Therefore, finding friends that understand their experiences becomes particularly important.

Through interviews with children who have survived cancer, Einberg et al. [11] establish a relational framework for integrating social interaction in the design of health promoting interventions in the form of peer support. They found that peer support in this context is based in enjoying joint activities that develop into friendship built on mutual care. This is accomplished through both emotional and practical interactions that deepen the relationships over time through trust and shared experiences [11]. Dimensions of interaction such as doing things together, showing trust and respect and helping each other, were found to be important in such a context. This is also the framework on which we base our perception of the concept of peer support.

Nevertheless, there are few DPS that are aimed at children. Giesbers et al. [15] study a forum based DPS for children between 12 and 18 years whose parents have cancer. Khair et al. [20] developed a social network for children in the age of 10 to 18 who suffer from hemophilia, again in the style of a forum. Webb et al. [32] describe an online forum project for adolescents with mental health difficulties. There are other, similar examples, but we were unable to find DPS for younger children.

Our target group is in the age of 8 to 12. These younger children may be unable to, or uncomfortable with expressing themselves in writing; young children tend to express themselves better in actions rather than words [9]. Basing a DPS for children in this age on discussion forums is thus not suitable. Also, play is more important than direct communication for children [37], which is not in line with discussion forum based DPS.

Social communication systems for children are the focus of several studies. Solutions for child-parent (e.g. [5; 37]) and child-child (e.g. [10; 35; 36]) communication have been developed to for example enable children to interact with distant parents. Davis et al. [5] develop the Virtual Box to mediate intimacy between members of separated families. Yarosh et al. [37] deploy the ShareTable to make it easier for children to initiate video communication with divorced parents. For child-child communication, Du et al. [10] create VideoPal for asynchronous video messaging between children in different countries. In an attempt to support unconstrained play between children using video communication, Yarosh et al. [35] evaluate four different setups with either computer or TV screens and identify challenges with managing visibility, maintaining the children's attention and intersubjectivity. These studies show that video communication supports the non-verbal communication that children require and is a type of technology suitable for children [10].

Of additional importance to our context is that children between 8 and 12 may not currently experience a need for peer support. The need may not manifest itself until they enter adolescence, or even later [22]. The challenge thus becomes to design social interaction in a way that is suitable for children and motivates use of the DPS for the possibility of future health promotion. The role of the DPS in the context of other healthcare activities is thus *strategic* and *salutogenic* [33]. For this purpose, the onboarding of the service takes place in the post-intensive treatment phase (Figure 1), and plays a continuous role in the transition to normal life. Wärnestål and Nygren [33] identified the Consultancy Nurse as a suitable agent for introducing the DPS to the children. As a strategic benefit in this context, the children's activity on the DPS can serve as a basis for clinical check-up conversations with caregivers about social interaction and well-being [33].

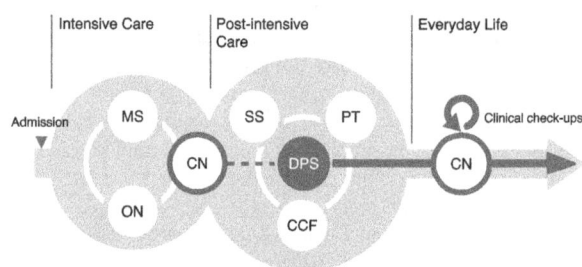

**Figure 1. Service onboarding opportunity mapped to treatment stages. MS = Medical Specialists, ON = Oncology Nurses, CN = Consultancy Nurses, SS = Sibling Support, CCF = Childhood Cancer Foundation, PT = Play Therapists, DPS = Digital Peer Support Service.**

## 2.2 Design Patterns

A design pattern is a tool to disclose design knowledge. It delineates a problem and its solution in a general but structured way [6]. Alexander (e.g. [1]) introduced the concept of design patterns for Architecture. Design patterns do not only support re-use of high-quality solutions, but are also intended to facilitate work for architects and accord users a language for communicating with architects [4]. The patterns present "good" solutions that can be applied to different contexts.

The design pattern concept has been embraced by Interaction Design and in a slightly adapted form by Software Engineering [6]. Interaction Design patterns are similar to Alexander's patterns. Alexander's original design patterns (cf. [1]) were given a telling name, a description of the problem context and an example of implementation. Borchers [4] suggests the following components for interaction design patterns: (1) a *context* in the design pattern hierarchy; (2) a *name* that describes the main idea; (3) the *problem* the pattern intends to solve; (4) an illustration of the problem and solution with *examples*; (5) a *solution*; and (6) a summarizing *diagram*. However, clarity should be prioritized over formal correct-ness [4] and the primary components to include are (1), (3), (4) and (5) [31].

A method for identifying design patterns has not been formalized, but the foundation of a pattern should always be in practice [6]. A well-defined pattern explains both how and why the solution is appropriate [6]. Alexander gives no empirical evidence of the validity of architectural design patterns, but argues that "good" patterns simply prove their validity by working [3]. However, Interaction Design patterns are usually verified through use [6] and this is illustrated by including an example of the pattern's implementation in the pattern description [3].

The concept of design patterns is closely related to participatory approaches. In this context, design patterns can be used as a vehicle for communication and a tool for users is design [7]. Though users may not always accept the suggested solution as the best [7], the patterns can initiate discussions and raise questions. Erickson [13] further argues that design patterns can make up a common language for all involved stakeholders and thus allow a higher degree of participation from all.

The idea of design patterns making up a an entire language is an essential aspect of the concept; Alexander presents 253 patterns, organized into hierarchies where some patterns are more comprehensive while others make up segments that help to complete the whole [13]. A pattern structure shows which patterns are related and adds value as a collection of design knowledge and experience [30]. Similarly, the context in which a pattern is used delineates if other, complementary patterns are also relevant or apply to the same problem [30]. Why a pattern is appropriate to the context is therefore important to clarify [6].

One way to organize design patterns is presented by Van Welie and Van Der Veer [30], who separate patterns into four levels: (1) posture, (2) experience, (3) task, and (4) action. Posture specifies what genre the application belongs to, if there are similar kinds of applications. Experience level patterns specify what the user goals and tasks are, and task patterns describe a series of interaction towards solving a problem. Finally, action patterns describe specific uses that are included in the higher-level patterns (for example buttons, selections etc.). Van Welie and Van Der Veer [30] further claim that most design starts from a goal – be it business, personal, or social goals. They therefore add a "starting point" to their model, which is not considered a level, but is included in the hierarchy: (0) business goals.

Interaction design patterns for social interaction for children have proven to be rare. Fails et al. [14] present configurations for collaboration over mobile devices. While not design patterns per se, they are presented similarly to patterns; they have a name, context and general description, along with examples of implementation. For example, the implementation of the configuration *content splitting*, where two connected mobile devices show different parts of the context, was preferred among the children for reading and sharing content [14]. Further, Zancanaro et al. [38] present the initial stages of research towards identifying design patterns and a design framework for teaching social competence to children with autism, though they do not specify the design patterns in their paper.

## 3. METHOD

Four design-oriented workshops were carried out and analyzed by (a) qualitative categorization, (b) explorative design, and (c) pattern identification. Step (a) was carried out between workshop 3 and 4, with an intermediate explorative design step (b) before the fourth workshop.

In the first three workshops, five children with a medical history of cancer teamed up in pairs with adult researchers and worked on design-related problems and questions introduced by a workshop facilitator [23; 33]. Each workshop was run twice: once with three

boys aged 11-12 and once with two girls aged 11 and 13. The girl who was 13 and outside our target age range of 8-12 had been 12 when she first joined the research project. The choice was also made to only include children in the upper age range of our target group. The children were aged 11-13, but could retrospectively represent children younger in age. Since they had all been 8 years old recently, they could think back on their experiences. Younger children, however, are not able to represent children older than themselves.

Each workshop lasted three hours including food and snack breaks. The workshops took place in a conference room at a local library. The three design workshops were progressions of each other in order to get a deeper understanding of the problems and design context. The first workshop was focused on establishing fictive child characters. The character construction process was triggered by questions (such as "where does your character live?", "what is his/her favorite hobbies or sports?", "what makes him/her happy?" etc.). These characters were used as proxies in the other two workshops when more sensitive subjects were broached. In the second workshop, the focus was to breathe life into these characters by placing them into narratives. The narratives captured stories of redemption, where the character started out in a negative or "bad" situation and ended up in a positive state through stories of friendship and social activities. The narratives were captured in the form of comic strips [23; 24; 34]. In the third workshop, the children and adults cooperated to design interactive, digital tools to support the stories created in the previous workshop. Comics were again used to communicate design ideas.

The work in the pairs during the workshop was conducted on an equal basis. Both partners contributed to the characters and comics. However, the researchers tried giving the children the most space and maintained the discussions with questions. Nevertheless, the children explicitly asked the researcher to contribute to for example the character creation. As such, there was clear cooperation in the pairs. As the work was conducted in pairs, each child was able to express themself to the same degree. There was no one who dominated the discourse. Further, by working in pairs we could keep an eye on the children's wellbeing and make sure that the subject did not unduly affect them.

The participating researchers analyzed the data from the workshops and created affinity diagrams. These diagrams were the basis for the identification of several conceptual ideas for various digital services focusing on aiding and facilitating social interaction and peer support. These concepts were brought back to the design studio where they were refined into conceptual paper prototypes and interface sketches in a collaborative team consisting of interaction designers, game designers, and researchers. Three concepts were chosen from the studio work, based on their embodiment of social peer interaction as described by Einberg et al. [11]: (1) an online community in the form of a virtual schoolyard where children can interact, visit "playhouses", and create their own collaborative spaces; (2) a photographic treasure hunt where users take pictures with their mobile phones on given themes or assignments and shares the pictures in the community; and (3) a two-way video camera game for remotely playing the parlor game Hot and Cold (also know as Hide the Key).

In the fourth workshop, seven children between the ages 10 and 12 participated. These children had not been part of the previous workshops and entered the design process as new testers and designers. The children did not have a medical history of cancer.

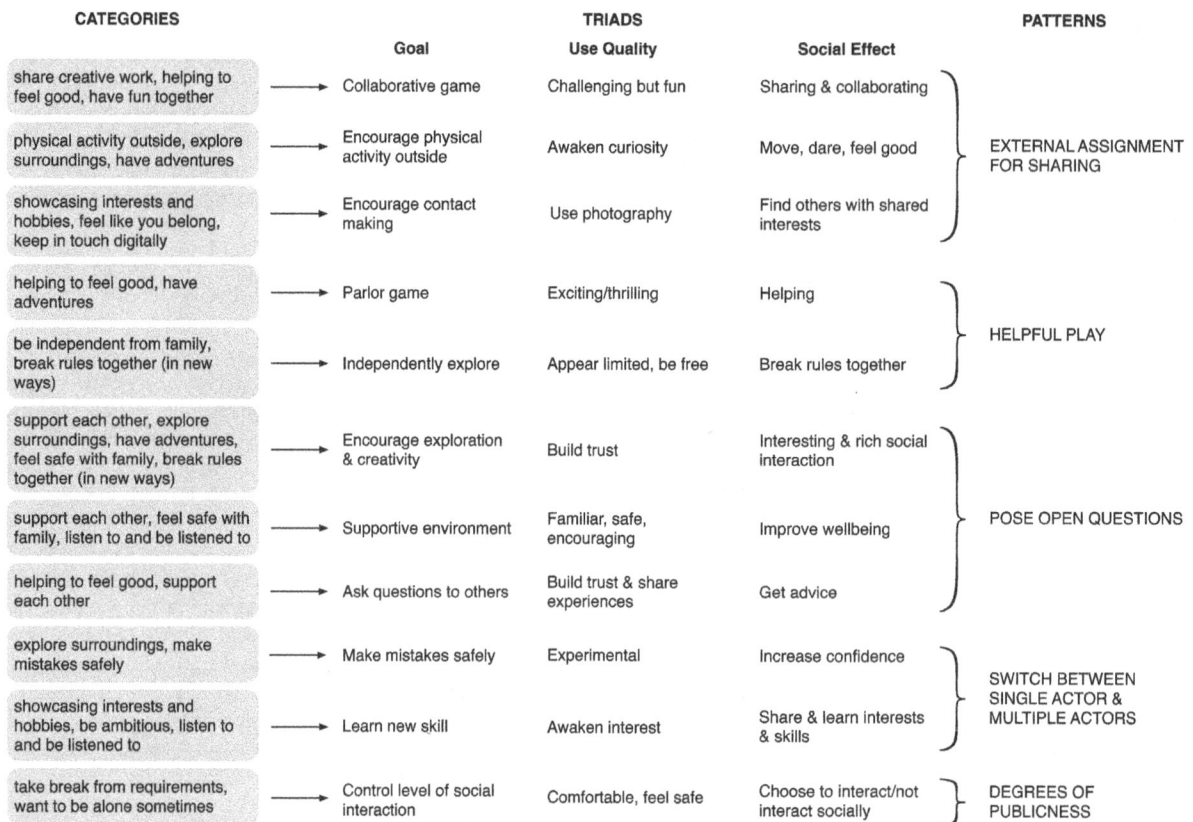

| CATEGORIES | TRIADS | | | PATTERNS |
|---|---|---|---|---|
| | Goal | Use Quality | Social Effect | |
| share creative work, helping to feel good, have fun together | Collaborative game | Challenging but fun | Sharing & collaborating | EXTERNAL ASSIGNMENT FOR SHARING |
| physical activity outside, explore surroundings, have adventures | Encourage physical activity outside | Awaken curiosity | Move, dare, feel good | |
| showcasing interests and hobbies, feel like you belong, keep in touch digitally | Encourage contact making | Use photography | Find others with shared interests | |
| helping to feel good, have adventures | Parlor game | Exciting/thrilling | Helping | HELPFUL PLAY |
| be independent from family, break rules together (in new ways) | Independently explore | Appear limited, be free | Break rules together | |
| support each other, explore surroundings, have adventures, feel safe with family, break rules together (in new ways) | Encourage exploration & creativity | Build trust | Interesting & rich social interaction | POSE OPEN QUESTIONS |
| support each other, feel safe with family, listen to and be listened to | Supportive environment | Familiar, safe, encouraging | Improve wellbeing | |
| helping to feel good, support each other | Ask questions to others | Build trust & share experiences | Get advice | |
| explore surroundings, make mistakes safely | Make mistakes safely | Experimental | Increase confidence | SWITCH BETWEEN SINGLE ACTOR & MULTIPLE ACTORS |
| showcasing interests and hobbies, be ambitious, listen to and be listened to | Learn new skill | Awaken interest | Share & learn interests & skills | |
| take break from requirements, want to be alone sometimes | Control level of social interaction | Comfortable, feel safe | Choose to interact/not interact socially | DEGREES OF PUBLICNESS |

Figure 2. Overview of the analysis that led to the patterns.

We chose to include healthy children in this stage for ethical reasons. Because we have a limited target group, it is difficult to include them in all stages of design without risking overusing them. Participation in research must not burden the participants, particularly children [16]. The feedback we needed at this stage related to concept feasibility, user experience and desirability. It was thus not unique to children with a medical history of cancer. Hence, we could include children without this medical history.

For 2 hours, the children worked in groups of 2-3 and gave feedback on the three conceptual applications that were the result of the previous workshops' analysis and synthesis work. The children were introduced to the concepts by lo-fi prototypes and sketches, along with a verbal explanation of what the idea behind each concept was. The children were then asked to give feedback on the usefulness and user experience, and were encouraged to provide modifications by verbally suggesting or sketching their ideas. The groups spent approximately 30 minutes on each of the three concepts. This workshop took place in a home environment.

All workshops were video recorded. The recordings were analyzed along with the characters, narratives and sketches.

## 3.1 Qualitative Categorization

Experiential aspects of peer support and friendship were noted throughout workshop 1–3 as a way to meaningfully organize the rich material collected. Each experiential aspect forms a data point as a potential base for a design pattern in the domain of digital peer support. By examining the implications of each aspect in an online, social setting, design problems and contexts could be identified. The data was then organized into clusters in terms of relatedness in a bottom-up fashion independently by two researchers and then cross-examined in a group discussion. Each cluster was named with a header that summarized the content of that cluster. The result is a collection of named clusters, or categories, each serving as a potential base for a design pattern targeting DPS and social interaction. Examples of such categories are: SHOWCASING INTERESTS AND HOBBIES, SHARE CREATIVE WORK, HELPING TO FEEL GOOD, etc. An overview of the categories that led to the subsequent patterns is available in Figure 2.

## 3.2 Pattern identification

Each category was examined in terms of goal or motive, perceived use quality, and social effect of the category contents. They were based on the concepts developed in and after workshop 3 and complemented with the data collected in workshop 4. Each category could be present in several goal, use quality and social effect triads. Likewise, each triad was based on more than one category. The categories could thus be tied to concrete design examples and interaction.

Examples of such goal, use quality and social effect triads are:

- a *challenging but fun* (use quality) assignment-based *collaborative game* (goal) as a way to *encourage sharing and collaboration* (social effect) of for example photos as social objects;

- a way to allow for *helping* (social effect) other players in an *exciting/thrilling* (use quality) *parlor game* (goal) situation;

- showing both user profile and created avatars in a virtual community to *build trust* (use quality) between users, but also *encourage exploration and creativity* (goal) to gain *interesting and rich social interaction* (social effect).

Roughly 30 triads were captured from the categories. Each triad forms the base for writing a design pattern. However, the triads vary in scope and potential effect on interaction design, and would not all be fruitful to pursue as design patterns. Eleven triads were selected, from which five patterns were developed. Figure 2 shows an overview of the triads that led to the patterns.

An additional pattern was developed as a direct result of the fourth design workshop. The pattern, DROP TO INVITE, was created based on the feedback from the healthy children in workshop 4. The children did not like to use written communication but were positive to drag-and-drop functionality they had used in various forms. This pattern does not specifically reference children who have had cancer, but is still relevant in the design of a DPS for these children. The pattern aims specifically at allowing invitations to social activities. Making this process work smoothly is essential for social interaction in an implementation of a DPS. In the next section we present how our six patterns are implemented in design iterations of the generated concept ideas.

# 4. DESIGN PATTERNS FOR SOCIAL INTERACTION

In this section we present our design patterns for social interaction for children. The patterns follow the style suggested by Borchers [4] with the exception of the diagram, which has been excluded.

## 4.1 External Assignment for Sharing

Users in an online community base their social interactions on sharing interests and similarities. However, not all users in the community share the same interests and do not know other users' interests beforehand. Furthermore, inherent shyness or lack of initiative might exist between members of the community.

◇◇◇

**For the design pattern EXTERNAL ASSIGNMENT FOR SHARING, the challenge is to encourage sharing and exploration of common interests – important aspects of social interaction.**

A solution to the problem is to externally specify assignments that users are meant to fulfill. Streamlining assignments to a specific theme or context can encourage not only participation, but encourage the creation of shareable material and thus the social interaction therefrom achieved. Making the user submitted assignment solutions public in some way is necessary for social interaction to be possible. Basing the assignments on a premise relating to one or more wanted behaviors can further encourage this behavior; an example is to have assignments that require physical activity, thus instigating an active behavior.

◇◇◇

This pattern has been applied in the mobile application prototype PhotoQuest (Figure 3). In the application, photographic missions are specified in different categories and the children are meant to cooperate in completing each quest. The different quests can for example take place outside, encouraging children to spend time out of doors. Each mission consists of several different photos and all uploaded photos are visible to all users.

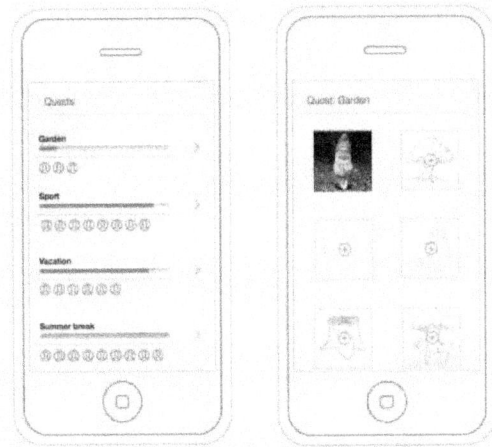

**Figure 3. Prototype of PhotoQuest, exemplifying EXTERNAL ASSIGNMENT FOR SHARING.**

There is a possibility for users to communicate, thus allowing social interaction to take place. However, as all users contribute to fulfilling each quest, they also interact implicitly through their contributions, even if no direct communication takes place. Further, using photographs, the children can express their interests and find others with similar interests to initiate interaction with.

This pattern is based on the indication from the first three design workshops where several of the participating children expressed an interest in photography. One of the girls said that she enjoys sharing photos with her friends. Moreover, some of the children used Instagram, which indicates an inclination to share their photography and interests with others. Our analysis also showed that sharing interests contributes to a feeling of belonging to a community. Further, particularly the boys expressed an inclination to be outside, to go on adventures and explore.

Initially, this design concept did not include making photographs public to all users, nor did we design the application specifically for cooperation. However, after applying this pattern, the concept was changed to include social interaction, aligning it more with the peer support concept. As such, we also altered the level of publicness (see 4.5 DEGREES OF PUBLICNESS) that the application has.

Related patterns: DEGREES OF PUBLICNESS

## 4.2 Helpful Play

An inherent part of friendship is helping each other, yet many social activities online encourage competition instead of cooperation and collaboration.

◇◇◇

**For the pattern HELPFUL PLAY, the challenge is to encourage helpfulness towards a common goal.**

One way to solve the design problem is to create a play context where the structure of play (i.e. the rules) is clear to the users but possible to divert from. For example, the users are given a task and asked to help each other in achieving it. They should then be able to give hints when appropriate and not only to the extent specified by the rules. The amount of autonomy given to the users directly affects their ability to aid one another. Further, in order to inspire cooperation, all participants should be rewarded upon success.

◇◇◇

The pattern HELPFUL PLAY has been applied to the prototype of a game with elements from the parlor game Hot and Cold (also called Hide the Key). It is a traditional children's game where one child hides something and another child tries to find it by querying how close they are. The mobile application concept Hot-'n-Cold (Figure 4) performs this game using video communication to be able to play over a great geographical distance and at the same time have an opportunity to get to know each other's surroundings. The children playing are aware of the rules of the game, but can choose to divert from the traditional hints of "hot" and "cold" and use more detailed aid should they wish or need to. When the hidden object has been found, both the hider and the seeker are rewarded points, thereby promoting reciprocity and eliminating the risk that the hider makes it more difficult for the seeker by withholding information required for the object's retrieval.

**Figure 4. Prototype of Hot-'n-Cold, exemplifying HELPFUL PLAY.**

This pattern originated from all four design workshops. There was a clear indication from all children that they liked helping others and wanted to make others feel good. Helping others also made them feel good. Moreover, one of the girls in the initial workshops mentioned that she liked to do mischief together with her friends. A similar aspect was brought up the fourth workshop when one of the children mentioned that she liked to use video communication with a friend after school when they were home alone. They would sometimes do things their parents would not allow, like eat candy. This concept of using digital communication to break rules together is an influencing factor for this pattern.

Related patterns: DEGREES OF PUBLICNESS

## 4.3 Pose Open Questions

In an online community where users have different interests and preferences, it can be difficult for new users to be introduced to the community and find others to interact with. Furthermore, there might be a wish to communicate with a larger subset of users than those the user is already intimately familiar with.

◊◊◊

**For the design pattern POSE OPEN QUESTIONS, the challenge is to reach all, or a subset of users in the attempt to (1) as a new member find friends and be introduced into the community, and (2) reach the expertise of the entire community.**

Creating a space for public requests and announcements can solve this problem. In this space, users are able to reach out to everyone in the community while still maintaining privacy and performing private communication with other users elsewhere. Having a dedicated space for public requests also gives users the control to choose themselves whether of not they want to see what others are posting.

◊◊◊

This pattern has been applied in the mobile application prototype The Query Box (Figure 5), where children can post video questions for others to answer. These questions can pertain to anything and the answers are rated by how good they are considered to be. The Query Box is a dedicated public space for questions, but the option to initiate private communication exists. The intent is for children to be able to reach and initiate contact with other children even if they are not acquainted with them already. Presumably, the children answering the questions will be interested in, have knowledge of, or similar questions on the same subject area.

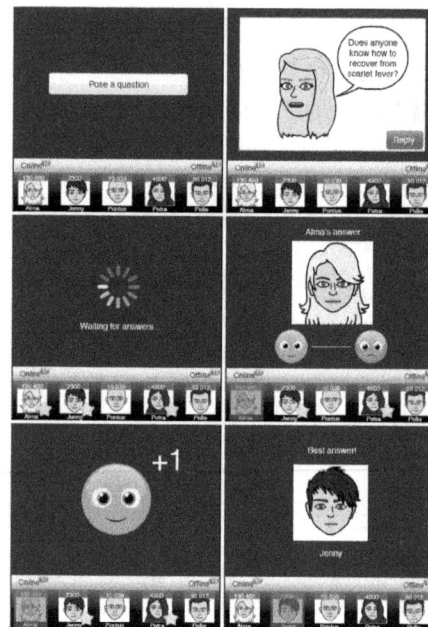

**Figure 5. Prototype of The Query Box, exemplifying POSE OPEN QUESTIONS.**

The concept of The Query Box originated directly from one of the children in the three initial design workshops. Throughout the pattern development, the concept has been amended to implement this design pattern fully. The pattern is for example based on the outcome from the first three design workshops, where support and feelings of safety were brought up as important categories. The children expressed that they felt safe with and were supported by their families. However, they also wanted to explore and have adventures. We thus saw indications that there needed to be a safe way to explore certain issues and subjects. This would also constitute an opportunity for them to support others.

Related patterns: DEGREES OF PUBLICNESS

## 4.4 Switch between Single Actor and Multiple Actors

In a learning situation, a user might be timid or disinclined to practice skills out of fear that the repercussions of mistakes are unpleasant and perceived by others. Further, not all users of an online community have the same skill level and would thus require different learning experiences.

◊◊◊

**For the pattern SWITCH BETWEEN SINGLE ACTOR AND MULTIPLE ACTORS, the challenge is to introduce information and skills to users in a way where mistakes do not have real-world consequences.**

A solution is to separate the online community into sections devoted to single actor and multiple actor interaction. In the single actor section it is possible to create a controlled environment where the users are led through scenarios or given specific information that is later required for participation in the multiple actors section. In the single actor section, users can practice without fear of consequences of mistakes that might occur in a multiple actor setting.

◊◊◊

We have created the concept of a DPS with single- and multiple actor sections. The single actor section is meant to be a controlled environment with linear narratives where the children practice social competence and similar skills. The children can switch to a multiple actor section where they implement their skills and interact with other children. In this way, they can practice skills they may be lacking in an environment where they are free to make mistakes without serious consequences.

Further, as a motivator for participation, the activities performed in the single actor setting affect the child's play in the multiple actors setting. This means that as the child progresses (levels up) in the single actor setting, they are given access to objects and locations in the multiple actors setting that they would not otherwise have access to. This would serve as motivation for the children to perform the exercises in the single actor setting and thus practice those important skills.

Indications from the design workshops were that some of the children were ambitious in school and worried about their grades. They said that they felt pressure to be good at school, popular with their friends and have extracurricular activities. They expressed worry about failing and making mistakes. The design workshops also highlighted a wish to explore and have adventures. In order to explore something, it has to be possible to take risks and make mistakes. This indicated a need for this pattern. If there was a safe place where the children could explore and practice skills, they can then utilize these skills with more confidence in social situations.

Related patterns: DEGREES OF PUBLICNESS

## 4.5 Degrees of Publicness

Online communities are inherently social, but users do not always want all communication to be available to all users of the community. Meanwhile, there are times when users need to contact all, or a subset of users they are unfamiliar with. There are also times when users do not wish for any social interaction to take place at all.

◊◊◊

**For the design pattern DEGREES OF PUBLICNESS, the challenge is to create a balance between public and private communication. Users do not want everything they post to be public, available to everyone, but there is also a need to reach all users of the community.**

A solution to the problem is to create areas in the community devoted to different degrees of publicness. The user is thus given control over when and what they want to communicate privately or publicly.

◊◊◊

We have for example applied this pattern in PhotoQuest (section 4.1) and in The Query Box (section 4.3). Further, we have developed the concept of a DPS that will have different spaces dedicated to different kinds of interaction. A public "square" will allow users to post publicly, while other formations around it will be set up to be private or semi-private areas for communication. There will also be a single actor section where no communication with other users will take place. In this way, users can choose how public they want to make their communication.

There were indications to promote both public and private communication in the design workshops. The children told us of their daily activities and interests. Many of these were social, active interests. All children had mobile phones, which they used to keep in touch with their friends and play games. However, in all workshops there were also indications that the children sometimes felt a need to be alone, to distance themselves. Also, in a discussion on privacy in social media, the boys in the third workshop agreed that they did not want everything posted for everyone to see – unless in was very funny.

Related patterns: POSE OPEN QUESTIONS, EXTERNAL ASSIGNMENT FOR SHARING, SWITCH BETWEEN SINGE ACTOR AND MULTIPLE ACTORS, HELPFUL PLAY

## 4.6 Drop to Invite

In an online community users need to be able to invite other users to collaborative activities.

◊◊◊

**For the pattern DROP TO INVITE, the challenge is how to initiate an activity between users.**

Use a drag-and-drop interface to drag the invited user to the chosen activity in order to send a request to start the activity. Activities that are possible to invite to should be clearly indicated.

◊◊◊

In our DPS concept, all users will have avatars. In order to invite users to games or other activities on the platform, they drag-and-drop the avatar of the user(s) they want to invite and wait for them to respond (Figure 6). When an avatar has been "picked up", all activities to which they can be invited will light up to indicate where they can be dropped.

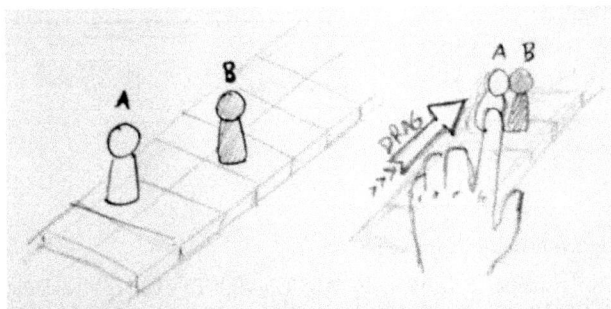

**Figure 6. Sketch of DROP TO INVITE implementation in the DPS concept.**

This pattern originated from the fourth workshop. The children in the workshop expressed a preference for a drag-and-drop interface over a textual interface. The boys in particular pointed out that textual chat interfaces were difficult to operate and understand.

# 5. DISCUSSION

The patterns presented in section 4 are examples of how social interaction can be designed. They are specifically derived from the work on designing a DPS for children with cancer. They are primarily, though not solely, relevant in the design of social interaction for children.

The presented examples of implementations of the design patterns are chiefly examples from mobile applications. While we consider the design patterns to be general enough to be applicable for most digital platforms, our specific choice of using mobile platforms was made as we wanted to encourage physical activity, preferably out of doors. A similar choice was made by Fails et al. [14].

The patterns DEGREES OF PUBLICNESS and DROP TO INVITE are of a different nature than the other patterns. The first is a general pattern, applicable to a wide range of genres other than DPS for children. It bears resemblance to patterns presented elsewhere, for example WORKSPACE WITH PRIVACY GRADIENT [2]. Patterns interacting with DEGREES OF PUBLICNESS can thus affect how the users interact socially (with what subset of users, with how many users, etc.). DROP TO INVITE is also a general pattern, although operating on a detailed interface level. It is related to traditional drag-and-drop interface techniques but is special since it consists of the social component of inviting another user to perform a collaborative action together (Figure 6). DROP TO INVITE is not specific to DPS. However, its relevance to DPS includes it among these patterns. That digital social interaction among children works smoothly is essential for the implementation of the other five patterns. If this does not work, the other patterns may not be possible to implement.

The two patterns DEGREES OF PUBLICNESS and DROP TO INVITE are considered complementary, since they do not directly relate to the creation of social interaction, though they are still relevant to the main patterns and to our implementation of a DPS.

## 5.1 Levels of Design Patterns

In section 2, we described a model for arranging patterns into hierarchies. In summary, the model contained: (0) business goals, (1) posture, (2) experience, (3) task, and (4) action [30].

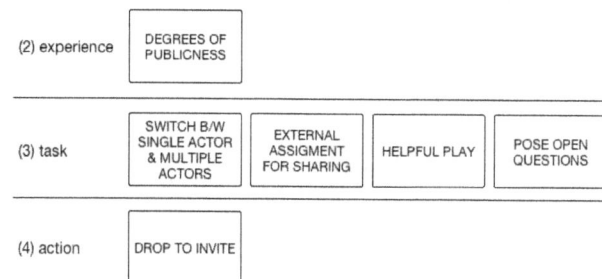

**Figure 7. Design pattern levels.**

The patterns EXTERNAL ASSIGNMENT FOR SHARING, HELPFUL PLAY, SWITCH BETWEEN SINGLE ACTOR AND MULTIPLE ACTORS and POSE OPEN QUESTIONS all fit into level (3) tasks. The patterns describe a path towards a goal, for example POSE OPEN QUESTIONS that describes how an online community can be designed to allow users to reach all other users of

the community. The pattern DROP TO INVITE, on the other hand, is an (4) action level pattern. This pattern specifies a specific unit of interaction, a specific action. The pattern DEGREES OF PUBLICNESS fits into level (2) experience. The pattern describes how the level of privacy can be designed to affect the user experience based on the users' goals.

Figure 7 summarizes the levels the design pattern organization. Currently, only the three lowest levels of patterns are represented and it would be a valuable addition to the pattern collection to identify higher-level patterns. These would map more closely to the digital peer support concept and show values that are unique to this context.

## 5.2 Using the Patterns in the Design of DPS

Children who have been under treatment for cancer for a long period of time have experiences that can in some respects make them more mature than other children their age; they have been through painful treatments and long periods of being seriously ill [22]. Meanwhile, they run the risk of missing out on crucial experiences that help develop for example social competence [22]. Hence, these children may need to practice basic social skills. We therefore applied the pattern SWITCH BETWEEN SINGLE ACTOR AND MULTIPLE ACTORS, and created the concept of a DPS with two separate sections: a single actor section where children can practice social skills in a controlled environment where they can make mistakes without fearing the consequences; and a multiple actor section where children interact with other children in various game and play situations.

Our concept further implements different levels of the DEGREE OF PUBLICNESS pattern, where some sections are public to all users, others are available to a by the user chosen subset of users. The single actor section is completely private. We utilize the EXTERNAL ASSIGNMENT FOR SHARING pattern to motivate children to share thoughts, feelings and interests with other children – a cornerstone in the framework for children's social interaction [11]. In our DPS concept, this is implemented in the PhotoQuest mobile application prototype. Our hope is that when sharing their interests with others, they will be able to find peers with similar interests and start building friendships.

Moreover, the pattern POSE OPEN QUESTIONS is implemented in the mobile application prototype The Query Box. It serves to introduce new members to the community and also to allow users to help each other, ask for help in return, and find common interests and experiences. By posting questions to all or a subset of users in the community, we hope that the children will answer each other's questions and in this way interact socially in a setting that encourages helpfulness and cooperation.

The pattern HELPFUL PLAY is implemented in a way that directly relates to helping each other – one dimension in the framework for children's social interaction [11]. In the Hot-'n-Cold mobile application prototype, children help each other to find objects they have hidden. Playfulness is an essential ingredient in creating reciprocal interaction among children [5]. Another aspect of this application is that the game, which takes place using video communication, will presumably be played out at the users' homes, meaning that they include the other player(s) in their personal space and share information about themselves. Again, this relates to building friendships and sharing personal information with others, and relies on the users having a high level of trust for each other.

Depending on the level of trust the user has to the DPS and the other users, they have control over the implementation of the DEGREE OF PUBLICNESS pattern. The user can choose to avoid the public areas in the community and interact on a low level of publicness, or choose to engage at a public level. Achieving trust occurs over a longer period of time [11]. Therefore, the children are given the possibility to control the privacy of their social interaction depending on how the pattern DEGREE OF PUBLICNESS is implemented.

Clearly, in our case the DEGREES OF PUBLICNESS pattern is essential for creating a DPS. Since peer support is a social concept, the children need to interact and share information with others. Having a completely private DPS is not possible. Yet, the children need to be able to practice skills. If they do not feel well enough to interact or are disinclined to be social, they should still be able to access the DPS. Therefore, there is a delicate balance in how the DEGREES OF PUBLICNESS pattern is applied in the design of a DPS for children cured from cancer.

Based on the identified design patterns, we can delineate some characteristics that become inherent to DPS for children. A common denominator between the implementations of the patterns DEGREES OF PUBLICNESS, HELPFUL PLAY and SWITCH BETWEEN SINGLE AND MULTIPLE ACTORS is giving the children control of their platform. Because the DPS is meant to be onboarded by the oncology nurse [33], the children can be certain that all users have a history of cancer. Having a common background is a condition for peer support. However, the children can control what kind of support they want. They can choose when to interact socially, when to communicate publicly and to what extent to follow the rules of play. This high level of user control we find to be essential in this kind of DPS . Naturally, in order to enable this control, it needs to be transparent to the user what state an activity has. This enables the users to shape what kind of social support they are receiving.

## 5.3 Reliability and Validity

As reliability and validity in qualitative design-oriented studies such as the one reported on herein are based on trustworthiness and a rigorous and relevant research process, we need to address these issues of the research (cf. [19; 39]).

The empirical base is multifaceted, since it comes from four sessions with (different) children in the target group. The conceptual artifacts and prototypes used in the study are co-created with children as well as designed by professional designers. The subjectivity of this study is limited to the pattern identification procedure and to the selection of prototypes that were brought to the children in the fourth workshop. Since two researchers carried out the identification procedure – first independently and then in collaboration – subjectivity is reduced. The selection of the three prototypes was made by examining experiential qualities based on a model of peer support and friendship in the domain of children surviving from cancer, which also strengthens the rigor of the research, as well as the objectivity of the result.

Relevance is addressed on two levels in this research. On a strategic level the project as a whole needs to be examined. The *need* and potential *positive effects on well-being* of peer support in the domain of cancer-surviving children is verified by several pieces of research from different fields (for example [28; 29; 34]). On the tactical level of design patterns presented in this study, and for the end-users in this domain, relevance is also ensured throughout the process by the

heavy reliance on end-user participation in all four workshops. Having the children take on various roles, such as informant, designer and tester, also strengthens the end-users' participation.

The transferability of the design patterns to other domains is not verified. However, since they reside on the lower levels of the hierarchy (see Section 5.1) they are not connected to specific applications and should therefore be possible to use as design assets in other online social contexts.

## 5.4 Future Research

Together, the design patterns presented in this paper only constitute a small part of a future pattern language for social interaction for children. They form a starting point for a larger body of work in defining a pattern language for facilitating children peer support for enhanced well-being. Furthermore, the design patterns presented are largely aimed at social interaction in an online community or a similar service. While they certainly promise suitability for other contexts, this has yet to be confirmed.

## 6. CONCLUSIONS

We have presented six design patterns for social interaction for children. The patterns have been illustrated with examples from implementations in design concepts and prototypes of DPS. An essential aspect in these patterns is giving the user transparency and control over the publicness of their social interaction. Therefore, the experience level pattern DEGREES OF PUBLICNESS is related to all the four task level patterns: SWITCH BETWEEN SINGLE ACTOR AND MULTIPLE ACTORS, HELPFUL PLAY, EXTERNAL ASSIGNMENT TO SHARE and POSE OPEN QUESTIONS. The final, action level pattern DROP TO INVITE describes a specific unit of interaction in the invitation of users to collaborative activities. The design patterns make up the beginning of a future design pattern language for DPS. Our intention is that these patterns can be beneficial for the design of social interaction in online communities for and together with children.

## 7. ACKNOWLEDGMENTS

We thank Eva-Lena Einberg for her contribution to planning, implementation and analysis. We thank Dr. Svetlana Yarosh for her valuable comments. Finally, we thank our children and adult research participants and gratefully acknowledge the grants from the Swedish Research Council, the Swedish Research Council Formas, the Swedish Childhood Cancer Society, the Knowledge Foundation, and the Swedish Governmental Agency for Innovation Systems (Vinnova).

## 8. REFERENCES

[1] Alexander, C., 1979. *The timeless way of building*. Oxford University Press.

[2] Arvola, M., 2006. Interaction design patterns for computers in sociable use. *INT J COMPUT APPL T 25*, 2, 128-139.

[3] Borchers, J.O., 2000. Interaction design patterns: twelve theses. In *Workshop, The Hague* Citeseer, 3.

[4] Borchers, J.O., 2001. A pattern approach to interaction design. *AI & SOCIETY 15*, 4, 359-376.

[5] Davis, H., Skov, M.B., Stougaard, M., and Vetere, F., 2007. Virtual box: supporting mediated family intimacy through virtual and physical play. In *Proc. of OzCHI* ACM, 151-159.

[6] Dearden, A. and Finlay, J., 2006. Pattern languages in HCI: A critical review. *Human–computer interaction 21*, 1, 49-102.

[7] Dearden, A., Finlay, J., Allgar, L., and Mcmanus, B., 2002. Evaluating pattern languages in participatory design. In *CHI EA '02* ACM, 664-665.

[8] Dennis, C.-L., 2003. Peer support within a health care context: a concept analysis. *Int J Nurs Stud 40*, 3, 321-332.

[9] Druin, A., 2002. The role of children in the design of new technology. *BEHAV INFORM TECHNOL 21*, 1, 1-25.

[10] Du, H., Inkpen, K., Chorianopoulos, K., Czerwinski, M., Johns, P., Hoff, A., Roseway, A., Morlidge, S., Tang, J., and Gross, T., 2011. VideoPal: exploring asynchronous video-messaging to enable cross-cultural friendships. In *Proc. of ECSCW* Springer, 273-292.

[11] Einberg, E., Svedberg, P., Enskär, K., and Nygren, J., 2013. Friendship from the perspective of children with experience of cancer: A focus group study. *EJON 17*, 6, 897-897.

[12] Enskär, K. and Berterö, C., 2010. Young adult survivors of childhood cancer; experiences affecting self-image, relationships, and present life. *Cancer nurs 33*, 1, E18-E24.

[13] Erickson, T., 2000. Lingua Francas for design: sacred places and pattern languages. In *Proc. of DIS* ACM, 357-368.

[14] Fails, J.A., Druin, A., and Guha, M.L., 2010. Mobile collaboration: collaboratively reading and creating children's stories on mobile devices. In *Proc. of IDC* ACM, 20-29.

[15] Giesbers, J., Verdonck-De Leeuw, I., Van Zuuren, F., Kleverlaan, N., and Van Der Linden, M., 2010. Coping with parental cancer: web-based peer support in children. *Psycho-Oncology 19*, 8, 887-892.

[16] Graham, A., Powell, M., Taylor, N., Anderson, D., and Fitzgerald, R., 2013. *Ethical Research Involving Children.* UNICEF Office of Research-Innocenti.

[17] Gustafsson, G., Heyman, M., and Vernby, Å., 2007. Childhood cancer incidence and survival in Sweden 1984-2005. *Karolinska Institute: Stockholm.*

[18] Herzer, M., Umfress, K., Aljadeff, G., Ghai, K., and Zakowski, S.G., 2009. Interactions with parents and friends among chronically ill children: examining social networks. *J Dev Behav Pediatr 30*, 6, 499-508.

[19] Hevner, A.R., March, S.T., Park, J., and Ram, S., 2004. Design science in information systems research. *MISQ 28*, 1, 75-105.

[20] Khair, K., Holland, M., and Carrington, S., 2012. Social networking for adolescents with severe haemophilia. *Haemophilia 18*, 3, e290-e296.

[21] Klemm, P. and Hardie, T., 2002. Depression in Internet and face-to-face cancer support groups: a pilot study. In *Oncology nursing forum* Onc Nurs Society, E45-E51.

[22] Li, H.C.W., Chung, O.K.J., and Chiu, S.Y., 2010. The impact of cancer on children's physical, emotional, and psychosocial well-being. *Cancer nurs 33*, 1, 47-54.

[23] Lindberg, S., 2013. Participatory design workshops with children with cancer: lessons learned. In *Proc. of IDC* ACM, 332-335.

[24] Moraveji, N., Li, J., Ding, J., O'kelley, P., and Woolf, S., 2007. Comicboarding: using comics as proxies for participatory design with children. In *Proc. of CHI* ACM, 1371-1374.

[25] Nesset, V. and Large, A., 2004. Children in the information technology design process: A review of theories and their applications. *LIBR INFORM SCI RES 26*, 2, 140-161.

[26] Oberholzer, A.E., Nel, E., Myburgh, C.P., and Poggenpoel, M., 2011. Exploring the needs and resources of children in a haematology-oncology unit. *Health SA Gesondheid 16*, 1.

[27] Potts, H.W., 2005. Online support groups: an overlooked resource for patients. *He@lth Information on the Internet 44*, 1, 6-8.

[28] Solomon, P., 2004. Peer support/peer provided services underlying processes, benefits, and critical ingredients. *Psychiatr Rehabil J 27*, 4, 392.

[29] Stinson, J.N., White, M., Breakey, V., Chong, A.L., Mak, I., Low, K.K., and Low, A.K., 2011. Perspectives on quality and content of information on the internet for adolescents with cancer. *Pediatr Blood Cancer 57*, 1, 97-104.

[30] Van Welie, M. and Van Der Veer, G.C., 2003. Pattern languages in interaction design: Structure and organization. In *Proc. of interact*, 1-5.

[31] Van Welie, M., Van Der Veer, G.C., and Eliëns, A., 2001. Patterns as tools for user interface design. In *Tools for Working with Guidelines* Springer, 313-324.

[32] Webb, M., Burns, J., and Collin, P., 2008. Providing online support for young people with mental health difficulties: challenges and opportunities explored. *Early Interv Psychiatry 2*, 2, 108-113.

[33] Wärnestål, P. and Nygren, J., 2013. Building an experience framework for a digital peer support service for children surviving from cancer. In *Proc. of IDC* ACM, 269-272.

[34] Wärnestål, P., Svedberg, P., and Nygren, J., 2014. Co-constructing Child Personas for Health-Promoting Services with Vulnerable Children. In *Proceedings of the Proc. of CHI* (Toronto, Canada, April 26-May 1 2014).

[35] Yarosh, S., Inkpen, K.M., and Brush, A., 2010. Video playdate: toward free play across distance. In *Proc. of CHI* ACM, 1251-1260.

[36] Yarosh, S. and Kwikkers, M.R., 2011. Supporting pretend and narrative play over videochat. In *Proc. of IDC* ACM, 217-220.

[37] Yarosh, S., Tang, A., Mokashi, S., and Abowd, G.D., 2013. almost touching: parent-child remote communication using the sharetable system. In *Proc. of CSCW* ACM, 181-192.

[38] Zancanaro, M., Gal, E., Parsons, S., Weiss, T., Bauminger, N., and Cobb, S., 2010. Teaching social competence: in search of design patterns. In *Proc. of IDC* ACM, 270-273.

[39] Zimmerman, J., Forlizzi, J., and Evenson, S., 2007. Research through design as a method for interaction design research in HCI. In *Proc. of CHI* ACM, 493-502.

# Investigating Interaction with Tabletops in Kindergarten Environments

Dietrich Kammer, René Dang
Technische Universität Dresden
01062, Dresden, Germany
dietrich.kammer@tu-dresden.de

Juliane Steinhauf
T-Systems Multimedia
Solutions GmbH
Riesaer Straße 5, D-01129 Dresden
juliane.steinhauf@t-systems.com

Rainer Groh
Technische Universität Dresden
01062, Dresden, Germany
rainer.groh@tu-dresden.de

## ABSTRACT

In this paper, we investigate interaction of children with interactive tabletops in kindergarten environments. In our understanding, such environments feature a certain degree of supervision, group play, as well as sole activities. In contrast to the traditional desktop PC workplace, interactive tabletops encourage communication and social interaction between children. In order to observe interaction and collaboration, we developed a suite of playful applications called VisMo, which we tailored to the needs and expectations of the target group. Our observational study with twelve Kindergarten children highlights pedagogical and usability aspects. We observed motivation and collaboration of the children and used a formal notation to transcribe their performed multi-touch gestures.

## Categories and Subject Descriptors

H.5.2 [**Information Interfaces and Presentation**]: User Interfaces – *Interaction styles (direct manipulation).* H.5.3 [**Information Interfaces and Presentation**]: Group and Organization Interfaces – *Synchronous interaction.*

## Keywords

Interface Design, Children, Education, Multi-touch.

## 1. INTRODUCTION

This paper focuses on Kindergarten children from age four to six. In this stage of development, creativity and social interaction need to be encouraged. Addressing the children's natural drive for movement and exercise is the best way to achieve this goal. The traditional desktop PC is a rigid environment that does not innately allow children to exercise communication skills and impedes a whole body experience while playing. Before the age of three, the PC is hardly accessible and holds little appeal to children. More graspable and immediate experiences are sought: baby phones, children's playbooks, and so forth.

The inherent qualities of multi-touch tabletops allow children to learn with all their senses. Therefore, we propose to introduce multi-touch tabletops to kindergarten environments. The objective is to familiarize children with a new medium, using

*IDC'14*, June 17–20, 2014, Aarhus, Denmark.
Copyright is held by the owner/author(s). Publication rights licensed to ACM.
ACM 978-1-4503-2272-0/14/06…$15.00.
http://dx.doi.org/10.1145/2593968.2593975

pedagogical valuable applications. The design of these applications should be engaging, interesting, and instructional, addressing all senses. The whole body experiences a tabletop device. Children can stand at the tabletop and move around, which is an advantage over the traditional desktop PC. However, this new technology requires a specific individual approach and skills. Little is understood about the way kindergarten children are able to interact with digital tabletops [1, 2]. This paper contributes an observational study of Kindergarten children, who interact with large-scale multi-touch tabletops. We collected data on the interaction techniques that the children employed and which social patterns emerged. To this end, we developed a suite of playful applications called VisMo, which addresses training and development of cognitive and motor skills. We first present related work and then introduce VisMo as well as our experimental design and study results.

## 2. RELATED WORK

In an experimental survey, Sim and Horton [3] investigated the performance and attitude of children in computer based versus paper based testing. In conclusion, Sim and Horton found that children as young as seven prefer using computers in their own assessment. However, performance did not seem to differ significantly between computer and paper based testing in the investigated group.

Khaled et al. describe the collaborative aspect of multi-touch play using two games [4]. Basic sorting tasks and collaborative constructing were used to observe active collaboration and parallelism of interaction. Unfamiliar players were hesitant to interact with the games and needed a formal introduction or another person interacting with the application. An important part of the entertainment were sound effects. The novelty of the technology was enjoyed, especially the possibility to trigger simultaneous events. However, lack of affordances made it unclear which parts of the interface were interactive. Technical issues such as latency or misinterpreted touch input were observed as well.

Rick et al. also investigated collaborative work with multi-touch devices with a particular focus on specific group dynamics [5]. The study shows that benefits and drawbacks of working together with a multi-touch device differ significantly for individual user pairings. In another work, Rick et al. performed an analysis of spatial orientation and user interaction with multi-touch devices [6]. Major findings were that the children use the entire tabletop surface to interact, but focus especially on the parts of the design closer to their relative position. Rick et al. also found that cooperative work on the design occurred;

however, the children often misattributed the actions of their social partner to themselves.

McKnight and Fitton explore the terminology for touch gestures, especially for the user group of children [7]. The study investigated how well children aged six and seven could transpose different text and audio instructions to four touch gestures. The test group of 13 children was able to perform the set of touch gestures and transfer metaphors from different contexts into a new environment. Hence, the design of an application should consider its influence on group dynamics and can be a tool to promote or suppress certain kinds of collaboration.

Mahmud et al. discuss the social gaming experience for older children (aged 7 to 11), incorporating psychophysiological measurements to enhance the gaming experience [8, 9]. The context is socially more binding than even traditional board games. Physiological feedback augmented the tabletop experience.

Zanchi et al. [10] developed eight tablet apps to teach preschool math. The goal was to develop a two-unit preschool math curriculum supplement that supports young children's learning of subitizing and equipartitioning. The created games support individual and collaborative play with peers and teachers. In addition to eight apps, they provide 101 non-digital assets (e.g. songs, finger plays and rhymes, books and others) as well as an interactive teacher's guide. This research provides guidelines for the design of tablet games and general multi-touch software that preschoolers can easily interact and learn with.

Jamil et al. [2] explored how students in India interact with multi-touch devices, focusing on collaboration strategies and touch input techniques. Collaborative work emerged between the pupils and simultaneous interaction served not just to solve the task, but also as an important tool to demonstrate understanding, learning, and knowledge between the peers. Another observation was that spatial positioning and close working were used dynamically and opportunistically to continue participation in the working process. The children also used various multi-finger input techniques for the same commands when touching and moving objects and drawing lines. The findings illustrate how children use multi-touch technologies and which spatial arrangements of collaboration appear in this context.

Our work contributes to the existing studies by focusing on the user group of Kindergarten children and tabletop systems. We also apply a formal coding scheme in order to precisely transcribe the multi-touch gestures performed by the children.

## 3. EXPERIMENTAL DESIGN

In order to explore the interaction of Kindergarten children with multi-touch tabletops, we created the VisMo application suite for training and development of cognitive and motor skills. We then conducted a user study to observe kindergarten children working with an interactive multi-touch tabletop.

### 3.1 Apparatus

The VisMo application was originally designed for Microsoft® PixelSense (former Microsoft Surface). It was subsequently adapted for the Samsung SUR40 with Microsoft® PixelSense™ technology. The SUR40 registers and processes up to 50 simultaneous touches, which allows multi-user scenarios. The possibility of using tangible objects to generate user inputs was another advantage provided by the multi-touch tabletop. For later productive use in kindergarten environments, the system has to be mobile enough to be relocated in the classroom. The

setup should allow children to stand at the multi-touch table and, most importantly, to move around. Transfer of new updates for VisMo applications onto the multi-touch table is easy via USB connection or wireless LAN. To improve the accessibility of the interactive surface, we modified the frame. Therefore, we removed the stand and positioned the device on an inverted table. Thus, our young participants could gain better access to all parts of the interface.

### 3.2 Tasks in VisMo

The VisMo application suite was developed in several iterations. We consulted tutors for early intervention regarding developmental deficits to check if our designs would fit the purpose.

Based on the goal to provide a tool for training and development of cognitive and motor skills, we created three different applications. By taking common tasks for such purposes found in physical exercise books into account, we designed the tasks *path tracking*, *shape tapping*, and *puzzle*. In the design process, we strived for a child-oriented graphical style in order to improve accessibility and acceptance. Playful learning should be possible with the offered tabletop applications. Visual metaphors from common tasks in the field of early intervention, such as grasslands, ponds, or flower fields, enrich the tasks. Each of the three applications are available for single and multiple users. Multi-user scenarios emphasize social aspects and communication. In preparation for the experiment, we conducted a preliminary test with eight kindergarten children to check the suitability for the intended user group. The games were immediately approached and played, however, we resolved some major issues with the puzzle task. Puzzle pieces needed to be created by the children by means of finger drawings. This approach proved to be error-prone and cumbersome. Hence, the application now provides the correct puzzle pieces.

#### 3.2.1 General Use

Placing dice tangibles on the tabletop starts each of the three applications (see Figure 1). Each side of the dice is associated with one of the applications in VisMo. Since it is possible to switch between the different applications at any moment, multiple persons using the application need to compromise. The modular structure of VisMo is extensible: a pool of various tasks controlled by multiple dice is imaginable. Different configurations for the same task are possible as well. Children learn from following the examples of their peers when playing with the multi-touch applications. Although competition and teamwork are both addressed, single user sessions are still possible.

**Figure 1. Dice tangibles with different byte codes on each side.**

### 3.2.2 Path Tracking

The focus of the path-tracking task is the training of motor skills. Fine motor skills develop fundamentally from age one to five. While drawing, children first produce large-scale paintings by movements in their arms. The forearm performs more fine-grained movements later on. However, by the age of five, the wrist should perform drawing as preparation for school enrollment. Multi-touch tables can assist children in improving their fine motor skills in a playful manner. In addition, cognitive skills and creativity are advanced. At an early stage, the reading direction should be introduced (from left to right). If properly configured, the path-tracking task of VisMo can assist in this endeavor.

Children have to move an object, modeled after a butterfly, to a corresponding target area, shaped like a flower. A random dipsy-doodle path or spiral increases the difficulty. The drag should be performed alongside this path. In the single user scenario, the child can track one path at a time or multiple paths simultaneously. Multiple user scenarios add collaborative aspects, a communicative component, as well as competition regarding the execution order, path ownership, and working space.

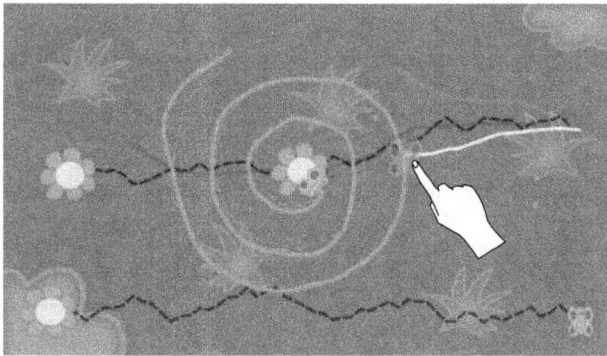

**Figure 2. User interface of VisMo's path-tracking application showing different kinds of task paths. The half opaque lines are failed attempts of dragging. Green paths display a finished drag and the white path is currently being traced.**

The path-tracking task consists of two phases. At first, one or more paths are displayed. The butterfly objects have to be placed on related flower areas. Dashed lines as seen in Figure 2 indicate the relation. Lifting the drag contact before the butterfly reaches the flower resets the target object. After solving all paths, the second phase begins. The second phase shows the score for the current set of paths. Dragging closer to the dashed lines yield a higher score. New rounds are started by touching anywhere within the score screen. Gestures needed for completion are touch and drag-and-drop.

### 3.2.3 Shape Tapping

The most attractive games that are already available on the PC include action. An example is catching birds or fish, which also trains fine motor skills. Hence, the second task allows children to catch objects in a collaborative game. The assigned task is the most simplistic of the entire set of applications. After activating up to four player slots in each of the surface corners, simple touching of the appearing objects collects them (see Figure 3). Hitting one object makes it disappear and creates a new one at a randomly chosen position. At the end of the game, indicators show how many objects of each type were collected in relation to the other players. The design of this application is mainly suited for multi-user interaction. Because competition is an engaging aspect, score indicators show how many shapes are collected. Even though there are just four player slots available, more children can play with the game by forming teams.

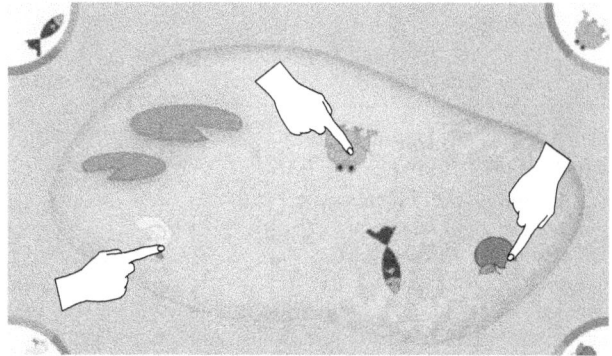

**Figure 3. VisMo's shape-tapping task offers up to four player slots for the collection of items.**

The shape-tapping task has the strongest playful nature. After a brief countdown, touching the hand icons in the four corners activates the player slots. Each corner has a related symbol (duck, apple, fish, and frog). As soon as the desired player count is setup, the symbols for each player start to spawn in the middle of the tabletop. The players then have to collect the assigned figures by touching them. Each collected figure disappears and a new one is spawned at a different position. After 15 seconds, the turn is over and scores are shown. Only a simple touch gesture is necessary to solve this task.

**Figure 4. Interface of the puzzle game, with predefined shapes that have to be fitted into the corresponding target areas.**

### 3.2.4 Puzzle

The last and most demanding application is the puzzle task. It shows a picture with six blank areas at startup. Those are marked with a black dotted line as seen in Figure 4. For each white space, a corresponding shape with random values for size, orientation, and position is created. The users then have to fit the puzzle pieces into the white spaces. If the center of a puzzle piece is over its target area and no touch down is registered on the object, it snaps to the center of the target area and translation is disabled. When a piece is fixed in position and the orientation is correct, rotation will be disabled as well. Adjusting the piece to the right size disables all manipulations and flags it as finished. As soon as all pieces are completed, the game can be restarted by touching the screen with new randomly scattered puzzle pieces. Available actions to solve the puzzle are dragging, rotating, scaling, and flick. In multi-user sessions, the children can manipulate the same shapes simultaneously. Thus, reasoning and compromise are indispensable in these sessions.

## 3.3 Hypotheses and Method

The following three hypotheses were the foundation of our observational study.

**H1 Motivation.** With child appropriate visualizations and a playful task design, the children are motivated and able to solve the given tasks in a maximum of 15 minutes. Dice tangibles can furthermore increase motivation for interaction with the tabletop. Frequent failures in execution may lower interest of the participant and can complicate the experiment.

**H2 Usability and Intuitiveness.** The test group can use the multi-touch tabletop intuitively. All relevant interface elements are reachable with low effort. The use of the hand as input device suggests natural gestures such as the tap gesture, which is similar to pointing at and touching objects. It is likely that children easily understand the drag-and-drop gesture and use it naturally.

**H3 Collaboration.** The children will mostly focus on their own work. However, collaborative interaction will also occur, especially in the form of indirect helping actions like pointing and verbal advice. Children will focus on nearby areas, but still use the entire tabletop surface. Tangibles are a collaborative element used together by the participants to control the application.

In order to evaluate the test sessions, we filmed each child during his or her turn from three different angles. The top view and a distance shot were used to analyze movement and interaction with the multi-touch tabletop. The third camera filmed the faces of the participants in order to analyze their emotions based on facial expressions and assess their center of attention. The participants were positioned at one of the long sides at the bottom of the screen as shown in Figure 5. Except for the opposite side of their initial position, the whole area around the table was free for movement.

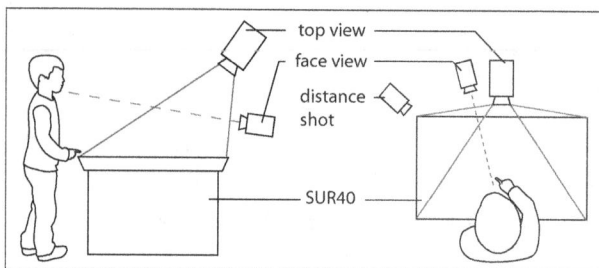

**Figure 5. Initial positioning of participants and camera setup.**

We tested a group of 12 children from the same Kindergarten (aged four to six) in a maximum of 10 minutes per single user sessions. Subsequently, we observed three of the children in a group session. In this session, we gave the die tangible to the children. They could use it to switch the task whenever they wanted. Because only one of the tangibles was available, the children needed to find a compromise regarding who should be in control.

Except one child, none of them had prior experience with multi-touch devices. Some did interact with a computer, but most had no experience with digital technologies. No filming permission was granted for two children; hence, the analysis of the video material covered just 10 of 12 children.

The test was conducted in the same room of our lab where the rest of the group waited, resembling a kindergarten environment

as close as possible. We constructed the test setup in one corner separated with movable walls from the rest of the room. Children currently not working at the multi-touch tabletop had different stations with activities.

Single sessions started with path tracking. Subsequently, the puzzle task was tested. Finally, the sessions were finished with the shape-tapping task. We did not randomize the order of the tasks because of the small group of participants. After the first task started, the experimenter instructed each child to try to interact with the multi-touch tabletop on its own. If they appeared too shy or did not know what to do, the experimenter explained the task. If they still struggled to solve the task, small hints for interacting were given. The same procedure was executed for the shape-tapping task. In the second application, the experimenter informed all children that it is a puzzle. Only in few cases, additional hints were necessary. General hints were given through verbal statements and pointing. For instance: "try to move the butterfly" or "collect the appearing figures". Instructional hints for interaction were only given verbally. For example: "drag the butterfly" or "touch the hand symbol to start".

## 4. FINDINGS

In this section, we present the major findings of our log-file analysis from the experiment, supplemented by observations from the video data and notes taken during the test sessions. Since only one of the authors rated the video material, we did not have to account for inter-rater inconsistencies. First, we examine participant's motivation for interacting with VisMo (H1). Second, we present our analysis about the general usability and intuitiveness for children interacting with the multi-touch tabletop and our application suite (H2). We also investigate which touch gestures the children used naturally. Third, we describe the observations from our group session regarding collaboration between children using a multi-touch application (H3).

## 4.1 Motivation (H1)

To determine the level of motivation, we combined several criteria. The defining criteria were concentration, fun, frustration, and ease of distraction. We examined all tasks separately from each other with the help of log files, notes from the observations, and video material.

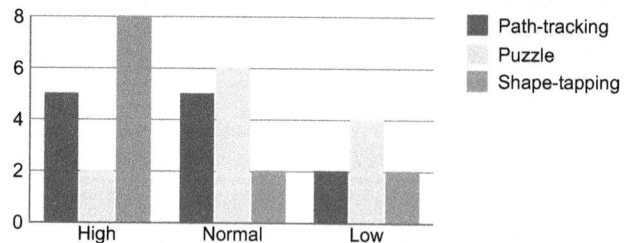

**Figure 6. Level of motivation for each child in the different applications of VisMo.**

Children who were highly concentrated and not easily diverted from the tasks are associated with the category *high motivation*. They also showed signs of increased enjoyment. When problems occurred, they exhibited tenacity and eagerness to fulfill the task. Most of them started to work independently without any external impulse. Children who worked concentrated at the multi-touch tabletop, but were distracted in some situations by the surroundings, belong to the second category, *normal motivation*. In several cases, they needed some motivation to get started. Overall, they worked on their own to solve the tasks. Children easily distracted by the background noises, other children, or the cameras, belong to the last category of *low motivation*. We observed stronger signs of frustration when they could not solve the tasks or the program did not work as expected. Some of them needed strong motivation by the experimenter or the caretaker to start interacting with the tabletop application. Most of the participants were either motivated or very motivated to interact with the multi-touch tabletop. Just a few got easily distracted or lost incentive. Figure 6 illustrates the number of children for each of those categories in the context of the different tasks.

Especially the puzzle task challenged the children. It was more complex and difficult as the other two tasks. As a result, the amount of low motivated children was highest in this task. Misinterpreted contacts on the surface led to erroneous system reactions. Those reactions could considerably trouble and frustrate the children. In some cases, the difficulty to execute the right commands was a motivating factor on its own. Hence, the higher demand in motor and cognitive skills predominated fun as motivating factor in the puzzle.

In contrast, the easiest task, shape tapping, was the most motivating of all three tasks. It was also the one with the strongest playful nature. After the participants understood the principle of this application, they showed signs of great enjoyment. Due to different reasons, only two children did not like the task as much as the others did. One of the kids from the low motivation category worked her way very fast throughout the VisMo applications. She tried to interact independently with the games and solved path tracking very fast on her own. Because she seemed to expect another game after shape tapping, she wanted to end this task. Motivation to play with the third application was lower than the curiosity about the next game. In the second case, the child in question was the last one in the single user sessions. While his turn was not finished yet, the other children left the room for lunch break. This caused the background noises to disappear. The child then wondered where the rest of his group went and wanted to end the test to rejoin them.

The path-tracking task was evenly motivating and highly motivating for the children. One of the low motivated children was very shy and seemed to be afraid of the situation. It needed strong support by the caretaker and the experimenter to begin experimenting with the multi-touch device. Spiral paths could raise frustration level since they are longer. Failing to complete the spiral paths could also be an inducement to try it over again or to try new input approaches.

Some children got distracted or were not very motivated. Still they all solved each task at least once. None of them except the last canceled a test run. The design of the tasks also helped to increase the acceptance of the target group. The different tasks also brought some variation to avoid boredom.

## 4.2 Usability and Intuitiveness (H2)

To better estimate the level of usability and intuitiveness, we focused on three aspects in the children's interaction with the multi-touch tabletop. We separately examined the intuitiveness that the participants showed, their overall accessibility to the device, and the used multi-touch gestures. Because of the different nature of the VisMo tasks, we analyzed them independently and later summarized the findings for the whole application.

### 4.2.1 Intuitiveness

In the first task (path tracking), each child was encouraged to explore the tabletop on its own without any further advice. Most of the children intuitively started to touch the screen and tried to interact with the surface. One child was very shy and needed strong external motivation to begin, but as soon as it started, it worked almost independently with the tabletop. Another one asked for permission to touch the display with the finger. It had the correct concept of interaction with the multi-touch device but needed assurance first. Three of the children could instantly solve the task. An interesting observation was that six participants tracked the given path without dragging the butterfly. They did not hit the butterfly at the beginning, lost it during the dragging process, or started tracking at the wrong end of the path. In any case, they did not notice that they had no contact on the movable object or they did not care.

| Age | Number of children | Ø trials per path | Standard deviation |
|-----|-----|-----|-----|
| 4 | 2 | 2.5 | 1 |
| 5 | 7 | 1.8 | 0.45 |
| 6 | 3 | 2.2 | 1 |
| 4-6 | 12 | 2 | 0.8 |

**Table 1. Average number of attempts for a path in different age groups.**

Table 1 shows the average amount of attempts needed to complete a path in the different age groups. As expected, the youngest participants needed the most attempts to complete one path with an average of 2.5 trials. The five-year-olds required about two trials for each path. The oldest kids needed a bit more than the five year olds did. A probable explanation is the fact that more six-year-olds had to solve a spiral path. Spirals were much more difficult to solve than straight paths. The larger test group of the five-year-olds better compensated this difficulty. Overall, the children needed about two trials for one path. For every two paths, the error rate was 46%. Losing the butterfly or tracking without the butterfly object were considered faulty trials. The following events caused loss of contacts and therefore resetting the task:

1. lifting contact during dragging to reposition arms
2. changing contact area during drag
3. slipping of the fingers

When the participants realized the failure, they tried different approaches to fulfill the tasks. Using more fingers for the drag and increasing the pressure on the display were the most common approaches. One child used the free hand to stabilize the dragging hand. Hence, it kept accurate control with higher pressure. Each child could at least solve one path. The playful design and visual indicators helped them to understand the task. Very few hints were necessary to initiate interaction.

The puzzle application presented the most demanding task. The experimenter explained that it as a puzzle. With knowledge of the first task, the children instantly started trying to drag objects around the screen. Depending on how long they needed to place two pieces correctly, the turn was finished before completion. This was due to the limited time for each session.

Table 2 shows an overview about the average correctly placed puzzle pieces and the needed time to position them correctly. It does not contain information about the last child, because the gathered data for the puzzle task was corrupt and due to no filming permission, the video material was not available. The values indicate that in our test the youngest participants were almost as fast as the oldest participants were. In the test, the random alignment of the puzzle pieces required the younger group just to translate them to the right position without rotation and scaling. After the first two pieces, they faced an increased difficulty for the remaining pieces, which needed more manipulations. Therefore, they had fewer total pieces solved at the end of their turn than the older children did.

The children tackled the rotation and scaling through trial and error, using many gestures intuitively. They easily understood the analogy between rotating a piece of paper and rotating the digital representatives. Scaling was the most challenging task for children of all ages in our test group. The experimenter gave the most hints for this kind of manipulation.

| Age | Number of children | Ø correct pieces | Standard deviation pieces | Ø time to place two pieces | Standard deviation time |
|---|---|---|---|---|---|
| 4 | 2 | 2.5 | 0.5 | 1m 31s | 59s |
| 5 | 6 | 4.7 | 1.9 | 1m 53s | 28s |
| 6 | 3 | 6 | 0 | 1m 11s | 42s |
| 4-6 | 11 | 4.6 | 1.8 | 1m 42s | 41s |

**Table 2. Average number of correctly places puzzle pieces in one session and time needed for two pieces in different age groups.**

Table 2 shows that the oldest children could solve the whole puzzle. It was much easier for them to position all objects at the right place in a short amount of time. One child even interacted with two different pieces at the same time. They also combined several modifications and thus reduced completion time further.

In order to ascertain the level of efficiency, we investigated how often the intended manipulations did what the children expected. Successful manipulations are all gestures that had the intended result, even if the performed gesture served a different purpose. For instance, a child wants to scale an object by clearly performing a tap gesture, achieving the scaling effect only by accident. Unsuccessful manipulations are those, which did not achieve the desired result, like scaling through tapping. The overall error rate is 31.5% across all age groups.

The last task was the easiest of all. In the first round, the children explored the game and acquainted themselves with its operation. The experimenter gave no advice until the children asked for it. Table 3 shows that all children could score higher in the second run. The oldest participants understood the concept most rapidly. However, everyone used the touch gesture intuitively to interact with the game objects.

| Age | Number of children | 1st run, shapes | 1st run, Standard deviation | 2nd run, shapes | 2nd run, Standard deviation |
|---|---|---|---|---|---|
| 4 | 2 | 2.5 | 0.5 | 6.5 | 0.5 |
| 5 | 6 | 2.5 | 1.3 | 5.7 | 1.4 |
| 6 | 3 | 5 | 3.7 | 7 | 2.9 |
| 4-6 | 11 | 3.2 | 2.4 | 6.2 | 1.9 |

**Table 3. Collected figures out of two runs in shape-tapping game for different age groups from 11 of 12 children**

In some cases, the objects could not be hit correctly because the hit box was too elusive. Especially the hand objects for player slot initiation and the fish figures had fine outlines. Sometimes the children hit the space between the fingers, which did not react to the contact. Still every child could solve the task and improve its performance with each additional turn. In addition, the low error rate indicates that the game was easy and intuitive to the children.

### 4.2.2 Accessibility

Using the video material and contact log files, we assessed the accessibility of the multi-touch workspace for the children. We classified the movement of the children (see Table 4). The results in this table are from the 10 children with permission to film. The log file analysis contains the available data from all 12 children.

We designed all tasks to be approachable from any side of the multi-touch tabletop. However, background images and interactive objects indicated a certain alignment. This did not affect children's interaction. In the group session, the visuals were upside down without the participants even noticing. Table 4 shows that the first two tasks induced little movement around the table. In the path-tracking task, most of the children stayed at their initial position and just moved a little bit to the left or right. Paths were positioned in the center of the screen. Not much movement was involved to reach them. Because the paths had to be traced continuously, the children did not reposition themselves during drag. Moving while dragging could easily cause failures. In the puzzle task, contact loss did not present a problem. Pieces could be released without causing failures.

| Kind of movement | Path-tracking | Puzzle | Shape-tapping |
|---|---|---|---|
| fixed position (centered) | 6 | 0 | 1 |
| slightly alongside long end | 3 | 2 | 4 |
| along long side | 0 | 7 | 1 |
| around the table | 1 | 1 | 4 |

**Table 4. Motion around the multi-touch table during each application.**

The interactive objects could spawn at any position on the screen. Children moved along the near end of the table to gain better access. Despite shorter arms, the vertical range was big enough to reach the far end of the table. Everything could be reached with lateral movement only. Most movement around the table occurred in the shape-tapping task. Even in solo sessions where all slots are available, children walked around the table to initialize the player slots. As soon as the collecting phase began, they returned to the starting position. We observed movement around the corners only a few times with four kids. In all three applications, the children increased touch range by leaning over or almost climbing on the tabletop.

The path-tracking task induces the least movement around the tabletop. Because the elements are generated in the center of the screen, the far end of the surface does not contain any relevant elements. The interactive objects were big enough for the children so they could reach them with ease.

In the puzzle task, contacts focused at the target areas. A contact peak at the bottom end is caused by the children's cloths and leaning over the edge. Otherwise, the majority of contacts is registered around target areas or between them. The most distant targets, sun and clouds, could be reached effortlessly. Along with the bush, they were the most correctly positioned ones. Like in the path-tracking task, each element had an adequate size for the children.

The shape-tapping task was logically and visually accessible from a 360° angle. However, due to the camera setup, the physical access was limited to 270°. The display of the spawning figures used the whole screen area. Hence, the participants needed to reach every area of the screen. The children moved along the near end most of the time. In few cases, they walked around the corner to initialize the fish or duck objects. Figure 7 shows the usage number for each of the four player slots and the associated figures. The nearest slot to the children was also the most activated. Each figure had at least two rounds. They initialized the left bottom slot seven times more often than the slots at the top. The duck and apple objects are closer to the viewing range and reach of action. It was easier to use them than to reach out for the far elements or walk around the table. The size of the elements was a problem for hand and fish objects. In few cases, they were hard to hit. As a result, the children developed further strategies to activate them on their own.

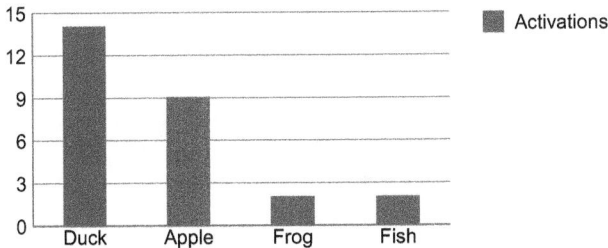

**Figure 7. Number of initializations for each player slot in solo sessions.**

In summary, we noticed that all children could gain access to every element on screen. In most cases, the multi-touch tabletop had no problems to detect the small fingers. In combination with the lowered mount, the children could interact with the SUR40 device without any physical drawbacks. For the given set of tasks, the touch input was handled well and induced enjoyment for the children.

### 4.2.3 Gestures

To determine the gestures used by the test group, we strongly focused on the video material. Therefore, the results presented in this section are from the 10 children we received permission to film.

We analyzed the gestures of the children to see what common touch gestures are intuitively used by them. To describe the gestures we use the formal notation for touch gestures GeforMT (Gesture Formalization for Multitouch) [12]. In GeForMT, simple gestures are usually expressed using a contact type such as fingers (F), hands (H), or undefined blobs (B) and a corresponding movement type such as freeforms (MOVE), static contacts (POINT, HOLD) or specific shapes (LINE, CIRCLE, SEMICIR-CLE). Hence, a simple tap or touch gesture with one finger is formally expressed as 1F(POINT), a circle drawn with two fingers as 2F(CIRCLE). Simultaneous actions are concatenated with an asterisk as in a scale gesture with two fingers: 1F(LINE) * 1F(LINE). Alternative gestures are listed using a vertical bar (|).

In order to classify the gestures in our study, we introduce additional attributes to the formal notation to determine the used hands and fingers. With such an extension, gestures can be distinguished using anatomic features. Advanced definitions for gestures can be specified in order to modify application behavior depending on finger combinations for similar gestures. For instance, a tap with the index finger of the left hand is described as

1F[LEFT.I](POINT), a tap where the index and the middle finger is involved can be formally described as 2F[LEFT.I,M](POINT). Table 5 shows the observed gestures. In addition to a pictogram of each class, it contains a description and the variations using the formal notation of GeForMT.

The children used the touch and drag-and-drop gestures intuitively. While using the tabletop, they found different variations for common multi-touch gestures. We observed the greatest variety of gestures in the puzzle task. Path tracking and shape tapping just used touch and drag. Still some variations of those gestures were observed throughout the experiment. Figure 8 shows how often each finger was used to perform a gesture. Fingers are sorted as if they are put in front of oneself. Multi is a representation of gestures being executed with three or more fingers at the same time. To execute simple gestures, the index finger of both hands (L.IF, R.IF) were used most frequently. Middle fingers (L.MF, R.MF) and thumbs (L.T, R.T) were also used exclusively as well in combination with the index and middle finger. Pinkie and ring finger did only contribute to gestures when used with a full hand. Another experiment [11] found out that the index finger is the most dominant over all age groups. Our analysis supports this finding for touch gestures in our test group. Note that we did not investigate the role of dominant and non-dominant hand in our study.

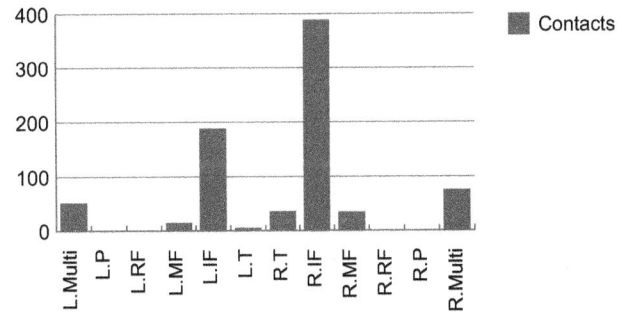

**Figure 8. Fingers involved in gesture execution.**

The overview shows the four different kinds of gestures used in our experiment. They include touch, drag, rotate, and scale. We also implemented flick gestures that were never used. In contrast, accidentally triggered flicks confused the children. They did not comprehend them as gestures and therefore never used them on purpose. Regardless of the side, touch gestures were performed in four different ways. Those were one, two or more fingers of one hand or two hands. Except for one, all children used the 1F[RIGHT.I](POINT) at least once. An advantage of this variant is that just a small space of the viewing area is covered by the finger. Thus aiming becomes a lot easier than with multiple fingers. However, using more than one finger can help hit fine objects better like hand and fish elements in the third task.

Gestures 2.1 and 2.2 depict the drag with either one or two hands. The alternative with the index finger of the right hand 1F[RIGHT.I](LINE) is again the most common amongst the participants. In the puzzle task, dragging with more than three fingers or complete hands could cause errors in the manipulation. Unintended contacts and sleeves on the screen caused the dragged objects to jump to random positions. All children except one tried to use less fingers when this problem occurred. They intuitively switched to the more accurate technique. Rotation and scaling only existed in the puzzle task. Overall, fewer children used the possible variations for those manipulations.

| Id | Depiction | Description and example extended GeForMT notation {used by x children} | Id | Depiction | Description and example extended GeForMT notation {used by x children} |
|---|---|---|---|---|---|
| 1.1 | | touch with one hand<br><br>1F[LEFT.I](POINT) {7}<br>1F[RIGHT.I](POINT) {9}<br>1F[RIGHT.M](POINT) {1}<br>2F[LEFT.I,M](POINT) {1}<br>2F[RIGHT.I,M](POINT) {1}<br>1B[LEFT](POINT) \| 1H[LEFT](POINT) {1}<br>1B[RIGHT](POINT) \| 1H[RIGHT](POINT) {2} | 3.2 | | rotate with one finger and fixed rotation center<br><br>1F[LEFT.I](SEMICIRCLE) {1}<br>1F[LEFT.D](SEMICIRCLE) {1}<br>1F[RIGHT.I](SEMICIRCLE) {3}<br>2F[LEFT.I,M](SEMICIRCLE) {1} |
| 1.2 | | touch with 2 hands<br><br>2B[LEFT-RIGHT] (POINT) \|<br>2H[LEFT-RIGHT] (POINT) {1} | 3.3 | | rotate with one hand and variable rotation center<br><br>1F[LEFT.I](SEMICIRCLE_CW) *<br>1F[LEFT.T](SEMICIRCLE_CW) {1}<br><br>1F[RIGHT.I] (SEMICIRCLE_CW) *<br>1F[RIGHT.T](SEMICIRCLE_CW) {5}<br><br>1B[LEFT](SEMICIRCLE) \|<br>1H[LEFT](SEMICIRCLE) {2}<br><br>1B[RIGHT] (SEMICIRCLE) \|<br>1H[RIGHT] (SEMICIRCLE) {2} |
| 2.1 | | drag with one hand<br>1F[LEFT.I](LINE) {4}<br>1F[LEFT.M](LINE) {1}<br>1F[RIGHT.T](LINE) {2}<br>1F[RIGHT.I](LINE) {9}<br>1F[RIGHT.M](LINE) {2}<br>2F[LEFT.I,M](LINE) {2}<br>2F[RIGHT.I,M](LINE) {2}<br>2F[RIGHT.I,T](LINE) {1}<br>1B[RIGHT](LINE(o)) \| 1H[RIGHT](LINE) {1} | 3.4 | | rotate with two hands and variable rotation center<br><br>1F[LEFT.I](SEMICIRCLE_CW) *<br>1F [RIGHT.I](SEMICIRCLE_CW) {2}<br><br>1F[LEFT.I](SEMICIRCLE_CW) *<br>1F [RIGHT.T](SEMICIRCLE_CW) {1}<br><br>1B[LEFT](SEMICIRCLE_CW) *<br>1B [RIGHT](SEMICIRCLE_CW) \|<br>1H [LEFT] (SEMICIRCLE_CW) *<br>1H [RIGHT] (SEMICIRCLE_CW) {3} |
| 2.2 | | drag with two hands<br><br>2F [LEFT.I-RIGHT.I](LINE) {2}<br><br>2F [LEFT.I-RIGHT.T](LINE) {1}<br><br>2B [LEFT-RIGHT](LINE) \|<br>2H[LEFT-RIGHT](LINE) {4} | 4.1 | | scale with one hand<br><br>1F[LEFT.I](LINE_SE) *<br>1F[LEFT.T] (LINE_NW) {1}<br><br>1F[LEFT.I] (LINE_E) *<br>1F[LEFT.M](LINE_W) {1}<br><br>1F[RIGHT.I](LINE_SW) *<br>1F[RIGHT.T](LINE_NE) {2}<br><br>1F[RIGHT.I](LINE_W) *<br>1F[RIGHT.M](LINE_E) {1} |
| 3.1 | | rotate with one finger and variable rotation center<br><br>1F[RIGHT.I](SEMICIRCLE) {3} | 4.2 | | scale with two hands<br><br>1F[LEFT.I](LINE_E) *<br>1F [RIGHT.I](LINE_W) {4}<br><br>1B[LEFT](LINE_W) *<br>1B[RIGHT](LINE_E) \| 1H[LEFT](LINE_W) *<br>1H[RIGHT](LINE_E) {5} |

**Table 5. List of recorded gestures**

It is likely that adding more tasks that require scaling and rotating would result in additional gestures and higher occurrence of the already recorded gestures. Two general cases had to be distinct for rotation gestures. In the first case, the rotational center is fixed. The target object cannot be translated anymore and every rotation is performed around the median point. This happens as soon as the puzzle pieces are at their correct target location. Three children used this method to rotate elements exclusively. Interestingly, rotations with fixed center and more than one finger did not occur. In the second case, the rotational center is variable, depending on contact position and finger count. Most children used rotations with two independent contacts. With gestures of the type 3.3 and 3.4 the control over object movement was higher as in gestures from type 3.1. One finger rotation with variable center can cause a translation of the object while rotating. With more contacts, this can be avoided. Fixing the rotational center with one finger holding the object and another finger performing a circular movement was never used. The formal notation would be: 1F(HOLD)+1F(SEMICIRCLE).

Scaling was the most difficult task for the children. Frequent erroneous interpretations of contacts caused unpredictable events. Due to failures, a correctly executed gesture could cause wrong behavior. Vice versa, wrong inputs could have a scaling effect. For example scaling with tap or double tap should not work. Because of additional contacts from sleeves, it worked nonetheless. This unpredictable behavior for scaling manipulations confused the children. Best results were performed with two hand scaling (4.2). This was also the most used category.

Despite the low complexity, touch and drag gestures have shown a high diversity regarding the execution. The complex rotation gestures had most variations. That is not surprising since they had the rotation center as an additional attribute. Drag and rotation correspond strongly to the manipulation of real paper shapes. The children easily understood the metaphor transfer to the digital world. Nevertheless, in this connection they did not understand that every contact on an object adds new control inputs. Using more fingers or bigger touch areas was an attempt to increase friction with the digital objects. Instead of better control, this could cause failures in manipulation processes. The possibility to execute multiple manipulations at the same time was a big advantage. If occasionally such a combination occurred, the children learned from this. Afterwards, they purposely combined rotation and dragging or scaling and rotating to increase performance. Many of the gestures used are similar to common touch gestures for smartphones or tablet PCs. The children discovered all of them on their own. Dragging and touch came naturally and even rotation was intuitively performed. Scaling gestures needed most hints, but were executed successfully as well.

## 4.3 Collaboration (H3)

In the group session, we allowed two boys and one girl to interact with the multi-touch tabletop and the VisMo application suite without interference or specific tasks by the experimenter. They got full control over the die tangible to select the different applications. Since they all observed the experimenter using the die to start the different applications in their single user sessions, no further instructions were needed. The color code for each task was understood very fast. The group then referred to tasks by their assigned color on the tangible. One of the children took the control tangible and kept it almost the whole time. At the beginning, he reacted to suggestions by the other children. The longer the session lasted, the more he used the tangible for his own desires. The puzzle was his favorite game and so he started it more often than the other games. His interests influenced task order significantly. In some games, he did not participate actively in the multi-touch interaction. The job to control the tangible and thus moderate the games seemed to be sufficient. He still helped to solve the task by verbal communication and pointing. The two children without the control device first asked the child with the tangible to select certain applications. After realizing that simple asking did not work anymore, one of the participants tried a new strategy. It wrapped its desire to start a particular game in a question. With that approach, it implicitly tried to get the child in control to do what it wanted. This method in fact did work very well.

At the beginning, one of the children was a bit shy and did not interact with the surface. It just watched the others play. Because they all knew the tasks from single user sessions, it is likely that this child was not as dominant as the others were. After a while, the child could assert itself and interaction with the multi-touch tabletop increased. In addition, the amount of communication between the children increased with the duration of the session.

In each game, the children claimed interactive objects for themselves. For the path-tracking task, these objects were the paths themselves. After announcing which path they claimed, only one child used the butterfly to drag it alongside the path. If more than one path was shown, they divided them amongst each other. In the puzzle task, the claimed objects were the puzzle pieces. After the claim of ownership was communicated to the others, the participants started to manipulate the pieces. They usually did not stop to use one object until it was placed correctly at its target

location. Regardless of the ownership of objects, the children sometimes tried to manipulate a puzzle piece, which was already in use of another child (see Figure 9). Motives for this behavior were the offer to help as well as the argument that they could solve it faster. This can be interpreted as help as well, because the final solution of the puzzle could be achieved sooner. Within the shape-tapping task, the interactive objects to be used by each child were assigned by the program. By activating a player slot, each participant had one kind of figures in its ownership. Although the multi-touch tabletop did not allow a mapping of finger contacts with the user who generated it, the children only tried to use their own figures. If just two slots were activated, the third child acted as a helper for the active players. Verbal hints, pointing, and even collecting figures for the others were used mechanisms. If someone had a better reach for an object they asked them for help.

**Figure 9. Two children manipulating one puzzle piece at the same time.**

The children focused on their individual interaction. However, they helped each other with words and actions. They showed others how gestures should be executed or pointed each other in the right direction. In the puzzle task, pointing to the target location of used puzzle pieces happened frequently. If a child did something wrong, this was communicated verbally and hints for the correct execution were given. The earlier mentioned interaction of two children with one puzzle pieces as seen in Figure 9 was a highly collaborative action. Since there was not any differentiation between contacts from one user or contacts from multiple users, problems could occur. One child trying to rotate a puzzle piece and another wanting to move it could be interpreted as scaling of the object by the system.

Since the children used the whole display area they moved around the table a lot. With all three children standing around the table, they crossed their working space very often. This did not seem to be a problem for them. They also told other children that they are in the way or pushed them a bit to get more room. Luckily, that always happened in a friendly manner. The children switched positions often during the group session.

The VisMo application suite strongly supported multi-user interaction. Each task was designed in a way that collaborative interaction was possible. The die tangible created a situation that needed compromise and common agreement. The children needed to make a compromise regarding the initiation of games. They found ways to get what they wanted even without having control over either the tangible or virtual objects. They also helped each other out when problems occurred. They communicated with one another very much during the test. Overall, they worked collaboratively to solve the different tasks and play together with the multi-touch tabletop.

## 5. CONCLUSIONS AND FUTURE WORK

The experiment we conducted showed that even preschool children could approach multi-touch tabletops very easily. With the child-oriented design of the interface and the chosen metaphors for the tasks, they got used to the interaction without significant problems. They naturally performed various multi-touch gestures and acquainted themselves to finger input with ease. No significant problems through physical drawbacks could be observed. The workspace was reachable by any child and overall input detection worked well. The children seemed to enjoy themselves and were motivated throughout the whole session. In the multi-user test, they showed collaboration and compromise to interact together in solving the tasks. In accordance with our research, multi-touch interaction is an easy way to control computer systems. Training the required skills required little time, even for younger users. An experimental comparison of performance between touch interaction and mouse-based interaction could examine which of both is more efficient. Similar experiments were already conducted for mouse and tangible-based interactions [13].

It is conceivable that children identify themselves with a special personal token as tangible in order to record high scores in the games. Such data can also be tracked and interpreted for therapeutic purposes. Using this data allows individual training for each child with regard to fine motor skills. VisMo is capable of accommodating multiple dice, to access diverse tasks. A pool of task dice can be used in a kindergarten environment to create variable training sessions and force the children to find compromise about execution order. In the long term, considerable evaluation is necessary in order to create a true pedagogically valuable program involving multi-touch tabletops in a kindergarten environment.

## 6. ACKNOWLEDGMENTS

René Dang, Jan Rößler, and Josefine Kretschmar designed and implemented the VisMo prototype in a student workshop. Thanks are due to T-Systems Multimedia Solutions GmbH for supplying the Microsoft Surface Device and providing technical assistance. Thanks are also due to our colleagues who supervised the student workshop. We would like to thank all children and their parents for participating in our study.

## REFERENCES

[1] A. N. Antle, A. F. Wise, A. Hall, S. Nowroozi, P. Tan, J. Warren, R. Eckersley und M. Fan, "Youtopia: A Collaborative, Tangible, Multi-touch, Sustainability Learning Activity," in *IDC '13 Proceedings of the 12th International Conference on Interaction Design and Children, pages 565-568*, New York, NY, USA, 2013.

[2] I. Jamil, M. Perry, K. O'Hara, A. Karnik, M. T. Marshall, S. Jha, S. Gupta und S. Subramanian, "Group interaction on interactive multi-touch tables by children in India," in *IDC '12 Proceedings of the 11th International Conference on Interaction Design and Children, pages 224-227*, Bremen, Germany, 2012.

[3] G. & H. M. Sim, "Performance and Attitude of Children in Computer Based Versus Paper Based Testing.," in *In P. Kommers & G. Richards (Eds.), Proceedings of World Conference on Educational Multimedia, Hypermedia and Telecommunications 2005, pages 3610-3614*, Montreal, Canada, 2005.

[4] R. Khaled, P. Barr, H. Johnston und R. Biddle, "Let's Clean Up This Mess: Exploring Multi-touch Collaborative Play," in *CHI '09 Extended Abstracts on Human Factors in Computing Systems (4 April 2009), pages 4441-4446*, Turabian / Chicago, 2009.

[5] J. Rick, P. Marshall und N. Yuill, "Beyond one-size-fits-all: how interactive tabletops support collaborative learning," in *IDC '11 Proceedings of the 10th International Conference on Interaction Design and Children , pages 109-117*, Ann Arbor, USA, 2011.

[6] J. Rick, A. Harris, P. Marshall, R. Fleck, N. Yuill und Y. Rogers, "Children Designing Together on a Multi-Touch Tabletop: An Analysis of Spatial Orientation and User Interactions," in *IDC '09 Proceedings of the 8th International Conference on Interaction Design and Children , New York, NY, USA*, 2009.

[7] L. McKnight und D. Fitton, "Touch-screen technology for children: giving the right instructions and getting the right responses," in *IDC '10 Proceedings of the 9th International Conference on Interaction Design and Children, pages 238-241 , Barcelona, Spain.*, 2010.

[8] A. Al Mahmud, O. Mubin, J. Octavia, C. Shahid, L. Yeo, P. Markopoulos und J. Martens, "aMAZEd : designing an affective social game for children.," in *Proceedings of the 6th international conference on Interaction design and children (IDC 2007) 6-8 June 2007, pages 53-56*, Aalborg, Denmark, 2007.

[9] A. Al Mahmud, O. Mubin, J. Octavia, S. Shahid, L. Yeo, P. Markopoulos und J.-B. a. A. D. Martens, "Affective Tabletop Game: A New Gaming Experience for Children," in *Second Annual IEEE International Workshop on Horizontal Interactive Human-Computer System, 2007. TABLETOP '07., pages 44-51*, Newport, RI, 2007.

[10] C. Zanchi, A. L. Presser und P. Vahey, "Next generation preschool math demo: tablet games for preschool classrooms," in *IDC '13 Proceedings of the 12th International Conference on Interaction Design and Children, pages 527-530*, New York, NY, USA, 2013.

[11] R. Raj und C.Marquis, "Finger Dominance," *The Journal of Hand Surgery: British & European Volume, Volume 24, Issue 4*, p. 429–430, August 1999.

[12] D. Kammer, J. Wojdziak, M. Keck und R. Groh, "Towards a Formalisation of Multitouch Gestures," in *Proceeding ITS '10 ACM International Conference on Interactive Tabletops and Surfaces*, New York, NY, USA, 2010.

[13] A. N. M. D. u. D. H. Antle, " „Hands on what?: comparing children's mouse-based and tangible-based interaction," in *IDC '09 Proceedings of the 8th International Conference on Interaction Design and Children, pages 80-88*, Milano, Como, Italy, 2009.

# Exploring Physical and Digital Identity with a Teenage Cohort

Lia Emanuel
CREATE Lab,
Department of Psychology
University of Bath
Bath, BA2 7AY, UK
+44 (0)12253 83137
L.Emanuel@bath.ac.uk

Danaë Stanton Fraser
CREATE Lab,
Department of Psychology
University of Bath
Bath, BA2 7AY, UK
+44 (0)12253 86023
D.Stantonfraser@bath.ac.uk

## ABSTRACT

The way we develop, use and visualize identity is rapidly evolving as research moves towards the capability to accurately link our digital and physical identities. With teenagers at the forefront of this hyper-connected world, this paper uses a systematic approach to contribute an in-depth understanding of teenagers' attitudes, values and concerns on privacy and identity information when considering both online and offline spaces. Using participatory design methods, we present three interactive workshops examining participant's perception of how their own online identities translated to the physical world, and the values and social considerations they hold around new or near-future identification techniques. We discuss how our deeper understanding of this age group's attitudes, values and concerns can be applied to designing socially acceptable identification technology and effective education on privacy and identity management among teens.

## Categories and Subject Descriptors

H.5.m [**Information interfaces and presentation (e.g., HCI)**]: Miscellaneous, K.4.2 [**Computers and Society**]: Social Issues.

## General Terms

Human Factors, Design

## Keywords

Teenagers, participatory design, values, identity, privacy, social acceptability

## 1. INTRODUCTION

Teenagers are spending more time than ever sharing information online [20]. This age group, often referred to as Digital Natives [23], is increasingly relying on online social network platforms to maintain and strengthen their social lives, as well as develop relationships [20]. Simultaneously, the increased availability of technology is enhancing their ability to represent who they are across both online and offline environments in novel and innovative ways [16]. Importantly, these current trends among teens' use of networked technology are predicted to be driving factors in how this group and the wider public will perceive and use identities over the

next 10 years [8]. There is a rich history of research on the concept of identity e.g. [4]. However, our perception and presentation of identity, or 'who we are', is rapidly changing [24]. We have the ability to represent multiple identities across both offline and online environments. Further, pervasive technologies have given us the capability to seamlessly move between these physical and digital personas. Therefore, it is unsurprising that we are now seeing new identification technologies and frameworks which incorporate this concept of identity existing across the physical and digital world [5, 25, 26]. As we advance to more sophisticated and novel ways to understand identity it is important to acknowledge not only how individuals use identity information, but also their values relating to how their identity information is used by others.

The IDC community has recently pointed out teenagers are one of the least understood user-groups [22, 33] in terms of understanding their distinct values and needs around the design and use of emerging technologies and online capabilities. We argue these developments around identification tools have implications for privacy and identity management among teens; the most likely demographic to be early adopters of technologies that will attempt to bridge the gap between the online and offline environments.

As part of a larger project, SuperIdentity [27], we report our work using participatory design to provide a richer understanding of the attitudes, practices and values teenagers place on their identity and privacy when online and offline spaces are considered a linked and unified environment. We first discuss the changing face of identity and privacy issues in relation to teenagers. We then describe how our approach of engaging with a teenage cohort over an extended period of time contributes to a more in-depth understanding of this age group's current values and expectations when they view different facets of online and offline identities becoming intertwined. We conclude by discussing how long term engagement with teens can lead to a co-design partnership in which the attitudes, values and concerns voiced in the current paper can be applied to designing socially acceptable identification technology, as well as raising awareness for good privacy and identity management practices among teens.

## 2. BACKGROUND

Modern identity takes on many facets. We refer to identity as defined by Saxby and Knight [24]; identity includes unique physical attributes such as biometrics, more biographical or descriptive characteristics such as our name, date of birth, and what cities we have lived in. In addition, identity includes personality attributes and behavior patterns. However, all of these facets of identity now also exist and represent who we are in the digital world, along with unique digital attributes of identity, such as an email or IP address.

How this wide range of personal information gets presented (e.g. identity management) and to what type of audience (e.g. private to public) is rapidly evolving as we accrue more digital identity data e.g. [8, 25].

Considered 'digital natives', teenagers spend the most time online, are more likely to disclose a wider variety of personal information online [7], and have the highest uptake of networked mobile technology usage [17] relative to any other age group. This all feeds into a unique mixture whereby teenagers conduct their social lives fluidly moving between online and offline interactions [16, 23]. However, much of the research examining teenagers' attitudes towards and use of identity has been anchored purely in the social navigation of online network spaces [2] or how they conceptualize privacy and security in online spaces only [6]. For a group whose reality is so immersed in the digital world [10, 23], it remains unclear if teenagers value and use identity attributes similarly across online and offline interaction spaces.

Considering online spaces in isolation, research suggests teens show a relatively high degree of awareness in the importance of identity and reputation management, and do take steps to protect their privacy [1, 2]. Work examining e-safety education initiatives has shown methods such as fear tactics, blocking online access, and techniques aimed at children (e.g., cartoons) have had limited success in delivering e-safety messages or having any impact on the behavior of teenagers [1, 6]. On the other hand, peer led e-safety programs have been shown to be effective [1], and may be a more suitable method considering teens tendency to seek online privacy and identity management advice from friends rather than adults, such as a parent or teacher [21]. However, our current knowledge with regards to teenagers' values and attitudes towards sharing information and privacy practices in online settings have largely been limited to survey and one-to-one interview techniques [2, 6, 20]. A more systematic and in-depth approach to understanding 'digital natives' values, attitudes, and behavior towards identity management and privacy is now more important than ever with personal information being increasingly collected and collated across online and offline environments.

Consumer awareness around how companies sell seemingly innocuous personal information to 3rd parties or tracking browsing behavior for advertising purposes has received recent attention [19]. Teens in particular report some of the lowest awareness, to disbelief, that companies or 3rd parties may use their personal information [20, 7]. Research initiatives are also constructing increasingly sophisticated identification frameworks [25, 27]. The SuperIdentity Project is one example of ongoing interdisciplinary research exploring how associations between identity attributes across both the physical and digital world can be connected and/or predicted via a model of identity [26]. In modeling identity we consider known facts about an individual, such as gender, job description, blog content etc. It is often possible to infer new facts from the known set; these inferences can be modeled as new links between facts about that individual [10]. For example, if a person's real name and employer are known, we could infer their email address with a certain level of confidence. By considering a breadth of identity measures across a range of domains – biographic, biometric, cybermetric and psychological – it is possible to bring together a core *SuperIdentity* [26], linking facets of identity across its many digital and physical world dimensions.

The applications for such an identity model could benefit end-user groups, such as law enforcement and intelligence, in improving the capacity to make an identification decision and reduce identity-related crime and fraud. However, of equal importance is the social acceptability, wider attitudes and concerns regarding the use of identity within such a model, which is where our interest lies. Especially in dealing with sensitive personal information, it is important that the design and the capabilities of identification systems are seen as socially and ethically acceptable to ultimately be usable [15].With teenagers at the forefront of those who are hyper-connected and straddle the digital-physical divide [8], we are working with this age group to better understand the social impact of these research driven identification techniques.

In this paper we report the process and results of three workshops which focused on participatory design, specifically value-sensitive design: a systematic approach to designing for human values in technology [9], with a cohort of teenagers. We suggest value-sensitive design methods are the ideal next step in better understanding not only teenagers' attitudes and concerns around identity and identity management in this rapidly changing landscape, but also how this trend may affect the way in which teenagers utilize and interact with technology. In addition, the highly interactive, 'hands on' value-elicitation approach reported has shown to be successful in fostering engagement and in-depth discussion with teenage groups [28, 29], and effective in its peer guided nature [1]. The purpose of these workshops was to better understand teenager's attitudes, values and concerns on privacy and identity information if online and offline spaces are considered a linked and unified environment. Similar to the approaches taken by Woelfer [31] and Yoo et al. [34] we used a combination of value-elicitation methods, both qualitative and quantitative. Each workshop used a different design activity, involving a mixture of sketching, avatar design, and verbal scenario techniques. Although the qualitative workshop data was our primary focus, survey data was taken to enable a mixed methods approach allowing the quantitative survey data to enrich the themes emerging from the design workshops.

The workshop activities allowed us to explore participants' perceptions of their own online identities, both in social network settings as well as in visual form, and how they perceived these identities translated to the physical world. We followed this up by asking the cohort to brainstorm and design new technologies that would allow them to dictate how they would represent and possibly bridge their offline and online identities.

The first workshop used a variation of the mapping method developed by Panteli et al, [18] which provided a metaphoric perspective for how participants interact and share information online by layering their experiences on a physical environment. This sketching exercise encouraged group interaction and discussion about identity in a way which aimed to draw out perceived contrasts, parallels and overlaps between online and offline interactions. This provided insight into how this age group views identity in different contexts and situations.

The second workshop used avatar design, a user made representation to interact in online or virtual environments, in which participants created their own avatar and evaluated a peer's anonymous avatar. The aim of this task was to see what identity information participants could gather from their peer's avatar. Unlike sharing photographs, the participants had complete control in providing as much or as little information about their true physical features in the avatar platform. Although there is a rich literature on identity and self-representation via avatars, including adolescent specific user groups, e.g. [12, 14], we were particularly interested in attitudes on the possibility that avatar designs may provide links to other forms of identity information. This workshop's method enabled us to explore both values and behavior around the choices this group makes sharing visual information online about their physical identity.

The third workshop used sketches and verbal scenario creation in which participants were asked to design new forms of future identification methods and technologies. Participants' designs acted as the value-elicitation to better understand the identity attributes and identification techniques this group was aware of and to articulate their values and social considerations around new or near-future technology. It is worth noting, we did not use these design activities as a means towards developing or designing 'solutions' for identity and privacy across digital and physical domains. Rather we used the design workshops as a way to facilitate an in-depth discussion with our teen cohort to gauge values, attitudes and concerns about identity information and privacy across online and offline spaces.

# 3. METHOD
## 3.1 Participants and Data Collection Context
Thirty-one students participated in the project, encouraged to take part in all three workshops (approx. 55% participated in all three). Students were recruited from two schools in the South West, UK; aged 13-18 years old. All participants provided informed consent to take part and parental consent was attained for participants under the age of 18. Participants were recruited by circulating fliers through contact teachers at each school for an ICT afterschool activity group being held bi-monthly. The workshops were held at the schools, within classrooms familiar to the participants and in similar year groups (e.g. no more than a 2 year difference in each group). A teacher was present to help gather the participants to the appropriate classroom before leaving the researcher to introduce and start the workshop activity. As an incentive for continuing participation across the project, a points scheme was used in which participants accrued points for each workshop attended and could trade these in for a £10 gift card.

## 3.2 Procedures
Three different workshops were run at each school during December 2012 - June 2013. The workshops consisted of a brief introduction explaining the activity an related instructions. In workshops involving drawing (1 and 3), participants worked around large tables, organically forming groups of 2-5 people but also in close enough proximity for groups to interact with each other. Each group was given large sheets of paper and color markers, spending approximately 30 minutes engaging in the drawing/designing activity. In workshop 2, the avatar design activity was held in computer classrooms, with participants working individually during the design portion. At the end of each design phase, the researcher led a 30 minute semi-structured discussion exploring concepts of identity and privacy in relation to participants' final designs and their design process. All workshops were audio recorded to capture participants' dialogue during the design activities and the semi-structured group discussion.

Following the first workshop participants were given access to a 2-page online survey to complete outside of the workshops over the course of the project. This survey collected additional information about the cohort's attitudes, practices, concerns and strategies around privacy and identity in online and offline environments. Survey questions included both discrete questions (e.g., on average how many hours a day do you spend online?) and scale rated questions (e.g., on a scale of 1, very rarely, to 5 very frequently; how often have you found that comments made online go beyond your intended audience?) as well as open ended questions (e.g., how do you feel about the use of CCTV?).

During the first workshop participants were asked to use markers and large sheets of paper to draw a floor plan that depicted how they visualize online social network sites (SNS) using a familiar physical environment (e.g. school, shopping center). While drawing their floor plan participants were encouraged to discuss and develop ideas with their peers. Participants were also asked to consider features they use in SNS and how they may map on to their floor plan, labeling what they thought was similar or different between the online and offline social spaces.

In the second workshop participants were told they would be creating an avatar anonymously. After designing their avatar, they were told they would be given a peer's avatar to analyze to see what identity information could be derived from the avatar. Prior to creating their avatars, participants were asked to fill out an abbreviated version of the Interpol Anti-Mortem form for missing persons (AMForm) [11] shortened to pertain to the avatar platform, *Voki Classroom* [30], which was used. Participants completed the form to best describe 17 of their own physical features. Following this participants were given approximately 20 minutes to create an avatar, being asked to create what they believed best represented who they are. Participants then used an identical AMform to describe 17 features of a peer's avatar (who remained anonymous). Finally participants were given the AM form of their avatar completed by a peer to compare against the AM form they filled out to describe themselves.

During the third workshop participants were asked to design new forms of identification (ID) that could be implemented in the future. The researcher began the workshop asking participants for examples of ID they may use, drawing attention to both online and offline forms of identification (e.g. passport, driver's license, usernames) and authentication (e.g. passwords to email/facebook accounts, PIN numbers). The researcher also introduced examples of near future technology being developed (e.g. face recognition on smartphones, RFID implants, inferred gait mapping) that used a wider array of identity attributes. Working in groups participants were asked to design an ID for the future and consider what type of personal information would be important to include, how their IDs would function, and how they would secure their personal information.

## 3.3 Analysis
All workshops were audio recorded and transcribed. The materials the participants created during the workshops, the transcribed discussions during design phases, the semi-structures discussions and the responses to the open-ended survey questions were analyzed using thematic analysis [3].

# 4. RESULTS
## 4.1 Mapping SNS
From the first workshop, a total of 10 map drawings were created. All groups used either areas of their school, such as a student common room, or their house as their physical space. We discuss the themes around teenagers' use of and attitudes towards identity across online and offline spaces that emerged from the drawings themselves, the in-depth discussion that was facilitated by the mapping exercise, alongside the participant's responses from the online survey.

### 4.1.1 Diversity of Socializing Spaces

The drawings of familiar physical spaces brought out the numerous different ways teenagers interact face-to-face. Sharing a secret with one person, organizing a group of people to meet up after school, or showing friends photos were common across many of the drawings. However, through layering how these interactions parallel to activity on SNS, participants revealed the diversity of SNS they use. Fifteen unique social interaction platforms were cited or labeled on drawings as being used by participants in the workshop. What this group defines as "SNS" encompasses a number of different interactive platforms, not just one or two different main stream networks (e.g. facebook, twitter). It became clear that participants use many different social platforms, such as private messaging applications (e.g. BBM, Kik), organizing meeting places (e.g. Foursquare), and sharing visual media (e.g. 4chan, YouTube) to fulfill very different facets of sharing information and interacting with people. The use of a variety of SNS appeared to allow participants to enjoy a diversity of interaction that more closely mirrored the choices they have to share information face-to-face.

Through drawing physical boundaries, rooms and arrangement of furniture to compartmentalize communication in a tangible physical space, it became apparent that this group similarly perceived different networks and online features to offer varying levels of privacy based on the target audience for participants' information. For instance, small confined spaces such as the toilets or small corridors were paralleled with private messaging, whereas large communal spaces were aligned with facebook wall posts (see Figure 1).

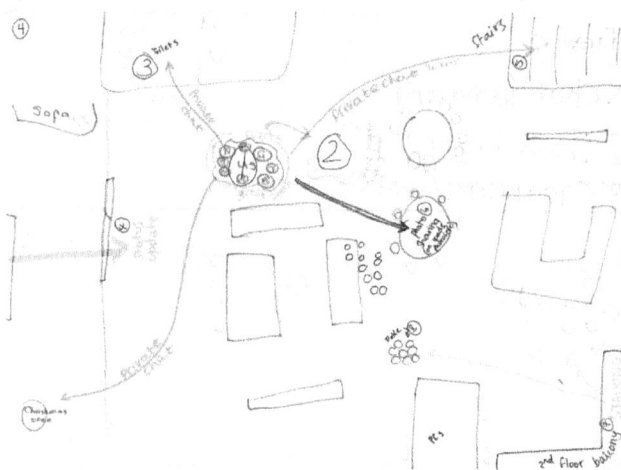

**Figure 1. Drawing from one group who used their student common room to map out SNS**

One group described how they organized social networks within their house as having Skype as their bedroom, because it is generally used for more private conversations and YouTube in their living room since it is more public and more people will see what you post or say. Similarly, awareness of the type of audience within certain networks was depicted, with an image sharing social network as the bathroom because, "*It is full of trolls that's why it is in the toilet*".

However, both physical and online spaces were not perceived as similar with regards to the level of control the group felt they had over the privacy of personal information once provided online. The majority of participants voiced the opinion that they felt that information had more permanence online, with one participant summing up the discussion by saying, "*offline people just chat and*

*it's done. If it's not [online], it will eventually die out. When it's online it's there for everyone, you can't delete it.*" Similarly, responses to the survey supported the beliefs drawn out of the group mapping exercise, with participants feeling they had slight to moderate control to delete or change personal information once posted online (rated M = 2.60, SD = 1.01), on a scale anchored 1, not at all, to 5 very much so.

### 4.1.2 Social Value

The majority of the physical space drawings included the labels of friends' names, and depicted people generally interacting in small groups. When asked to expand on what the group thought was similar and different about how they approach or get to know others online and offline, the majority of participants stated they primarily contacted and interacted with individuals on SNS that they knew offline. The main value of having an identity or presence on SNS to this group was largely toward the benefit of their face-to-face offline social life. In the online survey, socializing online was rated as the second most important online activity behind surfing/browsing and ahead of downloading media content. This was elaborated on in the workshop, with several participants stating their SNS presence was important for organizing, being included in social events and activities happening offline with known friends. The passive consumption of other's information was also highlighted as a unique facilitator of face-to-face interaction, "*I think it [SNS] does really help with communication, like sometimes it's easier to talk to someone if you know what they are into.*", and, "*snooping, looking things up about people is like my primary reason for using facebook*". This view raised in the mapping exercise was also evident in the survey with participants reporting spending significantly more time (once a day) passively checking content on SNS, relative to actively contributing information (once a week), t(13) = 4.69, p < .001. Our teen cohort was very aware that how they represent themselves on SNS platforms bleeds into their offline social lives, and state that maintaining a similar digital persona to their real-world persona actually benefits their social exchanges and relationships.

However, friends were also perceived to be the biggest threat to unintended sharing of personal information in online settings – a feeling that was not as prevalent in offline settings. During the workshop, through discussing how they compartmentalized interactions in their physical space participants were able to expand on concerns about control of personal information online and offline. Participants generally felt that they were fairly good at being careful about who they share potentially sensitive information with, but that 'friended' people who have access to their profile information, for example, were more likely to overshare their information. Further, the diverse SNS engaged with by this cohort was not seen to offer privacy protection in this instance, with overlapping networks of friends and the increasing emergence of services that link together different SNS accounts, making it more difficult to compartmentalize information online. Participants acknowledged this type of spread of information through friends was possible offline (e.g. "*overheard conversations*", "*gossipy friends*"). However, there was far less attention and discussion about the control and compartmentalization of personal information offline, suggesting this is less of a concern within the cohort.

### 4.1.3 Blurring Digital and Physical

Within participants' drawings there was one key aspect that appeared to blur the physical-digital divide. The majority of the physical environments utilize networked, often mobile, technology to depict how participants communicate with others. For instance, communicating via tablets and smartphones in participants' physical environments was depicted as a parallel with private messaging in online platforms. Similarly, one group drew talking with friends on Xbox live in their living room by microphone as a physical environment equivalent to group chat in online SNS. The prevalence of these devices being perceived as comparable forms of interaction in both physical and digital environments, suggests ubiquitous technology is one important facilitator in the blurring of cyber and physical spaces among teens.

However, there were some areas of bridging digital and physical spaces which were seen as concerning within the group. In discussing how the group perceived different levels of privacy, there was a pervasive feeling that anything placed online was going to be highly accessible to others. For instance, one participant stated: "*online just typing someone's name into google, their facebook account or any other account just pops up. You can easily access information about them. But in real life you just can't do that.*" However, the biggest concern about this level of access to personal information centered on the ability to link physical-base information, (e.g. a phone number or current location) to a cyber-persona (e.g. username or email address). This concern was echoed in the survey, in which 61% of responses to participants' biggest concerns regarding personal information online were specifically related to unknown individuals obtaining or misusing location, demographic and contact information. When posed the same question about offline environments, concern on the misuse of information (47% of responses) was lower and more generalized (e.g., "*personal information*", "*my information*") rather than specified to location or demographic details. This suggests attributing physical-based information to a cyber-persona is seen as less acceptable than attributing cyber-based information to a physical world persona by this cohort.

## 4.2  What Does Your Avatar Say About You

In this workshop, 15 avatars were created and analyzed by the cohort. When discussing how they approached the process of creating their avatar the majority of participants stated that they tried to make their avatars as similar to their actual physical features as they could. For instance, none chose to portray themselves with physically impossible features (e.g. purple skin or elves ears), none changed their gender, and very few changed distinguishing features such as hair color (23%) and eye color (7%). In fact, these types of characteristic features, such as hair, eyes and mouth were cited by participants as aspects they spent the most time on to get "just right" in relation to their actual features: "*Oh wow [participant name], yours looks just like you! It's the hair that gives it away*". Likewise, participants were generally unsurprised by the similarity between their own self-reported features on the Interpol AM form and those of their avatar's that were rated by a peer. Indeed, using Kappa coefficient [13] to determine if the agreement on the ratings of self and avatar features exceeded chance levels showed there was significant agreement for 77% of participants (all significant values $K \geq .44$; $p \leq .001$). Interestingly, the 33% who did not show similarity in self-avatar ratings above chance levels created avatars with highly stylized, cartoonish features, as opposed to more realistic features (as in Figure 2).

**Figure 2. Example avatar from workshop**

That is not to say exploration of different physical features didn't happen. Several participants described their avatar design process as testing out different looks, exploring the features and functions of the avatar platform, before trying to find features that were a more accurate portrayal of themselves. For instance, one participant said they spent about half their allotted time flipping through and 'trying on' features before "*entirely scraping that avatar*" to create their final more realistic avatar. When asked what features participants felt they were more creative with or deviated from their appearance, several stated more general alterations such as, "*I wanted to look a bit more cartoony*" and "*I made myself unbelievably good looking*". One participant highlighted there was a social benefit in creating avatars that more closely resembled their appearance: "*I have like 6 different avatars for different things but I keep them pretty similar [to me] so my friends know it's me*". Further, participants seemed to project this design approach onto the wider public, stating under certain circumstances they would trust the accuracy of an avatar as a reflection of its creator: "*If the avatar isn't unbelievably crazy looking…[it's] probably pretty spot on*".

However, there was a general feeling of skepticism that participant's avatars would provide valuable identity information to unfamiliar or unknown individuals online. For instance, participant's suggested that in the workshop exercise being in the same room and able to see who potentially created the avatar they were rating was an advantage they would not have just seeing an avatar online. Even when prompted further about aspects incorporated in their avatar that were not based on their physical features there was little concern around how that may relate back to them as a person. For example, one participant said they spent a lot of time choosing their avatar's clothing to include their favorite color, while others felt they spent a lot of time choosing a background picture to relate to their interests. Although the cohort agreed that aspects of their avatar design could link to other aspects of their identity or persona, many voiced the feeling that information regarding their interests was not particularly unique and could not be used to identify who they were offline.

## 4.3  Designing Future Identification Methods

The third workshop asked participants to consider what types of identification (ID) they could see being implemented in the future. In this type of future design scenario the cohort took a very imaginative view on the identification process. However, a number of underlying themes in this group's awareness and opinions of identification practices emerged. We briefly describe the five final ID designs the cohort created, before discussing the themes which came out of the design process, the group discussion and responses from the online survey.

### 4.3.1 The ID Designs

First, personalized tattoos were suggested in which the wearer could scan different tattoos made with traceable and irradiated ink (so they could be scanned through clothing). These tattoos would provide relevant identity information across different situations. The tattoos were described as unique to the individual with everyone having a personalized combination and style. The designers suggested the tattoos could also be made out of invisible ink to obscure patterns to the naked eye as a privacy measure.

Second, was the BeID system. The designers described the scenario that when an individual needed to be identified a micron-sized robot bee would 'sting' them, collecting their genetic information. The sample would then be taken to a centralized information center which matched the individual's genetic data to all other collected personal information on file. Notably, this group did not specify any privacy or security features for their identification system.

Third, a tongue sensor was designed as a personal security authorization method. The designer gave the example of access to a mobile phone, whereby the owner would lick their phone and the tongue scanner would pick up that person's unique tongue patterns to unlock the phone. This was the only design based on authorization. It held no identity information per se (e.g. you are either the correct individual or you are not), but potentially authorized access to further personal information on an individual's phone.

Fourth, the 'Hipster glasses' (Figure 3) were described as allowing the user to see detailed personal information on the lens of a pair of glasses about another individual. The glasses used facial recognition to identify a person and bring up all of their publicly available information. This group detailed certain settings that would authorize, via iris scan authentication, the wearer to receive more detailed information. For instance, a doctor could have access to a person's medical history, a police officer could access criminal history or a personal trainer could access a person's diet, weight and activity levels.

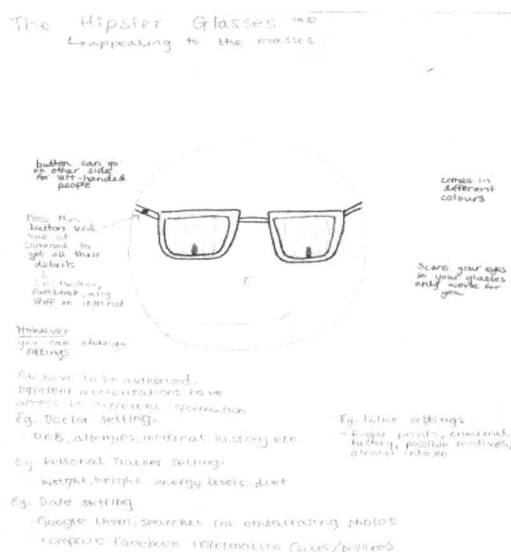

**Figure 3. Hipster Glasses ID design**

Last, ID jewelry was presented in which a chip and memory card was hidden within a piece of jewelry that would contain all of an individual's identification information. The user would scan the jewelry and provide a password or retina authentication to access and bring up necessary identity information. This group included a number of traditional security features, such as a small locking mechanism for the jewelry, as well as more technological features. Namely, the personal information could only be accessed if it was within a particular radius of the owner which was controlled by an RFID style chip implanted in the owner's tooth.

### 4.3.2 Biometric Focus

Throughout the design process and the group discussion participants viewed the use of biometrics as an obvious next step in the future of identification. Discussion of methods that would enable identification during the design phase was almost entirely on using biometric or biological means, such as blood sample, saliva, iris recognition, facial recognition and fingerprint scanning. Likewise, participants utilized biometrics as a security measure for accessing identity information. For instance, the ID jewelry and the Hipster Glasses relied on retina scanning to access information, and the Tongue scanner even introduced a new biometric in authorization via unique tongue patterns. The high frequency of biometric measures used in the ID designs echoes the positive feelings reported in the online survey when participants were asked how they felt about biometric measures being used for identification. All but one participants reported an accepting attitude, suggesting biometric identification was "*a good way to prevent fraud*" and "*made them feel safer*".

Participants also considered how more traditional tokens could be used in new ways or combined with biometric measures. In the initial design phase one group came up with an arm band that essentially turned the users arm into a USB stick when they needed to provide identity credentials. Another group suggested a smart card with the ability to hold a terabyte of information: "*Think if you could have like a terabit of information stored on your card, like your DNA sequence*". From the final designs, the personalized tattoos and the ID jewelry employed this token concept, whereby each could be scanned to provide identity credentials.

### 4.3.3 ID use across online and offline spaces

Across the five designs, participants reported relatively varied capabilities on how their ID designs could be used across both online and offline spaces. Both the BeID and the Tongue scanner designs were presented by the designers in a physical world setting, with no mention of online capabilities. When the larger group was asked if they could see the Tongue scanner technology being implemented in another broader ways only physical world applications were brought up, such as verifying identity at the airport. The designers of the two IDs that used scannable tokens, Personalized Tattoos and ID jewelry described scenarios where their designs could be used almost entirely in physical environments. Both design groups did agreed that the scanning properties could allow someone to log in to online services, for instance using their designed IDs in place of passwords. However, this online capability was online considered when directly prompted by the researcher. The Hipster Glasses design, akin to the concept of Google glass, was the only design presented in a way that relied heavily on matching identity based offline information (e.g. scanning facial features) to information related to that person online; "*You look at someone and press the button and then all their information comes up on the glasses. So on the normal setting you just get their twitter and facebook and anything [about them] on the internet.*"

### 4.3.4 Privacy: how and who can access information

In all of the presented designs dealing with identification, apart from the ID jewelry, identity information was not kept with the individual. In the ID jewelry, this feature was described as a means to secure personal information, *"obviously the bracelet could just stay [on your wrist] it wouldn't have to be removed, or very often anyway. It would be quite useful because it would be hard to lose... and disguised just as a normal piece of jewelry... so harder to steal"*. In the BeID, the Hipster Glasses and the Personalized Tattoo designs the actual identity information about a person was described as being stored on an external database or systems. For instance the BeID designers described their process as, *"So then the point sort of stings you and goes to an Info Centre, like they take themselves to the Info Centre and all your information is there."* In these three designs, the means to access or link a person with that information is kept with the individual (e.g. genetic material, retina scanning, and permanent ink patterns), but the actual information about them is not. These three groups also took on a relatively distinct perspective for who was accessing this personal information.

Two groups, the BeID and the personalized tattoo designers, explicitly presented their identification methods from a government/law enforcement perspective. The irradiated nature of the tattoos was presented within the scenario of ease of capture on CCTV and surveillance equipment, *"but it would be easy to trace and scan, like CCTV could pick it up"*. The BeID group made it clear who they envisaged operating their ID system when asked if someone tried to evade identification and smashed a bee; *"Then you owe the government millions of pounds"*. Although the Hipster glasses were presented in the scenario of ease of access to information for the individual user, the design revolved around gathering information about others. The designers presented scenarios where individuals in an authority position could access more sensitive data; *"there are settings which you have to be authorized to get, such as the doctor setting...and a police setting"*. However, the group did not elaborate on who decided authorization statuses or how an individual may protect their own information availability to others with these glasses. Participants responses to surveillance and identification techniques in the online survey mirror a similar level of acceptance as suggested through elaboration on their ID designs. When asked their feelings towards CCTV and related surveillance techniques, all participants were very positive about its current use. While 50% simply stated acceptance, 25% reported CCTV surveillance was beneficial if it was used appropriately, such as for legal or law enforcement purposes. A further 25% stated CCTV was valuable if used appropriately but did acknowledge feelings of discomfort, *"I think it is sometimes an invasion of privacy but it is there to keep people safe"*.

### 4.3.5 Values and Barriers on the uptake of new identification designs

Through each group's presentation and explanation of their new IDs, the cohort as a whole was very vocal in expressing and discussing acceptance and discomfort around the proposed functionality of their peers' designs. Negative perceptions of using the new technologies and techniques for identification were not generally based on the protection or privacy of information. Rather, lack of acceptance of certain features was largely grounded on personal discomfort, both physically and socially. During the design phase some biometric measures, such as DNA extracted from blood and saliva samples, were discarded quickly because they were perceived as painful; *"you would have to cut yourself each time you used it [blood sampling]"* or unhygienic; *"you would end up spitting on someone [using saliva sampling]"*. Socially normative behavior was also a driving factor in negative views on the implementation of some of the final designs. For instance, in the case of personalized tattoos one participant suggested tattoos were socially undesirable: *"Tattoos are definitely unattractive"*. Similarly, discussing the tongue scanner brought up the view that an individual would *"look weird"* licking their phone in public, even if it was more secure than a password.

Two design features in particular stood up very well against unacceptable or uncomfortable authentication methods. First, the tongue scanner was met with resistance from the group due to its perceived socially awkward and unhygienic method of authorization. However, the scenario of securing mobile phones specifically piqued the interest of this group. With the majority (60%) of the cohort reporting owning a smartphone, personal devices were reported as being highly personal and private in the online survey. Second, the high degree of customization in the wearable IDs was of particular interest to the cohort. Much of the discussion around these types of designs was building on the creative aspects and how the group could tailor the IDs to suit their individual style or tastes. This customizable aspect led several to eventually accept initially perceived negative qualities (e.g. implanting an RFID chip in a tooth for the ID jewelry).

## 5. DISCUSSION

The value-sensitive design methods in the present paper provoked considerable reflection and discussion with our teenage cohort in the way they view identity across many dimensions. Both the mapping SNS workshop and the Avatar designing workshop contributed insight into participants perceptions of their own online identity – how they use those identities, how they value private and public availability of their identity information – and the facilitators, benefits and concerns around how these identities may translate to the physical world. The designing a future ID workshop provided a broader approach by offering our cohort a unique way to express their level of awareness, values and social considerations around how they could ideally represent their identity through a variety of identification techniques.

The importance of relationship maintenance and reputation management in online spaces for teens is well documented [2, 16]. However, asking participants to consider how they share information and personify themselves layered across both online and offline environments yielded several insights into their values and behavior, as well as concerns. The variety of online spaces utilized by our participants, each for a subtly different purpose, allowed them to enjoy a diversity of interaction that more closely mirrored the choices they have to share information face-to-face. Similarly, the use of many different online social spaces also afforded participants a way to compartmentalize their identity information. Different spaces were used as a means for controlling the flow of information and indicated a relatively keen awareness of the potential audience consuming that information. In a sense, this reflects a relatively nuanced approach to privacy e.g. [2]. However, the variety of online SNS this age group engages with also provides a very rich identity foot print which affords subtly different snap shots of that person (e.g., video, images, voice, and textual/content information). Importantly, this type of selective sharing of information across diverse online platforms implies research can no longer be bound to just one main stream platform, such as facebook e.g., [35], to understand the full picture of how teens share or disclose identity information.

However even with using this compartmentalization strategy, participants felt there was a difference in their ability to control the privacy of their information online versus that ability offline. This feeling appeared to stem from two points. First was the permanence of personal information online, which was not present or perceived in offline disclosure. Second, participants' friends were seen as the biggest threat to teens' ability to control personal information. Both the qualitative and quantitative data suggested participants were highly confident in their ability to keep sensitive personal information private, across both online and offline spaces. However, it was primarily within online scenarios where friends and contacts were seen as more likely to 'overshare' participant's personal information.

Nonetheless, the social value or benefits gained among friend networks emerged as one of the main motivations for maintaining a similar digital persona to teens' physical persona. Similar to previous findings [20], our teen cohort reported that they primarily used online SNS to socialize with people they knew offline. In addition, participants were very aware of the high overlap in how they represented themselves online and offline among their friends. In both the mapping social networks and avatar workshops participants provided examples, such as improving face-to-face interaction or ensuring friends recognized them online, of the positive benefits they had experienced from keeping their offline and online self-representations similar.

Similar patterns of behavior were seen in the avatar workshop. The cohort's process of designing their avatar was creative but both the qualitative and quantitative data suggested the majority of the group created an avatar to resemble their actual features relatively closely. This is in line with McCue's [14] findings that adolescents showed a tendency to create avatars with realistic features as opposed to fantasy features. However, our findings uncovered an interesting contrast. Participants explicitly tried to design an avatar that accurately represented their appearance and were able to see that their peer's ratings of their avatar were quite similar to their own rating of their physical features. Yet, participants felt their avatars would not provide important or unique identity information in a public online setting. There was little to no concern voiced about the potential for an avatar representation online linking back to the participants offline. One possibility is that the greater control afforded to participants to be selective about the information related to their actual physical features led to lower levels of concern. Alternatively, the avatar platform used [30] was designed as a teaching aid to use avatars for teacher-student and student-student interaction on class assignments. Unlike other larger avatar platforms, such as Second Life, realistically the audience likely to see the participants' avatar was relatively small, and known to the participants offline.

However, this attitude was particularly interesting considering the tension brought up around the ability to link online and offline identity information. Overall, attributing physical-based information to a digital-persona was seen as less acceptable than attributing digital-based information to a physical world persona by this cohort. One example given by a participant was concern around the ability to infer and attribute physical based information (e.g. house address) to a digital-identity (e.g. email address) that was not expressly provided by the participant. This tension, which also emerged in the quantitative data, was voiced as a concern primarily due to the higher level of accessibility of personal information online versus offline.

The results suggest there is some tension around others ability to share or spread information from one online network to another. Particularly if this spread involves inferring physical world information, such as location or demographic details, and linking it to an online persona. However, participants were generally unconcerned that certain pieces of information could be derived from their avatar, such as interest, hobbies and general physical features. This may reflect the perception that some types of identity information are more or less sensitive than others. Yet it remains unclear how participants' attitudes and concerns may change when made aware of emerging identification techniques. The designing a future ID workshop began to address this question.

The envisioning aspect of the future ID workshop may have led participants to use design features that they found innovative or exciting, rather than reflective of their acceptance of such techniques were they implemented. For instance the BeID design is by no means realistic 'solution' for identification or identity management, nor do we believe the designs were necessarily seen this way by the participants themselves. However, this creative aspect of the participatory design activity did allow the group to articulate a number of values and attitudes they held around identification methods.

The cohort was very comfortable with using and creating new biometric indices. Biometric measures were the favored method among the group for both securing access to identity information as well as a means to identify an individual. The heavy use of biometric measures, almost an exclusively physical world identity attribute, may be one reason why all of the future ID designs apart from one were presented as functioning primarily in physical-world environments. On the other hand, the choice to maintain identity information in offline environments may further indicate tension around linking unique physical identity information to digital identities, and feelings of greater control of offline information that were voiced in the previous workshops.

We found teenagers also showed high usage of networked tokens, IDs working with existing surveillance practices and centralized identity databases (synonymous with dataveillance). This is in contrast with studies exploring adult user-groups. A relatively high level of resistance to ID methods incorporating government surveillance, dataveillance, and networked ID tokens has been documented among adult populations [32]. Within the present cohort, the wide use of these ID methods, biometric indices and the ease of discussing, largely the merits of, these techniques reflects some degree of acceptance. Teenagers are immersed in this type of technology, if not directly in their daily routine then through extensive media exposure, and therefore would perceive these methods as familiar or viable, unlike perhaps their adult counterparts [23]. However, the cohort's acceptance of these surveillance practices was largely dependent on the context in which it was used. For instance, if used for protection or by an authority figure. Future research needs to address values around privacy and identity management with this age group across a spectrum of contexts. A pertinent example which spans both online and offline spaces are teens' attitudes and concerns on the commercial (mis)use of identity. Likewise, values and trust around the concept of anonymity (e.g. the right to be forgotten, [24]) has yet to be explored in relation to teens view of acceptable uses of identity and identification technologies.

The current results provide a platform to begin to understand teenagers' values and concerns on the use of their identity information in light of the rapid evolution of identification technology spanning online and offline spaces [25, 26]. Namely, the reported workshops provide situations relevant to this age group to frame further examination of teens' attitudes and acceptance around how their identity is used. Specifically, further understanding values on technology with the capability of taking what was seen as relatively non-unique identity information and collating, inferring, and linking to other aspects of their identity [27]. For instance, mobile devices were portrayed as a favored way for participants to share information and facilitated interaction across both online and offline contexts. However, touchscreen devices can reveal identity information about the user via swipe gestures, such as gender, age, and height [26]. Through extended engagement with the teenage cohort, this mobile device example can be used to introduce how identity modeling makes it possible to infer or predict new identity information from a known set of facts [10], within a context that is relevant to the cohort. In this way, the cohort moves from participant to co-designer by feeding back on the acceptability of deriving identity information through identity modeling techniques, as well as suggest design features to improve and address negative or socially unacceptable features.

This use of participatory design methods to engage with teens also has implications for improving e-safety education and practices. The hands-on, interactive design workshops were an effective way of sparking interest on the topic of identity with teenagers. Importantly, this method led to enthusiastic engagement and provoked animated discussions. Through the semi-guided activities participants were able to articulate amongst their peers the main values and concerns they held while debating and exchanging advice on how they tended to make choices about sharing and using identity related information. This approach in raising awareness around disclosure practices is more in line with teen's tendency to go to peers for advice [21]. Together with the flexibility of using different activities to address different and ever evolving issues on identity management makes value-sensitive design methods a potentially valuable tool for e-safety education. Future research would benefit from further evaluation among both teens and teachers on the impact value-sensitive design methods has on changing identity management and privacy practices.

## 6. CONCLUSION

Constantly evolving pervasive technologies allows us to develop and move between different physical and digital personas. This makes better understanding the fusion of digital and physical identity a key priority in how the wider public will perceive and use identities over the next decade e.g., [8].With teenagers at the forefront of bridging the online-offline divide, the current findings suggest a number of key attitudes, values and concerns regarding identity across physical and digital spaces.

There were three main areas where we found teenagers perceived and largely use online and offline personas in a continuous way. First, similarly across both spaces, this group develops, uses and shares personal information across numerous and diverse social spaces, each allowing them to share a subtly different, and an overall rich representation of themselves. Second, through primarily having similar friend networks online and offline there was social value in maintaining similar personas across both spaces. Third, mobile devices were portrayed as a favored way for participants to share information and facilitated interaction regardless of online or offline context. Networked mobile technology may be at least one artifact that blurs and provides the strongest link between teenagers' digital and physical identities.

In contrast, two main points emerged which may indicate future tensions regarding the fusion of digital and physical identity. First, new identification frameworks should carefully consider the capabilities and security around inferring and attributing physical-based information to digital personas when not expressly given by the owner of the digital persona. Second, the concerns voiced about the reduced control over and ease of access to identity information was largely seen as a tension felt in online spaces only. Future research would benefit from focusing on design features and technology which address this latter issue, which in turn may reduce the tension around linking physical information to a digital persona.

Building off of previous survey and interview based studies [6]; the participatory design approach used in the present paper provided a rich and more comprehensive insight into teenagers' perception, experience and behavior with regards to identity and identification technology. In addition, our methodological approach contributes to the less developed area of participatory design methods for teen-CI [33], as well as highlighting the potential for value-sensitive design approach as an effective e-safety awareness tool. We can now move forward, using these outlined areas of similarities and tensions around *SuperIdentity* as a platform to engage with teens as co-designers of socially acceptable identification technology while developing awareness and good practice in privacy and identity management.

## 7. ACKNOWLEDGMENTS

This work was supported by EPSRC Grant (EP/J004995/1 SID: An Exploration of SuperIdentity). Colleagues on this grant are thanked for their helpful contributions to the current work. The authors would also like to thank Duncan Hodges for his engagement with the user-group, the students and schools taking part in the workshops. We also thank those who reviewed earlier versions of this paper for their helpful feedback.

## 8. REFERENCES

[1] Atkinson, S., Furnell, S. and Phippen, A. 2009. Investigating attitudes towards online safety and security, and evaluating a peer-led internet safety programme for 14-to-16-year-olds. Retrieved April 4, 2012. http://dera.ioe.ac.uk/1451/

[2] boyd, d. and Marwick, A. 2011. Social privacy in networked publics: Teens' attitudes, practices, and strategies. *A Decade in Internet Time: Symposium on the Dynamics of the Internet and Society.*

[3] Braun, V. and Clarke, V. 2006. Using thematic analysis in psychology. *Qualitative Research in Psychology* 3:2, 77-101.

[4] Brubaker, R. and Cooper, F. 2000. Beyond "identity". *Theory and Society 29*: 1-47.

[5] Collaborative information, Acquisition, Processing, Exploitation and Reporting (CAPER): for the prevention or organized crime. *Retrieved August 25, 2013.* www.fp7-caper.eu/

[6] Davis, K. and James, C. 2013. Tweens' conceptions of privacy online: implications for educators. *Learning, Media and Technology* 38:9, 4-25

[7] Eurobarometer 359 Special Report. 2011. Attitudes on data protection and electronic identity in the European Union. *TNS Opinion & Social and Directorate-General Communication.*

[8] Foresight Future Identities. 2013. *Final Project Report.* The Government Office for Science, London. Retrieved August 22,

2013. www.bis.gov.uk/foresight/our-work/policy-futures/identity

[9] Friedman, B., Kahn, P.H., Jr., and Borning, A. 2006. Value Sensitive Design and Information Systems. *In Human-Computer Interaction in Management Information Systems: Foundations.* P. Zhang and D. Galletta, Eds. M.E. Sharp Inc., New York.

[10] Hodges, D., Creese, S. and Goldsmith, M. 2012. A model for identity in the cyber and natural universes. *Proc. European Intelligence and Security Informatics Conference.* Odense, Denmark, EISIC'12, pp. 115-122.

[11] Interpol DVI forms (version 2002). Ante-Mortem (yellow) Victim Identification: Missing Person. *Retrieved Jan.15, 2013.* http://www.interpol.int/INTERPOL-expertise/Forensics/DVI-Pages/Forms

[12] Kafai, Y.B., Fields, D.A., and Cook, M.S. 2010. Your Second Selves: Player-designed avatars. *Games and Culture 5*(1), 23-42

[13] Landis, J. R., & Koch, G. G. (1977). The measurement of observer agreement for categorical data. *Biometrics* 33:159-174.

[14] McCue, C. 2008. Tweens avatars: What do online personas convey about their makers? *Proc. In Society for Information Technology & Teacher Education International Conference.* Las Vegas, NV, SITE'08: 1.

[15] Munson, S.A., Avrahami, D., Consolvo, S., Fogarty, J. Friedman, B., Smith I. 2012. Sunlight of Sunburn: A survey of attitudes toward online availability of US public records. *Information Polity*, 17(2), 99-114.

[16] Odom, W., Zimmerman, J., and Forlizzi, J. 2011. Teenagers and their virtual possessions: design opportunities and issues. *Proc. on Human Factors in Computing Systems.* Vancouver, BC, CHI'11, 1491-1500.

[17] Ofcom. 2012. Adults media use and attitudes report. Retrieved September 12, 2013. http://stakeholders.ofcom.org.uk/market-data-research/media-literacy/

[18] Panteli, N., Marder, B., and Davenport, J. H. 2013. Through the lens of age; situated identities online across different generations. *Proc. British Academy of Management.* BAM'13.

[19] Patel, K. 2012. How do you brand consumer privacy – Internet giants take their cases to the masses with ad campaign. AdAge Digital, *Retrieved December, 18 2013.* http://adage.com/article/digital/brand-consumer-privacy/232694/

[20] Pew (a). 2013. *Teens, Social Media and Privacy.* Washington, DC: Pew Research Center's Internet & American Life Project.

[21] Pew (b). 2013. *Where Teens Seek Online Privacy Advice.* Washington, DC: Pew Research Center's Internet & American Life Project.

[22] Poole, E.S. and Peyton. T. 2013. Interaction design research with adolescents: Methodological challenges and best practices. *Proc. Interaction Design and Children.* New York, NY IDC'13, 211-217.

[23] Prensky, M. 2001. Digital Natives, Digital Immigrants. *On the Horizon, 9*(5).

[24] Saxby, S. & Knight, A. 2013. Identity crisis: Global challenges of identity protection in a networked world. In *Law & Practice: Critical analysis and legal reasoning*, S. Kierkegaard, Ed. International association of IT Lawyers, Copenhagen, DK, 13-29.

[25] Secure Identity Across Borders Linked, (Stork). *Retrieved August 26, 2013.* www.eid-stork.eu/

[26] Stevenage, S.V., Whitty, M. and Saxby, S. 2013. Who am I?: SuperIdentity. *International Innovation*, Research Media Inc. 82-84.

[27] SuperIdentity project. *Retrieved August 23, 2013.* www.superidentity.org

[28] Thomas, L. and Briggs, P. 2013. Teenagers' attitudes and design values around identity management. *Proc. on Human Factors in Computing Systems.* Paris, France, CHI'13.

[29] Toth, N., Little, L., Read, J.C., Guo, Y., Fitton, D., Horton, M. 2012. Teenagers talking about energy: using narrative methods to inform design. *Proc. on Human Factors in Computing Systems.* Austin, TX, CHI'12, 2171-2176.

[30] Voki Classroom. 2013. Oddcast Inc., New York. http://www.voki.com/

[31] Woelfer, J.P. 2012. The role of music in the lives of homeless young people in Seattle WA and Vancouver BC. *Proc. on Human Factors in Computing Systems.* Austin, TX, CHI'12, 955-958.

[32] Wright, D., Gutwirth, S., Friedwald, M., De Hert, P., Langheinrich, M., and Moscribroda, A. 2009. Privacy, Trust and policy-making: Challenges and responses. *Computer Law and Security Review 25*, 69-83.

[33] Yarosh, S., Radu, I., Hunter, S., & Rosenbaum, E. 2011. Examining values: An analysis of nine years of IDC research. *Proc. of the Conference on Interaction Design and Children.* Ann Arbor, MI, IDC '11, 136-144.

[34] Yoo, D., Huldtgren, A., Woelfer, J.P., Hendry, D.G., Friedman, B. 2013. A value sensitive action-reflection model: Evolving co-design space with stakeholder and designer prompts. *Proc. on Human Factors in Computing Systems.* Paris, France, CHI'13, 419-428.

[35] Zhao, X., Salehi, N., Naranjit, S., Alwaalan, S., Voida, S. Cosley, D. 2013. The many faces of Facebook: Experiencing social media as performance, exhibition and personal archive. *Proc. on Human Factors in Computing Systems.* Paris, France, CHI'13, 1-10.

# Sparkles of Brilliance: Incorporating Cultural and Social Context in Co-design of Digital Artworks

Foad Hamidi
Lassonde School of Engineering,
Department of Computer
Science and Engineering,
York University
Toronto, ON M3J-1P3 Canada
fhamidi@cse.yorku.ca

Karla Saenz
Department of Design, Science,
Arte, and Technology
Universidad Iberoamericana,
Mexico City, C.P. 01219 Mexico
karla.saenz@uia.mx

Melanie Baljko
Lassonde School of Engineering,
Department of Computer
Science and Engineering,
York University
Toronto, ON M3J-1P3 Canada
mb@cse.yorku.ca

## ABSTRACT

Digital media have great potential as tools for self-expression and artistic exploration. We seek to enrich the discussion of challenges and benefits associated with using digital design methods and materials with children in developing countries through a case study. Our contributions to this discussion are based on our involvement in facilitating a two-day co-design workshop with 25 marginalized children in Oaxaca, Mexico. Together, we explored, designed and implemented digitally augmented paper artifacts based on traditional folk art from the children's native region. We analyzed the artworks and observed the children during the workshop to inform our research. Lessons learned include the importance of establishing trust though local contacts, incorporating relevant cultural and social elements, planning concrete outcomes and using technology appropriately. We hope that this detailed case study may serve as an exemplar, by providing insights and inspiration for other designers, researchers, and developers when planning, carrying out, and studying workshops.

**Author Keywords**
Co-design with Children; Intercultural Collaboration.

**ACM Classification Keywords**
H.5.2. User Interfaces

## INTRODUCTION

The emergence of accessible, both technically and economically, digital hardware and software tools, as well as, a global increase of interest in Making and Tinkering methods are bringing about a paradigm shift in design and production that some technology pundits call "the new industrial revolution" [1]. There is much potential to be explored in this area. Many initiatives have identified and explored possibilities of facilitating the use of technology for education and information sharing on a global scale [2]. A seemingly inevitable outcome of the combination of globalization and digital design "democratization" should be the proliferation of new global digital design ideas and perspectives: something that has been slow in coming!

We present the results of a case study in the form of a two-day digital media design workshop with children in Oaxaca, Mexico. The workshop aimed to provide the participants with a basic understanding of what technology is and its relationship to art and to facilitate the design of digitally augmented artifacts. The workshop was an example of intercultural collaboration, not only between the facilitators and the participants, but also among the facilitators themselves who came from different backgrounds. This characteristic is bound to become more common in research and educational efforts in an increasingly multicultural and heterogeneous global society [8]. Thus, we find it important to share our experiences working at a grassroots level.

The children who participated in the workshop are among the most marginalized and underserved children in Mexico with many families affected by social problems such as drug trafficking and sex work. These characteristics had important implications for the design of the workshop and it was essential to incorporate information about the cultural and social context in which the children are situated into the workshop design. One of the authors is from Mexico and has already worked with these children for several years. Her experience and relationship with the children was an essential part of the project and made it possible to come up with a plan that was relevant and informed, prior to conducting the workshop. The ultimate goal of this research effort is to come up with methodologies that not only facilitate creative expression and learning for children in similar contexts but bring about empowerment through creativity.

## BACKGROUND

### Learning and Agency

The traditional school system has been under great criticism in recent years. There has been a wide recognition of the diversity of intelligences and their effect on learning [7, 20]. Studies have identified the existence of multiple learning styles among children and have shown that achievement increases as teaching method matches the learning styles of children [6, 20].

*Constructivism*, an influential school of developmental psychology whose pioneers, Jean Piaget, John Dewey, and Maria Montessori regard children as constructing knowledge rather than being empty vessels and taking it in, emphasizes creating space for children to direct their own learning through experimentation and creative expression [12]. In this view, deep concentration through purposeful action is essential for learning for children. Seymour Papert applied these ideas to the design of tools to facilitate digital design for children at an early age and argued that the learning experience is positively transformed once children become engaged in projects that they design and execute themselves [17].

In recent years, innovative projects have demonstrated the potential of technology to educate and empower marginalized children. In the *Hole-in-the-Wall* project, [15] a computer connected to the Internet was embedded in a concrete wall in a slum in India. Access to the keyboard and mouse was restricted to children by placing guards that only small hands could pass through. No supervision was provided to the children and it was hypothesized that they will learn in an independent, self-motivated and collaborative manner. A computer literacy test, conducted after 248 days, reported a hike from 7% to 43%. This showed that the children could learn basic computing skills in the absence of teachers and curriculum, and with a fraction of the cost of setting up a class [15]. The study has since been emulated in 22 other locations throughout India with similar results [16]. While our methodology is different from Mitra et al., we are inspired by the results of questioning assumptions and using minimal technology to achieve great results. Another study of XO laptops distributed as part of the *One Laptop per Child* program to school children in Uruguay, identified positive effects such as increased interest in reading, writing, collaborating and learning from each other, as well as, accessing previously unavailable information resources, in the children [9].

### Co-design and Children

Several methodologies have been developed to facilitate digital design for children. *Cooperative Inquiry*, with roots in Participatory Design, is specifically developed to allow children to be design partners and collaborate with adults to come up with novel design ideas [5]. The method views children as potential designers and aims to facilitate their abilities to be design partners through accessible and intuitive methods. Cooperative Inquiry uses a series of techniques such as Bag of Stuff and Stickies to prototype and critique ideas. Bag of Stuff uses low-tech tools such as paper, pens and craft material to allow children to come up and express novel design ideas. Stickies uses small pieces of paper with adhesive glue on the back to express reasons for liking or disliking a design or to suggest new ideas about it. The ideas expressed initially on paper are to be followed up into actual implementation. Cooperative Inquiry is generally to be performed with child design partners frequently and over a long period of time.

Our method can be viewed as a different variation of Cooperative Inquiry in that it is highly inspired by it and shares the philosophy of viewing children as design partners. However, there are important differences. First, the main objective of our workshop was not to design a new interface for children, but to facilitate the design and creation of digitally augmented art works. Thus, in our approach the emphasis was on creative expression and aesthetics rather than problem solving or technological innovation. The focus and goal of our method is not to develop or evaluate user interfaces, although this could happen as a side effect, but to facilitate empowerment and learning through self-expression and creativity.

Second, the context in which we apply our method is different. The main implication of this is that resources, including time for facilitators and children to work together, are very limited. While in Cooperative Inquiry, the goal is to come up with design ideas that will be implemented in the future, for us the outcomes of the workshop were self-contained. In other words, while we initially used drawings as design proposals or interpretation of materials in the presentation, at the end, they turned into interactive artifacts and became one of the main outcomes of the workshop. This is essential because due to logistical reasons we cannot have frequent meetings with the children and, thus, for the workshop to be effective and meaningful for the children, we had to come up with concrete and self-contained results within such a short time.

Third, we had to take into account specific cultural and social barriers. The children did not have prior familiarity with computers (something that is increasingly rare in developed countries) and we had to provide scaffolding in the form of interactive presentations throughout the workshop. Finally, as with any project in a developing context, the question of sustainability was crucial to our designing the workshop. We will come back to questions of impact and sustainability in the discussion section. In a recent reexamination of Cooperative Inquiry, the developers of the method suggested its potential for modification for and application in developing world contexts [8].

Two other similar methods, Bonded Design and Informant Design, allow for children to be involved in the design process in different capacities. *Informant Design* incorporates children's input into design but does not view them as co-designers [18]. *Bonded Design* views children as design partners but also questions whether the hierarchies between adults and children can be overcome during the design process [11]. While our method has many similarities with Bonded Design, especially the emphasis on learning, in viewing children as full design partners we feel our approach is closer to Cooperative Inquiry and, perhaps, even goes further in viewing the children not only as design partners but actually as the main designers and the adults as facilitators or technical informants on how the children's ideas can be executed.

## AN INTERACTIVE DIGITAL ART WORKSHOP

### Workshop Background
The workshop was conceived through the coming together of two cultures and disciplines. The authors have different backgrounds: Computer Science and Interaction Design, on the one hand, and, Fine Arts, Public Art and Education, on the other. The idea for the workshop was formed through discussions around how technology and art can be combined and used for education and empowerment. The workshop was to focus on hands-on activities with concrete outcomes but be rooted in theory and foster reflection.

The aim of the workshop was two-folds: 1) to provide an introduction to what is technology and its relationship with art and creative expression; and 2) to facilitate the practice of knowledge learned through the hands-on design of digitally augmented artifacts. During the workshop, we observed the children closely and also analyzed their drawings, sketches and artworks post-workshop to inform our research.

### Setting and Participants
The participants consisted of 25 children between the ages of 5 to 13 (8 girls, 17 boys). One of the participants, a 7-year old boy had an unidentified speech impediment. Another boy of 12 had autism and did not communicate clearly, although he participated in many of the drawing activities. The children are amongst the most marginalized and vulnerable children in Mexico. The children live at the Casa Hogar Hijos de la Luna (Home of the Children of the Moon), which is a non-governmental organization (NGO) caring for children of impoverished families whose mothers are often involve in night-time employment and are not able to provide proper adequate care for their children. Many of the kids have experienced and witnessed violence and some have undergone abuse in the past.

The second author has worked with the children for several years and has a close relationship with many of them. In the past two years, she and her university students have spent several weeks each summer organizing an arts and craft festival called Yo Soy Arte (I am Art). The activities have included the creation of masks and traditional fantastical creatures called *alebrijes,* from papier-mâché and the writing, directing and acting in a theatrical play. This existing relationship was key to making the current technology-based workshop possible and effective.

The center is located in the suburbs of Oaxaca City, which is the center of Oaxaca state, a state in Mexico known for its rich folk art tradition and indigenous culture. From the beginning, we aimed to incorporate artistic and cultural elements familiar and relevant to the children in the workshop. In discussing possibilities for activities and projects during the workshop, we considered many artistic practices from carpet weaving to papier-mâché to mural painting. These were communicated to the children throughout the workshop and they chose which theme to focus on.

**Figure 1. The setting of the workshop.**

The workshop was held in a large room with a lot of sunshine and fresh air. The children sat on a large common table and were each given paper and simple crayons. Other than the first author's personal computer and a projector, no other computers or displays were available. Figure 1 shows the setting of the workshop.

### Material and Technique
A key consideration in designing any activity in a developing world context is *sustainability*: the question of what happens when the research or intervention teams leave? Our priority, especially for the hands-on activities, was to focus on design thinking and a method that could be applied to other contexts. Thus, it was essential not to focus on the tools but rather the method. Additionally, we wanted to incorporate existing and available material from the children's lives rather than introducing unnecessary technological gadgets and tools. The challenge, then, was how to engage the children and facilitate the creation of novel interactive designs using minimal computational material.

Drawing is one of the most accessible methods of communication for young children [21]. It makes sessions more interactive and is a good method to include participants, especially in a large workshop. Additionally, it provides a personal record for the children and a concrete and tangible outcome. The drawing phase of the workshop is essential because it helps internalize the concepts and gives the kids a chance to customize the ideas and take ownership of them. We used drawings in three capacities: as interpretations of concepts (e.g., technology, art festival, …), as proposals for digitally augmented artifacts and as functional digitally augmented paper artifacts. During the workshop, we had several drawing sessions. The third capacity is novel to our approach in the sense that the drawings were not ideas or only suggestions for future implementation, as we will describe in more detail in the outcomes section, the drawings *were* part of the implementation.

Many of the children who participated in the workshop do not have prior experience working with computers. While many of them knew what computers were and how you could access information, send and receive email and play games using them, only a couple of the children had actually used a computer before. Similarly, they had never used a smartphone or tablet. The implication of this was that we had to provide adequate scaffolding and context for the children to build on their design thinking. Thus, we came up with a simple theoretical model that was exemplified by concrete instantiations. We hypothesized that if we were successful in communicating the model effectively, the children could extend it and come up with new examples of its application.

The children had explored the theme of "art" in the previous years' festivals. They already had first-hand experience creating and showcasing artistic works. However, they had not explored the theme of technology before and so we did not spend time explaining and exploring the concept of art and focused on technology during this workshop.

Following, we will describe the workshop components in detail.

### Process: day 1

The workshop ran over two days and each day we worked with the children for approximately 4 hours. There were two short breaks, one for play and one for snacks, during each day. During the first day the following activities in the order mentioned were conducted.

**Meet and greet:** A key ingredient for successful intercultural collaboration is trust. The first author had not met the kids previously and did not speak their native language, Spanish. Therefore, it was essential for him to be introduced formally by the second author who had worked with the children before and had a close relationship with them. This *transfer of authority* is something that can be achieved by a simple introduction (preferably accompanied by a physical and symbolic act of greeting such as shake of hands, giving hugs, … depending on culture) and is very important to laying the foundation of a good relationship. The relationship was further established when the second author described where he was from, showing it on the map and so on.

**Overview of previous year's festival:** As mentioned previously, the children had participated in an art festival the year before and the next activity was for them to describe what was the favorite part of the festival. The purpose for this activity was two-fold: first, to identify possible ideas from the festival that could be extended by introducing digital material, and, second, to give a chance to the children to lead a dialogue and describe their activities and achievements to the adult facilitators. In our philosophy, children and adults should meet on equal planes and while letting children tell us about their world is not enough to break the hierarchies imposed between adults and children, especially if adults are

perceive as "experts", it is a good start. The use of such relationship building activities is recommended in previous research [2].

As the children were talking about their favorite parts of the festival, the second author wrote and categorized the ideas on a big sheet of paper that was hung on the wall. We came back to the sheet several times during the workshop as reference on possible projects to work on in the future. The section was followed by a drawing session where we asked the children to draw their favorites part(s) of the festival.

**An interactive presentation on technology and its relationship to us:** After talking about the art festival and the drawings the children made of their favorite parts, we conducted an interactive media-rich presentation on technology and its relationship to us. We used a style of presentation that uses a lot of metaphors, humor and personal stories. We have found that this technique, which we refer to as *poetic presentation*, allows for the engagement of diverse populations and age groups. During the presentation, we first explored the question of what is technology.

We used Marshal McLuhan's idea of "Technology as extension of man" [14] to expand this notion of technology to include tools that are not necessarily digital, for example wheels and candles and knives. This approach easily led to the question of what is the purpose of technology. Through questions and answers with the participants, we identified the purpose of making tools as objects designed to help people, make life more comfortable and allow people to express themselves (e.g., through musical instruments), etc. We also touched upon the idea that bad design can lead to accidents and problems (illustrated by a Charlie Chaplin clip from the Modern Times where a worker gets sucked into a factory machine).

This introduction was necessary to shift the children's understanding of technology as something to be consumed to something to be designed. This approach followed from our main goal to use digital design to engage the children in co-design and, thus, it was necessary to prepare them for hands-on activities that were to follow. In addition to being influenced by McLuhan's idea, the theory and design philosophy we use is highly influenced by Reflective Design that emphasize the importance of questioning underlying values in design and aiming to incorporate positive values in design [19].

In the presentation we also talked briefly about a simplified *Input-Process-Output* (IPO) model (originally formalized by IBM Corporation). We used the IPO model to help children break down components of an interactive design. We used metaphor and analogies to illustrate the model. For example, when a human encounters fire, their senses of sight and smell (i.e., input) alert their brain (i.e., processing unit) about the fire. Based on this input, the brain makes a decision (i.e., process) to move legs and vocalize a warning (i.e., output). This process is similar if we create a robot to detect fire. In the case of an encounter, the robot's sensors detect the fire (i.e., input), the microcontroller or computer inside makes a decision to act (i.e., process) and its actuators are activated so that it can move or alert others (i.e., output). As we were describing the example, two of the children suggested that in this case the wires would be like the nervous system because they carry the messages around. This confirmed that they had internalized the model and understood the metaphor and were able to extend it themselves. We showed a concrete technological example in the form of a wearable interface, *HugBug that* consists of a hat augmented with LED lights and a touch sensor. When the wearer of the hat hugs another person (activating the sensor) a light show in the hat is triggered.

After this session we had another drawing activity, where each child made drawings of their interpretation of technology and the examples they were shown.

**Design proposals for digitally augmented art works.** At this stage, we examined the drawings of favorite parts of the previous years art festival and identified several possible themes that could be further explored in the rest of the workshop. Our criteria for the themes were that they had to have a basis in the cultural context from which the children come from, they should be doable within a limited amount of time and the children must be interested in doing them. The possible themes identified were fantastical papier-mâché creatures called alebrijes, costumes and gadgets for super-heroes, a mural that tells a story and an interactive life tree with plants and flowers. After considering each possibility and taking into account the overwhelming preference of the kids, we decided to focus on the first option, alebrijes, in this workshop and consider the other themes for future ones.

*Alebrijes* are fantastical Mexican folk art papier-mâché sculptures that since their inception in the 1930's by the Mexican folk art legend Pedro Linares have become quintessential symbols of Oaxacan folk art [3]. The creatures are often times juxtaposition of different animal parts (e.g., elephant with wings) that are loved by children and despite their fearsome appearance are believed to be protectors from evil nightmares.

An appeal to choosing this topic for the workshop was that the children were already familiar with the creatures and did not need instruction on how to draw them. We asked them to draw their own alebrijes and indicate if they had lights, sensors, sound and other components where would they place them. We asked the children to use glitter to indicate glow and light if they wanted to.

After drawings were made, we concluded the first day's workshop. Note that until this point, the children had not used any new digital components in their drawings or activities. The outcome of the first day workshop was close to 50 drawings, most of which were interpretations of technology and some initial sketches of alebrijes. Six or seven of the younger children wanted to draw things

unrelated to the theme of the workshop, something that we did not encourage but allowed if they insisted.

**Figure 2. A wall covered by children's drawings of alebrijes**

**Process: day 2**
Refining the designs: The next day, we started the workshop by putting up the drawings from the day before and asking the children to describe the different parts to us. Some of the drawings were annotated with words like "light" or "sound". The purpose of this session was to introduce the concept of interactivity and apply it to the drawings of the alebrijes. Before that, however, we asked the children to spend some time refining their alebrijes designs with the view that these are going to be the main outcome of the workshop and something they could keep. While a few of the children, decided to build on the drawings they made the day before, many of the them decided to start afresh. At this stage, we encouraged each child to work on one drawing. In this version, we asked the children to not annotate on the drawing and only identify one spot on which they wanted to place an LED light. After about an hour and a half during which the children completed their designs, we put the final drawings on the wall (Figure 2) and identified each with the child's name.

**An interactive presentation on electricity and interaction:** At this point, we gave another interactive presentation on what is electricity and how to use it to make objects interactive.

To illustrate our point through a fun example, we introduced a new technology: the Makey Makey board [4]. While the underlying design of the board is complex for the children, the concept it exemplifies (that any conductive material including fruit, humans and water can be turned into a key on a keyboard) was very intuitive for the children and allowed them to experience interactivity and how electricity can affect it, first hand.

Using simple diagrams, we showed that a circuit is formed when two poles of an electric source are connected together. They experienced this when they held the ground (negative) wire connected to the Makey Makey and touched a banana that was connected to the positive wire, creating a closed circuit that triggered a sound effect on the computer. The children interacted with a simple sound effect software using the interface. They took turns playing and helped each other by making sure all the connections were made when each person was using the interface.

**Digitally augmenting the alebrijes.** Building on the play session with the Makey Makey, we described how an LED works and how it should be connected to a battery. We gave out a single blinking LED and a battery to each child. We instructed the children to first attach a second sheet of paper to the back of their drawings. Next, they had to make two small holes around the spot they wanted the LED light in. The two legs of the light were to be connected to the battery that was to be stuck to the back of the drawing. Finally, the second sheet of paper was glued so that you could only see the blinking drawing and not the underlying battery.

This process turned out to be harder than expected. A question was how do we make the battery and light stick together properly without soldering them. Many of the children wanted the light to have a switch so that it can become interactive and respond to touch. The solution to both problems came with the realization that if we leave the connection between the battery and LED loose, it can be activated when touched and effectively becomes a switch. We gave the children the choice between a permanent blinking light and one that is turned on by pressing a dot painted next to it. By the end of the session, there were 18 unique augmented drawings. Most of the children (10 out of 18) decided to make the LED lights sensitive to touch and loosened the connection to the battery. The drawings were different from each other not only in the shape, color and formation of the animal parts that formed the alebrijes but in the position of the light and whether they were permanently blinking or sensitive to touch.

Many more drawings had been made in addition to the augmented ones but some of the children did not finish putting in the LED lights. This was because they became restless and tired at the end and slowly lost interest. The workshop sessions were long and although we had breaks, some of the children, especially the younger ones became tired towards the end of the day. While 5 of the 7 children who did not finish their drawings were among the younger participants (5 to 8 years of age), at least 4 younger participants in the same age range did finish the work and stayed active until the end of the workshop.

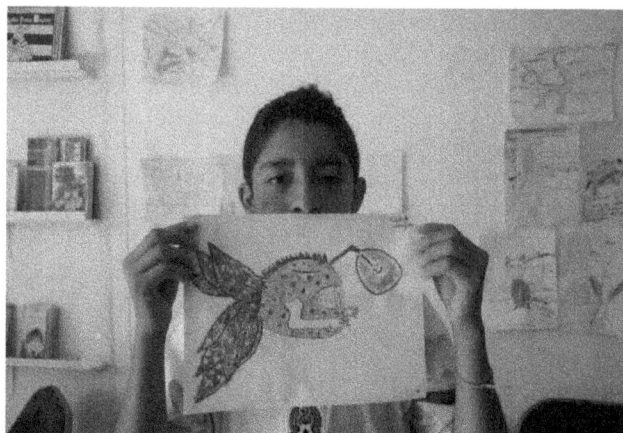

**Figure 3. A participant with his augmented alebrije.**

**Show-and-Tell:** We concluded the workshop by putting all drawings on a table. It was a beautiful sight for the children to see the fruits of their effort. The children had many questions about the lights (e.g., how long the battery is going to last? Would it blink at night?). The children were given a choice to keep their drawings or leave them in the common room where other people could see them. Many of the children were excited to show their work to parents (who occasionally visit them at the center) and the other care takers and adults at the center. The drawings encouraged social interaction between the children: they would examine their peers' work and comment on things they liked and didn't like. Also, all the children who finished putting lights into their prototypes were proud of their work and some wanted us to take their picture with their artwork (e.g., see Figure 3).

### Outcome

The 18 unique augmented alebrijes drawings are self-contained digital media art designs. They can also be viewed as proposals for future physical papier-mâché versions. While these (along with the other drawings made during the workshop) were the most concrete and tangible results of the workshop, they are an expression of an internal learning and creativity exercise that we believe the workshop facilitated.

In our mind, using simple and affordable digital technology, one LED light and a battery in this case, is a strength of the approach and shows how much can be achieved with little material. We believe the children's achievement in making designs that are personally meaningful for them with such limited instruction and material is remarkable.

The children were happy after the workshop and wanted us to come back to do more activities together, a positive sign that they enjoyed the sessions. We did not ask them directly whether they enjoyed the sessions to avoid putting pressure on them to respond positively to please us. Rather, we observed the joy and pride they took in their creations and their eagerness to show them to the other caregivers at the center, to each other and to us.

## DISCUSSION

Being acutely aware of the challenges and potential of conducting an intercultural co-design workshop is a humbling experience that is rewarded by the ingenuity and joy the children embody. Here, we share the lessons learned that were informed by observing the children during the workshop and analyzing their artworks and drawings after the workshop.

**Building relationships:** When conducting intercultural collaboration projects, the key ingredient is *trust*. We believe the success of our project was because of the trusting relationship that the children had developed with the second author who has worked with them on art projects for several years. We cannot overemphasize the importance of collaborating with someone who is situated within a culture in these projects. During the workshop, whenever there was need for clarity or direction, the children would defer to the second author who they knew and trusted. At the end of the workshop, they clearly enjoyed showing their final designs to her. In cases where collaboration at this level is not possible, at least having a local *Human Access Point* (HAP) is essential. In the field of Information and Communication Technologies for Development (ICT4D), HAP refers to a trusted member of the community for which the project is to be designed for [13]. Not only can a HAP provide invaluable feedback and suggestions on the design, but perhaps more importantly he or she can mitigate the trusting relationship with the community that is essential for any effective collaboration.

**Cultural and personal relevance:** Previously, "personal meaningfulness" of design activities in similar workshops, is identified as a prerequisite for deep engagement that is important for both learning and empowerment [9, 10]. We involved the children in the brainstorming that led to the activities of the workshop and observed consistent signs of pride and attachment in them not only towards the final outcome but to the collaborative process of the workshop as well.

We highly recommend that workshop facilitators make an effort to familiarize themselves with the culture of the region within which they plan to work and try to design culturally relevant activities. In our case, we found great sources of inspiration in the folk art and craft traditions of the folk artists and craft masters of Oaxaca and are honored that the outcome of the workshop turned out to be a fusion of an existing tradition and recent digital design methods and tools. From the outset, we wished to find a way to help the children appreciate their own culture and find value in the art and craft that they have inherited from their community. Of course, as with any activities planned with children, we had several backup plans, including working on cardboard robot models or futuristic gadgets, in case we could not identify other ideas successfully. However, we did not have to resort to these plans.

**Sustainability and impact:** One of the challenges of conducting projects in a developing world context is how to achieve sustainability and impact in such a short amount of time and with such little resources (especially, having limited time and ongoing contact). While these are big questions and this case study is just a start in developing methods or solutions, we will share some ideas and observations.

Three elements were present during the workshop: *the relationships, the process* and *the outcome.* With respect to the *relationship* between the facilitators and the children, we tried to embody our philosophy that the children are artists and designers too and our coming together is an encounter in which we respect each other for who we are and do not put pressure on the children by unrealistic expectations or plans for the future. At the end of the workshop, the children felt very comfortable talking with us and kept insisting that we come back for more workshops. With respect to the *process,* by limiting the technological tools used, we emphasized that the design process and design thinking are more important and useful resources than specific tools or technologies. The children quickly learned how to connect an LED light to a battery and furthermore learned how to "hack" the combination to create a push switch. Once the children learn how to question things, make decisions and weigh different choices and realize the value of their creativity and originality, they can use it in any context. Finally, with respect to *outcome* we made sure there were concrete expressions, in the form of the augmented drawings, of our collective experience during the two days. The children had vivid memories of the art festival of the previous year because they made tangible crafts and participated directly in the activities. We believe having a concrete outcome, such as the artifacts created in the workshop, provides the children with the experiential knowledge that their work matters and can last beyond the short workshop sessions.

The use of technology, although minimal, allowed us to achieve two results: 1) capture and sustain the children's attention throughout the workshop 2) give the children the ability to see technology as a tool whose design is not exclusive to factories or adults but can also be designed by them. Our claims about the impact of our approach should not be taken as a challenge to the idea (especially practiced by Cooperative Inquiry) that ongoing and frequent contact with children is not important to co-design. In fact, that would be an ideal setting where children and facilitators can establish a close relationship and deepen their understand of each other's method of thinking, feeling and experiencing. However, these conditions are not available to the children that we are working with who are, in fact, representative of a large number of children worldwide. If we plan to include these children in the worldwide design dialogue, something that is at the center of our research effort, we have to develop new techniques and modify existing ones to take into account these specific conditions.

## CONCLUSION

We have described and presented a case study involving a two-day workshop with marginalized children with Oaxaca, Mexico. The workshop was designed to facilitate creative expression through digital media and bring about learning of concepts pertaining to technology and interaction. We worked with 25 children ranging in age from 5 to 13. The children created 18 detailed drawings of *alebrijes,* fantastical creatures from the folk art of the region from which they were from, and augmented them with blinking LED lights.

The lessons learned during the workshop included realizing the importance of establishing trusting relationships through Human-Access Points, incorporating relevant cultural and social elements into the activities, planning concrete outcomes (e.g., tangible artifacts or toys) that provide a sense of completion and achievement to the children and using technology, but sparingly and sustainably. We plan to conduct more workshops with the children and also examine the effects of the project in the long-term. We hope that our lessons learned in this detailed case study would provide insights and inspiration for other designers, researchers, and developers when planning, carrying out, and studying similar workshops.

## REFERENCES

1. Anderson, C. (2012). *Makers: the new industrial revolution.* Random House.

2. Antle, A. N., and Bevans, A. (2012). Creative design: exploring value propositions with urban Nepalese children. *Advances in Computer Entertainment*, 465-468.

3. Bartra, E. (2000). Of Alebrijes and Ocumichos: Some Myths about Folk Art and Mexican Identity. *Primitivism and Identity in Latin America: Essays on Art, Literature, and Culture*, 53-73.

4. Collective, B. S. M., and Shaw, D. (2012). Makey Makey: improvising tangible and nature-based user interfaces. In *Proc. of TEI'12*, 367-370.

5. Druin, A. (1999). Cooperative inquiry: developing new technologies for children with children. In *Proc. of CHI'99*, 592-599.

6. Dunn, R., Beaudry, J., and Klavas, A. (2002). Survey of research on learning styles. *California Journal of Science Education*, 2(2), 75-98.

7. Gardner, H. (1985). *Frames of mind: The theory of multiple intelligences.* Basic books.

8. Guha, M. L., Druin, A., and Fails, J. A. (2012). Cooperative inquiry revisited: Reflections of the past and guidelines for the future of intergenerational co-design.

*International Journal of Child-Computer Interaction*, 1(1), 14-23.

9. Hourcade, J. P., Beitler, D., Cormenzana, F., and Flores, P. (2008). Early OLPC experiences in a rural Uruguayan school. In *Proc. of CHI'08*, 2503-2512.

10. Katterfeldt, E. S., Dittert, N., and Schelhowe, H. (2009). EduWear: smart textiles as ways of relating computing technology to everyday life. In *Proc. of IDC'09*, 9-17.

11. Large, A., Nesset, V., Beheshti, J., and Bowler, L. (2006). "Bonded design": A novel approach to intergenerational information technology design. *Library and Information Science Research* 28 (1), 64–82.

12. Lillard, A. (2007). *Montessori: The Science behind the genius.* Oxford University Press, Oxford.

13. Marsden, G., Maunder, A., and Parker, M. (2008). People are people, but technology is not technology. *Philosophical Transactions of the Royal Society A: Mathematical, Physical and Engineering Sciences*, 366(1881), 3795-3804.

14. McLuhan, M. (1994). *Understanding media: the extensions of man.* MIT Press, Cambridge, Mass.

15. Mitra, S. (2005). Self organizing systems for mass computer literacy: Findings from the "hole in the wall" experiments. *International Journal of Development Issues*, 4(1), 71-81.

16. Mitra, S., Dangwal, R., Chatterjee, S., Jha, S., Bisht, R. S., and Kapur, P. (2005). Acquisition of computing literacy on shared public computers: Children and the "hole in the wall". *Australasian Journal of Educational Technology*, 21(3), 407.

17. Papert, S. (1980). *Mindstorms: Children, computers, and powerful ideas.* Basic Books, Inc.

18. Scaife, M., Rogers, Y., Aldrich, F., and Davies, M. (1997). Designing for or designing with? Informant design for interactive learning environments. In *Proc. of CHI'97*, 343–350.

19. Sengers, P., Boehner, K., David, S., and Kaye, J. J. (2005). Reflective design. In *Proc. of Critical Computing*, 49-58.

20. Snyder, R.F. (2000). The relationship between learning styles/multiple intelligences and academic achievement of high school students. *The High School Journal*, 83, 11-20.

21. Xu, D., Read, J., Sim, G. and McManus, B., Experience it, draw it, rate it: capture children's experiences with their drawings. In *Proc. of IDC '09*, 266-270.

# Participatory Design Strategies to Enhance the Creative Contribution of Children with Special Needs

Laura Malinverni[1], Joan Mora-Guiard[1], Vanesa Padillo[2], Maria-Angeles Mairena[2], Amaia Hervás[2], Narcis Pares[1]

[1] Universitat Pompeu Fabra
Cognitive Media Technologies group,
ICT Department
c. Roc Boronat, 138
+34 93 542 2201
laura.malinverni, joan.mora,
narcis.pares@upf.edu

[2] Hospital Sant Joan de Déu
Unidad Especializada en Trastornos del Desarrollo (UETD)
Passeig Sant Joan de Déu, 2
08950 Esplugues de Llobregat
+34 93 253 21 00
vpadillo, mmairena, ahervas@hsjdbcn.org

## ABSTRACT

In recent years there has been an increasing awareness about the importance of involving children with special needs in the process of designing technology. Starting from this perspective, the paper presents the participatory design process carried out with children with autistic spectrum disorder for the design of a Kinect motion-based game aimed at fostering social initiation skills. By describing the strategies used for the design of the activities, we will suggest possible approaches aimed toward widening the space for contributions of children and including them at a more creative level. Within that, major emphasis will be dedicated to discussing the "empowering dimension" of participatory design activities as an instrument to enhance benefits both for design results and for the children themselves. Finally, the balance between structure and freedom in the design of the activities will be discussed.

## Categories and Subject Descriptors

H.5.2. **[Information Interfaces and Presentation (e.g., HCI]:** User Interfaces – theory and methods, user-centered design.

## General Terms

Design, Human Factors

## Keywords

Participatory Design, Design Method, Autistic Spectrum Disorder, Children, Empowerment.

## 1. INTRODUCTION

In the last decades there has been an increasing awareness about the importance of involving children in the process of designing technology [19]. This awareness is founded on the acknowledgement that children are an entirely different user population with their own culture, norms, complexities and preference [8].Their contributions are therefore crucial for the development of a technology that is capable of properly addressing their specific needs and interests. From this perspective, a number of different methods have been proposed to involve children in the design process, such as: user-centered design, contextual design, participatory design, informant design and cooperative inquiry [23].

Within this context, in recent years, an increasing interest has been posed on the possibilities of involving children with special needs into the design process. As Frauenberg points out, it is often this population that can benefit the most from design process that include them [13]. However, this approach can often present challenges related with properly defining the role that these children can assume in the design process. As Guha et al. point out, the appropriate level of involvement begins with researcher's expectations and it is influenced by the nature and the severity of the child's disability and the quality of the available support [15]. Defining the role of children represents a delicate issue since we move in the continuum between overwhelming the child and relegating him in a marginal role, in which his skills are not fully considered.

Starting from this perspective, this paper presents the participatory design (PD) process carried out with children with autistic spectrum disorder (ASD) for the design of a Kinect game aimed at fostering social initiation skills. During the unfolding of the workshop, the level of involvement of the children has been gradually redefined through the continuous observation of their responses. This iterative process of evaluation and adjustment of the proposed activities, together with the use of a set of narrative-based techniques, allowed widening the space for children contributions and including them at a more creative level.

The description of the gradual transformation of the level of involvement of children in the design process will offer a novel contribution to research oriented at involving children with special needs in participatory design. At the same time, the discussion of the tools and techniques used will provide specific suggestions and "concepts to think about" [19] when we design PD activities for children with special needs. Within that, major emphasis will be dedicated to discussing the "empowering dimension" of participatory design activities as an instrument to enhance benefits both for design results and for the children themselves. Finally the balance between structure and freedom in the design of the activities will be discussed.

*IDC'14*, June 17–20, 2014, Aarhus, Denmark.
Copyright is held by the owner/author(s). Publication rights licensed to ACM.
ACM 978-1-4503-2272-0/14/06…$15.00.
http://dx.doi.org/10.1145/2593968.2593981

## 2. PARTICIPATORY DESIGN WITH AUTISTIC CHILDREN

Autism is a neurodevelopment disorder characterized by delayed or abnormal functioning in social interaction, social communication and symbolic play and restrictive or repetitive interests and sensory abnormalities [3]. Within these, many researchers suggested that the social impairment may represent the most important deficit [28]. However, the use of appropriate educational interventions can improve quality of life of ASD children [25,27]. Given these premises a number of interactive systems have been developed to help ASD children to learn and practice social interaction skills [2,5,17,26,29,31].

Within this context, an increasing awareness has been placed on the importance of involving end-users in the design process to better understand their needs and preferences. Starting from this necessity, different approaches leading to different methods have been used, e.g.: children involvement as testers, participation via proxy, or direct involvement of children as informants [11].

The involvement of ASD children as informants has been reported by several authors [4,10,12,13,16,20], which propose different methods. Methods vary from efforts to get feedback from children about design choices [10,20], to the analysis of their preference [13], the creation of scenarios [20] or the observation of their behavior [13,16]. The incorporation of these methods permits integrating children's contributions directly into the initial design stages, allowing a deeper influence on the definition of the final product.

However, as Benton points out, much of the previous research in this area has focused on the benefits for design results rather than the potential benefits for the children themselves. When we involve children in a participatory design process, it is fundamental to carefully consider whether the defined activities are capable of engaging, motivating and inspiring them [19]. This means that, when we design with children, we don't have to take into account only the extent to which an activity can produce useful design results, but also to evaluate whether the activity can be enjoyable for children.

At the same time, another important aspect that we considered to be fundamental in the selection of activities for the PD process, is their "empowering dimension". This "empowerment dimension" should include the analysis of two main aspects: the extent to which children care about what they are doing (meaningfulness) and their perception about the relevance and importance of their contributions (feeling of competence). These aspects are particularly important when we work with children. According to Erikson's theory of psychosocial development, children between 6 and 12 years, need to experience situations in which they can demonstrate their competencies, tracking their achievements and feel that they are capable of doing stuff: if children are encouraged and reinforced they may start to feel industrious and confident [22]. This aspect is even more important when we collaborate with children with special needs, since this population tends to be underrepresented in decision-making processes and often, the focus on "needs" reduces the attention that can be placed on "skills". It is therefore fundamental to facilitate conditions in which they feel that their capabilities are recognized and that they are skilled for doing relevant and important things.

## 3. PROJECT DESCRIPTION

The project has been developed in the frame of the M4All European project. Its main goal is to develop a set of motion-based playful learning experiences for children with learning difficulties. Within this context, our goal is to develop a Kinect-based game for children with ASD to help them acquire simple abilities in social interaction. For this purpose we focus our design strategy on an informant model, aimed at involving different stakeholders during the different stages of the project [30]. According to this framework we structured the design process in two consequent stages. First, through collaboration with experts, we defined the educational goals of the project. Second, we carried out a participatory design with children to transform defined goals into an enjoyable playful experience.

### 3.1 Goals definition

To define the goals of the project we collaborated with experts of the "Specialized Unit on Developmental Disorders" (UETD) of the Sant Joan de Déu Children's Hospital in Barcelona. The requirements elicitation process was carried out through multiple meetings with the psychologists and psychiatrists of the UETD. A detailed description of the requirement elicitation process is reported in [21].

Through these meetings, we decided to focus the main goal of the project on promoting social initiation, understood as the promotion of behaviors such as approaching and asking for help to others, starting social communication and producing any verbal or gestural behavior for communicative goals. In order to achieve this goal the psychologists defined a short treatment plan based on four sessions. These four sessions are organized to progressively incorporate increasingly complex social initiation abilities to achieve interaction and collaboration with others. For this purpose the UETD professionals defined a set of objectives that constitute behavioral skills, which need to be addressed within traditional treatment related with fostering social initiation.

The main goal of the game was therefore to work as a mediator of social communication. This approach requires the design of situations that are either valuable for the children to feel the need to communicate about them, or that require the child to look for external collaboration. This main requirement posits the central necessity of merging the therapeutic techniques, used to facilitate social initiation, with the interests and preferences of children. To address this issue we planned five participatory design workshops aimed at integrating children perspective in the game design.

### 3.2 From goals to playful experience: defining the participatory design activities

The main goals of the PD were: (1) validate a set of initial design proposals derived from UETD professionals' requirements; (2) gather new ideas from children; (3) evaluate which aspects elicit higher level of motivation and interest in children. On a transversal view, PD activities were designed by taking into account two main aspects: the use of an educational design research approach in the definition of the activities and the creation of a feeling of continuity and progression between the different sessions.

#### 3.2.1 Educational design research approach

Educational design research is defined by Van den Akker as a research method focused on improving the effectiveness of educational interventions through progressive approximations. It is characterized by being an interventionist, iterative and process-oriented approach, which focuses its analysis on the integral phenomenon and not on the isolation of variables [32]. This approach implies adopting a research method based on continuous adjustments and iterations, which depends on the ongoing evaluation of the effectiveness and impact of the interventions.

Applying this approach to the design of PD activities implies embedding flexibility in the design of the structure of the workshops. This means to be able to constantly evaluate the impact of the proposed activities and to adjust them accordingly to ongoing observations. Mazzone et al., proposed two dimensions for evaluation of the PD activities: suitability and capability. Suitability is defined as the extent to which the proposed activities are capable of engaging, involving and inspiring children as active participants in the process. On the other hand, capability represents the extent to which the activities can produce useful results for the design [19]. At the same time we added a novel evaluation dimension into our analysis: the empowerment dimension. The evaluation of this dimension implies to consider the extent to which children care about what they are doing (meaningfulness) and their perception about the relevance and importance of their contributions (feeling of competence). .

The evaluation was carried out on two levels:

- During the session the engagement and contributions of the children were taken into account in order to define the effectiveness of the activities and eventually modify them (within-session adjustments).

- After each session, the opinions of the psychologist and the observations of the researchers were combined to improve the design of the following session (between-session adjustments).

### 3.2.2 Feeling of continuity and progression
Several examples of PD with children with ASD address the design of the activities as discrete units [13] that can often seem decontextualized and poorly related between them. We believe that a feeling of continuity and progression between the different activities would be beneficial to ground their contributions on a common terrain and to foster their involvement. To address this necessity we applied two main methods: (1) the use of an underlying narrative structure and (2) the use of personalized storage boxes.

#### 3.2.2.1 The narrative structure
The use of narrative in PD activities is a widely acknowledged practice, capable of supporting inquiry on specific issues, fostering engagement and facilitating collaboration with end-users [7]. This technique has often been used to provide a fictional layer, working as a pretext to address questions that otherwise could look odd or out of place [6,7]. However, in our case, instead of developing a narrative that is unrelated to the final application, we based the narrative structure on the backstory of the game, which was previously defined through the meeting with the psychologists. Following the Fictional Inquiry technique, workshop activities were structured around the plot of the backstory. Each workshop activity was designed to form part of a larger narrative structure and to address specific design questions. Two main techniques were used to promote a feeling of narrative continuity and progression:

1) Chapters and scene cards: Each workshop session was conceptualized as a chapter in the game backstory (see table 1). This structure was supported by the previous creation of "scene cards" in which the location, the child's targeted behavior and a series of possible conflicts were defined. Such method allowed organizing the workshop according to a progressively unfolding narrative, which we hypothesized, could help in grounding children's contributions on a common terrain and enhancing their attachment to the activities.

2) Cliffhangers: According to the chapter structure we used the narrative device of "cliffhangers" to foster the continuity between each workshop session. At the end of each session therefore the main character was confronted with a turning-point of the story, which would be solved only in the next workshop session. This device fostered children's curiosity since it helped to create a feeling of suspense about what would happen next.

#### 3.2.2.2 Storage material
Another device to strengthen the feeling of continuity of the experience and the attachment to the activities was the use of a personalized storage box for each child. At the beginning of the workshop each child was provided with a box aimed at containing both their own artworks (i.e. drawings) and the reward badges they received after completing each activity. These reward badges were designed to remind them about the main aspects of the carried out activities.

The use of a personalized box is a widely acknowledged practice both in art education and in expressive art therapies [9] since it doesn't only provides storage, but more importantly, allows keeping track of one's own progress. We hypothesized that the use of this device could help children feel their progress and competence through the unfolding of the workshops.

**Table 1: workshop sessions and chapters**

| SESSIONS | SCENE CARD | CHAPTER (Workshop activities) |
|---|---|---|
| 1 | *Location*: wood (planet Earth); day /*Targeted behavior*: start interaction | Introducing the main character |
| 2 | *Location*: wood (planet Earth); day /*Targeted behavior*: start interaction / *Conflict*: antagonists | Build a relation with the main character; help it |
| 3 | *Location*: wood (planet Earth); night /*Targeted behavior*: start a cooperative activity with a familiar adult | Help the character to build and fuel its spaceship; travel back to its planet |
| 4 | *Location*: alien's planet /*Targeted behavior*: joint attention / *Conflict*: antagonists | Help the character to find its friend |
| 5 | *Location*: alien's planet / *Targeted behavior*: turn taking /*Conflict*: antagonists | Meeting with the friend; celebration |

## 4. PARTICIPATORY DESIGN WORKSHOP
The workshop took place in a dedicated room of the Sant Joan de Déu Children's Hospital on a weekly basis. The participants selected by the UETD professionals were four children (A, B, C

& D) diagnosed within the Autism Spectrum Disorder, all males between 9 and 10 years old. All four children present normal cognitive capabilities, functional language and have been enrolled together in a previous social skill training group during one course in the UETD. Hence, they had a good bond with the therapist and between themselves. Child A presents some inabilities with oral expression, alteration of prosody, proneness to distraction and disconnection from the activities. Child B presents symptomatology of motor restlessness, impulsivity and difficulties in focusing attention. Child C presents good verbal expression competences and is participative and collaborative. However, he has an anxious socio-emotional base and a lack of ability to manage his emotions, which is controlled with medication. Child D presents symptoms associated to Attention deficit hyperactivity disorder (ADHD), specific learning problems and sleep problems, which are controlled with medication.

Despite their age did not fit with the target users (~5-6 years old), the UETD professionals considered that this developmental level (both in chronological and functional age) was more suitable for participatory design (PD) activities. Moreover, the UETD professionals considered that informing these children about the fact that they would be participating in the design of a videogame for younger children would have a beneficial effect at two main levels:

- firstly, by motivating them through the attribution of a role of responsibility and,
- secondly, by fostering the perspective-taking exercise of trying to figure out preferences of younger children.

A total of five sessions were carried out. During each session three researchers and a psychologist were present. All children were already familiar with the psychologist and the environment. Each session lasted for one hour and was designed to address specific aspects of the game design. For the analysis of each session direct observation and video analysis were used.

Direct observation was carried out by a psychologist and a researcher who took written field notes. Videos were analyzed after the sessions and relevant behaviors and utterances were transcribed. Material from video transcription and note taking was therefore coded by a researcher into two main categories:

- Design choices: understood as children's contributions to specific design aspects, such as: objects to appear in the environment, organizational aspects of the objects, color choices, etc.
- Affective aspects: understood as children's expressions related with how much they liked the activities and their level of enjoyment and motivation.

Data from this analysis was later discussed by the whole team and used to inform both the design of the game and the planning of the following PD activities. In the following sections we provide a short description of the used activities and relevant observations.

## 4.1 First session

The first session was aimed at introducing ourselves and the project to the children. We explained them that they would help us in designing a video game for younger children and that the aim of the game was to enjoy playing between friends. We started the session with the presentation of the game backstory: "a friendly alien arrives to the Earth by mistake; the child has to help it travel back to its planet to meet its friends again". After that we set-up a series of activities aimed at defining the alien's features. These

activities had two goals: (1) to investigate the possibility of including the customization of the alien as part of the game, and (2) to facilitate the involvement of the children in the workshop by establishing a relationship with the main character.

According to Fullerton, videogame characters cover two main functions: agency and empathy. Agency refers to the practical function of the character, while empathy is the potential for players to develop an emotional attachment to it [14]. Agency was already defined by the requirements of the UETD professionals; therefore we framed children's contributions around the definition of a believable and likeable character aimed toward fostering empathy. Children were asked to propose its name and were instructed that the alien can change its aspect depending on the food it eats. Hence, they proposed its food preference (Fig.1) and invented specific customizations related with the ingestion of specific food. To carry out these activities several low-tech materials were used such as: a little puppet theatre that worked as a scaled prototype of the virtual environment of the game (Fig. 2), causal tables of relations between food and effect and cut-outs of the different elements (Fig. 3). The materials were either produced by the researchers or derived from online resources of materials for special needs.

### 4.1.1 Observations

From the first session it was clear that the children were much more motivated, participative and creative than what we had been warned about and, hence, expected. A clear example of this was found in the use of causal tables. Causal tables were derived from resources of augmentative communication and based on a triptych structure. In these tables children had to indicate the initial state of the character, the food that it eats and the consequent transformation. A number of different models of causal tables were presented. Each one offered different levels of required completion, which ranged from having the initial and final state already defined (therefore allowing the children to choose only the food) to completely empty tables in which children were asked to fill all the stages. Children were instructed on how to fill each one of the tables and the different templates were made freely available to them. Children were asked to choose a preferred template to work with. Children generally preferred to work with empty tables, and ended up using a large amount of these. A possible explanation can be found in the fact that these templates allowed them to design a full new range of transformation possibilities. This observation suggested that children could better enjoy less constrained activities, since they were clearly more motivated by the possibility of inventing their own "worlds" and "situations". This allowed us to define the activities of the following sessions from a broader and more creative perspective.

At a design level the session allowed us to get a better understanding of two main aspects: (1) the fundamental role of the previous knowledge that children had on the language of cartoons and videogames as effective mediators of interaction metaphors and (2) the definition of the logic behind the transformation and customization of the character. The analysis of their proposals showed that character transformations should be highly discrete, self-evident and meaningful. Furthermore, the relation between food eating and transformation should be mainly based either on visual or on functional properties of the food (e.g. obtaining a "fire outfit" if the alien eats chili, turning its skin green if it eats lettuce, etc.). Children were especially motivated and engaged by transformations related with super-powers derived from their audiovisual culture (e.g. "super armor", "ice breath", etc.).

**Figure 1. Definition of food's preference using emotional expression**

**Figure 2. Puppet theatre**

**Figure 3. Causal tables and cut-outs**

## 4.2 Second session

The second session was aimed at observing the intuitiveness of the interaction with the Kinect device, define the character's behavior and design its spaceship. From the experience gained in the previous session we defined the activities in order to allow more freedom for children's creativity and contributions.

We introduced the activities as a second chapter of the story: the alien has already eaten and now it needs to plan how to go back to its planet. The session was divided into two main parts: a first part

dedicated to motor activity and a second part dedicated to drawing. To introduce the first part we started with a short warm-up activity based on reciprocal imitation of movements. After that, children were introduced to the game through the use of a Wizard-of-oz system which allowed starting a basic interaction with the elements (Fig.4). The set up of the Wizard of Oz was based on a Kinect camera and a standard television screen in order to emulate the final configuration of the game set-up. The child could see himself inserted in the virtual environment, in a third-person interaction paradigm typical of Kinect-based games (Fig. 4) [24]. An operator remotely controlled the interaction with the environment (e.g. activating the fall of a food when the child passed his hand over it) and grossly simulates the behavior of the alien (e.g. moving it toward the food). Being at an initial stage, neither animation, visual or sound effects were present. Children were invited to play in a single user mode while the others were involved in a drawing activity.

Subsequently, children were asked to start a short role-play activity in which, by turns, one child had to interpret the player and the other the alien. To guide this activity we used a step outline structure based on asking behavior related questions: e.g. "What would happen if the child did not pay attention to the character?" Meanwhile, the children that were not role-playing were asked to make a drawing of what they thought the spaceship of the character would look like.

### 4.2.1 Observations

The creation of a narrative thread between the different sessions and the central role assumed by the character allowed making it and its story a central reference for the contributions of the children (e.g. "this is the friend of the alien", "this is its spaceship", "it will seat here to drive"), facilitating conditions for a proper orchestration of the requirements and preferences of children. At the same time the use of a chapter structure fostered the curiosity of children on what would happen next.

From a design perspective the observation of their interaction with the virtual environments allowed us to find more intuitive ways to design the interaction. The use of role-play allowed us to define certain behaviors of the character and its expected reaction to the input of children. Children showed especially strong preference for highly expressive reactions in character behavior. Another important observed aspect was that one child felt uncomfortable seeing his own image represented on the screen. This finding suggested the possibility of adding a customization parameter to the application that would allow changing the visual representation of the player; e.g. from a fully detailed camera image to a plain simple silhouette.

**Figure 4. Child playing with a Wizard of Oz of the game**

## 4.3 Third session

The third session aimed at exploring which kind of situations require the collaboration of others and analyzing game mechanics related recovering and fueling the alien's spaceship. Unfortunately two children were unable to attend this third session and one child spent half the session going out of the room to see his father.

We tried to introduce the activities by explaining that the alien's spaceship was out of fuel and therefore they need to help him in fixing it. However, due to the changes in the dynamics caused by the absence of two children, the participants were poorly motivated to pay attention to the instructions. We therefore choose to quickly change the expected activities and involve the children in physical games that could be more suitable to deal with their lack of involvement. Through the use of low-tech materials, we made the children play a set of physical games proposed by the designers as possible mechanics to recover and fuel the spaceship. All the proposed mechanics were based on the need for collaboration to solve a certain task. For example, catching small "energy balls" (actually ping-pong balls) by putting their hands together as if forming a container-like structure. Finally, we asked them to rate the likeability of these physical games.

The quick change in the nature of the activity proved to be a good choice, since a climate of dialogue, enjoyment and participation was re-established. At a design level, even if we didn't manage to facilitate conditions for novel contributions, the session allowed us to evaluate the enjoyability of different game mechanics for this level. More importantly this experience showed the fundamental role of a flexible structure and the central necessity of researchers to be tuned and receptive to the affective state of children.

## 4.4 Fourth session

The fourth session aimed at exploring the visual aspects of the alien's planet and the game mechanics related to helping the character to find its friends. In contrast to the first session, in which the visual appearance of the environment was already provided to the children, we choose to avoid directing their contributions and give them the freedom to draw the planet as they imagined it (Fig. 5). Despite some authors suggest that children with ASD may feel distressed when confronted with a completely blank sheet of paper [20] , according to our previous observations we hypothesized that this method could be beneficial to foster their willingness to contribute and their feeling of competence.

Although they were all in the same room sharing the experience, children were asked to draw the planet on their own, without communicating their design choices to the others. This approach was chosen because, in the previous sessions, sometimes we had noticed a stronger leadership of one child who tended to influence the opinions of the others. After they had all finished their drawings, each child presented his drawings to the others. Then, we introduced a turning-point in the story: "a mysterious accident happened in the planet and all the spaceships of its inhabitants are now trapped". Through the use of directed design technique children were asked to suggest what is trapping the spaceships and how we can free them by collaborating between two children. A researcher drew their suggestions on a blackboard (Fig. 6).

### 4.4.1 Observations

This session was particularly productive and engaging for children. Several creative solutions were proposed for the design of the planet. By allowing a higher level of freedom in the imagination of children, this method was found to be particularly suitable in terms of engagement, if compared with the use of cut-out pre-designed materials (as in session 1). Children gave detailed explanations of their drawings, showing a certain level of excitement in explaining their ideas (e.g. asking us "Would you put this in the game?"). Two children asked whether they could to go show their drawings to their parents, suggesting a feeling of "being proud" of their artworks.

This activity however, in terms of its capability to provide concrete design solutions, caused some difficulties when integrating the highly different proposals. To overcome this issue we focused on extrapolating common features from children's proposals and give the planet an anachronistic appeal.

The directed design activity was highly effective in stimulating children collaboration. Several design ideas were proposed and children were highly motivated in specifying their ideas to allow the researchers understand them to draw them properly. Quite interestingly, during this activity, a misunderstanding with a word led the researcher to draw a "thorny sauce" ("salsa espinosa") instead of a "thorny bush" ("zarza espinosa"). This mistake produced great enjoyment in the children and facilitated the proposal of novel and less conventional ideas (e.g. "Spaceship are trapped in giant sandwiches and we need to collaborate to eat all the sandwich"). Furthermore, the "thorny sauce" anecdote became thereafter a sort of leitmotif for playful social interaction with the researcher, suggesting possible ideas about the design possibilities of "designerly mistakes".

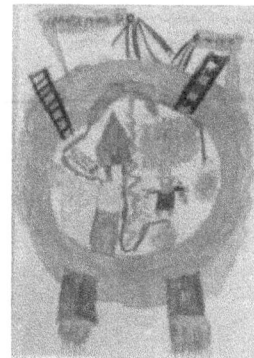

**Figure 5. Drawing of a planet produced by one child**

**Figure 6. Blackboard during directed design**

## 4.5 Fifth session

The fifth session had the objective of analyzing which elements of the whole gameplay received the biggest attention from children and defining idea for the resolution chapter. Children were asked to draw the story of the game in a storyboard format, on large squares of paper (Fig. 7), according to what they remembered of each chapter. After that each scene was summarized and drawn in the blackboard by a researcher through the directed design method. Finally we explained to them that the character had finally found its friend and was now going to celebrate the reunion. Children were asked to draw this last scene and directed design was used to visualize their proposals. In this context, the researcher also suggested some ideas to evaluate our initial proposal about how to design the final level.

### 4.5.1 Observations

The technique of the "recalling storyboard" was particularly effective in terms of its capability to quickly figure out, according to the children, which are the most relevant aspects of the game and therefore focus our design choices. However, the method was not particularly enjoyable for children and one of them refused to finish his storyboard, since he complained that he had already drawn these things. For future works it will be necessary to enhance the playful aspect of this activity in order to make it more appealing and engaging. At the same time, the use of directed design, allowed to modify our proposals. Our initial idea was to set the final level in a "jelly world". However children were not motivated by this idea and proposed urban environments. Therefore we decide to discard our proposal to include their interests and contributions in the design of the final level.

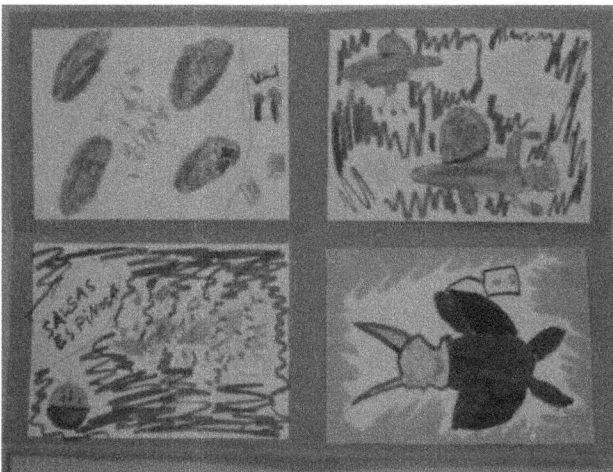

**Figure 7. "Recalling storyboard" produced by one child**

## 5. INTEGRATING CHILDREN'S CONTRIBUTIONS

The use of participatory design allowed us to understand the preferences of children, validating some initial design proposals, gathering new ideas and evaluating which aspects elicit a higher level of motivation and engagement. Within that, particularly useful insights came from the fundamental role of the audiovisual culture of children as a mediator for the interaction metaphors. Moreover, specifications about character behavior, enjoyable game mechanics, intuitiveness of the interaction, visual and narrative aspects were defined.

Since the project arose from specific requirements defined by the UETD professionals, the integration of children's contributions into the final design was carried out by using learning goals and technological constraints as criteria for selecting the design choices. However, the use of a narrative structure, both in requirements elicitation with psychologist and in the PD with children, facilitated a common directionality of the contributions. This therefore reduced the effort of merging different perspectives.

Currently a digital prototype of the game is under development (Fig. 8). This prototype will be evaluated together with the children that participated in the workshops in order to evaluate if our proposal meets their expectations and elicit novel feedback. This analysis will allow us to implement a new iteration that will then be tested with the target population (5-6 years old children with ASD) in order to evaluate the suitability of the experience for this target age and define eventual refinements. Finally, the game will be assessed for its effectiveness in promoting social initiation skills in the target population.

**Figure 8. First level prototype**

## 6. DISCUSSION

### 6.1 Entrusting and empowering ASD children's contributions

A particularly relevant finding was that children were much more engaged in activities that provided them enough space for personal interpretations and creative contributions. Such tendency was observed from the first session where children preferred to use blank papers instead of pre-designed templates for the exercise of "causal tables". It was also confirmed in the fourth session, where the use of blank paper to design the planet and the game's mechanics elicited a larger number of creative contributions.

This finding partially exceeded our initial expectations and contrasted with related works that report on the use of PD with high functioning autistic children. Related literature suggests the need for highly structured approaches for PD with ASD children and proposes activities in which children's contributions are often limited to very discrete and concrete aspects [12,16,20]. From this approach, we initially designed the first session according to a highly directive model, which clearly delimited the space for children's contributions to concrete elements (e.g. food selection, outfit of the character, etc.). However, from the beginning of the sessions it was clear that children were particularly participative and collaborative when faced with activities that give them the possibilities of proposing their own ideas and creations.

A possible explanation of this tendency can be found in the fact that these activities allowed children to feel proud of their productions and to have the perception that their contributions were relevant, valuable and unique. Indeed, children were very proactive in explaining novel ideas to the researchers and, at the end of some sessions they even asked to go to show their artworks to their parents.

Despite several studies point out the potential benefits of PD activities for the empowerment of ASD children [13], it is important to analyze how empowering some of the proposed activities really are. For example, many activities become repetitive exercises which are not only not empowering, but even diminish the present and future creative capabilities of children. We must therefore adopt a critical perspective when choosing these activities especially for ASD children. Such perspective requires analyzing the relation between the expectations of researchers, meaningfulness of the activity for the children and their perceived feeling of competence.

### 6.1.1 Researcher's expectations

As our experience suggests, our initial expectations were exceeded by the level of creative contributions of the children. Such findings indicate how possible bias in the initial expectations of the researcher can be detrimental for properly designing PD activities. It is therefore necessary to assume an approach that goes "beyond expectations". This implies being highly receptive to children's affective states and constantly adapting to the current situation and context. An effective strategy to address this aspect was the continuous evaluation of the meaningfulness of the activities, its suitability and the children's feeling of competence.

### 6.1.2 Meaningfulness and feeling of competence

Our observations showed how the use of the game backstory was particularly useful for making children care about what they were doing. The appeal of the alien's story fostered their interest for being active producers of its adventures. Several "sub-stories" were proposed even without the instructions of the researcher.

At the same time, the chapter structure and boxes showed to be effective in fostering children's feeling of competence. The possibility of tracking one's own achievement and seeing them recognized is fundamental to foster the feeling of competence [22]. The chapter structure facilitates conditions for which children can see their contributions reflected in the ongoing story. This feeling was strengthened by making their contributions explicit; e.g. "as you said last week, we have now incorporated this element".

The use of boxes was particularly useful for children self-tracking of their progress. Children quickly get used to storing their material in the boxes and often they take their previous works as reference for novel contributions. Indeed, a strong example was seen when in the last session a child became quite disappointed when he noticed that the large format storyboard did not fit in his box. This suggests the importance of having a container for all his artworks.

These observations showed how combining a meaningful context with the feeling of competence facilitated conditions for enabling children and researchers to create together. Moreover, they suggest the necessity of researchers to truly entrust the skills of children in order to allow them to feel capable and skilled. In this

context, an interesting finding, as the psychologist pointed out, was that, despite two of the children were not used to draw (as noted in their records), they all easily engaged with the activities based on drawing.

Such approach, oriented toward fostering the "empowerment dimension" of the activities, can enhance the potential benefits of PD activities both for the children themselves and for design purposes. Furthermore "the empowerment dimension" does not only influence the immediate response during the workshop but can also have long term implications related with children self-efficacy. The reinforcement of the idea that they are "capable of designing a videogame" highly motivated children, and two of them asked us for references and software to start developing their own videogames at home.

## 6.2 Designing activities: the balance between structure and freedom

The tension between structure and freedom represents a critical aspect in the design of all kinds of educational interventions [1]. Such relation acquires even greater importance when we design activities for children with ASD. As literature suggests highly unstructured activities may be distressing for these children [20]. However, as our experience suggests, excessive constrains can be counterproductive in terms of children participation and involvement.

Finding a proper balance between structure and freedom represents therefore a delicate task. It cannot be simplified to reducing the contributions of children to some very limited and discrete aspects, since this approach can reduce children's willingness to participate. To address this issue, during the workshop we implemented a set of transversal "structuring techniques" aimed at avoiding overwhelming them while giving them space for participation. Such techniques were: the use of the narrative structure, the constancy of the setting and the use of a visual schedule.

As previously stated the use of narrative showed to be an effective instrument both from the point of view of activity capability and in terms of children enjoyment and empowerment. Furthermore this method allowed us to find a proper balance between orienting children's contributions toward our design question, clearly defining the scope of the activities and giving enough space for creation. More concisely, through the use of narrative we had been able to provide children with scenarios that frame the activity without constraining their creativity. The shared experience that children had with storytelling [18] allowed them to move in a secure and known ground, which was at the same time structured enough to avoid being overwhelmed by starting from scratch, and sufficiently motivating to foster their engagement and willingness to contribute.

Another useful technique to facilitate the balance between structure and freedom was the clear definition of the setting. That is, that the time, space and norms in which the workshop took place should be maintained as constant as possible. A clear evidence of the importance of the constancy of the setting was the disruption of the usual dynamics produced by the absence of two children in the third session. This evidence is supported by traditional psychological practice, according to which this constancy strongly contributes to generate a secure and safe space to enable participation.

Finally, in the first session we used a visual schedule to inform the children about the upcoming activities. Despite we believed that this method would allow children to feel more secure by knowing what would happen, after the first session we decided to avoid the use of the schedule because we noticed that it was influencing children responses.

According to our experience the role of structure should not be interpreted as reducing the space for children's contributions. It is rather an instrument to generate conditions for which children can safely explore, play and create with the researchers.

# 7. CONCLUSIONS

The paper presented a participatory design workshop with ASD children aimed at integrating their contributions into the design of a Kinect-based game. The workshop had the goals of defining game mechanics that could be enjoyable for children and specifying game features.

At a methodological level the workshop was based on the use of the educational design research approach, understood as the continuous evaluation and adjustment of the proposed activity according to children responses. This method allowed us to widen the space for children's contributions and redefine their level of involvement, with benefits both from the design point of view and from the children themselves.

Such approach was supported by a careful evaluation of the "empowerment dimension" of the proposed activities, formalized as the extent to which children care about what they are doing (meaningfulness) and their perception about the relevance and importance of their contributions (feeling of competence). The analysis of this dimension allowed identifying some useful approach to strengthen children's empowerment and consequently fostering their participation. Main benefits were found in the use of narrative as an instrument both for empowering and providing a proper balance between structure and freedom. At the same time choices related with contextual and material aspects such as the constancy of the setting and the use of personal storage boxes, showed to be highly effective supports for PD activities with ASD children.

Our experience suggests the possible benefits of widening the space for children contributions. However, it is necessary to acknowledge that our findings are based on a reduced group of children and therefore cannot be generalized until additional follow-up studies are carried out. Nonetheless, a fundamental aspect that can be highlighted is that, when designing with children with ASD, it becomes crucial for researchers to be able to deal with a complex network of variables that range from socio-affective aspects to functional constraints. This approach requires going "beyond expectations". Moreover, it also requires being capable of assuming a situated perspective, in which understanding children's affective state represents a fundamental factor for properly designing activities that are both useful for design and enjoyable and empowering for children.

# 8. ACKNOWLEDGMENTS

We would like to thank the professionals of UETD for their support and collaboration and the four children who participated in the workshop.

# 9. REFERENCES

[1] Ackermann, E. 2004. Constructing knowledge and transforming the world. In M. Tokoro and L. Steels, eds., *A learning zone of one's own: Sharing representations and flow in collaborative learning environments*. IOS Press.

[2] Anamaria, P., Simut, R., Pintea, S., Saldien, J., et al. 2013. Can the social robot probo help children with autism to identify situation-based emotions? A series of single case experiments. *International Journal of Humanoid Robotics* 10, 3.

[3] Association., A.P. 2000. *Diagnostic and statistical manual of mental disorders*. 4th ed.

[4] Benton, L., Johnson, H., Ashwin, E., Brosnan, M., and Grawemeyer, B. 2012. Developing IDEAS : Supporting children with autism within a participatory design team. In *Proceedings of the SIGCHI Conference on Human Factors in Computing Systems* (CHI '12). ACM, New York, NY, USA, 2599-2608. DOI=10.1145/2207676.2208650 http://doi.acm.org/10.1145/2207676.2208650

[5] Cobb, S., Parsons, S., Millen, L., Eastgate, R., and Glover, T. 2010. Design and development of collaborative technology for children with autism: COSPATIAL. *INTED2010 International Technology, Education and Development Conference*.

[6] Dindler, C., Eriksson, E., Sejer, O., et al. 2005. Mission from Mars - A Method for Exploring User Requirements for Children in a Narrative Space. In *Proceedings of the 2005 conference on Interaction design and children (IDC '05)*. ACM, New York, NY, USA, 40-47. DOI=10.1145/1109540.1109546 http://doi.acm.org/10.1145/1109540.1109546

[7] Dindler, C. and Iversen, O.S. 2007. Fictional Inquiry— design collaboration in a shared narrative space. *CoDesign*. 3,4, 213-234

[8] Druin, A. 1999. The Role of Children in the Design of New Technology. *Behaviour and information technology*, 21,1, 1-25

[9] Farrell-Kirk, R. 2001. Secrets, symbols, synthesis, and safety: The role of boxes in art therapy. *American Journal of Art Therapy*, 39, 3.

[10] Frauenberger, C., Good, J., Alcorn, A., and Pain, H. 2012. Supporting the design contributions of children with autism spectrum conditions. In *Proceedings of the 11th International Conference on Interaction Design and Children (IDC '12)*. ACM, New York, NY, USA, 134-143. DOI=10.1145/2307096.2307112 http://doi.acm.org/10.1145/2307096.2307112

[11] Frauenberger, C., Good, J., and Alcorn, A. 2012. Challenges, opportunities and future perspectives in including children with disabilities in the design of interactive technology. In *Proceedings of the 11th International Conference on Interaction Design and Children (IDC '12)*. ACM, New York, NY, USA, 367-370. DOI=10.1145/2307096.2307171 http://doi.acm.org/10.1145/2307096.2307171

[12] Frauenberger, C., Good, J., and Keay-Bright, W. 2010. Phenomenology, a framework for participatory design. In *Proceedings of the 11th Biennial Participatory Design Conference on - PDC '10, 187*.

[13] Frauenberger, C., Good, J., and Keay-Bright, W. 2011. Designing technology for children with special needs: bridging perspectives through participatory design. *CoDesign* 7, 1, 1–28.

[14] Fullerton, T. 2008. *Game Design Workshop: A Playcentric Approach to Creating Innovative Games*. Morgan Kaufmann

[15] Guha, M.L., Druin, A., and Fails, J.A. 2008. Designing with and for children with special needs : An inclusionary model. In *Proceedings of the 7th international conference on Interaction design and children (IDC '08)*. ACM, New York, NY, USA, 61-64. DOI=10.1145/1463689.1463719 http://doi.acm.org/10.1145/1463689.1463719

[16] Keay-Bright, W. 2007. The Reactive Colours Project: Demonstrating Participatory and Collaborative Design Methods for the Creation of Software for Autistic Children. *Design Principles & Practices: An International Journal* 1, 2.

[17] Kozima, H., Nakagawa, C., and Yasuda, A. 2005. Interactive robots for communication-care: a case-study in autism therapy. In *Robot and Human Interactive Communication. ROMAN 2005. IEEE International Workshop*, 341-346. IEEE.

[18] Losh, M. and Capps, L. 2003. Narrative Ability in High-Functioning Children with Autism and Asperger's Syndrome. *Journal of Autism and Developmental Disorders*. 33, 3, 239 – 251.

[19] Mazzone, E., Tikkanen, R., Read, J.C., Iivari, N., and Beale, R. 2012. Integrating children ' s contributions in the interaction design process. *International Journal of Arts and Technology*. 5, 2, 319-346

[20] Millen, L., Cobb, S.V.G., Patel, H. 2010. Participatory design with children with autism. In *Proceedings 8th Intl. Conference on Disability, VR and Associated Technologies*, Valparaiso, Chile. 93–101.

[21] Mora, J., Malinverni, L., and Pares, N. 2014. Narrative-Based Elicitation: Orchestrating Contributions from Experts and Children. In *Proceedings of the SIGCHI Conference on Human Factors in Computing Systems (CHI '14)*.In press

[22] Muñoz Garcia, A. 2010. *Psicologia del desarrollo en la etapa de educacion primaria*. Ediciones Pirámide, S.A.

[23] Nesset, V. and Large, A. 2004. Children in the information technology design process: A review of theories and their applications. *Library & Information Science Research*, 26(2), 140-161.

[24] Parés, N. and Altimira, D. 2013. *Analyzing the Adequacy of Interaction Paradigms in Artificial Reality Experiences*. Human–Computer Interaction 28, 2, 77–114.

[25] Peeters, T. 2006. *L'autisme. De la compréhension à l'intervention*. Paris: Dunod.

[26] Porayska-Pomsta, K., Frauenberger, C., Pain, H., Rajendran, G., Smith, T., Menzies, R., Foster M.E. 2012. Developing technology for autism: an interdisciplinary approach. *Personal and Ubiquitous Computing*. 16, 2 , 117–127.

[27] Riviere, A. 2001. *Autismo: Orientaciones para la Intervención Educativa*. Ed. Trotta

[28] Roeyers, H. 1995. A peer-mediated proximity intervention to facilitate the social interactions of children with a pervasive developmental disorder. *British Journal of Special Education* 22, 161–164.

[29] Sansosti, F. and Powell-Smith, K. 2008. Using Computer-Presented social stories and video models to increase the social communication skills of children with high-functioning autism spectrum disorders. *Journal of Positive Behaviour Interventions*. 10, 3, 162–178.

[30] Scaife, M. and Rogers, Y. 1999. Kids as Informants : Telling us what we didn ' t know or confirming what we knew already ? In A. Druin, ed., *The design of children's technology*. 1–26.

[31] Strickland, D., Marcus, L., Mesibov, G., and Hogan, K. 1996. Brief report: Two case studies using virtual reality as a learning tool for autistic children. *Journal of Autism and Developmental Disorders*. 26, 6, 651-660.

[32] Van den Akker, J., Gravemeijer,K., McKenney,S., and Nieveen, N. 2006 *Educational design research*. Routledge.

# Play It Our Way: Customization of Game Rules in Children's Interactive Outdoor Games

Tetske Avontuur[1], Rian de Jong[1], Eveline Brink[1], Yves Florack[1], Iris Soute[2], Panos Markopoulos[2]

[1]User System Interaction Program, Department of Industrial Design, [2]Department of Industrial Design
Eindhoven University of Technology
P.O. Box 513, 5600 MB Eindhoven, The Netherlands
{t.p.avontuur}, {h.j.d.jong}, {e.brink}, {y.florack}, {i.a.c.soute}, {p.markopoulos}@tue.nl

## ABSTRACT

In traditional outdoor games, such as tag and hide-and-seek, children play in groups, and typically changes to the rules are negotiated fluidly, without disrupting the game flow. In contrast, games that are supported by interactive technology are usually rather static, not allowing for easy adaption towards the children's narrative and desired rules. We present an iterative design process in which 65 children aged 5-12 participated in different iterations, concluding with the design of GameBaker. GameBaker is an application that allows children to modify game rules for Head Up Games, outdoor collocated games supported by interactive handheld devices. We show how children: understand how setting different game rules allows them to modify the game, are able to relate these to how the game is played, and enjoy doing so. This research paves the way towards allowing children to take control of outdoor game technology, to create their own variation of games as they have done for centuries in traditional games.

## Categories and Subject Descriptors

H.5.2 [**Information Interfaces and Presentation**]: User Interfaces – *evaluation/methodology, user-centered design, prototyping.*

## General Terms

Design

## Keywords

Children, Customization, Head Up Games, Pervasive Gaming, Prototyping.

## 1. INTRODUCTION

Children are increasingly relying on interactive technology for play. The gaming industry provides an abundance of offerings targeting different ages and preferences, which entertain, engage, and even compel children to play them for longer. Physical toys are increasingly enhanced with interactivity, and while traditional non-interactive toys are appreciated by children, toys that are equipped with audio visual stimuli or even some basic computing capabilities are becoming widespread. Television and Internet add to the range of media that can entertain children and fill their time. Children's lives are deeply affected by these developments and

the day in the life of a child in the developed world seems to be pivoted on interaction with one technology followed by the next. While many of these technologies are designed with sensitivity to children's developmental needs and have demonstrable benefits for children, arguably, a great many are designed with the simple aim to be attractive and engaging, considering children primarily as consumers of products and content.

Several scholars have expressed concerns about how children spend their time with such entertainment technologies and their effect on e.g. children's health or social development and behavior [1,8,16]. Nevertheless, the literature on play has for long asserted that play is vital to children's development allowing cognitive, physical and social skills to develop [19]. Educational games (e.g. [2,6]) are an example of how the scientific community, as well as the industry, has approached this challenge. Countering trends towards a sedentary lifestyle, games that promote physical activity ([7,12,14,21]) have been designed and by now represent a considerably sized proportion of the gaming market. Games that support social interaction between players whether collocated or not have also attracted considerable interest (e.g. [11,15,25]) , and interacting with communities of remote players has become an essential feature of many computer games.

Despite these positive efforts, a worrying trend is that children play 'together and apart' [27]. Furthermore, play areas are often restricted to the small physical space before a screen, and social interaction is constrained to a narrow bandwidth of text communication or interacting with virtual characters in a virtual space. We argue that a lot of benefits are to be gained for children if interactivity manages to enhance traditional outdoor games, played by children in groups, supporting physical movement and face-to-face social interactions. Several games have been created to support this thesis. For example the genre of Head Up Games was created with this agenda in mind [23].

Traditional children's games are played in different cultures, by different groups of children and different constellations of ages, genders, physical abilities of the players. The official rules can be different from the way children actually play games [7]. Hughes defines rules dependent on the context and that children have an urge to play "nice". An important element of these games is that players dynamically adapt them. They change rules, create new ones, vary the game in creative ways throughout the game but also over longer periods of time, and create their own 'local' rules and variants of games [10]. This feature of traditional children's group games is in stark contrast to the closed narrative of video games, or of interactive toys, where a strictly defined action-reaction pattern limits interaction possibilities.

Our vision is similar to traditional outdoor games, to enable children to quickly adapt the interactive outdoor games, to change games, to create and adapt rules. To achieve this, we need to find ways in which technology can support children beyond the mere appropriation of an interactive technology. Technology should truly provide a pallet for them to create new forms of game play fitting their tastes, interests and play context, and that empowers them to engage with interactive games in a less passive way.

In this paper we show how our vision motivates some research questions about Head Up Games (HUGs). We go on to answer these questions in an iterative user centered design process, which is aimed at developing a platform for adapting HUGs. We discuss lessons learnt; how they contribute to the state of the art in Interaction Design and Children and how these efforts need to be pursued further to achieve the vision laid out above.

# 2. RELATED WORK

There is a growing interest on creating interactive gaming applications that can be played outdoors and/or motivate players to move more. The main idea for Head Up Games [23] is motivated by the observation that many interactive outdoor games are played using mobile technology such as smart phones, resulting in game play that forces the player to play *head down*. Interaction with such a device typically leaves little room for rich social interaction with other players, and does not allow for wildly running around. Head Up Games aim to trigger play behaviors as seen in traditional games, such as physical activity and face-to-face social interaction, while being supported, and not disrupted, by interactive technology. In many related fields similar goals are pursued; for example, though not primarily targeted at children, the genre of exertion games aims to motivate players to become physically active. A classic example of an exertion game is *Table Tennis for Three* [15]. Furthermore, Interactive Playgrounds, interactive installations that are physically bound to a playground, are similar in their ambitions and motivations to Head Up Games. A prime example of this genre is the Interactive Slide [20]. They differ in that HUGs aim to be nomadic, i.e. to be played without a fixed infrastructure, as traditional games can be played.

In all these related areas, there has not yet been an attempt to create technologies that will let children create, capture, and reenact new game rules. This may be because the idea of rule modifiability is not a core importance factor to those fields or simply because of the challenging nature of this task. The ambition to let children create their own games is shared with Open Ended Play research [3]. However, interactive toys created to support Open Ended Play do not encode or apply any game rules, so the games are only agreed with children and applied by them, remaining ephemeral and unsupported by technology.

In the digital domain there are numerous systems that support children to program their own games: a well-known example is Scratch [13] a visual programming environment targeted at children (8-10 years). Furthermore, several toolkits exist for children to build tangible artifacts (see [5]). Although children can indeed adapt and form their own creations using these systems and toolkits, the main aim is learning: learning a programming language, or electronics skills. Also, more importantly, the resulting games are tied to the digital domain and cannot be taken outdoors to play.

A range of Head Up Games [23] have been designed and the development of these games is supported by RaPIDO, a platform consisting of a programming library and a number of portable, interactive devices [24]. Earlier research has investigated in depth how to design and evaluate these games; however, the goal of creating adaptable game rules is a challenging one both technically and in terms of providing appropriate interaction mechanisms to children for doing so.

Toering et al [26] present a first attempt to support customization of HUGs supported by the Swinxs platform (www.swinxs.com). Using a deck of RFID-tagged cards, children could select to set some settings on the Swinxs game console, which would result in different games to be played. An evaluation involving 20 children, aged 11-13, showed that children are able to adjust the rules of Head Up Games without a graphical user interface and this increases their enjoyment of the game. However, the rule customization was limited to a few elements of the game and there was no ability to recall earlier settings.

# 3. DESIGNING GAMEBAKER

Our main aim is to enable children aged 7-11 to setup and adjust Head Up Games, in a way that approaches the natural behaviour of children in traditional games. We address this challenge by following a Research through Design [28] approach: through the act of iteratively designing prototypes and evaluating these with end-users we gain insight in the feasibility of this venture and understand how this could be attractive and engaging to children. Like any design challenge it can be answered in different forms; perhaps an obvious answer would be to provide programming tools that support the creation of HUGs by children. One could think of designing a custom-programming environment that targets children, addressing some of the cognitive challenges of novice programming, e.g. [13], [12], [14]. However, such a solution would arguably disrupt the game flow: finding a computer, hooking up the interactive devices for reprogramming and adjusting settings before going out to play again, does not seem a likely solution that would fit in the typical flow of outdoor play. Furthermore, enabling children to program does not necessarily imply their interest to do so. Moreover, it is not at all clear what it means to create a novel game, what functionalities should programming pertain to, and what context rule and game creation could take place in. To explain the last point, we argue that the notion of a single child programming his/her own game to be played by a group later, as a surrogate to adult game designers and developers, is not viable. Creating and adapting games for outdoor play has traditionally been a group activity tied to the location and context in which the game is played and it appears logical that HUGs should be adapted in a similar way.

## 3.1 Setup

An informant design approach [18] was followed, starting from creating and testing low fidelity prototypes, until GameBaker, a game configuration interface for HUGs was created. Children participated as informants and testers in all iterations.

The HUGs were implemented using the RaPIDO platform, which consists of a programming library and a number of handheld devices that facilitate interactive outdoor games. RaPIDO devices (see Figure 1) can vibrate, make sound, light up and communicate wirelessly with each other. Furthermore, they contain an RFID reader, an accelerometer, a rotary dial and a microphone. Characteristically, RaPIDO devices do not have a screen to avoid screen-based interaction which can easily get children to interact 'head down', hindering from moving around and interacting socially. The RaPIDO programming platform was designed to facilitate designers with a limited programming background to create new games. RaPIDO devices are currently programmed in C++ and Java using Eclipse and Processing. When the game code is changed, it has to be uploaded with a computer to each device individually.

Five design iterations (see section 3.4 - 3.8) were conducted to attempt to answer three main questions by proposing and testing appropriate interactive prototypes:

- Do children have the intrinsic motivation to modify game rules?

- How do children understand game rules implemented in the programmed behavior of RaPIDO devices?

- How do children understand the way rules, which are represented computationally, influence the actual play?

The answers to these questions are of course tied to design solutions that can be created for supporting the adaptation of game rules. We attempt to answer them by creating prototypes, evaluating them with children in context.

## 3.2 Target users
Our end users are children aged 7-11 playing Head Up Games on the RaPIDO platform. At this age abstract thinking is developed and children enjoy social and physical play [4]. However, children at this age still need guidance with reflecting and adult supervision tends to prolong game play and helps generating ideas [17]. So we chose set ups where an adult supervisor (in our cases these are teachers or scout leader) is present when the children play with the devices.

## 3.3 The BuzzTag game
We focused on the game *BuzzTag*, an adaptation of an earlier Head Up Game called *Save the Safe* [21]. The goal of this game is to acquire the 'buzz'. Each player has a HUGs device and at the start of the game, one of the devices starts to vibrate ('buzz'). The other players must steal the buzz from this player. They can do this by staying in close vicinity of the vibrating device for a set amount of time. The buzz is then automatically transferred to the other device. The player who has the buzz at the end of the game wins. If the game is played in teams, the entire team of the person who last had the buzz wins.

Throughout the study, we use *BuzzTag* as the game for our user tests. One reason for this choice is that the rules of the game are simple. This provides us with opportunity to add new parameters and rules. Also, because *BuzzTag* is a relatively simple game, we assume that children might be quickly bored with the game. This allows us to explore children's intrinsic motivation to adapt a game to make it more interesting.

**Figure 1: The RaPIDO devices**

## 3.4 Do children want to change HUG rules?
In our first iteration, a playtest was carried out aiming to understand how children learn to play a Head Up Game, how well they understand it, and whether they would be motivated to change the game to fit it more to their liking.

### 3.4.1 Procedure
Sixteen children (5-12 years old) took part in a playtest for *BuzzTag* at an after school care centre. Children were split in three groups, and each group played three rounds of *BuzzTag*. After the third round, we asked each group to explain the rules of the game to the next group applying a variation of the peer tutoring method [9].

### 3.4.2 Results
At first, following the initial explanations by the adults, children seemed unsure of the game rules. They were exploring the game and the interactive technology, for example: they experimented how to pass on the buzz by standing close or far, long or quick. Only during the third round, did most children understand the game fully and, developed game winning tactics. For example, one child would pretend to have the buzz to distract the others. After peer tutoring, one of the researchers had to amend the explanation of the game because not all children understood the instructions of their peers. One possible reason is that the peer tutoring was chaotic as multiple children would speak simultaneously and children did not pay attention to one another.

Younger children did not seem to fully understand the game and also seemed to be less active physically. This was expected, e.g., see [4] and [9] who suggest that younger children tend to be less physical in their play and have less ability for abstract thinking.

When we asked the children if they would want to change anything about the game, none of them were able to come up with something they wanted to change. They all said they did not want to change anything and could also not come up with opportunities for change.

### 3.4.3 Implications
None of the children were able to come up with game parameters that they would want to change. One explanation could be that they were unable to construct an abstraction of the game that would allow them to imagine variations of it. Another explanation could be that children are not as such motivated to change game rules. The second iteration set out to examine more closely the former possibility.

## 3.5 What is the mental model of HUGs in Children?
The goal of the second iteration was to examine if children can create a mental model of Head Up Games and to see whether children were able to understand that a game constitutes of several distinct parameters. To test this, we created three prototypes of a game adaptation interface and ran a play test in which the

children of the after school care (see previous iteration) were instructed to recreate the game they had played during the previous test. Most children had also participated in the previous test.

### 3.5.1 Three Game Adaptation Interface Designs
We prototyped three very diverse design concepts for changing game parameters: A) a game board, B) a decision tree and C) an iPad app. The prototypes supported some simple interactions but were essentially mock-ups with the researchers effecting children's choices in a Wizard of Oz manner.

Prototype A (Figure 2, left) resembles a board game, which children sit around. Game parameters are distributed around the edge of the board and children can change the value of each parameter by rotating a disc. In the middle of the board is a big

'Start' button that can be pushed at any time to start the game. Prototype B (Figure 2, middle) is a decision tree where each leaf represents the value of a parameter; children can hang cards on the leaves to choose the parameter values. Prototype C (Figure 2, right) is an iPad app with a touch-based interface that children can use to change parameters.

The parameters available in all prototypes were the *number of teams* that could be chosen (0, 2 or 3), the *length of the game* (short, normal, long), the *distance of buzz transfer* (close or far away), *tag return* (possibility to attain the buzz immediately after losing it) and *number of home bases* (0, 1 or 3). *Distance of buzz transfer* is how close a device should be before the buzz is transferred. In prototype A and B two additional parameters could be adjusted: the *number of players* (1-8), and *Team Choice Autonomy*. This difference in parameters was due to spatial and time constraints in building prototype C.

### 3.5.2 Expectations
We expected that all children would be able to understand and play the game; though we expected that the youngest children would have difficulty understanding the abstract notion of setting game parameters to vary game play, given that they have not fully developed the ability for abstract thought, e.g., see [4].

### 3.5.3 Procedure
We conducted this user study at the same after school care facility as the previous study. Sixteen children (5-10 years old) were divided into three groups. The groups were created by supervisors of the after school care to ensure that children in one group liked each other and to make sure that children would not have to leave halfway through the test.

First, each group was asked to recall what events took place during the previous test and to explain the game rules to us. Then the children were given the opportunity to play BuzzTag once to refresh their memory. Next, each group was given a different prototype. The group reconstructed the game they had just played by adjusting the parameters on the prototype. Finally, the children were asked to imagine what game parameters they would like to adjust, and set the values of these parameters in the interface accordingly, and what parameters they would like to change other than those shown in the prototypes.

### 3.5.4 Results and discussion
All children were able to accurately reconstruct the game they had played using the mock-up interface, which indicates that all concepts presented abstractions that were comprehensible to all players.

For prototype A, several children were able to interact with the prototypes themselves. One child took the lead, giving turns to the other children. However, for prototypes B and C, they seemed to need more guidance. For both prototypes, the adult would give turns to the children for interacting with the interface. For prototype B, children did not interact themselves so a researcher had to guide the children through each parameter, explain its meaning and show the possible settings. One possible reason for their difficulties could be that initially no parameters were presented but they have to be taken from a stack of cards. Also, not all children were able to physically reach the top of prototype B. Note that the children who interacted with prototype A were slightly older than those in the other group.

After reconstruction, we asked children to come up with new parameters. They came up with some realistic suggestions, e.g., having *invisible teams*. Children were able to come up with their own new ideas for the game, this indicates that they grasp the abstraction presented and are able to invent new parameters to describe game variations.

### 3.5.5 Implications
For the next iteration, we removed a couple of parameters for simplicity and ease of implementation. *Distance* was removed as the children did not understand what it meant. Also, increasing the *distance* means the buzz is lost too quickly, reducing the game experience. No tag return was removed because it was technically not possible to implement. Furthermore, children explicitly said they wanted to determine the exact length of the game. We therefore converted the *time* parameter into concrete numbers for future tests.

Children appreciated prototype B most. We attribute this to the fact that each parameter was shown big and centrally: all children were able to see all parameters at all times. With prototype C, the system state was shown in one screen but the children did not recognize that the screen was showing the chosen parameter values. However, they did understand the interactions through tapping on the touch screen immediately. With prototype A, the parameters were positioned around the board so a single child could not see the names and values of all parameters at a time.

Another issue was the difference in the fidelity of the prototypes. The board game interface was much more colourful than the other two. Also, we used an iPad mini in prototype C, which results in smaller visuals compared to prototypes A and B. These differences might have influenced children's responses to the interfaces. In the following iteration more attention was paid to ensure prototypes of uniform fidelity were compared.

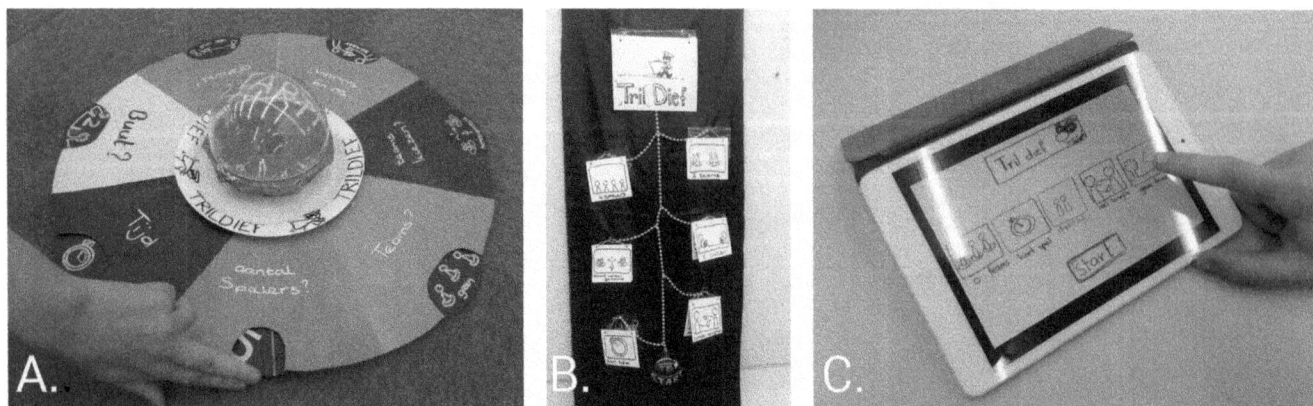

**Figure 2 left: Prototype A, board game with individual discs to change parameters. Middle: Prototype B, a decision tree. Choices are made with cards. It provides a constant overview. Right: Prototype C, application with pictogram based decisions choice.**

## 3.6 Do children want to adjust the game?

The previous iteration showed us that children understand how to describe a game in terms of parameters. However, it did not show whether children understand how changing parameter values influences game-play. Thus, we implemented the prototypes to enable the children to play the adjusted games. This also allows us to examine whether children have an intrinsic motivation to adjust game parameters.

For this iteration, we developed two prototypes and tested them with 11 children (8-10 years old). By comparing children's reactions to each prototype we assessed their relative strengths and weaknesses. Our observation focused on reactions between games and their willingness to play the game again.

### 3.6.1 Two Prototypes

Based on observations in the previous test, we extracted the strong features of the previous prototypes and integrated them into two new ones. Prototype B provided a clear overview of parameters to all children, we therefore chose to have prototypes that children could sit around. They should be able to see all parameters clearly from different angles. In prototype A, several children were able to interact with the prototype themselves. However, the interaction points were restricted. We chose to create another game board for prototype D with a more open interaction space. Because children clearly seemed to understand how to use a touch screen, we integrated this interaction mode in prototype E.

Prototype D (Figure 3, left) was a game board with different tokens that visualise different parameters, and a tablet. The tokens could be placed on the plateau and directly resembled the parameters they represented. On the tablet the explanation of each token was shown as well as the overview of all parameter values. When a token was positioned on the board a line would appear leading from the token to the tablet in the middle. This was constructed in a Wizard of Oz setup, by projecting an image on the game board, from a laptop. Each time the children placed a token, a researcher would draw the lines on the laptop which would be displayed immediately on the board.

Prototype E (Figure 3, right) was a suitcase. A touchscreen was built in the lid and to its left and right were vertical magnetic bars where tokens could be placed. The tokens were abstract circles and each token represented a parameter. After placing a token on the magnetic bar, the corresponding parameter and its possible values would be shown on the screen. After choosing a value, an overview was given of all chosen parameters. Interaction was again simulated in a Wizard of Oz setup with one researcher

sitting next to the suitcase with a laptop.

A parameter for *team visibility* was added after it had been suggested by one of our users in the previous study. If teams are invisible the players only know to which team they belonged after the game ends. The other available parameters were the *number of teams* (0, 2 or 3), *number of home bases* (0, 1 or 2), *visible buzz*, and *game length* (2, 3 or 4 minutes). This was the first test where *home bases* were introduced. Home bases are markers where children can gain points for their team. They have to hold their device in front of these markers while having the buzz to score a point. Furthermore, this time children could choose between two variants of the game: *BuzzTag* and *BuzzThief* (difference: the goal is either to lose or to gain the buzz). This was to see how children experience the game when the winning conditions change.

When a game was chosen it would have a set of default parameters (the basic games): 2 teams, visible teams, 0 *home bases*, invisible buzz, and a game length of 3 minutes. Parameters could be added or removed by placing or removing tokens. When a token is removed, the game reverts to the default settings for that parameter of the basic game.

### 3.6.2 Expectations

We expected the children to have some problems linking the parameters to the game. Choosing parameter values is an abstract process and we were unsure to what extent children can translate this to a concrete game. We expected them to have less trouble using prototype D as it provides a more direct mapping of parameters and the game than prototype E. We expected children to understand the impact of simple parameters. However, we expected them to have problems understanding *home bases* since adding these changes the nature of the game more than, say, changing the number of teams. We expected children to want to adjust the game and to be capable of inventing new parameters to make the game more fun.

### 3.6.3 Procedure

Ten children participated in this test (7- 10 years old) at the same after school care as the previous test, as children there were already familiar with us as well as the game. All children participated in at least one previous test. This means that if any interactions or parameters in the interface are unclear, it is less likely related to the children's understanding of the game itself and more likely related to the interface or their understanding of parameters.

We tested the two prototypes in two sessions (five children per session, though one child had to leave earlier in the first session).

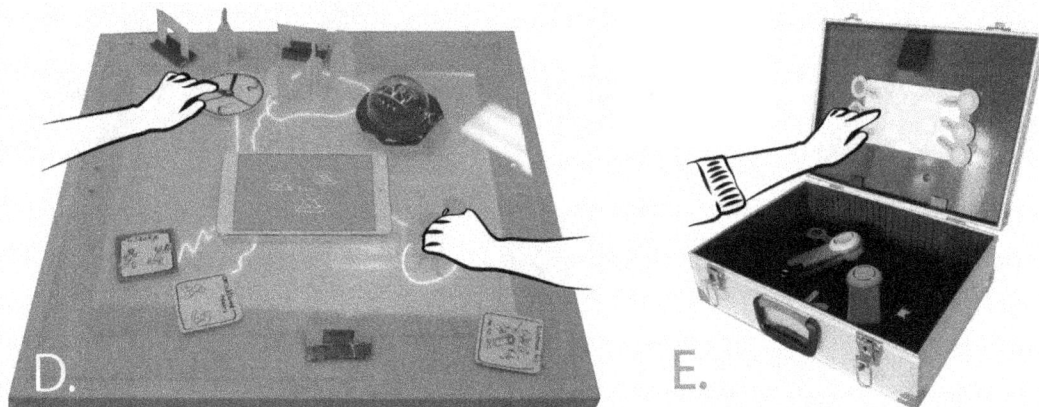

**Figure 3 Left: Prototype D, a game board with tokens representing different parameters. The tokens were used to select and adjust the Parameters Right: Prototype E, a suitcase with abstract tokens for parameter selection. The screen was used for adaptati**

At the beginning of the test, we asked each group what they remembered from last test to examine their mental model of the game. The children were then given the task to set up the game themselves and play the game according to their own settings. We then asked them to perform the same task on the second prototype. We ended with asking what they liked about each prototype and which prototype they preferred.

Though the interaction with the prototypes to set the parameters was working, technically there was no direct link between setting the parameters and transferring these to the game devices. Therefore, after the children finished adjusting the parameters, we manually uploaded these to the devices. This meant uploading the parameters one by one to one of the devices, after which this device automatically forwarded the settings to the other devices. This whole process took a few minutes, resulting in a delay between setting the parameters and starting to play the game.

### 3.6.4 Results and discussion
When children were given the opportunity to play the game the first time, they all responded enthusiastically. The second group was also enthusiastic about playing BuzzTag a second time. In the first group, two children expressed that they did not want to play the game a second time because they were bored but eventually agreed to play another time for the other two children.

We found that children do not take much time to adjust settings in between games. After a game was done, children would shout to each other one or two parameters that should be changed. They then quickly went to the prototype, changed the parameters and wanted to play again. However, because the implementation was yet incomplete there was a 5 minute time delay between setting parameters and the actual playing of the game.

The link between the interface and the RaPIDO devices did not seem clear to the children. After the children had set up the game and were already in the field to play, they were still asking questions about the game. They asked what game they were playing, how many teams there were and what the goal of the game was. It seems most likely that this confusion was caused by the time delay mentioned.

Children did not seem to understand that the number of players on the board should be equal to the number of players in the game in prototype D. The first group put some of the player tokens on the board but did not realize it should exactly represent the number of players in the game. The second group immediately put all available tokens on the board without any consideration about the meaning of each token. It was also unclear to them that they had to make teams by putting groups of tokens together. It is therefore possible that the user interface was unclear.

Regarding the children's understanding of parameters, neither group was enthusiastic about *home bases*. Neither of the groups would independently choose to use them. When we encouraged one group to play with the *home bases* it became clear that the children did not understand how they worked: they would ignore their base and play the game as they knew it before. Only after we brought their base to the children's attention, they started interacting with them. When asked later the children voiced two different understandings of the home bases: "you are safe there" and "you can get points".

Two parameters that also required explicit explanation of the researchers were *visibility of the buzz* and *visibility of teams*. Children asked what they meant at several different points in time. After explanation, they understood their meaning.

Children did not seem to grasp the concept of adding and removing parameters from a game. They thought that if they added a parameter to the game by placing a token, removing this token would not remove the parameter from the game. However, even after they understood the interactions, the children still seemed to be uncomfortable with removing parameters.

### 3.6.5 Implications
Despite the issues with understanding the interface, most children responded that they preferred prototype D over prototype E. When asked what they liked about it, the children said they enjoyed the direct feedback of prototype pertaining to the lines that would appear after a token was placed.

In each prototype, the tablet displayed an overview of the game settings. However, in both cases, children did not notice there was a game overview on the tablet until this was pointed out to them. This suggests having a more prominent game overview.

The children did not seem to grasp the notion of a basic game where parameters can be added and removed. Rather, they appeared to see the game as a whole, including all its parameters. This suggests making all parameters (active or not) visible in the interface.

## 3.7 Do children understand the mapping of game settings to game play?
In the fourth iteration, we want to examine to what extent children can set up and play a game independently and how to help players understand how changing a parameter can impact the game. We examine whether an improved interface enables children to better link the interface to the game played with the RaPIDO devices.

To answer these questions, we developed one prototype, named GameBaker. GameBaker was a suitcase based on the previous experiment. It contained a tablet on the inside of the lid and is depicted in Figure 5. The RaPIDO devices were placed in the bottom part of the suitcase. We kept the tablet integrated into the suitcase to provide a coherent user experience and hopefully strengthen the link between the interface and the RaPIDO devices.

**Figure 4: Prototype. Serves as a carrier for the devices and includes a touch screen in the lid to change parameters**

The interface of the suitcase consists of two parts. First, a screen is displayed with the title of the game and a short animation explaining the rules. One button, "choose game" leads to the screen where the values for each parameter can be adjusted. The chosen values are permanently visible at the bottom of the screen. By clicking on a parameter, a pop-up appears with all possible values, as displayed in Figure 5. Each time the value for a parameter is changed, the corresponding figure in the bottom jumps up and down for two seconds to inform the user of the changed value. The game can be started by tapping on the orange button in the bottom of the screen and the text "Play!" appears.

**Figure 5: The interface showing an overview of the parameters and possible values of the parameter "teams"**

A user-test of GameBaker was conducted at a scouting group in the Netherlands that was unfamiliar with Head Up Games. For this test, we selected six parameters: *number of players*, *number of teams*, *visibility of teams*, *visibility of the buzz*, *duration of the game* and *number of home bases*. The sixth parameter, *home bases*, was included because we wanted to examine if children do not choose it because it is too complicated or because it is not enjoyable. At the start of the test some default variables were already selected (4 players, 2 teams, invisible teams, 5 minutes, invisible buzz, and 2 or no home base).

### 3.7.1 Expectations
We assumed that the link between the interface and the RaPIDO devices would be clearer to the children than in the previous test. There are three reasons for this. First, we showed the suitcase to the children with the RaPIDO devices inside which we did not do before. Second, we presented the interface as a console and the RaPIDO devices as the controllers. This builds on children's existing mental models of video game systems. Third, we showed the children explicitly how the game is set up by using the interface ourselves instead of asking them to use the interface without having seen others interact with it as we did previously.

We expected children to be able to use the interface independently. However, we also expected that they would not know the values of all parameters. This expectation was based on previous observations where children would change two parameters and then immediately choose to play. This would also have a negative impact on the link between the interface and the RaPIDO devices as the children would not have a complete overview of the game settings.

### 3.7.2 Procedure
Eighteen children (8-11 years old) were divided into two groups of nine. Each group had different settings for *home bases* and our objective was to examine if children would understand the impact of this parameter on the game on its own merits.

We first showed each group an explanatory movie of the game. One group received an explanation of the game with two teams and without *home bases*; the other group received an explanation with two teams and two *home bases*: one for each team. The children were then allowed to play the game three times. As only seven RaPIDO devices were in working order, seven children

were able to play at a time, the remaining two players were substitutes, taking turns and swapping with other players after each game. This ensured all children could play an equal amount of time.

In the second part of the test we explained to the children that they were allowed to play BuzzTag again. This time, they were allowed to set up the game themselves and play the game twice according to their own chosen settings. Similar to the previous test, we needed to manually transfer the parameters to the RaPIDO devices.

#### 3.7.2.1 Results and discussion
The children seemed to understand the link between the interface and the devices and described the prototype as the controller of the devices, despite the fact that there still was a delay between setting the parameters and actual playing. They asked fewer questions regarding parameters than the children in previous iterations. Children now had a better overview of parameters. However, we observed that they did not actively look at all the individual settings in the overview and thus were not always aware of all specific details of a game. E.g. before the start of one game, they did not notice that teams were set to invisible until explicitly told.

Relatively few questions were asked while the children were in the field. However, the parameter *home base* still seemed complex. The group which played with *home bases* in the learning phase chose to use them again during the second part of the study, even though most children still did not seem to understand how they worked. They kept asking questions, even after explanation by a researcher. They were unsuccessful in collecting points because they did not know how to use the device in combination with their home base or because they were at the wrong base. A few children thought they would score points when the buzz was passed on. One reason could be that the sound for passing on the buzz and scoring a point was the same.

The children seemed capable of using the interface independently to change simple parameter values. However, for more complex parameters, they needed the researcher to encourage them to experience their impact on the game. Adult guidance also helps less dominant children to have a voice in choosing parameters. It also seems to help children focus on what they are doing as sometimes, parameter values are chosen without them realizing what a parameter implies.

### 3.7.3 Implications
As we observed that the delay between setting the parameters on the interface and actually playing the game disrupted the game experience, we decided to focus on this for our next iteration. Furthermore, the visuals of the *home bases* were unclear. Each home base had a different colour but this did not correspond with the team colour. This generated confusion. Also, the sound for passing on the buzz was the same as for scoring a point at a goal.

## 3.8 Are children motivated to adjust games?
Until now, we had not studied how the interface would be used without facilitation of the researchers. The current iteration aims to answer this question. Another issue that the previous iteration has not settled is if children have an intrinsic motivation to adjust games (in the previous iteration, researchers explicitly asked children if they wanted to change parameters). Therefore, the last user test was conducted with a scout group that had extensive experience with the RaPIDO platform, through their participation in earlier studies [22]. This diminishes the novelty and learning

effect and helps us to examine children's intrinsic motivation to change parameters. We asked the scout leader to guide the process to see how the platform would be used in context.

### 3.8.1 Prototype

In this final test, the same prototype was used as during the previous study. However, we modified the prototype to reduce the time needed to transfer the parameters to the game devices. Though we still could not implement a direct link between the prototype and the devices, we were able to set all parameters in one operation, from a laptop, reducing the delay to a few seconds instead of several minutes. We did this out of sight of the children, so for them it appeared to be an automatic process. Several small changes were made to increase the usability of the interface and the colour of the goals now corresponded to the teams. A short description about each parameter was added to see if children would understand the parameters better and to guide the scout leader if he decides to interact with the prototype himself.

### 3.8.2 Expectations

Because the children had previous experience with the RaPIDO platform and BuzzTag, we expected them to more rapidly get bored with the game than children in the other user tests. Because we shortened the delay between adjusting the game and the actual play, we expected the link between the GameBaker and the RaPIDO devices would be clear. We also expected that the test would feel more natural for the children because their own supervisor took the lead instead of a researcher.

### 3.8.3 Procedure

Twenty children were divided into three groups: two groups of seven children (7-10 years old) and one of six children (10-12 years old). Each group was given the opportunity to play the game and were afterwards given a choice whether or not they wanted to play again. We asked the scout leader to guide the process of selecting parameters while we observed the process. Afterwards an interview was conducted with the scout leader.

### 3.8.4 Results and discussion

The first two groups did not want to continue playing after two rounds of play: the children wanted to play something else. A possible reason for the first two groups to lose their motivation to play is that the groups had to take turns in playing. This increased the waiting time in between games and, it might be that they were out of patience. The third group, with the older children, did not have to wait in between games and played three games consecutively, after which they decided to stop playing. After this, we asked the children from the first two groups to play once more. In total five children wanted to play again. This number was fairly small; the scout leader attributed this to a dominant child not wanting to play.

We asked the scout leader to guide the play sessions at his discretion. He decided to take a clear lead in the decision process of setting the parameters and was initially the only person interacting with the interface. Only after the children had expressed they wanted to interact with the prototype themselves, the scout leader allowed them to do so. The younger children required more guidance than the older ones with the latter requiring hardly any guidance at all.

Contrary to our previous test the scout leader guided the group process of the children instead of a researcher. One advantage was that the scout leader knew the children. For example, there was one child who had a different opinion than the rest of the group regarding two parameters. The first time, the majority ruled that he would not get his way. The second time however, despite that the boy again was the only person having a different opinion, the scout leader decided that the boy could have his way. The scout leader knew that if he would choose again for the majority's opinion, this child would get very frustrated and probably would not want to play anymore. The other children did not seem to mind this overruling and all children felt satisfied with the chosen parameters. For situations as the one that was just described, a supervisor seems to add value compared to using just technology.

What is most promising however is that children asked the scout leader if they could change the parameters using the interface. Especially the older children (10-12) were more independent; they played and adjusted three games in a row. The fact that they themselves asked whether they could adjust it indicates that there might be an intrinsic motivation to change games and means that the interface seems easy enough for children to comfortably use.

One other indication that children want to change games is the fact that the older children independently chose to use home bases in the game. They felt this would make the game would more fun. We found that older children understood and enjoyed the *home bases* more than the younger children. When in play they discussed tactics and used them. This test was the first opportunity where this relatively complex parameter could be tested with both older and younger children. Also, the children had played a game similar to *BuzzTag* before. It might be the case that a more complex parameter such as *home bases* can only be appreciated after children have extensive experience with the basic game.

## 4. DISCUSSION

Throughout the design process, several questions were formulated and answered by building and evaluating different prototypes.

First, We examined the children's mental model of Head Up Games and specifically the game BuzzTag. Even though, during the first time they played some children seemed to be unsure how to play it, they still engaged. After playing three games, the children seemed to understand the game up to a level where they would start applying different tactics to win the game. They were able to recreate the game a week later. This means children form a mental model of a game through experience, which they can later explicitly recreate.

Secondly, we focused on the parameters that comprise a game. Can children understand basic parameters? How complex can these parameters be? And finally, do they understand how changing parameters influences game play? Children seemed to have clear understanding of basic parameters, such as number of players and number of teams. They can quickly relate that to themselves and see which outcomes are possible and how they impact the game. They understood when certain parameters were incongruent with each other and would actively change them to fix this ("you can't have three *home bases* with two teams"). This is an important finding as it shows that a game can be broken down into parameters that children can understand to the extent that they can change them and estimate their impact on the game. This abstraction of parameters is a useful tool that can be applied to other games as well.

The parameters used in this study are limited in number and complexity, except for one (*home base*). It would be interesting to see how children can deal with a higher number of parameters and more complex ones. The most complex parameter was now only chosen after experiencing it in a game at least once. Without having experienced it, children assumed that having *home bases* in a game would be less fun; however when letting children play one mandatory game with *home bases*, the children would choose them again later themselves. Still, when these were added to the game, it took longer for the game to be fully understood. Herein could lie a role for a supervisor (e.g. a scout leader in the scout group that participated in this study), who can help guide choices, and explain more complex parameters.

We also found that when a group of children aged 10-12 played with *home bases*, they seemed to understand them more quickly, enjoy them more and apply tactics more than the younger groups of children. They also took more initiative in changing the game than younger children. Older children have developed a more abstract level of thinking and can therefore understand complex parameters more easily. One implication of these findings is that games could be created comprised of simple and complex parameters. Children can then adjust the game based on their own level of thinking. This way, children can balance the game based on their own capabilities, resulting in a more enjoyable game.

The children were not always aware of the exact values for all parameters, neither do they scrutinise all settings and, as a result, they may be surprised during a game when something happens (as was the case with *invisible teams* during the fourth iteration). Children did not always understand a parameter beforehand, nor were they inclined to read the explanations. Often these parameters would become clear once the children have played with a parameter or when the supervisor has asked them to think about what it might mean. However, we believe that some additional help could be given by the system in the form of animations or sound. Because reading skills are still developing in our target age group, seeing might be better than reading.

During the third iteration, we presented the children a basic game where parameters could be added. This was not clear for children. They view the game as a whole where a parameter can be set and if they do not set or adjust it, it should not be absent, but instead be set to a default value. This means that any interface should support this line of thought.

The connection between the RaPIDO devices and the GameBaker interface should be clear. We found that the presentation of the platform as a whole is crucial in maintaining this mental connection. Children already have a notion of game systems as comprised of a console and controllers. We suggest using this existing mental model where the interface is the console and the RaPIDO devices are the controllers.

Also, the time between deciding to play and actually being able to play should be short as children change only one or two parameters and immediately want to play again. In the beginning, children would press start on the interface and run away onto the field before the game was completely set up. However, when we added a ten second countdown to the interface, the children waited before running away and did not express frustrations with waiting anymore.

We examined whether children are intrinsically motivated to adjust parameters in Head Up Games. Most children involved in our tests responded enthusiastically to playing the games but needed to be experienced with the game to be inclined to change parameters. When children were new to the games there might be a novelty effect increasing their enthusiasm for a particular game. At the same time, they are still learning how to play, and as a consequence are not yet able to change parameters This

observation is confirmed by observations in the third and fifth iteration; in these iterations children had previous experience with the RaPIDO devices. The novelty effect had worn off, up to a point where some children (fifth iteration) even found the games boring. However, when given the opportunity to adjust parameters they were eager to do so and as a result found the games engaging again.

This gives evidence that children are motivated to adjust game rules once they have fully explored the original game. Also, the group of children aged 10-12 was the only group that independently chose to add home bases to the game and understood how they worked. This is in concordance with the literature which states that children of this age are able to understand more complex [4]. Because older children understand more complex game rules and because they seem to have a motivation to change games, one game could be created with both simple and complex rules. The complex rules could then be used by older children to make the game more challenging to them.

Regarding the independence of the children in setting up and adjusting games, children wanted to interact with the interface themselves after having seen their supervisor interact. This also gives a positive indication for their motivation to change games. However, this research is insufficient to know if they will want to change games in the long term. The motivation to change games might be due to exploration of all parameters and their effects. Ideally the system should be placed in a natural environment, where over a longer period of time the amount of times the system gets placed with is monitored. This would require further development of the prototype with additional games.

## 5. CONCLUSION

Motivated by the vision of creating outdoor games that children can play together, being physically active, and interacting socially, we have argued for the importance of allowing children to customize games to fit their playing field, the group or the mix of players available, and their momentary preferences and social dynamics. Such adaptation happens fluently in traditional games, but is hampered by interactive technologies where the game remains immutable as delivered by technology designers with the children engaging in a fixed narrative and a predetermined set of rules. Supporting children in the process of creating their own games and game variants seems a crucial element of technology supported outdoor games for children.

The contribution of this paper is to present the iterative child centred design of GameBaker, an interface that children can use independently to adjust simple parameters while playing interactive outdoor games. GameBaker was designed to fit the context of outdoor play, where children are prepared to devote little time in between game play to control the technology, and where they interact as a group, negotiating, and designing their own play experience. Future work should explore how giving children the ability to adapt and create their own game is received by children, and what use of this functionality is made on the long term. Do children spontaneously adapt games? What usage patterns will emerge in the long run? Does adaptivity contribute to children engaging with these games rather than other sedentary and indoors activities? Future research will attempt to address these questions.

# 6. REFERENCES

[1] Anderson, C.A. and Bushman, B.J. Effects of Violent Video Games on Aggressive Behavior, Aggressive Cognition, Aggressive Affect, Physiological Arousal, and Prosocial Behavior: A Meta-Analytic Review of the Scientific Literature. *Psychological Science 12*, 5 (2001), 353–359.

[2] Barendregt, W., Lindström, B., Rietz-Leppänen, E., Holgersson, I., and Ottosson, T. Development and Evaluation of Fingu: A Mathematics iPad Game Using Multi-touch Interaction. *Proceedings of the 11th International Conference on Interaction Design and Children*, ACM (2012), 204–207.

[3] Bekker, T., Sturm, J., Wesselink, R., Groenendaal, B., and Eggen, B. Interactive play objects and the effects of open-ended play on social interaction and fun. *Proceedings of the 2008 International Conference in Advances on Computer Entertainment Technology*, ACM (2008), 389–392.

[4] Berk, L.E. *Child Development*. Pearson/Allyn and Bacon, 2006.

[5] Blikstein, P. Gears of Our Childhood: Constructionist Toolkits, Robotics, and Physical Computing, Past and Future. *Proceedings of the 12th International Conference on Interaction Design and Children*, ACM (2013), 173–182.

[6] Bodén, M., Dekker, A., Viller, S., and Matthews, B. Augmenting Play and Learning in the Primary Classroom. *Proceedings of the 12th International Conference on Interaction Design and Children*, ACM (2013), 228–236.

[7] Goldstein, K. Strategies in Couning Out. In *The Study of Games*. John Wiley & Sons, 1971.

[8] Gray, P. The decline of play and the rise of psychopathology in children and adolescents. *American Journal of Play 3*, 4 (2011), 443–463.

[9] Hughes, F.P. *Children, Play, and Development*. SAGE, 2009.

[10] Hughes, L. Beyond the rules of the game: why are Rooie Rules nice? In F.E. Manning, ed., *The world of play*. Leisure Press, 1983.

[11] Jansen, M. and Bekker, T. Swinxsbee: A Shared Interactive Play Object to Stimulate Children's Social Play Behaviour and Physical Exercise. In *Intelligent Technologies for Interactive Entertainment*. 2009, 90–101.

[12] Lund, H.H. and Pagliarini, L. RoboCup Jr. with LEGO MINDSTORMS. *IEEE International Conference on Robotics and Automation, 2000. Proceedings. ICRA '00*, (2000), 813–819 vol.1.

[13] Maloney, J., Resnick, M., Rusk, N., Silverman, B., and Eastmond, E. The Scratch Programming Language and Environment. *Trans. Comput. Educ. 10*, 4 (2010), 16:1–16:15.

[14] Millner, A. and Baafi, E. Modkit: Blending and Extending Approachable Platforms for Creating Computer Programs and Interactive Objects. *Proceedings of the 10th International Conference on Interaction Design and Children*, ACM (2011), 250–253.

[15] Mueller, F., Gibbs, M.R., and Vetere, F. Towards understanding how to design for social play in exertion games. *Personal and Ubiquitous Computing 14*, 5 (2010), 417–424.

[16] Rey-López, J.P., Vicente-Rodríguez, G., Biosca, M., and Moreno, L.A. Sedentary behaviour and obesity development in children and adolescents. *Nutrition, Metabolism and Cardiovascular Diseases 18*, 3 (2008), 242–251.

[17] Robertson, J. and Nicholson, K. Adventure Author: A Learning Environment to Support Creative Design. *Proceedings of the 6th International Conference on Interaction Design and Children*, ACM (2007), 37–44.

[18] Scaife, M., Rogers, Y., Aldrich, F., and Davies, M. Designing for or Designing with? Informant Design for Interactive Learning Environments. *Proceedings of the ACM SIGCHI Conference on Human Factors in Computing Systems*, ACM (1997), 343–350.

[19] Scarlett, W.G., Naudeau, S.C., Salonius-Pasternak, D., and Ponte, I.C. *Children's Play*. Sage Publications, Inc, 2004.

[20] Soler-Adillon, J., Ferrer, J., and Parés, N. A Novel Approach to Interactive Playgrounds: The Interactive Slide Project. *Proceedings of the 8th International Conference on Interaction Design and Children*, ACM (2009), 131–139.

[21] Soute, I., Kaptein, M., and Markopoulos, P. Evaluating outdoor play for children: virtual vs. tangible game objects in pervasive games. *Proceedings of the 8th International Conference on Interaction Design and Children*, ACM (2009), 250–253.

[22] Soute, I., Lagerström, S., and Markopoulos, P. Rapid Prototyping of Outdoor Games for Children in an Iterative Design Process. *Proceedings of the 12th International Conference on Interaction Design and Children*, ACM (2013), 74–83.

[23] Soute, I., Markopoulos, P., and Magielse, R. Head Up Games: Combining the Best of Both Worlds by Merging Traditional and Digital Play. *Personal Ubiquitous Comput. 14*, 5 (2010), 435–444.

[24] Soute, I. Head Up Games: on the design, creation and evaluation of interactive outdoor games for children. 2013. http://www.tue.nl/en/publication/ep/p/d/ep-uid/283744/.

[25] Tan, J.L., Goh, D.H.-L., Ang, R.P., and Huan, V.S. Child-centered interaction in the design of a game for social skills intervention. *Computers in Entertainment (CIE) 9*, 1 (2011), 2.

[26] Toering, E., Soute, I., and Markopoulos, P. Rule customization in head-up games. *Proceedings of the 3rd International Conference on Fun and Games*, (2010), 144–148.

[27] Turkle, S. Alone Together: Why We Expect More from Technology and Less from Each Other. *Journal of Social Work Practice 27*, 4 (2012), 471–474.

[28] Zimmerman, J., Forlizzi, J., and Evenson, S. Research through design as a method for interaction design research in HCI. *Proceedings of the SIGCHI conference on Human factors in computing systems*, ACM (2007), 493–502.

# Giving Ideas an Equal Chance: Inclusion and Representation in Participatory Design with Children

Janet C Read
University of Central Lancashire
Preston, UK
PR1 2HE
+44(0)1772 893285
jcread@uclan.ac.uk

Daniel Fitton
University of Central Lancashire
Preston, UK
PR1 2HE
+44(0)1772 893277
dbfitton@uclan.ac.uk

Matthew Horton
University of Central Lancashire
Preston, UK
PR1 2HE
+44(0)1772 895151
mplhorton@uclan.ac.uk

## ABSTRACT

Participatory Design (PD) in various guises is a popular approach with the Interaction Design and Children (IDC) community. In studying it as a method very little work has considered the fundamentals of participation, namely how children choose to participate and how their ideas are included and represented. This paper highlights ethical concerns about PD with children within the context of information needed to consent. In helping children understand participation in PD, a central aspect is the necessity to help children understand how their design ideas are used which itself challenges researchers to seek a fair and equitable process that is describable and defensible. The TRAck (tracking, representing and acknowledging) Method, is described as an initial process that could meet this need. This is evaluated, in two forms, in a PD study with 84 children. The TRAck Method encouraged careful scrutiny of designs and allowed the researchers to distil useful design ideas although these were maybe not the most imaginative. There is a trade off between the limitations of applying such a process to PD against the benefits of ensuring full-informed involvement of children.

## Categories and Subject Descriptors

H5.2 [**User Interfaces**]: Prototyping, User-centred design

## General Terms

Design, Human Factors, Theory,

## Keywords

Participatory Design, Child Computer Interaction, Ethics

## 1. INTRODUCTION

The Interaction Design and Children (IDC) community considers Participatory Design (PD) as an accepted, and often preferred, method for engaging with children in activities where new technologies for children are being developed. Since its inception in 2002, of the 195 long papers published at the annual IDC conference, 35 have included at least some aspects of participatory design (e.g. [16] [31]) (http://www.chici.org/resources). Many other papers on PD have been published at the annual CHI conference (e.g.[21], [7]).

Participatory design is predated by the ideal of inclusion of children as participants in research that has its roots in sociology. Hart's model of participation [13], describes a continuum that shows the deepening involvement of children as a factor that affects participation in the context of empowerment; thus at the extremes children are essentially not empowered at all (Rung 1 – Adult-led activities, in which a youth does as directed without understanding) or are fully empowered (Rung 8 – Youth-led activities, in which decision making is shared with youth and adults working as equal partners).

In research settings, when children act as participants, it is common practice to seek consent to gather data and to hold information about the study. This consent assumes that children are fully aware of the potential, and possibilities, for the data they will contribute. The extent to which a child can understand what he or she is consenting to is always a concern when researching with children. Many refer to children as not being able to give consent and typically assume that consent for their participation must be drawn from adults; this view is based on the belief that children cannot be "fully informed" so cannot give consent [24]. Fill information is, of course, never possible as one can never be sure where a piece of research will lead or what its effects may be.

When children participate with ideas for design within ICT settings, there might appear to be few concerns about data and the gathering of consent is often simply about gathering assent to take part. This is a result of the marrying of concerns about informed consent to the 'value' of the data gathered. Having full information about a study is also about an individual being empowered to understand what is going on, where the information gathered may be used and where the results and findings will be used. Inclusion of ideas, and the extent to which each child's contribution is collected, valued and used is also an important aspect. To date, in reported PD sessions, the IDC community, whilst typically paying attention to reporting the number of children, and their gender, has not been always clear about how children are informed to consent to participate and how each idea is included.

This paper adds understanding to this space by presenting an analysis method (TRAck) for the outcomes of participatory design sessions that could be described to children so they would understand how their ideas are used and that can therefore provide a starting point for moving the participation of children in PD sessions from Hart's Rung 3—where children are consulted but have limited means to feedback—to Rung 5 where they can know how and where their inputs go. TRAck is described in two forms and is considered most useful in large studies where many children from different places may contribute design ideas as it can be used to both ensure that all the ideas are considered in an equal way and it presents a defensible strategy, which could be explained to children, for the reduction from many ideas to a few ideas whilst ensuring fair representation.

The analysis method, TRAck (tracking, representing and acknowledging) is examined and demonstrated in the context of a PD case study of the design of a mobile product for teenagers that encouraged better use of electrical and other energy. The study involved 84 children aged between 11 and 15 from two different schools. TRAck was applied firstly as 1 design 1 idea (v1) and secondly as n designs n ideas (v2) and the results are compared and discussed. The paper critiques TRAck for its ability to identify ideas for future use and in the context of ensuring the most ethical and most high-level participation of children in PD work.

## 2. BACKGROUND

### 2.1 History and Origins of PD

Participatory design is a broad term that, in HCI, refers to the involvement of end users as informants in the design of technology. Participatory design has its roots in the participatory approaches to decision making that go back as far as Plato and the Athenian democracies. The principle was, and still is, that if people were given a voice then a) they would be more likely to be happy with a decision and b) that the people's voices had a value.

Participatory design emerged in various forms from two different needs The first, coming mainly from the US, was the need for technological rationalization where IBM and others sought to engage with users to ensure efficient design of systems with initiatives like joint application design. The second was the social and humanist approaches that considered user participation necessary for collective security and individual autonomy. This latter movement had support in the UK and Scandinavia with key contributions being socio-technical [23], and contributions from the Tavistock institution and Norwegian work experiments [29]. Participatory design in HCI has had several pioneers and has been used in several high profile projects [1], [22],

### 2.2 PD with Children

PD with children became fashionable in the late 1980s with influential work by Scaife et al. [28] and Druin et al. [10]. Different traditions of participation evolved along axes that partially mimic the two underlying principles, these being, children contributing to make better technology and children contributing their voices for empowerment. In the former model, the work on co-design by Druin [10] has been highly influential. The research lab at Maryland pioneered a co-design practice where small teams of children worked for several weeks on design projects with adult participants. In this model the children develop skills as designers and participate in a collaborative incremental process that leads ideas into a single design brief [35]. An alternative view, which is possibly more in line with what is understood as the Scandinavian approach, is lauded by Mazzone et al. [18] and others. This practice engages with large numbers of children in short bursts, often in a single event, and seeks to spread a broad net to capture many ideas as inspirations to be later used by an adult design team. Studies of participatory design with children tend to focus on the philosophical arguments around the involvement of children in the practice, on the examination of methods to facilitate children's involvement, and on the quality of the products and ideas that are generated during PD.

Philosophical debate focuses on the role of the children and on the extent to which they can participate in meaningful design activities. Early discussion has been outside the IDC community and has come from the social sciences where participation of children

has provoked discussion on the value of one-off participation of children as opposed to more sustained involvement with the concern being about empowerment [30]. The ethical commentator, Christensen, [4], voiced concerns about participation highlighting that although there cannot always be a symmetry of power with children, there should be great care taken to ensure ethical symmetry as a minimal requirement. Ethical symmetry assumes that children are treated with the same knowledge and ability to consent as adults would be rather than being considered a special case. In HCI, the Interaction Design and Children (IDC) community has begun dialogue on some of these themes. The roles of children as participants in HCI work has been modelled by Druin et al. [9], and participatory power imbalances were discussed by Read et al. [26] who delineated participatory design activities with children along an axis from informant through balanced to facilitated design The ethics of children's participation in design activities has also been examined by Read et al. [25] who made a case for children being given full information about the potential use of, and the funding for, the designs that they contribute.

In terms of methods for participatory design with children, several meta-methods have been described including co-design [5], design partners [8] and informant design. Each of these approaches varies in its motivations and focus but the core aspect of all is the engagement with the user group and the facilitation of design activities by research teams who deliberately seek to delegate the design activity and power to the participating user team.

The effectiveness of participatory design in terms of gathering ideas and inspirations from children has also been discussed within the IDC community. Here research seeks to explore the idea generation process [20] or to consider how PD can be used with specific user groups or specific design challenges [32]. User groups that have been shown to be able to participate in design activities include very young children [17] and teenagers [19].

### 2.3 Ideas, values and ethics

In the IDC literature very few researchers have documented how they have concerned themselves with the rights and feelings of children within the context of research using participatory design. Three studies stand out; one that is concerned with how ideas are seen to filter through the process, a second that foregrounds the values of the research team in the PD process and a third that challenges the research team to be especially honest and candid in their explanations to the children ahead of a PD event.

The first is the work by Guha et al. from 2004, entitled 'Mixing Ideas' [12] .This paper described how the authors adapted co-design methods for use in a single session with a young age group (aged 4 – 6). The central theme of this paper is that the children wanted to understand how their ideas were used. Tellingly the authors write that children were *'visibly upset' that their ideas were not being used and that children were 'not speaking and not contributing'* when they perceived that their ideas were not being listened to. The use of the children's ideas was the main feature of this work and the authors proposed a method by which ideas were mixed up, in small groups, and then mixed again and again until only one 'big idea' remained. The process took place in a consensus discussion with the participating children. The process was reported as having sparked imagination and ideas.

The second influential paper is by Iversen et al. in 2012 [16]. This paper, describing a design session for teenagers, deliberately put democratic behaviours and democracy at the front of the design session. In particular the researchers who were facilitating the design session are reported to have *'presented their interests'* to the teenagers ahead of the activity taking place. This action, of clearly letting the design participants know what the 'values' of the research team were, and the emphasis on the teenage designers being as informed as possible as to the nature of the task, is the only evidence found of such practice in participatory design studies with children. This is an example of value-centred design which explains itself as 'frontloaded ethics' [33; 34] and promotes an early look at the values that are incorporated in design. As written by Friedman et al. [11], *'Human values and ethical considerations no longer stand apart from the HCI community but are fundamentally part of our practice. This shift reflects, at least in part, the increasing impact and visibility that computer technologies have had on human lives'.*

The third work is from 2013 and is by Read et al. [27], in which the ethics of participation of children is examined. This paper suggests an approach in which the research team deliberately and critically examine why they are engaging with children and then ensure that the children have as much knowledge as possible in order to decide whether or not to participate. This process, when applied to design, implies that children should be informed about how their ideas will be used, where they might gain attribution for them, and what might happen should their idea ultimately result in monetary gains. Theoretically this takes a view of as 'ethical symmetry' [4], where children are not considered as any different to adults in terms of participation. It suggests that in all participatory work due consideration be given to ethical balances and to informed consent It is generally considered that the more meaningful participation is for children the more beneficial the activity is across all aspects [30], The IDC community has sought to report methods and approaches that value participation [15].

Collectively, these three papers spell out a research agenda for the IDC community suggesting three concerns that need attention. These concerns can be captured as follows:

- From Guha – Ideas need to be Accounted for - IA
- From Iversen – Participants need to be Told –PT
- From Read – Consent requires Information - IC

The remainder of this paper describes the implementation of a process that accounts for ideas (IA) in such a way that participants can be clearly advised (PT) about how their ideas are dealt with in order that they can give fully informed consent (IC) to participation. The following sections describe this process, show its application in a PD session and then discuss its potential.

# 3. DEMOCRATIC DESIGN PRACTICE

Democracies typically fall into two styles; one is a direct democracy where all participants have an equal and a direct say in decision-making, the second is a representative democracy in which all eligible citizens contribute by electing representatives who then carry their voices forward. This second model of democracy came about by necessity as populations became too large to allow each member a voice in each instance. The way individuals are represented is key to democratic action, and is one of the three practices (deliberation, participation and representation) that denominate democracy [6]. Representation is the creation of proxies to impersonate the desires of a participating population.

## 3.1 TRAck Method

The TRAck Method is described here as a means to ensure representation of ideas and tracking of ideas for PD sessions. A set of assumptions underpin the descriptions that follow. These are that:

| i) | There is a need to be able to articulate to children a method that satisfies them that their ideas are being considered |
|---|---|
| ii) | There may often be too many children participating in a design session for there to be a simple amalgam of ideas |
| iii) | The design team are able to agree, in advance, on a maximum number of key ideas that they are looking to take forward and identify as having come from the design session |
| iv) | There are available a team of experienced individuals who can examine the children's designs |
| v) | Any designs offered are sufficiently mature to convey at least one idea that can be taken forward |

The method is described in two versions (v1 and v2) – and these are each then examined in the case study that follows.

### 3.1.1 Terminology

In the narrative that follows *an idea* is considered to be something that could potentially be included in a final design specification prior to build. One design could have many ideas embedded in it and *a design* could be the work of one child, or of a group of children. A design can exist as a single image, or prototype, or could exist as a series of linked images or prototypes. For the purposes of discussion *a group* refers to a collection of individuals whose designs are linked in so much as they come from *a single cohort of children*, e.g. one school class and so merit representation. A *design activity* may be repeated with several groups to inform a single final product specification.

### 3.1.2 Stage 1 – Setting the Parameters

Having planned a design activity and having carried it out with a large enough cohort of children to make the merging and tracking of ideas problematic, the evaluators determine approximately how many ideas they are aiming to have at the end of the process, (in the example below, this number is ten) and also the approximate 'size' of competing teams (in the example described below this is between 3 and 5 – ideally these would be very similar or all the same). The designs from all the participating children are then placed into teams within the groups, with the *number of teams dictating the number of ideas that will be present at the finish*.

### 3.1.3 Stage 2 – Reporting Candidate Ideas

A set of reporting sheets are developed, one for each team, and each with as many spaces for *candidate ideas*, alongside each design, as there are designs in the team. Thus, if there are three designs in a team, each design has a space for three candidate ideas to be recorded, if there are five designs in a team, each has space for five candidate ideas to be reported (see figure 1).

Evaluators are then recruited to inspect the children's designs (this is situated in the work from Horn et al. [14] who stress the need for all ideas to be fairly considered and for consensual opinions). This group of evaluators individually inspects every design and lists as many candidate ideas as there is space to write ideas in the spaces on the reporting sheets. Once all the reporting sheets have been completed, the activity changes according to whether the 1:1 (v1) or n:n (v2) analysis method is being applied

### 3.1.4 Analysis using TRAck v1 - 1:1

Each evaluator selects one *candidate idea* from each design to take forward (in figure 1 this can be seen as a tick in the column headed individual). These ideas are then referred to as (that single evaluators) *selected ideas*. Note that there will always be as many selected ideas as there are individual designs coming into the process. The different evaluators then come together and consider each others selected ideas choosing from those the *most popular* ideas (based on how many evaluators chose that idea as their selected idea) and bring that idea forward as the 'winner' for that team of designs. At this stage there will be as many 'winners' as there are teams, and *each winning idea will represent a team* (which in turn will represent a group).

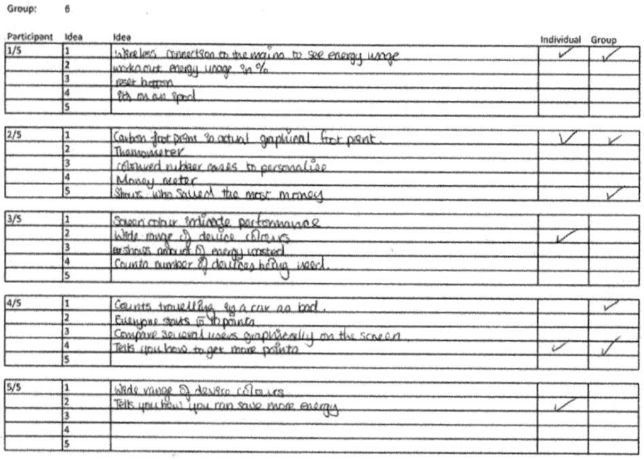

**Figure 1- Completed reporting sheet showing how 5 candidate ideas were transcribed and how 5 individual (1:1) and 5 group (n:n) were chosen to take forward.**

### 3.1.5 Analysis using TRAck v1 - n:n

In this version instead of the individual evaluator bringing forward one idea from each and every design, each evaluator brings forward *as many ideas from the 'team' as there are individual designs in the team* – thus, if there are five designs in the team then five ideas are brought forward to become the *selected ideas*. Theoretically these could all come from one design (whereas in v1 they have to come equally with one from each design). In figure 1 above it can be seen that designs 2 and 4 both contributed two ideas in this case. After each evaluator has determined his or her selected ideas (and again there will be as many selected ideas as there were designs coming into the process) the activity continues in the same way as in v1 with evaluators coming together and agreeing 'winners' *with one winning idea coming from each team*.

Both methods ensure that each design is considered and is only competing with ideas from similar groups and thus makes sure that each different 'group' of children is represented in the final design discussion space. It could be argued that v1 is more inclusive as every team brings an idea through to the 'vote off' but v2 has the advantage of possibly ensuring that should one design have all the great ideas, these ideas are not lost. Theoretically, v2 should result in better ideas than v1 but can still be considered to be representative.

## 3.2 Evaluating the TRAck Method

Three questions arise from the possible use of this method; these are;

a) Inclusivity: To what extent does this method ensure that all the children's ideas are acknowledged / considered?

b) Representation: How do the two models (v1, v2), for representation, differ?

c) Process - From the point of view of a design team, used to a more holistic approach, what is the effect of using this process by which ideas can be tracked?

These questions are examined in the case study that follows.

## 4. CASE STUDY

A participatory design study that took place over four days with four different groups of children in two different schools is described. The PD session aimed to gather designs for conveying energy use and was part of a three-year research project. The case study is written up in three parts, the first describes how the context was set for the pupils, the second describes what happened during the design session and describes the instruments used, and the third describes the use of TRAck to analyse the outputs.

## 4.1 Obstructed Theatre

The first stage in the design journey required the design team to understand what it was that they wanted from the pupils and to create a means by which these requirements could be conveyed without constraining design thinking. It is worth noting that the design team needed to create a successful usable product and so foremost in their thinking was the need to gather design ideas.

Probe questions that the design team explored were:

1. What is the team aiming to build?
2. What are the uncertainties of the design space?
3. What are the constraints that pupils will need to know?
4. What are the key functional requirements?

Having answered these questions the team determined to use the obstructed theatre [28] approach in order to ensure a consistent, inclusive, informative and open introduction to the design activities. This was considered important as the team were seeking to repeat the same design session with four different groups. Obstructed theatre is a method based on work by Briggs et al. [3] who took their inspiration from the use of pastiche scenarios in design [2]. It has been shown to work with children.

A script for the obstructed theatre was made as shown in Figure 2. This script conveyed the key responses to the probe questions:

1. The product will be a mobile / portable device that informs about energy use and is suited to teenagers.
2. The uncertainties are the shape, form and affordances of the product and how it should be interacted with.
3. The constraints are that it should be unobtrusive.
4. The key functional requirements are that the product alerts the owner to excessive energy use, conveys energy used, informs about energy uses of different things, and communicates with other similar devices.

In accordance with the practice, the theatre script was recorded by a teenage informant and accompanied with a Flash animation with stick figures that demonstrated the dramatic action.

## 4.2 Progressive Design Activities

Designs were gathered over four days in two different schools with two different year groups in each school. Each instance is referred to as a design session, thus there were four sessions (A, B, C and D). These are referenced in Table 2.

### 4.2.1 Participants

The two schools that participated in the study were standard government funded high schools and were typical of most such schools in the UK. One was partially sponsored by the Catholic Church (as are about 10% of all UK state funded schools) and the other had no religious affiliation. For the benefit of international readers of this paper it is very common for there to be Catholic High Schools in UK cities and larger towns – these schools take a small amount of funding from the Catholic Church and as such are able to include religious attendance / behaviour as part of their admissions criteria.

| SCRIPT |
|---|
| **Scene:** *Two hoodies in the garden – one (A) playing banjo, the other (B) on his phone* |
| **Shot:** *Of upper bodies* |
| *{opens to quiet activity – banjo and texting....A suddenly twitches his leg – in a surprised fashion)* |
| **Teen B:** what's up? |
| **Teen A:** s'okay – just my Oreo –hang on while I take a look.... |
| *(Teen A leans forward – out of vision a touch)* |
| **Teen B:** Oreo – as in biscuit? |
| **Teen A:** *(still messing around out of shot)* ha – nope it's summut me an Dee got given for the energy project... it's just let me know my energy use for the last couple of hours...... Organic energy object I think they call it! |
| **Teen B:** *(peering over)* it looks weird .... *(peering further)* what is it? |
| **Teen A:** it's some sort of new computer thing that moves and wibbles and what not ...... *(leans forward)* see you can squeeze it and fold it and that............. |
| **Teen B:** Sound..... what else does it do? |
| **Teen A:** well, when I do this it shows me how much gas, lekky and water I've used ........ *(moves his arms about)* and......... ........ I can see what Dee has used as well! |
| **Teen B:** cool |
| *(Teen A picks up his banjo again and plays a bit more)* |
| **Teen B:** you going out with Dee then? |
| *(Teen A doesn't respond)* |
| **Teen B:** are you? |
| **Teen A:** no! |
| *(Teen A picks up his banjo again and plays a bit more)* |
| **Teen B:** lookin' at your doofer seems she uses tons more lekky than you.... |
| **Teen A:** yeah.... I think she's got a Jacuzzi or something.. |
| **Teen B:** hey we should go try it out ........ do Jacuzzi's use a lot of lekky? |
| *(Teen B reaches to his phone as if to go to Google)* |
| **Teen B:** how d'you spell Jacuzzi? |
| **Teen A:** Jacuz |
| **Teen B:** slow down |
| **Teen A:** *(leaning towards his doofer again)* here – it's on here – I can put in the hours and the device and................. |
| **Teen B:** *(moving his phone away and leaning in)* that is something else... |
| *(Teen A carries on banjo playing.........)* |
| **Teen B:** shall we go chippy... |

**Figure 2 - Obstructed Theatre Script for the design session**

As a result these schools typically gather pupils in from a slightly larger catchment area than secular schools and typically do slightly better (on average) in academic achievement. They also tend to have a slightly more ethnically diverse pupil base. For this study, 84 (48 boys and 36 girls) children and teenagers from two schools and two-year groups in the UK contributed towards design ideas. These were pupils from design and technology and science classes. There was nothing extraordinary or out of the ordinary about the participating children.

### 4.2.2 Apparatus (Progressive Design Activities)

The design sessions were facilitated with the use of a pre printed A4 (roughly letter sized) design product made up of seven portrait-oriented pages with a small title on each page. It was not expected that all the pupils would complete all the pages but, having had experience in many school based design sessions, the research team had constructed this 'booklet' in order to ensure that the participating pupils were kept busy for the whole time that the study was being carried out (approximately one hour). The headings on the pages are detailed in Table 1 below and Figure 4 shows an example of three completed pages. At the top of page 1 it also said 'Use the spaces below to draw your designs'.

**Table 1 - The prompts as written on the design booklet**

| Page | Heading | Purpose |
|---|---|---|
| 1 | This is what the device is | To get a view of what the device looks like and some of its properties |
| 2 | This is how it tells me I'm doing well | To capture some ideas for the visualizations of 'doing well and doing bad' |
| 3 | This is how I check how I am doing | To gather some ideas about input and control aspects |
| 4 | This is how it looks when I use it to find out more information | To capture some ideas about how the information aspect might look |
| 5 | This is how it tells me I'm doing badly | To capture some ideas for the visualizations of 'doing well and doing bad' |
| 6 | This is how it looks when I meet my friends and compare how we are all doing | This was intended to capture some connectivity ideas |
| 7 | Anything else... | For any other points of interest |

### 4.2.3 Procedure

At the start of each design activity, which took place in a scheduled lesson, the research team began by ensuring that the pupils were aware of the aspects of the work. Pupils were told who was funding the study and were told that the findings from this design activity would feed into a research product. They were then told what that product would (potentially) ultimately be used for. Without having carried out the TRAck process, it was not possible at that point to assure the pupils that all their ideas would be used but it was pointed out that the intention was to examine a fair way of looking at all the ideas created. Pupils consented verbally to contribute their design ideas and were also advised that they could withhold them at the end if they so wished (no one did this). Following that, one of the facilitating team outlined the scope for the work by playing the obstructed theatre script so no examples were shown. Pupils were asked to annotate their drawings as appropriate so that the research team could understand them.

The designs were created collaboratively in self-organized *design groups* (DGs) using the pre-printed design booklets. The DGs were made up of two or three (occasionally four) pupils working together on a single output. There was no intention to control or manipulate gender therefore the DGs could be either single or mixed sex. Each session was facilitated by two or three academics from the research team and in each case the teacher was present, but not involved, for most of the session. The facilitators simply explained aspects of the task and ensured that the pupils stayed on task. They did not influence the design ideas and did not comment during the activity on any designs that were created. At the end of the sessions designs were collected up and marked with the makeup of the DG (boys and girls) and coded so they could be associated back to the session from which they originated.

## 4.3 Analysis of Designs

The analysis of the designs took place on a single afternoon in the university in a large room set aside for that purpose.

### 4.3.1 Participants

In the examination of the designs, four evaluators each independently examined every design for ideas. These evaluators comprised one professor of child computer interaction, one lecturer in interaction design, one research assistant in child computer interaction and one PhD student of human computer interaction. The evaluators were two males and two females. All four had experience of working in PD studies. Three of the four had been present at all or some of the design activities; the fourth had the procedure, purpose, and context of the design activity explained.

### 4.3.2 Apparatus

Pre-printed reporting sheets, one for each evaluator, were prepared; for an example see Figure 1. Also available for this activity were the 41 designs that had been created during the design sessions. These were identified with labels showing the team (1 – 10) and the identifier of the DG within that team (1, 2, 3, 4, or 5).

### 4.3.3 Procedure

Before any analysis took place, the children's designs were grouped in batches keeping the schools and year groups together. Table 2 shows how these four groups represented each school / year and shows the number of designs in each group. Each group was then subdivided so that there were ten teams created. This aligned to the idea of there being a desire to have ten ideas at the end of the process but also ensured that the teams were a sensible size, each comprising 3, 4 or 5 designs with 4 being the norm. In table 2, the figures in brackets after the team numbers show how many were in that team (e.g. team 6 had 5 designs, team 3 had 4).

**Table 2 - How the designs were grouped for analysis**

|  | Year 7 (ages 11–12) | Year 10 (ages14-15) |
|---|---|---|
| School 1 | A. Teams 1(4), 2(4) | B. Teams 3(4), 4(4), 5(3) |
| School 2 | C. Teams 6(5), 7(5), 8(5) | D. Teams 9((4), 10(3) |

As outlined earlier in this paper, the evaluators worked through the designs in stages. In stage one each evaluator looked at one design at a time and listed three, four or five (depending on the size of the team that that design belonged to) *candidate design ideas*. Each evaluator began looking at a different team's designs but all the teams were evaluated in order; thus evaluator R1 looked at team 1 through to 10, whilst R4 began with team 8 then did 9 and 10 before working through 1 to 7. Once all the designs had been looked at in this way the evaluators went through the teams and *selected ideas* from their candidate lists to take through as the best individual (1:1) choices (v1) and as the best group (n:n) choices (v2) following the process as described in section 3.

It is worth noting that two of the four (R2 and R3) did v2 then v1 and the other two (R1 and R4) did v1 then v2. Finally the four evaluators came together and determined the *winning ideas* from the selected ideas for, firstly v.1, and then v2.

## 5. RESULTS

The results are presented in two sections. The first section, gathering designs, describes the variety and the essence of the pupils' designs and includes data that gives an overview of the ideas generated across each team and reports some 'success' parameters of the PD session. This overview is taken from a synthesis of the ideas recorded by the four evaluators during the first stages of the analysis. The second section, evaluators choosing representatives, considers the results by comparing TRAck v1 and TRAck v2.

## 5.1 Gathering Designs

Each DG was able to create some designs for the device and all pupils completed page 1 of the design sheet. An example for page 1 is given in Figure 3 showing the detail and attention that was relatively typical in this design activity.

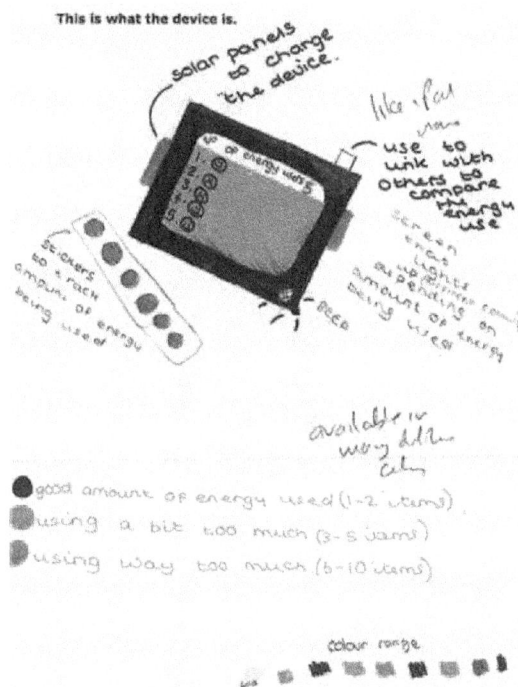

**Figure 3– Design 6/3 that ended up including one of the 'winning' ideas with its stickers.**

Most of the designs were adequately annotated but some had to have some small explanations added at the point of them being handed in. Figure 3, for example, shows 'available in many different colours' that was added in at the close of the session.

### 5.1.1 Progress through the task

All the teams completed at least the first three pages in the design booklet. Most of the teams completed five pages although not all the pages were completed consecutively (Figure 4 shows how one idea was developed). Several missed page four but went on to complete page five. There was some evidence to suggest that some pupils had hastily added content to the latter pages in order to 'finish the task'. Table 3 shows the progress through the activities (recorded as number of pages attempted) and the average number of *candidate ideas* noted by the evaluators for each of the four groups (A, B, C, D).

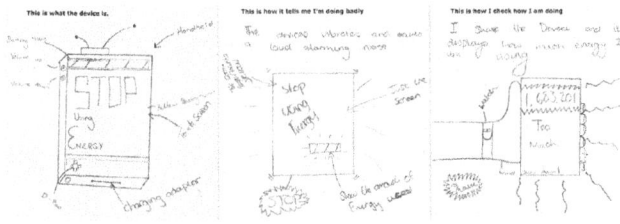

**Figure 4 – Design 5/2 showing how a design could be carried across the first three pages of the progressive design booklet. This was also a 'winner' with the idea of shaking the device being carried through to the end.**

Note that in Table 3, A and B were from one school, C and D from another and groups B and D were the older age groups. This table shows that the three design sessions produced roughly similar outputs; no one session was particularly poor in terms of completion of task or of idea generation.

**Table 3 The progress made during the four different design sessions -**

| Group | Average Progress through pages (where 7 implies all pages done)) | Percentage of Candidate ideas recorded by evaluators |
|---|---|---|
| A | 6.5 | 83 |
| B | 5.5 | 81 |
| C | 4.9 | 77 |
| D | 5.2 | 91 |

### 5.1.2 Counting Candidate Design Ideas

The principles of inclusion and representation within TRAck determined that for each design within a team, the evaluators could potentially list as many candidate ideas as there were designs in that particular team. Thus in a team with three design groups (DGs), as in team 10, a maximum of three ideas could be identified for each design. Thus a metric was designed as:

$$percentage\ of\ candidate\ ideas = 100\ \frac{n-i}{n}$$

*where i = the number of ideas identified by the evaluator and n is the number of design teams in the group.*

This percentage is applied as an average across all evaluators and all designs within a team in Table 3, and is further applied as a percentage across a team for an individual evaluator in table 4. For team 6, shown in figure 1, this percentage would be 76% for that evaluator as there were 19 candidate ideas listed against an allowable maximum of 25 (5 design groups in the team so potentially 5 candidate ideas from each = 25).

## 5.2 Evaluators Choosing Representatives

The TRAck process depends on the ability of the evaluators to identify ideas (see metric in 5.1.2). With the exception of one design, in the evaluation by R1, every evaluator was able to identify at least one idea from every design.

### 5.2.1 Stage 1 – Inclusion in Action

Table 4 shows the performance (shown as percentage of candidate ideas) of the four evaluators in terms of locating candidate ideas from the designs during the first stage of the process. The numbers in brackets next to the team number identify how many designs were in that team. The letter after the bracket identifies the group to which that team belonged.

**Table 4 - The performance of locating ideas**

| Team | R1 | R2 | R3 | R4 |
|---|---|---|---|---|
| 1(4)A | 75 | 88 | 94 | 56 |
| 2(4)A | 81 | 100 | 100 | 69 |
| 3(4)B | 50 | 75 | 88 | 56 |
| 4(4)B | 81 | 81 | 94 | 94 |
| 5(3)B | 100 | 89 | 100 | 100 |
| 6(5)C | 76 | 72 | 80 | 84 |
| 7(5)C | 76 | 60 | 84 | 56 |
| 8(5)C | 72 | 100 | 92 | 68 |
| 9(4)D | 81 | 88 | 100 | 69 |
| 10(3)D | 100 | 100 | 100 | 89 |
| *mean* | *79* | *85* | *93* | *74* |

Although not significant, it is noted that the mean percentage of candidate ideas recorded aligned to the experience of the each evaluator in participatory design sessions. R3 was the most experienced and R4 the least experienced both at facilitating and interpreting design sessions. R2 was the second most experienced in the group. The high numbers in this table show that all the evaluators put considerable effort into gathering as many design ideas as possible from the pupils' drawings indicating a high level of inclusion of ideas.

### 5.2.2 Stage 2 – Representation in Action

In the individual scenario (v1), it is clear that after the evaluator selected the ideas to go forward then each DG would be represented..

**Table 5 - Percentages of Ideas**

| Team | Representation in TRAck v2 | | | |
|---|---|---|---|---|
| | R1 | R2 | R3 | R4 |
| 1(4)A | 50 | 75 | 75 | 75 |
| 2(4)A | 75 | 100 | 75 | 50 |
| 3(4)B | 75 | 50 | 50 | 50 |
| 4(4)B | 75 | 75 | 75 | 100 |
| 5(3)B | 66 | 66 | 66 | 66 |
| 6(5)C | 60 | 60 | 60 | 60 |
| 7(5)C | 100 | 80 | 80 | 60 |
| 8(5)C | 80 | 80 | 60 | 80 |
| 9(4)D | 75 | 75 | 75 | 75 |
| 10(3)D | 66 | 100 | 100 | 66 |
| *mean* | *69* | *76* | *72* | *68* |

In the second scenario, (v2) it would be possible that representation would be significantly diminished, especially if all the ideas from one team came from one design group. This extreme loss of representation was not evidenced in the results but clearly some design groups lost their voice with this analysis. Table 5 shows how many designs were represented, from each team, after the individual evaluators made their group (v2) selections. In this table, for example from R1, team 1(4)A have 50% showing that of the four designs that came into this consideration, only two groups were represented when the TRAck v2 analysis was applied.

The individual DGs that were 'dropped' (i.e. had no contributions into TRAck v2) are listed in table 6.

**Table 6 – Teams ideas that were dropped**

| Rater | Teams dropped (Team and DG sub identifier) |
|---|---|
| R1 | 1/3, 1/4, 2/4, 3/2, 4/1, 5/3, 6/3, 6/5, 8/2, 9/1, 10/1 |
| R2 | 1/3, 3/2, 3/4, 4/2, 5/1, 6/1, 6/5, 7/2, 8/5, 9/4, |
| R3 | 1/4, 2/3, 3/2, 3/4, 4/2, 5/1, 6/1, 6/5, 7/5, 8/2, 8/4, 9/4, |
| R4 | 1/1, 2/1, 2/2, 3/2, 3/3, 5/3, 6/3, 6/5, 7/1, 7/4, 8/3, 9/4, 10/2 |

Ideas from 1/2, 3/1, 3/3, 4/3, 4/4, 5/2, 6/2, 6/4, 7/3, 8/1, 9/2, 9/3, 10/3 (13 designs) were retained by all of the evaluators and ideas from 1/1, 2/1, 2/2, 2/3, 2/4, 3/3, 4/1, 7/1, 7/2, 7/4, 7/5, 8/3, 8/4, 8/5 9/1, 10/1 and 10/2 (17 designs) were all kept by three evaluators This suggested that 30 of the designs would still have a good chance of being represented in the final idea list; only two designs were rejected by all four evaluators.

### 5.2.3 Stage 3 – Democracy in Action
The four evaluators agreed two sets of ideas to take forward. After this analysis there were 30 ideas that were the same from v1 and v2 and 11 that were different – thus 41 ideas were brought forward across the ten teams. From each team the evaluators then selected a single 'winning' v1 derived idea and a single 'winning' v2 derived idea. These ideas are listed in table 5.

## 5.3 Understanding TRAck
Reflecting on the evaluation of the TRAck Method, the three questions, posed earlier in the paper, are discussed here.

### 5.3.1 Inclusivity - To what extent does this method ensure that all the children's ideas are considered and valued?
It is clear that in this process, which was relatively lengthy, all the children's designs were at least looked at as each design was systematically scrutinized. It is possible that some ideas were not noticed and that some were lost, that will always be the case and can be attributed to either a poor articulation of the idea (i.e. the interpreter cannot see what it is about) or by the evaluator having already extracted 3, 4 or 5 ideas and the TRAck method not encouraging deeper investigation.

The team that carried out the studies in this paper, having previously taken a less rigorous approach to looking at design ideas, agreed that the process of TRAck had them all spending more time and more effort in considering the children's work.

**Table 7 - 'Winning' Ideas**

| Group | v1 'winner' | v2 'winner' |
|---|---|---|
| 1(4) | Shows green and red (1/1) | Display on a tea shirt (1/2) |
| 2(4) | A locket design (2/1) | A locket design (2/1) |
| 3(4) | The product bugs you on your phone (3/1) | The product bugs you on your phone (3/1) |
| 4(4) | Uses hypnosis to change behavior (4/1) | Uses hypnosis to change behavior (4/1) |
| 5(3) | Shake the device to get feedback (5/2) | Shake the device to get feedback (5/2) |
| 6(5) | Uses stickers on things that want tracking (6/3) | Uses stickers on things that want tracking (6/3) |
| 7(5) | The whole device turns red or green (7/5) | The whole device turns red or green (7/5) |
| 8(5) | Automatically switches off other devices (8/1) | Can spend points earned from device in shops (8/1) |
| 9(4) | *not able to select between four tied design ideas | Energy reduction targets are shown on the device (8/2) |
| 10(3) | *not able to select between two tied design ideas | Looks like a watch (10/1) |

By grouping ideas across the small teams, the TRAck Method ensured that each team was represented in the final list of ideas to go forward. Figure 5 shows the convergence and divergence (common features of design processes[1]) whilst each of the 41 design booklets conveying the participants' ideas were studied and up to 692 potential candidate ideas extracted, before reducing them down to 41 then further down to 10. This structured process attempts to be highly inclusive in that every design booklet was both considered (by 4 evaluators) and actively deconstructed into its components (candidate design ideas) before being considered for inclusion.

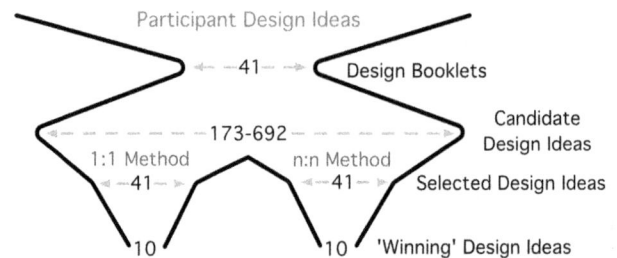

**Figure 5 - Convergence and Divergence within RAM**

### 5.3.2 Representation - How do the two models (v1, v2) for representation differ?
As can be seen in Table 7, the second version (v2), where one child / one set of children could potentially contribute more than one idea to the final 'round' resulted in a different set of ideas going forward. The idea of the t-shirt, getting points to spend, and

---

[1]  http://www.designcouncil.org.uk/about-design/How-designers-work/The-design-process/

the use of a watch would all have been lost given only the one idea per group. The case of team 8 is especially interesting as when judged individually (v1), the winning idea from 8/1 was that the device would 'switch off other things' but when multiple ideas were allowed from one design, a second idea from the same group 'to get points to spend in shops' emerged as a winner.

In more general terms, the process of ensuring representation in this way by using the TRAck Method did seem to lose something. Often the goal of design is to conceive a new and innovative solution and after completing the TRAck process the four evaluators reflected that they felt some of the most innovative ideas had been lost. This is particularly interesting as if all 4 evaluators had been in agreement on which these were they would, of course, have been the winning ideas. The TRAck Method therefore had a 'normalizing' effect whereby the *most* innovative ideas (as judged by individuals) may not have been carried forwards but those judged to have a high level of innovation by *all* researchers were.

### 5.3.3 Process - From the point of view of a design team, used to taking a much more holistic approach, does this method make any sense?

All members of the research team were able to go through the process. During the merging and agreement process there was much debate on what was being valued. It was evident that some interpretation was being applied but the discussion of this was in itself valuable and insightful. The team agreed that the TRAck Method ensured that every design had a chance of being in the final list of ideas and they also agreed that the method had them look very hard at some of the more farfetched ideas in order to get to some understanding.

The design ideas that were eventually filtered through were all useful. Specifically some of these have been incorporated into a functional product that is now in use. However, at the point of the evaluation taking place the design team also revisited each of the 41 design booklets to see what had been lost. The team discussed what would inspire design thinking from the sets of design ideas they had met. Three designs were highlighted as being particularly inspirational. Note that inspirational in this sense means they would possibly not be taken literally so for example 4/1 (violence) would not imply designing violence but the meta-idea of punishment was possibly a theme to take forward.

4/1 – which comprised a subliminal communicator, a walking tent, and violent punishment for bad behaviour.

9/2 – which incorporated room status controls, room control states, and always-visible data.

2/3 – a product on the underside of a shoe with a wristband control and a wired UI.

In thinking about 'lost' ideas the research team agreed that the process of listing ideas may have reduced designs to bullet points rather than allowing holistic thinking. It is interesting to note that from these three 'inspiring' designs, only one of these (9/2) was retained by all four evaluators (see table 6) but the other two were retained by three which does suggest some consistent thinking.

## 6. CONCLUSION

The TRAck Method allowed the research team to document how each child's ideas had been considered and also allowed representation of ideas from four different groups (two ages and two schools) into a single design brief. In those regards, TRAck supports a more inclusive and hence a more ethical approach to PD with children in so far as it makes defensible the process of idea use and also provides a means by which designs can be consid-

ered when many different children, with different ideas and abilities, are contributing. The TRAck method did generate some useful ideas and these could be incorporated into a final product.

The Scandinavian approach to PD, the empowerment of children, and the North American approach, the design of a product are thus both considered. TRAck provided a mechanism to help children 'climb the ladder of participation' by promoting inclusive and representative participation and will allow children to have more information in order that their consent could be more meaningful.

The TRAck Method, as a first attempt to provide for the tracking, representation and acknowledgement of children as idea generators in PD, enabled divergent and convergent consideration of all ideas through two democratic processes (v1 and v2) to begin an investigation of the impact of different forms of inclusion. The TRAck Method specifically sought to ensure ideas taken away from design sessions (for inclusion in later stages of a design process) were representative of all groups of participants and could be traced directly to a child's contribution. This traceability is important if, for example, a child wishes to withdraw consent from participation (and good practice for research governance).

Through this work some interesting trade-offs were explored, such as reducing the influence of the designer in order to ensure a more inclusive participatory design process where the designs that come through are those from the majority rather than those that are especially odd, and increasing the number of researchers involved in the design process to ensure a more democratic decision process.

It is hoped that the documentation of the case study presented here in its completeness will encourage researchers in IDC to consider how each stage of a PD process, the initial setting up, the use of materials, and the tracking of ideas can be reported.

Further work aims to apply TRAck with more unequal groups than in the present study and to further study the effects on the design process. To better understand children's empowerment, the research team will examine how the TRAck process can be easily conveyed to children and will seek to create tools that evaluate this effect on their understanding of participation. Comparative studies using TRAck methods and holistic design ideation will be considered in order to study what is lost from the design field when these democratic design processes are employed

## 7. ACKNOWLEDGMENTS

Our thanks to pupils from our two participating schools and their teachers, thanks also to EPSRC and the UK Funding Councils for supporting this research with grant EP/I000720/1.

## 8. REFERENCES

[1] Bjerknes, G., Ehn, P., and Kyng, M., 1987. *Computers and democracy:* A Scandinavian challenge Avebury, Aldershot.

[2] Blythe, M.A. and Wright, P.C., 2006. Pastiche scenarios: Fiction as a resource for user centred design. *Interacting with Computers* 18, 5, 1139-1164.

[3] Briggs, P. and Oliver, P.L., 2008. Biometric daemons: Authentication via electronic pets. In *Proc.* CHI 2008 ACM Press, Florence, Italy, 2423-2432

[4] Christensen, P. and Prout, A., 2002. Working with ethical symmetry in social research with children. *Childhood* 9, 4, 477 - 497.

[5] Churchman, C.W., 1968. *The systems approach.* Delaconte Press, New York.

[6] Davies, G.W.P. and Jegu, P., 1995. Ovide and teledemocracy. *Journal of Information Science* 21, 5, 383 -389.

[7] Dindler, C., Iversen, O.S., Smith, R., and Veerasawmy, R., 2010. Participatory design at the museum: Inquiring into children's everyday engagement in cultural heritage. In *Proc.* OZCHI'10, ACM, 1952239, 72-79.

[8] Druin, A., 1999. Cooperative inquiry: Developing new technologies for children with children. In CHI99 ACM Press, 592 - 599.

[9] Druin, A., 2002. The role of children in the design of new technology. *Behaviour and Information Technology* 21, 1, 1 - 25.

[10] Druin, A., Bederson, B., Boltman, A., Miura, A., Knotts-Callaghan, D., and Platt, M., 1999. Children as our technology design partners. In *The design of children's technology*, A. Druin Ed. Morgan Kaufmann, San Francisco, CA, 51 - 72.

[11] Friedman, B., 2004. Value sesnitive design. In *Berkshire encyclopedia of human computer interaction*, W.S. Bainbridge Ed. Berkshire Publishing Group, Great Barringham.

[12] Guha, M.L., Druin, A., Chipman, G., A, F.J., Simms, S., and Farber, A., 2004. Mixing ideas: A new technique for working with young children as design partners. In *Proc.* IDC 2004 ACM Press, College Park. Maryland, 35 - 42.

[13] Hart, R., 1997. *Children's participation: The theory and practice of involving young citizens in community development and environmental care.* UNICEF.

[14] Horn, D. and Salvendy, G., 2006. Consumer-based assessment of product creativity: A review and reappraisal. *Human Factors and Ergonomics in Manufacturing* 16, 2, 155 - 175.

[15] Horton, M., Read, J.C., Mazzone, E., Sim, G., and Fitton, D., 2012. School friendly participatory research activities with children. In *Proc.* CHI2012, ACM Press.

[16] Iversen, O.S. and Smith, R.S., 2012. Scandinavian participatory design: Dialogic curation with teenagers. In *Proc.* IDC'12, ACM, 106-115.

[17] Marco, J., Cerezo, E., Baldasarri, S., Mazzone, E., and Read, J.C., 2009. User-oriented design and tangible interaction for kindergarten children. . In *Proc.* IDC'09, ACM Press, Como, Italy, 190 - 193.

[18] Mazzone, E., Ivari, N., Tikkanen, R., Read, J.C., and Beale, R., 2010. Considering context, content, management, and engagement in design activities with children. In *Proc.* IDC2010 ACM Press, Barcelona, 108 - 117.

[19] Mazzone, E., Read, J.C., and Beale, R., 2008. Design with and for disaffected teenagers. In *Proc.* Nordichi 2008 ACM Press, Lund, Sweden 290-297.

[20] Mazzone, E., Read, J.C., and Beale, R., 2008. Understanding children's contributions during informant design. In *Proc.* BCS-HCI'08 BCS, 61 - 64.

[21] Moraveji, N., Li, J., Ding, J., O'kelley, P., and Woolf, S., 2007. Comicboarding: Using comics as proxies for participatory design with children. In *Proc.* CHI 2007 ACM Press, San Jose, CA, 1371 - 1372.

[22] Muller, M.J., 2003. Participatory design: The third space in hci. In *The human-computer interaction handbook*, A.J. Julie and S. Andrew Eds. L. Erlbaum Associates Inc., 1051-1068.

[23] Mumford, E., 1993. The ethics approach. *Commun. ACM* 36, 6, 82.

[24] Posch, I. and Fitzpatrick, G., 2012. First steps in the fablab: Experiences engaging children. In *Proc.* OZCHI'12 ACM, 497-500.

[25] Read, J.C. and Fredrikson, M., 2011. What do we take? What do we keep? What do we tell? Ethical concerns in the design of inclusive socially connected technology for children. In *Proc.* Ethicomp 2011 .

[26] Read, J.C., Gregory, P., Macfarlane, S.J., Mcmanus, B., Gray, P., and Patel, R., 2002. An investigation of participatory design with children - informant, balanced and facilitated design. In IProc. IDC'02 Shaker Publishing, Eindhoven, 53 - 64.

[27] Read, J.C., Horton, M., Sim, G., Gregory, P., Fitton, D., and Cassidy, B., 2013. Check: A tool to inform and encourage ethical practice in participatory design with children. In *Proc.* CHI2014 ACM, 2468391, 187-192..

[28] Read, J.C., Fitton, D., and Mazzone, E., 2010. Using obstructed theatre with child designers to convey requirements. In Proc. CHI2010 ACM Press, Atlanta, GA.

[29] Schuler, D. and Namioka, A., 1993. *Participatory design:* Principles and practices Lawrence Erlbaum, Hillsdale, NJ.

[30] Sinclair, R., 2004. Participation in practice: Making it meaningful, effective and sustainable. *Children and Society* 18, 106 - 118.

[31] Thang, B., Sluis-Thiescheffer, W., Bekker, T., Eggen, B., Vermeeren, A., and De Ridder, H., 2008. Comparing the creativity of children's design solutions based on expert assessment. In *Proc.* IDC 2008 ACM Press, Chicago.IL, 266 - 273.

[32] Theng, Y.L., Nasir, N.M., Thimbleby, H., Buchanan, G., Jones, M., Bainbridge, D., and Cassidy, N., 2000. Children as design partners and testers for a children's digital library. In *Proc.* ECDL2000 Springer Verlag, 249 - 253.

[33] Van Den Hoven, J., 2005. Design for values and values for design. *Information age,* 7 (2) 4 - 7.

[34] Van Den Hoven, J., 2008. Moral methodology and information technology. In *The handbook of information and computer ethics*, K.E. Himma and H.T. Tavani Eds. Wiley, New York, 49 - 69.

[35] Yip, J., Clegg, T., Bonsignore, E., Gelderblom, H., Rhodes, E., and Druin, A., 2013. Brownies or bags-of-stuff? Domain expertise in cooperative inquiry with children. In Proc. IDC2013. ACM Press, 201 - 210.

# Incorporating Peephole Interactions into Children's Second Language Learning Activities on Mobile Devices

Brenna McNally[1], Mona Leigh Guha[1], Leyla Norooz[1], Emily Rhodes[2], Leah Findlater[1]

[1] Human-Computer Interaction Lab
College of Information Studies
University of Maryland
College Park, MD 20742, USA
bmcnally@umd.edu, mona@cs.umd.edu,
leylan@umd.edu, leahkf@umd.edu

[2] Usability Lab
College of Arts and Sciences
University of Baltimore
Baltimore, MD 21201
emily@emilyrhodes.com

## ABSTRACT

Physical movement has the potential to enhance learning activities. To investigate how movement can be incorporated into children's mobile language learning, we designed and evaluated two versions of a German vocabulary game called *Scenic Words*. The first version used movement-based dynamic peephole navigation, which requires physical movement of the arms, while the second version used touch-based static peephole navigation, which only requires standard touchscreen interactions; static peepholes are the *status quo* interaction technique for navigation, commonly found, for example, in map applications and games. To compare the two types of navigation and to assess children's reactions to dynamic peepholes, we conducted an in-home study with 16 children (ages 8–9). The children participated in pairs but individually played each version of the game on a mobile device. While results showed that the more familiar static peepholes were the preferred interaction style overall, participants became accustomed to the movement-based dynamic peepholes during the study. Participants noted that the dynamic peephole interaction became easier over time, and that it had some advantages such as for dragging-and-dropping elements in the game.

## Categories and Subject Descriptors

H.5.2 [Information interfaces and presentation]: User interfaces – *user-centered design*.

## General Terms

Design, Human Factors.

## Keywords

Children, mobile, physical movement, peepholes, learning.

## 1. INTRODUCTION

Engaging in physical movement has been shown to enhance children's learning, for example, in gesturing while solving math problems [22] or learning new vocabulary [34]. Physical movement has also been incorporated into educational software with motion sensing technologies such as the Nintendo WiiMote [21] and the Microsoft Kinect [24].

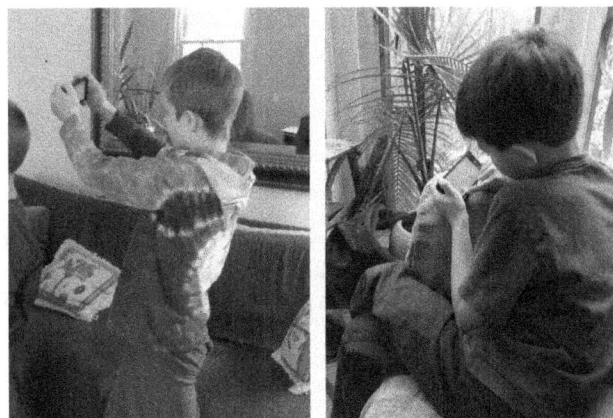

**Figure 1. Participants using the Scenic Words application to learn German vocabulary with movement-based dynamic peephole navigation (left) and touch-based static peephole navigation (right).**

We investigate how ubiquitous, off-the-shelf mobile devices can be used to support physical movement in children's second language learning activities. Current mobile devices can sense a variety of movement-based interactions through the touchscreen itself or with accelerometers, gyroscopes and even cameras. These devices are also increasingly accessible to today's youth: an international survey by the Groupe Speciale Mobile Association found that 65% of children ages 8 to 18 use a mobile phone, 27% of whom are smartphone users [19]. In the US, eight of ten children ages 5–8 have used smartphone or tablet devices [26]. This ready access to sensor-laden mobile devices gives us the opportunity to incorporate physical movement into learning activities, promoting the goal of learning anytime, anywhere.

Children's use of mobile device interaction techniques has been studied primarily in terms of stationary use. Focusing on the touchscreen, for example, studies have examined touch accuracy for tapping different objects [7, 5], issues children have with movement-based gestures (e.g., swipe and drag-and-drop) [8], and how children draw using gestural input with and without visual feedback [3]. These works noted a marked difference in performance between adults and children [7, 5], highlighting the importance of understanding and designing for children's interactions specifically.

In this paper, we investigate *peephole* interactions [18, 25, 35, 39] as a means of incorporating movement into a children's mobile learning application (Figure 1). Peepholes enable a mobile device to act as a lens into a virtual world. With *static peepholes* children explore a virtual scene by swiping the touchscreen to bring different areas into view; static peepholes are the status quo navigation technique found in many map applications and games. *Dynamic peepholes* are controlled more actively, by physically moving the device around as if it were a small window, while the virtual world remains still. While studies on peephole interaction with adults have explored performance and preference [35, 18, 25], to our knowledge no research has examined the design of such interaction with children.

We employed peephole interactions as a starting point to investigate the design of movement-based second language learning software for children. Our primary research questions were: (1) How do children explore and interact with static and dynamic peepholes? (2) Do dynamic peepholes have the potential to elicit movement in children's mobile interactions, toward our goal of augmenting learning activities?

We conducted a study with sixteen children aged 8–9 to compare use of a dynamic peephole interface (with arm movement) to a static peephole interface (touchscreen gestures only). To do so, we first designed and built a German vocabulary learning game, called *Scenic Words*, for a mobile phone platform. In Scenic Words, users discover words hidden in clouds in the sky and categorize these words by dragging them into labeled jars at the bottom of the scene. We created two versions of the game, one that uses static peephole navigation to move about the scene, and one that uses dynamic peephole navigation. Children then participated in pairs in an in-home study session that was designed to closely approximate a context where natural play would occur. For both types of peepholes, we looked at how participants positioned the device during use, how they explored the virtual space, their preferences, and how they performed on vocabulary recall and matching tests.

Results showed that the *status quo* static peepholes were the preferred interaction style overall. However, results also highlight the potential of using dynamic peepholes to elicit movement in children's mobile interaction. Participants became accustomed to the movement-based dynamic peephole navigation over the course of the study, noting that it became easier to use, and that it had some advantages over the static peepholes (e.g., for dragging-and-dropping elements in the game). The primary contributions of this work are insights into how children use dynamic and static peephole interaction techniques, how children think about each technique and why they prefer one technique over the other, and a comparison of vocabulary recall and matching in mobile learning activities that incorporate peephole interactions.

## 2. RELATED WORK
Many areas of literature inform the current work. We reviewed work on Mobile Assisted Language Learning, children's mobile interaction, movement and children's learning activities, and research (with adults) on peephole interactions.

### 2.1 Mobile Assisted Language Learning
Being fluent in multiple languages is becoming a critical skill for children in the US and elsewhere; the US National Standards for Foreign Language Education envisions a future where all students will be able to speak English and one other language to ensure they can communicate with a pluralistic American society and abroad [2]. Accordingly, Mobile Assisted Language Learning (MALL) is a growing field. MALL is a subset of M-learning— learning facilitated by mobile technologies that are potentially available anytime, anywhere [10, 29]. A review of MALL research from 2007-2012 found that these technologies have been used to explore many concepts in second language learning—such

as language learning outside the classroom and game-based learning— supporting the idea that MALL activities can enrich learners' second language acquisition [38].

Mobility of learning generates new modes of educational delivery: personalized, learner-centered, situated, collaborative, ubiquitous, and lifelong learning [37]. Kumar's work on mobile games with rural children in India used speech recognition to help them read content with understanding [30], and looked at how children voluntarily incorporate the use of mobile games to learn oral, written, and vocabulary concepts [31]. Mobile devices have also been used to support collaborative activities among peers with reading, improving collaboration and promoting motivation [32]. Educational delivery in MALL has the potential to aid learners in understanding a variety of language concepts.

### 2.2 Children's Mobile Interactions
The marked differences in performance found between how adults and children using touchscreen technologies suggest a need to study and design touch interactions specifically for children [5, 7].

Research on children's mobile device interaction has outlined several challenges and developed suggestions for overcoming them. For instance, in studying how to interpret children's gesture input on mobile devices, Anthony *et al.* [5] found that attempts to tap .25" square targets failed 30% of the time with children age 7-10. Touch accuracy could be improved by using larger targets or by increasing the active area around the target to allow slightly out-of-bounds targets to count as a hit [4, 5]. Work by Brown et al. [7] also noted that children had difficulty tapping small targets. Additionally, children in that study preferred to use individual strokes to create gestures, such as a square, rather than continuous strokes. We build off of these findings in the design of Scenic Words, for example, ensuring the touchscreen targets (clouds, jars) are larger than the recommended minimum size.

### 2.3 Movement in Children's Learning Technologies
Using technology to incorporate movement into children's learning activities can be accomplished in many ways. Mobile technologies that encourage users to move and explore their environments have been used to facilitate the investigation of scientific questions in real-world contexts [1, 28] and to bridge informal learning contexts such as parks and museums with formal classroom learning contexts [9, 27]. Movement has also been incorporated into shared storytelling activities to facilitate creating stories in varied contexts [14]. While these mobile learning technologies allowed movement, other research required the movement of the mobile devices in order for participants to complete objectives such as data collection [36].

Other learning technologies more directly tie physical movement to learning, which is also our focus. Antle [6], for example, explored how to teach children musical concepts such as harmony, melody, and rhythm through whole-body interfaces that create music. While this study was successful at teaching children musical concepts, certain interactions were not discoverable for some children and showed that there can be an initial learning period when including new movement-based interactions. Motion sensing technologies, such as the Nintendo WiiMote or the Microsoft Kinect, have also been explored for their ability to enhance learning. For instance, the Mathematical Imagery Trainer [21] leverages a WiiMote to teach proportional equivalence to children. In *The Potential of Kinect in Education* [24], Hsu discusses benefits such as interesting interaction types and

**Figure 2. The virtual world in Scenic Words, where users collect clouds displaying vocabulary words into jars displaying associated categories.**

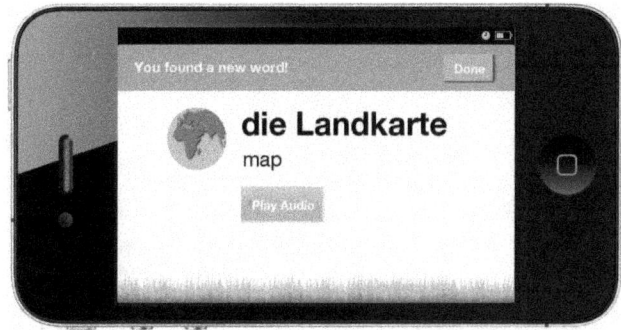

**Figure 3. The Word Card in Scenic Words, which appears when a cloud or bin is tapped.**

promoting learning via multi-sensory input as well as constraints such as large space requirements and calibration time. Xdigit [33], for example, is a gesture-based children's game for the Kinect whose goal is to enhance arithmetic learning. Dindler [11] explored using a Hydroscope, technically a large dynamic peephole device that users pushed along the floor to view a digital ocean, at a marine center to convey concepts about river beds and the properties of previously constructed fish. In contrast to these systems, mobile technologies (our focus) do not have large space requirements and users expect systems to work with minimal or no calibration.

## 2.4 Peephole Interaction Comparisons with Adults

Numerous studies with adults have investigated the differences between static peepholes (where the device remains still) and dynamic peepholes (where the user physically moves the device). Mehra et al. [35] found that dynamic peephole interactions were more natural than static peepholes as they allowed users to rely on spatial memory. Users were also able to complete tasks faster and more accurately with dynamic peepholes. Hürst and Bilyalov [25] compared the use of static and dynamic peephole navigation to explore 360-degree panoramic images, finding that dynamic peepholes were preferred and participants performed tasks better when using this condition. However, when participants were seated and unable to utilize the full rotation of the device, most opted for static peephole interactions.

Other results have been less straightforward and suggest that context may impact use of peephole interactions. Wenig et al. [39] conducted a field study of pedestrian navigation along a specific route, where participants used a static peephole, a dynamic peephole, or a static map image. While no significant difference was found between the two peephole conditions, they both outperformed the regular photographs. Grubert's work [17, 18], in contrast, found that peephole interactions alter between contexts. Static peepholes and magic lens peepholes, a version of peepholes that uses augmented reality to provide an overlay of information to what the user sees through a device, were evaluated by playing a find-and-select game at a public transportation stop. Findings in an initial study indicated that participants preferred magic lens interactions, while findings in a repeat study indicated that magic lens interactions were used and preferred less. The social context, such as one public transportation stop being a transit area and the other being a waiting area, could have influenced the participants' preference of interfaces [18].

While the literature on peephole interactions demonstrates affordances that may be context dependent, these interactions

have yet to be explored with children. Additionally, as children are still advancing through stages of development that are different from those of an adult, their interactions and preferences for the different peephole conditions may differ greatly.

## 3. SYSTEM DESIGN

We designed a mobile application named *Scenic Words*. The Scenic Words mobile application is a German vocabulary learning game designed for iPhone and iPod touch and intended for use by children ages 8 to 9. It is written in the Objective C programming language. We iteratively designed the game with children and built it to support the two different versions of navigation: dynamic and static peepholes.

## 3.1 Design Process

The Scenic Words application was developed using an iterative design process. Two Cooperative Inquiry [12, 13, 15, 20] design sessions were held at different points in the development process: one in the formative stage, and one in the evaluation stage of our iterative design process. The same children, ages 7 to 11, participated in both design sessions.

During the formative design session, the adult and child design partners worked in small groups to envision how they would use a peephole environment to learn a new language. For each group, three walls in a small room were covered in paper so that the virtual environment could be drawn, and mobile device outlines and art supplies were used to illustrate what would be displayed on the mobile devices as the virtual worlds were explored. Groups presented their ideas on the virtual world, how the mobile device would be used, and how learners would use this space to learn a foreign language. Design ideas from this session suggested that an application using peephole interactions to promote language learning activities should 1) combine realistic and imaginary elements in the virtual space, 2) teach a second language in small parts, 3) use a variety of physical movements, and 4) include game-like elements.

Following this initial design session we built the first iteration of the Scenic Words application. We incorporated findings from our literature review, such as making sure our touchscreen targets were large enough and increasing the active area, as well as the outcomes from the early design session, such as combining realistic and imaginary elements in the virtual space by having the children catch "clouds" in "jars".

We then presented the prototype application to adult and child design partners in a second design session, which focused on evaluation of a prototype within the iterative design process. Small groups were given mobile devices with a prototype of the Scenic Words application running, and were asked to give their

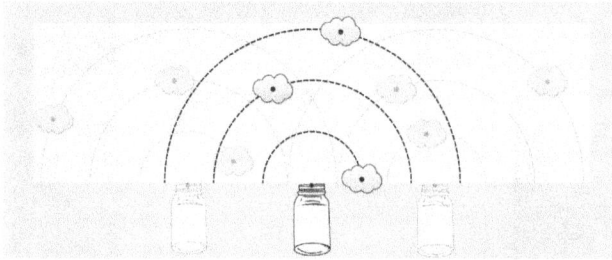

**Figure 4. To ensure that each user had to move clouds to jars from a variety of distances, clouds were randomly placed along three evenly spaced arcs that were centered at the corresponding category jar.**

feedback on both the dynamic and static conditions of gameplay. No direction was given regarding how to interact with the dynamic condition, and only one group was able to independently discern how to interact with the device to see the virtual space after exploring the application for about a minute. After an adult designer suggested, "now try using the app by standing and using your arms" there was a collective "oooh!" from the children, and the activity commenced in earnest. In addition to insights into how children are likely to explore the application and the direction they would need, the feedback from the evaluative session resulted in numerous simplifications to the application. Most notably, these simplifications included the removal of vocabulary word definitions because they were considered distracting and unnecessary in such a short activity.

## 3.2 Gameplay

The goal of Scenic Words is for the child to learn German vocabulary words. Clouds holding words are distributed across a sky and jars labeled with word categories (e.g., "school", "colors") appear on the ground; see Figure 2. Users earn points for correctly categorizing words by dragging clouds to the appropriate jars. For instance, the German word for "apple" would go in the jar labeled with the German word for "food", and a user's score would increase by one point.

Clouds and jars initially display only a question mark and are unmovable (Figure 2). To activate a cloud and jar, the user taps it to bring up a Word Card (Figure 3). A Word Card shows the new vocabulary word 1) in German, 2) in English, 3) with a picture of the item, and 4) with an audio clip of a native speaker saying the word. Once the user closes the Word Card, the now-activated cloud or jar displays the German word and, for clouds, the picture as well. From this point, the cloud can be moved and the jar can have items placed in it. The user makes a drag-and-drop interaction to move an activated cloud to a jar. The game ends when all nine clouds have been placed in the correct jars.

When the game loads, three jars (categories) and nine clouds (words) appear, such that there are three words for each category.

## 3.3 Navigation and Placement

To locate the word clouds and the category jars, the user must explore the virtual world with peephole interactions. In the static peephole version of the game, users swipe the touchscreen to explore the virtual world, scrolling the scene as they locate and categorize the clouds. The dynamic peephole version requires users to explore the same virtual space by physically moving their mobile device; touchscreen gestures do not scroll the scene. This dynamic peephole interaction was implemented through the use of the 3-axis accelerometer and the gyroscope that are built in to the

**Table 1. Pairs of participants were randomly assigned to an order. They were assigned either the static or dynamic condition first, paired with either word set 1 or word set 2.**

|  | Static First | Dynamic Second |
|---|---|---|
| Order 1 | Word Set (WS) 1 | WS 2 |
| Order 2 | WS 2 | WS 1 |
|  | **Dynamic First** | **Static Second** |
| Order 3 | WS 1 | WS 2 |
| Order 4 | WS 2 | WS 1 |

iPhone. Beyond these navigation differences, both versions of the game were the same.

To ensure that users would need to explore different areas of the scene and move clouds from a variety of locations to the jars, we controlled item placement as follows. Jars, corresponding to categories, were randomly assigned to the left, middle, or right position. The three clouds containing words associated with that jar were then randomly placed at three 1.2" (200 pixel) intervals from the top-center point of the jar, falling along three 180-degree arcs (Figure 4). The scene itself was 5.2 times wider than the screen and 3.1 times taller, where the device screen measured 2.94" x 1.96", respectively. The system was designed to shift the scene at approximately the same rate in both peephole conditions, that is, panning 4" in the static condition corresponds approximately to moving the device 4" in dynamic condition.

## 4. STUDY METHOD

To test Scenic Words in a context where we believe that children would use it in practice, we conducted in-home studies with eight pairs of children (sixteen participants in total). While we employed a mixed-methods approach, our focus was on use of peephole interactions *during* the language learning activity. Thus, this study was designed primarily to capture qualitative observations and self-report data, rather than precise performance measures of speed and accuracy in using peephole navigation.

German vocabulary was used for this study because courses in German are not available to students in the local public school system until high school, and we wanted to use a language with which participants would not have previous knowledge.

## 4.1 Pilot Tests of Method

Before we began the study, three potential methods for the in-home sessions were pilot tested with five children ages 8–9, three females and two males. We conducted three sessions such that the number of participants and presentation of the dynamic and static conditions varied as follows:

- Single participant
- Paired participants: Individual initial exploration of each condition, with each child having a device
- Paired participants: Joint initial exploration of each condition, with each child having a device

Having a single participant use Scenic Words and complete the study— including surveys, interviews, and the free recall tests— was an uncomplicated procedure. However, the feedback elicited from that participant during the survey and interview was terse and did not provide much insight into his interactions with the application. Testing the application with paired participants, where each child had the opportunity to explore each condition alone and then played again together, elicited more feedback as a dialogue developed between the participants regarding their use of the application. However, the relocation of the participants that this method required was logistically difficult and disruptive to the activities. Testing the application with paired participants where they played each condition together from start to finish elicited the most conversation between participants and with researchers, caused less disruption, and led to more unique interactions—such as using the device upside down. Accordingly, we chose this lattermost method for the study.

## 4.2 Participants

Sixteen children were recruited in pairs of two through advertisements to parents on listservs and through word of mouth. None had participated in the design sessions or pilot study. All children were 8 or 9 years old, with thirteen male and three female. All children had at least some previous experience using mobile touchscreen devices. Ten reported using these devices daily, while eight personally owned a mobile touchscreen device.

No children who had previous experience with German participated in the study, as German vocabulary learning was the focus of Scenic Words and we wanted to limit prior knowledge as much as possible. Nine of the participants had previously participated in second language learning activities, and reported varying degrees of fluency in eight languages including Spanish, French, Farsi, Arabic, Chinese, and American Sign Language.

## 4.3 Study Design

The study was designed as a 2×2 within-subjects factorial design with two factors:

- **Word Set:** Two sets of 9 vocabulary words
- **Peephole Type:** *Dynamic*, movement-based, or *static*, touch based, peephole interactions

To allow participants to learn new words when playing with each type of navigation, we created two word sets of nine words each (three words for each of three categories). The two word sets were then paired with the navigation conditions such that participants used word set 1 with dynamic peephole navigation and word set 2 with static peephole navigation or vice versa (Table 1). The orders of presentation for both factors were fully counterbalanced and pairs or participants were randomly assigned to an order.

The categories of German vocabulary words used in this study were chosen by consulting local curriculum for topic areas, such as "food". Vocabulary words that fell under the selected categories, such as "cheese" for "food", were then selected from a child's German language learning book [16] and were revised based on feedback from the second design session with children.

Each word set contained nine words: three vocabulary words in each of the three categories. Following the study, no statistically significant effects on the participants' recall or matching scores were found when comparing word set 1 to word set 2.

## 4.4 Procedure

Pairs of participants completed a single session that lasted from 45 minutes to an hour. Sessions began with a brief introduction to the project, a description of the Scenic Words game, and a survey on the participant's background. Parental permission and the children's assent were obtained, including for recording of audio, video, and photographs. Additionally, two researchers attended each session and recorded observational notes regarding the use of the system.

The static and dynamic peephole conditions were then presented in counterbalanced order. For each peephole condition,

**Table 2. Code set used to assess the participant's use of static and dynamic peephole conditions.**

| Navigation Styles | Expressed Likes and Dislikes |
| --- | --- |
| Attempt to interact with the background and cloud simultaneously | How long it took to complete the condition (like/ dislike) |
| Attempt to scroll background | Time to complete game being displayed (like/ dislike) |
| Tilt | Ability to drag (like/ dislike) |
| Body or arm rotation | Liked how easily words could be moved (like/ dislike) |
| Drag cloud and background separately | Disliked how tiring it was to complete the condition |
| Bump cloud against edges | Disliked Recalibrating |
| Unique interactions | Disliked Bouncing |
| Loss of navigation | Liked learning |
| Attempt to zoom | Liked Word Card elements |

| Device Locations | Social Interactions |
| --- | --- |
| Held up, free arms | Peeking |
| Held up, propped arms | Partner instruction |
| Held low in lap | Comparison of scores |
| Propped on a surface | |
| Flat on the floor | |

participants played the game twice, followed by a free recall test and a matching text. For the gameplay, we were interested in understanding the initial reactions of participants to the peephole conditions. As such, we provided no initial instruction on how to navigate the scene. If a participant became frustrated during the first attempt at a condition and remained stuck for more than 90 seconds, that attempt was abandoned and additional instruction was given. For the second repetition of the task in the dynamic condition, the instruction, "This time, I would like you to hold the device in front of you and use your arms to move around" was given to all participants, as pilot testing had shown that initial explorations of this condition varied and that this instruction was helpful in explaining how to explore the virtual space.

Once the game had been completed twice for a given peephole condition, the two participants were separated into different rooms and each completed the free recall and matching tests. During the free recall test participants were asked to write as many words as they could recall of the nine new words, either as pairs of words (German and English) or individual words (just German or just English). Participants were informed that spelling did not count, and that if they were not comfortable writing the researcher would write for them. The free recall test ended when the participant indicated that they did not recall any more words. For the matching test, participants were asked to draw a line between any of the nine German-English pairs of words that they remembered.

After both peephole conditions and associated tests were finished, each participant individually completed a follow-up survey, which asked about perceptions of static and dynamic peepholes and the Scenic Words application in general. Finally, the researchers led a joint semi-structured interview with both children regarding their attitudes and preferences toward the application.

## 5. ANALYSIS

Multiple forms of data were collected. As this was a mixed-methods study, the data were analyzed qualitatively and quantitatively. All user input on the device (*e.g.*, touch events, word placement, time in word card) and device movement were logged automatically by the Scenic Words software.

To analyze the video data, interview responses, and observational notes, we developed a code set following the iterative process described by Hruschka et al. [23]. A single researcher first reviewed two participants' data and developed an initial code set, refining it after discussion with two other researchers. The code set was then further refined after analyzing two additional participants' data. Finally, two researchers independently coded two more randomly selected participants' data, noting whether an interaction was either present or not present. Agreement was 100% across all codes with the exception of body or arm rotation, where one disagreement occurred and Cohen's kappa was 0.5. The final code set is shown in Table 2.

Navigation styles, likes or dislikes expressed by the participants, and social interactions were coded using researcher notes, relevant survey responses, and relevant interview responses. Changes in device position were coded based on the videos of the sessions. Videos were reviewed in full; however, due to technical issues for one pair of participants (trial 5), only 7 of the 8 sessions were videotaped and able to be reviewed. In addition to recording when and how the participant changed the position of the device in each condition, we noted whether the researcher had to intervene to correct the participant's position.

The results of the free recall test were assessed on a 0-2 point scale, looking at word pairs: 0 points for not recalling any part of the word pair, 1 point for partial recall of the word pair (e.g. the English word and part of the German word, just the English word), and 2 points for recalling the full word pair. Spelling did not count toward the assessment (e.g. groon in place of grün). Category words were omitted from all calculations as they were seen across both conditions, and were therefore more frequently encountered by participants in comparison to the word sets. Pairs of words on the matching test were marked correct, incorrect, or blank. We compared scores on both tests between the static and dynamic conditions using Wilcoxon's signed rank test.

# 6. FINDINGS

The focus of this study was to investigate peephole interaction in the context of language learning activities, rather than on measuring precise performance (speed, accuracy) with the two peephole techniques. Thus, while this section begins with a brief overview of performance, our primary focus is on physical device position, observation and self-report data of issues such as confusion and frustration, and interaction with the language elements of the game (e.g., word cards). Throughout this section we identify individual participants by combining the trial or pair number (Tx) and participant number within the pair (Px): T4P2, for example, refers to trial number 4, participant number 2.

## 6.1 Overall Time and Errors

Overall, it took a similar amount of time to complete the game in each peephole condition. Note that participant T2P1 is excluded from the measures of total time spent in the peephole conditions, time in word cards, and number of times audio was played. This participant played audio clips 329 times in the first instance of the first condition (static peepholes), which was at outlier at more than three standard deviations away from the mean number of audio plays for all participants in the first instance of the static condition ($M = 29$, $SD = 81.1$).

Participants spent an average of 3.8 minutes ($SD = 1.7$) to complete each static condition and an average of 3.6 minutes ($SD$

**Table 3. Comparisons of device position during gameplay.**

| Differences in Device Positions | Static (%) | Dynamic (%) |
|---|---|---|
| At least one position change | 21.4 | 64.3 |
| Dominant and final position match | 96.4 | 92.9 |
| Initial and final positions match, 1st use | 71.8 | 35.7 |
| Initial and final positions match, 2nd use | 85.7 | 78.6 |

$= 1.4$) to complete each dynamic condition. Participants spent more of their time reviewing word cards in dynamic condition, an average of 3.5 seconds ($SD = 4.25$) accounting for 26.2% of their time, than they did in static condition, which had an average of 2.7 seconds ($SD = 3.5$) accounting for 22.8% of their time. Thirteen incorrect word placements occurred in static condition, while seven occurred in the dynamic condition.

The time it took participants to complete each gameplay suggests the second use was easier to complete for both peephole conditions. The first use of static peepholes took participants an average of 4.6 minutes ($SD = 1.8$) to complete, while it only took 2.9 minutes ($SD = 0.9$) to complete the second time. Similarly, the first use of dynamic peepholes took participants an average of 4.3 minutes ($SD = 1.3$) for the first use and 3.2 minutes ($SD = 1.2$) for the second use.

The number of condition failures, where the researcher intervened after ~90s to stop the condition because the participant exhibited frustration or chose to stop the condition, was higher in the dynamic than the static condition: 8 versus 2 failures respectively.

## 6.2 Device Position

We examined how participants held the device during gameplay in each peephole condition to understand how participant behavior changes over time, perhaps with participants finding a preferred or optimized position over the course of the session. Videos were reviewed to code changes in device position, including initial, final, and dominant positions, with the dominant position being the position used the majority of the time.

We generally saw experimentation during the beginning of a session followed by settling in to one position for the duration of gameplay. Participant T7P2 was an exception with position shifts throughout gameplay in both conditions, but there was one position in each peephole condition that the participant kept returning to.

Gameplay with static peepholes was largely stable in regard to the position of the device (Table 2), with participants favoring positions where the device was propped on a surface or laid down flat on the floor. Six instances (21.4%) of at least one position change of the device during gameplay were seen. The dominant position of the device during gameplay matched the final position 96.4% of the time. In the first use of the static condition, initial and final positions were the same 71.1% of the time. During the second use, after participants had become acclimated to the peephole interaction required to complete the game, initial device position matched the final position 85.7% of the time. Three of the four differences in initial and final position of the device during the second use were changes from holding the device to placing it on a surface or the floor. The fourth was a change from laying the device on the floor to having it propped on a surface.

Dynamic peephole interactions required more exploration than static peephole interactions. Participants were much more likely to have shifts in the device position when using the game in the dynamic peephole condition (Table 3), and participants ultimately favored positions where the device was held up. There were eighteen instances (64.3%) of at least one position change during dynamic gameplay. The dominant position of the device during gameplay matched the final position 92.9% of the time. Researchers intervened twice to correct position, both during the gameplay using dynamic peepholes: once during the second use to remind a participant to "use their arms", and once during the first use when a participant kept having to move a device around a table, suggesting the participant push back her chair. That noted, in the first use of the condition, initial and final positions were only the same 35.7% of the time. The second use, after participants had become acclimated to the peephole interaction required to complete the game and received additional instruction, found that initial device position matched the final position 78.6% of the time. Position changes during the second use of the dynamic condition, after the participants had received additional instruction, fluctuated almost entirely between the two dominant positions: having the device held up with arms free, and having the device held up with propped arms.

## 6.3 Recall and Matching

For the recall tests, each question was assessed using a scale from 0 to 2 points, for a maximum test score of 18. For the matching tests, each question was marked as correct, incorrect, or blank, for a maximum test score of 9. For the free recall test, participants averaged similar scores in both peephole conditions: 5.4 points ($SD = 2.3$) with static peepholes and of 5.3 ($SD = 2.7$) with dynamic peepholes. For the matching test, participants averaged 4.1 ($SD = 2.2$) correct and .56 ($SD = .89$) incorrect answers with the static peephole condition. With the dynamic peephole condition, the average was 3.7 ($SD = 1.9$) correct and .56 ($SD = 1.2$) incorrect on the matching test. No statistically significant differences were found with Wilcoxon signed rank tests for any of these scores.

While no statistically significant effect on recall or matching was found when comparing static to dynamic peephole interaction techniques, it is encouraging to see how well participants were able to remember vocabulary from a new language after using the application for only a short time.

## 6.4 Preference Between Peephole Conditions

While survey responses to the question asking what version of the application participants preferred showed support for using static peepholes, a deeper look in to comments and use of the application suggest a less straightforward view of preferences. When surveyed, eleven participants preferred using the static condition, four participants preferred the dynamic condition, and participant T5P1 said he liked "both, because of the advantages and disadvantages of each condition".

Dragging interactions, which require a user to touch an interface element and maintain contact with the screen while moving the element, appear to be less complicated when using dynamic peepholes. With dynamic peepholes, participants could drag a cloud while viewing the virtual space by moving the device, whereas viewing the virtual space using static peepholes requires touch interaction. Although we did not explicitly ask participants about dragging interactions, six participants remarked on dragging the clouds during gameplay, the survey, or the interview. Five said that they disliked how dragging worked in the static condition and single participant disliked how dragging worked in the dynamic condition. T8P1, for example, terminated his use of static

condition saying, "I don't want to do this. I don't want to drag the clouds to the jars when it's far."

When looking at the overall ability to place words, and not just the drag interaction, participants were divided in their opinions. Comments about disliking how difficult it was to move words were mentioned by five participants regarding static peephole navigation by three participants regarding dynamic peephole navigation. Participants also expressed that they liked how easily words could be moved, which was expressed by four participants regarding the static peephole navigation and by seven regarding dynamic peephole navigation.

These conflicts may be due to unfamiliarity with dynamic peepholes. Dynamic Peepholes took the most getting used to, as evidenced by six participants noting that this condition was "easier the second time" or that they "got the hang of it". Participant T1P1, for example, ended up preferring the dynamic condition and he was quoted saying, "This is so much easier" even though, initially, this participant had some difficulty, saying "I'm stuck, can't really go up and down." T5P2 found the static peephole game easier to play because he "could move around easily and [he] knew exactly how to".

## 6.5 Interaction Styles During Peephole Use

Participants attempted to view the virtual world in different ways depending on whether they were using dynamic or static peepholes. When exploring gameplay with dynamic peephole interactions, participants attempted to use tilt or to scroll the background (as you would in the static condition), as well as variety of unique explorations. In the static condition, participants attempted multi-touch gestures to complete the game.

Overall, placing clouds required almost twice as many touchscreen interactions (e.g., taps, drags, swipes) in the static condition compared to the dynamic condition, with 735 and 385 total touchscreen interactions, respectively. One participant noted how tiring it was to complete the static condition. During the static condition, half of the participants attempted to interact with the background and the cloud simultaneously, using multi-touch gestures to drag the cloud while also scrolling the background. Most commonly, participants (8) would drag the cloud to the edge of the screen and use the bump of the cloud against the edge to scroll the background. Fewer participants (5) would drag the cloud partway, let go, and then drag the background separately.

During gameplay with dynamic peepholes, 87.5% of participants attempted to use a tilt interaction 71.4% attempted to scroll the background. Researchers most commonly noted these interactions during the first use of the condition, before the instruction to "use your arms" was given. There were numerous unique interactions noted by researchers as participants initially explored how to play the game using dynamic peephole interactions, such as turning the phone diagonally, upside down, an attempt at using 3 to 4 finger multi-touch gestures, and pushing the device backward and forward. Three participants disliked how tiring it was to complete the dynamic condition, such as T3P1 who said, "My arms hurt from holding [the device] out." However, other participants such as T8P2 noted the benefits of the moving condition, and preferred the physical interactions: "[Moving was] easier to touch [the cloud] and put it where you want it- like you're taking a picture."

## 6.6 Partner Interaction

We deliberately recruited children in pairs so that more dialogue would be elicited during gameplay and interviews. However, despite Scenic Words being a game that is used individually, partner interactions had the ability to influence the use of the application as well as convey items of interest. Additionally, children often play in social groups, even if they are using games intended for individual use. We coded for these interactions to understand how use may have been modified due to having a partner present.

Most sessions (6 of the 8) exhibited some form of partner instruction. There were verbal requests where one partner asked what should be done, such as T1P1 who asked his partner for direction on how to get clouds into the jars. There was also more direct instruction, such as participant T8P2 who played his partner's audio for him, or participant T4P2 who physically grabbed his partner's wrist during the dynamic condition to move it up and down and said, "look up". Peeking was noted in two groups, where one participant would look over the shoulder of their partner in order to observe some element of gameplay, such as how the audio was played. Game scores, based on points earned by correctly categorizing vocabulary, were displayed during gameplay and comparisons of scores between partners were noted in two groups, once as a casual remark and once as an expression of surprise that the partner was so far ahead.

Upon completion of gameplay the number of seconds it took the participant to complete the game was displayed to participants, causing some participants to feel as though they were in a race with their partner. Two participants in different sessions did not like time being displayed because it felt like they were racing each other as opposed to learning, including T6P1 who said, "The timer was like a race, so we won't memorize the words. It's not good for learning. It should be optional." However, five participants liked this feature, several noting their faster times between their first try at a condition to the second try, or the difference in their times between using the static and dynamic conditions.

## 7. DISCUSSION
In this work we investigated the design of a second language learning application for children called Scenic Words. Specifically, we investigated how children explore and interact with static and dynamic peepholes on a mobile device in an authentic context, and whether these interactions show potential for learning activities.

## 7.1 Incorporation of Peephole Interactions into Mobile Learning Activities for Children
We believe that incorporating movement into learning activities on mobile devices has the potential to benefit young learners, and that the results of this study support this notion. While mostly stating that they prefer static peepholes, several participants noted that the use of dynamic peepholes became easier over time, even with the short timeframe they used the application. This is to be expected, as static peephole interactions are more commonly found on mobile applications; therefore, users are likely more comfortable with static peepholes. Some participants also noted the benefits of using dynamic peepholes, such as only having to control the word with touch and being able to view the virtual space through moving. Using drag and drop interactions appeared to be easier in the dynamic condition. Given the interaction styles we noted, it could be useful to incorporate tilt in the dynamic condition and multi-touch gestures in the static condition.

More constrained measures, regarding user speed and accuracy with both peephole environments, would have the potential to provide additional information on how participants performed using the different interaction styles. However, we designed our study task to focus on language learning rather than interaction performance, and to measure performance with the interaction techniques we would need a more constrained task than those used in this study's vocabulary learning game.

Incorporating dynamic, movement-based peephole interaction into mobile applications poses challenges. Participants most often required additional instruction, the brief direction they were given during this study to "use their arms", to understand and make use of the dynamic peephole interaction technique to complete their tasks. This was reflected in how participants positioned the device during their use in each peephole condition, with device position being more stable when using static peepholes than dynamic peepholes. The tendency to resort to a single manner of positioning the devices also indicates that with additional practice with either peephole technique the mobile device may be positioned in a consistent manner during the entirety of use. Given this tendency it may also be beneficial to create virtual worlds that can be explored from a single position, such as the 180-degree scope used in Scenic Words.

## 7.2 Impact on Vocabulary Gain
One goal of this work was to examine if peephole interaction techniques, particularly movement-based dynamic peephole interactions, had an impact on participants' recall or matching scores. Although we did not find statistically significant differences between static and dynamic conditions on these scores, we are encouraged by how well participants were able to remember vocabulary from a new language after using the application for only a short time. We are also intrigued by trends that started to emerge, such as an increased number of errors in the static condition and a greater percent of total time being spent in word cards in the dynamic condition. However, to measure potential learning gains through using peephole interactions on mobile devices our scope would need to be expanded beyond a single session with immediate post-tests.

## 8. LIMITATIONS AND FUTURE WORK
We recognize that the study results are limited. We believe that these limitations are appropriate for an initial study, and that in future work many of these can be ameliorated. This was an initial study with sixteen children working in pairs of two, where we took a mixed-methods approach to analyzing our results. Future work using a larger sample size, a more equal distribution of genders, or more semantically meaningful gestures could lead to the ability to learn additional information, such as potential correlation between recall and matching tests and peephole type as well as more generalizable results.

Additionally, this study looked specifically at how children interact with static and dynamic peepholes when in their home. Given that prior work with peepholes have noted that context of use impacts how participants use the different peephole interactions, how children use peephole interactions may vary from our findings when the context is outside of the home. We hypothesize that how children use the Scenic Words application will vary from context to context; the use patterns we found in-home may be quite different from what we would see in schools or outside. Future work should explore how context changes how children the peephole interactions by investigating peepholes in different contexts.

Furthermore, the study method may have been a factor in our results. Participants completed each condition twice using the same word sets, and the familiarity with the vocabulary could, at least in part, explain why participants completed the second trial more quickly. Also, while we used immediate post-tests, full retention of vocabulary would need to be tested for at a later date, as testing immediately after the activity might lead to deceptively high recall rates. We also did not use a pre-test and instead asked participants if they knew any other languages and accepted from those responses that the participants did not know German. Future work should include a pre-test component as well as a delayed post-test component.

Finally, we recognize that limitations in the technologies that were used for this study may have had an effect on our results, as issues with recalibration during the dynamic condition and the "bouncing" effect of scrolling that wasn't completely smooth were noted by three of our participants.

Our observations suggest there may be other types of movement that could be explored in future work. The many ways children initially explored the virtual world using dynamic peephole navigation suggests a willingness to try a variety of interactions, such as multi-touch gestures, pushing the device backward and forward, turning the device upside- down, and turning the device diagonally. Again, since the dynamic peephole was a new interaction method, in contrast to the more familiar static peephole method, the relative success of the dynamic peepholes makes us optimistic in regard to future novel interaction methods.

# 9. CONCLUSION

In this work, we explored the possibilities of using dynamic and static peepholes on mobile devise to support children's second language learning. We found that participants completed the activity in similar amounts of time, preferring static peephole interactions but being willing to explore and becoming more accustomed to dynamic peephole interactions over time.

# 10. ACKNOWLEDGMENTS

We would like to thank the adult and child design partners at Kidsteam for their contributions to this work during the design sessions. We would like to thank Elizabeth Foss and Alex Kuhn for their help and recommendations on this work. Finally, we would also like to acknowledge the families, particularly the children, who participated in this study.

# 11. REFERENCES

[1] Ahn, J., Gubbels, M., Kim, J. and Wu, J. SINQ: Scientific INQuiry Learning using Social Media. In *Proc. CHI* (2012), 2081-2086.

[2] American Council on the Teaching of Foreign Languages. *National Standards for Foreign Language Education*. A Collaborative Project of the ACTFL, AATF, AATG, AATI, AATSP, ACL, ACTR, CLASS and NCJLT-ATJ. Web. 2014.

[3] Anthony, L., Brown, Q., Nias, J. and Tate, B. Examining the Need for Visual Feedback during Gesture Interaction on Mobile Touchscreen Devices for Kids. In *Proc. IDC* (2013), 157-164.

[4] Anthony, L., Brown, Q., Nias, J., Tate, B. and Mohan, S. Interaction and Recognition Challenges in Interpreting Children's Touch and Gesture Input on Mobile Devices. In *Proc. ITS* (2012), 225-234.

[5] Anthony, L., Brown, Q., Tate, B., Nias, J., Brewer, R. and Irwin, G. Designing Smarter Touch-Based Interfaces for Educational Contexts. *Journal of Personal and Ubiquitous Computing* (2013), 1-13.

[6] Antle, A., Corness, G. and Droumeva, M. What the body knows: Exploring the benefits of embodied metaphors in hybrid physical digital environments. *The Interdisciplinary Journal of Human-Computer Interaction*, 21, 1-2 (2009), 66-75.

[7] Brown, Q. and Anthony, L. Toward Comparing the Touchscreen Interaction Patterns of Kids and Adults. In *Proc. Proceedings of the SIGCHI Workshop on Educational Software, Interfaces and Technology* (2012).

[8] Brown, Q., Bonsignore, E., Hatley, L., Druin, A., Walsh, G., Foss, E., Brewer, R., Hammer, J. and Golub, E. Clear Panels: A Technique to Design Mobile Application Interactivity. In *Proc. DIS* (2010), 360-363.

[9] Cahill, C., Kuhn, A., Schmoll, S., Pompe, A. and Quintana, C. Zydeco: using mobile and web technologies to support seamless inquiry between museum and school contexts. In *Proc. IDC* (2010), 174-177.

[10] Chinnery, G. EMERGING TECHNOLOGIES: Going to the MALL: Mobile Assisted Language Learning. *Language Learning and Technology*, 10, 1 (2006), 9-16.

[11] Dindler, C., Krogh, P. G., Beck, S., Stenfelt, L., Nielsen, K. R. and Grønbæk, K. Peephole experiences: field experiments with mixed reality hydroscopes in a marine center. *Proceedings of the 2007 Conference on Designing for User eXperiences* (2007), p.20.

[12] Druin, A. Cooperative inquiry: developing new technologies for children with children. In *Proc. CHI* (1999) 592-599.

[13] Druin, A. The role of children in the design of new technology. *Behaviour and Information Technology*, 21, 1 (2002), 1-25.

[14] Fails, J., Druin, A. and Guha, M. L. Interactive Storytelling: Interacting with People, Environment, and Technology. *International Journal of Arts and Technology*, 7, 1 (June 9-12 2014), 112-124.

[15] Fails, J., Guha, M. and Druin, A. Methods and Techniques for Involving Children in the Design of New Technology for Children. *Human–Computer Interaction*, 6, 2 (2012), 85-166.

[16] Goodman, M. *Let's Learn German Picture Dictionary*. McGraw-Hill Companies, Inc, Hong Kong, 1991.

[17] Grubert, J., Morrison, A., Munz, H. and Reitmayr, G. Playing it Real: Magic Lens and Static Peephole Interfaces for Games in a Public Space. In *Proc. MobileHCI* (2012), 231-240.

[18] Grubert, J. and Schmalstieg, D. Playing it Real Again: A Repeated Evaluation of Magic Lens and Static Peephole Interfaces in Public Space. In *Proc. MobileHCI* (2013), 99-102.

[19] GSM Association and NTT DOCOMO *Children's use of mobile phones: An international comparison 2012*. Japan (2013).

[20] Guha, M. L., Druin, A. and Fails, J. A. Cooperative inquiry revisited: Reflections of the past and guidelines for the future of intergenerational co-design. *International Journal of Child-Computer Interaction*, 1, 1 (2013), 14-23.

[21] Howison, M., Trninic, D., Reinholz, D. and Abrahamson, D. The Mathematical Imagery Trainer: From Embodied Interaction to Conceptual Learning. In *Proc. CHI* (2011), 1989-1998.

[22] Howison, M., Trninic, D., Reinholz, D. and Abrahamson, D. The Mathematical Imagery Trainer: from embodied

interaction to conceptual learning. In *Proc. CHI* (2011), 1989-1998.

[23] Hruschka, D. J., Schwartz, D., John, D. C. S., Picone-Decaro, E., Jenkins, R. A. and Carey, J. W. Reliability in coding open-ended data: Lessons learned from HIV behavioral research. *Field Methods*, 16, 3 (2004), 307-331.

[24] Hsu, H. The Potential of Kinect in Education. *International Journal of Information and Education Technology*, 1, 5 (December 2011).

[25] Hürst, W. and Bilyalov, T. Dynamic versus Static Peephole Navigation of VR Panoramas on Handheld Devices. In *Proc. MUM* (2010), p.25.

[26] Kang, C. *Survey: For young children, mobile devices such as tablets, smartphones now a mainstay*. The Washington Post, Washington DC, 2013.

[27] Kuhn, A., Cahill, C., Quintana, C. and Schmoll, S. Using tags to encourage reflection and annotation on data during nomadic inquiry. In *Proc.CHI* (2011), 667-670.

[28] Kuhn, A., Cahill, C., Quintana, C. and Soloway, E. Scaffolding science inquiry in museums with Zydeco. In *Proc. CHI* (2010), 3373-3378.

[29] Kukulska-Hulme, A. and Shield, L. An overview of mobile assisted language learning: From content delivery to supported collaboration and interaction. *ReCALL*, 20, 03 (2008), 271-289.

[30] Kumar, A., Reddy, P., Tewari, A., Agrawal, R. and Kam, M. Improving Literacy in Developing Countries Using Speech Recognition-Supported Games on Mobile Devices. In *Proc. CHI* (2012), 1149-1158.

[31] Kumar, A., Tewari, A., Shroff, G., Chittamuru, D., Kam, M. and Canny, J. An Exploratory Study of Unsupervised Mobile Learning in Rural India. In *Proc. CHI* (2010), 743-752.

[32] Lan, Y.-J., Sung, Y.-T. and CHang, K.-E. A Mobile-Device-Supported Peer-Assisted Learning System for Collaborative Early EFL Reading. *Language Learning and Technology*, 11, 3 (2007), 130-151.

[33] Lee, E., Liu, X. and Zhang, X. "Xdigit: An Arithmetic Kinect Game to Enhance Math Learning Experiences." *Retrieved February* 14 (2012): 2013.

[34] Macedonia, M. and Kriegstein, K. Gestures Enhance Foreign Language Learning. *Biolinguistics*, 6, 3-4 (2012), 393-416.

[35] Mehra, S., Werkhoven, P. and Worring, M. Navigating on Handheld Displays: Dynamic versus Static Peephole Navigation. *ACM Transactions on Computer-Human Interaction (TOCHI)*, 13, 4 (2006), 448-457.

[36] Rogers, Y., Price, S., Fitzpatrick, G., Fleck, R., Harris, E., Smith, H., Randell, C., Muller, H., O'Malley, C., Stanton, D., Thompson, M. and Weal, M. Ambient wood: designing new forms of digital augmentation for learning outdoors. In *Proc. Proceedings of the 2004 conference on Interaction design and children: building a community* (2004), 3-10.

[37] Sharples, M., Taylor, J. and Vavoula, G. Towards a theory of mobile learning. *Proceedings of mLearn 2005*, 1, 1 (2005), 1-9.

[38] Viberg, O. and Grönlund, A. Mobile Assisted Language Learning: A Literature Review. In *Proc. Mobile and COntextual Learning (mLearn)* (2012), 9-12.

[39] Wenig, D., Nulpa, T., Malaka, R. and Lawo, M. An Evaluation of Peephole Interaction with Panoramic Photographs for Pedestrian Navigation. In *Proc. GI Zeitgeist* (2012), 23-32.

# Search Result Visualization with Characters for Children

Tatiana Gossen, Rene Müller, Sebastian Stober, Andreas Nürnberger
Data & Knowledge Engineering Group, Faculty of Computer Science
Otto von Guericke University Magdeburg, Germany
http://www.dke.ovgu.de/

## ABSTRACT

In this paper, we explore alternative ways to visualize search results for children. We propose a novel search result visualization using characters. The main idea is to represent each web document as a character where a character visually provides clues about the webpage's content. We focused on children between six and twelve as a target user group. Following the user-centered development approach, we conducted a preliminary user study to determine how children would represent a webpage as a sketch based on a given template of a character. Using the study results the first prototype of a search engine was developed. We evaluated the search interface on a touchpad and a touch table in a second user study and analyzed user's satisfaction and preferences.

## Categories and Subject Descriptors

H.5.2. [**User Interfaces**]; H.3.3. [**Information Search and Retrieval**]

## Keywords

Result visualization; Information retrieval; Search engine; Children; User-centered design.

## 1. INTRODUCTION

The number of children who use the Internet is increasing year by year [16, 32]. The German 2012 KIM study [32] reports that about 62% of the children of ages six to thirteen use the Internet, and 70% of those use search engines. They use the Internet for research related to their school activities (52%), for entertainment, e.g. online games (45%), and for information gathering related to celebrities (43%), news (35%) etc. According to [31], more than half of the children search the Internet mainly without an adult. Therefore, there are special search engines available that aim at supporting children during information acquisition.

In particular, they only retrieve child appropriate content in the WWW.

Another important aspect is the usability of those search engines. Search engines need to match the particular skills of children to increase their usability for this specific user group. The majority of the engines have a colorfully designed start page to attract children's attention (e.g. *kidrex.org, dipty.com, askkids.com, blinde-kuh.de, helles-koepfchen.de, quinturakids.com*). In every other aspect, existing web search engines for children still have a similar design as common search engines and do not always match the skills and abilities of children [12]. This may be a reason for children to experience difficulties during information acquisition. Not all children succeed in information inquiry and especially younger children experience difficulties [32].

We aim to increase the usability of web search engines for children. Therefore, we explore alternative ways to visualize search results for children and propose a novel approach. The main idea of this approach is to represent each web document as a character where a character visually provides clues about the webpage's content. The research questions addressed in this paper are: How would children map a web document to a character? How to visualize search results using characters? Does the character approach improve children's experience with search engines?

## 2. RELATED WORK

Information retrieval for children is a broad topic. A survey about information retrieval (IR) for children in general, where all the components – both user interface and algorithms – of an IR system are covered, is given in [15]. The survey explains the specifics of young users, i.e., their cognitive skills, fine motor skills, knowledge, memory and emotional states and how they differ from those of adults. It describes previous user studies about children's information-seeking behavior[1], e.g. [2, 3](seventh grade), [4](ages 9-12), [25](ages 8-12), [26](ages 8-10), [27](sixth grade), gives an overview of retrieval algorithms, e.g. [18], and search user interface (SUI) concepts, e.g. [24], and describes existing information retrieval systems for children, specifically web search engines and digital libraries, e.g. [23].

Overall, there are several conceptual challenges in the design of search systems for children. Children require emotional, language, cognitive, memory, interaction and rele-

---

[1]Information-seeking behavior is user's behavior during the process of information acquisition; it describes how people search for information [22, Chapter 3].

vance support [13]. This means that children can easily get frustrated, have difficulties to formulate queries due to a small vocabulary and errors in spelling, have difficulties with thinking abstractly, can process less information than adults, have difficulties with complex interactions and have difficulties to judge the relevance of the retrieved documents to their information need. In the following, we provide more details about the aspects that are in focus of our research.

## 2.1 SUIs for Primary School Children

Previous research suggests alternative ways for children to formulate a query like using a predefined term dictionary in *JuSe* [37], a set of tangible objects which represent the search terms in *TeddIR* [24], a visual querying interface in *Emma Search* [9] or browsing using categories represented by icons in the International Children's Digital Library [23].

Kammerer and Bohnacker [26] suggest an interface that allows manipulation of search query terms to explore alternative search result sets extracted from the original query. Thus, the proposed interface supports children by abstraction of their information needs in terms of keywords. *Coll-Age* [17] is a SUI that combines search results for children's web queries with additional child-oriented multimedia results which provide further relevance clues for children. Elliot et al. [10] and Glassey et al. [11] presented a mockup of the results presentation interface and used text size in a snippet as an indicator for result relevance.

To support children in interaction, the touch interface *ImagePile* [1] was proposed. It displays the results as a pile of images where the user navigates horizontally instead of the commonly used vertical scrolling. This coverflow visualization can be operated with simple click-and-point interactions, thus, making the usage easier for children whose fine motor skills are not fully developed yet.

Another SUI is the *Knowledge Journey (KJ)* [13, 14] that was designed for primary school children. It supports children in different ways, providing emotional, language, cognitive, memory and interaction support. KJ has acoustic tooltips, contains possibilities for both, searching through text input and navigating using menu categories, has a guidance figure for emotional support and a result storage func-

---

[3]http://blinde-kuh.de, accessed on 01.11.2013.

**Figure 1: 1st search result of the German search engine Blinde-Kuh[3] is shown. The surrogate contains meta information about web documents, e.g. the target age group in categories "S", "M", "L", "XL" for children from six to thirteen.**

tionality to support cognitive recall. KJ is also adaptable towards individual user characteristics allowing a flexible modiffcation of the SUI in terms of UI element properties like font size, but also UI element types and their properties.

To our knowledge, only the International Children's Digital Library [23] was co-designed with children (age six to eleven).

## 2.2 Presentation of Search Results

An important part of a SUI is the visualization of search results. Common presentation forms of search results that are currently in use are described in [22]. Usually search results are displayed as a vertical list of information summarizing the retrieved documents. An item in the result list consists of the web document's title, source (URL) along with a brief summary of a relevant portion of the document. This collection of information is also called document *surrogate* [22, Chapter 5]. The surrogate's content aims to provide relevance clues, i.e. help the searcher to judge the relevance[3] of the document before seeing it. Given a query, so called query-oriented summaries are provided, which contain text references to the terms within the query. Furthermore, query terms are highlighted to make them more visually salient, which enables a faster information access.

A summarization of preattentive techniques for visualization of information relevance is given in [7]. Preattentive techniques allow a user to unconsciously accumulate information before actively focusing on an information entity. They do not require much effort or attention of a user. Features such as the search results' position, orientation, color and intensity, size, animation, and stereoscopic depth have been discussed in terms of their effectiveness, comprehensibility, and visual interference and evaluated with adults. Based on the previous research, e.g. [28], animation, color and size are promising features for children. However, the usage of these features as relevance clues should be evaluated in future user studies.

Most search engines for children use a vertical list visualization of search results similar to common search engines. However, the surrogates of some search engines for children also contain a webpage's picture. Furthermore, surrogates in search engines for children may also contain information about rank, result's category, the target age group or reading level (e.g. see Fig. 1).

Previous SUIs for primary school children use three basic forms of search result visualization, i.e. a vertical list visualization of search results (e.g. *Emma Search*), coverflow (e.g. *Knowledge Journey*, *ImagePile*) or tiles (e.g. *International Children's Digital Library*). They also use a "standard" surrogate visualization as a block that contains a webpage picture or thumbnail, title and textual summary. To our knowledge, they was no research on how children would represent a webpage as a surrogate, what information they would consider to be important and how they would visualize it. This research is important to support children during relevance estimation. Therefore, in this work, we investigate an alternative visualization of search results for children with characters following a user-centered development approach.

---

[3]Relevance is a measure of how closely a given web document matches a user's information need. This judgment is done by the user and depends on different factors, e.g. his domain-knowledge, the context of the search, previously seen results.

## 2.3 Usage of Avatars

The idea to use characters for search result visualization is related to the usage of avatars in user interfaces. For example, the avatar idea was employed in music information research. Haro et al. [21] suggested to use a musical avatar to visualize a user's musical preferences. Musical preferences of a given user are mapped to the visual domain. Specifically, music genre, mood and other features are mapped to avatars head, eyes, mouth, hair, hat and instrument. Moreover, avatars have been used in SUIs for children in a role of a guidance figure that provides additional support for children, e.g. by spell checking [9, 13]. Children like to have a guidance figure, thus, an avatar creates an emotional bond with an SUI which increases children's willingness to accept its help during the search [13].

## 3. CHARACTER CONCEPT

### 3.1 Idea and Advantages

*Appropriate metaphor:* As proposed in [33], the idea to represent a webpage as a person or character is motivated by the fact that children often ask adults about information they would like to know. Vygotsky [39] describes this process in his social development theory. He argues that a child learns many important things through social interaction with a skillful tutor and social factors play a role in a child's cognitive development. A skillful tutor can be a parent, a relative, a person in the child's environment or another child, e.g. a schoolmate[4]. Therefore, information exchange between people can serve as a metaphor for searching for information on the Internet. Each webpage is a person that can explain some facts to a child.

*Visual clues:* It is also known that images better match the cognitive skills of children than written words [19]. Therefore, we suggest to visualize each search result as a character, where a character visually provides clues about the webpage's content.

*Motivation factor:* Furthermore, search result visualization with characters is playful and will bring children likely more joy than just textual labeling of search results. Therefore, this approach is a means of emotional support for children as positive disposition towards the system keeps them motivated.

### 3.2 Template Structure

We considered the following criteria for a character design to be important: simple and concise layout, adding features through layers is easy, cute and fun design.

*Simple and concise layout:* Characters can serve as a unique representation of a web document, i.e. each character is unique. However, this method is not feasible due to the huge size of the Internet. Another solution is to use a template of a character and map different webpage features to the template parts. In this way, a compromise between a characters' individuality and its adaptability for all pages can be found. By analyzing popular applications for children, a compromise solution was found. Nintendo has Wii avatars also called Mii[5] which are characterized by a template with a few degrees of freedom. All avatars have a sim-

---

[4]The theory of Vygotsky applies to pre-school and school age children [39].

[5]http://www.miicharacters.com/, accessed on 11.2013.

**Figure 2: Character development: design, rough drawing, fine drawing, vector graphics.**

ple 3D template which is enriched with features that make the figure customizable without large deviation from the basic template. Generated avatars look similar, however small face adjustments make them unique.

*Adding features through layers is easy:* A character template can be designed in different ways. The challenge in this work was to design a child-friendly character which is also adaptable. Therefore, we chose a comic look for the characters, similar to [21]. Characteristics of comic characters are easier to recognize because they are displayed superimposed [30]. Comic characters are a popular medium and well known to children. They have a simple look and bring both fun and game feeling, which is not achievable with realistic characters. Furthermore, we decided to create a 2D template of a character. A 2D template is simpler than a 3D one and allows the creation of a character with less computational effort.

*Cute and fun design:* In order to achieve a cute and fun design, we decided to use anime styles, specifically a Chibi [5] like character. Chibis' head size is large. It is equal to the size of the body. This makes the character look cute because of the resemblance with babies. The final process of character development is shown in Fig. 2. Vector graphics were created from the drawn pictures.

### 3.3 Visualized Features

The type of features that should be visualized with the character's help presents an open question. We propose to divide features into two categories: *explicit* and *implicit*. Explicit features come directly from the webpage's elements such as text, images, background color etc. Implicit features, on the other hand, have to be extracted from the webpage first, using diverse algorithms. Examples of implicit features are the webpage's topic, the age of the webpage (time of the last modification) or the webpage's complexity in terms of text size or reading level.

The number of features that should be visualized by a character presents an open question as well. The more features a character reflects, the harder it is to learn and recognize the coded information. According to Piaget [36], children in primary school age are in the concrete operational stage of their development. The concrete operational stage takes place from around ages 7 to 11. It is characterized as a stage where children learn to reason logically and have difficulties with abstract thinking. They can classify physical objects according to several features and order them along a single dimension such as e.g. size [35]. Children are also able to coordinate at most two dimensions of an object simultaneously [35]. Therefore, we suggest that the number of coded features for children of this age is limited to two.

# 4. WEBPAGE MAPPING BY CHILDREN

We conducted a first user study in order to investigate how children would represent webpages by a sketch based on a given coloring template of a character. Children's interest in painting was used as a motivation factor to participate in the study. Painting is known as an effective tool in the user interface development with children [8, 34, 40].

## 4.1 Tasks

We had two tasks. For the first task, children had to assign one or several colors to a topic. This information could later be used to decide on a colour coding of the webpage topics. We selected topics to support both educational and entertainment needs of children, as recommend in [28]. Specifically, we chose topics like games, sports, hobbies, leisure, news, science, nature, travel (geography) to also meet the information needs of children described in [29].

For the second task, children painted a sketch of a character in order for it to represent a specific webpage. For this, we selected web documents for children from different topics described above. Character templates and web documents were printed in A4 format. After studying the webpage, children drew a character that they would associate with the page. Children could paint as many webpages as they liked. Web documents were selected randomly for each child. We did not provide information about the webpages' topics to the participants. After each painting was finished, we asked the children to explain what they had drawn and why using a follow-up interview.

## 4.2 Results

The study was conducted in June 2013 during Magdeburg University Science day where the public is free to visit exhibits provided by the university researchers. This event always attracts much attention of parents with children. The children were approached and asked if they wish to participate in the study. Their parents signed the consent form and were free to visit other exhibits in the meantime. We used a large table in the hall for participants to paint. Children worked individually on their study assignments and were supervised by study conductors. Children used coloring markers and pencils for paintings.

18 Children participated in the user study, eleven boys and seven girls between six and thirteen (see Table 1). The first task was solved by 17 of 18 children. A six year old child could not solve the task because he did not understand the connection between a topic and a color. This conforms with human development theory of Piaget [36] that states that younger children have difficulties with abstract thinking.

The results of the first task show that the children could easily assign colors to half of the topics. These topics are nature, news, games and science (see Table 2). The children probably had differing associations with other topics and therefore the variety of colors is larger. In order to determine a color for topics with a small agreement among participants,

| topic | main color | % | total variety |
|---|---|---|---|
| nature | green | 59% | 4 |
| news | blue | 59% | 6 |
| science | blue | 47% | 6 |
| games | orange | 35% | 7 |
| sports | blue/black | 24% | 9 |
| leisure | black | 29% | 8 |
| hobbies | yellow | 29% | 10 |
| travel (geography) | blue | 17% | 9 |

**Table 2: Color distribution: 59% of the children assigned a green color to the nature topic, remaining participants suggested three other colors. For the sports topic there were two dominant colors that received an equal number of user's votes.**

we used topic colors that were chosen by a high percentage of participants (green, blue, orange). We assigned topics to one of the three groups (each group had a topic with a dominant color assignment) and sorted them by the degree of membership to education and entertainment topics. The dominant colors were interpolated on the remaining topics using a color gradient. The final color assignment is shown in Fig. 4.

For the second task, the participants were asked to paint a webpage using a character template. Four participants (among them also older ones) did not understand the task. One participant (thirteen years old) understood the task, had however no ideas what to draw. Furthermore, some older children did not know how to implement their ideas in pictures. In that case, children were given other webpages to work with. Fig. 3 depicts the most interesting paintings and the corresponding (German) webpages. In the following, we briefly summarize the explanations of the children regarding their paintings:

*Example 1 (Fig. 3a) Webpage about German family in Spain:* The colors of the character's t-shirt represent Germany and Spain. The blue head represents water [an island was mentioned in the text]. A green color was used because the text mentioned nature. The sun was painted on the pants because the webpage is about Spain. Gray color was used because of the mountains. "They are hiking in the mountains," the boy said [mountains were mentioned in the text].

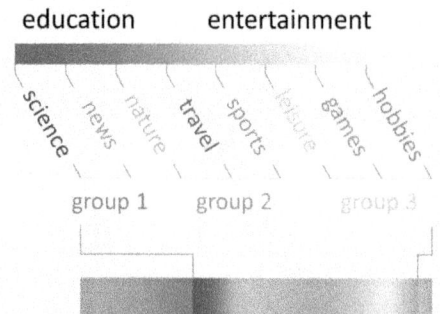

**Figure 4: Design of color distribution for topics.**

| Age | 6 | 7 | 8 | 9 | 10 | 11 | 12 | 13 | # | ∅age |
|---|---|---|---|---|---|---|---|---|---|---|
| Girls | 0 | 1 | 1 | 2 | 0 | 1 | 2 | 0 | 7 | 9,71 |
| Boys | 1 | 0 | 2 | 1 | 2 | 3 | 0 | 2 | 11 | 10 |
| Overall | 1 | 1 | 3 | 3 | 2 | 4 | 2 | 2 | 18 | 9,89 |

**Table 1: Demographic data of participants.**

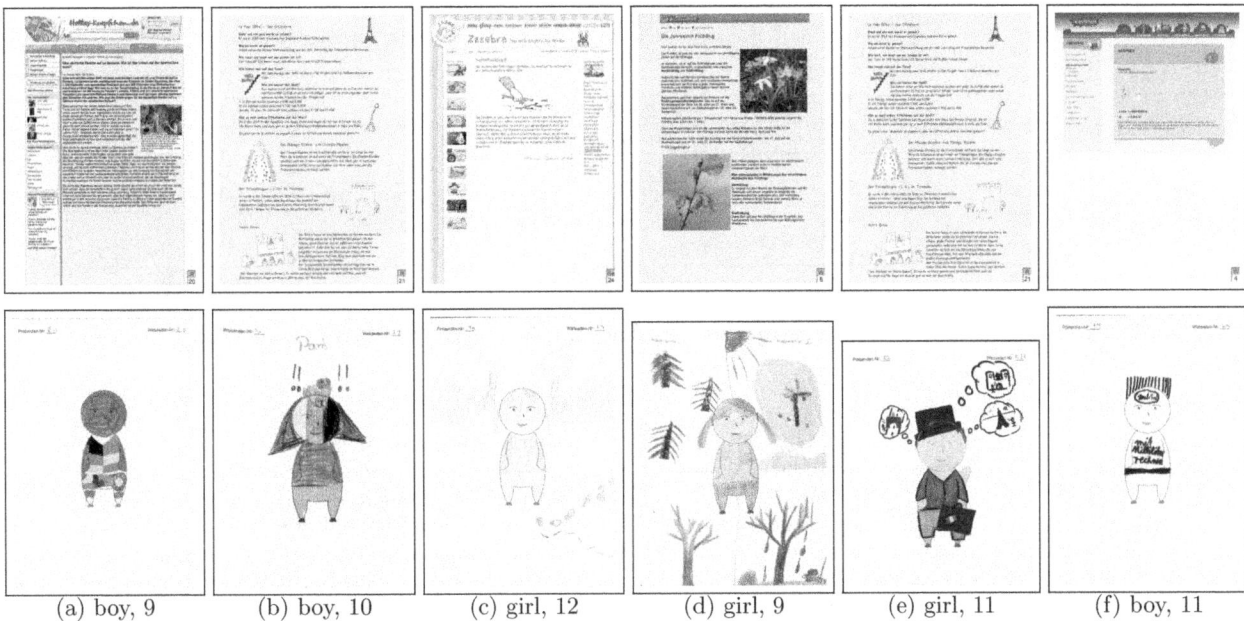

| (a) boy, 9 | (b) boy, 10 | (c) girl, 12 | (d) girl, 9 | (e) girl, 11 | (f) boy, 11 |

**Figure 3: Preliminary study: most interesting children's paintings and corresponding (German) webpages for children: story about German family in Spain, sightseeing in Paris, scavenger hunt, spring season, sightseeing in Paris, math.**

*Example 2 (Fig. 3b) Webpage about sightseeing in Paris:* The character has both "boy and girl" hair. The exclamation marks represent "information, a lot of text." The text header "Paris" was used because Paris is mentioned in the webpage's text. World atlas was painted on the head because Paris is "famous, known everywhere." "Blue (color on the t-shirt stands) for lots of information." "Yellow (color on the pants) because one becomes smarter." The boy also painted a brain to show that the reader gets "smarter and cheerful."

*Example 3 (Fig. 3c) Webpage about scavenger hunt [The website has a textual description of the game and a picture of a hand reaching for tree branches.]:* The character is a girl "just like that." The characters' clothing also has no special meaning. The girl painted trees and nature because the game described in the text is outside. She painted different paths and markings because the webpage's title is scavenger hunt.

*Example 4 (Fig. 3d) Webpage about spring season [The website has a text about spring and the beginning of spring and two images of snowdrop flower and pussy-willow]:* The girl painted four seasons as the character's background. The character is a girl because of "personal" reasons.

*Example 5 (Fig. 3e) Webpage about sightseeing in Paris:* The character has a skin color and hair "like a normal person." The character wears a blue jacket and jeans like "normal people". The character is "going to Paris." It has one baguette because a baguette is "typical for France." It also has a bag because one needs a bag for travelling. The french flag is painted on the bag. [Baguette, bag and flag are not explicitly mentioned in the text and are not present on the webpage's images.] The character imagines what he is going to visit in Paris. That is why thought bubbles are painted where each Paris sight is shown. [The images of the sights are similar to the ones on the webpage.]

*Example 6 (Fig. 3f) Webpage about mathematics, milliliter to liter conversion:* A thought bubble was painted on the character's forehead "so that children know they have to count". T-shirt has a text "milliliters conversion" taken from the webpage. The character has "normal" hair and pants.

Overall, children depicted explicit features of webpages such as text and images and implicit features such as objects or colors which to them represent the topic. Interestingly, many children tried to humanize the character by drawing hair or complexion. A summary of depicted features and techniques applied by children is shown in Table 3.

22% of the children embedded objects which were directly mentioned in the text or were a part of a webpages' image. For example, a squirrel was added to the character's surrounding because the web document contained text about squirrels. 17% of the children also incorporated text from web documents in their drawings (e.g. Fig. 3b,f).

44% of the children used colors and 33% depicted objects assosiated with words in text or webpage's images. For example, a character's head was painted in blue because the text contained information about water, and a sun was painted because the webpage was about Spain (Fig. 3a).

28% of the children drew outside the character. 17% of the children painted the character's surrounding to show the context (e.g. Fig. 3c,d). However, the characters itself do not provide any information about the webpages. The information about the webpage was drawn around the character. 11% of the children attached objects and features to the character, e.g. a lightsaber to depict a webpage about computer games. One child embedded the character in a scenario: Fig. 3e shows that the character is set in the context of Paris and travel. Therefore, Paris related objects such as baguette, and travel related objects such as hat and bag were painted. Thought bubbles were used to show that the

| feature category | webpage feature | technique | N | % | age |
|---|---|---|---|---|---|
| *explicit* | objects described in text/image | drawings | 4 | 22% | 7,8,13 |
| | text | incorporation | 3 | 17% | 10,11 |
| *implicit* | associations with word or image | usage of colors | 8 | 44% | 6,8,9,10,13 |
| | | drawing of objects | 6 | 33% | 6,8,9,10,11 |
| | context | objects/features are attached | 2 | 11% | 8,10 |
| | | painting of character's surrounding | 3 | 17% | 8,9,12 |
| | | character embedded in a scenario | 1 | 6% | 11 |
| | meta-information | usage of symbols | 1 | 6% | 10 |
| | emotions | usage of colors | 1 | 6% | 10 |

**Table 3: Depicted features and techniques applied by the children (n=18) during the study, participants' number and age.**

character is going to visit different sights in Paris, a bubble for each sight, because the webpage was about traveling to Paris.

One child (6%) employed many techniques. He depicted meta information about the webpage in his drawing using symbols (e.g. to express information complexity in Fig. 3b). The child also used colors in his other drawings, e.g. to describe emotions about the content. He used orange for fun to signal that the web document is about games and blue for cold to signal that the webpage is about winter song lyrics.

# 5. SEARCH USER INTERFACE

Most of the children that participated in the study were able to depict a webpage using a character. This encouraged us to continue along this design path and to make some decisions about the SUI design based on the study results. For the first prototype, we concentrated on the design of the characters and the SUI layout. For the character's design we used the ideas from the children's paintings such as thought bubble, the inclusion of a background, the use of color, the characters' humanization with hair and complexion, and the collapsing of character accessories into the subject categories.

We also considered webpage features that children paid attention to in the study. However, as too many coded features are considered to be difficult for children to comprehend, we decided for a character to depict two webpage features: One feature used by the majority of children in the user study was the association with words or images. For association we used topics. Topics are a level of abstraction, e.g. a set "bag, flag of Germany, flag of England, airplane, bus, train" can be summarized as a travel topic. The number of topics is significantly smaller than the possible number of low-level subjects. Therefore, it is easier and faster for children to learn the meaning of each topic representation.

We used a dual coding approach to depict topics. The topic information is visualized using the colors which were determined in the first user study. Characters representing different topics have a specific clothing color. We also used the idea from the user study about painting a character's surrounding to show the context. Characters representing different topics have a specific background (e.g. Fig. 6). For example, a character that belongs to the "Nature" topic has a landscape with trees around it (as seen in children's paintings Fig. 3c,d). Thus, topic information is dually coded with colors and background images.

Another feature was a representative picture from the webpage. For this, we used the children's idea about comic elements such as thought bubbles. Each character has a thought bubble with further explicit information about the webpage's content such as a representative picture from the webpage (see Fig. 5a, left). In order to distinguish between different characters which belong to the same topic, character elements such as hair, glasses, hat, shoes, eyes and lips shapes are used. Thus, a particular webpage has a distinctive combination of those elements.

The SUI itself (see Fig. 5) has an input field for textual queries. Under the input field a category bar is placed. A category bar consists of eight topics which are visualized as boxes. Boxes transmit both background and color information at the same time. This makes it easy to associate each search result with the corresponding topic. The category bar also provides information about which topic the search results belong to. In case a topic is not represented among the results, the box is faded.

We designed two versions of search result visualization using characters. The first one, called Alice (Fig. 5a), is an analogue of coverflow. Coverflow was found to be the best choice for younger children [13]. The selected element is clearly separated from the rest and a user can concentrate on one item at a time, thus resulting in a smaller cognitive load. The second version, called Tim (Fig. 5b), is an analogue of the list result visualization and is meant for older children. A vertical list of surrogates offers a fast overview of several results at once. By clicking on the snippet the result webpage is opened in the same window. The same window was chosen to better support the children's navigation in the search engine and to prevent backtracking [13].

For the backend we used Lucene[6] to create a search index. Our index contained 311 web documents[7] selected from webpages for children to assure a high quality of search results. In comparison, other research used 60 web documents for children [13], the Bing Search API [14] with general web documents or no information was provided about the backend (e.g. [9]). Each document was manually assigned to one of the eight topics. We also used the Readability.com[8] API to process web documents in order to show them in a clean and readable view (common format, no advertisement) which makes it easier for children to read. Our application also works with touchscreen devices. We think that touch

---

[6]`http://lucene.apache.org/`, accessed on 01.11.2013.
[7]A subset of these documents (25 documents) was used in the first user study.
[8]`http://readability.com/`, accessed on 01.11.2013.

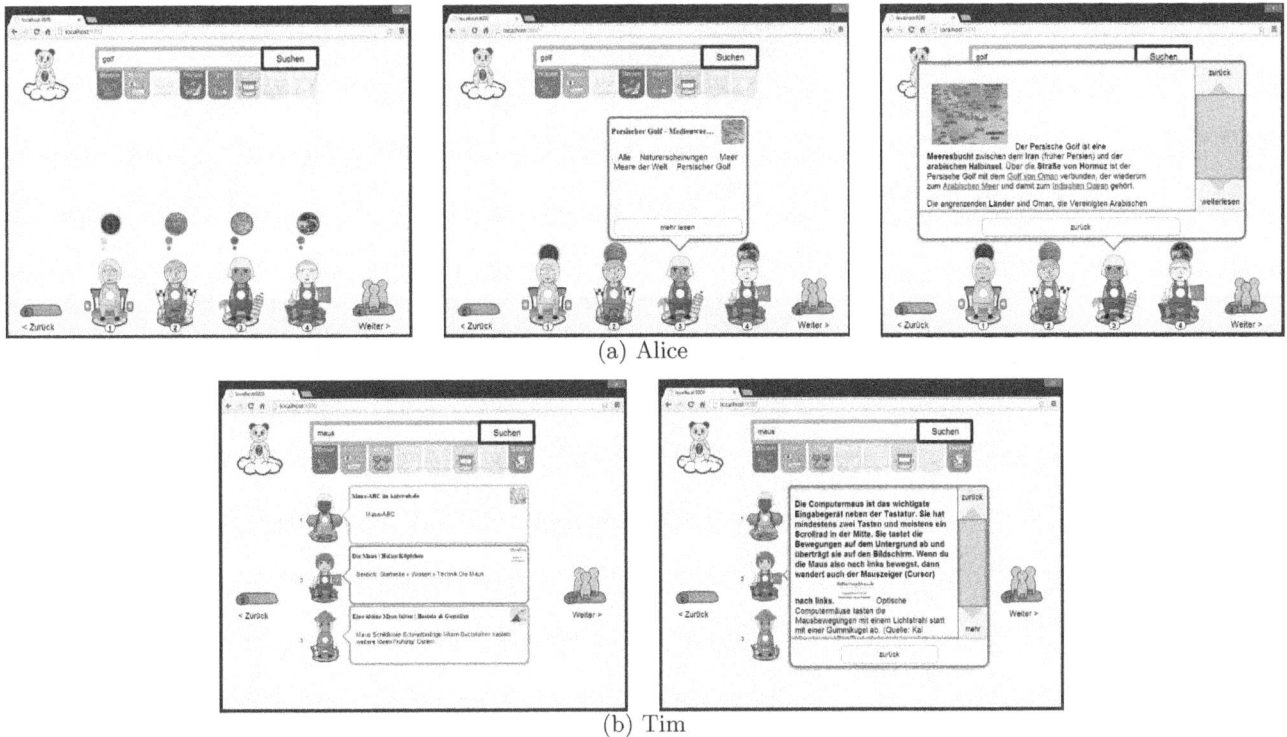

(a) Alice

(b) Tim

**Figure 5: Screenshot of the SUI with characters: a) horizontal result arrangement ("Alice"). Search for (German) "golf", first four results are shown (left), third result was clicked (middle), third result is opened (right); b) vertical result arrangement ("Tim"). Search for (German) "mouse", first three results are shown (left), second result is opened (right).**

**Figure 6: "Nature" topic design: character's surrounding to show the context, a pair of characters that represent two different webpages and a final character design.**

interaction is more natural for children than the usage of mouse. Touchscreen devices also become a part of our everyday life in the form of smartphones.

## 6. USER STUDY

The goal of this user study was to evaluate usability aspects of the SUI with characters. We had the following research questions: 1) Can children recognize topic information depicted by a character? 2) What is the children's attitude towards the new SUI? 3) What search engine would children prefer to use afterwards, with characters or the one they used before? 4) What search result visualization, Alice or Tim, do children prefer and why?

### 6.1 Study Design

Our user study was designed as follows: we used a pre-interview to gather children's demographic information,

their Internet and touch device experience. Then a lab experiment was performed using two versions of the SUI with characters, Alice and Tim. In order to reduce the bias due to the order in which the participants are using the UI, we applied a latin square design. Thus, half of the participants were asked to use Alice interface first and then to use Tim, whereas the other half did this in reverse sequence. Using each interface, children performed a task-oriented search, i.e. focusing on the completion of a particular task. In addition, we took notes about participants' unexpected behavior. After that, children were interviewed about UI features they liked most or disliked and what could be done to improve the SUI. Finally, we asked the participants what user search interface they preferred. The supervisors encouraged the participants to share their opinion to help the scientists build better search engines for children.

We used search tasks during the lab experiment as we believe a search task helps the participants to better explore the SUI in comparison to try-out sessions without a particular task. The search tasks were administered verbally. Children were asked to enter a pre-defined query for each task. The search tasks were designed to show the benefits of the visualization of topic information with characters: *Task 1:* Find out the location of the Persian Gulf (German "Persischer Golf") using the search query "golf". *Task 2:* Find out the names of three species of mice using the search query "mouse". The predefined queries were ambiguous. For example, in task 1, there were results about golf as a game and golf as a bay. Knowing the result topic, one was able to determine the relevance of a search result in a more efficient way. After a child entered a query, he or she was also asked to assign each of the first three search results to one of the eight topics.

Two touch devices were used in the user study, an Apple iPad and a 30-inch touchscreen tabletop Microsoft Surface 1.0. Each participant performed a lab experiment individually, either using the touchpad or the touch table. Children were randomly assigned to one of the devices. For efficiency reasons we conducted experiments on both devices in parallel with a supervisor each. The session lasted on average 30 minutes.

*Participants:* The study was conducted in July 2013 during children's university days. 22 children participated in the user study, twelve boys and ten girls between six and twelve (see Table 4).

| Age | 6 | 7 | 8 | 9 | 10 | 11 | 12 | # | ∅age |
|---|---|---|---|---|---|---|---|---|---|
| Girls | 0 | 2 | 2 | 1 | 2 | 4 | 1 | 12 | 9,58 |
| Boys | 2 | 3 | 2 | 1 | 0 | 2 | 0 | 10 | 8 |
| Overall | 2 | 5 | 4 | 2 | 2 | 6 | 1 | 22 | 8,86 |

**Table 4: Demographic data of participants.**

The distribution according to the frequency of the Internet usage is similar to the one in [32] In our study, 51% of six and seven year old children use the Internet very seldom or did not use it at all, whereas 88% of older children use the Internet at least once a week. However, in our study, we had more younger children who had Internet experience than in [32]. 68% of the children use the Internet without supervision. The distribution is uniform over the various age groups. Children use the Internet mostly to play online games (68%) and search for information mainly regarding homework (36%). In order to search for information, 68% of the children use Google.de, 23% use the search engine for children Blinde-Kuh.de. Less than 10% of the children also mentioned the search engines for children FragFinn.de and Helles-Koepfchen.de. Participants were familiar with touch devices: 68% of the children had used a touch device before, among them 50% of the six and seven year old children.

## 6.2 Study Results

*Character mapping:* The children were asked to assign each of the first three search results to one of the eight topics. In total, there were six search results with different topics given two interface versions and tasks. The largest recognition rate was 90%, i.e. 90% of the children correctly recognized that a search result belonged to the sports or travel topic. The leisure topic had the smallest recognition rate, it was recognized by 50% of the children. We observed, however, a positive learning effect: Using the second interface, three characters from the other three topics were correctly identified by all 22 subjects and the maximum error rate was only 25%. We noticed that the characters helped the children to be more efficient. Especially in the first task, they skipped the first characters with the wrong topic and directly selected the right result. However, more accurate data should be collected in the future.

*User satisfaction:* 76% of the children assessed our SUI with characters as easy to use. The rest of the participants (six and seven year old) gave a negative assessment because they had difficulties with reading texts and had to read too much. Younger children had difficulties with reading and

supervisors had to help them by reading the texts for them. Therefore, a text-to-speech function should be provided for those children. One twelve year old child wished that the results were sorted by the topic. He told us that he had attention difficulties (ADHS). The children assessed the arrangement of the elements on the screen (on a five-point scale[9]) as very good (29%) and good (57%). The Alice layout was criticized because too much free space was not used. The children assessed the presentation of results with characters (on a five-point scale) as very good (43%) and good (52%). The children assessed the design of the characters (on a five-point scale) as very good (52%) and good (33%). However, the participants opinion was divided. Whereas the younger children found the figures rather "funny" and "nice", the older participants would have preferred "more professional" figures and assessed the used ones as "odd". The children assessed the characters as being very helpful (57%) and helpful (24%) in topic recognition (on a five-point scale).

*Search engine preferences:* The new SUI received a positive response: 50% of the six and seven year old, 67% of the eight and nine year old, and 11% of the children between ten and twelve found it to better than the ones they used before. The rest of the participants between six and nine were unsure or found both to be equally good. Only the children between ten and twelve appeared to be more biased towards the conventional search engine Google (44%). However, the only explanation we received after asking for the preference reasons was "because Goolge is cool."

We also experienced that children have associated the search user interface with the used device or the search task difficulty, indicating the lack of abstraction. For the usability questions, supervisors had to emphasize the fact that children were asked about the SUI and not the devices or the search task.

*Layout preferences:* Comparing the two layouts (Fig. 5) the children preferred the Tim (52%) over the Alice (24%) layout, the rest of the children could not decide. The results are summarized in Fig. 7. Against our assumption, even younger children (six and seven year old) had a preference towards the Tim (33%) over the Alice (17%). However, 50% of the children were uncertain. The children did not like that in Alice they had to do one extra click to get to the webpage content. They preferred to see the textual summary right away and to be able to view several results at once as in the Tim layout. "One sees a bit of text right away and can have a look (at the web page) straight away." Children who chose the Alice liked the layout simplicity and visual attractiveness. Alice is "lovely", "easier", "does not have as much text (as Tim)".

*Touch and Devices:* Participants who used the Apple iPad rated search tasks to be more difficult than the ones who used the Microsoft Surface, especially for the second search task (iPad, 25% and Surface, 70% of the children found the task to be easy). For the second search task, one had to do more navigation effort of going to the next result pages in contrast to the first task, where the answer could already be found on the first result page. The screen size of the iPad is smaller than the one of the Microsoft Surface and it is harder to read the coded topic information. 86% of the children found the browsing of the search results to be easy.

---

[9]We used a Likert scale from very good to very bad. Each scale was visualized with smileys. This "Smileyometer" [38] was shown to the participants.

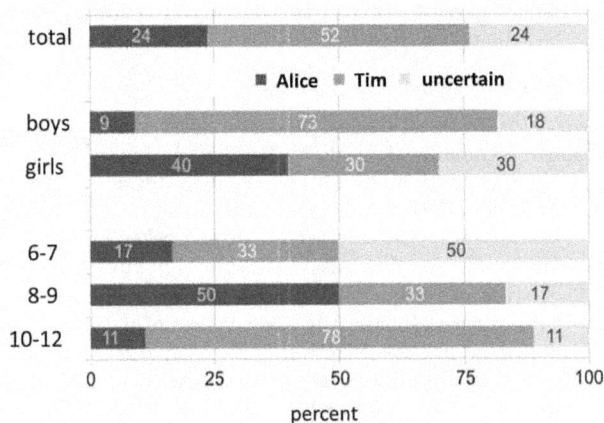

**Figure 7: Layout preferences grouped by gender and age: Alice versus Tim search result arrangement.**

Only some participants who used the iPad found it to be hard (however without explanation). We suppose that the small screen size of the iPad could have a negative impact on the result browsing. 81% of the participants found touch usage to be easy. Children who found touch to be difficult were between six and eight, told us however they already used touch devices before.

## 7. DISCUSSION

Both user studies (Sect. 4 and Sect. 6) show the potential of search result visualization with characters. We were able to determine children's view on web pages, what features of a web page are important for children and how they would visualize them. This takes us a step further in the direction to support children in relevance estimation described in [13], i.e. help children judge the relevance of a document based on its surrogate. The results of the second study indicate that the SUI we developed is mostly preferred by eight and nine year old children. We determined advantages and disadvantages of two possible layouts for search results, and a stronger preference towards the Tim layout.

This work has also some limitations. We used a wide age range of children in our studies. However, it helped us to determine the specific age of a target group that would use our SUI (eight and nine year old children). We can focus on these children in the future. We also left out the evaluation of the effectiveness of our SUI. We saw some indicators of higher effectiveness (children skipped irrelevant results without opening the web pages). However, a comparative user study to investigate children's performance using a SUI with characters and one without should be conducted.

Overall, the result visualization with characters presents many opportunities for information retrieval: Besides search result visualization, a character can be used in a query by example scenario (see [6, 20]), where the character represents an abstract search query. One can use a library for character's clothing, objects etc. for the user to chose from. A user creates a character using the library to provide an example for similar webpages he or she would like to find. Each feature of the created character serves as an abstract representation of a hypernym term for the query similar to [37]. Furthermore, a character can be used for personalized

ranking. A user creates his own profile using a character which reflects the users' interests.

## 8. CONCLUSION & OUTLOOK

We introduced a novel search result visualization for children using characters. The idea of this technique is to represent each web document as a character where a character visually provides clues about the web document's content. We believe that this technique has several advantages for children such as appropriate metaphor for a person a child can get answers from, visual clues are better than textual for children to comprehend, and a playful view is supposed to bring children more fun. Following a user-centered development approach, we first studied what webpage features children would depict using a given sketch of a character and how they would do this. We also showed how characters can be incorporated in a search user interface. We evaluated children's satisfaction while using the SUI with characters in a second user study and got promising results. In the future, it is also of interest to extend the number of depicted webpage features, e.g. by adding text complexity.

## 9. ACKNOWLEDGMENTS

We would like to thank all participants of the user study. We are very thankful to the reviewers for their appropriate and constructive suggestions on how to improve the paper.

## 10. REFERENCES

[1] S. Akkersdijk, M. Brandon, H. Jochmann-Mannak, D. Hiemstra, and T. Huibers. ImagePile: an Alternative for Vertical Results Lists of IR-Systems. *Technical Report TR-CTIT-11-11, University of Twente*, (ISSN 1381-3625), 2011.

[2] D. Bilal. Children's use of the yahooligans! web search engine: I. cognitive, physical, and affective behaviors on fact-based search tasks. *Journal of the American society for information science*, 51(7):646–665, 2000.

[3] D. Bilal and J. Kirby. Differences and similarities in information seeking: children and adults as Web users. *Inf. Processing & Management*, 38(5):649–670, 2002.

[4] C. Borgman, S. Hirsh, V. Walter, and A. Gallagher. Children's searching behavior on browsing and keyword online catalogs: the Science Library Catalog project. *J. of the American Society for Information Science*, 46(9):663–684, 1995.

[5] R. E. Brenner. *Understanding Manga and Anime*. Greenwood Publishing Group, 2007.

[6] N.-S. Chang and K.-S. Fu. Query-by-pictorial-example. *Software Engineering, IEEE Transactions on*, (6):519–524, 1980.

[7] M. Deller, A. Ebert, M. Bender, S. Agne, and H. Barthel. Preattentive visualization of information relevance. In *Proc. of the international workshop on Human-centered multimedia*, pages 47–56. ACM, 2007.

[8] J. Dinet and M. Kitajima. "draw me the web": impact of mental model of the web on information search performance of young users. In *23rd French Speaking Conference on Human-Computer Interaction*, 2011.

[9] C. Eickhoff, L. Azzopardi, D. Hiemstra, F. de Jong, A. de Vries, D. Dowie, S. Duarte, R. Glassey, K. Gyllstrom, F. Kruisinga, et al. Emse: Initial

evaluation of a child-friendly medical search system. In *IIiX Symposium*, 2012.

[10] D. Elliot, L. Azzopardi, R. Glassey, and T. Polajnar. Filtering and finding for children. In *Proc. of the ACM SIGIR Conf. on Research and Development in Information Retrieval, Geneva, Switzerland*, 2010.

[11] R. Glassey, D. Elliott, T. Polajnar, and L. Azzopardi. Interaction-based information filtering for children. In *Proc. of the IIiX Symposium*, pages 329–334. ACM, 2010.

[12] T. Gossen, J. Hempel, and A. Nürnberger. Find it if you can: usability case study of search engines for young users. *Personal and Ubiquitous Computing*, 17(8):1593–1603, 2013.

[13] T. Gossen, M. Nitsche, and A. Nürnberger. Knowledge journey: A web search interface for young users. In *Proc. of the Sixth Symposium on HCIR*. ACM, 2012.

[14] T. Gossen, M. Nitsche, J. Vos, and A. Nürnberger. Adaptation of a search user interface towards user needs - a prototype study with children & adults. In *Proc. of the 7th annual Symposium on HCIR*. ACM, 2013.

[15] T. Gossen and A. Nürnberger. Specifics of information retrieval for young users: A survey. *Inf. Processing & Management*, 49(4):739–756, 2013.

[16] A. Gutnick, M. Robb, L. Takeuchi, J. Kotler, L. Bernstein, and M. Levine. Always connected: The new digital media habits of young children. Technical report, The Joan Ganz Cooney Center at Sesame Workshop, 2011.

[17] K. Gyllstrom and M. Moens. A picture is worth a thousand search results: finding child-oriented multimedia results with collAge. In *Proc. of the 33rd international ACM SIGIR conf. on Research and development in information retrieval*, pages 731–732. ACM, 2010.

[18] K. Gyllstrom and M.-F. Moens. Wisdom of the Ages: Toward Delivering the Children's Web with the Link-based AgeRank Algorithm. Proc. of the International Conf. in Information and Knowledge Management (CIKM), 2010.

[19] D. Hackfort. *Studientext Entwicklungspsychologie 1: Theoretisches Bezugssystem, Funktionsbereiche, Interventionsmöglichkeiten*. Vandenhoeck & Ruprecht, 2003.

[20] H. Harb and L. Chen. A query by example music retrieval algorithm. In *Proc. of the 4th European Workshop on Image Analysis for Multimedia Interactive Services*, pages 122–128, 2003.

[21] M. Haro, A. Xambó, F. Fuhrmann, D. Bogdanov, E. Gómez, and P. Herrera. The musical avatar: a visualization of musical preferences by means of audio content description. In *Proc. of the 5th Audio Mostly Conf.: A Conference on Interaction with Sound*. ACM, 2010.

[22] M. Hearst. *Search user interfaces*. Cambridge University Press, 2009.

[23] H. Hutchinson, B. Bederson, and A. Druin. The evolution of the international children's digital library searching and browsing interface. In *Proc. of the 2006 conf. on Interaction design and children*, pages 105–112. ACM, 2006.

[24] M. Jansen, W. Bos, P. van der Vet, T. Huibers, and D. Hiemstra. TeddIR: tangible information retrieval for children. In *Proc. of the 9th Int. Conf. on Interaction Design and Children*, pages 282–285. ACM, 2010.

[25] H. Jochmann-Mannak, T. Huibers, L. Lentz, and T. Sanders. Children searching information on the Internet: Performance on children's interfaces compared to Google. *SIGIR'10 Workshop on accessible search systems*, pages 27–35, July 2010.

[26] Y. Kammerer and M. Bohnacker. Children's web search with Google: the effectiveness of natural language queries. In *Proc. of the 11th International Conf. on Interaction Design and Children*, IDC '12, pages 184–187, New York, NY, USA, 2012. ACM.

[27] A. Large and J. Beheshti. The Web as a classroom resource: Reactions from the users. *J. of the American Society for Information Science*, 51(12):1069–1080, 2000.

[28] A. Large, J. Beheshti, and T. Rahman. Design criteria for children's Web portals: The users speak out. *J. of the American Society for Information Science and Technology*, 53(2):79–94, 2002.

[29] S. Livingstone. Children's use of the internet: Reflections on the emerging research agenda. *New media & society*, 5(2):147, 2003.

[30] S. McCloud. *Understanding Comics: The Invisible Art*. Kitchen Sink Press, 1993.

[31] Medienpädagogischer Forschungsverbund Südwest. KIM-Studie 2010. Kinder+ Medien. *Computer+ Internet. Stuttgart*, 2011.

[32] Medienpädagogischer Forschungsverbund Südwest. KIM-Studie 2012. Kinder+ Medien. Computer+ Internet. 2013. Stuttgart.

[33] R. Müller. Suchmaschinen Interface für Kinder: Ein spielorientierter Ansatz mit Charakteren. Master's thesis, Otto von Guericke University, 2013.

[34] E. Nicol and E. Hornecker. Using children's drawings to elicit feedback on interactive museum prototypes. In *Proc. of the 11th Int. Conf. on Interaction Design and Children*, 2012.

[35] J. Ormrod and K. Davis. *Human learning*. Merrill, 1999.

[36] J. Piaget, B. Inhelder, and B. Inhelder. *The psychology of the child*, volume 5001. Basic Books, 1969.

[37] T. Polajnar, R. Glassey, K. Gyllstrom, and L. Azzopardi. Enabling picture-based querying and learning with the juse interface. In *Proc. of the 2nd Child Computer Interaction: Workshop on UI Technologies and Educational Pedagogy at CHI*, 2011.

[38] J. Read, S. MacFarlane, and C. Casey. Endurability, engagement and expectations: Measuring children's fun. In *Interaction Design and Children*, volume 2, pages 1–23. Shaker Publishing Eindhoven, 2002.

[39] L. S. Vygotsky. *Mind in Society*. Harvard University Press, 1978.

[40] D. Xu, J. C. Read, G. Sim, and B. McManus. Experience it, draw it, rate it: capture children's experiences with their drawings. In *Proc. of the 8th Int. Conf. on Interaction Design and Children*, 2009.

# A Diary Study of Children's User Experience with EBooks Using Flow Theory as Framework

Luca Colombo
University of Lugano - USI
Via Buffi 13, 6900 Lugano, Switzerland

luca.colombo@usi.ch

Monica Landoni
University of Lugano - USI
Via Buffi 13, 6900 Lugano, Switzerland

monica.landoni@usi.ch

## ABSTRACT

This paper describes a diary study aimed at evaluating the User Experience (UX) of 7 to 12 years old children when interacting with eBooks. The goal was to understand whether, in a context of leisure reading, enhanced eBooks provide a better reading experience than basic eBooks. We took inspiration from Csikszentmihalyi's Flow theory to define a benchmark for evaluating the reading experience, and then – by means of the Experience Sampling Method (ESM) and an adapted version of the Flow Short Scale (FKS) – we investigated and collected data on the reading experience of two groups of children: one group read an enhanced eBook while the other read a basic version of the same eBook. Following a mixed-method approach, with quantitative analysis we verified whether participants who read the enhanced eBook had a better reading experience, while with qualitative analysis we tried to understand why. The results showed that interactive and multimedia enrichments (read-aloud narration in particular) had a positive effect on children's experience with the enhanced eBook.

## Categories and Subject Descriptors

Human-centered computing ~ HCI design and evaluation methods

## General Terms

Human Factors

## Keywords

Child-Computer Interaction; leisure reading; ludic reading; electronic book; e-book; reading experience; User Experience; Experience Sampling Method.

*IDC'14*, June 17–20, 2014, Aarhus, Denmark.
Copyright is held by the owner/author(s). Publication rights licensed to ACM.
ACM 978-1-4503-2272-0/14/06 … $15.00.
http://dx.doi.org/10.1145/2593968.2593978

## 1. INTRODUCTION

Nowadays digital technology is an integral part of people's everyday life. Both children and adults interact with a multitude of digital devices over the course of the day, in a variety of situations and contexts. This, among other things, is transforming *leisure reading* – or *ludic reading* [40] – practices. Electronic book (eBook) readers, smartphones and tablet computers (tablets) with their high portability and their cutting edge displays made electronic reading (eReading) of long digital texts – such as novels or narratives – easier, and this contributed to consolidate the eBook phenomenon.

According to Wischenbart's "Global eBook" report [48] in 2013 in United States (US) and United Kingdom (UK) – the two largest eBook markets – eBooks have reached a market share of around 20% of trade sales – which goes up to 30% for fiction eBooks. According to the same report, US and UK eBook markets are now mature, and eBooks are transcending their initial niche in a number of countries in continental Europe. However, despite the global spread of eBooks and related technologies, there is a gap in the empirical research on digital leisure reading practices [24] thus *"more research is needed, especially research that focuses on children reading eBooks for pleasure, and the opinions and preferences of children"* [44].

Our study aims at filling this gap by investigating children's User Experience (UX) with eBooks – or *eReading experience*. In particular our goal is to understand whether *"enhanced"* eBooks provide a better reading experience compared to *"basic"* eBooks. In this paper, with enhanced eBook we identify all those eBooks enriched with multimedia and interactive elements while with basic eBook we mean digital facsimiles of print books (like most eBooks on the market). However the word "enhanced" should not be misunderstood: our view is that an eBook has to remain a book, thus the textual content must always be predominant.

Having clarified this point, our research question is: do multimedia and interactive enrichments have a positive effect on the leisure eReading experience (or they are just purposeless embellishments)? To answer this question after reviewing existing literature on the topic we will explore Csikszentmihalyi's concept of Flow [10, 39] and how it can be used as a benchmark for the evaluation of the reading experience. Building on this framework we will present the approach – based on the Experience Sampling Method (ESM) – that we used to evaluate eReading experience over time, in a natural context of use, with 7 to 12 years old children. Finally we will analyse the data and discuss the results we obtained, the limitations of this study and possible future developments.

## 1.1 Related Literature

As we wrote in the previous section, in this study we will compare the UX of an enhanced eBook and a basic eBook. One could argue that the outcome of the comparison will certainly be in favor of the more fascinating and captivating enhanced eBook, but this is less obvious than it might appear.

For instance Chiong et al. [3] – by means of a small-scale observational study with 3-6 year-old children – compared children's engagement when reading a print book, a basic eBook and an enhanced eBook. They observed that a majority (63%) of the children *"were as engaged reading the book as they were when reading the eBook (both types)"*. Jones & Brown [26] surveyed third-graders to investigate their engagement with electronic books in comparison to print books. Their conclusion was that *"the eBook format did not significantly increase comprehension, enjoyment, or engagement. The data clearly indicated that children prefer to have a choice of reading material and that the format was not as central to reading engagement as a connection with the story's characters and setting."* Maynard [37] conducted a pilot study to explore reading experiences of young children – aged 7 to 12 – and their families. She found that *"[compared to adults] child participants were more accepting of eBooks, with half preferring these and half preferring print books"* and that *"eBook readers might be beneficial for reluctant readers"*. All these studies assessed children's engagement with eBooks but the authors did not clearly define what engagement means in the context of their studies. In addition, the studies examined children's reading experience from an adult perspective by surveying and interviewing parents or by observing children and not by asking children directly (if not marginally). Lastly, all the studies – except Maynard's [37] – that we reported were conducted at school: not a typical context of leisure reading [8].

To date, Human-Computer Interaction (HCI) research on eBooks for children is rather limited and very little attention has been paid to children's UX with eBooks. Indeed most of the publications focus largely on the utilitarian/educational aspects of eReading such as text comprehension or literacy – for a synthesis of the research on the matter see the work of Zucker et al. [49].

As the review of related literature shows, it is not clear yet whether interactive and multimedia enrichments positively or negatively affect reading experience, both in terms of utilitarian (e.g. text comprehension, emergent literacy) and hedonic (e.g. reading engagement, absorption) aspects: this publication sets out to shed more light on the latter.

## 1.2 "Optimal" EReading Experience

As we wrote we aim at understanding whether "enhanced" eBooks provide a better eReading experience compared to "basic" eBooks. Colombo et al. [8] define eReading experience as *"a particular case of UX where the mediator is an eBook"*. The question is: how can we say that a reading experience is better than another one? Or else: when can we say that the eReading experience is good or – even better – "optimal"? This is a crucial question because by answering it we are going to define a benchmark for the evaluation of the eReading experience.

In the context of leisure reading we can say that we have an "optimal" reading experience when we metaphorically "get lost in a book", when we are completely engaged/absorbed in what we are reading, so absorbed that time flies without us noticing it and we lose awareness of the surroundings. According to Nell this state of *reading trance* is mediated by intense and focused attention [40].

Interestingly enough, the concept of "being lost in a book" shares more than one similarity with the concept of "being in flow" as outlined by Csikszentmihalyi [10, 39]. Although not originally intended as an explanation of engagement with eBooks, flow theory fits reading experience well, and resonates with reports of (optimal) leisure reading experiences – as already stressed by Mcquillan & Conde [38]. This may explain why reading is the most widely reported flow activity in the optimal experience literature [10, 38]. In addition according to Green et al. [17] *"the phenomenology of media enjoyment can be characterized as a flow-like state"*.

*Flow* – or *optimal experience* – is defined by Csikszentmihalyi [10] as a mental state of deep enjoyment and intense engagement in a certain activity, where most of a person's attention resources are devoted to accomplish that activity. According to the author, flow is characterized by eight major components: challenges/skills balance, clear goals and immediate feedback, merging of action and awareness, focused concentration, sense of potential control, autotelic – i.e. intrinsically rewarding – activity, loss of self-consciousness and distortion of time perception.

Flow not only fits reading experience well, but it can also provide a theoretical framework for investigating user experience with technology. For instance, some researchers attempted to explain *media enjoyment* using flow theory [45] while others took inspiration from flow characteristics to contribute with some recommendations on good interface design [2], to develop a set of heuristics for evaluating player enjoyment in games [46] or to investigate UX in online environments – for a review of the various studies on this last topic see Hoffman and Novak's work [22]. In general, flow captures the *holistic aspect* of UX and *"provides an important supplement to more traditional, fine grained variables, such as beliefs and attitudes"* [19].

Looking at the similarities between flow components and leisure reading characteristics, and at how UX research previously applied flow theory, flow seems to be a valid foundation for the evaluation of eReading experience. In other words, we deem "being in flow" as a good indicator of an "optimal" reading experience.

In the following section we provide more details on the study: who were the participants, where the study took place, how we evaluated eReading experience, which materials we used and what procedure we followed.

## 2. EVALUATION

For this study we chose a *between-subject* experimental design: one group of participants (*experimental group*) read an enhanced eBook while the other acted as (a sort of) *control group*: this group read the basic version of the same eBook (i.e. just text and images). The aim of the evaluation was to assess participant's "flow" in the eReading experience and then to compare the two groups to see which one featured a higher level of flow and, thus, to understand which book provided a better eReading experience. Our hypothesis was that participants in the experimental group would have had a better eReading experience.

## 2.1 Participants

Participants were volunteered from a population of primary/lower-secondary school pupils aged between 7 and 12 ($Md = 9$) from the Swiss canton of Ticino and the Italian region of

Lombardy (therefore all native Italian speakers). Even though the 7 to 12 age range might appear as relatively broad, it corresponds to the *concrete operational* stage of cognitive development [41]. De Leeuw et al. [33] well summarize the cognitive skills of children in this stage: "*In the first period (roughly 7 to 10) short term memory matures, but information processing is still twice as slow as in adulthood. Children learn to recognize the viewpoint of others and at the same time become more sensitive for disapproval. In the second period (roughly 10 to 12) memory is full-grown and processing speed increases. Basic reading and writing skills are acquired. Children have developed a social identity, and can put themselves in the other's place. Making friends becomes very important and they actively seek approval*". What is most relevant for this study is that basic reading and writing skills are acquired.

Thirty-two children (20 females, 12 males) were recruited using a combination of mailing lists, ads in public libraries/schools and snowball sampling to achieve a good mix in age and gender. Participation in the study was voluntary – upon active parental consent – and participants were randomly assigned to either the experimental or the control group. Below we report a summarized profile of the sample that took part in the experiment:

- eighteen children were regular users of tablets while six had never used them before;
- fourteen children could be regarded as strong readers (i.e. they had read more than 12 books in the last year) while six as weak readers (i.e. they had read less than 3 books in the last year);
- eight children had previously read the novel used for the experiment – nineteen if we include those who partially read it;
- twenty-eight children had never read an eBook before.

Having both regular and first-time users of tablets, and both children who had previously read or not the novel, allowed us to check for undesired effects due to novelty of the device or personal preferences, likes, or dislikes related to the novel – regardless of the eBook format.

## 2.2 Setting

With the inherent portability of eBook readers, smartphones and tablets, eBooks may be read in changing contexts and unpredictable situations. Many researchers agree that UX is context dependent [1, 32], thus traditional lab-based evaluation techniques tend to be inadequate as they omit this critical factor. For this reason, and to preserve a natural context of leisure reading, the evaluation was carried out *on the field*.

For that purpose we provided each participant with a tablet – on which we installed the eBook and the software to be used for the evaluation. They could have kept the device for all the time needed to read the novel – usually 1 or 2 weeks. In that period they were allowed to bring the tablet with them whenever and wherever they wanted.

Initial and follow-up interviews took place at our research facility when the device was first collected and then returned.

## 2.3 Method

In order to choose the proper evaluation method, we kept into account some peculiar aspects of the reading experience:

- *long duration*: for readers – especially younger ones – it usually takes from a few days to a few weeks to read an entire book;
- *fragmentation*: a book is almost never read from the beginning to the end at once, but reading experience is often fragmented over many sessions;
- *sequentiality and cumulativity*: each session usually starts from the point where the previous one ended, cumulating with all the previous ones in a sequential way;

These aspects – together with the variability of the context we discussed before – guided our decision on the UX evaluation method to use. In Children-Computer Interaction research three main approaches are used to investigate the user experience on the field (as suggested by Markopoulos et al. [35]): naturalistic observations, surveys and diaries.

In our case, observation methods would have been practically impossible to deploy due to the peculiarities of eReading experience we mentioned above: we should have followed each of the thirty-two participants throughout the day in a variety of places (e.g. at school, at home, at playgrounds, etc.) waiting for him/her to interact with the eBook. This was simply not feasible.

As for survey methods, we did not choose them because De Leeuw et al. [33] strongly advise against the use of recall surveys / retrospective questions with children in middle childhood: "*During middle childhood (7-12) memory and especially storage and retrieval of information are still developing [...] A general advice is to avoid retrospective questions as far as possible, especially when asking for non-standard events and details [...] young children (early middle childhood) have more difficulties to distinguish between imagined events and those actually perceived*". The same authors suggest using diary-based methods "*to overcome difficulties with questions that require complex memory processes, and cannot be answered from memory directly*" [33]. They also cite other studies in support of their statements: "*The diary method minimally appeals to cognitive processes and memory, and [uses] the 'here and now' type of question, which is especially appropriate for children (Amato & Ochiltree, 1989) [...] Otter (1993) showed that the use of the diary method with children, aged 9 years, to measure leisure-time reading yield good response quality, produce reliable and valid data responses. Even when the concepts of interest produce questions that burden children's memory, the use of diary method is by far superior compared to self-administered paper and pencil questionnaires (Otter, 1993)*".

For all these reasons we decided to use a diary-like method namely, *the Experience Sampling Method (ESM)*. Originally developed by Csikszentmihalyi [21] to investigate flow in everyday life, the ESM is an ecologically-valid contextualized data collection method in which participants' experience is repeatedly assessed in real-time through self-completion questionnaires. The ESM is widely used in flow research and is gaining popularity in the HCI field where it has been used for different purposes such as understanding people's information needs while on-the-go [4], building predictive user models [27], capturing users' feedback on mobile phone usage [15] or investigating quality of the experience in virtual environments [16]. – for more on the rationale of using the ESM in HCI research see Intille et al. [25] and Colombo [5] works.

One of the main drawbacks of the ESM is that it interrupts the experience being assessed. In an attempt to reduce this issue – which however does not affect the efficacy and validity of the method [11, 21] – we looked for a flow questionnaire that children can complete in less than 1-2 minutes. The questionnaire we used with the ESM is an adapted and translated version of the *Flow Short Scale (Flow-Kurz-Skala; FKS)* [12]. The FKS is a Likert scale consisting of 10 items through which respondents can evaluate their experience in relation to the components of flow. The FKS has already been validated and successfully used to evaluate UX with computer games [12, 47] and the web [34]. With the help of teachers and educators we adapted the FKS to the cognitive skills of primary school children by following De Leuww et al. guidelines [33] and by taking inspiration from Read & MacFarlane's *Fun Toolkit* [43]. Accordingly we rephrased some of the items to make them easier to understand for the children and we used 5-points pictorial Likert items (see Figure 2) instead of the 7-points Likert items of the original FKS.

## 2.4 Materials

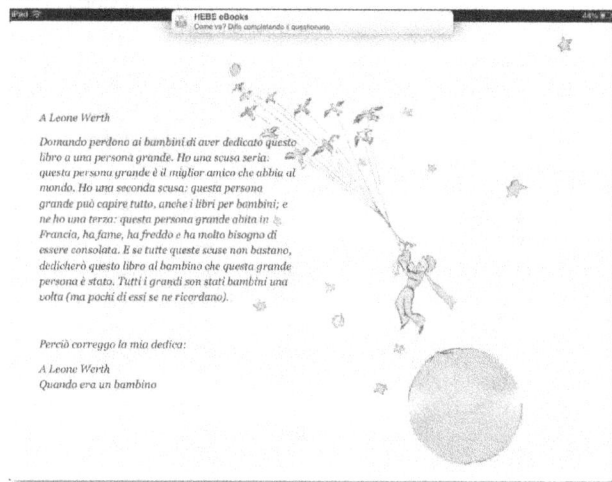

**Figure 1: A screenshot of the eBook with the ESM notification banner at the top of the screen**

In this study we employed tablets (i.e. iPads® 2) as reading devices. Even though they are not eBook readers in the strictest sense, working with tablets allowed us for more flexibility and a better support for interactive and multimedia content. On each tablet we installed the iOS 6.1.3 operating system and the iBooks 3.1 app.

Both the basic and the enhanced eBooks have been developed using a specific eBook authoring application (i.e. iBooks Author) and are based on "The Little Prince" novel. We chose this novel – with the advice of teachers and librarians – for its being suitable for children aged 7 to 12. The basic eBook is a digital facsimile of the print version of the novel – same text and same illustrations (see Figure 1). The enhanced eBook is a basic book enriched with video, audio, interactive and extra features. The enhanced eBook was designed by an intergenerational design team following the Cooperative Inquiry [18] method. A thorough and detailed description of the design process and of the characteristics of the eBook can be found in [6, 7]; here we report a shortlist of the features that we implemented in the enhanced eBook following the recommendations of the design team: sound effects, read-aloud narration, interactive images (e.g. drawing, coloring, moving objects around, etc.), videos that summarize parts of the text, puzzle games, an embedded in-line dictionary, descriptive cards and colored text.

To evaluate the eReading experience we developed an *ad-hoc ESM iOS app(lication)* that runs on the tablet participants used to read the eBook. As De Leeuw et al. [33] state *"[electronic diaries] produce good data quality (Kalfs, 1993). Van Hattum and de Leeuw showed that children are very good in computer-assisted self-interviews (CASI); even children from the age of 8 year successfully completed the questionnaire and enjoyed the process (Van Hattum & de Leeuw, 1999). The use of electronic diaries can motivate children because it gears to their experiences and minimize the burden of memory."*

The ESM app we developed works in the following way. When participants are reading the eBook some notifications are scheduled at pseudo-random intervals set by the experimenter – following the pilot study we set the range of variation from 15 to 25 minutes. At the scheduled times each notification is shown on the device in the form of a banner at the top of the screen (see Figure 1) followed by a sound. When the user answers a notification by tapping on it, an instance of the adapted FKS questionnaire is presented on the screen (see Figure 2). Once the user fills out and submits the questionnaire, the screen reverts back to the eBook page the user was reading. For every questionnaire submitted by the user, the application records the answers to each FKS Likert item in the form of a numerical value ranging from 1 to 5.

The application can also collect additional data through video recording and automatic logging. With video recording users have the opportunity to enrich information provided through the questionnaire with their personal thoughts about the experience – a sort of "additional comments" field. As for automatic logging, the device registers the current time, its geographic coordinates and its orientation in the space every time a notification is answered.

In order to provide a usable data collection instrument and to reduce its interference with the activity being assessed, in addition to what recommended in [14] and [29], we developed the ESM application with the following guidelines in mind: notifications to fill out the questionnaire should not be disruptive – i.e. the alert should be a subtle stimulus in the periphery of the attention; users should be allowed to answer to a notification whenever they prefer – yet within 20 min from when the notification was triggered; the time needed to fill out the questionnaire should be minimized to reduce activity interruption.

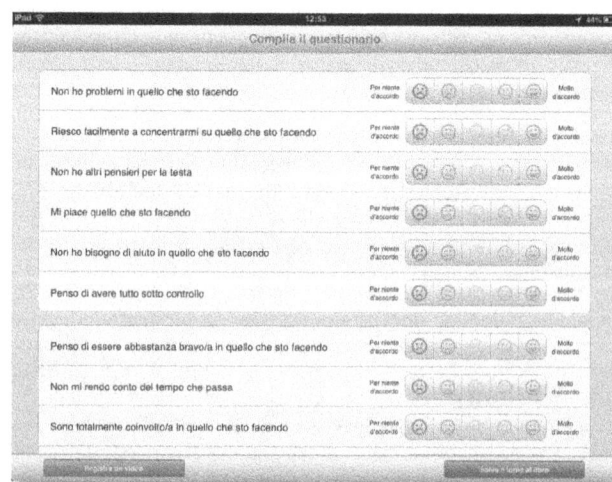

**Figure 2: A screenshot of the ESM application showing some items of the adapted FKS questionnaire**

## 2.5 Procedure

Prior to running the in situ evaluation we piloted the ESM app and the adapted FKS questionnaire on four children from the same population of the sample. This allowed us to set the proper interval between each notification, correct some small bugs in the software and review some of the items of the FSK to make them clearer. Before the study began we defined a procedural framework that we used throughout the study and that is reported in this section.

We coupled the diary study with initial and follow-up semi-structured interviews (a similar approach can be found in [9, 24 and 37]). The initial interview aimed at profiling participants while the follow-up interview aimed at gathering additional qualitative data on the eReading experience. Interviews lasted approximately 30 minutes but the interview format allowed participants to introduce new issues – which they regarded as important – to the discussion and thus to extend their duration.

When we first met the participants – each participant individually and accompanied by one parent – we explained to them and their parents the purpose of our study and we emphasized that it was not a test on their skills or a homework assignment. We also told them to be as objective as possible in answering the questionnaire, that there was not right or wrong answer and that they did not have to please us. We stressed that their participation was on a voluntary basis and that they could drop out from the experiment whenever they wanted. After the preamble we asked the parents to sign the consent to take part in the study, the privacy policy (as requested by our internal code of ethics when conducting user studies with children) and the free loan agreement for the tablets.

Then we gave the tablets to the children and we showed them all the features of the ESM application and how to use it. We read with them all the items of the FKS and we carefully checked that they understood the meaning of every single item. After that, we conducted the initial interview where we asked the children: Do you like reading? How many books do you usually read in a year? Where do you usually read? Did you already read this novel? Do you use a tablet at home and if yes how often? Did you ever read an eBook? What do you expect from the eBook?

Experience sampling was the core part of the study. As we wrote children kept the tablet until they finished to read the book and meanwhile they had to fill out and submit FKS questionnaires whenever they received a notification. Once they finished to read the book they had to attend a post-study meeting to return the tablet and to take part in the follow-up interview. The following questions were asked after the study: Did you read the entire eBook? How long did it take you to read it? How would you rate the eBook (poor, fair, good, very good, excellent)? Where did you read the eBook? What did you like the most? What did you like the less? What would you change/add in the eBook? Would you like to read a similar eBook? Would you suggest this book to your friends or classmates? Do you have any additional comments or thoughts? Finally we thanked the children – and their parents – for their participation and we asked if they wanted us to keep them informed on the results of the study.

In the next section we describe how we analyzed both quantitative and qualitative data and the result we obtained.

## 3. RESULTS

Following the recommendation of using a *mixed-method* approach in investigating UX [31] we collected and analyzed data both quantitatively and qualitatively. Maxwell [36] suggests that quantitative research should address "whether" and "to what extent" questions while qualitative research "how" and "why" questions. Accordingly, in this study quantitative analysis served to verify *whether* participants in the experimental group had a better (or worse) eReading experience compared to participants in the control group; while qualitative analysis served to understand *why* the UX with the enhanced eBook was better (or worse) – and thus to complement and supplement quantitative findings.

### 3.1 Quantitative Analysis

Starting from the data we collected through the ESM app (see Section 2.4) we computed a *flow score*. A flow score is simply the sum of the answers to the ten items of the FKS questionnaire. As each answer is a number that can range from 1 to 5, the flow score could range from a minimum of 10 to a maximum of 50; a higher score indicates a higher level of flow. Table 1 shows each participant's median flow score (and the median absolute deviation of the flow scores) together with age, sex, number of completed questionnaires and response rate (i.e. the number of completed questionnaires divided by the number of total notifications expressed as a percentage).

**Table 1: Age, sex, number of completed questionnaires, response rate, median flow score and median absolute deviation for each participant.**

| | Experimental Group | | | | | | | | | | | | | | | |
|---|---|---|---|---|---|---|---|---|---|---|---|---|---|---|---|---|
| Participant ID | P02 | P04 | P05 | P09 | P11 | P15 | P18 | P19 | P20 | P21 | P22 | P26 | P27 | P30 | P31 | P32 |
| Age | 7 | 7 | 10 | 7 | 12 | 10 | 10 | 9 | 10 | 12 | 8 | 8 | 8 | 10 | 10 | 9 |
| Sex | M | M | M | F | F | F | F | F | F | F | M | F | F | F | M | F |
| N° of completed questionnaires | 10 | 15 | 8 | 9 | 16 | 8 | 18 | 5 | 5 | 4 | 8 | 28 | 7 | 4 | 15 | 18 |
| Response rate | 30% | 23% | 21% | 23% | 38% | 12% | 26% | 10% | 16% | 17% | 40% | 40% | 44% | 9% | 33% | 55% |
| Median flow score | 47 | 50 | 48.5 | 50 | 50 | 46 | 45 | 46 | 43 | 45.5 | 49.5 | 48 | 48 | 46.5 | 48 | 49 |
| Median absolute deviation | 0.5 | 0 | 1.5 | 0 | 0 | 1 | 1.5 | 1 | 1 | 1 | 0.5 | 1 | 1 | 1 | 1 | 0.5 |

| | Control Group | | | | | | | | | | | | Excluded | | | |
|---|---|---|---|---|---|---|---|---|---|---|---|---|---|---|---|---|
| Participant ID | P01 | P06 | P07 | P12 | P13 | P14 | P16 | P17 | P23 | P24 | P28 | P29 | P03 | P08 | P10 | P25 |
| Age | 11 | 8 | 10 | 9 | 11 | 11 | 10 | 12 | 8 | 8 | 7 | 12 | 10 | 8 | 9 | 8 |
| Sex | F | F | M | M | F | M | F | F | F | M | M | F | F | F | M | F |
| N° of completed questionnaires | 18 | 4 | 9 | 17 | 14 | 5 | 5 | 10 | 7 | 20 | 8 | 7 | 2 | 27 | 1 | 0 |
| Response rate | 42% | 18% | 26% | 22% | 18% | 10% | 8% | 22% | 11% | 20% | 12% | 35% | 4% | 32% | 2% | 0% |
| Median flow score | 37 | 34 | 48 | 35 | 43.5 | 47 | 41 | 34 | 44 | 29 | 41 | 39 | 47.5 | 50 | 42 | |
| Median absolute deviation | 5 | 2 | 2 | 4 | 2 | 0 | 0 | 1 | 2 | 1.5 | 1 | 1 | 0.5 | 0 | - | |

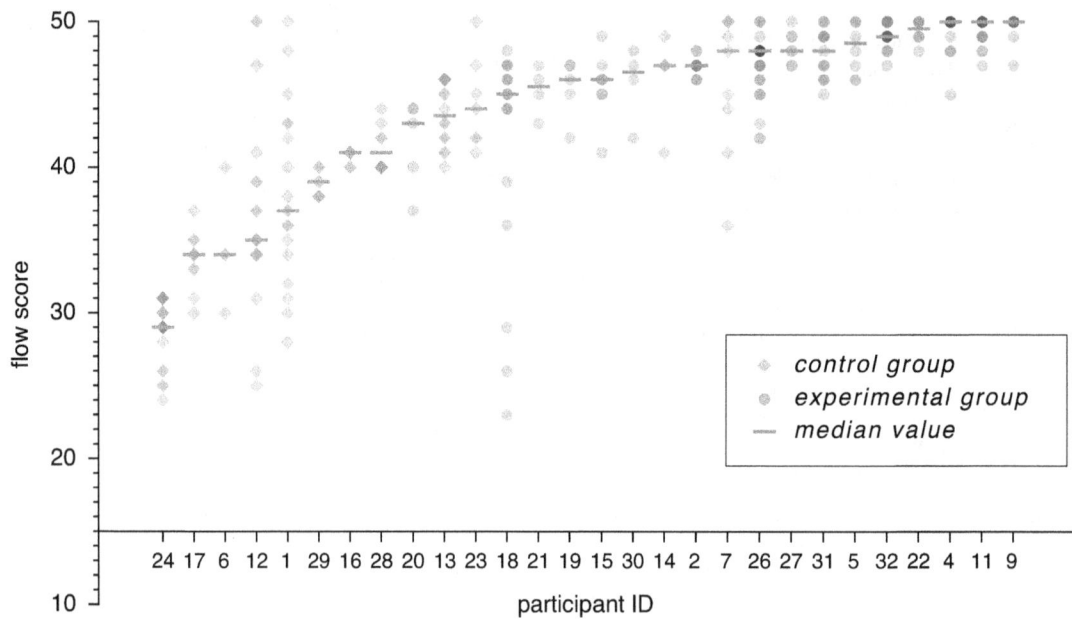

**Figure 3: Dot plot of the flow scores grouped by participant and sorted according to participant's median flow score. Aquamarine circles represent scores of the experimental group, orange diamonds represent scores of the control group. The darker is the mark, the higher is the number of occurrences of that particular value for the participant.**

Eighteen children were assigned to the experimental group (see the upper part of Table 1) and fourteen to the control group (see the lower part of Table 1) randomly. However four children (in gray in Table 1) were excluded from the comparison: P03, P10 and P25 due to a very low response rate – lower than 5% – and P08 because her pattern of responses showed a very strong acquiescence bias (i.e. the tendency to answer positively) [43]. As a side note we point out that, of the four excluded participants, two were from the experimental group (P03, P08) and two were from the control group (P10, P25): including them in the analysis would have added even more significance to the result – and increased the effect size – but we decided to take a conservative approach during the data-cleaning phase.

We followed a conservative approach also in organizing the data to allow the use of traditional inferential tests. To reduce the probability of Type I errors – and to avoid the problems of inflated N and unequal weighting – we employed *subject-level analysis*. This involves computing appropriate aggregate scores for each individual and analyzing these scores using the person as unit of analysis [30]. Since the data gathered through Likert scales is ordinal, we used the median to compute the aggregate scores (represented by horizontal dashes in Figure 3). For the same reason (as well as for the distribution-free nature of the data and the unequal and relatively small size of the groups) we used non-parametric inferential tests to check for differences between the two groups of participants – as advocated by Kaptein et al. [28].

The dot plot graph in Figure 3 shows all the flow scores we obtained during the experiment. Scores are grouped by participant, and participants are sorted according to their median flow score. Aquamarine circles represent the scores of the participants in the experimental group while orange diamonds represent the scores of the participants in the control group. A darker mark indicates a higher number of occurrences of that particular value for the participant.

A Mann-Whitney-Wilcoxon test was performed on the median flow scores to check whether there was a difference in the level of flow, between the experimental and the control group. The test showed that the flow scores of children in the experimental group ($Md = 48.00$) were significantly higher than the flow scores of children in the control group ($Md = 40.00$), $U = 17.00$, $z = -3.68$, $p < 0.05$, $r = -0.69$ (see Figure 4).

To identify potential *confounding factors*, participants were also grouped by: (A) regular, first-time and occasional user of tablets; (B) children who had or had not already read the novel (or who had partially read it); (C) weak, strong or average readers. We then compared the so obtained groups using a Kruskall-Wallis test, but in none of the cases significant differences were found: (A) $H(2) = 4.43$, $p > 0.05$; (B) $H(2) = 1.15$, $p > 0.05$; (C) $H(2) = 1.27$, $p > 0.05$.

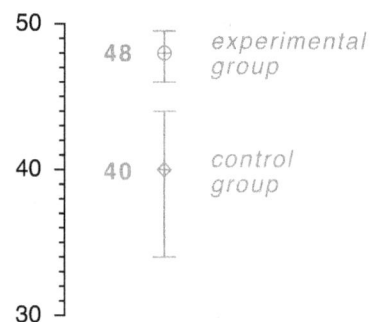

**Figure 4: Median flow scores of the experimental group and the control group. Whiskers represent approximate 95% confidence interval for the estimated population median (actual coverage is 97.9% for the experimental group and 96.1% for the control group)**

140

Also when we grouped participants according to age (D) or gender (E) inferential tests did not show significant differences between groups: (D) $H(2) = 1.25$, $p > 0.05$; (E) $U = 65.5$, $z = -1.32$, $p > 0.05$.

Finally we computed a Pearson correlation coefficient to check for the degree of linear dependence between participants' response rates and average flow scores, but the two variables did not show to correlate significantly: $r(28) = 0.25$, $p > 0.05$.

## 3.2 Qualitative Analysis

We pooled and analyzed data obtained through initial and follow-up interviews following a summative content analysis approach [23]. We generated codes by looking at the frequency and relevance of the issues raised by the children – i.e. those issues that occurred frequently or that were emphasized by the children. Two researchers independently hand-coded the data and disagreements were resolved by discussion in order to reach a consensus. As we did for the quantitative analysis we divided the children into the two groups but in this case none of the children was excluded. Here below we report the results of the analysis in terms of quasi-statistics [36].

In the initial interview we inquired children about their expectations regarding the eBook. Half of the children did not know what to answer; among those who answered many said to be expecting a better/different experience in comparison to reading print books; we asked them to try to be more specific but they struggled to provide a more articulated answer to this prospective question.

In the follow-up interview we asked participants about whether they finished or not to read the novel and whether they wanted to read another similar eBook and would suggest the eBook to someone else. In the experimental group (enhanced eBook) all the participants reported to have read the novel until the end, all of them wanted to read another similar eBook and all of them would have suggested the eBook to others. In the control group (basic eBook) four participants – out of fourteen – did not finish to read the novel (and none of them had read the novel before), four did not want to read another similar eBook and less than one third of the children would have suggested the eBook to others. We also asked to rate the eBook as poor, fair, good, very good, excellent: in the experimental group the eBook was rated as "excellent" by all the participants but two – who rated it as "very good"; in the control group the ratings were more distributed: we had three "excellent", six "very good", three "good", one "fair" and one "poor" ratings.

The last question we asked was about likes, dislikes and suggested improvements. As for the enhanced eBook read-aloud narration was by far the most appreciated feature – mentioned by the 50% of the participants – followed at some distance by puzzle games, videos and interactive images (in this order). Two participants did not like interactive images while others did not like sound effects or videos. Two children reported to have found inline dictionary definitions too complex, other two children suggested to improve the eBook by adding more dictionary definitions and descriptive cards while three children suggested to make dictionary definitions more child-friendly. As for the basic eBook: two participants lamented to have suffered eyestrain after prolonged use of the device, one child complained about the weight of the tablet while another evidenced the lack of clear indications about reader's progress through the book; three participants suggested, respectively, to add read-aloud narration, games and more images.

Very informative data was obtained from the unstructured phase of the interview. Four participants from the experimental group told us that they had the print version of the novel at home but they never started or finished to read it; three participants told us that they read some parts of the book together with their parents; three participants told us one more time that they really enjoyed read-aloud narration, two participants said that after having read the book they went back to replay videos and read-aloud narration; four children said that the interactive and multimedia elements made the eBook "less boring" than print books. For what concerns the control group, five participants spontaneously told us that they still prefer reading print books while two participants expressed their concern to use the tablet other than at home since the device could get broken or stolen.

Few children gave us some feedback also on the evaluation method used in this diary study: two of them found the ESM notifications bothersome while one (P10, who was excluded from the quantitative analysis) reported to have had difficulties in understanding some items of the questionnaire.

Overall only four participants recorded some videos (twelve videos in total) through the ESM app, and those videos did not add much to the information we obtained with the interviews: most of them contained children's enthusiastic comments about the enhanced eBook.

In the next session we discuss the implications of our findings, the limitations of this study and its possible future developments.

## 4. DISCUSSION

The decision to evaluate eReading experience on the field proven to be successful as it allowed us to preserve the natural context of use – a critical factor when evaluating user experience – and to get a better insight on eBooks and leisure reading. The Experience Sampling Method well adapted to the long-term, fragmented and sequential/cumulative nature of reading experience and – in combination with an adapted version of the Flow Short Scale – it allowed us to collect meaningful data about children's UX with the eBooks.

Despite the relatively small sample size and the rather low response rate, we collected enough data for hypothesis testing. As a matter of fact, comparison of the aggregated (i.e. median) flow scores showed that children's experience with the enhanced eBook was significantly ($p < 0.05$) better than children's experience with the basic eBook. Not only the result was significant but also the effect size was large ( $|r| > 0.5$). This gives even more relevance to the result if we consider the implicit acquiescence response bias that is common to observe with young respondents [43] . When we grouped the data according to other factors – such as children's age, gender, use of the device, reading habits, etc. – in none of the cases we obtained a significant result from the comparisons, in other words we did not find evidence that these factors have a direct influence on the observed variable (level of flow). As suggested by a reviewer we also tested whether in the present experiment a low response rate could have been an indicator of a higher level of flow (i.e. strong negative correlation), but the Pearson's $r$ did not indicated any significant correlation between these two variables.

In the light of the above we confirmed the hypothesis that participants in the experimental group would have had a better eReading experience. This could mean that, in a context of reading for pleasure – or at least in the context of this study – interactive and multimedia enrichments have a positive effect on the leisure eReading experience as they contribute to increase the level of flow of the children.

Results obtained from quantitative analysis were then complemented with qualitative findings: this allowed us, among other things, to understand why the UX with the enhanced eBook was better. As revealed by the initial interview, many children expected a better/different experience in comparison to reading print books. If we interpret this in the light of the fact that the basic eBook was a digital facsimile of the print book, we have a first insight on why participants in the control group reported a lower level of flow: the eBook simply failed to meet their expectations. After all what is the benefit in terms of UX of having eBooks that are nothing more than digital facsimiles of print book? As a matter of fact, most of the children who read the basic eBook spontaneously told us that they still prefer print books and this is reflected by the fact that almost one third of the participants in the control group did not finish to read the novel. By contrast, all children in the experimental group finished to read the eBook and showed a higher desire to repeat the activity (i.e. endurability [42]). This could have implications that go beyond the momentary or hedonic aspects: eBooks with a better reading experience might motivate children – reluctant readers especially, as suggested by Maynard [37] – to read more, with all the benefits that this entails in terms of literacy and educational attainments. In support of this speculation we emphasize that some participants in the experimental group who did not (finish to) read the print version of the novel despite owning a copy, did read the electronic enhanced version from the beginning to the end. Another participant from the experimental group (P03) told us that she did not like the story plot but still she read the eBook until the end because she liked to interact with it while reading the text. Quite the opposite happened with P25 who was assigned to the control group: she dropped out of the study after reading a few pages because – as she told us in the follow-up interview – she "did not like the book at all".

The results showed that read-aloud narration was by far the most appreciated feature among the ones we used to enhance the electronic book. P19 said that with read-aloud it was "quite like being at the theater" meaning that the experience was more encompassing, P32 reported that "reading the book with a narrative voice in the background makes you more immersed into the story". Read-aloud narration is nothing new: audiobooks have been around for years now. But the difference is in the way this feature can be implemented in an eBook. In the eBook we developed for this study the audio is synchronized with the text page by page and children could control the audio playback without having to switch to another application or device – as in the case of CD audiobooks – and thus without diverting their attention from the text page.

We argue that the seamless combination of visual reading with audio reading has the potential to make eReading a richer and more engaging experience. Indeed this combination enables a multi-modal reading experience allowing the readers to perceive the text through both vision and hearing, which requires them to devote more attentional resources to the activity of reading. As we wrote in Section 1.2, the idea of *attention saturation* is central to flow theory; hence we can understand why read-aloud narration was so appreciated by the readers and why it may result in an intensification of narrative transportation [20], namely in a higher likelihood of "getting lost in a book" – i.e. entering in a flow state.

We could extend the argument of flow and attention saturation to other eBook enhancements provided that they give a meaningful contribution to the text; otherwise they could distract the reader and compromise the eReading experience. This is reflected by the fact that not all the children in the experimental group liked the video, audio and interactive enrichments we added to the eBook.

It is also important that the various enhancements aim at providing an adequate level of challenge (also read as "opportunities for action" [39]) that meets the skills of the reader. For instance few children found the dictionary definitions too complex and suggested to make them more child-friendly – later we realized that these definitions should have been taken from a children's dictionary rather than from a common dictionary as we did. This is just one example of the importance of a good balance between the challenges of the activity and the person's skills – as flow theory suggests.

A final remark about ergonomic (e.g. eyestrain, weight of the device) and usability issues (e.g. lack of clear indications about reader's progress, complexity of inline definitions) that some participants reported us. The fact that children who read the basic eBook seemed to be more sensitive to these issues (most of the complain came from this group) might suggest a nexus of causality between user engagement and perceived ease of use. But according to Finneran and Zhang the opposite seems to be true [13] and this would confirm one more time the importance of ergonomic and usability aspects while designing for UX.

## 4.1 Limitations and Future Work

The sample we used in the evaluation was relatively small in size – still in line with the sample size of many HCI studies. Even though inferential statistics provided significant results – with a large effect size – the way we sampled the participants might limit the population to the specific context where the study was conducted. Thus we suggest caution in generalizing our results and we hope that other researchers can contribute with other studies and eventually refine and improve the methods and instruments we used in the present one.

Indeed being the first time that a combination of ESM and FKS is used with children, more work is needed to test their effectiveness when used with this specific population. For instance, our study confirmed that attrition is one of the main disadvantages of ESM (the average response rate in the present study was around 22%) and that acquiescence bias is often a problem when working with children. Research has to look for solutions for limiting – if not eliminating – these issues. As for FKS, we had to adapt and translate it to make it understandable for our participants. Given that it was applied and validated in a broad variety of contexts [34] we assumed its validity also in the context of this study, yet it may be useful to test for this assumption. Also, the self-video-recording feature we implemented in the ESM app did not work as we expected since very few children used it. Even if we could speculate on the reasons behind this (e.g. intimacy of the reading experience), it is clear that more work is needed in this sense.

For the future it would be interesting to explore some of the questions we have not addressed in this study, such as for instance: to what extent the various elements of the enhanced eBook (audio, video, interactivity, etc.) and their various combinations contribute to ameliorate children's UX with eBooks; or to what extent those elements impact on the amount of time spent reading the book.

Because of time and budget constraint we developed and evaluated only a couple of eBook prototypes based on a single novel. As the book choice and the plot of the novel inevitably have an influence on the reading experience [40], we plan for the future to replicate this study with eBooks based on different novels so that children will be free to choose which one to read.

Finally, despite having participants of various ages we did not look at how children's experience with enhanced eBooks changes according to their age, therefore it would be interesting to investigate this further and study how children of different ages interact with the various elements of an enhanced eBook.

# 5. CONCLUSIONS

In this paper we described how we evaluated 7 to 12 years old children eReading experience in a context of leisure reading by means of the Experience Sampling Method and an adapted version of the Flow Short Scale. Our study aimed at investigating children's eReading experience with eBooks. In particular our goal was to understand whether enhanced eBooks would have provided a better reading experience compared to basic eBooks. Our research question was: do multimedia and interactive enrichments have a positive effect on the leisure eReading experience or they are just purposeless embellishments? We compared the UX of children who read a basic eBook with the UX of children who read an enhanced version of the same eBook. The results showed that the level of flow was higher in the first case and thus we concluded that the enhanced eBook provided a better eReading experience. Through qualitative analysis we realized that the basic eBook failed to meet children's expectations about the experience while the enhanced eBook supported endurability and flow. These findings indicate that children's eReading experience would greatly benefit from multimedia and interactive enhancements – provided that they give a meaningful contribution to the storyline. The technology for doing this is there and appears to be mature: we just have to better exploit it.

# 6. ACKNOWLEDGMENTS

We would like to thank all the children who took part to the experiment and to their parents. A special thanks goes to our colleagues Elisa Rubegni for her precious contribution in the preparation of this paper and for the support during the study, and Marcello Paolo Scipioni for his comments and his invaluable help in reviewing the manuscript.

This work was supported by the Swiss National Science Foundation (HEBE project), Microsoft Research at Cambridge and the Faculty of Informatics at University of Lugano – USI.

# 7. REFERENCES

[1] Bargas-Avila, J.A. and Hornbæk, K. 2011. Old wine in new bottles or novel challenges? A Critical Analysis of Empirical Studies of User Experience. *Proceedings of the 2011 annual conference on Human factors in computing systems - CHI '11* (New York, NY, USA, 2011), 2689–2698.

[2] Bederson, B.B. 2004. Interfaces for staying in the flow. *Ubiquity*.

[3] Chiong, C., Ree, J., Takeuchi, L. and Erickson, I. 2012. *Print Books vs. E-books: comparing parent-child co-reading on print, basic, and enhanced e-book platforms*.

[4] Church, K. and Cherubini, M. 2010. Evaluating Mobile User Experience In-The-Wild: Prototypes, Playgrounds and Contextual Experience Sampling. *Proceedings of "Research in the Large" international workshop – UBICOMP10* (2010), 29–32.

[5] Colombo, L. 2012. Evaluating children's eReading experience through interactive and user-friendly experience sampling. *CHI 2012 workshop on "Theories, methods and case studies of longitudinal HCI research"* (2012).

[6] Colombo, L. and Landoni, M. 2013. Low-tech and high-tech prototyping for eBook co-design with children. *Proceedings of the 12th International Conference on Interaction Design and Children - IDC '13* (New York, New York, USA, 2013), 289–292.

[7] Colombo, L., Landoni, M. and Rubegni, E. 2014. Design Guidelines for More Engaging Electronic Books: Insights from a Cooperative Inquiry Study. *[Manuscript submitted for publication]* (2014).

[8] Colombo, L., Landoni, M. and Rubegni, E. 2012. Understanding reading experience to inform the design of ebooks for children. *Proceedings of the 11th International Conference on Interaction Design and Children - IDC '12* (New York, New York, USA, 2012), 272–275.

[9] Consolvo, S., Harrison, B., Smith, I., Chen, M.Y., Everitt, K., Froehlich, J. and Landay, J.A. 2007. Conducting In Situ Evaluations for and With Ubiquitous Computing Technologies. *International Journal of Human-Computer Interaction*. 22, 1-2 (2007), 103–118.

[10] Csikszentmihalyi, M. 2008. *Flow: The Psychology of Optimal Experience*. Harper Perennial.

[11] Delle Fave, A., Massimini, F. and Bassi, M. 2011. *Psychological Selection and Optimal Experience Across Cultures*. Springer Netherlands.

[12] Engeser, S. and Rheinberg, F. 2008. Flow, performance and moderators of challenge-skill balance. *Motivation and Emotion*. 32, 3 (2008), 158–172.

[13] Finneran, C.M. and Zhang, P. 2003. A person–artefact–task (PAT) model of flow antecedents in computer-mediated environments. *International Journal of Human-Computer Studies*. 59, 4 (2003), 475–496.

[14] Fischer, J.E. 2009. Experience-Sampling Tools: a Critical Review. *Mobile Living Labs 09: Methods and Tools for Evaluation in the Wild* (2009), 1–3.

[15] Froehlich, J., Chen, M.Y., Consolvo, S., Harrison, B. and Landay, J.A. 2007. MyExperience: A System for In situ Tracing and Capturing of User Feedback on Mobile Phones. *Proceedings of the 5th international conference on Mobile systems, applications and services - MobiSys '07* (New York, New York, USA, 2007), 57–70.

[16] Gaggioli, A., Bassi, M. and Delle Fave, A. 2003. Quality of Experience in Virtual Environments. *Being There: Concepts, effects and measurement of user presence in synthetic environments*. G. Riva, F. Davide, and W.A. IJsselsteijn, eds. Ios Press. 122–132.

[17] Green, M.C., Brock, T.C. and Kaufman, G.F. 2004. Understanding Media Enjoyment: The Role of Transportation Into Narrative Worlds. *Communication Theory*. 14, 4 (2004), 311–327.

[18] Guha, M.L., Druin, A. and Fails, J.A. 2012. Cooperative Inquiry revisited: Reflections of the past and guidelines for the future of intergenerational co-design. *International Journal of Child-Computer Interaction*. in press (2012).

[19] Guo, Y.M. and Poole, M.S. 2009. Antecedents of flow in online shopping: a test of alternative models. *Information Systems Journal*. 19, 4 (2009), 369–390.

[20] Have, I. and Stougaard Pedersen, B. 2013. Sonic mediatization of the book: affordances of the audiobook. *MedieKultur. Journal of media and communication research*. 29, 54 (2013), 123–140.

[21] Hektner, J.M., Csikszentmihalyi, M. and Schmidt, J.A. 2006. *Experience Sampling Method: Measuring the Quality of Everyday Life*. Sage Publications Inc.

[22] Hoffman, D.L. and Novak, T.P. 2009. Flow Online: Lessons Learned and Future Prospects. *Journal of Interactive Marketing*. 23, 1 (2009), 23–34.

[23] Hsieh, H.-F. and Shannon, S.E. 2005. Three approaches to qualitative content analysis. *Qualitative health research*. 15, 9 (2005), 1277–88.

[24] Hupfeld, A., Sellen, A., O'Hara, K. and Rodden, T. 2013. Leisure-Based Reading and the Place of E-Books in Everyday Life. *Proceedings of the 14th IFIP TC 13 International Conference on Human-Computer Interaction (INTERACT 2013)* (Berlin, Heidelberg, 2013), 1–18.

[25] Intille, S.S., Rondoni, J., Kukla, C., Ancona, I. and Bao, L. 2003. A context-aware experience sampling tool. *CHI '03 extended abstracts on Human factors in computer systems - CHI '03* (New York, New York, USA, 2003), 972–973.

[26] Jones, T. and Brown, C. 2011. Reading engagement: a comparison between e-books and traditional print books in an elementary classroom. *International Journal of Instruction*. 4, 2 (2011).

[27] Kapoor, A. and Horvitz, E. 2008. Experience sampling for building predictive user models. *Proceeding of the twenty-sixth annual CHI conference on Human factors in computing systems - CHI '08* (New York, New York, USA, 2008), 657–666.

[28] Kaptein, M.C., Nass, C. and Markopoulos, P. 2010. Powerful and consistent analysis of likert-type ratingscales. *Proceedings of the 28th international conference on Human factors in computing systems - CHI '10* (New York, New York, USA, 2010), 2391–2394.

[29] Khan, V.-J., Markopoulos, P. and Eggen, B.J.H. 2009. Features for the future Experience Sampling Tool. *Mobile Living Labs 09: Methods and Tools for Evaluation in the Wild* (2009), 31–34.

[30] Larson, R. and Delespaul, P.A.E.G. 1992. Analyzing Experience Sampling data: A guidebook for the perplexed. *The Experience of Psychopathology: Investigating Mental Disorders in their Natural Settings*. M.W. de Vries, ed. Cambridge University Press.

[31] Law, E.L.-C. 2011. The measurability and predictability of user experience. *Proceedings of the 3rd ACM SIGCHI symposium on Engineering interactive computing systems - EICS '11* (New York, New York, USA, 2011).

[32] Law, E.L.-C., Roto, V.H., Hassenzahl, M., Vermeeren, A.P.O.S. and Kort, J. 2009. Understanding, scoping and defining user experience. *Proceedings of the 27th international conference on Human factors in computing systems - CHI '09* (New York, New York, USA, 2009), 719–728.

[33] De Leeuw, E., Borgers, N. and Strijbos-smits, A. 2002. Children as Respondents: Developing, Evaluating, and Testing Questionnaires for Children. *International Conference on Questionnaire Development Evaluation and Testing Methods* (2002).

[34] Mahnke, R., Wagner, T. and Benlian, A. 2012. Flow Experience On The Web: Measurement Validation And Mixed Method Survey Of Flow Activities. *European Conference on Information Systems Proceedings - ECIS 2012* (2012).

[35] Markopoulos, P., Read, J.C., MacFarlane, S. and Hoysniemi, J. 2008. *Evaluating Children's Interactive Products: Principles and Practices for Interaction Designers*. Morgan Kaufmann Publishers Inc.

[36] Maxwell, J.A. 2010. Using Numbers in Qualitative Research. *Qualitative Inquiry*. 16, 6 (2010), 475–482.

[37] Maynard, S. 2010. The Impact of e-Books on Young Children's Reading Habits. *Publishing Research Quarterly*. 26, 4 (2010), 236–248.

[38] Mcquillan, J. and Conde, G. 1996. The Conditions of Flow in Reading: Two Studies of Optimal Experience. *Reading Psychology*. 17, 2 (Apr. 1996), 109–135.

[39] Nakamura, J. and Csikszentmihalyi, M. 2002. The Concept of Flow. *Handbook of Positive Psychology*. S.J. Lopez and C.R. Snyder, eds. Oxford University Press. 89–105.

[40] Nell, V. 1988. *Lost in a Book: The Psychology of Reading for Pleasure*. Yale University Press.

[41] Piaget, J. 2007. *The Child's Conception Of the World*. Rowman & Littlefield, 2007.

[42] Read, J.C. and MacFarlane, S. 2002. Endurability, Engagement and Expectations: Measuring Children's Fun. *Interaction Design and Children* (2002), 1–23.

[43] Read, J.C. and MacFarlane, S. 2006. Using the fun toolkit and other survey methods to gather opinions in child computer interaction. *Proceeding of the 2006 conference on Interaction design and children - IDC '06* (New York, New York, USA, 2006), 81–88.

[44] Schreurs, K. 2013. Children's E-books are Born: How E-books for Children are Leading E-book Development and Redefining the Reading Experience. *Partnership: the Canadian Journal of Library and Information Practice and Research*. 8, 2 (2013).

[45] Sherry, J.L. 2004. Flow and Media Enjoyment. *Communication Theory*. 14, 4 (2004), 328–347.

[46] Sweetser, P. and Wyeth, P. 2005. GameFlow: a model for evaluating player enjoyment in games. *Computers in Entertainment*. 3, 3 (2005).

[47] Weibel, D. and Wissmath, B. 2011. Immersion in Computer Games: The Role of Spatial Presence and Flow. *International Journal of Computer Games Technology*. 2011, (2011), 1–14.

[48] Wischenbart, R. 2013. *The Global eBook Report: Current Conditions & Future Projections*.

[49] Zucker, T.A., Moody, A.K. and McKenna, M.C. 2009. The Effects of Electronic Books on Pre-Kindergarten-to-Grade 5 Students' Literacy and Language Outcomes: A Research Synthesis. *Journal of Educational Computing Research*. 40, 1 (2009), 47–87.

# Waiting for Learning: Designing Interactive Educational Materials for Patient Waiting Areas

Zeina Atrash Leong
Northwestern Universtiy
Computer Science
2120 Campus Drive
Evanston, IL 60208 USA
zeina@u.northwestern.edu

Michael S. Horn
Northwestern University
Computer Science and Learning Sciences
2120 Campus Drive
Evanston, IL 60208 USA
michael-horn@northwestern.edu

## ABSTRACT

We describe the research and design of educational media for children in doctor's office waiting areas. Even though technology use for medical purposes has become increasingly prominent for doctors, administration, and patients, research on the use of interactive technology for health education is limited. In this project, we focus on clinics for Sickle Cell Disease treatment. These clinics treat patients of various ages and disease severity, but all patients make frequent, recurring visits for treatments and checkups. We describe our current research to better understand the behaviors and activities of patients as they wait in the clinic, their expectations and understandings of Sickle Cell Disease and its treatment, the educational material currently available, and our preliminary methods for developing interactive technologies for these environments. This reseach includes observations in pediatric clinic waiting areas, interviews with clinic staff, and preliminary user testing with our interactive designs.

This paper details our observations of waiting areas in two sickle cell clinics. We discuss our findings and their implications for design. We also describe the design of an augmented reality tablet application that we placed in the waiting area for user testing. We use this study to discuss further design iterations and directions for future work.

## Categories and Subject Descriptors

H.5.m [**Information interfaces and presentation (e.g., HCI)**]: Miscellaneous.

## Keywords

Health, education, interactive media, children, design

## 1. INTRODUCTION

The use of medical technologies has become increasingly popular both in and out of hospitals for doctors, adminis-

trators, and patients. However, research concerning the use of interactive technology for patient waiting areas is limited, especially with regards to the development of educational tools. We propose to take advantage of the time that patients spend in waiting areas to support health related learning activities using new forms of interactive technology. Our research investigates time that patients spent in waiting areas, the current education material provided in this space, and the design of new technologies to improve this experience for patients and their families. Our focus is on sickle cell treatment clinics in which patients receive blood transfusions and other treatments; here patients wait for treatments to begin and end – providing an opportunity for observations, development, and placement of materials. This paper describes an observation study involving over 500 patients, doctors, nurses, as well as other staff and patient family members. We also describe the initial design of a learning environment for children to learn about sickle cell disease in clinic waiting areas.

## 2. WAITING ROOMS

Little research has been done to understand the time patients and their families spent in waiting areas. There have been attempts to improve the waiting area experience for patients and their supporters, particularly in regards to design of the space. These efforts tend to focus on patient comfort and convenience through factors such as temperature, seating, coffee, what's on TV, or even wait time (e.g. [14, 9]).

Though there are many opportunities to redesign waiting areas for comfort, safety, and even entertainment, there are also opportunities to redesign the space to encourage learning. Studies have found that traditional educational material in waiting areas is often ineffective and goes unnoticed. Common materials include pamphlets and posters about diseases and disorders. A survey of surgery patients found that 79 percent of people waiting read the posters in the waiting areas, and that the longer people waited the more likely they were to read the posters [21]. However, further investigation found that most patients reported that the posters added anxiety to their visits [22], and that they didn't read or remember what the posters said [21]. Based on findings that suggest patients pay little attention to waiting area notice boards and posters, many conclude that the role of these materials and their presentation should be reevaluated [13, 21, 22].

# 3. SICKLE CELL DISEASE

We have selected Sickle Cell Disease as a focus for this work primarily because access to educational resources in the community is limited and patients often come from systematically underserved groups. Sickle cell is a chronic disease that the patients are born with and for which there is no cure. Due to the standard treatment protocols, patient visits also involve substantial amounts of down time as the children wait, allowing greater opportunity for testing and interaction with the material. Sickle Cell Disease, or SCD for short, is an inherited blood disorder in which the red blood cells become hard, sticky, and shaped like sickles. As these irregularly shaped cells move through the blood stream they clog the flow of blood. This can cause pain, strokes, infections, ulcers, internal damage, and anemia, among other symptoms [19].

All of these characteristics stem from an abnormality in the hemoglobin in the red blood cells. The hemoglobin, the part of the cell that delivers oxygen to the body, contain a defect in sickle cell patients. The sickle cell hemoglobin stick together, rather than float freely as they do in normal red blood cells. This causes them to form long chains and forces the red blood cell into non-circular shapes, typically forming something visually similar to a sickle shape. Though there are treatments for SCD, there is no cure. As a result patients with the disorder may practice a variety of different routines to manage their condition – for example, taking vitamins, or penicillin. Patients are also advised to drink plenty of water, to avoid extreme temperature conditions, and to limit stress or exertion. Extreme treatment for SCD can include blood transfusions in which patients visit clinics for many hours at a time [19].

# 4. RELATED WORK

Technology has come to play an important role in health care by supporting both patients and doctors through online communities, management systems, and even treatment options. Although not all study results are positive, technology has generally been shown to positively influence learning, self-care, and skill development as well as strengthen the established medical learning environment [10]. Health knowledge has expanded out of the clinic to the Internet, museums, virtual peers, and even into homes and mobile devices.

Technology use has been investigated throughout hospitals to ease patient management issues in areas such as hospital work, patient transfer, patient records, and doctor's charts (e.g. [8, 24]). Recently, there has been a shift towards improving the experience of patients, particularly in terms of educating them about their visit. For example, an information display can give patients the option to view the reason for their visit, their health profile, medications, and information of the staff working on their case [23]. Several studies have involved conversational agents to promote health knowledge and persuade patients to practice healthy behaviors [18] and to provide easy-to-understand discharge information [5]. However, most of these devices tend to discuss clinic visit details such as staff, medications, or test results and not the underlying causes of diseases and their symptoms.

As important as technology has become to hospital care, patients are increasingly reliant on technology when they are responsible for their own health outside of hospitals and medical offices. One very important use of technology in health is continuous education, awareness, and management while patients are outside of the hospital [7]. Virtual agents, multimodal surfaces, and a variety of other persuasive technologies are also used at home to help patients (e.g. [4, 15, 17, 6]). Many of these systems, such as Chic Clique, Fish N Steps, or Shakra have focused on health and wellness for children and teenagers [20, 11, 1]. Interfaces have become especially common in rehabilitation and therapy for speech [16], autism [3], and diabetes [2, 12]. These are only a few of the many examples of technology in the health realm.

Despite the extensive research on medical technology and educational health materials, none of these materials are designed for waiting areas to the best of our knowledge. Our goal in this work is to begin thinking about patient waiting areas as informal learning environments, much in the way that science museums offer visitors hands-on learning activities. We also attempt to make contributions to the content and form of the health education materials. Many virtual agents and health tracking applications have been developed to help manage health via diet, exercise, or medication adherence; however, none of these applications focus solely on the foundational biology of the body – cell structure, for example – to help patients understand their health. We attempt to go beyond textual descriptions to include interactive experiences with tangible manipulatives and augmented reality systems. These tools magnify characteristic details of the cells and root symptoms of the disease.

# 5. OBSERVATION & INTERVIEW STUDY

To ground our design work, we were interested in learning more about the education process for children with sickle cell disease. Therefore we interviewed a range of people that the patients with SCD encounter as part of their health care. We also conducted observations of the waiting areas to understand what patients and their families currently do while waiting, what options they have to occupy their time, how long they wait, and other details that may influence the design of material for the environment.

Finally, we collected a range of SCD education materials including pamphlets, books, CD's, and flyers that are handed out by the staff to the patients.

## 5.1 Participants

We conducted our study at two clinics: a large children's hospital in the Mid-Atlantic, and a small general hospital in the Midwest. During a patient's typical two to five hour long visit at either clinic, they are seen by nurses, physicians, nurse practitioners, social workers, genetic counselors, and psychiatrists. Blood transfusions also take place in both clinics; in either location, the patient is taken to a private area with a bed, seating, and a television. This area is separated by a wall on either side and a curtain at the entrance. Nurses' stations are at the entry of the transfusion center in both locations.

The Midwestern hospital has an SCD clinic with approximately 12 staff and 100 patients. The clinic is run one afternoon every other week. During routine checkups the staff try to limit patient time in the common waiting area and immediately take them to a clinic room. Once assigned a room, the staff rotates to see patients as they wait. The larger Mid-Atlantic clinic employs a 20 person staff and serves over

1,200 sickle cell patients. Here the clinic is run daily during regular business hours. During routine visits at this clinic, patients wait in a large room prior to their appointment, and often return to the waiting area at least once during their appointments. These clinics' locations, sizes, and populations served are quite diverse. These variations provide an interesting contrast for developing a generalizable design directions.

## 5.2 Methods

The observation portion of this study took place over two years between the two clinics. At the pediatric hematology and oncology clinic in the Mid-Atlantic, we observed over 200 family groups during approximately 38 hours in the main outpatient waiting area. In the Midwest clinic, observations totaled 10 hours between the main waiting area and the area where vitals are taken.

We did not video record or interact with patients or their families while conducting these observations. A researcher collected field notes, wait times, and age and gender estimates for patients and family members. The researcher also noted the behavior and demeanor of visitors as well as their interactions with objects, staff, and other patients.

The observations were interspersed with fourteen staff interviews including three physicians, six nurse practitioners, two social workers, one genetic counselor, and two administrators. These interviews were audio recorded and transcribed for analysis. With the exception of the administrative staff and one physician, all other participants worked almost exclusively with sickle cell patients; one physician was split between SCD and general hematology.

In addition, we interviewed a small number of patients and families to understand what patients take away from current educational materials and their general view on visiting the clinic. Three groups were interviewed: one 17 year old male patient and his mother; a 20 year old female patient; and a father, mother, and their 5 year old son and 7 year old daughter.

For both the family and staff, interviews lasted approximately thirty minutes. The interviews were done individually according the participant's schedule and generally took place in semi-private locations at the clinics.

## 6. FINDINGS

The Mid-Atlantic clinic averages 9 families entering the waiting area every hour with an average group size of 2.5 people. The average wait time for these families was 32 minutes. In the Midwestern clinic, approximately 8 patients go through the waiting room every hour between noon and 3 P.M. with an average wait time of 13.2 minutes and average group size of 2.36 people.

One of the first things we were interested in is what, if anything, people read while they were waiting. Of the roughly 500 people who were observed, less than 10 read books, magazines, or newspapers; all who did brought their own reading material with them. Over the course of our observations, three separate adults walked to the pamphlet area and looked at the flyers in the stand, and one of them picked up a pamphlet and took it back to his seat. In terms of digital media, one out of every two people used mobile technology while waiting, including cell phones, laptops, handheld gaming devices, or other mobile devices. Mobile technology use was especially common among teenagers and adults. We

only observed four people talking on their phones. TV's, art areas, and toys were popular among younger children and allowed them to play with others as they waited.

We were also interested in the frequency of clinic visits. Typical sickle cell patients visit between once a month to once a year for checkups, with a majority falling in the range of once every 3-6 months.

Every staff member mentioned self-care as their number one priority in patient education; this included information on how to stay healthy using diet and exercise, what to do in the case of SCD pain, and other details on how to manage personal health. Staff members also agreed that the current materials for teaching patients are usually written at the adult level, and used mostly as ways to "help hit high points" during appointments. Staff expected that parents are supporting children by transferring information in a way that suits the family once at home, though they recognize the limitations on parents' time during and after appointments. Most staff also agreed that teaching the patients about the biology of the disease, while interesting, would likely not influence self-care.

However, when discussing with the staff about how to improve patient compliance with health regimes, most suggested that better education and understanding would improve health outcomes and adherence to medications.

> "Everybody is pressed for time in the clinic. We may not have time to go over the details, but [the information] can help with compliance and staying healthier."

> "You have better compliance when you have better understanding and buy in from patients . . . "

> "If you understand why we're concerned, you're more likely to be concerned."

These discussions were interesting contrasts to the staff's strategies on educating their patients, usually focusing on the instructions to stay healthy. Many of the materials found in waiting areas or delivered to the patients were created by the local staff or other physicians and nurses that work with sickle cell patients.

This discrepancy lead to discussions about staff training, specifically in educating patients. Most medical training is centered about the human body and medical care. None of the questioned staff members had ever received formal education training, as this not routinely part of their extensive medical training. When asked how they learned to teach patients, most staff described picking up strategies from their mentors and co-workers.

Based on staff and patient interviews and a review of the available materials, we found that very little information is directed towards the children, especially at a younger age. When one patient was asked when he first learned about sickle cell he said "Never?" and went on to explain that he's always had it, and it was just part of his life knowing how it impacted his behavior. Since this is a disease diagnosed at birth much of the instruction is given to the parents early on. The transition of the information to the child is specific to every physician and family; there is no formal process. When the staff were asked how they begin to direct information to the patient rather than the parents they all explained that they just start talking and distributing materials to the child rather than the parent. There is no shift if types of materials used.

# 7. IMPLICATIONS FOR WAITING AREA DESIGN

Some key implications from our observations and interviews are discussed below.

**DI1.Collaborative** There is a requirement that all patients under the age of 18 attend appointments with an adult. Yet, with an average family group size over two, it implies that many patients are attending their appointments with additional family members such as second parents, siblings, or grandparents. This presents an opportunity for collaboration between and within patient groups who share an interest and potential motivation to learn. Moreover, our observations revealed that people in waiting areas frequently interact with one another as they wait. This could provide an opportunity for knowledge exchange and supporting discussions between children and adults.

**DI2.Engaging** Typical health education materials are neglected by patients and families, nor are they targeted at younger audiences; for our research it is important that our design engages patient groups, especially children. The primary goal of this project is not just to attract people as they wait for appointments but, more importantly, to help them to understand relevant health issues. Ideally education materials will keep people's attention and provide opportunities for discussion.

**DI3.Reusability** In many cases, patients visit the same clinic repeatedly throughout their lives for routine checkups. In the sickle cell community repeated visits are very common. Since these patients will be waiting frequently it is important that the material provide multiple opportunities for exploration over the course of months and years. The materials need to draw patients in to explore even after they have been used in multiple prior visits. The design should appeal to audiences of different ages and allow for a variety of different interaction patterns.

**DI4.Mobile Devices** Another potential aspect of design comes from the prominence of mobile devices. The majority of SCD patients and families spend most of their waiting time on mobile devices; a mode that is common and easily used to create educational experiences and opportunities for local community building. Having an experience that can travel with them as they continue to their appointment or leave the clinic provides additional opportunities for learning and conversation with physicians and staff, even other patients. Mobile devices also support patients in clinics where waiting does not occur in the main area. In the Midwest clinic, for example, the patients spend hours in the exam room waiting, but only a short period in the main area.

**DI5.Detailed Biological Explanations** While clinic staff have reported that they do not emphasize the biological details of the disease with patients, they do believe that this information would help with medication compliance and good health practices. It is difficult for staff to find the time to go into such detail during appointments, so if we can find a way to share that information at any time it may show some benefit. If the material explains the fundamental concept of the disease, then we might further explain why taking medications or other treatments correct or change those issues to improve health; for example, if we detail cell structure in sickle red blood cells and show its resulting effects on the body's blood flow, we can also detail the effects of medication on that structure and its corrections to the blood flow.

Ideally these explanations will help patients understand why they need to adhere to medical routines and result in better overall health.

# 8. DESIGN OVERVIEW

## 8.1 Implementation

We created a Sickle Cell Station consisting of three main features: a mobile application, a tangible blood vessel, and an information poster. These three features were designed to cover the implications listed in the previous section. Here we discuss the development and preliminary analysis of the mobile application and supporting poster.

For our initial iteration we focused on the basic principles underlying sickle cell disease including the difference in hemo-globin and the difference in blood flow with sickle cells. Materials used in this round of testing consisted of a tablet computer app, a physical blood cell model, and the poster. Each part of the design can be used independently, but they also reinforce one another conceptually.

We designed each component to support group interaction and collaboration. The tablet, tangible cells, and poster can all be shared by multiple users at once. In addition, the design anticipates that users will work with multiple components to explore the demonstrated phenomena.

Mobility is a more complex design issue for the station. Since we are trying to educate patients as they wait, we aim to provide an experience that patients will want to take advantage of during their visit to a clinic. For this reason, much of the station is not mobile; creating an experience that can only happen at the clinic and that patients will ideally look forward to. However, given the sporadic nature of some wait sessions (for example, being called to the clinic for vitals) we take advantage of the ubiquity of mobile devices so that patients can do some activities away from the waiting area, perhaps when they leave the clinic, or as they wait in an exam room. A tablet application provides a system that users can take with them, but also can be elaborated on at the local clinic station.

We attempted to make the exhibit engaging by creating an inviting design and demonstrating concepts without excessive amounts of information. We expect this allows users opportunities to notice and question details and encourage further investigation across the different materials at the sickle cell station.

Biological explanations are provided across the design. Hemo-globin and its impact on cell structure are highlighted on all branches of the station textually, physically, and visually. We anticipate that additions to the tablet application will give users an opportunity for deeper exploration as patients and their families become motivated to learn more.

### 8.1.1 Tangible Cells

We begin the design with the fundamental issue of sickle cell disease – the internal workings of hemoglobin. This is the key element for defining sickle cell disease so we use all three parts of the station to highlight the differences between normal and sickle hemoglobin. Hemoglobin floats freely in normal red blood cells but in sickle cells molecules bind with one another and form stiff chains. We use two tangible red blood cells (one normal and one sickle) made of fabric. The tangible normal cell is stuffed with beans, while the sickle cell is stuffed with beans as well as stiff strings of beads to replicate the hemoglobin structures of each cell respectively. Both cells are made from the same circle pattern measuring approximately six inches in diameter. However, when the sickle cell circle is filled with stiff rows of beads the shape becomes a longer narrower sickle shape approximately ten inches long; the strategy used to create the tangible cells was intended to replicate the natural process of cell sickling in the body. With only the tangible cells the user can feel the chains of hemoglobin in the sickle cell, while also being able to feel the loose hemoglobin of the normal cell. By itself, the tangible cell allows patients to begin understanding the mechanism behind SCD. These cells highlight biological details in a tangible form and also provide an inviting material to encourage its use.

### 8.1.2 Cell X-ray

We use a tablet application to generate an augmented reality of the hemoglobin over the tangible cells. This tangible representation is reinforced by the augmented reality view that visually shows both types of hemoglobin in its respective structures. On top of each cell is a tag for the augmented reality software to recognize the three dimensional orientation for image projection. The X-ray mode

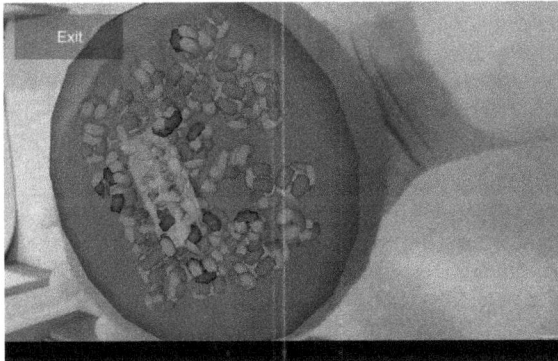

**Figure 1: Screenshot of the X-ray augmented reality tablet application, displaying hemoglobin structure overlaying the camera image of the tangible normal red blood cell.**

**Figure 2: Image of the X-ray app in use from the tablet application, displaying augmented reality image of hemoglobin structure over the tangible sickle cell.**

uses the Vuforia augmented reality software development kit (SDK) and its extension to the Unity game engine, allowing easy deployment to both the Android and iOS operating systems. The Vuforia extensions are used to track the physical red blood cell model in 3D space once it is in view of the tablet's camera. This information is then used to render a semi-transparent virtual model of the cell (see Figures 1 & 2). The virtual model shows the interior composition on top of the camera's image, making the physical cell appear transparent when viewed on the tablet. This is akin to an X-ray effect: when a user looks at the physical cell he/she only sees it's exterior, but when viewed through the tablet, additional details of the interior of the cell are now visible. This application runs in real-time – as the user pans and tilts the camera, or moves it closer or farther, the virtual model follows and allows the user to explore the cell from multiple angles and zoom levels.

To assist in tracking, Vuforia requires a unique tag to be placed on each physical object. In the case of our cells, we created labels for "Normal" and "Sickle" cells, placed in the center of the object for both tracking purposes as well as cell identification for the user. This provides the app with an estimate of the space in the image that the physical object occupies. The 3D representation of these cells is modeled using Blender, an open source 3D animation software package. This included specifying properties such as the textures, transparencies, colors, and interior contents. These models were then imported into the Unity engine for rendering. In reality, the hemoglobin in normal red blood cells have some freedom of movement. To create a more realistic image, we added C# code to define the rules for movement (rotation, velocity, and containment) of the hemoglobin in the blood cells.

### 8.1.3 Blood Flow Animation

Another key difference for sickle cell patients is blood flow. The shape of sickle cells causes various issues in the blood stream, primarily obstructions. A video shows a dynamic illustration of normal blood flow and compares it with one of a sickle cell patient.

The blood flow animation visualizes the movement of cells in a small section of the human circulatory system (Fig. 3). It includes several branches of blood vessels, with a cutaway view so that differences between sickle and blood cells are visible. The main concepts for this model are: normal and sickle cells have different shapes, and sickle cells (due to their shape) have more difficulty moving through constricted spaces slowing or blocking the smaller branches of the vessel. The animation was again developed using Blender. 3D models were built for individual blood cells, including both normal and sickle red blood cells, platelets, and white blood cells, as well as the vessel itself. Next, each cell type was defined as a particle system set to flow through the vessel. The sickle cells were configured to have higher resistance in the narrower portions of the vessel. An animation of the normal blood flow and the sickle cell flow were then created and added to the app. Lastly, a simple user interface was assembled to combine the two components in a single unified app. To rapidly prototype the UI, we used MIT App Inventor (http://appinventor.mit.edu/) to build an interface that allows for selection of the two components and handling the playing of the blood flow animations.

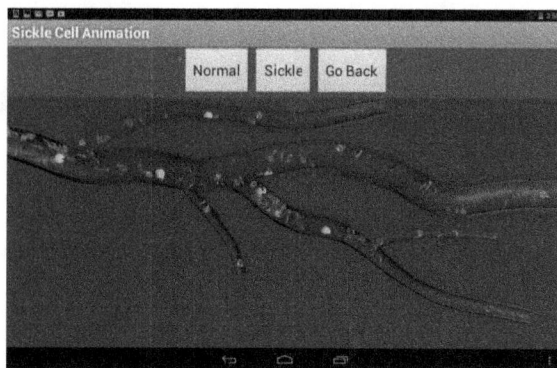

**Figure 3: Screenshot of the sickle cell blood flow animation from the tablet application.**

### 8.1.4 Information Poster

The station also includes an information poster measuring six feet by three feet (Figure 4). The poster illustrates a large blood vessel, and defines some basic principles and characteristics of the human circulatory system and issues related to sickle cell disease, including four types of blood cells, the shape and stiffness of sickle cells, and the cause of pain from sickle cells. This information is intended to build the understanding of blood by complementing the tangible and virtual materials and provide a written version of the information we are trying to share. For consistency, the image of the blood vessel is generated from the same Blender model used in the video application discussed in the previous section.

This poster contains text descriptions of sickle cell disease, the effects on the red blood cells and their hemoglobin, and short detail on treatments. It should be noted that this information is not described in either of the tablet applications.

## 9. USER TESTING

We conducted preliminary user testing on the base functions of the sickle cell station. Primarily we wanted to evaluate how people used the blood flow application, the X-ray application, and the poster.

### 9.1 Methods

Preliminary testing took place in the Mid-Atlantic clinic waiting area. Two flyers were posted in the waiting area to recruit participants on the day of testing: one outside the main entry door and the other on the back of the information poster in the testing area. The researcher also approached patient groups as they waited. We were not limiting users to sickle cell patients for testing since the material is designed for the general waiting area population.

A child-height table was set up in the back of the large waiting room. We spread the poster facing the rear wall of the room to create a barrier between the main area and the video recorded test area. We created this wall for two reasons: to ensure privacy during testing and consent-required video recording; and to make sure that the patients viewed the poster for the first time during testing. A video recorder was set up on a tripod focused on the table with the tangible cell models and tablet, which also meant it would capture and users' hand interactions. An additional audio recorder

was placed on the table for a secondary audio stream to validate transcriptions.

The groups were taken to the testing area and consented to video and audio recordings of their interactions with the station. They were then told the purpose of the testing and asked to use to material for as long or as little time as they would like. The researcher waited within view of the testing area and recorded notable interactions and conversations during testing. Following participants' use they were asked a few questions about their experience pertaining to usability and understanding of the materials.

### 9.2 Participants

In total six patient groups were recruited for testing. A patient group is defined as at least one parent and one child age 5-18 years. Each group consisted of a parent-child pair. However, in one instance the mother was called to the desk, so the child mostly participated alone. In another instance, the child was called up and the mother participated for the remaining time. Since these are common scenarios in the user population in the waiting area, we did not remove these sessions from our data set.

The children's ages ranged from 5 to 14 years, with an average of 7.7 years old. Four of the children were male, two were female. Five of the children participated with a female parent or guardian while one attended with a male parent. Three of the groups were African American, one group was Middle Eastern, and two groups were Caucasian.

Of the six groups, one of the children had heard of sickle cell before. Four of the adults had heard of the disease, but did not know much about it; one parent's knowledge is unknown. One mother of a sickle cell patient claimed to be an expert; her son had been to hospitals outside of the city for special programs and the Ronald McDonald program, among others; it should be noted that this mother was participating in the study with a different child.

### 9.3 Results

At this point in our design process we are interested in participants experience with usability and material engagement.

### 9.3.1 Usability

The groups had positive feedback about the station, saying the applications and poster were "cool" and they had "never seen anything like this". Every group managed to use both tablet applications independently, and only one technical error was uncovered during testing, discussed in detail later in this section. The tangible cells were used by multiple groups to feel the difference between the cells; one in a parents' explanation of why sickle cells get stuck. Three of the groups read some of the poster together, and compared the applications to the informative text. At least two groups referred to the images for identification and definitions of video details.

However, some groups had problems understanding the flow of the station as a whole. Half of the groups appeared to read the poster; this was determined by reading aloud or looking at the poster for more than a few seconds. As they approached the exhibit four of the groups immediately picked up the tablet before looking at the poster. However, the design of the station assumes that the information on the poster has been read prior. This was confusing for

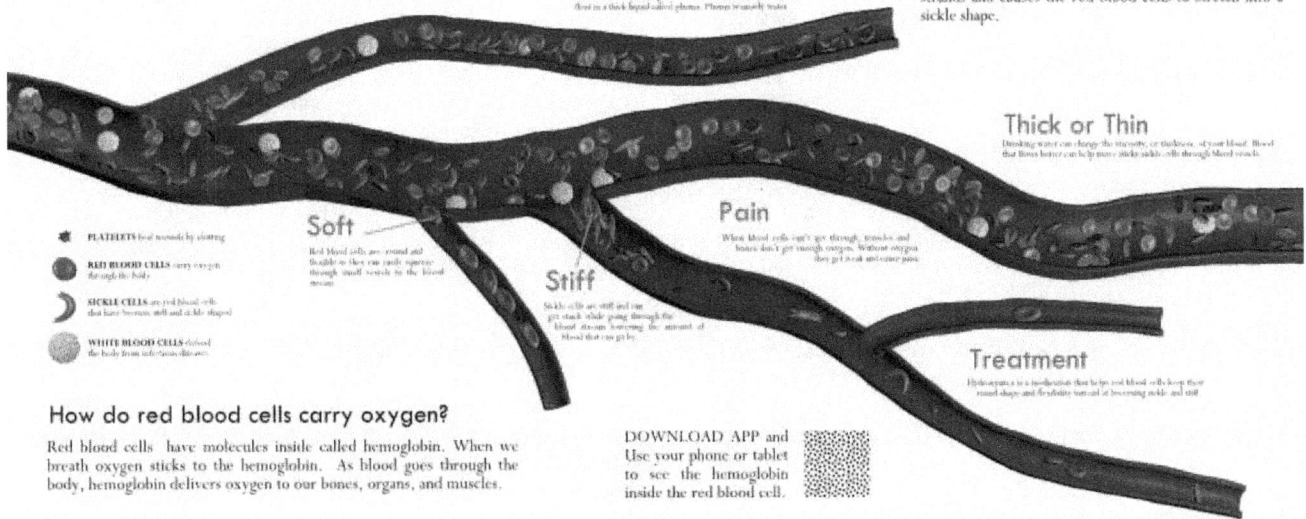

Figure 4: Informative poster.

many users as they attempted to use the X-ray application wondered what the "popcorns" in the cells were.

Holding the tablet computer camera steady above the AR tag also proved difficult for some users. One had trouble figuring out how to point the camera at the cells, even after given instructions; the camera would not focus on the tag resulting in no change to the application image.

One unexpected issue was discovered when one group used the tablet sitting down. Typically the application has been used while standing above a table – placing the tablet about ten inches away from the screen, and allowing the entire cell and its interior features to be visible. When the group used it while seated the tablet was approximately three inches above the cell, displaying a zoomed-in version of the hemoglobin to be displayed. While functional, this viewing distance focuses closely on the hemoglobin, but does not show the bigger picture of the cell, and makes the comparison of the hemoglobin structure less obvious. The mother in this group also pointed this out as a difficulty in getting the camera to focus on the label at such a close distance. The group never figured out to hold the tablet at a further distance during their testing, but still had meaningful conversation about the differences between the cells.

The tags on the tangible cells are written in QR type font for recognition; this makes it a bit difficult for the human eye to read. One mother asked her daughter to read it, but she couldn't make out the words. One young child pointed the tablet X-ray app at the poster after viewing the cells, implying that he expected a similar augmented reality of the blood vessel image, demonstrating his understanding of the tablet for augmented reality application. Unfortunately, this is a feature we designed the video application for in future iterations, but have yet to implement.

Otherwise, there were few technical issues with the usability of the systems. The design of the interfaces are attractive and interesting to the users, but the tasks are not clear and require additional instruction or a design with clearer use implications.

### 9.3.2 Engagement

The participants used the material for an average of 6.9 minutes (SD=0.12), with only one group using it for less than five minutes, and the longest lasting nearly eleven minutes.

Our first measure of engagement looked at the amount of discussion happening within groups. Four of the groups that worked in pairs had conversations about the material. We define these conversations as direct back-and-forth questioning or clarification between the parent and child.

Almost every user group alternated between the two tangible cells, the two videos, and the augmented reality feature (X-ray) comparing as they discussed the differences between them. For example, while using the X-ray application a mother asked her child "See the difference? Between the normal and the sickle cell one?..." as the child moved the camera from the sickle cell to the normal cell and back again. "One is jumbled up together, and this one is spread apart and moving" the child responded as they continued to look between the two. Similar instances occurred repeatedly with the video application, observing the blood clot caused by the sickle cells. "Its like they're trapped. Its like there's a door or something" pointing at the sickle cell video after having gone back and forth between the two. One girl held the tangible sickle cell and said "this one looks like a banana." The daughter went on to point out the stiff thread of beads in the sickle cell asking "Wait. What's this?" The mom explains, "That makes it have the [sickle] shape". The daughter then picks up the normal cell and says "this doesn't have it." In all three design aspects with comparable conditions the users noted and discussed differences.

We also used cross-references between the materials to measure engagement. That is, any time that one of the three parts of the station (tangible cells, virtual models, or poster) are used to support another; for example, if the patient is reading the poster and refers to the tangible cells to emphasize hemoglobin structure. We found cross-referencing to be common among the four families working in pairs. One mother read through the first part of the poster with her daughter asking her to read aloud specific parts. The mother then held the tangible normal cell and asked her child "this is like the blood you have; it's shaped like this. You can see it in the drawing... Do you see any that are shaped like this [sickle cell]?" The daughter then walked to the poster and pointed out several of the sickle cells. In another group, while watching the sickle video, one child asks "why are they getting stuck?" and the parent responds, picking up the tangible cell by the point on top "well these sickle cells are stiffer". They then switched to the normal cell video and continue their discussion comparing the normal cells to marbles in a tube.

Although the material highlights sickle cell disease, we were pleased to see other patients make the information relevant for themselves. Both the video and poster started conversations within groups that seemed relevant to the child, even if they didn't suffer from SCD. One example, a mother called her son over "...that's a vein filled with blood cells". The boy followed with "like my blood cells?.. that [shows] my blood pressure." In another instance, a father pointed out all the features that were relevant to his son who was currently undergoing chemotherapy, "See.. those are the white blood cells - the ones you're low on from the chemo." Many foundational concepts relating to the human body can be described using the same materials.

The expert mother said she had never been shown the inside of the cells before, elaborating that "There's a lot of information out there [about sickle cell disease]. But you have to go digging for it yourself. It's a lot footwork..." She had previously taken her son across to a neighboring city just to see a hospital exhibit on Sickle Cell. She continued to stress her enthusiasm for an exhibit so convenient for patients, especially using non-printed materials.

When asked about the cell structures in the follow up interview, one child described the hemoglobin as "all jumbled up... I thought it looked a lot like popcorn so I just kept thinking of that. These popcorns [in the sickle cell] are stuck together, like.. 'I can't let you go!'" Although this patient did not identify the hemoglobin by name, she showed an understanding of the basic cell structure which is the designs primary goal.

We found the conversations among participant groups to show an understanding of the content, and, moreover, often created meaningful ties to their own health care. Many collaborative conversations and inquiries were initiated from the materials, and users bridged highlights from each material to others to better understand or describe concepts of cell structure and blood flow. This evidence suggests the material provides an engaging experience for the users.

## 10.  DISCUSSION

Although technology has become an everyday part of health care at home and in hospitals, the focus is almost exclusively relegated to the management of records or health regimens. Chronic diseases that begin at birth pose an interesting problem for patients since there is no initial lesson; it's just a part of who they are. Our initial interviews suggest that current materials need reworking, especially if they intend to be used by children. Most information is either shared orally by a physician or given in writing using language geared to an adult audience; both are strategies that require parental involvement and may not be most engaging for children. In addition, the level of involvement of parents varies from family to family, again suggesting that children can benefit from materials that are more engaging and age appropriate to support direct and independent education if parental support is less available.

Our observations suggest that waiting areas are valuable settings for patient and family learning experiences. SCD patients and their families spend an average of 13 to 30 minutes in waiting areas before their appointments; some of this time could be spent learning about SCD in an engaging and interactive way. Family support in these environments is also noteworthy. Many families come together with the patients for various reasons, opening the possibility for collaborative learning experiences, much like those experiences shared by families in interactive museum exhibits. Physician interviews highlight expectations of knowledge sharing in the family, though our interviews suggest that this may not be a realistic expectation in all cases. The preliminary part of their time at the clinic provides an occasion to be free of other obligations and focus on working with their child to learn about relevant health issues.

Although we cannot draw any conclusions with such a small sample size, the results are promising for the design and purpose of our research. Based on the user testing we will reiterate our designs to include more information and instruction directly in the tablet applications. The material seemed engaging for our participant groups with relatively lengthy use times and meaningful conversation. The combination of materials allowed users to compare across different media and types of experiences, bridging the knowledge highlighted in each. Some patients even took the opportunity to relate the material to more personal situations. We hope this work will benefit not only the population of children with sickle cell and their support networks, but also become transferrable to other disease populations that face many of the same practices and issues for their own waiting area education designs.

We also hope that the design of the materials will help patients to understand the importance and purpose of medications and good health habits.

## 11.  FUTURE WORK

This project will continue to explore options for SCD providers to take advantage of the unique qualities of waiting areas, such as time, family support, and an abundance of mobile devices to create interesting and engaging tools for education and even health management. We plan to collect additional interviews directed towards patients' personal experiences with education including how and what information they receive from their doctors, the clinic, family or friends, and personal research. These interviews will also expand on the family relationship to education.

We have developed additional interactive material for the station, including a tangible blood vessel model measuring approximately eight feet long, which demonstrates many of the same characteristics as the blood flow videos. Tangible white blood cells, red blood cells, platelettes, and sickle cells are poured down the vessel replicating blood flow. A series of sensors along the vessel track the amount of oxygen delivered by the blood flow and reflect resulting oxygen levels in muscles using a light system. An in-depth user study is being conducted to evaluate the usability and understanding of the station as a whole and the materials individually. Naturalistic observations are also being collected to test the station's real world applicability in both clinics. During this process we are also conducting pre-test and post-test evaluations to elaborate on the children's and families' knowledge change after use of the material.

Future iterations of the design include improvements to both the app and the tangible blood vessel to demonstrate the effects of hydroxyurea, a common sickle cell medication, and hydration levels. In addition, we plan to continue all previously described testing in the Midwestern clinic to compare with the shorter wait periods and private wait locations.

As mentioned in the discussion, we hope to continue this work to better understand compliance issues with health care, but this is a long term project goal. Though a difficult process, long term follow ups with the help of the staff and medical records should help shed light on any behavior changes, as well as interviews with patients about their personal habits and understandings.

## 12. ACKNOWLEDGEMENTS

We thank Simone Ispa-Landa, Thrasos Pappas, Edd Taylor and Wesley Leong for their feedback, advice, and support as we develop this research. We also thank the hospitals and clinics whose staff and patient families are currently participating in these studies and developments.

## 13. REFERENCES

[1] I. Anderson, J. Maitland, S. Sherwood, L. Barkhuus, M. Chalmers, M. Hall, B. Brown, and H. Muller. Shakra: tracking and sharing daily activity levels with unaugmented mobile phones. *Mob. Netw. Appl.*, 12:185–199, March 2007.

[2] S. Ballegaard, T. Hansen, and M. Kyng. Healthcare in everyday life: designing healthcare services for daily life. In *Proceeding of the twenty-sixth annual SIGCHI conference on Human factors in computing systems*, pages 1807–1816. ACM, 2008.

[3] S. Benveniste, P. Jouvelot, E. Lecourt, and R. Michel. Designing wiimprovisation for mediation in group music therapy with children suffering from behavioral disorders. In *Proceedings of the 8th International Conference on Interaction Design and Children*, pages 18–26. ACM, 2009.

[4] T. Bickmore, L. Caruso, K. Clough-Gorr, and T. Heeren. [] it's just like you talk to a friend'relational agents for older adults. *Interacting with Computers*, 17(6):711–735, 2005.

[5] T. Bickmore, L. Pfeifer, and B. Jack. Taking the time to care: empowering low health literacy hospital patients with virtual nurse agents. In *Proceedings of the 27th international conference on Human factors in computing systems*, pages 1265–1274. ACM, 2009.

[6] F. Chen, E. Hekler, J. Hu, S. Li, and C. Zhao. Designing for context-aware health self-monitoring, feedback, and engagement. In *Proceedings of the ACM 2011 conference on Computer supported cooperative work*, pages 613–616. ACM, 2011.

[7] Y. Chen. Health information use in chronic care cycles. In *Proceedings of the ACM 2011 conference on Computer supported cooperative work*, pages 485–488. ACM, 2011.

[8] D. Gresh, D. Rabenhorst, A. Shabo, and S. Slavin. Prima: a case study of using information visualization techniques for patient record analysis. 2002.

[9] Htv changes waiting room experience. http://htvnetwork s.com/blog/htv-changes-waiting-room-experience/. [Retrieved on 17-Aug-2011].

[10] D. Lewis. Computer-based approaches to patient education. *Journal of the American Medical Informatics Association*, 6(4):272, 1999.

[11] J. Lin, L. Mamykina, S. Lindtner, G. Delajoux, and H. Strub. FishŠnŠsteps: Encouraging physical activity with an interactive computer game. *UbiComp 2006: Ubiquitous Computing*, pages 261–278, 2006.

[12] L. Mamykina, E. Mynatt, P. Davidson, and D. Greenblatt. Mahi: investigation of social scaffolding for reflective thinking in diabetes management. In *Proceeding of the twenty-sixth annual SIGCHI conference on Human factors in computing systems*, pages 477–486. ACM, 2008.

[13] B. McGrath and R. Tempier. Is the waiting room a classroom? *Psychiatric Services*, 54(7):1043, 2003.

[14] D. McQuillen and M. Derheim. Taking care of those who wait: Creating the ideal waiting room experience. http://www.eplabdigest.com/articles/Taking-Care-Tho se-Who-Wait-Creating-Ideal-Waiting-Room-Experience. [Retrieved on 17-Aug-2011].

[15] A. M. Piper. Supporting medical communication with a multimodal surface computer. In *Proceedings of the 28th of the international conference extended abstracts on Human factors in computing systems*, CHI EA '10, pages 2899–2902, New York, NY, USA, 2010. ACM.

[16] A. M. Piper, N. Weibel, and J. D. Hollan. Introducing multimodal paper-digital interfaces for speech-language therapy. In *Proceedings of the 12th international ACM SIGACCESS conference on Computers and accessibility*, ASSETS '10, pages 203–210, New York, NY, USA, 2010. ACM.

[17] S. Purpura, V. Schwanda, K. Williams, W. Stubler, and P. Sengers. Fit4life: the design of a persuasive technology promoting healthy behavior and ideal weight. In *Proceedings of the 2011 annual conference on Human factors in computing systems*, pages 423–432. ACM, 2011.

[18] D. Schulman and T. Bickmore. Persuading users through counseling dialogue with a conversational agent. In *Proceedings of the 4th International Conference on Persuasive Technology*, page 25. ACM, 2009.

[19] Sickle cell information center. http://scinfo.org/. [Retrieved on 17-Aug-2011].

[20] T. Toscos, A. Faber, S. An, and M. Gandhi. Chick clique: persuasive technology to motivate teenage girls to exercise. In *CHI'06 extended abstracts on Human factors in computing systems*, pages 1873–1878. ACM, 2006.

[21] K. Ward and K. Hawthorne. Do patients read health promotion posters in the waiting room? a study in one general practice. *The British Journal of General Practice*, 44(389):583, 1994.

[22] D. Wicke, R. Lorge, R. Coppin, and K. Jones. The effectiveness of waiting room notice-boards as a vehicle for health education. *Family Practice*, 11(3):292, 1994.

[23] L. Wilcox, D. Morris, D. Tan, and J. Gatewood. Designing patient-centric information displays for hospitals. In *Proceedings of the 28th international conference on Human factors in computing systems*, pages 2123–2132. ACM, 2010.

[24] X. Zhou, M. Ackerman, and K. Zheng. I just don't know why it's gone: maintaining informal information use in inpatient care. In *Proceedings of the 27th international conference on Human factors in computing systems*, pages 2061–2070. ACM, 2009.

# "It Helped me do my Science." A Case of Designing Social Media Technologies for Children in Science Learning

Jason Yip[1], June Ahn, Tamara Clegg, Elizabeth Bonsignore, Daniel Pauw, and Michael Gubbels

[1]Joan Ganz Cooney Center at Sesame Workshop, 1900 Broadway, New York, NY 10023, USA
jyip@sesame.org

University of Maryland - Human-Computer Interaction Lab
2117 Hornbake Bldg., South Wing College Park, MD 20742, USA
{juneahn, tclegg, ebonsign, dpauw, mgubbels}@umd.edu

## ABSTRACT

In this paper, we present the design evolution of two social media (SM) tools: *Scientific INQuiry* (SINQ), which transformed into *ScienceKit*. We detail our motivations for using SM tools in science learning and the design decisions we made over a 2-year, design-based research project. Our designs grew from our experiences using SM tools in the field and co-designing these systems with children. Our longitudinal case study and design narrative contribute to our understanding of the design and use of SM tools to support children's scientific inquiry. Specifically, we detail (1) the affordances and constraints we gleaned from the design evolution of SINQ to ScienceKit, (2) the potential of SM to guide learning behaviors, and (3) the role of SM for children and the community of adults and peers who support them.

## Categories and Subject Descriptors

K.3.1 [**Computer Uses in Education**]: Collaborative learning; Computer assisted instruction (CAI); H.5.2 [**User Interfaces**]: User-centered design

**General Terms:** Design, Human Factors.

**Keywords:** Social media, children, co-design, learning technologies, science learning.

## 1. INTRODUCTION

Children today are surrounded by social media (SM) platforms and mobile technologies. Questions abound about how young people use these platforms and devices, their influence on the social and learning experiences of youth, and how to design technologies that are uniquely appropriate for children's developmental contexts [3, 19, 21]. Likewise, our research team has worked for the last two years to understand the affordances of SM for children's science learning. We situate this work within the broader research literature that investigates the ways in which SM can enhance learning [20]. However, much of this research has been conducted with college students, with few studies of children's experiences [25, 28]. Very few studies have explicitly considered the role and effect of SM designs on children's learning. Grimes and Fields [21] note that there is a great need to understand the similarities and differences between the development of tools and platforms for younger children and those of teens and adults. After one takes design into account, a vital question emerges, "How do children respond to different site designs in interactions with influences of family, friends, schools, and other community influences?" (p. 54).

Our work responds to these issues by exploring how design decisions in SM tools relate to children's learning interactions. In this paper, we provide the design narrative of a 2-year design-based research project focused on the iterative development of two SM tools to promote and support scientific inquiry for children. Specifically, we explore the question: *How does the design of the user interface and experience of SM technologies support science inquiry learning?* Delving deeper, we aim to tease apart the *kinds* of inquiry experiences that various design aspects of the technology support.

Our case study describes the evolution of two SM apps for children, *Scientific INQuiry* (*SINQ*) [2] into *ScienceKit* [1]. We detail our motivations for using SM tools in science inquiry learning and the design decisions we made transitioning from a text-based interface (SINQ) to one that supported multimodal interactions (ScienceKit). Our design decisions grew from our experiences implementing the SM technologies in the field and co-designing with children [18]. Drawing on our analysis of this design process, we derived design implications regarding the affordances and constraints of SM platforms to support scientific inquiry in non-formal learning environments. We developed these design insights in the context of a non-formal learning environment, Kitchen Chemistry (KC), over a 2-year case study.

## 2. BACKGROUND

### 2.1 Designing Technology to Promote Inquiry

In the design of SINQ and ScienceKit, we focused on promoting scientific inquiry based on Chinn and Malhotra's [11] framework. Authentic inquiry challenges learners to generate their own research questions, select and invent variables to investigate, develop their own procedures to address questions, control multiple variables, find flaws in their results, engage in systematic observations, and plan multiple measures of independent and dependent variables, among other elaborate methods.

Our stance is that children's personal experiences in the everyday world can lead to authentic practices in science inquiry. We want to help children to consistently and frequently engage in scientific inquiry across the contexts of their lives (in and out of school). In essence, we aim to help them *scientize* their daily experiences. We define scientizing as helping learners develop their ability to recognize the relevance of science in their personal lives and to engage in scientific practices in those situations [16]. However, a

*IDC'14*, June 17–20, 2014, Aarhus, Denmark.
Copyright 2014 ACM 978-1-4503-2272-0/14/06...$15.00.
http://dx.doi.org/10.1145/2593968.2593969

major design challenge is developing learning environments, pedagogical practices, and technologies that can promote this type of everyday inquiry. Our study extends prior work that showed that SM technologies and learning cannot be separated from the sociocultural contexts in which learners reside and interact [23]. We examine how SM technologies can support the collaborations needed for children to engage in authentic scientific practices in a specific learning environment, *Kitchen Chemistry* (KC).

## 2.2 Technologies to Support Collaboration

Collaboration in learning must be nurtured and technologies can support or undermine the collaborative efforts of learners [35]. In the context of scientific inquiry, we aim to support collaborations that promote sharing ideas, questions, and hypotheses, building knowledge together, and drawing on the expertise of others [5].

### 2.2.1 Cognitive Supports for Collaboration

Prior research has focused on designing cognitive scaffolds for science learners' collaboration. Examples include the Web-based Inquiry Science Environment (WISE) and Computer Supported Intentional Learning Environment (CSILE, known later as Knowledge Forum). WISE is designed to leverage collaborative interaction and individual scaffolding in the forms of online discussions, peer review, and debates to help students build ideas around scientific phenomenon [29]. CSILE provides software-realized scaffolding to help learners build conceptual models, construct theories, and summarize their learning [33]. These platforms guide learners to collaborate with others, share ideas, and elaborate on these ideas in order to scaffold the learning of scientific concepts, or build mental models about a phenomenon. Of note, formal classrooms or groups of students were often the target context for which these platforms were designed. Inspired by this work, our first prototype, SINQ, largely extended these ideas of scaffolded, collaborative learning.

### 2.2.2 Social Supports for Collaboration

A separate stream of design and research has focused largely on technologies to support the social environments around which collaborative learning happens. This work has appeared most often in the field of Interaction Design and Children (IDC). Examples include the Scratch online community, Zydeco, and Tangible Flags. In the Scratch community, members can upload their programming projects for others to remix and extend [9]. Zydeco aims to bridge gaps between formal and informal learning environments [10], by enabling learners to tag observations in-situ (e.g., while in a museum), which they can later leverage during formal discussions in class. The Tangible Flags study highlighted how mobile technologies can enhance children's experiences in everyday contexts such as field trips [12]. We note that this stream of research has focused less on cognitive scaffolds, but more so on understanding and supporting the social environments within which children can learn about science. These efforts have compelled us to consider how children learn in informal, everyday environments and the unique ways that technology can support this learning process.

### 2.2.3 Social Media for Collaboration and Learning

Finally, our work is also motivated by research where learning is examined in already existing SM platforms. As platforms such as social network sites have risen in popularity, researchers have asked what relationships such platforms have to learning. Studies show that tools such as Twitter™ could be used to enhance student engagement [24], but that everyday use of platforms such as Facebook™ may be a negative distraction to earning grades [25]. Similar work has documented how students use Facebook™ to organize study groups or negotiate campus life [28, 34]. Many of these studies explore how to implement already existing SM platforms – with already present social and cultural norms – for the purposes of formal education. Moreover, inconsistent findings, where SM is found to be beneficial or harmful to learning, suggest a complex and nuanced relationship between technology and learning. *How* SM is designed and implemented is likely a vital factor for learning. We seek to explore these details in our work.

## 3. DESIGN-BASED APPROACH

In order to understand the role of SM technology in supporting collaboration and scientific inquiry, we followed a *design-based research* (DBR) approach [17]. DBR focuses on applying learning theories to progressively refine the design of a technology or intervention through a process of iterative development, implementation, and analytic feedback. In our DBR approach, we carefully considered the learning goals we thought were important for inquiry-based learning, developed and configured the tools that would attempt to meet those goals, integrated the tool into an authentic learning environment (KC), and examined what learning outcomes occurred. Based on the learning interactions we observed, we then iterated on the design of the technology and the learning environment.

## 3.1 SINQ and ScienceKit Social Media Tools

We first built SINQ as a mobile web application, in which the server and client were tightly coupled and co-dependent. The first prototypes of SINQ were primarily browser-based and text-heavy (Figure 1). As we integrated SINQ into non-formal settings and began co-designing with children, we transformed SINQ into ScienceKit. ScienceKit is a mobile, SM app similar to SINQ, with the consistent overarching goal of supporting inquiry-based learning in science. However, instead of a text- and browser-based interface, ScienceKit's design integrates multiple forms of multimedia (e.g., drawings, audio, video) to allow learners to document and share their everyday life experiences in science (Figure 2). In our design narrative, we highlight the inception of the prototypes, the design decisions we made, and the thematic outcomes of the implementation into KC.

## 3.2 Cooperative Inquiry Design Process

In the design portions of our DBR process, we collaborated with an intergenerational design team composed of children and design researchers in our lab called *Kidsteam*. Using a participatory design method known as Cooperative Inquiry [18], we worked closely with six to eight child designers (ages 7 – 11) and four to six adult design researchers. Cooperative Inquiry is an approach to designing technology with children as full partners, in which all members collaborate equally to develop prototypes, make decisions, evaluate designs, and elaborate on ideas. We chose to use Cooperative Inquiry because of children's inherent insights into developing technologies that are usable, functional, and aesthetically pleasing to other children. For the design of SINQ and ScienceKit from fall 2011 to spring 2013, we worked with the intergenerational design team for 11 sessions. Additionally, we solicited design ideas for ScienceKit from learners in KC.

## 3.3 Kitchen Chemistry: The Context

We implemented our SM tools in KC, a life-relevant learning environment in which children engage in scientific inquiry through the pursuit of personally meaningful goals [41]. Five aspects of KC help to support personally motivated inquiry learning [41]. First, children engage in *semi-structured activities* that support the development of skills and practice in both cooking and science. These activities prepare learners for *Choice Days*, a series of activities in which learners transform personal

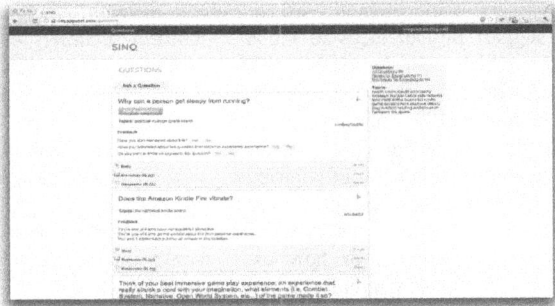

**Figure 1. The first prototype of SINQ**

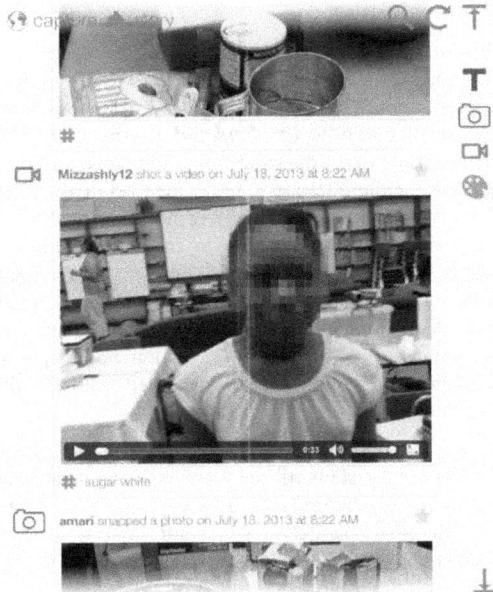

**Figure 2. The ScienceKit prototype**

food interests into their own science investigations. During all KC activities, learners engage in *whole-group discussions* that help to support evidence-based reasoning, argumentation, and integration of science knowledge into everyday practice. *Facilitators* guide children in all KC activities. Finally, children in KC use *mobile technologies* in the form of iPads™ and apps to collect data, write stories, and collaborate. It is here we situated our development and use of SM tools to support science inquiry learning.

Our design narrative details two implementations of KC: (1) an afterschool program in the spring of 2012, in which the learners used SINQ; and (2) a whole-week summer camp program in 2013, in which the learners used ScienceKit. All names of children and schools are pseudonyms. We conducted the afterschool implementation of KC at an independent Montessori school (The Green School) with six children between the ages of 8 – 11. During this time, children came to KC once a week, for a period of two to three hours, over a 12-week period. For the summer implementation, we worked with children from a lower socioeconomic status public elementary school (Springtown). For example, in 2011, over 80% of Springtown's student body received free or reduced meals. Seven children, ages 9 – 11, participated in the camp program for four consecutive days (Monday – Thursday, for 4.5 hours per day). Each implementation of KC was comprised of five to eight adult facilitators.

## 4. METHODS

We utilize a single-case study design [39] to present our DBR process and evolution of the SINQ and ScienceKit applications. This single-case represents a longitudinal case [39] that expands over two or more different points in time. A longitudinal single-case allows us to specify how the design of SINQ evolved into ScienceKit over time, given multiple KC implementations and co-design sessions. This case is bounded from the inception of SINQ in 2011 to the last implementation of ScienceKit in summer 2013. Our aim is to theorize how the design of SM tools for children relates to different learning interactions.

### 4.1 Data Collection and Analysis

To develop a deep narrative of our design process of these SM technologies, we collected a number of data sources from our two KC implementations and co-design sessions. In both KC implementations, we video recorded all sessions using multiple stationary cameras with table microphones. As facilitators, we acted as participant observers and maintained analytic memos of our experiences using the tools during KC. We also interviewed our KC learners about their usage of the SM tools. Finally, we collected software artifacts created by the learners (e.g., videos, questions) and analytics (e.g., timestamps, account logins, posts) from both tools. We conducted multiple co-design sessions, using a variety of techniques, depending on our design needs [38]. In design sessions, we collected all design artifacts, photos, video recordings, field notes, and analytic memos.

We began data analysis by reviewing videos of the KC sessions in which the SM tools were used. We triangulated analytic memos from our video reviews against our field notes [30]. We transcribed video excerpts that were significant to understanding how our design decisions affected the inquiry-based interactions. We used a hybrid inductive and deductive coding approach [36] to code interactions from our video transcriptions, while also comparing against our software artifact coding schema. Five of the authors open-coded data independently, noting specific themes for technology interactions, scientific inquiry-based interactions [11], collaborative behavior, and usability. Through an axial coding process, we compared and contrasted the open codes to identify emerging themes from the respective KC sessions, and developed additional codes for questioning, idea generation, and collaboration. We triangulated data from our analytic memos and software artifacts to ensure all pieces of evidence supported each other. Second, to analyze the co-design sessions, we used an inductive approach with constant comparative analysis [36] to develop codes on the design artifacts, notes, design layers, and presentations. Based on the codes, we developed categorical themes based on usability, aesthetics, and child interaction. Finally, we mapped these themes to the specific design decisions we made for SINQ and ScienceKit. In both sets of data, we conducted code checks and external audits with several reviewers who were not close to the project.

## 5. DESIGN NARRATIVE

We present our design narrative of our SM tools by first explaining two design iterations of SINQ. Second, we describe the thematic outcomes that arose from our implementation of SINQ in KC at The Green School. Third, we highlight the evaluation of SINQ and its affordances and constraints in science inquiry learning. Fourth, we explain the redesign of SINQ into ScienceKit, pinpointing changes in our interface design. Fifth, we illustrate the thematic outcomes of ScienceKit in our implementation of KC at Springtown. Finally, we outline how the design affordances of SINQ and ScienceKit contribute to different scientific inquiry practices across KC implementations.

## 5.1 SINQ: Social Media to Scaffold Inquiry

**First iteration – Contributions Scaffolding:** We began the design process of SINQ with an initial prototype in the fall of 2011. In SINQ, learners can contribute small snippets of inquiry: a question, hypothesis, or project idea. The system aggregates these contributions into coherent investigations for users to try out. SINQ's initial interaction design was heavily influenced by prior research on (a) defining the elements of scientific inquiry [11] and (b) the importance of scaffolding this inquiry process for learners [32]. From this foundation, we derived three interaction design goals for SINQ. First, we wanted users to capture and share the funds of knowledge that they bring from everyday life experiences [6], just as they would in a tool such as Facebook™. In doing so, we wanted them to connect these everyday experiences to modes of inquiry such as asking a question, forming a hypothesis, or devising a project to examine the question. Second, whenever a learner added a contribution like a question or hypothesis, the interface provided scaffolding that prompted them [32] to reflect on these aspects of inquiry.

Finally, users could submit micro-contributions, which SINQ then aggregated into larger, coherent projects. SINQ was designed to crowdsource the components of scientific inquiry in order to promote learners' conceptualization of it. One learner might contribute a question. Another learner might add a hypothesis; and yet another could add a project idea. We designed SINQ to enable users to contribute what was most salient and comfortable, but aggregated and guided these contributions to develop coherent project ideas. In this way, we hoped that learners could participate in ways that matched their interests and skill levels, but also readily observe how their small contributions connected together into a larger community endeavour.

**Second iteration – Social Scaffolding:** We brought this first iteration of SINQ to Kidsteam. In early co-design sessions, our child co-designers brainstormed ways to design social feedback mechanisms into SINQ. Many SM platforms rely on peer feedback mechanisms that offer untapped potential to experiment with learning interaction designs. For example, Facebook™ employs a "like" button that members can press if they like a status or post from a friend. In Twitter™, members can "favorite" a particular tweet or retweet a posting to their network. The use of ratings, averaged across members, is also prevalent in various platforms as a measure of the quality of products, services, or contributions. We aimed to understand how these design features could act not only as a form of social vetting, but also as a scaffolding mechanism during inquiry [22]. Through a design-strategy called sticky-noting [38], we asked the child design partners to think of a question they had about the world and write them on sticky-notes. The questions were posted around the room, and child design team members placed new sticky notes alongside questions they deemed high quality. On each note, design partners included reasons for their quality rating. In this way, the children reflected about why they would vote for a peer's contribution and the criteria that supported their "liking" of a question.

**Design Decisions for SINQ:** Based on our initial design goals to provide scaffolded support and low barriers for user contributions, coupled with feedback from our co-design sessions on social support, learner attribution, and collaboration, we made the following design decisions for SINQ's interface.

*1. Incremental contributions that scaffold steps of scientific inquiry:* Based on our knowledge of software scaffolding and

goals for inquiry-based learning [32], we designed SINQ as a way for learners to incrementally ask questions, develop hypotheses, and suggest project ideas to the SM platform. Learners could choose which contribution to make (questions, hypotheses, or project ideas). Learners could also come together to make small and incremental contributions on a single project idea. One idea could be built on multiple contributions and incremental steps. The gradual presentation of contributions was developed to guide learners through the complex inquiry process. In retrospect, a design consequence of our heavy focus on scaffolding was less attention to modality, or how users would interact with the platform. SINQ was initially a browser-based tool, with a text-heavy interface. The interaction-design focused on users expressing their cognitive process primarily via text input. This detail grew salient as our design-process evolved over time.

*2. Social vetting and feedback:* Analysis of the co-design session revealed three main criteria that children used to assess the quality of a peer's question: (1) **Wonder**, whether a person also wondered about the same question; (2) **Personal Connection**, whether a person could relate to the question from their personal life; and (3) **Novelty**, whether the question was deemed original or made the voter think about something they had not previously wondered about. We utilized these insights to transform generic voting mechanisms such as a *like* or *favorite* into specific voting criteria that could serve as a form of social scaffolding. We hoped that asking peers to assess and vote on the wonder, personal connection, or novelty of a question would spur learners to think about these criteria as they developed questions about the world to post in SINQ.

*3. Public and collaborative science learning:* We designed SINQ as a way to publicly show all the learners' ideas and authorship. Each learner had a personal account they could log into and post their contributions publicly. We built SINQ to aggregate contributions automatically into different categories that learners could search and filter through.

## 5.2 Thematic Outcomes for SINQ

We implemented this initial SINQ prototype with The Green School implementation of KC. The Green School participants mainly used SINQ to develop ideas for their Choice Day projects. The children tended to want to use SINQ individually, with a facilitator, and they accessed SINQ through a web browser on laptops or iPads™. Based on their interactions with SINQ, we observed the following themes in their interaction.

**Theme #1 – Idea generation and building:** The built-in scaffolds in SINQ helped to facilitate structured dialogue between the facilitators and learners. As the learners interacted with SINQ, some experienced difficulties coming up with an idea. For example, in video observations we found that one learner, Arman, often hesitated and needed explicit support to generate ideas. In one interaction, Mike (facilitator) randomly suggested that Arman think about "cinnamon goo". Arman quickly latched onto the idea and asked questions about the origins of cinnamon "powder" (i.e., ground cinnamon). As Mike explained that cinnamon powder resulted from grinding cinnamon sticks, Arman began to input his first question into SINQ, "How does cinnamon relate to cinnamon rolls?" As he typed this in, the interface prompted him: "Do you wonder about this?" Arman read the prompt aloud and responded to Mike, "Because cinnamon, actual cinnamon is a solid thing." The two then had a further discussion about cinnamon and its origins. From one prompt to another, Mike and Arman engaged in conversations that led Arman to consider the design of his Choice Day investigation around cinnamon and cinnamon rolls.

In contrast, another learner – Ben – immediately had an idea for an investigation he wanted to do for Choice Day: a "pizza ball" investigation that would create small pizza treats in the shape of a round ball. Despite Ben's certainty, SINQ still facilitated structured conversations between him and the facilitator with whom he worked. As Ben conversed with Charley (facilitator), he scanned the various prompts in the SINQ interface. Like Arman, Ben also read aloud the question, "What do you wonder about?" In response, Ben entered the following question into SINQ: "What would happen if you made a piz(z)aball [sic] when the dough rises and also when it doesn't." Ben then entered an hypothesis for his pizza ball investigation: "The pizzaball with the yeast in it will squeeze everything into the middle and come out when you bite into it, and the pizzaball without the yeast will do the opposite."

The design of SINQ and its structured prompts facilitated conversations between the adult and children through joint media engagement [37]. As learners voted questions up and down, SINQ prompted learners to consider, "Is this a novel question?" and "Can you relate to this question?" The ways in which prompts were integrated into SINQ's design afforded each of the KC learners who have been highlighted here time to reflect about the question with an adult.

**Theme #2 – Idea sharing:** Posting their ideas into SINQ in a public platform allowed the KC participants to interact with science inquiry learning in new ways. Seeing the process of question-development helped learners to consider how inquiry-based contributions could be made. For example, before entering their questions, both Arman and Ben scanned through SINQ for other questions learners had posted. They gained a sense of what was being posted, which helped them construct their own posts.

In addition, learners began to collaborate more with each other after scanning the posts. In one example, a learner Freddie worked with Tammy (facilitator) to develop his ideas for a green brownies investigation, or as Freddie called them, "Greenies." As they worked together to add questions, hypotheses, and project ideas for Greenies, Freddie noticed that another learner, Eric, recently voted up his SINQ question, "How should I make green brownies?" Another facilitator told him that Eric also had feedback for him. Interested in this feedback, Freddie approached Eric to learn more. Previously, the group often ostracized Eric for being too loud and talking out of turn in whole group discussions. However, while using SINQ, Eric could think from afar and post feedback for Freddie without being disruptive. Freddie was able to see that they had a common interest; Freddie wanted to make green brownies, while Eric wanted to make white brownies: "Whities." In this case, SINQ's design allowed learners to connect by publicly sharing ideas and their associated community votes.

Ideas and questions posted in SINQ allowed learners to share their experiences with their families. Many participants in KC had to be picked up by their parents from the afterschool setting. As parents arrived in the evening, learners frequently asked their parents to look at the questions they posted in SINQ. For instance, when Ben's father arrived to pick him up one day, Ben told him, "Look at my question. What would happen if you made pizza balls, well, made pizza balls when the dough rose. And also when it doesn't. Like you made two separate ones, one where the dough rises and one that doesn't. So you like take out the yeast." Ben's father asked him about the investigation and peered over his shoulder to see what Ben was entering into SINQ. Similarly, when Freddie's father arrived to pick him up, Freddie called out to him, stating that he was going to make chocolate brownies with green food dye. As Freddie read the ideas he proposed in SINQ, his father stated that green food coloring would only darken the brownies if

he used regular chocolate chips. Freddie realized this conundrum and changed his mind about using chocolate chips. The conversation shifted to focusing on how to lighten the color of the brownies so that they would absorb the green food coloring. Later, Freddie made sure his father had the login and password for SINQ to enable Freddie to continue to post his ideas at home.

In both situations, SINQ's design allowed learners to share their ideas amongst their KC peers; however, learners also wanted to share their contributions with their families in real-time. Parents likewise wanted to discuss the development of questions with their children. The way in which SINQ's design scaffolded the KC learners' investigation development into component questions, hypotheses, and project ideas allowed them to focus on sharing one aspect of the investigation with their parents at a time. Parents who did not have background knowledge of the investigations could then converse with their children about them.

**Theme #3 – Ownership of ideas:** SINQ allowed learners to post questions, hypotheses, and project ideas that were linked to a specific user account. As contributions and voting occurred, each post could be tracked back to a specific user profile. However, because of the nature of idea development, posting in SINQ did not always reflect the origin and authorship of the idea [15]. For instance, one learner, Donna, worked with Jason (facilitator) to develop her investigation for a hard candy called "Puffles". Sitting across from them were Anthony and Tammy (facilitator), who were also trying to come up with an idea for a separate investigation. In contrast to Donna, this was Anthony's first time using SINQ and he did not have an idea to start with. As Jason and Donna generated the hard candy Puffles idea, Anthony glanced over towards Donna's direction. Unbeknownst to Donna, Anthony started to converse with Tammy about a similar idea for hard candy. Before Donna was able to add her verbal expressions into SINQ, Anthony quickly entered a question into SINQ. The SINQ analytics data indicate that Anthony entered the question, "Why are candys hard? [sic]" before Donna could post her question, "How do you make a hard suger? [sic]" into SINQ. Later, as Jason and Donna discussed how the Puffles coating would be as hard as *"jawbreaker"* candy, Anthony indicated to Tammy he would like to do a project that would make, "like a *jawbreaker* thing". Immediately Donna overheard Anthony and Tammy's conversation and angrily accused Anthony, "You just take it [the idea] from me!" She exclaimed, "Puffles was my idea! Then why is he stealing it?"

The design of SINQ did not take into account that learners come into scientific inquiry at many different stages. Our findings indicate that the technology needed to provide support for learners to protect individual ideas during collaboration. Donna and Anthony's near-altercation underscored the importance of authorship, attribution, and the ability to truly own their ideas in a platform like SINQ, in which learners make small contributions towards a larger goal in the inquiry process.

## 5.3 Evaluation of SINQ and Redesign

We found that the SINQ's design influenced several beneficial learning behaviors with this specific group of children at The Green School. The cognitive scaffolding of SINQ allowed these learners to make contributions to the inquiry process in ways that were initially comfortable for each individual. The affordances of shared, public posts and carefully designed social voting mechanisms provided opportunities for learners to slow down, learn from others and gain social recognition for their contributions. They also served as artifacts around which new conversations and ideas could arise between learners and facilitators. In many ways, the mediated-interaction enabled in

SINQ often alleviated face-to-face tensions and breakdowns that occurred with this learner group [15]. In addition, the data culled from SINQ showed how different children entered into and followed individual, unique pathways through the inquiry process [4]. Some began by observing others' posts before embarking on their own inquiry, others started by developing project ideas before considering hypotheses, and yet others followed a formal process of designing questions, hypotheses, and projects.

The initial design iterations of SINQ and our subsequent KC implementation in The Green School provided several lessons. The application addressed the specific need to provide cognitive scaffolds to learners as they contributed smaller pieces of the inquiry process (e.g. a question, hypothesis, investigation idea). This cognitive focus influenced the interface, prompts to users, and the interaction design of the web application. SINQ was effective in the context of KC as learners constructed their own Choice Day food investigations. However, SINQ also required users to input text-only contributions about their cognitive process. Furthermore, facilitators in KC heavily guided the use of SINQ, often prompting the children to input their ideas.

## 5.4 ScienceKit: Mobile, Social Self Expression of Scientific Inquiry

In our third design session with the intergenerational design team – Kidsteam – the child design partners often noted that text-heavy SINQ was neither engaging nor fun to use. Many of the design suggestions were multimedia-based, such as adding color to the interface and integrating more engaging modes of interaction (e.g., video recording). While we could not employ every child design feature (e.g., digital mascot, ScienceKit game), we did note that children wanted to use integrated media to input evidence and information [40]. These design experiences led us to understand the importance of supporting both cognitive engagement and usability. For instance, in order for an SM app to support children's ability to scientize their everyday life experiences [16], children would need to easily capture elements of their daily life and share these contributions with peers and family. Current SM platforms such as Facebook™, Pinterest™, and Instagram™ allow users to capture and share multiple forms of media (e.g., photos, videos) easily. Similarly, from prior experience using *StoryKit* [8] and *Zydeco* [10] within the KC program, we had observed that free form usage of integrated media allowed learners to express science experiences in personally meaningful ways. Such technology also enabled learners to capture and record data in scientifically meaningful ways, e.g., through measurements and close observations [14].

Through several more iterations of design and development to improve usability and engagement, we refined SINQ into a renamed iOS™ native app called *ScienceKit*. We chose to use these technologies so that ScienceKit would be extensible by other researchers and application developers. This design process occurred from fall 2012 to spring 2013. Our experiences highlight our evolution of thought from an initial focus on cognitive scaffolding to also considering the importance of social engagement and personal expression in the learning process.

**Design decisions for ScienceKit**: Many of our early decisions from SINQ remained for ScienceKit. We still allowed for social vetting and feedback, incremental contributions that could be easily shared, and opportunities for individualized engagement and collaboration. However, based on our KC implementation of SINQ and our co-design sessions, we made the following new design decisions for ScienceKit.

*1. Media capture and sharing:* In our third design iteration, we sought to integrate the media-sharing and expressive features of tools such as StoryKit and Zydeco, with the cognitive scaffolding around scientific inquiry that was featured in SINQ. ScienceKit follows a similar interaction-design to the most recent iteration of SINQ, but allowed for more diverse media types. Learners could now capture and scientize their experiences in the form of photos, drawings, video, and textual contributions.

*2. Mobile experiences:* In addition, we evolved the interaction design from a primarily browser-based, text-heavy mode of interaction into truly mobile, multimedia-based participation in scientific inquiry. The browser interface on SINQ was more cumbersome, while a native app allowed for streamlined media integration. We envisioned children carrying these mobile tools into different types of daily experiences (e.g., classrooms, field trips, grocery shopping). They could use different multimedia tools (e.g., photos, videos) to record a science experience as it occurred, upload it to ScienceKit, and in the process pose a question, hypothesis, or project idea through the guided prompts.

*3. Timeline view:* In contrast to SINQ, learners' posts on ScienceKit could be seen in a timeline format. Similar to Instagram™ or Facebook™, a post in ScienceKit appears in a linear fashion, based on the time at which it was posted. Learners can scroll through in real time to see what others have posted. We wanted learners to see the progression of other participants' experiences through this timeline format.

*4. Collaborative tagging:* For each post, learners could tag the different participants they were working with. Since everyone (including the adults) had a personal profile, ScienceKit users could select which participants they were working with.

## 5.5 Thematic Outcomes for ScienceKit

We implemented ScienceKit in the summer of 2013 at Springtown Elementary School as a weeklong camp from Monday to Thursday. Seven children, ages 9 – 11, participated in the summer program. For this KC implementation, we used ScienceKit as the only mobile app for storytelling and data collection. Adult facilitators and child participants each had their own iPad™ linked to a personal account. Instead of limiting the learners' system use to idea generation for Choice Day (as they had done for the first KC implementation), participants used ScienceKit for all activities throughout the week.

**Theme #1 – Extended documentation:** We observed that learners wanted to document as much as they could with ScienceKit. Instead of just recording the data for their food science investigations, learners also documented whole group discussions and socializing times (e.g., breakfast). As the week progressed, different documentation roles emerged. We observed two types of recording, rapacious vs. selective recording [7]. For example, one learner, Judy, recorded almost the entire facilitator presentation in a whole group discussion. She held the iPad™ up, watching the camera recording, while peaking around at the live presentation. We also observed learners engaging in what we call "hidden camera" behaviors, in which they documented all aspects of their food investigations through extended recording. We observed children placing the iPads™ on tables, bookshelves, and other isolated spaces to let the camera record in the background, while they engaged in the food investigations. ScienceKit videos timed out after 10-minutes. Once the time was up, children would return to ScienceKit and post the extensive videos on the timeline. Some would start a new recording in an attempt to create a continuous record of the activity.

Conversely, children could also be quite selective about what they wanted to record in their process of scientific inquiry. In this selective role, learners carefully chose the importance of the media post. Learners would often take video recording while narrating. For example, a KC participant – DeMarco – took photos and short video clips of a semi-structured activity in which he and his friend James mixed oil, water, and eggs to observe emulsification. DeMarco quickly grabbed an iPad™ when his friend James mixed the eggs and narrated, "So James is mixin' up the egg so we can put it in the bottle." During this narration, DeMarco moved the camera between recording James mixing the egg, zooming in on the eggs, and finally showing off the bottle the eggs would be transferred into. Learners often did not do this in isolation. During a whole group discussion of a baking powder and baking soda experiment, the children spontaneously grabbed the iPads™ without adult prompting and huddled around together to record their observations in a similar, selective manner.

**Theme #2 – In-the-moment wondering:** Similar to SINQ, learners could post their questions, hypotheses, and project ideas in ScienceKit. However, the main difference that prompted interactions in ScienceKit versus those in SINQ was the multimodal design of the technology within a mobile platform, which supported its fluid integration into the culture of KC. By incorporating multimodal design into a mobile version of ScienceKit, learners gained the dual affordances of portability and in-situ freedom of expression [27]. Learners could carry their iPads™ around KC and ask questions at anytime. For example, during breakfast DeMarco wondered whether the breakfast cereal Apple Jacks™ contained real apples. Using ScienceKit, he created a video of himself with the cereal package asking the question, "I was having a question; does Apple Jacks really have apples in it?"

**Theme #3 – Expressions of play, self, and socialization:** Children's notions of play and scientific inquiry are often not separate, but integrated together [13]. The children used ScienceKit as a way to convey playfulness within their learning tasks. We have observed that these playful interactions through digital media can provide a way to make science learning personal and meaningful [14]. For example, children often took "selfies" of themselves with ScienceKit and interviewed their friends explaining their scientific experiments [7]. Also, instead of simply typing in their questions, children often created personal videos of themselves asking their questions and showing where their questions originated. Learners often interacted playfully with ScienceKit, by "photobombing" or inserting personal poses, even while collecting data and taking measurements. Learners also integrated their funds of knowledge from home life [6] into their personal expression with ScienceKit. KC functioned as a hybrid space [31] that allowed learners to integrate knowledge from home into science learning. For example, one learner, Allen, was a dedicated Minecraft™ gamer at home. He sketched many elements from Minecraft™ in ScienceKit throughout his Choice Day investigation, as he attempted to bridge his love of building in Minecraft™ with an emerging awareness of how to build a science investigation. These posts were quite popular with the other learners, who gave him numerous "stars" (votes) on these particular posts.

## 5.6 Evaluation of ScienceKit
We designed ScienceKit as an entirely mobile app that allowed learners to capture and record their daily lives through integrated media (e.g., photos, sketches, video). In contrast, SINQ was designed as a text-heavy, browser-based tool to provide cognitive support for developing questions, hypotheses, and project ideas.

The design decisions we made in ScienceKit profoundly changed the interaction and learning in the Springtown implementation.

First, creating ScienceKit as a fully mobile app with integrated media created more opportunities for documentation, expressions of self and play, and sharing with others. Learners in KC were not stationary; they constantly moved between different activities (e.g., whole-group discussions, Choice Day) and interactions with friends. As such, having a mobile tool ready for use to capture, record, and share findings fluidly allowed new kinds of interactions for learners that were different than SINQ, such as multiple styles of reporting. The affordance of quickly capturing a video of themselves asking questions or taking a photograph of an ingredient for later investigation gave the children unique opportunities to record in-the-moment thoughts and expressions.

Second, ScienceKit's timeline view allowed learners to observe several on-going investigations. With a dynamic timeline, learners could see data and recordings quickly populate. We observed learners growing excited as they saw different photos and recordings being posted at the same time as the investigation. However, in contrast to SINQ, which helped to organize data within structured question, hypotheses, and design idea categories, the children had difficulty searching for specific posts in ScienceKit. For example, during interviews, we asked the children to show one significant post in ScienceKit. We noted that similar to a Facebook™ timeline, the children needed to scroll through the timeline and had difficulty finding the specific posts they were proud of. In short, as the data recordings became more frequent, the children had a harder time finding the specific posts they wanted to share. However, with SINQ, the text-heavy posts were quickly categorized for easy access. This gave the children from The Green School a chance to show off their ideas quickly and clearly to their peers and family.

Overall, the design decisions for ScienceKit changed the experience of the technology usage. SINQ's focus as a cognitive scaffold into scientific inquiry helped learners to deconstruct complex interactions into more manageable and incremental contributions. SINQ was effectively utilized in idea generation activities for Choice Day preparation; however it is important to note that this concentrated use stemmed from pedagogical decisions, and not an inherent result of the technology. With the ScienceKit experience, we observed that idea generation occurred beyond moments in which learners had facilitator scaffolding. Questions such as DeMarco's, about apples in Apple Jacks™ breakfast cereal, are situated in personal experiences and in-the-moment interactions. The use of the mobile, integrated, and socially networked media afforded learners more access to scientize their daily lives due to quick access and sharing.

## 6. DISCUSSION AND IMPLICATIONS
This longitudinal case study and design narrative offers several contributions to our understanding of the design and use of SM for children's scientific inquiry learning. We focus our discussion on (1) the affordances and constraints of our SM tools, (2) the potential of SM to guide learning behaviors, and (3) the role of SM for children.

## 6.1 Design Affordances and Constraints
### 6.1.1 Cognitive scaffolding
First, our design for cognitive scaffolding in SINQ helped to focus learners on specific ways to engage in scientific inquiry. SM platforms, such as Twitter™, allow users to engage in many topics and discussions, ranging from politics and media to pop culture. However, for science learning, an expansive platform like

Twitter™ can tax a learner's cognitive load [26]. Instead, SINQ's design limited the children to three thinking points: questions, hypotheses, and project ideas. In this case, the affordance is that learners could concentrate and build on each other's contributions more seamlessly. We observed the children in The Green School building project ideas for Choice Day starting from initial wondering questions. By working together at the same time (e.g., Choice Day preparation), using the same medium of textual inputs (SINQ), and limiting thought processes to just questions, hypotheses, and project ideas, learners were able concentrate on the task of food investigation development. Such focused attention helped learners engage in scientific discussions with facilitators, share their contributions with peers and family members, and receive feedback on their ideas with others.

However, SINQ's cognitive scaffolding prevented learners from crafting a story from their activities. Although we designed SINQ for in-the-moment wondering, the children in The Green School implementation did not use SINQ for this purpose during their Choice Day investigations. Instead, whenever a child had a moment to wonder, they would often record their questions in storytelling apps like StoryKit as part of their cooking science experience. Our analysis suggests this is because the integrated media in StoryKit afforded more natural, intuitive question input. It became clear to us that SINQ's textual interface and cognitive supports helped learners to generate ideas when formally working with facilitators and each other; however this design feature was neither sustainable nor naturally integrated when it came to physical activities like cooking and science experimentation.

### 6.1.2 Personal expression

ScienceKit's design as a mobile tool for personal expression helped to change the dynamics of KC. One affordance of ScienceKit was that learners could scientize in-the-moment. For instance, ScienceKit's inherent mobility enabled learners to document as much of their experience of KC as they wanted. Documentation is one aspect of storytelling that supports personal expression [8]. We observed learners taking ScienceKit everywhere in the KC environment, such as to the kitchen, whole group discussions, semi-structured activities, and even the breakfast table. ScienceKit's design allowed learners to fluidly assume different kinds of reporter roles, ranging from recording specific science data to capturing the entire moments of discussion. They captured many kinds of data, such as peer social interactions and cooking science engagements. Learners could use ScienceKit to personally express how they wanted to record their engagements and what moments they thought were important.

Another affordance in personal expression was that learners' in-situ wondering could be quickly documented. We observed the children recording themselves with their thoughts, such as "Question is, do milk have sugar?" (video) and "How long does it take for chicken to cook in different oils??" (text). The ability for children to personally express themselves in multiple situations using integrated media informs our understanding of what they choose to notice and attend to at any given moment [1].

However, one limitation we found in ScienceKit when compared to SINQ was that we did not observe many of the idea building behaviors that we saw in SINQ. One reason is that the timeline in ScienceKit filled up quite fast. Even with only seven children using ScienceKit, we observed that its dynamic timeline interface quickly overpopulated to overwhelming volumes. Because ScienceKit's interface showed the full expanse of photos, videos, and sketches, learners had a difficult time scanning quickly through the contributions of other KC participants. The ScienceKit interface showed *everything* that learners recorded or documented, while SINQ scaffolded inquiry by being constrained to just showing questions, hypotheses, and design ideas. Seeing everything all at once made it very difficult for the children to focus on what to attend to and where to make contributions. While ScienceKit's interface color-coded the data into categories (e.g., photos, videos, questions, sketches), it was still difficult for the children to search for and find specific contributions.

## 6.2 Social Media and Learning Behaviors

This DBR study suggests that popular design features from SM platforms can offer promising ways to afford learning behaviors and experiences for children.

*New ways to participate*: Micro-contributions in SM can lower the barriers to entry for children to participate. In both SINQ and ScienceKit, children who had difficulties speaking in front of groups now had a means for making the same expressive contributions as children who spoke more frequently. In SINQ, we observed children who were disconnected through face-to-face interactions could connect online through information postings [15] In ScienceKit, we observed shy and reticent children participating through adding their ideas and personal media. The ability for children to scan through and see contributions from other children was an engaging behavior that can be leveraged for learning. When using both SINQ and ScienceKit, children spent time browsing other learners' posts. In SINQ, children could see what common ideas were contributed and could begin to collaborate. Overall, designers of SM tools for learning should consider the ways in which children browse through large amounts of contributions. This issue could be alleviated as designers devise innovative ways to display and aggregate streams of information for children.

*Modality can influence learning behavior*: Modality of interaction is a key, non-trivial design consideration. The evolution of SINQ's text-heavy and browser-based interface to ScienceKit's mobile, multi-modally interactive iOS™ app supported shifts in learning behaviors. The transition from browser-based to mobile app changed how the learners treated in-the-moment wondering and documentation behaviors. Text-heavy and multimodal designs each have advantages and disadvantages. In many ways, the design of ScienceKit aligned quite well to KC's focus on supporting scientizing of everyday life for children. However, if KC were more focused on content knowledge acquisition, it is difficult to unpack whether ScienceKit or SINQ would afford more beneficial features.

*Frameworks for learning*: Finally, design decisions for SM tools for learning need to be considered in concert with frameworks for learning. We demonstrate from this longitudinal case study that adhering solely to a cognitive scaffolding framework limited children's social, cultural, and playful learning efforts. However, using a framework of self-expression and play in our designs deterred learners from experiencing supportive guides and scaffolds needed for effective inquiry-based learning. In retrospect, we needed to integrate DBR processes to fully meld the two learning frameworks. Attending to balance of structure and freedom remains a challenging design space [14]. Tools from the Learning Sciences and Computer Supportive Collaborative Learning communities have done well in guiding learning, while tools from the IDC research community have much to say about deeply engaging children through play. This work, and other work such as Zydeco [10], are beginning to integrate such frameworks to develop tools that (a) promote promising learning behaviors, and (b) directly relate to the contexts of children's lives (e.g., their experiences in museums, homes, or afterschool programs).

## 6.3 Social Media and Children

We developed SINQ and ScienceKit as ways to promote science inquiry learning experiences for children. One observation we made regarding the children's learning behaviors and engagements is how excited they became when showing off their questions, design ideas, and creations to different stakeholders and community members. For instance, we found with SINQ that children wanted to share their questions and plans for Choice Day with their parents. The children spent several minutes pointing to the screen, allowing their parents to watch over their shoulders and see the questions they generated. In our ScienceKit implementation, learners took photos of teachers and interviewed school cafeteria workers about their food science projects. In both situations, because adult facilitators are an inherent aspect of KC culture that supports children's development of their personal food investigations, the children may have been accustomed to explaining their project ideas to other adults in their communities.

Therefore, consistent with Grimes and Field's [21] recommendations parents and stakeholders play a key role in design considerations of SM tools for learning and children. Multiple design dimensions for parents and community members are yet to be explored in SM tools, such as designing offline and online interactions that could exist to support children's learning. Although adolescents may often avoid SM platforms use where parents are also present, young children's participation in SM may be different enough that family integration into SM tools is worthy of examination. As a design recommendation, we suggest that design researchers explore how to integrate SM tools in the ways in which families interact with children, and to think intentionally about ways to promote joint media engagement [37].

## 7. LIMITATIONS

*Theoretical limitations:* We recognize that this is a single-case study of a DBR effort to develop SM tools for children and learning. As a qualitative case study, our goal is not to produce statistical generalizations [39]. Instead, the key to our study is to inform our understanding of SM learning tools via rich case description, and ascertain its transferability to other contexts.

*Changing conditions:* We also acknowledge the changing contexts of KC in the case study. The SINQ implementation occurred once a week, at an affluent independent Montessori school in a 12-week afterschool program. The ScienceKit implementation occurred as a four-day summer program in a lower socioeconomic status school. This study is limited in determining the extent to which switching from SINQ to ScienceKit impacted the behavior of the children, while also teasing apart differences in the child participants, school cultures, and socioeconomic influences. Our findings are not meant to be an isolated and blunt comparison between SINQ and ScienceKit and the children's behaviors. Instead, these findings are meant to advance our scholarly thinking about the design, implementation, and consequences of SM for children and learning.

## 8. CONCLUSIONS AND FUTURE WORK

Our design narrative offers several key contributions. We demonstrate how local design decisions, and the processes used to derive them (e.g. integrating learning theories with co-design with children), result in very particular SM tools. In addition, design decisions for the learning context (in this case, KC) impose another set of affordances and constraints. These factors interact to create learning interactions between children, facilitators, and other stakeholders (e.g. parents). In particular, our rich description highlights how particular features of SM (i.e. micro-contributions, social scaffolding, in-the-moment documenting) are aligned with our learning goals to help children scientize their daily lives. We argue that this DBR experience illuminates important avenues for future work. In particular, design work is needed to better articulate when and how technologies should balance structure (scaffolding) and freedom (expression) for different learning goals (e.g. content knowledge vs. scientizing). Moreover, DBR is needed to understand how to best leverage SM for children to mobilize diverse ecologies and contexts for learning. Future work is needed to understand how to design SM to help children engage in productive learning with parents, siblings, family members, teachers, and peers across formal and informal contexts. Specifically, we advocate for future DBR approaches that can bridge children's home, neighborhood, and school communities, and inform our efforts to integrate SM technologies into children's scientizing practices across their daily lives. As one of our ScienceKit users stated, "It (ScienceKit) helped me do my science."

## 9. ACKNOWLEDGEMENTS

We thank the Computing Innovation Fellows program for funding this work. We also thank the children, teachers, parents, and staff of The Green School and Springtown Elementary School for their participation. We also thank the Kidsteam child and adult partners for their help.

## 10. REFERENCES

[1] Ahn, J. et al. Submitted. Seeing the unseen learner: Designing and using social media to recognize children's science dispositions in action. (Submitted).

[2] Ahn, J. et al. 2012. SINQ: Scientific INQuiry learning using social media. *Extended Abstracts of ACM CHI 2012 Conference on Human Factors in Computing Systems* (New York, NY, USA, 2012), 2081–2086.

[3] Ahn, J. 2011. The effect of social network sites on adolescents' social and academic development: Current theories and controversies. *Journal of the American Society for Information Science and Technology.* 62, 8 (2011), 1435–1445.

[4] Ahn, J. et al. 2013. Using social media and learning analytics to understand how children engage in scientific inquiry. *Proceedings of Interaction Design and Children* (New York, NY, USA, 2013), 427–430.

[5] Barron, B. 2003. When smart groups fail. *The Journal of the Learning Sciences.* 12, 3 (2003), 307–359.

[6] Basu, S.J. and Calabrese-Barton, A. Developing a sustained interest in science among urban minority youth. *Journal of Research in Science Teaching.* 44, 3 (2007), 466–489.

[7] Bonsignore, E. et al. 2014. Selfies for science: Collaborative configurations around ScienceKit. *Proceedings of Computer Supported Collaborative Work* (2014).

[8] Bonsignore, E. et al. 2013. Sharing stories "in the wild": A mobile storytelling case study using StoryKit. *Transactions of Computer-Human Interaction (ToCHI).* 20, 3 (2013).

[9] Brennan, K. et al. 2010. Making projects, making friends: Online community as catalyst for interactive media creation. *New Directions for Youth Development,* 128 (2010), 75–83.

[10] Cahill, C. et al. 2011. Mobile learning in museums: How mobile supports for learning influence student behavior. *Proceedings of the 10th International Conference on Interaction Design and Children* (2011), 21–28.

[11] Chinn, C.A. and Malhotra, B.A. Epistemologically authentic inquiry in schools: A theoretical framework for evaluating inquiry tasks. *Science Education.* 86, 2 (2002), 175–218.

[12] Chipman, G. et al. 2006. A case study of Tangible Flags: A collaborative technology to enhance field trips. *Proceedings of*

*the 2006 Conference on Interaction Design and Children* (New York, NY, USA, 2006), 1–8.

[13] Clegg, T.L. et al. 2010. Playing with food: Moving from interests and goals into scientifically meaningful experiences. *Proceedings of the 9th International Conference of the Learning Sciences - Volume 1 (ICLS '10)* (2010), 1135–1142.

[14] Clegg, T.L. et al. 2012. Technology for promoting scientific practice and personal meaning in life-relevant learning. *Proceedings of the 11th International Conference on Interaction Design and Children (IDC '12)* (New York, NY, USA, 2012), 152–161.

[15] Clegg, T.L. et al. When face-to-face fails: Opportunities for social media to foster collaborative learning. *Proceedings of Computer Supported Collaborative Learning* (Madison, WI, 2013).

[16] Clegg, T.L. and Kolodner, J. 2014. Scientizing and cooking: Helping middle-school learners develop scientific dispositions. *Science Education*. 98, 1 (2014), 36–63.

[17] Collins, A. et al. 2004. Design research: Theoretical and methodological issues. *The Journal of the Learning Sciences*. 13, 1 (2004), 15–42.

[18] Druin, A. 1999. Cooperative Inquiry: Developing new technologies for children with children. *Proceedings of the SIGCHI Conference on Human Factors in Computing Systems (CHI 1999)* (New York, NY, USA, 1999), 592–599.

[19] Gelderblom, H. and Kotzé, P. 2009. Ten design lessons from the literature on child development and children's use of technology. *Proceedings of the 8th International Conference on Interaction Design and Children* (New York, NY, USA, 2009), 52–60.

[20] Greenhow, C. et al. Learning, teaching, and scholarship in a digital age Web 2.0 and classroom research: What path should we take now? *Educational Researcher*. 38, 4 (2009), 246–259.

[21] Grimes, S. and Fields, D. 2012. *Kids online: A new research agenda for understanding social networking forums*. The Joan Ganz Cooney Center at Sesame Workshop.

[22] Gubbels, M. et al. 2013. Scientific INQuiry (SINQ): Social media for everyday science learning. *Proceedings of the iConference 2013* (Fort Worth, TX, 2013), 1102 – 1105.

[23] John-Steiner, V. and Mahn, H. 1996. Sociocultural approaches to learning and development: A Vygotskian framework. *Educational Psychologist*. 31, 3-4 (1996), 191–206.

[24] Junco, R. et al. 2011. The effect of Twitter on college student engagement and grades. *Journal of Computer Assisted Learning*. 27, 2 (2011), 119–132.

[25] Junco, R. 2012. Too much face and not enough books: The relationship between multiple indices of Facebook use and academic performance. *Computers in Human Behavior*. 28, 1 (2012), 187–198.

[26] Kirschner, P.A. et al. 2006. Why minimal guidance during instruction does not work: An analysis of the failure of constructivist, discovery, problem-based, experiential, and inquiry-based teaching. *Educational Psychologist*. 41, 2 (2006), 75–86.

[27] Klopfer, E. et al. 2002. Environmental detectives: PDAs as a window into a virtual simulated world. *Wireless and Mobile Technologies in Education, 2002. Proceedings. IEEE International Workshop on* (2002), 95–98.

[28] Lampe, C. et al. 2011. Student use of Facebook for organizing collaborative classroom activities. *International Journal of Computer-Supported Collaborative Learning*. 6, 3 (Sep. 2011), 329–347.

[29] Linn, M. et al. 2003. WISE design for knowledge integration. *Science Education*. 87, 4 (2003), 517–538.

[30] Merriam, S.B. 2009. *Qualitative research: A guide to design and implementation*. John Wiley and Sons.

[31] Moje, E.B. et al. Working toward third space in content area literacy: An examination of everyday funds of knowledge and discourse. *Reading Research Quarterly*. 39, 1 (2004), 38–70.

[32] Quintana, C. et al. 2004. A scaffolding design framework for software to support science inquiry. *The Journal of the Learning Sciences*. 13, 3 (2004), 337–386.

[33] Scardamalia, M. and Bereiter, C. 1994. Computer support for knowledge-building communities. *The Journal of the Learning Sciences*. 3, 3 (1994), 265–283.

[34] Selwyn, N. 2009. Faceworking: Exploring students' education-related use of Facebook. *Learning, Media and Technology*. 34, 2 (2009), 157–174.

[35] Stahl, G. et al. 2006. Computer-supported collaborative learning: An historical perspective. *Cambridge handbook of the learning sciences*. R.K. Sawyer, ed. Cambridge University Press. 409 – 426.

[36] Strauss, A.L. and Corbin, J. 2007. *Basics of qualitative research: Techniques and procedures for developing grounded theory, 3rd ed.* SAGE Publications.

[37] Takeuchi, L. and Stevens, R. The new coviewing: Designing for learning through joint media engagement. *New York, NY: The Joan Ganz Cooney Center at Sesame Workshop* (2011).

[38] Walsh, G. et al. 2013. FACIT PD: Framework for analysis and creation of intergenerational techniques for participatory design. *Proceedings of the SIGCHI Conference on Human Factors in Computing Systems (CHI '13)* (New York, NY, 2013), 2893–2902.

[39] Yin, R.K. 2003. *Case study research: Design and methods*. SAGE.

[40] Yip, J.C. et al. 2013. Brownies or Bags-of-Stuff? Domain expertise in Cooperative Inquiry with children. *Proceedings of the 12th International Conference on Interaction Design and Children (IDC 2013)* (New York, NY, USA, 2013), 201–210.

[41] Yip, J.C. et al. 2012. Kitchen Chemistry: Supporting learners' decisions in science. *Tenth International Conference of the Learning Sciences* (Mahwah, NJ, USA, 2012), 103–110.

# Fiabot! Design and Evaluation of a Mobile Storytelling Application for Schools

Elisa Rubegni
Università della Svizzera italiana
via Buffi 13, Lugano
elisa.rubegni@usi.ch

Monica Landoni
Università della Svizzera italiana
via Buffi 13, Lugano
monica.landoni@usi.ch

## ABSTRACT

This paper contributes to the ongoing debate about how digital technology can be integrated into the formal education system. Within a longitudinal research study, which lasted four years, we conducted an investigation on how mobile technology can support educational activities as defined by a school curriculum. Among the topics included in the school curriculum, we focused on the literary field and developed a Digital StoryTelling (DST) application, Fiabot!, to support this activity. Here, we describe the design of the application and how we evaluated its impact on educational activities. The application was designed and evaluated in two primary schools. The study had the objectives of exploring whether Fiabot! supports children in achieving educational objectives defined by the curriculum, how this effectively supports teachers, and to what extent children like using it for the creation and sharing of their stories. Our findings show that the application has a positive impact on curriculum enactment and effectively supports the related educational activities. Overall, Fiabot! was demonstrated to be very effective in stimulating children's discussion of a story's plot and characters. Thus, Fiabot! supported children not only in being creative but also in organizing their work and exploring a digital media opportunity. This resulted in the development of new skills and the better grounding of previously acquired knowledge, while teachers also had the opportunity to expand their teaching skills and get a taste of ICT's potential in education.

## Categories and Subject Descriptors

H.5.2 [Information interfaces and presentation]: User interfaces – *Prototyping*

## Keywords

Child-Computer Interaction; Formal Learning; Mobile Learning; , Digital Storytelling .

## 1. INTRODUCTION

The last decade has seen growth in the use of digital technology in educational contexts. Digital media and artifacts change the nature of learning and teaching by substantially modifying the ways in which pupils and teachers access and manipulate information. This phenomenon has raised the interest of several communities;

now, it can be studied from different perspectives, including learning science and interaction design. Therefore, being a relatively recent field of study, many issues still need to be explored. We are contributing to this debate by carrying out a research project where we explored the extent to which digital technology can support primary school curriculum enactment and have investigated how to introduce it into existing practices. In order to address these issues, we organized a series of case studies in two primary schools. We focused on a specific area of the curriculum, such as the Local/First Language, and the subarea of literature and narrative genre. Among other linguistic competences, children have to learn how to write a narrative in different literary genres. Teachers train children by asking them to read and write stories that correspond to a specific genre in order to teach them its specific elements and structure. Often the creation of stories is done in groups since the development of social skills is an aspect included in the curriculum. In addition, this activity comprises the training of additional abilities included in the official program such as social skills, creativity, and media literacy. The study as a whole has produced several outcomes, including: a set of guidelines for the design of Digital StoryTelling (DST) intervention in schools [17], a model for illustrating the teacher's role—as the main curriculum implementer—in using digital media/devices in school [18], and a prototype of the DST application Fiabot!.

In this paper, we describe Fiabot! and the results of its evaluation in real educational contexts. In the next section, we present the background of our research project.

## 2. BACKGROUND

The interest that researchers and educators increasingly manifest in the introduction of digital storytelling in education is primarily linked to its potential for fostering educational benefits, thus complementing the role held traditionally by storytelling as a teaching and learning tool. According to Bruner [2], the narrative is a primitive function of human psychology and a fundamental aspect in the construction of meaning. In these perspectives, narrative is a way of mediating the construction of meaning and a child's organization of knowledge to express creativity and use the imagination. Indeed, human creativity rests upon real experience of the world. Considering the theory of imagination routed in the Cultural-Historical approach [22], each creation is founded on elements taken from reality that are already present in an individual's past experience. In addition, creative activities that are carried out in groups produce great benefits [13] in regard to teaching social skills [12]. Designing technology for a formal environment such as a primary school requires particular attention to the integration of the technological artifacts in the school curriculum. This does not imply an exclusive concern with the resulting artifact but does cover educational activities as well.

As argued by Lewis et al. [11], the design of educational technology is not limited to the system being developed; it includes the range of activities that the system can support and the learning benefits that students gain from completing them successfully. Some systems have been designed purposefully to encourage children's collaboration and foster the development of collaborative skills. For instance, Benford et al. [1] report an approach called "encouraging collaboration," which motivates children to work together and see the benefits of cooperative work. From this approach, systems such as *KidPad* and *Klump* [1] have been developed. Other systems have been designed to enhance the development of particular sets of attitudes, knowledge, and skills. For instance, some tools can assist the development of specific knowledge such as programming, e.g. *Storytelling Alice* [7]. Some interesting attempts have been made in the direction of mixing analog and digital content to create digital storytelling, as seen in the work of Halloran et al. [8] and the POGO Story World [4]. More recently there has been the CASTOR (Context Aware STORytelling) project [14], which is a mobile-based authoring system that allows children to collect and modify material on a single device, in this case, a tablet. These projects are multifaceted; they are also quite complex and can hardly be efficiently integrated into a school environment with respect to the timing and scope of an educational curriculum. Besides research prototypes, there are a variety of applications available on the market that allow children to produce interactive stories, e.g. StoryKit, Story Dice, YouFable, etc. However, these are entertainment-oriented and do not have the goal of supporting formal learning activities.

Our system, grounded in the curriculum and stakeholders' requirements, is focused on solving a specific issue. Indeed, we aimed to develop a feasible application that could support a specific activity and be harmonically integrated with other school activities.

## 3. THE RESEARCH PROJECT

The overall research project lasted four years and had the purpose of exploring **two main research aspects**:

i) understanding how technology can support school curriculum,
ii) investigating how to introduce that technology in the existing teaching/learning practices.

Indeed, the research started in 2009 and ended in 2013 with the evaluation of the prototype. We conducted the overall project by involving two primary schools in Lugano, Ticino region (the Italian-speaking area in Switzerland): the Leonardo da Vinci (LDV) and the Istituto Elvetico (IE). During the four-year study, we actively engaged the schools' stakeholders in the process: approx. 130 pupils (ages 6 to 11), 4 teachers, and 2 school directors. Overall the project consisted of three main stages:

1. Analysis of how storytelling activities are usually done in class, without the support of any digital technology;
2. Introduction of applications and digital devices in class for DST production; and
3. Design of a new DST tool and its evaluation in context.

In this paper we report on the work done and the findings obtained in stage 3 and we provide a brief overlook of stages 1 and 2: for more details on the first two phases the reader may refer to other publications ([17][18][19]).

## 3.1 The School Curriculum

School curricula are designed to support child development in clearly-outlined stages, with a focus on the sets of abilities and knowledge children are known to acquire throughout their educational trajectory. In addition, it is important to focus on the teacher as the real driver of school curriculum enactment. Thus, the design of any technology and intervention has to be conceptualized and shaped according to the curriculum and those who enable it. The Swiss government defines the primary school national curriculum in an official document [23]. This text specifies: the expected learning outcomes, the resources for each discipline and their organization, the educational strategies to be used, the teaching methods to be employed, the assessment procedures, and the procedures for managing the curriculum. The curriculum includes six main subjects: First Local Language, Second Language, Science-History-Geography, Art and Physical Expression, and Religion. Primary school is divided into five years and children start school in primary one when they are six years old.

As previously mentioned, we focus on a specific area of the curriculum: Local/First Language and, in particular, on the subarea of storytelling. In the creation of a narrative, children also develop other linguistic competences such as phonology, spelling, morph syntax, and lexicon. In accordance with the curriculum, each teacher has to dedicate two hours per week to this activity. The educational goals change according to the ages of the children and the school grade. Involving the school and its various stakeholders—in particular, teachers and students—is essential to effectively achieving the educational benefits defined in the curriculum. In addition, the inclusion of students' and teachers' voices in the design process acknowledges their role in the co-construction of innovations in educational practices and helps to address the research in terms of concrete curriculum needs. We decided to engage these two schools since their official curricula are identical for the part concerning the literary genre topic. Moreover, the teachers and directors were very open and positive about introducing technology in class, and their active participation greatly helped the exploration of new opportunities. One school was involved in all the three phases of the study, while the other took part in the study from the middle of the requirements elicitation until the end—phases two and three. We included a second institution in order to enrich and consolidate the requirements gathered from the study in the first school. Therefore, in this paper we report on the involvement of both schools in the last part of the project. Indeed, for the evaluation phase we selected two classes (grades 4 at IE and 5 at LDV) and carried out the study with children aged 9–11. According to the curriculum this is a particularly interesting group to work with because the children already had experience in using digital technology, and the development of literary genre skills is a priority. Thus, Fiabot! has been evaluated by 43 students and two teachers across two different but comparable institutions.

In the next section, the methodological approach taken within the overall project will be described and then the last phase will be focused upon.

## 3.2 Whole project methodological approach

From our perspective, the design of technology for improving an educational experience goes beyond the simple use of a digital device to support the learning process. Considering that the artifact has to be introduced into already existing practices, we needed to take a holistic perspective that looks at the overall learning experience, including the interaction between teachers, learners, and educational processes. Throughout the entire project, we applied a qualitative approach, and we used different methods and techniques in order to investigate the activity in detail and collect as much consistent information as possible, based on a methodological approach inspired by cooperative [6] and participatory design [20]. In the study, we considered students, teachers, school directors, head teachers, and technicians as the main stakeholders. We interviewed all the school stakeholders following the contextual inquiry [16] technique. After a first broad interview, we focused on the in-depth analysis of the activities of the teachers and pupils in class. According to the curriculum, a teacher has to dedicate two hours per week to the writing lab. Thus, we designed our research study according to their schedules in order to avoid any disruption to the class organization caused by our presence during this activity.

In the next section we provide more details on the project phases.

# 4. PROJECT PHASES

As mentioned above in the third section, the research project was split into three phases. In the following, we describe in brief the project stages in order to give an overview of our work as a whole ([17][18][19]).

## 4.1 Analysis of how storytelling activities are usually done in class, without the support of any digital technology

The aim of this phase was to elicit user requirements and understand how the teachers enacted the curriculum. In this phase, we analyzed the activity before the introduction of any technology. It was particularly useful to gather findings on how teachers enable the curriculum in a canonical situation. In particular, we investigated the learning styles, teaching strategies, and the children's attitudes when working in groups [20]. Teachers, as curriculum enactors, were interviewed before and after each session of the writing lab. The interviews with the teachers before the writing lab were aimed at understanding their skills and the children's abilities in using digital technology, as well as the pupils' knowledge on this specific topic. After each session, we asked teachers to reflect on the activity run within the lab, and we focused on specific issues: the quality of the stories created, the type of collaboration within the groups, how they used artifacts, and the production of content. Observations were also gathered during the activities and then analyzed to provide us with an insight into the pupils' and teachers' user experience in using the artifacts to achieve their goals. We observed human-artifact and human-human interactions in order to identify possibilities for design. Afterwards, we conducted a focus group with the pupils to explore the breakthroughs and breakdowns of the activity. The focus group findings were based on the children's self-perception of the positive and negative aspects of the story-creation experience. During the writing laboratories, the children worked in small groups of two to four members to create stories. As mentioned above, through the group work, children can also develop their social skills, which are important pedagogical objectives established in the curriculum.

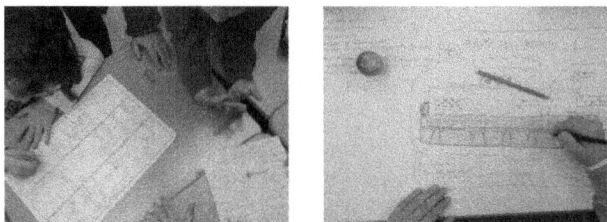

**Figure 1. Children create stories using only analogical artifacts, without digital technology.**

The stories had to follow a particular structure and content according to the literary genre that the teacher was explaining in that particular instance—e.g. fairy tales, fables, comics, etc. However, regardless of the type of narrative, the stories contained text and images (fig. 1).

## 4.2 Introduction of DST tools in class.

This phase has the objective of refining the requirements identified in the previous phase by directly introducing digital artifacts and applications into class activities. In the second phase, we used the technology probes [10] approach in order to refine the requirements elicited in the first phase. This approach is based on the use of digital technologies in class to support specific educational activities. During our research, we tested and evaluated many hardware and software solutions, from desktop computers to portable devices, such as the iPad™, and from web-based tools to desktop and mobile applications. We gathered data using the same approach used in phase one, through: a contextual inquiry with the teachers (before and after), a focus group with pupils after, and observation during the sessions.

This phase produced interesting insights in terms of the suitability of software and hardware to support educational benefits within a specific activity. These outcomes informed the research team about the opportunities and limits of the tools in a real context. Moreover, from the data analysis it emerged that the most suitable solutions are based on the use of portable/mobile devices. Thus, we decided to use the iPad™ to create our prototype.

**Figure 2. Phase two: children use laptops in class and desktop computers in the informatics lab.**

All these findings were elaborated and merged into a set of design recommendations [17] that drove the design of a DST application.

## 4.3 Design of a new DST tool and its evaluation in the field

The purpose of this phase is to elaborate the user requirements, and develop and evaluate the application to understand the impact of the tool on curriculum enactment. In phase three, we transformed the requirements into design parameters, and we built the application Fiabot!. Following the Houde and Hill approach [9], we developed low- and high-fidelity prototypes and went through many iterative cycles of design-evaluation-redesign. We will explain how we ran the final evaluation in more depth in section 6.

Considering the curriculum, and according to the teachers, we decided to target the application toward children aged 9–11, grades 4 and 5. At this age, the children have already studied the main features of narrative genres and are more focused on training their linguistic competences. Indeed, teachers asked children at these levels to practice the style, learn the structure (of the narrative type), and be creative in inventing a plot. These are the main educational objectives that have driven the design of the prototype that we present in the following section.

# 5. THE "FIABOT!" CONCEPT

"Fiabot!" is the name of the mobile application that we designed, prototyped, and tested in phase three. Fiabot! is an iPad application that enables the creation of interactive and multimedia stories. This application fits with class activities; thus, Fiabot! provides children with the opportunity to increase their ability to create a specific story genre. According to the curriculum and the teaching practices, Fiabot! provides indications of the structure and "ingredients" needed for each story type as well as reinterpreting and formalizing the workflow of the story creation.

In Fiabot! we propose for each literary genre a structure and a "list of ingredients" that inspire the children while they are creating the plot of a story and inventing the characters. These elements are well defined by the curriculum and stand as the basis of a teacher's explanation. The other important aspect is the workflow. This is not defined by the curriculum itself but is well established within the teaching practice. It should be noted that the same activity workflow emerged from all of the classes included in the study. Thus, on the basis of this activity process we defined three modules:

I)   Definition of story structure and plot;
II)  Media creation and editing;
III) Sharing within the class and publication of the story.

Each module corresponds to a specific step that the child, or the group, has to accomplish in order to create an interactive multimedia story. This structure was inspired by the observation of the activity in class, and, in addition, it overlaps with the Narrative Activity Model (NAM) [4]. The NAM articulates the narrative creation process in four stages: exploration, inspiration, production, and sharing.

Considering this model, each Fiabot! module can support a specific stage of the process: the first module supports the *exploration* and *inspiration* stages, the second the *production*, and the third the *sharing*.

The following section explains each module in detail.

**I) Definition of story structure and plot.**

According to the curriculum, each literary genre has a specific structure, plot, and content architecture. For each type of narrative Fiabot! provides a model of the structure to follow in order to create a complete story. This model is the same as the one used by the teacher during the face-to-face explanation. In addition, in Fiabot!, the ingredients needed to create the story are grouped according to the specific narrative genre. For instance, the fairy tale ingredients are: the antagonist(s), the protagonist(s), the protagonist helper(s), the antagonist helper(s), and the magic object(s). Children can specify detailed features for each of them (fig. 3). The defined ingredients will be shown on the story stage whenever, according to the structure of the story, they should be presented. For instance, a myth is made of a beginning (time, place, and explanation of the facts), development (characters plus a magic event), and a conclusion (the event modifies the reality, bringing things to the way they are at the moment).

This module supports the NAM phases of exploration and inspiration. Therefore, during *exploration*, pupils have a direct or mediated (by social relations or tools) interaction with the environment (e.g. a field trip, a book, or a movie). The input gathered in the experience is later elaborated on in the narrative process, while the *inspiration* phase is the moment in which children can understand the different aspects of their experience

and dissociate from it. In this phase, they can analyze and reflect upon what they have experienced by producing new content.

**Figure 3. The "list of ingredients" for creating a fairy tale.**

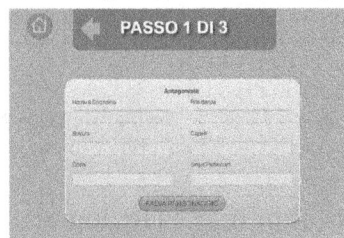

**Figure 4. Fiabot!'s box with details for each "ingredient".**

**II) Media creation and editing.**

One of the requirements of the curriculum is that children interpret and learn to use different media languages. In this module, children can create, import, and edit different media that can then be used in a story. The story contents can be very heterogeneous, i.e. images, photos, videos, music, audio, and animation. These can be found and created in different ways: using pen and paper, downloaded from the Internet, or produced using the native iPad application. All of these media can then be inserted into the story stage by importing them from the iPad photo gallery. Moreover, using the tablet camera it is possible to digitalize and import handmade drawings. All of this content can be used and mixed within the story in order to convey a unique, clear message (fig. 5).

**Figure 5. An example of part of a story that uses drawings imported into the tablet, a sketch done with an iPad app, and the icon of an audio file recorded with an iPad app.**

This module enables the *production* phase that corresponds to the association process and allows children to elaborate new content using different expression modalities. In this stage, children externalize the product of their imagination and express their emotions by producing a story. The story can take different forms, e.g. writing, drawing, and speech.

**III) Sharing in the class and publication of the story.**

As stated in the curriculum, the collaboration and understanding of social rules is quite relevant in the cognitive development of a child. Thus, sharing is an essential moment in this process. Indeed, even in phases one and two, the writing lab included a plenary presentation session during which all the students presented their stories to their classmates. With Fiabot! children can publish and share their stories with their classmates or a wider audience, such as other schools. Having the potential to show the results of their efforts is important for children, and it helps to improve agency and self-esteem. Stories can be delivered in different formats that are automatically generated by Fiabot!, e.g. website, video, newspaper, etc. The stories in different formats are published on a website accessible through a password; they are organized on a bookshelf and available for the children's families and other people who want to read them.

The third module supports the fourth phase, which is *sharing*. This last phase concludes the cycle that begins with exploration. The expression modality can go from verbal to bodily and be enhanced with other elements such as music.

Fiabot! has been through several iterative cycles, during which a few lo-fidelity prototypes were assessed and refined. As a result, we successfully produced the first version of Fiabot!, which was used for the evaluation of the study; it is presented in the following section.

# 6. EVALUATION OF FIABOT!

The Swiss primary school national curriculum defines: the expected learning outcomes, the resources for each discipline and their organization, the educational strategies to be used, the teaching methods to be employed, the assessment procedures, and the procedures for managing the curriculum. Teachers have to report whether or not a class has fulfilled the specific requirements. Fiabot!'s features are the explicit answer to the curriculum and users' needs: it is for mobile devices and supports the Swiss educational program's enactment. The evaluation session aimed to answer these questions:

A) To what extent can Fiabot! support children in achieving educational objectives defined by the curriculum?
B) How does Fiabot! effectively support teachers?
C) To what extent do children like using Fiabot! for the creation and sharing of their stories?

Thus, in order to assess the impact of Fiabot! on curriculum enactment, we had to design the evaluation session by looking at these topics as well as the organization of educational activities.

## 6.1 Methodological Approach

We explored these questions by involving both teachers and students. We applied various methods of data gathering and analysis in order to improve the validity of the study, such as: contextual inquiry, focus group, observation, and story evaluation.

Thus, the collected data covered the following areas of investigation: 1) improvement of curriculum enactment, 2) development of children's educational benefits, and 3) teaching practice enhancement. The contextual inquiry was conducted with the teachers (as in the previous phase) after the evaluation session with the purpose of investigating the perceived impact of Fiabot! on their teaching practices and on the children's activities in class.

The focus group with pupils was aimed at gathering their points of view in a collective discussion. We asked about their overall experience and whether or not they perceived themselves as having improved their skills. Data from the contextual inquiry and focus group were transcribed, coded, and analyzed. Coding and analysis were conducted in the vein of thematic analysis, standing mid-way between an inductive and deductive coding approach [5]. The transcribed data were initially coded in an inductive manner, identifying relevant data patterns that were then associated with themes. In a second wave, the relevant themes were grouped in relation to the three macro-categories mentioned

above. Data was reread to refine the emerging themes, and relationships between the themes were drawn in association with each macro-category. The analysis was done to evidence the themes and associations between them. In the final stage, the results were interpreted with regard to the outcomes of the other evaluation methods.

In addition, the observation allowed the researchers to gain an overview of the activities in class, and in particular, to observe interactions within the groups. Notes were transcribed and used to support the other set of data.

Teachers evaluated the stories according to a set of criteria inspired by the curriculum: Creativity, Collaboration, Media Literacy, and Consistency with the narrative genres.

This evaluation was aimed at indicating whether or not the children had achieved the learning targets defined by the current educational program, and how many children had accomplished them. In giving a score, teachers considered the quality of the outcomes (the stories) as well as the process of narrative creation. Moreover, the evaluation score was motivated by articulated feedback in which each teacher compared this result/process with the canonical activity without the support of any digital technology. The researchers assisted the teachers in the process of story evaluation. We observed that the teachers were consistent in their evaluations. Using the same criteria, each story was also evaluated by one researcher and another teacher. The three evaluations were quite homogeneous.

## 6.2 Evaluation Criteria

### 6.2.1 Creativity
The teachers specified that they usually evaluate the creativity of a story by looking at the originality of the plot and characters. They agreed on the creativity definition given by Vygotsky [21]: creativity is a process of combining past experience and reality. The teachers gave a high score to the stories that demonstrated an original combination of different elements and their elaboration, while stories that had no original elements or were merely a copy of a movie or book received a low score.

### 6.2.2 Collaboration
An important goal specified in the primary school curriculum concerns the development of affective and social education. In psychology, the benefit for children of developing collaborative behavior is well known [22]. Children have to develop social skills and learn how human and social organization works. Thus, starting from the first grade, teachers organize class activities to include group work. In our evaluation the score was higher when the children demonstrated the ability to distribute the tasks among themselves with the purpose of successfully achieving the educational objective and involving all the members of the group. When one or more children were not engaged in the activity, the group scored more negatively.

### 6.2.3 Media literacy
The Swiss curriculum provides a space for training students on media literacy mainly using a word processor and Internet browsing. Young people are considered digital natives [15] because of their natural ability to understand how digital media works and how to access online resources through self-acquired skills and competences. However, recently even Prensky reported on the younger generation's lack of "digital wisdom" [15] and in particular touched upon how poorly children are supported by existing educational curricula. Educating pupils and enhancing their media literacy is concerned not only with computer usage

and Internet browsing but also with the ability to create digital content and use it to communicate effectively.

Teachers gave positive feedback when children used digital content consistently within the story. Media can include voice, music, images, drawings, video, or animation and digitalized handmade drawings. In particular, teachers looked at the harmonization of this content within the narrative. A negative score was given for stories in which media was not a real added value or was used without any purpose.

### 6.2.4 Consistency with the narrative genres
In the curriculum, it is specified that children have to learn several literary genres: fairy tale, fable, tale, myth, and legend. Each genre has a precise structure and is made of specific "ingredients" that the child has to identify and learn to use in the creation of narratives. In the evaluation session we focused on the fairy tales genre since this was the main topic of focus in grades four and five. The fairy tales follow a structure with a beginning ("Once upon a time . . . ."), a middle, and an ending ("They lived happily ever after."). In addition, a fairy tale has these ingredients: the protagonist/hero, the anti-hero, the hero helper, the anti-hero helper, and the magic object/animal. A good story, worth a high score, had to include all the ingredients and be consistent with that specific structure. Teachers gave low scores to students who did not respect the required structure or omitted ingredients.

## 6.3 Using the Criteria
The teachers evaluated each story by providing a textual feedback and a score (from very poor (0) to very good (5)) for each of the above-mentioned criteria. In the assessment, both the outcomes (the fairy tales) and the process of creation were considered. The teachers' perspectives enabled us to understand the suitability of Fiabot! for accomplishing the curriculum objectives and to comprehend its impact on teaching practices and the children's learning processes. In addition, the children's viewpoints were useful in order to understand their experience in using Fiabot!.

In the subsequent sections, we present the setting where the evaluation took place and the procedures we followed.

## 6.4 Participants and Setting
The evaluation of Fiabot! was conducted within two schools. We engaged all of the school staff to design the study while the test was carried out in two classes. That involved two teachers (one in each school) and 43 children, in grades 4 and 5, aged 9–11. We decided to carry out the evaluation with a small number of teachers in order to conduct an in-depth analysis in two specific contexts. Moreover, working closely with the two teachers allowed us to gain their trust and confidence. In each class, we conducted two evaluation sessions—the second took place one month after the first one. Children were grouped in small teams of up to four members each. Each team was built to have a good balance in terms of specific pupils' abilities, covering: digital literacy, social skills, creativity, and knowledge of the curriculum topic. Thus, the teachers assigned children to groups using their deep knowledge of the children's skills, attitudes, and personalities so that the groups would have comparable strengths and abilities.

## 6.5 Procedure
Each evaluation session lasted for four days and was articulated in three stages:

i)   Children's training, 1 hour
ii)  Creation and sharing of the stories, 6 hours each day
iii) Focus group and contextual inquiry, 3 hours

i) Children's training.

The researcher trained the class on how to use Fiabot! for one hour, during which they also tried to create a short story. However, children in both classes already had experience in using the tablet as well as some tools for the shooting and editing of video and images, drawings, and audio recordings. Thus, the novelty effect was quite low. In the second session, the training was not replicated since the children already knew how to use Fiabot!.

ii) Creation and sharing of the stories.

The objective of the activity assigned to the children was to create a fairy tale using Fiabot!. The teacher explained to the children the objective and then organized them into groups. In the creation of the plot and the drawings children could use both digital and analog artifacts (pen and paper). Analog texts and drawings were then transformed into digital content by taking a picture of them with the tablet camera or by copying the text using a native text editor app. When all of the stories had been created, each group presented the narrative to their classmates in a plenary session. During the presentations the teachers made the evaluations using the predefined set of criteria.

iii) Focus group and contextual inquiry.

After the presentation of the story we separately conducted a focus group with the children and a contextual inquiry with the teachers.

At the end of the evaluation session the children had produced a total of 17 stories using Fiabot!.

## 7.  FINDINGS
We collected data using different methods and by taking different perspectives. Indeed, we analyzed the experience in the class from the points of view of the teachers, pupils, and researchers. Each perspective contributed to highlighting specific aspects and looking at particular facets. Data gathered through the contextual interview, the focus group, and the observation were treated separately and analyzed according to the specific method—i.e. interviews and notes were transcribed and coded. Afterwards, we looked at the whole corpus of data and organized it in order to answer our research questions. Here, we present the results of the study organized according to our three research questions.

## 7.1 A) To what extent can Fiabot! support children in achieving educational objectives defined by the curriculum?
As evidence of the impact of Fiabot! on supporting children to achieve educational objectives, we used teachers' assessments of the stories (following the four criteria introduced in 6.2), and their comments and notes. Each teacher evaluated the stories produced by the children in their class. In their assessment, they considered not only the final product, but also the process of production. Overall, the stories met the curriculum indications quite well and fulfilled many of the requirements and even the desiderata set by the teachers, which were in line with the school curriculum, both from the technical and pedagogical points of view. Indeed, as shown in the table (table 1), the scores were quite high. In the upcoming section, we discuss the assessment according to each criterion and quote some of the most relevant teacher comments.

### 7.1.1 Creativity
The evaluation of creativity was based on the ability of the children to combine elements of past experiences and reality.

Sixty percent of the stories obtained a very high score. Teachers in many cases appreciated the originality of the plot and in the choice of characters. As stated by teacher 1 (T1), *"I really liked how in the plot 'Virginia the vain' children integrated some episodes from one child's family with other elements that were invented. The plot is very consistent and these elements merged perfectly within the economy of the story. Another good example is the 'Luke and the savior' story. Children took inspiration from [The] Hunger Games but they didn't copy the game.*

**Table 1. Evaluations of student stories (N = 17)**

|  | Creativity | Collaboration | Media literacy | Narrative genres |
|---|---|---|---|---|
| Rebecca | 4 | 4 | 4 | 2 |
| The past in the future | 4 | 5 | 2.5 | 3 |
| The dragons and the family stone | 5 | 5 | 4.5 | 4.5 |
| Luke and the savior | 2 | 5 | 1 | 5 |
| Clouds and problems | 4.5 | 5 | 5 | 5 |
| Jonny and the giants | 1.5 | 5 | 4 | 4 |
| Everything happened in one night | 5 | 5 | 4 | 5 |
| The crown | 4.5 | 5 | 5 | 5 |
| Lucia's savior | 3.5 | 4 | 4 | 5 |
| Searching for the gold and silver tree | 5 | 5 | 5 | 5 |
| Virginia the vain | 4 | 5 | 4 | 3.5 |
| Romea and Giulietto | 2.5 | 4.5 | 5 | 4 |
| The adventure of two friends | 3 | 5 | 2 | 5 |
| The jewels of the Queen | 5 | 5 | 4.5 | 5 |
| Discovering the sweetie world | 5 | 5 | 5 | 5 |
| The kidnapped princess | 2 | 3.5 | 3 | 3.5 |
| The knight Aghoss | 3.5 | 4.5 | 5 | 4.5 |
| **Mean of rating** | **3.9** | **4.8** | **4** | **4.5** |

*They used the strategies of the game in the story by creating complex narrative mechanisms that were very intriguing for the audience. I have never seen this kind of connections [sic] before using Fiabot! In addition, I have noticed that there was an improvement in the level of discussion and engagement of pupils in creating the character of the story and the plot. It was quite surprising!".* The other teacher (T2) mentioned how module 1 of Fiabot! was useful in conceiving the narrative mechanisms before writing: *"In Fiabot! children are asked to define the characters/ingredients before the creation of the story. This allowed them to discuss about the plot as well as to talk about their experiences that might fit in the story. In addition the way*

*Fiabot! easily allowed them to explore Internet contents let them to [sic] find the information they needed for the plot."* As reported by all teachers in the interview, the originality of the plot was sometimes expressed through the unexpected behaviors of the story's characters or imaginative creatures made of a mix of different animals. For instance, in the *"The kidnapped princess"* story we can find both elements. *"Federica, the ant, spits poison from her mouth that dissolved the griffon."* The ant is hero Jack's helper and the griffon is a legendary animal, half lion and half eagle (see fig. 6).

**Figure 6. The drawing of the griffon inserted and used in the *The kidnapped princess* story.**

### 7.1.2 Collaboration

This criterion obtained the highest grade: 90% of the stories were valued with a score between 4.5 and 5. Teachers reported that the collaboration among children greatly improved with the use of Fiabot!, especially because it encouraged the organization of work within a group. T1: *"I have noticed that the workflow of Fiabot! imposed on the children to discuss about how to distribute the work within the group. Especially the first module—definition of story structure and plot—helped them to reflect on the type of story they wanted to create. They listed the tasks and then distributed the work according to the abilities of each member."* T2 on the same topic commented that: *"Fiabot! stimulated group discussion on the plot of the story and allowed a reflection of pupils on their abilities and skills. Children demonstrated a great maturity in focusing on the final objective and sometimes in overcoming personal wishes. In some cases, one member led the distribution of tasks. This depends on the children's temperament, and it is perfectly in line with other experiences we [have] had in class."* Nonetheless, two stories received a low score (3) because the process of organization was not effective, and one or more members were isolated from the group. Both teachers agreed that in these cases, the story was badly affected by the poor collaboration. Reflecting on the whole experience, teachers also commented that the positive feedback reinforced the children's belief that teamwork is a great asset in supporting educational achievements.

### 7.1.3 Media literacy

In their assessments, the teachers reported how the opportunity of using different media had a great impact on the quality of the stories as well as on supporting the creativity of the children.

T2 stated that *"In the story 'Everything happened in one night' the use of audio was amazing. Children created a blues ballad to describe the main characters of the story. In addition, the associated images of the characters gave a great added value to the audio and text: listening [to] the song while looking at the images had a great impact [fig. 7]. The options offered by Fiabot! in module 2—Media creation and editing—encouraged children to use different types of media. Children could experiment in creating, editing, and also merging different contents. They produced a large number of audio files and images and then, with the help of Fiabot!, selected and arranged these on the stage of the story. I found Fiabot! very effective in allowing children to edit and integrate media with the purpose of enhancing the communication of the message to the audience."*

T1 added, *"The opportunity offered by Fiabot! for creating, editing, and importing different media allowed the children to understand the different features of each of the contents. In addition, looking at the stories, it is evident how children explored the different languages in order to understand which was more suitable and added value to the story."*

**Figure 7. A screenshot of "Everything happened in one night."**

*In addition, I really appreciated how children spatially organized the media and combined handmade and digital images [fig. 7], text and sound [fig. 8]. This was possible, thanks to the Fiabot! flexibility in arranging contents on the stage of the story."*

**Figure 8. An example of the audio and images within the text.**

During the interviews, both teachers agreed on how much the children had improved their literacy skills while using the tablet to create text, images, and sound. Many times, they underlined how their literacy had remarkably improved and how Fiabot! had had a positive impact on the development of these skills.

### 7.1.4 Consistency with the narrative genres

The teachers also gave a very high score to the stories with regard to the consistency of the narrative within the fairy tale genre. Out of all the stories, 70.5% of them received a score higher than 4. Indeed, the teachers reported that they were very satisfied with how the children learned to create stories and how Fiabot! was a useful tool for reinforcing the recall of the content presented in class. T2 explained, *"I can affirm that Fiabot! helped children to consolidate their knowledge in this genre. For instance, when they had to conceive the ingredients in module 1 they discussed a lot about the possible characters and the plot. This module allowed them to brainstorm and then to focalize. In addition, during the discussion they used the appropriate language to indicate the characters and other elements of the story [in a way that has] never happened before. This indicates clearly that Fiabot! reinforced the recall of the information provided in the [initial] lecture and effectively supported the acquisition of this knowledge."* T1 added, *"I can see the benefit of using Fiabot! from the way they built the plot of the stories. They created correct narratives but they used the elements of the story in a creative and unusual way. For instance, the protagonist of one of the story [sic] is the crown, not a person, but a magic object! This choice is quite original and correct at the same time."*

As seen from the data analysis, the teachers were enthusiastic about the application. Fiabot! appears to support children in achieving educational objectives defined by the curriculum. Probably the biggest challenge for the children was to find the right balance between creating a complete fairy tale, being creative, using digital media for a purpose, and conveying the message of the narrative.

## 7.2 B) How does Fiabot! effectively support teachers?

The contextual inquiry done with the teachers, together with the researchers' observations, allowed us to better understand the role of Fiabot! in supporting the teachers in achieving the educational goals defined in the curriculum as well as in enhancing their teaching practices. Overall, the teachers and school administration really appreciated the way in which we conducted the study from the outset. Indeed, even if the narrative is part of the curriculum, we had to define the activity in terms of time, objectives, and practices. Starting from the initial stage of the study, the team and the school stakeholders worked very hard to refine our intervention in the school and integrate it within other running activities. As a result, the way in which we organized the activity was effective from the project perspective while simultaneously avoiding any disruption to other curriculum-related activities. As reported by T1, *"The integration of digital technology within the training of the first language was particularly useful especially for children who could explore the opportunity given by digital media and artifact on purpose."* T2 states, *"This practical activity well supported the explanation in class. In addition the use of Fiabot! introduced a new challenge such as to learn how to use media language in a coherent and creative way. In addition, it gave the possibility to recall the contents already discussed in class by creating a story."* The use of the tablet and digital media for a specific school activity, part of the curriculum, changed the children's perceptions of using digital artifacts. T1 stated: *"An important message that I tried to convey to the children is that tablets and mobile phones have a value and that [they] are not toys. After using Fiabot! children perceived clearly the importance of the tablet that could allow them to learn new things as being author of a multimedia story."* In addition, the use of Fiabot! improved the teachers' awareness of the possibility of using the tablet in other educational scenarios. T1: *"This experience encouraged me to expand the use of digital media in other class activities. For instance, I started to use video to show scientific phenomena in class. I found it very useful and I think that it could change significantly the way I teach."* Moreover, the use of Fiabot! engaged teachers in activities that enhanced their self-esteem. T1 said: *"Now that I understood how to create a multimedia story I feel more confident in using also other technology [such] as the smart board."* T2 reinforces this concept, adding: *"Technology helps us to keep focused and motivated, and enforces a positive attitude towards the use of digital media in class and the storytelling task."*

We asked teachers what their opinions were concerning the other advantages of using Fiabot! and T1 replied: *"Overall, children are more active in the creation of the story using Fiabot! than using other canonical artifacts. The tablet was very attractive, encouraged them to be more active and improved the level of engagement. In particular, the way Fiabot! gave the children the opportunity of being authors of something original and unique that could be shown to their friends and family. This was very satisfying for them."* T2 agreed that Fiabot! stimulated the agency in creating a multimedia story and improved the pupils' self-esteem: *"Stories in general were very rich and well done. Thus, pupils were satisfied of [sic] their work and felt [themselves] to be author[s] of multimedia contents. This helped me a lot to reinforce their self-esteem which is a fundamental element to which the elementary school is addressed."*

## 7.3 C) To what extent do children like using Fiabot! for the creation and sharing of their stories?

The focus group after the session helped us explore the experience from the children's points of view, as they could freely reflect on their experiences. The evidence we gathered is based on the children's self-perceptions. During the focus group we asked children to write down on Post-it notes their main issues regarding the different aspects that emerged during the discussion, e.g. their contribution to the activity, the part of the story s/he proposed, their most-liked experiences in using Fiabot!, their level of satisfaction, etc. Very interesting aspects emerged from the thematic coding analyses. Regarding their contribution, the most quoted items were connected either to the practical—e.g. *"writing," "drawings,"* or *"coordinating the group"*—or to the conceptual activities, e.g. *"creating the characters,"* or *"giving tips on the story plot."* Concerning their contribution to the story, the children quoted the "characters" (e.g. *"the evil witch as the antagonist,"* or *"the unicorn as the protagonist helper"*), a specific part of the plot (e.g. *"I have proposed the part of the story when the queen discovers her daughter's kidnapping,"* or *"the three riddles"*), and elements of story structures (e.g. *"the beginnings and the endings,"* or *"the middle part when Romea and Giulietto are in front of the infinite wall"*). Regarding their most-liked aspect of the assignment, children mentioned the plot (e.g. *"when the princess's hairs were [sic] covered with green mold"* or *"the part when the witch, the antagonist, has deceived the prince"*), elements of story structures (e.g. *"the beginning and the end"* or *"the conflict in the middle"*), and the practical activities (e.g. *"when I have recorded the character voices"* and *"the part where we wrote our idea on paper"*). In particular, they liked to create audio, images, and videos, and to integrate this content with text in the story (e.g. *"the funniest thing [ . . . ] was to make the voices of the character[s]"*). The children declared that providing a clear list of the elements of the structure—i.e. the beginning, middle, and ending—was one of the most interesting contributions of Fiabot!. In addition, when we asked about the quality of the collaboration within the group, the majority of the children described the group work as *"interesting"* and *"fun."* As suggested by Csikszentmihalyi, "Children can experience pleasure without any investment of psychic energy, whereas enjoyment happens only as a result of unusual investments of attention" [3]. Moreover, considering the richness of the narrative plots and the originality of the characters, it is quite evident how fruitful the children's collaboration was. During the focus group, children expressed their satisfaction with being the authors of a story—e.g. *"me and my classmate created a whole multimedia story as the professional"*—and they asked to show the stories to their parents to demonstrate that they had learned to create *"magic stories."* In general, the children were very enthusiastic and they never mentioned being tired or bored when using Fiabot!.

## 8. DISCUSSION

The main objective of this study is to contribute to the debate on how digital technology can be introduced in a formal context and support the enactment of educational curriculum. From the analysis of the data it emerged that Fiabot! met the curriculum requirements and improved the teaching and learning of literary

genres and other abilities connected to this activity (i.e. media literacy, social skills, and creativity). On the part of the teachers, we gathered positive feedback concerning how Fiabot! improved their awareness of the possibility of using the tablet in other educational scenarios and its effect on their self-esteem. On the children's side, we observed how children developed a combination of literacy skills by using Fiabot!, as well as how they achieved specific educational objectives as defined in the school curriculum. For instance, it was crucial to observe how children were correctly referring to each of the character's roles —e.g. *"I have invented that a bad donut is the antagonist while the sweet old lady is the protagonist"*—and the other elements of the story type as a direct result of Fiabot! reinforcing this terminology. For each of the three modules of Fiabot!, as described in section 5.1, we can recognize their specific contributions. In **Module 1**, the story structure and the ingredients were useful in supporting the children while they conceived the narrative mechanisms before writing. The discussion of the plot and characters allowed them to think about unexpected elements that made the story original. At the same time, the debate stimulated by Module 1 encouraged the pupils to also talk about their skills and to distribute tasks between group members accordingly. In addition, Module 1 supported the teaching strategy via the recall of the information already presented in class, such as the story structure and elements and the narrative mechanism.

**Module 2** contributed to the children's media "wisdom." This module allowed for exploration of the opportunity and limits of producing and using digital content, as well as how to use these elements to convey a specific message. The production and editing of digital media and the digital artifact itself raised a high level of interest among the pupils, who were extremely engaged with the activity. The children felt in control of the quality of the final product.

Finally, **Module 3** allowed the sharing of the story, contributing substantially to the children's self-esteem and their satisfaction with being authors. Indeed, the teachers had the opportunity to show other colleagues the results of this educational activity.

Fiabot! has not only helped to confirm and reinforce the theory that the children learned in class, but it has also enabled them to put it into practice and produce stories to be shared with their peers, teachers, and family. This gave them the opportunity to test their skills and have them recognized in a social context, making it a rewarding experience they really enjoyed. The children had previous experience creating stories without any digital device and found that using Fiabot! made it a more exciting challenge. Indeed, they had to learn a new semantic (the media language) and how to use it within a specific purpose, but at the end they were very satisfied. Being the authors of a multimedia story also improved their self-esteem.

## 9. IMPLICATIONS FOR FUTURE WORK

We are planning to explore other areas of the school curriculum and involve different communities of learners by adapting the methods and techniques we have applied in this project. Our experience shows that in order to effectively integrate technology in schools, it is important to have a holistic approach and respect the ecology of the school. This approach is essential for the design and even more so for the assessment of the impact of the new artifact. It was interesting to notice how using a school-related application on a game-oriented device, such as the available tablet, made both children and parents aware of its intrinsic educational value. This helped in promoting a positive change of attitude towards the adoption of tablets and technology in education, both in families and at the schools at large. A similar phenomenon took place among the teachers, too, in that those involved in the project felt encouraged to explore more ways and opportunities in which technology could add value to their teaching, starting with scientific subjects. It would be worth further exploring how the various actors in the process have benefited from being part of our study in terms of the development of new skills and changes in attitudes.

One of our main challenges was finding the right criteria for evaluation that would take into account the many facets of the experience and the tool we had designed. In addition, another issue we faced in the project concerned bringing together educational and technological objectives. It proved essential for the success of the project that all members of the research team were sensible to educational themes and contexts. This resulted in a very fruitful collaboration between school stakeholders and researchers, a truly bilateral exchange of ideas.

There remain open issues to be further explored in future projects, but we feel that our experience could provide a good starting point for forthcoming scientific investigations.

## 10. ACKNOWLEDGMENTS

We would like to thank the teachers, pupils, and school directors who have participated in the study. We are grateful to our colleagues, Luca Colombo, Marcello Scipioni, and Amalia Sabiescu for their valuable insights and contributions. A special thanks goes to Marcello Romanelli, who had a prominent role in the study's development. In addition, we wish to acknowledge the Hasler foundation, whose grant supported part of this study.

## 11. REFERENCES

[1] Benford, S., Bederson, B.B. Akesson, K., Bayon, V. Druin, A. Hansson, P., Hourcade, J.P., Ingram, R., Neale, H., O'Malley, C., Simsarian, K., Stanton, D., Sundblad, Y. and G. Taxén (2000) 'Designing storytelling technologies to encourage collaboration between young children', in *CHI 2000, ACM Conference on Human Factors in Computing Systems, CHI Letters*, 2 1 (2000), pp. 556–563

[2] Bruner, J.S. (1996). The culture of education. Cambridge MA: Harvard University Press

[3] Csikszentmihalyi, M. Flow: The Psychology of Optimal Experience. Harper Perennial, 2008

[4] Decortis F. and A. Rizzo (2002) New active tools for supporting narrative structures, in *Personal and Ubiquitous Computing*, 6(5-6), pp.416-429

[5] Fereday, J., & Muir-Cochrane, E. (2006). Demonstrating rigor using thematic analysis: A hybrid approach of inductive and deductive coding and theme development. *International Journal of Qualitative Methods*, 5(1), Article 7.

[6] Greenbaum, J., Kyng, M. Design at Work: Cooperative Design of Computer Systems, Lawrence Erlbaum, Hillsdale, NJ, 1991.

[7] Kelleher, C. and R. Pausch (2007) 'Using storytelling to motivate programming', in *Commun. ACM* 50, 7 (Jul. 2007), pp.58-64

[8] Halloran, J., Hornecker, E., Fitzpatrick, G., Weal, M., Millard, D., Michaelides, D., De Roure, D. (2006, June). The literacy fieldtrip: using UbiComp to support children's creative writing. In *Proceedings of the 2006 conference on Interaction design and children* (pp. 17-24). ACM

[9] Houde, S., & Hill, C. (1997). What do prototypes prototype? In M. Helander, T. Landauer, & P. Prabhu (Eds.), *Handbook of human-computer interaction* (2nd ed., pp. 367-381). Amsterdam: Elsevier Science.

[10] Hutchinson, H., Mackay, W., Westerlund, B., Bederson, B. B., Druin, A., Plaisant, C., et al. (2003). Technology probes: inspiring design for and with families. In *Proceedings of the conference on Human factors in computing systems* (pp. 17-24). Ft. Lauderdale, Florida, USA: ACM Press.

[11] Lewis, T., Petrina, S. & Hill, A. M.: 1998, 'Problem Posing – Adding a Creative Increment to Technological Problem Solving', *Journal of Industrial Teacher Education* **36(1)**, 5–35.

[12] Nicolopoulou, A. (1997). Children and narratives: toward an interpretive and sociocultural approach. In M. Bamberg, *Narrative development: six approaches* (pp. 179-216). London: Lawrence Erlbaum

[13] Papert, S. (1991) 'Situating Constructionism', in Idit Harel and Seymour Papert (eds.): *Constructionism*. Norwood, NJ: Ablex Publishing

[14] Pittarello, F., Bertani, L. (2012, June). CASTOR: learning to create context-sensitive and emotionally engaging narrations in-situ. In *Proceedings of the 11th International Conference on Interaction Design and Children* (pp. 1-10). ACM.

[15] Prensky, M. "Digital Wisdom and Homo Sapiens Digital," in Deconstructing Digital Natives: Young People, Technology and the New Literacies, M. Thomas, Ed. London: Routledge, 2011, pp. 15-30.

[16] Raven, M.E., and Flanders, A. (1996). "Using Contextual Inquiry to Learn About Your Audience." ACM SIGDOC Journal of Computer Documentation, Vol. 20, No. 1

[17] Rubegni, E., Colombo, L., Landoni, M., (2013) Supporting child creativity and sense making through Digital Storytelling at school, In: 27th International British Computer Society Human Computer Interaction Conference

[18] Rubegni, E., Landoni, M., (2013) *Modeling the role of teachers in introducing portable technology to the school curriculum,* In proceedings of ECCE '13. ACM, New York, NY, USA, Article 13, 8 pages.

[19] Rubegni, E. and Paolini, P. (2010) *Comparing canonical and digital-based narrative activities in a formal educational setting.* In: International Conference on Interaction Design and Children (IDC 2010). Barcelona, Spain, June 9–12, 2010, pp. 258-261

[20] Schuler, D., Namioka, A. (Eds.), Participatory Design: Principles and Practices, Lawrence Erlbaum, Hillsdale, NJ, 1993.

[21] Vygotsky, L.S. (2004; 1967). Imagination and creativity in childhood. Journal of Russian and east European psychology. Vol 42, no. 1

[22] Vygotsky, L. S. (1978) *Mind in Society: The Development of Higher Psychological Processes*. Cambridge, MA: Harvard University Press

[23] http://www4.ti.ch/decs/ds/usc/cosa-facciamo/programmi-ufficial

# Shake up the Schoolyard: Iterative Design Research for Public Playful Installations

Rob Tieben[1,2]        Linda de Valk[1]        Pepijn Rijnbout[1]        Tilde Bekker[1]        Ben Schouten[1]

1: Eindhoven University of Technology
Industrial Design, Playful Interactions
Den Dolech 2, 5612 AZ Eindhoven
the Netherlands

2: Fontys School of ICT
Serious Game Design
Rachelsmolen 1, 5612 MA, Eindhoven
the Netherlands

rob@robtieben.com        l.c.t.d.valk@tue.nl        p.rijnbout@tue.nl        m.m.bekker@tue.nl        bschouten@tue.nl

## ABSTRACT

Three different design research topics are presented in this article: how to design social and active play for teenagers, how to design for open-ended and emergent play, and how to evaluate interactive playful installations in situ. The Wiggle the Eye installation, five interactive wiggle benches and a central lamp, was iteratively developed and evaluated with more than 1000 users, at two high schools, one university and a design festival. The installation succeeded in inviting teenagers to play in a social way, yet the interaction design proved challenging: uncoordinated mass usage and a variety of external factors influenced the exploration and discovery process for the users. The presented insights serve as advice for everyone designing for teenagers, public spaces or playful interactions.

## Categories and Subject Descriptors

H.5.2 [**User Interfaces**]: Interaction styles (e.g., commands, menus, forms, direct manipulation), User-centered design.

## General Terms

Design, Human Factors.

## Keywords

Playful interactions; interactive installations; teenagers; public play; design research; in situ evaluations.

## 1. INTRODUCTION

*Imagine a high school; hundreds of teenagers walking out of the classrooms, sitting down to enjoy their lunch break. Talking, laughing, discussing the newest app. How can we design something that seduces them to move around and play? How can we create a playful experience that is enjoyable day after day, for all types of teenagers? And, how can we study such a design? How to implement, evaluate and analyze an interactive system in such a dynamic environment?*

The previous section sketches our design research interests. We are intrigued by three design research topics:

- Designing social and active play for teenagers. We want to design public installations that seduce teenagers to start playing, in a social and physically active way. We try to reduce the amount of passive sedentary moments during an average day, by inviting them to play and interact with peers [18]. The design challenge is how to design an installation specifically for teenagers, and to create a playful activity that connects to their daily life and interests.

- Designing for open-ended and emergent play. Open-ended play is play without predefined (game) rules, where players create and play with rules, meaning and interpretation [27]. We believe that open-ended play is suitable for all types of players, and can provide sustained and recurrent motivation for playing. How to design for this open play, and how to evaluate this type of play, are main questions for our research group.

- Evaluating interactive playful installations in situ: in order to understand playful interactions, they have to be evaluated with large groups of users, in real world situations. We try to optimize how we can study interactions that we cannot predict beforehand, interactions that are influenced by countless conditions - all the external and internal factors of an interactive complex system in a real world situation with users [15].

In this article, we present our 'lessons learned' about all three design research topics. We describe our iterative process for creating and studying an open-ended playful installation for teenagers, which we implemented at high schools, and evaluated with more than thousand users. We created an installation of wiggle benches for a schoolyard, accompanied by an interactive street light. Using sensors, vibration modules and the street light, we invited teenagers to explore, wiggle and play with the installation. We observed and evaluated their actions and iteratively explored multiple interaction designs on different locations. This process was iterative and extensive; we present the results and insights on a holistic level, in order to communicate an overview of insights and generalizable lessons learned. Due to space considerations, we cannot go into full detail for every iteration and evaluation; we want to take the reader along through this entire process, instead of diving into the - also interesting - details.

In this article, we first present related work on interactive designs for social and physical play, open-ended play and methodologies for in situ evaluations of such interactive installations. Following this, we explain our design research process and the specific challenges for designing and evaluating playful interactions for large groups of users in public areas. Then, we present the physical design of the installation, and more extensively the six iterations of interaction designs. We only report the evaluation results and insights on a holistic level: what did we learn in general about teenagers, public play, and this type of design research. Lastly, we make a few general conclusions, followed by a brief discussion.

## 2. RELATED WORK

### 2.1 Design Research for Playful Interactions

Using (insights from) play and games in design research is an emerging trend in the HCI community, and simultaneously the Game Research community is approaching the HCI philosophy more and more [e.g. 4, 5, 9]. The overlap of these disciplines has resulted in a large variety of design research fields: serious games, persuasive games, playful persuasion, and so on; accompanied by tools such as PLEX cards [10] and Lenses of Game Design [17].

In this large multi-disciplinary field, our research group focuses on Playful Interactions: designing and evaluating interactive objects and installations that use playful mechanisms to make people more socially and physically active [2]. We believe that if we successfully invite people to play in an open-ended and emergent way, then we can use this playful action to inherently achieve side-goals. In our group, we have explored and implemented this vision in many contexts: social interaction for elderly [16], physical activity for teenagers [25], social and physical play for children [28], and so on. Well-known examples that match our vision, by other designers and researchers, are the Interactive Slide [19], the Swing Scape [7] and the Piano Stairs[13]. These examples all use playful mechanisms to stimulate physical and social play.

We have gained three main insights from this related work: (1) the importance of inviting the user to start playing, combined with the trigger for performing the actions that we aim at. (2) Allowing and stimulating freedom in choice, so that users can and will create their own path, rules and goals. And (3) the awareness that different player types and social contexts result in differences in how people (want to) play. These insights are important when designing for playful interaction and have been used in the design of the Wiggle the Eye installation.

### 2.2 Design Research for Teenagers

Teenagers were, until recently, a mostly overlooked target group in the HCI community. In the last years, more attention has been given to this group, for example in several workshops [1, 6] and in publications [e.g. 14]. Our research group has published various articles about design research for teenagers, such as [20, 24].

Youth development psychology can tell us more about what interests teenagers. Youth from 12-16 is in the middle of the adolescence, the transition between childhood and adulthood. In this period, the teenagers rapidly develop on a physical, cognitive, emotional and social level, initiated by the puberty [3]. The cognitive, emotional and social changes focus among others on *exploration* and *development*: *self-reflection, identity development, self-concept* and *self-esteem* are important topics,

in addition to the *need for autonomy*, the forming of *cliques and crowds*, and the strong *peer conformity* and *pressure*. The teenagers explore, define and develop their own identity and their relation with others [3]. Daily activities and interests for teenagers confirm this; hence, when designing for teenagers it is important to create activities that connect to their daily life. In previous publications, we have sketched how to do this [e.g. 23].

In this article, we continue to improve these previous insights: we designed especially for teenagers, in the context of their real life.

## 3. DESIGN RESEARCH PROCESS

In our work, we follow a design research approach. We go through various iterations of design, evaluation and analysis; this process leads to rich, qualitative and situational insights [8].

As we focus on open and emergent play, we intentionally do not define any (game) rules for our playful installations beforehand. This creates an extra challenge: how to make design decisions that influence but do not explicitly direct user behavior? In previous work, we have proposed a link between design parameters and the emergent events that arise during interaction [15]. A designer can 'turn the knobs' by changing certain design parameters. These parameters then influence what happens at the emergent level. In our design research process, several 'turns of knobs' and their effect were explored to begin to understand how to design for emergent play.

Another challenge is the real-life context we design for. This requires practical thinking, flexibility and improvisation skills. We aim for our playful installations to become part of the everyday routine of teenagers at their high school, so we have to test them in situ. In this way, we were also able to focus on longer-term experiences with our installation, going beyond the initial novelty effect.

Evaluation of a multi-user installation in a real-life context provides yet another challenge: what is the optimal way to collect the relevant data, during a longer-term evaluation. The approach we used was inspired by similar studies, such as the work of Nielsen [11] and Peltonen [12].

The combination of these challenges asks for an iterative process with many explorations and evaluations, involving a large number of potential users. In this paper, we present the overview of our iterative process. We believe that, in the limited space we have, it is most important to discuss all iterations with the insights we gained and the progress we made along the way. Therefore, in the next sections we will only briefly describe the physical design and development of interaction designs, and focus on the qualitative results and insights.

## 4. INSTALLATION DESIGN

In this section, we will discuss the design and development of the physical installation.

### 4.1 Ideation & Concept Development

In order to formulate design requirements, we conducted user research: literature review, observations at schools and focus groups with teenagers [23]. This resulted in the following design requirements.

Design an installation that:

- Connects to the teenagers' daily life and activities: play with the installation should have a low-moderate intensity, allow social interaction, and fit in with the 'relaxing and hanging around' during the lunch break.

- Keeps renewing curiosity: triggers and possibilities for exploration should be renewed every week, to make users curious about the installation time after time.

- Allows open play: teenagers differ in their type of play, activity level, group composition, and so on. An installation that allows open play can cater to different types and styles of play, and therefore attract more users.

We closely integrate research and education in our universities: students receive design briefs and coaching based on our research projects. In the last years, students created over fifty concepts and prototypes [25]. Two of these concepts inspired us for this specific project: the Sway'It [21], a balancing seat that changes color depending on the user's actions, and the Teaseat [22], a set of connected seats where wiggling on one seat results in vibration and tilting of the other seat (see Figure 1). We were inspired by the combination of 'active sitting', social interaction and playfulness in these concepts.

After various creative sessions, we created the concept for our installation, called 'Wiggle the Eye'. Wiggle the Eye is an interactive installation that consists of multiple wiggle benches and one central interactive streetlight (See Figure 2). Teenagers can sit on the benches, and can wiggle while sitting, standing or jumping. Each bench contains a sensor and vibration motor, and responds to the users' actions; additionally, the user's actions also influence the other benches and the streetlight.

## 4.2 Design of installation

The concept was further developed through creative sessions and feasibility studies. Eventually, a first demonstrator for the seating element was developed: a wooden seating element on two springs, with an accelerometer and a vibration motor inside (see Figure 3, left). The streetlight started as a 'moving head' disco lamp: a lamp that resembles an eye, can rotate and tilt, and has different lighting options (Figure 3, right). Physical activity on the bench, such as wiggling, was measured by the accelerometer. This activity was translated in vibrations of the bench, and a response by the lamp.

We explored interaction possibilities and technology requirements with this first prototype, in order to create the requirements for the final installation design.

The final Wiggle the Eye installation (see Figure 4) consists of five wiggle benches with different sizes (3 small and 2 large). Every bench has two spring elements; an accelerometer that measures wiggling activity; a vibration motor that can vibrate continuously or with slow or fast pulses and a microcontroller that controlled the vibration engine and accelerometer. A central street light completes the installation: a five-meter high streetlight pole with on top a moving head disco lamp. The lamp is controlled by another microcontroller that defined position, color and intensity of the light. Each bench and the lamp contained an XBee module for wireless communication.

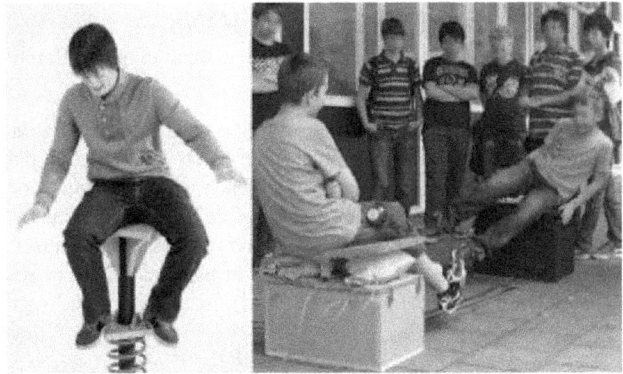

Figure 1. Two prototypes for 'active sitting'. Left: Sway'It by Fens. Right: Teaseat by Al Abdeli, Janssen, Kersteman and Scheffer.

Figure 2. Concept sketch of Wiggle the Eye prototype.

Figure 3. Left: One of the wiggle benches, containing a vibration motor and accelerometer. Right: Central street light, with a moving head lamp and variable light output.

Figure 4. The Wiggle the Eye installation, five interactive wiggle benches and a central street light.

# 5. DESIGN OF INTERACTIONS

In an iterative process we developed a total of six different interaction designs.

The software embedded in the Wiggle the Eye installation enabled us to program different interaction behaviors. Input parameters were (for each bench): 'is bench wiggling', 'duration of wiggling', and 'duration of non-wiggling'. Output parameters for each bench were vibration (short pulses, long pulses, continuous), and for the lamp 'position of light (aiming at bench / inside lamp / ground)', 'color of light', 'intensity of light', and 'pattern of light'.

All the interaction designs use the input and output parameters in a different way, in different spatial settings and contexts. Figure 6 and Figure 7 (on the next pages) show all six interaction designs: installation setup, a photo, interaction design, scenario of use, evaluation context and evaluation setup.

The six interaction designs vary on many design parameters; three important ones are *Control* (how do players influence the system), *Dynamics of Feedback* (how instant is the feedback from the system) and *Focus of Feedback* (where is the feedback visible) (See Figure 5).

| Interaction design | Control individual | Control collective | Dynamics of feedback Immediate | Dynamics of feedback complex | Focus of Feedback local | Focus of Feedback global |
|---|---|---|---|---|---|---|
| 1. Tease the Others | ✔ | ✗ | ✔ | ✗ | ✔ | ✔ |
| 2. Wiggle Pong | ✔ | ✗ | ✗ | ✔ | ✔ | ✗ |
| 3. Hey, Who Woke Me | ✔ | ✗ | ✗ | ✔ | ✔ | ✔ |
| 4. Joystick | ✔ | ✔ | ✗ | ✔ | ✗ | ✔ |
| 5. Energize me | ✗ | ✔ | ✗ | ✔ | ✗ | ✔ |
| 6. Simply Direct Me | ✔ | ✗ | ✔ | ✗ | ✔ | ✗ |

**Figure 5. The six interaction designs vary on the three design parameters.**

We distinguish the following aspects:

*Control: individual & collective*

In individual control, wiggling on one of the benches influences the system. In collective control, the actions on all benches together serve as input for the system.

*Dynamics of Feedback: immediate & complex*

Immediate feedback provides a direct and clearly perceivable result of a player's actions. Complex feedback delays this result, or integrates it in a more complex or ambiguous outcome.

*Focus of Feedback: local & global*

Local feedback is feedback focused at a specific location. Global feedback is not focused at a certain location, and is intended as output for all users.

Some interaction designs use both aspects of a parameter; e.g. in 'Joystick' a user can control one parameter of the lamp directly, which is individual control, but multiple users together can cooperate to control multiple parameters of the lamp, which is collective control.

# 6. EVALUATION OF WIGGLE THE EYE

Each iteration was evaluated with users. In this section, we discuss the results of these evaluations in two ways: brief specific insights for each interaction design iteration and general insights for the designed installation as a whole.

In the evaluations we used a combination of covert observations, informal interviews and group discussions to collect data. The overall process of evaluation developed iteratively from a general perspective to a more detailed focus. We started with open observation schemes, focusing on the interaction and behavior as a whole. Collected data was analyzed with this same focus. Further on in the evaluation period, we shifted our focus more to the group dynamics, the type of play, and the intensity of physical interactions. As we gained more understanding about play and interactions with the installation, our analysis shifted towards more focus on these aspects.

Table 1 presents a summary of evaluation findings for each interaction design iteration. Due to space limitations we will not discuss the findings of each iteration in detail.

If we look at the evaluations from a holistic perspective, we can summarize the following findings:

Overall, the installation was successful in eliciting social and active play. It attracted a lot of attention, users wiggled, interacted with each other and enjoyed themselves. During the in situ evaluations at high schools, the installation became an active sitting area. However, understanding and creating a (correct) mental model of the interaction design was sometimes difficult for the users. From these difficulties, we gained a number of interesting insights.

As we design for social settings, a lot of users are present at the same time. Evaluations showed a lot of mass exploration and interaction: multiple users interacting with the installation at the same time. In the first interaction scenarios, we focused on sequential interactions with one bench at a time (e.g. 'what happens if this bench moves and then this bench') but we did not consider simultaneous collective interactions with multiple or all benches (e.g. 'what if all benches move at the same time'). We expected this collective exploration to be somehow coordinated, but this did not happen. Instead we saw a lot of mass interaction leading to 'noise' in the interaction, which did not help the users in understanding the installation (i.e. the effect of their actions). From this we learned that when designing an interactive installation, both individual and collective control (*parameter 1*) are of importance. If there is no individual control (as in 'Energize me'), the installation is not suitable for individual users. On the other hand, when there is no collective control (as in all other scenarios), the installation is not suitable for mass interaction.

Output modalities should be extremely obvious; otherwise (new) users will not notice them. This can be achieved by implementing exaggerated and different output modalities. Also, these outputs should be both immediate and complex (*parameter 2*). An immediate output reaction motivates users to keep exploring. A complex output reaction serves as a trigger for longer & recurrent play. Moreover, both local and global feedback (*parameter 3*) are necessary. Without local feedback, users are not supported in understanding the installation. For instance, 'Joystick' does not incorporate local feedback, which makes it hard for users to understand the interaction design and create play possibilities with the installation. Without global feedback social interaction is barely elicited, as feedback is not shared among users. For example, 'Simply Direct Me' shows

## Interaction one: **Tease the Others**

| Installation setup: | Interaction design: | Evaluation context: |
|---|---|---|
| 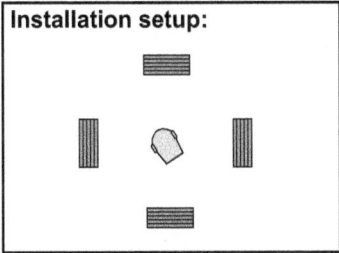 | The lamp moves in circles, from bench to bench. If a bench is wiggled while in the light, then both that bench and the opposite one vibrate. | Main hall of university, design workshop (n=80), three days, during public event (open house) and normal opening hours (n=30). |
|  | **Scenario of use:**<br>*Rose and Jamie are sitting on opposite benches. They wiggle a bit while talking - nothing happens. Then, Rose wiggles while the light shines at her: now, both benches start vibrating! Laughing, they tease each other, and then decide to wait until someone else joins them, so they can surprise that person by causing a vibration.* | **Evaluation setup:**<br>Informal evaluation (observations, interviews & group discussion) during:<br>- design workshop of 45 minutes; 2 groups of 40 prospective students (from high school)<br>- guided tours of 5 minutes; 2 groups of 20 prospective students (from high school)<br>- sporadic observations during 3 days of normal usage; ±30 observed users |

## Interaction two: **Wiggle Pong**

| Installation setup: | Interaction design: | Evaluation context: |
|---|---|---|
| 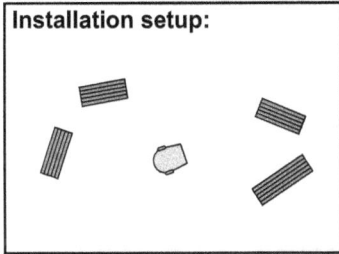 | The lamp moves in a semi-circle, from one group of benches to the other. If a bench is wiggled while in the light, then the light blinks, changes direction and moves back to the other group. If the other group 'bounces the light back' again, then the light's color intensity and movement speed increase. If nobody bounces the light back, then the light turns red and the game starts over again. | Three days of free use in university main hall (n=30). |
|  | **Scenario of use:**<br>*Michael and Judy are each sitting on a bench in one corner, and Eric is sitting on another. Eric wiggles while the light shines on him, and sees that the light blinks and moves towards Michael and Judy. They wiggle when the light reaches them, and the light moves back to Eric. Together, they discover that they can play Pong by wiggling at the right moment.* | **Evaluation setup:**<br>Informal evaluation (observations & interviews & group discussion) during:<br>- sporadic observations during three days of normal usage; ±30 observed users |

## Interaction three: **Hey, Who Woke Me**

| Installation setup: | Interaction design: | Evaluation context: |
|---|---|---|
| 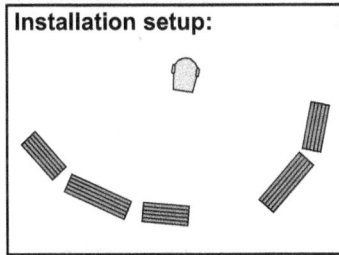 | In this interaction design the lamp is asleep and wiggling on the benches awakens it. The lamp moves towards an active bench, and makes that bench vibrate if someone is still wiggling while the light is on it. If players cause the lamp to move between groups without reaching the active bench, then the light becomes more irritated. At a certain level of irritation, the lamp makes all benches vibrate wildly, and then goes back to sleep. | two times one week at schoolyard of school #1 (n=750). |
|  | **Scenario of use:**<br>*Eva and Jon sit on the benches, and wiggle a bit. Slowly, the lamp seems to wake up, shines towards them, and then goes back to sleep. Curious, they wiggle harder. The lamp wakes faster this time, and makes their bench vibrate. Friends join, and together they try to stop the wiggling just before the light reaches a bench. The lamp moves faster, until eventually all benches start to vibrate. After this outburst, the lamp goes back to sleep, and fades out.* | **Evaluation setup:**<br>Three week evaluation at high school #1 (in June):<br>- daily covert observations during morning and lunch breaks<br>- weekly informal interviews with teenagers<br>- weekly interviews with caretakers and teachers<br>- 1st and 3rd week: scenario "Hey, who woke me?"<br>- 2nd week: scenario "Joystick" (see iteration four)<br>- last week, final year students not present due to exams (±150 students) |

**Figure 6. Interaction designs of Wiggle the Eye (part one).**

| Interaction four: **Joystick** | | |
|---|---|---|
| **Installation setup:**<br> | **Interaction design:**<br>Joystick is an interaction scenario in which every bench controls one dimension of the lamp and vibration modules (e.g. color, position X and Y, intensity, vibration on/off). Players have to work together to fully control the lamp. | **Evaluation context:**<br>One week at schoolyard of school #1 (n=750). |
| | **Scenario of use:**<br>*Mary sits on a bench, and starts wiggling a bit. She notices that the light becomes brighter, the harder she wiggles. She moves to another bench, and discovers that this one controls the left-right direction of the lamp. Smiling, she wiggles until the light shines directly into David's eyes* | **Evaluation setup:**<br>Three week evaluation at high school #1 (in June):<br>- daily covert observations during morning and lunch breaks<br>- weekly informal interviews with teenagers<br>- weekly interviews with caretakers and teachers<br>- 1st and 3rd week: scenario "Hey, who woke me?"<br>- 2nd week: scenario "Joystick" (see next iteration)<br>- last week, final year students not present due to exams (±150 students) |

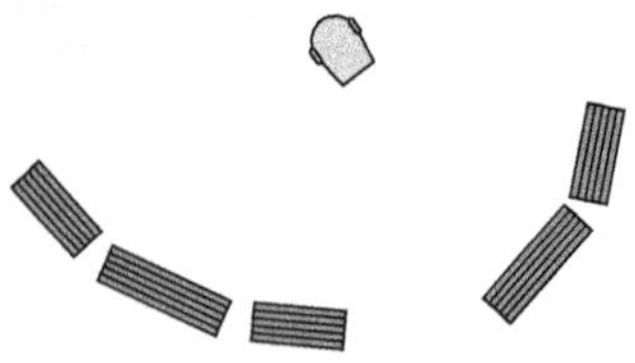

| Interaction five: **Energize me** | | |
|---|---|---|
| **Installation setup:**<br> | **Interaction design:**<br>In this interaction design the lamp is asleep, and wiggling on the benches awakens it. The total amount of wiggle-activity determines the activity of the lamp: if only one bench is being wiggled, then the lamp is moving slowly. Every one or two benches are coupled to a color (r/g/b); the brightness of that color indicates how active those benches are. If all five benches are wiggled simultaneously, then the lamp starts moving and blinking rapidly, and all benches vibrate. | **Evaluation context: .**<br>Four weeks at schoolyard of school #2 (n=370). |
| | **Scenario of use:**<br>*George and Simon are sitting on a bench, wiggling softly. They notice that the lamp is moving slowly, with a hardly visible blue color. Their friends join them, and wiggle at another bench: the lamp starts moving more rapidly, and the color becomes bright and purple. They spread out over all five benches, and start wiggling wildly. The lamp is shining red and blinking rapidly. After a bit, all five benches start to vibrate, which all friends find very funny.* | **Evaluation setup:**<br>Four week evaluation at high school #2 (in September):<br>- weekly covert observations during morning and lunch breaks<br>- weekly informal interview with teacher<br>- daily small diary study by one class (15 students, enjoyment & usage)<br>- all four weeks 'Energize me' scenario |

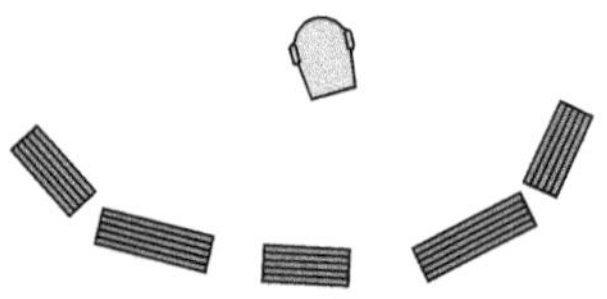

| Interaction six: **Simply Direct Me** | | |
|---|---|---|
| **Installation setup:**<br> | **Interaction design:**<br>Wiggling on a bench resulted in the lamp shining on that bench in a specific color (red/green/blue). If a bench was wiggled for three seconds simultaneously, then it started vibrating in one heavy pulse. If two or three benches were wiggled at the same time, then the chair with the fastest wiggling would be selected over the other(s). | **Evaluation context:**<br>Eleven days at exhibition (n=1100-1500). |
| | **Scenario of use:**<br>*Cristine approaches the benches, and sits down, curiously wiggling a bit. Immediately, a bright lamp shines on her in red. If she stops wiggling, the light turns off; if she wiggles faster, the light becomes brighter. After a few seconds of wiggling, her bench starts vibrating wildly, to the hilarity of Cristine.* | **Evaluation setup:**<br>- Eleven days at exhibition, with visitors (n=1100-1500)<br>- covert observation in three sessions of two hours, spread over the week (observed users = ±300)<br>- informal interviews with exhibition staff |

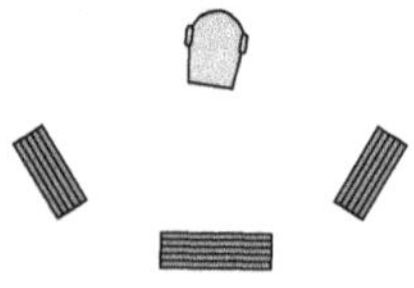

**Figure 7. Interaction designs of Wiggle the Eye (part two).**

how a lack of global feedback leads to a minimal amount of social interaction among users on different benches.

During the in situ evaluations, new users kept showing up, even after three weeks of evaluating. On the other hand, there were also users who already experienced the installation for three weeks and might expect different reactions or more complexity. Designing for this balance to satisfy both novel and experienced users was difficult.

These evaluations also gave us insights for performing *design research* in general. Evaluating these installations in the field opens up a lot of external factors that can all influence the observed user behavior. For example, each school and each schoolyard is different. One school might already have some cozy seating areas, while another school might not have any places to sit. This can affect the popularity of the installation, without saying much about the value of the interactivity. An outdoor installation adds extra challenges to the evaluation, as the weather conditions can have a large influence on the users' behavior. During our evaluations of 'Hey, Who Woke Me' and 'Joystick' the weather was extremely hot. As the installation was placed in the sun, some children preferred staying in the cooler shade during the breaks. The evaluation of 'Energize me' was affected by bad weather (i.e. a lot of rain in the first two weeks), which also demotivated users to start interacting with the installation and affected the novelty and exploration process. Lastly, we learned that in a real-life setting users are all over the place and social situations are very variable. If there are few users interacting with the installation, it is easy for them to explore its functionalities. If there are lots of users, the installation is popular, but it becomes much harder for the users to explore. In our evaluations, both situations occurred and not in a perfect timeline.

Overall, these factors make it difficult to get a grasp on the evaluations. More controlled research might eliminate some of those factors, but might also undo the real user contexts in which we evaluate our interactive installations. Furthermore, in this stage of our research it is still uncertain which factors are of importance. We believe that in order to be able to draw useful conclusions, one needs a broad scope in combination with an iterative process with multiple evaluations in different contexts (as is described in this paper).

**Table 1. Summary of the findings of our evaluations for each of the six interaction designs.**

| Interaction design | Summary of evaluation findings |
| --- | --- |
| 1. Tease the Others | Installation attracted a lot of attention, users sat down and started wiggling.<br>Users had trouble discovering the input-output relations.<br>Users moved on after a short period (<1 minute) of play.<br>Physical setup was not social enough due to distance between benches. |
| 2. Wiggle Pong | Users did not discover how to play the game.<br>Timed actions with this platform showed to be impractical and difficult.<br>Playing without knowing the rules was impossible. |
| 3. Hey, Who Woke Me | Benches were popular, installation became a social active sitting area for groups of students. Students were playing, talking, wiggling, standing and having fun.<br>Students understood that if they wiggled for a while, the benches would start to vibrate. The installation was so crowded that there were always 10+ users wiggling at the same time, preventing individual exploration.<br>There was very limited focus on the light.<br>Mental models were either too simple or too complex. |
| 4. Joystick | No students discovered how to control the installation using the benches; the crowdedness of the installation (10+ users sitting and wiggling at the same time) prevented individual users from seeing the result of their action.<br>Coordination in mass interaction hardly occurred; designing for mass interaction is hard.<br>Mental models were mostly 'it's broken! It doesn't vibrate anymore!'.<br>No play possibilities if users did not know the rules. |
| 5. Energize me | First two weeks, raining all day, limiting the novelty and exploration process.<br>Overall, benches were used less and calmer than at previous school.<br>Installation became a low-activity social sitting area; sporadically, all users started wiggling together to make the benches vibrate. Comments such as 'you have to wiggle way too hard before it vibrates!'.<br>Mass interaction was possible: a few times, 20+ users wiggling together to get vibration.<br>Threshold for enjoyable feedback (wild light & vibration) was too high; users on all benches had to wiggle before the result was rewarding enough. Individual feedback was too 'small', not rewarding for individual users to wiggle.<br>Diary study showed average daily enjoyment between 'Enjoyable' and 'Very Enjoyable', average daily duration between 'Not used' and 'Less than one minute'. |
| 6. Simply Direct Me | Easy to discover interaction possibilities for new users (wiggling = light; long wiggling = vibration).<br>Hardly social interaction between users on different benches.<br>Short play sessions (±1 minute). |

# 7. CONCLUSION

In this article, we presented our insights on three different design research topics: how to design social and active play for teenagers, how to design for open-ended and emergent play, and how to evaluate interactive playful installations in situ. These insights are useful for everyone designing for teenagers, public spaces or playful interactions. We described the process of iteratively developing and evaluating the Wiggle the Eye installation: five interactive wiggle benches and one central lamp, which are used to invite teenagers to play in a social and physical way. Six different interaction designs have been implemented; the installation has been evaluated at a university, two high schools and a design exhibition, with more than 1000 users in total.

We succeeded in eliciting playful and social active play; the installation design was very successful, the interaction design proved to be more difficult. The play possibilities were hard to discover for our users, mainly because mass exploration led to chaos, and not to collective coordinated exploration. We identified three important design parameters, each with two elements: individual and collective *control*, immediate and complex *dynamics of feedback*, and local and global *focus of feedback*. We investigated these parameters in context and learned that all elements have to be implemented for this type of play installations. Designers should design for both individual and collective control and find a balance in this. As mass exploration and interaction occurs a lot, designers should take into account that sequential interaction does not work as users do not wait on each other. Besides that, designers should not expect coordination in collective interactions. Concerning feedback, both immediate and complex outputs are essential. Immediate outputs motivate users to keep exploring whilst complex outputs serve as a trigger for longer and recurrent play. Furthermore, both local and global feedback is necessary. Local feedback supports the understanding of the installation. Global feedback supports social interaction as feedback is shared among users.

We presented several insights about evaluating in this complex environment, with all its external factors. Most of these factors cannot be manipulated (e.g. the weather), but awareness of these factors can support designers in planning their evaluation. Moreover, it is advisable to get to know the evaluation context beforehand to identify these possible influential factors. The necessity of doing design research in an iterative process has once again become clear: the users' creativity and experience, in real life situations, cannot be predicted - and designing for these user experiences cannot be done in the lab, but only in the wild.

# 8. ACKNOWLEDGMENTS

The authors would like to thank the students, teachers and management of De Rooi Pannen in Eindhoven and Mondial College in Nijmegen for their participation and support. We would also like to thank our colleagues, especially Janienke Sturm, Mark de Graaf and Berry Eggen for their input and feedback, and the Equipment & Prototype Center for their support in building the prototypes.

# 9. REFERENCES

[1] Behaviour Change Interventions: Teenagers, Technology & Design. (2013). Workshop at IDC2013, New York. Retrieved from http://research.northumbria.ac.uk/IDC2013_change/ on March 27, 2014.

[2] Bekker, M., Sturm, J., and Eggen, B. (2009). Designing playful interactions for social interaction and physical play. Personal and Ubiquitous Computing. 14, 5, 385-396.

[3] Berk,L.E.(2006).Development Through The Lifespan, 4th Int. ed.,Pearson Education (US), 2006, pp. 360-427.

[4] Chi Games & Entertainment Spotlight (2014), website, retrieved from http://chi2014.acm.org/spotlights/games-entertainment on March 27, 2014.

[5] Chi Play (2014), call for papers, retrieved from http://chiplay.org on March 27, 2014.

[6] Design for Cool workshop, during BHCI 2011, Newcastle.

[7] Grønbæk, K., Kortbek, K.J., Møller, C., Nielsen, J., and Stenfeldt, L. (2012). Designing playful interactive installations for urban environments - The swingscape experience. In Proceedings of Advances in Computer Entertainment (Kathmandu, Nepal, November 3-5, 2012). Springer, Berlin, 230-245.

[8] Hoven, E. van den, Frens, J., Aliakseyeu, D. Martens, J.B., Overbeeke, C.J., and Peters, P. (2007). Design research & tangible interaction. In Proceedings of the 1st international conference on Tangible and embedded interaction (Baton Rouge, Louisiana, February 15-17, 2007). ACM, New York, 109-115.

[9] Khaled, R., Dixon, D., & Deterding, S. (2011). Gamification - A Roundtable on Game Studies and HCI Perspectives. Panel during DIGRA'11. Slides retrieved from http://www.slideshare.net/dings/gamification-a-roundtable-on-game-studies-and-hci-perspectives

[10] Lucero, A. and Arrasvuori, J. (2010). PLEX Cards: a source of inspiration when designing for playfulness. In Proc. of Fun and Games '10. ACM, 28-37.

[11] Nielsen, R., Fritsch, J., Halskov, K., and Brynskov, M. (2009). Out of the box: exploring the richness of children's use of an interactive table. In Proceedings of the 8th International Conference on Interaction Design and Children (Como, Italy, June 03-05, 2009). ACM, New York, 61-69.

[12] Peltonen, P., Kurvinen, E., Salovaara, A., Jacucci, G., Ilmonen, T., Evans, J., Oulasvirta, A., and Saarikko, P. (2008). It's Mine, Don't Touch!: interactions at a large multi-touch display in a city centre. In Proceedings of the SIGCHI Conference on Human Factors in Computing Systems (Florence, Italy, April 05-10, 2008). ACM, New York, 1285-1294.

[13] Piano Stairs, website (2014), retrieved from http://www.thefuntheory.com/piano-staircase on March 27, 2014.

[14] Read, J.C., Fitton, D., Cowan, B., Beale, R., Guo, Y. and Horton, M. (2011) 'Understanding and designing cool technologies for teenagers', CHI 2011. Vancouver, BC, Canada, May 7-12, 2011. ACM pp. 1567-1572.

[15] Rijnbout, P., Valk, L. de, Vermeeren, A., Bekker, T., Graaf, M. de, Schouten, B. and Eggen, B. (2013). About

Experience and Emergence: A Framework for Decentralized Interactive Play Environments. INTETAIN 2013.

[16] Romero, N.A., Sturm, J., Bekker, M.M., De Valk, L. and Kruitwagen, S. (2010). Playful persuasion to support older adults' social and physical activities. Special Issue on Inclusive Design, Interacting with computers, 22(6), pp. 485-495.

[17] Schell, J. (2008). The Art of Game Design: A Book of Lenses. Morgan Kaufmann Publishers Inc., San Francisco, CA, USA.

[18] Sluis-Thiescheffer, R.J.W., Tieben, R., Sturm, J., Bekker, M.M. and Schouten B. (2013) An active lifestyle for youths through ambient persuasive technology: implementing activating concepts in a school environment. In Proceedings Games for Health 2013, October, The Netherlands, 293-308.

[19] Soler-Adillon , J., Ferrer, J., and Parés, N. (2009). A novel approach to interactive playgrounds: the interactive slide project. In Proceedings of the 8th International Conference on Interaction Design and Children (Como, Italy, June 03-05, 2009). ACM, New York, 131-139.

[20] Sturm, J., Tieben, R., Deen, M., Bekker, M.M. and Schouten, B.A.M. (2011). PlayFit: Designing playful activity interventions for teenagers. In Proceedings of DIGRA 2011.

[21] Sway'It. (2011). Internal project report by Fens.

[22] Teaseat. (2011). Internal project report by Al Abdeli, Janssen, Kersteman, and Scheffer.

[23] Tieben, R., Bekker, M.M., Sturm, J. and Schouten, B.A.M. (2011). Eliciting casual activity through playful exploration, communication, personalisation and expression. In Proceedings of CHI-Sparks 2011.

[24] Tieben, R., Sturm, J., Bekker, M.M. and Schouten, B.A.M. (2013). Eliciting recurring curiosity through playful interactions. In IDC 2013 workshop on Behaviour Change Interventions: Teenagers, technology and design at IDC 2013.

[25] Tieben, R., Sturm, J., Bekker, M.M., Schouten, B.A.M. (accepted). Playful Persuasion: designing for ambient playful interactions in public spaces. Journal for Ambient Intelligence and Smart Environments 2014.

[26] Toth, N., Little, L., Read, J.C., Fitton, D., and Horton, M. Understanding teen attitude towards energy consumption. Journal of Environmental Psychology, (2013) 34, 36-44

[27] Valk, L. de, Bekker, T., Eggen, B. (2013). Leaving room for improvisation: Towards a design approach for open-ended play. In Proceedings of IDC 2013, 12th International Conference on Interaction Design and Children (New York, USA, June 24-27, 2013), pp. 92-101.

[28] Valk, L. de, Rijnbout, P., Graaf, M. de, Bekker, T., Schouten, B., Eggen, B. (2013). GlowSteps – A decentralized interactive play environment for open-ended play. In Proceedings of ACE 2013, Advances in Computer Entertainment Technology (Twente, The Netherlands, November 12-15, 2013), pp. 528-531.

# CamQuest: Design and Evaluation of a Tablet Application for Educational Use in Preschools

Jennie Berggren
MSc Student at Industrial Design Engineering
Chalmers University of Technology
Sweden
+46 (0) 702 32 96 66
bjennie@student.chalmers.se

Catherine Hedler
MSc Student at Interaction Design and Technologies
Chalmers University of Technology
Sweden
+46 (0) 768 56 76 26
hedler@student.chalmers.se

## ABSTRACT

This paper describes the design, testing and evaluation of CamQuest, a tablet application intended for educational practice in preschools. CamQuest enables children to search for and photograph geometrical shapes in their surroundings with the tablet camera. In this paper, the results of three encounters with preschool children aged four to five are presented and discussed, as well as the design and concept of CamQuest. Each encounter with children was carried out with a different approach; testing, co-designing, and evaluating. The application can be used as a pedagogical tool, which enables preschool children to recognize and explore geometrical shapes in their environment through using digital media.

## Categories and Subject Descriptors

H.5.m [**Miscellaneous**]

## General Terms

Design

## Keywords

Ipad; application; tablet; preschool; education; children; collaboration; camera; geometry; geometrical shapes; spatial interaction; interaction design; digital media; GUI.

## 1. INTRODUCTION

The curriculum states that children in Swedish preschools should be introduced to digital media and technology [8]. As a consequence, the use of tablets in preschools has increased which in turn has led to related issues. Many preschool teachers lack in knowledge of how to work with the tablet in order to achieve an activity where the children can learn, and have not been educated on how the tablet can function as a pedagogical tool. In addition, there is a lack of proper applications developed for educational

use. Most applications used in Swedish preschools are based on one-player games, which results in individual play without involvement of other preschool children or teachers. Since collaboration is given a great significance in the curriculum [8], this type of use is not appropriate for preschools. The aim of CamQuest is to enable children to learn about two-dimensional geometrical shapes by exploring the surrounding environment by using the tablet camera together with fellow preschoolers.

This paper presents related work and describes the design and evaluation of the CamQuest prototype. We describe three studies of children aged four to five years old and discuss the results.

## 2. RELATED WORKS

Some related works that have been looked into are SketchCam [4], Tangicam [5] and Urban Alphabets [6]. SketchCam is a camera which is reduced to a single touch screen, enabling children to capture images by sketching directly on the screen with their fingers. Tangicam is a mobile device used for capturing and editing photos and videos. Instead of viewing the photos and recordings on a screen, the device can be connected to a DiamondTouch table. Urban Alphabets is an application for smartphones developed by a student at Media Lab Helsinki, where the user can photograph letters in the surroundings in order to create a personal alphabet.

We also looked into existing geometry applications for tablets, but were unable to find any application that uses the tablet camera as a tool for recognizing shapes in common surroundings. All of the applications consisted of screen based activities. Most of them were recommended for children aged five to ten, and very few applications aimed at preschool children were found.

## 3. CAMQUEST

CamQuest is a tablet application aimed for educational use in preschools that enables children to explore their surrounding environment by using a tablet. The name is derived from the words "camera" and "quest". The children are set out to find and photograph geometrical shapes with the tablet camera, which has an integrated image of the shape the children are supposed to search for. The integrated image provides guidance on what to look for, and helps the children to aim at the objects of interest. Four different shapes can be chosen; circle, square, rectangle, and triangle.

The purpose of CamQuest is to integrate the use of tablets in active play, where the children are not focused on the screen. Instead, we want the tablet to work as a link between them and the objects or shapes they search for. The application is supposed to enable children to interact with each other, and with the surrounding environment. Even though CamQuest can be used individually, our belief is that its full potential is reached when the children are engaged in collaboration. Because of this, the children were instructed to use the app in pairs during the study.

Since the application is intended for educational purposes, it relies on involvement of the teacher. For instance, CamQuest itself does not force the children to collaborate; it is up to the teacher to decide how the application should be used. To ensure that the teachers are informed about the pedagogical potential of CamQuest and how it can be used, a short text-based information guide is implemented in the application. In order to achieve a meaningful learning experience, the children would benefit from being introduced to the different geometrical shapes prior to using CamQuest. The photos taken by the children are saved in the tablet photo album, and can be used as a base for a presentation, discussion and reflection session held by the teacher in a larger group of children after the quest has been completed. Even though the application has been specifically developed for preschool use, we see possibilities for using it in other settings such as at home.

## 4. METHOD

In order to gain insight into how well CamQuest is received by children and to what extent the application is appropriate for educational use, three encounters with preschool children aged four to five were conducted during the development of the application. Each encounter was limited to one hour, and ten children were participating at a time. The children worked in pairs sharing one Ipad. A teacher was continuously involved in the planning and execution of the activities. Before and after each session the children were gathered for instructions and reflective discussions, which is an important routine in Swedish preschools that the children are used to. After each visit an interview was held with the teacher in order to gain important insights and feedback.

CamQuest was developed, tested and evaluated in an iterative process where the children were involved as testers and informants, in accordance with the different roles children can have in design of new technologies defined by Druin [2]. During the first encounter, the children were observed as testers of a low-tech prototype of CamQuest. Handling of tablet, need of guidance and level of collaboration are examples of important aspects that were taken under consideration during the observation. The second encounter involved the children as co-designers in a sketch workshop, where they were asked to make drawings of cameras, buttons and possible quests. They were also asked to design their own interface. A digital prototype was developed for the last encounter and tested by the children. Here, the children were given the role as informants, since they were asked questions about their experience of using CamQuest.

## 5. RESULTS

The participating children in the studies had very little previous experience in using a tablet for any other activity than playing games. Most of them had never used the camera application before. The children had previously been introduced to basic geometrical shapes, but they were not confident in using the correct terms and were unable to distinguish the different shapes from each other.

### 5.1 First Encounter: Testing and Observation

During the first encounter the children were initially gathered for a short introduction held by the teacher. Each couple was given a low-tech prototype to share. The prototype consisted of the Ipad

camera application, with a geometrical shape printed on overhead paper, which was taped onto the screen of the Ipad (see figure 1).

After the children had completed the quests of photographing the different shapes, they were gathered again to look at and reflect on all the photos as a group activity led by the teacher. Both the introductory and finishing group discussion were very valuable for the learning experience, but also for the sake of the children's motivation and amusement.

**Figure 1. The low-tech prototype used for early testing.**

The following conclusions could be made when analyzing the results from the first encounter:

- Using CamQuest made the children joyful, curious, eager and proud.
- The children embraced the new responsibility of being trusted with handling the Ipad on their own.
- The children managed to successfully collaborate with each other during the quests, by taking turns altering between two different roles; photographer and "searcher". The latter role includes searching for geometrical shapes, and bringing smaller objects to the photographer and holding them in front of the camera whilst the photo is taken.
- Most children held the tablet horizontally with both hands and pushed the trigger button with their right thumb.
- The different geometrical shapes varied in difficulty for the children. It was obvious from the amounts of photos taken of each shape that the circle was the easiest, followed by the square and the rectangle, while the triangle was the hardest shape to find.
- The children had difficulties in separating squares and rectangles from each other.

### 5.2 Second Encounter: Co-Design

During the second study a sketch workshop was held, where the children were asked to make drawings of cameras, buttons and possible quests. They also got to color the interface of the application according to their own preference. This provided us with an insight on how the children perceive cameras, and what they think the interface of the application should look like. The children mostly drew conventional cameras; a rectangular shape with a circular lens. Some children on the other hand, drew cameras similar to tablets. According to the drawings of buttons, those can vary a lot in both shape and function. When the children were asked what else they would like to search for in future quests, some of the things mentioned are: flags, letters, numbers, fruit, clothes, colors, and of course – poop.

When designing the interface, each child was given a template printed in black and white. All children colored the interface template in different colors, with the results ranging from very bright and colorful to completely black and grey (see figure 4). Many children also gave different colors to the trigger button and the buttons for selecting geometrical shape.

Figure 4. Some of the interfaces designed by the children.

When observing the children play with their creations we realized the importance of the shutter sound, since they added that sound themselves when taking imaginary photographs. This indicates that auditory feedback is of high significance regarding the children's perception and experience of using the tablet, and also the learning outcome from using the application. Therefore, sound clips of the name of each shape were added to the digital prototype tested during the third encounter described below.

## 5.3 Third Encounter: Evaluation

During the third encounter a first digital prototype of CamQuest was tested and evaluated, followed by short interviews with the children. When designing the graphical user interface of the prototype, the input from previous observations and workshops were taken under consideration. We strived to obtain simplicity both graphically and interactively, as simplicity is a significant parameter when designing successful technologies for children [7]. The application is made up of one single interface, which consists of the camera and a panel with buttons (see figure 5). The use of text has been totally excluded in favor of an icon based interface, since the amount of text in applications aimed at preschool children should be minimized. The buttons are given a generous size to make sure they are age appropriate [3]. When a geometrical shape is selected, an integrated image of the shape appears in the camera. The photo album can be accessed by tapping an image of the last taken picture, and by double-tapping the i-button on the bottom right the information for teachers and parents can be opened.

With the results from the first encounter in mind, the color of the integrated shape was changed from green to bright yellow to make it more distinguishable from the background (see figure 5). Since the children's color choices for the interface varied a lot, we decided to use a limited amount of gender neutral colors for the panel and the buttons: green and purple.

Figure 5. The CamQuest interface.

During the third encounter, it was obvious that the children's handling of the Ipad had improved compared to the observations made during the first encounter. On the contrary, one problem we noticed when the children were using the digital prototype was that some of the children felt uncomfortable with letting go of their two-handed grip (see figure 6). This made it difficult for them to reach the geometrical shapes at the top of the screen with their thumbs. This implies that the placement of the selectable shapes should be reconsidered.

Figure 6. A child using the digital prototype.

## 6. DISCUSSION

One important design decision we had to make when designing the application was whether or not to force collaboration on the users. Since the application is intended for educational purposes, it automatically relies on involvement of the teacher. We do not believe in forcing a specific way of using the app, since the advantage of an open-ended application is that it is unrestricted and versatile. In an educational context where children are at different stages of development and are learning things in different ways, it is more suitable with an open-ended application that can be used in several ways. An application with a more predefined method of use could in this case limit the educational potential.

During the evaluation of the digital prototype, it was noticeable that some children had problems with reaching and selecting the different shapes placed at the top of the screen, since they had a hard time holding the Ipad with one hand. Seeing this, a more user-friendly design of the graphical user interface could be to place the shapes vertically on the left side instead.

We found that observation was very useful as a method for understanding how the children interacted with, understood, and experienced CamQuest. Observing children in their natural environment and analyzing their behavior turned out to be more useful than interviewing them. We think asking children in this age to reflect on their own behavior yields less useful results, since their responses often contradicted our observations. This was also true when evaluating the digital prototype.

The main advantage with co-design as a design method is that the designers can gain greater understanding and important insights about a user group that is very different from themselves. It makes the children feel more secure and confident in the presence of the designers, which in our case lead to a more natural and unaffected behavior in both ways. There were however not many direct design decisions based on the results from the co-design workshop.

Despite the lack of measurable data regarding learning outcomes of using CamQuest, we allow ourselves to draw some conclusions based on our findings. We found that the children gained both confidence and knowledge, not only from being involved in the design process but also when it comes to their accomplishments with the application and the Ipad. From using the application in combination with other activities related to geometry, the children were able to transfer the knowledge about geometrical shapes to other contexts separated from the tablet. For example, the children started to ask the teachers for "rectangle papers" to draw on. Being able to distinguish between the names and the shapes provides the children with a vocabulary to use when discussing basic mathematical concepts. We believe that the transfer was successful because the fact that the combination of reality and tablet provided the children with a relatable context that is meaningful to them, something that is also comparable to Druin's findings on mobile technologies and learning [1]. This adds to the children's motivation and understanding of the concept of geometrical shapes.

According to the teacher, the children continued to work with CamQuest for a longer time compared to when they are given the Ipad to play a game by themselves. We think that one reason to this could be that the activity is diverse and therefore motivates the children. We found that the children enjoyed each part of it; the introduction, performing the quest together with a fellow preschooler, and reflecting on the photos with the teacher afterwards in a concluding group gathering. When CamQuest is used in this way; in pairs and as a group activity; the children

practice collaboration, communication and problem solving. They are also given the opportunity to develop skills in presentation, discussion and reflection during the final gathering. The variation in these different activities enables the children to experience through different senses and to learn by varied subtasks.

The purpose of this study was primarily to design and test the app specifically in the preschool context, but it would be interesting in further work to measure the actual learning outcome and the long time impact on the children regarding social interaction and collaboration.

## 7. CONCLUSION

CamQuest has potential to change the common attitudes towards the use of tablets in preschools, and to promote the advantages of using the tablet as a pedagogical tool. The application enables preschool children to recognize and explore geometrical shapes in their environment through using digital media. The application also supports group activity led by the teacher, and social interaction and collaboration among the children.

There are many reasons to why we find CamQuest highly suitable for educational use in preschools. The simplicity of CamQuest not only appeals to the children, but also provides pedagogical benefits. Teachers can set their own educational goals adapted to children's specific needs. Thanks to its open-endedness, the application also provides good opportunities for varied use, for example both indoors and outdoors. When tablets and applications are used in this manner, we are convinced that tablets can provide a useful and valuable complement to the educational tools in preschools.

## 8. ACKNOWLEDGMENTS

We thank preschool teacher Annkin Höglund Marchiafava for important insights and feedback, and the children at Älgen, Hallens förskola. We would also like to thank Victor Carlsson who programmed the digital prototype.

## 9. REFERENCES

[1] Druin, A. Mobile Technology for Children: Designing for Interaction and Learning. Burlington: Morgan Kaufmann Publishing, (2009).

[2] Druin, A. The Role of Children in the Design of New Technology. *Behaviour and Information Technology*, 21(1), (2002), 1-25.

[3] Hourcade J.P. Interaction design and children. *Foundations and Trends in Human–Computer Interaction*, 1(4), (2007), 277-392.

[4] Labrune, J-B., Mackay, W. SketchCam: Creative Photography for Children. *IDC 2007*, ACM Press (2007), 153-156.

[5] Labrune, J-B., Mackay, W. Tangicam: Exploring Observation Tools for Children. *IDC 2005*, ACM Press (2005), 95-102.

[6] Media Lab Helsinki
http://mlab.taik.fi/students/

[7] Resnick, M., and Silverman, B. Some Reflections on Designing Construction Kits for Kids. *IDC 2005*, (2005), 117-122.

[8] Skolverket. Curriculum for the Preschool Lpfö 98. (2011), 10. http://www.skolverket.se/publikationer?id=2704.

# Connecting Children to Nature with Technology: Sowing the Seeds for Pro-environmental Behaviour

Bronwyn J. Cumbo[1], Jeni Paay[2], Jesper Kjeldskov[2], Brent C. Jacobs[1]

[1] Institute for Sustainable Futures
University of Technology
Level 11, UTS Building 10
235 Jones St
Ultimo, NSW, Australia 2007
{bronwyn.cumbo, brent.jacobs}@uts.edu.au

[2] Centre for Socio-Interactive Design,
Department of Computer Science
Aalborg University
Selma Lagerlöfs Vej 300
Aalborg East, Denmark, 9220
{jeni, jesper}@cs.aau.dk

## ABSTRACT

Regular interactions with nature are vital for the development and well-being of children and also to build attachment and value for natural environments that potentially promote pro-environmental behaviour in later life. In this paper, we report on a study designed to identify opportunities for digital technology to support children's connectedness to the natural environment, thereby encouraging positive environmental attitudes in children, as well as healthy physical play. Through participatory engagement with a group of 15 Danish children (aged 8-12) and their parents, using focus groups and follow up interviews, we explore what motivates children to undertake everyday recreational activities, focusing on activities undertaken in nature, and how these interactions influence meaning associated with their local natural place. The contribution of this paper is a deeper understanding of what motivates children to interact with nature, and a discussion of how technology may enhance this interaction.

## Categories and Subject Descriptors

H.5.2 [**Information Interfaces And Presentation** (e.g., HCI)]: User Interfaces - *User Centred Design.*

## General Terms

Design, Human Factors.

## Keywords

Participatory engagement, child-centred design, nature, place attachment, pro-environmental behaviour.

## 1. INTRODUCTION

Regular, playful interactions in the natural environment have many health and well-being benefits for children [8], and build a place attachment and value for the preservation of natural environments [4]. Rising urbanization, safety concerns of parents, loss of 'free time', and popularity of indoor online recreation have led to a significant reduction in time children spend outdoors in nature over the last 40 years [7]. This shift has been linked to an increase in anxiety and depression amongst children, lowered levels of self-efficacy in nature, and reduced awareness and value for its preservation [7, 8].

Pervasive and emerging technologies have the potential to motivate children to experience more frequent and meaningful interactions with local natural environments by designing opportunities for interactions between children, parents and technology "in the wild". Many children have regular access to powerful digital devices containing GPS, access to online information and networks and audio-visual recorders that motivate children to interact and share how they relate to the physical environment [10]. Elements of this technology can also be applied to counteract some of the barriers to independent outdoor play in children [14]. This study provides a deeper understanding of how children currently view and interact with nature to propose opportunities where technology can play a role in enhancing this connection.

The majority of examples of mobile and ubiquitous technologies designed for outdoor use with children have been oriented toward formal education [2, 9]. Applying technology to extend the learning space beyond the classroom has been shown to motivate more self-directed learning and improved outcomes for a wider range of students [2]. Additionally, systems are increasingly being designed for leisure contexts to motivate children to connect with people and places in their free time. These have been shown to effectively motivate children in social interactions [13, 14], and encourage creative ownership of outdoor environments [14]. In HCI literature there is a general understanding of how technology can successfully engage and motivate children, however, an understanding of how technology influences a child's meaning and attachment for physical places, specifically local, natural places is, as yet, unknown. This is the gap we address with our current research project.

This paper reports on explorations into understanding children's current connections to their local natural environments. Through this we will identify the potential for technology to facilitate more regular, meaningful interactions between children and local nature, with the intention of building place attachment and value for the preservation of these natural areas. We describe our research investigations, specifically two focus groups and follow up interviews, with a group of 15 Danish children (8-12 years) and their parents, to investigate what motivates children to engage in everyday activities, including interactions with local natural environments, and how these interactions influenced the meaning and attachment they have for nature.

## 2. WHAT IS NATURE?

Nature is traditionally defined as the living and non-living elements that occur 'naturally' without human influence [12], however over 95 per cent of the earth's surface is now influenced by human activities [3]. For the purpose of this research, we will adopt a broader definition of nature as "the continuum of human-environment influence, ranging from total human designed space to 'pure' wilderness" [3]

# 3. PLACE ATTACHMENT

Building place attachments contributes to the establishment of identity, sense of belonging and overall well-being of children [4]. Children develop positive or negative associations with the physical places they interact with from a very young age, favouring places where they undertake repetitive, social, and child-directed activities [7]. Repetitive, social and child-centered interactions in local parks and playgrounds develop a child's capacity for independent thought, movement and social behavior [7]. The role of 'child-directed' experiences in building attachments is significant, as it is through these activities that a child has capacity to make meaning of the space, and their relationship with each other on a broader scale.

The location and scale of place attachments evolve throughout a child's development. Middle school children (aged 8-12 years) expand their level of exploration from the home and backyard to the local neighbourhood [4]. Children tend to build attachments for natural places as they provide an unpredictable and ever changing play-scape of sights, sounds, smells and tactile experiences that satisfy a child's physiological, creative, cognitive and social explorations [4, 6].

## 3.1 Rising Disconnect with Nature

Opportunities for regular, social, child-centred interactions in nature required to build place attachment are diminishing [7, 8]. Rising urbanization has reduced access to natural areas for many children, and social anxiety and safety concerns are preventing parents from allowing their children to explore the local neighbourhood without adult supervision [7, 8]. 'Free time' available to children after school and on weekends is more frequently being consumed by organized, extra-curricular activities, removing the time available for child-centered playful interactions [7]. In addition, most children are spending an increasing amount of time engaging in indoor, online recreation that enables independent, social, child-centred experiences [7, 8]. Addressing the rising disconnect with nature, therefore requires an understanding of how to both *motivate* and *enable* regular, child-centred engagement.

## 3.2 Role of Technology

Mobile and ubiquitous computing have been applied across many fields to reconnect people to the physical environment. Well-designed examples are inherently engaging and promote embodied, context-specific experiences providing richer experiences for individuals (e.g. geocaching) [2]. Although the majority of interactive, outdoor technologies for children have been designed for formal educational settings, some recent designs have inspired more playful interactions in children to address the need for positive experiences in physical outdoors. [e.g. 13, 14]. Emerging technologies, e.g. tangible computing and sensors and actuators, have the potential to encourage even more direct interactions with the physical environment.

The aim of our overall study is to investigate the role that technology may play in engaging children with their local nature to form place attachments, and evaluating an interactive system to understand how it may achieve that. The initial stages of the investigation, reported in this paper, consequently involve understanding children's current experiences and connections with local nature, and the key *motivators* that inspire these interactions.

# 4. THE STUDY

Research was conducted with 15 Danish children (8-12 years) each with an accompanying parent, from two different primary schools in Aalborg, Denmark. Six boys and nine girls participated in the study, which involved two separate research inquiries: a focus group and a follow-up interview. Parents participated in the focus group and the interviews. The two main researchers spoke only English, the children spoke only Danish. To overcome the language barrier, eight assistant researchers from Aalborg University and the parents, who spoke both Danish and English, helped with translations between the children and the main researchers.

## 4.1 Data Collection

### 4.1.1 Focus Groups

The fifteen children were divided into two focus groups of ninety minutes duration, held on different days at different locations, for the two schools. The aim of the focus group was to introduce the project and investigate key motivators that inspire interest in a child, specifically toward the natural environment. Fictional inquiry [5] was applied to engage children in the task, introducing a "visitor" from a foreign country (Australia) who was unable to speak the language and unaware of local behaviours. The children were encouraged to explain their "world" to the "visitor" through local interpreters.

**Figure 1. Drawing activity in children's group**

The session began with an ice-breaker activity between children, parents and researchers. Parents and children were then separated into two groups, in two separate rooms.

In a group, children were asked to: a) draw a picture of something you enjoy doing with your parents (see Figure 1); and b) draw a picture of an activity you enjoy doing in nature. Each task was followed by a brief presentation by the child in Danish (translation mediated by an assistant researcher), which facilitated further discussion and questioning to gather insights into the types of activities that children enjoy, and elements that motivate them, as they explained their pictures to the "visitor".

In a separate focus group, parents undertook two activities: a) list elements that motivate your child to take part in an activity (followed by a discussion to compare the motivators among children); and b) describe a positive experience you have shared with your children in nature, (followed by a discussion of these positive experiences to identify the key elements that motivated their child to take part in that activity). Motivational elements identified were then organized into an affinity diagram.

Finally, the two groups came together for a short time, where children explained their drawings to their parents, and parents commented to the researchers on the children's views, and motivations.

### 4.1.2 Follow-up Interviews
Each child-parent unit then participated in a 30-minute semi-structured follow-up interview, aimed at understanding the meaning and connection children felt for local parks and forests, and the motivating factors that led to interactions with nature. Each child participated in two separate activities in the interview, during which parents played the role of 'translator' between the researcher and their child.

Children were presented with a series of photographs of various natural scenes and landscapes within urban, rural and wilderness areas, and asked to identify the photo that represented the type of nature they visited most often, the frequency of visits, activities, and motivational factors that led to this interaction.

As a final activity, children were asked if they had a 'special place' in the nature they visit most often. If they could identify a special place, they were asked to draw this place and include all the elements that held significant meaning for the child. Children were given ten minutes to draw this place and were then asked why this place held significant meaning for them, and what motivated and enabled the types of interactions that led to this meaning.

### 4.1.3 Data Analysis
Data collected from the focus group and follow up interviews included video and audio recordings of all sessions, notes on the session written in English by an assistant researcher, drawings produced by the children, and two affinity diagrams produced during the parents' focus group session. Audio files were translated and transcribed in detail by the assistant researchers. Text and images were coded and analyzed to identify the common and contrasting motivators that led to interactions in local nature.

## 5. FINDINGS
Drawings depicting activities children enjoyed doing with their parents included going shopping with mum, going to a pizzeria together, going to the pet store and learning about the animals with dad, going sailing with dad, mountain biking with dad, playing ball with dad in the backyard, going to the beach with the family, being tickled by dad, and baking a cake with parents. Drawings showing what they enjoy doing in nature included: making a bonfire in the forest with the school class, picnic in the

**Figure 2: Child's drawing of her special place in nature.**

forest with friends, going to the beach with friends, fishing for crabs with sisters, swimming in the sea, and making a tree house in the forest (Figure 2).

A series of key motivators were identified through both drawing tasks, which included: opportunities to learn, special attention from parents, connecting with animals, feeling peaceful, comfortable and safe, new experiences and social opportunities. An interesting element of these drawings was the role parents played in motivating and enabling children to engage in everyday activities and activities in nature. Children were motivated to engage in activities when parents took time to do small things exclusively with them, creating an experience where they get to feel "special" for a day. Child experiences in nature were generally everyday and local, but often motivated by opportunities to socialize with friends, rather than parents. However, parents were frequently the enablers of these experiences, providing children with the idea, transport or financial support to engage in these activities.

The affinity diagrams produced during the focus groups with parents in response to "My child is motivated by…" elicited the following main themes: *Having fun* (activities should be fun); *Being social* (children like to mix with others); *Drawing and creating* (children like to use their imagination to create both tangible and abstract things); *Rewards* (either physical or virtual - effort or skill should be rewarded); *Being outside* (especially relevant when playing with others); *Competition* (preferably in groups cooperating to win, or against parents); *Achievable wins* (children are easily discouraged if it is too hard to win); *Family time* (children like spending time with their family); *Skills and learning* (children will spend time gaining new or enhanced skills); and *Narrative* (children like stories, and being involved in them). In the discussion part of the session two additional concepts emerged: *One-on-one time* (children really like it when they have sole access to one parent, making them feel special); *Divergence from everyday routines* (children generally have quite routine lives - even a small divergence from the routine is seen as exciting and memorable).

From the follow-up interviews we gained a deeper understanding of the common motivators that connect children with their local, natural environment. In the following quote a child participant (girl, 10 years) describes an experience she undertakes regularly with her friends in her local natural area, a forest behind her local school.

*My favourite part of the forest is to go to the tree-house we (my friends and I) built together. We have hidden it amongst the leaves in the forest so no one can find it. It's very different to other tree houses… (When we are there) we race each other to see who can climb the tree first, and who can take the hardest route. We play a lot of games here that we make up…Every Friday we get off school early, and go and have our lunch up there. Only the four of us (girls) that made the tree house know where it is. It's secret.* [Girl participant, 10 years old].

The experience described by this girl highlights a range of motivators for connecting with nature such as opportunities to socialize with friends, problem solve and learn, engage in physical activity, and team work/collaboration. By hiding their creation from others the children are exercising imaginative play, creating a world separate from others. By completing this tree house and having a place to play together, the child has expressed a strong sense of accomplishment and independence, free from the common constrains of adult-directed activities.

# DISCUSSION & CONCLUSIONS

In this study, the role in the design of new technology for the children has been as "informants" [5] to understand current practice. The children have been involved in talking and drawing to communicate to researchers their relationship to nature and participation in recreational activities. During focus groups and interview sessions the parents of the children also played an important role in that communication, acting not only as language interpreters but also as interpreters giving context to the children's responses.

Although this is early work, the outcomes of this study have identified important considerations for designing technology to motivate children to engage with their local nature. Previous research, along with our findings here, have identified that independent, child-directed interactions are essential for motivating the types of experiences in nature that build meaning and attachment. Our findings have revealed great diversity in the *types* of independent, child-directed activities that engage children with nature, including opportunities for abstract or tangible expressions of creativity, learning or collaborations with peers. However, the validity of these initial findings requires more investigation. During the next stage of research we will explore in depth the types of common and contrasting motivators that engage children with nature, and ways technology can be designed to enhance these motivational elements.

The context for our research is unique, as we intend to inspire child-nature interactions within an informal context (during their free time, outside school hours) instead of within an institutional framework. Thus, interactions with nature are facilitated by *motivation,* and also *enablement*. The range of barriers preventing children from engaging with nature is an issue of far greater significance in an informal context, than a formal or institutionally supported context. During school or organized outdoor programs, children are operating in the same space, and timeframe, with a consistent objective, enabling them to take part in any activity. Once removed from these formal structures, children face a range of barriers to engaging with nature, such as capacity to coordinate free time to play together, lack of independent access to natural areas and safety concerns of parents, which may prevent the most motivated child from engaging with nature. In the next phase, we intend to investigate the role of technology in overcoming the barriers to engagement with nature present in informal contexts, a novel contribution to the field of child-computer interaction. Outcomes of this preliminary study suggest that parents may be significant 'enablers' of child-nature interactions. Technology may have an important role in assisting parents enable their children to engage in meaningful interactions with local nature.

Although some of these are not new understandings for designing interactions for children, we think it is worth presenting them as issues that were interwoven with children's' perceptions of their natural environment, motivating them to spend time there.

# 6. FUTURE WORK

In our future research we intend to apply the model of Ecological Inquiry [11], an interventionist approach to social practice, place and technology through the co-design of technologies 'in-situ', to investigate how technology may motivate children to engage with their local nature. We also intend to expand the Ecological Inquiry model to include 'barriers to engagement' with local nature, and explore potential applications of technology to address these barriers. For example, the safety concerns of parents may be addressed by increasing community connectedness, or enabling child monitoring practices. Understanding what motivates and enables children to engage with local nature may have long-term applications for urban planners and policy makers responsible for natural urban spaces.

# 7. ACKNOWLEDGMENTS

Our thanks to the children and parents that participated in this study, and Informatics students from Aalborg University: Daniel Kappers, Simon Iversen, Richard Trondheim, Christian Pilgaard, Adam Gistrup, Dennis Dalgaard, Frederick Nielsen and Casper Sorensen.

# 8. REFERENCES

[1] Baskin, Y. 1997. *The Work of Nature: How the diversity of life sustains us*. Island Press, Washington.

[2] Brown, E. (Ed.). 2010. *Education in the wild: contextual and location-based mobile learning in action*. A report from the STELLAR Alpine Rendez-Vous workshop series.

[3] Carver, S., Evans, A.J. and Fritz, S. 2002. Wilderness Attribute Mapping in the United Kingdom. *International Journal of Wilderness 8*, 1 (2002), 24-29.

[4] Chawla, L. 1992. Childhood Place Attachments. In Altman, I. & Low, S.M. (Eds.). *Place Attachment*. Plenum, London.

[5] Dindler, C., Eriksson, E., Iversen, O., Lykjke-Olesen, A. and Ludvigsen, M. 2005. Mission from Mars - A Method for Exploring User Requirements for Children in a Narrative Space. In *Proc. IDC '05*, ACM (2005), 40-47.

[6] Druin, A. 2002. The Role of Children in the Design of New Technology. *Behaviour and Information Technology*, 21, 1 (2002), 1-25.

[7] Kellert, S. R. 2002. Experiencing Nature: Affective, Cognitive, and Evaluative Development. In Kahn P. & Kellert, S.R. (Eds.) *Children and Nature: Psychological, Sociocultural, and Evolutionary Investigations*. The MIT Press, Cambridge, MA.

[8] Louv, R. 2005. *Last Child in the Woods: Saving our Children from Nature Deficit Disorder*. Algonquin Books, Chapel Hill, USA.

[9] Rogers, Y., Price, S., Fitzpatrick, G., Fleck, R., Harris, E., Smith, H., Randell, C., Muller, H., O'Malley, C., Stanton, D., Thompson, M., and Weal, M. 2004. Ambient wood: designing new forms of digital augmentation for learning outdoors. In *Proc. IDC '04*, ACM (2004), 3-10.

[10] Ryokai, K. 2013. Off the Paved Paths: Exploring Nature with a Mobile Augmented Reality Learning Tool. *International Journal of Mobile Computer Interaction 5*, 2 (2013), 21-49.

[11] Smith, R., Iversen, O., Hjermitslev, T. and Lynggaard, A. 2013. Towards an ecological inquiry in child-computer interaction. In *Proc. IDC '13*, ACM (2013), 183-192.

[12] Tuan, Y-F. 1978. Children and the Natural Environment. In Altman, I. & Wohlwill (Eds.) Children and the Environment, Springer, New York.

[13] Verhaegh, J., Soute, I., Kessels, A. and Markopoulos, P. 2006. On the design of Camelot, an outdoor game for children. In *Proc. IDC '06*, ACM (2006), 9-16.

[14] Williams, M., Jones, O., Fleuriot, C. and Wood, L. 2005. Children and Emerging Wireless Technologies: Investigating the Potential for Spatial Practice. In Proc. CHI '05, ACM (2005), 819-828.

# Connected Messages: A Maker Approach to Interactive Community Murals with Youth

Orkan Telhan
University of Pennsylvania
205 South 34th St.
Philadelphia, PA 19104
+1 (215) 573-6089
otelhan@design.upenn.edu

Yasmin B. Kafai
University of Pennsylvania
3700 Walnut Street 405
Philadelphia, PA 19106
+1 (215) 746-3468
kafai@upenn.edu

Richard Lee Davis
Stanford University
520 Galvez Mall
Stanford, CA 94305
+1 (570) 335-8507
rldavis@stanford.edu

K-Fai Steele
Free Library of Philadelphia
1901 Vine Street, Room 5A (TOPSS)
Philadelphia, PA 19103
+1 (215) 686-5372
steelek@freelibrary.org

Barrie M. Adleberg
University of Pennsylvania
3700 Walnut Street
Philadelphia, PA 19106
+1 (703) 507-3404
adleberg@upenn.edu

## ABSTRACT

Connected Messages brings together traditions of engaging youth in designing interactive murals with themes relevant to their lives and new low-cost networking technologies of connecting local groups with global audiences. We describe the design of a community mural that functions like a public display, which can be remotely programmed through an online interface. The implementation with Maker Mentors in five Free Library branches with over 1,000 youth focused on different aspects of youth maker agency in accessing, participating, and expressing their ideas. In the discussion, we review key dimensions expanding youth and Maker Mentor participation in community-relevant designs.

## Categories and Subject Descriptors

K.3.1. [**Computers and Education**]: Computer Uses in Education

## General Terms: Design. Human Factors.

## Keywords: Public display, community engagement, maker culture

## 1. INTRODUCTION

Maker activities, popular in fabrication spaces, children's museums, science centers, community organizations and maker faires (Honey & Kanter, 2013), have focused mostly on personally-relevant designs such as robots, toys, and clothing. While these designs are often created with support of others and shared with others, they leave aside the potentially rich area of community-relevant designs that could engage not only local participants but also connect to global audiences. Community-relevant designs can introduce a new genre of maker activities that is not only concerned about teaching a particular skill set but also about fostering a sense of community. One popular application of community-relevant designs are murals found in many cities that often depict historical events, consist of messages, images or scenes built by individuals or groups who intend to preserve the spirit of the community (Golden et al. 2002).

While most communities change over time, murals are designed often to be fixed representations and thus lack the dynamic nature of digital public displays such as large-scale permanent projections and media facades. Digital public displays have the potential to allow communities to express themselves in more dynamic ways because they combine permanent display with real-time participation and bridge the personal and the local with online communities. Efforts here range from the pioneering work by Brignull and Rogers (2003) on *Opionizer* that led participants voice and share their ideas, to Peltonen et al.'s (2008) *CityWall* projects that led children display their designs, and to Hsi and Eisenberg's (2012) recent *Math on a Sphere* project which provided children with a programming language to create and share designs for spherical displays in public science centers. Digital public displays, while inviting contributions and interactions, often lack the sense of intimacy, community voice, and identity that traditional murals possess. Relatively modest, low-cost, DIY public displays can be as effective as expensive infrastructures such as video walls, plasma screens, or interactive surfaces in creating intimate and meaningful interactions. Seitinger et al. (2009)'s *Urban Pixels*—a display system made of low-cost, programmable, networked and unbounded light sources—uses wireless light emitting units that can integrate to urban environments in different configurations to create different visual patterns on the facades of buildings. Here, users can selectively activate individual pixels by turning them on or off or control them remotely in groups using their phones and customize the look and feel of the display. Taylor and Cheverest (2012) discuss an even more low-cost display strategy that combines printed and digital postcards that would allow photo sharing during a village fair. In the spirit of public bulletin boards, the project utilizes simple postcard designs to lower the barriers of participation in rural communities. Here, hand made designs created by the locals and digital postcards sent by remote participants are brought together to build a display that fosters a sense of belonging within the community.

It is within this larger landscape of interactive, participatory, and public displays that we situate the design and implementation of a community mural, called *Connected Messages,* that combines the empowering nature of city murals with the dynamic qualities of digital displays. In the design of our interactive community mural, we pursued a maker approach that fostered a do-it-together mentality, to build on a sense of ownership by encouraging youth to realize their public image together. We report on the design and implementation of *Connected Messages* with youth ages 6-19 and a group of Maker Corps Mentors in Philadelphia Free Library branches. This work draws on Philadelphia's longstanding tradition as "The City of Murals" (Golden et al. 2014) where over 3,600 murals have transformed the city into a canvas, highlighting the community-building power of collaborative art. We examined two aspects of the approach in more detail: youth' maker agency and maker mentor support in accessing, participating, and expressing their community ideas and concerns by asking the following questions: What impacts youth participation in and expression of community themes at different sites? How can mentors support youth voice, making, and technical learning in community-relevant designs? In the discussion, we address how this maker approach to public displays can allow for not only increased community engagement but also provides the opportunity to incorporate more computational engagement.

## 2. DESIGNING CONNECTED MESSAGES

The *Connected Messages* mural consisted of the following components: (1) physical foam boards for displaying and connecting message boxes created by participants, (2) tile-like message boxes made by youth with one LED, and (3) a website that displayed a virtual representation of the mural and allowed the LEDs to be controlled. Each 'blank' *Connected Messages* board (see Figure 1) consisted of a 4x4' piece of foam board purchased at a local art supply store, strips of adhesive copper tape laid out in an overlapping grid, an Electric Imp hardware module, a 16x8 LED matrix controller, and a 4G modem that connected the board to the internet. Youth decorated the lids using markers and installed a single white LED in the box using two conductive copper traces. When these traces were connected to 3.3 volts, the LED inside the box would turn on and illuminate the design on the lid. Once the box was pinned to the copper-tape grid on the board, the LEDs in the boxes could be turned on and off from the main website. These board and materials were installed in five library branches across Philadelphia.

Figure 1. Foam board with copper traces (upper left), Electric Imp and a modem (upper right), back of tile boxes with copper connectors (lower left), and tile boxes with designs on board (lower right).

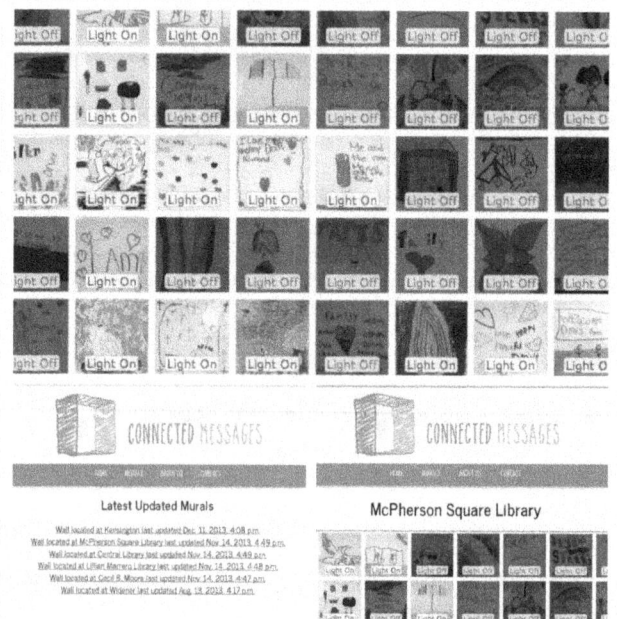

Figure 2. Connected Messages website interface.

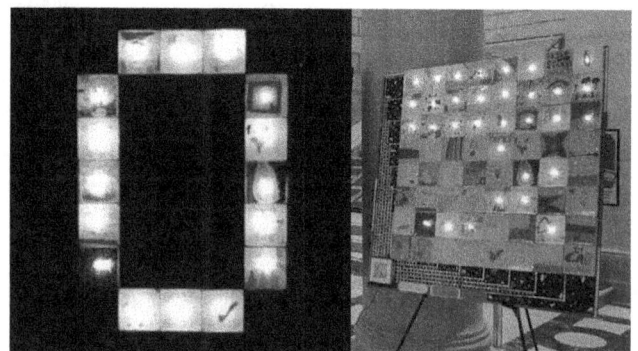

Figure 3. Connected Messages: Letter "O" scrolling (left) and selected lights on (right).

## 3. MAKING CONNECTED MESSAGES

The *Connected Messages* murals were set up and designed during the summer of 2013 in five Free Library locations in underserved neighborhoods across North and West Philadelphia. The mural activities were led by five Maker Mentors, a team that consisted of three men and two women, ages 21-31, with backgrounds as working artists and undergraduate students (Chemistry, Industrial Design and Engineering majors). The Mentors were trained as part of a Maker Ed Initiative grant to lead workshops in electronics, arts, and crafting. The research team together with the Maker Mentors designed and constructed the boards and materials, which were then delivered to each site. Our evaluation focused on observations of youth maker activities in library branches and debriefing interviews conducted with Maker Mentors.

### 3.1. Observations of Youth Makers

A total of 1,036 total youth participants, between ages 6-19 years, participated in *Connected Messages* activities, their daily participation fluctuating from three to thirty participants. Youth and mentors at each location developed a theme for their board based on conversations relating to the themes (e.g., bravery, kindness, acceptance, anti-bullying) of Lady Gaga's Born Brave Bus Tour, which visited Philadelphia in March 2013. The most striking differences were found in themes for the boxes adopted in each site. While all of them started from Lady Gaga tour themes, the mentors realized in order to imbue a true sense of ownership in the project, the making had to be personalized. One library location—embedded within a nonprofit whose mission is to reduce the recidivism of adjudicated African-American youth—created boxes that addressed recent school closings versus new prison construction, their perspectives on the Trayvon Martin trial, and choosing positivity and creative outlets over perpetuating violence. As the mentor explained, "[The participants] took each problem as an interesting challenge and made it their own. It was easier to scaffold their learning to the point where I could be almost completely hands-off during their making."

The sites also differed substantially in terms of participation, access, themes, and completion of the community mural designs and illustrated some of the challenges in implementing such maker projects across different sites, albeit in the same city. Participation varied and depended on the nature of implementation and instructor expertise at each Connected Messages site. At one branch, the board was filled within one week. The Maker Mentor, an artist with no maker or computing background, described his tactics in encouraging engagement in likeness to his artistic process: "Drawing and painting is all creative problem solving, If you can step up and get closer and see the smaller parts, it make it much more tangible to someone who is uncomfortable with their own skills." In contrast, the Maker mentor at another library location had a strong technology background. At this site, several of the participants got to the point where they were able to scan their designs to flash drives and upload them for the website. While many youth were interested in how the board and the website functioned, they never dug deeper into the technical back-end. He recounted, "The coolest part is the breakthrough—when we had to do documentation for it, they all worked on Mozilla and they would help piece together the html and the website." No matter which technical orientation, at all sites youth and mentors alike found it gratifying when the boards lit up.

Access to the boards also differed significantly across sites and thus impacted community involvement. The site that locked their board in a conference room and opened it three times a week was the last to finish and the maker mentor had to mount many of the boxes herself. In contrast, the site that displayed the board in a prominent, high traffic area for optimal visibility generated more interest in the project. The mentor recalled that creative process became very personal to participants, "in the end some got into heated debates over who could present our work to the community." *Connected Messages* culminated in a local Maker Celebration, which brought together all five board plus a blank one, which visitors of the Celebration could complete with their own messages. Over 50 youth presenters and over 100 additional attendees gathered in the lobby of the Central Library to display their messages of community. Participants had the opportunity to share the meaning behind their postcards, as well as the technological knowledge they accumulated over the summer by helping attendees create their own postcards. One of the boards was also connected to the Internet and visitors could type in a message and see it scroll across the LEDs.

### 3.2. Reflections of Mentor Makers

At the completion of *Connected Messages*, we interviewed the five Maker Mentors about their experiences in supporting learning, production and expression of community voice, and their own learning. Mentors encouraged participants to explore the project in self-directed, inquiry-based approaches that allowed for differing levels of engagement. One mentor described his style as informal; "I'm for more of just exploration, getting into the nitty gritty, not necessarily a top-down approach but just guiding kids through what they're interested in." Several Maker Mentors recalled that youth described their neighborhoods of North and West Philadelphia in a way that echoed census statistics on drug abuse, violence, and low education: "It was a bit sad to hear their initial responses of *not safe, no good*." In response, mentors often shifted the conversation to a more asset-based approach that focused on positive aspects, "One of them wanted to make a box about recycling, not because the community is all that trash-conscious, but because it's something he wanted to say he feels is important to making a community healthy." By challenging a negative, dominant narrative and supporting curiosity, youth were able to expose personal stories about their communities. One mentor described that the process became organic, "I quickly learned that kid input and project driving needed to be a priority of mine… Informal exploration time allowed me to connect with my kids a bit more." A learning outcome of Connected Messages was a basic understanding of simple circuits. A mentor explained, "I think the majority understood the idea that the leads on the board all were positive/negative and how that had to operate." In attempts to spark more interest he continued, "I took off the barcode box [showed them the hardware] just so they could see what was under the hood." In future iterations of the project, mentors agreed that exposure to back-end, hardware construction would be a great impetus for deeper learning.

## 4. DISCUSSION & NEXT STEPS

In our evaluation of designing and implementing *Connected Messages* we found that providing youth with agency in building the physical mural fostered their participating and expressing community ideas and concerns. We utilized a maker-oriented approach and provided each participant the basic components to build a "pixel" message box that became the building block for expressing ideas about community and composing a larger public display. In this process, message boxes began to gain secondary meanings based on their neighboring tiles and more importantly started to embrace a more collective role of combining individual efforts with a group sensibility. This also succeeded in drawing in participants and establishing an audience, which has been a key issue for many communal displays (Agamanolis 2003). It was, however, less obvious how to engage members in the making of the technical backend of the board and web site.

In re-designing our approach, materials, and processes used in Connected Messages, one challenge for us is to design an interaction process that unfolds from simple to the complex in multiple stages that are parallel to the learning objectives. We could definitely engage youth more in the process of laying out the boards, introduction to soldering and materials and give them more time to play with/see what other sites are doing (engage in peer production, peer learning via the internet). A good parallel to this is Eisenberg's Math on a Sphere, where people can write basic programs in LOGO and see the output displayed on a giant, public sphere (Hsi & Eisenberg, 2012), participants could learn to write simple programs to send or receive HTTP requests to control the mural. A curriculum could be developed that taught kids python by having them program simple animations and games for the board. Furthermore, we could engage youth in learning how to write word filters that screen out offensive terms.

Perhaps an even more important measure of community engagement, is that *Connected Messages* continues to be a successful program and community object in five libraries because of its accessibility and flexibility in allowing all community members to engage in a dialogue based on community selected themes. It has provided an opportunity for the community to create personally meaningful parts of a larger object, much in the way that their personal voice serves as a piece of their community as a whole.

# 5. ACKNOWLEDGMENTS

This work was supported by a grant (#1238172) from the National Science Foundation to Yasmin Kafai, Orkan Telhan and Karen Elinich. Any opinions, findings, and conclusions or recommendations expressed in this paper are those of the authors and do not necessarily reflect the views of the National Science Foundation or the University of Pennsylvania. The authors wish to thank to the Free Library of Philadelphia and the MakerCorps members of the Maker Jawn initiative.

# 6. REFERENCES

[1] Honey, Margaret, and David E. Kanter (Eds.) (2013). *Design, Make, Play: Growing the Next Generation of STEM Innovators*. New York, NY: Routledge.

[2] Golden, J., & D. Updike, D. (2014). *Philadelphia Mural Arts @ 30*. Philadelphia, PA: Temple University Press.

[3] Brignull, H., Izadi, S., Fitzpatrick, G., Rogers, Y., & Rodden, T. (2004). The introduction of a shared interactive surface into a communal space. In *Proceedings of the 2004 ACM conference on Computer supported cooperative work* (pp. 49-58). New York, NY: ACM.

[4] Peltonen, P., Salovaara, A., Jacucci, G., Ilmonen, T., Ardito, C., Saarikko, P., & Batra, V. (2007). Extending large-scale event participation with user-created mobile media on a public display. In *Proceedings of the 6th international conference on Mobile and ubiquitous multimedia* (pp. 131-138). New York, NY: ACM.

[5] Hsi, S., & Eisenberg, M. (2012). Math on a sphere: using public displays to support children's creativity and computational thinking on 3D surfaces. In*Proceedings of the 11th International Conference on Interaction Design and Children* (pp. 248-251). New York, NY: ACM.

[6] Seitinger, S., Perry, D. S., & Mitchell, W. J. (2009). Urban pixels: painting the city with light. In *Proceedings of the SIGCHI Conference on Human Factors in Computing Systems* (pp. 839-848). New York, NY: ACM.

[7] Taylor, N., & Cheverst, K. (2008). This might be stupid, but...: participatory design with community displays and postcards. In *Proceedings of the 20th Australasian Conference on Computer-Human Interaction: Designing for Habitus and Habitat* (pp. 41-48). New York, NY: ACM.

[8] Golden, J., & D. Updike, D. (2014). *Philadelphia Mural Arts @ 30*. Philadelphia, PA: Temple University Press

[9] Agamanolis, S. (2004). Designing Displays for Human Connectedness. In K. O'Hara, M. Perry, E. Churchill, and D. Russell (Eds.), *Public and Situated Displays* (pp. 309–334). Dordrecht, Netherlands: Kluwer.

# Design and Evaluation of Interactive Musical Fruit

Cumhur Erkut, Stefania Serafin, Jonas Fehr, Henrique M.R. Fernandes Figueira,
Theis B. Hansen, Nicholas J. Kirwan, and Mariam R. Zakarian
Aalborg University Copenhagen, Medialogy
A.C. Meyers Vænge 15
DK-2450 Copenhagen SV, Denmark
+45 9940 258
{cer,sts}@create.aau.dk, {jfehr,hferna,tbha,nkirwa,mrza}13@student.aau.dk

## ABSTRACT

In this paper we describe the design and evaluation of a novel, tangible user interface for interaction with sound, to be implemented in a museum setting. Our work-in-progress is part of a larger concept for an installation prioritizing a collaborative, explorative, multimodal experience. Focus has been centered on novice children, in order to accommodate all potential users of the museum, and to minimize the risk of excluding users based on skill or previous musical know-how. We have developed four instances of a multimodal device for interacting with sounds via a tangible interface, and called them Interactive Musical Fruits (IMFs). The IMF consists of an embedded processing system, which can detect its orientation. Qualitative testing with children has been performed, to better evaluate the current design state. Positive feedback from the test subjects upholds the validity and the potential of the IMF as an interface in a museum context. However, further research is required to improve the interactive and collaborative aspects of the device, as well as the aural and visual properties of the IMF.

## Categories and Subject Descriptors

H.5.2 Information Interfaces and Presentation (e.g., HCI): User Interfaces – *evaluation/methodology, interaction styles, user-centered design*. K.3.0 Computers and Education: General.

## General Terms

Performance, Design, Experimentation, Security, Human Factors.

## Keywords

Tangible and embodied interaction, musical instrument, IMU.

## 1. INTRODUCTION

We present our ongoing work on an interactive musical installation, which aims to provide the visitors an experience of making music together, without necessarily having musical skills or expertise. Our framework builds upon a *tree metaphor*, and consists at the moment of four tangible interfaces (*fruits*) that are connected to a central unit (*trunk*, used for synchronization) via *branches*.

The concept, created for The Danish Music Museum in Copenhagen, is illustrated on Fig. 1. The museum is in the process of moving to a new facility where a dedicated room will be used for new musical initiatives. In a brief, they expressed an interest in including users from all age groups. The museum as a setting comes with certain inherent constraints, such as the development of immediately understandable and intuitive designs, as one cannot expect the visitors to spend any considerable amount of time on learning to use a new interface. Prior knowledge of music cannot be assumed as a prerequisite; novices (e.g. children) have to be catered for. Finally, the museum emphasizes the following learning goal: all current and past musical instruments, however sophisticated or advanced in form and function, consist of elementary interactions initiated by human action. This is a strong call for us to revisit *embodied interaction* and *action-sound* relations as background material and design inspiration.

The rest of our contribution is as follows. After providing a brief background on the concepts outlined above, we describe our design process in Section 3, together with the implementation of both hardware and software. The next section focuses on testing, Section 5 presents a discussion of the results, and we conclude the paper in Section 6.

**Figure 1. Our concept. © Mariam R. Zakarian, 2013.**

## 2. BACKGROUND

In [3], a comparative overview of several contemporary, collaborative interface designs related to music-making for novices is provided. Felts & Lyon update this line of work annually in their "Gentle Introduction to NIME" tutorial series; the interested reader is referred to their tutorials for extensive references on easy user interfaces for music and interactive sound installations. Many of the conclusions, in particular those relating to collaborative interfaces, have been very relevant to our work. For instance, an interface that is *novel to all users* is beneficial in ensuring that users with different musical abilities can have the same starting point [3]. Similarly, *identical interfaces* for all users make it possible to quickly comprehend other user's input, once one has understood the use of one's own device. This is a way of shifting focus from the single interface to collaboration, and making it possible to learn from each other as well.

One way of creating an explorative, collaborative musical interface is to focus on a tangible design [4], which provides good opportunities for discovery and participation among users. Bakker and her colleagues [2] note that physical objects, unlike purely virtual ones, can help facilitate bridging the gap between the abstract and the concrete for children, e.g. as is the case when working with an abacus to learn math. Tangible interfaces can provide rich sensorimotor engagement and ease of understanding, which can in turn enhance the experience of music and stimulate discovery and participation [2]. In their investigation of using embodied metaphors in design, Bakker et al. note that even small children (of age four) are capable of understanding musical expressions such as volume and tempo, their vocabulary however is too restricted to articulate what they hear. One way to alleviate this problem is to avoid using language in exploration, and to allow children to explain via movement [2].

Besides embodied metaphors, the IDC community identifies a need for a wide set of expertise in building technologies with innovative forms of interaction [1], and emphasizes that breadth of expertise is key in building interactive technologies, which are tied to different content areas including music composition [1]. One such area is *sketching in hardware* by using modular, reconfigurable systems originating from the domain of designing and evaluating digital musical instruments [5, 6].

## 3. DESIGN AND IMPLEMENTATION

Our early ideas on design and implementation are presented in a short video at http://www.youtube.com/watch?v=-dJyK_y2CUg. Here, we provide an overview and update.

### 3.1 Physical Design

The main concept of the design is an interactive installation in the shape of a tree. Interactive musical fruits (IMFs) with individually assigned sounds are the interfaces, with which the guests of the museum can interact. The resulting soundscape contains a central background theme, on top of which the sounds of individual fruits are layered.

The fruits are essentially tangible interfaces containing a degree of abstraction, which are easily created through rapid prototyping, and are physically identical. We have gravitated towards an interface, which is free from musical associations. A spherical shape can be related to the shape of many different fruits, so we have adapted this shape for the prototype design. Both the *dodecahedron* and *icosahedron* were considered as simple abstractions of the sphere, as both can be unfolded into a two-dimensional plane. However, the *icosahedron* has more naturally

connected edges, making it structurally more stable and more practical for rapid prototyping with the laser cutter. Prototypes were used to test the structure and gave a beneficial insight into how to encapsulate the electronic components in the fruits.

Suspending the fruits was a central part of the development of the interface. There was the need for attaching the prototype to a reference point, as the sensors inside the fruit deliver information about the interface's orientation. Through mounting the fruit to a fixed point it was possible to use the orientation to calculate the position in a two dimensional space. For a quick solution, we chose to use installation tubes for electrical wiring as a support mechanism for the prototype. The flexible properties of the tubes make it possible to move the fruit in space while also serving as a transport channel for the cable.

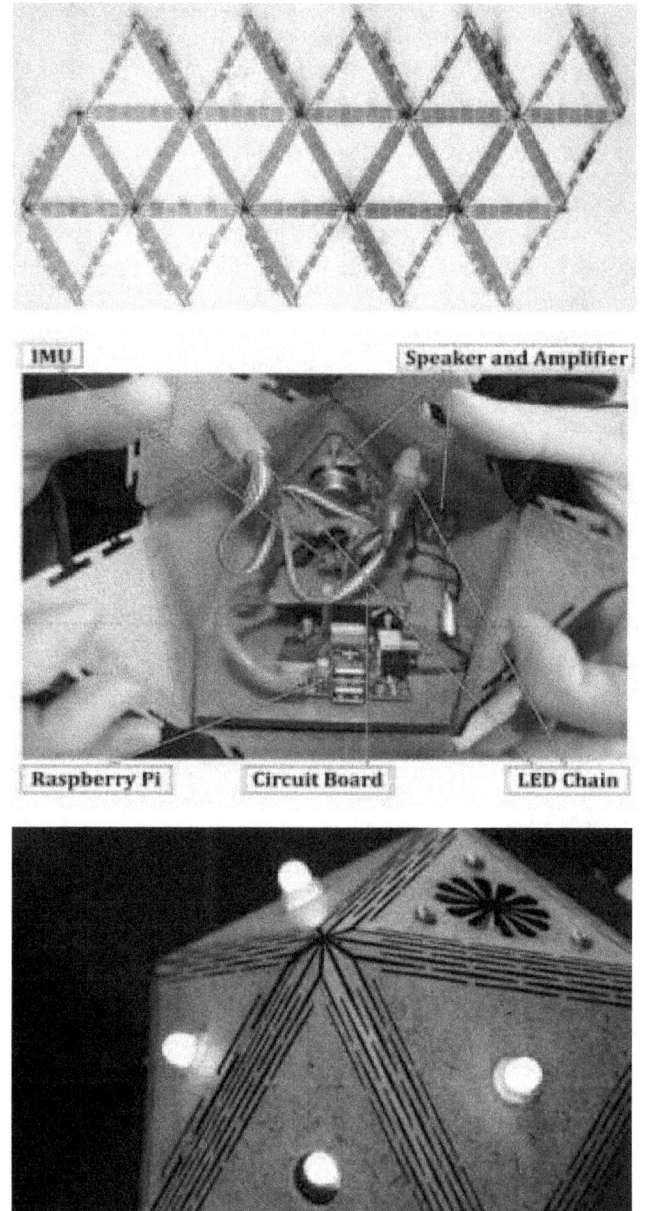

Figure 2. (Top) The icosahedron on planar plywood for laser cutting. (Middle) Inserting electronics. (Bottom) The 3D prototype. Photographs © Mariam R. Zakarian, 2013.

## 3.2 Implementation

Each fruit contains embedded sound synthesis and processing, which is controlled through movement. At the core of the system is a Raspberry Pi, a compact computer (Fig. 2, middle). Connected to this is an MPU-9150 *inertial measurement unit* (IMU), which collects orientation data. Visual feedback is provided by an addressable, multi-color LED chain. Audio feedback is provided by a small amplifier and speaker with a stereo 3.5mm jack input. Finally, the circuit board enables both the IMU and the LED chain to be physically integrated into the system. With the electronic components in place, the sides of the prototype are hinged together, and the result is illustrated on Fig. 2 (bottom).

## 3.3 Interaction and sound design

To encourage explorative gestures with the interface, we have decided to use its orientation data on two axes. This solution makes it possible to comprehend that moving the fruit to the same point will result in the same sound. Choosing left-right and up-down movements limit the parameters and the possible gestures in the IMF. This restricted control, however, contributes to making the interface more straightforward, accessible and easy to understand as far as *multimodal feedback* is concerned. More dynamic and compound gestures, considering acceleration and speed of the movement, can also be integrated into the interface in the future.

Three different sound generators were used in an attempt to implement easy-to-learn and limited control interfaces: i) a *granular synthesizer*, allowing the user to play very complex sounds using simple control implementations, ii) a sample looper, where movements control the playback speed and the volume of the sound, and iii) a plucked string simulation where the amount of played notes is randomly chosen from a pentatonic scale. Table 1 presents how the 2D actions are mapped to control, and eventually to auditory feedback.

The main sound generation and manipulation is facilitated by Pure Data (PD). Input from the IMU is received, scaled and routed to sound-generating and light-controlling parts of the program. Open Sound Control (OSC) protocol for remote messages is also supported.

**Table 1. Action-control-sound mappings**

| Synth | Left/right | Up/down | Complexity |
|-------|-----------|---------|-----------|
| Granular | Playhead position | Playhead jumps | Intermediate |
| Sampler | Speed/Pitch Change | Volume | Low |
| String | Range and physical damping | Note density and feedback | High |

## 4. TESTING

In a preliminary test, 14 participants from our university provided material for us to discover common gestures, which could be connected to musical attributes such as volume, pitch, tempo, rhythmic patterns, and timbre. The participants were videotaped while exploring the prototypes within a think-aloud protocol (examples available at http://www.youtube.com/watch?v=-dJyK_y2CUg). The exploration and comments differed a lot, therefore intuitive gestures were difficult to discern. The clearest indication of a gesture-sound mapping was the up and down movement related to volume change. While we have used this

mapping in our next test, it is also likely that the flexible support tubes were more suggestive of vertical motion than horizontal, and have influenced the way the participants moved the IMF.

Our next test was with children about 12 years of age, considering our focus on novice users. Our test centered on the following questions: i) How do children *interact with and respond to our prototype*? ii) Do they interact with the prototype as *we expected* or will they show us new ways for further development? iii) How do they react on different sounds? Is abstract design a constraint?

8 children from a local school were recruited for testing. The children were presented with a short introduction to the project in two testing areas: A large room and an adjacent, smaller room. Audio was recorded from both testing areas. During testing, the gestures of the children were observed as they interacted with the prototype. They were then interviewed by the design team members. Finally, they were invited to free play with the interfaces. The free play is depicted on Fig. 3.

**Figure 3. Free play after tests.**

In interviews, additional questions were sometimes necessary to gauge how much the child comprehended, and because of this, the challenge during the interviews was finding the balance between stimulating the individual to answer, while at the same time avoiding influencing the answer. The interviews were conducted in the native language of the children.

The questions can be divided into three groups. The first block aimed at judging the child's musical knowledge and preference as well as getting more confident and familiar with each other. The second block aimed to assess if the child can comprehend what is being controlled and if they can describe what they hear. The focus of the test was to understand how the test subjects interact and play with the prototype. Finally, the last block was regarding the user's overall impression of the prototype. Each child was asked which sound synthesizers he/she preferred and was encouraged to suggest changes for further development.

## 5. RESULTS

Almost all the children said they listen to pop music, some mentioning specific artists. Some reported musical skills, but none of them an interest in making music. Four out of the eight participants stated that they play or have played an instrument casually. Our observations suggest that prior knowledge of music is not needed for interacting with the fruit, and even with more advanced musical knowledge no difference in interaction was observed.

Most of the children were careful while interacting with the prototype in the beginning, but after encouragement they became less inhibited and moved it more confidently. A gentle, tapping motion was observed frequently, as when playing with a basketball. As they tapped the prototype, it bounced and returned by the elastic force of the branch. The children rarely took the fruit in both hands to move it in space, in order to scan for specific sounds. Some of them moved the prototype to extreme positions after being asked to investigate how it works. The majority of the time, the prototype was in continuous movement. The changing sound did not seem to provoke different gestures without different movements being requested by the interviewers.

## 5.1 Action-sound

All the children discovered that moving the prototype up and down had an effect on the sound. It is not possible to conclude from the test results if the children were able to understand if the sideways movements also influenced the sound, as they had to specifically be requested to perform this movement before they consciously did. Referring to Table 1, for the granular synthesizer it was not possible for the children to comprehend the mapping of gesture to sound, but several recognized that moving the fruit to the same place resulted in the same sound. Almost all the children were able to detect the speed change in the sampler. Only a few mentioned the volume as well. The third synthesizer seemed more straightforward and almost everybody recognized changes in the temporal density. Two users also mentioned the difference in sound related to moving the fruit side to side. Two of the children were reproducing specific sounds as an aid to explain the function.

## 5.2 Sound associations

All the participants except one mentioned a string instrument for the third synthesizer, and more than half of them associated it with a guitar. The other two patches resulted in a greater variety of answers. The granular synthesizer produced descriptions such as a parakeet, robot, an alarm clock, electronic or alien-sounds. One of the children described the sounds using a metaphor indicating playing conditions: boring and funny. The sampler (with playback speed changes) was often described with the sound's mechanics, for instance, sounding like it is being slowed down or sped up. Similar sounds were used as description, such as an airplane sound or an accident in a movie. The abstract association with a dream was also mentioned.

Describing an abstract sound is a difficult task, even for musically trained adults. Therefore, our test subjects often could not answer related questions verbally. However, some explained by direct vocalization. This is similar to what has been reported in [2].

## 5.3 Preferences

There were differences in sound preferences; some preferred the sampler and some the string synthesizer. Similarly, a large variance was observed in how the prototype was perceived in both shape and look. Several associations included special balls (ball/cube with corners), something from space (meteor, flying saucer), ornament, or just a specially folded box. None of the children mentioned the expected fruit. This matches our intention to keep the shape as abstract as possible.

## 5.4 Free play

The children displayed a clear interest in trying the prototype out of their own free will, long after the test. During this free play, it was observed that more than one child could play with the prototype at the same time. Some children used it to tease others, by holding the prototype over their heads and out of reach, as they tried to jump and grab it. Others used it as a football, bouncing it between them. One child mentioned that it could be fun to use the prototype as a swing you could sit on. It was also mentioned that the prototype is fun even without sound. The suggestions we have gathered provide us with insight that could be accommodated in future iterations.

## 6. CONCLUSIONS

In the pursuit of designing a musical installation for a museum, we have developed a tangible user interface for sound exploration. Starting from concept generation, we have aimed for an engaging interface that is abstract enough to invite both novices and experienced musicians. Key aspects we have addressed in design and implementation include *modularity, mobility, versatility* and *customizability*, as well as setting the *basic framework for the development of a collaborative system*. While it is true that collaboration is not investigated here and seems incidental to the reported results, our focus on the identical interfaces motivated us to investigate our design space on one interface before many. We hope that the short video at http://www.youtube.com/watch?v=-dJyK_y2CUg helps explaining our design rationale.

The overall positive response from the children during the user testing confirms that our design is progressing in the right direction. Clearly, there are aspects that need further work, especially regarding interaction. Further research is required to provide novices with a more straightforward and easy-to-use interface, as well as tailoring its use towards an explorative experience. Whether this experience is related more to sound or music is debatable; but following E. Varèse's definition of music as organized sound, we believe that exploring the relation between action, sound, and music is a relevant domain of inquiry, given the pedagogical goals of our brief. We are more interested in how the children construct this relation than what the interface does or how the sound models work. Yet, since sound is integral to our design, it will also be a major focus of further development. Likewise, the development and implementation of visuals and the actual tree interface will be concentrated on. As noted during testing, participants found the IMF interesting and stated that they would use it in a museum setting. This is a promising tendency and the concept will be developed and refined in the near future.

## 7. REFERENCES

[1] Alper, M., Hourcade, J.P. and Gilutz, S. 2012. Interactive technologies for children with special needs. *Proc. IDC'12 Workshop* (Bremen, Germany, 2012), 363-366.

[2] Bakker, S., Antle, A.N. and van den Hoven, E. 2012. Embodied metaphors in tangible interaction design. *Personal and Ubiquitous Computing*. 16, 4 (Apr. 2012), 433–449.

[3] Blaine, T. and Fels, S. 2003. Collaborative Musical Experiences for Novices. *Journal of New Music Research*. 32, 4 (2003), 411–428.

[4] Ishii, H. 2008. Tangible user interfaces. In *The Human-Computer Interaction Handbook*. Lawrence Erlbaum Associates (2008), 469-487

[5] Overholt, D. and Møbius, N.D. 2014. Embedded audio without beeps: synthesis and sound effects from cheap to steep. *Proc. Intl. Conf. Tangible, Embedded and Embodied Interaction* (Feb. 2014, Munich, Germany), 361-364.

[6] Rasamimanana, N., Bevilacqua, F., Schnell, et. al. 2011. Modular musical objects towards embodied control of digital music. *Proc. Intl. Conf. Tangible, Embedded and Embodied Interaction* (Funchal, Portugal, Jan. 2011), 9–12.

# Understanding Child-Defined Gestures and Children's Mental Models for Touchscreen Tabletop Interaction

Karen Rust[1], Meethu Malu[2], Lisa Anthony[3], Leah K. Findlater[1]

[1] College of Information Studies | HCIL
[2] Department of Computer Science | HCIL
University of Maryland, College Park, MD
{k579, meethu, leahkf}@umd.edu

[3] Department of CISE
University of Florida
Gainesville, FL USA 32611
lanthony@cise.ufl.edu

## ABSTRACT

Creating a pre-defined set of touchscreen gestures that caters to all users and age groups is difficult. To inform the design of intuitive and easy to use gestures specifically for children, we adapted a user-defined gesture study by Wobbrock et al. [12] that had been designed for adults. We then compared gestures created on an interactive tabletop by 12 children and 14 adults. Our study indicates that previous touchscreen experience strongly influences the gestures created by both groups; that adults and children create similar gestures; and that the adaptations we made allowed us to successfully elicit user-defined gestures from both children and adults. These findings will aid designers in better supporting touchscreen gestures for children, and provide a basis for further user-defined gesture studies with children.

## Categories and Subject Descriptors

H.5.m. Information interfaces and presentation (*e.g.*, HCI): Miscellaneous.

## General Terms

Design, Experimentation, Human Factors.

## Keywords

Children, interactive tabletop, touchscreens, user-defined gestures.

## 1. INTRODUCTION

Interactive touchscreens have become ubiquitous. In the United States, an estimated eight out of ten children use mobile devices regularly [7]. Larger touchscreens such as interactive tabletops are also being adopted, particularly in educational contexts such as classrooms [11] and museums [6]. However, the vast majority of research on touchscreen gestural interaction has focused on adults, for example, investigating user consistency [2], user preferences [9], and gesture intuitiveness [12]. To date, research on children's touchscreen interaction is limited, despite unique challenges that children encounter both in performing gestures and in having gestures registered and interpreted correctly by these devices [1].

A common method for gaining insight into users' mental models and preferences with respect to gestures is the *user-defined gesture* approach popularized by Wobbrock et al. [12]. In their study, adult participants created one-handed and two-handed gestures for *referents* (actions) on an interactive tabletop (e.g., opening an application, deleting an object). Participants were first

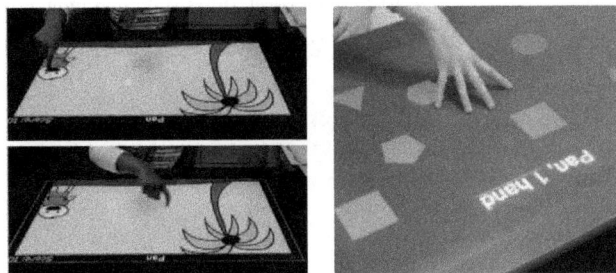

Figure 1: A sample gesture (*pan*) from our study (left) and Wobbrock et al.'s [12] study (right). Our child-centric protocol uses more concrete on-screen representations.

shown an effect (a video clip of a change in the interface) and then asked to create a gesture that would cause that effect. Analyzing these gestures and the creation process, exposed through a think-aloud protocol, can provide insight into gesture mechanics, mental models, and user preferences. The user-defined gestures method yields gestures that are preferred to those created by designers [9]. However, this method has only been employed with children to a limited extent, to study whole-body gestural interaction [5]; touchscreen gestures have not been examined. This gap is important to address because touchscreen interaction studies with adults do not always generalize to children, who have different motor and cognitive capabilities [1].

Even considering other approaches, only a few studies have examined children's touchscreen interaction (e.g., [1,6,8,11]). For example, Anthony et al. [1] identified differences in how children and adults articulated standard gestures on mobile devices (e.g., tapping, tracing). McKnight and Fitton [8] investigated young children's ability to understand touchscreen terminology such as "tap," "press and hold," and "slide," finding that children are more prone to accidental or unintended touches. Hinrichs and Carpendale [6] examined use of a touchscreen tabletop in a museum setting by children and adults, and found that people may use different gestures for the same action depending on age, context, and overall intention. Rick et al. [11] reported design considerations for group use of a tabletop in the classroom, such as equity of participation and use of touch space. In contrast to these studies, we consider a more open-ended gesture elicitation approach focusing on how children *design* new gesture-based interactions, allowing us to infer preferences and characterize assumptions that children bring to touchscreens.

To inform the design of touchscreen gestures for children, we first employed an iterative design process with six participants to adapt Wobbrock et al.'s [12] study protocol to better support children (Figures 1 and 2). We then employed this modified protocol to compare gestures created by 12 children and 14 adults on an interactive tabletop. The contributions of this paper are: (1) a set of changes to the user-defined gesture protocol to accommodate the unique needs of children; (2) a characterization of differences and similarities between children's and adults' gestures; and (3) a comparison of mental models for gestural interaction between adults and children. These findings can be used to design better touchscreen gestural interactions for children and as a basis for further user-defined gesture studies with children.

## 2. ADAPTATION OF USER-DEFINED GESTURE PROTOCOL FOR CHILDREN

Experimental protocols designed for adults do not always apply to children [3,4]. We closely adapted Wobbrock et al.'s [12] original user-defined touchscreen gesture protocol to work with children. Our method is in contrast to Connell et al.'s [5], which included Wizard-of-Oz interaction that responded to children's whole-body gestures. Instead, we retained Wobbrock et al.'s [12] more open-ended approach of not providing feedback.

To adapt the protocol, we first conducted an iterative design session with six children (aged 7 to 11). We divided the children into two groups of three. Each group went through the original protocol on a Microsoft PixelSense tabletop. We noted when participants lost focus, were confused, or made suggestions. The final set of modifications, below, was derived (a) from this design session, (b) from our experience conducting studies with children, and, finally, (c) from two pilot sessions we conducted of the protocol (one adult and one child). The final adaptations were:

**Facilitator.** The original study used automated audio and video to guide participants. To better support child participants, we introduced a facilitator. The facilitator could replay video examples, repeat instructions, and answer questions.

**Referents.** Session length was a concern for child participants in terms of attention and focus; in addition, some referents in the original study were very similar or conceptually complex. We combined, renamed, or cut referents to create a more child-friendly list. We also added three referents to reflect actions that children might do on a touchscreen device—*app switch, make a note* (annotate), and *share* (e.g., by email)—and two collaborative referents to reflect that children often use tabletops in a collaborative context—*give* and *my space* (i.e., delineate physical space). These changes reduced the original set from 27 to 20 referents, including: one *practice* referent (*flip*), 17 *individual* user referents, and the two new *collaborative* referents. The *individual* referents were *app switch, back, bigger, copy, help, make a note, move, next, pan, pick many, pick one, remove, share, smaller, tools, turn,* and *undo*. Examples of renaming referents include *maximize* to *bigger*, and *previous* to *back*. A modified referent description example is changing "*Pan. Pretend you are moving the screen to reveal off screen content.*" to "*The gesture is called pan. You are looking at picture that is too large to fit on the screen. How would you move the picture to see the hidden part?*"

**Effective Abstraction.** The original study used abstract visuals, which children in the iterative design session found confusing. We redesigned them to be more concrete, without being so specific as to lead participants to perform a particular gesture (Figure 1).

**Novelty Effect.** The children were distracted by the novelty of an interactive tabletop and spent several minutes at first playing with it to understand what it could do. To mitigate this novelty effect, we added an initial 5-minute "play" period during which children used a drawing program before moving on to the "real" tasks.

**Gesture Feedback.** The original study did not show any visual feedback while participants gestured. Our child participants found this lack of feedback confusing and were unsure if their gestures

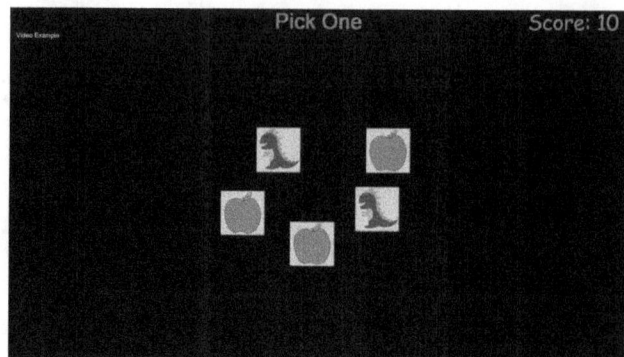

**Figure 2. Screenshot of experiment software showing the *pick one* (select) referent. As a gamification element, the score in the top-right corner increased by 5 points after every referent.**

were registered. We added visual feedback by displaying a green border around the edge of the screen when the user touched it.

**Number of Hands.** The original study prompted users to create both one-handed and two-handed gestures for each referent, but participants strongly preferred one-handed gestures [12]. Therefore, we chose to only prompt participants for one gesture per referent and did not specify how many hands to use.

**Likert Scale.** The original study used 7-point Likert scales to rate each gesture on suitability and ease of use. Such questionnaires can be difficult for children to use [10], so we employed the 5-point Smiley-o-meter scale instead [10].

**Gamification.** Gamification has been shown to be useful for maintaining children's engagement with empirical protocols and does not compromise data integrity [3]. As such, in our study, participants received five points per referent and a prize at the end based on total points (Figure 2).

## 3. METHOD

Following the iterative protocol design process, we conducted a study to compare children's versus adults' gestures on a tabletop.

### 3.1 Participants

Twenty-six participants (12 children and 14 adults) were recruited via email lists and word-of-mouth; none had participated in the iterative design or pilot sessions. Adults (9 females) ranged in age from 19 to 60 ($M = 34$, $SD = 16.0$), while children (4 females) were recruited to be 8 to 11 years old ($M = 9.4$, $SD = 1.2$). This age group was selected because children within this range have been shown to be clearly different than adults in terms of touchscreen use patterns [1]. Touchscreen experience was high in both groups: only two participants in each group did not have access to a touchscreen device at home, and only three adults and two children self-reported as beginner touchscreen users.

### 3.2 Apparatus

We adapted Wobbrock et al.'s [12] custom experiment software, written in C#, for use on a 40" diagonal Microsoft PixelSense tabletop running Windows 7 (screen resolution 1920×1080); see Figure 2. Sessions were recorded with two video cameras: one placed to the side to capture the horizontal plane of the screen and the participant from the waist up, and the second placed above the screen to capture the participant's arms and hands.

### 3.3 Procedure

Following the adaptations described in Section 2, the same procedure was used for adult and child participants. Participants first used a drawing application to overcome novelty and to practice the think-aloud protocol. The facilitator then opened the experiment software and walked the participant through the practice referent, after which the 17 individual referents were presented in random order. For each referent, the facilitator read a brief description, then played a video demonstrating the effect (4 to 11 seconds long). The first frame of the video was then shown again, and the facilitator prompted the participant to think aloud and envision an appropriate gesture that would cause the effect they had seen. The participant then performed their new gesture and rated it on Smiley-o-meter scales [10] for suitability ("The gesture I picked is a good match for the action.") and ease of use ("The gesture I picked is easy to do."). The two collaborative referents, which we do not report on (see Section 3.4), were presented at the end of the session and did not affect earlier tasks.

In terms of gamification, participants received a prize after completing the 17 individual referents based on points earned for completing each referent, and could trade in that prize for a different one if desired after the collaborative referents. The session ended with a survey on the participant's touchscreen experience, administered verbally for children.

## 3.4  Video Analysis

We analyzed 442 gestures (17 per participant); this data excludes the two collaborative gestures, which we observed to be particularly confusing for both age groups. In about 1% of cases (5 gestures), the participant became distracted by the object in the video example or went off-task despite facilitator intervention and protocol explanation. For example, P3 [child, male] focused on the texture of a tile rather than the referent's effect for *undo*. We discarded such data, leaving 437 gestures. The experiment software also logged touches on the screen, but we did not analyze this data because we were unable to accurately separate intended (hand) from unintended (arm, sleeve) touches.

We qualitatively coded the videos and think-aloud comments along five *objective* dimensions (e.g., which hands or fingers were used) and 13 *subjective* dimensions that included gesture type (e.g., tap or swipe) and mental models (e.g., rationale, and whether a menu, widget, or button was referenced). The initial code set was created based on prior work [12] and our analysis of two randomly selected videos (one child and one adult). We then used an iterative process to refine the subjective codes: two independent coders analyzed two more videos and met to discuss and refine the codes before randomly dividing and coding all remaining videos. To assess inter-rater reliability, we randomly selected two of these videos (one child and one adult) to be coded by both researchers with the final code set and calculated Cohen's kappa for each subjective coding dimension. We do not report on the dimensions for which reliability was low (kappa < 0.50); for the remaining eight dimensions, kappa ranged from 0.57 to 1.0 ($M = 0.78$, $SD = 0.18$).

## 4.  RESULTS

Adults and children exhibited similar gesture creation patterns. For frequencies across all gestures, we report percentages out of 236 total gestures for adults and 201 total gestures for children.

## 4.1  Gesture Types

For the majority of gestures, both adults and children employed standard touchscreen gestures (tap, drag, swipe, pinch, rotate), rather than creating entirely new gestures. These standard gestures were used in 96% of all gestures, and the pattern of gesture types

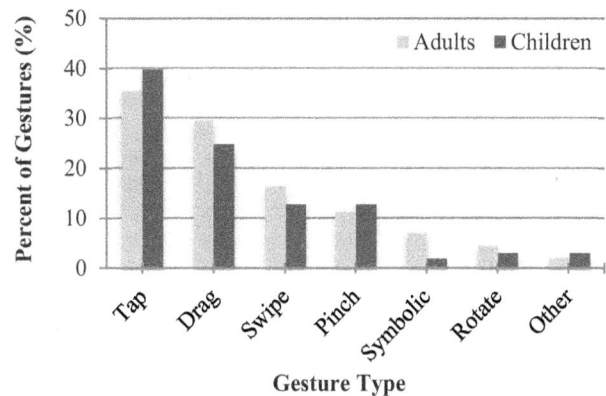

**Figure 3. Types of gestures created by adults and children, showing similar patterns across both groups. Complex gestures could be coded as exhibiting more than one type ($N = 236$ adult gestures and 201 child gestures).**

employed was similar for each participant group (Figure 3). Besides these standard gestures, participants also created symbolic gestures, such as drawing an undo arrow, writing an "X" for remove, and drawing a question mark for help. Ten adults performed a symbolic gesture compared to only four children. This result suggests that gestures for children should include direct physical manipulation rather than being symbolic.

## 4.2  Gesture Mechanics

Each gesture was coded for the number of hands, number of fingers, and individual fingers used. Almost all gestures were performed with one hand: 93% of adult gestures and 92% of child gestures. For these one-handed gestures, children tended to use only one finger more often than adults: 75% of child gestures and 62% of adult gestures (Table 1). For both groups, one-handed gestures with two fingers were much less frequent, accounting for only 15% of adult gestures and 7% of child gestures. Of the adults, 86% (12/14) used two fingers for at least one one-handed gesture, while 75% (9/12) of children did so.

There were differences in individual finger usage across adults and children as well. Adults used their middle finger in 28% of gestures, compared to 18% of child gestures. Though the percentage of gestures using a particular finger was similar for both adult and child gestures, more individual adult participants used the middle, ring, and pinky fingers than child participants did. More adult participants used a wider range of fingers than child participants did. Overall, users performed one-handed gestures using the index or middle fingers the most.

## 4.3  Mental Models

We inferred mental models of touchscreen interaction from think-aloud comments. As mentioned above, the majority of gestures

| Number of Fingers | | | Individual Finger Usage | | |
|---|---|---|---|---|---|
| | Adults | Children | | Adults | Children |
| 1 | 62% | 75% | Index | 94% | 95% |
| 2 | 15% | 7% | Middle | 29% | 18% |
| 3 | 6% | 2% | Ring | 16% | 12% |
| 4 | 3% | 2% | Pinky | 11% | 8% |
| 5 | 6% | 6% | Thumb | 17% | 15% |

**Table 1. Percent of all one-handed adult and child gestures in terms of number of fingers and individual fingers used. Adults were more likely than children to use more than one finger. ($N = 236$ adult and 201 child gestures).**

created were based on standard touchscreen interactions. This reliance, however, was not always evident in the think-aloud comments, perhaps because the mapping from participants' past touchscreen experience to the study tasks was immediate enough not to compel elaboration. Participants verbally referenced a touchscreen device for only 5% of adult gestures and 7% of child gestures. As P20 [adult, male] said, "*It's all kind of going back to what touchscreen things [are] already out there. Because they've [touchscreens] been out for enough now, it's kind of just become the prevalent idea that everything has the same sort of function.*"

We also examined references to WIMP (windows, icons, menus, pointers) interfaces. Note that five referents included a WIMP element in the video example, though not in the static image over which participants gestured (*app switch, share, tools, make a note,* and *help*; the last three are similar to [12]). In total, for 27% of child gestures and 15% of adult gestures the participant mentioned using a WIMP element. While creating a gesture for *copy*, for example, P24 [child, male] said, "*Normally, there's, on my computer at school, when I move my mouse over to that corner, if then, then I pull it out it'll turn the whole screen blue and then when I right-click it it'll normally say 'What do you want to do?' I'll press 'copy,' 'take' then 'make two'.*" The top three referents for which participants mentioned using a WIMP element were *tools* 63% (15/24 instances), *app switch* 58% (15/26 instances), and *help* 52% (13/25 instances); note that two gesture instances for *tools* and one for *help* were excluded due to user confusion.

### 4.4 Ease of Use and Suitability

Participants rated each gesture on a scale from 1 (low) to 5 (high) for suitability and ease of use. For suitability, the average ratings were 4.1 (*SD* = 1.0) and 4.0 (*SD* = 0.9) for children. For ease of use, the average ratings were 4.5 (*SD* = 0.8) for adults and 4.0 (*SD* = 1.0) for children. These ratings also support the main message of this study: that both age groups are similar in their gesture creation patterns and mental models of gestures.

### 5. DISCUSSION

We adapted Wobbrock et al.'s [12] user-defined gesture protocol for use with children, including reducing and renaming referents, introducing a facilitator to guide participants through the protocol, and incorporating gamification elements. In general, these adaptations allowed us to successfully elicit user-defined gestures from both children and adults. One modification for future studies, however, would be to use more of an interview dynamic rather than only think-aloud protocol, especially for children. For example, some children were far less likely to elaborate unprompted than adults, commenting, e.g., "I would do this [gesturing]" (P52 [child, female]), without explaining further.

Many similar findings exist between our study and the Wobbrock et al. [12] study (e.g., references to WIMP interfaces). However, participants in their study were novice touchscreen users, and, since then, touchscreens have become ubiquitous. All participants in our study had touchscreen experience, and the influence of this experience was evident in the gestures they created. This finding suggests that touchscreen interaction is now mature enough that users have internalized certain standardized gestures. Designers should capitalize on these standards wherever possible.

Participants performed standard navigational and manipulative gestures (e.g., tap, swipe) and overwhelmingly used one hand and one finger to complete gestures. These findings show that, despite differences between adults and children, simple one-handed, one-finger gestures are the most frequently created for a variety of

actions. However, there are times when both groups used a one-handed gesture with two-fingers for gesture types such as rotate or pinch. Designers should work to design systems that use simple, direct manipulation gestures using one or two fingers.

Overall, in our study, both adults and children tended to create gestures based on existing touchscreen interactions and created simple gestures that were repurposed for a variety of tasks.

### 6. LIMITATIONS AND FUTURE WORK

This study provides a basis for further user-defined gesture studies with children, but more work remains to be done. One limitation of our study is the focus on one age group (8 to 11 year olds). While this age group is the oldest group still clearly different from adults in terms of touchscreen use [1], future work should include younger children and teenagers to uncover differences between age groups. Another limitation is that participants in both groups had high touchscreen experience. Finally, while interactive tabletops are used in classrooms and public spaces, the results from our study may not reflect interactions on smaller smartphone or tablet devices. For example, screen size may affect direct manipulation gestures, such as resizing an object. Future studies should investigate this potential influence on children's gestures.

### 7. REFERENCES

1. Anthony, L., Brown, Q., Nias, J., Tate, B., and Mohan, S. Interaction and Recognition Challenges in Interpreting Children's Touch and Gesture Input on Mobile Devices. *Proc. ACM ITS'2012*, ACM Press (2012), 225–234.

2. Anthony, L., Vatavu, R.-D., and Wobbrock, J.O. Understanding the Consistency of Users' Pen and Finger Stroke Gesture Articulation. *Proc. GI'2013*, Canadian Information Processing Society (2013), 87–94.

3. Brewer, R., Anthony, L., Brown, Q., Irwin, G., Nias, J., and Tate, B. Using gamification to motivate children to complete empirical studies in lab environments. *Proc. IDC'2013*, ACM Press (2013), 388–391.

4. Brown, Q., Anthony, L., Brewer, R., Irwin, G., Nias, J., and Tate, B. Challenges of Replicating Empirical Studies with Children in HCI. *Proc. RepliCHI'2013*, CEUR Workshop Proceedings (2013), 53–57.

5. Connell, S., Kuo, P.-Y., Liu, L., and Piper, A.M. A Wizard-of-Oz elicitation study examining child-defined gestures with a whole-body interface. *Proc. IDC'2013*, ACM Press (2013), 277–280.

6. Hinrichs, U. and Carpendale, S. Gestures in the wild: studying multi-touch gesture sequences on interactive tabletop exhibits. *Proc. CHI'2011*, ACM Press (2011), 3023–3032.

7. Kang, C. Survey: For young children, mobile devices such as tablets, smart phones now a mainstay. *The Washington Post*, 2013. http://www.washingtonpost.com/7e386f3c-3f1f-11e3-a624-41d661b0bb78_story.html.

8. Mcknight, L. and Fitton, D. Touch-screen Technology for Children: Giving the Right Instructions and Getting the Right Responses. *Proc. IDC'2010*, ACM Press (2010), 238–241.

9. Morris, M.R., Wobbrock, J.O., and Wilson, A.D. Understanding users' preferences for surface gestures. *Proc. GI'2010*, Canadian Information Processing Society (2010), 261–268.

10. Read, J.C. and MacFarlane, S. Using the fun toolkit and other survey methods to gather opinions in child computer interaction. *Proc. IDC'2006*, ACM Press (2006), 81–88.

11. Rick, J., Harris, A., Marshall, P., Fleck, R., Yuill, N., and Rogers, Y. Children designing together on a multi-touch tabletop: An analysis of spatial orientation and user interactions. *Proc. IDC'2009*, ACM Press (2009), 106–114.

12. Wobbrock, J.O., Morris, M.R., and Wilson, A.D. User-defined gestures for surface computing. *Proc. CHI'2009*, ACM Press (2009), 1083–1092.

# Jigsaw Together: A Distributed Collaborative Game for Players with Diverse Skills and Preferences

Dimitris Grammenos, Antonis Chatziantoniou
ICS-FORTH
N. Plastira 100, Vassilika Vouton, Heraklion, Crete
GR-700 13 Greece
gramenos@ics.forth.gr; hatjiant@ics.forth.gr

## ABSTRACT

Presently it is very hard (or even impossible) to allow multiple players with highly diverse characteristics (including age, skills, and preferences) to collaboratively share and play a single jigsaw puzzle. Towards this end, the work presented in this paper aims to expand the capabilities of digital jigsaw puzzles in 3 directions: (a) multi-playability by a large number of players; (b) accessibility by people with hand-motor and visual impairments; and (c) concurrent playability by people with highly diverse characteristics. In this context, we present an electronic puzzle game which supports single player as well as distributed multiplayer sessions by people with diverse characteristics. The paper introduces the background against which the work is based and describes the key design features of the resulting game's user interface and gameplay.

## Categories and Subject Descriptors

H.5.2 [H.5 INFORMATION INTERFACES AND PRESENTATION]: User Interfaces, K.8.0 [PERSONAL COMPUTING]: General - Games

## General Terms

Design, Human Factors

## Keywords

Universal Access, multiplayer games, collaborative interfaces

## 1. INTRODUCTION

Jigsaw puzzles constitute a popular pastime for people of all ages. At a high level, a jigsaw puzzle is a two-dimensional image cut in several smaller pieces. The number and shape of the pieces may vary, directly affecting the perceived game difficulty. The game's goal and mechanics are quite simple. Initially the pieces are randomly arranged. The player has to rotate and move them around trying to reassemble the original image. Today, in addition to the numerous physical jigsaw puzzles available, the game is also offered on most existing digital platforms, ranging from PCs and game consoles, to tablets and mobile phones. A simple search

in iTunes and the Google Play returns several hundreds of results, while there are also a huge number of on-line versions of the game. At first glance, this vast abundance of game instances creates the impression that this is an oversaturated domain with little or no space for innovation and improvement. Nevertheless, a more thorough study reveals that almost all electronic jigsaw puzzles faithfully reproduce the physical and functional characteristics of the original game, without taking real advantage of their digital form (beyond some obvious options, e.g. user selection of the puzzle image and of the shape and number of pieces). Thus, on the one hand, there is little differentiation among them, but, most importantly, there are some fundamental limitations that they all share.

Jigsaw puzzles mainly challenge 3 types of skills:

(a) *Fine motor skills*: To complete a puzzle the muscles of the hand, fingers and thumb must all be used in coordination with the eyes. In digital puzzles, fine motor skills are also required which may differ depending on the input methods used (e.g., mouse, or multitouch screen).

(b) *Cognitive skills*: Problem solving and management, planning, decisions-making, reasoning, short-memory.

(c) *Visual perceptual skills*: Visual spatial relations, visual closure, eye movement, visual memory, visual attention and the ability to transition around a central fixation with peripheral vision.

Depending on its characteristics, a single jigsaw puzzle instance requires a different combination and level of each of those skills and thus eventually appeals to a rather limited group of potential players. For example, most manufacturers recommend[1] that puzzles for children 2-3 years old should have 4-12 pieces, for 3-5 years 12-50 pieces, etc., while adults prefer puzzles with more than 500 pieces. In addition to the required skills, the player's preference regarding the puzzle's image plays an important role, and may considerably vary depending on player profile (e.g., age, gender, culture). Physical puzzle games inherently support collaborative play with virtually any number of participants, while their electronic counterparts have a clear disadvantage in this respect as they are severely limited by the input method used (i.e., mouse or touch), as well as by the size of the available screen. Regarding people with hand-motor impairments, both physical and digital puzzle games maybe hard or impossible to play, while for the blind, physical puzzles may be accessible if tactile information resides on them.

---

[1] http://puzzles.about.com/od/jigsawpuzzles/p/jigsaw_puzzle.htm

From the above, it becomes evident that presently it is very hard (or even impossible) to allow multiple people with highly diverse characteristics (including age, skills, and preferences) to collaboratively share and play a single jigsaw puzzle. Towards this end, the work presented in this paper aims to expand the capabilities of digital jigsaw puzzles in 3 directions: (a) multi-playability by a large number of players; (b) accessibility by people with hand-motor and visual impairments; and (c) concurrent playability by people with highly diverse characteristics.

## 2. BACKGROUND & RELATED WORK

The work presented in this paper builds upon the concepts of Universally Accessible Games [8] and of Parallel Game Universes [5], as on the one hand it aims to provide access to the jigsaw game to individual players with diverse characteristics, while on the other hand to integrate appropriate solutions for allowing them to play the game concurrently (cooperatively and competitively). As long as it concerns making games accessible to gamers with disabilities and other impairments there are various sets of guidelines and advice, as for example the ones provided by gameaccessibilityguidelines.com [4], the "Includification guide to game accessibility by the AbleGamers" Foundation [1] and BBC's "Accessible Games Standard" [2] aiming to ensure that any games used on BBC sites are accessible. Furthermore, Westin et al. [12] provide a comprehensive overview of published research literature between 2005 and 2010 on game accessibility.

A particularly challenging task when creating Universally Accessible Games, relates to supporting multiplayer sessions. To this end, the theory of Parallel Game Universes [5] suggests to allow each player to play in a different "game universe" and then devise ways to project each universe onto the other(s). A "game universe" is an instance of the game after it has been adapted to best suit the requirements and needs of a particular gamer playing under particular conditions. To achieve that, a "transition function" is required in order to translate the events of one universe into the other in a format that is suitable and meaningful in the receptor universe.

There are a few existing games that share some common ground with the presented work, either due to their accessibility characteristics or due to their theme (i.e., puzzle games) and mechanics. For instance, UA-Chess [6] is a chess game supporting concurrent accessibility, even in two player matches (both local and Internet-mediated), for people with diverse disabilities including low vision, blindness, hand-motor impairments and mild memory or cognitive impairments. Most of the methods and techniques used are directly applicable to other types of digital puzzle games. Access Invaders [7] and Terrestrial Invaders [8] are two Space Invaders-like games that also follow the Universally Accessible Games paradigm, integrating several accessibility features that can be switched on and off, both off-line and on-the-fly, offering profile-based adaptation and also instantiating the concept of Parallel Game Universes. More recently, BBC has also embraced the principles of Universally Accessible Games during the development of four web-based games related to its "Something Special" TV programme [9]. The games are designed to be enjoyable and developmentally valuable to very young children (2-6 years old) with profound and multiple special needs, including conditions such as low functioning autism and cerebral palsy.

As long as it concerns puzzle games accessible by people with motor impairments, Judy Lynn Software[2] has developed a puzzle game for iOS that implements scanning and supports switch adapters, in addition to the multitouch interface. The game is modeled after wooden puzzles with cutouts. The user is requested to place the given puzzle pieces to the proper cutouts one at a time. The puzzle pieces can be moved around by using 3 different methods: 1-switch (auto scan), 2-switches (step scanning) and drag and drop (direct selection). There are also a few puzzle games supporting non-visual interaction. For example, TapBeats [11] is a musical rhythm game for Android based on audio cues which also implements a gesture system that utilizes text-to-speech and haptic feedback to allow blind and low-vision users to interact with the game's menu screens using a mobile phone touchscreen. Carvalho et al. [3] have created a multimodal puzzle game for the Android platform supporting an audio mode for blind people. Some similar apps are available for iOS and Android devices (e.g., Kinito Music Puzzle[3]; Musical Puzzle HD[4]; Audio Puzzle[5]).

Finally, in terms of allowing people of different age and skills to work on a puzzle at the same time, an example comes from the physical instantiation of the game where there are so called "family puzzles" (e.g., by Springbok[6]) which include pieces in three different sizes: small for adults, medium for older kids, and extra-large for young children and seniors.

## 3. GAME DESIGN

During the design and development phases of the game formative evaluation sessions were held with representative players with diverse profiles to help shape the user interface and gameplay in terms of accessibility, usability and fun. This section presents the outcomes of this process.

Prior to playing the game, some key attributes can be adjusted to better fit the player's profile, such as the cut-out shapes of the pieces, the minimum distance and variation in the rotation between two matching sides to be considered as connected, whether the pieces are rotated or not, etc.

When the game starts, players can browse a collection of images and select one to play with. Upon selection, they can choose the number of the pieces that the image will break into.

### 3.1 Multi-playability

Jigsaw Together supports distributed collaborative multiplayer sessions, i.e., multiple people trying to complete a single puzzle using multiple (stationary or mobile) computers at the same time (Figure 1). In this case, a player can start a multiplayer session in any one of the available devices and – at any time – additional gamers can join in. Every time a new player joins (or exits) the game, the puzzle pieces are distributed among the available devices. Any number of players (at most as many as the pieces) can play. Single puzzle pieces or even partially completed parts of the puzzle can be transferred from one player's screen to

[2] https://www.judylynn.com/

[3] http://www.deliriumstudios.com/kinitomusicpuzzle

[4] http://www.pianoid.com/mp/

[5] http://audiopuzzle.com/games/

[6] http://www.springbok-puzzles.com/category/400-piece-family-jigsaw-puzzles

another's simply by being tossed out of its bounds. The game ends when the puzzle is completed in any one of the available screens.

**Figure 1. Playing the distributed multiplayer version of the game on 3 different devices (kiosk, table & tablet).**

## 3.2 Accessibility

Jigsaw Together supports multiple input modalities, as it can be played using a multitouch screen, a mouse, mid-air hand gestures (using MS Kinect) and switches in combination with scanning techniques. Furthermore, the game includes a special non-visual mode that is accessible to the blind. Beyond the gameplay elements (i.e., the puzzle pieces), all game menus and options are also accessible using any of the supported modalities.

For people with hand-motor disabilities two different approaches have been developed which employ hierarchical scanning techniques [8]. In both approaches the first step is to select a puzzle piece. This is accomplished by sequentially shifting the focus among the available puzzle pieces either manually (i.e., by pressing a switch) or automatically (i.e., on fixed time intervals) and then pressing another switch when the desired item has the focus. Subsequently, depending on the approach followed a different set of actions is supported:

**Figure 2. Scanning approach A: Free piece movement where the "move upwards" icon has the focus.**

*Approach A: Free piece movement* (Figure 2). A circular menu appears around the selected piece from where the user can pick an action to execute, such moving, rotating and unselecting the piece. In order to minimize visual clutter, all menu items except the one that has the focus are rendered as semi-transparent. If a piece's side is moved near a matching one, the two pieces connect. When two or more pieces are connected they operate as a single piece. In multiplayer mode, additional functions are offered through the circular menu for sending the selected piece to another player.

*Approach B: Direct matching of the sides of two pieces* (Figure 3). This approach frees players from the burden of having to meticulously move the pieces around, as they can directly select a candidate matching side for the selected piece. Subsequently, the focus is passed to the remaining pieces from which the user must select a second matching candidate by repeating the same procedure. If the two selected sides match, then the respective pieces are connected, otherwise, the second piece is automatically deselected. As in Approach A, when two or more pieces are connected together, they are handled as a single piece and only the unconnected sides are iterated. In the multiplayer mode, additional options are offered through the circular menu for sending the selected piece to another player.

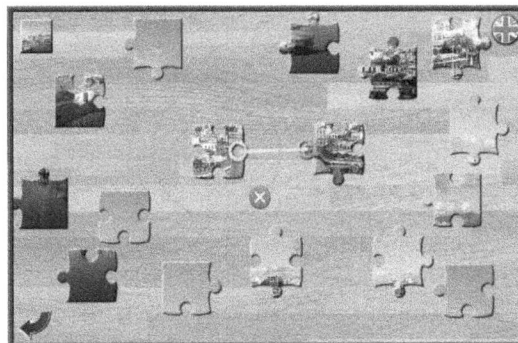

**Figure 3. Scanning approach B:**
**Direct matching between the sides of two pieces.**

For blind players, the game works as a musical puzzle sharing some similarities with the game created by Carvalho [2012] and the various related apps, but also integrating accessibility characteristics for non-visual use, as for example audio feedback and a simplified user interface that employs gestures and taps on a touch screen as in the case of the Slide Rule [10]. The puzzle pieces (song segments or notes) are placed in a random order. At any given time the whole screen represents the currently selected piece. By single tapping, the user can listen to it. By double tapping the user denotes that the selected piece is the one that should be appended in the currently completed part of the puzzle. By swiping right or left the next available piece is selected. Different feedback sounds are associated with success or failure when trying to place a piece in the completed part. The four screen corners work as function buttons. The top left plays the partially completed puzzle, the top right plays the full song or notes sequence. When the puzzle is completed, the song begins to play, and the user can double tap the screen to start over with another puzzle. In multiplayer mode, the user can send the current piece to another player by double tapping the bottom left and right corners. Different difficulty levels are supported. For example, at the easiest level, puzzle pieces are rendered through consecutive notes played by the same instrument. At the next difficulty level non-consecutive notes are used, while at the hardest level the notes are played by different instruments. Additionally, like in other existing audio puzzles games instead of single notes the pieces may contain musical phrases or the segments of a song.

## 3.3 Concurrent playability by people with highly diverse characteristics

Following the concept of Parallel Game Universes [5], Jigsaw Together allows players to fully customize their individual game sessions even when playing in multi-player mode. This effectively means that many people can collaboratively solve a single puzzle while playing using different devices among which the key attributes of the game, as well as the user interface, may considerably vary. For example, two parents, one of whom is blind, can cooperative play with their very young child. In this case, e.g., the child plays a 4-piece puzzle of an animal image using a tablet; the blind parent plays the non-visual music version with 8 pieces on a smart phone; and the other parent is using a laptop to complete a puzzle of a landscape comprising 16 pieces. When a piece is sent from one player to another, then it "conforms" to the characteristics of the corresponding game universe. For example, if the child sends a piece to the non-blind parent, then it is automatically broken in 4 pieces of the landscape (Figure 4). In the opposite situation, when the parent sends one piece to the child, 3 more pieces are automatically attached to it before leaving the screen. In order to be able to cater for such challenging situations, the application is highly parameterized and follows some strict protocols that define the communication and correspondences between different instances of the same puzzle. Of course there are still some limitations that cannot be overcome, e.g., regarding the number of pieces in each "universe" so as to be able to make meaningful translations when a piece is transferred from one to the other.

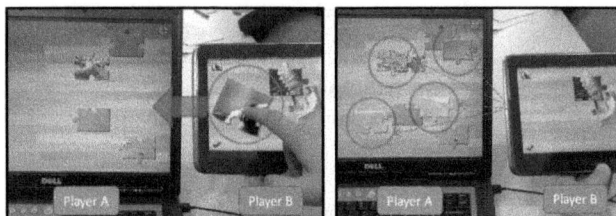

**Figure 4. Sharing the same puzzle using a different image and number of pieces per player. When the selected piece of Player B (left image) is sent to player's A screen, it breaks into 4 pieces that also display a different image (right image).**

## 4. CONCLUSION & FUTURE WORK

This paper presented a multiplayer collaborative game designed to be able to accommodate players with diverse skills and preferences even when playing together. In this context, our fundamental motivation was to create a working prototype demonstrating the fact that through appropriate design considerations and utilizing a modest amount of resources it is possible to create fully functional games that can cater for universally accessible "shared" fun experiences. Such approaches can considerably broaden the scope and target groups of digital games and open up new opportunities for innovation in the field.

Preliminary findings from informal evaluation sessions that were held with diverse representative players during the design and development phases of the game indicate that the suggested approach is valid and that the resulting game is much enjoyed and appreciated. To this end, our next steps include the extensive and formal usability, accessibility and experience evaluation of the single-player mode on multiple setups with people of varying ages with no disabilities, with hand-motor or visual impairments, as well as of the multiplayer version of the game with 2 or more concurrent players with highly diverse profiles.

Additionally, a distributed competitive multiplayer version is being developed, where each player tries to complete the "same[7]" puzzle before all the others.

## 5. ACKNOWLEDGMENTS

This work has been supported by the FORTH-ICS RTD Programme "Ambient Intelligence and Smart Environments".

## 6. REFERENCES

[1] AbleGamers Foundation, 2013. Includification: A practical guide to game accessibility. Retrieved August 12, 2013, from http://www.includification.com/AbleGamers_Includifi cation.pdf

[2] BBC, 2014. Accessible Games Standard v1.0. Retrieved January 10, 2014 from http://www.bbc.co.uk/guidelines/ futuremedia/accessibility/games.shtml

[3] Carvalho, J., Duarte,L., and Carriço, L. 2012. Audio-Based Mobile Puzzle Gaming for Blind People. In *Proceedings of Mobile Accessibility Workshop at MobileHCI 2012*.

[4] gameaccessibilityguidelines.com, 2012. Game accessibility guidelines. Retrieved September 10, 2012, from http://gameaccessibilityguidelines.com/

[5] Grammenos, D. 2014. From Game Accessibility to Universally Accessible Games. In *Fun for All: Translation and Accessibility Practices in Video Games*, Mangiron, C., Orero, P., O'Hagan, M., eds., Peter Lang AG, International Academic Publishers, Bern, Switcherland, 21-44.

[6] Grammenos, D., Savidis, A., and Stephanidis, C. 2005. UA-Chess: A universally accessible board game. In *Proceedings of HCI International 2005*. Mahwah, New Jersey: Lawrence Erlbaum Associates. [CD-ROM].

[7] Grammenos, D., Savidis, A., Georgalis, Y., and Stephanidis, C. 2006. Access Invaders: Developing a universally accessible action game. In *Proceedings of ICCHP 2006*. Springer, Berlin, 388–395.

[8] Grammenos, D., Savidis, A. and Stephanidis, C. 2009. Designing universally accessible games. *Comput.Entertain.*, 7(1), 1-29.

[9] Hamilton, I. 2011. Something Special: Out and About the Users. BBC Internet Blog. Retrieved October 25, 2011, from http://www.bbc.co.uk/blogs/bbcinternet/2011/10/something_ special_makaton_out_about_universal.html

[10] Kane, S., K. Bigham, J., P. and Wobbrock, J. O. 2008. Slide rule: making mobile touch screens accessible to blind people using multi-touch interaction techniques. In *Proceedings of ASSETS '08*. ACM, New York, NY, USA, 73-80.

[11] Kim, J., Ricaurte, J. 2011. TapBeats: Accessible and Mobile Casual Gaming. In *Proceedings of ASSETS '11*. ACM, New York, NY, USA, 285-286.

[12] Westin, T., Bierre, K., Gramenos, D., and Hinn, M. 2011. Advances in game accessibility from 2005 to 2010. *In Proceedings of UAHCI '11*. Springer-Verlag, Berlin, Heidelberg, 400-409.

---

[7] Quotes are used since e.g., the "same" puzzle for a 3-year and a 20-year old player may have 4 and 32 pieces respectively.

# ChiroBot: Modular-Robotic Manipulation via Spatial Hand Gestures

Jasjeet Singh Seehra
C – Design Lab
Purdue University
jseehra@purdue.edu

Ansh Verma
C – Design Lab
Purdue University
verma25@purdue.edu

Karthik Ramani
C – Design Lab
Purdue University
ramani@purdue.edu

## ABSTRACT

We introduce ChiroBot, a cyber-physical construction kit that allows users to create custom robots out of craft material, easily assemble the robots using joint modules and control them using hand gestures. These hand-crafted robots are assembled using our modules packaged with actuator, wireless communication and controller electronics. These modules eliminate the need for expertise in electronics and enable a plug and play system that directly encourages users to explore by quick prototyping. We designed a glove embedded with sensors to enable the user to control the robots using hand gestures. We present different usage scenarios to demonstrate the system's versatility such as vehicular robot, humanoid puppet, robotic arm, and other combinations. This paper describes the ChiroBot system, interaction methods, few sample creations, and proposes possible "play value".

## Categories and Subject Descriptors:

H.5.2 [**Information Interfaces and Presentation**]: User Interfaces—Input devices and strategies, interaction styles; K.3.1 [**Computers and Education**]: Computers Uses in Education

## General Terms

Design, Experimentation, Human Factors

## Keywords

Modular robot, gestural interface, Play-Value, Constructionism

## 1. INTRODUCTION

Handicraft has been a way to demonstrate one's skills, knowledge, thoughts, experiences, perceptions and emotions [14]. The process of building and constructing functional prototypes has been shown to actively engage users particularly when they see their creation as an extension of their self-concept. Studies show that people relate to self-constructed robots as emotional and intellectual companions [4]. Present day technology has the potential to enable the user to combine craft and electronics to provide new affordances for creative expression. Animation of such user constructed robots can be made intuitive with the help of gestures as *"Gestures are integrated on actionable, cognitive and ultimately biological levels" (pg. 3)* [12].

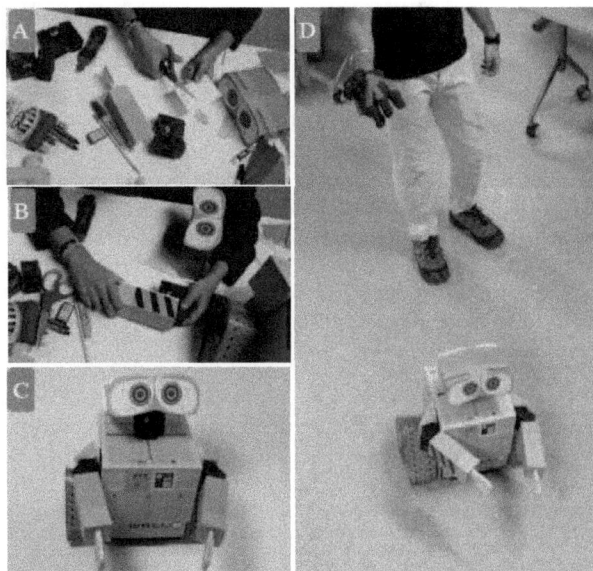

Figure 1. ChiroBot System (A) Using craft material to make robot (B) Assembly of wireless modules with craft using Velcro (C) Final robot (D) Playing with robot using hand gestures

Amalgamation of craft and technology normally require expertise in motor control, packaging, communication, wiring and programming. A simple system that takes away these complexities can allow to boost play value. To this end, we introduce ChiroBot (Chironomia + Robotics) to explore the intersections of three important trends: (1) expression of user's creativity through handicraft, (2) encapsulating the technology into modules, and (3) hand gesture as a controlling mechanism to interact with them. These robots can be crafted using materials like cardboard and foam core coupled with our designed wireless modules which provides more affordances for handicraft design. A tablet application helps the user to configure the robot they built. The robot-system is then controlled using a glove based device using hand gestures. The glove is integrated with flex sensors and inertial sensors that read signals to understand the pose of the hand. This gestural affordance engages the user by giving them an opportunity to control their play-things in a natural manner.

## 2. RELATED WORK

ChiroBot draws its inspiration from a multitude of fields, namely tangible interfaces, customized personal robots, puppetry and gestural interaction. Here we mention some of the influential work in these fields that motivated the ChiroBot system.

Customized robots were built using craft and lego parts and programmed via a graphical programming to create artistic robots [1]. Building robots using pre-defined shapes has been widely commercialized via Lego Mindstorms [6] and EZ-Robot[1]. Techniques have been developed to animate constructive systems and plush toys, using kinetic memory - the ability to record and playback physical motion [2, 3]. The systems in these kits are generally designed to make objects with fewer (1 – 4) motor actuated joints. The majority of these prior works have a set of predefined physical shapes and ways to assemble them that restrict design freedom. Handicraft objects on the other hand provide more freedom to explore imagination.

The control techniques in the above-mentioned kits generally uses either a graphical programming system or a record and playback technique. Some other techniques to control mobile robots have also been developed using captured gestures [11]. Capturing hand gesture using camera or sensors has now become a popular method to interact and control different virtual and tangible objects [5]. Dipietro [7] provided a comprehensive survey of the various Glove-Based Systems. Many different designs of glove based input devices have been explained, leveraging the anatomy of the hand. Some are discrete to the finger whereas others are upper limb garment prototypes. Various technologies have been used to implement the prototypes – Magnetic, Ultrasonic, Optical and Inertial. Other commercial products are also introduced in the market that use a glove-based input device e.g. Peregrine game glove and Mechdyne's Pinch glove [7].

## 3. ChiroBot

The design goals for ChiroBot was to convert art forms created using cardboard/craft materials into interactive robots. We attempt to take away the technical complexity and allow expansion of design, construction and creativity. The system was thus designed based on the following design goals:

DG1. *Versatile and easy connection technique:* The system should allow the user to easily attach craft material.

DG2. *Easy to use:* The system should be simple enough to be used by people of all ages specially children.

DG3. *Safe and robust:* As the system is to be used by children, the device should be safe and work reliably.

DG4. *Adequate & smooth movement:* The system should be able to recreate most motions (both fixed angle and continuous motion) smoothly to provide an enjoyable experience.

DG5. *Scalable:* In the spirit of a modular design, every individual component should be physically and computationally complete and extensible.

DG6. *Expressive*: Encourage exploration of a topic without prescribing "right" and "wrong" activities.

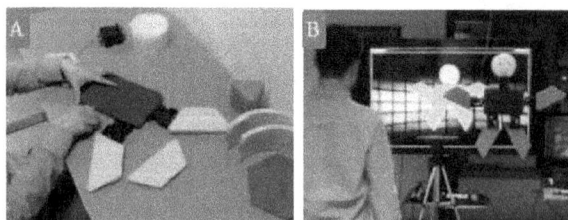

**Figure 2. Initial Prototype (A) Assembly of active and passive parts (B) Control of robot with body gestures using Kinect**

## 3.1 Early Design Phase

To achieve the goals stated earlier, we developed an initial prototype comprised of a set of actuators and basic shapes such as triangle, rectangle, trapezoid and circle. This initial prototype was controlled using body and hand gestures detected from a Kinect or Leap motion camera (Figure 2). Based on a pilot study performed with the system and after talking to different puppeteers who actively conduct workshops for kids, we found that users preferred a system that could easily be attached to pre-existing familiar material. Further, the users also showed strong inclination towards untethered systems.

We thus redesigned the system to have independent wireless modules whose position and configuration could be allotted once by the user using a mobile / tablet application. To make the control of the system mobile and gesture controlled a flex sensor and IMU (Inertial Measurement Unit) based glove was developed. To explore the versatility of the construction, we provide the user with a set of 9 such independent modules as a set.

## 3.2 Module Design

The joints are modules which get easily attached to the craft material using Velcro (DG1) as it is a widely popular temporary fastener among artisans and puppeteers. These modules are currently made of 3D printed material. To obtain a high torque and smooth motion Herkulex DRS-101[2] motors are used. The motor parameters are adjusted to obtain a smooth and non-jerky motion (DG4). These modules contain an XBee[3] module for wireless communication and an Arduino nano[4] (Figure 3).

The motor, wires and electronics are enclosed in a shell like casing to make the device safe for use for kids (DG2, DG3). To

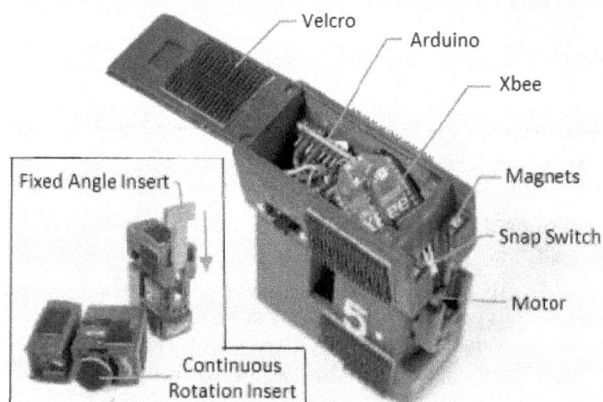

**Figure 3. Electronics in the Joints and Inserts used for different types of motion**

**Table 1. LED Indication**

| State | Red LED | Green LED | State | Red LED | Green LED |
|---|---|---|---|---|---|
| Active Motion | ● | ● | Motor Error | ● | ● |
| Waiting to start | ● | ●● | Wrong Insert | ●● | ● |

*Note: 2 LEDs in a cell indicate blinking*

[2] http://www.dongburobot.com/jsp/cms/view.jsp?code=100788
[3] http://www.digi.com/xbee
[4] http://arduino.cc/en/Main/arduinoBoardNano

[1] http://www.ez-robot.com/

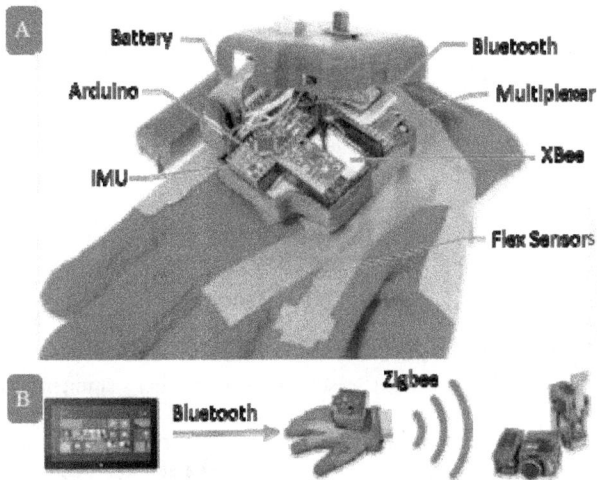

**Figure 4. (A) Electronics in the Glove Controller (B) Communication Protocol**

allow the device to have both angular motion and continuous rotation (basic forms of one degree of freedom electric joints), an insert is used to lock the upper and lower halves of the module. These inserts are held in place with the help of magnets. A snap switch is used to prevent damage to the module in case the fixed angle insert is in place but the joint is being used for continuous rotation. Two LED lights are used to provide the user with the visual feedback of the state of the device (Table 1). Each module is powered using a standard 9V battery.

## 3.3 Controller Design

In order for the interface to be as natural as possible, we leverage the dexterity of the user by developing a glove-based controller. There are seven flex sensors, which were multiplexed by a 16-channel CD74HC4067 MUX breakout board. These sensors are synergistically coupled with an IMU device to read the analog values which are used to capture the hand pose of the user. The flex sensors are placed on the thumb (Interphalangeal, Metacarpophalangeal joints) index and middle fingers (Proximal Interphalangeal and Metacarpophalangeal joints) due to the greater dexterity of these fingers [13]. A sensor is also placed on the pinky finger for differentiating normal control gestures from global gestures. An LED based visual feedback system is incorporated to make the user aware of the state of the IMU and controller (Figure 4A). The communication between the tablet application and the controller takes place via Bluetooth as it is compatible with tablets. XBee (Zigbee communication protocol) is used to create a Personalized Area Network for communicating between the controller and the modules. (Figure 4B).

## 4. INTERACTIONS

We created a sample of popular objects to explore the versatility of our system. With the help of our developed glove controller, these objects are being controlled by the means of hand gestures. The gestures can be classified as global and class-specific.

Global gestures (Figure 5A) are valid irrespective of the class of object selected by the user. The global gestures are:

*Shake:* This gesture is used to start the system. After shaking the hand, user is expected to keep their hand flat for 2 seconds so that the system starts from the origin position and the user has more control over it.

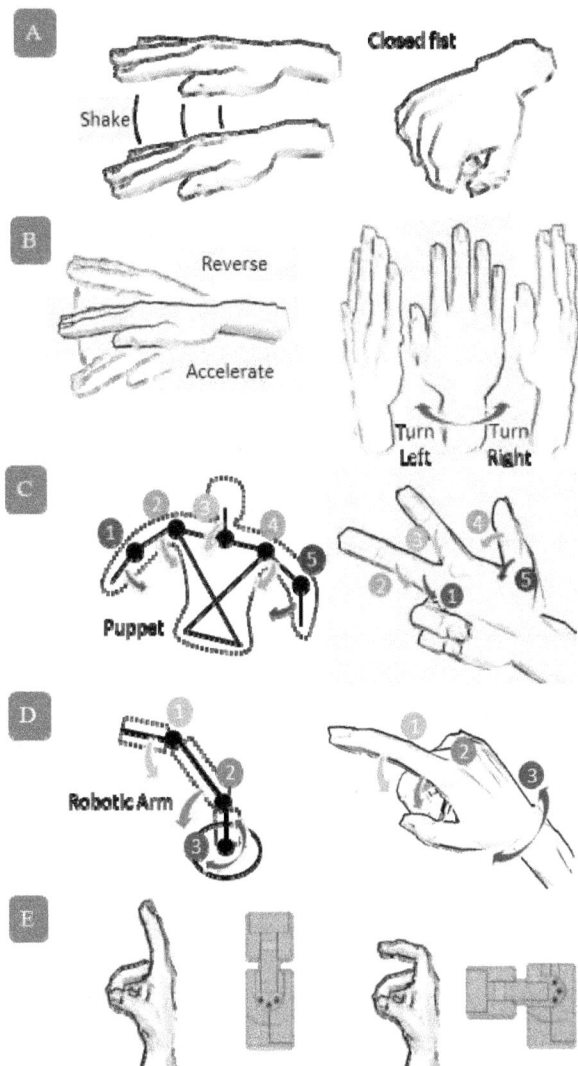

**Figure 5. Control Gestures for Chirobot: (A) Global gestures (B) Gestures for controlling Vehicular Robot (C) Gestures for manipulating Puppets (D) Gestures for Robotic Arm (E) Fixed angle rotation of module mapped to PIP joint of index finger**

*Closed fist:* This gesture is used for an emergency stop. Whenever this gesture is performed in any orientation of the hand, the system comes to a standstill. The shake gesture is then required to restart the system.

The specific control of each class of robots is divided into the relaxed hand state where the object is in rest and active hand state where the object performs the motion based on the mapping (Figure 5E). These specific mapping is displayed to the user on the tablet interface. Some of the classes of robots created by us are:

*Vehicular Robots:* These types of robots consist of 2, 3 and 4 wheeled robots. The speed is mapped based on the principle of a joystick where the speed is proportional to the angular displacement of the hand from the relaxed (flat) position (Figure 5B).

*Puppet Shaped Robots:* The user has the freedom to control either the top or bottom of the puppet. For controlling this class, the person makes use of the thumb, index, middle finger and their hand orientation. This mapping is similar to one of the common hand mapping used for controlling hand puppets [9] (Figure 5C).

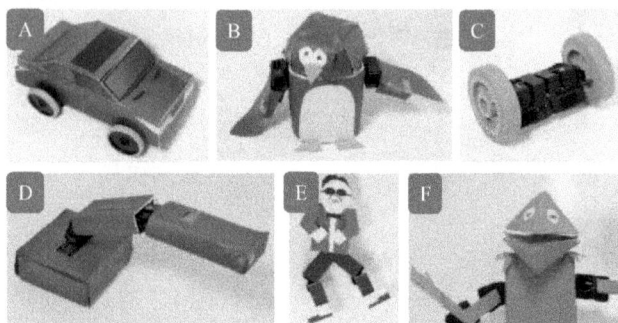

**Figure 6. Robot Creations (A) Car (B) Penguin (C) 2 Wheel Car (D) Robot Arm (E) Psy – Gangam Style (F) Kermit**

*Robotic Arm:* As index finger is the most decoupled from the rest of the hand, the robot arm is controlled using the index finger and hand orientation of the hand [13] (Figure 5D).

*Other Objects:* Along with these three classes, the user has the freedom to create combinations of these classes (DG5, DG6) (Figure 6).

To understand the class of the robot and joint mapping we use a tablet application. This is a simple interface where the user selects the class of the object. This operation has to be done only once at the beginning after the user constructs their object. The interface is built using Unity3D[5] game engine and can be installed on any tablet or mobile device. Seven sample class of objects have been created in this interface which is a combination of the above mentioned families.

Note that, (1) construction can be done using everyday objects, (2) the user has the freedom of both continuous and fixed rotation with the joints created, and (3) each robot family can be extended to create a multitude of robots. Thus, the possibility of objects that can be created and controlled using this system is practically limitless.

## 5. IMPLICATION

*Play Value:* Our system provides aspects like fantasy, challenge and construction to the user [10]. We predict that our system provides active involvement, aspects of free play, physically and mentally active and a socially associative involvement.

*Constructionism and robotics in education:* Our system enables children to learn important rudimentary engineering skills through the process of creation. Robotic technologies make it possible for children to practice and learn many necessary skills such as collaboration, cognitive skills, self-confidence, perception and spatial understanding [5], and our system supports this ideology.

*Cognitive Load:* In a heavy menu driven application; the user develops a 'split attention effect [8]: dividing their attention between the task and the control mechanism. By leveraging proprioception of the hardware coupled with a visual feedback (LED display), we hypothesize that the user will be more immersed in the task rather than dividing a greater attention for the control mechanism.

*Potential Improvement and Future Work:* Because of the size of the modules, the overall size of the robots tends to be bulky. In a more customized implementation, we could fabricate components with a smaller footprint and integrate them into a more power efficient system with a smaller form factor. We are also working on controlling multiple creations together using a single controller. We intend to determine the usability of this framework by conducting a user study.

---

⁵ https://unity3d.com

## 6. CONCLUSION

We present the ChiroBot, a system that enables the user to craft functional electromechanical prototypes and control them using hand gestures. The demonstrated system, we believe, is an instance of a more general framework that will allow users to creatively build and explore electromechanical systems without the need for expertise in underlying complex electronics. Our immediate goal is to evaluate the performance of our system in terms of responsiveness and intuitiveness of gestural control. Our broad overarching intent is to investigate and understand how our framework can facilitate creative thinking in an educational setting.

## 7. ACKNOWLEDGMENTS

We would like to thank Christina Cantrill for her comments on puppetry and our fellow C-Design lab members for their critiques and support, especially Ke Huo and Paul Jafvert. We would also like to acknowledge support from the Donald W. Feddersen Professorship, and in part by the National Science Foundation CPS grant 1329979 and CMMI grant 1235232.

## 8. REFERENCES

[1] Rusk, Natalie, et al. "New pathways into robotics: Strategies for broadening participation." Journal of Science Education and Technology 17.1 (2008): 59-69.

[2] Sugiura, Yuta, et al. "PINOKY: a ring that animates your plush toys." Proceedings of the SIGCHI Conference on Human Factors in Computing Systems. ACM, 2012.

[3] Raffle, Hayes Solos, Amanda J. Parkes, and Hiroshi Ishii. "Topobo: a constructive assembly system with kinetic memory." Proceedings of the SIGCHI conference on Human factors in computing systems. ACM, 2004.

[4] Groom, Victoria, et al. "I am my robot: The impact of robot-building and robot form on operators." Human-Robot Interaction (HRI), 2009 4th ACM/IEEE International Conference on. IEEE, 2009.

[5] Alimisis, Dimitris, and Chronis Kynigos. "Constructionism and Robotics in education." Teacher Education on Robotic-Enhanced Constructivist Pedagogical Methods (2009): 11-26.

[6] Shaer, Orit, and Eva Hornecker. "Tangible user interfaces: past, present, and future directions." Foundations and Trends in Human-Computer Interaction 3.1–2 (2010): 1-137.

[7] Dipietro, Laura, Angelo M. Sabatini, and Paolo Dario. "A survey of glove-based systems and their applications." Systems, Man, and Cybernetics, Part C: Applications and Reviews, IEEE Transactions on 38.4 (2008): 461-482.

[8] Hollender, Nina, et al. "Integrating cognitive load theory and concepts of human–computer interaction." Computers in Human Behavior 26.6 (2010): 1278-1288.

[9] Engler, Larry, and Carol Fijan. Making puppets come alive: how to learn and teach hand puppetry. Courier Dover Publications, 2012.

[10] Kudrowitz, Barry M., and David R. Wallace. "The play pyramid: A play classification and ideation tool for toy design." International Journal of Arts and Technology 3.1 (2010): 36-56.

[11] Iba, Soshi, et al. "An architecture for gesture-based control of mobile robots." Intelligent Robots and Systems, 1999. IROS'99. Proceedings. 1999 IEEE/RSJ International Conference on. Vol. 2. IEEE, 1999.

[12] McNeill, David. *Gesture and thought*. University of Chicago Press, 2008

[13] Ingram, James N., et al. "The statistics of natural hand movements." Experimental brain research 188.2 (2008): 223-236

[14] Pöllänen, Sinikka Hannele. "Beyond craft and art: a pedagogical model for craft as self-expression." International Journal of Education through Art 7.2 (2011): 111-125

# Affective Communication Aid using Wearable Devices based on Biosignals

Yuji Takano
University of Tsukuba
1-1-1 Tennodai
Tsukuba, Japan
yuji@ai.iit.tsukuba.ac.jp

Kenji Suzuki
University of Tsukuba/JST
1-1-1 Tennodai
Tsukuba, Japan
kenji@ieee.org

## ABSTRACT

We propose a novel wearable interface for sharing facial expressions between children with autism spectrum disorders (ASD) and their parents, therapists, and caregivers. The developed interface is capable of recognizing facial expressions based on physiological signal patterns taken from facial bioelectrical signals and displaying the results in real time. The physiological signals are measured from the forehead and both sides of the head. We verified that the proposed classification method is robust against facial movements, blinking, and the head posture. This compact interface can support the perception of facial expressions between children with ASD and others to help improve their communication.

## Categories and Subject Descriptors

I.5.5 [**Implementation**]: Interactive systems; K.4.2 [**Social Issues**]: Assistive technologies for persons with disabilities

## General Terms

Measurement

## Keywords

Facial expression, Smile sharing, Autism Spectrum Disorder

## 1. INTRODUCTION

In this paper, we propose a novel interaction method for sharing children's facial expressions with their parents in order to facilitate communication. In human communication, facial expressions carry some of the most important non-verbal information. Facial expressions include psychological information, such as emotions, which are very important aspects of communication. People can read a person's thoughts simply by observing their expression. Psychological studies have found that facial expressions can project emotions such as disgust, sadness, happiness, fear, anger, and surprise [2]. Expressing these emotions is a universal communication skill common to all humankind and does not much depend on culture. Understanding facial expressions correctly is very important for communication with other people. Daily communication between parents and children is very important to building their relationship and has a key role in children's mental and social development. However, there are some cases where it is difficult for parents or caregivers to consistently recognize their children's facial expressions. For example, children with autism spectrum disorders (ASD) have difficulties with communicating and socially interacting through facial expressions, even with their parents. Autism comprises a wide range of neurodevelopmental disorders, and its intensity differs greatly in individuals. Therefore, setting a clear boundary between healthy and autistic people is difficult, and the mechanisms of autism have not yet been clarified. A typical example of the communication difficulty in the case of autism includes the lack of facial expressions and eye contact [5, 9]. Facial expressions play an important role in communication with others, and we want to know when and how much their facial expression changes based on events in their daily lives. Previously, we reported on the relationship between smiles and positive social behavior [4]. The smiles of children with ASD can be quantitatively measured and analyzed by using a wearable device [6]. There are many situations where reading and understanding a child's facial expressions are desirable.

Various classification methods of facial expressions have been proposed based on different features. The facial action coding system (FACS) [3] describes facial expressions based on physical and anatomical criteria, and many researchers have embraced FACS to classify facial expressions [8]. There are also many approaches to capturing facial expressions. One method is to extract physical variations in facial features from video by means of image processing. This is a non-contact method that is the most commonly used to recognize facial expressions; it is also easy to use, with little effort needed to install the equipment. However, it has the disadvantage of spatial limitations as it depends on the camera position and field of view, and its accuracy is affected by the head posture, so the target user has to face the camera constantly. For use in actual situations outside a controlled environment, there is little possibility of the subject staying in the same position constantly, especially for children who are moving and playing around. Thus, using image processing is difficult. Another possible approach is to use motion-capture technology to extract the three-dimensional shape of the face from the markers' coordinates and measure the physical features more properly. However, placing the

*IDC'14*, June 17–20, 2014, Aarhus, Denmark.
Copyright 2014 ACM 978-1-4503-2272-0/14/06 ...$15.00.
http://dx.doi.org/10.1145/2593968.2610455.

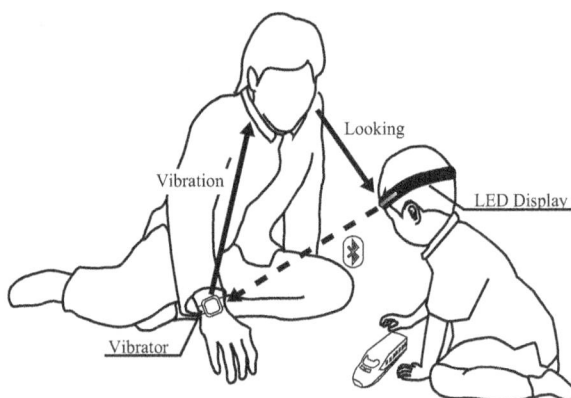

Figure 1: Smile sharing: proposed interaction paradigm

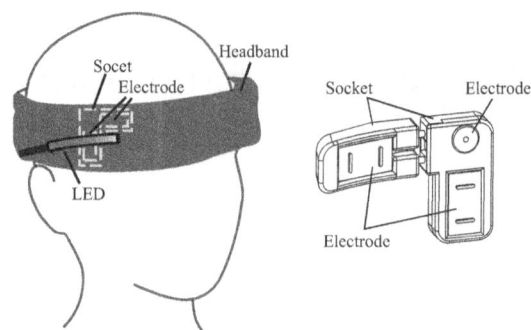

Figure 2: Overview of head-mounted interface

markers requires preparation, which makes this approach laborious, and the markers can be easily occluded. Thus, the development of a method for capturing facial expressions that is easy to use and does not depend on spatial orientation is still a difficult challenge. We have been developing a tool to detect the facial expressions of a person who has difficulty with expressing their intent in an accurate and continuous manner through the use of a wearable device. This allows users to not only capture the facial expression but also share them with others, even if the face is not always observable by sensors installed in the environment, such as cameras or depth sensors. In this paper, we propose the concept of smile sharing, where a wearable device—namely, an affective communication aid—is used that meets the above criteria to communicate facial expressions. We evaluated the device to verify its performance through several case studies.

## 2. METHODOLOGY

The proposed system provides a novel method of interaction, particularly between children and their parents, that considers use in daily life. Figure 1 shows a conceptual diagram of the proposed interaction frame. We first describe the method for capturing and classifying the facial expressions independent of spatial orientation and then the sharing of the facial expressions.

### 2.1 Wearable Interface

Our proposed wearable interface can capture facial expressions independent of the spatial orientation. To realize this system, we use surface electromyography (sEMG) on the forefront and sides of the face. sEMG can be captured by using small electrodes to measure the bioelectrical signals emitted from muscles that are activated to generate facial expressions. Conventionally, the electrodes must be accurately pasted on the skin on top of facial muscles, including the orbicular muscles of the mouth and eyes, for sEMG measurement of the face. However, pasting electrodes on the skin has some disadvantages: The process takes a long time, and the electrodes are prone to interference from facial movements. A possible approach to overcoming these obstacles is measuring sEMG on the sides of face, i.e., distal EMG [6]. We have previously shown that distal electrode locations on areas of low facial mobility have a strong amplitude and are correlated to signals captured in the traditional

positions on top of facial muscles. In this study, we measured sEMG on the sides of the head and forehead to reduce inhibition against physical variations of the face and developed an easy-to-wear interface. We used patterns of acquired sEMG signals to classify the facial expressions. By regarding facial expressions as specific patterns of activity by several facial muscles, the interface can classify them without needing to identify individual muscle activity. A support vector machine (SVM) was used for pattern classification and to differentiate smiles from other facial expressions.

### 2.2 Smile Sharing

We propose a method for sharing facial expressions so that a child's ambiguous or hidden expressions can be perceived in real time. In the current implementation, we only classify the child's smile and communicate it to their parents through various modalities. A smile is a facial expression that represents happiness [1], and the perception of smiling facilitates communication between children and their parents. Specifically, perceiving a child's smile helps in understanding what makes the child happy. By knowing what a child is interested in, the parents can communicate with him or her more intensely and feel more encouraged in their understanding. For smile sharing, we used both light-emitting and vibration devices. Using a light-emitting device helps the parents perceive a child's smile even if the child turns away his or her face. The parents can also perceive the child's smile by using a wrist-mounted vibration device even if they are not relatively close, which can happen when playing. These methods are also viable for autistic children and their parents when the parents cannot look at their child's face directly.

## 3. SYSTEM CONFIGURATION

The system consists of an interface unit and signal processing unit. The interface unit measures signals and outputs the classification results. The signal processing unit classifies facial expressions based on the measured sEMG signals and sends the result to the interface unit via Bluetooth wireless communication.

### 3.1 Interface unit

We developed two different wearable interfaces: head-mounted and wrist-mounted devices. Figure 2 shows an overview of the head-mounted interface. The wrist-mounted interface is a simple vibration device that simply vibrates when the smile is detected by the head-mounted interface.

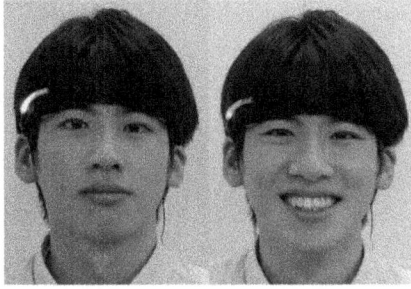

Figure 3: Appearances of LED interface

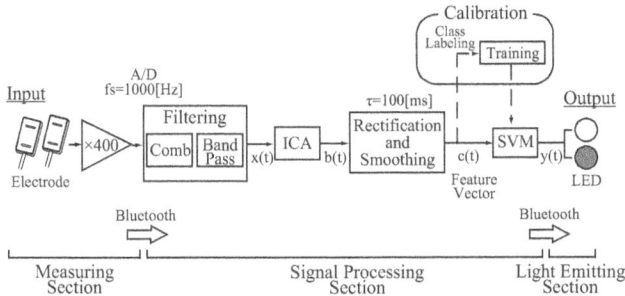

Figure 4: Overview of facial recognition by using head-mounted interface

The head-mounted interface is used both to acquire facial sEMG and to display the resulting facial expression classification. It comprises dry electrodes and an LED embedded in a headband. sEMG is acquired by the interface and sent to the signal processing unit through Bluetooth wireless communication. We decided to use dry electrodes in the interface, although they are prone to noise contamination in the case of unstable contact with the skin, because they are much easier to apply on the skin and enable fast measurement of sEMG with minimal preparation time. The headband is made of elastic material, and the position of the electrodes inside the headband is adjustable. Therefore, the interface can manage different head sizes and shapes, and it holds the dry electrodes steady in place to provide better stability. Figure 3 shows the appearance of the LED, and the LED colors of the interface are white and red. The LED emits a red light if the wearer is smiling and a white light for any other facial expression. The LED is fitted in a small tube as shown in Figure 3 to make it easily noticeable by others.

The wrist-mounted interface comprises a vibration motor and presents the facial expression of the headband wearer through vibration. This interface vibrates if the person wearing the head-mounted interface is smiling. By using this interface, parents can perceive their child's smile even if they cannot look at his or her face directly. In particular, the wrist-mounted interface can help the parents of autistic children perceive their child's smile.

## 3.2 Signal processing unit

The signal processing unit handles digital filtering and pattern recognition processes. The sEMG signals acquired from the interface unit are pre-processed and then classified

by the SVM based on their patterns. Figure 4 shows an overview of the signal processing. The sEMG signals are acquired every 1 ms, and the facial recognition is performed within a certain time window ($\tau = 150$ ms). sEMG signals vary depending on individual differences and electrode position. The system first needs to be calibrated for each user by recording some facial expressions in advance and learning the wearer's signal pattern and intensity. However, it is difficult for children with ASD to participate in this calibration session. In such cases, the system user simply gives the period of smiling time as a reference, which is used as the basis for smile recognition.

## 4. EXPERIMENT

We conducted two experiments to evaluate the performance of the proposed system. In this section, we present the classification accuracy and robustness against head motion of the system.

## 4.1 Evaluation of classification accuracy

In order to evaluate the classification accuracy of the proposed system, we compared it to the human cognitive ability to recognize smiling in an experimental setting. We recorded videos of three people (persons A–C); each alternately smiled and had a neutral expression for two or three times over about 20 s while wearing the headband interface. Nine subjects (eight male, one female) in their twenties and thirties were recruited for the experiment. Informed consent was obtained from the participants in advance. Videos of the smiling/neutral faces (A–C) were shown to the subjects, and they were asked to mark the smile intervals by clicking a button to indicate the start and stop of smiles. We covered the LED in the videos to avoid influencing the subject's judgment. We calculated the maximum, minimum, and median values of precision and recall based on the classifications by the subjects and proposed system. Figure 5 shows the results.

As shown in the figure, the precision of each subject was above 0.95, but the recall varied among subjects depending on who created the facial expressions. The differences in recall may have been due to the different facial features, some of which are more difficult to recognize than others. This made it more difficult to set a threshold for smiling (as for subject B), which lowered the recall. However, in terms of classification accuracy, the results were positive because the precision average was sufficient for potential applications. We also calculated the intra-class correlation coefficient to evaluate the degree of coincidence between the classification by the interface and the judgment of the subjects. The average intra-class correlation coefficient was more than 0.936, which is also sufficient.

## 4.2 Evaluation of robustness

We then conducted an experiment to investigate the robustness of the system against head motion artifacts. In this experiment, we investigated whether the system is capable of classifying facial expressions when there are disturbances such as head motions. The classification accuracy against head nodding (forward and back head movement), head tilting (left and right head tilting), head shaking (right and left rotation), and blinking was checked to evaluate the robustness of the system. The three motions we investigated (nod, tilt, and shake) correspond to all possible motions

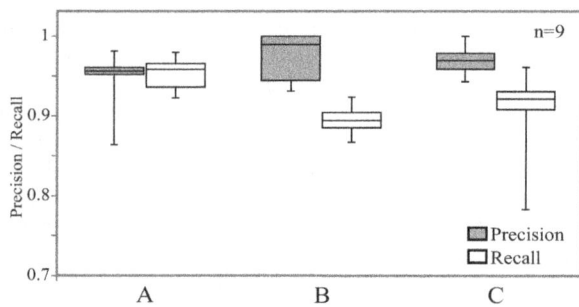

**Figure 5: Maximum, minimum, and median values of precision and recall**

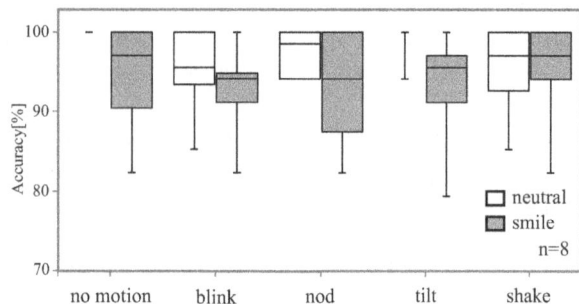

**Figure 6: Maximum, minimum, and median values of robustness**

(roll, pitch, and yaw); therefore, a positive result means that the system is likely to be robust against any combination of head motions. We asked the eight subjects to perform this experiment while wearing the headband. Each subject performed each motion for about 5 s while smiling or having a neutral face. *Blink* represents 10 blinks, and *Nod* and *Tile* were done twice each. *Shake* represents random head shaking along the yaw axis. Figure 6 shows the maximum, minimum, and median values of the classification accuracy for each motion in the experiment. The results showed that the system classified neutral expression with no motion with a probability of 100%. The system was able to classify the neutral expression of most subjects with an accuracy of more than 95% even when there were some disturbances. In the case of smiles, there were some cases where the smile was occasionally not detected properly. In the most prominent case, subjects reported that it was difficult to smile and blink at the same time, which probably contributed to the classification accuracy for blinking being lower than others. However, the interface was capable of classifying smiles by the majority of the subjects with an accuracy of more than 90%.

## 5. DISCUSSION AND CONCLUSIONS

In this study, we considered the scenario of daily communication between children and their parents and focused on facial expressions, which are non-verbal information that is important to facilitating communication. We proposed wearable interfaces to classify facial expressions based on facial muscle activities and share them through light and vibration. We evaluated the classification accuracy and robustness of the system through experiments and verified that

the acquired signals from the sides of the head and forehead can be used for facial expression classification. Through several experiments, we verified the classification accuracy of the developed system. The results demonstrated that the interface can be used in real environments with some disturbances to classify facial expressions with high accuracy and to present smiles in real-time. Further investigation will include the implementation of adaptive filtering to remove motion artifacts.

So far, we have presented the concept of a novel interaction design between children and their parents and developed interfaces that enable the realization of such interaction. We have already conducted a feasibility study with children having ASD during robot-assisted activities and confirmed that the proposed device is acceptable [7]. In the future, we plan to conduct a user study with children and families to verify that the interfaces can support the sharing and perception of facial expressions in the given scenario.

## 6. REFERENCES

[1] P. Ekman. An argument for basic emotions. *Cognition and Emotion*, 6(3):169–200, 1992.

[2] P. Ekman. *Emotions Revealed: Recognizing Faces and Feelings to Improve Communication and Emotional Life*. Times Books, 2003.

[3] P. Ekman and W. Friesen. *Facial Action Coding System: A Technique for the Measurement of Facial Movement*. Consulting Psychologists Press, 1978.

[4] A. Funahashi, A. Gruebler, T. Aoki, H. Kadone, and K. Suzuki. The smiles of a child with autism spectrum disorder during an animal-assisted activity may facilitate social positive behaviors - quantitative analysis with smile-detecting interface. *J Autism Dev Disord*, 44(3):685–693, 2014.

[5] K. Gray and B. Tonge. Are there early features of autism in infants and preschool children? *J Paediatr Child Health*, 37(3):221–226, June 2001.

[6] A. Gruebler and K. Suzuki. Design of a wearable device for reading positive expressions from facial emg signals. *IEEE Trans. on Affective Comput.*, (in press).

[7] M. Hirokawa, A. Funahashi, and K. Suzuki. A doll-type interface for real-time humanoid teleoperation in robot-assisted activity: A case study. In *ACM/IEEE Intl. Conf. on Human-Robot Interaction*, pages 174–175, 2014.

[8] J. J. Lien, T. Kanade, J. F. Cohn, and C. C. Li. Automated facial expression recognition based on facs action units. In *IEEE. Published in the Proceedings of FG'98*, April 1998.

[9] F. R. Volkmar and L. C. Mayes. Gaze behavior in autism. *Development and Psychopathology*, 2(1):61–69, January 1990.

# Screen Time for Children

**Steven LeMay**
Usability Matters Inc.
215 Spadina Ave., #550
Toronto, ON, M5T 2C7, CANADA
steven@usabilitymatters.com

**Terry Costantino**
Usability Matters Inc.
215 Spadina Ave., #550
Toronto, ON, M5T 2C7, CANADA
terry@usabilitymatters.com

**Sheilah O'Connor**
**Eda Conte-Pitcher**
North York Central Library
Toronto Public Library
5120 Yonge Street
Toronto, ON, M2N 5N9, CAN
soconnor@torontopubliclibrary.ca
econte@torontopubliclibrary.ca

## ABSTRACT

When setting out to redevelop its online offerings for children, The Toronto Public Library needed to establish a position on the controversial issue of screen time for children. Given the concerns about the appropriateness, benefits and potential harms of screen time for young children, the question of what if anything the library should be providing online for children aged 5 years and under needed to be answered. This paper examines how an answer to this key question was achieved and the implications of this decision for the design of online services for children.

## Categories and Subject Descriptors

H.1.2 [**Models and Principles**]: User/Machine Systems

K.4.2 [**Computers and Society**]: Social Issues

## General Terms

Design, Human Factors.

## Keywords

Children, Public Libraries, Screen Time, Websites, Apps, Literacy, Early Childhood Development

## 1. INTRODUCTION

In 2013, the Toronto Public Library {TPL} began a redevelopment of their online offerings for children, beginning with children aged 5 and under with older children and teens to follow. Given the concerns about the appropriateness, benefits and potential harms of screen time for children, one of the key questions for the redevelopment is what if anything the library should be providing online for this age group. This paper examines how an answer to this key question was achieved and the implications of this decision for the design of online services for children.

## 2. BACKGROUND

### 2.1 About the Toronto Public Library

The Toronto Public Library (TPL) is the largest public library system in North America. It serves a population of over 2.6 million people, has an annual circulation of over 33 million items, and over 18 million total visits per year. On a per capita basis, it

far exceeds its North American peers in circulation, visits and square footage of library space [1]. These numbers serve to point out the enormous popularity of the TPL among the city's population.

With almost 26 million website visits in 2012, the library's popularity also extends to its online presence [1].

### 2.2 Ready for Reading

One of the library's key services is its' programs for children. For preschoolers, the library has created a series of services and resources entitled Ready for Reading which aim to promote early literacy and a lifelong love of books. The fun, play-based approach involves reading storybooks, singing, movement, finger-plays and rhymes. Ready for Reading incorporates the breadth of the library's expertise: its' collections, expert staff, storytime programs, and branch spaces for kids. The program also includes an award winning printed resource guide that encourages early literacy through play-based learning. All of these efforts have built upon and extended the work of the American Library Association in its Every Child Ready to Read efforts [2,3,4].

Missing from the Ready for Reading program, however, is an online component that achieves the same fun and engagement to meet early literacy objectives. Usability Matters was engaged to work with TPL to fill this gap through an extensive strategy, research and design process. One of the key concerns from the outset was screen time for children.

### 2.3 Screen time

The controversial question of whether time in front of screens is beneficial or detrimental to children has been studied since televisions began entering homes in the mid twentieth century. As new screen-based technologies have been added over the years, questions have persisted and, with the proliferation of mobile devices, concerns are being raised anew leading some public health organizations to recommended limitations or outright prohibition of screen time for young children on traditional media such as television [5,6].

To determine a position on screen time for children under 5, the TPL undertook a review of the literature. Additionally, while interviewing parents, Usability Matters investigated their thoughts and practices regarding screen time. Findings from this research are outlined in the next sections, Secondary Research and Primary Research.

## 3. SECONDARY RESEARCH

In its survey of current research, the TPL found that while there is a great deal of literature on the watching of television and videos, studies on interactions with newer touchscreen and smartphone devices is only beginning to emerge. Additionally, available research is largely U.S.-based; Canadian research in the area of screen time is limited and no research from outside North America was included in the review.

Key highlights from the review of current literature include:

- There is conflicting evidence about the impact of screen time. There is no evidence that educational media aimed at kids 2 and under helps with cognitive development and some evidence that it does not. Limiting screen time for children is therefore widely recommended. The Canadian and American paediatric societies discourage screen-based activities for children under 2 and a limit of 2 hours per day for children older than 2 [5,6].

- There is concern that media usage comes at the expense of the direct human interactions that are essential for language and cognitive development [1,2]. Language is not learned by observing conversations but through direct interaction. A key objective of screen-based media for children should therefore be to foster positive interactions between adults and children. It should be child-driven but have a clear interactive role for parents or other adults - not just co-viewing but joint engagement [7].

- Not all screen time is equal. In fact, the amount of screen time may be less important than the kind of screen time. Passive viewing of television and videos is fundamentally different from technology that requires navigation, tap and touch interactions, game play, whole body engagement and the participation of others [8,9].

- The digital divide exists. There is unequal access to technology between higher and lower income families especially with newer technologies [10]. While touch screens may be better suited to the cognitive capacities of toddlers than the more complex hand-eye coordination required to use a mouse, inequality of access to this technology is prevalent [11].

Findings were gathered in the form of a briefing paper for use by internal stakeholders and the steering committee charged with oversight and guidance of the project team's efforts.

## 4. PRIMARY RESEARCH

To gain insights into the needs of parents, caregivers and early childhood educators, Usability Matters conducted a series of 12 interviews. Most interviews were conducted in library branches, often with children present. Others were conducted by phone or at schools. The interviews were exploratory and included discussion of screen time among other topics.

Parents were recruited through a casual friends and family search. This was identified as a shortcoming later in the process when a series of personas was developed to guide the design process. To better match the desired audience described through the personas, it would have been beneficial for the interviews to have included parents that the library seeks to attract, not just those already engaged with the library, especially parents with lower literacy or English as a second language. Future research to evaluate the design will address this gap.

## 4.1 What we heard from interviewees

There was wide recognition among interviewees that screen time is an important issue in early childhood development. Some

parents were well informed on the subject or described using their own best judgment and all suggested that they have spoken to other parents about it.

However, in practice there was no clear consensus. Some parents allowed no screen time at all, some described clearly defined – sometimes elaborate – restrictions and some placed no restrictions on screen time at all. Parents were well aware of this lack of consensus and knew that screen time practices were different in the homes of their children's friends.

> "They had no screen time at all for the first 3 years".
> - Parent

> "My children get a limited amount of screen time every second day" - Parent

> "He has ADHD so he really enjoys using the computer… doing puzzles … but we find that it's difficult because we say you can have one hour, then we say your hour's almost up, 5 minute warning, 2 minute warning then ROAR!" - Parent

> "We have screen time but we also practice piano and we listen to music and do dancing so watching television is not the only thing we do. Screen time is not the be-all and end-all. If you spend too much time in front of a screen, your brain kind of turns sideways." - Parent

> "The iPad is such a temptation. It's not hard to find educational things but it's hard to moderate it." - Parent

> "When I'm sitting one-on-one with a child, they'll tell me 'Oh, I was playing this game on my Mom's phone'." - Early childhood educator

> "We stay away from technologies because we want to encourage that face-to-face, one-on-one interaction… We do not have computers or iPads in our programs."
> - Administrator, early childhood education programs

### 4.1.1 Tension between the real world and best practices

The interviews revealed a tension between the best practices advocated by respected sources and the real-world screen time practices of some parents. This points to an opportunity for the TPL. Through its Ready for Reading program, the library is uniquely positioned to offer alternatives to screen time and more importantly to model the best practices, including screen time best practices, that support early literacy.

## 5. TPL POSITION

### 5.1 How we got there

A number of key themes emerged from the interviews, including parents' thoughts about screen time, that could shape what the library will offer online for parents, caregivers and educators, but a position on screen time was required to determine what, if anything, TPL should offer online for children 5 and under.

To help TPL reach a position, Usability Matters conducted a workshop with the project's steering committee consisting of directors and key personnel from across the library. The briefing paper outlining the screen time findings from the secondary research was circulated in advance to establish a common understanding of the problem domain.

The workshop began with a short discussion of the findings from the briefing paper and the interviews. Usability Matters then drew a large 4-quadrant diagram for all in the room to see (Figure 1). The horizontal axis represented the choice of screen time for children alone vs. together with parents and caregivers. The vertical axis presented a choice of passive viewing vs. active engagement, with a few words indicating a loose definition of each.

Recognizing that these aren't simple binary choices but rather a continuum, a selection of child friendly websites was shown and the committee was asked as a group to map where on the continuum of passive to active each of the websites belonged. This initial exercise primed the committee members with an understanding of the model. Thus prepared, we turned to the question of what the library should offer online for children.

### 5.1.1 Children 2 Years and Under

Beginning with the age group 2 years and under, the committee was asked if they would support providing online offerings in each of the four combinations: passive and alone; passive and together; active and alone; active and together. Each answer in turn was written on the diagram in the corresponding quadrant and in each case, the answer was a confident no (Figure 1).

The second age group, 2 to 5 years, was then addressed in the same manner. In this case, the answers were more nuanced.

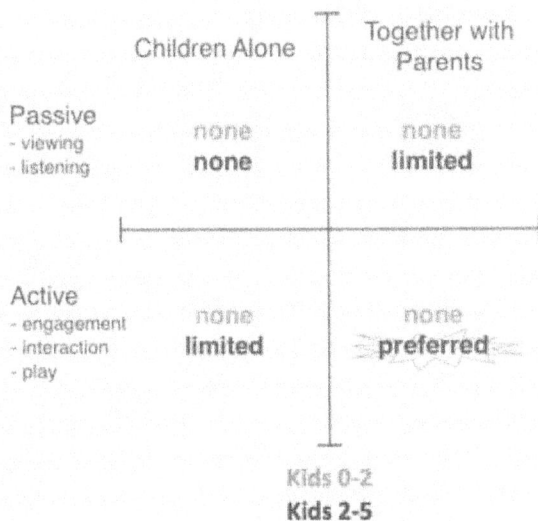

Figure 1: 4-quadrant workshop exercise completed for the 2 age groups

### 5.1.2 Children 2 to 5 Years

For children aged 2 to 5, the literature clearly recommends active interaction and joint engagement between children and caregivers. This aligns extremely well with the very popular storytime programs that the library offers in its branches. Online content and features should be just as fun and engaging as the in-branch experience and therefore the combination of active and together is preferred.

The conclusion for passive and alone was no, but with some reservations. Parents had clearly described a need for something worthwhile to keep their child occupied for just a few minutes while the parent completed a task such as taking a shower or preparing a meal. However, the literature just as clearly recommends that passive viewing be strictly limited. The library's position would therefore be that this content is available elsewhere and while the library should not speak against it, the library should not add to it.

Passive and together was deemed more appropriate than passive and alone but any such features or content should be limited.

Similarly, active and alone is preferred to any passive viewing but it is missing the key joint engagement that best fosters early language skills. Online content and features should encourage active participation and should favour joint engagement over engagement alone.

## 5.2 What it means for the design

The four-quadrant exercise and the broader screen time research have a number of important implications for the design.

The real target audience for content and features for children aged 2 and under is their parents, caregivers and educators rather than the children themselves.

Joint engagement is at the heart of the library's in-branch story time programs and through them the library has earned a solid reputation for its early-years literacy efforts. Any online offerings should connect parents and children with these library programs that have joint engagement at their core.

Any digital content should be just as fun and engaging as the in-branch experience. It should focus on joint engagement and encourage the activities that are positive to early childhood development – talk, read, sing, play and write [2].

Parents are eager for great book recommendations and librarians are a trusted source for these recommendations. The library should capitalize on its expertise and respected reputation by helping parents find recommended materials online, especially books that children and parents will love. For children over 2, this should extend to e-books such as those included in the Tumblebooks service, audiobooks and e-materials in general. Achieving this fundamental aim of connecting parents and children with great materials is more important than entertaining children online.

The digital divide is a reality and the library plays a significant role in helping to bridge it by providing free access to computers and computer-skill training in its branches. The digital divide with apps, however, is wider. Therefore any interactive screen-based features and content for children should be web-based to minimize the effects of the digital divide. Apps can follow at a later date.

## 6. FUTURE

With a direction regarding screen time in hand, the project team has been able to assemble a list of desired features and content. The project team's efforts have now moved into the interaction design. Interaction design is now underway. Visual design and development will begin shortly and a rapid iterative prototyping process is anticipated.

## 6.1 Evaluation

Working with iterative prototypes will afford the opportunity for multiple rounds of usability testing with each of the target audiences – children aged 2 to 5, parents, caregivers and educators. The initial prototype is currently underway and the first set of usability test will be conducted in early May 2014.

Testing with people relying on assistive technologies related to visual and other impairments is also anticipated in the coming months.

## 6.2 Kids 6 to 12

Following immediately on the heels of this effort will be a similarly structured strategy, research, design, development and testing process that addresses the library's online offerings for children aged 6 to 12.

## 6.3 Possible Impacts Beyond this Project

There have been discussions, outside of the context of this project, of including iPads and e-materials in story time programs. The library also has dedicated computers for young children with a selection of featured e-materials in some branches. It is foreseeable that the steering committee's decision on screen time could have an impact on these in-branch uses of technology.

Additional impacts could be experienced in selecting new materials for the library's collection. Collection policies for young children's e-materials especially may need to focus on joint engagement between parent and child and avoid altogether any e-materials for children under 2.

## 7. ACKNOWLEDGMENTS

Our thanks to the individuals involved in the project, including Toronto Public Library staff, especially the members of the children and youth steering committee and the project advisory group. Thanks too to the library's members, especially those who participated directly through interviews or observation, and to Usability Matters and its staff.

## 8. REFERENCES

[1] Glass, E., Palmer, K. and Pyper, J., 2012. 2012 Annual Performance Measures and Strategic Plan Update. http://www.torontopubliclibrary.ca/content/about-the-library/pdfs/board/meetings/2013/apr29/15.pdf

[2] Toronto Public Library, 2012. Let's Get Ready for Reading Guide, http://www.torontopubliclibrary.ca/ready-for-reading/lets-get-ready-for-reading.jsp

[3] Ontario Library Association, 2013. OPL Service Award, Minister's Award for Innovation, https://www.accessola.org/Documents/OLA/About/Awards/Ministry_PLSA_2013/Toronto%20Public%20Library.pdf

[4] Public Library Association, 2011. Every Child Ready to Read, http://www.everychildreadytoread.org

[5] Canadian Paediatric Society, 2011. Tips for limiting screen time at home, http://www.caringforkids.cps.ca/handouts/limiting_screen_time_at_home

[6] Strasburger, V. C., Hogan, M. J., Mulligan, D. A., Ameenuddin, N., Christakis, D. A., Cross, C., ... & Swanson, W. S. L., 2013. Children, adolescents, and the media. In *Pediatrics*, 132.5, 958-961.

[7] Takeuchi, L., Stevens, R., and The Joan Ganz Cooney Centre, 2011. The New Coviewing: Designing for Learning through Joint Media Engagement, http://www.joanganzcooneycenter.org/publication/the-new-coviewing-designing-for-learning-through-joint-media-engagement/

[8] Kleeman, D. and The Fred Rogers Center, 2011. Beyond Screentime. http://www.fredrogerscenter.org/blog/beyond-screen-time/

[9] Radich, J. 2013. Technology and interactive media as tools in early childhood programs serving children from birth through age 8. In *Every Child*, 19.4, 18.

[10] Rideout, V. and Common Sense Media. 2011. Zero to eight: children's media use in America. *Common Sense Media.* http://www.commonsensemedia.org/research/zero-to-eight-childrens-media-use-in-america

[11] Schuler, C., and The Joan Ganz Cooney Centre, 2012, iLearn II: An Analysis of the Education Category on Apple's App Store. http://www.joanganzcooneycenter.org/publication/ilearn-ii-an-analysis-of-the-education-category-on-apples-app-store/

# Power Puppet: Science and Technology Education through Puppet Building

Firaz Peer
Georgia Institute of Technology
Atlanta, GA 30332
firazpeer@gatech.edu

Michael Nitsche
Georgia Institute of Technology
Atlanta, GA 30332
michael.nitsche@lmc.gatech.edu

Lauren (La) Schaffer
Georgia Institute of Technology
Atlanta, GA 30332
la.schaffer@gatech.edu

## ABSTRACT

In this paper, we describe our approach to designing electronic puppet-building workshops for middle to early high school students. Power Puppet uses traditional puppet building materials - paper and cloth as the main resources, together with simple circuits elements such as LED's, batteries and magnets. We document our process of designing puppet-building workshops that include STEM education criteria. We collaborated with the Center for Puppetry Arts to design these workshops in such a way that part of the making will include basic electronic input and output components. We aim to open this tradition up for larger audiences to enhance hardware CS education in STEM fields.

## Categories and Subject Descriptors

H.5.2 [**Information Interfaces and Presentation**]: User Interfaces – *prototyping* K.3.2 [**Computers and Education**]: Computer and Information Science Education – *computer science education*

## General Terms

Design, Documentation, Performance.

## Keywords

Electronic Puppets, Workshops, Puppet Making, Conductive Materials, Basic Electronics, STEM Education, Curriculum

## 1. INTRODUCTION

Puppetry as an expressive art form is over 4000 years old and - just like any other artistic format - has adapted to various technologies and practices. As a result, it provides a wide range of designs and technologies to build and control puppets. It has been used in scientific research to tackle control mechanisms in advanced robotics [14], interface design [15], and network optimization [12], among other areas. But it also has been applied to digital media and design through storytelling, improvisation, and public engagement [2], to describe the relationship between user and avatar [23], and in educational projects [13]. At the same time, traditional puppetry has started to explore and theorize its relation to the digital, gradually building frameworks to include it better [22].

*IDC'14*, June 17–20, 2014, Aarhus, Denmark.
Copyright © 2014 ACM 978-1-4503-2272-0/14/06…$15.00.
http://dx.doi.org/10.1145/2593968.2610457

The Power Puppet project builds on this convening field. Its goal is to teach middle school to early high school students basic circuit building in the setting of a puppet building workshop. As students build their puppets, including control mechanisms (like rods and strings) and expressive elements (like joints and materials), they also create basic circuits that operate in combination with the puppet that houses them. This does not break with puppetry tradition, as the inclusion of digital control components have been applied to puppet design and revolutionary input devices such as the Waldo were co-designed by puppeteers like Jim Henson. This paper reports on the first stage of the project: designing and preparing the workshops.

## 2. WHY ELECTRONIC PUPPETS?

There are a range of successful projects in Computer Science for software related STEM education (ALICE, Scratch, countless game-based projects). However the list of hardware-related projects is much shorter [4], [20]. This stands in contrast with the growing needs to educate a new generation into the age of ubiquitous computing, where hardware construction of computational devices is becoming as relevant as their software programming.

Atlanta is an international center for puppetry; it not only hosts the world-renowned Center for Puppetry Arts but is also home to a number of puppeteering troupes and performers. Many of these artists also provide educational programs in their performances as part of their puppet making. Puppets as educational tools are in use in formal as well as informal education settings in Atlanta. For example, each young audience show at the Center for Puppetry Arts includes a Make-Your-Own-Puppet workshop. These workshops offer basic puppet building opportunities to its visitors. Different workshops are offered to different audiences: short basic construction workshops encourage younger audiences to build mainly paper puppets that relate to the current stage productions; more elaborate courses are directed at older K12 students and include different materials (foam) and practices (hot glue guns); finally, specialized workshops on puppet building and control are provided to mainly adults and often cover specialized areas (such as marionette control or shadow puppetry). The craft of puppet design and construction is a lifelong learning process and offers many entry points to engage students and involve them in new design experiences.

Puppet making, thus, is a typical art and craft practice and well supported in Atlanta. Notably, it is a practice embraced across genders, age groups, and educational backgrounds. It offers a gateway to reach precisely those new audiences interested in creative making but deterred by a purely CS-technological perspective.

## 3. RELATED WORK

Since Froebel established the first kindergarten in 1837, and developed a set of toys with the explicit goal of helping young children in learning concepts such as number, size, shape, and color, other educators, such as Maria Montessori, have created a wide range of manipulative materials that engage children in learning through playful explorations [3].

Continuing in this tradition of playful explorations, Leah Buechley and other researchers at the High-Low Tech group at the MIT Media Lab have conducted workshops that teach participants to design circuits on paper, producing a small set of interactive projects [16]. In Pulp based computing [7] the authors describe a series of techniques for embedding electro-active inks, conductive threads and smart materials directly into paper during the papermaking process, thereby creating seamless composites that are capable of supporting new and unexpected application domains in ubiquitous and pervasive computing at affordable costs. In [10] the authors describe ways to produce electronic origami using thermochromic and conductive ink that changes color when electricity is applied. Saul et al. [21] describe a family of interactive devices like paper robots, paper speakers and paper lamps made from paper and simple electronics.

With a Kit of No Parts [18], Perner-Wilson describes an approach to building electronics from a diverse palette of craft materials, which the author argues are more personal, understandable and accessible than the construction of technology from a kit of pre-determined parts. "Personal materials" like these have proven their value in research workshops that use the intimacy of such materials to the student as "new technologies can be taught in ways that open students to the potentialities for self-empowerment and playful exploration of taboos or serious issues within contexts that are creative and artful" [1]. Furthermore, projects like these have proven effective for the engagement of new student groups, particularly women and girls, in hardware prototyping technology through craft [6].

## 4. OUR APPROACH

A key inspiration for our approach is Buechley's combination of craft and computing [5] and related work on the use of soft circuits in education [11], [17]. Buechley's initial work was an expansion of existing techniques through new technology. In Buechley's case, this included the development of the LilyPad, a prototyping board that simplified building soft circuits in cloth, with the aim of reaching newer audiences. Challenges reaching newer audiences, such as women or underrepresented minorities remain as long as technology education aims to teach for technology's sake. STEM robotics programs are often taught without a view to the context for these technologies. Students use LEGO Mindstorms to learn about robotics - not about the underlying context and the cultural role of the mechanisms they build. Consequently, these programs reach mainly students already interested in technology but they fail to reach out further [8].

The second challenge is continued "black boxing" of many educational technological tool sets [9],[19]. Commercial kits like Mindstorms hide the underlying functionality of their parts and black boxing is in the nature of these kits as marketed to educators. Their commercial viability depends on limited access.

Each state in the US has a different set of standards and expectations when it comes to science education. To make matters worse, public, private, and charter schools within each state also have their own sets of guidelines that they enforce. To simplify our approach, we decided to use the physical science curriculum published by GeorgiaStandards.org to design our workshop exercises. We looked at the learning outcomes and performance goals mentioned in these documents, and designed our individual exercises around it. According to Georgia Performance Standards Framework for Physical Science [GeorgiaStandards.org], eighth grade students should be able to

1. Draw a diagram of a circuit that will light a bulb, given an electric wire, a battery cell and a bulb.
2. Draw a diagram of a series circuit with 2 bulbs.
3. Draw a diagram of a parallel circuit with 2 bulbs.
4. Identify an advantage of a series circuit.
5. Identify an advantage of a parallel circuit.

We used this as a guideline when deciding which electronic components to use in our exploration. With these standards in mind, we built interactive puppets and installations with paper and cloth that made use of conductive tape, conductive thread, batteries, LED's, washers and magnets. We believe such materials have a lower barrier to entry compared to electronic circuit building kits like LittleBits, Arduino LilyPad and BlinkM's in terms of cost and availability while at the same time allowing us to build a variety of simple interactive pieces.

## 5. PUPPET PROTOTYPES

Jean Piaget observed that children acquire knowledge by acting on the world around them. We started off by building basic series and parallel circuits with conductive tape, batteries and LED's laid out on paper. This method is included to allow students to realize abstract concepts such as polarity and flow of electricity in more concrete and tangible ways. The circuits can be put together in minutes, so students can easily make multiple test circuits for a variety of applications.

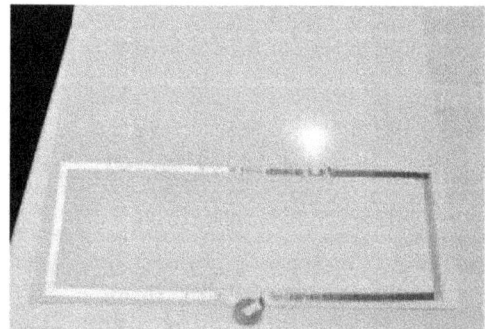

**Figure 1: Series circuit with conductive tape**

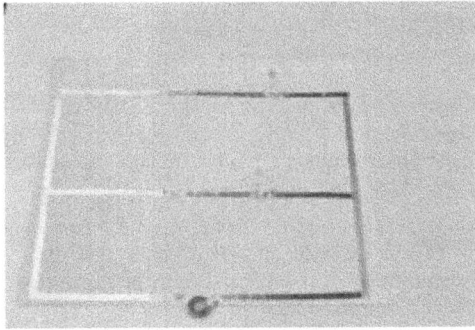

**Figure 2: Parallel circuits with conductive tape**

We used this as a base to add on more interactive elements to the circuit. We constructed origami puppets with two LED's for the eyes, connected in series. In order to make the connections between the conductive tape and the origami puppets, we fixed magnets onto the conductive tape as shown. By using paper clips and washers as leads in the origami puppets, we snapped connections into place.

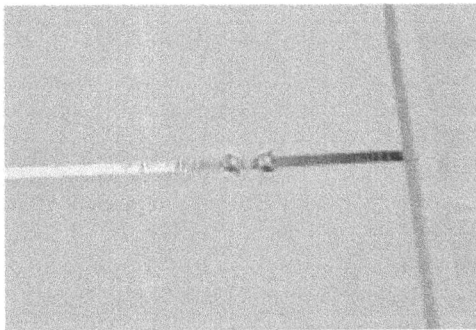

**Figure 3: Fixing magnets on the conductive tape**

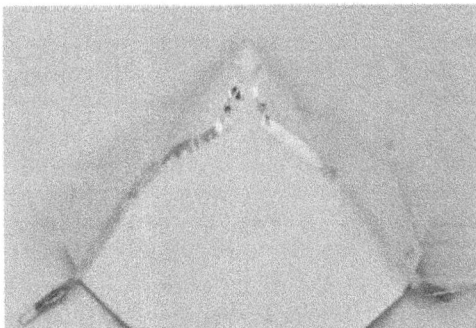

**Figure 4: Internals of the origami puppet**

**Figure 5: Placing the origami puppet on the circuit**

Our next task was to incorporate these basic electronic components into more elaborate paper and cloth puppets. We attended workshops at the Center for Puppetry Arts to learn puppet making from the experts. The materials included 1" foam sheets, non-stretch fabric, plastics dowels, cardstock, felt, various craft pieces for decoration (buttons, yarn, eyes, etc.), craft glue, hot glue, a bowl of water in case of burns, scissors, and markers. The puppet-building process was simple enough for our target age group to accomplish, though the hot glue will require some supervision. These puppets came together in a way that allowed for easy access for inclusion of technology, and they are durable and complex enough to offer many options for applications of students' ideas.

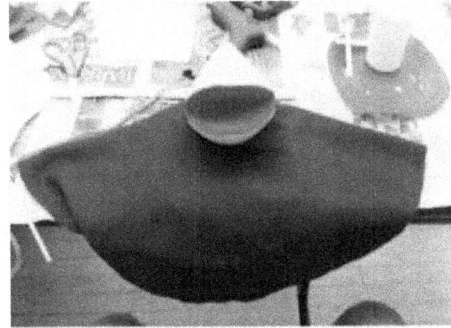

**Figure 6: Making cloth puppets at the Center for Puppetry Arts**

Once we had a better understanding of how the puppets were made, we took them back to the lab to wire them up with LED's and conductive thread to embed possible electronic circuits. To encourage collaborative play, we experiment with distributing the circuit across two puppets by putting the battery in one, and the LED's onto the other so that they light up only when the two puppets come in contact with each other to complete the circuit.

The final part of the design process was to invite the puppetry workshop organizers over to our lab so they could give us feedback on our concepts and to check the kinds of interactions that are permissible for children attending the puppet building workshops. Although they appreciated our use of technology to improve puppet interaction, they were concerned about our concept of collaborative play. Our design had conductive materials in the mouth of one puppet and the hand of the other, so the circuit is complete when one puppet bites the other on the arm. We were informed about how the center tries to consciously avoid interactions like biting, punching, pushing and poking while designing their plays for younger audiences. It would therefore, behoove us to follow similar guidelines when including technology in our puppet interactions.

## 6. FUTURE WORK

Going forward, our aim is to use the paper and cloth puppets designed at the center as a base for us to build our technological exploration upon. This approach has the two-fold advantage of

1. Leaving puppet building in the hands of the experts, while we concentrate on the technical aspects of the workshop
2. Allowing us to more easily integrate our electronics workshop with the puppet building one, so students can learn it as a whole and not two distinct parts.

We will continue to work with our current collaborators at the Center for Puppetry Arts to organize a final workshop for evaluation. This evaluation will consist of retrospective pre and post test attitudes surveys and pre / post content knowledge assessments. It will use pre / post surveys to assess attitudes towards computing and self-efficacy.

# 7. CONCLUSION

Our goal behind building these Power Puppets is to design a series of workshops that will introduce students to the concept of building interactive paper and cloth puppets. The workshops are not a goal in and of themselves, but the means to an end, namely enabling students to take control and solve problems, and build creative working hardware prototypes. Given how pervasive technology has become, it is vital that we prepare children to not only use technology but to be reflective about how it works on the hardware level as well. We hope these exercises and workshops give children the necessary hands on experience to equip them with the basics of puppet building and electronic circuits, from which they can develop more creative and imaginative contraptions that will lead to a future based on imagination and creativity.

# 8. REFERENCES

[1] Berzowska, J. and Coelho, M. 2006. SMOKS. *CHI '06 extended abstracts on Human factors in computing systems - CHI EA '06* (New York, New York, USA, Apr. 2006), 538.

[2] Bottoni, P. et al. 2008. CoPuppet : Collaborative Interaction in VirtualPuppetry. *Transdisciplinary Digital Art. Sound, Vision and the New Screen.* 326–341.

[3] Brosterman, N. and Togashi, K. 1997. *Inventing kindergarten.*

[4] Buechley, L. et al. 2007. Towards a curriculum for electronic textiles in the high school classroom. *ACM SIGCSE Bulletin.* 39, 3 (Jun. 2007), 28.

[5] Buechley, L. and Eisenberg, M. 2009. Fabric PCBs, electronic sequins, and socket buttons: techniques for e-textile craft. *Personal and Ubiquitous Computing.* 13, 2 (Aug. 2009), 133–150.

[6] Buechley, L. and Perner-Wilson, H. 2012. Crafting technology. *ACM Transactions on Computer-Human Interaction.* 19, 3 (Oct. 2012), 1–21.

[7] Coelho, M. 2009. Pulp-Based Computing : A Framework for Building Computers Out of Paper. (2009), 3527–3528.

[8] Cruz-Martín, A. et al. 2012. A LEGO Mindstorms NXT approach for teaching at Data Acquisition, Control Systems Engineering and Real-Time Systems undergraduate courses. *Computers & Education.* 59, 3 (Nov. 2012), 974–988.

[9] Hertz, G. 2009. Methodologies of Reuse in the Media Arts: Exploring Black Boxes, Tactics and Archaeologies. *Digital Arts and Culture 2009.* (Dec. 2009).

[10] Kaihou, T. and Wakita, A. 2013. Electronic origami with the color-changing function. *Proceedings of the second international workshop on Smart material interfaces: another step to a material future - SMI '13* (New York, New York, USA, Dec. 2013), 7–12.

[11] Kuznetsov, S. et al. 2011. Breaking boundaries. *Proceedings of the 2011 annual conference on Human factors in computing systems - CHI '11* (New York, New York, USA, May 2011), 2957.

[12] Mapes, D.P. et al. 2011. Geppetto: An Environment for the Efficient Control and Transmission of Digital Puppetry. *International Conference on Virtual and Mixed Reality: Systems and Applications.* 270–278.

[13] Marshall, P. et al. 2004. PUPPET: Playing and learning in a virtual world. *International Journal of Continuing Engineering Education and Life-Long Learning.*

[14] Martin, P. and Johnson, E. 2011. Constructing and implementing motion programs for robotic marionettes. *Automatic Control, IEEE ....* 56, 4 (2011), 902–907.

[15] Mazalek, A. et al. 2011. I'm in the game: Embodied puppet interface improves avatar control. *Proceedings of the fifth international conference on Tangible, embedded, and embodied interaction (TEI '11).* (2011), 129–136.

[16] Mellis, D.A. et al. 2013. Microcontrollers as Material : Crafting Circuits with Paper , Conductive Ink , Electronic Components , and an " Untoolkit ." (2013), 83–90.

[17] Peppler, K. 2013. STEAM-Powered Computing Education: Using E-Textiles to Integrate the Arts and STEM. *Computer.* 46, 9 (Sep. 2013), 38–43.

[18] Perner-Wilson, H. 2011. *A Kit of No Parts.* Massachusetts Institute of Technology.

[19] Resnick, M. and Rosenbaum, E. 1993. Designing for Tinkerability. *M. Honey & D.E. Hunter (Eds.) Design, make, play* (Routledge, London, 1993), 163–181.

[20] Resnick, M. and Silverman, B. 2005. Some reflections on designing construction kits for kids. *Proceeding of the 2005 conference on Interaction design and children - IDC '05.* (2005), 117–122.

[21] Saul, G. et al. 2010. Interactive paper devices. *Proceedings of the fourth international conference on Tangible, embedded, and embodied interaction - TEI '10* (New York, New York, USA, Jan. 2010), 205.

[22] Tillis, S. 1999. The Art of Puppetry in the Age of Media Production. *TDR/The Drama Review.* 43, 3 (Sep. 1999), 182–195.

[23] Walser, R. 1990. Elements of a Cyberspace Playhouse. *Proceedings of the National Computer Graphics Association* (Anaheim, CA, 1990).

# Motivating Children's Initiations with Novelty and Surprise: Initial Design Recommendations for Autism

Alyssa M. Alcorn, Helen Pain
University of Edinburgh School of Informatics
Edinburgh, EH8 9AB, UK
{aalcorn, helen}@inf.ed.ac.uk

Judith Good
University of Sussex Department of Informatics
Brighton, BN1 9QJ, UK
j.good@sussex.ac.uk

## ABSTRACT

Data from the ECHOES *virtual environment* (VE) suggests that young children with *autism spectrum conditions* (ASC) may be motivated to initiate repeatedly and positively about novelty and expectation-violations (i.e. *discrepancies*) in a VE. This is of interest because initiating communication is developmentally important but difficult to encourage—it must be unprompted in order to "count". Also, the ASC literature would predict that discrepancies should be distressing, not motivating. Based on this unexpected but positive finding, we are exploring the possibility of embedding discrepancies into VEs to support children's initiation practice. As a first step, we propose 6 empirically-derived design principles for including discrepancies as motivators, while still maintaining the VE's overall integrity.

## Categories and Subject Descriptors

H.1.2 [**User/Machine Systems**]: Human factors; H.5.1 [**Multimedia Information Systems**]: Artificial, augmented, and virtual realities; H.5.2 [User Interfaces]: User-centered design; K.3.1 [Computer Uses in Education]: Computer-assisted instruction (CAI); K.4.2 [**Social Issues**]: Assistive technologies for persons with disabilities---*autism*.

## General Terms

Design; Experimentation; Human Factors

## Keywords

Autism; ASC; children; social communication; initiation; virtual environments; discrepancy; novelty; surprise; HCI; design

## 1.  INTRODUCTION & BACKGROUND

Young children with *autism spectrum conditions* (ASC) are a distinct group with respect to interaction design. Designing for this group differs from designing for "young children" generally due to two central issues: the characteristics of autism, and the end goals designers may be trying to achieve. The ASCs are a set of pervasive developmental disorders, with core features of difficulty with communication and with social interaction, plus the presence of restricted, repetitive behaviours and interests [1]. These characteristics of ASC drive the divergence from common design goals for young *typically developing* (TD) children.

Indeed, a sizeable proportion of all ASC-specific technologies target skills that TD children may acquire early in life with little or no explicit instruction. Thus, there is a need for design strategies that engage with both ASC-specific characteristics and the social and pedagogical goals relevant to this group.

### 1.1 Motivating initiations

Many technologies for ASC aim to support practice of basic communication skills, such as preferentially orienting to people [2], or identifying facial expressions [3]. The rationale for using technologies to teach these skills is that they can provide a more finely controllable, repeatable method of instruction than practicing with a person, and can be personalised to individual children [4]. Children *initiating* communication has proved a particularly desirable but difficult target. Initiation appears difficult for this group to acquire compared to *responding* to others' communication [1]. Initiation is difficult to target from a research perspective because it definitionally means that the child's behaviour has not been prompted by the partner, nor is it directly contingent on immediate past communication with that partner. So, how do researchers foster initiation practice if directly prompting children means that their actions no longer "count"?

One approach has been to embed indirect "demands" for initiation in a child's environment, e.g. by providing an incorrectly-sized or broken object for doing a task [5], or placing an object out-of-reach, forcing a request for help. While anecdotally successful at motivating initiation [5, 6], the question remains whether similar strategies can be applied in technology-based contexts. Some success has been observed in relation to the ECHOES *virtual environment* (VE) [7]. Re-analysis of ECHOES data suggests a new potential strategy for motivating young children with ASC to initiate a range of positive communications with social partners.

### 1.2 The ECHOES project

The ECHOES VE blends foundational social skills practice with exploratory, playful interactions. It comprises a set of non-competitive learning activities set in a "Magic Garden" and accessed through a multi-touch screen. Activities have minimal language, emphasising sensory elements and discovery of cause-and-effect relationships. Andy, a childlike *virtual character* (VC), is present as a playmate and guide, able to both react to the child's actions and execute deliberative plans. A popular example activity is "ball sorting", where Andy demonstrated putting bouncy balls into boxes of the same colours. Children were invited to help, receiving a visual reward as each box was filled (see Figure 1).

A researcher managed the sessions (e.g. choosing new activities) through a graphical interface on a second monitor and was available as a social partner for the child. Their role was defined as that of responder and supporter, *not* an instructor directing the child's use of the system. Researchers noted that intermittent software errors[1] unpredictably altered the behaviour of both the VE and VC, breaking down the cause-and-effect relationships and otherwise violating child expectations about how the environment and its contents "should" behave. For example, Andy sometimes made mistakes in an activity he had previously demonstrated for the child. There were multiple instances of children clearly detecting and reacting to occurrences of the type in Figure 1.

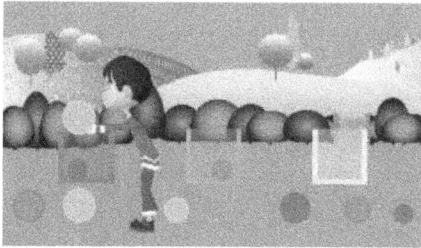

**Figure 1. Andy sorts a ball into the wrong box.**

Some reactions were non-social (e.g. self-narration), but many were spontaneous *initiations* to a partner, such as shared positive affect, commenting, and pointing to direct their attention. Re-examining the ECHOES video data [7] identified a broad pattern of *discrepancy-child reaction pairs* (DR pairs). These are the phenomenon of children detecting and reacting (socially or non-socially) to instances in which a current aspect of the environment is mismatched with the child's knowledge of, or expectations about, the behaviour of that environment. "Mismatches" may be due to *novel* aspects, meaning the child does not yet have expectations about their properties, or alternately, to *surprises,* or violations of established expectation(s). A child might react to the mistake in Figure 1 because Andy has previously done the task correctly (i.e. it is a *surprise*). Conversely, Andy's first demonstration of ball sorting may be detected as *novel*, because the child needed to form a new expectation about this action. Novel and surprising aspects are collectively referred to as *discrepancies.* See Alcorn et al. for more information about discrepancies and the types of DR pairs, including examples and a description of the coding process and its results [7].

A detailed analysis of 347 minutes of video data from a subset of ECHOES participants (M=7, F=1, mean developmental age 3 yrs, 9 mo.) showed that DR pairs occurred across all participants, who varied considerably in degree of intellectual disability, interests, and personality (see [7]). To be included in the analysis, participants needed phrase-level language use or better, and at least 30 minutes of video from activities that included the VC.

There were 236 unique discrepancies, yielding 308 observable reactions[2]. 71.11% of these were initiations to a partner. Reactions were overwhelmingly positive or neutral, with only a few instances of verbal frustration in relation to un-resolvable discrepancies (see 3.3). There were *zero instances* of serious distress (e.g. children shouting, crying, attempting to escape or otherwise "melting down") in relation to any part of the ECHOES VE or sessions. Overall, ECHOES appears to offer good (if unintentional) proof-of-principle that discrepancies can motivate young children with ASC to initiate positively to social partners.

---

[1] Errors in the sense of the system executing the "wrong" action with respect to activity goals, usual object behaviour, etc.

[2] The reaction total includes instances of children making multiple initiations about the *same* discrepancy, and thus is higher than the number of unique discrepancies in the dataset.

## 1.3 Reconciling RRB & discrepancy-detection

These findings seem to contradict the "core" ASC characteristic of *restricted and repetitive behaviours* (RRB), sometimes described as a "need for sameness" (e.g. [1]). There may be insistence on specific routines, unusually intense and narrow interests, and experience of changes as highly disruptive. The ASC literature would *not* predict that this group would show (positive) interest in, or *enjoy,* novel and surprising aspects, let alone share these with another person—repeatedly. So, what exactly is happening in ECHOES? Why do we see giggling instead of crying?

The simplest conclusion is that there *is* no conflict between the literature and the current findings. Instead, ECHOES fortuitously struck a productive balance between sameness and (unplanned) discrepancies. The VE appears to have violated expectations and/or introduced novel aspects in such a manner as to attract interest and be "worth communicating about", while still keeping *enough* sameness not to be overly confusing or threatening.

## 1.4 Discrepancy-detection as a design strategy

This demonstration of a productive balance in ECHOES suggests a more general design strategy for motivating young children with ASC to initiate *within* and *about* VEs (or similar technologies): *deliberately* embedding attractive novel aspects, pattern-violations and other alterations in order to attract child interest and motivate their initiations. Collectively, these are referred to as *discrepancy-detection opportunities* (DDOs). However, the example of ECHOES suggests that DDOs cannot be crammed into a system higgledy-piggledy; they must be balanced with aspects that are held constant and expectations that are *not* violated. Design recommendations are essential to maintaining this balancing act. The current paper distils what appears to have "gone right" in ECHOES with respect to balancing DDOs and predictability, grouping this information around six core concepts and introducing preliminary, high-level recommendations for incorporating DDOs into future interactive technologies.

## 2.     ASSUMED CONTEXT OF DESIGN

The high-level design recommendations in this paper are likely to be valid for contexts broadly similar to ECHOES in terms of their goals, general style of child-system interaction, manner of use, and child user group (see 1.2). They assume an exploratory environment with non-competitive activities, oriented toward play and interaction rather than performance. Activities may offer embedded skills practice, but not explicit content teaching or drill-and-practice. The child is assumed to use the environment multiple times, permitting her/him to develop expectations about it. An adult is assumed to be continuously available during use, able to respond to the child or assist where necessary. This role should be largely reactive, with the child primarily acting on the system and driving social interactions with the adult, if any.

These recommendations also make a crucial assumption about *why* designers may wish to include deliberate DDOs: that the end goal is always to *encourage children's spontaneous initiations.* Children's discrepancy-detection is neither considered inherently valuable, nor treated as a stand-alone task. It is of value to the design only where it motivates subsequent communication.

## 3.     INITIAL RECOMMENDATIONS

These recommendations aim to help designers motivate child initiations via DDOs and to ensure that children's overall system experience is positive and emotionally manageable. While it is "good practice" to design systems and interactions that are coherent, comprehensible, and largely predictable to users, the current goal is more complex: to create a system *coherent and predictable enough* that its behaviour can be a talking point rather than a threat for children with ASC—even as it repeatedly violates their expectations. The task is thus to identify the fruitful middle zone between complete "sameness" and unmanageable chaos.

ECHOES appears to have successfully balanced novelty, surprise, and the "need for sameness"—even though this was not an original design goal. *Most* aspects of the VE (background, sounds, objects) and the sessions (researchers, duration, room) remained largely similar over weeks of use, i.e. they had high *integrity*. Based on analysis of the number, type, and distribution of DR pairs in the ECHOES data [7], the authors offer several high-level recommendations for successfully embedding *deliberate* DDOs in future technology designs, grouped around six key concepts. We recommend that designs with embedded DDOs should:

1. Maintain high *integrity* in the environment and in individual activities, such that "usual" rules and relationships are clearly established and largely maintained over time.
2. Allow *flexibility* of interaction within activities such that children are never "forced" to interact with a DDO that they may find disinteresting, incomprehensible, or stressful.
3. Ensure that DDOs that alter or prevent customary actions are always *resolvable,* and do not create unachievable goals or the perception of the environment being completely "broken".
4. Offer a *variety* of DDOs to accommodate child interests.
5. Include DDOs at a *frequency* that is regular, but will not make them a major proportion of the child-system interaction.
6. Offer DDOs that are *ambiguous* communicative motivators, rather than DDOs that make implicit demands for the child to initiate using specific behaviours or for specific purposes.

## 3.1 Integrity

An environment with high *integrity* maintains a level of consistency that makes it *possible* for a child to determine what is new, different, or missing (i.e. to detect discrepancies). For this user group, the required consistency is high. *Most* aspects should be held constant most of the time. The environment should appear to be a lawful place with occasional changes and mistakes, not one with constantly changing rules or no rules at all. The child should be able to explore and to develop clear expectations about the content, patterns and functions of the environment (i.e. to establish a mental model against which to compare later experiences). He may need to play each activity at least once in an "original" form to develop these expectations, before surprises are introduced. Forming expectations means establishing how and when one's actions affect the environment. Cause-and-effect relationships must be clear and reasonably simple, with a 1:1 correspondence between actions and results. Ideally, results should be immediate, or minimally delayed.

Systems with multiple activities must have a certain level of integrity, to make sure that children can tell activities apart, understand which "rules" may apply, and be sure of their current goal. This recommendation is included specifically because it was a weakness of ECHOES, which did not adequately signal different activities in a consistent, language-free way. One background plus re-use of objects to "keep things simple" meant that many activities *looked* similar, despite differing goals and

object properties. This created frequent confusion when children tried to perform object actions that "should work" only to find that the objects were "broken" (i.e. actions were currently disabled), or looked for objects that "should" be there, but were not a part of the activity. ECHOES participants initiated about these expectation-violations insistently but calmly. However, the potential for these situations to create frustration and negative affect remains.

We advise that activities should be easily differentiable *from the child's viewpoint* (i.e. in terms of appearance and goals—not only by name). Where several activities are related (e.g. activities with same core goal, varying in difficulty) this should also be apparent *from the child's viewpoint.* Designers should not choose DDOs that affect activity-identifying features and introduce confusion about which activity is being played (e.g. do not remove a "signalling" piece of scenery as a surprise). Also, DDOs should not fundamentally alter, or prevent attainment of, core activity goals. When activities are very simple with limited objects and actions, an altered core goal effectively creates a new activity.

## 3.2 Flexibility

In ECHOES, it was rare for multiple parts of an activity or the environment to be concurrently affected by a discrepancy. Novel aspects were always presented alongside familiar ones. AI planner or graphical rendering errors generally only disrupted one object type at a time (or Andy), leaving the rest of an activity "intact" and operating as usual. Children who did not wish to engage with particular aspects could act on unaffected (or less-affected) ones. Those encountering (objectively) new or different aspects could switch their attention elsewhere without any other apparent reaction, continuing the overall flow of play. This *flexibility* of action (i.e. never being "forced" to engage with a DDO) may be a reason why ECHOES discrepancies were manageable. The opportunity to detect any given discrepancy lay with the child, as did the option to share it, laugh at it, *or ignore it.*

Based on these observations, designers are advised to enable flexibility of action by including DDOs that affect only *part* of the environment at a time, rather than having global effects, and by ensuring that there is *more than one possible action or focus of attention in the environment* that the child can switch between. A flexible "order of operations" is one way to do this, e.g. making activities modular with repeated "units" of action, rather than unique actions or actions in a set sequence. These suggestions aim to help children feel safe, and prevent disrupting their experiences to the extent of feeling overwhelmed or angry.

## 3.3 Resolvability

This principle requires DDOs that alter or prevent customary actions to be *resolvable* within the environment, and to avoid impasses in which activity goals are unachievable or the environment appears "broken" and unresponsive. *Resolving* a discrepancy may include direct child action (e.g. doing the action after the virtual character made a mistake), or may require adult intervention (e.g. demonstrating the correct action, giving a command through a system control panel). Re-starting an activity or the system should also automatically resolve or "reset" altered aspects (i.e. they should not persist across uses). DDOs that totally halt the "flow" of activity and demand a specific action or adult intervention should be relatively rare, as genuine system malfunctions may already provide events of that type. Finally, note that not all discrepancies require resolution. This principle applies only to surprises that alter or prevent customary actions. It does not make sense to talk about "resolving" a novel aspect.

## 3.4 Variety

When designing for young children with ASC in general, ECHOES findings suggest incorporating a wide *variety* of DDOs, including "something for everyone", whether a child needs hands-on interaction, notices novelty but not surprises, or only likes sound effects. Each child can detect and react to *some* opportunities, meaning that the overall design strategy can still be of benefit even when individual users' patterns of interest and activity are quite different. This recommendation stems from the ECHOES observation that particular discrepancies of great interest to some children were *completely unnoticed* by others. There was strikingly little overlap between children in the sets of discrepancies they detected, plus wide variation in their *breadth* of interest (a range from 8 to 21 types of discrepant aspects). Only *one* aspect motivated all children to initiate: discovering that a usually responsive object was now unresponsive.

The lack of overlap would be problematic *if* children had reacted positively to "favourite" discrepancies and been upset by others. This was not the case: they laughed and shared excitement about favourites, with visible but more neutral reactions elsewhere. The lack of negative reactions to discrepancy may be related to *flexibility* of interaction: In ECHOES, children almost always had options within the VE, and were not "forced" to interact with or resolve specific [potentially disinteresting or threatening] aspects. Without this flexibility, negative reactions might increase.

## 3.5 Frequency of DDOs

As noted in 3.4, there was relatively little overlap in the aspects children detected as discrepant—what fascinated some was invisible to others. The highly *subjective* nature of discrepancy means that designers can include a fairly high number of DDOs without worrying about creating chaos—only some of them will "exist" to any one child. Current ECHOES videos can help us to estimate how many DDOs to use in the future. Children detected 236 unique discrepancies (129 surprises and 107 novel aspects) in 347 minutes of video. On average, this is a surprise detected every 2.7 minutes and a novel aspect every 3.2 minutes. A 12-minute session could thus include *at least* 4-5 surprises *and at least* 3-4 novel aspects while still maintaining high overall integrity. "At least" is emphasized as it is highly unlikely that a child would take up all opportunities. Designers need to include enough DDOs, with enough variety, for every child to be interested in a subset of them (e.g. planning 10 surprises and 8 novelties in a session, expecting that children may react to half).

## 3.6 Ambiguity

A strong potential benefit of deliberate DDOs as a design strategy is that they enable interesting and open-ended communicative *opportunities,* to which the child can react for any purpose, using any relevant behaviour. For example, after observing Andy make a mistake (Figure 1) it is equally relevant and appropriate to initiate by correcting him, by commenting and pointing, or by sharing laughter with the researcher. The alternative to such ambiguous motivators is embedding specific communicative *demands,* (e.g. giving a child a broken pencil with which to write her name "demands" an initiation to request another; see [5, 6]). The *flexibility* principle grants children some freedom of action. *Ambiguity* seeks to enable freedom of *re*action. With respect to facilitating initiation, these ambiguous opportunities seem more like "daily life" situations than do specific demands, possibly forming a more likely basis for skill generalisation (as yet an untested hypothesis). From a research standpoint, ambiguous DDOs offer a valuable window into the interests and attentional focus of young children with ASC, illuminating the often-significant gaps between the adult designer's intentions and the child's experience of the interaction.

## 4. ONGOING & FUTURE WORK

Previous work [7] has established discrepancy-detection as a promising phenomenon. This paper takes the first steps toward developing it as a design strategy. Many unknowns remain regarding the relative motivational effectiveness of specific discrepancies and the types of initiations which result. Ongoing work with the ECHOES dataset seeks to answer these questions and to generate more specific, low-level recommendations. A parallel line of analysis is investigating patterns of discrepancy-detection within and across children, developing a small set of design personae representing different styles of child-system interaction as a resource for personalising technologies at a "profile" level, rather than the one-size-fits-all approach here.

The next phase of research will be to implement these recommendations in new activities and test how they work in practice. Ideally, this will broadly replicate the existing patterns of DR pairs, provide proof-of-principle that DDOs can motivate communication, and yield information about the extent to which this phenomenon generalises across participants and contexts of use. The end goal of the current and planned work is a robust and flexible collection of design strategies applicable to motivating initiations in interactive technologies for ASC.

## 5. ACKNOWLEDGMENTS

This research is part of a PhD by the first author, funded by The University of Edinburgh and SICSA. It includes materials from the ECHOES project (ESRC/EPSRC TEL; RES-139-25-0395). Thanks to the ECHOES team (see www.echoes2.org) and participating schools, staff and children.

## 6. REFERENCES

[1] DSM-5: *Diagnostic and Statistical Manual of Mental Disorders*. American Psychiatric Association, Washington DC. (2013).

[2] Fletcher-Watson, S., McConachie, H., O'Hare, A., Pain, H., & Hammond, S. (2012). Click-East: Teaching Social Attention Skills to Young Children with Autism using an iPad App. (ITASD, Valencia, Spain).

[3] Baron-Cohen, S., Golan, O., Chapman, E., & Grander, Y. (2007). Transported to a world of emotion. *Psychologist*, 20(2):76.

[4] Rajendran, G. (2013). Virtual environments and autism: a developmental psychopathological approach. *J. of Computer Assisted Learning. 29*(4), 334-347.

[5] Constable, C. (1983). Creating communicative context. In Winitz, H., editor, Treating language disorders: for clinicians by clinicians. University Park Press, Baltimore, MD.

[6] Howlin, P. (1998). Children with autism and Asperger syndrome: a guide for practitioners and carers. John Wiley, Chichester.

[7] Alcorn, A.M., Pain, H., Good, J. (2013). Discrepancies in a virtual learning environment: something "worth communicating about" for young children with ASC? (IDC '13, New York).

# MakeScape Lite: A Prototype Learning Environment for Making and Design

Brian A. Danielak, Adam Mechtley,
Matthew Berland
University of Wisconsin–Madison
Department of Curriclum and Instruction
225 N. Mills St. Madison, WI 53706
{danielak, mechtley, mberland}@wisc.edu

Leilah Lyons, Rebecca Eydt
New York Hall of Science
47-01 111th St.
Corona, NY, 11368
{llyons, reydt}@nysci.org

## ABSTRACT
We describe the development and user testing of an iPad prototype for a new museum-based, interactive tabletop computer game called *MakeScape Lite*. The game lets learners—who have no prior formal experience in circuitry—build virtual circuits in a fantasy challenge scenario to (1) learn some basic circuitry concepts and (2) engage in basic engineering practices, such as problem identification, design, and iteration. In phase 1 of testing, we explored how children socially interacted to develop design goals when the game lacked explicit guidance about what to do. In phase 2, which we discuss here, we iterated the prototype with partially worked examples to offer more explicit guidance to children. We then studied video and game log data of students playtesting the game.

## Categories and Subject Descriptors
K.3.1 [**Computers Uses in Education**]: *Collaborative learning*;

## Keywords
*MakeScape*, constructionism, engineering education, informal learning, design-based research.

## 1. INTRODUCTION AND RATIONALE
Many recent educational reform documents in the US have pressed for a focus on enhancing scientific and technological literacy of young people [9]. Among other things, it is frequently argued that in order to participate meaningfully in a society that is rich in technological artifacts, people should develop not only an understanding of the concepts underlying technologies, but also familiarity with the practices and values found in the social groups where these technologies are used and created.

In this regard, a good deal of work in recent decades has focused on enhancing the abilities of young people to participate in computer programming. For example, *Scratch* was initially developed to provide a platform for young people to express themselves, and was made freely available in specialized community centers, or Computer Clubhouses [11]. In addition to the successes Scratch has had in scaling to wider audiences, its associated research program has helped to advance theoretical aspects of designing such experiences for youth.

In spite of these inroads, however, there still exist few bridges for young people to pursue *physical* computing. For example, while it has been suggested that *Scratch* can serve as an effective stepping stone for more advanced computer programming tools [12], there are few ways for middle-school-aged young people to develop incipient expertise required for the creation of custom electronics and circuits. Although Arduino has substantially lowered the entry barrier for novice electrical engineers [10], newcomers focused on tinkering and exploration can still easily damage its components.

One tool that currently bridges this gap for young people is Elenco Electronics' *Snap Circuits*, an educational toy that uses real components and formal semiotic markers of circuitry, without requiring users to solder interconnections. Kits contain a number of pre-wired components that can be snapped into a breadboard, much like LEGO bricks, in order to create working circuits. Depending upon the particular components included, each kit also contains instructions for various projects, such as alarms or radios. Although products such as *Snap Circuits* provide an opportunity for interested young people to learn about the basics of circuitry, they do not, as designed artifacts, embed motivation for activity in themselves.

Computer games, on the other hand, are predicated on inspiring motivation in their players. We posit there is room for computer-game-based learning environments to serve as a stepping-stone into the world of custom circuitry because they can provide "embodied learning experiences" [5, 6] and environments where the learning content has "situated meaning" [13].

Consequently, we describe a prototype of a museum-based computer game—*MakeScape Lite*—wherein players must explore basic concepts of circuitry in order to probe the game's underlying rules, as well as to accomplish in-game tasks. As a virtual space, *MakeScape Lite* enables the rapid exploration and prototyping of circuit construction. Students get framed practice engaging in basic engineering practices, such as problem identification, design, and iteration. In what follows, we describe results from two iterative user studies on an iPad-based prototype of *MakeScape Lite*.

## 2. DESIGNING MAKESCAPE LITE

In order to motivate the creation and modification of circuits in a way that can be easily understood by a range of potential users, the game employs a playful fantasy world. Specifically, the conceit of the game (largely implicit in this iteration) is that players take on the role of explorers in a newly discovered, aquatic cave ecosystem where their duty is to catalogue the species they encounter. Luminescent creatures in the game are attracted to different color combinations of light, and explorers can build light-emitting diode (LED) circuits as lures. This decision was adopted with the purposes of both motivating activity (i.e. players build circuits because they are the principal means of attracting creatures) and providing structure to guide experimentation (i.e. patterns of association between creatures and lights can help children form and test hypotheses about novel creatures). For example, we proposed that creatures could vary across a number of dimensions (e.g., color, morphology) that correspond to different properties of the lights (e.g., color, number of lights), and, as a result, part of the challenge entails learning how these patterns correspond in order to make predictions and execute plans related to luring specific organisms.

In this regard, a principal challenge for us has been to specify what learning goals are suitable in the game's use context, given that the creation of circuits potentially entails a range of complex concepts of electricity that have been a source of persistent problems among physical science educators of adolescents and young adults [3, 4, 7, 14]. We plan to deploy the final product—*MakeScape*—as an exhibit at a museum situated in a diverse urban community, which introduces a few unique challenges. First, the community the museum serves is very multicultural, such that proficiency in English cannot be assumed. Second, although interactive exhibits commonly command a greater duration of visitors' attention than do traditional exhibits, we likely have a small amount of contact time with which to work. Third, as has been remarked elsewhere [1, 2], the inclusion of several modes of interaction (particularly when they are of equal salience) can obscure the phenomena that designers intend to foreground. Learners might get so engaged in the fantasy world that they miss the engineering focus.

As such, we have elected to focus only on aspects of simple circuits, of which only a subset was incorporated in this iteration. Specifically, the current phase of prototyping only allowed differences in the number and colors of lights, though later iterations could incorporate timers to control blinking, for example. Moreover, the principal concept explored in this iteration concerned simply the need to create a closed circuit with a power source.[1] Consequently, quantitative reasoning aspects of resistance and current have not yet been incorporated, and the only circuit components were batteries and lights. Future iterations will introduce further elements as needed, such as resistors and timers. Additionally, in order to facilitate electrical engineering *literacy*, we elected to use semiotic markers of the discipline, such as symbols on circuit diagrams.

Fundamentally, we have adopted *constructionism* as a guiding framework for this project [8]. In short, we expect that

participants' learning processes are enhanced not only when they are responsible for the construction of their own knowledge (in contrast to, e.g., receiving information from an expert), but also when they represent their knowledge in the form of externally accessible artifacts. This facet has the added benefit of facilitating players' learning from one another. For example, the goal is for the final museum exhibit to be played on a multi-user, interactive tabletop surface using physical manipulatives (i.e. "blocks") with fiducial markers, each corresponding to a different component featuring a visual representation of its diagrammatic symbol.

In line with the constructionist design, our goal is ultimately to create an experience, which—in contrast to traditional modes of learning about electricity and circuitry—is focused on creating circuits in order to accomplish specific tasks. In short, rather than introduce abstract concepts which learners then apply in the planning and construction of circuits, we aim to offer players the opportunity to create and test circuits with minimal costs of failure. Rather than *learning in order to make circuits*, we aim to allow players to *make circuits in order to learn about them*. In this regard, we hypothesize there to be two primary modes of user interaction with the game, rapid experimentation and deliberative planning, each of which supports learning in different ways. For instance, our decision to represent light nodes with accompanying color selection context menus was intended to allow players to quickly change the colors of lights in order to get immediate feedback, which in turn was hypothesized to contribute to players' understanding of the lights' function in the game's goal structure.

Because we did not yet have final hardware for this stage of work, *MakeScape Lite* was created for the iPad. Consequently, the nodes were represented virtually in the game, rather than with physical objects. Figure 1 illustrates examples of the virtual nodes used.

**Figure 1. Graphical representations of battery nodes (left) amd LED nodes (right).**

Because *MakeScape Lite* features virtual blocks instead of physical ones, we also used mechanics of touching, pinching, and dragging to translate and rotate nodes. Players can draw lines between virtual, on-screen terminals attached to the nodes in order to make connections between positive and negative connectors. These connections are then represented by lines with scrolling arrows to indicate the flow of the current from one node to another. The speed and color of the scrolling animation differs to indicate whether the connection is live (i.e. transmitting power on a complete circuit). (Similarly, the nodes change colors based on these states.) Players can also trace lines with their fingers transverse to existing "wires" in order to break or "cut" a connection.

## 3. PROTOTYPE USER STUDY

### 3.1 Prototype Description

The foremost problem identified from the first round of play testing (which consisted of four children in a mixed-sex, mixed-age group) was that players needed more scaffolds in order to advance their comprehension of the game's goal structure (from (1) non-comprehension of goals, through (2) understanding of the

---

[1] Formally, this iteration allowed the creation of certain circuits that would not be valid in the real world. LEDs, for example, did not need to be paired with resistors, while in most real-world circuits LEDs require a current-limiting resistor.

need to attract fish, and ultimately to (3) an understanding of the patterned relationships between creatures and light). In short, there was simply not enough of a *game* in place to properly direct and motivate activity for an extended period of time. This problem was addressed through a couple of related modifications intended to focus players' attention on *planning* rather than on figuring out what the goals were.

First, creatures were made to emit heart particles while en route to a desired, active light source, and they were removed from the play area (i.e. collected) when they arrived at a destination. This change was intended to decrease cognitive load by reducing ambiguity in feedback. Second, a journal was added to the user interface, accessible via an iconic button in the upper right corner of the screen (see Figure 2). The journal contained clues to help establish a goal structure and facilitate movement toward the third level of comprehension identified in the first study. Specifically, a "sticky note" contained a verbal clue about the relationship between the creatures and the lights, and a progress grid recorded collected creatures and their totals. The grid was arranged in such a way as to organize the mapping between creature color/light color, and creature morphology/light count, which was conjectured to decrease cognitive load in progress monitoring. In short, the purpose of the journal was to provide a compact, non-invasive way to communicate some in-game hints to players. In order to more clearly observe the ways in which players might use the journal to form specific conjectures, we intentionally left some combinations unrepresented.

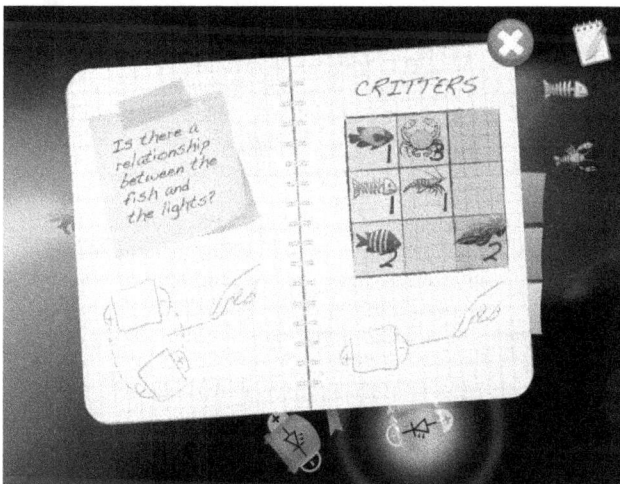

**Figure 2. The toggleable collection journal provides contextual information to players. Here, numbers indicate the number of creatures of that type a player has caught.**

In iteration 2, we also introduced a logging system to help capture participants' in-game activity with sufficient granularity. The logging system allowed us to record time-stamped entries for each basic action players took (e.g., connecting two specific nodes, disconnecting two specific nodes, moving a node, changing a light color, and opening/closing the journal). The logger also records game state every 2 seconds, including the state of the player's circuit graph and all creatures in the play area.

## 3.2 Method
As in our first test, participants consisted of a convenience sample of children recruited from a local parents' group. Specifically, the second round of testing consisted of two friends—a 12- and a 13-

year-old male (12M and 13M)—each of whom sat at a large, rectangular table with his own iPad.

Participants sat next to one another during the session and were videorecorded while they played. The game started with three lights and one battery, though one light was connected to the battery in a simple circuit. In addition to the video recording data, logs were collected from their devices after the session concluded. After playing, participants were given a brief, open-ended survey followed by a short group discussion. The survey asked about participants' gaming habits, their goals, what they had to learn in order to achieve these goals, what they found unclear, and whether the game reminded them of anything from real life.

## 3.3 Results
Participants were quick to start exploring the game. However, there was surprisingly little interaction between the participants, who were very focused on their respective game screens, with 13M glancing to his side only 3 times during the session. Rather than describe the whole session serially here, it is useful to talk about each participant in turn, as they each seemed to use the game in very different ways.

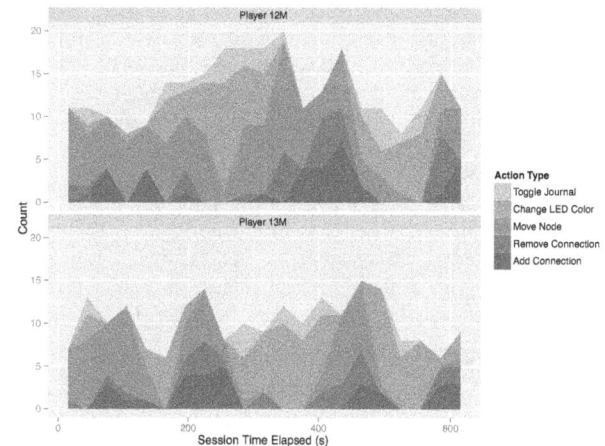

**Figure 3. Comparison of players' activity logs. Player 12M's log is on top, 13M's is on the bottom.**

A glance at 12M's action log shows that he initially focused a great deal on moving nodes around the play area (see Figure 3, top). As a consequence of this experimentation, however, he had disconnected the exemplar in the first 11 seconds, and did not begin to collect any fish until around 1:13, by which time he had created a new complete circuit. Within a few seconds of his first accessing the journal (0:36, 8 second duration), he changed an LED color. At 2:43, however, he opened the journal again (9 seconds duration) and then rapidly began to experiment with changing LED colors (8 changes within a 6-second period). By the end of his play session he had collected 181 individual creatures representing each of the classes present in the prototype.

12M's focus on goals was also apparent in his survey responses. He described both the purpose and the learning requirements in terms of our third-level understanding identified in study one. Specifically, he wrote that the purpose of the game was to "find which fish react with what light or lights," while also indicating that, in order to achieve this goal, he had to "find which fish went with what light." Moreover, he noted that "[in] the journal there were only 6 fish [and he] saw 9 slots," which he found confusing.

The video and log data reflect his adoption of the journal as a tool for progress monitoring. To wit, he opened it 14 times (average duration 4.9 seconds) to find out which creatures he was missing, and created proper configurations to attract missing creatures (including trying to create configurations for combinations absent from the prototype). In this regard, there is some evidence that he identified *testing* as the purpose of the game, and *planning* and *evaluation* as the skills needed to facilitate this goal.

In contrast, 13M appeared to be more focused on repetition of an optimal play strategy than on planning, testing, and evaluating. While he opened the log 7 times (average duration 3.5 seconds), he did not appear to use it to pursue specific creatures as much as to monitor collection counts. For example, when asked during the follow-up what they tried to do after they felt like they had collected all the creatures, 12M indicated attempting novel color combinations, while 13M said, "try and collect as many as I could, or try and collect all on one screen."

A glance at 13M's log reveals how exploitation of a single strategy can emerge from a more tentative play style. His more cautious initial interactions resulted in preservation of the exemplar circuit's connections for a longer period of time (e.g., he did not disable the example circuit until 0:29). Consequently, he had collected his first creature within 10 seconds of starting the session. In the end, he had collected 164 individual creatures representing each of the classes present. Interestingly, in comparison with 12M, more of 13M's points were distributed among creatures with higher light counts (and thus requiring more complex circuits). This disparity can be explained, however, by the long periods of time where he did little but change LED colors, which allowed his circuits to remain active (possibly due to fewer accidental disconnections). As Figures 3 shows, he interacted with the connections and nodes much less than did 12M, instead focusing on changing light colors.

## 4. DISCUSSION & FINDINGS

A key finding this study revealed was that some facilities for rapid experimentation detract focus from exploring the desired circuitry concepts when they can enable exploitation of optimal strategies. In particular, the ability to simply change colors of connected LED nodes allowed players to quickly get feedback on fish behaviors, but it also meant they devoted less time to connecting and disconnecting circuits. It is plausible this behavior is a side effect of not only the differing durations of the feedback loops for each mechanic, but also problems with the gesture-based interface. As such, circuit making became, by comparison, a more deliberative process. This pattern can be seen in Figure 3 in particular, which shows cycles predominated by either manipulation of nodes and connections, or by changing light colors and monitoring creature counts. In short, the task became simply to create a functional circuit and then play with it. Future iterations will need to more carefully investigate how or if this phenomenon relates to players' mastery of engineering practices and concepts. We expect there is a balance to maintain between artificially reinforcing the concepts of circuit creation and allowing players to painlessly pursue the game's goals.

## 5. ACKNOWLEDGMENTS

This material is based upon work supported by the National Science Foundation Graduate Research Fellowship under Grant No. DGE-0718123, as well as by the National Science Foundation under Grant No. REE 1263814. Any opinions, findings, and conclusions or recommendations expressed in this material are those of the authors and do not necessarily reflect the views of the National Science Foundation.

## 6. REFERENCES

[1]  Allen, S. 2004. Designs for learning: Studying science museum exhibits that do more than entertain. *Science Education.* 88, S1 (2004), S17–S33.

[2]  Allen, S. and Gutwill, J. 2004. Designing With Multiple Interactives: Five Common Pitfalls. *Curator: The Museum Journal.* 47, 2 (2004), 199–212.

[3]  Cohen, R. et al. 1983. Potential difference and current in simple electric circuits: A study of students' concepts. *American Journal of Physics.* 51, 5 (May 1983), 407–412.

[4]  Engelhardt, P.V. and Beichner, R.J. 2003. Students' understanding of direct current resistive electrical circuits. *American Journal of Physics.* 72, 1 (Dec. 2003), 98–115.

[5]  Gee, J.P. 2004. *Situated language and learning: a critique of traditional schooling.* Routledge.

[6]  Gee, J.P. 2003. *What video games have to teach us about learning and literacy.* Palgrave Macmillan.

[7]  Gentner, D.R. and Gentner, D. 1983. Flowing Waters or Teeming Crowds: Mental Models of Electricity. *Mental Models.* D. Gentner and A.L. Stevens, eds. Erlbaum. 99–129.

[8]  Papert, S. and Harel, I. 1991. Situating Constructionism. *Constructionism: Research Reports and Essays, 1985-1990.* I. Harel and S. Papert, eds. Ablex Pub. Corp. 1–11.

[9]  Pearson, G. et al. 2002. *Technically speaking: Why all Americans need to know more about technology.* National Academy Press.

[10] Recktenwald, G.W. and Hall, D.E. 2011. Using Arduino as a platform for programming, design and measurement in a freshman engineering course. *Proceedings of 118th American Society of Engineering Education Annual Conference & Exposition* (Vancouver, B.C., Canada, 2011).

[11] Resnick, M. et al. 1999. High technology and low-income communities: prospects for the positive use of advanced information technology. D.A. Schön et al., eds. MIT Press. 263–286.

[12] Resnick, M. et al. 2009. Scratch: Programming for All. *Commun. ACM.* 52, 11 (Nov. 2009), 60–67.

[13] Shaffer, D.W. et al. 2005. Video Games and the Future of Learning. *The Phi Delta Kappan.* 87, 2 (Oct. 2005), 104–111.

[14] Stetzer, M.R. et al. 2013. New insights into student understanding of complete circuits and the conservation of current. *American Journal of Physics.* 81, 2 (Jan. 2013), 134–143.

# Stamp-On in a Museum:
# Helping Children's Scientific Inquiry

Keita Muratsu
Kobe University
3-11, Tsurukabuto, Nada-ku
Kobe, Hyogo, Japan
115d101d@stu.kobe-u.ac.jp

Ayako Ishiyama
Tama Art University
2-1713, Yarimizu
Hachioji, Tokyo, Japan
ishiyama@tamabi.ac.jp

Fusako Kusunoki
Tama Art University
2-1713, Yarimizu
Hachioji, Tokyo, Japan
kusunoki@tamabi.ac.jp

Shigenori Inagaki
Kobe University
3-11, Tsurukabuto, Nada-ku
Kobe, Hyogo, Japan
inagakis@kobe-u.ac.jp

Takao Terano
Tokyo Institute of Technology
4259, Nagatsuta, Midori-ku
Yokohama, Kanagawa
terano@dis.titech.ac.jp

## ABSTRACT

This study proposes a mobile support system "Stamp-On" to promote elementary school children' scientific inquiry into museum exhibits. The unique characteristic of Stamp-On is its use of a stamp-shaped interface to connect exhibits and mobile device content in an extremely simple way. In this paper, we first describe the principles and implementation of the Stamp-On system. Then, we evaluate the performance of the Stamp-On system at a various rock exhibitions. For the evaluation, 35 Japanese sixth-grade elementary school children (aged 11-12) used the Stamp-On system. We recorded the actions and utterances of one of them during their scientific inquiry process. To clarify the effectiveness of Stamp-On, we have analysed the following two factors in the scientific inquiry processes: 1) observing subjects attentively and 2) interpreting information obtained through the observation. Based on these analyses, we conclude that Stamp-On is effective to promote scientific inquiry among children.

## Categories and Subject Descriptors

H.5.2 [**Information System**]: Information Interface and presentation – *User Interfaces*

## General Terms

Design, Experimentation

## Keywords

Mobile device, museum, tangible, scientific inquiry

## 1. INTRODUCTION

In science education, children need assistance in scientific inquiry in both formal and informal settings [1, 2, 3] because inquiry is an authentic scientific practice and children should be engaged in the inquiry process [4, 5, 6]. Factors composing scientific inquiry include observing subjects attentively and interpreting the data information obtained through observation [7, 8]. To support scientific inquiry, mobile exhibition support systems used by children visiting museums have been developed and evaluated in recent years [9, 10]. However, the interfaces of these mobile systems in the literature are hard for every child to use. For example, even if these systems can be operated simply, multiple steps are required to display the content in many cases. In this study, we developed Stamp-On, a mobile exhibition support system to promote scientific inquiry among children visiting museums. The unique characteristic of Stamp-On is its use of a simple process to guide visitors toward scientific inquiry without misidentifying the exhibits. The main purpose of this study is to examine the effectiveness of the Stamp-On system to promote elementary school children's scientific inquiry into museum exhibits. The rest of the paper is organized as follows: Section 2 gives an overview of the Stamp-On system; Sections 3 and 4 describe our museum experiments, results, and discussions; and section 5 follows with concluding remarks.

## 2. A BRIEF DESCRIPTION OF THE STAMP-ON SYSTEM

### 2.1 An Overview of Basic Functions and the Interface

Stamp-On is a stand-alone system run on an iPad mini with the newly developed stamp-shaped interface. The stamp is equipped with small metal chips as used in stylus pens. The metal patterns represent coded information related to the object to be explained. Figure 1 shows an overview of Stamp-On. The system consists of an iPad mini and stamps; tangible objects in the shape of stamps are physically connected to the exhibits. When a child presses a Stamp-On to the iPad mini screen, the iPad mini acquires an ID, after which content connected to the ID is displayed on the screen. As referred to above, the unique characteristic of Stamp-On is that these linked stamps make it possible to connect exhibits to content in an extremely simple way. Because of this characteristic, children are able to conduct an inquiry without misidentifying the exhibits. The multi-touch technology of iPad and Android devices is used for the stamps. In this study, the bottom of the stamps (Figure 2) includes 10 types of electrification patterns. When the user picks up the stamp and presses it onto the iPad mini screen, the iPad mini detects the pattern and displays an explanation corresponding to the exhibit.

## 2.2 Contents for the Experimental Evaluation

Eight representative types of rocks found in Hyogo Prefecture, Japan, were used to evaluate Stamp-On. Children had to observe these rocks using three hints and the names of the rocks displayed on the iPad mini. They then identified specific rocks. The three hints related to the condition of the rock's surface ("surface hint"), the rock's colour ("colour hint"), and a magnified photograph of the rock's surface ("magnified photograph hint"). For example, based on hints in the tuff (Figure 3), children can obtain the following information: the surface of the rock is fine and smooth with a beautiful layered structure. To confirm their identification of the rocks, the child presses the stamp attached to the rock they have chosen against the rectangular 'answer' button shown in the lower part of Figure 3. If the answer is correct, the screen displays the word 'correct', and then provides a description of the rock. A quiz on the rock is also given.

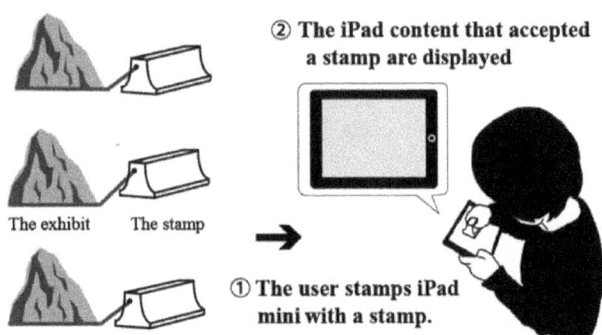

Figure 1. Overview of the Stamp-On system

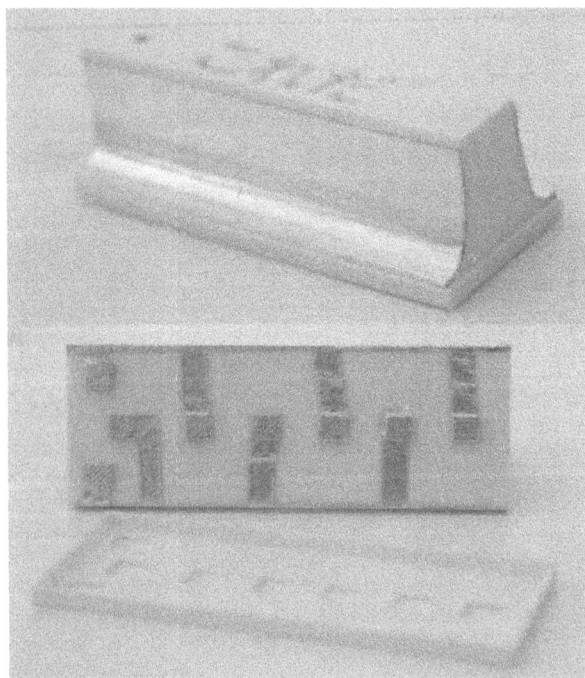

Figure 2. Top and bottom of the stamp.

## 3. EVALUATION AT A MUSEUM

The purpose of the evaluation is to determine that Stamp-On promoted scientific inquiry among participants. We thus recorded the actions and utterances of one participant during the observation. The participants were 35 Japanese sixth-grade elementary school children (aged 11–12) with no prior experience of using Stamp-On. The experiment process was as follows. First, the 35 participants were separated into groups of six children, with each group being asked to observe rocks based on the three hints and the names of the rocks displayed on the iPad mini, and then to identify specific rocks. One iPad mini was distributed to each participant during the rock observation and identification. Eight types of rocks were displayed in the exhibition, and the time allocated to the observation and identification was approximately 10 minutes. Figure 4 shows a child pressing a stamp to an iPad mini. The child picked up the stamp attached to a rock in both hands, and then pressed it against the rectangular 'answer' button.

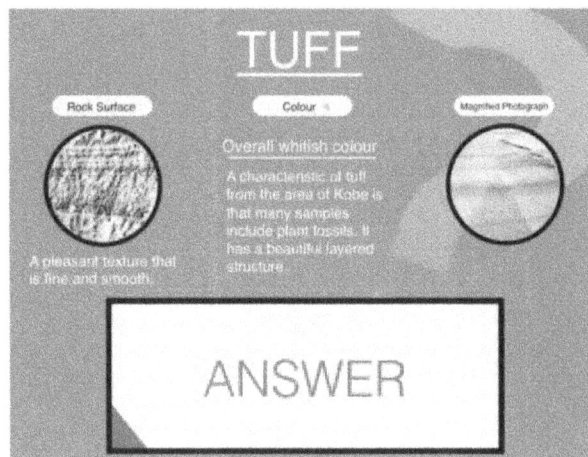

Figure 3. Screen displaying the surface, colour, and magnified photograph hints.

Figure 4. Child pressing a stamp onto the iPad mini.

## 4. EXPERIMENT AND DISCUSSION

### 4.1 Data Source and Methods of Analysis

To determine that Stamp-On promoted scientific inquiry among participants, one child was randomly selected from among the 35 participants. The actions and utterances of the participant were recorded during the experiment as the data source. The actions were recorded using a video camera and the utterances recorded with a wireless microphone. The recording of actions and utterances lasted approximately 10 minutes.

The utterances were first transcribed and then compared with the recorded actions to match the participant's actions and utterances. These were then used to determine that the following two factors comprising scientific inquiry were present: observing subjects attentively and interpreting the information obtained through observation.

## 4.2  Results and Discussions

Table 1 presents the actions and utterances of Participant 1 (P1) when observing a tuff. Four actions corresponding to the first factor, observing subjects attentively, were confirmed, notably actions 03, 06, 09, and 10. In action 03, P1 moved her face closer to the tuff from the front (a distance of 30 cm) and stared at it. In action 06, P1 observed the pelitic schist from the front, without moving her eyes (3 sec). In action 09, P1 observed the rhyolitic welded tuff from the front (2 sec). During three of these actions, P1 attentively observed the upper front surface of the exhibited rock. In contrast, in action 10, P1 lowered her face to the left, level with

**Table 1. Actions and utterances of Participant 1 (P1) during the rock observation.**

| Time (sec) | iPad mini display | Action | Utterance |
|---|---|---|---|
| 0 | Surface hint (The surface has a pleasant texture that is fine and smooth) | 01 P1 quickly heads to the location of the exhibited tuff while reading the surface hint. | 01  It's [the rock] probably over here. |
| | | 02 After standing in front of the tuff and quickly touching the front side two or three times with her right index finger, P1 slowly looks over the exhibited rock from left to right (approximately 3 sec). | 02 This one [the tuff] is made up of layers, so it's sedimentary. |
| | | 03 <u>P1 moves her face closer to the tuff from the front (distance of 30 cm) and stares at it.</u> | |
| 15 | Colour hint (This rock contains many plant fossils and has a beautiful layered structure) | 04 P1 taps the screen with her right index finger to open the colour hint. | |
| | | 05 While viewing the screen with the surface and colour hints, P1 slowly moves to the location where the pelitic schist is exhibited (5 sec). | |
| | | 06 <u>P1 observes the pelitic schist from the front, without moving her eyes (3 sec).</u> | |
| 30 | Magnified photograph hint (Photograph showing the layered structure of tuff) | 07 P1 places her elbow on the desk, displays the magnified photograph hint, and looks over the exhibited rock (2 sec). | 03 Is that it? No, maybe not… |
| | | 08 P1 runs to the exhibited rhyolitic welded tuff (6 sec). | |
| | | 09 <u>P1 observes the rhyolitic welded tuff from the front (2 sec).</u> | |
| 45 | | 10 <u>P1 lowers her face to the left, level with the exhibited rock, and then moves closer to the rock (10 cm) to observe it (4 sec).</u> | 04 I think it's this one. Wait, no… |
| | | 11 P1 looks at the screen with three hints (5 sec). | |
| 60 | | 12 P1 moves in front of the exhibited tuff while reading the colour hint aloud (10 sec), and observes the tuff from the front (2 sec). | 05 It has plant fossils. It has a layered structure. |
| | | 13 P1 puts the iPad mini on the table where the rock is exhibited. She presses the stamp on it while smiling. | 06 Ah, it's this, this one! |
| 75 | Screen confirming the correct identification of tuff and an explanation. | 14 P1 picks up the iPad mini and reads the screen that confirms her correct response and gives an explanation. She looks concentrated (5 sec) | 07 Hmm, it's 'tuff' [in English]. |
| 90 | Quiz screen (Does tuff have a rough or smooth texture?) | 15 P1 smiles and sways (approximately 3 sec). She displays the quiz screen and reads the quiz (4 sec). | 08 Okay! I found it! Can I touch the rock? |
| | | 16 <u>P1 confirms the texture of the tuff by rubbing its surface four times from the top to the bottom, with her right index, middle, and ring fingers (approximately 3 sec)</u> | 09 <u>It's smooth.</u> |
| | | 17 P1 pushes the "smooth texture" answer button. | |
| 105 | Screen displayed after answering the quiz correctly | 18 P1 smiles while looking at the screen (approximately 3 sec). | 10 I picked the rock up. |

*Note.* The underlined portions are actions and utterances corresponding to the scientific inquiry process.

the exhibited rock, to observe the rock from the side and then moved closer to the rock (10 cm) to observe it (4 sec). It is thought that P1 looked at the side of the rock because the colour hint stated that the rock had a layered structure, which encouraged P1 to observe the characteristics of the rock from different angles. We can speculate that action 10 provided the best viewpoint for observation and was desirable in the context of carrying out a scientific inquiry.

Action 16 and utterance 09 were confirmed to correspond to the second practice of interpreting information obtained through observation. P1 collected information to respond to a question in the quiz as to whether the surface of tuff is rough or smooth when touched. In action 16, P1 confirms the texture of the tuff by rubbing its surface 4 times from the top to the bottom with her right index, middle, and ring fingers (approximately 3 sec). She also spoke while performing this action, saying, 'It's smooth'. Therefore, utterance 09 may be perceived as an interpretation of the rock's surface based on the information obtained through action 16.

We can speculate that the following aspects of Stamp-On are beneficial, as confirmed in the scientific inquiry process manifested through P1's actions and utterances. First, because the stamps are linked to actual rocks, there was low risk that participants would misidentify the rocks while conducting the scientific inquiry. Second, viewpoints for rock observation could be given to participants through rock-related hints provided by Stamp-On.

## 5. CONCLUDING REMARKS

The purpose of this study was to examine the effectiveness of the Stamp-On system to promote elementary school children's scientific inquiry into museum exhibits. The unique characteristic of Stamp-On is its use of a simple process to guide visitors towards inquiry without misidentifying the exhibits. From the results of the evaluation, two factors in the inquiry process were confirmed in the child's actions and utterance. From these results, we conclude that Stamp-On may promote scientific inquiry among children.

Our future work includes clarifying the effectiveness of the Stamp-On system with more participant subjects, and further improving the Stamp-On system.

## 6. ACKNOWLEDGEMENTS

This research was supported by JSPS KAKENHI Grant Number 24240100 and 24650521.

## 7. REFERENCES

[1] Metz, K. E. 2004. Children's understanding of scientific inquiry: Their conceptualization of uncertainly in investigations of their own design. *Cognition and instruction 22*, 2, 219-290.

[2] National Research Council. 2009. *Learning science in informal environments: People, place, and pursuits.* Washington, DC: The National Academy Press.

[3] Metz, K. E. 2011. Disentangling robust developmental constraints from the instructionally mutable: Young children's epistemic reasoning about a study of their own design. *Journal of the Learning Sciences 20*, 1, 50-110.

[4] Lederman, J., Lederman, N., Bartos, S., Bartels, S., Meyer, A., and Schwartz, R. 2013. Meaningful assessment of learners' understandings about scientific inquiry: The views about scientific inquiry (VASI) questionnaire. *Journal of Research in Science Teaching 51*, 1, 65-83.

[5] Abd-El-Khalick, F., BouJaoude, S., Duschl, R, Ledeman, N, G., Mamlok-Naaman, R., Hofstein, A., Niaz, M., Treagust, D., and Tuan, H. 2004. Inquiry in science education: International perspectives. *Science Education 88*, 3, 397-419.

[6] Duschl, R., Schweingruber, H., and Shouse, A. (Eds.). 2007. *Taking science to school: Learning and teaching science in grades K-8*. Washington, DC: The National Academies Press, 2007

[7] National Academy of Sciences. 2012. *A framework for K-12 science education: Practices, crosscutting concepts, and core ideas.* Washington, DC: The National Academy Press.

[8] NGSS Lead States. 2013. *Next generation science standards: For states, by states.* Washington, DC: The National Academy Press.

[9] Ceipidor, U. B., Medaglia, C. M., Perrone, A., Maesico, M., and Romano, G. 2009. A museum mobile game for children using QR-codes. *Proceedings of the 8th International Conference on Interaction Design and Children.* Como, Italy: ACM, 282-283.

[10] Cahill, C., Kuhn, A., Schmoll, S., Lo, W., McNally, B., and Quintana, C. 2011. Mobile learning in museums: How mobile supports for learning influence student behaviour. *Proceedings of the 10th International Conference on Interaction Design and Children.* Ann Arbor, USA: ACM, 21-28.

# Children as Co-Researchers: More than Just a Role-Play

Fenne van Doorn
Delft University of Technology
Faculty Industrial Design Engineering
Landbergstraat 15, 2628 CE Delft, NL
+31-15-2781685
F.A.P.vanDoorn@TUDelft.nl

Mathieu Gielen
Delft University of Technology
Faculty Industrial Design Engineering
Landbergstraat 15, 2628 CE Delft, NL
+31-15-2782749
M.A.Gielen@TUDelft.nl

Pieter Jan Stappers
Delft University of Technology
Faculty Industrial Design Engineering
Landbergstraat 15, 2628 CE Delft, NL
+31-15-2783029
P.J.Stappers@TUDelft.nl

## ABSTRACT

Co-research is a method that engages participants in contextual user research by giving them the role of researcher. This method aids to capture their input in the fuzzy front end of the design process. A previous study [5] showed that children can act as co-researchers to gather contextual knowledge. In that study 20 children aged 9-12 interviewed their peers or their grandparents. One of the findings from that study was that the professional role of the co-researcher is a motivating and influencing factor, which we want to enhance in a follow-up study. Another finding was that the way of reporting (audio-recording and notes in a research booklet) could be improved.

In the present study 28 children (aged 9/10) acted as co-researchers by interviewing their peers. The goal of this study was to enhance the professional role of the children and to experiment with different recording devices, in order to explore the methodological consequences.

Using co-research gives an opportunity to go to places that are less accessible to lead researchers, like the child's room, and looking at it through the children's perspective. Making a choice between audio recorders and video cameras depends on the research set up and topic, in this case video added a lot of context since we were interested in personal belongings and a tour though their bedroom. It was found that giving mobile phones to coresearchers in order to record their interviews is not advisable; the quality of the audio is not that good and switching between making pictures and explaining them on audio is hard for them.

## Categories and Subject Descriptors

H.5.2 [**Information Interfaces and Presentation**]: User-centered design

**General Terms**: Design, Human Factors

**Keywords**: Co-research, contextual user research, design roles, children

*IDC'14*, June 17–20, 2014, Aarhus, Denmark.
ACM 978-1-4503-2272-0/14/06 …$15.00.
http://dx.doi.org/10.1145/2593968.2610461

## 1. INTRODUCTION

### 1.1 Children are experts

PD (Participatory Design) attempts to actively involve all stakeholders in the design process. Users are important stakeholders, because they are the "experts of their experience" [4]. Just as adults, children have their own wishes and needs and it is important to keep those in mind when designing technology aimed at children. Children's experiences and thoughts are valuable input in the design process to ensure the end product fits their needs. Therefore, we need to involve them from the start of the design process. Techniques for that, used in the field of Child Computer Interaction are for example: Cooperative Inquiry [1], Cultural probes [2] and Contextmapping [4]. This paper focuses on co-research, a method to give children the role of researcher to conduct research with their peers or key-persons in order to generate contextual knowledge [5].

### 1.2 Co-research

The model shown in Figure 1 explains the co-research principle [5]. It displays from left to right: a designer, a researcher, a collaborator (or co-researchers) and his/her participant(s). The collaborator can be from the same target group as the participants (as in figure 1), or a key-person who is not part of the intended target group but knows somebody who is (for example a child is the key-person to his/her grandparent who belongs to an elderly target group). The main difference between these situations is that the collaborators from the same target group can reflect on the other as well as on themselves, in contrast to the key-persons who only reflect on the data from the participants.

**Figure 1. Co-research model [5]**

Similar co-research methods are used in other fields of research, like social and political sciences, to empower people under study by giving them a voice in research that is influencing their lives [3].

The translation of co-research to the field of contextual design research can be of added value because, next to empowerment this method can be used to gather different kinds of insights and motivate and train collaborators [5]:

- Co-researchers can use their network to get access to peers or key-persons.

- Conversations between peers generate different content than conversations between a participant and a researcher.

- By listening to others and hearing different people talk about the same subject, the co-researchers reflect on their own experiences and develop a grounded opinion of their own.

## 1.3 Previous study

In a previous study [5], children got the role of co-researchers to investigate intergenerational contact and opportunities to design technology that could make children and elderly become physically active together. In that study, 20 children aged 9-12 acted as co-researchers by interviewing their grandparents or peers. The project consisted of 4 meetings with groups of 4-5 children and a lead researcher. In the first meeting the children were introduced to the project and thought of questions to ask in the interviews they were going to perform. These questions were used in the development of a research booklet for the children to guide them in performing their interviews.

The second meeting was a training session in which they used the research booklet to practice interviewing on each other. After the training each child conducted interviews with 2 grandparents or peers. Subsequently, the groups of children came together for a feedback session in which they reported on their interview and made personas together. The final step was a creative session with the whole class to think of new ideas, building on the insights they gathered in the interviews.

This study showed that listening to children's conversations, without the direct interference of adults, gives an inspiring glimpse into their world. Besides that, the children developed useful skills, like asking questions, empathizing with and listening to others [5].

## 1.4 Recommendations

The professional role of the co-researchers turned out to be an important factor of the co-research method. The co-researchers take their role very serious, which makes them feel important and responsible. One aspect of this professional feeling is the audio recorder, a device most of the children never used before, and the fact that they can keep it for a week. It is interesting to investigate if other factors can increase the feeling of professionalism as well.

The audio recorder only captures sound, which already gives a lot of context in the form of conversations, whisperings and background noises, but video might give an even richer output since it adds image. Audio recorders are not at hand for every researcher. Therefore, experimenting with mobile phones, which researchers and participants more commonly own, is interesting. Also the combination of audio recording, photography and video, which a mobile phone can make, might give added value.

## 2. STUDY

The main goal of this co-research case study was to enhance the professional role of the children and to experiment with recording devices to see the methodological consequences. This study was part of the ProFit project, funded by the European Union under the Interreg IVB North West Europe program and undertaken in cooperation with the Delft City Council to improve opportunities for children's outdoor play and exercise. The topic of this case study was to investigate opportunities to use technology in order to combine children's own possessions and public playground equipment. The gathered user insights will be used as the starting point of a design assignment for students in order to design new playground technologies and equipment for children. However, this paper will report about methodological findings and will not go into detail about the topic.

In order to test the methodological consequences of the recommendations that derived from the mentioned case study, a new study was set-up in the following manner:

- Three different conditions were created, in which the children used different kinds of recording devices: audio recorders (just as in the previous case), video cameras, and mobile phones to record audio and make pictures. Some children in the previous study complained about writing in the research booklets because this slows down the interview. By adding photos and video the emphasis is no longer on writing. However, the co-researchers still need to write down keywords in their research booklets, in order to remember the interviews and being able to reflect on their findings in the feedback session a couple of days after conducting the interviews.

- More professional tools are introduced: the video cameras, mobile phones, tripods and research bags. The project is concluded with handing out research certificates, stating that the children successfully participated as co-researchers. Next to that, the overall attitude of the lead researchers towards the children is more professional and always focused on the value of their expertise.

The creative session at the end of the project is removed from the procedure since the main goal for the children is to do the interviews and to get to know and understand their peers.

## 2.1 Procedure

One class from a primary school in Delft participated in this study. This class consisted of 28 children aged 9-10 years. As in the original study, this project started with a kick-off. The whole class got a presentation about the project and engaged in a discussion about what research is. The main message towards the children was that they are experts and that we need them to gather important data. We wanted them to feel important and responsible. The children asked a lot of questions and seemed interested and eager to start.

After the group discussion their teacher divided the children in 5 groups of 5 or 6 children. Two lead researchers each guided their own groups. The goal of this first meeting was to get familiar with the research subject (borrowing, lending and using personal belongings together) and to think of questions to put in the research booklet. We started with an icebreaker in which they had to guess an object the other child had written down. We wanted them to experience that by asking the right questions you can find out information that you need and we also wanted the children to understand their expertise. They know and understand their peers better; if the lead researchers would ask the questions they would need more time to figure out the object. The final step of the first meeting was to think of questions that can be incorporated in the research booklets.

The research booklets (figure 2) consisted of: interview tips and explanations, questions to ask, encouragements and a final question in which the roles were reversed and the interviewer became the participant, in order to reflect on the interview. The booklet ended with a question the co-researchers could fill in after the second interview to compare the two interviews as preparation for the feedback session.

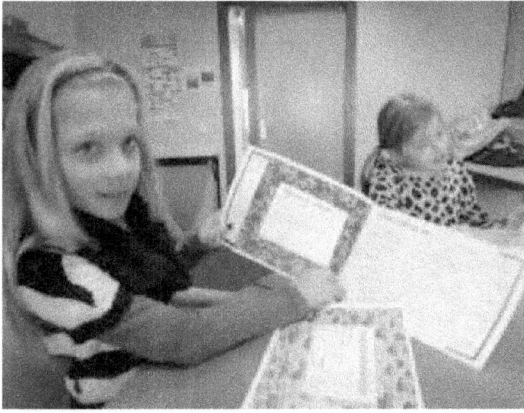

**Figure 2. Practicing with the research booklets.**

The second meeting with the small groups of children, one week later, was a training session in which the children received interview instructions and practiced with the research booklets by interviewing each other. During these practice interviews the lead researchers guided the children on what follow-up questions to ask. The tips the children found most important, or personal tips that were given during the rehearsal interview, could be added in a special area in the margin of the research booklet. The inner pages are smaller than the cover of the booklet in order for the tips to be visible during each question. Another important part of the session was filling in a research plan with the children about the choice of their participants and the timing and location of the interviews. It is important that the children choose participants they now very well and that the interviews take place at the participant's house since the questions were about personal belongings and include a tour through their bedroom. At the end of this training session, each child received a bag with a recording device (video camera, audio recorder or mobile phone), two research booklets, a pen and in some cases a small tripod (figure 3). After the training the children got one week to perform 1 or 2 interviews.

**Figure 3. Co-researchers explore their video recorders.**

After conducting the interviews, the groups of children and lead researchers came together for a final feedback-session. At the start, the children turned in their recording device and research booklets. They reported on their interviews and combined their findings by dividing their participants into different categories and making those into personas by using specially designed templates (figure 4). The templates are filled up with insights and anecdotes from their participants but also from other people they know. The personas create distance to the real participants, making it easier to share personal insights and anecdotes [5]. At the end of the feedback session all children were rewarded with a co-researchers certificate.

**Figure 4. Co-researchers show a filled-in persona template.**

## 2.2 Analysis

All the group sessions and interviews were transcribed. From these transcriptions, interesting quotes were highlighted and turned into statement cards by adding an interpretation of their meaning. Then these statement cards were clustered into different topics.

## 3. FINDINGS

## 3.1 Experimenting with recording devices

Having three different recording devices (audio recorders, video recorders and mobile phones) caused some discussion between the groups. Almost all children wanted to use one of the mobile phones; it took some time to show the possibilities of the video and audio recorders, in order for every child to be satisfied. The children with mobile phones used the audio recording and photography options, since it did not have enough memory to make video recordings of two interviews lasting at least half an hour. It turned out that the audio recordings of the mobile phones were of least quality and that the focus of the children who used the mobile phones was on making photos, which made them forget to tell stories that belong to the photos. Therefore mobile phones are not advisable.

Video cameras were used to give the children an increased feeling of professionalism and to get images accompanying the audio. In this case this worked well because they were showing personal belongings to the camera. A side effect of using video camera was that some children appointed a cameraman, an extra person who was sometimes distractive.

*Girl: "Our cameraman is using your dolphin as a wrecking ball"*

*Friend: "Noooo!"*

*Girl: "He is very annoying"*

When the co-researchers operated the camera themselves or placed it on the tripod it worked well. You can actually see the children, their facial expression, their (sometimes messy) rooms, what's hanging on their walls and how they interact with each other. It also gave the children the opportunity to emphasize certain objects or aspects by zooming in on them.

When using video you don't rely solely on the children's stories. Seeing their room also forces them to be honest, for example in the quote below from a brother with a very messy room:

*Boy: "Some children don't take good care of their things, do you have an example of that?"*

*Brother: "Euh... yes... If you are going to film my room later, you will see that I'm not that careful with my things."*

Some of the video interviews are more formal than the audio recordings because the children are more conscious of being filmed. In the end the choice to use a video or audio recorder depends on the subject of the research. In this case it was about objects within children's private spaces and within their family homes, so video added a lot of context that would be hard to enter and observe as an adult researcher.

A few co-researchers recorded extra material, for example videos of playing a computer game and the way home from school and audio recordings of breakfast in the morning and beatboxing. These additional recordings raise the level of empathy. They give a glimpse of the children's lives in an unguided way, which makes it new and surprising for the lead researcher. In this respect, the recorders functioned as collectors of more or less random probes into their lives.

## 3.2 Professional role of the co-researcher

Through the emphasis laid upon their expertise in every step of the process, the co-researchers come to feel they make an important contribution. Using their input for the research booklets and designing detailed and good looking booklets, templates and forms is appreciated by the children. The recording devices, tripods and research bags also emphasize their professional role. Most of the children appreciated the research certificate they received at the end of the project.

However, most important is to incorporate the children's expert role in the attitude of the lead researcher. It should not be deployed as a procedural gimmick for motivational purposes, but truly be at the core of the lead researcher's interest. Only then does it get naturally woven into the set-up and execution of all the interaction between researcher and co-researchers. By believing in it, the lead researcher mentions it more and uses it to motivate and compliment the children. This is also a good way to bring back focus when they tend to get off track. An indirect example of the finding that the children felt like experts is that one of the mothers told us that her son came home after the kick-off session telling her that he was the expert and that he therefore needed to do the interviews.

## 3.3 Other findings

Next to testing the improvements, we found out other striking differences between the sessions, of which two will be mentioned:

### Switching roles

The final page in the research booklet included an assignment to switch roles, giving the participant the opportunity to ask some reflecting questions to the co-researcher. For some children it did not have the effect that we intended with this assignment: reflecting on the interview together, in order to prepare the co-researcher for the feedback session.

A couple of duos skipped some of the other questions, but all children did this particular assignment. They liked switching roles for a minute. The goal of this assignment was to let the co-researcher reflect on the interview and on his/her skills, about what went well and what could be improved. An unforeseen and unwanted side effect was that switching roles gave the original interviewer the opportunity to evaluate the participant instead of his own performance.

*Co-researcher: "You did not understand some of the things, that is a big difference with the previous interview I did, that person did understand."*

Next to that, even though some children gave some beautiful reflections and conclusions, the "similarities" and "differences", that were asked to reflect upon, were taken very literally, like "he is a boy and I am a girl" or "we have the same parents".

### Group size

Another difference between the two studies was the group size. Groups of 4-5 worked well in the previous study, this time we used groups of 5-6. It turned out that a group of 6 is too big. It is hard to divide attention between all the group members, to listen to all their stories, to react adequately and to keep them focused.

## 4. DISCUSSION AND CONCLUSIONS

This paper focuses on contextual design research, getting informed and inspired by children in order to design for them.

Three different recording devices were used in order to record the individual interviews the co-researchers conducted with peers. It turned out that mobile phones are not advisable; the quality of the audio is not as good as when using audio recorders and switching between making pictures and explaining them on audio is hard.

Making a choice between audio recorders and video cameras depends on the research set up and topic, in this case video added a lot of context since we were interested in personal belongings and a tour through the children's rooms.

Using co-research gives an opportunity to go to places that are less accessible to lead researchers, like the child's room and looking at it through the children's perspective. Giving co-researchers control over a recording device that they find interesting, over a period of a week, yielded extra recordings of their daily life situations and play. These slices of life added to the broader empathic understanding of these children beyond the scope of the interviews they held.

## 5. ACKNOWLEDGEMENTS

This research is part of the Profit project, which is funded by the European Union, under the Interreg IVB North West Europe program. We would like to thank the involved primary school and especially the teachers and children of group 6 for participating in this study. We are also grateful to the Delft City Council for their cooperation throughout the project.

## 6. REFERENCES

[1] Druin, A., Cooperative Inquiry: Developing New Technologies for Children with Children, *CHI 99*, 1999

[2] Gaver, W., Dunne, T., and Pacenti, E., Cultural Probes, *Interactions*, 6, 1(1999), 21-29.

[3] McLaughlin, H., Involving Young Service Users as Co-Researchers: Possibilities, Benefits and Costs, *British Journal of Social Work*, 36.8 (2006): 1395-1410.

[4] Sleeswijk Visser, F., Stappers, P., van der Lugt, R., and Sanders, E. B. N. Contextmapping: experiences from practice. *Codesign*, 1, 2 (2005), 119-149.

[5] Van Doorn, F., Stappers, P., J., Gielen, M., Design Research by proxy: using children as researchers to conduct contextual design research. *CHI 13*, 2013

# Considering Visual Programming Environments for Documenting Physical Computing Artifacts

Eva-Sophie Katterfeldt
Digital Media in Education (dimeb)
Department of Computer Science, TZI
University of Bremen, Germany
evak@tzi.de

Heidi Schelhowe
Digital Media in Education (dimeb)
Department of Computer Science, TZI
University of Bremen, Germany
schelhowe@tzi.de

## ABSTRACT

In online communities makers share and give feedback on DIY projects. Such feedback could also help novices who get stuck in their projects. However, documenting work in progress is little considered in current tools. We therefore developed a How-To related web platform for documenting work in progress and studied how children (aged 13-18) used it to document their physical computing projects during workshops. The evaluation outcome questions the appropriateness of our web platform and reveals the benefits of visual programming environments for documenting physical computing artifacts. Suggestions are given how to extend visual programming environments into minimalistic documentation tools that provide ways for children to successfully share their work in progress with other makers.

## Categories and Subject Descriptors

K.3.2 [**Computers and Education**]: Computer and Information Science Education

## Keywords

Documentation; Visual Programming; Physical Computing; DIY; Children

## 1. INTRODUCTION

The maker movement brings about easily accessible resources to a wide audience, comprising hardware kits as well as informal learning material such as How-To tutorials and videos created and shared by amateurs. They offer informal learning approaches to sometimes complex issues such as physical computing. However, most of the work presented on maker platforms (e.g. [7, 5]) shows successfully finished projects. We presume, that learning from each other can benefit from sharing unfinished projects, including projects that got stuck and failures. This seems especially relevant

when young novices want to start making and learn something new, but face a lot of obstacles.

To benefit from other makers' help and to contribute to this maker movement, the state of a project needs to be communicated, including visions and/or current problems. To be able to communicate and share a work in progress in an online maker community, or to resume own projects later, requires having documentation at hand. It needs to be comprehensible and give a comprehensive picture, including the artifacts appearance, functionality, its authors' motivation, problems, attempts undertaken etc. But documenting work you are engaged in is laborious and not much fun because it interrupts hands-on construction activities. We are interested in how to support children (mostly teenagers), who are beginners in physical computing, to document their work in progress. Initially, we wanted to find out how a documentation tool could be designed and used for this purpose. To investigate this we developed a web platform that follows the common "How-to" format and evaluated how children used it to document their physical computing projects.

After giving some background on documentation tools and physical computing in maker and IDC contexts, we introduce the web platform, its functionality and design. The evaluation setting and methods are described. The outcome of the evaluation is presented, shifting the focus of this paper towards another kind of tool—visual programming environments—that seem more suitable for children's documentation of physical computing constructions. This is followed by a further look into work related to the outcomes, before we discuss the results and conclude the paper.

## 2. BACKGROUND

### 2.1 Documenting and Sharing

The maker movement creates a vast amount of informal learning resources. Many come from DIYers who document and share their projects online to learn from each other. They usually create this documentation in a very concrete and informal way, e.g. by means of How-To instructions which consist of pictures with text (similar to storyboarding) and demonstrate hands-on "how to" construct an artifact [19]. The How-To format is very popular, and is used on platforms like Instructables [7]. Variations of this picture-text format can be found. Diy.org [5] wants to encourage children to make and share DIY projects. Projects can be documented in a gallery style with pictures or links to videos and a description. The platform is targeted at presenting finished projects. The mobile app How.do [6] transfers the

How-To principle to mobile devices. Users can upload photos or videos of the project steps. Instead of typing text, descriptions can be audio recorded. Using a handheld device for documenting projects seems well integrated into the making process.

These very general formats are suitable for documenting diverse DIY projects and are not explicitly designed for documenting physical computing projects. They focus on documenting outcomes, not work in progress.

## 2.2 Constructing Physical Computing Artifacts

Technology development has not only contributed to the maker culture in the form of Web 2.0 communities: physical computing technologies such as Arduino [2] have become accessible to people not trained as engineers or programmers in recent years, and many educational Construction Kits [10] for children are based on Arduino components. Such kits are used in various educational settings with children who engage in hands-on experiences, inventing personally meaningful computing artifacts (e.g.[11, 4, 3]).

### 2.2.1 Visual Programming Languages

Physical computing construction kits require programming. Most tools that target children and novices use visual programming languages (VPLs). The basic elements of a VPL are graphic symbols which represent programming commands. The symbols can be composed into an executable program. The graphical symbols simplify the syntax [12]. Only certain combinations of symbols are allowed by the programming software, so that syntactic rules are inherent. A prominent example of a visual programming environment (VPE) with a VPL for kids is Scratch [16], including releases for programming Arduino [9].

## 3. THE WEB PLATFORM

In order to provide a flexible tool that facilitates documenting work in progress as well as project processes and not just project outcomes, we developed a web platform (referred to as WP hereafter). It was designed as a web community (accessible only by workshop participants) and implemented some principles derived from the How-To format. E.g., each WP item (similar to a step in a How-To) can contain one or more pictures, descriptions and file (e.g. program code) or video attachments. Pictures can be uploaded or directly captured from a webcam and annotated. Items can be commented by other users. How many items one creates to document the current state of a project is optional. On the project overview page, thumbnails of single steps can be aligned or grouped arbitrarily (fig. 1). Instead of displaying single steps linearly like common How-Tos do, individual ways (with dead end branches) of a project can be visualized. Therefore, non-linear development processes can also be documented, different solutions can be shown as different branches, and several items can be grouped as a project step.

The tool offers specific features for physical computing projects. When creating an item, standard pictures of hardware components (e.g. LEDs, sensors) can be selected from an image gallery, and file attachments allow for uploading program code. Items can be assigned to categories according to their focus (hardware development, programming, project idea, etc.). The assigned category determines the frame color of the step thumbnail shown on the project overview

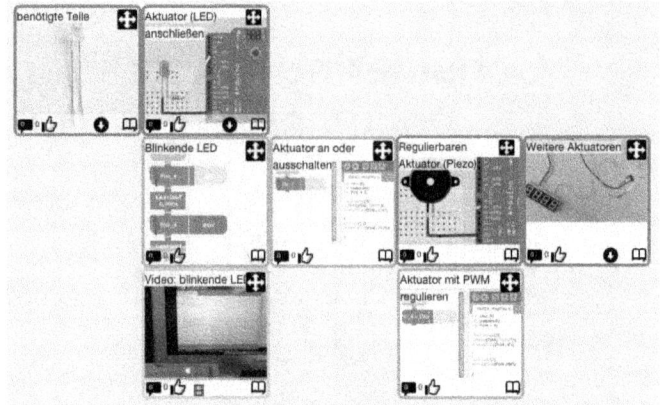

**Figure 1: Sample project overview page of the web platform showing non-linearly aligned item thumbs.**

page. The design of the tool was influenced by insights gained through running physical computing workshops for children for more than six years [18] following Constructionist [15] principles. Children did not actively participate in the design phase, but the workshops described below were meant to generate feedback for a redesign of the WP.

## 4. EVALUATION

The evaluation aimed to find out how children make use of the tool, whether the chosen format and features were suitable and perceived as useful, and how the artifacts were represented. The latter issue was examined in a content analysis of project documentations created by kids, while the previous issues were investigated in-depth in a case study.

### 4.1 Context and Setting

The tool was used and evaluated in the context of three TechKreativ Arduino workshops [18, 4]: a weekly 2-hour workshop during five weeks run as an after-school activity with 7 tenth-graders (3f/4m) and a tutor, and two four-day-long full-day workshops at a summer camp with 15 children (aged 13-18) with two tutors each. After an initial brainstorming about smart objects and a brief introduction to the technology and programming, groups of two to four participants set their project goals and worked on them for the rest of the workshop (project examples in fig. 3). The tutors tried to intervene as little as possible, and assisted the participants only when needed. The material included Arduino and Arduino LilyPad boards, switches, sensors and actuators, wires, resistors, crafting material and computers with a VPE with access to the WP. The children were encouraged to use the WP for their own needs, e.g. to create a documentation for others and for themselves for resuming projects later, or to look up solutions from others' projects.

The children used the visual programming environment (VPE) Amici [1] to program their artifacts. Amici offers a graphical interface to program Arduino boards (fig. 2). It is based on a block metaphor where graphical blocks represent programming commands. The block syntax is translated into textual Arduino programming code automatically. When choosing blocks to program sensors and actuators, the user is asked to select graphical icons representing the hardware sensors or actuators and pins, which are then visible

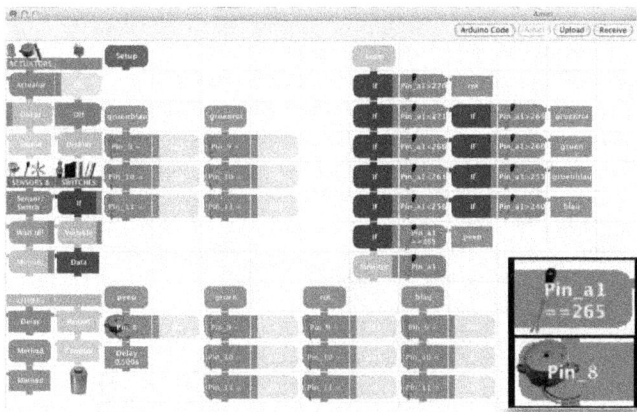

Figure 2: Amici code (for the "smart cup") with close-ups of blocks showing hardware icons.

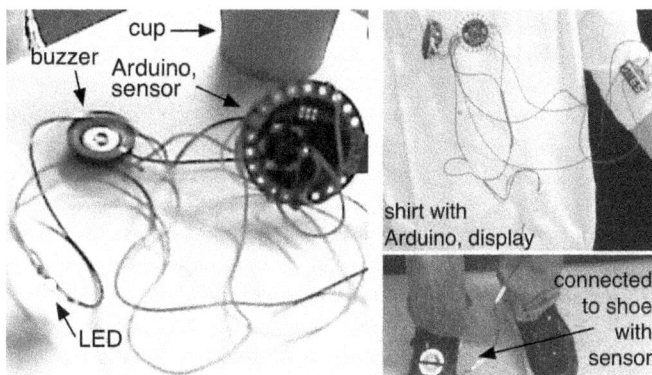

Figure 3: L: "Smart cup" before assembly. R: Close-ups of a "step-counter-shirt".

on the block. Variables and methods (i.e. functions created by the programmer) can be declared with custom names.

## 4.2 Case Study

At the weekly after-school workshop an in-depth case study was conducted with a project group of four pupils (2m/2f). They were inventing, constructing and programming a "smart cup" that showed the right drinking temperature (fig. 3 left). This project group was selected for the case study because this workshop was run on a weekly basis, making documentation appropriate for remembering the current state. When compared to other kids, the members of this group attended all sessions, were equally mixed in terms of gender and at an average age.

During and after all sessions brief field notes were taken by a tutor. One week after the last session, a semi-structured group interview was conducted by the tutor with the case study project members in an informal gathering. Its purpose was to find out how the participants perceived the tool and its features in general, why they chose to document certain artifact characteristics and use certain media types, and how they would redesign it. Screenshots of the WP features and the interviewees' project documentation were provided to facilitate the discussion and to scribble suggestions for redesign.

## 4.3 Methods for Content Analysis

The interview and field notes were analyzed with a content-structured qualitative content analysis [13]. The interview of the case study was transcribed and coded together with the field notes by one coder in two rounds. The findings were summarized according to coding categories.

Additionally, all eight project documentations created with the How-To were analyzed with scaling-structuring content analysis [13]. The purpose of this analysis was to gain insights about which specific media types were used to document different characteristics of the artifacts. The coding was done as described above. The final categories represented different characteristics (in/formal, static, dynamic) of the artifact, pragmatic aspects (such as context, authors, intention), and media types. E.g., a photograph of the hardware setup was coded as "hardware" and "iconic graphics". Results were summarized quantitatively on a percentage basis by documentation and item type. They, together with the field notes, served as contextual material for the interview evaluation.

## 5. OUTCOME

Unfortunately, use of the WP to document project states was very limited (5 project documentations with 8 items in total). E.g., at the summer camp only two documentations were created. Using the tool imposed additional effort, as it was not naturally integrated in the construction process.

The document analysis also showed that the image upload and webcam function of the WP was the documentation feature most used (5 items) besides program code upload (all items). Very few descriptive texts were added (2 items). Formulating descriptions seemed to be challenging especially for the younger children (according to the field notes). Features like image annotation and categorization of steps were not used. Also the project overview page was hardly considered. Some just updated the latest WP item to the current project state instead of creating a new item.

The kids of the after-school case study uploaded visual program code after each session and sometimes webcam captures of the built-up hardware configuration, a sketch, or of themselves. In the interview they told that they had taken pictures of the wired hardware components (like in fig. 3 left) to be able to build it up again, but that they had not used nor needed it at the next workshop session. Instead, they realized that they had found all the necessary information in the visual program code immediately: "Actually [...] the program was sufficient where you could see what was connected where" one boy concluded. Asked what other information they considered relevant for external makers to reproduce the project, they argued that, besides a detailed picture, they would say what the artifact was supposed to be and describe incidents that occurred.

Due to these rather unexpected findings, we analyzed 16 Amici programs (documented in the WP plus others created by kids in similar workshops, see also fig. 2). The same analyzing procedure and categories used for the WP document analysis were applied. It was found that about one third of the analyzed programs did not only contain characteristics of the program and hardware setup. By means of method declarations and program code file names, information about the appearance, behavior or purpose and context of the artifact (e.g., "future", "blink", colors) were mentioned. The outcomes also confirmed us about design decisions made for Amici previously [18].

## 6. RELATED WORK ON VPES

Attempts to implement additional value into VPEs for children and novices have been made by others. Some VPEs for Arduino have features which are suitable for documenting hardware setups, similar to the ones of the Amici VPE. Examples are ModKit [14], Minibloq [8] and S4A [9]. S4A builds on Scratch, which is connected to a community website. Programs can be uploaded directly from the IDE [16]. Extensions have been suggested for encouraging Scratch programmers to reflect on their intentions [17]. However, these tools are not comprehensive in the sense that they allow users to document all facets of their artifacts, including "soft" characteristics such as appearance, purpose or functionality.

## 7. DISCUSSION

The WP proved to be less suitable for documenting the artifacts than expected. This was probably due to the fact that they required extra effort and because using it interrupts the construction process. Surprisingly, the evaluation pointed to VPEs potential not only for programming, but also for documenting. The children found the program files sufficient to rebuild their project configuration, especially because they could read the hardware configuration at a glance from the VPE program. Direct access to a webcam proved to be very suitable to facilitate the integration of pragmatic aspects (e.g., context and authors) and informal characteristics like the artifact's appearance or sketches.

A VPE is well integrated into the construction process, since its usage is essential for activating a programmable artifact. With a VPE like Amici, mostly formal characteristics of the artifact are represented, although some hints about its appearance or the authors intentions were indicated by method and file names. We suggest that documentation tools for physical computing targeting children and novices start from VPEs. Short text fields and image fields with webcam access can enhance a VPE to facilitate the documentation of artifact attributes such as appearance or the authors' intentions. Also a version control panel could be useful to go back to earlier programs and track changes, but still focus on the current state.

The tool was evaluated at tutored technology workshops. Being a case study, only one project group was interviewed and looked at in-depth. We did not verify whether the documentations are comprehensible for young makers who have not participated in such a workshop. More research is needed to verify the results with such makers, including their motivation to document projects.

## 8. CONCLUSION

This paper has presented a study of how children use a How-To related web platform to document their physical computing projects in the context of three workshops. Surprisingly, the evaluation shifted the focus from the initial WP to the VPE the children used to program their artifacts. A VPE has inherent potential for project documentation since its programs were perceived as sufficient and practicable by the kids. The visual programs created with such a VPE contain adequate information to rebuild the current state of a project. Creating programs is an essential part of the construction process and therefore such a tool is already part of the artifact construction.

We argue for VPEs as basic documentation tools for children constructing physical computing artifacts. To enable a comprehensive picture of the artifact covering its informal and pragmatic characteristics, we suggest integrating image fields with webcam access and small text fields.

This work paves the way for tools for children that allow them to more conveniently document on-going physical computing projects and eventually share them in maker communities. We have started implementing the recommended features in Amici. For future work, it needs be evaluated. Further, export and upload features (e.g., export into common web formats) are required to make the VPE a useful tool that helps children to share projects in a maker culture.

## 9. REFERENCES

[1] Amici. http://dimeb.de/eduwear. 2014.

[2] Arduino. http://arduino.cc. 2014.

[3] Creative technologies. http://castilla.verkstad.cc. 2014.

[4] Dimeb TechKreativ workshops. http://www.techkreativ.de. 2014.

[5] Diy. http://diy.org. 2014.

[6] How.do. http://how.do. 2014.

[7] Instructables. http://instructables.com. 2014.

[8] Minibloq. http://blog.minibloq.org/. 2014.

[9] S4A. http://s4a.cat/. Acc. 14-01-06.

[10] Blikstein, P. Gears of our childhood: Constructionist toolkits, robotics, and physical computing, past and future. In *Proc. of IDC*, ACM (2013), 173–182.

[11] Buechley, L., Peppler, K. A., Eisenberg, M., and Kafai, Y. B., Eds. *Textile Messages: Dispatches from the World of E-textiles and Education*. Peter Lang, 2013.

[12] Kelleher, C., and Pausch, R. Lowering the barriers to programming: A taxonomy of programming environments and languages for novice programmers. *ACM Comput. Surv. 37*, 2 (2005), 83–137.

[13] Mayring, P. *Qualitative Inhaltsanalyse: Grundlagen und Techniken*. Beltz, Weinheim [u.a.], 2010.

[14] Millner, A., and Baafi, E. Modkit: blending and extending approachable platforms for creating computer programs and interactive objects. In *Proc. of IDC*, ACM (2011), 250–253.

[15] Papert, S. *Mindstorms: children, computers, and powerful ideas*. Basic Books, New York, NY, 1980.

[16] Resnick, M., Maloney, J., Monroy-Hernandez, A., Rusk, N., Eastmond, E., Brennan, K., Millner, A., Rosenbaum, E., Silver, J., Silverman, B., and Kafai, Y. Scratch: Programming for all. *Commun. ACM 52*, 11 (Nov. 2009), 60–67.

[17] Rosenbaum, E. Jots: reflective learning in scratch. In *Proc. of IDC*, ACM (2009), 284–285.

[18] Schelhowe, H., Katterfeldt, E.-S., Dittert, N., and Reichel, M. EduWear: e-textiles in youth sports and theatre. In *Textile Messages*, L. Buechley, K. A. Peppler, M. Eisenberg, and Y. B. Kafai, Eds. Peter Lang, 2013, 95–103.

[19] Torrey, C., Churchill, E. F., and McDonald, D. W. Learning how: the search for craft knowledge on the internet. In *Proc. of CHI*, ACM (2009), 1371–1380.

# A Study Of Auti: A Socially Assistive Robotic Toy

Helen Andreae
VUW
P. O. Box 600
Wellington, NZ
+64 21 188 7257
Helen@andreaedesign.com

Peter Andreae
VUW
P. O. Box 600
Wellington, NZ
+64 4 463 5834
Peter.Andreae@vuw.ac.nz

Jason Low
VUW
P. O. Box 600
Wellington, NZ
+64 4 463 6721
Jason.Low@vuw.ac.nz

Deidre Brown
VUW
P. O. Box 600
Wellington, NZ
+64 4 463 4720
Deidre.Brown@vuw.ac.nz

## ABSTRACT

This paper presents an evaluation of the effectiveness of a new socially-assistive robot, Auti, in encouraging physical and verbal interactions in children with autism. It aims to encourage positive play behaviors such as gentle speaking and touching, with positive reinforcement through movement responses, and to discourage challenging behaviors, such as screaming or hitting through the removal of the reinforcing movements. This study evaluates the design by comparing a fully-interactive Auti to an active-only version, which does the same movements but does not respond to the child. Results from 18 participants indicate that the Interactive Auti does encourage positive behaviors more than the Active-only version. However, further design is needed around addressing problematic behaviors.

## Categories and Subject Descriptors

K.4.2 [**Computers and Society**]: Social Issues – *assistive technologies for persons with disabilities.*

J.4 [**Social And Behavioural Sciences**]: Psychology

## General Terms

Design, Experimentation, Human Factors.

## Keywords

Socially Assistive Robots, Toys, Autism, ABA Therapy.

## 1. INTRODUCTION

Autism is a prevalent and growing developmental disorder. One in 50 children in America are diagnosed with an autism spectrum disorder (ASD). Individuals present with deficits in three areas: impaired social interaction, impaired communication, and repetitive and restrictive behaviours and interests. Difficulties with social interactions, such as understanding and controlling body language, are a large part of the presentation of ASD. The etiology of ASD is still unclear. There are multiple approaches seeking to explain the disorder from various research perspectives, ranging from genetic and neurobiological approaches to cognitive and social theories. The disorder's heterogeneous nature is likely to reflect multiple etiologies resulting in similar behavioural presentations.

Considering the lack of an evidence-based unifying theory and the variability in the presentation of the disorder, it is not surprising that there are many available treatments – the survey in [4] identified 111 different autism treatments. Although many autism treatments are controversial and not yet backed by experimental evidence, Applied Behaviour Analysis (ABA) is well researched, with 40 years of development, and experiments have shown clearly positive results. It is considered the most effective therapy for ASD [8]. ABA is an approach to therapy arising out of the behaviourist perspective of psychology and is, in essence, the application of operant conditioning. When applying ABA to a case of autism, the behaviours of the child are analysed and specific goals are set to help improve behaviour [7]. Therapists will prompt a desired behaviour. If the child responds, the reward is offered; thus reinforcing the desired behaviours. If the prompts are disregarded, rewards are withheld [12].

The use of robotics in teaching children with autism is a recent area of exploration. The emerging field of socially-assistive robots addresses robots that help develop or aid social interactions for a range of users such as the elderly, stroke patients, and those with cognitive disorders [3]. It is important to investigate this area, as it may offer a more economical and readily available way to assist those with autism.

Children with ASD tend to show a preference for interacting with inanimate objects over people [1]. Socially-assistive robots are particularly interesting for teaching those with ASD as robots may offer an intermediate step between inanimate objects and people, because robots have a mixture of characteristics of inanimate objects and human agents. Robots may allow some elements of social interaction without confusing the child with an overwhelming onslaught of social stimuli. Also, by pairing the social stimuli with stimuli that are already attractive to the child, robots can draw more overall attention. Further, Diehl *et al*'s [2] analysis of current research found the literature suggests that agents with robotic characteristics are preferred over both passive toys and humans, at least initially. They also found that robots could be effective in eliciting behaviours, although the research was predominantly theoretical. Interestingly, they only found one robot that provided reinforcement for behaviours to teach a skill. So they concluded that this is an area that merits more research, particularly given that ABA-based therapies are dominant in the treatment of autism.

Although evidence for robots being a successful medium for teaching children with ASD is building [6, 13], the research is still new and has limitations. Many studies in robotics have particularly low participant numbers, typically between 1 and 5.

*IDC'14*, June 17–20, 2014, Aarhus, Denmark.
Copyright is held by the authors. Publication rights licensed to ACM.
ACM 978-1-4503-2272-0/14/06···$15.00.
http://dx.doi.org/10.1145/2593968.2610463

Also, as pointed out in [11], much of the robotic research is from an engineering perspective which has different priorities and methods from psychology. The majority of the studies are characterised by having few or no human controls, no qualifying diagnostic tests for the participants, and are focused on the robots' performance rather than the children's. To find how children are being affected, there is a need for more careful studies in this area.

Auti, the focus of this study, is a socially-assistive, robotic toy designed to help encourage positive play behaviours and discourage problematic behaviours (See Autitoy.com). Auti employs ABA principles, applying reinforcement through movements when positive play behaviours like talking, patting or initiations occur; and removing reinforcement by stopping when challenging behaviours like screaming, hitting or throwing occur.

Auti was designed from the start for children with autism, taking into consideration the role of the face, sensory difficulties, and difficulties with imaginative play. Auti has contrasting textures – fluffy soft fur and smooth legs – to encourage sensory exploration. Its form reflects 'cute' elements which have been shown to help engage and focus attention[9]. To alleviate anxiety or confusion caused by facial stimuli, the toy does not have a face. The lack of a face, in conjunction with Auti not looking like any particular animal, also helps remove external expectations of how the toy should be played with, making it easier for a larger range of play to be accepted and encouraged. It also means that children do not have to understand Auti as a representation of something else to be able to play with it. Auti does however move with animal characteristics to make it easy for children who do understand representation to play with it as if it were an animal.

Auti can move each of its four limbs independently in movements which combine up-down and in-out motion. It can detect different types of physical interaction. Gentle physical contact is detected using a proximity sensor that is triggered when a person's body comes close enough to touch the fur. Auti responds to gentle touching or speaking with one of six distinct movement responses. Shouting, screaming or rough physical interactions result in the toy freezing for 5 seconds.

After it has finished its response, Auti enters a resting state unless it is reactivated. The aim of this state is to encourage initiation – little movements indicate that the toy is still responsive, but requires the child to initiate interaction with touch or voice. If Auti is upside-down, it waggles its limbs gently until it is turned back over. Auti also has a remote control that an instructor can use as a manual back-up to control Auti in the event that any sensor fails. During the experiments, the sound detection was done manually through the remote, since reliable automatic detection of someone talking quietly close-up versus someone shouting from a distance is extremely difficult.

This current study explores the effectiveness of applying reinforcement through the medium of Auti. The study also asks how the children classify Auti (as an animate entity or as an object). The first hypothesis of this study is that the children using Auti will display more targeted positive behaviours and less targeted challenging behaviours than the control condition. The second hypothesis is that the children using Auti will use more anthropomorphic/zoomorphic language and display more social behavioural interactions than the children in the control condition.

## 2. Method

The study assessed the children over a 2 ½ - 3 hour structured play session during which children played with three toys. The protocol was flexible to simulate how a child might play in a standard home environment. If the child wanted to keep playing with Auti or one of the other toys or if they really wanted a break, the protocol was adapted. The children were split into two conditions. The first condition used the full Interactive Auti, which responds to a child's behaviour as described above. The second condition used Auti running an active (but not interactive) program. Active Auti ignores all sensors, and cycles through its movements randomly so that no distinguishable pattern can be predicted. Active Auti performs the different movements in the same frequencies as Interactive Auti does during average interactive play. At the end, children in the active condition were given Interactive Auti to see if there were any differences in their play behaviours – providing both between-subject and within-subject comparisons.

### 2.1 Participants

Participants consisted of 18 children with an autism diagnosis between the ages of 4 years 6 months and 8 years 2 months. Four participants were female. All participants had a formal autism diagnosis from a paediatrician and this diagnosis was confirmed with the Gilliam Autism Rating Scale Second Edition (GARS-2). Nine participants were assigned to each condition and were matched across the conditions according to their ages, their scores on the GARS-2 test, the Peabody Picture Vocabulary Test (PPVT) and the colour progressive matrices test (CPM). Table 1 shows how the means and standard deviations of matching criteria along with the significance value from the between-subjects t-tests. The table also shows that there was no significant difference between the way the groups interacted with a walking puppy toy (WP) which was used to compare the children's general play behaviors.

**Table 1. Group differences**

|  | Int. μ | Int.σ | Act. μ | Act.σ | Sig. |
|---|---|---|---|---|---|
| GARS-2 | 90.89 | 15.35 | 90.00 | 16.03 | .91 |
| PPVT | 97.40 | 34.86 | 89.60 | 26.65 | .70 |
| CPM | 13.56 | 13.82 | 14.78 | 14.61 | .86 |
| AGE | 6.44 | 1.25 | 6.50 | 1.23 | .92 |
| WP | 50.78 | 57.08 | 58.44 | 50.30 | .77 |

### 2.2 Procedure

Before the main experiment, the instructor conducted a 45-minute interview with the parents and a half hour interview with the children where background information and data for matching was collected. The trials took place in the child's home to ensure that the children were in an environment where they felt comfortable, removing the difficulties some children have with new places. Video cameras were set up in the room from two angles and turned on before the toys were introduced.

To gauge how the child played with standard active toys, the instructor initially gave them a walking puppy toy to play with for up to 10 minutes. The toy was a modified 'Furreal Friends Walkin' Puppy', the modifications removed the all the puppy sounds as well as the 'pat switch', resulting in a dog toy which walked indefinitely when turned on.

Auti was then introduced and the dog was taken away. The child had three play periods with Auti over an hour and a half. For the first 15 minutes, attention was directed toward Auti. The child was then allowed to keep playing with Auti or choose another preferred activity. After 10 to 20 minutes, they were then redirected back to Auti. This was repeated twice, resulting in three

Auti-focused times. This flexible protocol was used so the child felt they were in control and because behavioural shaping only works if the child desires the 'reward'.

Throughout the first section of the play time (~15min), Auti was referred to as an 'it', unless the child referred to Auti as an animal or a he/she. In which case, the instructor then responded in kind from that point. In the second two sections, "support toys" of a brush, a blanket and blocks were introduced and the instructor referred to Auti as a 'he' to see if this changed how the child classified the toy.

The children in the control condition were also given the interactive version of Auti for up to 10 minutes to see if their behaviours were different. After the last session playing with Interactive Auti, Auti was taken away and a realistic looking "sleeping dog" (Perfect Petzzz® chocolate lab) was put by the child to see if any behaviours seen with Auti were generalised.

The video recordings were coded for positive and negative physical and verbal interactions and their causes (own initiative vs. prompted by instructor). One "physical interaction" was counted every time the child touched and released the toy. For longer interactions, one "physical interaction" was recorded every 2 seconds the child was in contact with the toy. One "verbal interaction" was counted for every continuous verbalization followed by a break. The coding also recorded how the children classified Auti, and whether they engaged in extended play with the toy. Classification was counted every time the child referred to the toy using anthropomorphic or zoomorphic language or they behaved towards the toy as if it were 'alive'. Extended play was recorded when a child went beyond simple action-response play. This was counted the first time a new extended play occurred, or if the extended play had not occurred for 3 minutes.

## 3. Results

In all the analysis below, the interactions prompted by the instructor were disregarded. Because the skew and kurtosis of the collected data were outside of the normal range, and Kolmogorov-Smirnov normality tests came back as significant, the data was analysed with a Generalized Linear Model (GLM) using a Poisson regression with a log link function, which is a common non-parametric test for count data. Significance in GLM is tested using The Wald statistic (a particular form of a $X^2$ statistic) on the slope coefficient of the GLM.

**Positive and Negative Interactions**.

As the hypotheses predicted, significantly more positive verbal and physical interactions occurred with Interactive Auti than with Active Auti ($p \leq .001$) (Table 2). This was also the case for the children who played with both toys. Paired sample t-tests showed they displayed significantly more positive interactions when playing with the Interactive Auti than they did when they played with the Active Auti ($p = .05$) (Table 3). The comparisons are still statistically significant when the positive interactions are broken down into the verbal and physical interactions. This was also the case for children who played with both toys.

There was no significant difference between the number of negative interactions displayed in the Interactive condition and the Active condition, nor when the physical and verbal interactions were analysed separately were any significant results found. (Table 2) This was also the same for the challenging behaviours displayed by the children who played with both versions of Auti.

### Classification and Extended play occurrences

A significant difference was found between the number of times the children categorised the Auti as 'animal like' in the Interactive and the Active conditions ($p \leq .001$), with more occurrences in the Interactive condition. There were however no significant differences in classification occurrences with children who played with both toys (Table 4). Instances of extended play occurred significantly more in the Interactive than the Active condition ($p \leq .001$) There were however no significant differences in the number of times the children who played with both Auti's extended their play (Table 3).

**Table 2. Between-subject means and test statistics**

|          | Int. μ | Int.σ  | Act. μ | Act.σ  | $X^2$  | Sig. |
|----------|--------|--------|--------|--------|--------|------|
| +total   | 222.89 | 151.68 | 98.11  | 111.22 | 412.84 | .001 |
| +physical| 197.33 | 137.26 | 98.11  | 111.22 | 287.99 | .001 |
| +verbal  | 25.56  | 36.23  | 0      | 0      | -      | -    |
| -total   | 4.33   | 7.67   | 4.67   | 8.27   | .11    | .73  |
| Classific.| 8.56  | 11.00  | 1.44   | 2.24   | 35.19  | .001 |
| Extension| 5.89   | 8.58   | 1.89   | 2.42   | 16.64  | .001 |

**Table 3. Within-subject means and test statistics**

|          | Int. μ | Int.σ | Act. μ | Act.σ | $t$   | Sig. |
|----------|--------|-------|--------|-------|-------|------|
| +total   | 122.00 | 94.22 | 40.67  | 54.45 | 3.77  | .05  |
| +physical| 108.89 | 87.32 | 40.67  | 54.45 | 23.35 | .01  |
| +verbal  | 13.11  | 13.46 | 0      | 0     | -     | -    |
| -total   | .22    | .44   | .44    | 8.40  | 1.48  | .18  |
| Classific| 7.22   | 15.80 | 1.44   | 2.24  | 1.06  | .32  |
| Extension| 3.33   | 3.91  | 1.89   | 2.42  | 1.13  | .29  |

## 4. Discussion

The primary aim of this study was to explore whether ABA principles of reinforcement, applied through a robotic toy, could be effective in encouraging and discouraging targeted behaviours in children with autism. The results of the experiment confirm that positive behaviours can be encouraged through a robotic toy. The high variability in the data is not particularly surprising given the heterogeneous nature of ASD. Different presentations of the disorder are likely to significantly affect the way in which children play with the toy.

As this study hypothesized, the children with Interactive Auti displayed significantly more targeted positive behaviours than with Active Auti. This was particularly prominent in the verbal interactions where no verbal engagement was observed in the control condition. This aligns with the research on ABA: offering a reward for behaviour will help elicit it. Moreover, it tells us that rewards delivered though the medium of a robot can be effective. Though this may seem an obvious result, given that children with autism respond to stimuli a-typically, it would be an unreasonable assumption to consider this obvious. The experiments also tell us that responsive movements of a robotic toy are enough of a reward compared to non-responsive movements to encourage positive interactions. This is an important point, not just for Auti but for all such robotic toys, considering the review in [2], which pointed out the lack of research and development around robotics incorporating ABA principles.

The main experiment addresses between-subject comparisons. But it was also interesting that, in spite of fatigue and exposure to the non-interactive version, the children who played with Interactive Auti after Active Auti also displayed significantly more positive interactions with Interactive Auti. It would be interesting to see if within-subject experiments that controlled for order effects had the same results.

There are limitations to the interactions displayed by the children. Of the positive verbal interactions, 10 of the 18 children interacted only using the word 'hello', which was the word the instructor used to demonstrate the interaction. Physical interactions were similarly repetitive. It is possible that the varieties of interactions could be increased, if Auti could distinguish more finely between different types of positive interactions. The analysis part of ABA is crucial to its effectiveness [10]. Currently, no robots, including Auti, are able to analyse and address behaviours with the skill of a human. However, this level of analysis is not necessary as the robots are the medium for teaching, not the teacher. Still, the more types of interactions robots can distinguish or sense, the more behaviours a program can target.

The negative interactions did not significantly differ between the conditions. There are several possible reasons why the negative interactions did not decrease. Firstly, children seemed to be confused by the toy stopping. They did not appear to know whether it was purposely meant to stop or whether they had broken it. And since challenging behaviours seldom occurred, they had little opportunity to learn the pattern of the toy's responses. Secondly, children may not have viewed the movements as a strongly rewarding; so they didn't care if they were removed. Thirdly, reducing challenging behaviours can be more complex than eliciting new behaviors. ABA has had good results when dealing with challenging behaviours, but employs careful analysis and develops targeted strategies.

Like the study in [5], this study found that more animal-like classifications occurred with the Interactive toy than with the Active one. This result is of interest for two reasons. It helps us understand how the children view the toy, and it raises the possibility of using Auti, or other robotic toys, in similar ways to how animals are used in Animal Assisted Therapy (AAT). Although the results show that the children are distinguishing between the Interactive and Active Auti, and acting more socially toward Interactive Auti, the results do not compare their interactions to their interactions with an actual animal. Some of our observations make it clear that at least some of the children were not classifying Auti as an animal: 10 of 18 children behaved differently toward the sleeping dog (which they initially thought was alive) than they did toward the Interactive Auti. Considering the difficulties children with ASD have generalising, it is not safe to assume that they are making links between Auti and animals. All that can be said is that children interact differently with the Interactive Auti and it is closer to animals than Active Auti is.

It was noticed, that children with different levels of functioning appeared to play with the toys differently: low functioning children explored the toys sensorily – touching it to their faces, feeling the vibration of the motors and holding the smooth legs while they moved – but did not engage with the action-response interactions. Those in the mid range, tended to interact with the action-response interactions, but their interactions often became repetitive. The higher functioning range moved more easily into extended play, pretending to feed the toy, or building houses for it. However, many did struggle with coming up with ideas as to what to do. These observations would fit with the cognitive theories of ASD.

This study found that 61% of children displayed identical behaviours or expectations with the sleeping dog as they did with Interactive Auti. This may indicate that some children were able to generalise the skills they learned from Auti. For some this was more clearly the case since they verbalized their expectations: "Why won't this one do the same thing?" However, some children may have been generalising the instructor's expectations for play which they had learned when Auti was demonstrated. This would indicate that they were generalising skills learned from the instructor rather than from Auti, which is an important distinction.

The lack of a face was also commented on by the parents and may have impacted both the extended play and the categorization of the toy. Three parents felt that no face was positive, one commenting that the no face meant that the toy didn't 'invade' her child's space. Six parents felt that no face resulted in their children not knowing how to interact with the toy. The rest of the parents thought it was fine either way, though all parents liked the idea of the face being an optional attachment like Mr. Potato Head. The thinking in the original design had been that less preconceived associations with Auti would make it easier to play with Auti in any manner. But it may be that associations that help inform children how to play with the toy would make it easier to engage with the toy particularly at initial stages. An experiment looking at how a face impacted the categorization of the toy and the extended play would be beneficial.

# 4. REFERENCES

[1] Celani, G. 2002. Human, Animals and Inanimate Objects What do People with Autism Like? *Autism*. 6, 1 93–102.

[2] Diehl, J. et al. 2011. The clinical use of robots for individuals with Autism Spectrum Disorders: A critical review. *Res. Autism Spect. Dis*. 6, (2011), 249–262.

[3] Feil-Seifer, D. and Mataric, M. 2005. Defining Socially Assistive Robotics. (2005).

[4] Green, V.A. et al. 2006. Internet survey of treatments used by parents of children with autism. *Res.Dev. Disabil*. 27, 1, 70-84.

[5] Kahn, P. et al. 2004. Robotic Pets in the Lives of Preschool Children. *CHI '04 Extended Abstracts on Human Factors in Computing Systems* (, NY, USA, 2004), 1449–1452.

[6] Kim, E. et al. 2012. Social Robots as Embedded Reinforcers of Social Behavior in Children with Autism. *J. Autism Dev. Disord*.

[7] Lovaas, O.I. 1987. Behavioral treatment and normal educational and intellectual functioning in young autistic children. *J. consult. clin. psych*. 55, 1 (Feb. 1987), 3–9.

[8] Matson, J.L. et al. 2012. Applied behavior analysis in Autism Spectrum Disorders: Recent developments, strengths, and pitfalls. *Res. Autism Spect. Disord*. 6, (2012), 144–150.

[9] Nittono, H. et al. 2012. The Power of Kawaii: Viewing Cute Images Promotes a Careful Behavior and Narrows Attentional Focus. *PLoS ONE*. 7, 9 (Sep. 2012), e46362.

[10] Pierce, W.D. and Epling, W. 1980. What happened to analysis in applied behavior analysis? *The Behavior Analyst*. 3, 1 , 1–9.

[11] Scassellati, B. et al. 2012. Robots for Use in Autism Reasearch. *Annu. Rev. Biomed. Eng*. (2012).

[12] Smith, T. 2001. Discrete Trial Training in the Treatment of Autism. *Focus Autism Other Dev. Disabl*, 16, 2, 86.

[13] Stanton, C. et al. 2008. Robotic Animals Might Aid in the Social Development of Children with Autism. 271–278

# Design With the Deaf: Do Deaf Children Need Their Own Approach When Designing Technology?

Leigh Ellen Potter
Griffith University
170 Kessels Road
Nathan, Queensland, Australia
+61 7 3735 5191
l.potter@griffith.edu.au

Jessica Korte
Griffith University
170 Kessels Road
Nathan, Queensland, Australia
+61 7 3735 5191
jessica.korte@griffithuni.edu.au

Sue Nielsen
Griffith University
170 Kessels Road
Nathan, Queensland, Australia
+61 7 3735 5025
s.nielsen@griffith.edu.au

## ABSTRACT

In this paper, we focus on the question of design of technology for Deaf children, and whether the needs of these children are different from their hearing counterparts in a technology design setting. We present findings from literature together with our own observations to determine if there are distinguishing characteristics for Deaf children that may influence design sessions with them. We found that Deaf children generally have reduced literacy and slower academic progress, reduced social and emotional development, reduced empathy and a level of nervousness in novel situations, delayed language development, and limited or delayed spoken language. We also found that Deaf children are active and innovative in approaching communication, have sensitive visual attention in their peripheral vision, enhanced attention to small visual changes, and a capacity for visual learning. Finally, cultural issues within the Deaf community mean that Deaf children should be free to interact on their own terms in a design situation. We suggest that these differences merit the development of a design approach specific to the needs of Deaf children.

## Categories and Subject Descriptors

H.5.2 User Interfaces (User-centered design)

## General Terms

Design, Human Factors

## Keywords

Child Computer Interaction; Deaf Children; Prototyping

## 1. INTRODUCTION

The study of the interaction between children and information technology has gradually emerged as a distinct research area - Child Computer Interaction - within the broader Human Computer Interaction community [15]. The area is concerned with how children use interactive products [11] and includes (but is not limited to) research in design, participation, and evaluation techniques specific to children and technology. We are specifically interested in developing an approach that will work well for Deaf children. Recently we have been asked why we would look to develop an approach in this area specifically for

Deaf children – why not simply use design best practice? This paper endeavours to answer the question "Do Deaf children need a special approach when designing technology?"

This paper discusses preliminary work in progress within the Seek and Sign project, which was established to develop technologies to enhance the communication environments of very young Deaf and hard of hearing children and explore the issues in design with that client group. The focus for this paper is the element of design of technology for Deaf children, and whether the needs of these children are different from their hearing counterparts.

In order to answer this question, we will look first to the literature to determine if there are distinguishing characteristics for Deaf children. We will also present our own observations from working with Deaf children. In doing so we will outline the characteristics of Deaf children that have been identified or observed that may affect their ability to participate in the design of technology.

## 2. A NOTE ON LANGUAGE AND CULTURE

Deaf Australia provides definitions for terminology to describe people with hearing loss as follows:

"deaf (with a small letter, d) is a general term used to describe people who have a physical condition of hearing loss of varying degrees irrespective of which communication mode they use such as Auslan and lip reading for example. Deaf (with a capital D) is used to describe those people who use Auslan (Australian Sign Language) to communicate, and identify themselves as members of the signing Deaf community. These people may also identify themselves as "Culturally Deaf." They are more likely to have been born deaf or become deaf early in life, are pre-lingually deaf and use sign language as a primary or preferred mode of communication.

Hard of hearing is the term used to describe those who have a hearing loss, usually acquired post-lingually and whose communication mode is usually by speech. This term also covers those people who have become deafened later in their life" [17].

This paper will follow the conventions of Deaf Australia and use the term ""deaf" when referring to all Deaf and hard of hearing groups at once."

## 3. HOW ARE DEAF CHILDREN DESCRIBED IN LITERATURE?

A range of design techniques have been used for design with children generally, including observations, questionnaires, surveys, storytelling, workshops, roleplaying, and prototyping [21], and many approaches for working with children have been developed, such as the cooperative inquiry approach [6], co-design sessions [15], and Guha, Druin, and Fails [9] inclusionary model for children with special needs. The choice of method for a design session is dependent on the skills of the specific design session participants, the aims of the session, and the attributes of the product to be designed. We contend that when the children who will be involved in the design session are deaf, the nature of their abilities requires the consideration of additional factors. In order to answer whether that contention is true, we need to explore the actual characteristics of Deaf children and identify the additional factors for consideration.

As with any child the skills possessed will depend on the individual participating. However some more general attributes have been identified specific to deaf children. A large percentage of deaf children are born to hearing parents, with statistics reported ranging from 70% to 90% [8]. In Australia, that figure is reported at 95% [5]. While the deaf children of deaf signing parents acquire sign language at a comparable rate and with similar milestones as hearing children acquire verbal language, deaf children of hearing parents acquire language more slowly, leading to ongoing learning difficulties [12]. These children go on to experience reduced levels of literacy as compared to their hearing counterparts [20, 23]. This suggests that when designing for these children, a design team needs to establish the development level of the child and be prepared to use tools and techniques that are suitable for that level.

The importance of cultural characteristics is clear from the definition for Deaf people provided by Deaf Australia. It is critical that a design approach for Deaf children engages them 'on their own terms', allowing them to express themselves in the way that is most comfortable for them.

Intellectually, deaf children have similar characteristics for perception, learning and memory to hearing children [22]. Despite this, deaf children frequently lag behind hearing children in academic areas, including reading, comprehension, written language, mathematics, and speech and language [22]. The delay in language development then leads to reduced levels of literacy [14], however deaf children can be active and innovative in approaching communication by incorporating drawing and writing to communicate when they do not have spoken or signed language [24]. This suggests that a design approach for these children needs to be flexible and tangible allowing the children to engage innovatively.

In addition to potential literacy delays, general and spoken language may be limited or delayed for Deaf children [13]. Not all deaf children can communicate verbally, however they do use facial expression and body movement, which can provide valuable feedback. The structure of design sessions involving deaf children should be flexible and communication support should be available [4]. Participatory approaches involving deaf children also require flexibility [1]. Any design approach for working with Deaf children must be focused beyond the written or spoken word. Tactile and visual interaction may be a means for facilitating communication in design. The approach must allow for the general communication challenges that will exist when working with the children.

Many Deaf children of hearing parents experience elevated levels of behavioural and attention problems, with these problems occurring both at home and at school [16]. Barker, Quittner,

Fink, Eisenberg, Tobey and Niparko [2] suggest that this may be in part due to language difficulties and to the challenges and frustrations involved in communication between a hearing parent and Deaf child. They found a link between language skills and the ability of the child to sustain attention to a task. This suggest that a design approach for Deaf children would need to facilitate communication between the children and the design team and operate with a language that the children are comfortable with in order to maintain the attention of the child.

Deaf children may exhibit reduced social and emotional development in terms of communication, understanding of both situations and other people, and flexibility [3, 20]. For these reasons, Deaf children must be given the scope and opportunity to express themselves freely, without the expectation of typical social mores or niceties, and any design process must facilitate this.

People who are Deaf progressively develop more sensitive visual attention in their peripheral vision than their hearing counterparts as they get older [10], and this change to visual attention starts in childhood. Mitchell and Quittner [16] suggested a connection between the attention difficulties they observed in Deaf children with "distracting or "competing" visual stimulation in the environment". Hirschorn (2011) suggests that classrooms need to be designed to suit this through smaller class sizes, arranged seating, and predictability within the environment. She also suggests that the characteristic may affect the way Deaf children deal with written information, as words in their periphery vision may attract their attention instead of words in their main field of focus. These same considerations for visual attention should be supported within a design approach.

Deaf children use visual-spatial cognitive perception and processing [7]. Parasnis [18] suggests that the acquisition of sign language is a critical factor for the further development of visual spatial skills for these children. These skills provide an opportunity for developing an innovative design approach that would capitalize on the visual nature of Deaf children.

# 4. OUR OBSERVATIONS OF DEAF CHILDREN

The Seek and Sign project is focused on the use of technology to support young Deaf children as they acquire sign language [19]. The project has used a number of different techniques, including separate observations of both Deaf and hearing children's interactions with applications, discussions with parents and teachers of Deaf children, cooperative design prototyping sessions with Deaf children for the development of game based applications to help children learn signs in Australian Sign Language, or Auslan, and exploration of technologies that may be suitable for recognition of sign language gestures. The key participants in the project are the children themselves and a decision was made early in the development of Seek and Sign to actively involve children in the design process. There is "recognition of the fact that children's views differ from those of adults" (Rabiee et al. 2005), and when developing technology for children we feel that it is important to gather the child's ideas, not only those of the supervising adult. The importance of recognizing the child's view is made more critical in an area where different methods of communication may be used, and where there is potential for distortions from interpretation and reinterpretation between children, carers, and the design team [5].

We have observed hearing and Deaf children as they have interacted with the applications developed as part of the project, as well as observing Deaf children's interactions with technology more generally. Early design sessions with Deaf children have involved a child-as-informant approach to requirements elicitation, as described within the Cooperative Inquiry approach [6]. These sessions are informing the development of an approach that will facilitate the participation of Deaf children as design partners.

In the course of the cooperative design prototyping and observation sessions that have been conducted across the life of the Seek and Sign project with Deaf children, we have observed a range of characteristics that the children displayed. While we encountered several issues that could be general to all children, there were some challenges that were specific to their needs as Deaf children. We have observed many of the characteristics that are reported in literature, including language and literacy delays (which affect the use of written language when working with the children), attention problems, and differences with visual processing. It is perhaps unsurprising that the primary challenge in dealing with Deaf children was around communication.

Communication is arguably one of the most important facets in a participative design process, and when the participants are essentially speaking different languages challenges are inevitable. This is compounded when dealing with Deaf children who have a communication deficit through a lack of mastery of language. When working with the children we experienced difficulties with feedback during prototype design sessions, both with the children providing feedback and with the designer eliciting input and feedback. Initially, some children were reluctant to speak during early sessions, and would not share thoughts at all unless prompted. There also appeared to be contradictions in their interaction, such as one example where a child's behavior of singing and making noises for elements within the interface, seemed contrary to his stated opinion, that he didn't want the interface to make sounds. Design techniques for working with Deaf children need to be flexible enough to support communication in whatever medium is most comfortable for the child.

We observed a degree of initial nervousness in Deaf children when they were introduced to the prototyping sessions. Whereas hearing children were comfortable with interacting with the game, the Deaf children were hesitant to explore the game to its fullest, as evidenced by their reluctance to click on buttons during the early part of the sessions. This seems to be due to overall nervousness due to being placed in an unfamiliar situation, rather than a reluctance to play, and applied to both introverted and extroverted participants. With increased familiarity (with the game and prototyping approach) they demonstrated the same confident and animated approach as their hearing counterparts. This may suggest the need for a technique within a design approach that bridges hesitancy.

We observed examples of attention and behavioural issues with some of the children, such as sessions when children would fight over who had control of a computer mouse, or an instance when a child displayed hyperactive behavior and was more interested in clicking on everything in the prototype and making up stories about the items on screen than trying to learn the signs. While it could be argued that this is typical of many children regardless of their hearing, it has been found that Deaf children have a higher level of behavioural and attention problems and a design approach

must be flexible in order to deal with this. In the example above, the child's story telling provides an opportunity for a designer to capture the child's thoughts in a novel way, and a flexible design approach needs to allow for this in a fluid way.

We found that working with the children in pairs when developing a computer based prototype was effective for dealing with potential behavioural problems as this minimised fighting between the children and made it easier to direct their efforts and attention. In pairs, the children tended to support each other in a constructive fashion, as evidenced by the children answering one another's questions relating to the technology in use, or in pointing out interaction options to each other. A design approach that can facilitate team or small group settings could capitalize on these benefits.

The Deaf children were generally visually acute. Even very minor changes, such as the addition of a button to a screen or a minor change to the background, were very obvious to them and were noticed immediately. Such changes caused the children to fixate on the change itself, rather than the expressed goal of the prototyping session. A design approach should allow for this, both in terms of capitalizing on the potential opportunities offered by their level of observation, and in minimizing any potential negative impact of minor changes.

A second aspect of their visual attention that affected their interaction with designers was their ability to be distracted by their surroundings – a finding commonly reported in parent forums and consistent with findings related to visual attention in literature. Changes occurring in their peripheral vision will catch their attention and distract them, such as movements seen through windows. They can also be distracted by someone sitting near them if their position is such that they are in the child's peripheral vision. Clearly these aspects must be included within a design approach for Deaf children. The children were also observed to delight in animated graphics and buttons within the prototypes. This is perhaps unsurprising given the nature of their visual attention.

In addition to their visual nature, they often seemed to learn visually. The grandmother of one participant commented that her grandson from "a very early age could easily find objects and find his way around shopping centres, even after having been there only once." She also noted that he was "much more attentive to the environment than other children who probably cruise through on the basis of what they hear."

## 5. CONCLUSION

Within this paper we have looked at the characteristics of Deaf children reported in literature that may influence their ability to be active participants in a design process, and presented our own observations from working with Deaf children. We were seeking to answer the question "Do Deaf children need a special approach when designing technology?" The findings in literature and our observations suggest that Deaf children differ from their hearing counterparts in several areas, and that the combination of these differences warrants an approach that is tailored to their needs.

The characteristics discussed in this paper relate to the development of Deaf children. Academic development characteristics are represented in reduced literacy and slower academic progress. Emotional and social characteristics are represented in reduced social and emotional development, reduced empathy, and a level of nervousness in novel situations. Deaf children demonstrate delayed language development, and limited or delayed general or spoken language, however Deaf children are also active and innovative in approaching communication. Deaf children have sensitive visual attention in their peripheral vision, enhanced attention to small visual changes, and a capacity for visual learning. Finally, cultural issues within the Deaf community mean that Deaf children should be free to interact on their own terms in a design situation.

The choice of methods for the design of a new technology should be based on the skills of the participants. The characteristics of Deaf children that have been identified suggest that a design approach specific to the needs of Deaf children is warranted. We intend to develop a design approach that will support communication between all parties in the design process. This approach must support Deaf children independent of their level of literacy, facilitate language support appropriate for them, capitalise on their visual abilities, and allow creative expression.

# 6. REFERENCES

[1] Allsop, M. J., Holt, R. J., Levesley, M. C. and Bhakta, B. 2010. The engagement of children with disabilities in health-related technology design processes: Identifying methodology. *Disability and Rehabilitation: Assistive Technology*, 5 (1), (Jan. 2010), 1-13.

[2] Barker, D. H., Quittner, A. L., Fink, N. E., Eisenberg, L. S., Tobey, E. A. and Niparko, J. K. 2009. Predicting behavior problems in deaf and hearing children: The influences of language, attention, and parent–child communication. *Development and Psychopathology*, 21 (2), (Aug. 2009), 373-392.

[3] Calderon, R. and Greenberg, M. 2005 *Social and emotional development of deaf children: Family, school, and program effects*. Oxford University Press.

[4] Cavet, J. and Sloper, P. 2004. Participation of disabled children in individual decisions about their lives and in public decisions about service development. *Children & Society*, 18 (4), (2004), 278-290.

[5] Deaf Children Australia, D. S. Q. 2008. *Annual Report 2007/2008*. Deaf Children Australia, Melbourne, Australia.

[6] Druin, A. 1999. Cooperative Inquiry: Developing new technologies for children with children. In *Proceedings of the CHI 99* (Pittsburgh, PA, May 1999). ACM, New York, NY, May 1999.

[7] Ebrahim, F. 2006. Comparing creative thinking abilities and reasoning ability of deaf and hearing children. *Roeper Review*, 28 (3), (Spring 2006), 140-147.

[8] GRI 2008. *Regional and national summary report of data from 2007-08 annual survey of deaf and hard of hearing children and youth*. Gallaudet Research Institute, Gallaudet University, Washington, DC.

[9] Guha, M. L., Druin, A. and Fails, J. A. 2008. Designing with and for children with special needs: An inclusionary model. In *Proceedings of the 7th International Conference on Interaction Design & Children* (Chicago, USA, June 11-13, 2008), New York, NY, June 2008.

[10] Hirshorn, E. 2011. *Visual Language and Visual Learning (Research Brief 3)*. Science of Learning Center, Washington DC.

[11] Markopoulos, P., Read, J. C., Hoysniemi, J. and MacFarlane, S. 2008. Child Computer Interaction: Advances in methodological research. *Cognition, Technology & Work*, 10 (2), (Mar. 2007), 79-81.

[12] Masataka, N. 2000 *The role of modality and input in the earliest stage of language acquisition: Studies of Japanese Sign Language*. Psychology Press, City.

[13] Mayberry, R. I. 2010 *Early language acquisition and adult language ability: What sign language reveals about the critical period for language*. Oxford University Press, City.

[14] Mayer, C. 2007. What really matters in the early literacy development of deaf children. *Journal of Deaf Studies and Deaf Education*, 12 (4), (Jun. 2007), 21.

[15] Mazzone, E., Read, J. C. and Beale, R. 2011. Towards a framework of co-design sessions with children. In *Proceedings of the INTERACT 2011: 13th IFIP TC 13 International Conference* (Portugal, 2011). ACM, New York, NY, September 2011.

[16] Mitchell, T. V. and Quittner, A. L. 1996. Mulitimethod study of attention and behavior problems in hearing-impaired children. *Journal of Clinical Child Psychology*, 25 (1), (1996), 83-96.

[17] Myers, M. D. 2009. *Qualitative Research in Business and Management*. SAGE Publications, London.

[18] Parasnis, I., Samar, V. J., Bettger, J. G. and Sathe, K. 1996. Does deafness lead to enhancement of visual spatial cognition in children? Negative evidence from deaf nonsigners. *Journal of Deaf Studies and Deaf Education*, 1 (2), (1996), 145-152.

[19] Potter, L. E., Korte, J. and Nielsen, S. 2012. Sign my world: lessons learned from prototyping sessions with young deaf children. In *Proceedings of the the 24th Australian Computer-Human Interaction Conference* (Melbourne, Australia, November 2012). ACM, New York, NY, December 2012.

[20] Sass-Lehrer, M. and Bodner-Johnson, B. 2003 *Early Intervention: Current Approaches to Family-Centred Programming*. Oxford University Press, City.

[21] Sluis-Thiescheffer, R. J. W., Bekker, M. M., Eggen, J. H., Vermeeren, A. P. O. S. and de Ridder, H. 2011. Development and application of a framework for comparing early design methods for young children. *Interacting with Computers*, 23 (1), (Jan. 2011), 70-84.

[22] Taylor, R., Smiley, L. and Richards, S. 2009. *Exceptional Students: Preparing teachers for the 21st century*. McGraw-Hill, US.

[23] Traxler, C. B. 2000. The Stanford Achievement Test, 9th Edition: National norming and performance standards for deaf and hard-of-hearing students. *Journal of Deaf Studies and Deaf Education*, 5 (4), (2000), 337-348.

[24] Williams, C. 2004. Emergent literacy of deaf children. *Journal of Deaf Studies and Deaf Education*, 9 (4), (Fall 2004), 352-365.

# Applying the CHECk tool to Participatory Design Sessions with Children

Maarten Van Mechelen
Bieke Zaman
Karin Slegers
CUO | Social Spaces, iMinds, KU Leuven
Parkstraat 45/3605, 3000 Leuven, Belgium
maarten.vanmechelen@soc.kuleuven.be
bieke.zaman@soc.kuleuven.be
karin.slegers@soc.kuleuven.be

Gavin Sim
Peggy Gregory
Matthew Horton
ChiCI Group, UCLan
Preston, PR1 2HE, UK
GRSim@uclan.ac.uk
AJGregory@uclan.ac.uk
MPLHorton@uclan.ac.uk

## ABSTRACT

To encourage ethical practices in participatory design with children the CHECk tool was created. This paper reports on an expert review of the CHECk tool and a validating case study. Four main challenges to the CHECk tool are identified: (1) *how to* inform children on the research and their role herein, (2) distinguishing between project values and designer or researcher's personal values, (3) accounting for the dynamic nature and social constructedness of values in design, and (4) the emergence of values in all stakeholders including child design partners. We advocate complementing CHECk with interactive storytelling and show how this narrative can be used to not only inform participation and achieve ethical symmetry, but also to negotiate values with child design partners.

## Categories and Subject Descriptors

K 4.1 [Public Policy Issues] ethics

## General Terms

Human Factors

## Keywords

CCI; Participatory Design; Value Sensitive Design; ethics

## 1. INTRODUCTION

Within the area of Child Computer Interaction (CCI) children have participated in the design of technology for over two decades using a variety of established methods, e.g. [1][6].

Technology has moral impacts on users and their environment, it shapes their lives and practices in important ways. Technology is therefore not merely enabling but constitutive. On the other hand, users may appropriate technology for purposes other than those intended in design and, by doing so, technology's functionality is adjusted and changed. Such an interactional position holds that values are not solely designed into technology, nor are they solely conveyed by social drivers and forces, it works both ways [12].

Since technology should no longer be considered value-neutral, an increasing body of HCI (and CCI) research has concerned itself with understanding how to explore values more explicitly during design and evaluation. At the same time, a number of approaches for systematically considering human values in information technology have emerged, in particular value sensitive design [7][3]. Furthermore, in related fields such as participatory design attempts have been made to rekindle values in what is called a more authentic approach towards participatory design [10]. In this paper we rely on Rokeach's [15] notion of values as something that a person or a group of persons consider(s) important in life, as have many others, e.g. [7][10].

To encourage ethical practice in participatory design with children a value checklist referred to as CHECk was created for use prior to and at the start of design activites [13]. CHECk, consists of two checklists, CHECk 1 and 2, designed to help CCI researchers to critically consider their values when involving children in design projects, and to examine how best to explain participatory design activities to children to aid informed consent [13].

In this paper, we advocate complementing CHECk with interactive storytelling and using this narrative to not only better inform participation and achieve ethical symmetry, but also to negotiate values concerning the project and its outcomes with our child design partners. This way, CHECk becomes a vehicle to open up dialogue and to establish a shared narrative space, that is, a common ground where adults and children can meet.

## 2. EXAMINING VALUES AND PARTICIPATION

Examining your own values as a researcher or designer prior to any design activity is a *condition sine qua non* to better inform child design partners. Using tools like CHECk fits in a broader general trend in the HCI and CCI community that has often been referred to as the third wave of HCI research [3]. This transition came with a turn to design and culture as new theoretical concerns, indicating a trend towards more critical reflection [11]. It has called for accountability in the ethnomethodological sense in that researchers and designers are increasingly expected to explicitly account for what they are examining, designing and the procedures followed to perform these practices [8]. It does not only call for a responsibility to account for the values that are being designed for, but also for a reflexivity regarding the fact that interaction designers and researchers themselves bring values to the design process [15]. Design and research teams therefore need adequate codes or tools.

However, ethical questions that arise when involving children as design partners are not always considered in a standard ethics review (e.g. ownership of ideas). In addition, informed consent documents usually target parents rather than informing both adults and children. Finally, there is an urge for an added layer of ethical discussion, indicating personal responsibility to do more than just the minimum.

In order to support CCI researchers and designers to become accountable for the values that they design for, Read et al. have developed CHECk, a tool to encourage reflexivity, consisting of two checklists [13]. The first checklist, CHECk 1, focuses on examining values by asking six questions to be answered prior to any design activity. The questions challenge the designer or researcher to consider the appropriateness of both the technical solution and the involvement of children. The aim is to become more explicit about the values that drive the work, pushing designers and researchers to the extremes of honesty.

The second checklist, CHECk 2, aims to examine the value of participation to the child design partners. Child design partners should be informed about what they will be doing during the design activities, how their contributions will be disseminated and, although difficult, who has credit for the ideas they come up with during these design activities. The main goal of CHECk 2 is achieving ethical symmetry, that is, full consent from the children instead of only consent by adults [5]. By answering the questions, designers and researchers can make sure children can understand their research.

In this paper, we will investigate CHECk's effectiveness to facilitate critical reflection about ethical issues in CCI and to achieve ethical symmetry in participatory design sessions with children. Furthermore, by complementing CHECk with interactive storytelling and creating a shared narrative space were adults and children can meet, we will explore how the tool can be used as a starting point not only to inform but also to negotiate values with child design partners.

## 3. CASE STUDY

Our study consisted of two parts. Firstly, the first author of this paper performed an expert critique of the CHECk tool. Reflections were discussed in follow-up iterations with the co-authors. Based on the results of the expert review, an extended CHECk tool was suggested. Secondly, the extended CHECk tool was empirically evaluated in a concrete case study that dealt with the design of tangible, digital tools to foster pro-social behavior off- and online within a class group. More particularly, the goal was to strengthen social cohesion and prevent (cyber)bullying. Data were gathered in co-design sessions that took place in two schools in Flanders, Belgium, with a group of 49 children aged 9 to 10.

### 3.1 Reviewing the CHECk Tool

The results of the expert review on CHECk identified both strengths and opportunities for improvements. Although CHECk was judged to be a useful tool for examining values and participation prior to and at the start of design activities with children, we also identified four challenges that can be tackled to exploit the full potential of the tool.

Firstly, CHECk focuses on 'what' to tell child design partners but no explanation is given on 'how' to best tell it. This is an important issue since the CHECk tool aims to facilitate a better understanding by children about what the project is about and how they will be involved and contribute to it. Therefore, one should carefully consider in what form to bring the information to the children.

Secondly, designers and researchers involved in a project do not necessarily have a 'shared' point of view. A distinction should be

made between values that are explicitly supported and adopted in a given investigation or project and designer or researcher's personal values (cf. self-disclosure) [3]. Designers and researchers also bring values to the design process through 'seeing as' and through making design judgment [10]. These personal values do not necessarily correspond with the more general project values.

Thirdly, designers and researchers do not necessarily have a 'fixed' point of view about the project. Their values may be dynamic, they can change as part of the design process due to interactions with other stakeholders as well as the technology being developed, and several viewpoints may co-exist depending on the context [9][10][12]. The use of groups in participatory design furthermore reflects a theoretical commitment to the notion that meanings are socially and collectively produced [4]. Therefore, CHECk, as an ethical probe, should account for changes in values about the project and the technology being developed.

Lastly, CHECk does not fully account for children's values. Only researchers and designers are prompted to examine their values prior to any design activities. Child design partners on the other hand are not given the opportunity to express their values on participation or to negotiate their views on ethical questions such as ownership of ideas. We suggest that, in order to develop ethical practice in participatory design with children, dialogue is required, not only between researchers but also between researchers and child design partners

We argue that interactive storytelling may offer interesting opportunities for the challenges listed above and in particular for how to bring the information to the children and how to account for children's values. Building a story around the design challenge and making the project more tangible by adding persona like characters and a realistic plot may be useful for increasing involvement and helping children better understand the value of participation. Establishing a shared narrative space between adults, as outsiders to children's life-world, and children, creates a common ground to meet on [1][6]. When telling the story, children should be prompted to reflect on the design challenge, the values at stake and the consequences of participation. This way, the narrative becomes a stepping stone to open up dialogue with child design partners. Giving a voice to children who are typically not consulted in research practices and ethical considerations may destabilize existing power structures [17].

In sum, the expert review has revealed four areas for improvements to extend CHECk 1 and 2: (1) considering *how* to inform children on the research and their role herein, (2) distinguishing between project values and designer or researcher's personal values, (3) accounting for the dynamic nature and social constructedness of values in design, and (4) the emergence of values in all stakeholders including child design partners. We advocate complementing CHECk with interactive storytelling and using this narrative to not only inform participation and achieve ethical symmetry, but also to negotiate values with our child design partners [5].

### 3.2 Answering the CHECk Questions

In accordance to the CHECk protocol [13], we answered the questions of the two checklists.

#### 3.2.1 CHECK 1 questions
*1. What are we aiming to design?*

Tangible, digital tools to stimulate pro-social behavior, off- and online, within a class context to prevent (cyber)bullying from happening in the first place.

*2. Why this product?*

Excuse: Bullying behavior, off- and online, is still a widespread problem often related to existing social contexts such as the class. Since (cyber)bullying is a group process in which bystanders play an unmistakable role, we target the whole class as a particular social group.

Honest: We had to choose a target group and a societal problem within an ongoing project. Since preventing and coping with (cyber)bullying is a hot topic in Flanders and abroad, we saw interesting academic opportunities.

*3. What platform or technologies are we planning to use?*

Not yet decided, but our aim is to develop tangible, digital tools that can be used in and around the classroom throughout the year.

*4. Why this platform or technology?*

Excuse: tangible interaction offers interesting opportunities to bridge the gap between the off- and online world of children, and to stimulate pro-social behavior on both levels. Furthermore, tangible, digital tools can easily be embedded in a classroom for structural use throughout the year.

Honest: we wanted to do something with tangible interaction, since it offers more possibilities from a technological innovation point of view compared with a mobile application.

*5. Which children will we design with?*

Fourth graders (i.e. 9- to 10-year-olds) living in Flanders Belgium.

*6. Why these children?*

Excuse: According to literature, 9- to 10-year-olds are an interesting target group for prevention due to the growing influence of peers and the early uptake of social media.

Honest: One of the researchers involved in the project was looking for an additional case for his PhD research. Therefore, we chose the exact same target group.

### 3.2.2 CHECk 2 questions
*1.1 Why are we doing this project (i.e., summary of CHECK 1)?*

By designing tangible, digital tools to foster pro-social behavior off- and online within a class group, we hope to prevent (cyber)bullying. The societal relevance of the problem provides interesting academic opportunities. Also, tangible interaction is an interesting topic from a technological innovation point of view. Finally, 9- to 10-year-olds are an interesting age group for prevention and this target group could also be aligned with an ongoing PhD research.

*1.2 What do we tell the children?*

We are looking for ways to enhance the class atmosphere and to make sure everybody gets along. We therefore aim to build some kind of technology that you, the children, can use in and around the class throughout the year.

*2.1 Who is funding the project?*

IWT, the Agency for Innovation by Science and Technology in Flanders, Belgium.

*2.2 What do we tell the children?*

We are researchers working at the University of Leuven, this means the university pays us to do research.

*3.1 What might happen in the long term?*

By means of multi-modality analysis we will analyze and interpret the results (i.e., artifacts and explanations). The results will be taken forward to fuel the design process and complement the viewpoints of adults. The final design may be implemented in different schools and released in the market.

*3.2 What do we tell the children?*

Some of your ideas may actually be used but most likely not just one idea but a mix of different ideas from you, the children, as well as ideas from parents, teachers, etc. With all these ideas in mind, we will invent something that we might sell to schools throughout Belgium.

*4.1.What might we publish?*

Reflections on methodology and results of the participatory design activities with children.

*4.2.What do we tell the children?*

We will write about the activities we will be doing together and the ideas you come up with during these activities. These writings will be published in specialist magazines.

## 3.3 Extending CHECk with Storyline

In the case study, we aimed to evaluate the suggestions for improving the CHECk tool that followed from the expert evaluation. To realize this, we extended CHECk with an interactive storyline. As a starting point for our narrative, we used the results of CHECk 2. The first part of the narrative was about us, about what it means to be a design researcher. The second part contextualized the design challenge by telling a partly fictional story about a schoolteacher, Miss Anneleen. The 23 9-10-year-old boys and girls in her class are having a difficult time. The children don't get along very well and the atmosphere in the class is below zero. A lot of detailed examples were included in the narrative, such as:

*"Some children always play together during breaks, while excluding others who would really like to join them."*

The teacher tried many things to change the atmosphere for the better, but without success. Therefore, she contacted her brother, a researcher at the university, and asked him for help. Since the brother did not know what to do either, he decided to ask children in other schools to help him solve the problem of the bad atmosphere. Together with these children and a colleague he wants to invent something 'magical' to be used in class to enhance the atmosphere and the team spirit. With this story, our aim was to establish a common ground to meet on and to provide a clear end-goal.

## 3.4 Negotiating Values

The narrative became the leitmotif of the design activities with children. In total 4 design sessions were arranged with the children over a number of weeks. During this first meeting, we also gave the children a sensitizing package [16] with four assignments. Unfortunately there is no room to elaborate on each of the assignments, but in one of the assignments we asked them to draw a class with a bad atmosphere, a class they definitely don't want to be part of. This was an individual assignment carried out at home. The results of this were then used to inform the narrative within the second design session. This way, the design challenge became much more tangible and tailored to children's life-world, creating feelings of ownership and a better understanding of the problem.

When we met the children for the first time in their classroom, we did not tell the story in a one-way fashion. Rather, we combined it with an interactive introduction about us, being researchers and what that means. We asked the children what they think it is that researchers do and why. Next, we introduced the problem of Miss Anneleen and we asked the children about their opinions. We then revealed the purpose of our visit, being asked by Miss Anneleen to help her solving the problem of the bad atmosphere in her class and that we needed their help. Some children were a bit skeptical in the beginning and wondered if the story was real. However, because of the many details and the story's realism, the children got excited right away.

Next, we used the answers of CHECk 2 to negotiate and inform participation. We asked questions such as *"What should we do if our ideas actually solve the problems in Anneleen's class?"* and *"What if we earn money with an invention based on our ideas?"* Formulating these and other questions, we tend to use *'our'* and not *'your'* ideas, since the designer or researcher facilitating the activities will actively contribute as well. These questions evoked interesting debates, for example between a boy wanting to buy a PlayStation for class use and a girl proposing to use the money to help children in other schools.

*"I think, that uh, we should use the money to help children in other schools as well, and so, that the class atmosphere can improve their as well, in all schools in Belgium."*

While making these suggestions, children's values were implicitly expressed. Some of the children's opinions notably changed during the discussions with their peers and the researchers. When we finally proposed to use the money, if we would make any money at all, for additional research on the topic they simultaneously yelled *"Yes!"*. In other words, an overall consensus was reached. Instead of being passive listeners, the children behaved as active participants from the very start. Due to this process, feelings of problem ownership emerged and children gradually uncovered and identified their personal values. This is considered to be an important step for building mutual trust between adults and child design partners. These values were documented by writing down children's reactions and by making a report immediately afterwards.

## 4. REFLECTIONS AND CONCLUSION

Complementing CHECk with interactive storytelling has been shown to be an effective way as to 'how' to inform participation and achieve ethical symmetry, but with it came new challenges. The subtle paradox of using a half lie (i.e., a made up story) to strengthen ethics and transparency in participatory design with children and the question of how to control the risk of possible influences from researchers on children's answer for final consensus should both be topics for further research.

Besides these challenges, interactive storytelling enabled us to create a shared narrative space. The shared narrative became the leitmotif, structuring the design activities and providing a clear end-goal for our child design partners. Since the story was fueled by children's input, it became tailored to their life-world, creating feelings of problem ownership and mutual trust.

By constantly probing children to think about and discuss their underlying motives (e.g. a group discussion about ownership of ideas, why questions embedded in drawing assignments, etc.), children's values emerged and developed recursively. Although CHECk was intended as an ethical probe to be used prior to and at the start of design activities, it became a vehicle for eliciting and negotiating values throughout the project.

## 5. ACKNOWLEDGMENTS

This study is part of (1) the EMSOC project (Emowerment in a Social Media Culture), funded by IWT (Angecy for Innovation by Science and Technology) and (2) a PhD research funded by the MAD-faculty (UHasselt).

## 6. REFERENCES

[1] Bekker, M., Beusmans, J., Keyson, D. & Lloyd, P. (2003). KidReporter: a user requirements gathering technique for de-signing with children. *Interacting with Computers*, 15(2), 187-202.

[2] Bødker, S. (2006). When 2nd wave HCI meets 3rd wave challenges. In *Proc. of the 4th Nordic conf. on HCI: changing roles* (NordiCHI '06), ACM, NY

[3] Borning, A. & Muller, M. (2012). Next Steps for Value Sensitive Design. CHI'12 Proceedings of the Conference on *Human Factors in Computing Systems*. ACM, NY.

[4] Buckingham, D. (2009). 'Creative' visual methods in media research: possibilities, problems and proposals. *Media, Culture and Society,* 31, 633-652.

[5] Christensen, P. & Prout, A. (2002). Working with ethical symmetry in social research with children. *Childhood*, 9(4), 477 - 497.

[6] Dindler, C., Eriksson, E., Iversen, O.S., Lykke-Olesen, A. & Ludvigsen, M. (2005). Mission from Mars: a method for exploring user requirements for children in a narrative space. *Proceedings of the 2005 conference on Interaction design & children* (IDC '05). ACM, NY, 40-47.

[7] Friedman, B., Peter Kahn, J., & Borning, A. (2006). Value sensitive design and information systems. In P. Zhang & D. Galletta (Eds.), *Human-Computer Interaction in Management Information Systems: Foundations*. M.E. Sharpe, NY.

[8] Hallnäs, L., & Redström, J. (2002). From use to presence: On the expressions & aesthetics of every-day computational things. *ACM Transactions on Computer-Human Interaction,* 9(2), 106-124.

[9] Halloran, J., Hornecker, E., & Stringer, M. (2009). The value of values: Resourcing co-design of ubiquitous computing. Co-Design, 4(5), 245-273.

[10] Iversen, O.S., Halskov, K., Leong, T.W. (2010). Rekindling Values in Participatory Design. *PDC '10 Proceedings of the 11th Biennial Participatory Design Conference*. ACM, NY.

[11] Löwgren. J., & Stolterman, E. (2004) *Thoughtful Interaction Design*. MIT Press, Cambridge.

[12] Manders-Huits, N. (2011). What Values in Design? The Challenge of Incorporating Moral Values into Design. *Science and Engeneering Ethics,* 17(20), 271-287.

[13] Read, J., Horton, M., Sim, G., Gregory, P., Fitton, D., Cassidy, B. (2013). CHECk: A Tool to Inform and Encourage Ethical Practice in Participatory Design with Children. *CHI '13 Extended Abstracts on Human Factors in Computing Systems*. ACM, NY.

[14] Rokeach, M. (1973). *The Nature of Human Values*. Free Press, NY.

[15] Sengers, P., Boehner, K., David, S. and Kaye J. (2005). Reflective design. *Proceedings of the 4th decennial conference on Critical computing: between sense and sensibility*. ACM, NY.

[16] Sleeswijk Visser, F., Stappers, P.J., van der Lugt, R., Sanders, E.B.N. (2005). Contextmapping: Experiences from practice. *CoDesign: International Journal of CoCreation in Design and Arts*, 1(2), 119-149.

[17] Vines, J., Clarke, R., Wright, P., McCarthy, J., Oliver, P. (2013). Configuring participation: on how we involve people in design. *Proceedings of the SIGCHI Conference on Human Factors in Computing Systems,* 429-438. ACM, NY.

# Low-fidelity Prototyping Tablet Applications for Children

Etienne Bertou
Department of Communication & Information Sciences,
Tilburg University
Warandelaan 2
5037 AB Tilburg
e.m.bertou@tilburguniversity.edu

Suleman Shahid
Tilburg center for Cognition and Communication
Sciences, Tilburg University
Warandelaan 2
5037 AB Tilburg
s.shahid@uvt.nl

## ABSTRACT

Children are using computer technology at increasingly younger ages and have become a potential end-user group for tablet applications. The possibilities for incorporating this user group in the early design evaluation with prototyping are still being explored. We compared three low-fidelity prototyping approaches and concluded that one approach to low-fi prototyping was particularly more suitable for early design evaluation of tablet apps with 7 – 8 year olds.

## Categories and Subject Descriptors

H.5.2 [**User Interfaces**]: Prototyping.

## General Terms

Design, Experimentation, Human Factors.

## Keywords

Low-fidelity Prototyping; Usability; Early Design Evaluation; Evaluating with Children; Tablet Computers.

## 1. INTRODUCTION

With the adoption of touch-screen technology children are able to use computer technology at increasingly younger ages [1]. As children differ greatly from adults, adapting observational methods for involving users to facilitate early design evaluation has become a priority. One early design evaluation method that is found to be effective and efficient with young children is prototyping [2]. While the benefits of low-fidelity prototyping are widely recognized, low-fidelity prototyping approaches for touch-screen applications for young children are a relatively underexplored research area.

### 1.1 Low-fi prototyping with children

In general, paper and other low-fi materials are used to validate the concept, main functionality, navigational flow and other aspects of tablet applications that are costly to develop during task-based evaluation. Still, there are many different methods for creating a low-fi prototype. Some approaches allow for the rearranging of interface elements during the evaluation [3], while other approaches use cards with the different interface states put

*IDC'14*, June 17–20, 2014, Aarhus, Denmark.
Copyright is held by the owner/author(s). Publication rights licensed to ACM.
ACM 978-1-4503-2272-0/14/06…$15.00.
http://dx.doi.org/10.1145/2593968.2610466

in sequence [4]. It is also possible to incorporate the tablet in the evaluation. A native photo managing application can be used for putting pictures of the sketched interfaces in the correct order for completing predetermined tasks [5].

As there are major differences between these approaches it stands to reason that not all prototypes are appropriate for early design evaluation with young children. Exploration of the design space is a priority in the early design phase, so a prototyping approach that leads to 1) the uncovering of more real issues and 2) generation of more valid changes is considered more suitable. Prototype evaluation methods often rely on participants verbalizing their reasoning during task-based evaluation. A shorter evaluation time is preferable if the same results are yielded as this will lead to quicker prototyping iterations. Additionally the attention span of 7 – 8 year olds is limited and severely affected by prolonged multi-tasking [6].

Other determinants of effective prototyping are the fun children experience during evaluation, how easy they find the evaluation and to what extent they find the prototype realistic. Fun is considered a very important determinant, as it is the main motivation for children to interact with technology [7] and helps children verbalize their thoughts. Easiness is directly related to the appropriateness of the prototype approach [8], as an overall easier evaluation leads to quicker uncovering of unexpected difficulties. Lastly, when a prototype is not considered realistic, it is difficult to determine whether participants are evaluating the intended application or the model itself, in which case deriving accurate information from an evaluation becomes a challenge.

## 2. STUDY

### 2.1 Materials

Two novel tablet games for children were sketched as to create an authentic prototype evaluation. The games allowed for creating and sharing pieces of art. As the games were developed for the Apple iPad, we adhered strictly to the Apple design guidelines for interface design [9]. TekenTablet is a drawing application and with the Muzikalo app children can play musical instruments. The applications had similar home- and category selection screens, and their navigational structure was almost identical. Furthermore, it was ensured the navigational structure resembled that of popular tablet games for children [10][11] and common ways of gesture-based interaction were used for navigation. Both games used tapping for navigating to a new interface state, horizontal and vertical swiping for scrolling content and the drag and drop gesture to reposition on-screen elements. The native virtual keyboard was used in both apps. Both applications posed the same challenges for the low-fi prototyping approaches. For each game three tasks were designed to make participants use this range of gestures to navigate during evaluation.

Multiple prototypes were created using different prototyping approaches (Figure 1, 2). The first approach used a cardboard background on which loose interface elements were rearranged to recreate interface states (Background). Content that would fall outside of the viewport was initially hidden by folding the paper. In the second approach full interface cards and multiple layers of cardboard were used to simulate navigational flow and the device- and viewport constraints (Blinder).

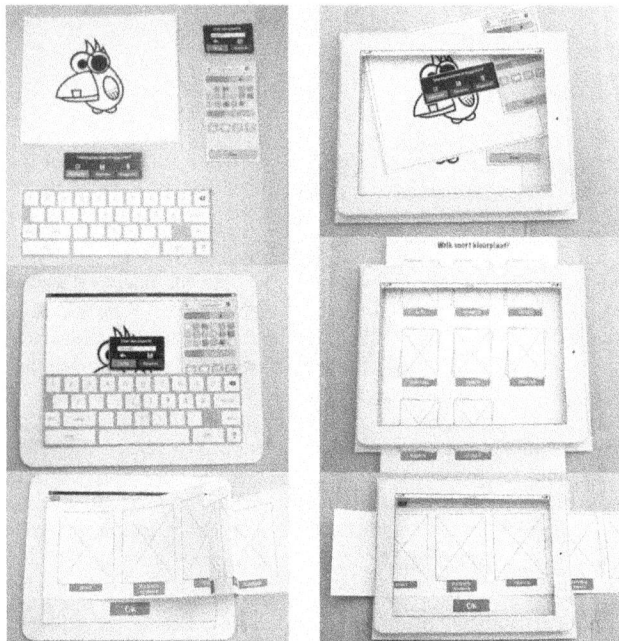

Figure 1. Background (left) and Blinder (right) prototypes.

In the third prototyping approach, photos of the interface states were arranged in the native photo managing application iPhoto (Paper-in-screen). All interface states for completing the tasks were sketched in grey-scale using illustrator software. The designs were printed and processed into the appropriate interface elements for each prototype approach.

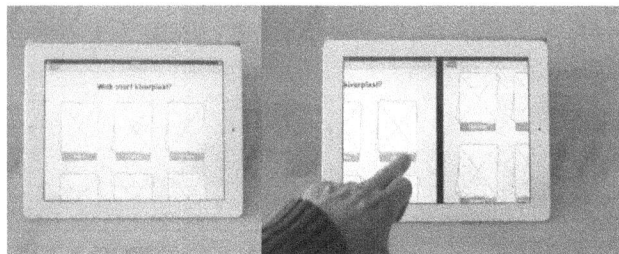

Figure 2. With Paper-in-screen the native photo-managing application is used.

To aid participants in verbalizing their thoughts during prototype evaluation and keeping them more focused, a Problem Identification Card was used [12]. It featured pictures representing possible problems such as "I am confused" or "It is taking too long". The pictures we used were adapted from the Picture Exchange Communication System-Method [13].

## 2.2 Instrumentation

In a post-evaluation interview the participants' attitudes towards the evaluation were recorded. A distinction was made between experienced Fun (the experienced joy and pleasantness during the evaluation), Easiness (the perceived difficulties when completing the tasks and the required effort) and Realism (the extent to which evaluating the applications felt genuine or "authentic" to evaluating an actual tablet application). To start the post-evaluation interview the same two questions were always used, after which the researcher adapted the dialogue to the answers of the participants until the topic was covered to a satisfying degree. After each discussion participants were asked to grade the evaluation for that particular topic on a five-point rating scale. A smileyometer – with smileys ranging from very unhappy (1) to very happy (5) – was used. Evaluation time and audio were also recorded for later analysis.

## 2.3 Participants

24 Children – 12 boys and 12 girls – from the southern part of the Netherlands participated in the evaluation. All participants were between the ages of 7 and 8 ($M = 7.5$, $SD = 0.51$), attended either grade 4 or 5 in a Dutch elementary school and could read and write basic Dutch sentences. 20 Children (83.3%) had used a tablet computer. Most participants used tablet computers frequently (65%) and over half of them would play longer than thirty minutes per session. All children mentioned playing computer games as their main motivation for using the device.

## 2.4 Experimental Design

A counterbalanced within-between subject design was employed to reduce the possible effect of individual differences between participants skewing the results of the evaluation. Carry-over effects, gender and familiarization with the application were also taken into account. Children evaluated Tekentablet (A) and Muzikalo (B) using a prototype that was created with one of three prototyping approaches: Background (1), Blinder (2), or Paper-in-screen (3). Participants would never evaluate two prototypes created with the same approach. The effect of the order in which children evaluated the applications was also considered (Table 1).

Table 1. Order of evaluation of Applications (Tekentablet = A, Muzikalo = B) in relation to Prototype Approaches (Background = 1, Blinder = 2, Paper-in-screen = 3).

| Prototype / Application | 1-2 | 1-3 | 2-1 | 2-3 | 3-1 | 3-2 |
|---|---|---|---|---|---|---|
| A – B | A1-B2 | A1-B3 | A2-B1 | A2-B3 | A3-B1 | A3-B1 |
| B – A | B1-A2 | B1-A3 | B2-A1 | B2-A3 | B3-A1 | B3-A2 |

12 children started by evaluating Tekentablet, while the other half evaluated Muzikalo first. This resulted in a total of 48 evaluations: 16 evaluations per prototyping approach and 24 evaluations per application. A distribution of 12 girls and 12 boys over order of prototyping approaches (Background, Blinder, Paper-in-screen) and Applications (A-B or B-A) was eventually established.

## 3. ANALYSIS & RESULTS

For analyzing the data collected during evaluation, grounded theory [14] methods for conceptualizing, categorizing and enumeration were employed. An inductive coding approach for analyzing the Issues Found and Changes Generated resulted in a distribution over the categories Concept (concepts, terminology, main user requirements), Layout (interface layout, content), Navigation (structure, taskflow), Control (input methods, gesture-based interaction) and Other. Levene's test was used to confirm homogeneity of variance within groups, validating the use of parametric tests for analysis of variance and Bonferroni post-hoc criterion for significance.

For analyzing the understanding of gestures and the evaluation experience, findings were extracted from the recordings and notes on interaction with the prototype taken during the evaluation. We identified the prominent observations per gesture per prototype approach. Statistics were computed for the ratings given for Fun, Easiness and Realism and Mark for the overall experience.

## 3.1 Issues Found

One-way Anova showed the average number of found issues with Background, Blinder and Paper-in-screen prototype approaches differed significantly $F(2,47) = 3.29$, $p < .05$. Bonferroni post-hoc criterion showed that with a Background prototype, more issues were found than with a Paper-in-screen approach. A significant difference was found specifically for the number of issues with Control $F(2,47) = 11.35$, $p < .05$. Bonferroni post-hoc criterion for significance showed that more issues were found related to Control with the Background approach than with both Blinder and Paper-in-screen. For the number of issues in the categories Concept, Navigation, Layout and Other, no significant differences were found between prototype approaches, $F < 2.59$, $p > .09$.

## 3.2 Generated Changes

One-way Anova showed that the average number of generated changes related to Concept was higher for Blinder than for Background prototyping approaches $F(2,47) = 4.15$, $p < .05$. For Navigation more changes were generated with Blinder than with both Background and Paper-in-screen approaches $F(2,47) = 19.90$, $p < .05$. Also, the total number of changes generated during evaluation was higher with the Blinder prototype than with both the Background and Paper-in-screen prototype $F(2,47) = 7.70$, $p < .05$. For all other categories no significant differences between averages could be confirmed $F < 1.00$, $p > .38$.

## 3.3 Attitude and Evaluation Experience

No difference was found between prototype approaches for the time required for evaluating the applications, $F = .59$, $p = .56$. One-way ANOVA showed that average scores for the reported Easiness differed per prototyping approach, $F(2,47) = 5.99$, $p < .05$. Bonferroni post-hoc analysis confirmed that evaluation was found to be Easier with the Blinder prototype ($M = 4.50$, $SD = .63$) than with the Background prototype ($M = 3.38$, $SD = 1.03$). For Fun, Realism and overall Mark for the evaluation no statistical differences were found between approaches, $F < 3.6$, $p > .07$.

## 3.4 Understanding of Gestures

For the number of times children would immediately understand what gestures to use per prototype approach, Fisher's exact tests provided evidence that the observed distribution differed significantly from the expected distribution over prototyping approaches for the swiping gesture, $p < .05$. For understanding drag and drop gestures and using the virtual keyboard no significant difference was found, $p > .60$. No statistics were computed for tapping, as it was fully understood by all participants.

In the Background approach the content that was folded to simulate viewport constraints was often misunderstood (Figure 3). Children would argue that the content was not there, navigate to the home screen to try alternative routes and even pick up the paper, unfold it and point at the required category. Also, with the

Background prototype rearranging the loose elements took a long time when switching interface states. During evaluation, children were very careful not to rearrange the elements by accident. As a side-effect they would sometimes refrain from dragging & dropping interface elements altogether before the researcher asked them to continue, even when it was understood as a requirement for completing a task.

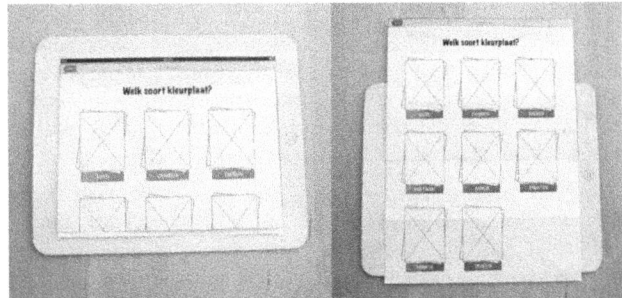

**Figure 3. Participants did not use swiping gestures to reach content outside of the screen with the Background approach.**

With the Paper-in-screen approach problems were found with all gesture-based interaction. The photo managing application responded to the touch as if the participant was using the application for its intended purpose, which interrupted the evaluation on many occasions. On a double-tap the application zoomed in and whenever an accidental pinch occurred, the gallery overview was displayed. This behavior, although perfectly valid for its purpose, was unexpected and made children uncomfortable.

Aside from these differences, with each prototyping approach children understood the basic concept of navigating the prototypes. Dragging elements for accomplishing tasks, as well as using the virtual keyboard for entering text, were clear with all three approaches.

## 4. DISCUSSION & CONCLUSION

It was expected that with all prototype approaches approximately the same amount and type of issues would be uncovered. However, more issues were found with the Background prototyping approach due to an increased number of issues found with gesture-based navigation. This was caused by a misunderstanding of the folding technique that was used for simulating swiping with the Background prototype; most children picked up the paper and unfolded it to get to content outside of the viewport. A possible explanation for this behavior is that when the researcher placed the folded top layer on the background, participants had already seen the content underneath.

The Background prototyping approach allowed children to physically rearrange interface elements. This increased the number of skills involved and provided a greater degree of freedom, which might have led to more generated changes. However, children would be hesitant to use the loose paper elements to illustrate changes to the design. Participants mentioned being afraid of unintentionally moving the wrong piece of paper or misplacing it. Furthermore, as the researcher continuously had to recreate the interface from scratch during navigation the participant's train of thought was continuously disrupted. Children easily lost focus while the researcher built the next interface state, resulting in a more chaotic evaluation and a decrease in proposed prototype changes.

Evaluating using the Blinder prototypes was found to be easier than with the Background prototypes. The researcher did not need as much time to prepare interface states and all required gesture-based interaction was understood perfectly. This led to a much smoother evaluation. As a result, more focus could be directed towards identifying usability issues and exploring the design space.

The Blinder approach facilitated discussion between the researcher and the participant very well. More potential changes to the interface that are fundamental to explore during the early design phase (e.g. used concepts and navigational flow) were suggested. The participant and researcher could easily review multiple interface states at the same time, which was not the case with the other approaches. Participants would comfortably navigate to a previous interface state for describing their ideas or suggest omitting certain interface states as a whole.

Using the Paper-in-screen prototype was considered more difficult. Children rely heavily on visual feedback during evaluation [15] and participants felt uncomfortable when the responsive interface of the photo managing application showed behavior that did not match their expectations. Participants became very careful not to touch the tablet in the wrong way, and handling the device distracted from evaluating the application. Using a photo managing application that does not respond to gestures for photo-manipulation might have been less distracting.

With the Paper-in-screen prototype, children generally performed the correct gestures for completing the tasks. This might be due to the children already being familiar with the mobile tablet experience and operating system. While the Paper-in-screen method was specifically developed to facilitate a more authentic evaluation, children did not find the representation of the Paper-in-screen prototype more realistic. The difficulties in interacting with the prototype can very well be the reason why the prototyping method was not considered more realistic, even though the actual device was involved in the evaluation.

In conclusion, not all low-fi prototyping approaches are similarly useful for evaluating gesture-based applications with young children. While prototyping itself has shown to be an appropriate early design evaluation method for 7 – 8 year olds, traditional techniques using loose interface elements for simulating in-page interaction were found to be less suitable. With the Blinder prototype the researcher and participant were able to come up with more conceptual and navigational changes to the applications. We recommend the use of full interface cards, and can confirm the use of multiple layers is beneficial in communicating screen constraints.

Another interesting aspect of the evaluation was the alternative usage of the Problem Identification Card in this study. The images on the card helped children in verbalizing their thoughts. Whenever participants used an image on the card for identifying an issue, they could explain the issue much better. An unexpected side effect was that children would also incorporate the terms used to identify the pictures in their feedback. This reduced the need for the researchers to interpret and use the children's terms in discussing the issues.

Further research might be directed towards the possibilities of low-fi prototyping approaches for more complex gesture-based interaction. Multi-touch gestures and prolonged touches will be difficult to evaluate and the appropriate behavior of the interface will be complex to mimic using low-fi materials alone. Developing a tool that facilitates this interaction while still being as accessible as low-fi prototyping might prove very valuable.

## 5. REFERENCES

[1] Druin, A. 2002. *The Role of Children in the Design of New Technologies.* Behaviour and Information Technology (BIT), 21(1), 1-25

[2] Sluis-Thiescheffer, R. J. W., Bekker, M. M., Eggen, J. H., Vermeeren, A. P. O. S., & Ridder, H. 2011. *Development and application of a framework for comparing early design methods for young children.* Interacting with Computers, 23(1), 70-84.

[3] Snyder, C. 2003. *Paper Prototyping: The Fast and Easy Way to Design and Refine User Interfaces (Interactive Technologies) (1ˢᵗ ed.).* San Francisco: Morgan Kaufmann Publishers.

[4] Weiss, S. 2002. *Handheld Usability.* New York: John Wiley & Sons.

[5] Bolchini, D., Pulido, D., & Faiola, A. 2009. *FEATURE: "Paper in screen" prototyping: an agile technique to anticipate the mobile experience.* interactions, 16(4), 29-33.

[6] Magimairaj, B. M., & Montgomery, J. W. 2012. *Children's verbal working memory: Relative importance of storage, general processing speed, and domain-general controlled attention.* Acta Psychologica, 140(3), 196-207.

[7] Inkpen, K. (1997) *Three Important Research Agendas for Educational Multimedia: Learning, Children and Gender.* Paper presented at the Educational Multimedia, Calgary.Forman, G. 2003.

[8] Fawcett, S., & Rabinowitz, P. 2013. *Selecting an Appropriate Design for the Evaluation.* Retrieved 4 May, 2013, from http://ctb.ku.edu/en/tablecontents/chapter37_section4_main.aspx

[9] Apple. 2012. *iOS Interface Guidelines.* Retrieved November 12, 2012, from http://developer.apple.com/library/ios/ - documentation/UserExperience/Conceptual/MobileHIG/

[10] WeWantToKnow AS. 2012. *DragonBox Algebra 5+* Retrieved November 13, 2012, from https://play.google.com/store/apps/details?id=com.wewanttoknow.DragonBoxPlus

[11] Disney. 2012. *Where's My Water?* Retrieved November 13, 2012, from https://play.google.com/store/apps/details?id=com.disney.WMWLite

[12] Barendregt, W., & Bekker, M. M. 2005. *Development and Evaluation of the Picture Cards Method.* Workshop Interaction Design for Children. Paper presented at the IFIP 9th INTERACT Conference, Rome, Italy.

[13] Bondy, A., & Frost, L. 1994. *The picture exchange communication system.* Focus on autistic behaviour, 9, 1-19

[14] Corbin, J., & Strauss, A. 2008. *Basics of Qualitative Research. Techniques and Procedures for Developing Grounded Theory. (3 ed.):* Sage Publications, Inc.

[15] Anthony, L., Brown, Q., Nias, J., & Tate, B. 2013. *Examining the need for visual feedback during gesture interaction on mobile touchscreen devices for kids.* Proceedings of the 12th International Conference on Interaction Design and Children, New York, New York

# An Owl in the Classroom: Development of an Interactive Storytelling Application for Preschoolers

Iris Soute and Henk Nijmeijer
Eindhoven University of Technology
Den Dolech 2, 5612 AZ Eindhoven, the Netherlands
{i.a.c.soute, h.nijmeijer}@tue.nl

## Abstract

In research there is a considerable interest in developing interactive educational systems. However, the typical classroom remains a rather low-tech environment. Allowing teachers to create, adapt and share interactive learning applications might increase the uptake of technology in the classroom. In this paper a study is presented that explores the deployment of a robot-storytelling application for preschoolers, while simultaneously investigating the teacher's requirements for a toolkit to create stories for the robot. The results suggest that a robot-storytelling application can be a valuable addition to the classroom and that indeed a toolkit for creating stories would increase its usefulness in the curriculum.

## Categories and Subject Descriptors

H.5.2 [**Information Interfaces** and Presentation]: **User Interfaces** – user-centered design, prototyping.

## General Terms

Design, Human Factors.

## Keywords

Children, Teachers, Education, Robotics, End-user development.

## 1. INTRODUCTION

Though within research there is a considerable interest in applying technology in education, so far the typical classroom remains a rather low-tech environment. One of the factors that influences the adoption of technology in the classroom is the ability for teachers to 'shape their own curricula' with it [1]. However, typically, applications available are pushed on the market with 'fixed' content – with very little means to adapt the content post-production. So, from the outset designing technology with the intention to support adaption by a teacher might possibly increase the adoption rate. It makes sense too, as teachers are the domain experts in education and are best informed on the capabilities and learning potential of their students. Also, as education is moving more and more towards 'personalized learning' teachers need to be equipped with tools that allow creation and curation of personalized learning experiences.

Thus, in the design process of educational technology the teachers must be seen as one of the major stakeholders. However, in most research projects emphasize is put on the child, as the learner, and

the teacher is deemed less important [5, 9]. Furthermore, designers should take on the role of *meta-designers*; instead of focusing primarily on the learning experience, they should focus on supporting the teacher to create a learning experience.

Enabling end-users to develop their own content is not a novel idea, and is studied extensively in the field of end-user development [2]. Though most research is targeted at users professionally working with computers (e.g. data scientists, working with Excel on a daily basis), more recently researchers are broadening the scope to include professionals such as teachers and physiotherapists to provide end-user development (EUD) environments for tangible and embodied technology (e.g. [6]). We argue that, before teachers can inform designers on how they would use technology in the classroom, they need to experience it first: i.e. see it in action in the classroom. A complicating factor in the design process for educational technology is that teachers typically have very little time to be involved in the design process.

In this paper we investigate the first step in developing technology that is designed for teachers to create learning experiences for young children (4-6 years), using a robot platform as a carrier and requiring minimal effort of the teacher during the process. First, in the next section the initial design process is described in which a robot-storytelling application was built. Next, the study, aimed at eliciting user-requirements for an end-user development environment is presented. Finally, in the conclusion a reflection on the process and application is given.

## 2. INITIAL DESIGN PROCESS

As a carrier for this project, we selected a small robot, an owl, manufactured by the start-up company WittyWorx[1] (see Figure 1). The robot is approximately 30cm in height, can move in six directions (e.g. shake or nod his head, move up and down) and has OLED eyes. Combining movement, sound and different eye configurations, the robot can express a range of emotions (see Figure 2). A group of four interaction designers brainstormed and prototyped several applications for the robot over the course of one week. These applications were presented to the teacher, who immediately took a liking to an application in which the robot interactively tells a story.

In contrast to many interactive story telling applications developed in the IDC field (see [4] for an overview) that enable children to create their own stories, the robot interactively reads a story to a child, more resembling an e-book. It is generally accepted that being read stories is important for children to develop language and literary skills, to grow their vocabulary, to gain knowledge and cultural awareness, etc. [7].

In the interview, the teacher envisioned a need for such an application, illustrating it with the following scenario: in

---

[1] http://www.wittyworx.com

preschool the teacher often reads aloud stories, engaging children in the story, but she also encourages the children to explore books individually. For this, a typical (Dutch) preschool classroom has a so-called 'book corner' – a small area in the classroom dedicated to books and reading. Children 'read' books individually here. Obviously, as pre-school children do not read yet, children mostly look at picture books, or once in a while are read to by older school children from other classes. However, the problem with this corner is that children find it boring and have trouble staying focused for a longer period of time. Therefor, the teacher saw added value to having a robot telling a story, keeping the children engaged by requiring interaction to progress the storytelling.

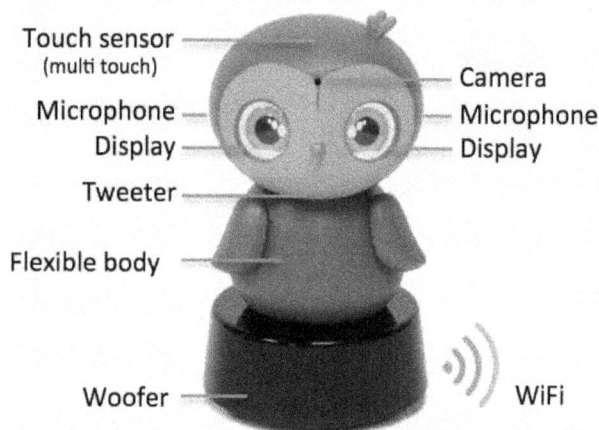

**Figure 1: The IxI play robot**

**Figure 2: Selection of expressions**

As discussed previously, a robot-storytelling application would be of greater use if adaptable by the teacher – so that he/she can create stories that match for example the current curriculum, or a particular interesting topic for a child. To investigate in what way the creation of stories could be best supported and also because the robot interaction was new for the children and teacher, a first version of the storytelling application was built, without the ability to create stories, for the teacher to gain experience with it in the class.

## 3. STORY TELLING APPLICATION

Based on the teacher's recommendations, two books were selected as source material, taking from the books both story line as well as images that corresponded with parts of the story (see Figure 3). The images are printed on cards that contain visual markers, enabling the robot to identify each card using its camera. Six cards were created per story.

A robot-storytelling session occurs as follows: a child is given a set of cards. The robot reads aloud a part of a story and then prompts the child to select the card showing the image that belongs to that particular part of the story and show that to the robot. The prompt is an auditory cue (a 'ping'); at this point the robot does not offer additional verbal cues. If the child selects the

correct card, the robot acknowledges this by excitedly nodding his head and continues with the story. If a wrong card is selected, the robot shakes his head, and verbally prompts the child to try again ("No, that is not the correct card. Please try again."). If the child would again select a wrong card, the robot verbally reveals the correct card, by indicating the color of the card (each card is lined with a distinct color) ("The correct card is the card with the yellow edge"). Other than these two supporting sentences, the robot offers no additional verbal cues and sticks verbatim to the story line as it is in the original book.

**Figure 3: Selection of cards with images of the story**

With regard to movements: during the storytelling the robot blinks its eyes at random intervals. Also, the robot executes random movements during story telling. However, after the prompt, the robot stops the random movements and waits for the child to present a card.

The application was pilot tested with two children (age 5 and 6), which verified that children understood the interaction and a few minor technical issues were revealed and fixed.

## 4. STUDY

The main aim of our study was to expose teachers to the robot, as it would be used in a regular school context, with the intention to identify requirements for an environment that would allow teachers to create their own stories for the robot. As a secondary aim we were interested in exploring the children's reaction to the robot and the storytelling application.

### 4.1 Setup

#### 4.1.1 Participants

24 children, aged 4-6, from a pre-school class in the Netherlands participated in this study, as well as the two teachers (both female) of this class - one teacher taught Mondays and Tuesdays, the other the rest of the week. Beforehand, the parents were asked for consent for their children's participation.

#### 4.1.2 Procedure

The main aim of the study was to confront the teachers with the robot in their regular context, to enable them to reflect how they would integrate the use of the robot in their daily routine. Therefor, the sessions took place at school; the importance of testing the robot "in the wild" is generally acknowledged [10], as there are so many external factors that can influence the actual use of the robot. All children of the class were allowed to interact with the robot, though, due to time constraints, the teachers could only be present in six sessions. The sessions in which the teacher could not be present were afterwards discussed using the observation log that was kept during the sessions.

The robot was placed outside the classroom, in a common area in between classrooms. It was set on a small table, with a child sitting in front of it on a small chair (see Figure 4). The laptop, that controlled the robot movement and interaction, was placed within reach of the researcher, but not in the direct field of view of the children.

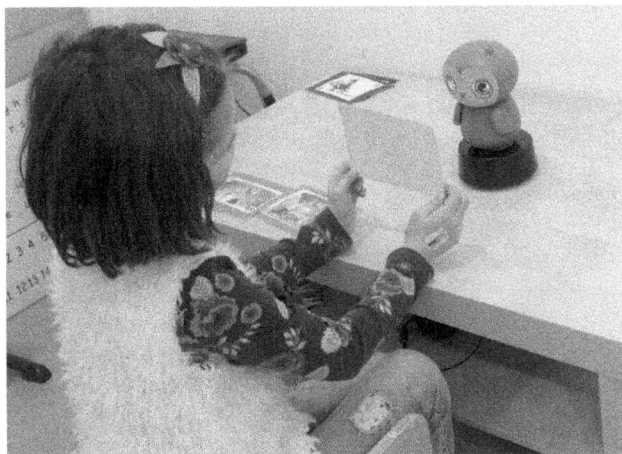

**Figure 4: Preschooler showing a card to the robot for identification**

Before the sessions each teacher was introduced to the robot and given a demonstration of the storytelling application. After this, the teacher immediately reflected on how she expected that children would react to the robot.

The sessions with the children took place during three days in one week. On the first morning the children were introduced to the robot, and were told what to expect. Next, children were arranged in pairs of two at the teacher's discretion, and these pairs participated in the evaluation throughout the morning, temporarily leaving the regular routine. Whenever the schedule allowed, the teacher would join the evaluation, assuming a passive, observing, role.

At the start of a session, the children were shortly re-introduced to the robot. They were assured that at all times they were allowed to quit the session, using a common phrase also used in class to stop unwanted situations. Next they were allowed to pick one of the two stories and the researcher would shortly discuss with the children the cards corresponding with that story. Then the robot would start telling the story and children were asked to show the appropriate cards, according to the story line. A session took between three to eight minutes and one researcher was present to guide and observe the process. No metrics of the child's performance were logged. Events such as children needing help, or an unexpected reaction of a child were recorded in an observation log.

At the end of each day the researcher interviewed the teacher that was present that day. During the semi-structured interview, the observations made by the researcher of each child's session were discussed. Furthermore, the teacher's own observation of the use of the system was discussed.

## 4.2 Results and Discussion

Though the initial plan was to evaluate the robot with pairs of children, after five sessions it became clear that this would not be the optimal setting for use. The teacher had assumed that when working in pairs, children would collaborate and help each other out – but this did not happen at all. In contrast, we observed that at the start of the story children would agree on turn taking, each child patiently waiting for his/her turn, without helping the other

out when he/she would get stuck. We also observed that children would (unintentionally) distract each other: a movement or sound would cause a child to shift focus from the robot to the other child. As the robot has no means of detecting such shifts in focus, he would continue his story, resulting in the child missing part of the storyline. The teacher and researcher agreed to continue the tests with single users, not pairs.

The sessions in which the teachers were present gave them much insight in the robot's use, and the interviews afterwards provided valuable information: even though the teachers had had a demonstration of the robot before the sessions, seeing it in action with children provided new insights. Interestingly, after observing the children the teachers became aware of the fact that the application trained a skill that they had not anticipated beforehand. Namely, they argued it practices the skill of 'listening comprehension', i.e. a child must comprehend the auditory information to transform it to visual information. The teachers valued this highly, as they deemed it a preparatory skill for 'reading comprehension' skills – a skill that becomes very important in later classes.

Furthermore, in relation to the children's performance: in a toolkit for creating stories, the teachers would like the possibility to differentiate in the level of support or scaffolding the robot gives. For some children, the amount of support given now was sufficient; other children would have benefitted if the robot had provided more guidance or support. For example, extending the auditory cues with verbal prompts with more information when a card must be selected, e.g. by letting the robot ask a question, to give more guidance in identifying a card. As the teacher knows a child's capabilities best, she would like to be able to set this per child. Also, as the idea is that this application is used unsupervised, the teacher would like to receive a summary of the child's performance after the session, e.g. indicating the correct and incorrect number of cards and the time it took to complete the session.

When asked how often they would use such a robot in class, they answered that they probably would use it on a daily basis. However, they envisioned that they would create approximately two stories per month. They expected that not all teachers would be eager to *create* stories, but would be happy to use stories created by other teachers. Furthermore, they mentioned that the use of the robot would definitely not replace the story reading sessions of the teacher; rather they saw it as a supplementary activity to increase the number of reading sessions in an engaging way.

Though no exact metrics on performance were logged, we found that all children were able to finish their story within reasonable time. Still, the range of how well children performed was quite broad: some children did need help from the researcher, while others flawlessly went through the session, not needing help at all. This seemed not to be related to age: some of the four year olds performed better (in terms of speed and identifying correct cards) than some of the six year olds. When reviewing the researcher's notes of each session with the teacher, the teacher confirmed that generally a child's behavior and performance was in line with what she expected from that child, based on classroom behavior.

Causes for needing help originated from several sources: not understanding what was expected, most particularly the first time the robot prompted for a card. In general, one demonstration was enough to remedy this. Another reason for needing help was when a child was distracted during the storytelling. Then, he/she would (obviously) find it difficult to identify the correct card. The researcher would help out, as there was no means to have the robot repeat that particular part of the story. Furthermore, there was one technical issue that sometimes caused the robot's camera to lose focus, resulting in a prolonged time for card identification. The children did not seem too perturbed by this.

Regarding the interactive behavior of the robot, after the first day we identified behavior that had gone unnoticed during the development of the application: namely that when the robot was given a command for a movement, any subsequent movement commands given *during* that movement would be completely disregarded, but other cues would go through (such as the audio cue for the prompt). Only after completing a movement, the robot would be accepting commands for new movements. As a result, when a child would be very fast in identifying and showing a card, it could happen that the auditory cue was given during the execution of a previous random movement. If the correct card was presented while the robot was still moving, the "acknowledging" movement would be sent to the robot, but the story would immediately continue disregarding the acknowledgment. We observed this happening with one child, who consistently very rapidly identified each card, and never received the "acknowledging" movement. Though he did not mention anything and kept on performing well, he did seem a bit confused whether he was doing it right. In contrast, in observing the other children we saw that the "acknowledging" movement was engaging and fun and they immediately understood that they had identified the correct card.

We observed that this robot was appropriate for use for this age group and children were attracted by its 'cute' looks. Furthermore, the interaction of the robot seemed appealing; we observed several instances were children 'mirrored' the movements of the robot, enjoying the interaction. This is inline with findings of other studies in Child-Robot interaction for preschoolers [3].

## 5. CONCLUSION AND FUTURE WORK

Though a single study is too limited to result in conclusive findings, a few tentative remarks can be made. First, the use of a robot as storytelling medium was engaging for the children; especially the movements seem to be a very natural way to interact with children. However, this study also suggests that such interactions must be carefully designed, as a badly timed movement can negatively influence the user experience.

Furthermore, it indeed turned out to be valuable to expose the teachers to the robot as a means of identifying user requirements for an end-user development toolkit. Seeing the robot in action in context allowed the teachers to reflect better on possible usage scenarios and their requirements for an eventual toolkit. Moreover, the study was set up in such a way that it did not require a heavy time commitment of the teacher, suggesting that, in the case that involving teachers as co-designers is not a viable option, the approach followed here is a good alternative.

Finally, the study suggests that a toolkit is indeed needed to better support each child's capabilities and create additional content. Though the question of what functionality an eventual toolkit should support was addresses, future research should investigate *how* a toolkit can be implemented in a way appropriate for teachers, also with respect to how the robot interactions are to be designed by the teacher. Earlier work in EUD for computer based learning systems, such as [8], suggest that it is indeed feasible to develop tools and methods that allow teachers to create

educational content. This work extends that line of research by moving from a desktop environment to robot-enhanced learning experience, opening up interesting challenges in interaction design such as programming movements and designing robot-child interaction by non-technical users. As Tetteroo et al. [11] suggest, such design issues pose a real challenge, which are still relatively unexplored.

## 6. ACKNOWLEDGMENTS

Our thanks go to all the children and teachers involved in this project. Furthermore, we are very grateful to Linda de Valk, Daniel Tetteroo and Nikos Batalas for contributing to the initial design. Finally, we would like to thank WittyWorx for making available their robot for this research.

We acknowledge the support of the Innovation-Oriented Research Programme 'Integral Product Creation and Realization (IOP IPCR)' of the Netherlands Ministry of Economic Affairs.

## 7. REFERENCES

[1] Cuban, L. 2009. *Oversold and Underused: Computers in the Classroom*. Harvard University Press.

[2] Fischer, G. 2009. End-User Development and Meta-design: Foundations for Cultures of Participation. *End-User Development*. V. Pipek, M. Rosson, B. de Ruyter, and V. Wulf, eds. Springer Berlin / Heidelberg. 3–14.

[3] Fridin, M. 2014. Kindergarten social assistive robot: First meeting and ethical issues. *Computers in Human Behavior*. 30, (Jan. 2014), 262–272.

[4] Garzotto, F. 2014. Interactive storytelling for children: a survey. *International Journal of Arts and Technology*. 7, 1 (Jan. 2014), 5–16.

[5] Good, J. and Robertson, J. 2006. CARSS: A framework for learner-centred design with children. *International Journal of Artificial Intelligence in Education*. 16, 4 (2006), 381–413.

[6] Hochstenbach-Waelen, A., Timmermans, A., Seelen, H., Tetteroo, D. and Markopoulos, P. 2012. Tag-exercise Creator: Towards End-user Development for Tangible Interaction in Rehabilitation Training. *Proceedings of the 4th ACM SIGCHI Symposium on Engineering Interactive Computing Systems* (New York, NY, USA, 2012), 293–298.

[7] Isbell, R., Sobol, J., Lindauer, L. and Lowrance, A. 2004. The Effects of Storytelling and Story Reading on the Oral Language Complexity and Story Comprehension of Young Children. *Early Childhood Education Journal*. 32, 3 (Dec. 2004), 157–163.

[8] Marchiori, E.J., Torrente, J., del Blanco, Á., Moreno-Ger, P., Sancho, P. and Fernández-Manjón, B. 2012. A narrative metaphor to facilitate educational game authoring. *Computers & Education*. 58, 1 (Jan. 2012), 590–599.

[9] Robertson, J., Macvean, A. and Howland, K. 2012. Embedding Technology in the Classroom: The Train the Teacher Model. *Proceedings of the 11th International Conference on Interaction Design and Children* (New York, NY, USA, 2012), 20–29.

[10] Salter, T., Werry, I. and Michaud, F. 2008. Going into the wild in child–robot interaction studies: issues in social robotic development. *Intelligent Service Robotics*. 1, 2 (Apr. 2008), 93–108.

[11] Tetteroo, D., Soute, I. and Markopoulos, P. 2013. Five Key Challenges in End-user Development for Tangible and Embodied Interaction. *Proceedings of the 15th ACM on International Conference on Multimodal Interaction* (New York, NY, USA, 2013), 247–254

# KIKIWAKE: Participatory Design of Language Play Game for Children to Promote Creative Activity based on Recognition of Japanese Phonology

**Takahiro Nakadai**
Tokyo University of Science
2641, Yamazaki
Noda, Chiba, Japan
bzluey.g@ed.tus.ac.jp

**Tomoki Taguchi**
Tokyo University of Science
2641, Yamazaki
Noda, Chiba, Japan
j7512639@ed.tus.ac.jp

**Ryohei Egusa**
Kobe University
3-11, Tsurukabuto, Nada
Kobe, Hyogo, Japan
126d103d@stu.kobe-u.ac.jp

**Miki Namatame**
Tsukuba University of Technology
4-3-15, Amakubo
Tsukuba, Ibaraki, Japan
miki@a.tsukuba-tech.ac.jp

**Masanori Sugimoto**
Hokkaido University
Kita 15, Nishi8, Kita-ku
Sapporo, Hokkaido, Japan
sugi@ist.hokudai.ac.jp

**Fusako Kusunoki**
Tama Art University
2-1723, Yarimizu
Hachioji, Tokyo, Japan
kusunoki@tamabi.ac.jp

**Etsuji Yamaguchi**
Kobe University
3-11, Tsurukabuto, Nada
Kobe, Hyogo, Japan
etsuji@opal.kobe-u.ac.jp

**Shigenori Inagaki**
Kobe University
3-11, Tsurukabuto, Nada
Kobe, Hyogo, Japan
inagakis@kobe-u.ac.jp

**Yoshiaki Takeda**
Kobe University
3-11, Tsurukabuto, Nada
Kobe, Hyogo, Japan
takedayo@kobe-u.ac.jp

**Hiroshi Mizoguchi**
Tokyo University of Science
2641, Yamazaki
Noda, Chiba, Japan
hm@rs.noda.tus.ac.jp

## ABSTRACT

This study proposes a system for supporting the Shotoku Taishi game, which is a language play game that uses the voice of children. The Shotoku Taishi game is a group game in which multiple people presenting a problem vocalize different words at the same time and the respondents are required to guess what the combination of the words is. The authors developed and implemented a system using a microphone array to extract the voice of a specific person presenting a problem in this game. The participants were 36 elementary school students whose native language was Japanese. The results showed that the participants were enjoying the Shotoku Taishi game and that this group activity was a creative activity that deepened their awareness of the Japanese language.

## Categories and Subject Descriptors

K.3.2 [**Computing Milieux**]: Computer and Information Science Education - *Information Systems Education*

## General Terms

Design, Experimentation

## Keywords

Sound Source Separation, Microphone Array, Science Education

## 1. INTRODUCTION

Language play activities are essential for helping an individual to learn a language [1]. Therefore, the development of a system that supports voice-based language play games can greatly help children to learn a language. However, there have not been many technical advances in the development of voice-based games with an interactive design for children, except for games using equipment that converts natural voice or games using voice inputs [2, 3]. This study proposes a system for supporting language play games using the voice of children.

There are different types of language play games. Well-known language play games include tongue twister and palindrome. The Shotoku Taishi game is one such language play game popular in Japan. It is a voice-based group game, and its flow is described below.

First, participants are divided into a group that presents a problem and a group that solves the problem. A problem is composed of multiple words. Next, each member of the group that presents a problem is assigned a word and, all members vocalize their respective words simultaneously. The members of the responding group listen to an audio composed of a mixture of multiple vocalizations and guess who vocalized which word. Then, the responses are checked and points are awarded if the responses match the combination of words vocalized by the group presenting the problem. Because it is difficult to accurately distinguish words, the members of the responding group must pay close attention to the slightest difference in sound, particularly to vowels. The Shotoku Taishi game is not only fun to play but also considered to be a means to encourage children to pay attention to the characteristics of the Japanese language, that is, to identify the vowels/consonants in the syllables of words.

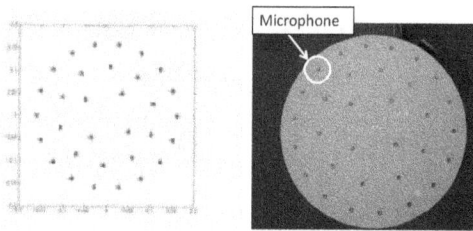

Figure 1. Optimal arrangement of the microphone array.

We developed a system for supporting the Shotoku Taishi game; the system uses a microphone array to extract the voices of individual members of the group presenting the problem from audio composed of a mixture of voices of these members [4]. The use of this system offers the following advantages. First, participants can repeatedly listen to the audio at the same quality. Second, the extent of extraction is varied so that gradually, individual members presenting the problem and their vocalized words can be distinguished. Therefore, children can concentrate on the vocalization, and when they prepare their own problems, their creativity can be triggered to recognize the characteristics of the Japanese language.

In this study, the Shotoku Taishi game was played using this system to investigate the awareness of participants regarding the characteristics of the Japanese language during and after participating in the game. The participants were 36 elementary school students whose native language was Japanese. The purpose of the study was to determine whether the experience of playing the Shotoku Taishi game using the system was a pleasant one for participants and to clarify whether their awareness regarding the characteristics of the Japanese language was improved by the use of the proposed system.

# 2. HARDWARE SYSTEM USED FOR THE GAME

## 2.1 Design of Microphone Array

There are several signal processing methods for the output of a microphone array. We selected the method called delay-and-sum beamforming (DSBF) [5] because it is robust in practical environments. The DSBF method can be used to locally capture a sound at an objective angle to form a beam of high sensitivity. The performance of this method is heavily dependent on the microphone arrangement. Therefore, we designed an optimal microphone array by performing a simulation [6], as shown in Figure 1.

## 2.2 Signal Processing

The microphone array reduces the non-objective sound and accentuates the objective sound. However, a listener cannot recognize any sound clearly because the processing accentuates the sound relatively. To eliminate the non-objective sound, we apply frequency band selection (FBS) [7] after the microphone array signal processing.

The above method was used in conjunction with a sound source identification apparatus by Sasaki et al. First, two voices are accentuated using DSBF. Next, to select the desired accentuated frequency components, the frequency bands of the two voices are compared. Finally, the selected frequency components are retained, and all others eliminated. This signal processing method can separate the voice of each talker clearly.

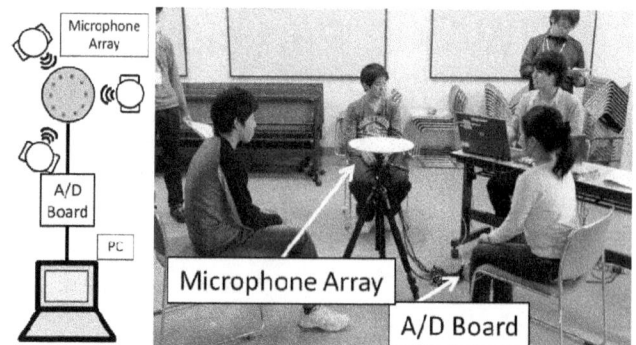

Figure 2. Hardware components and states of the game.

# 3. EVALUATION

## 3.1 Evaluation Method

The participants were 36 students (grade 6, 11 to 12 years of age) attending an elementary school affiliated with a national university.

The outline of the game is as follows. The game was played by nine members, who were divided into three groups of three members each. Figure 3 shows a flowchart of the game. The game was divided into the following four processes: 1. preparation of the first problem; 2. presentation of the problem and response with a solution (1st round); 3. preparation of the second problem; and 4. presentation of the problem and response with a solution (2nd round). Each group prepared problems twice during the game and asked another group to respond with solutions to them. Each problem was composed of three words. The respondents had to provide solutions by describing what they heard when the three people who presented the problem vocalized words simultaneously (hereinafter referred to as the "mixed voice"). Respondents were provided with two hints before they responded with solutions. The first hint was the mixed voice processed by DSBF (accentuated voice) and the other hint was the mixed voice processed by FBS (separated voice). The microphone array–based system was used for carrying out the abovementioned voice processing. Respondents were required to present solutions to problems by using as few hints as possible. Problems were formulated through a discussion held within the group that prepared the problems. Particularly, during the preparation of the second problem, the problems presented by other groups during the first round were referenced, and each group conducted a brainstorming session to discuss their next problem. The brainstorming sessions entailed preparing paper cards with as many candidate problems as they can come up with; words were combined so that they would be difficult to identify individually even after voice processing, and then, these cards were sorted and integrated. The entire game duration was 55 min. The data source for the purpose of evaluation included the above cards prepared during the brainstorming sessions and freely written descriptions by participants on the positive aspects of the game as well as parameters considered while preparing problems. Furthermore, 16 participants were randomly selected and interviewed. The questions asked during the interview pertained to the intention behind preparation of the problems. The duration of the interview was approximately 3 min per person.

Implementation date: November 2, 2013.

**Table 1: Representative examples of opinions given by participants: positive aspects of the game and parameters considered while preparing problems**

| | |
|---|---|
| Positive aspects | |
| | It was fun for the three of us to work together and put much effort into the preparation of problems. |
| | There were some difficult problems but I was very happy when I could solve them. |
| | The funniest part was when we had no idea what was being spoken, and it was fun to struggle a lot to solve them. |
| | It was fun to present our problems and to have them solved. |
| Parameters considered | |
| | We made an effort to use similar words with similar number of characters. |
| | We sometimes brought the same characters to the beginning of the words. |
| | We selected words from different genres (attributes) but with similar sounds. |
| | We used lengthy (in terms of the number of characters) and unexpected problems. |
| | We presented words by saying them quickly while hiding our lips and facing down. |
| | We varied the loudness of our voice. |

**Table 2: Interview: Intention behind preparing problems**

E1: What parameters did you consider (while formulating the problems)?

P1: We considered sounds made by animals, such as "Nyā" (mewing of cats), "Ki-ki-ki" (screeching of bats), and "U-ki-ki" (chattering of apes). Because "Nyā" is quite impressionable, we thought that it would be more difficult to distinguish between "Ki-ki-ki" and "U-ki-ki." In addition, because "Ki-ki-ki" and "U-ki-ki" were similar, we thought it would be difficult to distinguish them even if "Nyā" was identified.

E1: What kind of problems did you create as a group?

P1: The first problem created by our group was "Pa-ri-n, Pa-n, Tya-ri-n" (onomatopoetic words), and the second problem was a combination of greetings, "good bye, how are you, and what is your name," in French.

E1: What parameters did you consider while formulating the problems?

P1: When we were observing other groups, we realized that distinct Japanese vowels were easily recognizable but using dull sounds and vowel combinations made distinguishing difficult, so we decided to use a lot of these.

E2: What kinds of problems did you come up with?

P2: For the first problem, we used all words ending with the same sound, "Do-n": "U-do-n" (noodles), "Sa-ra-U-do-n" (Nagasaki dish of noodles with various toppings), and "Ka-tsu-Do-n" (rice bowl with pork cutlet). The second problem was "Pa-pa," "Ha-ha," and "Ma-ma," whose vowels are all the same.

E2: What made you think of considering these parameters?

P2: We thought that if all words had the same vowel, some would became inaudible and others would sound like a different word with the same vowel, which could possibly make them indistinguishable. In addition, with all words ending with the sound, "Do-n," we thought that the sound was vigorous and stood out above all else, and when three words were mixed, we thought only "Do-n" would be audible and the rest would be difficult to distinguish.

E2: If you were to formulate another problem, what parameters would you consider?

P2: We would consider words that sound the same but are actually different. We like what another group just did: changing one character to create a combination of words such as "Africa," "America," and so on.

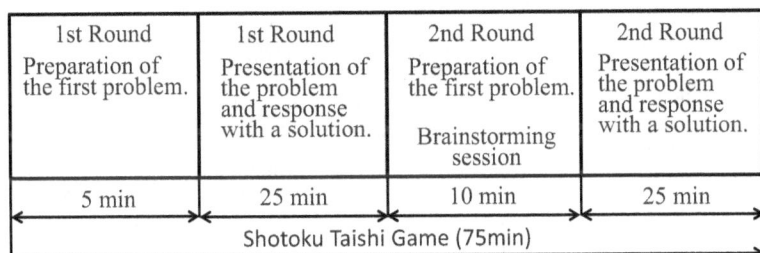

| 1st Round | 1st Round | 2nd Round | 2nd Round |
|---|---|---|---|
| Preparation of the first problem. | Presentation of the problem and response with a solution. | Preparation of the first problem.<br><br>Brainstorming session | Presentation of the problem and response with a solution. |
| 5 min | 25 min | 10 min | 25 min |

Shotoku Taishi Game (75min)

**Figure 3. Flowchart of the Shotoku Taishi game.**

**Figure 4. Participants preparing problems.**

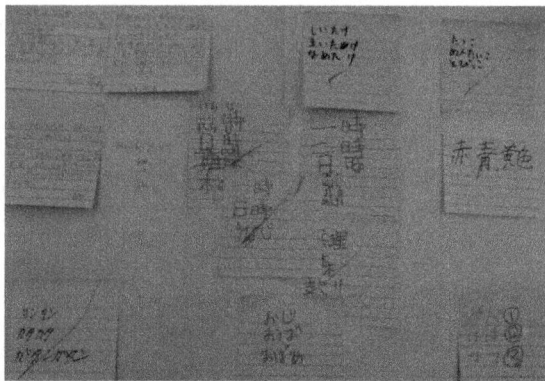

**Figure 5. Worksheets used for preparing problems.**

## 3.2 Evaluation Results

Figure 4 shows an example of worksheets used by participants as they consulted each other while they prepared the problems. The participants of this group individually prepared problems and sorted them according to their properties. More specifically, they was a problem of three words having identical vowels, a problem of three words having the same attributes (food and color), and a problem using onomatopoetic words. Furthermore, traces of sophisticated processes used to prepare problems through consultation, such as changing the problem that started off as a combination of "Ichi-ji" (one o'clock), "Ni-ji" (two o'clock) and "Nichi-ji" (date and time), by replacing "Ichi-ji" with "Una-ji" (nape) (shown at the center of Figure 5). In the end, the combination of "Pa-pa" (father), "Ha-ha" (mother), and "Ma-ma" (synonym of mother) was selected (shown at the bottom of Figure 5). This worksheet revealed that the participants were focusing on certain properties of Japanese words as they prepared the problems. Furthermore, with regard to the properties of the three words adopted for each problem, the worksheet also suggested that the participants considered selecting words with the same vowels to be appropriate.

According to participants' opinions about the game after it was completed, 34 out of 36 participants evaluated the game positively, saying, "it was amusing," or "it was fun." The remaining two participants also mentioned the positive aspects and characteristics of the system and they did not provide any negative evaluations of the game. The representative responses listed in Table 1 are obtained by summarizing the positive aspects of the game and parameters considered while preparing problems. Preparing problems as a group and tackling the problems presented by other groups were revealed to be aspects that were fun for the participants. Furthermore, it was also revealed that by understanding the characteristics of the system, they selected the properties of words for a problem and the tone of their voices.

Table 2 presents a representative example of the outcome obtained from interviews on what their intentions were when they prepared the problems. P1 was aware of the similarities and vigor of sounds when preparing the first problem but then focused on the dull sounds and contracted sounds (forming one syllable using a consonant, semi-vowel, and vowel; sounds similar to diphthongs such as "ae") for the preparation of the second problem. This focus on the contracted sounds may be interesting because it takes into consideration the characteristics of the Japanese language, in which words are fundamentally composed of syllables that have a vowel or a consonant and vowel. P2 prepared the first problem

while being aware of the vigor of sounds, but for the preparation of the second problem, he prepared the problem with focus on creating words using the same vowel. This idea is based on the fact that using three words with the same vowel would make it difficult to distinguish the words that are phonologically similar. The change in the awareness of the participants from the first round to the second round of questions during the game is evident.

## 4. CONCLUSION

Playing the Shotoku Taishi game using the proposed system revealed that participants enjoyed playing the game and that the awareness of participants regarding the phonological and syllabic characteristics of the Japanese language deepened. In particular, with regard to the latter, the participants prepared combinations of words that would be difficult for the system to clarify, considering that the system gradually clarified the persons that presented a problem and the vocalized words. This activity was shown to be a creative process wherein the participants prepared problems while re-recognizing characteristics of the Japanese language, which they regularly use.

## 5. ACKNOWLEDGEMENTS

This work was supported in part by Grants-in-Aid for Scientific Research (B) (Nos. 24300290 and 23300303).

## 6. REFERENCES

[1] Guy Cook. 2000. Language Play, Language Learning (Oxford Applied Linguistics). Oxford University Press.

[2] Oscar. M., Jordi. B., Jordi. J. 2010. KaleiVoiceKids: Interactive Real-Time Voice Transformation for Children. In Proceedings of the 9th International Conference on Interaction Design and Children. pp.234-237.

[3] P. Hämäläinen., T. Mäki-Patola., V. Pulkki., M. Airas. 2004 Musical Computer Games Played by Singing. In proceedings of the 7th International Conference on Digital Audio Effects. pp. 367-371.

[4] Taguchi, T., Goseki, M., Egusa, R., Namatame, M., Sugimoto, M., Kusunoki, F., Yamaguchi, E., Inagaki, S., Takeda, Y., & Mizoguchi, H. 2013. KIKIWAKE: sound source separation system for children-computer interaction. In CHI '13 Extended Abstracts on Human Factors in Computing Systems pp.757-762.

[5] Vu, N. V., Ye, H., Whittington, J., Devlin, J., and Mason, M. 2010. Small footprint implementation of dual-microphone delay-and-sum beamforming for in-car speech enhancement. *Proc. ICASSP* pp.1482–1485.

[6] Taguchi, T., Goseki, M., Takemura, H., Nakase, I., Fukui, K., Kusunoki, F., Inagaki, S., and Mizoguchi, H. 2012. Investigation on optimal arrangement of microphone array with 3-dimensional directivity. *International Symposium on Nonlinear Theory and its Applications*, pp.251-254.

[7] Sasaki, Y., Kagami, S., and Mizoguchi, H. 2006. Multiple sound source mapping for a mobile robot by self-motion triangulation. *Proc. 2006 IEEE/RSJ International Conference on Intelligent Robots and Systems*, pp.380–385.

# Exploring Challenging Group Dynamics in Participatory Design with Children

**Maarten Van Mechelen**
CUO | Social Spaces
iMinds, KU Leuven | MAD-faculty
Parkstraat 45/3605
3000 Leuven, Belgium
maarten.vanmechelen@soc.kuleuven.be

**Mathieu Gielen**
Department of Industrial Engineering
Delft University of Technology
Landbergstraat 15
2628 CE Delft, The Netherlands
m.a.gielen@tudelft.nl

**Vero vanden Abeele**
e-Medialab, GroepT
KU Leuven association
Vesaliusstraat 13
3000 Leuven, Belgium
vero.vanden.abeele@groept.be

**Ann Laenen**
LUCA Faculty of the Arts
KU Leuven association
Koningsstraat 328
1030 Brussel, Belgium
ann.laenen@kuleuven.be

**Bieke Zaman**
CUO | Social Spaces
iMinds, KU Leuven
Parkstraat 45/3605
3000 Leuven, Belgium
bieke.zaman@soc.kuleuven.be

## ABSTRACT

This paper presents a structured way to evaluate challenging group or 'co-design dynamics' in participatory design processes with children. In the form of a critical reflection on a project in which 103 children were involved as design partners, we describe the most prevalent co-design dynamics. For example, some groups rush too quickly towards consensus to safeguard group cohesiveness instead of examining other choice alternatives (i.e., groupthink). Besides 'groupthink' we describe five more challenging co-design dynamics: 'laughing out loud', 'free riding', 'unequal power', 'apart together' and 'destructive conflict'. We argue that balancing these dynamics has a positive impact on the dialectic process of developing values and ideas in participatory design, as well as on children's motivation. Therefore, the CCI community could benefit from our in-depth exploration and categorization of challenging group dynamics when co-designing technology with children.

## Categories and Subject Descriptors

H.5.2 User Interfaces, Theory and methods, User-centered design

## General Terms

Design; Performance

## Keywords

CCI; Co-design; Group dynamics; Values; Participatory design

## 1. INTRODUCTION

Participatory design has urged us to consider 'users' as co-designers of their technology and of the practices that may be reified in that technology. Within the area of Child Computer Interaction (CCI) children have participated in the design of technology for over two decades using a variety of established methods [3][12]. These methods typically involve children in dyads or groups, rather than individually. The use of groups in

*IDC'14*, June 17–20, 2014, Aarhus, Denmark.
Copyright 2014 ACM 978-1-4503-2272-0/14/06…$15.00.
http://dx.doi.org/10.1145/2593968.2610469

participatory design reflects a theoretical commitment to the notion that meanings are socially and collectively produced [1].

## 1.1 Negotiating values

Recently, attempts have been made to rekindle values in what is called a more authentic approach towards participatory design [10]. During design activities, children's values may be implicitly expressed as something they care about and find important. Values do not progress stepwise in one direction. Rather they emerge, develop and ground recursively and dialogically over the course of the design process [10]. The way we work with values in participatory design with children is centered on dialogue. Therefore, one of our core tasks as researchers is to orchestrate this dialogue with and among children and to make sure value conflicts are transcended and translated into meaningful design concepts. Special attention should thereby be given to group dynamics that may impact this dialogical process.

## 1.2 Group dynamics

Within the area of CCI, authors have only recently started to acknowledge the importance of facilitating group dynamics in co-design with children, e.g. [17]. Focusing on group dynamics is believed to have a positive impact on children's motivation as well as on the development of creative solutions [2]. Nevertheless, the concept 'group dynamics' remains generally poorly defined within the field, and little solutions to overcome challenging group dynamics have been suggested. Also, the majority of CCI authors tends to focus primarily on remediating asymmetrical power relationships between adults and children, e.g. [4][7][12]. Therefore, the CCI community would benefit from an in-depth exploration and categorization of challenging group dynamics when co-designing technology with children.

The term group dynamics was first coined by social psychologist Kurt Lewin (1945) and refers to a system of behaviors and psychological processes occurring within a social group (i.e. intragroup dynamics), or between social groups (i.e. intergroup dynamics) [5]. In this paper, we refer to 'co-design dynamics' as a system of intragroup dynamics occurring within a group of children sharing a common design goal.

In the form of a critical reflection, this paper presents a structured way to account for challenging co-design dynamics within groups of children. In section 2 we describe a project in which children were involved as design partners. In section 3 we reflect upon these co-design activities, presenting the most prevalent dynamics we encountered during the project, and in section 4 we discuss our categorization of challenging co-design dynamics and touch upon topics for further research.

# 2. CASE STUDY

The study took place in three schools in Flanders, Belgium. All children were in the fourth grade of elementary school, aged 9 to 10. Each class, ranging from 19 to 30 children, was divided in a morning- and afternoon group. In sum, 103 children were involved. At the beginning of each co-design session, these morning- and afternoon groups were split up in two to three gender-mixed subgroups of four to six boys and girls. Literature has shown this to be the most optimal group size [9]. Also, many authors suggest that heterogeneous groups are more capable of coming up with diverse ideas [4][14]. Therefore, with the help of the children's teachers, these subgroups were formed heterogeneously, based on criteria such as intelligence, communication skills, gender and creative abilities.

Over a period of two months, four co-design sessions were organized in each school on the theme of arts and culture education. We thereby divided our general design theme into subtopics, one for each co-design session:

Session 1: organizing a fun and engaging class excursion.

Session 2: making schoolwork both fun and engaging.

Session 3: designing a fun and engaging website for learning.

Session 4: inventing magical technology to assist schoolchildren on a museum visit.

## 2.1 General procedure

We used a blend of two different approaches to co-design: 'Cooperative Inquiry' [4] and the 'Contextmapping' procedure as described by [15]. The goal of Cooperative Inquiry is to support intergenerational design teams in understanding what children as technology users do now, what they might do tomorrow and what they envision for the future [4]. Contextmapping on the other hand is a systematic approach to elicit contextual information of product use. Generative techniques are often used in Contextmapping. The basic principle thereby is to let people make designerly artifacts and tell a story about what they have made [13][14].

Two researchers were involved in each co-design session: one facilitator who interacted with the children and one fly-on-the-wall observer making notes. In addition, the whole session was recorded on video and a report was written immediately afterwards. Each session lasted for about 150 minutes and typically consisted of the following stages:

### 2.1.1 Sensitizing

By means of an individual assignment we triggered children's reflection in a playful and creative way before the actual co-design session. Approximately one week ahead of each session, we introduced an assignment in the children's classrooms. They then continued working on it at home. In one such assignment, 'Future Classroom', we asked the children to draw or prototype their ideal classroom of the future. In the co-design session that followed (i.e. session 2: making schoolwork both fun and engaging), the children discussed their drawings or paper prototypes for the first 10 to 15 minutes. Through this 'warm-up', children were better able to access their experiences and values and to express their ideas regarding the co-design session's topics. This is in line with [15] to whom we refer for more detailed information on sensitizing.

### 2.1.2 Introduction and warm up

The session took place in an available (class-)room in the school. First, the children were divided into two to three teams of four to six boys and girls depending on the class size. Then, the adult facilitator explained the co-design session's topic as well as the rules such as 'listen to each other', 'there are no bad ideas', and 'you may walk around but stick to your team'. The latter activities took about 10 to 15 minutes. Next, the facilitator warmed up the children for another 10 to 15 minutes by discussing the results of the preceding sensitizing assignment. During these discussions, children's values were implicitly expressed as something they care about and find important. This way, a problem space was identified that children felt is worth tackling.

### 2.1.3 Ideation and selection

The facilitator handed out post-its and markers and explained the rules for ideation (i.e. defer judgment, encourage wild ideas, build on the ideas of others and go for quantity) [16]. The children were then encouraged to brainstorm, writing down as many ideas as possible on post-its. Although brainstorming's effectiveness has been questioned, the technique should not be evaluated in isolation here, since we combined it with individual reflection (cf. sensitizing) and low-tech prototyping (cf. elaboration) [16]. Each design team had five minutes to brainstorm ideas. Then they were asked to group similar ideas together. Finally, each team member could vote for his or her favorite ideas by means of three little stickers (i.e., sticky dot voting) [6]. Only one vote could be given to one of their own ideas. The most popular ideas were taken to the next stage for further development.

### 2.1.4 Elaboration through making

In this phase, children elaborated hands-on on the selected ideas. The facilitator explicitly asked the teams to mix the three previously selected ideas into one 'big idea' [7]. They could either visualize their big idea through a collage or make a paper prototype out of it. For this purpose, each team had a generative toolkit [13] at their disposal made up of two-dimensional components ranging from figurative to abstract (e.g. paper shapes, stickers and color photographs). The teams had about 45 to 55 minutes to visualize or prototype their big idea. Again, since space is limited, we refer to [15] for a more detailed description on the use of generative toolkits.

### 2.1.5 Presentation and discussion

In approximately five minutes, the teams prepared a presentation about their design. When one team was presenting their collage or prototype and the ideas and values embedded in it, the other teams functioned as a jury. After the presentation, the jury could ask critical questions about the design. We stressed that the jury should focus on the design's quality rather than on the form of the presentation. The facilitator moderated this dialogue between jury and design teams and asked some additional open-ended 'why' questions inspired by UX laddering as described by [18]. Thereby, the deep reasons and values behind certain design decisions were revealed. After each team had presented and discussed their collage or prototype, a short wrap-up followed and the session ended. Presentation and discussion took about 15 minutes per team.

## 2.2 Analysis

We qualitatively analyzed the data by means of open and axial coding. The raw data consisted of observation notes, reports written after the sessions, co-design artifacts, video footage and transcripts from the presentations and discussions.

# 3. CO-DESIGN DYNAMICS

The framework presented below is not exhaustive and although some of these challenging dynamics may not seem novel at first sight, they have rarely been addressed explicitly in CCI and in literature on co-design methods.

## 3.1 Unequal power

Some co-design groups quite openly followed the opinions and ideas of the most dominant or charismatic team member. These children were enjoying a higher status and had a tremendous impact on the group process, either positively or negatively. They might for example capitalize on the situation to force their ideas and values on the group and undermine team effectiveness. A co-design dynamic that we label as 'unequal power' in analogy with social psychologist [5]. This makes it difficult for children with a lower status to voice their opinions, limiting their influence in the group. Many times, these children appeared to be rather shy in contrast to the more dominant, high-power children. Thus, group members with more power than others have a higher likelihood of swaying any final decision by direct or indirect pressure as well as through the time they are allotted for discussion.

## 3.2 Free riding

The results showed that some children took advantage of the work of others in the team. These children may have felt less accountable to contribute, so they devoted less effort. A dynamic that we label as 'free riding' in analogy with a particular kind of social loafing described by social psychologists [16] as *"the reduced social motivation that occurs when certain members decide to let the others contribute and choose not to fully participate"*. Free riding may easily manifest itself during co-design activities. For example, one particular child took a free ride almost every co-design session, no matter what group he was in. He hardly did anything and sometimes he was even counterproductive by making jokes about the others who became visibly agitated. Surprisingly, he tried to take credit for the ideas during presentation by intervening repeatedly when someone else was talking. Although this was a rather extreme and rare case of free riding, milder forms were very common.

## 3.3 Laughing out loud

In some cases we noticed co-design groups ganging up on the task. They were having a good time, but there was an unwillingness to take the task at hand serious. In such groups, the atmosphere was rather disruptive instead of constructive. This may be due to a lack of intrinsic motivation and problem ownership. When team members do not gradually uncover and identify their values, it may become problematic to identify a problem space they feel is worth tackling as a group.

Sometimes, this tendency towards an unserious atmosphere was a gradually evolving process. At the start of one particular co-design session, only two out of five group members were giggling while coming up with rather silly and irrelevant ideas. After a while, this behavior affected the other children in the group and once the session was half way, their priorities as a group had shifted from finding a design solution to having a good time.

## 3.4 Apart together

Some of the group's designs were a disconnected mix of rather individual designs lacking an overall design vision. Instead of mixing ideas and working toward one integrated design, the children followed their idiosyncratic interests and only in the end they combined the individual designs quite literally. In one such example, each of the group's members invented a piece of 'magical technology' to guide schoolchildren during a museum visit. By drawing ropes between them, they combined these individual designs afterwards. Among the individual designs were a 'minimize device' to make souvenirs from artworks and historical buildings, 'holographic video glasses' that could project a virtual guide in front of you and an 'electronic notebook' with an integrated 'ask a question' dice game. When presenting, it became clear they had not negotiated their personal values and ideas profoundly. As a consequence their final design lacked an overall design vision. Children from other teams confirmed this after the presentation. They literally questioned the feasibility of the idea, already anticipating that all these components together would weight a lot so that it would be impossible to carry it while walking in the museum. Different and contradictory answers followed. It was obvious the team members had not thought profoundly about this matter. This may be due to a lack of communication within the team, but it may also depend largely on the developmental characteristics of child participants this age.

## 3.5 Deconstructive conflict

We noticed that some children had a difficult time letting go of their initially chosen ideas. This complicated negotiating ideas with other team members during the selection phase. Children were not always capable of managing such conflict or differing voices productively, leading to a polarization within the team. Such negative or competitive behaviors between team members may reduce trust and it is being known in other fields such as social psychology and cooperative learning that the lack of trust reduces group cooperation [5] [11]. Based on our observations, this also holds true for co-design activities with children. Although conflict may be an essential process to move teams towards necessary change and creative breakthroughs, it must be managed. If not, conflict easily becomes destructive, causing defensive behavior, inflexibility, contempt and an unwillingness to work together.

## 3.6 Groupthink

The dynamic of groupthink occurred in some teams with high group cohesiveness. Psychologist Irving Janis coined the term 'groupthink' to describe a phenomenon in which *"the group ends up being dumber than its individual members"* [14]. In our study, groupthink happened when children were reluctant to criticize each other's ideas. They then kept on adding functionalities to please everyone and eventually ended up with a design featuring too much functionality. Although a strong, overall design vision was lacking, this was not the result of any problems in the collaboration process as for instance was the case in the Apart Together dynamic.

A technology-enriched fur coat, designed by one of the teams is a striking example. At first sight, the children collaborated successfully and no tensions were observed. However, during prototyping they kept on adding overlapping functionalities to their technology-enriched fur coat. It seems like they wanted to please every team member to safeguard the positive atmosphere in the group. In doing so, they got more and more off track and they gradually lost sight of the design goal, ending up with a design doing too many things at once. This was made explicit by the opening sentence of their presentation, in which they announced their design as the *"Everything Fur Coat"*. This emphasis on concurrence seeking instead of fully surveying choice alternatives subsequently increases the possibility of poor decision-making, as confirmed by social psychologists [5]. Value conflicts in such groups are often neglected rather then negotiated and transcended, which makes it less likely for creative breakthroughs to emerge.

## 4. DISCUSSION AND FUTURE WORK

The goal of this paper was to present a structured way to evaluate six challenging co-design dynamics that may occur in participatory design practices with children. The categorization is not exhaustive and only includes the most prevalent challenging dynamics encountered so far. We believe that balancing these dynamics has a positive impact on the dialectic process of developing values and ideas in participatory design, as well as on children's motivation. The CCI community could thus benefit from our in-depth exploration and categorization of challenging group dynamics when co-designing technology with children.

These dynamics may be closely linked. For example, a group may fall into the 'groupthink trap' because the viewpoints of a dominant and charismatic child (cf. unequal power) are agreed upon too soon without critical examination of other alternatives. Groups rushing too quickly towards consensus and agreement could actually benefit from a mild form of conflict. Although conflict is often perceived as a negative force while cooperation is at the other end of the continuum, their impact on group performance is more nuanced than that. In fact, conflict can be a positive force because it can create energy around sharing diverse information and viewpoints. The challenge is to avoid groups moving from constructive to dysfunctional and destructive conflicts [5]. In future work, we will further investigate these complex interrelationships.

Currently, we are looking more deeply into other fields such as educational pedagogy and in particular conceptual approaches to Cooperative Learning have gained our interest, e.g. [11]. We have been translating solutions from an educational into a co-design context. For instance, by having children take on different roles as 'timekeeper', 'inspiration general', 'material guard', and so on, positive interdependence will be enhanced. The idea is that if children value their group members as a result of cohesiveness-building activities and are dependent on one another, they are likely to encourage and help one another to succeed, because they perceive that their effort is important for the entire group [11]. In future work, we will further translate solutions from an educational into a co-design context and validate promising solutions rigorously.

## 5. CONCLUSIONS

In this paper, we have defined 'co-design dynamics' as a system of intragroup dynamics occurring within groups of children sharing a common design goal. These dynamics clearly impact the dialectic process of developing values and ideas in participatory design. These challenges, however, have rarely been addressed in the field of CCI and in the literature on co-design methods.

The dynamics encountered in our study are the 'apart together' phenomenon (i.e., working individually and only combining results quite literally in the end), 'free riding' (i.e., reduced effort by some individuals when working in a co-design team and taking advantage of the others), 'unequal power' (i.e., some children come to the co-design tasks with higher status than others and vice versa), the 'laughing out loud' phenomenon (i.e., an unwillingness to take the task at hand serious as a group), 'destructive conflict' (i.e., escalating disagreements about which ideas too work on further) and 'groupthink' (i.e., rushing too quickly towards consensus neglecting choice alternatives). We strongly believe that focusing on these dynamics is essential to better engage with values in participatory design [10]. Therefore, the CCI community could benefit from our in-depth exploration

and categorization when co-designing technology with children. In future work, we will further investigate how these challenging co-design dynamics are interrelated and how they can be balanced and remediated into positive forces.

## 6. REFERENCES

[1] Buckingham, D., 2009. Creative visual methods in media research: possibilities, problems and proposals. *Media, Culture & Society,* 31(4), 633-652.

[2] Cross, N. & Cross, A.C., 1995. Observations of teamwork and social processes in design. *Design Studies,* 16, 143-170.

[3] Dindler, C. et al., 2005. Mission from Mars: a method for exploring user requirements for children in a narrative space. *Proceedings of the IDC 2005 conference.* ACM, NY.

[4] Druin, A., 2002. The role of children in the design of new technology. *Behaviour & Information Technology,* 21,1-25.

[5] Franz, T.M., 2012. *Group Dynamics and Team Interventions.* Wiley-Blackwell, Chichester.

[6] Gray, D., 2010. *Gamestorming: A Playbook for Innovators, Rulebreakers, and Changemakers.* O'Reilly, Sebastopol.

[7] Guha, M.L., Druin, A. & Fails, J.A., 2013. Cooperative Inquiry revisited: Reflections of the past and guidelines for the future of intergenerational co-design. *International Journal of Child-Computer Interaction.*

[8] Halloran, J., Hornecker, E., & Stringer, M., 2009. The value of values: Resourcing co-design of ubiquitous computing. *Co-Design,* 4(5), 245-273.

[9] Heary, C.M. & Hennessy, E., 2002. The Use of Focus Group Interviews in Pediatric Health Care Research. *Journal of Pediatric Psychology,* 27(1), 47-57.

[10] Iversen, O.S., Halskov, K., Leong T.W., 2010. Rekindling Values in Participatory Design. *PDC '10 Proceedings of the 11th Biennial Participatory Design Conference.* ACM, NY.

[11] Johnson, D.W. & Johnson, R.T., 2005. New Developments in Social Interdependence Theory. *Genetic, Social and General Psychology Monographs,* 131(4), 285-358.

[12] Mazzone, E. et al., 2010. Considering context, content, management, and engagement in design activities with children. *Proc. of the 9th Int. Conf. on Interaction Design & Children.* IDC '10. ACM, NY.

[13] Sanders, E., 2000. Generative Tools for CoDesigning. In S. Scrivener, L. Ball, & A. Woodcock, eds. *Proceedings of CoDesigning 2000.* Springer, 3-12.

[14] Sawyer, K., 2008. *Group Genius: The Creative Power of Collaboration.* Basic Books, NY.

[15] Sleeswijk Visser, F. et al., 2005. Contextmapping: Experiences from practice. CoDesign, G(2), 119-149.

[16] Sutton, R.I. & Hargadon, A., 1996. Brainstorming Groups in Context: Effectiveness in a Product Design Firm. *Administrative Science Quarterly,* 41(4), 685-718.

[17] Vaajakallio, K., Mattelmäki, T. & Lee, J.-J., 2010. Co-design lessons with children. *Interactions,* 17(4), 26–29.

[18] Zaman, B. & Van den Abeele, V., 2010. Laddering with young children in User eXperience evaluations. *Proc. of the 9th Int. Conf. on Interaction Design & Children.* ACM, NY.

# Detecting Handwriting Errors with Visual Feedback in Early Childhood for Chinese Characters

Will W.W. Tang    Hong Va Leong    Grace Ngai    Stephen C.F. Chan

Department of Computing
The Hong Kong Polytechnic University
Hong Kong
{cswwtang,cshleong,csgngai,csschan}@comp.polyu.edu.hk

## ABSTRACT

This paper presents KID, an *interactive app* on a smart device, designed to facilitate and encourage young children to learn and practice Chinese characters. It relies on pen dynamics to extract the strokes and map the written character to the proper one. The stroke orientation is also analyzed for ordering and spatial alignment features that pinpoint common errors. A visual pictorial feedback is then provided to motivate children and to arouse their interest. We iterate the prototype design and implementation upon collecting feedback from focus group interviews, from where the system is greeted with positive comments.

## Categories and Subject Descriptors

H.1.2 [**User/Machine Systems**]: Human factors, Human information processing, Software psychology.

## General Terms

Design, Human Factors, Languages.

## Keywords

Learning to write, stroke analysis, stroke alignment, pictographic feedback.

## 1. INTRODUCTION

Early childhood education is an important sector of education. In Hong Kong, an increasing amount of public educational resource has been allocated towards early childhood education. The availability of ubiquitous computing devices has also led to the development of increasing numbers of technology-enabled education methodologies and platforms, with the main focus being on languages (English and Chinese) and Arithmetic.

Oriental languages, and Chinese in particular, possess a complex structure. While Latin languages are composed of a linear sequence of basic alphabetical components, written Chinese exhibits a two-dimensional pictographic composition nature, in which the basic ingredients, *strokes*, can be spatially arranged in many different ways. To maintain literacy, children learn to write at an early age. In Hong Kong, for example, formal reading and writing starts before elementary school, with most kindergarten children starting to learn penmanship as early as age 3 or 4. By the time they are in elementary school, children regularly spend as much as 50% of their time in handwriting tasks (Tseng &

Chow, 2000), and a failure to achieve handwriting competency has been shown to have long-term effects on self-esteem (Feder & Majnemer, 2007), not to mention the impact on elementary study.

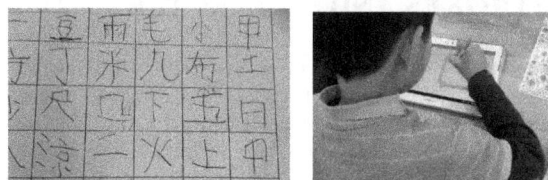

**Figure 1. Sample of graded penmanship from elementary school child, with teacher-annotated errors (left). A child playing with KID (right).**

The most common learning approach is learning by practicing: teachers ask students to write the characters on a gridded sheet of paper, such that each character falls neatly within one gridded square, as shown in Figure 1 left. They are "graded" according to the correctness of the written character, whether they exceed the boundary of the grid, whether they are too big or too small, or presence of any obvious irregularity. Grading by hand is tedious and oftentimes subjective and inconsistent. The feedback is also delayed, which means that children often practice incorrect methods of writing for extended periods of time before they are identified and corrected. Finally, the feedback inflicts negative feeling upon the children, especially when the evaluation is not positive. There is certain software for children to practice Chinese character writing, in following an animated stroke sequence in a manner similar to practicing using the Latin copybook, and scoring in whether the stroke order is followed correctly.

**Figure 2. Visual feedback from KID. A correctly written "cow" character (left) generates a proper-looking cow (second to left). An improperly written character (center) is annotated with the error (second right) and generates a crooked-looking cow (far right).**

This paper presents a potential solution to this problem through an app called KID (**K**indergarten **I**nteractive **D**emo-app) in Figure 1 right. It shares some commonality with the calligraphy (Huang et al., 2012). KID runs on an Android tablet and will detect the child's written strokes and determine whether the character is correct. Errors in incorrect characters are highlighted to provide immediate feedback. To motivate the children and to add an element of fun, correctly written characters are "rewarded" with their corresponding pictorial form displayed. Incorrect characters produce a pictorial with missing features or misalignment. This reinforces their learning with immediate, interesting and rewarding feedback. Figure 2 shows an example for the Chinese character "cow" (牛). The character on the left is correct, producing a graphic of a normal-looking cow. The character on the center is badly written, so the computer circles the error (rightmost character) and produces a crooked-looking cow.

The contributions of our paper can be summarized as (1) KID, which facilitates children to learn and practice Chinese writing; (2) algorithms for efficiently evaluating the correctness of written character; (3) positive reinforcement feedback to motivate learning; (4) decent user interface design based upon focus group interviews; and (5) preliminary field studies with positive results.

## 2. STROKES AND CHARACTERS

Although Chinese characters are made up of simple strokes, just like English words are made up of a sequence of alphabets, the same stroke can appear differently in different characters. Furthermore, English words are linear in structure, but Chinese characters are constrained in a two-dimensional square-shaped space and the strokes can be placed in different positions. This additional degree of freedom makes the mastering of Chinese characters much more difficult as the spatial information must be considered and reflected correctly. Many Japanese and Korean characters are also derived from Chinese and thus share a large common intersection. The ISO-10646 UTF standard considers these three languages collectively as the CJK languages.

KID represents each Chinese character as a sequence of strokes. In common input algorithms in mobile phones, there are 5 basic strokes. While it is appropriate for adult users, its lack of discriminative power on a sequence of strokes to identify a character make it unsuitable for character recognition for children. In KID, the more precise 6-basic strokes and 23-compound strokes input system (Chen, 2008) is adopted for its ability to represent most Chinese characters uniquely. The 6 basic strokes are similar to those in the 5-stroke system: *horizontal* ( − ), *vertical* ( | ), *press down* subsuming *dot* ( \ . ) and *throw away* ( / ), *rise* ( ' ) going from bottom towards top and *hook* ( \ ) going from bottom towards top. For example, the character "cow" (牛) is represented by the stroke order of *throw away*, *horizontal*, *horizontal* and *vertical*. Since stroke-based systems do not consider the position of the strokes, a few characters would be represented by the same stroke sequences. The character "noon" (午) has the same stroke representation as "cow" (牛). However, this kind of collision or isomorphism reduces drastically with the increase in number of character strokes.

## 3. KID: AN APP FOR CHILD LEARNING

In KID, we adopt a dictionary with 60 common Chinese characters as recommended by the kindergartens operated under the Hong Kong Christian Service. The first KID prototype used a subset of 10 common characters, with various pictorial formats, including "deformed" graphics that correspond to incorrectly written characters. The characters are selected because they are neither too simple (the character "human" 人 with just two strokes would not be selected) nor too complex, and because they are nouns that lead to easy exposition in pictorial form. In our next stage of work, we will populate KID with the remaining 50

characters and extend it to include more characters as appropriate. The list of characters selected is shown in Table 1.

**Table 1. Characters with pictorial forms in KID.**

| Character | 豆 | 口 | 牛 | 羊 | 果 |
|---|---|---|---|---|---|
| Meaning | bean | mouth | cow | sheep | fruit |
| Character | 草 | 土 | 火 | 雨 | 門 |
| Meaning | grass | earth | fire | rain | door |

### 3.1 System Design

The raw input to KID being captured is a sequence of points produced by the child using a pointing device (a stylus), each point in the form of a tuple <x, y, pressure, time>, indicating the position and the sensed stylus pressure on the tablet. When the stylus is lifted above the tablet, the absence of captured points for the period indicates the pen-lift time, which provides additional information towards the writing style analysis. The set of consecutive points will be merged into a line. Successive connected lines are structured into a stroke. The strokes are then composed into a character.

In order to perform the mapping more efficiently and accurately, we need to handle imprecision in each of the steps. The first step is to recognize a trace from the set of points captured by the touch screen device. We adopt a moving window to smoothen the trace until there is a sharp turn (Huang et al., 2012). The collection of successive lines oriented in a similar manner is considered as a simple stroke. Successive simple strokes are then considered as a whole for consolidation into a compound stroke. This information is then used to determine the stroke level errors committed.

We use the character "cow" (牛) as depicted in Figure 2 as an example. The first stroke is written as a slightly concave curve going to the left. The variation in orientation indicates the stability of the stroke, quality or even correctness. The second stroke (the top *horizontal* stroke) should touch the first stroke, but it does not. The third stroke (the second *horizontal* stroke) should be straight, but it is written as a line inclined at 20 degrees, indicating instability in orientation and a badly written character.

The collection of strokes is then processed against a dictionary of characters for the best matching one. A first filtering step is to use the concatenated stroke order (a sequence) as an index into the dictionary for one or more exactly matched characters. To cater for characters with incorrect, missing or superfluous strokes, we perform character stroke matching for characters whose stroke count falls within a pre-defined tolerance level, e.g., ± 2 strokes. Using a dynamic programming approach based on the edit-distance measure, we compare the sequence of input strokes and the strokes of a particular character. The set of characters producing the smallest edit distance are considered the candidate set. Discrepancy revealed by the edit-distance matrix provides us the feedback information on the error(s) committed by the child, e.g., an insertion error may indicate the presence of extra strokes. The information is then displayed visually for feedback.

The next step is to resolve the possibility of multiple matching cases, such as two characters that are represented by the same stroke sequence. We take into account the spatial relationship between the strokes of a character to indicate the structure of the character. We build up a *stroke spatial relationship matrix* for each character. Each element $S_{ij}$ indicates the spatial relationship between stroke $i$ and stroke $j$, whether they intersect or they touch. The spatial relationship matrix for characters "cow" (牛) and "noon" (午) is shown in Figure 3, where a blank entry means the strokes are *unrelated*, **t** means *touching* and **c** means *crossing*. This matrix is symmetric and relatively sparse.

**Figure 3. Determining spatial relationships of strokes.**

This matrix allows us to disambiguate seemingly isomorphic characters. A stroke that fails to intersect another stroke when there should be an intersection is easily detected by this spatial relationship matrix. A poorly written character like the one in Figure 2 could be evaluated, where the entry $S_{12}$ in the written character became a blank. The spatial relationship matrix provides a simplified spatial analysis on all the strokes with respect to their proper positions in an actual character. It is highly resilient to character shape distortion error, a very common problem for children.

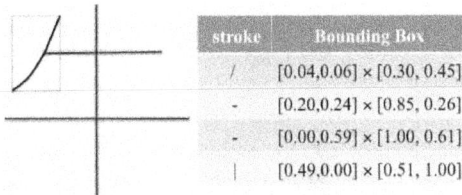

| stroke | Bounding Box |
|---|---|
| / | $[0.04, 0.06] \times [0.30, 0.45]$ |
| - | $[0.20, 0.24] \times [0.85, 0.26]$ |
| - | $[0.00, 0.59] \times [1.00, 0.61]$ |
| \| | $[0.49, 0.00] \times [0.51, 1.00]$ |

**Figure 4. Using bounding boxes for spatial analysis.**

In order to more precisely evaluate how well the written character conforms to the "template" character, we measure the actual spatial location of the strokes for the written character and the candidate character. For each character in our dictionary, we associate a bounding box for each of the strokes, normalized with respect to the extent of the character in $[0,1]^2 \times [0,1]^2$. Figure 4 shows an example for the character "cow" (牛). In a well-written character, the location of the input stroke and the candidate stroke should be close enough. We proceed by computing the bounding box for the input character and the locations of the strokes are then normalized with respect to this character bounding box. We measure the distance between the centers of the bounding boxes of the strokes. If the individual distance and the total distance for all the strokes are below pre-established thresholds, we assume that the strokes of the two characters match in location. This allows KID to detect mistakes resulting from misplacement of strokes that do not touch or cross other strokes, and also allows the extent of each stroke to be compared for the writing quality.

## 3.2 User Interface

KID has two modes of display. The first is the traditional teaching mode, as would normally be found in similar contemporary software, but with enriched features. The second mode is the pictorial feedback mode to provide more visual feedback and motivate children for better learning. This is depicted in Figure 5.

In the traditional teaching mode, after a child writes the character, KID analyzes the quality of each stroke. When strokes of inferior quality are detected, e.g., lack of "straightness", or uneven pressure along a stroke, a reference "desirable" stroke will be displayed over the problematic stroke (Figure 5 center and right), so that the child knows that there is room for improvement on his/her stroke. If the stroke type is incorrect, the offending stroke is marked in red (Figure 5 right). Similarly, misaligned strokes with spatial error will be marked with a correct reference line. For example, Figure 2 shows a red circle where there is a too-large gap between the first two strokes of the character "cow" (牛). In either case, a correct character will be displayed for comparison. If the strokes are in wrong order, not only the character will be displayed, but also the correct stroke order displayed along side the character (Figure 5 right).

**Figure 5. Screenshots from KID in operation**

The pictorial feedback mode applies concepts of metaphoric congruence transfer (Maurer, 2006, Huang et al., 2012) and uses a spatial metaphor between the written character and a pictorial image linked to the character to provide visual feedback on errors. When the character is written correctly, a "cute" pictorial representation of the character is displayed with an affirmative sound. However, when a missing stroke is detected, the same image is displayed but with some features missing, e.g., missing eyes or missing feet, depending on where the missing stroke is, together with a denial sound. Extra strokes lead to the same image with displaced features and denial sound, e.g., a cow with a horn. Incorrect stroke order or type will cause the image to become twisted, like the one in Figure 2 right. When an error is reported, the correct character will be displayed, and an animation displays the proper writing stroke order, stroke by stroke.

## 3.3 Deployment

We implement the KID prototype on an Android tablet (a Samsung Note 10.1 in our case) with a digitizer surface. To ensure natural writing movement, the touch feature for the tablet is disabled, so that only stylus strokes will be recognized. The digitizer surface can detect the pressure applied to the stylus as well as when the stylus is hovering (i.e., not touching) the writing surface, which allows us to monitor writing defects such as hesitation and uneven pressure for in-depth analysis.

## 4. EVALUATION

We built the first prototype, KID-1, based on our past experience in developing software with input from frontline teachers (Ngai et al., 2013). We performed a preliminary evaluation on KID-1 to gauge its usability and acceptance among children and their parents, through user exploration and focus group interviews (Lazar et al., 2010). We sought further understanding of the intended user's point-of-view when designing our system features and user interface.

We invited two children, aged 6 and 7, for a pilot exploration with KID-1. They were asked to write the 10 Chinese characters in each of the two modes. Their accompanying parents were asked to observe their performance, and more importantly, their reaction towards KID-1. They would also ask their own children which mode they preferred, whether they enjoyed the system, and the part of the system that they did not like. We conducted focus group interviews with the parents to uncover the difficulties that their children encountered, based on their observation of their children's performance, as well as talking to their children. We also listened carefully to the parents' idea on the potential cause of the difficulties, and possible suggestions.

From the focus group interview, as well as our own observation of the children, both children liked the electronic platform and remained engaged throughout the experiment. However, they did not know where to write on the relatively big screen in the first instance. Parents commented that they may write really big or really small characters, adding on the "unsure" writing position. Thus, KID-2 includes an outline bounding box within which the children are supposed to write their character, similar to how they would usually write a character within a gridded box on paper.

Unlike the passive gridded paper, with which children would not feel frustrated as they had no expectation for receiving interactive feedback, they got frustrated with KID if no correct writing form could be displayed when they believed they had written correctly and did not know what / how to correct. There is a discrepancy between what they thought was correct and what was really correct. As such, we have tuned the tolerance level on the stroke type classification for better alignment of user expectation in our modification with more informative feedback. We would also like to reduce the gap between system intelligence and human-perceived system intelligence.

Another issue brought up by the children was that of partial credit. Children generally felt that they should be rewarded if they got their work mostly right, e.g., the character is correct except that the stroke order is not quite correct, or just one stroke is not quite straight but a little misaligned. In other words, a good score of 9 (out of 10) points would be expected! However, KID-1 kept on displaying distorted images with a denial sound. This was perceived as negative feedback and made them unhappy.

We also recognized that the binary pictorial feedback was not sufficient to differentiate between almost-properly-written versus poorly-written characters. There is a degree of transition, when a child gradually improved his/her writing. If a child kept on improving, continually receiving the abnormal image would be quite demoralizing.

To remedy this, we give a grand score to a whole exercise of written character practice on the 10 selected characters. If the overall score is higher than a threshold, a "mostly correct" reward is given. The reward can be of multiple levels, depending on the degree of attainment. In the future, we also plan to reward better writing with nicer visualization, such as adding animations when the level of attainment is high. This is where the bounding box spatial algorithm would be more useful.

We then conducted a second evaluation with the same children for the improved prototype KID-2. They seemed more engaged and enjoyed writing more. They liked the demonstrative animation of how to write the character strokes correctly. With the bounding box introduced, they often wrote the upper left part of the character larger than the other parts, due to a lack of sense of space. This resulted in characters that were out-of-bounds or disproportionate. Parents suggested that a 3×3 grid could be laid in the background to help, and more feedback would be helpful for poorly written characters until improvement is achieved.

In summary, our initial evaluation brings us important feedback to improve on the system features as well as the user interface design.

We believe that the first round of interview has enabled us to build a more useful and user-friendly KID to teach children the challenging task of learning Chinese characters, as evidenced by results in the second evaluation.

## 5. CONCLUSION AND FUTURE WORK

Based on the preliminary evaluation, our KID-1 prototype drew upon user feedbacks for improvement. The focus group interview and evaluation by subjects served to unearth issues and suggest possible solution in implementing an improved KID-2, which is greeted with positive feedback in engaging children to learn to write Chinese character by providing real-time multimodal visual and audio interaction that they would not have received in paper-based exercises. Currently, the study is only of a small scale, thereby limiting the confidence on the findings.

We would like to extend KID-2 further with animation, a larger set of vocabulary, and user design feedback for usability. More dimensions in providing visual feedback will be explored, for better accuracy and better motivation for children. We would also like to extend our analysis towards the writing characteristic from the collected data to build a model for children learning to write Chinese characters. This intelligent tutoring approach enables us to detect abnormalities in writing and automatically devise corresponding training modules for the children. Statistical results and evaluation would also be provided to inform their parents of potential learning problems.

Upon building a more comprehensive KID, we would like to conduct large-scale experiments on kindergarten children. Eventually, we would like to explore its usability on children with dyslexia, making use of the writing model that we build and additional data collected specifically with these children.

## 6. ACKNOWLEDGMENTS

This research is supported in part by the Research Grant Council and the Hong Kong Polytechnic University under Grant numbers PolyU 5235/11E and PolyU 5248/10E.

## 7. REFERENCES

[1] Chen, G.S. et al. (2008) Stroke order computer-based assessment with fuzzy measure scoring. *WSEAS Transactions on Information Science and Applications*, **5**(2):62–68.

[2] Feder, K.P. & Majnemer, A. (2007) Handwriting development, competency, and intervention. *Development Medicine and Child Neurology*, **49**:312–317.

[3] Huang, M.X. et al. (2012) MelodicBrush: A novel system for cross-modal digital art creation linking calligraphy and music. In *Proc. of Designing Interactive System Conference* (DIS'12), pp 418–427.

[4] Lazar, J., Feng, J.H. & Hochheiser, H. (2010) *Research Methods in Human-Computer Interaction*. Chichester, UK. Wiley.

[5] Maurer, D, Pathman, T & Mondloch, C.J. (2006) The shape of boubas: Sound-shape correspondences in toddlers and adults. *Developmental Science*, **9**(3):316–322.

[6] Ngai, G. et al. (2013) Designing i*CATch: A multipurpose, education-friendly construction kit for physical and wearable computing. *ACM Transactions on Computing Education*, **13**(2):7-36.

[7] Ramachandran, V.S. & Hubbard, E.M. (2001) Synaesthesia: A window into perception, thought and language. *Journal of Consciousness Studies*, **8**:3–34.

[8] Tseng, M.H. & Chow, S.M.K. (2000) Perceptual-motor function of school-age children with slow handwriting speed. *American Journal of Occupational Therapy*, **54**:83–88.

# Adapting Design Probes to Explore Health Management Practices in Pediatric Type 1 Diabetes

Damyanka Tsvyatkova
Computer Science & Information Systems
IDC, University of Limerick
Limerick, Ireland
Damyanka.Tsvyatkova@ul.ie

Cristiano Storni
Computer Science & Information Systems
IDC, University of Limerick
Limerick, Ireland
Cristiano.Storni@ul.ie

## ABSTRACT

We used Design Probes (DP) as a communication tool supporting designers to learn about users, collecting self-documentation data from children and parents about their everyday chronic disease management. DP are also applied as alternative strategies to perform ethnographic study in a domestic environment and to elicit inspirational data for the design of an educational interactive eBook for newly diagnosed children with type 1 diabetes mellitus (T1DM). Eight probe activities were designed for children between the ages of 8-12 years who have diabetes and their caregivers, which were then distributed to seven families. The main issue discussed in this paper is the adaptation of the DP to the users (children and parents) and the results produced by participants who used them.

## Categories and Subject Descriptors

H5.2. **Information Interfaces** and Presentation (e.g., HCI): User Interfaces (Evaluation/methodology, User-centered approach)

## General Terms

Design

## Keywords

Design Probes, User-Centred Design, Participatory Design, Child-Computer Interaction, children with type 1 diabetes.

## 1. INTRODUCTION

In this paper we report on our use of Design Probes (DP) to explore, familiarize and better understand young users' needs, issues and perspectives regarding self-care practices in pediatric Type 1 Diabetes Mellitus (T1DM). The goal of this investigation is to inform the design and development of an educational interactive eBook for newly diagnosed children and their families. The development of the probes was informed by a series of exploratory semi-structured interviews conducted with parents/guardians who have experience with pediatric diabetes [8]. Through such explorations, we have identified a series of personal barriers, self-care needs, and difficulties in dealing with the disease on a daily basis often outside the attention of the medical team [8]. In particular, we found that affected families discussed negative emotions toward diabetes presented by their children and complained about the lack of a proper education and educational materials supporting newly diagnosed young individuals with T1DM [8]. Since this topic was recurrent, we decided to focus our attention on these educational issues as we

*IDC'14*, June 17–20, 2014, Aarhus, Denmark.
Copyright 2014 ACM 978-1-4503-2272-0/14/06…$15.00.
http://dx.doi.org/10.1145/2593968.2610471

explore the role of interactive eBooks in supporting better understanding and sense making.

Gaining first-hand experience of such issues is however very difficult: extensive ethnographic observations are difficult in domestic settings, especially in relation to such a sensitive topic; our interviews with parents were greatly informative, but children were reluctant to talk about their experience (parents were concerned that talking about diabetes was going to upset some of the children). Diabetes management is however constant and ubiquitous [7]; pediatric diabetes involves a series actors (parents, child, nurses, doctors and their perspectives) and different sites (home, school, playground, hospital, and their practices, etc). In the attempt to learn more about the perspective of the children, and the practices in the home and inform/inspire our design intervention, we decided to develop some DPs.

We developed eight activities, supporting materials and instructions. Seven of these activities were intended for children aged 8 to 12 years who have T1DM and one was for their parents. Seven families used DP materials for a month and then the sets were collected and analyzed. In this paper we would like to report and reflect on the use of our probes. In particular we aim to show and explain how the DP materials were adapted to the peculiar target audience, and how the probes were used and appropriated by the children and their families.

## 2. DESIGN PROBES

DP can be seen as an unobtrusive way of collecting data, reducing the distance that separates the designer from the domestic settings they are designing for, especially in sensitive settings [1]. DPs include materials supporting self-documentation and a series of activities (physical objects and tasks) encouraging creative and subjective responses by the users that help with representing their own experience, daily lives, needs, and attitudes [2][5]. The set with designed objects is distributed to participants for a period of time and then returned to researchers. As often discussed [10], the goal is not to establish facts about diabetes, but rather to develop an understanding of their perspective so that our design would better relate and resonate with the user's actions, intentions, emotions and environment [5].

Design probes were originally introduced as cultural probes by Gaver and colleagues [2]. In its original formulation, probes were a way to express the growing skepticism toward the rational(ist) method to collect design requirements, and to explore new tools that would trigger subjective and creative responses rather than objective and universal ones. In order to design innovative technologies for the elderly, the original packs by Gaver et al [2] offered a range of materials (postcards, map, disposable camera and photo album) to freely document the daily life of the elderly. Probes were intentionally designed to elicit ideas and inspirations in researchers [2]. Mattelmäki [5] who worked extensively on design probes from the tradition of Participatory Design (PD), pointed out that DPs "are an approach of user-centred design for understanding human phenomena and exploring design opportunities". She emphasized three characteristics of DPs as an approach to User Centered Design (UCD). DPs support user participation by self-documentation (e.g. support PD). They focused attention on the users as they examined their personal context and environment (e.g. user's work places, homes, hostels, sensitive care settings, etc.). DP's exploratory character supports creativity and interpretation by users and designers [5].

There are only a few examples [4, 6, 9] of educationally-focused design probe studies for children, and in two of these cases children assisted in the development of the probe materials, objects and activities [6, 9]. In the design stage of game development, Moser et al [6] mixed qualitative and quantitative probe materials to collect data "to capture experiences" with games. The purpose of qualitative materials (e.g. postcards, collage and maps) was to explore children's game interests, gaming behaviors and requirements, while the quantitative material (e.g. diary) helped designers to create child personas for different mini-games [6]. Wyeth and Diercke [9] used PD in a school environment to design educational activities for children between 11 and 13 years of age. The aim was to gain insights and inspirations for children's educational software [9]. Nokia 7650 mobile phones were used as a digital cultural probe for collecting photos and audio clips by children to share their home life and after-school activities, and to design technology supporting education in the real-world outside classroom settings [4].

## 3. DESIGN AND RESPONSES

We adapted our packets of design objects into sets with an awareness of the children's personality and maturation as well as the different stages of their cognitive and physical development [3]. As mentioned, parents shared valuable data related to the life of their children, their struggles, their activities at home and at school, information related to educational practices at clinic and domestic settings, and so on [8]. By analyzing this collected data we assumed that a design of an eBook may help parents and newly diagnosed children in their diabetes education as the technology can be used in both the clinic and home settings [8]. The data also helped us to devise and select the activities in the set of probes.

Seven probes were designed for children between 8 and 12 years of age, and one for their parents. For each probe, a large colorful box was used for the materials, labels and instructions (clear and expressed in a child-appropriate language suitable for the age-group). All activities in the probe set were understandable for children used to having pre-structured materials. The aim was to encourage children's creative thinking and to help them to express their unique interests and needs, to document their own self-care practices, feelings and experiences with diabetes.

Below we describe the intended purpose of using each probe material, how they ware adapted as well as some examples of generated data.

## 3.1 Disposable camera

For this activity we had a disposable camera, a series of sticky labels with numbers (1 to 22) and a list with 22 picture requests for the children (Figure 1, first image). The purpose of this probe was to learn more about the children's point of interests, how diabetes influenced different daily activities e.g. sports, visiting places, meeting with people, playing outside with friends, things that they like or dislike, such as books, food, toys, etc. The second image (Figure 1) is a picture of an animated/cartoon movie that

participant 2 enjoys watching. The third image is picture of a toy that the child (participant 1) doesn't like. Knowing more about children's preferences will help us to develop story characters and content for the eBook. Unfortunately, many photographs were of poor quality because of the children's inexperience with the use of disposable (not digital) cameras. For instance, even with the clear instructions many had problems in activating the flash (key for taking pictures indoors), moving the advance wheel to wind forward to the next picture, and to determine the distance between the object and camera (disposable cameras have no screen).

Figure 1: *Disposable camera* with examples of responses

## 3.2 Technology Gadget Design

In this activity, children were asked to design a technological gadget that could help them in their daily life. Safe art and craft materials as pipe cleaners (regular and short), buttons, beads, feathers and foam blocks (Figure 2, first image) allowed children to explore their creativity and imagination whilst developing solid objects. This activity was particularly appreciated and seen as fun. Children produced their own concepts explaining the functions of their gadget, how it can be used, and what it would do. The concrete objects that were developed were: a non-invasive glucometer-bracelet (glucometer is a devise for measuring blood glucose level) (Figure 2, second image) and a combination of a glucometer and an insulin pump (a medical device that constantly delivers insulin to the body) (Figure 2, third and fourth images). The glucometer takes data from the blood and sends it to the pump for the automatic adjustment of insulin in the body.

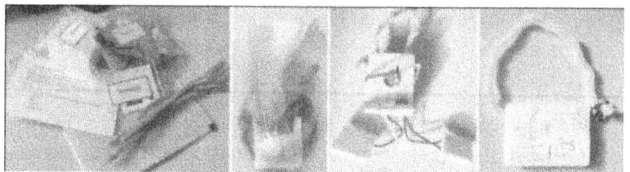

Figure 2: *Technology gadget design* probe with responses

## 3.3 Send a Postcard

*"My wife and myself share the care."* (Parent 9)

*"The only thing which bothers her was she never got to go to sleepovers...My mother lives in the north and she wants to stay there like sometimes in the summer and then maybe go on home. No problem but I can't leave her own, I didn't want to give my mum that responsibility."* (Parent 5)

Taking into account parents' concerns about shared care responsibility in the family, we decided to use postcards as a tool to learn more about the children and their relationship with other family members, teachers, friends, relatives, etc. In the pack we had seven illustrated postcards with stamped envelopes, glue, a pack full of decorative material and a list with 'common' people (your doctor, your granny, your teacher, your cousin, your classmate, Santa Clause and us) to send the postcard to. Analysis shows that most of the postcards are addressed to children's friends and only few to their relatives. Diabetes requires control and can be frightening for people who don't know how to deal with T1DM in children. Sharing responsibility demands knowledge and practical skills in diabetes care in both children and the adults who will care for them.

## 3.4 Design Collage/Poster

This idea was taken from one parent who discussed how designing a poster for the World Diabetes Day positively changed the attitude and life of her daughter. Trying to provoke children's interest and curiosity with the topic (diabetes), this probe contained art and craft materials (Figure 3, first image) that children used to develop their own collage/poster for an imaginary World Diabetes Day that they will present in class (Figure 3, second and third image).

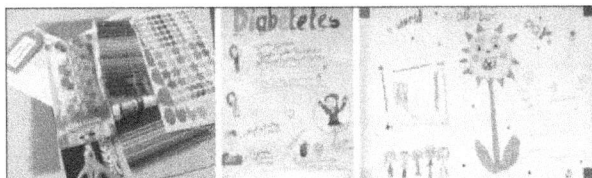

**Figure 3:** *Design collage/poster* **probe with some responses**

Wyeth and Diercke [9] also used a collage in their DP pack but they didn't get any responses from the young users. Contrary to that experience, we observed that designing a poster/collage for the World Diabetes Day was one of the favorite activities for children who participated in this study (Table 1). All children used the poster to explain technologies used in diabetes management (glucometers, injections, and insulin pumps), famous people with diabetes, and facts about diabetes and some of their feelings. This helped the children to articulate what they would like others to know about their diabetes; they seek out "positive role models" as an example of how they can achieve their dreams despite diabetes.

## 3.5 Kid's diary

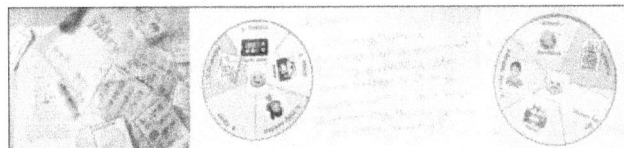

**Figure 4:** *Kids diary* **probe with examples of responses**

Trying to escape the tedious and boring activity of diary writing (we found that traditional method of keeping diary keeping is not motivating enough [9]) so we devised a graphical diary to provoke comments and reflections about self-monitoring and autonomy in children. We designed a template called "circle of activities" with five sectors. For each sector, we had a deck of available images that the children could use to stick on the segment appropriate to their activity (Figure 4, first image). The goal was to characterize diabetes related events (e.g. an accident) based on the five sectors: place when the event occurred, people who participated in that event, physical activity related to the event, used tools, and feelings. For example, they can use the image of a pump or of an insulin pen to describe the tool they used to inject insulin; they can use the image of a home or school to show the place where the insulin was taken. For participation or help, they were provided with the images of teacher, parent, etc. We also used different images related to sports and physical activities linked with the event in question, and finally for the feelings segment, we gave to them images representing hunger, dry skin, drowsiness, etc. A pack with small faces (ranging from sad to smiling) was also provided to help characterize the emotional state attached to that particular event. Children were also invited to decorate the diary and write supportive or other information they wish to share (Figure 4, second and third images). Only two participants used this activity. We found that the emotional state corresponds to the children's problems with low or high glucose levels in the blood. Children detect some of the symptoms related to their state and gave explanation for this reason "...for my birthday I ate some sweets and my blood went a bit high..." (Figure 4, second image).

## 3.6 Super Hero and a story of his/her power

Children were asked to use modelling clay to model a figurine of a Super Hero who will help and support them in diabetes management. To help them to develop the character and to write a story for the superhero, we provided them with a series of questions (Figure 5, first image) regarding the name of the hero, his/her work and power, and how does superhero help all children with diabetes.

**Figure 5:** *Super Hero* **probe with some responses**

The aim of this activity was to get inspiration and hopefully develop one of the characters in the interactive educational eBook that we have in mind. Four children modeled a figurine of their superhero and answered the questions. Produced results were extremely rich. One of the stories described "Hypo-Hyper Man" as a scientist. During the day he is trying to find a cure for diabetes and by the night he is protecting children who are having high or low blood glucose levels.

## 3.7 Design your own recipe book

**Figure 6:** *Design your own recipe book* **probe with responses**

Parents struggle with managing the child diet (especially avoiding sugar and balancing carbohydrate intake). As reaffirmed in the exploratory interviews with parents [8], diet is one of the most difficult parts of diabetes management. Some of the parents use recipe books to help them with the ingredients and with counting carbohydrates (a key factor in a diabetes diet as carbohydrates are broken down into sugar by the body). With this probe we gave an opportunity for children to design their own recipe book (Figure 6, second and third images) as the collected data will help to develop interactive game elements in the eBook for healthy food. The book had four dividers for breakfast, lunch, dinner and snacks, and a nice recipe template to be filled (Figure 6, first image). Unfortunately, only one child worked with this activity sharing her recipes.

## 3.8 My problem solving diary

Parents are very busy, working very hard to manage the activities of their family and constantly care for their diabetic child. We had only one activity for the parents and this was aimed at collecting stories about emerging problems and how they are dealt with. In the diary each page has five sections (Figure 7, first image) as parents were asked to write their own concerns about diabetes care, feelings, emotional reactions, personal control of the situation, steps they take in solving identified problems, and lessons learned (Figure 7, second, third and fourth image). The parent's diary gave rich examples of the constant stress provoked by different issues related to the health of their children; struggles to make the right decision and lessons learned dealing with the problems. Most of the provided examples revolved around: sharing responsibilities with family members and institutions (schools and playschools), holiday traveling and diabetes, GP appointments, pump settings, high or low blood glucose levels, helplessness and tiredness described by parents trying to control diabetes.

**Figure 7:** *My problem solving diary* **probe with responses**

## 4. DISTRIBUTION AND REFLECTION

The recruitment of participants for our probes was performed among the parents who were already interviewed and who expressed their interest in continuing with this study. We had seven volunteering families, those parents who have children with diabetes between 8-12 years of age. After four weeks, a total of five boxes were returned. One of the authors met each volunteer to collect the sets and to learn how the materials and objects were used with a short follow up interview. All returned boxes with probes materials (Table 1) were analyzed with the aim to learn more about the young participants.

**Table 1: Responses**

| Activity | Responses |
| --- | --- |
| Disposable camera | 3 |
| Technology Gadget design | 4 |
| Send a Postcard | 3 |
| Design Collage/Poster | 5 |
| Kids diary | 2 |
| Super Hero and a story of his/her power | 4 |
| Design your own Recipe book | 1 |
| My problem solving diary | 4 |

According to Table 1, the design of a poster/collage about an imaginary world diabetes day is the favorite activity. The design of a Technological Gadget, the development of a Superhero and My problem solving diary were also pretty successful and generated lots of engagement. Children liked to work with materials to build their pieces with accurate features, but they had less interest in keeping diaries and designing their own recipe book. We can explain this lack of enthusiasm in using these materials because in diabetes management parents and children constantly keep a food journal and blood glucose log. Food restriction related to diabetes, the scheduling of meals and children's preferences cause parents constant concern about their children's diet.

This study suggests that applying the DP method is a promising way to collect data from children with chronic illnesses in private settings. Using DP we adapted objects and activities into sets for children who have type 1 diabetes to be appropriate to the children's ages, to be focused on young user's needs (e.g. design your own Recipe Book), shared care with close relatives (e.g. send a postcard), their individuality (e.g. disposable camera) and experiences in self-care management (e.g. kid's diary, super hero and a story of his/her power, technology gadget design and design collage/poster). Our materials were playful and intriguing, provoking a dialogue between designer and users, easy to use, having detailed descriptions and clear instructions, affording user's involvement and participation in the design process. DPs

helped to foster children's imagination and, in some cases, to increase their willingness to describe and discuss the world from their perspective, despite their negative feelings toward the illness.

## 5. LIMITATIONS AND FUTURE WORK

The collection of the probe materials was a problem; it took a few months to arrange a time to meet parents. We found one limitation related to the amount of activities in the probe set. Eight activities for a month were a little ambitious assuming that parents did not have the time to help and encourage children to use the materials. Our analysis of the DPs results highlighted the success of the idea of a Superhero, which is currently the focus of a series of design workshops for diabetic and healthy children entitled "Superhero is sick". Here children-generated scenarios are explored to fine-tune the language and narratives to be developed in our design. DPs further suggested the integration of game elements as well as the inclusion of references to real famous people who have diabetes.

## 6. CONCLUSION

In this paper we report on the use of design probes to explore pediatric diabetes management with children between 8 and 12 years of age. The main part of this paper concerns outlining our probes and how the participants used them. The reason for choosing DPs was to gain insights about everyday activities in non-clinically controlled settings (e.g. school, home and other domestic environment) but also and more importantly the subjective and creative responses of the affected children with the hope to develop a perspective, a language and an orientation for our design. The valuable knowledge obtained in this study will be used for the next stage of UCD, to elaborate design ideas for low fidelity prototypes to be tested.

## 7. ACKNOWLEDGMENTS

This research is financed by the Irish Research Council (IRC).

## 8. REFERENCES

[1] Crabtree, A., Hemmings, T., Rodden, T., Cheverst, K., Clarke, K., Dewsbury, G., Hughes, J. and Rouncefield, M. 2003. 'Designing with care: Adapting cultural probes to inform design in sensitive settings'. *In Proceedings of the 2004 Australasian Conference on Computer-Human Interaction (OZCHI2004)*. 4-13.

[2] Gaver, B., Dunne, T., and Pacenti, E. 1999. 'Cultural Probes'. *Interactions*. 6(1). 21-29.

[3] Hourcade, J. P. 2007. 'Interaction Design and Children'. *Foundations and Trends in Human–Computer Interaction*. 1(4). 277–392.

[4] Iversen, O.S. and Nielsen, C. 2003. Using digital cultural probes in design with children. *In Proceedings of the 2003 conference on Interaction design and children* (IDC '03). ACM, New York, NY, USA, 154-154.

[5] Mattelmäki, T. 2006. *Design probes*. Helsinki: University of Art and Design.

[6] Moser, C., Fuchsberger, V. and Tscheligi, M. 2011. 'Using Probes to create Child Personas for Games'. *In Proceedings of the 8th International Conference on Advances in Computer Entertainment Technology*. Lisbon, Portugal. 8-11 Nov. ACM, New York.

[7] Storni, C. 2013. 'Patients' lay expertise in chronic self-care: a case study in type 1 diabetes'. *Health Expectations*. 1-12.

[8] Tsvyatkova, D. and Storni, C. 2014. 'Investigating issues related to pediatric diabetes education: problems and barriers'. Accepted for *PervasiveHealth 2014*.

[9] Wyeth, P. and Diercke, C. 2006. 'Designing cultural probes for children'. *In Proceedings of the 18th Australia conference on Computer-Human Interaction: Design: Activities, Artefacts and Environments* (OZCHI '06). ACM, New York, NY, USA. 385-388.

[10] Wallace, J., McCarthy, J., Wright, P. C., & Olivier, P. 2013. 'Making Design Probes Work'. *In Proceedings of the SIGCHI Conference on Human Factors in Computing Systems*. Paris, France. New York: ACM. 3441-3450.

# Design Guidelines for More Engaging Electronic Books: Insights from a Cooperative Inquiry Study

### Luca Colombo
University of Lugano - USI
Via Buffi 13, 6900 Lugano,
Switzerland
+41 58 666 43 15

luca.colombo@usi.ch

### Monica Landoni
University of Lugano - USI
Via Buffi 13, 6900 Lugano,
Switzerland
+41 58 666 43 00

monica.landoni@usi.ch

### Elisa Rubegni
University of Lugano - USI
Via Buffi 13, 6900 Lugano,
Switzerland
+41 58 666 47 13

elisa.rubegni@usi.ch

## ABSTRACT
This paper presents the results of a cooperative inquiry study aimed at developing a prototype of enhanced eBook for leisure reading. Together with a group of 9 to 11 years old children we explored various design ideas and, starting from these ideas, we developed the eBook prototype and elaborated a shortlist of recommendations. The paper aims to extend the research on the design of children's eBooks with a set of six guidelines that are intended to help designers in creating better and more engaging eBooks.

## Categories and Subject Descriptors
Human-centered computing ~ Participatory design

## Keywords
Child-Computer Interaction; User Experience; reading experience; prototyping; eBook; e-book; leisure reading; reading for pleasure; co-design.

## 1. INTRODUCTION
It was 1972 when Alan Kay in his paper entitled *"A Personal Computer for Children of All Ages"* [9] envisioned the *Dynabook*, a sort of ancestor of today's electronic books (eBooks) and electronic readers. Part of his vision was that technology might *"provide us with a better 'book', one which is active (like the child) rather than passive"* before stating that *"This new medium will not 'save the world' from disaster. Just as with the book, it brings a new set of horizons and a new set of problems."*

Since then more than 40 years have passed, yet in our – and other researchers' [18] – opinion these horizons and problems have been only partially explored and addressed. As a matter of fact,

despite the exponential growth of the eBook market and the familiarity children have with technology, for the time being most eBooks are just a digital transposition of their paper counterpart and we feel that the potential of new reading devices – such as tablet computers – has yet to be fully exploited.

The goal of the work here presented was to design a prototype of a children's eBook that could create a better user experience, specifically an eBook that could result more engaging for young readers. Our focus was on children in the concrete operational stage [15] and on a context of reading for pleasure – or leisure reading (for a definition of *leisure reading* see [1]).

In this paper we will describe how we designed the eBook prototype and we will suggest some design guidelines for Human-Computer Interaction (HCI) researchers and practitioners concerned with the design of eBooks for children.

## 2. RELATED LITERATURE
Most of the research to date on eBooks for children looked at the utilitarian/educational aspects of electronic reading (eReading) such as text comprehension or emergent literacy – for a synthesis of the studies on the matter see the work of Zucker et al. [21]. Moreover, most of the studies have been merely *summative* – i.e. determining how good an eBook is – with only a minority which have been *formative* in nature – i.e. providing guidance for the design of eBooks. Among these studies, is the one from Wilson et al. [20] who developed a set of design guidelines obtained through a "series of evaluations conducted on a variety of eBooks". Those guidelines have a fairly strong empirical support, yet they have been proposed more than 10 years ago and – in line with the main trend in HCI research at the time – they are merely focused on preventing usability problems rather than on creating a better user experience. In addition, these guidelines are targeted to an adult population and they have not been created with children in mind.

Guidelines specifically for children's eBooks can be found in the work of Shamir and Korat (as cited in [16]) who elaborated a shortlist of high level design features for educational eBooks: *"(a) oral reading with text highlights that illuminate the nature of print; (b) hotspot activation aligned with text; (c) a dictionary option that allows repeated action by the child; and (d) a game mode separate from text mode"* These guidelines are somewhat interesting and can be a source of inspiration for our study, however they are specifically developed for educational eBooks and aimed at supporting children's emergent literacy. Instead our study pays more attention to leisure eBooks and on how to support readers' engagement.

To our knowledge there is little research in this area. In fact, the review of the literature showed that previous research mainly focused on the usability of eBooks for adults and/or on the utilitarian/educational aspects of children's eReading, while generally little attention has been paid to leisure reading. By focusing on this specific context and on the user, our work aims at filling the gap in the HCI literature on leisure reading and at extending the research on the design of children's eBooks.

## 3. COOPERATIVE INQUIRY

Research already showed the benefits of including children in the design process [14], therefore our assumption is that we can design better eBooks by actively involving children as design partners. What differentiates the various participatory design approaches – besides the different philosophies behind them – is the degree of user involvement throughout the design process. According to Nesset and Large [14] *Cooperative Inquiry (CI)* is the method which entails the higher degree of involvement, and this is the main reason why we decided to use it. CI is a combination of techniques from different design methods, and it is *"grounded in HCI research and theories of cooperative design involving a multi-disciplinary partnership with children, field research, and iterative low and high-tech prototyping"* [14].

### 3.1 Participants

CI advocates a design partnership in which adults and children are equal stakeholders in the design process [6]. Therefore we built an intergenerational design team composed by 10 children (7 females and 3 males in the 9 to 11 age range), 3 HCI researchers – i.e. the authors of this paper (who led the design sessions) – and 2 librarians (who helped in the role of facilitators and also provided logistic support).

Children were volunteered from a population of regular users of a children's library. We provided each child with a tablet to keep for the entire length of the partnership, this in order to let them use the device at home, become more familiar with it and have an experience with eBooks in various formats.

### 3.2 Materials

When we started the project we had to choose for which platform/eReader the eBook prototype should have been developed. Even though it is not an eBook reader in the strictest sense, we chose to use a tablet computer – i.e. iPad® – to have more freedom both for what concerns the format of the eBook and the features it could implement – traditional eBook readers have more restrictions in this sense. IPads® were also introduced in the late stage of the prototyping workflow, and used in combination with a presentation software – i.e. Keynote® – as prototyping tools.

### 3.3 Setting

During the three months of the study the design team met once a week for one hour and a half. The meetings took place in a children's library in Lugano (Switzerland). We chose this location in order to work in an informal environment that was, at the same time, a location familiar to the participants.

### 3.4 Approach

In the first meeting we welcomed children, explained them the purpose of the study, gave to each of them a tablet, and answered all their questions. In the second meeting – after children spent one week to read various eBooks in different formats – we did a brainstorming to elicit "likes and dislikes" of current eBooks and to propose new ideas on how to improve them (see *sticky note critiquing* [19]).

In the following phase the design team was divided into 2 groups and each of them worked to develop a paper mockup of an eBook based on the ideas emerged in the previous phase – but children were free to introduce new ideas. After some design sessions, once the paper mockups reached a satisfactory level, the two groups worked to translate the paper mockups into interactive prototypes. We alternated paper prototyping and tablet prototyping sessions – for more details and a discussion on the advantages and disadvantages of each approach see [3]. Children were trained on how to use the Keynote® app and then, together with the adult designers, they worked to realize slideshows that mimicked a real eBook on the iPad®.

To further refine and elaborate the design ideas emerged in the previous stages, the paper mockups were disassembled and each group used the various resulting parts to create new prototypes (see *mixing ideas* technique [19]). The so obtained prototypes informed the final phase of design, where the two groups worked to add the new design ideas in the interactive prototypes previously realized.

### 3.5 Outcomes

The result of the cooperative inquiry study we just described was a set of increasingly elaborated eBook prototypes. Taking inspiration from the ideas reflected in the prototypes, the authors developed a *beta* – i.e. feature complete – version of an *enhanced* eBook based on *"The Little Prince"* novel. The eBook has been realized using a specific eBook authoring application (i.e. iBooks Author) and existing guidelines on hypertext usability for children [4], eBook production [20], children's interaction with mobile devices [11] and device-specific interaction [8] were taken into account.

In the next section we will discuss the six guidelines we derived from the most salient ideas emerged during the Cooperative Inquiry study. For each of the guidelines we will describe how they have been implemented in the final prototype and the rationale behind them.

## 4. DESIGN GUIDELINES FOR MORE ENGAGING EBOOKS

The design guidelines presented in this section have been derived from the ideas that – according to the intergenerational design team – would be more effective in enabling a more engaging reading experience. These guidelines do not aim at being prescriptive. Less ambitiously we see them as a source of inspiration for researchers and practitioners for the future design of children's electronic books for leisure reading. For this reason we voluntarily left them quite general in their scope.

*I. "It (i.e. the eBook) should not be 'boring'": use audiovisual enrichments to allow for different reading paths*

Not surprisingly children wanted to have an eBook that is not "boring", and to this end the design team suggested: (a) videos that summarize parts of the text and (b) sound effects linked with words and images. Videos would allow for a non-linear multi-path reading experience – e.g. children could skip some parts of the text or they could recall what they just read – while sound effects can be used by readers both as a diversion from the reading activity or, in alternative, as a support for their imagination [7]. On the whole the idea is that audiovisual elements should be used to supplement and enhance rather than replace text [20] – i.e. to add redundancy to the textual information – thus allowing for different modes of fruition.

## II. "It should have a touch of 'Pathos': provide read-aloud narration of the text

Most children have been accustomed to read-aloud narration since a very young age (with parents reading bedtime stories to them) and it seems that its appeal does not cease when children grow older. In fact our young design partners – who were primary school pupils – included this feature in the eBook prototypes they developed.

Reading aloud is nothing new, and audiobooks have been around for years now – long before tablets and eReaders – but technology is contributing to a *digital renaissance* of read-aloud narration [7]. Electronic books allow for more control over the narration playback and for a synchronized combination of visual reading with audio reading. This creates a multi-modal reading experience that, in turn, may result in an intensification of narrative transportation [7] (see also the concept of *flow* in reading [12]). Moreover, previous research showed that the provision of narration may increase text comprehension [5, 21] and according to Verhallen & Bus (as cited in [17]) *"the temporal contiguity of audio (narration, music) with visual information (illustrations) appears to draw children's visual attention to pictures and print in ways that concretize the text, making it more real for them and more memorable".*

## III. "It should be playful": use interactivity to add value to the eBook and make it more playful.

Wilson et al. [20] argued that *"interactivity can increase a reader's sense of engagement with the book and enhance the material's likeability".* In line with this, the design team suggested to transform the various illustrations in objects one can interact with so that the reading experience can become more lively and playful. Therefore we included features such as coloring pages (see Figure 1) and puzzle games (see Figure 2) to the eBook. Children stressed that interactive enhancements should not be implemented just for the sake of interactivity – e.g. trivial touch-and-response animations – but they should add some "value" to the story and enhance the reading experience in a playful way – e.g. a puzzle that has to be solved in order to reveal some hidden text. In addition to increasing engagement, meaningful interactive enhancements may also support reading comprehension – whereas incongruent enhancements may hinder it [21].

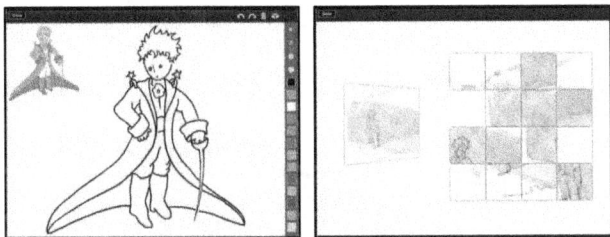

**Figure 1 (left): An example of a coloring page: by clicking on an outlined illustration children can paint it; Figure 2 (right): One of the puzzle games we implemented in the enhanced eBook prototype.**

## IV. "It should not be too difficult to read": provide in-line dictionary definitions and illustrated descriptive cards

In our view text must withstand as the core of the eBook (see Guideline VI) and many children emphasized the importance of having an eBook that is easy to read (in terms of text comprehension). Writing is (obviously) a writers' duty, yet interaction designers can give their contribution: text can be made interactive with in-line dictionary definitions (see Figure 3) or illustrated descriptive cards (see Figure 4).

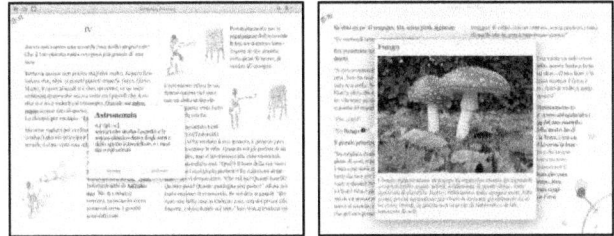

**Figure 3 (left): An example of an in-line dictionary definition for the word "astronomy"; Figure 4 (right): An example of an illustrated descriptive card for the word "mushroom".**

By doing so we enable children to tailor the reading to their skills and this in turn may facilitate *weak readers'* text comprehension or it may allow *strong readers* to expand their reading experience. A good balance between the challenges of a text and a reader's skills is an antecedent of ludic reading [13] and a key condition for *flow* (i.e. intense engagement in a text [12]) to occur. We do not mention here the educational benefits that reading with in-line dictionary entails as they have been already investigated by Korat & Shamir [10].

## V. "It should be colorful": use colors to differentiate the various parts in the text

**Figures 5 and 6: Few examples of how colors have been used to differentiate the various parts in the text**

This might sound as the most trivial and obvious guideline since children's printed books already make an extensive use of colors both for the text and the illustrations. However, surprisingly – in a negative way – colors are seldom used in electronic books and in some cases even illustrations are rendered in black and white. In the *beta* eBook we developed some text was colored to make it more aesthetically appealing (see Figures 5 and 6), but also to facilitate readers in recognizing different part of it – such as direct speeches of different characters. A meaningful use of colors may also help readers to identify patterns in the book, thus simplifying the interaction with the text and enhancing readability.

## VI. "It has to remain a book though": use non-textual elements with care and moderation

During a brainstorming session – in one of the early meetings – many children asked us whether some of the highly-interactive eBook applications we provided them could have still been considered "books". They were puzzled because those eBooks had little to do with the concept of "book" they had in mind: interactive, multimedia and/or game-like elements were prevailing over the text and the act of reading was confined to an incidental activity. Therefore the design team's suggested that text must withstand as the core component of an eBook. As we already stressed, non-textual elements should enhance, not replace text: they should not be the only source of engagement, they should rather foster readers' engagement with the text.

# 5. CONCLUSIONS

In this paper we proposed some recommendations for designing better and more engaging eBooks for children. They were informed by the ideas of an intergenerational design team. Cooperative Inquiry proved to be an effective method for our purposes: the long-term partnership with children co-designers allowed us to explore many ideas and, consequently, to condensate the most salient ones into a set of six guidelines.

In general, some of these guidelines seem to suggest that the eBook should be designed to be flexible enough and to allow children to tailor the reading experience on their persona in order to reach a balance between the challenges of the reading activity and their skills. *Gamification* (i.e. using game design elements in non-game contexts) is another important aspect in a context of leisure reading, but designers should exercise caution when adding features to enhanced eBooks. This because the story told by the text is, or should be, the core of the book and the main source of children's engagement with it: therefore any design solution or enhancement should contribute in this sense.

Our recent work of evaluation [2] seems to indicate the efficacy of our design guidelines, still further research is needed to better understand children's experience with enhanced eBooks (for instance eBooks based on different novels or targeted to a different age-group) or the interplay between the story itself and the various multimedia/interactive elements. Our hope is that these guidelines will inspire researchers and practitioners to create eBooks which are – as Alan Kay wrote – *"active (like the child) rather than passive"* [9].

# 6. ACKNOWLEDGMENTS

We would like to thank the children who have been our design partners over the last year and all the teachers and librarians who helped us in the study.

This work is supported by Swiss National Science Foundation (HEBE project), Microsoft Research at Cambridge and the Faculty of Informatics at University of Lugano – USI.

# 7. REFERENCES

[1] Clark, C. and Rumbold, K. 2006. Reading for Pleasure: A Research Overview.

[2] Colombo, L. and Landoni, M. 2014. A Diary Study of Children's User Experience with EBooks Using Flow Theory as Framework. Proceedings of the 13th International Conference on Interaction Design and Children - IDC '14 (New York, New York, USA, 2014).

[3] Colombo, L. and Landoni, M. 2013. Low-tech and high-tech prototyping for eBook co-design with children. Proceedings of the 12th International Conference on Interaction Design and Children - IDC '13 (New York, New York, USA, 2013), 289–292.

[4] Gilutz, S. and Nielsen, J. 2002. Usability of websites for children: 70 design guidelines.

[5] Grimshaw, S., Dungworth, N., McKnight, C. and Morris, A. 2007. Electronic books: children's reading and comprehension. British Journal of Educational Technology. 38, 4 (2007), 583–599.

[6] Guha, M.L., Druin, A. and Fails, J.A. 2012. Cooperative Inquiry revisited: Reflections of the past and guidelines for the future of intergenerational co-design. International Journal of Child-Computer Interaction. in press (2012).

[7] Have, I. and Stougaard Pedersen, B. 2013. Sonic mediatization of the book: affordances of the audiobook. MedieKultur. Journal of media and communication research. 29, 54 (2013), 123–140.

[8] iOS User Experience guidelines: 2013. https://developer.apple.com/library/ios/documentation/userexperience/conceptual/mobilehig/UEBestPractices/UEBestPractices.html. Accessed: 2013-09-05.

[9] Kay, A.C. 1972. A Personal Computer for Children of All Ages. Proceedings of the ACM annual conference - Volume 1 (New York, NY, USA, 1972).

[10] Korat, O. and Shamir, A. 2008. The educational electronic book as a tool for supporting children's emergent literacy in low versus middle SES groups. Computers & Education. 50, 1 (2008), 110–124.

[11] McKnight, L. and Cassidy, B. 2010. Children's Interaction with Mobile Touch-Screen Devices: Experiences and Guidelines for Design. International Journal of Mobile Human Computer Interaction. 2, 2 (2010), 1–18.

[12] Mcquillan, J. and Conde, G. 1996. The Conditions of Flow in Reading: Two Studies of Optimal Experience. Reading Psychology. 17, 2 (Apr. 1996), 109–135.

[13] Nell, V. 1988. Lost in a Book: The Psychology of Reading for Pleasure. Yale University Press.

[14] Nesset, V. and Large, A. 2004. Children in the information technology design process: A review of theories and their applications. Library & Information Science Research. 26, 2 (2004), 140–161.

[15] Piaget, J. 2007. The Child's Conception Of the World. Rowman & Littlefield, 2007.

[16] Roskos, K., Brueck, J. and Widman, S. 2009. Investigating Analytic Tools for e-Book Design in Early Literacy Learning. Journal of Interactive Online Learning. 8, 3 (2009), 218–240.

[17] Roskos, K., Burstein, K., Shang, Y. and Gray, E. 2014. Young Children's Engagement With E-Books at School: Does Device Matter? SAGE Open. 4, 1 (2014).

[18] Schreurs, K. 2013. Children's E-books are Born: How E-books for Children are Leading E-book Development and Redefining the Reading Experience. Partnership: the Canadian Journal of Library and Information Practice and Research. 8, 2 (2013).

[19] Walsh, G., Foss, E., Yip, J. and Druin, A. 2013. FACIT PD: A Framework for Analysis and Creation of Intergenerational Techniques for Participatory Design. Proceedings of the SIGCHI Conference on Human Factors in Computing Systems - CHI '13 (New York, New York, USA, 2013), 2893–2902.

[20] Wilson, R., Landoni, M. and Gibb, F. 2002. Guidelines for Designing Electronic Books. Proceedings of the 6th European Conference on Research and Advanced Technology for Digital Libraries – ECDL (2002), 47–60.

[21] Zucker, T.A., Moody, A.K. and McKenna, M.C. 2009. The Effects of Electronic Books on Pre-Kindergarten-to-Grade 5 Students' Literacy and Language Outcomes: A Research Synthesis. Journal of Educational Computing Research. 40, 1 (2009), 47–87.

# Do Interactions Speak Louder than Words?
## Dialogic Reading of an Interactive Tablet-based E-book with Children between 16 Months and Three Years of Age

Hendrik Knoche
Department of Media Technology
Sofiendalsvej 11
9200 Aalborg SV, DK
hk@create.aau.dk

Niklas Ammitzbøll Rasmussen
Department of Media Technology
Sofiendalsvej 11
9200 Aalborg SV, DK
nara10@student.aau.dk

Kasper Boldreel
Department of Media Technology
Sofiendalsvej 11
9200 Aalborg SV, DK
kboldr10@student.aau.dk

Joachim Lykke Østergaard Olesen
Department of Media Technology
Sofiendalsvej 11
9200 Aalborg SV, DK
jloo10@student.aau.dk

Anders Etzerodt Salling Pedersen
Department of Media Technology
Sofiendalsvej 11
9200 Aalborg SV, DK
apeder10@ student.aau.dk

## ABSTRACT

Dialogic reading, in which the reader prompts the child to speak while listening to the story being read, represents a promising way to boost children's lingual development but it is unclear how content interactivity and agency affect the technique. We used video interaction analysis to investigate the effect of interactive elements on speech production of 12 children between the ages of 16 and 33 months when engaged in individual dialogic reading sessions with a tablet-based e-book. Interaction with interactive elements did not reduce the children's responses to dialogic reading prompts. Spontaneous utterances were longer than prompted ones and the children's engagement with interactive elements or sounds coming from the application most often triggered these spontaneous utterances.

## Categories and Subject Descriptors

H.5.2 [Information Interfaces and Presentation] User Interfaces

## Keywords

Dialogic reading; interactive e-book; tablet; speech production

## 1. INTRODUCTION

Early language development provides the basis for a child's competence in language and literacy. Late talkers not only perform worse in behavioral tests of spoken and written language but also show decreased neurological activity suggesting longer term effects on linguistic performance during their school years [6]. Studies on dialogic reading, in which the reader takes an interactive approach and prompts the child to engage in speech

*IDC'14*, June 17–20, 2014, Aarhus, Denmark.
Copyright © 2014 ACM 978-1-4503-2272-0/14/06…$15.00.
http://dx.doi.org/10.1145/2593968.2610473

production in relation to the book, have shown promising results both for expressive and receptive language skill acquisition [5]. Tablet computers now constitute a platform ready to be taken to the bedside for nighttime reading - a common venue for child-parent reading activities - and they are becoming part of the inventory in daycare centers, another venue in which many children are exposed to and experience reading. A number of interactive or e-books specifically aimed at pre-school children have become available but whether reading activities aimed at increasing language acquisition are enhanced or disturbed by interactive elements remains unclear. According to a survey, parents find interactive elements potentially detrimental in shared reading situations [8]. How does the child's agency in manipulating the interactive elements in the book affect their responses in a dialogic reading situation?

To this end, we observed 12 children in one-on-one dialogic reading sessions of an interactive book on a tablet. The application contained interactive elements that allowed for pointing or dragging, which resulted in animations or visual state changes; were muted or had sound; and worked once or repeatedly. The paper focusses on how the interactive elements impacted dialogic reading in terms of the adults prompting behavior and the children's response frequencies and lengths.

## 2. BACKGROUND

A range of studies has shown positive correlations between the frequency of shared book reading and children's acquisition of language skills [2]. Dialogic reading is one example of a more concise approach to shared reading - see for example Whitehurst's seminal work on picture book reading [9] in which the adult encourages the child to talk about and discuss the contents of the book. Mol *et al.*'s meta-analysis on dialogic reading showed significant gains in vocabulary and language development [5]. For 2-3-year olds Zevenbergen & Whitehurst included the following activities in dialogic reading: asking open-ended and what questions with follow-ups to child's responses, confirming and praising the child's utterance, repeating what the child says and expanding on this, helping the child as needed, following the child's interest and creating an enjoyable experience for the child [10]. In Whitehurst's original description [9] of the technique the ideal facilitation follows a PEER-sequence: The facilitator *prompts* the child to say something ("What is the lion doing?"), *evaluates* the child's response ("Yes, the lion is eating..."), *expands* it through rephrasing and/or adding information ("...a big sausage."), and *repeats* the prompt ("Can you say sausage?").

To the best of our knowledge, no studies have investigated how using a digital interactive book on tablets or computers instead of paper impacts dialogic reading in general and our target age group in particular. The only available account we found about how interactive elements impact shared reading was Valaa & Takeuchi's large-scale survey of parents of 3 to 5 year olds. Parents found the following features or parts of interactive books to be the most distracting: videos (66%), games (63%), and hotspots/animations 48%. The latter refers to (potentially) highlighted interactive elements that can be triggered to: emit sound, move, or cause changes in state of the interactive book [8]. However, it remains unclear whether the results apply to dialogic reading and the survey does not provide information about how detrimental an impact these interactive elements have on reading acquisition as 42% of parents found them beneficial.

Children have reduced fine motor skills compared to adults, which affects their ability to interact with interactive elements through touch screens [3] and these elements need to be both big enough and adequately distanced from each other. In terms of target sizes for 7 to 10-year-olds Anthony *et al.*'s identified squares of 6mm sides for pointing accuracy with a 20% miss rate, which they deemed acceptable [1]. Sesame Workshop developed a set of practitioner design guidelines for apps and games on tablet computers [7]. According to them tapping and dragging are the two most intuitive touch screen gestures but finger-on-screen continuity might pose a problem for drawing, dragging and swiping. Unfortunately, they neither offer concrete guidelines regarding target sizes, distances and gesture accuracy nor information about how the abilities change with age but they do acknowledge large differences between 2- and 4-year olds. Joiner *et al.* provided evidence for poorer performance of 5-6-year olds compared to 10 year olds, particularly when it came to dragging. Since we could not find previous work on pointing accuracy in the age range under consideration we conducted an initial test into target sizes with an 18-month old child interacting with both a tablet and a book being prompted to point at objects. From video recordings we found that precision varied and even for large objects could be up to two centimeters.

# 3. STUDY

## 3.1 Participants
Twelve children (5 male, 7 female) aged between 16 and 33 months (average 24, SD=5.6) took part in the study. Three caregivers (1 male, 2 female) familiar with and refreshed on dialogic reading facilitated the sessions in a daycare center, a familiar location to the children. One of them (male) read to six the other two (female) read to three children each. Subsequently we will use the terms caregiver and facilitator interchangeably.

## 3.2 Material
We converted a children's picture book to a tablet-based e-book that covered two animal protagonists exploring the world. Our factorial design covered eight scenes, which included all combinations of:

- *gesture* - touch or drag interaction, which resulted in (1-4 second) animations and/or displacement of elements,

- *sound* - whether the gesture triggered a (1 to 6 second) sound feedback or not

- *repetition* - whether the gestures worked repeatedly on the interactive elements or only once.

All interactive elements had a white outline and a shadow visually lifting them into the foreground.

## 3.3 Procedure
Caregivers facilitated the sessions in a dedicated room over the course of one day. The caregiver sat on a beanbag with the child seated on his/her lap and held the tablet (c in Figure 1). An experimenter assisted in case of technical errors - situated out of sight behind the child between two high-definition camcorders (a) (*c.f.* Figure 1). A high quality audio recorder (b) recorded the audio. We conducted debrief interviews with two caregivers after they had facilitated all sessions.

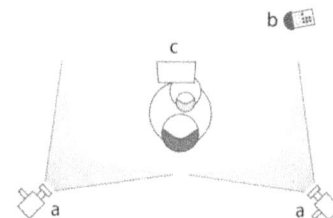

**Figure 1: Physical setup of the dialogic reading sessions with two cameras behind the facilitating child minder holding the tablet and the child on their lap**

## 3.4 Analysis
For the analysis of the recorded footage we relied on Jordan & Henderson's Video Interaction Analysis [4]. We initially took a grounded approach to establish categories of events from which to analyze the material. After having watched one full session and generating a first set of codes independently two researchers created a merged set of codes. Three researchers then applied this coding scheme to the entire corpus. For a child's utterance we logged its *length* in words, *discernibility* (yes/no), *spontaneity* (whether the utterance related to the most recent prompt), and its *reason*, for example whether it related to a prompt or an interaction in the interface. For the children's interactions with the app we logged *how* they interacted and whether these interactions were *successful*. For the adults we logged: the *type* of prompt according to the PEER model, prompt *details*, for example whether it prompted for a location or label and *encouragements* of the child to interact. We logged all adult interactions with the application, for example, when showing the child how to interact. Moreover, we logged application errors that occurred, e.g. in out-of-synch renditions of audio, which occurred in 72 cases with more than two seconds delay due to poor wireless internet connectivity.

The coding from the 65 minutes of recorded footage contained a total of 1408 logged events, including 108 prompted and 96 spontaneous word utterances and 77 verbal non-word utterances. We coded utterances as spontaneous if they had no obvious causal relationship with the caregiver's dialogic reading prompts.

For the subsequent analysis we used the following dependent variables on an overall and per-scene basis. We took the number of prompted word responses and divided them by the number of prompts that the adult had issued for each child (*response/prompt ratio*). For both spontaneous and prompted utterances we computed *length of utterance* in words. Spontaneous utterances (words and non-words) were computed on a per minute basis since the caregivers spent between 26 and 60 seconds in the scenes. Furthermore, we looked into the *prompts per minute* the facilitator had used.

We computed for each child and scene the number of touch screen *interactions* they had *per minute* (*ipm*) and the ratio to the interactions the adult had (child/adult agency ratio, *caar*). This provided us with an estimate of the child's agency vis-à-vis the application and allowed for controlling for the difference in styles the caregivers had in using the application during the dialogic reading. The male caregiver who read to six children controlled the application himself most (*ipm* average of his children was 2) whereas the other two caregivers encouraged and had the children interact with the application more (*ipm* averages of 3 and 5.5).

# 4. RESULTS

We found a strong positive correlation (r(10)=.74, p<.01) between the children's age and their response/prompt ratio. Older children responded more often to dialogic reading prompts. There was a nonsignificant correlation 0.1 between age and the utterance length of the children's responses. The response/prompt ratio (ranging from zero to 1.1) and utterance length (from 0 to 3.4 words) across all scenes are summarized in Figure 2. The children's spontaneous utterances were significantly longer (2.5 words) than the ones responding to a prompt (1.8 words) - according to a paired t-test for the children that had replied to prompts and talked spontaneously t(5)=3.11, p=.026. The large difference was due to a number of closed question prompts from the caregivers, which resulted in yes/no replies from the children. When we excluded simple yes/no responses for both prompted and spontaneous utterances the difference was smaller (prompted 2.4, spontaneous 2.7 words) but still significant. We found no significant correlations between the children's age and the length of their spontaneous and prompted responses but there was a positive trend between age and the length of spontaneous utterances but no such trend with the length of prompted responses (see the trend lines in Figure 4). Older children produced longer spontaneous utterances than younger ones. But when prompted the older children's utterance were of similar average length.

The children interacted with the application on average 2.4 times per minute. Younger children interacted as much with the application as the older ones did. To check whether the children would respond less often or more mono-syllabic when interacting

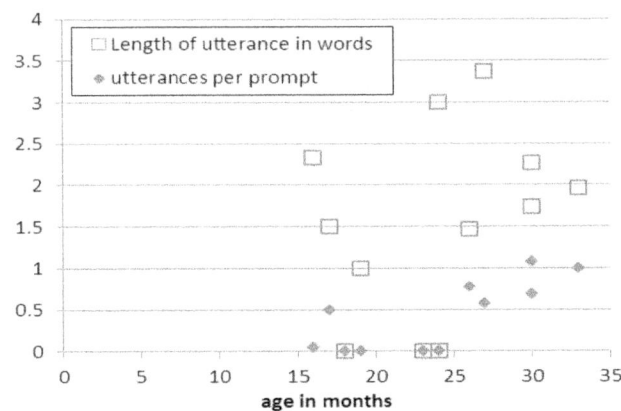

Figure 4: Average length of utterances by age

more with the application we included age in a multiple regression analysis along with *imp* as predictors of the children's *average utterance length* and their response/prompt ratio. We found no significant effects and Figure 3 plots the child's *ipm* against their average utterance length and their response/prompt ratio. In other words, there was no evidence that increased interaction with interactive elements reduced the children's responses to prompts nor the length of t responses.

To test the independent variables from our factorial design we ran multiple regressions on children's (both spontaneous and prompted) utterance lengths and their response/prompt ratio. We found no signficant contribution of *gesture*, *sound* or *repetition* as predictors with age, *ipm* and *caar* included in the regression as controls. Of the control variables only age was a significant predictor for the response/prompt ratio. However, the multiple regression, which included the same set of predictors and controls on spontaneous utterances (per minute), showed that both age ($\beta$=.16 t(90)=4.57, p<.001.) and *caar* ($\beta$=.28, t(90)=2, p<.049) were significant predictors. Older children and those that interacted more with the application than their caregivers spoke more often spontaneously. The scenes in which the children could repeat actions did not yield significantly more interactions than the scenes not allowing for repetition.

The children derived most fun from the animations and sounds. Of the 39 times the children laughed or giggled, most were triggered by animations (12) and sounds (11). Of the 96 spontaneous utterances the largest number happened because of or in relation to interactions with the application (22) and sound (12). A follow-up regression comparing utterance lenghts of these

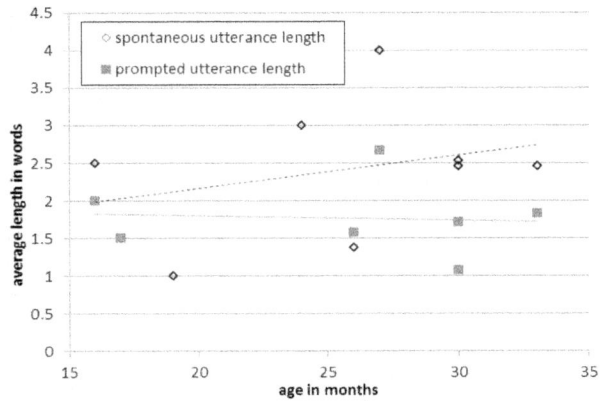

Figure 2: Utterance frequency and average length by age

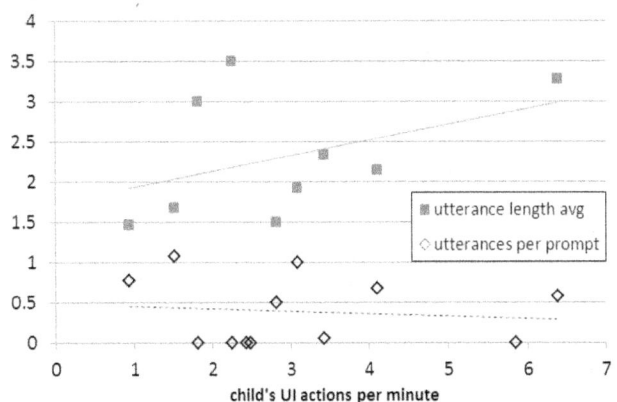

Figure 3: Response ratio and utterance length by the child's UI actions per minute

two with all other triggers of spontaneous utterances showed that these two triggers resulted in significantly longer utterances. The longest spontaneous sentences were evoked by *sound* (3.5 words) and when commenting "*it wants to be down here*" or asking about pointing or dragging *interactions* "can you put it there?" (2.9). Most of the spontaneous utterances around interactions occured in the last scene, which had no sound but various animals could be repeatedly dragged and re-positioned anywhere on the screen. The prompted utterances that fared better than average (1.8 words) were the ones in which the children described an *action* (2.4), *labeled* an object or character (2.3) or talked about a *sound* that was made (2).

The adults prompted the children on average 2.3 times per minute and between zero to 12 times in the different scenes. We tested *gesture*, *sound* and *repetition* impacted on the adult's prompting frequency by entering them along with *ipm*, *caar*, and age as predictors in a stepwise regression in which factors with the smallest p-value (<.05) were entered first. Only *age* and *sound* significantly predicted *prompts per minute*. The adults prompted more frequently when the children were older ($\beta=.14$, $t(90)=2.77$, $p<.01$) and in scenes that did not contain sound ($\beta=.56$, $t(90)=2.02$, $p<.05$.). This was mirrored during the debrief interviews with the caregivers. The caregiver who had prompted least suggested including music and narration while the most prompting caregiver feared that narration would weaken the contact with the child. Both disliked interactive elements not supported by text, as they did not know what to tell about them.

## 5. DISCUSSION

The initial concern that children might talk less often or with shorter responses when engaged with interactive elements was not warranted in our sessions. The children who interacted with the application more than the caregivers (larger *caar*) made more spontaneous utterances, too. However, since caar represents a covariate this finding would need more controlled follow-up research to provide causal conclusions.

The engaging effect of sound does not come as a surprise with the number of books available that supplement the visual reading experience with sounds. While sound in the scenes resulted in fewer prompts from the caregivers, it stimulated longer spontaneous utterances from the children. We used only sounds shorter than six seconds and further studies need to include the limits at which sound might begin to have detrimental effects, which the survey results from Vaala & Takeuch suggest.

The sizes of targets and difficulties with dragging might pose a usability problem but we found that these problems fostered verbal exchanges in line with the goal of dialogic reading.

We decided against using one facilitator unfamiliar to the children and relied instead on caregivers they knew. However, we found that facilitation by different adults varied a lot both in terms of dialogic reading and how much they allowed or encouraged the children to interact with the application. While dialogic reading represents an interactive, child-driven situation with large differences between children, we would still advocate for using one trained facilitator to keep this condition more controlled. The fact that the children's spontaneous utterances were longer than the prompted ones was partially due to some caregivers' prompts. This raises an important concern for training, which Zevenbergen and Whitehurst originally addressed with two workshops. Although our caregivers were all familiar with and had received a refresher before the session, they might have facilitated the

sessions differently with more training. When engaged in dialogic reading with e-books facilitators might benefit from having access to example prompts as some of the closed questions we observed resulted in short yes/no answers and the caregivers disliked interactive elements not supported by the storyline. Similarly, initial work on teaching facilitators dialogic reading involved example and training sequences.

## 6. CONCLUSION

The children's agency in manipulating interactive elements did not adversely affect their responses to dialogic reading prompts. Interactive elements did provide triggers for children to speak in addition to dialogic reading prompts in shared e-book readings sessions. Sounds and being able to move objects and characters around produced longer spontaneous utterances in comparison to responses to dialogic reading prompts. Open-ended interactions worked particularly well and future research should explore concepts for spontaneity more in the context of dialogic reading.

## 7. ACKNOWLEDGMENTS

We thank Ditte Aarup Johnson for artwork and storyline from "Tulle og Skralle på eventyr" and the children and caregivers from Aarhus community center for participating in the study.

## 8. REFERENCES

1. Anthony, L., Brown, Q., Nias, J., Tate, B., and Mohan, S. Interaction and recognition challenges in interpreting children's touch and gesture input on mobile devices. Proceedings of the 2012 ACM international conference on Interactive tabletops and surfaces, ACM (2012), 225–234.

2. Hargrave, A.C. and Sénéchal, M. A book reading intervention with preschool children who have limited vocabularies: The benefits of regular reading and dialogic reading. Early Childhood Research Quarterly 15, 1 (2000), 75–90.

3. Hourcade, J.P. It's too small! Implications of children's developing motor skills on graphical user interfaces. (2003).

4. Jordan, B. and Henderson, A. Interaction analysis: Foundations and practice. The journal of the learning sciences 4, 1 (1995), 39–103.

5. Mol, S.E., Bus, A.G., de Jong, M.T., and Smeets, D.J. Added value of dialogic parent–child book readings: A meta-analysis. Early Education and Development 19, 1 (2008), 7–26.

6. Preston, J.L., Frost, S.J., Mencl, W.E., et al. Early and late talkers: school-age language, literacy and neurolinguistic differences. Brain 133, 8 (2010), 2185–2195.

7. Sesame Workshop. Best Practices: Designing Touch - Tablet Experiences for Preschoolers. http://www.sesameworkshop.org/assets/1191/src/Best%20Pra ctices%20Document%2011-26-12.pdf.

8. Vaala, S. and Takeuchi, L. Co-Reading with Children on Ipads: Parents' Perceptions and Practices. The Joan Ganz Cooney Center, 2012.

9. Whitehurst, G.J., Falco, F.L., Lonigan, C.J., et al. Accelerating language development through picture book reading. Developmental Psychology 24, 4 (1988), 552.

10. Zevenbergen, A. and Whitehurst, G. Dialogic reading: A shared picture book reading intervention for preschoolers. On reading books to children, (2003), 177–200.

# Building an Internet of School Things Ecosystem – A National Collaborative Experience

**Chris Joyce**
CREATE Lab
Centre for Digital Entertainment
University of Bath
cfj21@bath.ac.uk

**Han Pham**
ICRI-Cities
Intel Labs Europe
London
han.pham@intel.com

**Danae Stanton Fraser**
CREATE Lab
Department of Psychology
University of Bath
d.stantonfraser@bath.ac.uk

**Stephen Payne**
Department of Computer Science
University of Bath
s.j.payne@bath.ac.uk

**David Crellin**
ScienceScope
Writhlington School, Radstock
david@auc.co.uk

**Sean McDougall**
Stakeholder Design
4 St Andrew's Close, Hereford
sean@stakeholderdesign.com

## ABSTRACT

Over the course of the next 10 years, the Internet of Things (IoT) is set to have a transformational effect on the everyday technologies which surround us. Access to the data produced by these devices opens an interesting space to practice discovery based learning. This paper outlines a participatory design approach taken to develop an IoT-based ecosystem which was deployed in 8 schools across England. In particular, we describe how we designed and developed the system and reflect on some of the early experiences of students and teachers. We found that schools were willing to adopt the IoT technology within certain bounds and we outline best practices uncovered when introducing technologies to schools.

## Categories and Subject Descriptors

H.5.2 [**Information Interfaces and Presentation**]: User Interfaces.
K.3.1 [**Computers and Education**]: Computer Uses in Education.

## General Terms

Design

## Keywords

Participatory Design; Discovery Based Learning; Education; STEM Learning; Internet of Things (IoT)

## 1. INTRODUCTION

### 1.1 The Internet of Things

The IoT, a collection of physical sensors and actuators, which communicate via the internet, encompasses a variety of applications from personal exercise tracking devices, home

heating systems and weather stations to performance indicators built into industrial machines. Its emergence in recent years provides an exciting space not only for industrialists looking to streamline their production costs [3] or for computer science researchers looking to develop ever more exotic transport protocols [8] but also for educators and students.

The emergence of the IoT has led to urban data becoming increasingly available, which allows new ways of understanding and visualising the connected city via its digital traces and data, both historical and real time [2]. The Internet of School Things (IoST) aims to build an ecosystem where students and educators can gain a deeper, empirically-based understanding of their environments and can actuate change through the use of the IoT.

In this paper we discuss our approach to innovating visualisations and interactions using participatory design with both teachers and students to create Project DISTANCE: Demonstrating the Internet of School Things - a National Collaborative Experience.

### 1.2 DISTANCE

DISTANCE originated as a consortium made up of 5 commercial partners, 4 universities and 8 schools with the shared vision that children are the creators of future digital data economy rather than just passive consumers.

This project explores the emerging ecosystem of IoT in schools helping teachers, students and businesses to share certain types of data openly. Students and teachers will be taught to measure and share data, using new IoT technologies, in ways that help make learning fun and enable students to investigate and address real-world, applied challenges using open urban data. This builds on projects such as the Participate Schools [4] and NQuire [6] where students carry out discovery-based learning with the help of supporting mobile and web technologies. Unlike its forerunners, the DISTANCE project is developing a co-created ecosystem which supports the collection of data from devices both within and outside the control of the individual.

In order to facilitate students' role as creators using the IoT an extensible technical and social ecosystem needs to be put in place integrating hardware, data, and associated content and services. This ecosystem should provide easy access to information, facilitate the interpretation of this data and empower students to take action on their interpretations.

## 2. METHODOLOGY AND PROCESS

### 2.1 Participants

Students and teachers from 8 schools spread across England took part in participatory design sessions run between June 2013 and February 2014. Primary, Middle and Secondary Schools all took part in the project. Teaching sessions took place within key stage 2 & 3 classes (students aged between 9 & 13, US equivalent of 4th-7th grades). Key stage 4 students (ages 14-16) also participated in the visioning sessions. Teachers from Maths, Science, Design & Technology and Geography departments took part in the design of the hardware, software and curriculum as well as subsequent teaching with the technology. Participating schools were selected to represent geographical, socio-economic, and domain-diversity across the UK, including schools in Lancashire, Birmingham, Suffolk, London, Peterborough, Liverpool and Bath and North East Somerset. This diversity was also represented in the range of prior experience with sensing technologies within the participating schools, from those with bespoke insulation sensors provided by previous innovation projects to other schools with only rudimentary provision of digital resources. The range of participant schools also translated into a range of teaching environments which varied from standard 60-minute classes of 30 students to bespoke "superlabs" of 200 students, as well as lunchtime learning clubs. In order to create appropriate technologies and content for these diverse contexts we used a participatory design approach which we will describe in the following section.

### 2.2 Methods Used

We used an iterative, mixed methodology across the eight-month design and pilot phase, including open-ended interviews, focus groups, training sessions, classroom observation, and shadowing. The participatory design process was defined as three phases aligned with the progressive maturity of the project: Conceptual (initial phase to explore baseline school cultures, expectations and use cases), Pre-pilot curriculum design (to further adapt envisioned use cases) & Iterative, in situ design (through action research). These sessions were iterative progressive stages, rather than distinct elements, tailored to the progress and needs of each partner school. In each, a slight variation of methodologies was used, including formal group design workshops, informal one-on-one design sessions, physical prototyping of digital data networks, teacher-led usability reviews, and illustrative comic strips to articulate students' emergent conceptual frameworks of the IoT.

#### 2.2.1 Conceptual

Participatory design requires an understanding of the predisposition, assumptions and contexts of the co-designing group. As we were co-designing ways to introduce and sustain an emergent educational technology, this understanding was particularly important in order to ground the unfamiliar concepts of the IoT within a meaningful and appropriate framework. This phase of the design process included more than fifteen two-hour progressive visioning workshops across the 8 schools.

Considering that the IoST could encourage a shift in current organisational hierarchies, the initial workshops were structured to allow students and teachers to ideate separately, to allow for the intentional creation of a safe, peer-to-peer environment for risk-taking. Once the initial use case concepts were generated, subsequent design workshops brought together both students and teachers across all year groups. The "Conceptual" design phase allowed the team to identify IoT educational use cases that were both relevant and salient. The majority of the paper focuses on the following design phases, which refined these for actioning as curriculum or software within actual classroom settings.

#### 2.2.2 Pre-teaching Curriculum

Prior to the deployment of the technology, a 4-hour participatory design curriculum development workshop was run in one of the schools with 6 teachers from the Science, Design & Technology and Mathematics departments alongside two of the consortium's researchers. A number of data-sensing and broadcasting devices were brought along and shown in action so that the teachers would obtain a realistic impression of the devices capabilities.

Three pre-prepared exemplar lesson plans were discussed and enhanced and a new set of lesson plans were co-created to meet the requirement of providing enough scope to sustain 14 hours of teaching time to be carried out over seven two-hour sessions. A delivery timetable for the resultant lesson plans and support materials was agreed upon, ensuring teachers had adequate run-in time. An audio and video record was made of this event and transcribed to ensure all the requirements were captured.

#### 2.2.3 In-Situ Design

Researchers helped facilitate and document the initial teaching sessions creating field notes, audio and video recordings. Teachers were interviewed before, during and after particular sessions and the findings were fed back into the development process. Improvements to the design of the curriculum and software were available for piloting in the upcoming sessions, where possible.

## 3. WHAT WE LEARNED FROM DEPLOYING THE IoST

### 3.1 Contexts That Motivate Students

A context-based approach, which was initially introduced in the UK with the aim to engage less academic students with science, uses applications of science in the real world as the starting point for the development of scientific ideas. Bennett et al [1] conducted a systematic review of the literature surrounding the use of context in secondary science suggesting this approach yields considerable benefits in terms of attitudes to school science and reduces the difference of attitudes towards the subject between genders. In order to engage students with the IoST we looked at applying a context-based approach when introducing the technology into schools. Initially the consortium identified four thematic areas around which to frame the IoST: Weather, Mobility, Health and Energy. We then used participatory design to define more specific contexts which would appeal and be relevant to students and teachers alike. The first phase of the design process focused on generating the most relevant ideas from the schools for use cases.

By providing safe spaces for discussions the team was able to elicit and understand the diverse personal contexts that could be used when applying the IoST to real-world challenges and in creating further engagement with the IoST in the future. For example, students in the second phase of the visioning workshops were asked to envision what type of data would be hosted by DISTANCE for personal safety. They began by identifying the hyperlocal context in which it was relevant to the school, i.e., a shift in the timetable causing a situation in which the students could feel unsafe returning from school. Next, students considered what contextual data could be relevant to exploring school safety and which could be collected for their school (e.g. perceptions of safety, statistics on prior crime, mapping lighting zones to and from school). Students also explored what data could be both possible and valuable to access and share across the network of schools in the DISTANCE hub (e.g. commute distances, comparison of travel modes, availability of public transport). Finally, students ideated how this data could be aggregated to create a hypothetical school-based "danger" sensor.

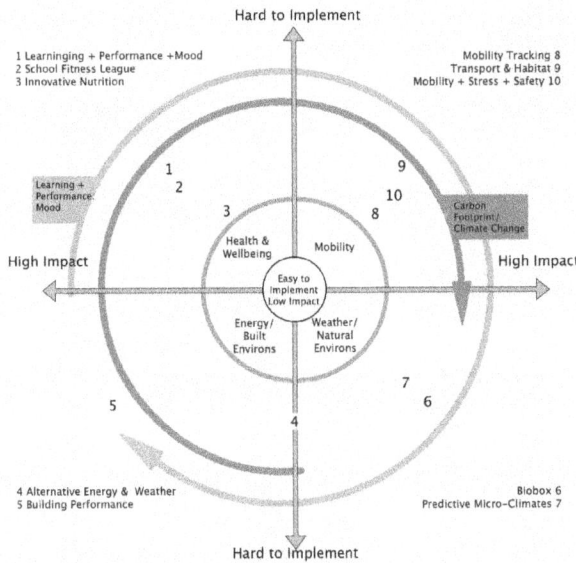

**Figure 1: Map of key ideas from visioning workshop.**

Figure 1 shows a map of key ideas generated by the schools during this two-month phase. Eventually, this was refined by the research team into 11 use cases which carried over to the Pre-teaching Curriculum design phase.

## 3.2 Giving Schools Tools to Visualise Data

A key part in the establishment of an IoST ecosystem was the development of platform(s), which allowed students and teachers to visualise, interpret and interact with the large amount of urban data available. Interviews with teachers and in-situ observation of students provided a number of key insights listed below.

### 3.2.1 Access to Contextual Data

The desire to explore contextual data, first observed in the visioning workshops, was further highlighted in practice when students started to compare data from their own school, which has a familiar context, to that of other participating schools. For instance, when students were trying to predict if the climate in Birmingham was warmer than in Bury Saint Edmunds, factors such as elevation, urbanisation and distance from the sea had to be taken into account alongside weather data. Initially, Google Earth was used in a separate window to provide this information. However an improved solution was developed which incorporated placing mapping and other information, such as descriptive statistics, side-by-side with the sensed data (Figure 2).

### 3.2.2 Reading from Graphs

A design decision was made to keep the onscreen clutter to a minimum by limiting the number of gridlines used when graphing the data. A consequence of this was that it was difficult to get an exact reading from the graph. For this reason a hover behaviour was introduced to present the x & y values (sensor & date/time) as a tooltip when a data point was highlighted (Figure 2). Initially the sensor value was presented next to the data point and the date/time was placed above it at the very top of the graph.

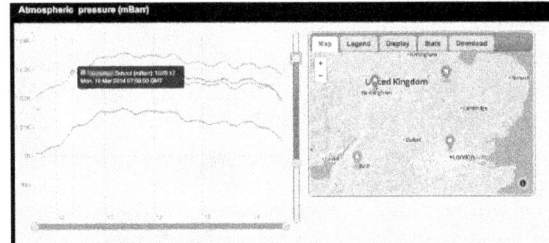

**Figure 2: Displaying Data with Context and Hover function within DISTANCE Exploratory (App)**

However this lead to the graph being misread by a number of students with the date/time being confused for the sensor value. This was then redesigned so that data series name, sensor value and unit were provided on the first line of the tooltip and the date and time on the next line, which the students then found to be very intuitive. Teacher feedback was mixed as the hover behavior deviated from the standard paper-based experience of graphs, in which students practice the skill of reading values from axes. This skill is valued by teachers and is assessed in state exams. Teachers, however, readily acknowledged its practicality in allowing students to quickly interpret complex data, reducing drudgery and increasing enjoyment and playful exploration.

## 3.3 The Right Time

To develop familiarity with technology, teachers require free time in advance of lessons to explore new resources. Many teachers already have full schedules which constitutes a barrier to the adoption of new technologies. This highlights the need for intuitive, efficient technologies that allow discovery-based learning for both teachers and students in-situ. This would allow a progressive adoption of the technology without requiring intensive training or expertise. In this project we tried to address this issue by providing a number of intuitive and interactive tools to visualise and interpret data, as outlined in previous sections, alongside curriculum-related and context-based resources, such as lesson plans, presentations and worksheets which teachers could use with the new technology. However, in interviews carried out with teachers, it was suggested that more lightweight, upfront resources, such as tutorial videos showing how to make use of the technology could be used during the lesson to encourage student-led learning and problem solving and help establish a more collaborative learning hierarchy.

## 3.4 The Right Place

Key Stage 3 (US approximate equivalence of 6th-8th grade) is a space where schools in the UK are most comfortable in experimenting with novel technologies, in part due to the absence of state exams. Consequently it is not surprising that a large proportion of the teaching which made use of IoST technologies took place here. One of the challenges in moving the use of the technology to other year groups is that teachers are concerned that the risk of obtaining an unexpected result is greater than with a tried and tested existing protocol. Time would then need to be invested into understanding how the unexpected result was arrived at rather than invested into content that is likely to be assessed. This is an inherent risk of discovery-based learning and not exclusive to the IoT. For instance, Tan et al report that 311 out of 485 teachers identified "Graphs/results obtained were different from theory" as a factor which deterred them from using dataloggers [7]. The Data Portal app has attempted to address this by enabling teachers to refer back to pertinent data selections via its permalink system (Figure 3). This allows students to access data and graphs that have been previously deemed relevant and illustrative of a theory.

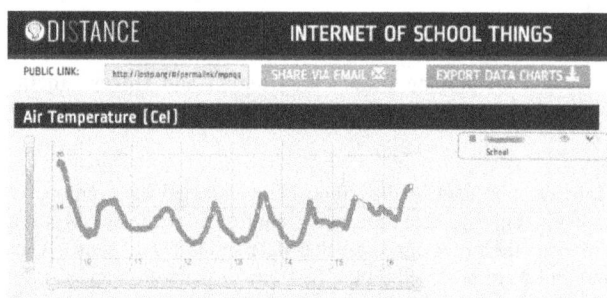

**Figure 3: Use of permalinks in Data Portal app allows easy referral to data selections.**

## 4. CHALLENGES AND OPPORTUNITIES

Creating an ecosystem where environmental data is readily available provides a new learning experience, which allows students and teachers to dive directly into the data being generated, stimulates open discussion and discovery and shifts time away from setup to higher-level learning activities in the classroom. A participatory approach to building a prototype ecosystem, encompassing hardware, software and services, was useful to begin to understand the specific needs of this context in order to reduce friction and increase engagement. The vision of encouraging educators, students and businesses to share data openly meant that how we designed the tools, using a collaborative and participatory approach, was fundamental in allowing schools to scale this idea on their own initiative. We found the process created value for schools, not only in terms of the tangible outcomes of curriculum content and software, but also in a greater sense of ownership over data, the development of a school-based digital identity within open educational data use and an increased flexibility to incorporate discovery-based learning. A unique aspect of this project is not just a focus on interactions in the digital environment, but the cross-over into physical environments, computing and other learning tools to create extended learning environments within and beyond the classroom. The hands-on nature of practical science lessons has been shown to enhance the learning experiences of students. [5] There is a danger that collecting data using sensors with a fixed position (and consequently very little need to directly manipulate them) will result in a drop in engagement and motivation. This needs to be examined and, if it proves to be the case, steps should be taken to include physical interaction where appropriate.

Sessions designed as part of the Weather Use Case already address this where students examine the measurement apparatus by trying to 'trick' a weather station. Building session materials which take into account the upkeep and periodic re-calibration of sensors would seamlessly embed these activities while also sustaining the infrastructure of the IoST. Facilitating student and teacher driven hardware development would also contribute to a hands-on experience. Strategies, tools and support materials need to be developed to ensure that IoST can continue to grow, fed by the teachers' engagement to secure its legacy as a transformative technology.

## 5. ACKNOWLEDGEMENTS

The research reported in this paper was funded by a Technology Strategy Board contract which was won by a consortium made up of Intel, ScienceScope, the Open University, Xively, Birmingham Urban Climate Lab (BUCL), Centre for Advanced Spatial Analysis (CASA), Mission Explore and Stakeholder design. Chris Joyce is a doctoral student from the EPSRC Centre for Digital Entertainment & the CREATE lab at the University of Bath funded partly by ScienceScope.

## 6. REFERENCES

[1] Bennett, J., Lubben, F., and Hogarth, S. 2007. Bringing Science to Life: A Synthesis of the Research Evidence on the Effects of Context-Based and STS Approaches to Science Teaching. *Science Education 9 (3)*, 347-370.

[2] Ferreira, A.C., Silva, L.T., and Ramos, R.R. 2012. Urban Observatories, Tools for Monitoring Cities. In *8th IASME/WSEAS International Conference on Energy, Environment, Ecosystems and Sustainable Development (EEESD'12)*.

[3] Haller, S., Karnouskos, S., and Schroth, C. 2009. *The Internet of Things in an Enterprise Context.* Domingue, J., Fensel, D., and Traverso, P. (Eds.): FIS 2008, LNCS 5468, Springer-Vertlag Berlin Heidelberg, 14-28.

[4] Kanjo, E., Benford, S., Paxton, M., Chamberlain, A., Stanton Fraser, D., Woodgate, D., Crellin, D., and Woolard, A. 2018. MobGeoSen: Facilitating Personal Geosensor Data Collection and Visualization using Mobile Phones. *Per Ubiquit Comput 12*, 599-607.

[5] Martin, S., Stanton Fraser, D., Fraser, M., Woodgate, D., and Crellin, D. 2010. The impact of hand held mobile technologies upon children's motivation and learning. In *9th World Conference on Mobile and Contextual Learning* (Malta, October 01, 2010).

[6] Mulholland, P., Anastopoulou, S., Collins, T., Feisst, M., Gaved, M., Kerawalla, L., Paxton, M., Scanlon, E., Sharples, M. and Wright, M. 2012. nQuire: Technological Support for Personal Inquiry Learning. *IEE Transactions on Learning Technologies 5 (2)*, 157-169.

[7] Tan, D.K.C., Hedberg, J.G., Seng, K.T., and Choo, S.W. 2005. Dataloggers and Inquiry Science. In *2005 Redesigning Pedagogy Conference: Research, Policy, Practice* (Singapore).

[8] Tan, L. and Wang, N. 2010. Future Internet: The Internet of Things. In *2010 3rd International Conference on Advanced Computer Theory and Engineering* (ICACTE).

# TangiPlan: Designing an Assistive Technology to Enhance Executive Functioning Among Children with ADHD

Orad Weisberg[1], Ayelet Gal-Oz[1], Ruth Berkowitz[2], Noa Weiss[2], Oran Peretz[1], Shlomi Azoulai[1], Daphne Kopleman-Rubin[2], Oren Zuckerman[1]

[1]Media Innovation Lab, Sammy Ofer School of Communications, The Interdisciplinary Center (IDC) Herzliya
[2]LD & ADHD Unit, School of Psychology, The Interdisciplinary Center (IDC) Herzliya
{oweisberg, goayelet, daphnekr, orenz}@idc.ac.il,
{rruthberko, noaw22, oranperetz, azshlomi}@gmail.com

## ABSTRACT

Children with Attention Deficit and Hyperactivity Disorder (ADHD) experience a deficit in cognitive processes responsible for purposeful goal-directed behaviors, known as executive functioning (EF). In an effort to improve EF, we are developing TangiPlan – a set of tangible connected objects that represent tasks children perform during their morning routine. We describe the initial stages of a user-centered design process, consisting of interviews with both domain experts and potential users, followed by paper prototyping. Based on our findings, we formulated preliminary design principles for EF assistive technology: facilitate organization, time management and planning; involve caregivers in the process, but strive to reduce conflict; implement intervention techniques suggested by experts; avoid distraction by mobile phones; avoid intrusion. We discuss the benefits of implementing these principles with a tangible interface, present our prototype design, and describe future directions.

## Categories and Subject Descriptors

H.5.2 [**Information Interfaces and Presentation**]: User Interfaces – *Prototyping, User-centered design.* K.4.2 [**Computers and Society**]: Social Issues – *Assistive technologies for persons with disabilities.*

## Keywords

ADHD; Executive Functions; Time Management; Children; Tangible; Assistive Technology.

## 1. INTRODUCTION

Attention Deficit and Hyperactivity Disorder (ADHD), estimated at 3%-7% in school-age children, is reflected in a persistent pattern of inattention and/or hyperactivity-impulsivity [1]. Inattention may manifest in academic, occupational, or social situations. Individuals with this disorder may fail to give close attention to details or may make careless mistakes in schoolwork or other tasks. They may also have difficulties sustaining attention in tasks, and often find it hard to persist with a task until

completion. They are easily distracted and often forgetful in daily activities [1].

Central to the meaning of ADHD is a deficit in cognitive processes responsible for ongoing, purposeful, goal-directed behaviors, known as Executive Functioning (EF) [7, 16]. EF includes inhibition (self-control, self-regulation), cognitive flexibility and working memory [11], problem-solving, reasoning and planning [3]. Behavioral manifestations of poor EF are Organization, Time Management, and Planning (OTMP) difficulties, which adversely affect children's functioning and persist through adulthood [2].

Besides medication, treatment for ADHD typically is directed at enhancing cognitive and learning skills [e.g. 17], emphasize social and emotional functioning [e.g. 6] or both [10]. Since OTMP problems reflect a performance rather than skill deficit, successful interventions include behavior modification that rewards goal-based behaviors, which can increase the occurrence of these behaviors and ostensibly reinforce the behavior chain linked to goal attainment as well [5].

We set out to design an assistive technology, aimed to help middle school children with ADHD improve EF. We based our prototype, called TangiPlan, on strategies employed by ADHD clinicians. TangiPlan is currently being designed in an iterative process. In this paper we describe the initial stages of the design process, consisting of interviews with domain experts and users, followed by paper-prototyping. We present preliminary design principles, and explain how we are implementing them into a tangible prototype.

## 2. RELATED WORK

Several assistive technologies aimed to enhance executive functioning were presented in recent years, though not specifically targeting children with ADHD. ProcedurePal [4] is a smartphone application for rehearsing common daily tasks. Tasks are defined and divided into smaller steps, each represented by an image. Users view the images to learn how to perform the task. TaskTracker [9] is a smartphone application enabling users to define tasks for themselves, set alarms and motivational messages, and then track actual progress. Basic Calendar [12] is a smartphone application that enables task-tracking through a customized calendar interface. It also enables others to remotely add tasks for the user. Time Timer (http://www.timetimer.com) is a physical timer with a red disc that disappears as time elapses, making it easier to visualize how much time is left for completing a task. Watchminder (http://watchminder.com) is a vibrating wrist watch for setting alarms.

While these systems address various aspects of executive functions, some of them are intrusive, often displaying reminders and alarms. It is unclear whether children with ADHD would be willing to use such systems. Furthermore, when the system is a smartphone application, children with ADHD might get distracted by other applications on their phone. Hence, we strive to develop a non-intrusive tangible system.

## 3. SYSTEM DESIGN PROCESS
### 3.1 Interviewing Domain Experts
Our first step was consulting experts in the field of ADHD.

#### 3.1.1 Participants
Three highly experienced educational psychologists and a psychiatrist, all specializing in treating children with ADHD, were interviewed.

#### 3.1.2 Method
Participants were asked to list common challenges that middle school children with ADHD are facing, and describe current intervention and treatment techniques.

#### 3.1.3 Results and Discussion
Participants explained that children with ADHD experience academic, behavioral, emotional, and social difficulties. However, many intervention programs focus only on learning skills. A prevalent challenge concerns lack of efficiency in maintaining daily routines, due to a deficit in executive functioning. This challenge is equally prevalent among boys and girls. Therefore, we decided to focus on enhancing efficiency in daily routines. Currently, in order to increase efficiency, children are advised to: (1) Plan a daily schedule and allocate time for each activity. (2) Separate complicated tasks into smaller, more manageable ones. (3) Write to-do lists and reminders. (4) Ask for assistance from caregivers or friends. (5) Use a stop-watch to track task completion time. Participants also stressed the importance of caregiver involvement – caregivers are known to play a crucial role in children's motivation and ability to overcome challenges.

### 3.2 Interviewing Potential Users
Our second step was interviewing potential users in order to learn more about their challenges with daily routines, and particularly how they attempt to overcome these challenges.

#### 3.2.1 Participants
Six child-parent pairs (children: 4 males, 2 females; parents: 1 father, 5 mothers) were interviewed. All children were 12 years old, and currently receiving treatment for ADHD. They were referred to the study by their psychologist.

#### 3.2.2 Method
Interviews were conducted at families' homes. Parent and child were interviewed separately for approximately 30 minutes each. The interviews were recorded; the audio recordings were later transcribed. Two researchers independently analyzed the transcriptions to identify emerging common themes.

#### 3.2.3 Results and Discussion
Similarly to experts, parents described a lack of efficiency in children's ability to follow daily routines (*"He goes around the house without planning ahead; he just goes from one room to another"*). The morning routine was considered particularly important (*"If his morning starts badly, he would be on edge all day"*). Furthermore, this specific routine was relatively similar among all participants. Therefore, we decided to focus on the morning routine. Inefficiency often results in wasting too much time on one task, then having to rush through the remaining tasks (*"He can spend 10 minutes tying his shoes, and would only carry on when I call him"*). Most parents said they constantly have to monitor their children, rush them when necessary, and verify they don't forget anything. Consequently, the atmosphere in the house could become tense and unpleasant (*"I want to start my day without my mom shouting at me"*).

Morning inefficiency appears to bother parents more than children (*"When I forget my key I say to myself 'I am so stupid', but two minutes later I forget all about it"*). Some parents are extremely bothered, so even though they wish their children would become independent, they perform tasks for them to ensure successful completion (*"I never organize my school bag; my mom does that for me"*). Interestingly, children don't mind keeping their parents involved in their morning routine, mainly because this involvement compels them to be ready on time (*"The only thing that makes me go out of bed is mom standing at the door"*).

When asked which techniques are employed to increase efficiency, most children explained that they tried writing notes, but found it tedious and irrelevant (*"Why should I write notes on paper when I have my mobile device? That's stupid"*). Most of them tried setting reminders and various timers on their phone, but perceived those as annoying (*"I'm tired and cranky in the morning, I don't want something beeping at me all the time"*). Moreover, mobile phones could potentially become a distraction (*"If I open my phone and see I have new massages, there is no way I can ignore them. I can spend 5-10 minutes in conversation and mom gets angry at me"*). Accordingly, most children are not allowed to use their mobile phone in the morning.

Based on the interviews with both experts and users, we formulated preliminary design principles for an EF assistive technology: (1) Facilitate organization, time management and planning. (2) Involve caregivers in the process, as they are the main agents of change, but strive to reduce conflict. (3) Implement intervention techniques suggested by experts. (4) Avoid distraction by mobile phones. (5) Avoid intrusion.

### 3.3 Initial Design
Our third step was implementing the design principles in TangiPlan – a system of tangible connected objects. Each object represents a task that needs to be performed in the morning. Using TangiPlan consists of two main stages: planning and execution.

*Planning:* during this stage, which occurs at the previous evening, parent and child divide the morning routine into small tasks, and allocate time for completing each one. This strategy corresponds with the suggestions of experts for increasing efficiency. Once the list of tasks is ready, the child pairs each task with a tangible object, and then places each object at the location where the task is supposed to be performed. The benefits of using a tangible interface are three-fold: first, avoiding potential distraction by mobile phones. Second, the tangible objects act as physical non-intrusive reminders for performing the corresponding tasks. Third, the tangible objects are location-specific, and location has been shown to enhance cognitive processes like memory and learning

[8, 13, 14]. Thus, the use of location-specific tangible objects potentially has cognitive advantages.

*Execution:* during this stage, which occurs the next morning, the child activates each object at the beginning of the task, and deactivates it when the task is complete. While active, the object intuitively indicates elapsing time, assisting the child with time-management. The order of performing the various tasks is flexible: a certain task could be performed first one day, and last another day. This flexibility allows the child to change the internal order of tasks according to external circumstances, as well as maintain a sense of autonomy. Autonomy has been shown to positively affect task perseverance among youth with ADHD [15].

The tangible objects are connected to a web-based interface to enable real-time monitoring of task-completion. Real-time monitoring enables parents to remain informed from a distance, hopefully reducing conflict. Moreover, real-time monitoring can remind children to complete overlooked tasks before leaving the house. In the long run, the system could provide analytical performance-based information, for example suggestions to allocate more or less time to a certain task.

## 3.4 Paper Prototyping

Our fourth step was creating a paper prototype of the system in order to validate our initial design. The paper prototype consisted of simple cardboard cubes, 3cmX3cmX4cm in size. These are the minimal dimensions required for the desired electronic components. We also created a document for pairing tasks with objects. The document consisted of a table with four columns: number, name of task, time per task, remarks.

Our research questions were: (1) Can users pair morning tasks with tangible objects? (2) On average, how many tasks are included in the morning routine of a child with ADHD? (3) Where would children choose to place the objects?

### 3.4.1 Participants

Three child-parent pairs participated in the study. They were recruited from the sample that was previously interviewed, based on availability. All children were males and parents were females.

### 3.4.2 Method

A research assistant visited participants in their home, and presented them with the paper prototype. First, participants were asked to pair tasks with objects, using the table. Then, the child placed the cardboard cubes in the locations where corresponding tasks would be performed the next morning. Lastly, parents and children were interviewed regarding this experience and their general impression of TangiPlan. The interviews were recorded; the recordings were later transcribed and independently analyzed by two researchers to identify emerging common themes.

### 3.4.3 Results and Discussion

Overall, the results were promising: parents and children liked the general concept, and found it relatively easy to pair tasks with cardboard cubes. They usually listed 12-15 tasks in the table, having learned from past experience to divide the morning routine into micro-tasks, for example: *"wear shoes"*, *"take house keys"*.

The cardboard cubes were placed by children in various locations around the house, for example: near the sink in the bathroom or inside a shoe (see Figure 1). We learned that the tangible objects

should be durable. Moreover, several cubes were placed in shared spaces, which are also used by parents and siblings as part of their own morning routine. Therefore, we should prevent accidental activation, and refrain from disturbing other family members.

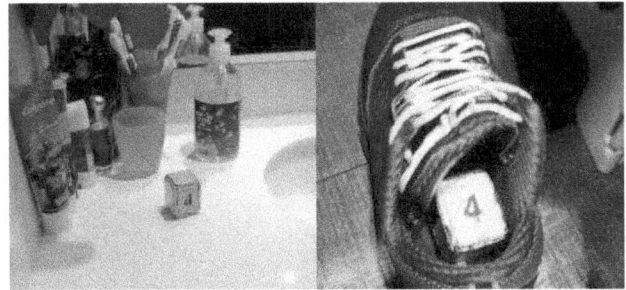

**Figure 1. Locations where the tangible objects of TangiPlan would be placed: near the sink (left) and inside a shoe (right).**

## 3.5 The TangiPlan Prototype Design

Our fifth step was designing the tangible objects. They were designed as a 3D pyramid, the wide base ensuring steadiness. A nano-Arduino board, a WiFi board, a LED matrix, and a battery are embedded inside the object. The entire front panel is transparent to allow LED lighting to be easily observed from several angles (see Figure 2).

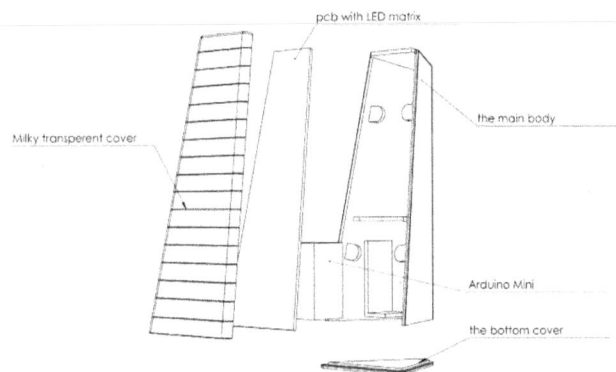

**Figure 2. Design of the tangible object of TangiPlan.**

The TangiPlan system is comprised of multiple objects, each intended to represent a single task in the child's morning routine. All objects are identical to allow interchangeability between them, and thus flexibility. Our main goal is facilitating organization, time-management and planning. Organization is supported by physically placing objects at intended locations for performing tasks. Time-management is supported by the interaction with the object – as time elapses, white light flows across the front cover from top to bottom, resembling a "digital hourglass". When the allocated time for a task is up, red light begins to flow in the opposite direction. Planning is supported by pairing tasks with objects, and allocating time intervals for completing each task.

We are currently designing additional interactions to support the remaining design principles and considerations. For example, objects will light up only after manual activation by the child, thus remaining relatively unnoticeable for other family members.

Future work includes designing additional components of the system, implementation of a web-based interface and analytical tools, as well as conducting user studies to evaluate the usability and effectiveness of TangiPlan.

## 4. CONCLUSION

Children with ADHD experience a deficit in executive functioning (EF). We set out to design an EF assistive technology, intended to improve efficiency during morning routines. Our first step was consulting experts to learn which strategies they currently employ. Our second step was interviewing potential users to learn more about their specific challenges. Based on our findings, we formulated preliminary design principles for an EF assistive technology: (1) Facilitate organization, time management and planning. (2) Involve caregivers in the process, but strive to reduce conflict. (3) Implement intervention techniques suggested by experts. (4) Avoid distraction by mobile phones. (5) Avoid intrusion. Our third step was implementing these principles in an initial design. We chose a tangible interface, which offers unique benefits for children with ADHD: association with location, minimal distraction and intrusion. Our fourth step was validating the initial design with a paper prototype. Our fifth step was designing 3D tangible objects to represent tasks children perform during their morning routine.

## 5. ACKNOWLEDGMENTS

We would like to thank Prof. Mario Mikulincer for initiating the collaboration that led to this research; Ms. Tamar Gal for her assistance with market research and transcribing interview recordings; the experts and families who participated in our studies, for offering their time and valuable insights.

## 6. REFERENCES

[1] American Psychiatric Association. 2013. *Diagnostic and statistical manual of mental disorders.* 5th Ed. American Psychiatric Publishing, Arlington, VA.

[2] Barkley, R. A., and Fischer, M. 2011. Predicting impairment in major life activities and occupational functioning in hyperactive children as adults: Self-reported executive function (EF) deficits versus EF tests. *Dev. Neuropsychol.* 36(2), 137-161. DOI= 10.1080/87565641.2010.549877.

[3] Blair, C., and Razza, R. P. 2007. Relating effortful control, executive function, and false belief understanding to emerging math and literacy ability in kindergarten. *Child. Dev.* 78(2), 647-663. DOI= 10.1111/j.1467-8624.2007.01019.x.

[4] Carrington, P., Kuber, R., Anthony, L., Hurst, A., and Prasad, S. 2012. Developing an interface to support procedural memory training using a participatory-based approach. In *Proceedings of the 26th Annual BCS Interaction Specialist Group Conference on People and Computers* (Birmingham, UK, September 12 - 14, 2012). BCS-HCI '12. British Computer Society, Swinton, UK, 333-338.

[5] DuPaul, G. J., and Stoner, G. D. 2004. *ADHD in the schools: Assessment and intervention strategies.* Guilford Press, New York, NY.

[6] Freilich, R., and Shechtman, Z. 2010. The contribution of art therapy to the social, emotional, and academic adjustment of children with learning disabilities. *Art. Psychother.* 37(2), 97-105. DOI= 10.1016/j.aip.2010.02.003.

[7] Gioia, G. A., Isquith, P. K., Kenworthy, L., and Barton, R. M. 2002. Profiles of everyday executive function in acquired and developmental disorders. *Child. Neuropsychol.* 8(2), 121-137. DOI= 10.1076/chin.8.2.121.8727.

[8] Godden, D. R., and Baddely, A. D. 1975. Context-dependent memory in two natural environments: On land and underwater. *Brit. J. Psychol.* 66(3), 325-331. DOI= 10.1111/j.2044-8295.1975.tb01468.x.

[9] Hribar, V. E. 2011. The TaskTracker: Assistive technology for task completion. In *Proceedings of the 13th international ACM SIGACCESS Conference on Computers and Accessibility* (Dundee, Scotland, UK, October 24 – 26, 2011). ASSETS '11. ACM, New York, NY, 327-328. DOI= 10.1145/2049536.2049631.

[10] Kopelman-Rubin, D., Brunstein Klomek, A., Al-Yagon, M., Mufson, L., Apter, A., and Mikulincer, M. 2012. Psychological intervention for adolescents diagnosed with learning disorders-I Can Succeed (ICS) treatment model, feasibility and acceptability. *I JRLD.* 1(1), 37-54.

[11] Miyake, A., Friedman, N. P., Emerson, M. J., Witzki, A. H., Howerter, A., and Wager, T. D. 2000. The unity and diversity of executive functions and their contributions to complex 'Frontal Lobe' tasks: A latent variable analysis. *Cognitive. Psychol.* 4(1), 49-100. DOI= 10.1006/cogp.1999.0734.

[12] Molinero, A. A., Hernández, F. J., Zorrilla, A. M., and Zapirain, B. G. 2012. Technological solution for improving time management skills using an android application for children with ADD. In *Proceedings of the 4th international conference on Ambient Assisted Living and Home Care* (Vitoria-Gasteiz, Spain, December 3 - 5, 2012). IWAAL'12. Springer-Verlag Berlin, Heidelberg, 431-434. DOI= 10.1007/978-3-642-35395-6_58.

[13] Nadel, L., and Willner, J. 1980. Context and conditioning: A place for space. *Physiol. Psychol.* 8(2), 218-228. DOI= 10.3758/BF03332853.

[14] Smith, S. M., and Vela, E. 2001. Environmental context-dependent memory: A review and meta-analysis. *Psychon. B. Rev.* 8(2), 203-220. DOI= 10.3758/BF03196157.

[15] Thomassin, K., and Suveg, C. 2012. Parental autonomy support moderates the link between ADHD symptomatology and task perseverance. *Child. Psychiat. Hum. D.* 43(6), 958-967. DOI= 10.1007/s10578-012-0306-1.

[16] Welsh, M. C. 2002. Developmental and clinical variations in executive functions. In *Developmental variations in learning: Applications to social, executive function, language, and reading skills,* D. L. Molfese, and V. J. Molfese, Eds. Lawrence Erlbaum Associates, Mahawah, NJ, 139-185.

[17] Wexler, J., Vaughn, S., Roberts, G., and Denton, C. A. 2010. The efficacy of repeated reading and wide reading practice for high school students with severe reading disabilities. *Learning Disabilities Research & Practice.* 25(1), 2-10. DOI= 10.1111/j.1540-5826.2009.00296.

# ExciteTray: Developing an Assistive Technology to Promote Self-Feeding Among Young Children

Ayelet Gal-Oz[1], Orad Weisberg[1], Tal Keren-Capelovitch[2], Yair Uziel[1], Ronit Slyper[1],
Patrice L. (Tamar) Weiss[2], Oren Zuckerman[1]

[1]Media Innovation Lab, Sammy Ofer School of Communications, The Interdisciplinary Center (IDC) Herzliya
[2]Department of Occupational Therapy, University of Haifa

goayelet@idc.ac.il, oweisberg@idc.ac.il, tlnzvkrn@netvision.net.il, yair.uziel@post.idc.ac.il,
rys@cs.cmu.edu, tamar@research.haifa.ac.il, orenz@idc.ac.il

## ABSTRACT

Typically developing children usually master self-feeding by the age of three years. However, children with Cerebral Palsy and other developmental disabilities encounter great difficulties acquiring this instrumental ability. In an effort to motivate young eaters in the process of acquiring self-feeding abilities, we set out to develop ExciteTray – a customized self-feeding assistive technology. We describe the initial stages of an iterative design process consisting of interviews with domain experts, rapid-prototyping, and evaluations with children. Based on our findings, we formulated preliminary design principles for a self-feeding assistive technology: draw attention without causing distraction; motivate the child during the various stages of self-feeding; facilitate face-to-face interaction between caregiver and child; adapt feedback to the cognitive and motor ability of each child. We explain how these principles were implemented in a prototype, discuss safety considerations and describe future work.

## Categories and Subject Descriptors

H.5.2 [**Information Interfaces and Presentation**]: User Interfaces – *Prototyping, User-centered design.* K.4.2 [**Computers and Society**]: Social Issues – *Assistive technologies for persons with disabilities.*

## General Terms

Design, Human Factors.

## Keywords

Food; Self-Feeding; Children; Caregiver; Assistive Technology; Cerebral Palsy.

## 1. INTRODUCTION

Eating is a complex process with physiological, biomechanical, and behavioral aspects involving the whole body [12]. Food items must be identified and located, grasped to be brought to the mouth, ingested, chewed, swallowed and digested. Disruption of any one of these steps may lead to malnutrition, poor growth, developmental delay and loss of general health and well-being.

Eating and feeding are also emotional and social experiences for both caregiver and child, with opportunities for communication and intimacy but which may also entail struggle and conflict [1].

Self-feeding involves a complex, multi-dimensional process with sub-systems that are expected to dynamically self-organize as children shift to higher levels of independent performance [15]. The self-feeding process is mastered by a typically developing child by the age of three years [7, 12, 14]. In contrast, children with Cerebral Palsy (CP) and other developmental disabilities have great difficulty in becoming independent in this vital skill.

CP describes a group of developmental disorders of movement and posture leading to activity restriction that is attributed to disturbances occurring in the fetal or infant brain [13]. Motor impairment may be accompanied by a seizure disorder and by disturbances of sensation, cognition, communication and behavior [2]. Children with CP often have significant feeding and eating difficulties due to impairments in oral-motor control, posture and movement [4] or their difficulty in consuming different textures of food [16].

We set out to develop a customized self-feeding assistive technology, aimed to motivate very young children with CP throughout the gradual process of acquiring independent eating skills. The technology – ExciteTray – is currently in its second prototype stage. The iterative design and prototyping process consists of interviews with domain experts, rapid-prototyping, and evaluations of children while they eat with the tray. In this paper we describe the design principles formulated thus far, present our initial prototypes and discuss findings from a user study.

## 2. RELATED WORK

Food-related interactions have been recognized as a challenge for the HCI community, because physical, physiological, cognitive and social factors have to be taken into account [5]. It is particularly challenging to design such interactions for young children due to developmental and safety concerns.

EducaTableware [10] are interactive tableware devices (fork or cup) intended to make eating more enjoyable by emitting sounds when a child eats or drinks. Sensing Fork [8, 9] is a fork-type sensing device, which detects children's eating actions and chosen food items. This device is connected to a smartphone that analyzes sensor data, and provides feedback through a game application. Playful Bottle [3] is an augmented water bottle that uses a smartphone to track water intake. It aims to encourage drinking by using water intake as input for a mobile game. Playful Tray [11] aims to reduce meal completion time with a weight-sensitive tray that tracks children's eating actions. These are then used as input for an interactive game embedded within the tray.

While these systems address various challenges experienced by children while eating and drinking, they have not been adapted to the unique requirements of children with developmental disabilities such as CP. Furthermore, many systems draw attention to a screen-based game, thereby reducing face-to-face interaction between caregiver and child during meals. In contrast, we strive to develop a system that preserves face-to-face interactions rather than shift the child's or caregiver's attention towards a screen.

## 3. SYSTEM DESIGN PROCESS

ExciteTray is being designed by an interdisciplinary team that includes an occupational therapist specializing in CP management, a rehabilitation technology researcher, and HCI researchers and practitioners. We set out to develop an assistive technology that motivates young children in the process of acquiring self-feeding skills.

### 3.1 Interviews with Domain Experts

Our first step was interviewing expert clinicians who treat children with developmental disabilities.

#### 3.1.1 Participants

Participants were staff members of a rehabilitation daycare center for young children (8-36 months old): the director of the center, a senior care-giver, an occupational therapist, and an assistant. All participants feed children with developmental disabilities, including CP, on a daily basis.

#### 3.1.2 Method

Interviews were conducted at the daycare center while participants were not actively caring for the children. Participants were interviewed separately, for approximately 20 minutes each, regarding the challenges they face in feeding children, and types of feedback they give during meals. The interviews were recorded with the consent of participants. The recordings were later transcribed and independently analyzed by two researchers to identify emerging common themes.

#### 3.1.3 Results and Discussion

Participants described a typical meal at the daycare center as a shared experience, where all children sit at a communal table and eat their meal at the same time. Each staff member is in charge of 1 or 2 children. Children with developmental disabilities have difficulty in focusing only on eating, so staff members often need to draw their attention to the plate, and verbally motivate them throughout the meal. Considering that children have a wide range of motor and cognitive impairments, caregivers must adapt "verbal rewards" according to the individual needs of each child. It was agreed by all participants that the most common challenge in the self-feeding process is using a utensil to scoop food from the plate.

In addition, it was evident that the act of feeding has considerable implications beyond nutrition; this daily interaction with caregivers is an intimate, bonding experience that provides social and emotional support for the children. This daily interaction also enables caregivers to monitor individual progress.

Based on these findings, we formulated five preliminary design principles for a self-feeding assistive technology: (1) Draw attention to the plate. (2) Motivate the child during the various stages of self-feeding. (3) Avoid or prevent distractions, to the child and to others. (4) Facilitate face-to-face interaction between caregiver and child. (5) Adapt feedback to the individual cognitive and motor ability of each child.

### 3.2 Initial Prototype

The first iteration of the prototype consisted of a standard food tray that was augmented with 10 LEDs, mounted in a row just below the surface near its upper edge (see Figure 1, left). The LEDs were programmed to display animations including blinking and side-to-side wave. The lights are intended to draw the child's attention towards the plate (design principle 1), and act as a digital reward for specific self-feeding actions (design principle 2). The visual feedback is not overly distracting (design principle 3). The LEDs are activated by the caregiver, using a custom remote switch. This allows caregivers to trigger the visual feedback as appropriate, and to adapt the feedback to the cognitive and motor ability of each child (design principles 4 and 5).

The tray was built with an Arduino prototyping microcontroller, powered by 4 AA batteries. Ten LEDs in various colors were wired for individual control (see Figure 1, right). A black cloth and a bag of soft material were attached to the back of the tray to cover the electronics.

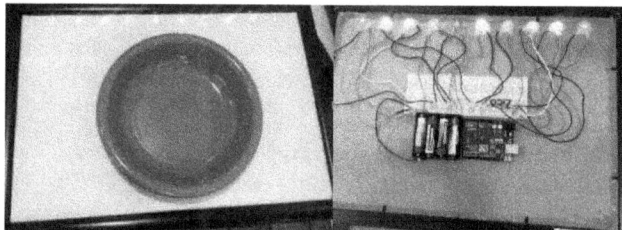

**Figure 1. Version 1 of the ExciteTray prototype. Left: top side. Right: bottom side (uncovered).**

We minimized potential risks related to the use of the tray with the following measures:

- The tray is battery-operated and does not require high-voltage electricity.
- All electronics were completely isolated, preventing the child from any direct contact with these parts.
- The LEDs on the top side of the tray cannot become heated and are not dangerous in any way; but, as a general precaution, they were covered with clear tape so the caregiver or child could not touch them directly.
- The tray's materials include wood, plastic and glue that are safe for children, with no toxic materials.
- The tray was designed with protective plastic and cloth covering over the LEDs, electronic parts, and batteries to protect those parts from the spilling of any liquids or moist foods during the meal.

### 3.3 User Study

A user study was conducted in order to validate the preliminary design principles, and to evaluate children's self-feeding behavior while using the tray. The study focused on the action of scooping food from the plate. This specific action was selected because it was previously described by experts as especially difficult for children.

In the field of occupational therapy, understanding typical development is the foundation to understanding and detecting diversity or disability [6]. Similarly, we need to understand how typically developing children respond to ExciteTray, as a baseline that will allow us to understand the responses of children with CP. Therefore, the user study reported here was conducted with typically developing children.

### 3.3.1 Participants
Four typically developing children (2 boys, 2 girls), 16-24 months old, participated in the study. Parents signed informed consent forms for their children prior to participating in the study.

### 3.3.2 Method
The study was conducted by a senior occupational therapist, experienced in feeding children of this age group. She conducted a feeding session using ExciteTray with each child at his or her home. All sessions were videotaped. Parents prepared food for their child and remained nearby. They were instructed not to react to the tray themselves, to prevent them from influencing their child. At the beginning of the session, the therapist demonstrated to the child how the tray works, and explained that "every time you scoop food from the plate, the tray will light up". This explanation was intended to clarify the cause-and-effect relationship between the scooping event and the lighting up of the tray. Using a "Wizard of Oz" methodology, the therapist operated the tray herself with the remote switch. She activated the LEDs whenever scooping occurred. The session ended when all food was consumed, or when the child signaled that he or she had finished the meal (usually after 3 to 6 minutes).

### 3.3.3 Results and Discussion
Video recordings were independently analyzed by two researchers. We present the results according to the five design principles we aimed to validate:

*Do children pay attention to the tray?* Directing one's gaze towards the tray was the main indication of paying attention to the tray. One boy and one girl consistently directed their gaze towards the tray whenever it lit up. The boy (the oldest participant, who had the highest level of ability) also said "lights", and "tested" the tray's feedback by delaying the insertion of the spoon to his mouth. These two behaviors were only observed once. In contrast, the other two participants only directed their gaze towards the tray sporadically, often missing occurrences when it lit up. In sum, it appears that the lights do not draw enough attention towards the plate.

*Does the tray motivate self-feeding?* Even when the lights were noticed by the children, they did not appear to be sufficiently motivating to serve as digital rewards.

*Does the tray distract children from eating?* Noticing the tray light up did not distract any of the children from self-feeding, they simply looked at the lights as they kept scooping food and bringing it towards their mouth.

*Does the tray facilitate face-to-face interaction between caregiver and child?* The therapist served as the caregiver during the study. Even though she was in charge of operating the tray using the remote switch, she was able to focus on the children and communicate with them during the sessions. For example, she called their name if they were distracted by a loud noise outside,

or encouraged them to eat more. The children often looked at her as they ate, establishing eye contact, and responded to her when she talked to them. In sum, it appears that ExciteTray does not obstruct the interaction between caregiver and child.

*Can a caregiver adapt the feedback to the individual abilities of each child?* The caregiver used a remote switch to activate the LEDs when desired, in this case when scooping occurred. The visual feedback could be activated to reward any other self-feeding action. This enables caregivers to adapt the feedback to various ability levels, for example: reward simple actions while feeding children with a low level of ability, and more complex actions while feeding children with a higher level of ability.

## 3.4 Second Prototype
Overall, the results of our initial user study were promising. We observed face-to-face interaction between caregiver and child while using the tray. In addition, the tray was revealed as easy to operate at the discretion of the caregiver, thus adaptable to different levels of ability, and it did not distract children from eating. However, the LED feedback did not draw enough attention to the plate, and did not seem to be sufficiently motivating. Following these findings, we redesigned the tray. In the second iteration of the ExciteTray prototype the LEDs have been placed in a circular display at the center of the tray, surrounding the plate area (see Figure 2). The LEDs were covered by a clear acrylic layer, producing a more dominant yet soothing visual effect. In addition, we added a sunken plate-holder area, to ensure that the plate is leveled with the tray surface and does not block the child's view of the lights. Our next step is examining whether the new design is indeed more engaging for typically developing children. Once this step is accomplished, we will conduct in-depth studies with children with CP.

**Figure 2. Version 2 of the ExciteTray prototype.**

## 4. FUTURE WORK
We plan to continue with the prototype development process, and to incorporate sensors for automatic detection of specific self-feeding related behaviors (e.g. scooping, lifting). We also plan to develop tools for caregivers to assign specific feedback to each behavior. In that manner, detected behaviors will be automatically rewarded with pre-selected feedback. Since manual operation will no longer be required, caregivers could focus on the interaction with the child, or could supervise the feeding of several children simultaneously, as is often required in daycare settings.

The sensor for automatic detection of self-feeding behaviors will be a digital spoon that communicates with ExciteTray. The spoon will be used to both detect and measure eating-related movements, thereby providing caregivers with diagnostic data regarding each child. To date, insufficient information is available regarding the skills required to enable a child to eat independently, nor the factors that impinge upon or delay independence. Little data exists concerning the biomechanics of grasping utensils or the food and bringing it to the mouth, control over the activity kinetics and issues related to motor planning and learning. The digital spoon could provide caregivers with this valuable information.

# 5. CONCLUSION

Children with developmental disabilities encounter great difficulties acquiring self-feeding abilities. We set out to develop an assistive technology aimed to motivate them in the process of mastering self-feeding. In this paper we described the initial design and implementation of "ExciteTray" – an early-stage prototype of a digital food tray, which rewards self-feeding with visual feedback in the form of colorful lights. ExciteTray was designed based on principles derived from interviews with domain experts: (1) draw the child's attention to the plate; (2) motivate the child during the various stages of self-feeding; (3) avoid or prevent distractions; (4) facilitate face-to-face interaction between caregiver and child; (5) allow caregivers to adapt the feedback to the individual cognitive and motor ability of each child. A prototype based on these principles was evaluated in a preliminary user study, following which a second version of the prototype was created. The second version of ExciteTray was designed to draw greater attention towards the plate, and to be more engaging for children. Future work includes additional user studies, as well as automatic detection and measurement of self-feeding behaviors using a digital spoon.

# 6. ACKNOWLEDGMENTS

This research was supported by the I-CORE Program of the Planning and Budgeting Committee and The Israel Science Foundation (grant no. 1716/12). We would like to thank the staff of the daycare center and the families who participated in our studies, for offering their time and valuable insights.

# 7. REFERENCES

[1] Arverdson, J. C., and Brodsky, L., Eds. 1993. Pediatric swallowing and feeding: Assessment and management. Singular Publishing Group Inc., San Diego, CA.

[2] Bax, M., Goldstein, M., Rosenbaum, P., Leviton, A., Paneth, N., Dan, B., Jacobsson, B., and Damiano, D. 2005. Proposed definition and classification of cerebral palsy. Dev. Med. Child. Neurol. 47(8), 571-576. DOI= 10.1017/S001216220500112X.

[3] Chiu, M-C., Chang, S-P., Chang, Y-C., Chu, H-H., Chen, C. C-H., Hsiao, F-H., Ko, J-C. 2009. Playful Bottle: A mobile social persuasion system to motivate healthy water intake. In Proceeding of the 11th International Conference on Ubiquitous Computing (Orlando, Florida, USA, September 30 - October 03, 2009). UbiComp '09. ACM, New York, NY, 185-194. DOI= 10.1145/1620545.1620574.

[4] Cokrill, H. 2009. Feeding. In Finnie's handling the young child with cerebral palsy at home, E. Bower, Ed. Butterworth Heinemann Elsevier, UK, 149-164.

[5] Comber, R., Ganglbauer, E., Choi, J. H-J., Hoonhout, J., Rogers, Y., O'Hara, K., and Maitland, J. 2012. Food and interaction design: Designing for food in everyday life. In Extended Abstracts on Human Factors in Computing Systems (Austin, Texas, USA, May 5 - 10, 2012). CHI EA '12. ACM, New York, NY, 2767-2770. DOI= 10.1145/2212776.2212716.

[6] Delaney, A. L., and Arvedson, J. C. 2008. Development of swallowing and feeding: Prenatal through first year of life. Dev. Disabil. Res. Rev. 14(2), 105-117. DOI= 10.1002/ddrr.16.

[7] Illingworth, R. S. 1980. The Development of the Infant and young child: Abnormal and normal (7th ed.). Churchill Livingstone, London, UK.

[8] Kadomura, A., Li, K. C-Y., Chen, A. Y-C., Chu, H-H., Tsukada, K., and Siio, I. 2013. Sensing Fork and persuasive game for improving eating behavior. In Proceedings of the ACM Conference on Pervasive and Ubiquitous Computing Adjunct Publication (Zurich, Switzerland, September 8 - 12, 2013). UbiComp '13 Adjunct. ACM, New York, NY, 71-74. DOI= 10.1145/2494091.2494112.

[9] Kadomura, A., Li, K. C-Y., Chen, A. Y-C., Nakamori, R., Tsukada, K., Siio, I., and Chu, H-H. 2013. Sensing Fork: Eating behavior detection utensil and mobile persuasive game. In Extended Abstracts on Human Factors in Computing Systems (Paris, France, April 27 - May 2, 2013). CHI EA '13. ACM, New York, NY, 1551-1556. DOI= 10.1145/2468356.2468634.

[10] Kadomura, A., Tsukada, K., and Siio, I. 2013. EducaTableware: Computer-augmented tableware to enhance the eating experiences. In Extended Abstracts on Human Factors in Computing Systems (Paris, France, April 27 - May 2, 2013). CHI EA '13. ACM, New York, NY, 3071-3074. DOI= 10.1145/2468356.2479613.

[11] Lo, J-L., Lin, T-Y., Chu, H-H., Chou, H-C., Chen, J-H., Hsu, J. Y-J., and Huang, P. 2007. Playful Tray: Adopting ubicomp and persuasive techniques into play-based occupational therapy for reducing poor eating behavior in young children. In Proceeding of the 9th International Conference on Ubiquitous Computing (Innsbruck, Austria, September 16 - 19, 2007). UbiComp '07. Springer-Verlag, Berlin, Heidelberg, 38-55.

[12] Morris, S. E., and Klein, M. D. 1987. Pre-feeding skills: A comprehensive resource for feeding development. Communication Skill Builders, Tucson, AR.

[13] Rosenbaum, P., Paneth, N., Leviton, A., Goldestein, M., and Bax, M. 2007. A report: The definition and classification of cerebral palsy April 2006. Dev. Med. Child. Neurol. 49(s109), 8-14. DOI= 10.1111/j.1469-8749.2007.tb12610.x.

[14] Sugden, D., and Wade, M. 2013. Typical and atypical motor development. Mac Keith Press, London, UK.

[15] Thelen, E., Kelso, J. A. S., and Fogel, A. 1987. Self-organization system and infant motor development. Dev. Rev. 7(1), 39-65. DOI= 10.1016/0273-2297(87)90004-9.

[16] Weir, K. A., Bell, K. L., Caristo, F., Ware, R. S., Davies, P. S., Fahey, M., Rawicki, B., and Boyd, R. N. 2013. Reported eating ability of young children with cerebral palsy: Is there an association with gross motor function?. Arch. Phys. Med. Rehab. 94(3), 495-502. DOI= 10.1016/j.apmr.2012.10.007.

# Understanding and Fostering Children's Storytelling During Game Narrative Design

Laura Benton, Asimina Vasalou, Daniel Gooch
London Knowledge Lab, Institute of Education
London, UK
l.benton@ioe.ac.uk, a.vasalou@ioe.ac.uk,
d.gooch@ioe.ac.uk

Rilla Khaled
Dept. of Digital Games, University of Malta
Msida, Malta
r.khaled@um.edu.mt

## ABSTRACT

Children typically have extensive expertise and experiences of computer games, which can enable them to make valuable contributions when involved in the design of games. Within this paper we discuss our approach to the involvement of children in the game design process, specifically to inform a game narrative. We describe two design workshops with children, which focused on the design of the narrative within a literacy game based on the Day of the Dead festival. We describe how the knowledge that resulted from these workshops furthered our understanding of children's storytelling schema and preferences for games as well as their approach to story creation and expression during the game design process. We also discuss how our findings informed an initial set of design principles for guiding narrative design within children's games as well as recommendations for including storytelling design activities within the technology design process.

## Categories and Subject Descriptors

H.5.2. User Interfaces: User-centered design.

## General Terms

Design, Human Factors.

## Keywords

Children; Game Narrative Design; Storytelling; Design Process.

## 1. INTRODUCTION

Children have been involved in the design of new technology through approaches such as informant and participatory design for well over a decade. They are considered 'experts' in being children and it is acknowledged that their individual expertise and experiences can enable them to make valuable contributions to the technology design process [4, 5]. In the case of computer games, in particular, children typically have extensive experiences [2], with gaming forming a significant part of children's culture [9]. This experience potentially offers a wealth of knowledge that children could contribute to the game design process, particularly as identifying ways to ensure children's enjoyment of playing the resultant game is seen as a key focus of this process [12].

Previous research has obtained children's input on specific game design features such as for instance game characters, background graphics, game menus and rules. Even though many researchers

have discussed the benefits of involving children in the design of games, several challenges have also been noted. As Duh et al. [7] argued, focusing on the design of specific game functionality can overlook important knowledge about children's experiences, presumptions and cultural values and beliefs that are important to consider within the game design context. Furthermore, although having experiences in a particular area can mean that children may have extremely valuable knowledge and ideas to contribute to the game design process, this can also impact on their pre-conceived notions of what a computer game should include [4], potentially constraining their idea generation to solely producing ideas that they believe the designers are expecting. Indeed, researchers have discussed common situations where children have directly copied from the example ideas provided during design workshops or where they have copied other children's ideas within the group [10, 14]. This imitation, or 'recycling', of design ideas can additionally be observed in terms of the integration of features from existing technology the children are familiar with and have previous experience using [10]. Moreover, in the specific case of learning games, children's ideas often fail to fit with the educational aims of the game as a result of their lack of domain knowledge [15, 16].

In putting these challenges in context, Druin [5] has argued that we should not expect children to be able to successfully contribute to all aspects of the design and development process. Children are more able to contribute "what excites and bores them, what helps them learn, and what can be used in their homes or schools" [5] rather than detailed specifications of technological features. Therefore it is important that researchers carefully consider what they mean when claiming to *involve* child participants in design. Druin's observations are echoed by Fallman [7] who has argued more broadly that design researchers often aim at generating *knowledge* about participants "by involving typical design activities in the research process". The developed product becomes "more of a means than an end" [7]. In line with this view, children's ideas and input have formed the basis for generative research in the context of game design [2, 11, 13].. Danielsson and Wiberg [2] identified the importance of ensuring that educational games for teenagers were not too boring, childish or prejudiced and one design session resulted in a set of guidelines which could be used to verify this. In a second example, during the design of a game aimed at developing emotion regulation for teenagers at a pupil referral unit, Mazzone et al. [11] set out to gather knowledge relating to "the vocabulary, the interests, and the abilities of the pupils" as well as an "understanding of their contexts".

In line with this approach, in this paper we discuss the outcomes of two design workshops with children that took place in the context of an ongoing research project aiming to design a new literacy game for children between the ages of 9-11. Narratives are an important and motivating component of games. As Tan et al. [15] claim, the integration of narrative elements into games to increase children's engagement is now a common technique. In elaborating a storytelling component for our game, we initially chose a fantasy-based design concept foregrounding the relationship between life and death, and its celebration. Death is often a topic of fascination for children and was thus expected to contribute to the motivation of playing the game. We envisioned our game to deliver its literacy content through a series of interactive activities embedded within this shared narrative.

In advancing our design work, we recognised the potentially challenging and sensitive nature of our design concept for our target age group, which could prompt some children to reflect on their own attitudes towards mortality and ideas about life after death. Additionally, in considering game narrative design more broadly, children and adults may understand these narratives differently due to their previously acquired schemata [6]. Even very young children are able to comprehend narrative structures, and involving the children in the narrative design could ensure the resulting game is "contextually, temporally and culturally relevant to their life experiences" [6]. Therefore, our research aim was twofold: (1) to examine children's sense making in the context of our game narrative as well as understand how they construct and tell stories more broadly and (2) to explore how to best support children's storytelling within design activities during the game design process. We chose to investigate these aims through design workshops involving low-tech art materials rather than ask the children to create their own games. This was to mitigate against the children becoming overly focused on other less relevant game mechanics, which may occur during a game creation activity.

The remainder of this paper explores what we learned about the children's approach to storytelling within the context of the narrative design for a literacy game. Based on our findings we contribute a set of design principles for children's games, and storytelling technologies more broadly as well as recommendations for supporting storytelling design activities involving children during the game design process.

## 2. METHODS

### 2.1 Participants

We undertook two design workshops with two classes (year five and six) at a single mainstream primary school in south-east London, located in a socially and ethnically diverse area. The children were all within our target age group (9-11 years). A total of 37 children participated (20 boys and 17 girls), with 22 children from the year five class (aged 9-10) and 15 children from the year six class (aged 10-11). The children were divided into groups of four or five, with a total of five groups in the year five class and four groups in the year six class.

### 2.2 Procedure

Each workshop lasted approximately one hour and was facilitated by three to four researchers, including one fully qualified teacher with specific experience of teaching children with reading/writing difficulties. The children's class teacher was also present throughout the session.It was explained to the class that we were designing a learning game for reading and writing based on the Day of the Dead (a Mexican festival celebrating the lives of relatives/friends who have passed away) and that we needed their ideas for developing the characters and stories within the game. The children were first introduced to the festival as a class by showing them an animated film based on the story of a child's experience of this festival. This provided the children with an overview of the visual style of the festival. One researcher then told a story about a girl and her dog, through which the children

were introduced to the specific customs and traditions associated with the festival.

Within their groups the children were asked to create their own characters for a story about this festival, one living character and one dead. Each group was provided with two paper templates (see Figure 1), which they could fill in with information about each character such as their hobbies/interests, job, and relationship to the other character. Example templates, based on the story that was told to the children earlier, were displayed on an interactive whiteboard as a prompt for groups who were struggling to think of ideas for their characters. Once the children had agreed on their two characters they were then provided with modelling clay as well as a selection of other art materials and asked to build or draw each of their characters. Next the children were asked to create a story about their characters, focusing on why and how one character wants to contact the other character, what they want to say to them and to think about how the story could end. Each group was provided with a blank paper storyboard on which they could document their ideas for their story. Lastly each group was given a Flip video camera and asked to capture their story on this to enable the researchers to share the children's story ideas with the game development team. Due to the setup of the workshop it was not possible to video record the sessions, therefore each of the researchers took written notes to document their observations across teams.

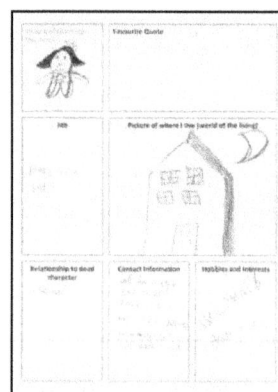

**Figure 1 – Example Character Template**

## 3. FINDINGS

In order to explore the children's approach to storytelling within a game context, a thematic analysis [1] was undertaken on the workshop data. The data included all of the materials produced by the children as well as the researchers' written notes. The analysis aimed to identify relevant themes in terms of the children's approach to understanding the specific game focus and related topics through storytelling as well as how they created and shared their stories through the different design activities. These themes are discussed in detail below.

### 3.1 Understanding children's sense making through storytelling

The original brief set at the beginning of the workshops was for the stories to focus on the communication between the living and dead characters, which five groups successfully managed. The other groups' stories ended up having a slightly different primary focus. Our analysis identified some general themes that occurred across multiple stories. Some groups focused on the *relationship between the two characters* and described a shared experience that they had had together, such as going on an adventure. These were often in the form of missions set by one of the characters that they had to complete and related most directly to the game design context. Some of these stories integrated aspects that the children were familiar with from their everyday lives, particularly family life and friendship, for example: "*Lucas was really upset and jumps up and down on his bed and breaks it, which his mum is really annoyed about and says 'that cost £150 you will have to pay for that now'.*" Within the written notes of the workshop, one researcher also noted that one boy had particular trouble making up characters and instead only talked about characters based on his family and what they do at home.

In addition we identified what we have termed *'nonsensical' story elements*. Example nonsensical ideas included "*a cocker-spaniel loving skeleton called Zorgon*" (see Figure 2), "*his other hobbies include being a hat critic and chihuahuas*" and "*the pirate lives in a caravan and is grandfather to an FBI agent who owns a bullet-proof tuxedo*". These forms of nonsensical story elements, random inclusions that often appear from nowhere and have little relation to reality, requiring the reader/listener to use their own imagination to fill in the gaps, are quite common and appealing features of children's stories. For example, they frequently feature in children's books, such as those written by the well-known author and poet Dr. Seuss.

**Figure 2 – A child's drawing of Zorgon the cocker-spaniel loving skeleton**

Other groups' stories focused on how the living character *enters the world of the dead*. Some children became fascinated with how the dead character had died. They therefore focused their story around this character's death, which in some cases was quite violent, and the emotional response of the living character to this.

Within two groups the theme of *religion* was highlighted. In these groups it was clear that some of the children had religious backgrounds and for them the Day of the Dead festival was associated with religion and their idea of god and heaven/hell. This made prayer the obvious means of communication and they saw the 'world of the dead' as heaven.

## 3.2 Supporting story creation and expression

Within the workshops the children were provided with various tools to plan their stories, which they were encouraged, but not required, to use. Seven of the groups utilised the *character profile paper templates* that allowed them to specify characteristics, relationships and preferences of their story characters and enabled them to develop a backstory. The use of *clay modelling* to develop the visual appearance of their characters was extremely popular (see Figure 3), with eight out of the nine groups using the clay. In addition to this three groups drew out their characters using *pencil and paper*. The *paper storyboard grids* were designed to be used flexibly, with seven of the groups using them to varying extents, some drawing their story, some documenting with text and others using a mix of both. Three of the groups used the storyboards minimally in their story planning and four of the groups used the storyboards more extensively, the remaining groups did not use

them at all. There was evidence of four groups using some level of *verbal improvisation* when filming their story, with some children modifying their original story plan and others generating the majority of the storyline from scratch during this phase.

**Figure 3 – Children creating their clay model characters**

As with the creation of the stories, there were also clear differences between the groups in how they chose to express their final stories. Two groups acted out the majority of their story, six groups used their clay models to help them tell the story, two groups incorporated dancing and/or song within the telling of their story and four groups used their drawings and/or storyboards to aid them in verbally narrating or explaining their story.

## 4. DISCUSSION

The findings presented above have provided a basis for a set of initial design implications to help guide the development of narratives within children's games, as well as recommendations for supporting children's storytelling within design activities during their involvement in the game design process.

## 4.1 Initial design implications

### 4.1.1 Fostering imagination through nonsense

The incorporation of nonsensical and fantasy-based narrative elements within the stories highlighted the children's enjoyment and engagement with this type of narrative content. It also raised the possibility of using this content in order to inspire children's imagination. Integrating nonsensical content within game narratives provides opportunities for children to use their creativity and imagination to 'fill in the gaps' within different stories encountered during the gameplay. It can also provoke curiosity or surprise through the narrative that can support enjoyment and engagement within the game.

### 4.1.2 Providing space to explore the unfamiliar

Although the subject of the characters' death was not positioned as the focus of the story during the workshops, a number of the groups explicitly chose to centre their stories on how one character died. It is possible that the children's engagement with the more macabre elements of the design task (such as the violent way a character died) could be due to the more taboo nature of this topic appealing to children of this age group. Our workshops appeared to provide the children with a safe environment for exploring and grasping more adult topics such as mortality, which could be incorporated into the game narrative. Experiencing emotions associated with topics such as this within a secure environment is important for children to learn how to deal with death in the real world. Therefore whilst topics such as mortality should be handled with care, game designers should not completely avoid the inclusion of more macabre narrative components, as this is a key area of potential appeal and learning for children. Lastly the findings raised the need to consider the handling of certain game topics such as the Day of the Dead sensitively, particularly within the context of religion. It may be necessary to avoid religious associations and connotations where possible to ensure the game narrative does not directly conflict with a child's individual religious beliefs.

### 4.1.3 Social rules and structures
Children created stories that presented relational dynamics between characters based on familiar social structures, rules and experiences from their own social environment. Identifying these recognizable social rules and structures, and reflecting them in the game narrative, may therefore help to support children's comprehension and connection with a game and its educational content. However, it is important to note that game narratives can also provide valuable opportunities for children to learn about unfamiliar social rules and relationships, but that these may be more appropriate to introduce at later points within the narrative when children feel secure with other aspects of the game context.

## 4.2 Recommendations for supporting children's storytelling within design activities
The flexibility of the workshops helped to provide more creative freedom for the children to plan their stories in a way that best matched their preferred approach to story creation and expression. Some children preferred to document their ideas in detail on paper to ensure they did not forget anything and were highly engaged in the creation of detailed drawings or clay models. Whereas others appeared to be at their most creative and engaged when spontaneously generating story ideas in front of the camera and sharing them verbally. Previous research incorporating storytelling-based design activities with children during the game design process typically requires all child participants to share their stories using the same modalities, e.g. [3, 8]. Based on our findings, future work may consider incorporating a number of different options and modalities that further enable the space for personal expression, including audio-visual as well as tangible modalities. Considering the effectiveness of our design approach to support children in telling stories, we believe that multimodality can enable a range of children with different creative and communication styles/preferences to participate, as a consequence giving researchers better insight into the particular questions they want to address.

## 5. CONCLUSION
To conclude we reflect on our findings in the context of Druin's [5] consideration of what children are best able to contribute to the technology design process. Through our design research we have increased our understanding of children's storytelling to provide an engaging experience for children through game narratives as well as how to support their involvement in the game design process within storytelling activities by understanding how they construct and tell stories. This has resulted in an initial set of design guidelines for children's game narrative design in relation to existing social structures, fostering imagination and exploring unfamiliar content as well as recommendations for a multimodal approach to storytelling design activities. Within future work we intend to build on these findings by conducting similar activities specifically with children who have literacy difficulties, to establish how game narratives can best promote their confidence and engagement with game-based literacy activities. We will then use the workshop outcomes to guide development of our game characters, ensuring their background stories report information the children felt was important such as how they died and their relationships with other characters as well as allow the children to discover further nonsensical facts about them through the game play. We hope that this work will be a useful basis for designers

of children's games, and that they will be able to use this a starting point to further extend our proposed design guidelines and recommendations.

## 6. ACKNOWLEDGMENTS
This research was funded by the EU FP7 ICT project iLearnRW (project number: 318803). We thank all of the children for sharing their stories and their teachers for supporting the workshops.

## 7. REFERENCES
[1] Braun, V. and Clarke, V. Using thematic analysis in psychology. *Qualitative Research in Psychology.* 3, 2 (2006), 77–101.

[2] Danielsson, K. and Wiberg, C. Participatory design of learning media: Designing educational computer games with and for teenagers. *Interactive Technology & Smart Education.* 3, 4 (2006), 275–291.

[3] Dindler, C. and Iversen, O.S. Fictional Inquiry - design collaboration in a shared narrative space. *CoDesign.* 3, 4 (2007), 213–234.

[4] Druin, A. Cooperative inquiry: developing new technologies for children with children. *Proc. CHI 1999*, ACM (1999), 592–599.

[5] Druin, A. The role of children in the design of new technology. *Behaviour and IT.* 21, 1 (2002), 1–25.

[6] Duh, H.B., Yew Yee, S.L.C., Gu, Y.X. and Chen, V.H.H. A Narrative-Driven Design Approach for Casual Games with Children. *Proc. SIGGRAPH 2010*, ACM (2010), 19–24.

[7] Fallman, D. Why Research-Oriented Design Isn't Design-Oriented Research: On the Tensions Between Design and Research in an Implicit Design Discipline. *Knowledge, Technology & Policy.* 20, 3 (2007), 193–200.

[8] Giaccardi, E. et al. Embodied Narratives : A Performative Co-Design Technique. *Proc. DIS 2012*, ACM Press (2012), 1–10.

[9] Kafai, Y.B. and Carter Ching, C. Meaningful contexts for mathematical learning: The potential of game making activities. *Proc. ICLS 1996.* International Society of the Learning Sciences (1996), 164-171.

[10] Kuure, L. Halkola, E., Iivari, N., Kinnula, M., and Molin-Juustila, T. Children Imitate! Appreciating recycling in participatory design with children. *Proc PDC 2010*, ACM (2010), 131–140.

[11] Mazzone, E., Read, J.C. and Beale, R. Design with and for disaffected teenagers. *Proc. NordiCHI 2008*, ACM (2008), 290-297.

[12] Moser, C. 2012. Child-centered game development (CCGD): developing games with children at school. *Personal and Ubiquitous Computing.* 17, 8 (2012), 1647–1661.

[13] Nousiainen, T. *Children's Involvement in the Design of Game-Based Learning Environments.* Doctoral Thesis (2008).

[14] Read, J.C., Horton, M. and Mazzone, E. The Design of Digital Tools for the Primary Writing Classroom Involving Children in Product Development. *Proc. ED-Media 2005*, AACE (2005), 1029–1035.

[15] Tan, J.L. Goh, D. H. L., Ang, R. P., and Huan, V. S. Child-centered interaction in the design of a game for social skills intervention. *Computers in Entertainment.* 9, 1 ( 2011), 1–17.

[16] Vasalou, A., Ingram, G. and Khaled, R. User-centered research in the early stages of a learning game. *Proc DIS 2012*, ACM (2012), 116–125.

# Interactive and Live Performance Design with Children

Karen Rust[1], Elizabeth Foss[2], Elizabeth Bonsignore[3], Brenna McNally[4],
Chelsea Hordatt, Meethu Malu, Bie Mei and Hubert Kofi Gumbs
Human-Computer Interaction Lab, University of Maryland
2117 Hornbake Library, South Wing, College Park, MD, 20742
kr579@umd.edu[1]; efoss@umd.edu[2]; ebonsign@umd.edu[3]; bmcnally@umd.edu[4]

## ABSTRACT

Performative Experience Design (PED) is an extension of experience design focusing on the unique time-bound encounter between performers and spectators. Technology is purposefully designed to enhance the experience between audience and performers. PED has been studied with adult participants; however, it has not been explored with children. We conducted a Cooperative Inquiry session to explore 1) how children want to interact with live performances; 2) how they seek to change a story in live performances; and 3) a specific technique that might facilitate designing for such interactions. We present our initial findings regarding children's perceptions of what constitutes live performance and the ways in which children want to use technology to interact with, direct, and respond to narrative structures and characters within live performances. We include a discussion of the features of a specific co-design technique for supporting the ideation process of our child designers.

## Categories and Subject Descriptors

H5.2. [Information Interfaces and Presentation]: User Interfaces – User-centered design

## General Terms

Design, Human Factors

## Keywords

Children, Cooperative Inquiry, co-design, interactive theatre, live performance, Performance Experience Design

## 1. INTRODUCTION

Given the proliferation of pervasive technologies (e.g., mobile, wearable), design approaches to support new kinds of user experience known as pervasive or mixed reality experiences [1] are increasingly of interest to HCI researchers [1,2]. Researchers are establishing new frameworks to guide designers in ways to include spectators (or audience) and performers in meaningful interactions in public spaces [1,2,7]. For example, [1] used an urban street game, *Uncle Roy All Around Us*, to develop design recommendations for using mobile technologies to frame the experience of live performances for bystanders and players, thereby reducing some of the risk inherent with strangers interacting in public spaces. Design work in the area of live performance is also known as Performative Experience Design (PED). PED is an extension of experience design focusing the unique time-bound encounter between performers and spectators,

*IDC'14*, June 17–20, 2014, Aarhus, Denmark.
Copyright 2014 ACM 978-1-4503-2272-0/14/06…$15.00.
http://dx.doi.org/10.1145/2593968.2610478

Figure 1. Technology used in unconventional and conventional ways to interact with a performance. A child directed actors using a slider remote on her shoe (left); another called performers (right).

in which technology is purposefully designed to enhance the experience [7]. These works provide a foundation for understanding how new technologies are breaking "the fourth wall" through which audiences passively experience live performances in traditional, proscenium arch-based theaters. However, these studies focused on the user experience of adults, not children. In contrast, child development studies have shown that children possess a natural predilection toward mixed reality as well as performative play as a means for learning and literacy development [e.g., 3,5]. Our exploratory study aims to build on mixed reality and PED design research for adults to understand children's perceptions of interactive live performance and the consequent live performance designs they are inclined to develop.

In this paper, we present our initial findings regarding children's perceptions of what constitutes interactive, live performance and the ways in which they want to use various technologies to interact with, direct, and respond to the narrative structures and characters within live performances. We worked to explore the questions raised by PED of "how can we understand the dynamic of performative experience between spectator, performer, and device within HCI? How do we reason about interactions with this new dynamic, and how do we design for them?" [7]. We investigated children's ideas through a single design session using techniques that focused on the physical interactions that are possible during live, interactive performances. We found that children 1) tend to limit live performances to musicals and plays held in a space with a clear distinction between stage and audience; 2) are hesitant to break the fourth wall, wanting to remain part of the audience; and 3) believe all audience members need to have a fair and equal chance of interacting with or providing input to a performance.

## 2. METHODS

### 2.1 Cooperative Inquiry and "Big Props"

Children have their own unique opinions and needs that are different from adults so it is important to include children as fundamental stakeholders throughout the design process. [6] Cooperative Inquiry is a design method in which adults and children work as equal partners in an intergenerational design team to solve design problems [6]. Within the Cooperative Inquiry method there are a number of techniques researchers can use to elicit design ideas or feedback from the team. One technique used to facilitate design work when considering how to encourage physical movement is Big Props [8]. For Big Props, small groups of design partners use an assortment of physically large items, such as umbrellas, cardboard boxes, or tablecloths to develop interactions and movements for dynamic situations. We conducted a design session using Big Props because we were specifically concerned with how children approach physical interactions between an audience and the performers.

## 2.2  Design Session Structure

The structure of our design session mirrored previous Cooperative Inquiry sessions [6]. First, all child and adult co-design partners individually answer the question of the day (QoD). This question is developed around the content of the session's activity and helps the partners begin thinking about the design context for the session. The QoD for the interactive theater session was, "What kind of performances have you seen with real people?"

For the co-design task, the team split into three small groups of both adults and children. Seven children, ages 7-11, were grouped by similar ages (i.e., two 7-8 year olds were paired together, as were two 9 year olds and three 10-11 year olds). We used a modified version of the Big Props technique: rather than using typical props, we used readily available pieces of technology (e.g. a flashlight, smartphone, game and television controllers, stopwatch, etc.). The team used these technology props to focus their design ideas on the *interaction* with the performers, rather than having them concentrate on creating new technologies. Each small group received one bag filled with four to six different technology props and were told the technology props did not have to function as expected. The design task given to the groups was "How would you involve audiences in live performances using technology?" Teams also had to demonstrate how they would use the technology props to change each of two predetermined stories.

We purposefully selected a short, traditional tale, and a larger, broader narrative to see what trends would emerge from both. The first story was *Hansel and Gretel*. We gave a brief overview of *Hansel and Gretel* to refresh children's memories. The second story was *Harry Potter*. Here, the children could pick any aspect or story within *Harry Potter*. We chose two stories that varied in aspects such as length, complexity, and genre in order to explore what common themes would emerge across differing stories.

Each group considered how they would interact with the first story using technology and then presented their ideas to the entire team. After these presentations the bags of technology were rotated; the groups created technology interactions for the second story; and their ideas were again presented to the full team. For each presentation, an adult design partner noted the ideas each group presented on a whiteboard. This allowed us to formulate the *Big Ideas* generated from the design session, where a researcher uses the raw notes transcribed on the large whiteboard to identify common themes or unique ideas. One adult presented these ideas to the team and discussed them at the end of the session.

## 2.3  Data Collection and Analysis

At least one adult in each group took participant-observation notes guided by our research questions. Researchers noted how the child co-designers might 1) repurpose or otherwise appropriate the technology; 2) change the story; 3) combine technologies; 4) interact physically with the technology and/or elements of the

story as they enacted it; and 5) engage in any other interesting interactions. Segments of the session and all presentations were also photographed and video recorded.

Immediately after the session, the adult researchers used their field notes to collaboratively code for major themes surrounding how children could affect live performances [4]. During this debriefing session, the adults shared and compared their experiences from their separate small group interactions and their interpretations of the session's outcomes. From this collaborative open-coding process [4], the following major themes arose: controlling performers' behavior; audience factions and voting; audience distance and interaction mediated only via their technology; and telling happier stories. A core group of co-authors conducted a second round of thematic analysis on these themes, during which they grouped similar design ideas together [4].

## 3.  FINDINGS
## 3.1  Reflections on Technique

Although our intention in modifying the Big Props technique was to retain the inherent physicality of the technique, it was occasionally difficult to elicit physical responses from the design team after substituting with technology props. The adult partners found that they had to instigate acting out scenes, as the child partners appeared more comfortable discussing their ideas from a passive, rather than active, perspective. This may have been a result of their more traditional fourth-wall understanding of audience-performer interaction (detailed in the following section). While the children desired the ability to impact the performance, they did not want to become directly involved as performers.

## 3.2  Perceptions of Live Performance

To frame the QoD for the child designers, we presented live performance as any experience in which performers are in front of those watching in real-life. From their responses to the QoD, we found the child partners had a conventional understanding of live performance. The most common answer was a play in a theater, with a distinct divide between audience and performers. No child talked about audience participation. They omitted many different types of performances such as comedy shows, concerts, dance performances, etc. In particular, the children focused on the specific plays and musicals, professional or amateur, they had seen, such as *Peter Pan*, *Hamlet*, or a school play. Some children mentioned the type of performance they had seen, such as opera.

## 3.3  Technology Mappings

The child partners made direct and conventional mappings when using familiar technology props. For example, children used remote controls to affect events and characters in the storyline. Video game controllers manipulated performers directly as if avatars in a game. The youngest children repurposed a television remote as a "secret remote" to set off a bomb. The remote contained buttons for the number one through nine: for larger numbers, there was a bigger explosion. Other conventional mappings included using a flashlight as a beam of light to blind a spider, watching the performance on a smartphone screen, calling the performers on stage with a mobile phone, and wearing headphones to hear what the performers were saying on stage.

Although many of the ways in which the child designers appropriated the technology props were direct mappings to typical uses, they generated a much wider variety of audience interaction options when using a prop with multiple functions in everyday life or whose functions were unfamiliar or amorphous. For example, in the *Harry Potter* scenario, a laser pointer and flashlight enabled performers to act out the game "Quidditch." The laser pen became a light-based "Snitch" that performers playing "Seekers" chased. Likewise, the larger beam shining from a flashlight became a "Quaffle" that performers followed and "caught" as audience members moved the light. Similarly, another group used an old-fashioned aerial antenna as a searching tool (to find the witch from *Hansel and Gretel*). Other alternative mappings included using a stopwatch to store magical spells and transforming a calculator cover into a vehicle for characters in the story. Technologies such as a stopwatch, flashlight, and laser pointer have distinct purposes in everyday life but more amorphous affordances as interaction devices between audience and performer. These technology props do not present specific interaction functions as do game controllers or remotes. Consequently, our child design partners seemed to generate a wider variety of interactions with technology props with more nebulous functions than they did with props with more established functions (i.e., flashlight vs. game controller; antenna vs. remote).

Other unique ways our child designers repurposed technology props were likely the result of unfamiliarity with their uses in everyday life. For example, one bag of technology included a presentation remote (one that advances slides in a computer-based presentation). When an adult design partner asked the children in the group what the object was, they responded that they did not know. Despite its conventional buttons, one child ignored these features, attaching the remote to her shoe. She explained that the number of stomps determined which effect took place (e.g. one stomp caused a spider to appear and attack Hansel and Gretel).

## 3.4 Technology Distribution and Fairness

Child design partners described technologies as intentionally distributed to the audience in a variety of ways and combinations, specifically: 1) randomly given to "lucky" audience members; 2) given on a first come, first serve basis; 3) distributed to every audience member; and 4) passed on to from one audience member to another. In each of these ways, technology, or the means to be a participant-spectator, is *given* to an audience member at the performance venue, rather than having an audience member attend a performance with an existing technology with the freedom to decide whether or not to participate. That is, the child design partners did not presume that potential participant-spectators would have technology available to interact (e.g., mobile phones) before they entered the live performance. If there were factions in the audience (or different roles to fulfill), the audience members who came earliest to the performance could choose what faction they wanted to be a part of or what aspect of the performance they wanted to control based on which technology they chose. Once a limit of available technology or available audience roles was reached, all other members of the audience would be assigned a faction or role randomly. When there was a limit to the number of audience members who could receive an interactive performance technology, the technology would be randomly assigned. In one case, a child designer specified that the technology was hidden under chairs and audience members had to find them.

For each distribution method there was an element of fairness and politeness. Technology was randomly assigned when there was a limit on the amount of technology available. Another idea was to share or pass the technology from one audience member to the next, with audience members given a specific time limit to control their interaction. The idea of politeness also emerged as a small group explained using a smartphone as small screen in front of them so they could see the performance if someone sitting in front

of them was too tall, and to be able to listen to the performance on headphones if a person wanted it to be louder.

## 4. DISCUSSION

### 4.1 The Audience as Directors

Our child design partners sought some aspect of control over the story, wanting to *influence* story narratives, but entirely new story elements and storylines themselves were rare. In only one instance did the children use technology to change a scene and therefore change the plot, in this case when the outcome was undesirable (e.g. Dumbledore dying in the *Harry Potter* series). Instead, the child designers focused on existing characters and story facts. Their emphasis on what actions characters should carry out may have resulted from how we delivered the design prompt. We did not explicitly tell our child design partners they could go beyond the bounds of each story's realm.

Rather than making sweeping plot changes, our child design partners concentrated on directing performers in ways that would help their favorite characters. Directing the performers could have resulted from the technology devices used during the session, as a number of remotes were included. As noted earlier (section 3.3), the children used familiar objects in familiar ways, such as with the Xbox controller to control a character like a video game avatar. In these cases, the child partners used the technology to help protagonists and hinder antagonists. Children identified with the "good guys" in each story (i.e., Hansel and Gretel, Dumbledore from the *Harry Potter* series) while wanting to attack, foil, or control the "bad guy" (i.e., the witch in *Hansel and Gretel*, Voldemort from the *Harry Potter* series). For example, one group used a stopwatch to hold spells for Harry Potter to make it easier for him to cast spells and used a remote control to force Voldemort to dance.

The children talked about how audience members may disagree about directions for performers. Although the audience could direct the performers, the performers explicitly retained the freedom to decide whether or not to respond to audience control. It may be that children trust in performers and familiar theater etiquette to ensure that performers will only respond to audience input that leads to a positive audience experience. Furthermore, while the child designers enjoyed having a voice, they did not see their direction or interaction as the most important aspect of the experience; enjoying the performance was more important.

### 4.2 Audience Experience

Another focus was the experience an audience member would have during the performance. Our child partners did not want to merely observe, but also to attend a memorable and entertaining event. To contribute to their experience, all of the small groups designed wearable devices for the audience (Figure 1).

Even so, audience members – with or without wearable devices to enhance their experience – acted only as participants to facilitate and direct. They did not actively become performers themselves. Only one group gave audience members the option to join performers onstage or not. Limited physical movement and a focus on watching the performance from a distinct, separate area from the performance area underscored our observation that the children were unwilling to break the fourth-wall and resisted becoming performers themselves. The setting the child partners envisioned implicitly had a large audience. This observation simultaneously links to their original notions of conventional in-theater performances and extends their idea of being part of an exciting, mass participation event.

In all cases, communication between the audience and the performers was one-directional. The audience communicated to the performers. There was no performer-to-audience or intra-audience communication, and a technology device, such a remote control, mediated all communication. When an audience member talked directly to a performer, it was only one at a time and through a mobile phone. In the instance where audience members could go on stage, they went as a character from the performance. Additionally, the child's interaction with other performers was limited to a short amount of time on stage consisting mostly of physical actions with little to no dialogue.

## 4.3 Democratization

Our child design partners made it very clear during the design session that any technology system had to be fair and respond to numerous audience members. For example, a technology system acted as a polling device. If the majority of the audience voted for a performer to do one action versus another, the performer would have to do the most popular action. The majority-rule allows audience members to trust the system, because no single audience member is preferred over another. Alternately, a technology required the audience to take turns to decide the next action. The children insisted that each audience faction had a turn to give input. When choosing an action, individual audience members had a variety of pre-determined actions to choose. This format is similar to the "choose your own adventure" books where the reader can pick which storyline they want from a list of options. In this case, however, the most popular choice wins.

In addition to all audience members being heard by performers, all performers were required to be represented within the audience. Generally, groups of audience members would be randomly assigned a character to control. One group of children, however, stated that an individual audience member could control a specific character. For this one-to-one audience-character mapping, characters were assigned on a first-come, first serve basis. The group explained that the audience members most interested in the performance would come early and be able to be the only person to control a specific character or pick which faction of the audience they wanted to be in.

## 5. LIMITATIONS

While we have uncovered several themes and expectations that children have when designing for live, interactive, mixed reality performances, our study was limited to a single, initial 90-minute design session with seven child designers. Our observations are exploratory and can benefit from further investigation. Additional design sessions could 1) focus on the types and directionality of interaction (e.g., intra-audience or performer to audience); or 2) tease apart nuances regarding specific affordances of technology props that elicit unique designs for audience-performer or audience-storyline interaction.

In addition, some of the children's design responses may have stemmed from the way in which the prompts were delivered. For example, we did not explicitly state that they could design live interactions that went beyond a story's known boundaries. Design responses may also have stemmed from the technology props, which were selected for convenience and variety. Based on the observed limits on the design ideas of the children when using well-known and single-purpose technologies, further exploration using amorphous design props, unknown/ rare technologies, or a wider variety of technologies might result in differently designed interactions between audiences and performers.

Our goal for this first session was to learn how children perceived live performance and we did not want to lead the child designers with ideas that did not originate from them. However, in future sessions, it would be informative to make such options explicit, in order to gather more data related to our findings regarding issues like politeness (e.g., will performers be directed to change a well-known story when some audience members demand it?).

## 6. CONCLUSION

We worked with children ages 7-11 as design partners using the Cooperative Inquiry method and a modified Big Props technique to explore how children would use technology props to interact with a live performance within the context of PED. This exploratory study has contributed to our understanding of children's perceptions of live performance and the ways they want to interact with it, thus helping to answer questions raised by PED [7]. We found that children want a meaningful and entertaining experience where everyone has an equal and fair way to interact with the performance and that children want to remain a part of the audience, with a distinct divide between audience and performers. These initial findings also inform our development of design techniques that incorporate technology prototypes, in that we observed that child designers who used unconventional or unfamiliar technology props tended to generate more novel ideas and interactions for live performance. We look forward to exploring PED with children in future work with the goal of extending existing frameworks such as [2,7] specifically for young participants.

## 7. ACKNOWLEDGMENTS

We would like to thank all of our Kidsteam design partners.

## 8. REFERENCES

[1] Benford, S., Crabtree, A., Reeves, S., Sheridan, J., Dix, A., Flintham, M., & Drozd, A. (2006). The Frame of the Game: Blurring the Boundary between Fiction and Reality in Mobile Experiences. In *Proc. CHI 2006*, ACM Press, 427–436.

[2] Benford, S., & Giannachi, G. (2008). Temporal trajectories in shared interactive narratives. In *Proc. CHI 2008*, ACM Press, 73–82.

[3] Cassell, J., & Ryokai, K. (2001). Making Space for Voice: Technologies to Support Children's Fantasy and Storytelling. *Pers. and Ubiq. Computing, 5*(3), 169–190.

[4] Corbin, J., & Strauss, A. (2008). *Basics of qualitative research: techniques and procedures for developing grounded theory (3rd ed.).* LA, CA: Sage.

[5] Cuthbertson, A., Hatton, S., Minyard, G., Piver, H., Todd, C., & Birchfield, D. (2007). Mediated education in a creative arts context: research and practice at Whittier Elementary School. In *Proc. IDC 2007*, ACM Press, 65–72.

[6] Guha, M.L., Druin, A., & Fails, J.A. (2013). Cooperative Inquiry revisited: Reflections of the past and guidelines for the future of intergenerational co-design. *IJCCI, 1*(1), 14-23.

[7] Spence, J., Frohlich, D. M., & Andrews, S. (2013). Performative experience design. In *CHI 2013 Ext. Abstracts (alt.chi)*, ACM Press, 2049–2058.

[8] Walsh, G., Foss E., Yip, J., & Druin, A. (2013). FACIT PD: A framework for analysis and creation of intergenerational design techniques. In *Proc CHI 2013*, ACM, 2893-290.

# Designing Digital Media for Creative Mathematical Learning

Chronis Kynigos
Educational Technology Lab, UoA & Computer Technology Institute
University of Athens Campus, 15784
0030 210 7277508
kynigos@cti.gr

Foteini Moustaki
Educational Technology Lab, UoA & Computer Technology Institute
University of Athens Campus, 15784
0030 210 7277508
fotmous@ppp.uoa.gr

## ABSTRACT

Although "creativity" has been included in lifelong competencies, designing tools and pedagogies for fostering creativity in classroom has been in the last years a field that appears quite overwhelmed. The reason for that mostly stems from the lack of a clear definition of what creativity is or even from the wide range of descriptions for the specificities of situations inside which creativity arises. Among others, the interplay between problem solving and problem posing has been considered an indicator of creativity. This short paper describes the design of a web platform that entails a constructionist medium and two on-line shared workspaces. Empirical research with these tools attempts to enhance our understanding on they may support students in jointly figuring out how to fix a program for a 3D mathematical artifact and use it as a building block for creative constructions.

## Keywords

Creativity, problem-solving, problem-posing, meaning making, half-baked microworlds

## 1. FRAMEWORK

The last years, educational researchers have turned their interest on how to design technological tools that may specifically foster *creativity*, not only for some specially gifted children, but for all children. Creativity is a term policy-makers have been flagging as a lifelong competency in the frame of a new entrepreneurial culture. Even from 2000, NCTM [1] has included in its proposed math standards and expectations for the upcoming years, the ability of every student to use mathematics to solve problems creatively and resourcefully, preparing for the new levels of mathematical thinking required in the workplaces. EC [2], more recently, has set the goal of cultivating creative skills for all in and attempt for a more knowledge-based society and new jobs in an economy that favors innovations. Towards this direction, ICTs are considered to play a crucial role, allowing the development of e-skills and adequate media literacy levels for all EC citizens.

Educationalists, for twenty or more years, have been designing within the constructionist paradigm, ICTs to be used by students as expressive and explorative media, engaging them in rich mathematical meaning making processes [3]. Such digital tools afford programming, dynamic manipulations and visualizations of complex situations driven by underlying mathematical rules - all usually offered through multiply connected representations. Although, these have been quite innovative technologies, designing artefacts and classroom pedagogies that can result in fostering creativity for all students (and not just for the talented ones) has been proven a rather tall order. Creativity has been approached in an extensive number of ways, which led multiple researchers to suggest that the term "creativity" and the situations through which it may arise can't be specifically defined [4, 5].

To this end, the factors considered to be important when designing for creative mathematical thinking range from making sure that the students gain a good understanding of mathematics itself, to having deep experiences in doing mathematics, to establishing specific norms inside a mathematics classrooms [6, 7].

In this short paper, however, we suggest designing artefacts and pedagogies that may offer opportunities for problem-posing and problem-posing activities, as means for fostering creative mathematical thinking [7]. We call those artefacts "half-baked microworlds" [8]. These are a special kind of microworld [9] as they are designed to be buggy or incomplete, aiming to challenge students to change them and make sense of the reasons for their unsatisfactory behavior. Considering the shaping of mathematical meaning making as a social activity, we design those artefacts to be questionable and improvable, with an intend to encourage students' participation in collectives. Jointly tinkering the artefacts as members of a community [10], we expect the students to debug the half-baked microworlds, reconstruct them and integrate their own ideas on how they should work.

Within such a community, the improved artefacts that the students make public and share on-line serve as "boundary objects" [11], i.e. artifacts obviating the need for any member of the community to understand what is already understood by another, but also becoming key in a mechanism through which the members of the community shape their collaborative activities and engage in joint meaning making processes [12].

In this short paper, we describe instances in which such a community used on-line shared workspaces to pose and solve mathematical problems coming from its members' explorations with the "Twisted Rectangle" half-baked microworld. We discuss the affordances of the designed tools and how the participation in collectives and the joint tinkering of programmable artefacts created situations for creative mathematical thinking [13].

## 2. THE METAFORA PLATFORM

The Metafora System [14] is a web platform that offers two main shared workspaces for collaborating and communicating on-line.

The first one, the "Planning Tool", is designed to allow groups of students to structure a common plan of work (Figure 1). Through this synchronous on-line tool, students can jointly decide on the actions to take, in the different phases of their explorations, so as to address the mathematical problem in hand. For each action there is an available card, which the students place in the shared workspace and connect it to others in order to depict any temporal or cause-effect relations. Apart from phases like "Explore", "Model", "Evaluate", there are also cards that depict the group's stances. For example, when "Exploring" a particular situation, the students may decide that they will need to be "Open-minded" so as to make sure every angle is covered. The Plan is available at any time and the students may go back and change it when they decide to follow a different direction in their explorations.

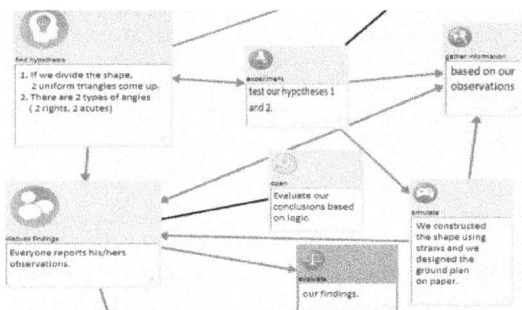

**Figure 1. The Plan a Group of students created and revised**

To discuss about their Plan, the students may use and instant chat or "LASAD", a similar WYSIWIS environment (Figure 2). LASAD is a "Discussion Tool" that allows groups of students -or even individuals- to synchronously communicate on-line. To do so, there is available a set of pre-defined text-boxes from which the students choose their contributions. The title on the top of the box describes the type of the contribution they post, while drop-down lists allow them to further explain their idea. Linking contributions together, the students create a discussion map.

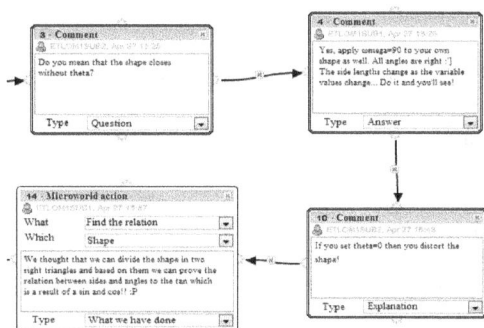

**Figure 2. Four linked LASAD contributions**

However, through LASAD and the Planning Tool, the students may share their whole work with the microworlds. Received microworlds, open in new tabs, allowing the students to view both their own and the others' versions of the microworld they are working with. In its early state, this functionality was performed manually, as the students were asked to copy-paste elements of their microworld they wished to make public within the community.

"3d Math" (http://etl.ppp.uoa.gr/malt) is one of METAFORA's on-line authoring tools for mathematical learning. It is a 3D Logo-based Turtle Geometry tool integrating affordances for dynamic manipulations of variable values and dynamic camera perusal. [15, 16]. The 3D figures created within 3d Math, are results of programming commands that drive a turtle. The turtle's consecutive turns in 3d space and position changes leave a linear trace behind, generating the figure. The dragging of a number-line variation tool affords dynamic "real-time" manipulations of the figure. This can be achieved as the variation tool controls the values of the variables in the program that initially created the figure (Figure 3).

**Figure 3. The Twisted Rectangle half-baked microworld in 3d Math**

Building and manipulating geometrical objects in 3d Math is not solely restricted to looking at the 3d world from static 2d views. A Camera Controller affords a dynamic change of the viewpoint. Navigating around, inside and through their constructions students can visualize 3d space and conceptualize mathematical notions related to stereometry. Thus, 3d Math can be used as an authoring tool for developing 3d geometry half-baked microworlds, such as the "Twisted Rectangle" (Figure 3).

The Twisted Rectangle is a "buggy" 3d rectangle that has one segment twisting on a plane vertical to the one defined by the other three. It is designed to be an open-shape, aiming at challenging students to explore the mathematical relationships among the shape's lengths and angles as they attempt to close it.

## 3. METHODOLOGY AND CONTEXT

The study described was implemented for 26 school hours in a Lower Secondary Education School in Athens (1st Experimental Middle School) with ten 9th grade students (14 years old). The students were divided in two Groups, each consisting of two to three Subgroups. In each Subgroup there were two and sometimes three students, gathered around the same PC and working with the same 3d Math microworld. Communication with the Subgroups sitting in other parts of the classroom took place through LASAD and the Planning Tool, while for the initial construction of the Plan all Group members sat together in front of a common PC.

The research approach was based on the idea of studying learning in authentic settings through design experiments [17]. Design experiments entail the engineering of tools and tasks in advance and the systematic studying of if and how these means support forms of learning in real classrooms. To this end, the researchers (also acting as the classroom teachers) chose not to intervene in the students' discussions and experimentations. Posing meaningful questions, they attempted to encourage them to continue their exploration and to communicate their ideas with the others members of their Groups and Subgroups through Metafora.

The data collected from cameras and a screen-capture software (HyperCam), recording the students' interactions with the Metafora System, were verbatim transcribed. The corpus of the data was completed by the students' LASAD maps, Plans, microworlds and the researchers' field notes. In analysing the data, we searched for instances in which the students, using the Metafora System, engaged in problem-posing and problem-solving processes. Our attempt was to identify how affordances of the tools may support these processes, possibly leading to creative mathematical thinking.

## 4. THE DESIGNED ACTIVITIES

The students were given the "Twisted Rectangle" half-baked microworld, designed in a way that one of its vertexes was obviously 'broken', i.e. two of the corresponding segments were not connecting (Figure 3). Working in Subgroups, they were asked to try to "make the shape close". This entailed exploring the shape's geometrical properties and finding the relationships among the shape's elements that needed to be expressed in turtle turns and displacements in the Logo program so as to fix this "buggy behavior". After completing the bug fix, the students in the Subgroups were asked to create their own constructions using the "Twisted Rectangle" as a building block. As members of a larger Group, they were expected to prepare a common Plan of work, discuss their ideas and share Logo program or parts of their constructions with the other Subgroups through LASAD, so as to create meaningful for them complicated artefacts.

## 5. RESULTS

### 5.1 Posing Mathematical Problems to explore

Implementing mathematical problem-solving and problem-posing strategies interchangeably was a process that the students started just from the beginning of their explorations. After opening up the "Twisted Rectangle" microworld and playing with simulation, they came across a question that was then explicitly asked by the teachers and the researchers: "How can you make this shape become a closed one?".

To address this quite generic problem, the students initially used the "Planning Tool". By placing and connecting "Activity" cards, they managed to translate the whole problem and its solving process into a diagram of actions. The cards were used to describe more eloquently the posed problem and the expected results to signify that the problem has been solved. Although this seemed to be a clearly problem solving technique, the students also engaged in problem-posing processes.

The "Find Hypotheses" card that they added (Figure 4), served as a venue for breaking the generic problem into simpler ones, possibly more manageable for them. The two new problems that the students came to pose were: "how to use only two variables to make the shape close" and "how to relate to each other the three variables to make the shape close". The first of the sub-problems

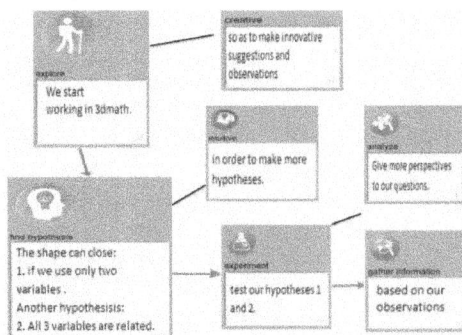

**Figure 4. The Plan a Group of students devised to address the problem with the open Twisted Rectangle**

seemed to be a special case of the generic one. Manipulating two of the three variables, by making the third one equal to zero, generated a simpler and more familiar problem. It was a problem that didn't correspond any longer to 3d shape, but to a shape projected in a 2d plane. For 9th grade students, whose learning of trigonometry was limited and only for the 2d space, this new posed problem constituted a smaller "bite", fit to the mathematical knowledge they had been taught at school.

The second sub-problem was the original problem's *mathematical* translation. Although, the original question was asked in the context of "3d Math", it was not a clearly mathematical one. It didn't entail any mathematical terms (like "angles", "triangle sides" and "lengths"), but more-or-less, everyday language terms. In this "Find Hypotheses" card (Figure 4), the students restated the question, turning it into a more domain-specific problem that they could work with using the available resources. Looking for mathematical "relations among three variables", was a problem appropriate for 3d Math and its functionalities (programming using variables) and at the same time a problem one step more complicated than the first one.

Problem posing was a process that went on for students as they implemented their Plan and seemed to appear in-between problem-solving strategies. Experimenting with 3d Math, and through the "information they gathered" after their "observations" didn't bring the desired results for some time. The students moved then to LASAD seeking for peer-to-peer evaluation of the outcomes of their explorations and joint decisions on how to continue as a group (Figure 2).

Again, this workspace was used as a venue for reshaping, this time, the initial subproblem. Instead of having just two variables (eliminating the third one by making it equal to zero), the students went one step further by suggesting another simplification: attributing a specific value to one more variable. However, this new special case with two out of the three variables being equal to 0 or 90 (these were angle variables), was tested in 3d Math and rejected. Attempting to solve the problem through this second special case, led into having a "distorted shape" (Figure 2).

After several dead-end approaches, one subgroup of students used some straws –for which they had asked a researcher in a previous session- to represent the Twisted Rectangle and a piece of paper to create a 2d plane beneath it (Figure 5).

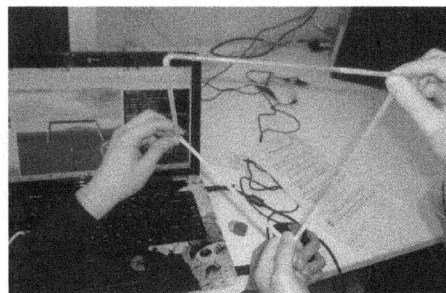

**Figure 5. Same problem with different resources**

Folding a part of the paper around the straws, they identified one more plane that they should take into consideration for closing the shape. This was a major breakthrough for the students, which resulted in creating projections of the shape in two separate planes. The problem of "how the three variables may relate to each other" was then turned into a simple and familiar for them trigonometry problem between two right triangles. To explain how the initial problem was cut down into pieces, they changed the "Find Hypotheses" card in their Plan indicating the solving strategy they followed (Figure 1).

## 5.2 Novel constructions

Having finished with the bug-fixing phase, the two Subgroups used the experience they had gained during their experimentations to create novel constructions using the Twisted Rectangle as a building block. Having created a "participating in collectives" culture, the subgroups of students shared separate artefacts in LASAD and discussed on how to combine them into a jointly constructed one (Figure 6).

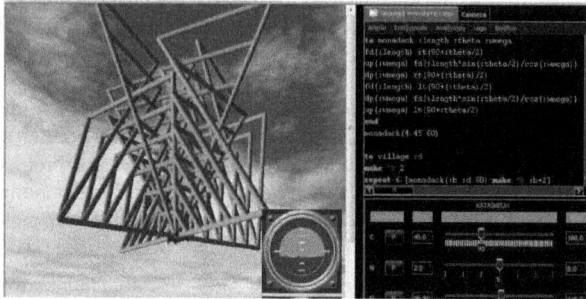

**Figure 6. The "ice-cream cone" construction**

The integration of the artifacts initiated a new process in which the students engaged in two types of activities. The first one related to making sense of the artifact received and of the way it was constructed. The second one referred to how to combine it with their own so as to generate a more elaborated artefact.

## 6. Discussion

Understanding creativity as a term that has been coined through different approaches, we used in this paper the students' problem solving and posing strategies to explain how they came to create novel and interesting artefacts as they worked with an web-platform. Our specific focus was on evaluating the design of the platform that included two on-line shared workspaces and a half-baked microworld with a buggy behaviour. The open-ended problem of "How to close the open shape" was thus chosen to call for planning of actions in advance, discussing in collectives and exploring mathematical ideas to fix the 3d shape.

As the students worked with the Platform's tools to address the problem, we signified several occasions in which they used interchangeably problem-solving and problem-posing strategies. Those were related to: cutting down the initial problem to smaller and more manageable pieces, translating it using terms close to the resources available for solving the problem, reshaping the problem creating special cases of the general problem, sharing the outcomes of the posed problems and assessing others' attempts, recognising situations in which the restated problem didn't lead to any results with regard to solving it, generating larger problems that combining the solutions of smaller ones.

The experience leaves us with a sense of needing to find out more about how to design affordances of tools that may create situations for problem-solving and problem-posing opportunities, aiming at studying if and how these may constitute a more solid indicator for the appearance of creativity.

## 7. ACKNOWLEDGMENTS

MC SQUARED (EC-FP7/2007-2013- N610467). The publication reflects only the author's views and Union is not liable for any use that may be made of the information contained therein.

## 8. REFERENCES

[1] National Council of Teachers of Mathematics (NCTM) 2000. Principles and Standards for School Mathematics. Reston, VA: NCTM.

[2] European Commission. 2010. EC Green Paper. Unlocking the potential of cultural and creative industries. COM - 183.

[3] Noss, R. and Hoyles, C. 1996. Windows on Mathematical Meanings: Learning Cultures and Computers. Dordrecht: Kluwer Academic Publishers.

[4] Mann, E. 2006. Creativity: The essence of mathematics. *Journal for the Education of the Gifted, 30*, 236–230.

[5] Sriraman, B. 2005. Are giftedness and creativity synonyms in mathematics? *Journal of Secondary Gifted Education, 17*(1), 20–36.

[6] Leikin, R. 2009. Exploring mathematical creativity using multiple solution tasks. In R. Leikin, A. Berman, and B. Koichu (Eds.), *Creativity in mathematics and the education of gifted students* (pp. 129-145). Rotterdam, the Netherlands: Sense Publishers.

[7] Silver, E. A. 1997. Fostering creativity through instruction rich in mathematical problem solving and problem posing. *ZDM*, 3, 75-80.

[8] Kynigos, C. 2007. Half–Baked Logo microworlds as boundary objects in integrated design. *Informatics in Education, 6*(2), 335–358.

[9] Sarama, J., and Clements, D. 2002. Design of Microworlds in Mathematics and Science Education, *Journal of Educational Computing Research.* 27(1), 1-3.

[10] Resnick, M. 1996. Distributed constructionism. In D. C. Edelson, & E. A. Domeshek (Eds.), *Proceedings of the 1996 international conference on Learning sciences*, (280-284).

[11] Star S. L. 1989. The structure of ill-structured solutions" boundary objects and heterogeneous distributed problem solving. In L. Gasser and M.N, Huhns (Eds) *Distributed artificial intelligence, Vol. 2*, 37-54.

[12] Kynigos, C. 2012. Constructionism: theory of learning or theory of design? *Proceedings of the 12th International Congress on Mathematical Education*, Seoul, S. Korea.

[13] Eisenberg, M., Elumeze, N., MacFerrin, M. & Buechley, L. 2009. Children's programming, reconsidered: settings, stuff, and surfaces. *In P. Paolini & F. Garzotto (eds.)*, IDC 2009.

[14] Dragon, T., McLaren, B., Mavrikis, M., Harrer, A., Kynigos, C., Wegerif, R., et al. 2012. Metafora: A web-based platform for learning to learn together in science and mathematics. *IEEE Transactions on Learning Technologies* .

[15] Latsi, M., & Kynigos, C. 2012. Experiencing 3d simulated space through different perspectives. *Research on e-Learning and ICT in Education: Technological, Pedagogical and Instructional Issues.* Springer Science + Business Media, Part III, p. 183-196.

[16] Moustaki, F., & Kynigos, C. 2011. Engineering students' visualization and reasoning processes while interacting with a 3d digital environment. In B. Ubuz (Ed.), *Proceedings of the 35th PME Conference. Vol. 3*, 257-264. Ankara, Turkey.

[17] Cobb, P., Confrey, J., diSessa, A., Lehrer, P., & Schauble, L. 2003. Design experiments in educational research. *Educational Researcher , 32* (1), 9–13.

# Craft, Click and Play: Crafted Video-Games, a New Approach for Physical-Digital Entertainment

Jesús Ibáñez Martínez
Madeira-ITI, University of Madeira
9020-105 Funchal, Madeira, Portugal
jesus.ibanez@m-iti.org

## ABSTRACT

In this paper we present a novel approach for kids' entertainment along with a related technology that makes it possible (as well as a set of use cases that demonstrate its potential). Our approach employs both physical and digital elements. Instead of mixing the physical and digital worlds in the same interface, both worlds are employed separately. In a few words, the kids play with typical physical elements in a creative way for crafting a game scenario in the real world. Then, the result of this physical playtime is transferred to a digital device (particularly a tablet or smartphone) by taking a picture of it. Particular game elements (and its role) are recognised based on their colour. As a result, a digital game is automatically built from the photograph of their physical creations. Two key features of our approach are simplicity and immediacy. The kids can create new whole entertaining experiences very easily (from the technological point of view). The kids are not only responsible for creating the scenarios, but also for defining the game rules and controlling its compliance (as it happens in traditional physical games). The approach aims to foster kids' creativity, socialization, responsibility, conflict resolution, flexibility, and their manual and artistic skills.

## Categories and Subject Descriptors

K.8.0 [**Personal Computing**]: General---games.

## General Terms

Design, Human Factors.

## Keywords

Crafting, Games, Children, Interaction Design, Apps.

## 1. INTRODUCTION

Some interesting initiatives that combine physical and digital elements in games exist. That is the case, for instance, of augmented reality games [3] and mixed reality games [4]. Some groups work on extending the elements of physical games with electronic components [1]. Other groups research on the creation of tangible games on tabletop devices by using diverse technologies such as RFID [2] and visual fiducials [5].

Like all these approaches, ours employs both physical and digital elements. However, our approach differs from all of them in several aspects. For instance, augmented and mixed reality games add a digital layer to the physical elements (or to a representation of the world). Both worlds, digital and physical, are mixed in real time. Thus, the kids interact with digital devices during the whole playtime. Our approach, instead, decouples both worlds (real and digital) and promotes that the kids play with natural physical elements. First, the kids creatively play with physical elements. Then, they play with digital elements.

Both physical games augmented with electronic components and augmented tabletop games require special (and in some cases expensive) technology. Our approach, on the contrary, only requires a state of the art mobile phone or tablet. Moreover, creating new games with current approaches is a non trivial task for kids. However, by employing our approach, the kids can create new games very easily (from the technological point of view).

## 2. TECHNOLOGY

In this section we describe the technology we have created in order to support the proposed approach. The technology is an App that allows the creation of new video-games from pictures of crafted scenarios. It works on Android devices and adapts itself to different screen and camera resolutions.

The App allows any number of moveable **interactive objects**. In the current version of the App, these objects are displayed as small coloured circles. There are several different interactive mechanisms to move the interactive objects. The kids can select the one they prefer for each concrete game/scenario. The current version of the App supports the following **interaction techniques**: tilt (tilt the device so that the object falls as if gravity would affect it), push (tap, hold and pull forward to throw the object), slingshot (tap, hold and pull back to slingshot the object) and follow the finger (tap the screen and the ball starts moving towards the finger location).

The App is able to recognise a number of **colours** in the scenario picture (the current version of the App recognises: blue, red, green, orange, yellow, white and black). Each of those recognisable colours is assigned a **role** in the game (thus, when crafting the physical scenarios, the kids should take into account the role of each colour). The roles are generic enough so that the kids can give them their real concrete meaning in the universe they define (i.e. each role can have different meanings in different games/scenarios). In turn, each role is assigned an **action** that will take place or not depending on certain conditions. The conditions depend on the location of the interactive object relative to the elements of the specific roles. Thus, colours are assigned to roles, and roles are assigned to actions. The App includes by default values for those assignments but they can be redefined as needed or preferred.

Next we summarise the roles our App supports and the actions assigned to them by default:

**Good**: this role corresponds to something that is, in a generic sense, positive for your interactive object (such as something that your object can eat, something that your object can beat, somewhere where you object can rest, etc).
*Action*: visually change the colour of an element with the role "good" when it is reached by an interactive object. Note that this is just visual feedback to make it clear that the object have reached that good element. The semantic meaning of this action is given by the kids and it depends on the particular game/scenario.

**Bad**: this role refers to something that is negative for your interactive object (monster, hole in the floor, etc).
*Action*: visually highlight that an element with the role "bad" has collided with an object.

**Solid**: this role corresponds to something that the interactive objects can not pass through (wall, floor, closed door, etc).
*Action*: the object stops when it collides with a solid element.

**Interactive objects**: apart from the elements contained in the picture (the ones recognized by their colour), the other players' interactive objects are elements of the game with a corresponding role and related action.
*Action*: the object stops when it reaches another interactive object; the objects are animated for a very short time to provide visual feedback about the collision.

Note that we avoided including other more specific roles such as entrance and exit. Instead, we rely on the kids' responsibility in order to deal with this kind of issue. For instance, they can write "entrance" and "exit" in particular locations of the labyrinth when crafting it, so that other kids know where to put the interactive objects when starting the video game and where they should get to exit/win.

## 3. CASES OF USE

In this section, we present a few examples of games we have already physically crafted and digitally tested in the App. The examples illustrate three different kinds of situation our approach facilitates.

### 3.1 Typical videogames

Here we show a typical kind of videogame (labyrinth game) that can be created very easily by using our approach. A labyrinth can be physically crafted by one or several kids and its digital counterpart is well suited for being played by one player. An appropriate interaction technique for this kind of videogame is the accelerometer (tilt). Actually, this is the interaction mechanism usually employed in labyrinth videogames when played in mobile devices.

One of the simplest and quickest ways to create a new labyrinth is by drawing it. Figure 1 shows a labyrinth drawn with a blue marker on a piece of paper. By using our App, once the player takes a picture of the drawn labyrinth with the tablet's camera, the picture appears as the scenario of a new digital video game. The user should take a ball out of the labyrinth by using the

accelerometer to control the ball. In that case, blue colour is assigned the solid role in the App. The App allows the user to choose among three different kinds of view: the original picture (Figure 1, top), the scenario recognised by the App from the picture (Figure 1, bottom left), and a mixed view that shows the original picture highlighting the elements recognised by the App (Figure 1, bottom right). The first view is the most enjoyable one, as it gives the player the impression that he is playing on a real scenario. The other two views are useful right after taking the picture of a physical scenario, as they allow checking whether the scenario is well recognised by the App from the picture.

**Figure 1. The App provides three views: original picture (top), recognised scenario (bottom left) and mixed view (bottom right).**

As shown through the previous example, the creation of new scenarios is very easy. That allows the user to focus on the design process. The users can create more artistic (Figure 2, left) and personalised (Figure 2, right) games in a simple manner.

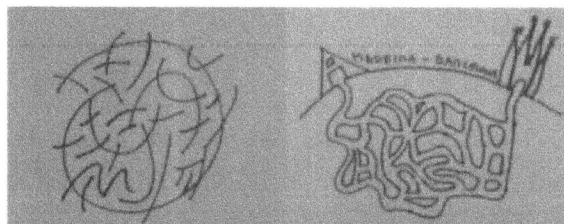

**Figure 2. More artistic and personalized scenarios.**

**Figure 3. A labyrinth can be collaboratively created with Lego pieces. A photograph of it can be played in our App.**

Apart from drawing, a labyrinth scenario can be crafted with any other coloured materials. For instance, Lego pieces are very adequate for the collaborative creation of a new scenario. Several kids can sit or lie around a Lego platform and collaboratively create a new labyrinth such as shown in Figure 3 (top). Figure 3 (bottom left) shows a kid playing with a physical labyrinth created with yellow Lego pieces placed on a blue Lego platform. A wooden ball is used in that case. Figure 3 (bottom right) shows another kid playing with the digital counterpart of the same scenario. In that case, the yellow colour (instead of the blue one) is assigned the solid role in the App. Note that the kinds of interaction employed in both the physical and the digital versions of this particular labyrinth are similar (tilt).

This example illustrates also another quality of our approach. It confers persistence to otherwise ephemeral creations. Lego constructions have normally a short life. A just finished construction will be deconstructed as soon as its pieces are required for a new construction. Our approach gives certain persistence to physical creations by converting them into digital games.

Finally, as shown in Figure 4, a labyrinth can be created by using a mixture of different kinds of materials. By combing a few elements, a simple scenario can be easily crafted by (and for) very young children (Figure 4, left). Older children can add more elements to get a more elaborated scenario (Figure 4, right). Note that, in those cases, the blue and red colours were assigned the solid and bad roles in the video game respectively. The goal of the game is to take a ball out of the labyrinth by using the accelerometer to control the ball and avoiding the red elements.

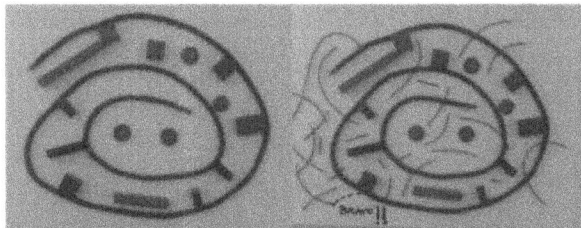

**Figure 4. Mixture of materials. Left: cotton cord, buttons and Lego pieces. Right: adds pieces of thin plastic cord.**

## 3.2 Traditional physical games

This case illustrates how certain classic physical games can be easily converted to digital games. "Las chapas" is a traditional outdoor game that used to be played on the street by kids of earlier generations in Spain. Now, this physical game is still being played in some Spanish primary schools as an activity framed into the physical education subject.

The game elements are basically some bottle caps ("chapa" is the Spanish word to refer to a bottle cap) and a circuit drawn on the floor by the kids themselves. The circuit was traditionally drawn with chalks. Now, in the schools, the circuit is normally created with coloured adhesive tape.

Once the circuit is created, the game consists essentially of a bottle cap race. First, all the bottle caps (one per kid) are put on the start line. Then, the kids take turns hitting their bottle cap with their index finger (following a pre-defined order). If a bottle cap goes outside the circuit, it should be put back on the point from where it left the circuit. The first one reaching the finish line is the winner.

Figure 5 (left) shows two kids playing the traditional physical game. Figure 5 (right) shows a picture of the circuit that can be played as a videogame in our App. The blue colour is assigned the solid role. As a consequence, the interactive objects (one ball per player representing its bottle cap) cannot get out of the circuit. Thus, the elements outside the circuit do not mind (whatever their colours are), since they cannot be reached by the interactive objects (as the objects cannot pass through the blue limits of the circuit). The most appropriate interaction techniques for this game are push and slingshot.

**Figure 5. "Las chapas", a traditional Spanish game that can be easily converted into a digital game in our App.**

## 3.3 New games

This case shows how our approach facilitates the creation of new games. We describe the process we followed in order to design a new game which can be played both physically and digitally. Our initial idea was to design a game vaguely inspired by sports where several players use the same ball for scoring into the opponent goal. We started by sketching a game scenario in a piece of paper (Figure 6). Our intention was rapidly sketching a first scenario so we could play the game in the tablet to validate the idea.

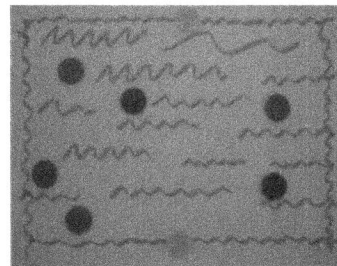

**Figure 6. Sketch of the initial idea for the new game.**

The rules we envisioned for the game are as follows. The game is intended to be played by two players. There are two goals in the scenario, each per player. The goals are the two yellow buttons located on opposite extremes of the scenario. Both players play with the same ball. In other words, both players share the same interactive object in the video game. The objective of the game is reaching the opponent's goal. First, the ball is located in the centre of the scenario. Then, the players take turns hitting the shared ball, trying to approximate the ball towards the opponent's goal. The ball collides with the blue lines. Once a player hits the ball, if it reaches the opponent's goal, the player wins (the opponent looses) and the game finishes. Otherwise, if the ball reaches a red element, the player looses (the opponent wins) and the game finishes. If not, if the ball reaches a green element, the player is allowed to hit the ball again. In any other case, the turn passes to the opponent (the opponent will hit the ball).

We took a picture of the sketched scenario and played the game in the tablet. The blue, green and red colours were assigned the solid, good and bad roles in the App respectively. The interaction technique we considered appropriate for this game is slingshot. By playing the game, we realised that one of its rules was not suitable for the scenario. If players take turns alternatively and each player hits the ball once per turn, the game duration was too long. Thus, we changed that rule so that each player hits the ball three consecutive times per turn. With this slight change, the playability improved greatly. The games were shorter and more enjoyable.

As we enjoyed the video game, we wanted to play it in other scenarios. In order to facilitate the generation of variations of the scenario, we crafted a version of the physical scenario where all its elements are moveable. In particular, we created magnetic coloured elements by combining both coloured foam and cuttable magnets. Then we could easily create new scenarios for the video game just by repositioning the elements on a metallic surface (such as a dishwasher door) and taking them a picture (Figure 7).

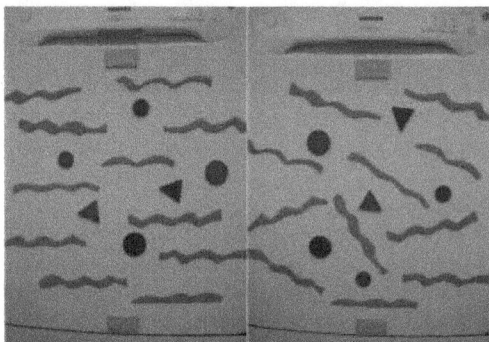

Figure 7. The use of moveable magnetic elements facilitates the creation of scenarios for the video game.

After some time playing the digital game, we wanted to play a physical version of it. Thus, we arranged the magnetic scenario elements on a horizontal metallic surface (see Figure 8). We used a wooden coloured ball as interactive object. For throwing the ball, each player should blow to it through a drinking straw. When the ball collides with the magnetic elements it rebounds due to the elements height.

Figure 8. First version of the new physical game.

After a short time, we refined the design of the physical game so that it is more adequate and coherent from the interactive and aesthetic point of views. The new scenario recreates a water world with elements such as islands, marine animals and waves (see Figure 9). Instead of balls, we use crafted paper sailboats as interactive objects. This change is coherent with the physical interaction technique (blowing). Two interactive objects (instead of one) are now employed, and the goals are treasures. The interactive objects are pirate sailboats that try to obtain the opponent's treasure. The sailboats are not magnetic, the rest of elements are. The kids can relocate the elements from game to

game. The green elements are islands where the pirates can rest, and fishes the pirates can hook to eat. The red ones are dangerous elements (shark, giant octopus). And the blue ones are waves the sailboats collide with.

Figure 9. Refinement of the new physical game.

## 4. CONCLUSIONS

We aim to provide kids with elements and mechanisms that allow them to create their own play. By using the presented technology, the kids can create new whole entertaining experiences very easily. They are responsible for creating the game scenarios, but also for defining the game rules and controlling its compliance.

Our strategy is to provide a very simple approach that allows the creation of many different games. The technology is intentionally simple. We intend to provide the minimum interactive elements and general game roles to represent a playable digital version of a physical scenario. The use cases that we have presented in the paper demonstrate the great potential of the current technology. We are working on the extension of the model with a few new game roles that expand the repertoire of types of game the kids can invent.

## 5. REFERENCES

[1] Dertien, E., Dijkstra, J., Mader, A., and Reidsma, D. 2012. Making a Toy Educative Using Electronics. In *Proceedings of Advances in Computer Entertainment - 9th International Conference*. ACE 2012. Lecture Notes in Computer Science 7624, Springer, 477-480.

[2] Deshmukh, S., and Baru, V. B. 2013. Applications of RFID in Interactive Board Games. In Proceedings of International Conference on Recent Trends in engineering & Technology (ICRTET'2013). Special Issue of International Journal of Electronics, Communication & Soft Computing Science & Engineering, ISSN: 2277-9477

[3] Huynh, D. T., Raveendrany, K., Xuz, Y., Spreenx, K., and MacIntyre, B. 2009. Art of Defense: A Collaborative Handheld Augmented Reality Board Game. In *Proceedings of the 2009 ACM SIGGRAPH Symposium on Video Games* (Sandbox '09), Stephen N. Spencer (Ed.). ACM, New York, NY, USA, 135-142.

[4] Khoo, E.T., and Cheok, A.D. 2006. Age Invaders: Inter-generational Mixed Reality Family Game. *The International Journal of Virtual Reality*, 5, 2 (2006), 45-50

[5] Marco, J., Cerezo, E., and Baldassarri, S. 2012. ToyVision: A Toolkit for Prototyping Tabletop Tangible Games. In *Proceedings of the 4th ACM SIGCHI symposium on Engineering interactive computing systems* (EICS '12). ACM, New York, NY, USA, 71-80.

# Head Mounted Displays and Deaf Children: Facilitating Sign Language in Challenging Learning Environments

**Michael Jones**
Dept. of Computer Science
Brigham Young U.
Provo, UT
michael.jones@byu.edu

**M. Jeannette Lawler**
Dept. of Physics and
Astronomy
Brigham Young U.
Provo, UT

**Eric Hintz**
Dept. of Physics and
Astronomy
Brigham Young U.
Provo, UT

**Nathan Bench**
Dept. of Computer Science
Brigham Young U.
Provo, UT

**Fred Mangrubang**
Dept. of Education
Gallaudet U.
Washington D.C.

**Mallory Trullender**
Mantua Elementary School
Fairfax, VA

## ABSTRACT

Head-mounted displays (HMDs) are evaluated as a tool to facilitate student-teacher interaction in sign language. Deaf or hard-of-hearing children who communicate in sign language receive all instruction visually. In normal deaf educational settings the child must split visual attention between signed narration and visual aids. Settings in which visual aids are distributed over a large visual area are particularly difficult. Sign language displayed in HMDs may allow a deaf child to keep the signed narration in sight, even when not looking directly at the person signing. Children from the community who communicate primarily in American Sign Language (ASL) participated in two phases of a study designed to evaluate the comfort and utility of viewing ASL in an HMD.

## Categories and Subject Descriptors

H.5.2 [**Information Interfaces and Presentation**]: User Interfaces; H.1.2 [**Information Systems**]: User/Machine Systems

## 1. INTRODUCTION

Spoken and signed languages are each difficult to use in certain environments. For example, spoken languages are difficult to use in noisy environments, but headphones with speakers and directional microphones allow people to communicate more easily. Signed languages are visual rather than auditory, and they are difficult to use in a different set of environments than spoken languages. However, as with spoken languages, technology can facilitate communication in these settings.

There is much we do not know about how deaf and hard of hearing children learn and there is even less we know about how deaf children experience sign language in HMDs. The driving principle behind our work is to deliver instruction in sign language rather than in written captions. This is particularly important for young children who are learning sign language as their first language.

Compared to spoken language acquisition by children who hear, a child who is deaf or hard-of-hearing often experiences significant acquisition delays with their first language [5]. It is estimated that 95% of school-age deaf and hard of hearing children are born to hearing parents [6]. These children often do not begin learning sign language until entering school and may only receive fluent language input during school hours.

Improved sign language learning may lead to increased learning in a second language such as English. Research shows "that children who learn through their first (minority) language for as long as possible not only tend to have improved final achievement, but also their English language skills tend to develop to a higher level than those who were taught through their second language with some first language support" [4].

In this paper we explore the configuration of and potential benefits of head-mounted displays for education done in sign language in difficult environments. Difficulties arise when students cannot see or are not looking directly at the signer. Our purpose is to evaluate the comfort and utility of viewing sign language in an HMD as perceived by a child who communicates primarily in sign language through the use of ASL video presented through an HMD. This may enable both teachers and deaf children to interact in new ways by allowing students to view instruction wherever they may look.

## 2. RELATED WORK

Methods have been developed for delivering written English captions to deaf or hard-of-hearing students in the classroom (such as C-Print [8]). While these methods are effective for children with strong English (or any other written language) reading skills, they are not effective for children with poor reading skills. Over 30 years of educational testing in the United States, the average reading level is below the fourth grade level (which included children ages 9-10 in the United States). It included hearing children in grades K through 12. The fourth grade level is normalized against the reading level of their hearing peers. [7].

Several groups have explored methods for deliving captions in a planetarium setting. A planetarium is a particularly difficult environment to present ASL. One of the early, well documented efforts is reported by DeGraff and Hamil [2]. DeGraff and Hamil used a slide projector to project captions near the horizon of the planetarium dome. Daniel [1] details a slightly different way of using captions in a live show. The words are either projected near the object of interest on the dome or a green arrow directs student's eyes to the relevant area of the dome.

In Grice [3] we find the beginnings of a more modern approach to captioning systems. This is a major move into devices for planetariums and theaters. The first device they tested were Virtual Vision glasses that showed captions over the right eye in a small screen. Grice reported that most people put these away after a few minutes and experienced a "dizzying effect." Grice experimented with an LED display system that was mounted behind the audience. This system would display the captions in reversed text. For the demo, Plexiglas was mounted on specific seats that would then reflect the captions back to the viewer correctly. Finally, Grice tested a Vacuum Fluorescent Display (VFD). This is a box that attached to a seat in front of the individual and had captions run across the screen. The planetarium installed four VFD captioning systems that could each support three people.

It was apparent during our review that very little work has been done using HMDs in Deaf education. Most work focused on using captions to address the issue of relaying information to deaf participants. However, this approach does not cater to younger deaf children as their reading skills have not fully developed.

## 3. METHODS AND RESULTS

We conducted a two-phase evaluation of comfort and utility for HMDs used to convey ASL to children in logistically challenging informal education environments. A total of 18 deaf or hard-of-hearing students who communicate primarily in sign language participated in this portion of the study. In the first phase, 8 participants provided subjective feedback after watching a short astronomy based video on a screen with ASL narration viewed through an HMD. We provided software for repositioning the ASL video in the display and recorded changes made by each subject. In the second phase, 10 participants watched a 20-minute planetarium show with the narration provided in ASL. Five watched the narration projected directly onto the planetarium dome and 5 watched the narration in an HMD.

Test subjects were drawn from a local deaf school and a summer university program for high school students. In each case we limit the study to children who are deaf or hard-of-hearing and who communicate primarily in ASL. All of the participants were between 13-18 years of age.

Because the participants in this study communicate in ASL, care was taken to minimize linguistic barriers. Interactions with the participants were direct ASL-to-ASL communications without any intervening interpreter. Deaf and hard-of-hearing individuals who use ASL as their native lan-

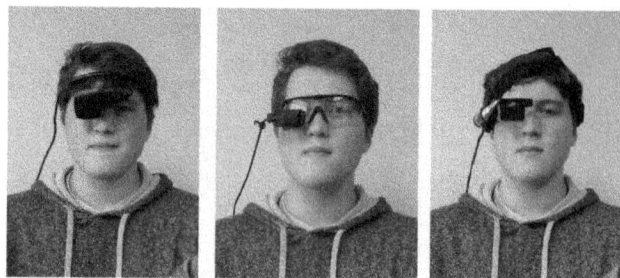

**Figure 1: The three HDMs used in evaluations. The displays are all monocular and include fully occlusive on the left, partially occlusive in the middle, and see-through with a half-silvered mirror on the right.**

| Table 1: | | | | |
|---|---|---|---|---|
| Display | fov | Res. | Color | Weight |
| Virt. Realities VR1 | 40° | 800x600 | 24 bits | 3 oz. |
| Vusix Tac-eye | 29.5° | 800x600 | 8 bits | 1.81 oz. |
| Laster PMD-G3 | 50° | 800x600 | 24 bits | 3 oz. |

guage but who are not part of the investigation team were recruited to interact with and interview participants in order to avoid bias.

A video record was kept for all interactions with the subjects. Cameras were positioned to allow us to view sign language used by both the interviewers and the participants during interviews and focus groups. Cameras were also used to record interactions between the subject and the HMD hardware. The videos were later translated into English and coded both for verbal content and subject actions by both ASL-speaking and English-speaking investigators.

In each evaluation the subject could adjust the size, position, and brightness of the ASL signer video. Initially, participants adjusted the video using a laptop keyboard, but this required looking at the keyboard, which proved distracting while trying to watch ASL and a video at the same time. We later modified the system to use a video game controller rather than the laptop keyboard to collect the positioning data. All adjustments were logged for later analysis.

### 3.1 Displays

The three displays used in our evaluations are shown for comparison in Figure 1. We used only monocular displays to maximize the amount of light reaching the eye and because adding stereoscopic 3D to the display does not necessarily improve comprehension when viewing sign language. The display on the left of Figure 1 is a fully occlusive Virtual Realities VR1. The center display is a Vusix Tac-eye partially occlusive display. The display on the right is a Laster PMD-G2 see-through display with a half-silvered mirror that blocks some incoming light. Table 1 contains the diagonal viewing angle, resolution, color depth, and weight for each display. Viewing sign language at a resolution of 800x600 is not likely to negatively impact comprehension. Weaver et al.'s study [9] of ASL comprehension and video resolution found that novice signers could observe and reproduce specific signs with equal success when learning those signs from video rendered at 640x480, 320x240, or 160x120 on a mobile phone screen.

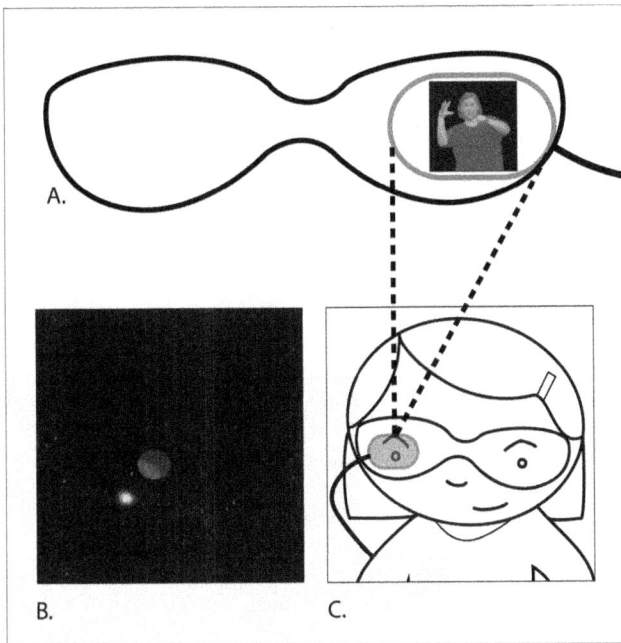

Figure 2: Example of what was seen in an HMD by a participant. A) Shows the ASL interpreter in the HMD view. B) Scene from the video watched on a screen. C) Illustration of a child wearing an HMD.

All three displays listed in Table 1 were too large, bulky, and heavy for use by children. The Laster offered the largest viewing angle but had a small eye box. The eye box is the volume of space in which the display is correctly aligned with the eye to allow viewing of the full image. A few participants spent quite a bit of time adjusting the display to make sure that the full field of view was visible.

## 3.2 Evaluation

The first phase of evaluation was conducted using video shown on a flat screen in a room. Four female and four male participants, ages 15 through 18 were recruited from a university summer camp for youth who are deaf. Each of the subjects watched a five-minute video while the narration in ASL was delivered through an HMD (Figure 2).

The individual subjects were interviewed about their experience. Eight children from the first phase were brought together into two mixed-gender groups of four to participate in a focus group. In both the individual and the focus group interviews participants were asked to discuss their opinions both of the concept and its execution. We encouraged them to tell us when, where, and how they thought an HMD could be used. We also asked about issues of design and comfort.

We coded both the transcripts and the video recordings of the interviews and the focus groups. Open coding of the transcripts allows us to identify themes from intentionally open-ended questions. We defined codes for the video recordings that related to comfort and utility. Video recordings of interviews and focus group discussions were translated from ASL to English by a deaf interpreter. All transcripts and video recordings were coded by three members of the research team.

The second phase was conducted in the planetarium so we could spread visual information over an entire viewable hemisphere in a controlled environment. Ten participants ages 13-15 were recruited from a local school for the Deaf. Spreading visual information out over the entire planetarium dome creates a logistically challenging environment for ASL instruction. The duration of the planetarium show allowed us to observe the use of the displays for comfort and utility over a longer period of time. In this phase we showed a video called "New Horizons" which was produced specifically for projection onto the dome of a planetarium. We obtained the English transcript of the narration for the show and asked a Certified Deaf Interpreter (CDI) to translate the narration into ASL.

### 3.2.1 Themes from First Evaluation

The primary codes found among all participants are split focus, fit and position, signer position, occlusion, and attention. Among all groups, position and fit was the most common theme with split focus as the second most common. The position and fit theme includes comments related to the position and fit of the HMD itself on the participants' head or face. The split focus theme contains comments related to splitting visual focus between the signer in the HMD and the external world. Each theme is addressed below.

*Signer Position.* We provided two ways for subjects to change the position of the signer. Subjects could move the signer in the display and subjects could move the display itself. The majority of the participants had the HMD positioned on the top-right of the right lens of the glasses with one exception: One participant being left-eye dominant preferred the top to middle-left of the left lens.

Once the HMD was properly positioned on the glasses, subjects exhibited a slight preference to moving the sign language presenter down and toward to the center of the subjects' field of view. This preference was evident in both the subjects' comments and in the positioning log. Some subjects turned or tilted their heads in order to place the signer at the center of their field of view. Subjects may have turned their heads to reposition the signer because they did not know how to adjust either the HMD itself or the position of the signer in the video.

*Split attention.* Subjects talked about the challenge of splitting their visual focus between the signer in the HMD and either the video or the people around them. All of the subjects mentioned splitting visual focus between the signer and the screen. Two made positive comments which are given in the subsequent section. Comments from the other six, three male and three female, indicated difficulties focusing on both the interpreter in the HMD and the movie projected onto the screen. A male subject reported, "I feel like it is separate, and it is jarring to look back and forth."

In contrast, two female participants stated that they liked being able to see both the signer and the visual presentation at the same time. One said, "I liked the HMD; it was good. I liked being able to see the screen and the interpreter–to see the speech and the sign interpreter on the screens. I liked that. It was neat."

*HMD Fit.* Subjects described discomfort related to the fit of the HMD. These issues are concerned primarily with occlusion and with issues related to weight and balance. The Vuzix Tac-eye is designed for military and tactical use where ruggedness and durability are more important than weight

**Table 2: Recorded final adjustment of signer position in an HMD.**

| Subject | Eye | Horizontal | Vertical |
|---|---|---|---|
| 1 | right | - 2.25 | 0 |
| 2 | left | 5.625 | 0 |
| 3 | right | 1.125 | 2.8125 |
| 4 | right | 0 | 0 |
| 6 | right | 0 | 0.5625 |
| 7 | right | -1.6875 | 0 |
| 8 | right | -2.25 | -3.375 |
| 9 | right | -1.125 | 0 |

and balance. Adding some weight to the frame of the glasses may have corrected the balance problem but would have added more weight to the HMD unit. In a comment typical of others, a female subject said, "It felt uneven having to compensate for my head being pulled to the side."

We observed some participants, that used the Laster display, continued to make adjustments with their hands to steady the display in proper viewing position. This may be due to the small eye box found on the Laster display.

### 3.2.2 Adjustments of Signer Position

Subjects could use software controls to reposition and re-size video of the ASL signer. All adjustments were recorded for later analysis and a summary of repositioning data is shown in Table 2. The data suggests a bias toward viewing the signer in the center of the field of view. In the table, negative numbers represent movement to the viewers' left and positive numbers represent movement to the viewers' right. For example, movement in the negative direction by a a subject viewing ASL with the right eye indicates movement toward the center of the subject's field of view. Adjustments by subjects 1,2,7,8 and 9 moved the signer toward the center of the field of view while adjustments by subject 3 moved the signer away from the center. Vertical adjustments were less common. The data in Table 2 only includes changes made in software. Subjects also repositioned the signer in their field of view by tilting their heads and physically moving the display on their face.

## 4. CONCLUSIONS

We identified two sources of discomfort in using HMDs to view ASL by children who are deaf or hard-of-hearing and who communicate primarily in ASL. First, the displays we used were too large and bulky for children to use effectively. Second, participants struggled to split their attention between the signer in the HMD and the external world. This may be due to the design of HMDs tested, their utility, and the novelty of the device. In addition to these limiting factors, finding the appropriate number of deaf children from our community was an issue. Future recruitment from other Deaf communities outside our area will be necessary to broaden the pool of potential participants.

We consistently found a slight preference to position the signer in the center of the field of view but this was not a universal preference. This was demonstrated both in the ASL position data and the physical adjustment of the HMD on the participants head. Placing the signer in the center of the field of view may allow the subject to switch between vi-

sual inputs with minimal eye movement thereby minimizing the effort and latency involved with shifting visual attention between the signer and what is being presented in the environment.

Based on the feedback we received and from our observations, a smaller and lighter HMD designed for the geometry of a child's head should be developed. In addition, the use of participatory design will be paramount to maximize the potential of a child specific HMD design. The outlook for the successful use of HMDs for deaf children in educational settings is promising and should be explored.

## 5. REFERENCES

[1] L. Daniel. Planetarium for the deaf. *Planetarian*, 3(1), 1974.

[2] J. V. DeGraff and F. Hamil. Seeing stars. *Planetarian*, 1(2), 1972.

[3] N. Grice. Resources for making astronomy more accessible for blind and visually impaired students. *Astronomy Education Review*, 5:154, 2006.

[4] P. Knight and R. Swanwick. *Working with Deaf Pupils: Sign Bilingual Policy into Practice*. Routledge, 2002.

[5] M. Marschark and P. Hauser. *How Deaf Children Learn: What Parents and Teachers Need to Know*. Perspectives on Deafness. Oxford University Press, USA, 2011.

[6] R. E. Mitchell and M. A. Karchmer. Chasing the mythical ten percent: Parental hearing status of deaf and hard of hearing students in the united states. *Sign Language Studies*, 4:138–163, 2004.

[7] S. Qi and R. E. Mitchell. Large-scale academic achievement testing of deaf and hard-of-hearing students: Past, present, and future. *Journal of Deaf Studies and Deaf Education*, 2011.

[8] Rochester Institute of Technology. C-print computer software, 2014. Accessed January 2014.

[9] K. A. Weaver, T. Starner, and H. Hamilton. An evaluation of video intelligibility for novice american sign language learners on a mobile device. In *Proceedings of the 12th international ACM SIGACCESS conference on Computers and accessibility*, pages 107–114. ACM, 2010.

# 3D Printed Tactile Picture Books for Children with Visual Impairments: A Design Probe

**Abigale Stangl**
ATLAS
University of Colorado
Boulder, CO 80309 USA
abigale.stangl@colorado.edu

**Jeeeun Kim**
Computer Science
University of Colorado
Boulder, CO 80309 USA
jeeeun.kim@colorado.edu

**Tom Yeh**
Computer Science
University of Colorado
Boulder, CO 80309 USA
tom.yeh@colorado.edu

## ABSTRACT

Young children with visual impairments greatly benefit from tactile graphics (illustrations, images, puzzles, objects) during their learning processes. In this paper we present insight about using a 3D printed tactile picture book as a design probe. This has allowed us to identify and engage stakeholders in our research on improving the technical and human processes required for creating 3D printed tactile pictures, and cultivate a community of practice around these processes. We also contribute insight about how our in-person and digital methods of interacting with teachers, parents, and other professionals dedicated to supporting children with visual impairments contributes to research practices.

## Categories and Subject Descriptors

D.3.3 [ Design]:

## General Terms

Documentation, Design, Experimentation, Human Factors,

## Keywords

Tactile Graphics, Tactile Picture books, Design Probe, Blind, Children, Communities of Practice

## 1. INTRODUCTION

For children who are born with or who acquire visual impairments (VI), reading requires an additional layer of three-dimensional tactile information so that the child can feel the shapes of the objects. Tactile pictures make the content of a book relatable and legible. The creation of tactile pictures requires visual pictures or experiences to be transcribed such that a child natively relates to the content, or associate the represented object with the real world. Conversely, tactile picture books aid in the development of a child's tactile acuity and mobility, their sense of seeing or feeling of their environment, as well as their confidence to explore and build relationships and associations through touch.

In this paper we present our initial steps towards creating a digital library of 3D printed tactile picture books, as an effort to make tactile graphics more accessible to parents, teachers, advocacy organizations, and designers committed supporting children with VI, as well as making tactile graphic creation practices more accessible. We discuss how the use of social media and online communication facilitated a 3D printed picture book to become a

*IDC'14*, June 17–20, 2014, Aarhus, Denmark.
Copyright 2014 ACM 978-1-4503-2272-0/14/06···$15.00.
http://dx.doi.org/10.1145/2593968.2610482

design probe to solicit feedback from a user-population that is typically difficult to access due to their limitation of time and proximity. [2]. Additionally, we share insight gained about the need space from these respondents and how this information informs future design work towards the goal of creating a 3D tactile picture book library. We build on previous research about how 3D printing and other automated methods of creating tactile graphics and measuring feedback may provide benefit to a variety of stakeholders; these benefits including the creation of affordable, replicable, and personalized tactile picture books.

## 2. FOUNDATIONAL RESERCH

Our research began with the suspicion that 3D printing will become beneficial to the community committed supporting children with VI. To investigate this suspicion, we formed a partnership with a preschool for young children with VI to identify the unique needs of the children and their families, the role teachers of the visually impaired (TVIs) can play in a child and her family's life, and the environments and materials that support their learning, as well as how and why tactile graphics are typically made for children with VI. We volunteered in classrooms, assisted with a summer camp, and interviewed TVIs and parents about their general practices of making tactile books.

During this formative research we noted that parents feel like there is a limited selection of tactile picture books, either due to availability at their child's school or library, that they are expensive, or because of their child's unique needs [11]. Of the parents that have created tactile books, making their own books was not a common practice due to the time and effort it took to make the books. While there are resources and guidelines [6] [9] available to parents and teachers interested in creating tactile graphics, there are few forums for teachers, parents, and artists to share how they apply these guidelines to their craft or the actual materials they created. These factors present immediate barrier of entry for many parents with children with VI wanting to access or create tactile graphics. Parents often depend on their child's TVI to learn about learning resources for their child, national organizations like the National Federation of the Blind (NFB), and occasionally social media sites like Pinterest for inspiration.

We also attended the Tactile Graphics Conference put on by the National Federation of the Blind (NFB). This quinquennial conference attracts around 200 artists, TVIs and transcriptionists from all over the world to gather and share their knowledge. At this event, we observed that the practitioners, governmental representatives, and companies that attend were more oriented at sharing resources and knowledge about resources than emerging methods of production. We also learned that there are few formalized studies on their creation methods or field tests.

Parents and TVI's do share information about resources on list serves like the NFB-Members list, Blindkid list, BVI-Parents list, etc., however much of the content pertains to parents exchanging advice about how to handle difficult scenarios or access resources, as opposed to providing information about their practices creating tactile picture graphics. An analysis of posts on the list serves mentioned above showed that the phrase "Tactile Graphics" was only referenced 15 times during one year. None of these instances contained information on specific craft practices or 3D printing.

Becoming familiar with the existing communication resources within the community was very beneficial to our general understanding of the community, the environment, and the personnel necessary to create an advantageous learning environment for children with VI. Yet, we noted that this research was very time consuming and expensive. Parents and TVIs are very busy and have limited time to attend special trainings and meetings outside of their teaching role. In some cases there are tactile graphics specialists to create individualized content for children and support the teachers, but this is rare due to budget allocations. We also found that TVI's and parent's exposures to graphic creation and 3D printing were limited.

In turn, we identified four unique design ideas surrounding the use of 3D printers to reduce this barrier to entry and to increase knowledge sharing between stakeholders about the child's learning milestones [8]. These include: 1) Content for an 3D tactile book digital library, with downloadable 3D picture books and a community forum, where for people can share their experiences and needs while creating tactile graphics; 2) A communication device between parents and TVIs that focuses on sharing observations of learning milestones; 3) Software that enables parents or TVIs to input data about a child's needs and interests, in turn producing a books suggestion and kit of parts to 3D print; 4) Touch-receptive sensors to recognize a child's engagement with the book's surface. [3].

These design ideas and the preceding research create a closed-loop approach to improving access to tactile picture books and resources to create these tactile graphics. (Figure 1).

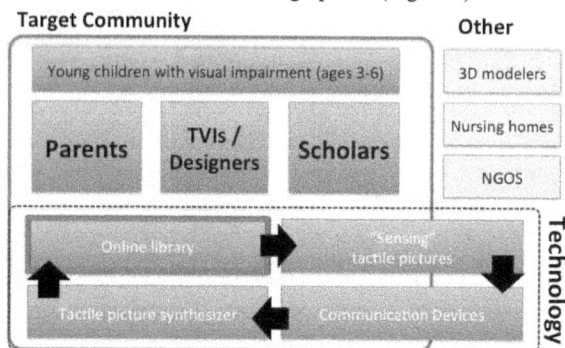

**Figure 1. Target Community**

We choose to focus on creating a 3D picture book library first because it makes content readily, supports a community that has a need for specialized, child specific learning aids, and to use emerging technology as an incentive for parents to become engaged in learning how to design tactile picture books for their children and support emergent literacy skills. We realized that the aim of creating a public forum for the community to share and exchange resources on designing printing 3D tactile picture books complements the development of the other design ideas.

## 3. CONTENT CREATION

Given the lack of publically available and easily replicable tactile picture books, and the complexity of creating tactile graphics, our first aim was to create enjoyable and relevant books for our readers. To develop the initial content for the library, we began an iterative and user-centered process. Throughout the process of developing the first 3D printed book, we continued direct outreach and participation in the community and conducted several rounds of in-person and online outreach efforts to solicit feedback. Subsequently we used a 3D printed picture as a design probe to reach a broader audience. This revealed the challenges and advantages associated with 3D printing as seen by our respondents, which will inform future research on 3D modeling and printing as well building a community of practice. [4]

### 3.1 Iterative Book Design

**Figure 2. 3D tactile model of the original picture**

The first 3D printed tactile picture book we created was a transcription of the classic book, "Goodnight Moon", by Margaret Wise Brown, illustrated by Clement Hurd. We obtained permission from the publisher of this book. The focus of the initial prototype was to learn about the 3D printing process and the strength, texture, malleability of the 3D printed pages. (Figure 2).

We transcribed the image by combining several perspectives in an effort make objects distinct to touch. For example, we represent the bed in an orthogonal view, while objects around the room are presented in plan or sectional view depending on what representation communicates the tactile information best. [10] We showed the book to four TVIs to get initial feedback. Their responses focused on how to simplify the image by focusing on the level of abstraction of the image.

Our second attempt at obtaining feedback about the book involved submitting it to the Typhlo & Tactus Tactile Book Competition. Our entree was accepted into the competition and was selected as one of the top five submissions and was sent onto a competition at the international level. Through involvement in this competition we received feedback from the judges, who said "very interesting possibilities" and "keep exploring it." We received feedback that the plastic models are harder to interpret than rich textures, and similar to the previous feedback from the TVIs, the judges recommended that *"only one or very few objects"* should be shown per page, since our trial to replicate all objects shown at the original page makes the page too complicated. (Figure 3).

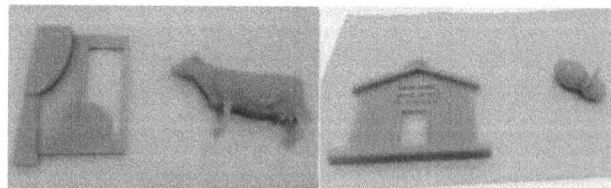

**Figure 3. The Design Prototype**

## 4. DIGITAL COMMUNITY

The acceptance of our work in this competition prompted us to create a webpage to provide a forum for people within our intended user-group to inquire about our methods; we published a photo gallery of the tactile version Goodnight Moon. We also reached out do various 3D modeling practitioners via Twitter, one of whom works at OpenSCAD and develops a 3D braille creator. OpenSCAD is a free software for creating solid 3D CAD models. Via Twitter we started communicating about our work and posted photos to show how we wanted to use his software. He retweeted this photo, which was subsequently retweeted 5 times, and favorited 3 times. While these numbers are not large, we saw almost three times the traffic on our website. Additionally, one of the twitter followers is a publisher of copyright-free children books. He shared our project on his website, which increased visitorship to our website two-fold since we published the tactile version of *Goodnight Moon* to our website.

## 5. DESIGN PROBE

Harkening back to the difficulty of gaining the attention of people through on the ground efforts, we saw this increased visitorship as an opportunity to obtain feedback from a wider audience. On our website we offered single 3D printed pages to solicit feedback. 3D printing afforded us ease in replicability, a key challenge in creating tactile graphics [5]. To date, we have received 28 requests to date and we have printed and sent nearly 60 design probes (Figure 4). Directly after we receive an inquiry, we send two pages from Goodnight Moon and request general feedback.

## 6. FINDINGS

All of the individuals who inquired about the 3D printed picture book pages (design probes) indicated an interest in 3D printing of tactile graphics and picture books. The respondents were self-identified stakeholders who want to improve opportunities for children and others with sensory, cognitive, or other physical disabilities, including visual impairment, dementia, and autism—a range of interest broader than our initial intent. Many of our requestors did not mention who they are exactly, but implicitly indicated they are parents of blind kids, by saying *"I have a son who is blind..."*, indicate they are professor, by saying *"I teach Cognitive and Developmental Psychology to..."*, etc.

Scholars: We received inquiries from scholars from different fields of study (developmental psychology, art and design, photography, and cognitive science). The majority of them work directly with people with VI and wanted information to discriminate to others within their professional community. Some indicated their specific domain interest, including: interactive mapping, tactile perception research, design research. Other scholars requested the design probes to display at upcoming events to promote the use of 3D printers or advanced methods within the domain of STEM education for people with disabilities. One of the respondents was looking for new methods to inspire students to focus on diverse populations. *"Our students opt for careers working with special needs youth. The tactile nature of these books would appeal to the students as hands-on learners."*

TVI's: TVIs who requested pages identified time as the biggest hindrances to their work, and spoke of this issue in respect to making tactile graphics *"I teach beginning braille readers and it takes forever to make the tactual pictures for books."* Speaking directly about 3D printing, one teacher shared, *"We had the opportunity to see a 3D printer at a conference, but had not seen it used as shown in your pictures. We did not pursued a 3D printer is the time required and the difficulty of programming for making the 3D forms."* The benefits of supporting TVI's in efficiently and effectively creating tactile graphics were further articulated by one TVI who explained their role in parents' lives. *"We have the capability to change the written material into Braille, which many of our parents would not be able to do. 3D printing could enhance our ability to provide for parents."*

Braille Transcriptionists and Designers: To date we have received three inquiries from braille transcriptionist and designers who work for public schools, who are searching for new ways to create tactile graphics, and who want to learn how to use 3D printers to create custom models. They report that they are working on behalf of students in need of this technology, are excited about the promise of 3D printing. *"We also have 3D printers at several of our schools and I am seeing great promise for the possibility of producing our own 3D tactile books in the future."* They also disclosed their current practices and needs for 3D printing. *"I currently use Swell Touch paper to make raised-line images or try to find pre-made, small scale models,"* and describe themselves as a bridge of information to others in their profession. *"I promise I would share your book with others. I'd just love to see (feel) it!"*

Parents: We received seven inquiries from parents of young children, five of whom have children with a visual impairment, one with a child with autism, and one with sighted "mechanically inclined children." The commonality between all respondents was the fact that they were looking for resources to keep their children's attention in the reading experience, a key factor in developing emergent literacy skills [1] Several of the parents indicated that they are seeking ways to motivate their children to engage in the reading experience. *"She is struggling with motivation to learn Braille. I think tactile picture books will help her develop tactile discrimination and get her interested in Braille."* Several requests indicated that by sending them the tactile picture book pages they would be exposed to 3D printing and become empowered to learn more about the 3D printing process. *"There are no 3D printers in our world! But if I had a copy of this book, there would be!"*

Other Community: We received a range of additional requests from people that identified themselves with other communities and see an application of our work. For example a unit manager a long term nursing center working with residents with dementia was looking for sensory items for their residents. Another respondent works for an NGO that provides arts and accessibility services to people with disabilities and wanted to use 3D printing. Other respondents indicated working for their town libraries.

## 7. DISCUSSION

By creating a platform for respondents to contact us, and by using a design probe we received a much greater range and depth of feedback than we were able to obtain through initial fieldwork and in-person participation in the community. We attribute this finding a method that accommodates TVI and parents need to be efficient with their time and do things on their own schedule. While most of the information the design probe provided related to our requesters needs, the 3D printed pages of Goodnight Moon provided general design feedback about the specific models, disclosed some of the complexities around creating tactile graphics, and validated the exploration of using 3D printing for these purposes. Many respondents were surprised about the quality of the 3D printing, for example the detail of the cow and mouse as shown in Figure 4. Respondents also liked that we represented different perspectives to distinguish characteristics about an objects, such as an upright mouse and side view of the cow. They did wanted more detail on some of the objects, such as a tail of mouse, which is the key character of the animal, as well as vivid and contrasting colors on the model. Many respondents indicated that parts of the 3D models are easily removed from the base page, indicating that our current 3D models are not designed robust enough. This feedback challenges us to find the correct level of abstraction to express the key characters of objects precisely, while creating models simple enough to minimize other trivial features. We will continue to refine our models and send out design probes to solicit more feedback.

From the highest level, this work was motivated by the desire to gain information about how and why people create tactile graphics and how 3D printing can facilitate these processes, in an effort to find ways to support parents and teachers of children with VI with emergent literacy needs. While pursuing the idea of developing an online library, and the content (books), the potential of using social media to access this hard to reach population became ostensible as an effective practice, as well as using these digital connections to direct people to our website and build a community of practice [4] around *"making"* with and for the visually impaired. By using this digital social networking tool, people were directed to our website, which enabled us to reach our intended user group in a way that suited their needs and motivations, as opposed to requesting them to break their routines. The use of the design probes and website provided a casual yet accessible communication channel between researcher and the community. We hypothesize that this approach will yield fruitful results in efforts to further understanding the need space and establish relationships by sharing their findings during interaction each other. Our aim is to help participants feel like they are contributing to their own community, while providing them a bank of growing resources to help in their self-directed endeavors (as opposed to research subjects). Considering the participants' time and resource limitations, we also aim to consolidate various disparate resources to build open virtual/online community in a forum they are already using (the internet and social media).

Throughout our work with this community, we have noted a value of openness in the exchange of information. This furthers our hypothesis that there is an opportunity to create platform where people can share ideas and further knowledge sharing. From scholars to TVI's, stakeholders readily share insight about the creation of tactile graphics. As one TVI said, *"We have some very talented Teachers of the Visually Impaired on our team that could both utilize what you have developed and hopefully develop programs to share back to your group."*

## 8. FUTURE WORK

In section 2 of this paper we displayed a holistic loop of our design ideas, by pursuing the *"Online Library"* design idea creating preliminary content for the library, we were able to gather important information from respondents. All of the information we obtain from respondents about their wants and need concerning using 3D printers for the creation of tactile graphics will contribute to the four designs indicated.

Using social media and online communication and design probes will continue to influence our method in how to reach participants. As we continue to refine our design probes, we hope that feedback will become more and more specific. We plan to embed solar sensors and/or conductive paint onto the surface of the 3D printed models to obtain immediate feedback (finger touch spots) about what part of the images attract a child's attention.

These *"Sensing Tactile Pictures,"* will provide parents, teachers, and researchers feedback about their child's engagement with the book that may otherwise go undetected.

We will continue to explore how social media as well as in person communication can expand our reach and validate this work. We will include using more hashtags in our social media posting, contributing anonymous feedback from users on our site, providing direct responses to our respondents, and developing relationships to continue to understand the existing design practices. We will ask respondents to classify the types of experiences they have, as well as what learning milestones their activities were contributing to for a child. This metadata will further our analysis of how to create a *"Communication Device"* that shares ideas between parents and TVIs. Furthermore, have also started building the technical infrastructure for the 3D Tactile Library, which will start to host users feedback and make more books available on different smart devices. As we develop the *"Tactile Picture Synthesizer,"* we will confer with the findings above. In particular, we will consider the challenges of learning to use 3D modeling software and the 3D printers indicated by TVIs, which prints barriers of entry to many novice users.

## REFERENCES

[1] Bus, A. G., (2003). *Joint Caregiver-Child Storybook Reading: A Route to Literacy Development*, Handbook of Early Literacy Research., Vol.1, ISBN/UPC 9781572306530, The Guilford Press

[2] Ferrell, K. A., Mason, L., Young, J., & Cooney, J. *Forty Years of Literacy Research in Blindness and Visual Impairment*. Technical Report. Greeley, CO: University of Northern Colorado, National Center on Low-Incidence Disabilities

[3] Kim, J., Stangl, A., Eisenberg, A., & Yeh, T. (2014). *Tactile Picture Books for Young Children with Visual Impairment*, TEI'14

[4] Lave, J. & Wenger, E., (1990). *Situated Learning: Legitimate Peripheral Participation*. Cambridge: Cambridge University Press. First published in 1990 as Institute for Research on Learning report 90-0013

[5] Lipson, H. & Kurman, M., (2013). *Fabricated: The New World of 3D Printing*, Wisely

[6] Philippe C., (2009). *The Typhlo & Tactus Guide to Children's Book with tactile illustrations*, Les Doigts Qui Revent

[7] RNIB http://www.rnib.org.uk

[8] Stangl, A., Kim, J., & Yeh, T., (2014). *Technology to Support Emergent Literacy Skills in Young Children with VI*, CHI'14

[9] Suzette, W., (2013). *Guide to Designing Tactile Illustrations for Children's Books*, American Printing House for the Blind

[10] Swaminathan, R., Grossberg, M. D., & Nayar, S. K., (2003) *A Perspective on Distortions*, IEEE Computer Society Conference on Computer Vision and Pattern Recognition CVPR'03

[11] Tactile Library for the Blind and Partially Sighted, http://www.tactilelibrary.com

# Meta-Designing Interactive Outdoor Games for Children: A Case Study.

Susanne Lagerström[1,2], Iris Soute[2], Yves Florack[2], Panos Markopoulos[2]

[1]Department of Communications and Networking,
Aalto University, School of Electrical Engineering,
Otakaari 5A, 02150 Espoo, Finland

[2]Department of Industrial Design
Eindhoven University of Technology
Den Dolech 2, 5612AZ Eindhoven, The Netherlands

susanne.lagerstrom@gmail.com, i.a.c.soute@tue.nl, y.florack@tue.nl, p.markopoulos@tue.nl

## ABSTRACT

The growth of tangible and embodied interfaces has lead them to expand from research labs to everyday life. This has raised the question of end-user development and the user requirements for an environment supporting development. This paper researches the user requirements for a toolkit to create interactive outdoor games for children, by adults with no programming skills. We present a case study in which adults designed such games and tested them with children. For the design and testing of the games, RaPIDO, a platform specially designed for prototyping interactive technology, was used. Based on this experience we identify requirements for a toolkit to support the creation of interactive outdoor games.

## Categories and Subject Descriptors

H.5.2 [**Information Interfaces** and Presentation]: **User Interfaces** – evaluation/methodology, user-centered design, prototyping.

## General Terms

Design, Human Factors

## Keywords

End-user development; meta-design; children; interactive outdoor games

## 1. INTRODUCTION

Adaptation and personalization of interactive devices is a growing trend in the field of Human Computer Interaction [5]. It has consequently been proposed that end-users themselves should be enabled to create and adapt systems to their personal needs and likes [8]. A well known example of a system that lets children create their own content, is Scratch [9]. Similarly, offerings such as LEGO Mindstorms [3] allow children to create interactive

systems. Typically, these systems have a learning goal: to teach children how to program. Furthermore, these systems are generally designed for indoor use, and are usually not suitable for outdoor play - which is our particular research interest.

The continuing miniaturization of technology has enabled designers and engineers to create interactive technology that can easily be taken outdoors and create novel user experiences. In particular, pervasive (outdoor) gaming is receiving growing interest in research [2,6,10,13]. Still, the trend for supporting adaptation and personalization is less common for tangible and/or mobile interactive technology [14].

We argue that, especially where outdoor gaming is concerned, there is a need for supporting non-technical schooled people to create and/or adapt games. Caretakers of children, such as scout leaders and teachers are natural designers of games for children. Scout leaders currently already design and create non-digital games for the children to play. For instance, they create different versions of *Capture the Flag*, such as a soccer version, in which famous soccer players replace all original military roles. Scout leaders have a unique understanding in what kind of games children prefer to play. Also, the ability to constantly adapt and change games, allows for games to 'grow' with the children, matching their interests as these evolve over time.

Interactive technology brings novel and enjoyable play experiences to outdoor games [13]. Currently, however, the development process of such games requires a considerable amount of time and software skills; time and skills that, e.g., scout leaders typically do not possess. This research examines how interactive applications could support adults, with little or no programming skills, to create interactive outdoor games for children.

In this paper we first discuss related work in end-user development of interactive systems. We propose arguments for why current practices in end-user development may not be suitable in the design of games in the class of interest. Next, we present a case study where two interactive, outdoor games for children are iteratively designed and evaluated by adults using RaPIDO [12], a platform that enables the easy prototyping of interactive outdoor games. Finally, we discuss our main findings on user requirements for a toolkit for creating interactive outdoor games, and conclude with a reflection on how this work might also be valuable for other research areas.

## 2. END-USER CUSTOMIZATION OF TANGIBLE INTERACTIVE TECHNOLOGY

As interactive systems continue to evolve, they become easier to use for end-users who are typically not schooled in computer programming. Research in end-user development (EUD) [8] focuses on how to best support these users to adapt computer tools to integrate in their everyday life, the main focus being on users that are *information workers* [7], i.e. users that use computers and software in their professional context, but are not trained software engineers. A typical example of such a user is a financial expert, who uses spreadsheet software on a daily basis. Though such a user is not trained in programming, he/she might write scripts to ease his/her routine tasks. Research in end-user development (at earlier times under the label of end-user programming) has often considered the need of the domain expert who is a non programmer, e.g., see [4]

Less emphasis has been put on researching the challenges and opportunities that end-user adaption of *tangible* interactive systems brings for non-information workers, such as physiotherapists, and teachers. A notable exception is offered by Tetteroo et al. [14], who identify five key challenges that end-users face when adopting tangible interfaces in their daily routine. Challenges include: integrating the virtual with the physical; supporting end-users in designing interactivity; and EUD in a social-technical context. Tetteroo et al. also argue that due to the needed engineering skills and the effort it takes to design interactive applications, end-users do not have the time, nor do they have a fundamental interest in mastering the skills needed to do so. Therefore they argue that there is a need for toolkits that make it even easier to engage in end-user development.

In the last 10 years, several toolkits have been developed targeting the simplified world of engineering, e.g. the Arduino platform [1] makes it relatively easy for novices to create interactive systems. Modular hardware is offered with a programming environment and software libraries, and a range of extensible hardware is available to further adapt the system. Furthermore, it is supported with an active online community promoting tutorials and examples of how to build interactive applications. For non programmers and especially for people engaging in discretionary end-user programming (i.e. not as part of work), the disadvantage of most of the mentioned platforms, is the need to learn coding and basic engineering. We examine related challenges in a case study that follows end-users in their design process of an interactive game for children.

## 3. CASE STUDY SETUP

This case study examines how non discretionary end-user developers engage with designing games, and in doing so it aims to establish the user requirements for a toolkit for end-user development of interactive outdoor games. This tool would be targeted at adults, with no programming experience, to design games for children using the RaPIDO platform. The RaPIDO platform [12] consists of a set of devices that support various interaction styles that are useful in outdoor interactive games, such as tactile and auditory feedback, sensors for detecting motion and distance. Currently, the RaPIDO platform offers a software API to program games, but it requires advanced software skills to use it.

## 3.1 Participants

The participants in this study were five scout leaders, aged 20-24 of a scouting organization in the Netherlands. During the process of designing the games, children (7-10 years old) have participated as testers. We obtained consent from the parents of the children for their children participating in the sessions, and also for gathering video and photo material.

The scout leaders had previous experience designing non-digital games for children, such as tailor-made versions of Capture-the-Flag. However, they had no experience with programming.

## 3.2 Procedure

In total, four sessions were organized with the scout leaders, in which they iteratively designed two games. In the first two sessions the scout leaders (re-) designed the games, in the third and the fourth session these games were tested by the children.

As the scout leaders had no programming experience, they *designed* the game rules, which we subsequently programmed for the RaPIDO platform. We chose for this approach as we were less interested in the actual programmed result, but more in the process surrounding the creation of games – and how an eventual tool would best support that.

## 3.3 Design sessions

Four scout leaders, 2 women and 2 men, participated in the first game designing session. From these scout leaders 3 out of 4 participated in a previous study and were therefore familiar with the devices and the games. In the second design session two scout leaders, 1 woman and 1 man, participated.

In the first session (Figure 1) we interviewed the scout leaders about their normal way of creating games for the children. Furthermore, the scout leaders were (re) acquainted with RaPIDO by playing an existing game. Then, the design process started, in which we kept our own interference to a minimum. First, we asked the scout leaders to individually write down as many games as they could come up with. Next, ideas were discussed and merged in to two game designs, which we implemented on RaPIDO after the session. In the second design session the scout leaders played these games and brainstormed on improvements.

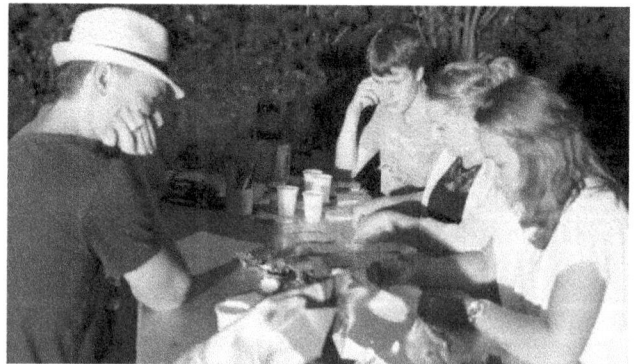

**Figure 1. First designing session with scout leaders**

We noted that when designing the games the scout leaders were thinking about the added value of technology. They tried to focus on games that needed the technology and ruled out some game ideas that would not have a need for technology. They were also reasoning about how the children would experience the game.

We observed that the scout leaders know how to come up with conceptually good game ideas. Often they did not consider the interaction between the device and the player. For example, they did not always think about how the user would get feedback in different situations, e.g. advancing from one level to the next. However they did think about some details in the game e.g. using vibration to show a player that a tag has been read, when not wanting to show it to other players. Unsurprisingly, they had difficulty envisioning the use of some of the technology. This relates to the fact that, though the scout leaders were aware of what the devices could *do*, they were not aware of *how* it was technically implemented, and how best to use the technology to support the game design. For example, they were aware that the devices could show RGB colors using four RGB LEDs. However, due to technical limitations, only one color can be selected at a time. In their game design, the scout leaders envisioned each led showing a different color. Once they realized this was not possible, they could not think of alternatives, and eventually it had to be us suggesting to them to switch the LEDs consecutively on and off, so that each could show its designated color, which left the game design relatively intact.

## 3.4  Game test sessions

In the next two sessions the games designed by the scout leaders (and implemented by us) were tested by children (Figure 2). In the first test session, 5 scout leaders, 3 men and 2 women, attended to the meeting. 9 children (8 boys, 1 girl, 7-10 years) also attended the scout meeting. In the second session 3 scout leaders, 1 man 2 women, attended to the meeting. 6 children, all boys, attended to this meeting, one of them had not attended in the previous session nor the evaluation made earlier [13].

In the game testing sessions the scout leaders would play the games with the children. We would only act as observers and in case of problems help them with the devices. We gave them instructions on how to handle the devices and a recap of how the games work before the children arrived.

After playing with the children, the scout leaders had some ideas on how to change the games, both regarding the interaction with the game and new game rules. For instance when they found that the children were learning the correct order of tags that needed to be found in one of the games, they wanted to randomize the order of tags. They also asked for color collecting assignments, which previously had been shown on paper cards, to be shown on the devices themselves.

**Figure 2. Designing and testing session
with scout leaders and children**

We observed that it was easy for the scout leaders to handle the devices in terms of initiating games. However, explaining the games to the children proved more difficult than normally. Aside from explaining the game rules, now they had to explain the interaction with devices and the game flow as well, which they were not yet familiar enough with.

## 4.  DISCUSSION

The main goal of this study was to study the process of designing games in order to establish the user requirements for a toolkit targeted at adults, with no programming experience, to design outdoor games for children.

## 4.1  Findings for User Requirements

In the sessions with the scout leaders, the main focus was to look at how the target-user can create games from the ground up, conceptualizing the game interactions, possible storyline and, in this case, what technologies would be used.

Concerning the user requirements for a toolkit to create interactive outdoor games, the design, reflection and testing sessions provided some insights for a potential list of requirements.

First of all, there was definitely a need for helping them understand what is possible with technology. For example, during the designing sessions, the scout leaders found it challenging to include the technology in their designs, not knowing the opportunities they had, nor having any practical examples to compare to. They could implement technological aspects they had seen put into practice before, but coming up with new ideas, seemed challenging for them. Peer support, online resources are ways to provide this awareness, or perhaps an explicit account of different possibilities.

Second, scout leaders have no background in interaction design, so it is not surprising that they had trouble designing detailed interactivity aspects, such as user feedback. For example, in the first game design session, the scout leaders incorporated scanning an RFID tag in one game. From a users' perspective it is easier if a successful scanning action is confirmed by, say, an auditory cue. However, such cues were not taken into account in the design. Upon testing in the second session, the scout leaders clearly missed such feedback and wanted it to be implemented.

Tetteroo et al. [14] also state that, in general, end-users are not used to designing interactivity and there for they need support in this. At the moment there is a lack of design guidelines for end-users who want to create their own solutions. Therefore, Tetteroo argues that meta-designers should not only provide a toolkit for end-users, but they should also be provided guidance in how to meaningfully design interactivity, or even add detailed interactivity aspects automatically (e.g., automatically inserting an audio cue for every scanned tag)

Third, during the testing sessions, it seemed to be difficult for the scout leaders to explain the games and the interactions to the children. By adding a possibility within a toolkit to demonstrate aspects of a game, it would probably help the scout leaders explain the game. One of the scout leaders also remarked that usually with games without technology, they show the children how it is done beforehand. Taking this into consideration throughout the design process of a game, we hypothesise that this will provide the scout leader with the capability to better communicate and translate the game to the children. In principle, this aspect can also be used during the design phase, to test and evaluate the design with.

Finally, there was a need for being able to set up a game with e.g. number of players, teams, time-limit, etc. or the need to change parameters between games. Also, during play it could be handy for the scout leaders to monitor the game, i.e. see some game parameters in real-time (e.g. scores, time left to play etc.) During one of the testing sessions there was definitely a need to adjust settings for one game, as it was becoming boring for the children.

## 4.2 Reflections on the Method Used

In general we think that the method used in this study worked well with our target group, the scout leaders. The scout leaders designed two games that both they and the children liked to play. As the scout leaders did not have experience programming the RaPIDO devices, we have done this for them. We did implement some details of games that were not specifically designed by the scout leaders – in particular details that, when not implemented, would make a game totally unplayable. However, we kept this 'interference' to a minimum; the general design of the game originated from the scout leaders. As such, this process gave us a good insight in how the scout leaders would engage in the design process and what kind of designs they are capable of.

Compared to using co-design, where the user is given the position of 'expert of his/her experience' by providing tools for ideation and expression" [11], as a method for this research, we believe that our approach was more suitable for this specific study. If we had co-designed the games with the scout leaders, we could have assumed the role as technology and game design experts and would have had more influence on the game design, which would have given a distorted image of how scout leaders would have designed games without our presence.

## 5. CONCLUSION

Adults, such as scout leaders, often have a good insight on what kind of games the children like and may therefore be good, and perhaps even better than interaction designers, at designing the game concepts for these kind of games. However, these people rarely have experience in interaction design or programming, which we argue is needed for being able to design interactive games with a good game flow and which match with the game concept. Therefore we strongly believe that there is a need for a toolkit that supports and structures the creation of interactive outdoor games. The main idea of such a toolkit would be to give non-programmers and people who do not have experience in interaction design a chance to design and/or tweak interactive outdoor games.

Even though the target group in this research was very specific, we believe that the findings in this research could also be transferred to other Tangible and Embodied Interfaces. As (embedded) technology is becoming more and more established in everyday life, it becomes important that users are able to adapt functionality to their preferences, to encourage adoption of said technology. Especially professionals, who are not educated in technology, taking up technology in their work context, could benefit from tools to adapt technology. For example, a toolkit, tailored to the capabilities of a teacher, would enable the teacher to use technology in a meaningful way. This research is a first step in showing how the development of such toolkits could be executed.

## 6. ACKNOWLEDGEMENTS
We would like to thank the children and scout leaders of Scouting Steensel, the Netherlands for excellent cooperation.

## 7. REFERENCES

[1] Arduino. Arduino website. 2014. www.arduino.cc.

[2] Benford, S., Crabtree, A., Flintham, M., et al. Can you see me now? *ACM Trans. Comput.-Hum. Interact. 13*, 1 (2006), 100–133.

[3] Blikstein, P. Gears of Our Childhood: Constructionist Toolkits, Robotics, and Physical Computing, Past and Future. *Proceedings of the 12th International Conference on Interaction Design and Children*, ACM (2013), 173–182.

[4] Bonnie A. Nardi. *A small matter of programming: perspectives on end user computing.* MIT press, 1993.

[5] Fischer, G. User Modeling in Human-Computer Interaction. User Modeling and User-Adapted Interaction 11, 1-2 (2001), 65–86.

[6] Fujiki, Y., Kazakos, K., Puri, C., Pavlidis, I., Starren, J., and Levine, J. NEAT-o-games: ubiquitous activity-based gaming. *CHI '07 extended abstracts on Human factors in computing systems*, ACM (2007), 2369–2374.

[7] Ko, A.J., Abraham, R., Beckwith, L., et al. The state of the art in end-user software engineering. *ACM Comput. Surv. 43*, 3 (2011), 21:1–21:44.

[8] Lieberman, H., Paternò, F., Klann, M., and Wulf, V. End-User Development: An Emerging Paradigm. In H. Lieberman, F. Paternò and V. Wulf, eds., End User Development. Springer Netherlands, Dordrecht, 2006, 1–8.

[9] Maloney, J., Resnick, M., Rusk, N., Silverman, B., and Eastmond, E. The Scratch Programming Language and Environment. *Trans. Comput. Educ. 10*, 4 (2010), 16:1–16:15.

[10] Rogers, Y., Price, S., Fitzpatrick, G., et al. Ambient wood: designing new forms of digital augmentation for learning outdoors. *Proc. of IDC '04*, ACM (2004), 3–10.

[11] Sanders, E. and Stappers, P.J. (2008). Co-creation and the new landscape of design. CoDesign. Vol. 4, No. 1. 5-18.

[12] Soute, I., Aartsen, H., and Bangaru, C. On Developing a Platform for Mobile Outdoor Gaming for Children. In D.V. Keyson, M.L. Maher, N. Streitz, et al., eds., *Ambient Intelligence*. Springer Berlin Heidelberg, Berlin, Heidelberg, 2011, 200–204.

[13] Soute, I., Lagerstrom, S., and Markopoulos, P. Rapid prototyping of outdoor games for children in an iterative design process. *Proceedings of the 12th International Conference on Interaction Design and Children*, ACM (2013), 74–83.

[14] Tetteroo, D., Soute, I., and Markopoulos, P. Five Key Challenges in End-user Development for Tangible and Embodied Interaction. *Proceedings of the 15th ACM on International Conference on Multimodal Interaction*, ACM (2013), 247–254.

# The Effects of Visual Contextual Structures on Children's Imagination in Story Authoring Interfaces

Sharon Lynn Chu and Francis Quek
TAMU Embodied Interaction Lab (TEIL)
Texas A&M University
College Station, TX
[sharilyn; quek]@tamu.edu

## ABSTRACT

This paper investigates how the presentation of contextual visual images may influence a child's imagination during the use of authoring systems to create digital content. This issue is particularly significant to understand what supports the child's creativity in authoring systems in creative storytelling. We address specifically children aged 8 to 10 because of the 'Fourth-Grade Slump' phenomenon whereby children experience a decrease in creative engagement at this period. We carried out a study in which children used a storytelling system that allows the user to physically enact stories in a digitally-augmented space contextualized by either a contextual background image or a blank screen. Using methods of video coding and analysis, we uncovered themes relating differences between children's enactment in the presence of a digital background and without in terms of both the process and product of storytelling. We discuss implications that the themes have for the design of story authoring systems for children.

## Categories and Subject Descriptors

H.5.2 [**Information Interfaces and Presentation**]: User Interfaces (Screen Design)

## General Terms

Design, Human Factors

## Keywords

Creativity, Digitality, Children, Imagination, Perception

## 1. INTRODUCTION

The affordances of both physical toys and digital interfaces have tremendous power to transport children into worlds of imaginary pretend play. An 8-year-old playing with a stick may imagine herself to be a knight, pirate, or even her favorite superhero. She imagines freely and creates stories in her 'mind's eye', projecting mental imagery on artifacts in her environment. If we place this child in a room with a pirate-ship wallpaper motif however, her imagination may become constrained to pretend play as a pirate.

Likewise, a child playing a digital game with the Wii game controller or the Kinect is acting within a situation where the context is given. Psychological research in design fixation has shown that the provision of external structures can prime the individual's imagination or idea generation [1, 2]. How does that affect the design of authoring interfaces for children?

Authoring interfaces provide a digital environment for children to create in. They frame the creative process of the child as the latter engages in idea generation and expression. In the domain of creative storytelling that we focus on, research has looked at the technical implementation of systems, the proposition of new interaction concepts, or the study of a particular technology to support learning, social connectedness, motivation, etc. Examples of story authoring systems include POGO [3], StoryMat [4] and Story-Room [5]. Yet, little research has been done to understand the specific requirements for designing digital interfaces in such authoring systems. The design of the system's interface is typically arbitrary to a large extent. Our research aims to provide guidelines as to the design of story authoring interfaces for elementary school children. We investigate how the presentation of contextual visual images may influence a child's imagination during the story creation process and the stories produced.

Many existing story authoring systems for children such as those mentioned above have been developed to leverage the child's capacity to readily engage in pretend play. In fact, Chu & Quek [6, 7] proposed the concept of performative authoring whereby the child physically enacts out to construct or tell a story, thus providing a transparent creation medium as opposed to, for instance, writing which requires technical skills. This paper presents a study in which children used a storytelling system that creates a digitally-augmented space where the user can enact stories contextualized by varying visual presentations.

## 2. BACKGROUND & CONTEXT

We focus on children aged 8 to 11 (3rd – 5th grade) because children of that age range undergo a period of cognitive, social and emotional development, and are susceptible to a phenomenon called the 'Fourth-grade slump' [8], whereby children experience a sudden decline in creative engagement. One possible explanation that has been advanced for the decline is the intensification of social awareness in the child, which causes the child to self-evaluate her output more negatively. This in turn leads to a drop in the child's self-efficacy, and a consequent decline in motivation to engage in creative activities [9, 10].

In contrast to theories of design fixation [11], theories of embodied cognition have suggested that external representations such as visual images are helpful for people to think. McNeill [12] proposed that external objects can be appropriated as 'material carriers' to represent thought objects, in essence bringing the person's perceptual and spatial abilities to participate in her thinking process. This suggests the positive participation of perception in the creative process. Empirical evidence has been presented to that effect showing that features of the physical environment can mediate creative performance [13].

In line with fixation theories however, Neblett et al. [14] found that the presence of physical objects of particular shapes made available for perception and manipulation was functionally equivalent to simply visualizing or projecting the shapes in one's mind, resulting in no difference in outcomes. Anderson & Helstrup [15] saw that physical synthesis could generate more patterns, but the patterns were not necessarily more creative. In this sense, the presentation of perceived structures may not translate to benefits.

Given the conflicting theories, it is difficult to determine whether the provision of visual contextual structures may support or hinder the child's story creation process. Bipolar explanations for possible outcomes include: the **'design fixation'/'stimulus' hypothesis**, whereby the perceived structures either have an overpowering effect on cognition or triggers the creation of new lines of association among the child's memory structures; the **'lack of raw materials'/'structures influx' hypothesis**, whereby the child either does not have sufficient experiences from which to draw or has a large store of memory structures that creates an influx of connections to be actualized in the creative act; the **'offloading'/'automatic retrieval' hypothesis**, whereby the external representations either help the child to reduce cognitive load therefore facilitating her retrieval of memory structures or cause the 'automatic' retrieval of schema (memory structures) associated with the task preventing the child to readily recombine other farther structures; and the **'cognitive dissonance' hypothesis** [16] stating that people may show poorer performance in creativity when imagined and perceived stimuli are mismatched/misaligned.

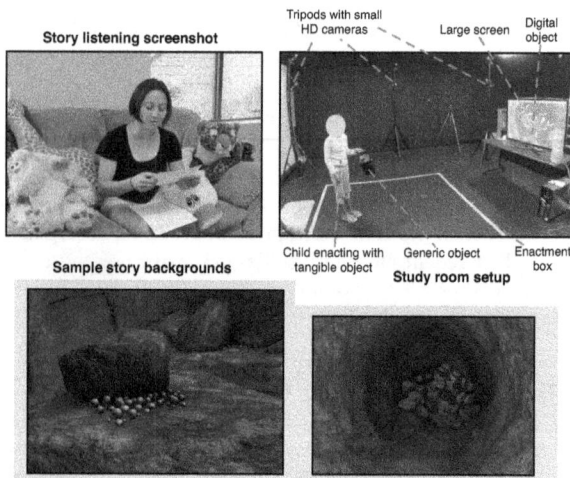

**Figure 1. System-related pictures**

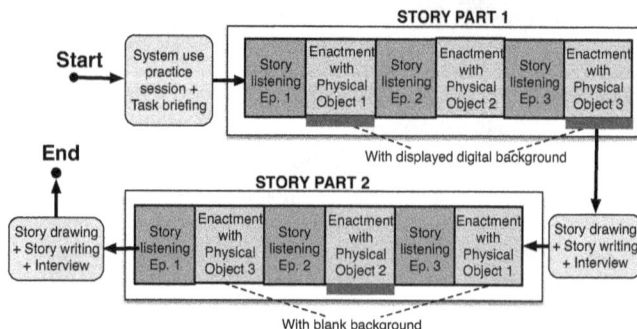

**Figure 2. Design of study conducted**

Our research question is as follows: <u>How do contextual visual structures in story authoring systems affect the child's process of creative storytelling and the nature of the creative product?</u>

## 3. THE STUDY

We ran a study in the form of a digital storytelling workshop in a studio space for children aged 8 to 11 (3 boys and 3 girls) whose parents voluntarily signed them up. Story backgrounds shown on a large display (see Figure 1 top right) were chosen as the form of contextual visual structures to be provided. This configuration is a common feature in many interactive systems for children. An interactive digital story authoring system was developed to help in the conduct of the study. The system has two modes: 1. Story listening, and 2. Story creation. In the story listening mode, the system plays a video of a story reader narrating a story (Figure 1 top left). In the story creation mode, the system allows the child to tell a story using enactment with a generic tangible object. The use of the tangible object enables the child to interact with an analogous digital version of the object on the screen, e.g., moving a tangible toy lantern in the 'enactment box' will correspondingly move a digital 3D model of a lantern onscreen. In this story creation mode, either a background image or a blank screen can be displayed together with the digital object model on the screen.

The study was carried out as illustrated in Figure 2: using the digital storytelling system, the child participant first watched the narration of a novel story of three dwarves going into a cave to find resources for their town. The story consisted of two parts, each part consisting of three segments or episodes. The three episodes in each story part were crafted to tell the same events (i.e. dwarves cooking, dwarves digging, dwarves shooing away enemies). The story was paused after each episode and the system was switched to creation mode. The child was asked to continue the story using enactment. All children engaged in two kinds of study sessions: enactment with a background image and with a blank screen. If a background image was displayed during enactment episodes of Story Part 1 for a participant, a blank screen was displayed for story creation in Part 2. In total the study took 1.5 hours, with each story listening episode lasting around 3 mins and each story creation session lasting about 2 – 3 mins. The children indicated to the researcher when they were done enacting their story part. All enactment sessions were video recorded.

## 4. DATA ANALYSIS

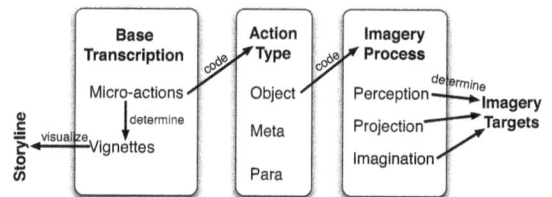

**Figure 3. Data analysis of story enactment videos**

The overall analysis approach of the enactment videos is shown in Figure 3: **(1)** Using the Inqscribe software [17], the base transcription was done based on Chu & Quek's MAIA approach [18], in which the videos are transcribed first at the level of *micro-actions* (atomic actions including the use of voice), and second at the level of *vignettes*, meaningful groups of micro-actions telling a story piece; **(2)** Each micro-action is coded using a variant of McNeill's [19] reference chain analysis scheme into three levels: *object*- (referencing the story that the child is telling, e.g., rocking the frying pan to enact a cooking action), *meta*- (referencing the process of telling the story, e.g., pausing in mid-action to think about the next step in the story being told), and *para-* (referencing objects and persons in the immediate environment unrelated to either the story being told or the process of telling the story); **(3)** 'Object-level' actions that indicated simulated interactions with some sort of story environment element were coded into three categories based on Kirsh's [20] spectrum. Kirsh classifies the use of external structures participating in cognitive processes depending on its level of dependence on what may be readily perceived in the environment. In *Perception*, the mental imagery is anchored completely in perceived external structures. In *Projection*, imagined structures retrieved from memory are anchored on external structures, similarly to one wearing 'augmented reality' glasses. In *Imagination,* mental imagery is wholly retrieved from memory, and is independent from any perceived external structure. The utility of Kirsh's model is that it provides us with a way to analyze and understand the mechanism by which the child imagines and creates her enacted story.

# 5. FINDINGS

We describe and discuss below themes uncovered in our analysis in terms of the process of story creation and the stories produced. The findings are summarized in Figure 4.

| With Background | Without Background |
|---|---|
| Translation + Augmentation of digital stimuli | Augmentation of any environmental stimuli |
| Projection from environmental structures | Projection from memory |
| Creativity flow | Reduced story focus |
| Greater motivation | More structured storyline |
| More typical storyline | More elaborate storyline |

**Figure 4. Summary of findings**

**PROCESS: Transformed Imagination:** There were differences in terms of the types of objects that the child's imagination targeted depending on the background condition. In the case with the digital background, the child would appropriate the perceived digital structures, e.g., mushrooms on the cave banks (refer to Figure 1), move them elsewhere on the screen or out into the world onto a different anchor, e.g., the tangible object. This transformation of perceived structures were not limited to translation or movement only, but also included augmentation of the state of the structures, e.g., the mushrooms being chopped up and cooked instead of raw. However, in the sessions without the contextual backgrounds, the child augmented any perceived structure in the environment (the tangible object, the blank screen, the floor, etc.) with structures retrieved from memory. Processes of appropriation, translation and augmentation were not needed.

**PROCESS: Story Focus:** We found that the child had a harder time getting started and staying on task in storytelling without the perceived stimulus of the digital background. To a large extent, sessions without digital backgrounds were punctuated with more periods of play or non-story relevant actions than sessions with digital backgrounds. 'Meta-level' and 'Para-level' micro-actions were significantly more prevalent. The child would often drift in and out of the story mode (e.g., to examine the tangible objects or to play with the technology) instead of having an unbroken block of storytelling activity. This is detrimental given that enactment has been identified as episodes of 'flow of creativity' [6, 21], and has formed the rationale for many children's storytelling systems.

**PROCESS: Motivation, Interest and Excitement:** Apart from the excitement of the children by the interactive capabilities of the storytelling system with regards to the tracking of the tangible objects, we observed that the provision of the digital backgrounds consistently caused greater interest in the child to engage in story creation. The fewer number of micro-actions until the first story-relevant micro-action on average for many of the children, as well as comments during the post-interviews, provide evidence of the motivational effect of the digital structures.

**PRODUCT: Affordance-based Imagination:** The types of actions that the child performed in the digital background sessions were usually more typical of the situation presented in the story episode than in the no-digital background sessions. For instance, the first event of the child's story tended to consist of an action that plays off the key contextual digital element (e.g., scoop up mushrooms) when digital structures were present, whereas with no digital structures the first story event was often one that sets some form of context or background to the child's story (e.g., declaring "I'm hungry", planning to get more food). The overall storyline as well was usually more typical of the schema of the story situation (e.g., gather food, cook food, eat food). More imagined actions and objects outside of the typical schema of the story narration were seen in the no-digital background condition (e.g., spotting ants, getting burnt, walking in a tired manner). We call the child's imagination in the with-digital background sessions 'affordance-based' as the ideas that the child retrieved to include in the story were more often than not associated with what the perceived digital structures directly provided.

**PRODUCT: Structured narrative:** The stories told in the sessions without digital backgrounds were observed to generally follow more of the narrative structure with a beginning, middle and end than those from the with-digital background sessions. The no-digital background storylines tended to start with speech uttered by the story character, the child's own narration, or character action that sets the context of the story (e.g., "I'm a miner", the character walking to the mines, the character being hungry). Although a clear climax was not always immediately evident, the child typically provided a closure or wrap up of some sort to the story (e.g., the character assessing the food cooked as "yummy", the character walking out of the scene to the next). With digital backgrounds present, the storylines were more focused on interaction with the elements perceived instead of producing an actual story that is normally defined by the narrative arc.

# 6. IMPLICATIONS FOR DESIGN

We investigated the role of contextual digital structures in story authoring systems for children to inform the design of interfaces that optimize support for the creative process of the child. Our findings indicate that there are clear tradeoffs. On the one hand, these structures act as prompts for task and story engagement for some children. On the other hand, they may harm the quality of the stories or creative products that a typical child can produce. Amabile's [22] componential model highlights the importance of motivation, creativity-relevant skills and content knowledge for creativity. Given the 'Fourth-Grade Slump' phenomenon that we described in Section 2, motivation is a key component that should be considered for our 8 to 10 year-old target age group. Compromises may have to be made in design decisions when considering the level of perceived support to provide in an interface. For example, if contextual digital representations are excluded in the design of a system so as to maximize support for the child's creativity-relevant skills and content knowledge, one may want to incorporate a separate feature designed to increase the motivation of the child to be involved in the creative activity.

The stories constructed by our participants in the with-digital-background were less elaborate and exhibited poorer structure in the form of a less apparent narrative arc. The reason for this may be Kirsh's [20] observation that projecting mental imagery onto perceptual structures incurs a 'cost' for the viewer to deconstruct the background structure and to transform its elements. In the no-background-image case, the child does not have to overcome this 'cost' in order to employ prior experience both in content and understanding of narrative structure.

One possible way to alleviate the 'cost' and making contextual structures effective is to reduce the 'size' of the unit of the provided contextual structure. Investigating the design of physical objects for children's story enactments, Chu & Quek [23] proposed that the affordances of objects may lie on a spectrum of cultural-specificity ranging from very similar to very arbitrary to real-life referent objects. Similarly, we can think of the background and no-background conditions in our study as two poles along a continuum of 'atomization' of perceived digital elements. We made use of a 'whole' background in our study. In the background condition, all visual pieces are rigidly embedded in a whole image with semiotic roles for each element. In the no-background condition, only the animated objects are present, disconnected from any specification of its meaning. We can imagine a continuum of visual representations with varying commitment to 'whole construction' that a child may use (e.g., tires and vehicle bodies → whole fire engines → fire engines at the scene of a large fire, as different points on the continuum). Where representations lay on this continuum may help to satisfy the trade-off requirements of degrees of visual support for motivation and creativity.

## 7. CONCLUSION

Our findings are necessarily limited to the context of the choices that we made in the design of the study and system, e.g., despite efforts to construct similar and comparable story episodes for each study condition, minor differences and other factors beyond our control may have influenced children's creative processes. Possible directions for future research are numerous: presented digital structures can be manipulated to be smaller units to test our 'atomization' premise; contextual representations can be extended to be not only perceived in the visual sense but in terms of other sensory modalities like hearing; apart from story backgrounds that we studied, other types of contextual structures commonly used in system interfaces for children can be manipulated, e.g., pre-generated characters.

Our research studied the impact that contextual digital structures may have on the process of how children imagine stories and the actual stories produced. The five themes uncovered show that the design of interfaces with respect to the child's imagination is more complex than one may expect, and is worthy of thorough study.

## 8. REFERENCES

1. Smith, S.M., T.B. Ward, and J.S. Schumacher, *Constraining effects of examples in a creative generation task.* Memory & Cognition, 1993. **21**(6): p. 837-845.

2. Jansson, D.G. and S.M. Smith, *Design fixation.* Design studies, 1991. **12**(1): p. 3-11.

3. Polazzi, L. *The Pogo active tools: Narrative logic, time and space in children storytelling.* in *Interaction without frontiers: Joint AFIHM-BCS conference on Human-Computer Interaction.* 2001. Cépaduès-Éditions.

4. Ryokai, K. and J. Cassell. *StoryMat: A Play Space for Collaborative Storytelling.* in *CHI.* 1999. Pittsburg: ACM.

5. Alborzi, H., et al. *Designing StoryRooms: Interactive Storytelling Spaces for Children.* in *Designing Interactive Systems (DIS).* 2000. NY: ACM.

6. Chu, S., Q. F., and J. Tanenbaum. *Performative Authoring: Nurturing Storytelling in Children through Imaginative Enactment.* in *International Conference on Interactive and Digital Storytelling (ICIDS).* 2013. Istanbul, Turkey: Springer.

7. Chu, S. and F. Quek. *An Enactment-based Approach to Creativity Support.* in *IDC '13 Workshop on Interactive Technologies that Enhance Children's Creativity.* 2013. New York, NY: ACM.

8. Torrance, E.P., *Understanding the Fourth Grade Slump in Creative Thinking*, in *Cooperative Research Project.* 1967, US Department of Health, Education and Welfare. p. 444.

9. Chu, S., et al. *The Effects of Physicality on the Child's Imagination.* in *Creativity and Cognition '13.* 2013. Sydney: Australia: ACM.

10. Chu, S.L., F. Quek, and X. Lin. *Studying Medium Effects on Children's Creative Processes.* in *Creativity and Cognition.* 2011. Atlanta, GA: ACM.

11. Smith, S.M., J.S. Linsey, and A. Kerne, *Using evolved analogies to overcome creative design fixation*, in *Design Creativity 2010.* 2011, Springer: London. p. 35-39.

12. McNeill, D., *Hand and Mind: What Gestures Reveal about thought.* 1992, Chicago: University of Chicago Press.

13. McCoy, J.M. and G.W. Evans, *The potential role of the physical environment in fostering creativity.* Creativity Research Journal, , 2002. **14**(3-4): p. 409-426.

14. Neblett, D.R., R.A. Finke, and H. Ginsburg, *Creative visual discoveries in physical and mental synthesis*, in *Creative imagery, Discoveries and inventions in visualization*, R.F. (1990), Editor. 1989, Lawrence Erlbaum, Inc.: Hillsdale, NJ.

15. Anderson, R.E. and T. Helstrup, *Visual discovery in mind and on paper.* Memory & Cognition, 1993. **21**(3): p. 283-293.

16. Finke, R.A., *Creative imagery: Discoveries and inventions in visualization.* 1990, Hillsdale, NJ: Lawrence Erlbaum, Inc.

17. Inquirium LLC. *Inqscribe: Digital media transcription software.* 2013; Available from: http://www.inqscribe.com/.

18. Chu, S. and F. Quek. *MAIA: A Methodology for Assessing Imagination in Action.* in *CHI 2013 Workshop on Evaluation Methods for Creativity Support Environments.* 2013. Paris, France: ACM.

19. McNeill, D., et al., *MIND-MERGING*, in *Expressing Oneself / Expressing One's Self: Communication, Language, Cognition, and Identity: A Festschrift in honor of Robert M. Krauss (11/8/07)*, E. Moresella, Ed. 2008, Taylor & Francis.

20. Kirsh, D. *Projection, Problem Space and Anchoring.* in *31st Annual Conference of the Cognitive Science Society.* 2009. Austin, TX: Cognitive Science Society.

21. Chu, S. and F. Quek. *An Enactment-based Approach to Creativity Support.* in *Workshop on Interactive Technologies that Enhance Children's Creativity at IDC '13.* 2013. New York City, NY.

22. Amabile, T.M., *The Social Psychology of Creativity.* 1983, New York Springer-Verlag.

23. Chu, S. and F. Quek. *Things to Imagine With: Designing for the Child's Creativity.* in *Interaction Design & Children '13.* 2013. New York City: NY: ACM.

# Towards a Constructively Aligned Approach to Teaching Interaction Design & Children

Eva Eriksson
Division of Interaction Design
Department of Applied IT
Chalmers University of Technology
Gothenburg, Sweden
eva.eriksson@chalmers.se

Olof Torgersson
Division of Interaction Design
Department of Applied IT
University of Gothenburg
Gothenburg, Sweden
olof.torgersson@ait.gu.se

## ABSTRACT

This paper proposes the principles of constructive alignment as foundation for course design within Interaction Design and Children (IDC). While the field has existed for over a decade, there is still no settled curriculum for teaching it. The paper demonstrates how intended learning outcomes in combination with related work and research on teaching IDC can be used to develop a course in IDC, and exemplify this with a brief description of the development of a recently completed course. The contribution of this paper is to support anyone who intends to start teaching in this area, to stimulate discussion in the community, and contribute to an emerging curriculum for Interaction Design and Children.

## Categories and Subject Descriptors

H5.2. Information interfaces and presentation: User Interfaces – Theory and Methods

## General Terms

Design

## Keywords

Interaction design and children, teaching, curriculum, CCI.

## 1. INTRODUCTION

IDC - Interaction Design and Children (or CCI - Child Computer Interaction) is a growing area in both research and design, and the community has more than quadrupled in size over the last eight years [14]. Despite this extensive growth, there is still no settled curriculum for what to teach in the field of IDC, and very little discussion on how to do it. This can be illustrated by a survey of the proceedings of all the IDC conferences so far, where only 3 papers were found dealing with development of teaching for IDC; one work in progress paper at IDC'13 [6], one workshop at IDC'11 [7] and one position paper from that same workshop [13]. To improve the design practice in the IDC area, we believe that it is necessary to not only study and improve methodology in a research context, but also how to transfer the gained knowledge to new generations of designers, to ensure its use in design. This topic is investigated in the two year project DEVICE: Design for Vulnerable generations – Children and Elderly, where a

*IDC'14*, June 17–20, 2014, Aarhus, Denmark.
Copyright 2014 ACM 978-1-4503-2272-0/14/06...$15.00.
http://dx.doi.org/10.1145/2593968.2610485

combination of current best practices from academia and industry, design explorations and teaching experiments are used to suggest an approach to teaching design for and with children and elderly [6].

In this paper we briefly present the development of one pilot study from the DEVICE project; a master level course on interaction design and children. The course development is based upon the work within the project, related work [e.g. 7, 13], and on the principles of constructive alignment [4], which is a major current pedagogical trend within higher education. This means that the design of the course is based on a set of intended learning outcomes for students, describing the skills they should be able to demonstrate upon completing the course. The paper is an effort to stimulate the discussion on what a curriculum for teaching IDC could be and to contribute to the community by presenting our experiences and material that others can draw from when teaching IDC. In line with this, all the material from the course is publicly available at http://ixdcth.se/courses/2013/ciu235/ for anyone interested in investigating the material or to adapt it for use in teaching.

## 2. BACKGROUND

Based on an inventory of several courses, Gilutz et al suggest the following eight topics as critical to teaching IDC in a multidisciplinary context [7]: *Communication* (facilitating various forms of interpersonal communication, children's media use and literacy), *Psychology* (Human development, learning theories, motivation), *HCI* (general), *Children's HCI* (History and current trends), *Pedagogies, Technologies, Experiences* (Designing for play, education, development, health, and communication), and *Design* (Methods and adaptation). This is elaborated further by Read [13], who suggests two different curricula, one for undergraduate students, and one for postgraduate students. The undergraduate curriculum, titled *Designing cool stuff for children working, learning and playing,* aims to introduce designing interactive technology for children and to provide skills to evaluate interactive technologies for children by demonstrating how children act around and use interactive technologies [13]. In the postgraduate curriculum, titled *Child Computer Interaction*, Read suggests that the aim is to introduce students to the theory and practice of Child Computer Interaction, to give them skills to be critical and reflective designers of interactive technology for children, and to equip students with tools and techniques for carrying out and design safe, ethical research studies with child participants in the field of HCI and CCI [13].

This brief overview of related work on teaching in IDC exemplifies discussion on topics to be covered, rather than expected learning outcomes and what to include within the suggested topics. In the next section we describe an IDC course development taking on the perspective of constructive alignment as well some suggestions regarding content.

## 3. COURSE DESIGN

A 7.5 ECTS credit project course was given within the Interaction Design and Technologies (ID&T) master's program at Chalmers University of Technology in Gothenburg, Sweden. The program is based on four pedagogical ideas. Firstly, a mix of theory and practice, applied in constructively aligned courses. Secondly, a mix of given and open problems; the former to practice application of certain skills the latter to practice problem solving and innovation. Thirdly, a large amount of project work where students work in mixed groups in a studio environment, similar to the situation in real life. Fourthly, students are trained to present their work to the public, as exhibitions, or taking part in conferences and contests. These principles are based on current pedagogical research, see for instance [11] pp 57-70 and were taken into account when designing the course. That the course was designed to fit within the ID&T program meant that all students could be assumed to have taken a basic course in Human-Computer Interaction, one in Interaction Design Methodology and a course on Prototyping Techniques, in extension to their various bachelor backgrounds in e.g. engineering or design.

### 3.1 Intended Learning Outcomes

The course was designed along the principles of constructive alignment. Using constructive alignment, the teaching system should align activities and methods to the learning objectives (intended learning outcomes) to facilitate for students to construct meaning (knowledge) [4]. The intended learning outcomes should be stated in such a way that it becomes clear to students what skills and knowledge they should be able to demonstrate after the course and the teaching should then be designed to facilitate for students to reach them. Thus, when defining a course in interaction design and children, the intended learning outcomes becomes the natural starting point describing the teacher's intent with the course. Since the purpose of the course is to teach the essentials of interaction design for children, the learning outcomes can also be seen as a description of the core skills needed by practitioners in the field according to the authors' opinions.

The learning outcomes for the course are divided into 3 categories, *Knowledge and understanding*, *Skills and abilities* and *Judgment and approach*:

*Knowledge and Understanding*

- K1 Describe stages of child development relevant for design
- K2 Describe methods for working with interaction design and children
- K3 Describe the similarities and differences of children and other intended user groups
- K4 Describe considerations for involving children in the design process

*Skills and abilities*

- S1 Create designs specifically adopted for children
- S2 Design with regards to both children and caretakers
- S3 Modify design methods to fit the context and needs of children
- S4 Identify needs and requirements for children and caretakers

*Judgment and approach*

- J1 Evaluate designs taking into account the needs of children

- J2 Make an informed evaluation of the ethical and societal impacts of a design
- J3 Criticize designs and design processes with respect to the needs of children

When defining the criteria for *knowledge and understanding* the focus was to catch the most central theoretical knowledge on which to base a design process. The criteria for *skills and abilities* focus on what the designer should be able to do in a design process. The criteria for *judgment and approach* are intended to capture that students should be able to make a critical analysis of (a proposed) design, taking the needs and perspectives of children into account as well as performing evaluation with children. Once the intended learning outcomes have been settled, the focus of the rest of the course design process becomes to define tasks and material that ensure that the students fulfill the outcomes upon completing the course. A brief description of the results from this process follows below.

### 3.2 Literature

The core literature used in the course was the paper "Interaction design and children" by Hourcade [9], which covers a lot of the basics of the field. To cover aspects of evaluation and ethics, parts of the book "Evaluating Children's Interactive Products" by Markopoulos et al [12] was used. In addition to this a number of research papers by authors such as Druin [5], Antle [1], Bekker et al [3], Walsh et al [17], Kärnä et al [10] Read & MacFarlane [15], Resnick & Silverman [16] and Guha et al [8] were included in the course literature to add additional material and depth. Finally, the students were also introduced to the Developmentally Situated Design (DSD) cards [2] since these represent a valuable and useful compilation of knowledge directly useful in design for children. The students were further encouraged to find additional literature related to the topics of the course and to their projects.

### 3.3 Teaching Modalities

Following the common approach of the ID&T program, the course applied a combination of teaching methods and a mix of theory and practice to stimulate the students' learning. To practice presentation and feedback skills, presentations were held twice.

#### 3.3.1 Lectures and Exercises

The course lasted for eight weeks during which one whole day the first seven weeks was scheduled for the course. In addition to the scheduled time students were expected to work on their own for roughly one and a half day each week. The eighth week was an examination week during which the students had the opportunity to work on their project reports to hand in for grading. Each scheduled day contained a mixture of activities. Typically, there was a lecture on some parts of the course contents, followed by an exercise on the same topic, to enforce learning and to mix theory with practice. The topics of the lectures of the course were:

- Child Development
- Ethics and Regulations
- Pedagogical perspectives
- Design for and with Children
- Design for Children with Disabilities
- Evaluation with children
- Design for Formal vs Informal Learning Contexts
- Principles of Screen and Web Design for Children
- Case studies

The reasoning behind the order of the presentation of the material was to first present important characteristics of children relevant for design, then methods for working with design for and with children and finally present specific guidelines that can be useful when designing and evaluating for the target group.

### 3.3.2 Literature Seminars

The course contained 3 mandatory literature seminars, which lasted for about 2 hours each. In the first seminar the focus was to get some touch on the foundations of the field of Interaction design and children. Two foundational papers were chosen [9, 5], and the students were to prepare either a research trend presentation based on chapter 7 in Hourcade or a presentation of Druin. The second seminar was more focused on inspiring the students in the areas of design and selection of methods to use when co-designing with the children. The students were to read four papers [16, 10, 17, 3], list advantages and disadvantages with each approach, and be prepared to argue for or against any of the four papers and their approach. The third seminar focused on evaluation, and was based on [1, 15, 8], the students were to consider the different approaches to evaluating children's participation in a design process.

### 3.3.3 Design Project

A major part of the course was a design project running throughout the course. The aim of the project was to provide all students with practical hands-on experience from planning and executing design for and with children. The project was done in groups of 2-3 students and the task was open-ended, with no specific restrictions on what kind of topic to address.

During the project students had to have at least three encounters with children for observation, co-design and evaluation. The purpose of the first session was to learn more about the target group. The purpose of the second encounter was to practice co-design with children and get input for design. For the final evaluation session the students needed that the project had resulted in a prototype that could be evaluated with children. This could, but did not have to, be a hi-fi working prototype. The encounters took place in the children's ordinary environment.

The project groups had weekly supervision meetings with a teacher to follow up progress and discuss problems and ideas. The supervision mostly concerned how to plan and structure activities with the children, and how to inform the parents. The students seemed to be confident in the design and technology parts, but lacked the experience and needed support on what was possible to do with the children and how to go about performing the methods.

The course was graded on the group project only, but the students had to attend seminars, exercises and also hand in two individual exercises. All students received written feedback on their projects, exercises and individual hand-ins.

## 4. OUTCOME

19 students took the course. Of these, 18 were students at the ID&T program and one majoring in Industrial design.

### 4.1 Student Projects

The course ended up with seven different projects. The student projects varied from applications for smartphones and tablets to physical interaction toys, and ranged from partly developed prototypes to fully implemented designs. CamQuest is an example of an app, and is an attempt to change the common attitudes towards the use of tablets in preschools, and to promote the advantages of using the tablet as a pedagogical tool. The aim is to enable children to learn about two-dimensional geometrical shapes by exploring and taking photos of the surrounding

environment by using the tablet camera together with fellow preschoolers, see Fig 1a.

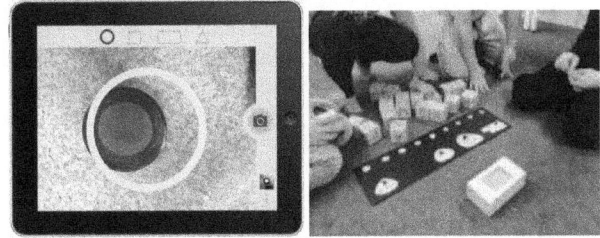

**Figure 1: a) Interface of CamQuest b) Evaluation of Blocks**

An example of a more tangible project is Blocks, which consists of augmented alphabet blocks with screen based and auditory feedback, see Fig 1b. The challenge is to spell words, presented by a voice, by using alphabet blocks. It is a learning tool designed to nurture the cognitive and social development of 6-7 years olds. This learning tool combines technology and tangible aspects to garner positive effects (in terms of learning) from both realms.

### 4.2 Course Evaluation

The course was evaluated through a meeting in the middle of the course, again when the course was completed, using a questionnaire developed for DEVICE, and with a meeting about two months after the course. 17 students completed the questionnaire at the final presentation, consisting of 9 multiple-choice questions and 3 open questions to leave comments and suggestions for improvements to the course.

The multiple-choice questions asked about the students general impressions of the course and teaching, what they had learned and so on. Overall, the results on the content and learning experience were positive. Some re-occurring themes could be found in the answers to the open questions. Most notably students really appreciated the direct involvement working with the children and the knowledge and understanding gained from this. Regarding what they learned, many commented about that they had gained an understanding of children, but also generally about the need for understanding users. Related to some of the above is also that many students appreciated that the course covered material on child development theories. Students also liked the theory covered in the literature and the literature seminars. Other things appreciated by the students were also the exercises, the project and design methods. One thing that the students missed was considerations regarding gender issues.

## 5. DISCUSSION

The intended learning outcomes describes the author's view of what a course in IDC could cover in that it describes what students should learn. Of course, what these learning outcomes should be is an open question and one of the aims of the present paper is to stimulate a discussion around these issues. We acknowledge that depending on the goal of the course and the school in which it is taught, different methods and content may be used to teach IDC [7]. The conducted research on related work and best practices in academia and industry have been useful as input on what to teach to fulfill certain learning outcomes and were also useful as input when defining the learning outcomes. When defining a course based on intended learning outcomes it of course becomes important to verify that the course content actually ensures that the learning outcomes are met. A first analysis shows that most of the learning outcomes were met, for instance K1 was met through literature [9] and a lecture, and J1 through a lecture, literature [12] and several practical tasks.

What students appreciated most of all in the course were the forced encounters with children. Meeting the children and working together with them was a most efficient eye-opener that also served to make all the different parts of the course come together. In the meetings with the children, the students could really see how and what they had learned about theory and methods became directly useful. The authors agree with [13], that one essential question that influence choices regarding the course design, as well as the motivation of the students, is how and if the course will be examined. The time to get insight into this field is limited with one course, why we suggest to focus on what has been learnt and to what extent the students have developed their knowledge and understanding within IDC in accordance with the intended learning outcomes rather than judging the novelty and quality of the designs. For future editions, the course could be extended to topics such as media use, theories of play, gender issues, and ergonomics.

## 6. CONCLUSION

This paper proposes the principles of constructive alignment as an approach for course design in IDC, exemplified by a brief description of the development of a master's level course. The work is based on two years research performed by the DEVICE project on development of design teaching for children (and elderly) as well as on current pedagogical research on how to teach interaction design. A set of intended learning outcomes were used as the basis for the course design. Despite the fact that the field of interaction design and children has been around for at least ten years, rather little work has been done on development of teaching curriculum for the field. This paper can serve as an inspiration for others developing courses in the same area. To facilitate this all the material used in the course is freely available online. It is the hope of the authors that the work can serve as a starting point for discussions on further development of curricula for teaching IDC.

## 7. ACKNOWLEDGMENTS

The DEVICE project is supported by the Lifelong Learning Programme (Erasmus) of the European Union. This publication reflects the views only of the author, and the Commission cannot be held responsible for any use that may be made of the information contained therein.

## 8. REFERENCES

[1] Antle A. 2007. The CTI framework: informing the design of tangible systems for children. In Proceedings of TEI'07. ACM, New York, NY, USA.

[2] Bekker T. and Antle A. 2011. Developmentally situated design (DSD): making theoretical knowledge accessible to designers of children's technology. In *Proceedings of* CHI '11. ACM, New York, NY, USA, 2531-2540.

[3] Bekker T., Sturm J., Eggen B. 2010. Designing Playful interactions for social interaction and physical play. Personal Ubiquitous comput. 14, 5 (July 2010), 385-396

[4] Biggs J. 2003. Teaching for Quality Learning at University, 2nd edition, Open University Press, Maiden UK.

[5] Druin A. 2002. The Role of Children in the Design of New Technology. Behav Inform Technol, 21 (1), 1-25.

[6] Ferrarini C., Eriksson E., Montanari R, and Sims R. 2013. The DEVICE project: development of educational programs with a specific focus on design for children. In *Proceedings of* IDC '13. ACM, New York, NY, USA, 360-363.

[7] Gilutz S., Bekker T., Fisch S, and Blikstein P. 2011. Teaching interaction design & children within diverse disciplinary curricula. In *Proceedings of* IDC '11. ACM, New York, NY, USA, 257-259

[8] Guha M.L., Druin A., Fails JA. 2010. Investigating the impact of design processes on children. In Proceedings of IDC'10. ACM, New York, USA, 198-201.

[9] Hourcade JP. 2008. Interaction Design and Children. Found. Trends Hum.-Comput. Interact. 1, 4 (April 2008), 277-392.

[10] Kärnä E, Nuutinen J, Pihlainen-Bednarik K, Vellonen V. 2010. Designing technologies with children with special needs: Children in the Centre (CiC) framework. In Proceedings of IDC '10. ACM New York.

[11] Lundgren S. Teaching and Learning Aesthetics of Interaction. 2010. PhD thesis Department of Applied IT, Chalmers University of Technology, Gothenburg, Sweden.

[12] Markopoulos P., Read J., MacFarlane S., and Hoysniemi J. 2008. Evaluating Children's Interactive Products: Principles and Practices for Interaction Designers. Morgan Kaufmann Publishers Inc., San Francisco, CA, USA.

[13] Read J. 2011. Creating a child computer interaction curriculum. In Proceedings of IDC '11. ACM, New York, NY, USA, 268-270.

[14] Read J., Druin A., Markopopoulis P. 2011: A Community for Child Computer Interaction. CHI 2011, May 7–12, 2011, Vancouver, BC, Canada.

[15] Read J. & MacFarlane S., 2006. Using the fun toolkit and other survey methods to gather opinions in child computer interaction. In Proceedings of IDC '06. ACM, New York.

[16] Resnick M., Silverman B. 2005. Some reflections on designing construction kits for kids. In Proceedings of IDC'05. ACM, New York.

[17] Walsh G., Foss E., Yip J, Druin A. 2013. FACIT PD: a framework for analysis and creation of intergenerational techniques for participatory design. In Proceedings of CHI'13 ACM, New York, NY, USA, 2893-2902

# Using Digital Game as Clinical Screening Test to Detect Color Deficiency in Young Children

Linh-Chi Nguyen
Keio-NUS CUTE Center
Interactive & Digital Media Institute
National University of Singapore
idmnlc@nus.edu.sg

Weiquan Lu
Keio-NUS CUTE Center
Interactive & Digital Media Institute
National University of Singapore
lu.weiquan@nus.edu.sg

Ellen Yi-Luen Do
Keio-NUS CUTE Center
Interactive & Digital Media Institute
National University of Singapore
ellendo@nus.edu.sg

Audrey Chia
Singapore National Eye Center
11 Third Hospital Avenue
Singapore 168751
audrey.chia.w.l@snec.co.sg

Yuan Wang
Keio-NUS CUTE Center
Interactive & Digital Media Institute
National University of Singapore
idmwy@nus.edu.sg

## ABSTRACT

Digital games as education tools for children have been studied in the past. However, the use of digital games in clinical environments such as for children's healthcare is still rare in the research community. This paper reports on the development of a digital tablet game called "Dodo's catching adventure" which examines the use of games in visual color-deficiency screening for young children. A user study was conducted at a National Eye Centre. Results of the study show that the digital game demonstrates sensitivity and specificity on Red-Green color deficiency detection, and is comparable to the two gold standards in color deficiency tests, namely the Ishihara and Farnsworth D15. Furthermore, children found the game to be more enjoyable than the Ishihara test. This provides evidence for the feasibility of using such games as diagnosis tools for early childhood health conditions.

## Author Keywords

Digital game, color deficiency test, children game

## ACM Classification Keywords

H.5.2 User Interfaces, K.8.0 Games

## General Terms

Colorblind, children game

## INTRODUCTION

Computer and videogames can be very engaging for children [10]. Such games play a significant role in children's development. A recent study showed that 82% of American children are avid gamer players, and by the age of two, a child has already has the capability to play many computer games [22]. Children appreciate computer games for their novelty, similar to other forms of entertainment such as comic books and cartoons, as such activities provide extreme experiences [10]. With their ability to engage young children, it seems that computer games have the potential to be used for situations for children in the healthcare settings, such as in eye health screening.

However, it is interesting to note that (to the best of our knowledge), none of the validated color visions test for children are in the form of a digital game. The conduct of color screening tests for young children have traditionally been wrought with difficulty since it often requires advanced verbal or cognitive skills [9]. Such tests may also reinforce the social stigma regarding such color deficiencies, since children may become discouraged if they compare their performance with their normal vision peers. By using digital game technology via a screen-based activity, our game ("Dodo's catching adventure," or Dodo game for short) is designed to detect color vision defects effectively in children from two and a half to six years of age, through a fun and relaxed manner.

## THE NEED OF COLOR VISION DEFICIENCY TESTS FOR YOUNG CHILDREN AND ITS CURRENT LIMITATIONS

Congenital Dyschromatopsia affects 8% to 10% of males and 0.4% to 0.5% of females [5,7,17,18]. In Red-Green color deficiency (Deuteranopia or Protanopia) are relatively common, while Blue-Yellow color blindness (Tritanopia), are extremely rare [5,17].

Isochromatic plates, arrangement tests, anomaloscopes, and lantern tests are commonly used in clinical practice today [2,20]. The Ishihara test and the Farnsworth D15 test are currently the most widely used screening tests. Ishihara is used to detect Red-Green color deficiency and total color deficiency. The test contains plates with circular dots of different colors forming a number character that would be invisible to a person with color deficiency but visible to a normal vision person, or vice versa. The D15 test is used

**Figure 1: Dodo game's starting screen on a tablet computer**

worldwide to select applicants for employment in occupations that require good color vision. In the test, participants are asked to arrange sixteen color caps in a logical rainbow order [4, 11].

Color vision tests for young children are important [1,8,20]. However, approximately 40% of color vision deficient people are unaware of their condition [8]. Color vision testing for young children remains a challenge for clinicians because many screening tests require a relatively high cognitive demand on children, especially on those younger than 5 years old [6,9,19]. In fact, both the Ishihara and D15 tests are not suitable of children under the age of 5 [6,20]. Computer-based tests do not solve this cognitive limitation [1,17,23]. While there exist screening tests specially designed for young children, they are not as effective as Ishihara and D15, and they require special communication from the examiner, therefore the result may not be objective [9,15,17,18,21].

## DODO GAME DESIGN

Dodo game's main target users are young children. Hence, the game adopts a color matching game type with audio support, which is suitable for young children. The game is designed with bright color tones against a white background to ensure minimal interference with game object. It contains colorful graphics and interesting characters in order to engage young children. Dodo game is currently available on iPads and PC platforms (Figure1).

In this game, players are asked to tap the screen to pick an object with similar color profiles. The Dodo game includes 4 sub-games: Sub-game 1 (Ladybug game) is designed to test total color deficiency. However, both Red-Green and Blue- Yellow color deficiency sufferers can also fail this game; Sub-game 2 (Fish game) is used for testing Blue-Yellow color deficiency, Sub-game 3 (Butterfly game) is used for testing Red-Green color deficiency and the Sub-game 4 (Owl game) is a classification test for two types of Red-Green color deficiency: deuteranopia and protanopia. Each sub-game consists of six quick stages where each player is asked to pick one object out of four objects that looks the most similar in color to the a sample object. Objects in each game can be grouped into four groups: a sample object, normal vision objects, color-blind objects and neutral objects. At the start of each sub-game, the blinking sample object (e.g., a butterfly) appears in a speech

**Figure 2: Sub-game 3 layout**

bubble next to the Dodo character with the "Pick This" text and audio. Then, four groups of objects appear on the screen for the player to pick the most similar one. The player will pick either normal vision selectable objects or color-blind selectable objects or neutral objects, depending on his/her color vision.

The game's win-lose condition is independent on whether the players have color deficiencies. The player would be prompted to play the game again if his/her choices were the neutral (control) objects indicating that the player does not fully understand the rules of the game, or that the player is being uncooperative. Otherwise, the player will always win the game. At the end of the game the screen always displays the message "You Win!" This is designed intentionally to not discourage color deficient children. The color deficiency test results can be accessed by clicking on the information icon located on the top right of the screen.

### Design method

Based on Gestalt principles, such as the law of similarity in visual perception, humans naturally tend to group similar objects by shape, color, size or brightness together [25]. The design method of Dodo game is based on the assumption that differences in hue and saturation of objects would direct players with color deficiency to group objects differently than those with normal vision.

When a color deficient individual cannot distinguish the hue of objects (since they look alike), they can only notice the difference of object's saturation and brightness (Figure 4). The key feature of the game design is to compensate for the low resolution in the recognition of hues, as colorblind individuals tend to be more sensitive to the differences in saturation [16]. An individual with normal vision can hardly notice the difference of saturation between the sample object and the normal vision object, and will naturally choose this object when he/she is asked to pick an object similar to the sample object. Figure 4 shows a color

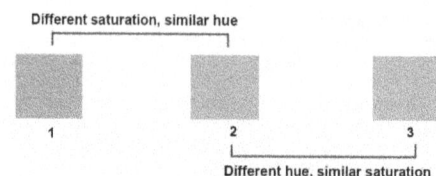

**Figure 4: Dodo game design concept**

profile of the sample object (2), the color-blind selectable object (3) and the normal vision selectable object (1) in sub-game 3. When being asked to pick the object similar to a sample object (2), a Red-Green color deficient person sees the hues of all objects are nearly alike, hence they will choose (3) with similar saturation. A normal vision person will choose (1) with similar hue. All the sub-games are designed based on the same principle for different types of color deficiencies.

The color design was adopted from the Ishihara PC based version with isocromatic data for Red–Green color deficiency established by Lakowski [15,17]. Vischeck color deficiency vision simulation was used to simulate the color rendering of objects to color deficiency color vision for color-blind selectable objects [13]. Figure 5 shows how Sub-game 3 appears when viewed by a normal vision person and the Red-Green color deficient person respectively, using the Vischeck computer simulation.

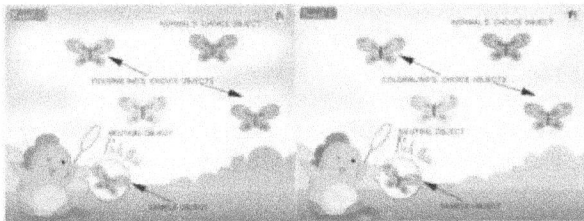

**Figure 5: Sub-game 3 in normal vision (left) and in Red-Green color deficient vision simulated by Vischeck (right)**

### Dodo game's criteria
Both Ishihara and D15 do not provide a clear grading and give little indications of severity based on the number of mistakes. Therefore, Dodo game follows this grading convention. In terms of the number of errors that a player is allowed to make, the percentage to distinguish between mild and strong color deficiency is set to be more than 50%. Therefore in Red-Green color deficient detection, if the ratio is above 10/18 errors, the player will be a strong color deficient. Players that make between 4-9/18 errors would be classified as having slight/mild color deficiency.

### Pre-test on adults to verify design method
A pre-test was conducted on six male adults, including three Red-Green color deficient individuals, and three normal vision individuals, all tested using the Ishihara test. The reason for this pre-test, was that adult players could comprehend and communicate with researchers directly, thus preventing any confusion or negative results caused by a lack of understanding. A pre-test result would be useful to determine if our current prototype was functional, and the pre-test would help researchers fine-tune the different elements. The tests were conducted under good room lightening, and both eyes were tested simultaneously. A PC version of Dodo game on a 13 inch Macbook laptop was used in this pilot study. Color calibration was performed before each participant was asked to play the game. All the participants were able to play the game from the start of the

test. Dodo game was successful in detecting color deficient subjects with no false positives.

### Observation of Dodo game's usability on toddlers and pre-school children
In the game development process, we asked a small group of young children to play Dodo game. They were all detected as having normal color vision as indicated by the Dodo game. All of the children were able to play and win the game easily in the first trial with minimal instruction. None of the children realized that the Dodo game was a screening test.

### USER STUDY
An ideal color vision test should reliably detect, categorize and grade the severity of color vision deficiencies. Currently, the two gold standard tests, Ishihara and the D15, are the most used color vision test in optometry clinics [7,11]. Dodo game's target users were children from two to six years old. However, such young color deficient subjects were not available for recruitment because the current clinical practice usually does not ask children at that age to do colorblind tests at hospitals. Thus, as the two gold standard tests are not recommended for children under six years old, there did not exist a ground-truth to evaluate the game's reliability with the target group. Optometrists at Singapore National Eye Centre suggested using Ishihara test and the Farnsworth D15 test (D15) to compare Dodo game's effectiveness on Red-Green color deficiency detection. During the six-month user study, we were not able to recruit Blue-Yellow (Tritanopia) color deficiency participants due to the rarity of such sufferers.

A within-subjects repeated measures user study was supervised by optometrists at the National Eye Centre. Thirty-two subjects (N=32, Mean Age = 11.42, 1 Female) were recruited. All the tests were conducted under good indoor lighting in a clinical environment with both eyes tested simultaneously. The iPad version of Dodo game was used in this study. The screen brightness was kept balanced at the default setting (auto brightness). Sixteen of subjects were Red-Green color deficient, as detected by Ishihara test. The control group consisted of sixteen normal color vision participants. The average playtime of Dodo game was 3.14 minutes to finish four sub-games.

### Sensitivity and specificity
Using the Ishihara test results as reference (which detected all sixteen colorblind subjects), D15 mis-classified four subjects as normal (25%), while Dodo game mis-classified three subjects as normal (18%). All tests classified the normal subjects correctly.

### Comparing enjoyment level of Dodo game to the two gold standard tests
For enjoyment measuring, we modified a related sub-scale of Intrinsic Motivation Inventory (IMI) with 7 questions, using a seven-point Likert scale [12]. Three tests were counterbalanced to avoid order effects, with the same questionnaires administered after participants completed

each tests. Using repeated measures ANOVA, we analyzed the results. In terms of Enjoyment, the results showed a significant main effect (F[2,62] = 4.01, $p < .05$).

Using paired samples $t$-tests between Ishihara and D15 (t[31] = -1.24, $p$=.23), D15 and Dodo game (t[31] = -1.55, $p$ = .13), Ishihara and Dodo game (t[31] = -2.925, $p$<.01), Dodo game was significantly more enjoyable than Ishihara.

## DISCUSSION, CONCLUSION AND FUTURE WORK

The results suggested that Dodo game had slightly better sensitivity than D15, but less than Ishihara. In terms of enjoyment, Dodo game was significantly more enjoyable than Ishihara, while being on par with D15.

The results give support for the potential use of Dodo game as a new approach for the use of digital games to screen children at pediatric clinics or at home. As a new clinical tool for color vision screening, it is compatible with the two gold standard Ishihara and D15 tests in sensitivity and specificity. Portable, easy and fun - the game may be a good choice for color vision screening for children below the ages of five. Future work will involve the fine-tuning of Dodo game, and testing it with a larger population of young children.

## ACKNOWLEDGMENTS

This research is supported by the Singapore National Research Foundation under its International Research Center Keio-NUS CUTE Center @ Singapore Funding Initiative and administered by the IDM Program Office.

## REFERENCES

1. Arden, G., Gundoz, K., Perry, S. Color vision testing with a computer graphics system: Preliminary results, *Documenta Ophthalmologica 69* (1998), 167-174.
2. Birch, J. A practical guide for color-vision examination: Report of the Standardization Committee of the International Research Group on Color-Vision deficiencies. *Ophthalmic Physiol Opt 5* (1985) 265–285.
3. Birch, J. Efficiency of the Ishihara test for identifying red-green color vision deficiency. *Ophthalmic Physiol Opt 17*, 5 (1997), 403–8.
4. Birch, J. Use of the Farnsworth—Munsell 100-Hue test in the examination of congenital color vision defects, Ophthalmic and Physiological Optics, Wiley Online Library, 1998.
5. Chia, A., Gazzard, G., Tong, L., Zhang, X., Sim, EL., Fong, A., Saw, S.M. Red-Green color blindness in Singaporean children. *Clinical & Experimental Ophthalmology 36* 5 (2008) , 464–7.
6. Choi, S.Y., Hwang, J.M. Ishihara test in 3- to 6-year-old children, *Jpn J Ophthalmol 53* 5 (2009), 455-7
7. Cole, B.L. The new Richmond HRR pseudoisochromatic test for colour vision is better than Ishihara test, *Clin Exp Optom 89* 2 (2006), 73-80
8. Color vision screening: a critical appraisal of the literature, New Zealand Health Technology Assessment (NZHTA) NZHTA Report 7 nzhta.chmeds.ac.nz/publications/nzhta7.pdf
9. Cotter S.A., Lee, French A.L. Evaluation of a new color vision test: 'Color Vision Testing Made Easy. *Optom Vis Sci 76* (1999), 631–6.
10. Crawford, C. The Art of Computer Game Design McGraw-Hill (1984) www.stanford.edu/class/sts145/Library/Crawford%20on%20Game%20Design.pdf
11. Dain, S.J.Clinical colour vision tests, *Clin Exp Optom 87* 4-5 (2004), 276-293
12. Deci, E.L., Ryan, R.M. Intrinsic Motivation Inventory. http://www.selfdeterminationtheory.org/questionnaires/10-questionnaires/50
13. Dougherty, B., Wade, A. Vischeck simulates colour-blind vision. www.vischeck.com
14. Grammenos, D., Savidis, A., Stephanidis, C. Designing universally accessible games. *Comput Entertain 7*, 1 (2009), 1-29.
15. Hoffmann, A., Menozzi, M. Applying the Ishihara test to a PC-based screening system, *Displays 20* 1 (1998), 39-47
16. Kohei, M. Color Universal Design (CUD) How to make figures and presentations that are friendly to Colorblind people. http://jfly.iam.u-tokyo.ac.jp/color/#see
17. Lakowski, R. Theory and practice of color vision testing. A review. Part 1 *Br J Industr Med 26* (1969), 173–288.
18. Ling, B.Y., Dain, S.J. Color vision in children and the Lanthony New Color Test. *Visual Neuroscience 25* (2008), 441-444.
19. Mäntyjärvi, M. Color vision testing in pre-school-aged children, *Ophthalmologica 202* 3 (1991), 147-151.
20. Melamud, A., Hagstrom, S., Traboulsi, E. I., Color vision testing, *Ophthalmic Genetics 25* 3 (2004), 159–187.
21. Neitz, M., Neitz, J. A new mass screening test for color-vision deficiencies in children, Color Research & Application, Special Issue: In *Proc of the International Color Vision Society 26* S1 (2001), 239-249.
22. NPD Group. Among American kids ages 2-17, 82 percent report that are gamers. Press Release (Dec 2) Port Washington, New York, 2009.
23. Pardo, P.J. PeÂrez, A.L., Suero, A.L. A new color vision test in a PC-based screening system, *Displays 21* 5 (2002), 203-6
24. Prensky, M. *Digital Game-Based Learning*, chapter 5: Fun, Play and Games: What Makes Games Engaging, 2001.
25. Soegaard, M. Gestalt principles of form perception. www.interaction-design.org/encyclopedia/gestalt_principles_of_form_perception.html

# SmartHolder: Sensing and Raising Families' Awareness of Tooth Brushing Habits

Ana Caraban, Maria José Ferreira, Vítor Belim, Olga Lyra, Evangelos Karapanos

Madeira Interactive Technologies Institute, University of Madeira
Campus da Penteada, 9020-105 Funchal Portugal
{ana.caraban, mjrf85, d3str4v4d0, lyra.olga, e.karapanos}@gmail.com

## ABSTRACT

With an increasing emphasis on behavior change technologies, interest has grown over time also on the role of HCI in motivating healthy tooth brushing habits on children. In this paper we present the design and development of *SmartHolder*, a toothbrush holder that senses the frequency and duration of toothbrush practices and motivates healthy tooth brushing habits, through raising family members' awareness of each other's practices. Wed first present two preliminary studies about children's and adults' tooth brushing behaviors and how these are influenced by social interactions within the family. We conclude through a presentation of early conceptual designs as well as an initial working prototype of *SmartHolder*.

## Categories and Subject Descriptors

Persuasive technology, children, tooth brushing.

## Keywords

H5.2. Information interfaces and presentation (e.g., HCI): User Interfaces.

## INTRODUCTION

Regular brushing of teeth is essential in maintaining oral hygiene and preventing from chronic diseases [1, 2]. Tooth decay, toothache and bleeding gums stand out among the common oral problems but, poor oral hygiene can even have detrimental effects to chronic conditions such as diabetes and heart disease and has also been linked to mouth cancer and early labor [1, 2, 3].

Despite its importance, individuals often fail to adhere to healthy tooth brushing habits. This is often rooted in a lack of motivation to perform an unattractive task, or in the absence of an established routine [1]. While establishing such routines from early childhood has proven particularly important [1], parents are often struggling to educate their children about the importance of maintaining healthy tooth brushing habits. To help overcome this situation, different approaches have been developed to change brushing behaviors and create engagement (especially children), from colorful and musical toothbrushes to technological solutions that sense and provide feedback on individuals' tooth brushing habits.

In our line of work we attempt to motivate healthy tooth brushing habits through tapping to the social mechanisms of families.

Grounded upon the theoretical framework of Social Translucence [13], we argue that increasing the transparency of tooth brushing behaviors among family members will increase individuals' motivation and accountability in adhering to desired behaviors. We discuss the design and development of *SmartHolder*, a prototype that senses the frequency and duration of tooth brushing practices and attempts to raise family members' awareness of each others' behaviors. In the current paper we present our early attempts towards this direction with two studies that attempted to inquire into the drivers and barriers towards adhering to healthy tooth brushing behaviors and present our early prototypes.

## RELATED WORK

Engaging children in tooth brushing practices is not a new trend. Playful products such as colorful toothbrushes and tasteful toothpastes have been some of the early solutions towards this goal. More recently, technological products have filled the market. For instance, Spinbrush[1] and Squeaky Clean Teeth[2] are toothbrushes that play a song while tooth brushing for the minimum recommended time (i.e., 2 minutes) with the goal of sustaining children's interest in the activity. Beam Brush[3] also logs users' behaviors and allows them to review using a mobile app. Oral-B SmartSeries 5000[4] provides a visual display with feedback about time as well pressure control.

Recent research efforts have gone a step further. Playful Toothbrush [5] is an ubicomp technology that attempts to assist parents in educating kindergarten children on proper tooth brushing practices. The prototype uses a vision-based motion tracker that recognizes different tooth brushing strokes and an interactive game that highlights the teeth that are yet to be brushed. Alonso et al. [6] developed a prototype that provides haptic feedback with the goal of learning to perform a complex tooth brushing technique. Nakajima et al. [7] proposed a virtual aquarium that motivates individuals to adhere to 3-minute tooth brushing practice. Gerling et al. [8] and Soler et al. [9] proposed serious games as educational tools in raising awareness of the importance of tooth brushing and educating children on proper tooth brushing behaviors. Finally, Hachisu and Kajimoto [10] proposed a solution that manipulates the auditory sensation of tooth brushing with the goal of augmenting the experience of progressive cleanliness.

### Theoretical foundations

The vast majority of the technological solutions described earlier have relied on providing just-in-time motivational feedback with

---

[1] http://www.spinbrush.com/toothtunes.html
[2] http://neyeni.net/16051/squeaky-clean-teeth.html
[3] http://www.beamtoothbrush.com/
[4] http://www.oralb.com/products/professional-care-smart-series-5000/

the goal of increasing adherence to desired behaviors or performance within. In line with Fogg's behavior model for persuasive design, they attempt to increase children's awareness and motivation for frequent or appropriate tooth brushing, to increase children's (perceived) ability to perform the task, or to provide the triggers that encourage behavior change during appropriate moments.

An aspect missing from these applications is the role of the family in inducing behavior change on children. An extensive body of work in behavior change applications has pointed out the strong influence that social ties have in reinforcing or changing behavior [12]. Especially close social ties, such as families, have profound influence on their members' behaviors, through effective and advanced social strategies such as playful nudging and maintaining an awareness of each others' behaviors. Over time, these practices enable families to develop common routines and establish social norms. As such, technological interventions may be more effective if they integrate with families' existing social practices.

A theoretical framework that can be particularly fruitful for the design of such systems is the *Social Translucence* framework [13], which prescribes how individuals modify their behaviors when they become aware that these are visible by others. Social Translucence identifies three critical properties of systems acting towards this goal. The first is *visibility*; the system should make meaningful information about each others' behaviors visible to others (e.g. has a child brushed her teeth this evening?). Secondly, *awareness* refers not only to the fact that parents become aware of the child's behavior, but also to that the child becomes aware that her parents are aware (mutual awareness). Social Translucence argues that through this process, a critical property is established – *accountability*, which increases the likelihood of the child's conformity to the desired behaviors.

One should note two things. First, a socially translucent technology should not aim to replace families' existing means for behavior change but rather to best integrate with them. Second, a socially translucent technology should make no value judgments on the child's behaviors – it is up to the parents to appropriate the feedback of the technology and establish norms and practices around it, such as playful nudging and positive reinforcement.

The Social Translucence framework has been extensively applied in the design of collaborative systems [13], and more recently in the design of behavior change systems. For instance, Barreto et al. [4,11] used the Social Translucence framework to study how families' communication and coordination practices influenced energy consumption practices in a household. They found that even with aggregate information (i.e. overall household consumption), families had a rich understanding of the practices and appliances that led to an increase in consumption, and employed creative social practices to influence each other.

With SmartHolder we aim to focus on the role of social interactions in motivating proper tooth-brushing, understanding which contributions could stand out and differentiate from the previous individual behavior change work mentioned.

## PRELIMINARY STUDIES

The following section presents two studies, a survey and a set of interviews, that tried to inquire into children's and adults' practices of tooth brushing (such as the perceived frequency and duration), the motives and the barriers towards adhering to desired

practices, as well as how social interactions among family members affect individuals' tooth brushing practices.

## Survey

A survey aimed at gaining insights into individuals' tooth brushing behaviors. A total of 61 participants completed the survey. Their mean age was 24 years old (min=7, max=59). Fourteen (23%) of the participants were children between seven and nine years old. Children completed the survey on paper and were recruited in a school with prior authorization (mean age=7, min=7, max=9).

To avoid memory biases we employed a similar procedure to the Day Reconstruction Method ( [13], see [15] for an alternative). Rather than asking them to report on their typical behaviors, we asked them to recall the past day and report when and for how long they brushed their teeth, along with other information about these events.

## Findings

### Tooth brushing practices

Overall, individual's self-reported habits are better than expected. In fact, 97% of participants reported brushing their teeth two or more times a day, the minimum frequency recommended by experts [3] the average number in our sample was three per day. However, while participants' reported frequency of tooth brushing may be judged adequate by experts, the majority of the them (61%) reported that they would like to increase the frequency of tooth brushing by 1 time/day (43%) or 2 or more times/day (14%).

The median perceived duration was 2 minutes and 37 seconds; only 59% of participants reported brushing their teeth for 120 seconds or more, the duration recommended by experts [3].

We found that individuals with age lower than 18 years old (N=21, Mean=146 seconds, SD=108 seconds) spent less time brushing their teeth than adults (N=61, Mean=177.15 seconds, SD=216.19 seconds, t(79)=- 6.19, p=0.5). An even stronger effect was found in the perceived frequency of tooth brushing with children and teenagers displaying less frequent behaviors (N=21, Mean= 2.05, SD=0.740) than the adult participants (N=61, Mean=2.90, t(79) = -3.61, p<0.01).

As expected, children of nine or lower were not aware of the time spent brushing their teeth, but they were conscious about their tooth brushing frequency. Only 43% of the children reported a tooth frequency of twice a day (or more), the minimum recommended practice.

### Barriers against healthy tooth brushing practices

We identified five primary barriers against adopting healthy tooth brushing practices: individuals' lack of motivation coupled with the unattractiveness of the task (39%), time constrains (blaming the frenetic lifestyles and rotating schedules, preventing the execution of the "task that in itself requires some time" - 21%), missing routines (17%) and the lack of information about health consequences (12%).

### Intra-family awareness and influence

In total, 59% of survey respondents reported being aware of other family members' tooth brushing practices. They attributed this mostly to common routines (16%), such as leaving home at the same time and taking meals together. About 9% of the respondents reported this awareness coming through discussion as they attempt to remind each other to brush their teeth, while respondents reported that subtle cues such as the sound of tooth brushing as well as the tooth brushes being wet often raises this awareness.

Almost all of respondents (90%) reported that they often attempt to influence other family members' tooth brushing habits, with the primary practice (in 77% of the cases) being contextual reminders, such as reminding others to join them when brushing their teeth.

All children below nine reported that they brush their teeth accompanied by a family member. The majority of them (71%) admitted being forced by their parents to brush. However, when asked about the importance of oral hygiene, we found young children to be well informed about the reasons why one should maintain good oral hygiene.

## Limitations

While this study provided some interesting preliminary results, one may note a possible self-selection bias, especially in our adult population. This might have affected the results as individuals concerned about oral hygiene, and consequently more likely to adhere to healthy behaviors, could be more likely to respond to the survey.

## Interviews

The interviews aimed at a deeper inquiry into children's and adults' practices and the social interactions among family members. We interviewed a total of 29 individuals from 11 families, from which 8 were children (ages between 3 and 14 years old). We started by inviting all family members to complete a Day Reconstruction diary [14] one day prior to the interview. This diary asked participants to reconstruct all activities an individual performed during the past day, from the moment of waking up till the moment he or she went to sleep. This provided us with a rich, situated account of one particular day of the family and served as input to the interview. Interviews took place with all family members present and lasted approximately 20 minutes. We ended by walking through a typical tooth-brushing event in the actual space.

## Findings

Overall, the interviews corroborated the findings of the survey with lack of motivation, time constrains and missing routine being critical barriers in individuals' adherence to healthy tooth brushing practices. While some individuals demonstrated lack of awareness on what constitutes a healthy practice ("[P22] I think I own a good oral health... I do not feel like brushing my teeth more than once a day, one is enough...", "[P7] I brush my teeth once a day. Perhaps my oral hygiene could be better"), the majority of participants knew what a healthy practice is, but often failed to adhere to it, attributing this to lack of motivation ("[P7] "People do not have patience, they can even have time to brush their teeth but have no motivation", "[P25] Sometimes I am too lazy to brush my teeth"), time constraints ("[P6] Sometimes people are always in a rush and do not give importance to brush teeth"), or the lack of an established routine ("[P5] I do not have a good tooth brushing routine but at this time I find difficult to change it. I use to try to brush more often but after a few days I tend to forget").

Parents reported employing a number of strategies to help them and their children engage with the task, such as listening to music ("[P6] I turn the radio on every morning and only turn it off when I am leaving home. I think it motivates me to perform my daily practices and I end up leaving home in a good mood"), providing incentives to children ("P28] "Kids do not feel achieving something when brushing their teeth so we try reward techniques

like: if you brush you can choose the movie"), making the task more playful for their children through selecting fun toothbrushes and toothpastes ("P[15] I have a toothbrush with some drawings that I like", "[P26] I like to brush my teeth because I have toothpaste that is very tasty. That toothpaste is cool to swallow" (4 years old), embedding the task in daily rituals ("[P20] "When we are almost done eating mummy asks what we should do next and then we scream brush our teeth!"), brushing their teeth at the same time with other family members ("P[26] I brush my teeth with my brother, it's more fun", "[P6] (...) When children are home, I brush my teeth and wait in the bathroom while they brush theirs."), or simply nudging them ("[P10] (...) with my son, I have to remind him every day. Sometimes he forgets but in others he is too lazy! He needs to get used to it while he is young".

## Summary of findings

Overall, the results from the survey and the interviews revealed some interesting findings: tooth brushing is a behavior that can be accomplished more easily in the long term when grounded upon a strong, established routine. This proved to be a hard task and individuals try to incorporate means of playfulness to increase engagement, especially when children are involved. Despite the difficulty to keep supervision and being aware of others family members' behaviors (primarily with dual-income families and rotating work schedules) individuals exhibit concerns about others behaviors, and feelings of accountability quickly manifest. As expected, this sense of responsibility showed to be stronger between families that possess a good family dynamic and feel comfortable in sharing their daily practices.

A number of interesting implications for design and concepts emerged from the studies. We believe that for effective behavior change the system should hold three main characteristics:

a) A playful, appealing system (visually and functionally) - a playful system is more likely to engage individuals in prolonged periods of time [14, 16] than one that focuses merely on information presentation, helping to create a routine and joust lack of motivation.

b) Increases transparency – Rather than merely presenting information to individuals, the system should opt to make this information available and visible to all family members through comprehensive explanation about the current behavior, helping increase awareness among them, especially when families hold different schedules. We believe that individuals are more likely to become interested and care about their behaviors if they are face often to them.

c) Enhances positive communication – Rather that inducing negative self-perceptions coupled with feelings of accountability and guilt, the system should induce positive and playful among family members.

## WORKING PROTOTYPE

We decided to incorporate an awareness system in a common object, visible to all family members without adding external resources to their environment. We present a functional prototype of the proposed solution: a toothbrush holder that senses families' toothbrush behavior and provides situated, just-in-time feedback through visual cues and support families to communicate and coordinate on desired practices.

The design process followed three steps. Firstly, we examined different metrics relating to the frequency, the duration and the performance of tooth brushing. Based on our survey and interview results, we decided to focus on frequency and duration as this was most often what individuals were concerned about, what families coordinated upon, and since we noticed that estimating the duration of tooth brushing was not an easy task for individuals.

Secondly, we developed a number of designs taking in account the bathroom space and behaviors within, based on our interviews and activity walkthroughs with the interviewed families, leading us to different forms and feedback displays that were modeled into cardboard prototypes as well as virtual 3D prototypes.

**Figure 1. Two early conceptual designs**

Thirdly, we developed a first working prototype of *SmartHolder* using 3D printing, an Arduino platform and a set of sensors and actuators. *SmartHolder* is a usual toothbrush holder that senses when each toothbrush is (or not) present through an infrared emitter and receptor. This allows us to log when and for how long each individual uses his toothbrush and provide feedback accordingly.

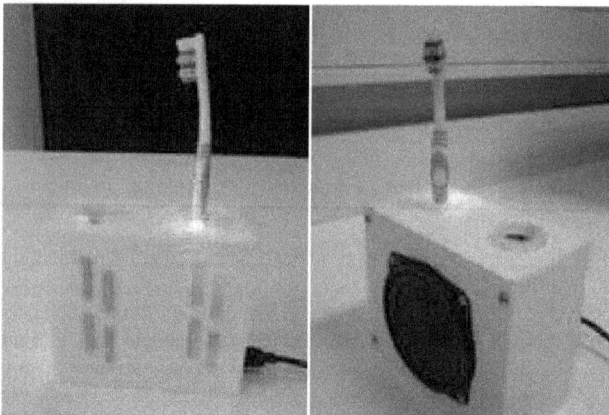

**Figure 2. SmartHolder indicating the user of the right side had brushed at least twice for 2 minutes. When no activity is detected (left side), the system do not provide any feedback.**

On the top of the holder, each hole is surrounded by a semi-transparent ring that provides feedback about the user tooth brushing frequency. The ring lights up green if a user has brushed her teeth at least 2 times during the last 24 hours, yellow if only once and red for none. After 32 hours the led does not light up, assuming that the respective user is not in the household. On the front side of the holder four led lights per user provide instance awareness of tooth brushing duration, with each led lighting up once 30 seconds of tooth brushing having elapsed, recommending a total duration of 2 minutes. These led lights are trigged by a motion sensor, thus providing ambient awareness as individuals enter the bathroom. Music and micro-learning audio-clips are played throughout tooth brushing, according to users' preferences and time of the day helping increase engagement and willingness in the practice. An algorithm as well as a crowd sourcing

community for the duration and evolution of audio content is currently being developed.

## CONCLUSION

Data relating to oral hygiene habits have shown alarming results through time, and the importance of acquiring healthy habits early on during one's life has been repeatedly stressed. With this work, we aimed at a socially translucent technology that aims at leveraging families existing social mechanisms rather than replace them. Using Social Translucence [13] as a theoretical framework we designed and prototyped a toothbrush holder that senses the frequency and duration of all family members' tooth brushing practices, and makes this visible into the familial environment. Our future work aims at further iterating on the prototype and conducting a longitudinal field study.

## REFERENCES

1. Dental Health Fundation, Retrieved on 16 March 2014 from: http://www.dentalhealth.ie/dentalhealth/teeth/effective toothb.html
2. Choo A., et al. (2001) Oral hygiene measures and promotion: review and considerations, Australian dental journal, 166-173.
3. Colgate, Retrieved from: http://www.colgate.pt.
4. Barreto, M., Karapanos, E., Nunes, N. (2011) Social translucence as a theoretical framework for sustainable HCI, INTERACT 2011.
5. Chang, Y., et al. (2008) Playful toothbrush: ubicomp technology for teaching tooth brushing to kindergarten children, in CHI'2008.
6. Alonso, M.B., Stienstra, J., and Dijkstra, R. (2014) Brush and learn: transforming tooth brushing behavior through interactive materiality, a design exploration, in TEI'14.
7. Nakajima, T., Lehdonvirta, V., Tokunaga, E., Kimura, H. (2008) Reflecting human behavior to motivate desirable lifestyle, In DIS'08.
8. Gerling, K. M., Klauser, M., Masuch, M. (2010) Serious Interface Design for Dental Health: WiiMote-based Tangible Interaction for School Children, In Mensch & Computer.
9. Soler, C., Zacarías, A., Lucero, A. (2009) Molarcropolis: a mobile persuasive game to raise oral health and dental hygiene awareness, In ACE'09.
10. Hachisu, T., Kajimoto, H. (2012) Augmentation of toothbrush by modulating sounds resulting from brushing, In ACE'12.
11. Barreto, M., Szóstek, A., & Karapanos, E. (2013). An initial model for designing Socially Translucent systems for Behavior Change. In Proceedings of the Biannual Conference of the Italian Chapter of SIGCHI (p. 8). ACM.
12. Consolvo, S., Everitt, K., Smith, I., Landay, J.A. (2006) Design Requirements for Technologies that Encourage Physical Activity, in CHI'06.
13. Erickson, T., and Kellogg, W.A. (2000) Social Translucence: An Approach to Designing Systems that Support Social Processes, ACM TOCHI.
14. Karapanos, E., Zimmerman, J., Forlizzi, J., Martens, J.B. (2009) User experience over time: an initial framework, In CHI'09.
15. Gouveia, R., and Karapanos, E. (2013) Footprint tracker: supporting diary studies with lifelogging, In CHI'13.
16. Lyra, O., Karapanos, E., Gouveia, R., Nisi, V., & Nunes, N. J. (2013). Engaging children in longitudinal behavioral studies through playful technologies. In Proceedings of the 12th International Conference on Interaction Design and Children (pp. 396-399). ACM.

# Action! Co-Designing Interactive Technology with Immigrant Teens

**Karen E. Fisher**
Information School
University of Washington
Seattle, WA 98195 USA
+1 206.685.9937
fisher@uw.edu

**Ann Peterson Bishop**
Graduate School of Library &
Information Science
University of Illinois USA
abishop@illinois.edu

**Lassana Magassa**
Information School
University of Washington USA
lmagassa@uw.edu

**Phil Fawcett**
Microsoft Research USA
philfa@microsoft.com

## ABSTRACT

In the minds and hands of young people lie the capacity to change the world. Our work, InfoMe, is about understanding (a) how immigrant and refugee youth help others in everyday life—elders, friends, complete strangers—through information and technology, and (b) how these behaviors can be supported through youths' designs for interactive technologies and services. We reflect on our work developing the Teen Design Day methodology with youth from Africa and Asia, and consider our approach in relation to others for supporting interaction design with youth. Teen Design Days is a scalable, portable methodology used in situ that enables investigators to explore concepts, test ideas, and create designs with youth, while meeting their developmental needs in safe settings and in culturally and gender appropriate ways.

## Categories and Subject Descriptors

C.4. [**Computer Systems Organization**]: Performance of Systems – *design studies*. [H.1.2 [**Information Systems**]: User/Machine Systems – *human factors*. K.4.0 [**Computers and Society**]: General.

## General Terms

Design, Human Factors, Theory.

## Keywords

Burma; Design Thinking; East Africa; Immigrants; InfoMe; Information Behavior; Information Mediaries; Social Networks; Somalia; Teen Design Days; Teenagers; Viet Nam; Youth.

## 1. INTRODUCTION

*"Another time, I helped a girl who had a big problem because she offered someone to use her phone and that person ran away with her phone. Even though I never knew this girl, I was very humble to assist her by using my phone to call the cops and being a witness for her. I learned by helping this person, one day someone would be there to help me."* Pure Honey, 17, Female, Ethiopia

*"I usually go to my dad's appointments because I have to help him about what the doctor says and explain information the doctor gives."* Amai, 16, Female, Kenya

Why do teens help other people—even complete strangers—with everyday life situations using information and technology? How can these behaviors be supported through designing interactive technologies? How can more researchers be engaged with teens?

Digital Youth are defined as people who have grown up without having to adapt to digital technologies because they have always been a ubiquitous part of their lives. Logically, the younger the child, the more immersed s/he is in a digitally pervasive culture, and excellent design work has been accomplished with children not yet in their teens [11, 13, 19]. But older youth are also rapidly adopting digital media and devices at a significant rate.

The need for research on interactive technology design with teenagers is clear [10, 22]. And it is important for interactive technology designers to understand the unique qualities of teens: their cognitive and emotional state; their developmental stage at the intersection of childhood and adulthood; their lifeworlds and culture; their terminology; their experience with technology; and their physical and social environments. The basic lack of methodological expertise is commonly acknowledged, as few design projects, and few studies of the design process, focus on teens. While our understanding of specific methodological aspects of interactive technology design with teens is limited, with many gaps and uncertainties; conversely, creative and thoughtful techniques are being explored [e.g., 15].

Several researchers in the IDC community recently shared papers on specific issues in collaborative teen design: motivating teen participation in design [17]; and selecting an appropriate site for youth design work and establishing the values and ethics of design work with teens [14]. Of particular relevance to our work with immigrant teens and their role as information and technology help-givers in everyday life is work that explores designing for families and communities in the diaspora [3, 24], for the interactions between community-based social agencies and their immigrant clients [5], and for the design of technology to support healthy behavior in vulnerable families [18, 21, 23]. But the basic question remains: *how may designers best collaborate with teens?*

Our IDC Note shares our experiences with teens and design. As social scientists of the human-information experience, our InfoMe ("information mediary") research focuses on understanding the nature of how and why youth—ethnic minority and refugee youth in particular—use information and technology to provide others with vitally needed everyday life assistance. This question is based on a progressive body of work [9, 20] and most recently, a study for the Institute of Museum and Library Services and the Bill & Melinda Gates Foundation of 50,000 public library computer users in the U.S. That study showed that two-thirds of users were searching online and carrying out tasks on behalf of someone else [1]. Regression analysis identified these InfoMes as young (ages 14-18), non-white, and non-native English speakers. Thus, it appears that ethnic minority youth are key for surfacing the needs of their respective populations and passing on needed information to otherwise hidden users (especially non-English speaking, non-users of libraries). Understanding the information behavior of InfoMes, thus, is crucial for identifying the greater range of how digital devices, web applications, and information services can help in immigrant communities. These findings also support work on the challenging lives of immigrant youth [4, 16].

## 2. InfoMe

The InfoMe programme is guided by the following questions:

- How do youth surface the needs of others, provide information and technical help, and create, remix, manage, curate, and search for information?

- How do elders and others engage with youth and benefit from provided assistance?

- How can these behaviors be uncovered and integrated with design thinking [2], in order to translate teen InfoMe experiences into ideas for interactive technology design?

Funded by the Institute of Museum and Library Services and Microsoft Inc., InfoMe's mixed methodology includes: (1) Teen Design Days (TDD)—an award-winning method used with immigrant youth in Seattle, Washington (USA); (2) a paper-based survey (n=575) in six Seattle high schools; and (3) TDD Train-the-Trainer Workshops with designers, researchers, and youth professionals geared to adapting the TDD methodology for use with youth in different places and contexts.

TDD methodology and findings are shared in other reports and video [7, 8]. In essence, it is a high-energy, scalable, portable method for engaging and studying youth that is conducted in varied field settings across two or more days in workshop format.

Basic TDD components include regular "light and lively" activities (short games of physical activity that are tied to the TDD theme and encourage creative thinking), instruction, discussion, group design work and hands-on creation of artifacts, youth presentations, and celebrations joined by family, community representatives, funders, TDD staff, and others. In our remaining space, we present how our TDD method approaches some of the issues noted in the teen design community, such as setting, recruitment, teen motivation, structures for collaborative design, and the role of adults vs. teens. We share our reflections for moving forward, based on our experiences as well as our peer debriefings with researchers at other labs, conferences, and workshops in cognate fields.

## 3. FEATURES OF TEEN DESIGN DAYS
### 3.1 Basic Structure
The core of TDD is meeting the key developmental needs of teens—physical activity, competence and achievement, self-definition, creative expression, positive social interaction, structure, and clear limits [6]. TDD attend to both cultural and

gender differences and emphasize having fun. TDD stand out for working with a relatively large number of youth (n=12-24) over a series of days in a non-lab community setting. Our typical researcher to teen ration is 1 facilitator to 5 youth. We thread design periods through each day.

Youth are recruited with the assistance of a community liaison who shares information about the community's experiences leading to their settling in Seattle; identifies potential teen participants; sets up a venue for our team to both recruit youth and conduct TDD workshops; and helps translate and explain human subject protection forms as well as TDD goals and procedures to families. Because youth are paid cash, TDD are oversubscribed.

Another TDD hallmark is that they are held in safe, informal community settings (to reduce association with school formalities), close to where the youth live, during large blocks of time when the youth are not in school. Flexible space is important: TDD require moveable tables and chairs, as well as space for sharing meals and incorporating physical activity. We bring everything—all the supplies, including design kits, paperwork, and snacks. Meals are typically delivered from local caterers owned or frequented by youths' families.

Video-recording, audio and stills are taken of most every TDD activity. Consent and assent forms include these permissions and youth show few signs of observer effect about being recorded. Indeed, teens view access to their TDD photos as an incentive. Because of the TDD design elements and complex inclusion of youth, industry, academic, government and non-government organization partners, our materials are being expanded to include a Creative Commons license governing intellectual property rights.

### 3.2 Participating Youth
Our ideal number of youth participating is 16-18; divided into 4-5 working groups with at least one adult facilitator. One TDD staff serves as a "runner," attending to ad hoc matters. We've been asked to host as many as 60-100 teens, but haven't the requisite staff/facilities nor are convinced those sizes are feasible.

TDDs typically engage youth from mixed cultures, aged 14-19. While youth are sometimes from one country, such as Burma, or one region such as Eastern Africa, it'd be a gross generalization to assume that youth have shared experiences. Within Eastern Africa, for example, youth may speak any of several languages and have very different immigration or refugee experiences coming to the U.S. Thus, unlike many youth co-design projects, TDD youth are diverse in language ability; age; socio-economic span; and their personal histories and experience with technology.

### 3.3 Focus on Teens' Help-Giving Behavior
Once youth arrive and settle in at TDD with ice-breakers, they develop together a set of expectations, e.g., "respect others" and "everyone participates." The TDD method for understanding InfoMe behavior begins with establishing concepts and eliciting drawings and stories, in order to uncover the youths' use of terminology and their lived experiences. Teen stories also provide early creative content for dramatic play, appropriate cultural probes, and later design. Thus far we've used similar instructions at TDDs: draw a diagram or write a story of how you help people with information and technology. One lesson we learned is that nuances in the preceding conceptual discussion affect the teens' stories and diagrams and subsequent TDD work. Another is that asking for *both* a drawing and a picture might generate more productive and clearer output from teens.

Specifically, TDD1 (March 2013), with 11 youth from East Africa and Viet Nam, ages 14-19 (6 boys, 5 girls) was influenced by (1) language from the facilitators of technology playing a de facto role in InfoMe behavior; and (2) difficulty explaining the concept social network versus social media. Youth returned with diagrams that reflected their digital social media—e.g., Twitter and Instagram—worlds. At TDD2 (June 2013) with 23 youth (ages 15-18; 9 boys, 15 girls) from East Africa and Nepal, we refrained from privileging "technology" in the opening discussion and used "social circles" in the diagram instruction. Next morning, youth returned with a broader range of less-technology focused diagrams and stories, more youth had elected to write stories, and a few youth chose do both—story+diagram illustration.

The resulting data provided insights into the participants' lives. An example is provided at this paper's outset—the stolen cell phone and how the teen offered hers to the victim to contact help, albeit aware of the risk of her own phone being stolen. In sharing stories, youth reflect on their experiences with information and technology and become primed for engaging with design. Youth also share how they curate information, such as writing ideas and notes on paper, devices, and skin (hands, forearms).

## 3.4 Interactive Design with Youth

TDD differs from much a lot of co-design work in that it is as much about teen development and community capacity-building as it is about design; thus, our methodology has roots in community-based participatory research [12]. We provide opportunities for individual expression, growth and learning. At the same time, TDD produces design insights that recognize a *community-wide system* of *general everyday help-giving and help-getting*, rather than focusing on a single device, organization, application, or website. We've learned to base our hands-on, low-tech prototyping around a focal point proposed by TDD adults, yet left open enough for teen appropriation and expression. "Staying on the sidelines" is one way to depict the role we have as adult facilitators in TDD design sessions.

TDD2 included two design tasks. The first was to create "your ideal cell phone," since mobiles were more common and desirable than laptops or tablets among our teens. They focused and were inspired by their current mobile use and desires for new features. Because of teens' heavy use of mobiles, we included an introduction to TouchDevelop, a programming tool for smart phones. The second design task was to "create any tool or service that would aid you in your role as an InfoMe." With about 2 hours in which to work, teen groups of 4-5 with one adult facilitator were given a table-sized piece of paper and markers, as well as a design kit with craft supplies (each kit costs ~$50). First came group brainstorming, with each member jotting and sketching ideas on the paper, which everyone saw as they talked. Next, each group came up with a single idea for further development, often merging ideas from individual group members. Then they moved from 2D to 3D work, using craft supplies—e.g., paper, popsicle sticks, pipe cleaners, stickers, wiki sticks, clay, cardboard, and felt. In the second hour, the groups presented their 3D designs. A facilitator, using large paper taped to the walls, collected feedback from everyone on each design. Teens used sticky notes to record their "likes, dislikes, and suggestions for improvement."

InfoMe tool prototypes included a wristwatch cell phone, a multimedia information kiosk at bus stops, and a free van for the elderly equipped with "comfy seats" and information monitors that would take the seniors from their homes to various information and educational hubs (including museums and classes) in the city and home again.

Similar to other design projects reported in the literature and noted above, we have found teens to be competent partners in design. They also helped refine TDD processes. At the end of each day, we reflect with participants about (1) what went well, (2) what could have gone better (didn't go so well), and (3) what could be changed for next time/day. On the final day, the teens receive an evaluation sheet that asks them to reflect on the experience as a whole and provide feedback that can be used to determine if session goals were met and suggest improvements for future TDD iterations. Thus, we learned during TDD1 that we needed to spend more time with the youth exploring the concepts they would be designing around. In TDD2, we discovered that the light and lively activities rejuvenated teens and helped them stay on task, and could be further linked to InfoMe behavior. In TDD3, in April 2014, we will ask teens to combine stories and pictures to depict their information worlds. We also hope to improve our work by offering less talk and more active exploration and play.

## 4. CONCLUSIONS

InfoMe is an example of how research programmes are about sometimes digging deep, at other times casting broadly. Both are needed to understand a big picture and make a difference over a lifetime of effort that involves a multi-disciplinary cast to inform and enrich the journey en route.

To summarize key lessons that might help others, we recommend:

- Provide cash, fun, convenience, and autonomy to motivate teens;

- Follow precepts for addressing teen developmental needs;

- Use teens' stories, skits, and drawings to stimulate and complement design work;

- Choose settings that get teens away from formal school influences; and

- Expect the unexpected, be flexible, and embrace messiness.

We've also learned the importance of crafting strong partnerships with varied stakeholders. These include: (1) community-based organization staff, who suggest and describe youth populations for study, facilitate youth recruitment and access to facilities, guide engagement with parents, and hope to learn from TDD; (2) industry and universities that sponsor our work and provide consultants and resources for TDD design and programming activities (as well as video-recording); and government funding agencies looking for rigorous and useful research results to guide their policy making and increase their impact.

A TDD hallmark is the hope for creating short-term, mid-term and hopefully, long-term impacts on youth, to build teens' capacity and contribute to their families and community. In this regard, our work fits into the larger frame of the intersection between design and constructive social change, along the lines of IDEO.org and AIGA's Design for Good platform (http://www.aiga.org/design-for-good/). We've learned that small mindful ways to "do good" include over-catering so the youth can bring extra food home. In our workshops, youth are coached to really see and appreciate how they help others in their community. Larger commitments include supporting teens' participation in national conferences to build their communication skills, give them a sense of accomplishment and self-confidence, and provide them with the chance to travel and experience professional work activities.

While still learning about teens and design, we believe that worldwide, youth are one of society's biggest assets. As educators and designers, we've found that a great deal can be accomplished when a youth-focused, action-oriented, and fun process is employed. Once the basic elements of communal respect and openness are established, much can be created, developed and shared to promote broader individual, familial, community, and societal benefits. As TDD youth shout in unison at the start of each new session: 1-2-3 Action!

## 5. ACKNOWLEDGEMENTS

We wish to thank Microsoft Research, Microsoft Global Community Affairs, Institute of Museum & Library Services, University of Washington, King County Library System, Seattle Public Library, YMCA of Greater Seattle, Horn of Africa Services, Northwest Communities of Burma, Vietnamese Friendship Association, and most importantly, all the youth who participate and totally rock!

## 6. REFERENCES

[1] Becker, S., Crandall, M. D., Fisher, K. E., Kinney, B., Landry, C., and Rocha, A. 2010. *Opportunity for all: How the American Public Benefits from Internet Access at U.S. Libraries*. Institute of Museum and Library Services, Washington, DC.

[2] Brown, T. 2008. Design thinking. *Harv. Bus. Rev.* 86, 6 (2008), 8-92.

[3] Brown, D. and Grinter. 2012, R. E. Takes a transnational network to raise a child: the case of migrant parents and left-behind Jamaican teens. In *Proceedings of the 2012 ACM Conference on Ubiquitous Computing* (UbiComp '12). ACM, New York, NY, 123-132.

[4] Chu, C. M. 1999. Immigrant Children Mediators (ICM): Bridging the literacy gap in immigrant communities. *New Rev. Children's Lit. Lib.* 5 (1999), 85-94.

[5] Clarke, R., Wright, P., and McCarthy, J. 2012. Sharing narrative and experience: digital stories and portraits at a women's centre. In *CHI '12 Extended Abstracts on Human Factors in Computing Systems* (CHI EA '12). ACM, New York, NY, USA, 1505-1510.

[6] Davidson, J. and Koppenhaver, D. 1992. *Adolescent Literacy*. 2d ed. Garland, New York, NY.

[7] Fawcett, P., Fisher, K. E., Bishop, A., & Magassa, L. 2013. Using design thinking to empower ethnic minority immigrant youth in their roles as technology and information mediaries. *CHI 2013 Changing Perspectives. ACM SIGCHI Conference on Human Factors in Computing Systems*. 27 April – 2 May, 2013, Paris, France.

[8] Fisher, K. E., Bishop, A., Magassa, L., & Fawcett, P. 2013. InfoMe @ teen design days: A multi-variable, design thinking approach to community development. *ICTD 2013: International Conference on Information and Communication Technologies for Development*. December 7-10, 2013, Cape Town, South Africa. ACM. http://dx.doi.org/10.1145/2517899.2517914

[9] Fisher, K. E., Durrance, J. C., & Hinton, M. B. 2004. Information grounds and the use of need-based services by immigrants in Queens, NY: A context-based, outcome evaluation approach. *Journal of the American Society for Information Science & Technology*, 55,8 (2004), 754-766.

[10] Fitton, D., Read, J. C., and Horton, M. 2013. The challenge of working with teens as participants in interaction design. In *CHI '13 Extended Abstracts on Human Factors in Computing Systems* (CHI EA '13). ACM, NY, 205-210.

[11] Guha, M.L., Druin, A. and Fails, J.A. 2013. Cooperative inquiry revisited. *Int. J. of Child-Comp. Interact,* 1, 1 (2013).

[12] Hacker, K. 2013. *Community-Based Participatory Research*. Sage, Thousand Oaks, CA.

[13] Hourcade, J. P. 2008. Interactive design and children. *Found. Trends in Hum-Comp. Int*, 1, 4 (2007), 277-392.

[14] Iversen, O. S. and Smith, R. C. 2012. Scandinavian participatory design. In *Proceedings of the 11th International Conference on Interaction Design and Children* (IDC '12). ACM, New York, NY, USA, 106-115.

[15] Katterfeldt, E. S., Zeising, A., and Schelhowe, H. 2012. Designing digital media for teen-aged apprentices. In *Proceedings of the 11th International Conference on Interaction Design and Children* (IDC '12). ACM, New York, NY, USA, 196-199.

[16] Katz, V. S. 2014. *Kids in the Middle: How Children of Immigrants Negotiate Community Iinteractions for their Families*. New Brunswick, NJ: Rutgers University Press.

[17] Krog Hansen, E. I. and Iversen. O. S. 2013. You are the real experts! In *Proceedings of the 12th International Conference on Interaction Design and Children* (IDC '13). ACM, New York, NY, USA, 328-331.

[18] Little, L., Bell, B., Defeyter, G., Read, J. C., Fitton, D., and Horton, M. 2013. Behaviour change interventions: teenagers, technology and design. In *Proceedings of the 12th International Conference on Interaction Design and Children* (IDC '13). ACM, New York, NY, USA, 610-612.

[19] Markopoulos, P., Read, J. C., MacFarlane, S., and Hoysniemi, J. 2008. *Evaluating Children's Interactive Products*. Morgan Kaufmann Publishers, San Francisco, CA.

[20] [DELETED FOR BLIND REVIEW]

[21] Miller, A. D., Pater, J., and Mynatt, E. D. 2013. Design strategies for youth-focused pervasive social health games. In *Proceedings of the 7th International Conference on Pervasive Computing Technologies for Healthcare* (PervasiveHealth '13). ICST (Institute for Computer Sciences, Social-Informatics and Telecommunications Engineering), ICST, Brussels, Belgium, Belgium, 9-16.

[22] Read, J. C., Horton, M., Iversen, O., Fitton, D., and Little, L. 2013. Methods of working with teenagers in interaction design. *In CHI '13 Extended Abstracts on Human Factors in Computing Systems* (CHI EA '13). ACM, NY, 3243-3246.

[23] Siek, K. A., LaMarche, J. S., and Maitland, J. 2009. Bridging the information gap. In *Proceedings of the 21st Annual Conference of the Australian Computer-Human Interaction Special Interest Group: Design: Open 24/7* (OZCHI '09). ACM, New York, NY, USA, 89-96.

[24] Wyche, S. P. and Chetty, M. 2013. "I want to imagine how that place looks." In *Proceedings of the SIGCHI Conference on Human Factors in Computing Systems* (CHI '13). ACM, New York, NY, 2755-2764.

# RaBit EscApe: A Board Game for Computational Thinking

Panagiotis Apostolellis
Computer Science Dept.
Virginia Tech
Blacksburg, VA 24060
panaga@vt.edu

Michael Stewart
Computer Science Dept.
Virginia Tech
Blacksburg, VA 24060
tgm@vt.edu

Chris Frisina
Computer Science Dept.
Virginia Tech
Blacksburg, VA 24060
special@vt.edu

Dennis Kafura
Computer Science Dept.
Virginia Tech
Blacksburg, VA 24060
kafura@cs.vt.edu

## ABSTRACT

Computational thinking (CT) is increasingly seen as a core litera-cy skill for the modern world on par with the long-established skills of reading, writing, and arithmetic. To promote the learning of CT at a young age we capitalized on children's interest in play. We designed RabBit EscApe, a board game that challenges chil-dren, ages 6-10, to orient tangible, magnetized manipulatives to complete or create paths. We also ran an informal study to inves-tigate the effectiveness of the game in fostering children's prob-lem-solving capacity during collaborative game play. We used the results to inform our instructional interaction design that we think will better support the learning activities and help children hone the involved CT skills. Overall, we believe in the power of such games to challenge children to grow their understanding of CT in a focused and engaging activity.

## Categories and Subject Descriptors

K.3.2 [**Computer and Information Science Education**]: Com-puter science education; K.3.1 [**Computer Uses in Education**]: Collaborative learning.

## Keywords

Computational thinking; tangible games; education.

## 1. INTRODUCTION

Every generation of adults and parents tries to prepare their youth for a successful and happy adult life. The preparations we teach our children evolve with our societies. In today's world of ever more pervasive technology, we consider technological skills and understanding of systems to be critical competencies for our chil-dren's future. Computational Thinking (CT) is a current area of inquiry around what it takes for the 21st century citizen to func-tion in an environment where interacting with technology is re-quired for much more than work or recreation, but also to act on other necessities. To help produce future generations with these competencies, we believe that we should start teaching these con-cepts at a young age, and continue using a spiral curriculum [4] to reintroduce elements of CT in different subjects and different

years. In order to be successful with children as young as age 6, and when repeatedly encountering these themes, it is important for the activities to be engaging, pedagogically sound, and well- (but not over-) structured.

The overarching goal is to equip children with the necessary prob-lem-solving skills to cope with the abundance of challenges in our increasingly technologically demanding era. Being able to solve hard problems through computation is a considerable qualification for their future everyday and professional lives, as well as a "cog-nitive pillar" of literacy [7]. There are many opportunities in chil-dren's lives for leveraging this type of thinking and helping them develop the necessary skills, which have recently been included under the umbrella of CT. Traditional games like Scrabble and chess are examples of appropriate vehicles for evoking the higher-order skills that are necessary for effective problem-solving [11].

Additionally, games are motivating for children and promote learning in an engaging and entertaining manner. We created a physical board game to underpin the skills and attitudes of CT. We argue that the game is a pedagogically sound sandbox for enabling children to engage in CT through collaborative problem-solving. We have taken into account previous work both in com-puter and tangible games and how they leverage the involved CT skills for successful game play. In the following sections, we pre-sent RabBit EscApe, an educational tangible board game that supports CT through collaborative game play.

## 2. RELATED WORK

### 2.1 Computational Thinking Pedagogy

Since Wing's influential work [19], the research around Computa-tional Thinking (CT) has exploded into myriad lines of divergent pursuits. Following prior work such as the Great Principles of Computing [6] on the topic of defining either prerequisites for computer science (CS) or its transferable skills, and coinciding with other work attempting to broaden participation in CS, Wing et al. have demonstrated the immensity of the research space around CT. Much of this work has offered working definitions of CT [1, 2, 5], but none has become the standard.

Despite the current diversity of views, various institutions have committed to agendas supportive of "computational thinking." We chose the Operational Definition of Computational Thinking for K-12 Education by the International Society for Technology in Education (ISTE) [9] as our operational definition for this work. We thought this to be an appropriate definition due its relevance to our target group, but also its clarity regarding the expectations, skills, and attitudes involved. According to this definition, "CT is a problem-solving process that includes (but is not limited to) the following characteristics":

- Formulating problems in a way that enables us to use a computer and other tools to help solve them
- Logically organizing and analyzing data
- Representing data through abstractions such as models and simulations
- Automating solutions through algorithmic thinking (a series of ordered steps)
- Identifying, analyzing, and implementing possible solutions with the goal of achieving the most efficient and effective combination of steps and resources
- Generalizing and transferring this problem solving process to a wide variety of problems

In support of the aforementioned skills, ISTE suggests that students should be able to express five specific attitudes and dispositions, which are presented in the RabBit EscApe section discussing how our game satisfies each one of them.

## 2.2 Tangible Educational Games for CT

It is natural to want to extend the enthusiasm and promise of educational games to every domain; CT should be no exception. To offer an environment in which play and, hopefully, fun result in learning CT would be ideal. However, unlike many other domains, the definition and scope of CT is still in flux, making it challenging to argue (or at least to have agreement) that a given activity would support CT.

Indeed, based on the notion of learning by doing, researchers at MIT Media Laboratory have coined the term objects-to-think-with as a means to leverage the power of computation in the exploration process [13, 14]. LEGO/Logo is maybe the most famous offspring of this approach where students are learning to program by controlling enhanced LEGO structures (equipped with motors and sensors). Resnick et al. proposed "digital manipulatives" as a continuation of this work where students are called to control through Logo programming other tangible artifacts like blocks, balls, beads, and badges [13]. On the other hand, we were interested in investigating how low-cost games with easy to manufacture components can be leveraged to provide CT exposure to very young children (less than 10 years old).

Along these lines, Berland and Lee explored the CT that might be taught in the commercialized board game Pandemic [3]. As Pandemic is essentially a cooperative multiplayer game with a graph-theoretical representation of several major cities in the world, some implications of the involved CT concepts stem from the fact that the game mechanic is the opponent rather than the other human players. The aspects of CT the authors chose to focus on were conditional logic, distributed processing, debugging, simulation, and algorithm building. One of the things Berland and Lee propose in their work is that maybe board game designers should focus on intentionally designing their games as a means to encourage CT. We too think that there is great potential in exploring the challenges of instructional design in turning a tabletop game into a tool for developing computational thinking. This was our basic motivation for exploring existing board games and eventually developing our own.

## 3. RABBIT ESCAPE

RabBit EscApe is a board game with tangible wooden pieces intended for ages 6 and up. As shown from previous work, tangible wooden blocks like the Froebel blocks [10] are engaging and educational for this age group, contributing to children's emotional, social, and physical development through play. The game was inspired by the combination of the magnetic tile game Picasso-Tiles [15] and the work from Weller et al. on objects-to-think-computationally-with using the Posey construction kit and a Pac-man-style game to teach state machine representations to children [17]. In our approach we decided to avoid using any electronic medium like computers or sensors in an attempt to reach younger ages, which are accustomed to fiddling with tangible objects but are not yet ready to make connections between physical objects and virtual representations.

### 3.1 Description

The game is comprised of fourteen different shapes of wooden pieces half an inch thick which we call bits; each bit is equipped with small magnets which are encased in different sides of the bit and can attract or repel each other depending on polarity. By putting two bits together, you can make a block, which is usually a square, rectangle, or hexagon. Magnets are placed either at the middle of a bit's side or near one of the side's corners to allow a variety of path formations. From the fourteen different shapes, there are twenty-nine unique bits due to varying magnet placement and polarity combinations. We also provide a selection of boards with a path comprised of all, or a subset, of these 29 bits. Boards are of different levels of difficulty depending on the combination of pieces and the ambiguity in block formations.

The goal of the game is to put the bits together (matching opposing polarity) on the predefined path and help the rabbit (a separate token) escape from the fierce apes (i.e., separate pieces that need to be repelled from the path). Hence the name of the game RabBit EscApe! Figure 1a depicts the path of Level A as it was designed on the computer, and Figure 1b is a photograph of the actual board with most pieces placed in the right place.

**Figure 1: (a) Designed completed board for Level A; (b) Physical construction with most bits in the right place**

What makes the game especially challenging, and appropriate for practicing CT skills, is the correct identification of the bit properties and their subsequent utilization to construct the blocks and then the whole path. These properties, acting similar to data properties in abstract CS terms, are: a) the size of each bit, b) the position of the magnet on the bit, c) the polarity of each magnet, and d) the orientation of the bit (or whole block). Players must combine all these attributes in order to put the bits next to each other in such a manner that they stick together at the right place, while also repelling the enemies positioned around the board.

### 3.2 Gameplay Alternatives

The possible suggested activities for teaching CT with the game are described briefly below, although we understand that there are many variations that can derive from these suggestions.

### 3.2.1 Collaborative

Players are given a predefined number of bits and a board and need to complete the board with all the pieces. Team players need to negotiate about path building, by collaboratively evaluating the board state and available bits. Distributed computation [17] is apparent when the players interpret the staged pieces and converse to construct a rule-based plan and complete the path. Distributed CT was also indicated as one of the distinguishing properties of CT compared to CS, according to the National Research Council [5].

### 3.2.2 Competitive

Players or teams are playing against each other and have to complete the most of the path but starting from opposite ends, working toward the middle. They roll the dice and can place as many bits as the number rolled. This activity demands well organized planning, since making the wrong choice will render the board impossible to complete. This competitive mode demands efficient modeling skills since opponents would need to simulate the construction of a large portion of the board with the available pieces, to avoid the cost of negotiating retraction of a previous block or bit placement. Both model building and simulation (forming and contrasting hypotheses) have been defined as foundational aspects of CT and revealed increased benefits compared to traditional methods of instruction [18].

### 3.2.3 Board Construction

With an entry point on one side of the board and finish on an exit point at another side, a team can use all the bits or a random subset and make a custom path on an empty board. They have to do this by drawing the blocks on the board but without placing the bits. They will need to create a mental model of the path, taking each "used" bit out before moving on, until they believe they have drawn the whole path. Another team can then use this custom board to play the game in either of the first two ways. Like the competitive activity, this construction method demands well organized planning to combine bit properties in order to make a playable board. Considering bits and their properties to be the data, players need to construct sets of pieces as part of the path using conditional logic during the process similarly to writing an algorithm (e.g. "If I place this bit here, then this block has a minus on the bottom and needs a big square piece with a plus on the top"). This activity in particular demands the complex skill of combining different requirements to build a set of steps that will lead to an efficient solution of a problem and has been defined as procedural or algorithmic thinking [12], considered a core concept of CT [5].

## 3.3 CT in RabBit EscApe

RabBit EscApe satisfies most of the characteristics of the Operational Definition of CT for K-12 Education as defined by the ISTE [9]. Considering the game mechanics and supported activities, students playing the game should be able to:

**Logically organize and analyze data.** Bits have to be organized in blocks and block combinations that are meaningful according to bit properties and the path's form; pattern recognition is important in this process for identifying which bits create blocks that can fit the path printed on the board while also attracting adjacent blocks or repelling ape blocks (demands analyzing the board based on possible bit combinations and organizing them on the path).

**Automate solutions through algorithmic thinking (a series of ordered steps).** Board construction setup demands that players devise some kind of strategy for correctly utilizing bits and matching the polarity and magnet position; for this purpose they need to come up with some kind of "recipe" for putting bits together while drawing the path on the board, also accounting for the remaining pieces (demands some kind of procedural thinking).

**Identify, analyze, and implement possible solutions with the goal of achieving the most efficient and effective combination of steps and resources.** In all game setups, especially Collaborative and Competitive, players need to correctly identify the combination of blocks and bits by analyzing the path's comprising shapes and then simulate possible solutions for effectively completing the board, with the least number of bits and in the minimum time (efficiency).

Additionally, the game supports all dispositions and attitudes that are essential dimensions of CT, as expressed by the definition:

- **Confidence in dealing with complexity:** Puzzles are inherently complex systems and without an operational strategy for dealing with complexity, the task might prove too challenging. RabBit EscApe introduces added complexity due to the additional puzzle piece properties that need to be accounted for. Confidence is built through successive iterations and attempts during the scaffolded activities, as discussed under the Discussion.

- **Persistence in working with difficult problems:** Deriving from the previous attitude, students are called to overcome initial frustration and persist in finding the solution. In our informal study (see: Discussion), two groups finished the game with one wrong bit placement, but still persevered to start over and get the whole path completed correctly.

- **Tolerance for ambiguity:** All three of the suggested activities include some degree of ambiguity deriving from either the complexity of the board and the amount of clues provided (e.g. including block divisions or a "cheat sheet"), or from the collaborative or competitive nature of the game (i.e. no two players have the same understanding about, nor expectations for the game).

- **The ability to deal with open-ended problems:** Being able to cultivate the previous attitude naturally leads to practicing their ability to deal with open-ended problems. Especially in Board Construction, players must have a good understanding of the game mechanics and bit properties, and be able to deal with the messy process of modeling a new path with minimal constraints.

- **The ability to communicate and work with others to achieve a common goal or solution:** All three modes of play have been designed to encourage or demand some form of collaboration or competition. This requires players to externalize their mental models and rectify any misconceptions. Even in the Competitive activity, students have to express their intentions through negotiations with the opponent(s), as a means to achieve their goals.

## 4. DISCUSSION

Although we did not have sufficient time to complete a rigorous evaluation of RabBit EscApe, we ran an informal study at an elementary school with two groups of three students each, aged between 8 and 10 years. We discovered that scaffolding is a necessary step in enabling children to get the most out of such a game. Scaffolding includes levels of increasing difficulty, starting from making a single block and moving on to more complicated shapes. At some points kids will have the option to construct the different shapes using more than one combination of bits, and will have to incrementally take into account other piece properties and examine the implications of their choices. This mental modeling of the different affordances of each piece will enable children to be more efficient in the actual game activities, without demanding extra cognitive load to process them during gameplay.

Another idea to aid the bit selection and usage process is to provide a separate "cheat sheet" with all pieces and their count, next to the actual game boards. Players can cross out any pieces that have been used with a marker in order to keep track of what has been used and what is still available. This cheat sheet can be used during the initial sessions and then progressively removed, letting the users depend on their ability to recognize the physical pieces. This is a common process of scaffolding in instructional design, also called fading, because the additional information (scaffold) is removed (faded) over time [8].

These introductory puzzles can also assist in dealing with some observed instances of under-specification. We suggest that children should have a very clear understanding of the piece properties and the constraints that they introduce. Thus, we should help them form some kind of algorithmic representation including all the properties that bits should have in any given position, and show them how to apply it in similar situations. This can be achieved through guiding questions that will lead children to evaluate the different properties of any missing piece on the board. Questions like "How big should this piece be?", "How should it attach to adjacent blocks?", and "What polarity should the magnets have?" will help them construct mental functions of bit and path properties that need to be evaluated at every point.

Social interactions are important in the conversion of the game attributes (i.e., path shape on board, bit properties, remaining bits) to mental functions. Students should be encouraged to question each other's assumptions while moving from the initial introductory puzzles to more complex game boards, to prevent an adversarial tone. Because the game could become quite difficult, depending on the path and pieces provided, we found it helpful to include a "more knowledgeable other" in the form of a guide, who could intervene before frustration overwhelmed the students. This guide, in conjunction with the students' interpersonal interactions, keeps the activity in their "zone of proximal development" [16].

While further, rigorous evaluation is necessary, we agree with one of our reviewers that RabBit EscApe "seems novel and engaging, and likely to be of interest to many other researchers, and to spark interesting debates."

## 5. CONCLUSION

A significant leap must be made to educate our youth as society continues to develop computational systems with which they must interact Along these lines, we have developed RabBit EscApe to teach CT in a relatively explicit way, intentionally moving the focus of the game away from mathematical concepts, which are predominant in other CT game setups. Having run a study to observe children's interactions with each other and our game, we believe there is a promising avenue for low-tech, tangible games for teaching CT to children aged 6-10 years in an engaging way. Our next step includes running a formal study to assess the game for its appropriateness in cultivating CT skills, and verify if the designed strategies support these skills in a successful manner.

## 6. ACKNOWLEDGEMENTS

We would like to thank the Institute for Creativity, Arts, and Technology (ICAT, http://www.icat.vt.edu) at Virginia Tech for their generous support of this project.

## 7. REFERENCES

[1] Allan, W., Coulter, B., Denner, J., Erickson, J., Lee, I., Malyn-Smith, J. and Martin, F. Computational thinking for youth. *White Paper for the ITEST Small Working Group on Computational Thinking (CT)*, 2010.

[2] Barr, V. and Stephenson, C. Bringing computational thinking to k-12: what is involved and what is the role of the computer science education community? *Inroads*, 2(1):48–54, 2011.

[3] Berland, M and Lee, V.R. Collaborative strategic board games as a site for distributed computational thinking. *International Journal of Game-Based Learning*, 1(2):65, 2011.

[4] Bruner, J.S. The process of education. *American Journal of Physics*, 31:468–469, 1963.

[5] National Research Council. Report of a Workshop on the Scope and Nature of Computational Thinking. *National Academies Press*, 2010.

[6] Denning, P.J. Great principles of computing. *Communications of the ACM*, 46(11):15–20, 2003.

[7] DiSessa, A.A. *Changing minds: Computers, learning and literacy*. The MIT Press, 2001.

[8] Driscoll, M.P. *Psychology of Learning for Instruction (3rd Edition)*. Pearson, 2004.

[9] ISTE. *Operational definition of computational thinking of the international society for technology in education*. https://www.iste.org/learn/computational-thinking/ct-operational-definition

[10] Liebschner, J. *A child's work: Freedom and play in Froebel's educational theory and practice*. Lutterworth Press Cambridge, 1992.

[11] Newell, A., Simon, H.A., et al. *Human problem solving*, volume 14. Prentice-Hall Englewood Cliffs, NJ, 1972.

[12] Papert, S. Mindstorms: *Children, computers, and powerful ideas*. Basic Books, Inc., 1980.

[13] Resnick, M., Martin, F., Berg, R., Borovoy, R., Colella, V., Kramer, K., and Silverman, B. Digital manipulatives: new toys to think with. In *Proceedings of the SIGCHI conference on Human factors in computing systems*, 281–287. ACM Press/Addison-Wesley Publishing Co., 1998.

[14] Schweikardt, E. and Gross, M.D. Roblocks: a robotic construction kit for mathematics and science education. In *Proceedings of the 8th international conference on Multimodal interfaces*, 72–75. ACM, 2006.

[15] Picasso Tiles. *Picasso tiles 3d*. http://www.picassotiles.com/

[16] Vygotsky, L. *Mind in society: The development of higher psychological processes*. Harvard University Press, 1978.

[17] Weller, M.P., Do, E. Y.-L., and Gross, M. D. Escape machine: teaching computational thinking with a tangible state machine game. In *Proceedings of the 7th international conference on Interaction design and children*, 282–289. ACM, 2008.

[18] Wilensky, U. and Reisman K. Thinking like a wolf, a sheep, or a firefly: Learning biology through constructing and testing computational theories—an embodied modeling approach. *Cognition and instruction*, 24(2):171–209, 2006.

[19] Wing, J.M. Computational thinking and thinking about computing. *Philosophical Transactions of the Royal Society A: Mathematical, Physical and Engineering Sciences*, 366(1881):3717–3725, 2008.

# FabCode: Visual Programming Environment for Digital Fabrication

**Harshit Agrawal**
Indian Institute of Technology
Guwahati
Department of Design
harshit.rnnh@gmail.com

**Rishika Jain**
Indian Institute of Technology
Guwahati
Department of Design
rishika.j92@gmail.com

**Prabhat Humar**
Indian Institute of Technology
Guwahati
Department of Design
prabhat1992@gmail.com

**Pradeep Yammiyavar**
Indian Institute of Technology Guwahati
Department of Design
pradeep@iitg.ernet.in

## ABSTRACT

In this paper, we introduce FabCode, a visual programming environment using which one can create designs that can be manufactured using digital fabrication techniques like 3D printing and laser cutting. This project is primarily about making accessible and enhancing the kinds of 'thinking' that the computational medium is capable of supporting and spreading. FabCode is situated in the context of design and engineering of objects, and is based on the premise that programming 3D models for personal fabrication would enable practice of computational thinking for the same. Children will learn as they work on personally meaningful projects—building, describing, printing and playing with things, and debugging and discussing their processes and outcomes. It will be a child-centered, constructionist tool for FabLabs.

## Categories and Subject Descriptors

D.3.3 [**Programming Languages**]: Language Constructs and Features

## Keywords

Constructionism, Digital Fabrication, Computational Thinking, 3D Modeling, Visual Programming, Blockly

## 1. INTRUCTION

Digital fabrication is inherently an iterative process based on the established iterative cycle of creative learning [1]. Digital fabrication and "making" have been argued to be a new and major chapter in this process of bringing powerful ideas, literacies, and expressive tools to children. What Logo did for geometry and programming – bringing complex mathematics within the reach of schoolchildren – fabrication labs can do for design and engineering [2]. Computational design and digital fabrication offer many compelling opportunities for personal creative expression through programming [6].

FabCode could serve as a 'Mathland' [3] inspired by LOGO, because through programming designs of objects, one can let math do the making. All objects can then possibly serve as objects-to-think-with [4] while playing with them, and in the process of making them by considering aspects such as their mechanical functions, needs fulfilled by them, and attributes.

Computational Thinking involves defining, understanding, and solving problems, reasoning at multiple levels of abstraction, understanding and applying automation, and analyzing the appropriateness of the abstractions made [5]. Computational thinking shares with engineering thinking in the general ways in which we might approach designing and evaluating a large, complex system that operates within the constraints of the real world. Computational design offers a number of benefits that can extend traditional design techniques. These benefits include: precision and automation, generativity and randomness, parameterization [6].

Papert has explained his pedagogical philosophy thus: "constructionism boils down to demanding that everything be understood by being constructed" [7]. With objects, the starting points are concrete and grounded. FabCode can support thinking in 'mind sized bites' [3], where programmers start with one specific case, entirely understood, develop intuition and then gradually generalize, level by level, in a way that they still fully understand the program at each level of abstraction. Deconstruction of objects and associated notions may lead to breaking of black-boxes, followed by investigation and reconstruction or re-invention of tangible objects through new methods and techniques. In this manner, our platform could be a realization of the computational medium acting as a material-to-think- with.

Also, Piaget and other developmental psychologists have emphasized the importance of using physical objects for children's cognitive development, which is a major part of the iterative cycle of digital fabrication [8, 9]. The benefits of digital fabrication and FabLabs for children have been well established through research projects like FabLab@School [10].

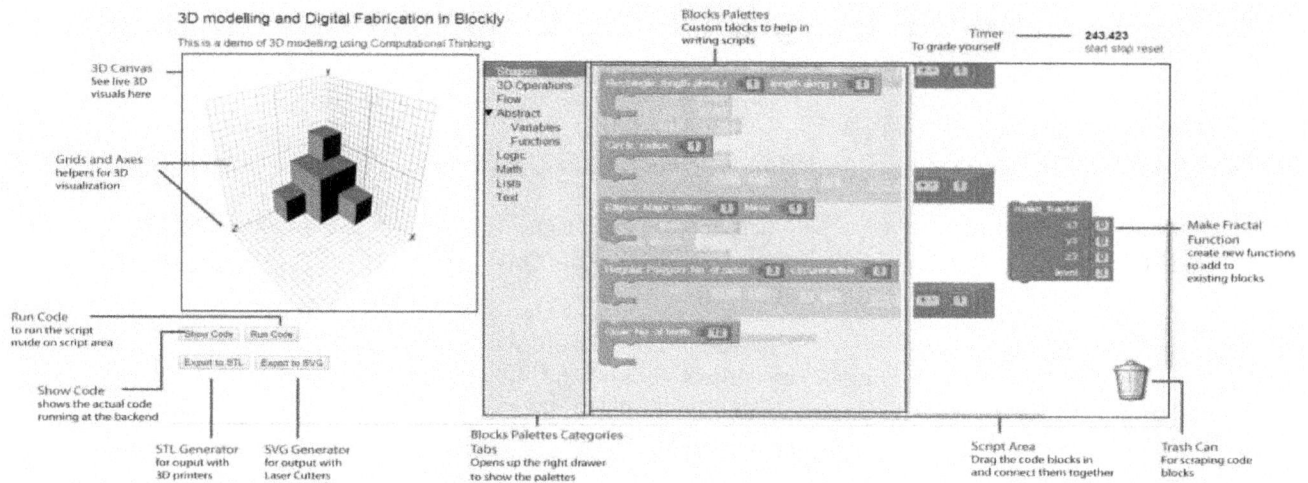

**Fig 1. FabCode interface with labeling of different parts. A fractal is constructed here combining the blocks of FabCode**

Programming tools such as Scratch [11] and NetLogo [12] have been instrumental and fundamental in encouraging children to think and create new things computationally. Scratch, linked learning of programming concepts and computational thinking skills to a personally meaningful output that kids could create in the form of animations, games and other kind of media. Correspondingly, FabCode aims to bring forth the computer as a new material for learning [13] and making by situating digital

literacy in the context of creation of physical objects through 3D digital design and fabrication.

## 2. Existing Software
We studied existing software in two domains:

- Modeling software

- Software that combine computational design and digital fabrication

The software currently available for creating models for digital fabrication can be roughly put in two categories: tools for beginners with a low threshold and tools for professional users with a high ceiling [14]. Tools for amateur users include Google SketchUp [15], Tinkercad[16], and Autodesk 123D Design [17]. 3D objects are created by combining and modifying basic shapes, such as cubes, spheres, cylinders, and planes. The functionality to modify the shapes by altering the underlying geometrical figures is limited, thereby limiting understanding of the link between 2D shapes and 3D ones. Sketch It, Make It is a 2D CAD tool that allows users to constrain their designs through gestures made using a digital drawing tablet [18]. These software have their limitations in bringing clarity to how 3D shapes are constructed from 2 D shapes. They are also limited in the detail of design that can be modeled. The tools of these software do not have an inherent aim of linking computational thinking and programing constructs with designing of models.

On the other hand, there are 3D modeling tools for professional 3D modeling like SolidWorks [19], Rhinoceros [20] or Autodesk Inventor [21]. They allow for developing sophisticated 3D objects, but seem to be less suitable for beginners. There are also professional tools that are explicitly developed for computational design like Grasshopper, a third-party add-on for the Rhinoceros 3D modeling tool [22]. In the context of digital fabrication, one of the most important elements of these tools is their ability to

import and export a wide variety of file formats, thus facilitating the transitions between a digital design and the required file type for a specific fabrication tool. Despite their power, and due to their high cost and complex feature set, these professional tools are extremely difficult for amateurs to access and use. Successfully using them in a FabLab context requires prior knowledge.

Platforms with the aim of making computational designing (programming driven) for digital fabrication to be accessible to novice users have been built. FlatCAD seeks to connect programming and digital fabrication and allows users to build customized construction kits with a laser cutter by programming in FlatLang, a novice-oriented programming language modeled on Logo [23]. Codeable Objects allows for novice programers to create design for fabrication using the laser cutter and the vinyl cutter [6]. Both these support 2D designs and only. They could be put together for constructing 3D structures, but these platforms do not provide for modeling shapes in 3D directly, thereby having limited capability. The existing environments, especially the ones aimed at beginners, do not have an inherent intention of encouraging users to think and work computationally to create the designs that they want to. There has been little concrete attempt at creating a scalable platform that links the two skills- that of programing with design and engineering.

## 3. FABCODE
FabCode is an online platform where users can use visual programming language to create models for digital fabrication. FabCode derives its design principles from the guiding principles for designing construction kits as laid out by Resnick et al [24]. These include: learning through designing, having low floor and wide walls and supporting many paths for designing the same object. FabCode, being an online environment will also make it simple for users to share their designs that are personally meaningful to them, a component of effective learning as proposed in the theory of Constructionism.

### 3.1 Features of current interface
#### 3.1.1 Single-Window User Interface
A single window multi pane design ensures that key components are always visible, and interface navigation is eased. To invite coding, the command palette is always visible, wherein the

commands are divided into categories, and their ordering and color coding helps keep the different commands visible, comprehensible and accessible [25]. The render area in FabCode can be rotated, zoomed in and out, panned across for viewing different views. A timer is also provided to time how long it takes you to create something if you want to see it [Fig 1].

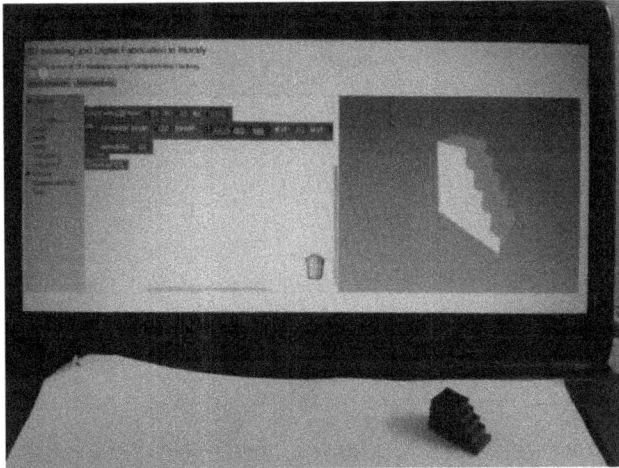

**Figure 2. A looping program written to generate the model of a staircase in an earlier version of FabCode. The 3D printed model as created from the STL file that FabCode produced is shown, thereby showing the cycle of writing a program for modeling, seeing the virtual model, then 3D printing it for iteration and studying its tangible features**

### 3.1.2 Block-based programming
FabCode's interface was built using the Blockly API [26]. It is a graphical programming editor which removes the hassle of mastering syntax of programming languages before one can code. To this visual programming interface, we add our own blocks for the purpose of creating shapes and performing operations to generate 3D geometries. These can be easily understood by the user. Each block has a tooltip message attached to it to explain to novice users the functionality of each block, if need be. These blocks include 2 categories- shapes which comprise of rectangle, circle, ellipse, n-sided regular polygon and gear and 3D Operations which consists of bulge (extrude), move to, rotate around axis and intersection, subtraction, joining of solids. Contrary to most novice CAD environments, we decided not to provide ready-made 3D models to users. Therefore, we skipped giving blocks of cuboid, sphere, cylinder, pyramid etc., instead encouraging the user to think of how these can be made from the blocks provided. Users can make static or functional objects using blocks like gear block in combination with other parts. The interface also has a 'show code' option where a person would be able to see the actual underlying JavaScript code running [Fig 1].

### 3.1.3 Tinkerability
FabCode, like Scratch, is tinkerable because it lets users experiment with commands and code snippets the way one might tinker with mechanical or electronic components.

### 3.1.4 Low threshold, High ceiling and wide walls
Sets of tools and materials like clay, paints and canvas, etc. have their respective barriers and accessibilities. In computational design, many barriers do not exist, and new powerful tools are available. We make these tools available through programming.

Block-based programming, pre-defined starting tool set and pre-platform activities will help provide structures-to-think-with and lower the threshold to the generation of complex objects. Logo was designed for children. Our platform will potentially grow with children into adulthood. They will add tools to toolsets by making those tools as functions first. They can then move to more complex designs by black-boxing self-designed functions which can create models through passing of parameters. Sharing of user-made functions as tools will enable more complex creations through collaboration. FabCode also has the characteristics of wide walls- supporting different ways of expression or many paths towards the same object.

## 3.2 Development
To have it be capable of supporting extensive 3D modeling, FabCode's functioning is written using three.js, a lightweight cross-browser JavaScript library/API used to create and display 3D computer graphics on a Web browser [27]. Blockly has various visual programming 'blocks' built into it that implement programming constructs like variable defining, loops, math operations, conditional statements etc. We have built various new blocks that help model 2D and 3D designs and convert these designs to file formats that are supported by digital fabrication machines, STL for 3D printing and SVG for laser cutters [Fig 1].

## 3.3 FabCode Workflow
To explain the entire workflow and to bring clarity to how we are linking computational thinking and modeling of objects, let us take an example of modeling a spiral staircase. To be able to model a spiral staircase in FabCode, one has to understand the design of a staircase by applying computational thinking skills of decomposition, pattern recognition, pattern generalization, abstraction and algorithm design. A user would have to understand the pattern of how each step is placed in relation to the previous step such that they form a spiral. They would then have to device an efficient algorithm to represent this pattern using the tools of programing that FabCode provides. For example, one would write a loop program for doing this. Using programing as a tool to design can result in users making more abstract designs by designing algorithms such that they could create a staircase with different base polygons- like a hexagon staircase. FabCode provides for creation of new functions that become a part of the blocks palette. Thus, one could create a generic function using which one could create a spiral staircase with different sided polygons as base. All this would require a coming together of different ideas and concepts! [Fig 2].

## 4. FUTURE WORK
### 4.1 Evaluation
We plan to evaluate FabCode in terms of the usability of the functions provided and the effectiveness of FabCode in reaching its intended goal of encouraging computational thinking of objects.

For the former, the usability and effectiveness of FabCode will be evaluated with users and the results will be used to give direction to the design of FabCode. Right now, we have made blocks based on the existing modeling software and its nomenclature, but we need to validate their usability in our context. For the latter, we will record the designs that users create along with the 'code' they write to generate it. Analyzing this, we aim to see if our direction has been effective in getting users to think computationally and in an efficient manner. Considering most of the designs that users create would have been possible to model in a variety of ways, we will aim to see if the user has used 'brute' ways of modeling rather than thinking of an efficient algorithm.

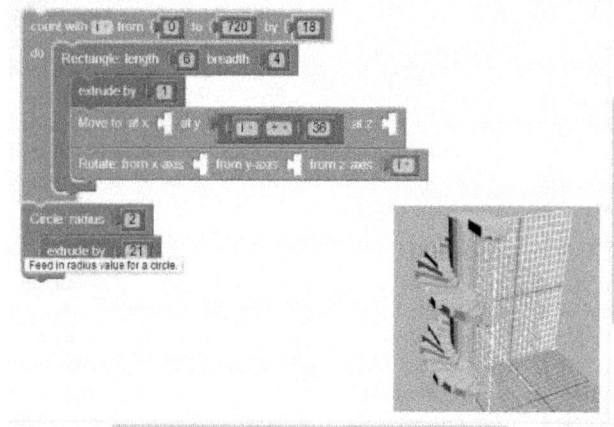

**Figure 3. Creating a spiral staircase model (code on left and rendered model in sub- image)**

## 4.2 Activity Design

We plan to design activities that fit well into curricula of STEAM disciplines. We see FabCode's and the activities' active deployment in maker spaces and places like FabLab@School. FabLab@School already aims to integrate its activities in the curriculum and we will iterate upon our activities so that they can be easily integrated.

## 5. CONCLUSION

FabCode is an attempt at making a platform wherein programing for physical objects acts as a tool to encourage computational thinking and build engineering and design skills. We want to situate FabCode such that it facilitate imagination and investigation of ideas, not acting just as just a validator of imagined ideas but as a material-to-think-with.

## 6. REFERENCES

[1] Resnick, Mitchel. "Sowing the Seeds for a More Creative Society." Learning & Leading with Technology 35.4 (2008): 18-22.

[2] Blikstein, Paulo. "Digital Fabrication and 'Making'in Education: The Democratization of Invention." FabLabs: Of Machines, Makers and Inventors(2013): 1-21.

[3] Eisenberg, M. (2003). Mindstuff: Educational Technology Beyond the Computer. In Convergence, Summer 2003.

[4] Papert, S. (1980). Mindstorms : children, computers, and powerful ideas. NewYork: Basic Books.

[5] http://www.hindawi.com/journals/tswj/2014/428080/

[6] Jacobs, Jennifer, and Leah Buechley. "Codeable objects: computational design and digital fabrication for novice programmers." Proceedings of the 2013 ACM annual conference on Human factors in computing systems. ACM, 2013.

[7] Papert, S. 1980. Constructionism vs. Instructionism. Proceedings from Japanese Educators Conference. http://www.papert.org/articles/const_inst/

[8] Piaget, J. (1962). Play, dreams, and imitation in childhood. New York: Norton.

[9] Ginsburg, Herbert P., and Sylvia Opper. *Piaget's theory of intellectual development* . Prentice-Hall, Inc, 1988.

[10] Blikstein, Paulo, and Dennis Krannich. "The makers' movement and FabLabs in education: experiences, technologies, and research." Proceedings of the 12th International Conference on Interaction Design and Children. ACM, 2013.

[11] Resnick, Mitchel, et al. "Scratch: programming for all." Communications of the ACM 52.11 (2009): 60-67.

[12] Tisue, Seth, and Uri Wilensky. "Netlogo: A simple environment for modeling complexity." International Conference on Complex Systems. 2004.

[13] Resnick, M. 2006. Computer as Paintbrush: Technology, Play, and the Creative Society. In D. Singer, Golikoff, R., and Hirsh-Pasek, K. (Eds.), Play = Learning: How Play Motivates and Enhances Children's Cognitive and Social-Emotional Growth. Oxford University Press.

[14] Zeising, Anja, Eva-Sophie Katterfeldt, and Heidi Schelhowe. "Considering Constructionism for Digital Fabrication Software Design."

[15] http://www.sketchup.com/

[16] https://tinkercad.com/

[17] http://www.123dapp.com/design

[18] Johnson, Gabe, et al. "Sketch it, make it: sketching precise drawings for laser cutting." CHI'12 Extended Abstracts on Human Factors in Computing Systems. ACM, 2012.

[19] http://www.solidworks.com/

[20] http://www.rhino3d.com/

[21] http://www.autodesk.com/products/autodesk-inventor-family/overview

[22] http://www.grasshopper3d.com/

[23] Johnson, Gabe. "FlatCAD and FlatLang: Kits by code." VL/HCC. 2008.

[24] Resnick, Mitchel, and Brian Silverman. "Some reflections on designing construction kits for kids." Proceedings of the 2005 conference on Interaction design and children. ACM, 2005.

[25] Maloney, J., Resnick, M., Rusk, N., Silverman, B., and Eastmond, E. 2010. The scratch program- ming language and environment. ACM Trans. Comput. Educ. 10, 4, Article 16 (November 2010), 15 pages. DOI = 10.1145/1868358.1868363. http://doi.acm.org/10.1145/1868358.1868363.

[26] https://code.google.com/p/blockly/

[27] http://threejs.org/

# Frog Pond: A Code-First Learning Environment on Evolution and Natural Selection

Michael S. Horn, Corey Brady, Arthur Hjorth, Aditi Wagh, Uri Wilensky
Northwestern University
Learning Sciences and Computer Science
2120 Campus Drive, Evanston, Illinois 60208 USA

{michael-horn, cbrady, uri}@northwestern.edu,
{arthur.hjorth, aditiwagh2012}@u.northwestern.edu

## ABSTRACT

Understanding processes of evolution and natural selection is both important and challenging for learners. We describe a "code-first" learning environment called Frog Pond designed to introduce natural selection to elementary and middle school aged learners. Learners use NetTango, a blocks-based programming interface to NetLogo, to control frogs inhabiting a lily pond. Simple programs result in changes to the frog population over successive generations. Our approach foregrounds computational thinking as a bridge to understanding evolution as an emergent phenomenon.

## Categories and Subject Descriptors

H.5.m [**Information interfaces and presentation (e.g., HCI)**]: Miscellaneous.

## Keywords

Children; agent-based modeling; code-first environment; evolution; natural selection; design; learning.

## 1. INTRODUCTION

Understanding processes of evolution and natural selection is both important and challenging for learners [9, 15]. We present a learning environment called Frog Pond designed to introduce natural selection to elementary and middle school aged learners. With Frog Pond learners use NetTango [4], a blocks-based programming interface to NetLogo [21], to control the actions of colorful frogs inhabiting a lily pond environment (Figure 1). Chains of simple block with names like `hop`, `left`, `right`, and `hatch` form programs that can result in changes to the frog population over successive generations—in particular, frogs can become bigger or smaller (or both) depending on selection pressures exerted by the environment and frogs' behaviors. Importantly, children never program these outcomes directly; they never write code that explicitly says, "make the frogs get bigger". Instead, outcomes *emerge* as the aggregate result of hundreds of individual frogs enacting rules from the same program. These outcomes can be surprising and counterintuitive, but because they

result from programs that learners create themselves, our hope is to encourage explanations that attribute change to emergence resulting from individual interactions ("bigger frogs are better hunters, so they get to reproduce more and have babies that are also big"). In this way our intention is to foreground *computational thinking* [10, 11, 27] as a bridge to understanding evolution as an emergent phenomenon.

With this goal in mind, we designed Frog Pond as a *code-first* learning environment (e.g. [20]). By this we mean three things. First, the primary way to interact with Frog Pond is by creating programs. Second, the programming interface is designed to be very easy to learn and use. And, finally, it is possible to create very short programs that nonetheless result in several distinct evolutionary outcomes. To achieve these design objectives, we have been conducting a design-based research study in which we have iteratively developed and refined prototypes over the past year and a half. As part of this process, we have tested versions of Frog Pond with visitors in a natural history museum. In this paper, we describe our resulting design and share findings from our most recent round of testing with museum visitors. Our findings suggest that Frog Pond enables learners to quickly build programs that lead to population-level changes. This provides an opportunity to reflect on mechanisms underlying evolutionary effects.

## 2. BACKGROUND

Understanding evolution is notoriously difficult for learners [2, 15, 23]. Developmental and cognitive psychologists have identified cognitive biases such as teleology and essentialism that hinder student understandings of evolution (see [15]). Other researchers have argued that students' unfamiliarity with emergent processes in general is problematic [2]. Wilensky and Resnick [22] note that in trying to understand complex systems such as evolution, students will often exhibit *slippage between levels* as they attribute properties or behaviors at the individual level to the population as a whole (or vice versa). For instance, when reasoning about natural selection, students might believe that changes in the population are the result of changes to individual organisms over the course of their own lifespans.

Emergent phenomena are often simulated using computational *agent-based models* (ABMs). In these models, individual computational agents have properties and can enact behavioral rules as the simulation runs. For example, the NetLogo modeling environment [21] is widely used in middle schools, high schools, and universities. By emphasizing the behavior of individual actors in a system, ABMs can help students draw on their own bodily and sensory experiences in the world [16, 24, 25].

This project builds on more than fifteen years of work on evolution education using the NetLogo modeling environment [21]. This line of work has sought to present evolution as a set of emergent phenomena characterized by individual-level mechanisms that lead to population level effects. In the *SimEvolution project*, middle and high school students explored agent-based models of classic evolutionary phenomena such as peppered moths and genetic drift. In the EACH project [1], high school and undergraduate students explored and built models that assessed the advantages and disadvantages of selfish behavior and how cooperation could evolve. In the BEAGLE project [23] students use both agent-based modeling and participatory simulations to explore core mechanisms of evolution. These projects resulted in increased understanding of evolution and mechanisms that can lead to population-level changes. In the past few years, there have been efforts to include elementary students in this type of modeling [3, 5]. For example, *Evolution Readiness* [5] is a curriculum that uses interactive computer-based models and activities to help elementary students learn about evolution and natural selection.

While experimenting with a pre-existing agent-based model can be a powerful learning experience, there has been steady attention in involving K-12 students in programming their own models [6, 7, 26, 18]. Proponents argue that programming can expose underlying mechanisms and relationships [12, 17, 24] and can help students develop more personal connections in making sense of math and science [8, 17]. This emphasis on programming is also consistent with Constructionist theories of learning in the sense that students are engaged in building external artifacts that reflect internal conceptual structures and thereby make their thinking available for "debugging" [11]. Some of these recent projects have involved text-based programming languages and some have used graphical programming. Text-based languages are expressive and powerful, but they can sometimes be daunting to students and teachers, particularly at lower grade levels [28]. Blocks-based languages, on the other hand, while perhaps more inviting, can limit the complexity of programs and models that learners can create.

Several programming environments have been developed that attempt to preserve the advantages of agent-based modeling while being more accessible to younger learners. StarLogo TNG uses a domain-general blocks-based programming interface to allow learners to construct a wide range of models [7]. However, as it is a fully-featured modeling environment, the task of programming models can still be involved.

An alternative approach involves offering high-level primitives that are specific to a domain of interest. For example, Modelling4All [6] is an environment that allows for the construction of models from micro-behaviors. Modelling4All has been used to design museum exhibits and other short-duration learning experiences. Another example of this approach is DeltaTick [18, 26], a blocks-based programming available for NetLogo. DeltaTick enables designers to create blocks that are semantically close to the modeled domains. Building on DeltaTick, Wagh and Wilensky have involved middle school students in constructing models of evolution in a project called EvoBuild [18]. With EvoBuild, students model within-species variation by adding traits and manipulating the distribution of its variations in populations. Students can also assign rules to individuals by using behavior-based primitives such as "reproduce" or "die" that generate evolutionary outcomes over time.

To a certain extent these two efforts (addressing younger students and involving students in building models) have traded off against each other. For instance, the work of Dickes and Sengupta [3] have provided considerable scaffolding for younger students to explore models while model creation has been primarily tried with older students. In this project, our emphasis is on increasing the accessibility of programming even further, thus enabling young students to program their own models and grapple with evolutionary effects.

## 3. DESIGN OVERVIEW

We implemented Frog Pond using HTML5, CSS, and the Dart programming language. The use of these cross-platform web technologies allows the environment to run on several different types of devices including tablet computers, laptops, and multi-touch tabletops. Frog Pond is now available through app stores for some platforms. To reduce the visual separation between the code and its effect on the frogs, the programming workspace is superimposed directly on the pond. The workspace consists of a menu bar at the bottom of the screen from which users can select programming blocks; a toolbar with buttons for starting, stopping, fast-forwarding and restarting programs; and the user's current program (Figure 1). This language is similar to other blocks-based languages like Scratch [13], Blockly (code.google.com/p/blockly/), and Open Blocks [14], but it includes several interactive features designed to make it easier for inexperienced users to get started.

There are four distinct evolutionary outcomes that learners can generate with Frog Pond depending on the programs that they build. The easiest result to achieve is for frogs to get smaller over successive generations. This happens with programs similar to the one shown in Figure 2 (left). The important ingredients are a hatch block that allows frogs to reproduce and a hop block that moves frogs forward on their lily pads. If a frog hops off a lily pad, the app plays a "splash" sound effect and the frog is removed from

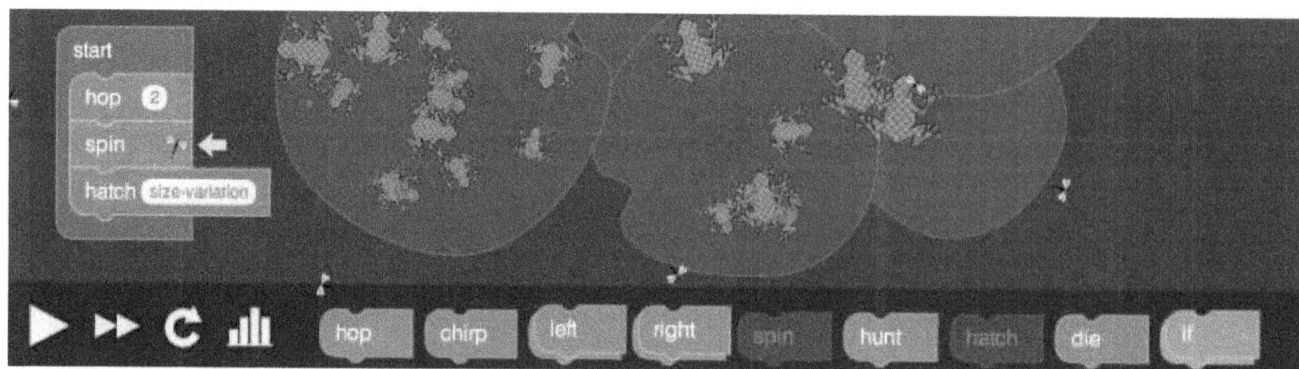

Figure 1. With Frog Pond learners use blocks-based programming to control colorful frogs in a pond.

the simulation. This mechanism creates a selection pressure that favors smaller frogs that take shorter hops. The second outcome results in an opposite effect: the frogs get bigger over successive generations (Figure 2, right). One way to achieve this outcome is to allow frogs to starve to death. Programs then need to include a hunt block (which cause frogs to "hunt" for food by sitting and waiting for a fly to pass into their field of view) and conditional logic that causes starving frogs to die. Bigger frogs see farther and have longer tongues, so larger size now conveys a survival advantage. The third outcome extends the second program, but creates a situation with countervailing selection pressures. This balances out the advantage of being large (due to tongue length) with the advantage of being small (due to hop distance). A final outcome extends the second outcome by creating regions in the environment that differentially favor larger or smaller frog populations. This is accomplished by dragging lily pads around the screen to form larger and smaller islands that frogs inhabit.

# 4. EVALUATION

We produced the current version of Frog Pond through iterative cycles of development and testing in a natural history museum. In our testing sessions, we recruited museum visitors between the ages of 9 and 16. When possible we invited pairs of children to use the software together. Families engaged with the environment for a 15-20 minute period. We collected a variety of data from theses sessions, including a demographic survey, video and audio recordings of the interactive sessions, and researcher field notes.

## 4.1 Findings

**Accessibility and a low-threshold**. In testing with our latest version *all* of our users were able to create and run programs within the first 1-2 minutes of encountering the Frog Pond. Of course, many of these early "programs" were extremely simple constructions, serving more to explore the space of functionality of the available blocks, rather than expressing intentions to produce emergent effects or to solve one of the programming challenges. Nevertheless, this rapid progress from introduction to the environment to first program execution in noteworthy, particularly since some of these initial programs actually did produce interesting emergent effects when they were run.

**Advantages of the code-first environment**. In part because the

programming and simulation environments of Frog Pond are merged on a single screen, it was common for learners to attempt to interact with frogs using direct touch or drag gestures. However, the failure of these gestures to produce a response may have cued exploration of particular programming blocks. For instance, after failing to drag a frog that was facing the edge of a lilypad, one user tried using the right block as her first programming command. Observing the ways in which participants attempted to manipulate Frog Pond as they learned the logic of the environment provided us with several key insights. For instance, several users dragged a programming block directly onto a frog. Interpreting this gesture as a temporary command (e.g., as a way to preview a block's functionality) might be a useful feature that could support users in learning about the blocks. However, the design of Frog Pond seemed to create a clear distinction between such "one-off" commands on the one hand, and the program blocks that constitute the frogs' nature on the other. For children of a wide variety of ages, the code-first environment seemed to support reasoning about collective behavior through programming and thinking about patterns of behavior as a heritable trait.

**Emergence and "runtime surprises"**. In spite of the increase in transparency in the code achieved through the blocks-based interface, the environment consistently provided "runtime surprises" for users. We attribute these surprises to two causes, each of which carries value for grappling with evolution and its mechanisms. The first of these has to do with the fact that a user's program is executed in a repeat loop. This is closely connected with the idea that the program is a behavioral trait of the organism; it is repeatedly executed and constitutes the frogs' relation to their environment. Because the user creates the program while observing inert frogs in initial locations and orientations, the effects on frogs as these situations change can be a surprise. The second cause for surprise has to do with the idea that the programmatic behaviors are transmitted to offspring. In users' experimentation with the environment, this emerges most clearly in their experience with the hatch block. Most of our users initially created programs that did not include reproduction; however, introducing and running a program that included the hatch block produced surprised laughter in multiple cases.

**Effective engagement with evolutionary phenomena through programming**. In our testing to date, we have limited ourselves to

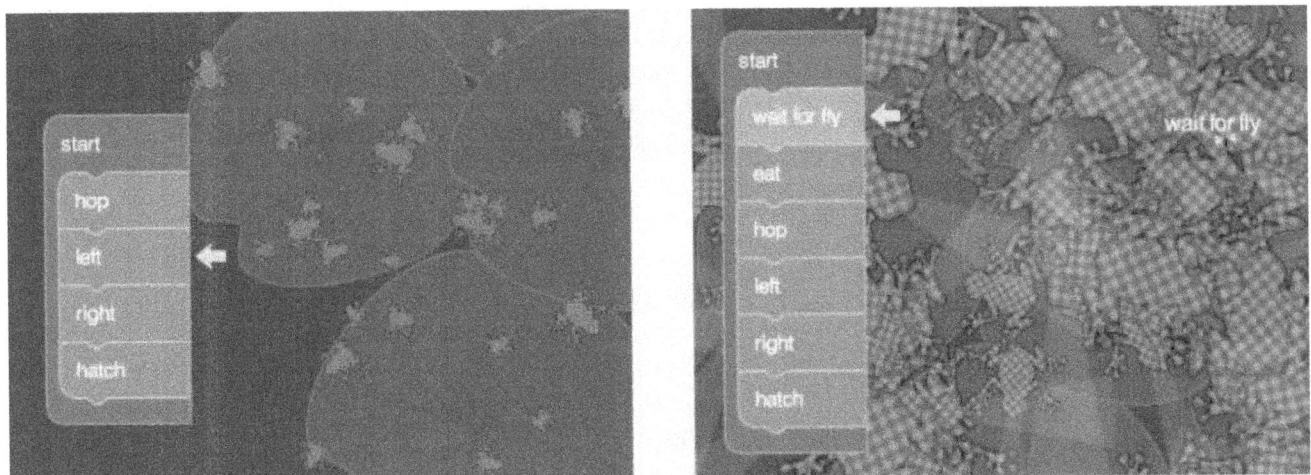

Figure 2. Frog Pond can produce four distinct evolutionary outcomes depending on users' programs: (a) frogs get smaller over time (left); (b) frogs get larger over time (right).

15 to 20 minute sessions. In this time, middle-school aged programming novices were able to produce one or more of the target evolutionary outcomes described in the design section above: most often, the small-frogs and big-frogs outcomes. In assessing the significance of this feature of the environment, we consider not only the emergent phenomena produced by users through their code but also the ways in which Frog Pond motivated reasoning about the mechanisms that led to those emergent effects. This meant that all of our users created or copied a program that yielded a clear change in the distribution of frog body sizes within a few minutes of engaging with Frog Pond. At that point, our users were faced with the challenge of making sense of this emergent result. Here, we saw different levels of success in learner explanations.

## 5. CONCLUSION AND FUTURE WORK

While our preliminary results are promising there is substantial work left to be done. In particular, we hope to test with a broader audience in a diverse range of settings including elementary school and middle school classrooms. In this way we will be able to understand how far leaners can go with this relatively constrained modeling environment.

## 6. ACKNOWLEDGMENTS

Amartya Banerjee contributed to this project. This work was supported by the National Science Foundation (grant DRL-1109834). Any opinions, findings, or recommendations are those of the authors and do not necessarily reflect the views of the NSF.

## 7. REFERENCES

[1] Centola, D., Wilensky, U., & McKenzie, E. (2000). Survival of the groupiest: Facilitating students' understanding of the multiple levels of fitness through multi-agent modeling—The EACH project. *The Interjournal Complex Systems, 337.*

[2] Chi, M.T.H., Kristensen, A.K., & Roscoe, R. (2012). Misunderstanding emergent causal mechanism in natural selection. In K. Rosengren, S. Brem, & G. Sinatra (Eds.), *Evolution Challenges: Integrating Research and Practice in Teaching and Learning about Evolution* (pp. 145-173). Oxford University Press.

[3] Dickes, A.C., & Sengupta, P. (2012). Learning Natural Selection in 4th Grade With Multi-Agent-Based Computational Models. *Research in Science Education,* 1-33.

[4] Horn, M.S., & Wilensky, U. (2011). NetTango [computer software]. Evanston, IL: Center for Connected Learning and Computer-Based Modeling, Northwestern University.

[5] Horwitz, P., McIntyre, C. A., Lord, T. L., O'Dwyer, L. M., & Staudt, C. (2013). Teaching "Evolution readiness" to fourth graders. *Evolution: Education and Outreach, 6*(1), 21.

[6] Kahn, K., Noble, H., Hjorth, A., & Sampaio, F.F (2012). Three-minute Constructionist Experiences. In *Proc. Constructionism.*

[7] Klopfer, E., Scheintaub, H., Huang, W., & Wendel, D. (2009). StarLogo TNG. In *Artificial Life Models in Software,* 151-182.

[8] Levy, S. T., & Wilensky, U. (2009). Crossing levels and representations: The Connected Chemistry (CC1) curriculum. *Journal of Science Education and Technology, 18*(3), 224-242.

[9] Miller, J.D., Scott, E.C., & Okamoto, S. (2006). Public acceptance of evolution. *Science, 313,* 765-766.

[10] National Research Council. (2011). *Report of a Workshop of Pedagogical Aspects of Computational Thinking.* Washington, D.C.: The National Academies Press.

[11] Papert, S. (1980). *Mindstorms: Children, computers, and powerful ideas.* New York: Basic books.

[12] Parnafes, O., & diSessa, A. (2004). Relations between types of reasoning and computational representations. *International Journal of Computers for Mathematical Learning, 9*(3), 251-280.

[13] Resnick, M., Maloney, J., Monroy-Hernández, A., Rusk, N., Eastmond, E., Brennan, K., Millner, A., Rosenbaum, E., Silver, J., Sliverman, B. & Kafai, Y. (2009). Scratch: programming for all. *Communications of the ACM, 52*(11), 60-67.

[14] Roque, R.V. (2007). OpenBlocks: an extendable framework for graphical block programming systems (Doctoral dissertation, Massachusetts Institute of Technology).

[15] Rosengren, K. S., Brem, S. K., Evans, E. M., & Sinatra, G. M. (Eds.). (2012). *Evolution challenges: Integrating research and practice in teaching and learning about evolution.* Oxford.

[16] Sengupta, P., & Wilensky, U. (2009). Learning electricity with NIELS: Thinking with electrons and thinking in levels. *International Journal of Computers for Mathematical Learning, 14*(1), 21-50.

[17] Sherin, B., diSessa, A., & Hammer, D. (1993). Dynaturtle revisited: Learning physics through collaborative design of a computer model. *Interactive Learning Environments, 3*(2), 91-118.

[18] Wagh, A. & Wilensky, U. (2012). Evolution in blocks: Building models of evolution using blocks. In *Proc. Constructionism 2012.*

[19] Wagh. A. & Wilensky, U. (2012). Breeding birds to learn about artificial selection: Two birds with one stone? In *Proc. International Conference of the Learning Sciences (ICLS'12).*

[20] Weintrop, D., & Wilensky, U. (2013). RoboBuilder: A Computational Thinking Game. In *Proc. ACM Technical Symposium on Computer Science Education,* 736-736.

[21] Wilensky, U. (1999). NetLogo [computer software]. Evanston, IL: Center for Connected Learning and Computer-Based Modeling, Northwestern University. http://ccl.northwestern.edu/netlogo.

[22] Wilensky, U., & Resnick, M. (1999). Thinking in Levels: A Dynamic Systems Approach to Making Sense of the World. *Journal of Science Education and Technology, 8*(1), 3-19.

[23] Wilensky, U., & Novak, M. (2010). Understanding evolution as an emergent process: learning with agent-based models of evolutionary dynamics. In R.S. Taylor & M. Ferrari (Eds.), *Epistemology and Science Education: Understanding the Evolution vs. Intelligent Design Controversy.* Routledge.

[24] Wilensky, U., & Papert, S. (2010). Restructurations: Reformulations of Knowledge Disciplines through new representational forms. In *Proc. Constructionism 2010.*

[25] Wilensky, U. & Reisman, K. (2006). Thinking like a wolf, a sheep or a firefly: Learning biology through constructing and testing computational theories. *Cognition and Instruction, 24*(2), 171-209.

[26] Wilkerson-Jerde, M. & Wilensky, U. (2010). Deltatick: Using agent-based modeling to learn the calculus of complex systems. In *Proc. Constructionism 2010.*

[27] Wing, J. M. (2006). Computational thinking. *Communications of the ACM, 49*(3), 33-35.

[28] Xiang, L., & Passmore, C. (2010). The Use of an Agent-Based Programmable Modeling Tool in 8th Grade Students' Model-Based Inquiry. *Journal of the Research Center for Educational Technology, 6*(2), 130-147.

**Closing Panel**

# How can Interaction with Digital Creative Tools Support Child Development?

**Allison Druin**
University of Maryland

**Marilyn Fleer**
Monash University

**Brian David Johnson**
Intel

**Paulo Blikstein**
Stanford University

**Janet C Read**
University of Central Lancashire

**Mitch Resnick**
MIT Media Lab

**Bo Stjerne Thomsen**
The LEGO Foundation

The last session at this year's conference is an interactive panel discussion facilitated by Prof. Mitch Resnick from MIT Media Lab. The closing panel consists of leading university and industry researchers with strong opinions about digital technology and its relation to children and childhood. The topic for this session is the general question for this year's conference: 'How can interaction with digital creative tools support child development?' The panel reflects on theoretical frameworks and challenges for the design of new digital technologies for a new generation of children, discussing new trajectories to support children's learning, well-being, and sense-making. Panelists draw upon ideas from the papers,

demos, tutorials, and keynotes presented at the IDC 2014 conference. IDC delegates have the opportunity to join the conversation, posing their own questions and comments. The closing panel concludes IDC 2014 by sharing ideas on how we can build tomorrow's technology – together.

**Categories and Subject Descriptors**

H.5.2 [Information Interfaces and Presentation]: User Interfaces – Theory and Methods, User-Centered Design

**Keywords**
Digital Creative Tools; Child Development

# Author Index

www.ingramcontent.com/pod-product-compliance
Lightning Source LLC
Chambersburg PA
CBHW080711220326
41598CB00033B/5380